ENCYCLOPEDIA OF THE AMERICAN INDIAN IN THE TWENTIETH CENTURY

ENCYCLOPEDIA OF THE AMERICAN INDIAN IN THE TWENTIETH CENTURY

ALEXANDER EWEN AND
JEFFREY WOLLOCK

UNIVERSITY OF NEW MEXICO PRESS
ALBUQUERQUE

© 2015 by Alexander Ewen and Jeffrey Wollock
Maps © 2013 by Infobase Learning
All rights reserved. Published 2015
Printed in the United States of America

20 19 18 17 16 15   1 2 3 4 5 6

LIBRARY OF CONGRESS CATALOGING-IN-PUBLICATION DATA

Ewen, Alexander.
Encyclopedia of the American Indian in the twentieth century /
Alexander Ewen and Jeffrey Wollock. — First edition.
     pages cm
Includes bibliographical references and index.
ISBN 978-0-8263-5595-9 (cloth : alk. paper)
1. Indians of North America—History—20th century—Encyclopedias.
2. Indians of North America—Biography—Encyclopedias.
I. Wollock, Jeffrey, 1946–
II. Title.
E77.W84 2015
970.004′97—dc23
          2015002923

Cover illustration: Karl E. Moon & Co., photographer. "*The Pottery painter,*" *Isleta*. Photograph, c1906.
Library of Congress Prints and Photographs Division, Washington, D.C., 20540 USA. LCCN: 2010651720.

Composed in Adobe Garamond Pro 10/12. Display type is Gill Sans Standard

In memory of
Ingrid Washinawatok El-Issa
(Flying Eagle Woman),
1957–1999
and
Tonya Gonnella Frichner
(Gawanahs)
1947–2015

CONTENTS

ACKNOWLEDGMENTS

A book of this kind would not have been possible without the help of many people. We would like to thank:

- Jennifer Goodman Wollock for her writing and research assistance on some 20 articles, including most of the biographies of American Indians in science.
- Cora Lee Palmer, for writing and research on the biographies of Native dancers as well as the articles on powwows and lacrosse.
- Mark Michaels, whose research on the New Age and Indians was of great value to us in the preparation of that article.
- Richard Campo, for extensive research for the article on crime and criminality.
- Jacqueline Sheridan for her research for the article American Indians in World War II.
- Xan Finnerty for turning us on to Link Wray.
- Ronnie Farley, for all of the photographic research.
- Steven Van Zandt, without whose support this book would not have been possible.
- Adam Clayton, Bono, Larry Mullen, and The Edge for their long-standing, generous support, as well as Michael Johnson and SIR New York. Special thanks to Herbert Kurz.
- The Solidarity Foundation for its support.

Our debts to Rosemary Richmond and the American Indian Community House, and the late Tonya Gonnella Frichner and the American Indian Law Alliance are too deep and varied to be counted.

Many other people generously gave us the benefit of their time, skills, resources, and memories. We thank Tom Holm, professor of American Indian studies, University of Arizona (Tucson), for his personal reminiscences of Robert K. Thomas; Robert N. Wells, Munsil Professor of Government, St. Lawrence University, for valuable information on Indians and higher education; G. Hubert Matthews, professor of linguistics, Montana State University at Billings, for his memories of Red Thunder Cloud (Carlos Westez); Miffy Shunatona Hines, New York, for information on her father, Joe Shunatona; Francine Locke Bray, Indianapolis, for valuable leads on Wesley Robertson; Stephen Mitchell, principal of Burrillville High School, Harrisville,

Rhode Island, for his memories of Lucy Nicola; Irene Wilkie and Robert Bruce, Rolla, North Dakota, for information on Robert E. Bruce; David Vecchioli for information on Spopee; Gene Hightower, Ph.D., Argosy University, for suggesting an article on Indians in psychology.

We would also like to acknowledge the assistance of various institutions around the country and their staffs. These include the New York Public Library, with its great American Indian collection in the Reference Division, as well as the many resources of its Performing Arts Library at Lincoln Center; the Jones Library, Amherst, Massachusetts, for the use of its Charles Eastman collection; Dan Smith of the Local History Division of the Onondaga County Public Library in Syracuse, New York, for his help in finding some scarce items of Iroquois history; Mary Davis of the Huntington Free Library, Bronx, New York, for her valuable comments and suggestions; the Kansas City, Kansas, Public Library, for its collection of press clippings on the Conley sisters; Mike De Leo of the Silas Bronson Library, Waterbury, Connecticut; Linda Smucker of the Muskingum County Pioneer Historical Society, Zanesville, Ohio; Jane Bentley, librarian of the San Diego Museum of Man, for help in tracing the elusive Constance Goddard Du Bois; Geoffrey Reynolds, archivist of Hope College in Holland, Michigan; Jeffrey LaMonica, archival technician of the Department of History, Presbyterian Church (USA), Philadelphia, and Delphine Nelson of Educational Services, Comanche Nation, both for help in finding data on James Ottipoby and his family.

Additional thanks go to Lizka Segal, archival assistant at the University of Colorado at Boulder, for documents on Robert K. Thomas, and Dawn Pilcher, librarian and archivist of NAES College, Chicago, for additional information on Thomas; Alessandro Pezzati, archivist, University of Pennsylvania Museum, Philadelphia, for material on Louis Shotridge and Don Whistler, as well as Western History Collection at the University of Oklahoma, Norman, for information on Don Whistler; the National Archives (Pacific Northwest Region), Seattle, for help with Archie Phinney and George P. LaVatta; the Ohio State University Archives, Columbus, for information on Lucille Johnson Marsh; Lois Webb, Librarian, Bacone

College, for help with Mary Stone McLendon (Ataloa); and Randy Talley of the Office of Public Relations, University of Science and Arts of Oklahoma, Chickasha, for information on Te Ata (Mary Thompson Fisher).

We would also like to thank the staffs of the American Indian Science and Engineering Society and the General Federation of Women's Clubs Archive, Washington, D.C.

We are grateful for the expertise of staff members of many historical societies, museums, and governments, notably Barbara Landis of the Cumberland County Historical Society, Carlisle, Pennsylvania, for information on many Carlisle students; Brian Shovers, reference historian, Montana Historical Society, Helena, for material on Two Guns White Calf; the Oregon History Center Research Library, Portland, Oregon, for information on Elizabeth Bender Cloud; Alfreda Irwin, historian of the Chautauqua Institution, Chautauqua, New York, for information on Mabel Powers; Cynthia Monroe of the Nebraska State Historical Society for information on Melvin Gilmore; Susan Dingle, reference specialist at the State Historical Society of North Dakota, for information on Mary Louise Bottineau Baldwin; the staff of the library and archives of the Oklahoma Historical Society, Oklahoma City, for information on many Oklahoma Indians; the library staff of the Buffalo and Erie County Historical Society, Buffalo, New York; the staff members of the Florida Room at the State of Florida Historical Resources Division, Tallahassee, for information on the Seminole and Mikasuki; Kerry Chartkoff, state capitol historian, Lansing, Michigan, for material on Cora Anderson; Claudia Stoebe; and Carl Ballenas, local historian of Queens, New York, for information on Mary Chinquilla.

We are grateful for the help of many tribal institutions and their staffs, in particular Vera Hernandez, program coordinator, Enrollment Support Services, and Waneeta Bennett of the Turtle Mountain Heritage Center for material on Robert and Fred Bruce; Sharon Giles, director, and Anita Stevens of the Sac and Fox Nation Library; Loretta Metaxin of the Cultural Heritage Office of the Oneida Tribe of Wisconsin; Jody Beaulieu, director of library and archives, Red Lake Board of Chippewa Indians, Minnesota; the Yakama Indian Nation, Toppenish, Washington, for information on Chief Yowlachie; and Marilyn Molotier of the Yakama Agency Museum for her help with Nipo Strongheart.

Last but not least, we would like to thank the staff of Facts On File, our copy editor, Elin Woodger, who made many valuable contributions to the book, our editor, Nicole Bowen, without whose patience, dedication, and support this book could not have been possible, and of course John Byram and Maya Allen-Gallegos of the University of New Mexico Press, and Stephany Evans of Fine Print Literary Management.

The authors have made every effort to ensure factual, orthographical, and typographical accuracy, but it is perhaps too much to hope that a work of this scope and size can be entirely free of error. We take full responsibility for any such errors or omissions. The interpretations of the facts are solely those of the authors.

Authors' Note

Maintaining consistency and correctness in the use of names of American Indian confederacies, tribes, groups, subtribal groups, and bands presents a challenge.

The name by which a Native group refers to itself in its own language is often not the name that is familiar to the public. In addition, the familiar name of the tribe is often also the official name by which it has been legally known for a very long time. Although a few tribes have legally exchanged their familiar name for one in their own language, these changes have been so recent that we feel it would be confusing, in a work covering the whole of the 20th century, to use the Native-language name in historical contexts where it was not used.

Furthermore, based on cultural, linguistic, geographic, or historical considerations, a Native-language name often refers to a grouping that is either broader or narrower than the one denoted by a corresponding familiar name, although they overlap in some respects. Each name has its own particular usefulness, but to substitute one for the other, across the board, can only create additional confusion.

For the sake of clarity and consistency therefore, we have opted, except in a few appropriate contexts, to retain the more familiar historical names. Sometimes other versions of names are provided in parentheses afterward. Traditional and popular names for tribes will be found in the tribal index at the back of the book.

INTRODUCTION

At the start of the 21st century, there were about 300 Indian tribes in the United States, each with its own history. Can a single book do justice to all those histories, or even to the collective history of the American Indian in the 20th century? Of course not. Yet in a short, convenient form, this book gathers together biographies and concise analyses of major events, organizations, and important general topics, to provide an overview of the history of American Indians in the 20th century. The overall outline and the significant features of the history of Indians in the 20th century emerge in an easily accessible format. Whatever one's view on the relationship of the American Indian to the United States, this book provides a particular vantage point, sharing elements in common with general American history but also much that is absolutely unique. It is a history that general American history tends to keep in the background, and it challenges some of America's most deep-seated myths.

To get an overall picture of American Indian history in the 20th century is not easy. While excellent studies have been written on individual tribes and individual topics, there are few books that attempt to give an overview of the whole century (Mary Davis's *Native America in the Twentieth Century: An Encyclopedia* and Peter Iverson's *"We Are Still Here": American Indians in the Twentieth Century* are notable exceptions); even the specialized studies are fewer in number than one might expect. Furthermore, Indian tribes are distinct from one another; almost no statement holds true for all. It is always difficult to achieve a synthesis of the most recent history at such short distance. The greatest difficulty, however, in compiling a composite history of Native Americans is understanding how their modern history often contradicts the myths of American history.

American history has typically viewed the Indian as part of the country's heritage—a vanishing part ever receding into the past. That is probably why Indian history of earlier centuries is far more studied than is 20th-century Indian history. It is also why some nonspecialists to whom we mentioned this project seemed almost unable to conceive of an American Indian history as something distinct from an ethnographic study.

At the beginning of the 20th century, Indians were largely passive victims of irrational and continually shifting federal policies that were ultimately aimed at their complete assimilation into mainstream American society. In hindsight, if there is a unifying theme to all the diversity, the history of American Indians in the 20th century is the story of how they gradually emerged as protagonists of their own drama, masters of their own fate. Instead of disappearing, they have continued against great odds to develop vigorously, creatively, and in ways undreamt of by most observers at the beginning of the century. And this story is not lacking in heroes.

Indians have certainly not vanished. Over the course of the 20th century, the Native population increased at least eightfold, and even the number of federally recognized tribes, to say nothing of other Native communities, has grown. The stated aim of federal Indian policy for the first six decades of the 20th century—to eliminate the political existence of tribes and dissolve reservations—has been defeated.

But numbers cannot tell the whole story. At the beginning of the 19th century, "pulverizing the tribal mass," as President Theodore Roosevelt put it, was the official policy. Tribal lands were broken up, and by 1930, two-thirds of the total had been lost. The best and the brightest of Indian youth were put through a system of education designed to absorb them into mainstream white culture, to turn their talents and aspirations away from their tribes. Native religions were to be wiped out. The goals were total assimilation, the complete suppression of all indigenous cultures, and the termination of all reservations and the tribes themselves. This policy was pursued with determination by the best of the administrators, with corruption by the worst: There were disagreements about how and at what rate to do it, but no alternative was ever officially considered until the late 1920s.

Indians served with distinction in World War I, in numbers far out of proportion to their population in the United States. The war brought a brief phase of prosperity to Indian ranchers and farmers, but with the armistice this prosperity collapsed. The granting of U.S. citizenship to the remaining noncitizen Indians in 1924 was largely propelled by the service of Indians in the war. (The states of Arizona and New Mexico would not yield until 1948, and Maine would hold back until 1954.) This was a civil rights victory, though some traditional communities chose to reject citizenship. However, corruption and land loss continued through the 1920s, with such dreadful effects that finally both Indians and the general public had had enough. The Hoover administration ushered in an era of earnest reform in 1929, though at first with limited practical success. Paternalism and the ideology of assimilation still reigned, but in a more benign form.

The Great Depression of the 1930s hit some Indians in the same way it hit most Americans: Individual small-scale Indian farmers in the dust bowl, such as the Prairie Potawatomi, were affected as badly as their white neighbors were. But paradoxically, the Great Depression was, on the whole, a rather good time for Indians. During the prosperous 1920s, except for a few oil-rich individuals, Indians had been the poorest of the poor. With President Franklin Roosevelt and Bureau of Indian Affairs (BIA) commissioner John Collier in power, programs such as the Indian Civilian Conservation Corps and the Works Progress Administration Indian Arts and Crafts Board formed a safety net and improved Indian life and morale to some extent. Even more important, the general ideology shifted, and, for the first time, the BIA administration had as its goals the preservation of Indian culture, an end to the depletion of land and indeed a beginning to some land recovery, and greater self-government (although often in forms alien to the cultures). New, pioneering legal interpretations were put forth by the Department of the Interior (of which the BIA was part), which, at least in theory, opened up paths more compatible with what tribes understood as their rights to existence under treaties or under the principle of inherent sovereignty.

Yet Collier's Indian Reorganization Act (1934) was controversial and left an ambiguous legacy, mainly because it undercut a number of ancient, traditional governments and, by organizing tribal governments to be more compatible with the overall U.S. system, made them more susceptible to outside manipulation.

With America's entry into World War II at the end of 1941, the Indian response was similar to that of the previous war. However, this war went on much longer, and far more people were involved. Indian participation in the war effort turned out to be a great natural boost to assimilation, spurring the Termination policy of the late 1940s and the 1950s, a deliberate attempt to roll back the achievements of the New Deal era and settle the Indian problem by legislating tribes out of existence. The new Indian Claims Commission pointed toward the same goal, making it possible for tribes to collect compensation—but not to recover land.

During this time, though, the Indians proved stronger. Though damage was done and several tribes were actually terminated, within a decade the tide of Termination had largely been stemmed, thanks in large measure to the National Congress of American Indians and a fledgling movement of determined Indian youth—the Red Power movement. And indeed, all tribes terminated in that era have since been reconstituted. A lasting effect of these policies, however, was the considerable urbanization of Indians, about half of whom, as the century neared its close, lived in cities; as well as the establishment of effective political pan-Indianism, best exemplified by the National Congress of American Indians.

Termination coincided with the period of postwar megaprojects: massive oil, gas, water, mineral, and timber exploitations that caused immense damage to some Native communities. Thanks to the Indian Reorganization Act, massive exploitation had become possible by entirely legal means, with the help of tribal governments. This approach would be continued by corporate America after Termination's defeat.

The modern era of Indian history really began in the 1960s. There was no overnight change: It had required much preparation, and the ingredients had long been brewing. First, there was now a sophisticated, educated, organized, and dedicated group of older Indians who had come up during the New Deal, many of whom had worked for the Collier administration. Second, there was a large contingent of disaffected youth, some educated, some not, but all waking up to the need to connect with their cultures and their people and to stop the Termination process. Third, there was the persistence of the traditional elders and their influence on the youth. Throughout the century, traditional culture had persisted to some degree: There were still elders, ancient languages were still spoken, and the younger generations were now eager to learn. Fourth, there was a continuing development of pan-Indianism—the mutual enriching of traditional cultures, strategies, and points of view through increasingly diverse conferences and organizations. For the first time there was the participation of some staunch traditionalists—Hopi and Iroquois in particular—who until now had fought their own fights but had enjoyed no particular national leadership role. This combination coalesced into a broad movement that would fight for Indian rights.

Through the whole process of 20th-century Indian history, education played a leavening role. Indeed, education is one of the greatest success stories of the 20th century for Indian people. It now became important not for assimilation, but to put new skills to use for the communities, to help them hold on to what they had and push ahead to what they still needed. Through the 1960s and beyond, losses continued: Dams and mines forced the relocation of communities, productive lands were devastated, and vital waters were poisoned.

The capstone of the youth movement and the new militancy was the American Indian Movement (AIM). Modeled in many ways on the Black Panthers and the general youth rebellion of the 1960s, AIM was largely the product of urban Indian youth from families relocated during Termination. The 1970s also saw the rise of sophisticated tribal leaders who wanted a "piece of the action" of corporate America. Under the leadership of a new group of young Native intellectuals, the younger generation grew in theoretical and legal sophistication. They began thinking of Indians as existing in a state of "internal colonialism." The international perspective on Indian sovereignty—something suppressed during the 19th and early 20th century—came back to life, and a dialogue of indigenous peoples from around the world began.

Riders in South Dakota commemorate the centennial of the Wounded Knee Massacre of 1890. *(Ronnie Farley)*

From the 1970s through the 1990s, poverty and social problems continued. Starting in the 1980s, legalized gambling began to improve the financial position of many tribes, though for the most part only modestly because federal funding was decreased through the same period. Yet as more and more programs and responsibilities were transferred from the Bureau of Indian Affairs to the individual tribal governments, Indian tribes were becoming skilled political players and were finding the strength to turn back outright attacks. Indeed, the more publicly they spoke out, not only on issues of special concern to them, but on those that affected everyone—especially the environment—the more influence and authority they seemed to have.

By the end of the 20th century, tribes were becoming their own agents, taking on more and more responsibility, while the power of the Bureau of Indian Affairs continued to diminish. The tribe did not wither away; it proved its viability in the American system of government. As of the time of the publication of this book in the early 21st century, it may be too early to tell what implications the new era of globalization and free trade holds for tribal sovereignty, but these issues are

sure to emerge in coming years. The government may try to buy off the tribes, but many people have already realized that this would only be a new form of termination. In any case, the current situation is not at all what historians of 1901 would ever have expected. Indians have survived and increased in number; they have tremendously increased their sophistication for operating in the modern world; they have not only maintained traditional cultures and languages to a remarkable degree, they are continually gaining respect for their traditional world view, which at the beginning of the 20th century was either ridiculed or treated as sentimental nostalgia. They have not vanished with the buffalo; in fact, the buffalo are also increasing.

This book aims to provide the greatest access to biography of Indians in the 20th century thus far available. Much of the material is based on original research and is unobtainable in any other reference work. Much can be found elsewhere, but not in as handy or comprehensive a form. Although it is impossible in a book of this small compass to cover the whole subject, it is hoped that this one has succeeded in presenting a concise and representative overview.

Two special features increase the value of this encyclopedia: The first is the cross-referencing of articles throughout, which makes the work not just an aggregation of articles, but an interwoven whole. One can start virtually anywhere and, by following the cross-references, see in deepening perspective how a particular person or topic fits within the larger field of American Indian, American, and even world history of the 20th century. The second special feature is the listing of further reading at the end of most articles, allowing the curious reader to step outside the boundaries of this book into the larger literature on whatever subject. Every effort has been made to include even the most recent publications. The reader will find that these two features work together to enhance the effectiveness of this encyclopedia as a reference tool.

A to Z
ENTRIES

Abeita, Pablo (1871–1940) *Isleta Pueblo governor, prominent leader of the All-Pueblo Council*
Pablo Abeita was born on February 10, 1871, in Isleta Pueblo. Noticing his aptitude for learning, a local Catholic priest had him enrolled in a Jesuit school in Old Albuquerque. After transferring to St. Michael's College in Santa Fe, Abeita returned home in 1889. He was appointed to serve on the Isleta Council, thus beginning his lifelong role as a Pueblo leader. In 1900, he became a typesetter for the Albuquerque *Morning Democrat* (now the *Journal*), and two years later, a commercial clerk. In 1905, he joined the Indian Service, as the BUREAU OF INDIAN AFFAIRS was known at the time, becoming a farm instructor. In 1907, he left the post to run his family's general store in Isleta.

A few years later, Abeita was appointed judge of the Court of Indian Offenses, a judicial body under the Indian Service that had jurisdiction over crimes on Indian reservations. He held this position from 1913 until 1923. He was chosen to chair the All-Pueblo Council when it was reestablished, and in November 1922, when the council began to elect its members, he was elected secretary, a post he held until shortly before his death. The council was instrumental in fighting the DANCE ORDERS of Indian Commissioner CHARLES HENRY BURKE, which sought to outlaw Indian ceremonies, as well as the BURSUM BILL, which tried to extend legal protections to non-Indian squatters on Pueblo lands. The role of the council in piloting the first successful Indian-based movement of the 20th century marked an important turning point in Indian affairs.

Bold and outspoken, Abeita gave a speech on May 29, 1940, at the dedication of the Francisco Coronado Monument in Bernalillo, New Mexico, in which he broke from the other guests and criticized the Spanish conquistador, arguing that "white man's history was ninety percent wrong." A popular and well-respected leader, Abeita served Isleta in every major official capacity. He was elected governor several times. Among Abeita's admirers was the famous journalist Ernie Pyle, who wrote that Abeita was "smart" and "spoke better English than I do." Pablo Abeita died on December 17, 1940.

See also COLLIER, JOHN.

Further Reading
Guggino, Patricia Burke. "Pablo Abeita." Unpublished M.A. thesis, University of New Mexico, 1995.
Sando, Joe S. *Pueblo Profiles: Cultural Identity through Centuries of Change*, 41–49. Santa Fe, N.Mex.: Clear Light Publishers, 1998.

Adams, Hank (1943–) *Assiniboine–Dakota Sioux tribal activist, influential writer on Indian rights*
Born in Poplar, Montana, on the Fort Peck Reservation, on May 16, 1943, Hank Adams, an Assiniboine–Dakota Sioux, was raised on the Quinault reservation on Washington's Olympic Peninsula. After attending Moclips High School, where he was student-body president, editor of the school newspaper and annual, and a starting football and basketball player, he enrolled at the University of Washington, but left in 1963 after two years. During this time, he also worked on and off as a laborer and a clam digger and in a sawmill.

Adams began his activism when he refused to be drafted into the U.S. armed forces, citing broken Indian treaties. He did eventually serve in the army, however. He began to work on fishing rights in the Northwest, becoming the chair of the NATIONAL INDIAN YOUTH COUNCIL's (NIYC) Washington State Project in 1963 (see HUNTING AND FISHING RIGHTS). Influenced by the confrontational tactics advocated by NIYC's CLYDE WARRIOR, Adams helped organize a march on the Washington State capital of Olympia in which actor Marlon Brando, comedian Dick Gregory, and more than 1,000 Indians took part. He followed that by organizing "fish-ins" with JANET McCLOUD on the Nisqually and Puyallup

Rivers, publicity events that became the scene of violent confrontations between Indians and state law enforcement officials. Between 1964 and 1965, Adams also served as research secretary for the NATIONAL CONGRESS OF AMERICAN INDIANS (NCAI), at that time headed by VINE DELORIA, JR.

After being drafted again and serving a two-year stint in the army, where he was editor of the post newspaper, Adams became director of the Quileute Tribe Community Action Program. He then joined the 12-member steering committee of the Poor People's Campaign, a grassroots coalition chaired by Martin Luther King, Jr. Working alongside King, Reverend Ralph D. Abernathy, consumer advocate Ralph Nader, and Senator Robert F. Kennedy, Adams became a major force in bringing Indian issues into line with the broad civil rights movement of the time. The militant stance of Adams's "Red Muslims," as they were known, was a departure from the mainstream efforts of groups such as the ASSOCIATION ON AMERICAN INDIAN AFFAIRS and NCAI and led to an important shift in Indian politics—as well as concrete political results (see BENNETT, ROBERT LAFOLLETTE). Adams helped Senator Kennedy draft a critical report on the Indian educational policies of the day, *Indian Education: A National Tragedy*, leading to increased federal funding for Indian children (see EDUCATIONAL POLICY, AMERICAN INDIANS AND). Kennedy toured a number of Indian reservations in 1968, holding hearings on the state of Indian affairs and Indian education, and the plight of Indians became an important issue in his presidential campaign.

After Robert Kennedy's assassination in June, Adams continued to work through the Poor People's Campaign to try to influence the highly charged 1968 election, organizing a sit-in in Interior Secretary Stewart Udall's office at the conclusion of the Poor People's March on Washington. Adams persuaded Senator George McGovern to sponsor a series of reform initiatives, including an overhaul of the BUREAU OF INDIAN AFFAIRS (BIA), but the legislation did not succeed.

Adams returned to Washington State to make an unsuccessful run for a congressional seat before becoming director of the Survival of American Indians Association, based in Tacoma. From 1969 until 1972, he edited the association's newsletter, *The Renegade: A Strategy Journal of Indian Opinion*, which focused on treaty and fishing rights. In January 1971, Adams was shot and seriously wounded by an unknown assailant while at a fish-in. He recovered in time to help plan the TRAIL OF BROKEN TREATIES, participating in the 1972 takeover of BIA headquarters in Washington, D.C. The Trail had been conceived by ROBERT PHILLIP BURNETTE, with REUBEN SNAKE and Adams as cochairs.

For the Trail, Adams wrote the Twenty Points, a set of demands that reflected a modern stance on Indian sovereignty. In many respects a reformulation of the "Position Paper on Indian Affairs," which Adams had written for his run for Congress, the Twenty Points advocated a return to the treaty relationship that was formerly held between the federal government and Indians. It also advocated a repeal of the proviso of the 1871 Appropriations Act that forbade any further treaty-making between the U.S. government and Indians (see SOVEREIGNTY, INDIGENOUS AND TRIBAL). The call for the establishment of a new federal commission to review past treaty violations and be empowered to make new treaties with Indians set the tone for the coming demands of the AMERICAN INDIAN MOVEMENT (AIM). None of the three originators of the Trail were members of AIM, but they were overshadowed by the flamboyant AIM leaders who ended up taking the credit for the Trail and who carried Adams's confrontational tactics even further.

In 1973, Adams helped to negotiate a settlement of the standoff at WOUNDED KNEE. In the mid-1970s, he chaired the Treaties Task Force for the AMERICAN INDIAN POLICY REVIEW COMMISSION. After that, he began to distance himself from the national political scene, returning again to the fishing rights struggles on the Northwest Coast. He was briefly back in the spotlight when, with RUSSELL MEANS on a trip to Nicaragua in 1985 to investigate the plight of the Miskito Indians, his group was attacked by the Sandinista military; Adams was unhurt.

Hank Adams was one of the most influential Indian activists of the 1960s. With his effective organizing skills and clear articulation of Indian sovereignty, he provided a focus for the RED POWER movement, which would reach its zenith under AIM in the early 1970s.

Further Reading

Akwesasne Notes. *Trail of Broken Treaties: BIA, I'm Not Your Indian Anymore*. Rooseveltown, N.Y.: Akwesasne Notes, Mohawk Nation, 1972.

Indian Country Today, January 11, 2006. Tributes by various notables on Adams's receipt of the 2006 American Indian Visionary Award.

Smith, Paul Chaat, and Robert A. Warrior. *Like a Hurricane*. New York: New Press, 1996.

Wilkinson, Charles F. *Blood Struggle: The Rise of Modern Indian Nations*. New York: W. W. Norton, 2005.

Advisory Council on Indian Affairs
See COMMITTEE OF ONE HUNDRED.

agriculture, traditional   *See* INDIGENOUS ECONOMICS.

Akers, Dorothy Smith (Dolly Akers, Day Eagle Woman) (1901–1986) *Assiniboine tribal leader, state legislator*
Dorothy Akers was the first Assiniboine and the first woman to lead the Fort Peck tribal governing board, as well as the first Indian to serve in the Montana state legislature. Born in Wolf Point, Montana, on March 23, 1901, the daughter of William Henry and Nellie Trexler Smith, Dolly Smith was educated at the Sherman Institute in Riverside, California. Before her marriage in 1917 to rancher George M. Cusker, she was a welfare worker. During his illness and after his death in 1941, she

managed their 1,400-acre ranch herself. Later she married John Akers, also a rancher.

In 1932, Dolly Cusker was elected Democratic representative to the Montana state legislature from Roosevelt County, the first Indian woman and the only woman member in the state legislature at that time. When elected, she was given the name Day Eagle Woman, and relatives gave away horses in her honor. She chaired the Federal Relations Committee. During her first term she was appointed Governor Frank Cooney's special representative to Secretary of the Interior Harold Ickes to request that the public welfare act of 1934 include the Indians of Montana.

In the 1950s, Dolly Akers became the first woman in 20 years to be elected to the Fort Peck Tribal Council. Later she became the first woman in her tribe and one of the first women of any tribe to serve as tribal chair. Although removed at a disputatious council meeting in September 1958, she was reinstated by Bureau of Indian Affairs commissioner Glenn Leonidas Emmons in January 1959.

Akers was the governor's delegate to the White House Conference on Children and Youth in 1960. By then a Republican, she was a close friend of Arizona senator Barry Goldwater and worked on his 1964 presidential campaign. In 1968, she was the Montana state chair of Indians for President Richard Nixon.

In 1963, Akers became a registered lobbyist for the Fort Peck Reservation in the Montana legislature; the following year she became area vice president for the National Congress of American Indians. From 1969 to 1979, she served as secretary of the Montana State Intertribal Policy Board, coordinating the seven Montana Indian reservations.

Dolly Akers died on June 5, 1986, at her daughter's home in Rimini, Montana, after an illness of several months.

Akwesasne, siege of (1979–1981)

The siege of Akwesasne was an armed confrontation, lasting from 1979 until 1981, between Mohawk of the Akwesasne Reservation and police from New York State, which was attempting to exert jurisdiction over Mohawk lands.

The conflict had its roots in the previous century when, in 1802, New York State appointed three Mohawk "headmen" to administer the affairs of the tribe and, more important, to transfer land from the Mohawk to the state. This violated the Non-Intercourse Act of 1790, which, in order to clamp down on numerous frauds occurring after the Revolutionary War, specifically forbade states from acquiring land directly from Indians and required that all purchases be made or approved by the federal government.

Throughout the 19th century, Mohawk land holdings were considerably reduced. By the end of that century, Akwesasne, also known as the St. Regis Reservation, a tiny slip of land on the Saint Lawrence River 50 miles west of Plattsburg, was all that remained. In 1935 and 1948, the Mohawk voted to oust the three-man tribal council created by the state of New York. The state, however, refused to recognize any new government. In 1948, local courts went so far as to rule that the Mohawk, as a tribe, did not exist in the state. The ruling held that there were only individual Indians, who were subject to state laws.

By the late 1960s, a revitalizing movement led by Ray Fadden had managed to reestablish the Longhouse Religion and tribal government at Akwesasne. (The Longhouse Religion is the traditional religion of the Iroquois Confederacy, known as "the People of the Longhouse," from the long wooden structures the Iroquois used to live in. In the early 19th century, this ancient religion was revitalized by the Seneca prophet Handsome Lake, and today most, though not all, of the Longhouse Iroquois follow the Code of Handsome Lake.) Attempts by the Immigration Department to cut off the easy access that individual Mohawk had to their relatives in nearby Canada had sparked a resurgence of political activity culminating in the Cornwall Bridge Blockade in 1968 and the establishment that same year of a national newspaper, *Akwesasne Notes* (see journalism). Moreover, a group of energetic younger chiefs, led by Tom Porter and Jake Swamp, began to take their place in the Longhouse during the early 1970s. They agitated against neighboring industrial plants, built during the 1960s, which were seriously polluting the reservation. After the tribal council was recognized by the Bureau of Indian Affairs (BIA) as the official government of the Mohawk in 1971, the reservation became increasingly divided between two camps: one that adhered to the traditional Longhouse Religion and followed the traditional system of chiefs and clan mothers, and another that was beholden to the tribal council with their large amounts of federal money.

New York State, in the meantime, began to be concerned over its lack of title to the vast Mohawk lands seized a century before. The state watched uneasily as the Penobscot and Passamaquoddy land claims in Maine—based on the violation of the same Non-Intercourse Act of 1790—successfully made their way through the federal court system (see Stevens, John W.). In 1975, seizure of land near Moss Lake, New York, by dissident Mohawk from Canada led to armed confrontations between the state and Indians. The state was aligned with the Akwesasne tribal council it had created, which, in contrast to the traditionals, could be counted on not to mount a land claims fight.

Since 1972, the BIA had funded a police force that worked for the Mohawk tribal council. In 1978, the BIA began to aid secret negotiations between the tribal council and New York, in the hope that the trustees would agree to a settlement of the Mohawk land claim.

The siege of Akwesasne was triggered by events that began on May 22, 1979, when traditional Mohawk chief Loran Thompson and his friend Joe Swamp discovered a group of youths, working on behalf of the tribal council, cutting trees on Thompson's land for the purpose of building a fence to demarcate the reservation. The chief confiscated the chainsaws but let the youths leave. However, that night tribal council police, joined by state police, arrested Thompson for assault and kidnapping and in the process badly beat both the chief and an elderly woman who had tried to defend him. The action incensed the traditionals, hundreds of whom surrounded the tribal council building one week later, disarmed the tribal police, and ousted the tribal council.

New York State took this opportunity to try to extend its jurisdiction over the reservation and break the traditional government, issuing arrest warrants for most of the traditional leaders. When the traditionals refused to appear in court, hundreds of state police, backed by vigilantes and Mohawk aligned with the tribal council, gathered during the summer on the outskirts of a small peninsula on the reservation—Raquett Point, where the traditional leaders had sought safety—to try to arrest them by force if necessary. The traditionals, in the meantime, began to draw support from other Iroquois nations, who sent Onondaga chief OREN LYONS, JR., and Seneca writer JOHN C. MOHAWK to try to negotiate a peaceful compromise with the state. Through the work of longtime Mohawk activist Lorraine Canoe and other members of the large Indian community in New York City, as well as the statewide Indian support group Rights for American Indians Now (RAIN), which had been formed in the wake of the Moss Lake controversy, outside support helped to turn the traditional encampment into a heavily armed, highly defended, and well-supplied stronghold.

It quickly became apparent to the state that any assault—even if it could be accomplished successfully— would lead to a tremendous loss of life. The state eventually settled for a long siege, trusting that, as with the OCCUPATIONS OF ALCATRAZ ISLAND and WOUNDED KNEE a few years earlier, the authorities could wait the Indians out. However, this was neither a group of young college students, as with Alcatraz, nor a collection of hotheaded urban radicals like the AMERICAN INDIAN MOVEMENT. The siege only strengthened the Mohawk community under the leadership of their chiefs and clan mothers and led to a renewed sense of unity and purpose.

By winter 1981, after having spent more than $10 million trying to keep up the siege, the state finally dismissed the indictments against the traditionals and conceded to the traditional government. The aftermath of the siege brought the Mohawk, and the Longhouse government of the Iroquois in general, to the height of their power in modern times. They had essentially achieved the independence for which they had fought since the days of Deskaheh (see GENERAL, ALEXANDER). Although the Mohawk were to accomplish much in the next few years (including building the Akwesasne Freedom School, one of the most successful cultural revival programs in the United States), the achievements of the siege would later begin slowly to evaporate with the invasion of the GAMING industry and the development of the Warrior Society (see SHENANDOAH, LEON).

Further Reading

Garte, Edna. "Where the Partridge Drums." *Journal of American Indian Education* 21, no. 1 (November 1981): 24–30.

Ismaelillo, and Robin Wright. *Native Peoples in Struggle: Cases from the Fourth Russell Tribunal and Other International Forums.* Bombay, N.Y.: E.R.I.N. Publications, 1982.

Matthiessen, Peter. "Akwesasne." In *Indian Country*, 127–163. New York: Viking Press, 1984.

Weyler, Rex. *Blood of the Land: The Government and Corporate War against the American Indian Movement.* Philadelphia: New Society Publishers, 1992 [1982].

Alaska Native Brotherhood   *See* ALASKA NATIVE LAND CLAIMS SETTLEMENT ACT.

Alaska Native Land Claims Settlement Act (ANCSA) (1971)

The Alaska Native Land Claims Settlement Act (ANCSA) was legislation, passed in 1971, that transferred title to the lands within Alaska from Alaska Natives to the state and federal governments in return for a sum of money and 40 million acres in federal land grants.

Throughout most of the early 20th century, the vast bulk of Alaskan lands had remained relatively untouched by non-Natives. Attempts to extend the policy of Allotment to the territory, through the Alaska Allotment Act of 1906, failed due to lack of demand for Native lands and the poor quality of the soil, which made standard 160-acre allotments impractical. The creation of the Alaska Native Brotherhood (ANB) in 1912, with the help of the BUREAU OF INDIAN AFFAIRS (BIA) and Presbyterian missionaries at the Sitka Training School (now Sheldon Jackson State College), marked an important step in Alaska Native politics. Its founders included one Tsimshian and 12 Tlingit Indians, and although the organization was largely confined to Indians in southeastern Alaska and had little support from Eskimos (Inupiat, Yup'ik) or Aleut, it would be the main Alaskan Native political body until the 1960s.

Like other pan-Indian organizations of the day, the ANB favored the rapid assimilation of Alaska Natives into white mainstream culture. The group advocated the abolishment of Native customs such as the potlach, as well as promoting Christianization, citizenship, and the right to vote, hold property, and be free from discrimination.

The ANB grew to include chapters in Juneau and Douglas, as well as numerous Native villages in southeastern Alaska. An Alaska Native Sisterhood was also established. In 1923, the ANB began to publish its newsletter, the *Alaska Fisherman*. During the 1920s and 1930s, under William L. Paul, Sr., a mixed-blood Tlingit and Carlisle Indian Industrial School graduate, the organization achieved some success, exempting Alaska from the INDIAN REORGANIZATION ACT of 1934, mobilizing its members to boycott segregated movie theaters, defending the rights of Alaska Natives to vote in territorial elections, and agitating for the protection of indigenous salmon stocks. After World War II, the organization favored many of the policies of TERMINATION advocated by DILLON SEYMOUR MYER, including the closing of the Alaska Bureau of Indian Affairs and the transfer of health services from the BIA to the U.S. Public Health Service.

World War II dramatically changed the lifestyles of many

Alaska Natives who became a part of the war effort. Aleut and other Alaska Natives helped to repel Japanese attempts to conquer the Aleutian Islands in 1942. Much of the coastline of Alaska became militarized, a situation that continued during the Cold War, when relations with indigenous peoples across the Bering Strait were cut off.

The admission of Alaska to statehood in 1958 brought about a growing need for mobilization of Alaska Natives to protect their lands from being ceded to the new state. The act of 1958 had allowed the newly formed state to select more than 102 million acres of land from the public domain within its borders, virtually all of which was unceded Native land. New groups arose to challenge Alaska's selection of lands, such as the Tanana-Yukon Dena' Nene' Henash, formed in 1962. Composed of the chiefs of Athapascan villages in the Yukon River basin, the group asked the U.S. Department of the Interior to withdraw from public domain tracts of land around the villages so they could not be taken by the state. The ASSOCIATION ON AMERICAN INDIAN AFFAIRS formed an affiliate, the Alaska Native Rights Association, to combat state land grabs as well.

These organizations, as well as the Alaska Native Brotherhood, which was seen as too assimilationist, were largely superseded as a political force in the state by the formation of the Alaska Federation of Natives (AFN) in 1965. Organized by Emil Notti, president of the Cook Inlet Native Association, the federation sought to include all Alaska Natives and managed to create a united front through its determination to protect Native lands. The AFN's point of view was promoted by the *Tundra Times*, a newspaper founded in 1962 by HOWARD ROCK initially to stop the Point Hope nuclear tests.

The discovery of oil in Alaska during the 1960s required that the state's questionable land title be resolved and led directly to negotiations with the AFN that created ANCSA in 1971. Under ANCSA, in return for relinquishing all outstanding land claims and eliminating existing reservations, Alaska Natives received 40 million acres in federal land grants; 4 million acres to be set aside for Native corporations in cities, as well as cemeteries, historic sites, and other uses; a $462 million cash payment; and another $500 million in future payments for mineral rights. The act set up 12 regional corporations, and the Alaska Natives within each region were given shares in the corporation they resided in. A 13th corporation was set up for nonresident natives. The regional corporation held the valuable subsurface mineral rights to the lands they were assigned. The act also reorganized the Native villages in Alaska into village corporations, in which Native villagers were given shares as well. The village corporation held the surface mineral rights.

Although hailed as a victory at the time, it became clear that the transformation of Indian communities into corporations was simply a modern twist on the Allotment policy. While Alaska Native Americans may have owned shares in their respective corporations, children born after the act were effectively disenfranchised, as they did not receive shares and could only gain them through inheritance. The regional

corporations began to exploit the mineral wealth, which frequently brought them into conflict with village corporations, many of which preferred to leave the land pristine. The fiscal drain of maintaining a corporation, and the lawyers and accountants it entailed, began to bankrupt some of the village corporations. Some of the regional corporations also began to fail. After 1991, the stock in the corporations was also sold on the marketplace, thus stirring a fear that someday the corporations might be taken over or might declare bankruptcy, thereby forcing the Alaska Natives to leave their homes.

ANCSA was amended on January 20, 1988, after a vigorous lobbying movement to repair its flaws. Although the new law (PL 100-241) makes the sale of stock more complicated, it does not prevent it from being sold to non-Indians nor does it ensure continued Native control or ownership of the corporations. It does not issue stock to those born after 1971, although corporations may, if they so desire, issue new shares out of their own holdings. ANCSA did not prevent Native stock from entering the market in 1991; the act's basic flaws remained unchanged. In the end, ANCSA took away millions of acres of land belonging to the Alaska Natives; in effect, it was the largest transfer of land by Native peoples to the United States in the 20th century. It remains to be seen whether, in the long run, Alaska Natives will be able to hold on to the land they have left.

Further Reading

Chance, Norman A. *The Inupiat and Arctic Alaska: An Ethnography of Development.* New York: Holt, Rinehart and Winston, 1990.

CIRI Foundation Web site. Available online. URL: http://www.thecirifoundation.org. Accessed October 20, 2004.

McClanahan, Alexandra J. *Growing up Native in Alaska.* Anchorage, Alaska: CIRI Foundation, 2000.

Mitchell, Donald Craig. *Sold American: The Story of Alaska Natives and Their Land, 1867–1959.* Fairbanks: University of Alaska Press, 2003.

West, W. Richard, Jr., and A. Lazarus, Jr. "The Alaska Native Claims Settlement Act: A Flawed Victory." *Law and Contemporary Problems* 40, no. 1 (Winter 1976): 132–165.

Alcatraz Island, occupation of (1969–1971)

In late 1969, a group known as INDIANS OF ALL TRIBES led an unarmed takeover of the abandoned prison on Alcatraz Island in San Francisco Bay. Begun on November 20, 1969, the occupation lasted more than 16 months and became the catalyst for the RED POWER MOVEMENT of the early 1970s.

Alcatraz, a notorious federal penitentiary, had been closed since 1963. A small group of Bay Area Sioux first occupied the island on March 8, 1964. Led by Allen Cottier, president of the Bay Area Council of American Indians, together with Richard McKenzie and Walter Means, who brought his son, RUSSELL MEANS, along with him, the Sioux argued that Article Six of the 1868 Treaty of Fort Laramie entitled them to stake claims on abandoned federal property. After peacefully occupying

Chippewa and Bay Area community leader Adam Fortunate Eagle headed the initial attempt to occupy Alcatraz Island in 1969. *(AP/Wideworld)*

the island for a few hours, the Indians left when they were threatened with arrest.

After that dramatic action, the local Bay Area Indian community worked on a number of proposals to the federal and local governments in hope that the island would some day be turned over to them. In late 1969, however, two events galvanized the community to action: The San Francisco Board of Supervisors voted to turn Alcatraz over to the Hunt family of Texas for commercial development, and the San Francisco Indian Center burned down, leaving local Indians with no place to meet and hold events.

Among those who had joined the Sioux in the 1964 occupation was ADAM FORTUNATE EAGLE, a successful Chippewa businessman who lived in the Bay Area. A general consensus had formed among the local Indians that only an occupation of the island would prevent it from being handed to the Hunts, and as chairman of the United Bay Area Council, a regional umbrella group, Fortunate Eagle led the planning.

He enlisted RICHARD OAKES, a student leader at San Francisco State University, to head the occupation. The first attempt at landing, on the morning of November 9, was aborted when the charter company reneged at the last minute on its agreement to provide boats, though one Indian was able to swim to the island from a hastily borrowed sailing ship. That night a second attempt managed to land Oakes and 13 other Indians, including three women.

The first occupiers left the island the next day after securing a promise from the General Services Administration (GSA), which managed the island, that there would be negotiations over the island's future. When these negotiations did not materialize, the Indians landed again on November 20, this time determined to stay. Led again by Oakes, the occupation force of about 90 Indians, including more than 30 women and a dozen young children, landed in the middle of the night and proceeded to make themselves at home in the unoccupied cell blocks. The large number of people on the island, as well as the strong support from the mainland, made the GSA reluctant to use force. An attempt by the Coast Guard to blockade the island was abandoned after only three days.

The first council on the island, like most of the occupiers, was composed almost exclusively of young students. It included Oakes; Seminole Al Miller; Winnebago (Ho-Chunk) Ross Hardin; Eskimo Bob Nelford; Luiseño Dennis Turner; Cherokee James Baugh; and a young professor from the University of California, Los Angeles, Cahuilla Ed Castillo. The new council offered to pay the government $24 in beads and trinkets for the island (the same amount the Dutch paid for Manhattan) while issuing a series of demands concerning Native sovereignty and the conditions of Indians around the country. The group also hoped to build an Indian cultural center, a college, and an ecological center, and intended to make the island a spiritual home for the local Indian people.

The takeover electrified Indians across the country, many of whom traveled to San Francisco to join the swelling ranks of occupiers, and inspired attempts to duplicate the feat, including an abortive occupation of Ellis Island off New York City. Among those who would join the occupation were Shoshone-Bannock La Nada Means, who became an articulate negotiator; WILMA MANKILLER (Cherokee); GRACE THORPE (Sac and Fox); MAD BEAR ANDERSON (Tuscarora); and JOHN TRUDELL (Santee Sioux [Dakota]), who organized an independent radio station. The occupation also drew tremendous support from the Bay Area's non-Indian community, who supplied the occupiers with food, water, and money and who petitioned the government in favor of the Indians' demands.

The federal government, unsure of how to act, decided on a strategy of waiting out the activists. In May 1970, they cut water and electricity to the island. The occupation, begun with such great enthusiasm, began to disintegrate through dissension, first with friction between the young occupiers and the local Indian community, then among the occupiers themselves. Attempts to enforce unity and discipline led to the creation of a police force that did little except increase tensions. Oakes departed after his stepdaughter was critically injured in an accident in January 1970. When five buildings were destroyed by fire, the press, which until then had been largely supportive, began to turn against the occupation.

By the time federal marshals seized the island on June 11, 1971, only 15 occupiers remained, and the issue had largely disappeared from the national consciousness. Despite its failure to gain the island for Indian people—though it did prevent its commercial exploitation—the Alcatraz occupation, which had been conceived by moderate elements of the local Indian community, nonetheless provided the blueprint for the Red Power Movement across the country, thereby galvanizing organizations such as the AMERICAN INDIAN MOVEMENT and inspiring takeovers such as the TRAIL OF BROKEN TREATIES and the occupation of WOUNDED KNEE.

Further Reading

Fortunate Eagle, Adam. *Alcatraz! Alcatraz!: The Indian Occupation of 1969–1971.* Berkeley, Calif.: Heyday Books, 1992.

———. *Heart of the Rock: The Indian Invasion of Alcatraz.* Norman: University of Oklahoma Press, 2002.
Johnson, Troy R. *The Occupation of Alcatraz Island: Indian Self-Determination and the Rise of Indian Activism.* Urbana: University of Illinois Press, 1996.
Johnson, Troy, Joane Nagel, and Duane Champagne, eds. *American Indian Activism: Alcatraz to the Longest Walk.* Urbana: University of Illinois Press, 1997.
Smith, Paul Chaat, and Robert A. Warrior. *Like a Hurricane.* New York: New Press, 1996.
Strange, Carolyn, and Tina Loo. "Holding the Rock: The 'Indianization' of Alcatraz Island, 1969–1999." *The Public Historian* 23, no. 1 (Winter 2001): 55–74.

Film

Alcatraz Is Not an Island. Directed by James M. Fortier. San Francisco: Diamond Island Productions, 2001.

alcoholism, American Indians and

The introduction of alcoholic beverages to the North American continent ranks as one of the most destructive factors in the onslaught against Native people, and alcohol abuse remains a leading health problem among Indians today. Unfortunately the effects of alcohol on Indian culture were so pervasive that the stereotype of the "drunken Indian"—the idea that a large segment if not the majority of Indians were alcoholics—became ingrained in the American public mind through the first three-quarters of the 20th century. Highly publicized victims of alcohol abuse, such as war hero IRA HAMILTON HAYES, served to reinforce public perception of Indians as a conquered people who were culturally and biologically more susceptible to alcohol, less able to metabolize it, and more likely to become drunk.

In the last two decades of the 20th century, new pathological and historical studies shed some light on Indian consumption of alcoholic beverages. The most important of these summarizing masses of previous data was published by the Indian Health Service in 1989, and a more recent update was published by Philip A. May in 1996. Although the studies confirm the notion that alcohol abuse is a serious problem for certain Indian tribes, they also indicate that, on the whole, Indian people are less likely to consume alcohol than the general public.

It is now known that the incidence of alcohol consumption varies greatly from tribe to tribe. A study carried out by May on the Navajo (Dineh) reservation in 1984 indicated that on average, far fewer Navajo adults drink than non-Indian adults. However, the Indian Health Service report seems to show that of those Indians who do drink, the prevalence of abuse is much greater than that among non-Indians. Compounding the problem, according to the same study, is the fact that Indians who do drink tend to begin at an earlier age than their non-Indian counterparts, and that among Indian youth, the rate of alcohol abuse is greater than that of non-Indian youth.

A 1994 study by Stephen J. Kunitz and Jerrold E. Levy

found that "binge drinking" is more common among Indians, and that Indians are more susceptible to diabetes, cirrhosis of the liver, fetal alcohol syndrome, and other alcohol-related diseases than are non-Indians. The Indian Health Service study found that Indians are between five and seven times more likely to die of alcoholism and alcohol-related deaths than other Americans. Tempering these statistics somewhat is the fact that the western and southwestern states, where Indians are most likely to live, have a much higher drinking rate in general than the rest of the country, and in some areas the high statistical rates of Indian alcohol abuse are matched by their non-Indian neighbors.

A 1976 paper by L. J. Bennion and T. K. Li in the *New England Journal of Medicine* scientifically refuted the idea that Indian people are biologically more susceptible to alcohol or less able to metabolize it. In a book published in 1996, William Unran showed that the patterns of Indian alcohol consumption may have been shaped by historical forces and federal policy, a history that differs from that of non-Indians and contributes to both the problem and the perception of abuse.

Before contact with Europeans, with the exception of a few tribes in the Southeast and Southwest, alcoholic beverages were unknown to the Indians of what is now the United States. On the other hand, the early American settlers were among the hardest drinkers in history. The men of the United States drank an average of half a pint of hard liquor per day, and binge drinking was a socially acceptable form of recreation on the American frontier until the temperance movement of the 19th century. Not only did the first settlers generally set a poor example, but early trappers and traders, and even the federal government, often used liquor to their advantage in dealing with Indians, fostering such an addiction to the product among certain Indian tribes that whiskey became a medium of exchange between the peoples.

During the late 19th and early 20th centuries, federal policy changed as reformers (generally allied to the temperance movement) sought to integrate Indians into the general society. Alcohol was banned from Indian reservations; however, "border towns," towns just outside reservation boundaries, quickly sprang up to circumvent the ban. The necessity of traveling off the reservation to drink only encouraged the pattern of binge drinking and became heavily responsible for the greater alcohol-related mortality rates (through automobile accidents, exposure, and alcohol poisoning) that have been prevalent among Indians.

The federal policy of ASSIMILATION, which sought to stamp out traditional Indian cultures and economies, and which consigned most Indians to desperate poverty during this time, undoubtedly contributed further to the use of alcohol. Border towns such as Gallup, New Mexico, and Gordon, Nebraska, which existed almost exclusively to serve Indians liquor, were, unfortunately for many Americans, their only glimpse of Indian people, leading to a skewed vision of Indian life.

Throughout the latter half of the 20th century, Indian communities mounted significant efforts to counter alcohol abuse (see, for example, DODGE WAUNEKA, ANNIE), though

their success has yet to be determined. Arrests for driving while intoxicated and other liquor offenses showed little improvement, although arrests for public drunkenness declined significantly from 1987 through 1996. Between 1979 and 1987, the age-adjusted alcoholism death rate for American Indians and Alaska Natives decreased 47 percent, from 59.0 deaths per 100,000 population to 31.1 deaths. However, after that time, the death rates shot back up. The 1996 rate was 48.7 deaths per 100,000 population. Data from the Centers for Disease Control for 2004 indicated that the alcoholism death rate had not declined much since 1996. The 2004–2006 rate was 43.0 per 100,000. As of 2004, accidents, most of which were alcohol-related, were the third leading cause of death among Indians, following heart disease and cancer. Cirrhosis of the liver and other chronic liver diseases killed Indians at more than two and one-half times the rate of non-Indians and constituted the fifth leading cause of death after diabetes. High rates of homicide and suicide on many reservations are also linked to alcohol use. The problems of alcohol abuse are prevalent throughout American society, and it is a leading cause of death in the general population as well. This scourge, labeled "Indian Kryptonite" by Oneida comedian CHARLIE HILL, continues to be one of the most serious problems facing Indian communities today.

See also CRIME AND CRIMINALITY AMONG AMERICAN INDIANS; DEMOGRAPHICS; HEALTH, AMERICAN INDIAN.

Further Reading

Bennion, L. J., and T. K. Li. "Alcohol Metabolism in American Indians and Whites. Lack of Racial Differences in Metabolic Rate and Liver Alcohol Dehydrogenase." *New England Journal of Medicine* 294, no. 1 (1 January 1976): 9–13.

Dorris, Michael. *The Broken Cord: A Family's Ongoing Struggle with Fetal Alcohol Syndrome*. New York: Harper & Row, 1989.

Indian Health Service. *Trends in Indian Health*. Washington, D.C.: U.S. Department of Health and Human Services, 1990.

Kunitz, Stephen J., and Jerrold E. Levy. *Drinking Careers: A Twenty-Five Year Study of Three Navajo Populations*. New Haven, Conn.: Yale University Press, 1994.

Leland, Joy. *Firewater Myths: North American Indian Drinking and Alcohol Addiction*. New Brunswick, N.J.: Rutgers Center of Alcohol Studies, 1976.

———. "The Epidemiology of Alcohol Abuse among American Indians: The Mythical and Real Properties." *Journal of American Indian Culture and Research* 18, no. 2 (1994): 121–143.

———. "The Prevention of Alcohol and Other Substance Abuse among American Indians: A Review and Analysis of the Literature." In *The Challenge of Participatory Research: Preventing of Alcohol-Related Problems in Ethnic Communities*, edited by Phyllis Langton, 185–243. Washington, D.C.: NIAAA & CSAP, monograph no. 3, 1995.

May, Philip A. "Overview of Alcohol Abuse: Epidemiology for American Indian Populations." In *Changing Numbers, Changing Needs: American Indian Demography and Public Health*, edited by G. Sandefur, R. R. Runfuss, and B. Cohen, 235–261. Washington, D.C.: National Academy Press, 1996.

Unrau, William E. *White Man's Wicked Water: The Alcohol Trade and Prohibition in Indian Country, 1802–1892.* Lawrence: University Press of Kansas, 1996.

Alexie, Sherman (1966–) *Spokane–Coeur d'Alene poet, novelist*

Sherman Alexie was born on October 7, 1966, on the Spokane reservation in Wellpinet, Washington. His father, Sherman Joseph Alexie, was a Coeur d'Alene, and his mother, Lillian Cox Alexie, a Spokane. Alexie grew up on the reservation and attended Reardan High School, where he was a star basketball player. He later attended Gonzaga University before transferring to Washington State, where his English professor, the poet Alex Kuo, encouraged him to write. His first works of poetry and short fiction were published in *Hanging Loose* magazine in 1990. It was this initial success that inspired him to quit drinking and concentrate on his writing.

Alexie's first small collection of fiction and poetry, *The Business of Fancydancing* (1992), was favorably reviewed in the *New York Times*, and his second collection of poems, *I Would Steal Horses* (1992), won the Slipstream Press's fifth annual chapbook contest. Alexie received a grant from the National Endowment for the Arts in 1992, and his work began to be featured in prominent magazines such as *Esquire* and *Vanity Fair*.

In 1993, Alexie released a collection of short stories, *First Indian on the Moon*. His next story collection, *The Lone Ranger and Tonto Fistfight in Heaven* (1994), dubbed "eerily humorous" by one reviewer, won him national praise. In 1998, the collection became the basis for the popular movie *Smoke Signals*, directed by Cheyenne-Arapaho filmmaker Chris Eyre and starring Adam Beach, Irene Bedard, and GARY DALE FARMER. Alexie's next work, *Reservation Blues: A Novel* (1995), about the adventures of a Catholic Indian rock 'n' roll band, confirmed his status as one of Native America's leading writers. Alexie also continued to write poetry, publishing *Water Flowing Home* in 1995 and *The Summer of Black Widows* in 1996.

Outspoken and controversial, Alexie has frequently attacked non-Indians who write about Indians, essentially arguing that only through the experience of being Indian can one legitimately understand Indians themselves. Although his works have been praised for exploding common Indian stereotypes, other critics have argued that he is merely substituting a newer, hipper stereotype rather than providing an accurate picture of Indian life.

Like JOHN TRUDELL and JOY HARJO, Alexie has expanded into music, teaming up with guitarist Jim Boyd, formerly of XIT, to produce an album called *Reservation Blues: The Soundtrack* (1997). In 1996, Alexie published *Indian Killer*, a novel about a serial killer loose in Seattle. In 1998, he published a chapbook of poetry, *The Man Who Loves Salmon*, and in 2000, produced a collection of stories, *The Toughest Indian in the World*. Also in 2000, he released a collection of poems and prose, *One Stick Song*. In 2002, Alexie directed a film version of *The Business of Fancydancing*. In 2003, he published his fourth collection of short stories, *Ten Little Indians*, and in 2005, *Dangerous Astronomy*, a book of poems. *Flight: A Novel* followed in 2007, and in that same year he won the National Book Award for Young People's Literature for *The Absolutely True Diary of a Part-Time Indian*.

One of Native America's most acclaimed poets and short story writers, Alexie is also a committed peace activist who has spoken against American intervention in the Middle East and other parts of the world.

Further Reading

Grassian, Daniel. *Understanding Sherman Alexie*. Columbia: University of South Carolina Press, 2005.

Alford, Thomas Wildcat (Gaynwah-piahsika, Gaynwah) (1860–1938) *Absentee Shawnee missionary, political leader*

Thomas Wildcat Alford was born in Indian Territory (now Oklahoma) in 1860. At 10 days old, he was given the name Gaynwah-piahsika (later shortened to Gaynwah), which means leader of a file or herd. His mother was said to be a great-granddaughter of Shawnee chief Tecumseh. His father was a counselor to one of the Shawnee chiefs.

Alford and his parents belonged to a group of Shawnee bands known as the Absentee Shawnee. By a treaty with the Shawnee in 1854, allotments of land were designated for the Shawnee who remained in Kansas, and provisions were made for "absentee members" in case they should return within five years; however, the absentees never took this offer. The group now known as the Absentee Shawnee descended in part from Shawnee bands in Ohio and Alabama that had moved to Spanish territory in Missouri and Texas in the late 18th century to escape conflicts with the United States. Driven out of east Texas in 1839 after Chief Bowles and his Cherokee were defeated by Texans led by Mirabeau Buonaparte Lamar, president of the Republic of Texas, the Shawnee bands settled on the Canadian River in what is now Oklahoma, where they were joined by the "absentees" from Kansas. In 1872, the Absentee Shawnee were recognized and their lands were confirmed by the U.S. government. They remain the most traditional of the Shawnee, preserving customs and ceremonies in their most complete form.

Alford had a traditional upbringing until the age of 12, when he began attending a mission school. He then went to Hampton Institute, the first federal boarding school to establish a program for Indians (1879; see PRATT, RICHARD HENRY); while there, he converted to Christianity. In 1882, Alford became one of the school's first three Indian graduates. He then returned to Indian Territory, but his Christianity led to conflict with the traditionals. For five years, he served as principal of the federal Shawnee school, where he also worked to educate adults. Later he taught at the Chilocco School.

Alford helped Special Agent Nathan S. Porter of the Indian Service (as the BUREAU OF INDIAN AFFAIRS was then known) to survey and allot tribal lands, and he was the first Absentee Shawnee to accept a fee-simple ALLOTMENT. (Allotment was a federal policy in force between 1887 and 1934, which mandated the subdivision of tribally held lands into small "allotments" that were then distributed to individual tribal members.)

The Absentee Shawnee government was abolished by the United States in 1893. White Turkey, the last hereditary chief of the Thawikila group of Shawnee, died in 1899; Big Jim, chief of the Kishpokotha Shawnee and Pekowitha Shawnee, died the following year. Alford's friend John King, who should have succeeded White Turkey, declined to accept the position because (in Alford's words) it had become nothing more than an empty honor. As a member of the tribe's business committee, King had some genuine authority. Alford chaired the business committee, the nearest thing the Absentee Shawnee had to a tribal government. He led an effort against what he called the "injustices of the Allotment system," going to Washington to represent his people.

Over the course of his life, Alford was an interpreter, teacher, surveyor, adviser, advocate, and representative of the tribe. In his speeches and publicity activities, he often pointed out the similarities between the traditional Shawnee code and Christianity, especially as exemplified in the life of their great leader Tecumseh, a comparison made with somewhat different emphasis by naturalist and Indian advocate ERNEST THOMPSON SETON. Alford wrote "Shawnee Domestic and Tribal Life," a chapter in W. A. Galloway's *Old Chillicothe* (1934), and a book, *Civilization* (as told to Florence Drake, 1936), one of the best modern accounts of traditional Shawnee culture. Thomas Alford died in 1938.

Further Reading

Alford, Thomas Wildcat. *Civilization and the Story of the Absentee Shawnees*. Norman: University of Oklahoma Press, 1979.

Allen, Paula Gunn (1939–2008) *Laguna Pueblo-Sioux poet, novelist, nonfiction writer*

Born Paula Marie Francis on October 24, 1939, in Cubero, New Mexico, Paula Gunn Allen was the daughter of a mother of mixed Laguna Pueblo, Sioux, and Scottish ancestry and a father of Lebanese descent. She grew up at Laguna Pueblo, then attended St. Vincent's Academy in Albuquerque. After the seventh grade, she attended a mission school in the town of San Fidel, New Mexico. Allen began her college education at Colorado Women's College in Denver but interrupted her studies to marry. She subsequently obtained a B.A. in 1966, an M.F.A. in 1968 at the University of Oregon, and a Ph.D. at the University of New Mexico in 1976. While completing her

doctorate, she taught at the University of New Mexico and at De Anza Community College in San Francisco.

Allen subsequently taught at Fort Lewis College in Durango, Colorado; the College of San Mateo; San Diego State University; San Francisco State University (where she directed the Native American Studies Program); the University of New Mexico, Albuquerque; and the University of California at Berkeley (where she was Professor of Native American and Ethnic Studies). She then became professor of English, creative writing, and American Indian studies at the University of California at Los Angeles (UCLA).

Allen's first work, a collection of poems entitled *The Blind Lion* (1974), focused on the "female journey to spiritual transcendence," a theme she would return to in *Skin and Bones* (1988). She explored the Native symbol of the "Spider Woman" and the quest for meaning in her novel *The Woman Who Owned the Shadows* (1983), a mixture of myth and tradition interwoven with contemporary questions of identity and gender relationships.

As professor of literature at UCLA, Allen published a number of scholarly essays, brought together in *The Sacred Hoop: Recovering the Feminine in American Indian Traditions* (1986), which cemented her status as one of the leading Native American feminists in the United States. In 1990, her anthology of Native women writers, *Spider Woman's Granddaughters* (1989), won the Columbus Foundation American Book Award. This was followed by a collection of stories and essays, *Grandmothers of the Light: A Medicine Woman's Sourcebook*, in 1991 and an anthology, *Song of the Turtle: American Indian Literature 1974–1994*, in 1996. She retired from her position as professor of English, creative writing, and American Indian studies at UCLA in 1999. In 2004, Allen published a biography of Pocahontas, which tells the story of the famous Indian maiden from a Native perspective. Paula Gunn Allen died on May 29, 2008.

Further Reading

Donovan, Kathleen M. *Feminist Readings of Native American Literature: Coming to Voice*. Tucson: University of Arizona Press, 1998.

Keating, Ana Louise. *Women Reading Women Writing: Self-Invention in Paula Gunn Allen, Gloria Anzaldua, and Audre Lorde*. Philadelphia: Temple University Press, 1996.

Allotment (1887–1934)

Allotment was a U.S. federal policy, beginning in 1887 and lasting until 1934, of breaking up tribal landholdings, with the goal of converting Indians from a subsistence economy to an agricultural economy. Under this policy, Indian lands, traditionally held in common by all the members of the tribe, would be subdivided into "allotments," usually of 160 acres, which would then be distributed to individual tribal members. After a period during which these allotments remained under federal trust, the allottees would be granted ownership in "fee simple"—that is, in the manner in which most Americans own private property (see LAND TENURE). Any remaining "surplus" lands still belonging to the tribe in common would be sold off to non-Indians or opened for settlement. The policy also intended an aggressive educational and vocational component to help Indians adjust to the transition.

The idea of allotting Indian lands was advocated as early as the colonial period, but although the option of owning individual parcels was incorporated into many 19th-century treaties, the vast majority of tribes refused to allow their lands to be allotted, preferring to manage them according to their traditional customs. By the late 19th century, however, hunger for Indian lands had grown, especially among western politicians, settlers, ranchers, and loggers who were openly clamoring for the end of the reservation system and in many cases even calling for the extermination of Indian tribes that stood in the way of settlement. Humanitarian reformers increasingly came to believe that the Indians' only hope for survival was to attempt to integrate their landholdings into the American system, which embodies numerous protections for private property. In addition, Allotment was seen by these reformers as a means of assimilating Indians into the American culture, dissolving tribal governments, eradicating Native religions, and in short, transforming the unique fabric of Indian life into the mainstream American experience (see ASSIMILATION).

The policy was inaugurated with the General Allotment Act of 1887, also known as the Dawes Act, after its sponsor Massachusetts senator Henry L. Dawes. Under the act, the president was authorized to survey a reservation, prepare a tribal census, then divide the tribally held land into 160-acre allotments for heads of families, 80-acre allotments for single individuals over the age of 18, and 40-acre allotments for unmarried persons under 18. The amount of land could be doubled if the land was suitable only for grazing. In order to prevent fraudulent or coerced transfers of the allotments to non-Indians, the legislation placed these allotments under trust for 25 years, during which the lands could not be sold, encumbered, or taxed. After that, the allottee or his or her heirs would receive a "patent-in-fee" (title to the land) and become eligible for U.S. citizenship. Lands not allotted were declared "surplus" and sold, and ostensibly the income would be returned to the tribe. But since this money could only be appropriated by Congress, the tribe in many cases never received it.

At the beginning of the process, Indian tribes still held title to approximately 138 million acres, or more than 10 percent of the continental United States, and with the exception of 11,000 acres, all of it was tribally owned. Most reservation Indians bitterly opposed the new policy; the act, however, gave them no choice once their reservation was slated for allotment.

The first INDIAN RESERVATIONS to be allotted were the ones most sought after by non-Indians and included the Santee Dakota (Sioux), Winnebago, and Omaha lands in Eastern Nebraska, as well as the Yankton Nakota (Sioux) and Sisseton Dakota (Sioux) reservations in the Dakotas. Soon after the Allotment policy began, more than 20 million acres of land were deemed "surplus" and opened for settlement. The

allotment of the reduced reservations proceeded more slowly, and as late as 1900, little more than 5 million acres had been allotted. However, the pace of allotment increased dramatically with the ascension of FRANCIS ELLINGTON LEUPP to the office of commissioner of the Indian Bureau in 1905. Between 1905 and 1912, both Leupp and his successor and protégé, ROBERT GROSVENOR VALENTINE, oversaw the allotment of approximately 24 million acres of Indian land. By 1913, more than 32 million acres of Indian lands were held by allottees, and only 35 million acres remained in tribal hands.

Leupp also supported an important amendment to the Dawes Act, the Burke Act of 1906. The Burke Act allowed the commissioner to remove the trust protections from an allottee's land if that person was declared "competent" to manage his or her own affairs, and it also allowed the commissioner to extend the trust period if necessary. Under Valentine and CATO SELLS, the Burke Act was used to establish controversial "Competency Commissions" that would travel from reservation to reservation, often forcing Indians to accept the removal of trust protections from their allotments.

Another important revision of the Dawes Act occurred in 1891 when it was amended to allow for the leasing of allotted lands to permit the young, the old, and those otherwise unable to work their lands to derive income from them.

In 1898, the CURTIS ACT extended Allotment to the Five Civilized Tribes (as the Oklahoma Cherokee, Choctaw, Chickasaw, Creek, and Seminole were known), who had until then managed to keep themselves exempt from the Dawes Act.

As had been predicted by the opponents of Allotment, allotted lands that lost their trust protection were quickly grabbed up by non-Indians. In 1903, whites purchased 44,494 acres of heirship allotments. That figure tripled the next year to 122,222 acres and remained steady over the next six years, averaging 95,000 acres lost per year. Despite these losses, the Allotment process continued. By 1920, more than 35 million acres of tribal lands had passed into allotments. As the trust periods began to expire and more Indians were declared "competent," the allotments were rapidly alienated (sold or stolen).

By 1934, when Allotment was ended by the INDIAN REORGANIZATION ACT, Indians held only a little more than 51 million acres of land, approximately 34 million acres tribally held and 17 million still in the hands of the allottees. While many reservations were never allotted, in almost every case these were in arid, isolated locations with no land of agricultural or ranching value. Indeed, fully half of the remaining Indian land base was desert or semidesert in character. Moreover, of the 51 million acres remaining, 11.5 million acres of grazing land and 2.5 million acres of the best farming land were under lease to non-Indians. Because of the complex heirship laws, in 1934 an additional 7 million acres were held in probate and could not be used by their owners.

Although Allotment was the product of liberal reformers, it dealt a devastating blow to Indian life and is generally regarded as a dismal failure. Despite the stated goal of turning Indians into ranchers and farmers, the policy did the opposite, destroying the successful adjustments many tribes had been making in agricultural and ranching operations—often in large communal operations that were run along traditional lines. Indian agriculture and ranching actually deteriorated after 1900. Moreover, the vocational and educational training that was a cornerstone of the original idea was never adequate, since most allotted land was held by adults, whereas education was directed to children. Thus, Indians were generally left to fend for themselves in trying to cope with the tremendous dislocations that occurred when the process began. By 1934, the policy had created an army of 100,000 landless and largely homeless Indians.

Worse, Allotment was a font of corruption and fraud that proved impervious to reform. In some cases, almost entire reservations, such as the White Earth Reservation (see BEAULIEU, GUS H.) and the Omaha Reservation, were illegally transferred to large ranchers, lumber companies, or real estate syndicates. Leasing of Indian allotments became a major source of collusion between local whites and officials of the BUREAU OF INDIAN AFFAIRS, as well as contributing further to the destruction of Indian farming and ranching. In oil-rich Oklahoma, the scale of looting was so great and reached such frenzied proportions that murder of Indian allottees to seize their lands was by no means uncommon (see OSAGE REIGN OF TERROR). The policy also opened the door to railroad magnates, oilmen, and other powerful interests, who liberally helped themselves to choice parts of Indian reservations with the assistance of a pliant Congress.

The net effect of the Allotment policy was the transfer of almost two-thirds of the existing Indian land base from Indian hands to non-Indians, the "checkerboarding" of many reservations that made them impossible to use efficiently, and the further impoverishment of most Indian people. The social consequences of Allotment were no less disastrous, damaging if not destroying the social integrity of tribes and breaking down family cohesion. Harshly criticized by the MERIAM REPORT in 1928, the policy was finally overturned by commissioner JOHN COLLIER six years later. By the end of the 20th century, more than 6 million acres of allotted land still existed. In most cases, however, the ownership of each parcel has passed to numerous heirs, leaving the lands so subdivided that they are unusable or must be leased out.

Further Reading

Banner, Stuart. *How the Indians Lost Their Land: Law and Power on the Frontier*, ch. 8, 257–290. Cambridge, Mass.: Harvard University Press, 2005.

Kickingbird, Kirke, and Karen Ducheneaux. *One Hundred Million Acres*. New York: Macmillan, 1973.

LaVelle, John P. "The General Allotment Act 'Eligibility' Hoax: Distortions of Law, Policy and History in the Derogation of Indian Tribes." *Wicazo Sa Review* 14, no. 1 (Spring 1999): 251–302.

McDonnell, Janet A. *The Dispossession of the American Indian, 1887–1934*. Bloomington: Indiana University Press, 1991.

Otis, D. S. *The Dawes Act and the Allotment of Indian Lands*. Norman: University of Oklahoma Press, 1973.

American Indian Association *See* ST. JAMES, RED FOX; TIPI ORDER OF AMERICA; URBANIZATION, AMERICAN INDIANS AND.

American Indian Chicago Conference (1961)

On June 12–18, 1961, a landmark meeting was held at the University of Chicago, sponsored by the NATIONAL CONGRESS OF AMERICAN INDIANS (NCAI), the University of Chicago, and the Emil Schwartzhaupt Foundation, and facilitated by anthropologist SOL TAX. Others involved in the planning were Robert Rietz, director of the Chicago Indian Center; Nancy Lurie, an anthropologist from the University of Michigan; HELEN WHITE PETERSON of NCAI; and the anthropologist Albert Wahrhaftig. There were 467 registered participants, perhaps 700 altogether, representing somewhere between 80 and 90 recognized or unrecognized tribes or bands. At the time, it was the largest and most tribally diverse assembly of Indians that had ever come together for a common goal.

Indian representatives included reservation, nonreservation, and urban Indians, professionals and traditionals, from federally recognized and nonfederally recognized tribes, and many antagonistic factions within these. Nevertheless, there was general agreement among the vast majority of Indians that the TERMINATION policy of the 1950s had been a failure and that a new policy had to be developed. As the 1960 presidential election drew near, it occurred to Tax that if Indians of the widest diversity were given the opportunity to draw up a statement of purpose, it would serve as a valuable guide to future Indian policy and an important means for educating the public. Termination had been a failure because it was based on the double ideological illusion that lands held in common were a "waste" of national wealth (a theory derived ultimately from John Locke) and that Indians were a "vanishing race" (rationalized by ideas drawn from Charles Darwin). The reality was, as Tax put it, that "the vanishing Indian is here to stay."

The Chicago Conference had links with another project with which Tax was involved, the summer workshops at Boulder, Colorado (see THOMAS, ROBERT KNOX). Many others were involved in both. D'ARCY MCNICKLE, as both director of the summer workshops and chair of the conference steering committee, planned the first week of the 1961 workshop to coincide with the conference, and some workshop participants were among the students and recent graduates who attended as observers. CLYDE WARRIOR, who would play an important role at the conference, was a very active student participant in both the 1961 and 1962 workshops.

In advance of the conference, McNickle drew up a working draft of a statement of goals, which was widely circulated among Indian tribes and organizations. Preliminary regional meetings were then held in various parts of the country to discuss it. Based on the responses, McNickle prepared a 30-page "Declaration of Indian Purpose," submitted to the first plenary session at Chicago, and chaired the committee that drafted the final text of the document. Much of the draft was written by the militant youth caucus led by HERBERT CHARLES

BLATCHFORD, Clyde Warrior, and MEL THOM. It was a statement that aimed for the first time to present a unified Native American position on the relations of Native peoples to the federal government.

The meeting was largely conducted by D'Arcy McNickle; Helen Peterson; Clarence Wesley, president of NCAI; and other NCAI people. It adhered to a democratic, though not a traditional Native, process. WILLIAM RICKARD, representing the Indian Defense League of America, played the role of gadfly at the conference by bringing up controversial issues, such as the recognition of treaty rights, traditional sovereignty, traditional Native religion, and acceptance of nonfederally recognized communities, that might otherwise not have been addressed. As chairman of the eastern regional planning meeting at Haverford College, member of the Indian steering committee for Chicago, and leader of the Long House League of North America—an organization that had revived the Iroquois tradition of providing a kind of guidance for small eastern communities from areas such as New Jersey, Virginia, New England—Rickard saw to it that representatives of traditional perspectives and from nonfederally recognized and nonreservation communities—mainly eastern tribes—participated in the planning sessions and were invited to the conference. The traditionals withdrew their support only at the end.

Rickard came to the meeting with the perspective of an Iroquois traditional, further energized by a recent visit to the traditional Hopi in Arizona. He was repeatedly frustrated by the moderate approach of the NCAI, particularly its JOHN COLLIER–era emphasis on U.S. citizenship and participation in democracy (see PETERSON, HELEN WHITE, and CLOUD, ELIZABETH BENDER ROE) instead of the traditionals' emphasis on Native sovereignty and citizenship in a Native nation. Rickard's emphasis on traditional sovereignty made a tremendous impression on many younger participants.

The NCAI was the first national pan-Indian organization founded by and for Indians. Its founders were the cream of the New Deal BUREAU OF INDIAN AFFAIRS bureaucracy, who by 1944 had seen trouble ahead and organized to preserve the hard-earned political gains tribes had won within the Collier system. They worked as a pan-Indian group, mostly with tribes that had no deep government tradition. Rickard found their approach boring and their agenda off-base and nontraditional. Yet without the work the NCAI had done since 1944, Termination would have gone much further than it did. Moreover, they were the only existing organization with the reputation and experience to make such a conference happen.

The Iroquois, on the other hand, had a long tradition of sophisticated political organization and, having escaped most federal jurisdiction, were not suffering from the same destruction of traditional community institutions. Having always worked through their own institutions and in light of their own history, however, they were fairly isolated from national Indian politics.

The Chicago Conference and the outspokenness of Rickard, Warrior, Thom, and Blatchford helped trigger the first quantum leap in Indian affairs since Collier's early days as head of the BIA. Fired up by Rickard and others, those most impatient with the conventional approach, exemplified by McNickle, an old Collier BIA man, and characterized by anthropologist Nancy Lurie as "relatively younger Indian people who considered the Declaration correct but too mildly stated and in any case requiring organization and action to achieve Indian purposes," met in Gallup, New Mexico, a short time later to found the NATIONAL INDIAN YOUTH COUNCIL (NIYC).

GERALD WILKINSON, later director of NIYC, reminisced: "By the end of the conference, something profound had happened to all the Indians there. . . . They could see that Indians were in a sense one people and were becoming more so. With the Pan-Indian Movement . . . in the 1960s and 1970s, it is easy to forget the profundity of the revolution that occurred in Chicago." It was the realization of the youth that by acting together they had political power, and thus the Chicago Conference marks the beginning of the RED POWER era.

Further Reading

Ablon, Joan. "The American Indian Chicago Conference." *Journal of American Indian Education* 1, no. 2 (January 1962): 17–23.

Clarkin, Thomas. *Federal Indian Policy in the Kennedy and Johnson Administrations, 1961–1969.* Albuquerque: University of New Mexico Press, 2001.

Hauptman, Laurence M., and Jack Campisi. "The Voice of Eastern Indians: The American Indian Chicago Conference of 1961 and the Movement for Federal Recognition." *Proceedings of the American Philosophical Society* 132, no. 4 (December 1988): 316–329.

Lurie, Nancy. "American Indian Chicago Conference." *Current Anthropology* 2, no. 5 (1961): 478–500.

American Indian Defense Association

See COLLIER, JOHN.

American Indian Federation (AIF) (1934–1940)

The American Indian Federation (AIF) originated in 1934, when several Indian groups that had already opposed BUREAU OF INDIAN AFFAIRS (BIA) commissioner JOHN COLLIER's work in the 1920s for increased tribal autonomy and land acquisition joined forces with such leaders as Navajo JACOB CASIMERA MORGAN and other critics of the Collier administration. Membership consisted of three groups: assimilated Indians who were successfully managing their property; missionized converts to conservative Protestant denominations; and disciples of CARLOS MONTEZUMA, who wanted to eliminate the BIA. The organization included some carryovers from the old SOCIETY OF AMERICAN INDIANS, notably THOMAS L. SLOAN, who was the AIF's attorney. Except for a brief period around 1936, dues-paying members probably never numbered more than a few hundred, but it was a vocal organization with excellent press contacts.

The AIF's main purpose was to stymie and discredit

Collier's policies, and it was the only national Indian organization to do so. Morgan, the first national vice chairman, used opposition to livestock reduction to help defeat the INDIAN REORGANIZATION ACT (IRA) on the Navajo Reservation (1935). Culling the vast sheep herds to prevent overgrazing, a conservation measure advocated by John Collier and the BIA, was deeply unpopular among the Navajo (Dineh), and Morgan succeeded in turning these bitter feelings against Collier's attempts to reform Indian governments through the IRA. Among his allies were Protestant missionaries, the Indian Rights Association, some traders, many returned students, and even some traditional leaders. Most important of all was Senator Dennis Chavez of New Mexico, who was against Collier's policies philosophically and also opposed expansion of the Navajo Reservation eastward. In the late 1930s, the AIF tried to secure a foothold on the Flathead Reservation in Montana.

The AIF opposed extension of the IRA to Oklahoma and was active in the campaign to repeal the IRA itself. By 1936, the organization had acquired 4,664 dues-paying members by proposing to lobby Congress for a bill to allot or "detribalize" the trust funds and guarantee each Indian $3,000 a year. Denounced by Secretary of the Interior Harold Ickes as a "swindle," the proposal was nevertheless given a hearing in 1939 by Senator Burton K. Wheeler, chair of the Senate Indian Affairs committee, now hostile to Collier.

Thirty AIF delegates met at the organization's first major convention in Salt Lake City on July 23–25, 1936. They were led by Joseph Bruner (1872–1957), a Creek who was also active in the Society of Oklahoma Indians; O. K. Chandler (1884–1952), a mixed-blood Cherokee who had been superintendent of the Quapaw Agency at Miami, Oklahoma; and Rev. Delos K. Lone Wolf (1870–1945), a Kiowa. They attacked Collier for opening up the gates to communism within the IRA, encouraging the decline of Christianity among Indians, and appointing radicals to his staff. They even circulated some Nazi propaganda. Collier saw this as a vendetta led by Chandler because in 1929, due to illegal trade with the Indians at Quapaw, Chandler's civil service status had been revoked.

When the pro-German senator Wheeler brought Indian witnesses in to testify about the incompetence or communistic tendencies of Collier and his colleagues, AIF was eager to cooperate. One witness was Seneca Alice Lee Jemison (1901–1964), whose articles had stirred up much negative opinion against Collier, particularly among church and missionary groups. In a hearing in June 1940 on Senate bill 2103, exempting some Indian groups from the IRA—a bill the AIF supported—Jemison cited, as an example of the bureau's alleged atheist-communist contempt for Christianity, a laudatory review, published in the BIA magazine, *Indians at Work*, of OLIVER LA FARGE's novel *The Enemy Gods*, which tells the story of a young Navajo who eventually rejects his Christian upbringing and returns to the traditional Navajo religion. The review had been written by young bureau employee D'ARCY McNICKLE. Collier accepted responsibility for it.

Ultimately, the AIF took its accusations to the Dies Committee, predecessor of the House Committee on Un-American Activities. However, evidence that Collier had been gathering since 1936 showed unmistakably that the AIF had ties to the pro-Nazi German-American Bund. Several of Jemison's contacts were indicted, resulting in the end of the AIF.

Further Reading

Deloria, Vine, and Clifford M. Lytle. *The Nations Within: The Past and Future of American Indian Sovereignty*. Austin: University of Texas Press, 1998.

Gracey, Marci Barnes. "Joseph Bruner and the American Indian Federation: An Alternative View of Indian Rights." In *Alternative Oklahoma: Contrarian Views of the Sooner State*, edited by Davis D. Joyce, 63–86. Norman: University of Oklahoma Press, 2007.

Hauptman, Laurence M. "The American Indian Federation and the Indian New Deal: A Reinterpretation." *Pacific Historical Review* 52 (1983): 378–402.

American Indian Movement (AIM)

The American Indian Movement (AIM) was a militant pan-Indian organization whose acts of showmanship and defiance transformed the Indian political landscape during the 1970s. Founded in July 1968 by a group of Chippewa (Anishinabe), including DENNIS JAMES BANKS, CLYDE BELLE-COURTE, George Mitchell, Eddie Benton Benai, and Mary Jane Wilson, the group was modeled after the Black Panthers' street patrols, to curb endemic police brutality against Indians in the Minneapolis area. To a large extent, AIM was an outgrowth of the TERMINATION policies of the 1950s and 1960s, which fostered a massive relocation program, leading to the rapid URBANIZATION of American Indians. Although militant activism had been practiced before, notably by the NATIONAL INDIAN YOUTH COUNCIL and the Iroquois under WILLIAM RICKARD and MAD BEAR ANDERSON, AIM became the first nationwide militant Indian movement, and it eventually hardened its tactics to include armed self-defense.

The street patrols were effective in reducing police brutality, even though AIM members such as Bellecourt were repeatedly beaten by the police for their efforts. As a social service and legal rights organization, AIM attracted support from church groups, community groups funded through the Office of Economic Opportunity, and even grants from corporations such as the Northern States Power Company. In 1970, AIM began the first of a succession of "freedom schools" that would spring up across the country (see EDUCATIONAL POLICY, AMERICAN INDIANS AND).

AIM was inspired by the 19-month occupation of Alcatraz (see ALCATRAZ ISLAND, OCCUPATION OF) lasting from November 1969 to June 1971, to take a more confrontational approach to solving local problems. When RUSSELL MEANS joined the organization in 1969, AIM gained someone whose dedication to national Indian issues and mastery of the media would enable the group to transform itself from a community-based organization to a powerful political movement in only a few short years. Another important addition to AIM was

JOHN TRUDELL, a masterful organizer who joined the organization in spring 1970. Unlike most other political organizers, the leaders of AIM, virtually all of whom were assimilated urban Indians, began to seek out spiritual advisers to help direct the movement. In 1970, they recruited LEONARD CROW DOG as well.

In fall 1970 and in spring 1971, AIM established a camp on Mount Rushmore, in the Black Hills of South Dakota, an area that had long been claimed and held sacred by the Sioux. Also during this time, Means led a dramatic takeover of the *Mayflower II*, a replica of the ship that carried the first Pilgrims and berthed in Plymouth, Massachusetts, on Thanksgiving Day 1970. AIM continued to show a flair for media events and demonstrations, but it was their success in winning justice for the murder of RAYMOND YELLOW THUNDER, who was brutally murdered in Gordon, Nebraska, in February 1972, that caught the attention of Indians nationwide. A successful demonstration in March that same year endeared AIM to the traditionalists of the Lakota reservation at Pine Ridge, South Dakota, who normally had little to do with urban Indians.

The organization was quiet over the next few months after its efforts to help the Chippewa of Leech Lake were rebuffed in April 1972. But in October 1972, AIM joined the TRAIL OF BROKEN TREATIES. AIM was only one of several participating organizations, but after the occupation of the BUREAU OF INDIAN AFFAIRS (BIA) headquarters that ended the demonstration, AIM's charismatic leaders left the event with most of the publicity. The group then returned to South Dakota, again to seek justice for a murdered Indian, Wesley Bad Heart Bull, but this time the demonstration ended in a melee with the police. This incident, known as the CUSTER RIOT, would once more bring AIM together with the traditional Lakota of Pine Ridge, under the leadership of their talented organizer, PEDRO BISSONETTE. The two groups formed an alliance to try to bring down the repressive government of Pine Ridge tribal chairman RICHARD WILSON. In an effort to publicize their grievances they chose to occupy the village of WOUNDED KNEE. The occupation, which lasted more than two months, and the long trial that followed it catapulted AIM to the forefront of Indian politics.

In some respects, AIM was not so much an organization as a loose movement led by various leaders who often worked independently of each other and sometimes clashed. AIM also attracted a seamy element of the Indian and non-Indian community who tarnished the reputation of the group even when it was achieving its greatest victories. The 1974 BOX CANYON MURDER in California did particular damage to AIM's prestige. The FBI, through their notorious COINTELPRO program, were also doing their best to discredit the movement by planting provocateurs and informers in the group. (COINTELPRO was an extralegal FBI operation established in the early 1960s to discredit the Civil Rights movement using tactics such as blackmail, disinformation, and occasionally violence.)

The showdown between AIM and the FBI turned violent in June 1975 when a shootout on the Pine Ridge Reservation left two FBI agents and an Indian dead and led to a massive manhunt for the killers, one of whom was believed by the FBI to be AIM member LEONARD PELTIER. In February 1976, another AIM member, ANNA MAE AQUASH, was found murdered on Pine Ridge. Between 1973 and 1975, more than 60 people were killed on the Pine Ridge Reservation. Most of these were AIM supporters, such as Pedro Bissonette, who was shot by a policeman. Russell Means was also shot by a policeman in 1975 but survived.

The FBI campaign also used the law to harass AIM members, and by 1976 most of them were in jail, in court, or in hiding. The movement began to disintegrate, and most of its leaders began to drop out. Backlash against AIM had a serious effect on federal Indian policy as, for example, in the relative lack of success of the AMERICAN INDIAN POLICY REVIEW COMMISSION. Although AIM chapters continued to function into the 1990s in Minneapolis and Denver, nationally the organization no longer exists. An offshoot of AIM, the INTERNATIONAL INDIAN TREATY COUNCIL, remains active, organizing indigenous peoples in other countries.

AIM was the culmination of the RED POWER MOVEMENT that began in the early 1960s. While its direct achievements are few, and while in many instances, such as its occupation of an electronics factory on the Navajo Reservation in 1975 (see MACDONALD, PETER), AIM's actions hurt more than they helped, its indirect achievements were enormous. AIM generated a resurgence of pride among Indians, and in particular Indian youth. The group also transformed the Indian political landscape, brushing aside aging groups such as the NATIONAL CONGRESS OF AMERICAN INDIANS and forcing a rapid dramatic change in federal Indian policy. AIM's call for self-determination led to this transformation, although not in the way they had planned. The Indian Self-Determination Act of 1975 was the culmination of an effort by the administrations of Presidents Richard Nixon and Gerald Ford to accommodate the rising tide of discontent, ending the stranglehold of the federal government over Indian tribes.

AIM also transformed the way America viewed Indians. Instead of an invisible people who were a part of the American heritage, and thus seen exclusively as being in the past, AIM put before the American public a modern Indian: proud, angry, and still very much alive.

See also BRUCE, LOUIS ROOK, JR.; THOMPSON, MORRIS.

Further Reading

Banks, Dennis, and Richard Erdoes. *Ojibwa Warrior: Dennis Banks and the Rise of the American Indian Movement.* Norman: University of Oklahoma Press, 2004.

Churchill, Ward, and Jim Vander Wall. *Agents of Repression: The FBI's Secret Wars against the Black Panther Party and the American Indian Movement.* Boston: South End Press, 1988.

The FBI Files on the American Indian Movement and Wounded Knee (1969–1977). 26 microfilm reels. Lexis Nexis.

Matthiessen, Peter. *In the Spirit of Crazy Horse.* New York: Viking, 1992.

Smith, Paul Chaat, and Robert Allen Warrior. *Like a Hurricane: The American Indian Movement from Alcatraz to Wounded Knee.* New York: New Press, 1996.

Weyler, Rex. *Blood of the Land: The Government and Corporate War against the American Indian Movement.* New York: Everest House, 1982.

American Indian Policy Review Commission (AIPRC)

The American Indian Policy Review Commission (AIPRC) was set up by Congress in the mid-1970s to thoroughly investigate all aspects of American Indian policy in the United States as a basis for drawing up legislation to improve life for all Indians. Though the original plan was well conceived, the AIPRC would fall far short of its goals, due to an unfavorable climate in Congress.

Demonstrators occupied the BUREAU OF INDIAN AFFAIRS (BIA) on November 2, 1972 (see TRAIL OF BROKEN TREATIES), and in February 1973 there was an armed standoff at WOUNDED KNEE, South Dakota. In opening remarks at a hearing on Wounded Knee on June 16, 1973, Senator James G. Abourezk of South Dakota, chair of the Senate subcommittee on Indian Affairs, criticized Congress's neglect of Indian problems. On the same day, he introduced Senate Joint Resolution 133, which aimed to set up an American Indian Policy Review Commission to allow Congress to comprehensively study the history and legal basis of federal-Indian relations "to support the formulation of more positive and effective national Indian policies and programs." A companion bill was sponsored by Congressman Lloyd Meeds as House Joint Resolution 881.

Abourezk was mindful of the MERIAM REPORT of 1928, the most comprehensive study up to that time and one that had led to tremendous changes in Indian policy through the INDIAN NEW DEAL (see INDIAN REORGANIZATION ACT). Now there was a general consensus within the American Indian community that during WORLD WAR II and the TERMINATION period, the great New Deal Indian legislation had been distorted in its execution and administration. A new study was sorely needed in order to bring about a fundamentally just Indian policy. From the start, brilliant American Indian thinkers such as VINE DELORIA, JR., and K. KIRKE KICKINGBIRD were involved in formulating this vision.

The proposal was for an even more comprehensive study in which, unlike the Meriam Report, Indians would play a leading part. Moreover, whereas the Meriam Report had been an executive branch study, this would be congressional. The formulators of the bill aimed to steer clear of the executive branch because they did not want the BIA directly involved. They did want to include in the study both urban Indians (at that time already 50 percent of the Native population) and nonfederally recognized tribes, neither of which were under BIA jurisdiction. Finally, they wanted the studies to focus on law and federal treaties rather than on administration.

Thanks to the considerable leverage Abourezk enjoyed in Congress, the AIPRC was authorized by an act passed on January 1, 1975. Congressional conservatives, though unable to block passage, did manage to weaken the legislation. Whereas Abourezk had originally wanted the commission to be made up of a large and representative group of Indian leaders, the bill as passed provided for only five Native members, in part because of the Interior Committee's fear that a larger number would make it possible for the AMERICAN INDIAN MOVEMENT (AIM) to be represented. The small number of Indian slots imposed very special selection criteria. Only three could be from federally recognized tribes, one had to be from a nonfederally recognized tribe, and the fifth had to come from an urban community. There was a broad feeling that neither of the recognized tribal representatives could be Sioux (Dakota, Lakota, Nakota) or Navajo (Dineh) because, being by far the most populous, either of these two groups would destroy the balance of representation.

Selection was an informal process. The final list, drawn up with a large amount of community input from all over the country, contained 200 names, out of which six members of Congress selected the five Native commissioners. Theoretically, these would represent the spectrum of Native American viewpoints, but in reality this was impossible. In the end, those selected were all effective lobbyists with Washington experience.

In addition to the five Indians, the commission consisted of three senators and three congressmen, all selected by Congress. The members were: Senators Lee W. Metcalf (Montana), James Abourezk (South Dakota), and Mark O. Hatfield (Oregon), as well as Congressmen Lloyd Meeds (Washington), Sidney R. Yates (Illinois), and Sam Steiger (Arizona). On March 5, 1975, Abourezk was designated as chairperson, and the congressional members selected the five Indian members. Federally recognized tribes were represented by ADA ELIZABETH DEER (Menominee, Wisconsin), Jake Whitecrow (Quapaw-Seneca, Oklahoma), and John Borbridge (Tlingit-Haida, Alaska). Nonfederally recognized tribes were represented by Adolph Dial (Lumbee, North Carolina), and urban Indians by LOUIS ROOK BRUCE, JR. (Mohawk-Sioux, New York).

Because the commission was structured on the basis of representation rather than to mandate specific recommendations, the act provided structure through nine task forces to investigate: (1) trust responsibility and federal-Indian relationships, including treaty review; (2) tribal government; (3) federal administration and structure of Indian affairs; (4) federal, state, and tribal jurisdiction; (5) Indian education; (6) Indian health; (7) reservation development; (8) urban, rural nonreservation, terminated, and nonfederally recognized Indians; and (9) Indian law revision, consolidation, and codification.

As the commission proceeded, it was decided to limit the focus of Task Force 8 to urban and rural nonreservation Indians and to create an additional Task Force 10 for terminated and nonfederally recognized Indians. A new task force (11) on alcohol and drug abuse was also created, relieving Task Force 6 (health) of this large topic. All task forces were to submit reports to the commission by August 1976. Each task force consisted of three persons, at least two of whom had to be of

Indian descent. In commission meetings, it was decided to add a specialist to each task force to take over major administrative responsibilities.

Selection of the task forces took place from July through September 1975. Out of an original pool of 460 nominees, 44 were chosen, and the selection generally tended to reflect "traditional" Indian cultural values. Although the NATIONAL TRIBAL CHAIRMAN'S ASSOCIATION (NTCA) filed a suit claiming that the task force selection was unrepresentative of a large percentage of the Indian population, the suit was rejected by the federal court.

The commission's work was hindered by a growing backlash in Congress against activities of the American Indian Movement, particularly the shootout between members of AIM and the FBI at Pine Ridge in summer 1975 (see PELTIER, LEONARD). A major obstacle, however, was that Congress had set aside only $2.5 million for the commission's work. The AIPRC had been conceived amid the crisis of the early 1970s by Native intellectuals working with Senator Abourezk on a fundamental job of rethinking from the ground up. The selection of commission and task force members, difficult as it was, still had some resemblance to what the bill's framers had in mind. But opponents in Congress could reduce the effectiveness of the final report by limiting the amount of money and time available for task force hearings. This would prevent the truly thorough studies mandated by the commission's charter and generate hurried and superficial recommendations, lacking the historical perspective mandated by the charter.

A problem area for the task forces was the method of data collection, mainly through hearings in local communities. This provided good information on community concerns, but the lack of hard data would seriously compromise the validity of the commission's eventual recommendations.

The commissioners were in a corner; they simply had to do the best they could with very limited resources. Nevertheless, the draft reports, going into the 1976 elections, gradually allowed the commissioners to see the American Indian population for the first time as a national political constituency—a fact recognized by both conservative and liberal members. The conservative members drew up minority rebuttal reports, leading to a split within the commission. This put further pressures on the task forces, and the final result was a far cry from what had originally been envisioned, and by no means an adequate basis for developing an Indian policy for the 21st century.

Further Reading

Brown, Anthony D. *New Directions in Federal Indian Policy: A Review of the American Indian Policy Review Commission*. Los Angeles: American Indian Studies Center, University of California, Los Angeles, 1979.
Kickingbird, Kirke. "American Indian Policy Review Commission: A Prospect for Future Change in Federal Indian Policy." *American Indian Law Review* 3 (1975): 243–253.
Meeds, Lloyd. "The Indian Policy Review Commission." In *American Indians and the Law*, edited by Lawrence Rosen, 9–24. New Brunswick, N.J.: Transaction Books, 1978. (Originally issued as vol. 40, no. 1, of *Law and Contemporary Problems*.)

American Indian Religious Freedom Act (AIRFA) (1978)

The American Indian Religious Freedom Act (AIRFA) was legislation enacted to safeguard the practice of Native religions. Traditional Native religions, as well as the NATIVE AMERICAN CHURCH and other pan-Indian religions, had been under attack by Christian groups and government officials since the 19th century. Although in the 1930s, BUREAU OF INDIAN AFFAIRS commissioner JOHN COLLIER ended overt attempts to ban Indian religions and christianize Indians, the federal policy since the late 19th century, Native religions were still subject to interference and harassment. In particular, Indian sacred sites, burial grounds, and the use of sacred plants such as peyote, were not accorded protection under the law. After agitation on the part of national Indian leaders, Congress passed AIRFA in 1978. Although the act clearly protects the right of American Indians, Alaska Natives, Aleut, and native Hawaiians to their traditional religions, including access to sites, possession of sacred objects, and the freedom to conduct their ceremonies in the manner they see fit, it has failed to prevent states from aggressively enforcing laws that infringe on Indian beliefs. In particular, Indian prisoners may still be denied the right to possess ceremonial objects, conduct ceremonies, and use peyote. Also, the Supreme Court has held that sacred sites, such as MOUNT GRAHAM, are not protected from development that is in the public interest, and the government can prevent the destruction of these sites only if the development is specifically intended to impair the religion. The Court has ruled that AIRFA is simply a policy statement, not enforceable legislation, and as such merely offers guidelines.

See also RELIGIOUS FREEDOM, AMERICAN INDIAN.

Further Reading

Feldman, Alice E. "Othering Knowledge and Unknowing Law: Oppositional Narratives in the Struggle for American Indian Religious Freedom." *Social & Legal Studies* 9, no. 4 (2000): 557–582.
Harjo, Suzanne Shown. "American Indian Religious Freedom Act at 25." *Native American Policy: Network Journal of the Native American Studies Association (NASA)* 14, no. 2 (Fall 2003): 43.

American Indian Science and Engineering Society (AISES)

The American Indian Science and Engineering Society (AISES) was founded in Boulder, Colorado, in 1977 by a group of American Indian scientists, engineers, and educators, including FRANK CHARLES DUKEPOO, a Hopi-Laguna geneticist; CAROL METCALF GARDIPE, a Penobscot-Passamaquoddy geophysicist; and ALFRED QÖYAWAYMA, a Hopi engineer who became its first chairman. AISES's chief goal is to remedy the low enrollment, low graduation numbers, and high dropout rates of Indian college students, as compared to other ethnic groups, and to address the great underrepresentation of American Indians in science and technological fields. NORBERT S. HILL, JR., an Oneida educator, served as director from 1983 to 1998. By 2008, AISES had more than 5,000 members.

AISES encourages American Indians and Alaska Natives to consider careers in science, engineering, business, medicine, and other related fields. It offers financial, academic, and cultural support to Native students from middle school through the graduate level; trains teachers to develop culturally appropriate curricula for Indian students; maintains chapters on the college and professional level; sponsors student science fairs, summer internships, and college preparatory programs; and publishes a quarterly journal, *Winds of Change*.

Anderson, Cora Reynolds (1882–1950) *Chippewa politician, state legislator*

The first woman to serve in the Michigan House of Representatives and the only woman ever elected to the state legislature from Michigan's Upper Peninsula, Cora Reynolds was born in L'Anse, Michigan, on April 10, 1882. She was of French-English and Keweenaw Bay Chippewa descent. After graduation from L'Anse High School in 1899, she attended the Graves Normal School in Petoskey for a term and then taught school at the Methodist Episcopal Mission (later called the Zeba Indian Mission or Foot-school) at L'Anse. Following this, she took a year of special training at the Haskell Institute (now Haskell Indian Nations University), after which she taught in the Skanee, Michigan, school for two terms. On December 25, 1903, she married Charles H. Anderson, a Skanee farmer and lumberman.

A Republican, Cora Anderson was elected without opposition on November 4, 1924, to represent Michigan's Iron District (Baraga, Iron, Keweenaw, and Ontonagon counties) in the state House of Representatives. She served through 1926.

Anderson had a long-standing interest in welfare work, particularly public health issues in Baraga County, and was instrumental in securing the first public health nurse in the county, Jennie Knevles, R.N., whose salary was paid out of the proceeds of Christmas Seal sales (which Anderson also ran) for the treatment of tuberculosis. She also assisted her husband in prohibition work, making the county and state dry. She joined the Grange in Kalamazoo in 1910, was an officer in the state Grange for eight years, and was the Upper Peninsula state Grange Master for four years. A Methodist Episcopal church member, she was active in church and literary societies. Cora Reynolds Anderson died on March 11, 1950, in L'Anse. She was later inducted into the Historical Division of the Michigan Women's Hall of Fame, Michigan State University, Lansing.

Anderson, Mad Bear (Wallace Anderson)
(1927–1985) *Tuscarora activist*

A Tuscarora activist during the 1950s and 1960s and forerunner of the militancy of the RED POWER MOVEMENT, Wallace

Tuscarora activist Mad Bear Anderson is pictured here in 1958 on the Tuscarora reservation in New York State, on which the State Power Authority planned to build a reservoir. *(AP/Wideworld)*

Anderson was born in Buffalo, New York, on November 9, 1927, and raised on the Tuscarora Indian reservation near Niagara Falls. A member of the Bear Clan, his mother nicknamed him Mad Bear for his quick temper as a youth. During World War II, he joined the U.S. Navy at the age of 16, piloting landing craft in the invasions of Saipan and Okinawa. After serving in Korea, he worked in the merchant marine until New York State's attempt to annex a part of the Tuscarora reservation converted him to a life of militant activism.

In 1958, Robert Moses, head of the New York State Power Authority, decided to use one-fifth of the Tuscarora reservation as a storage reservoir for the giant St. Lawrence Seaway project. Led by WILLIAM RICKARD; his father, CLINTON RICKARD; and Elton Green, the Tuscarora managed to somewhat mitigate the size of the reservoir, originally slated to cover 1,383 acres of Tuscarora land, in the end compromising by allowing the flooding of only 560 acres. This effectively handed the powerful Moses, who had bulldozed whole neighborhoods and towns with his many massive development projects, one of the few defeats of his career. Anderson himself was arrested twice by police for participating in demonstrations blocking Power Authority construction workers.

The next year, Anderson helped lead a revolt of the traditional Iroquois on the Six Nations Reserve in Ontario against their Canadian-appointed government officials. On March 29, 1959, he attempted a citizen's arrest of GLENN LEONIDAS

EMMONS, the notorious commissioner of the BUREAU OF INDIAN AFFAIRS, a tactic that would be copied by RUSSELL MEANS and RICHARD OAKES a decade later. In July that same year, Anderson caused a sensation by leading a delegation of Indians, including Miccosukee who were fighting for recognition of their land rights, to Cuba, where they met with Fidel Castro (see TIGER, WILLIAM BUFFALO).

In 1964, Anderson aided William Rickard in organizing the North American Indian Unity Caravans, which were influential in reviving Native traditions among younger Indians; Anderson led many of the caravans himself. He briefly joined the occupation of ALCATRAZ ISLAND in 1969, later bringing traditional healer Peter Mitten to a hospital to help bring Richard Oakes out of a coma he had suffered after a barroom brawl.

Unlike HANK ADAMS or CLYDE WARRIOR, Anderson preferred working alone to building a movement. His chief impact throughout his life was to inspire others to take a more militant stance toward solving Indian problems. He participated in the TRAIL OF BROKEN TREATIES but was eventually overshadowed by the rise of the AMERICAN INDIAN MOVEMENT (AIM), a younger group of militants who possessed an even greater flair for the dramatic. Nonetheless, Anderson continued to champion Indian causes through speaking engagements and travels across the world, though his later years were plagued by illness. Mad Bear Anderson died on December 20, 1985, in Sanborn, New York.

Further Reading

Boyd, Doug. *Mad Bear: Spirit, Healing, and the Sacred in the Life of a Native American Medicine Man*. New York: Simon & Schuster, 1994.

Kersey, Harry A. "The Havana Connection: Buffalo Tiger, Fidel Castro, and the Origin of Miccosukee Tribal Sovereignty, 1959–1962." *American Indian Quarterly* 25, no. 4 (Fall 2001): 491–507.

anthropologists and American Indians

By the start of the 20th century, quite a few Native people were already working in anthropology and ethnology, among them FRANCIS LA FLESCHE (Omaha), JOHN NAPOLEON BRINTON HEWITT (Tuscarora), JAMES R. MURIE (Pawnee), MARIE LOUISE BOTTINEAU BALDWIN (Chippewa), WILLIAM JONES (Fox), and ARTHUR C. PARKER (Seneca). LOUIS SHOTRIDGE (Chilkat Tlingit) did ethnographic fieldwork in Alaska for the University of Pennsylvania Museum from 1912 to 1932.

By the 1890s, anthropologist FRANZ BOAS had realized that the prevalent low estimations by Western scholars of the Indian race and cultures were simply wrong. Earlier theories asserted either major racial differences, implying that Native survival was impossible, or a one-directional scheme of "stages of civilization," implying that assimilation was inevitable. Influenced by Boas, anthropologists now appreciated Native cultures and saw in them things "worth saving." They could show that policies imposing extreme cultural change were ignorant and counterproductive, and opposition to such policies could now be based not on romantic sentimentality but on sound social science.

This new attitude came from being more open-minded and attentive to the Indians themselves. Among early non-Indian researchers especially open to the Native world view were CONSTANCE GODDARD DU BOIS, MELVIN RANDOLPH GILMORE, GEORGE BIRD GRINNELL, and Boas's student FRANK GOULDSMITH SPECK. Annoyed with the assimilationism (see ASSIMILATION) promoted by the SOCIETY OF AMERICAN INDIANS, Speck encouraged Indians to study anthropology so as to better appreciate the value of their own cultures and help preserve them. Among his Native students were GLADYS TANTAQUIDGEON and MOLLY SPOTTED ELK.

With Progressive Era reformers seeking to base "good government" on science rather than religion or politics, authorities like Boas and psychologist G. Stanley Hall (1844–1924) had a noticeable policy influence. Under Indian commissioners FRANCIS ELLINGTON LEUPP (1904–09) and ROBERT GROSVENOR VALENTINE (1909–12), overt repression of Indian culture eased somewhat: "I like the Indian for what is Indian in him," said Leupp. But the change was superficial, given that the institutionalized land- and culture-destroying ALLOTMENT program intensified at this very time. Nevertheless, it was the first glimmer of a more respectful official attitude toward Native culture, referred to by JOHN COLLIER, in a 1923 letter to the *New York Times*, as "the brief illumination and uprising of common sense which occurred under . . . Indian Commissioner Leupp. . . ."

While Leupp's successors Valentine and CATO SELLS hired some personnel with sociological or social-work training, they made little use of anthropologists. However, archaeologist WARREN KING MOOREHEAD, of the Board of Indian Commissioners, lobbied Valentine to set up a Bureau of Indian Arts and Industries within the Office of Indian Affairs, led by himself and with a small staff of people with "ethnological" experience. Though the plan was not adopted, it foreshadowed the INDIAN ARTS AND CRAFTS BOARD.

By 1918, only seven institutions in the United States had anthropology departments; 39 others gave some instruction. That year, seven anthropologists, Indian and non-Indian, testified against the Hayden Bill, which would prohibit all use of peyote, on grounds of Indian cultural and religious freedom. James Mooney (1861–1921), who had studied the cultural use of peyote for almost three decades and experimented with it himself, gave the most notable testimony; he would later assist in the formation of the NATIVE AMERICAN CHURCH. For this, the government ejected him from the Kiowa Reservation and would not allow him back, even at the urging of the Smithsonian Institution.

When Indian Commissioner CHARLES HENRY BURKE issued the 1923 DANCE ORDERS, many anthropologists wrote protest letters to newspapers. According to John Collier, however, during the crucial Indian rights struggles of the 1920s, only two anthropologists really worked to restore tribal authority and to end Allotment: Theodore L. Kroeber, who became a board member of Collier's American Indian Defense

Association in 1924, and John P. Harrington, of the Bureau of American Ethnology. The ethnologist F. W. Hodge, a friend of ERNEST THOMPSON SETON, also lent his support (see RELIGIOUS FREEDOM, AMERICAN INDIAN).

Nine anthropologists served on the COMMITTEE OF ONE HUNDRED (1923)—a panel formed to discuss government Indian policy—including Kroeber, Clark Wissler, and Parker, who headed the committee. Herbert J. Spinden, curator of primitive art at the Brooklyn Museum and president of the Eastern Association on Indian Affairs (see ASSOCIATION ON AMERICAN INDIAN AFFAIRS), was active on the American Anthropological Association's Standing Committee on Indian Affairs in the 1920s. While there was virtually no anthropological involvement in the MERIAM REPORT (1928), Commissioner CHARLES JAMES RHOADS hired anthropologist OLIVER LA FARGE (1929) as his adviser.

On becoming commissioner of Indian affairs in 1933, Collier advocated the use of social science to improve Indian administration. In 1934, he consulted with leading anthropologists and ethnologists and sought cooperation from both the American Anthropological Association and the anthropology section of the American Association for the Advancement of Science. He invited La Farge to participate in the hearings on the INDIAN REORGANIZATION ACT and asked other anthropologists to testify by way of a questionnaire on specific areas of Indian life. Among those who did were John R. Swanton, Ralph Linton, La Farge, Harrington, Kroeber, and Boas.

In January 1936, Collier established an applied anthropology unit under H. Scudder Mekeel of Harvard University. (Mekeel hoped to employ applied anthropologists in every branch of the BUREAU OF INDIAN AFFAIRS (BIA), but there was never adequate funding.) The unit was intended to help field agents in "cultural translation" between Western political assumptions (such as majority vote and "loyal opposition"), embodied in the model constitutions, and the cultural values of each tribe. Old-line BIA employees resented the anthropologists, however, and the program was not a success. The unit was dismantled in late 1937.

Anthropologists also worked in the education branch (for example, La Farge and Edward Sapir developed an alphabet for the Navajo language) and with Indian farmers in studies for the Department of Agriculture's Soil Conservation Service and Bureau of Agricultural Economics. In his book *Raw Material* (1943), La Farge advocated a "wedding between ethnology and politics." As adviser to Commissioner Rhoads, he had tried, unsuccessfully, to set up a working relationship with the Bureau of American Ethnology. In the Collier years, La Farge drew anthropologists Eduard C. Lindeman, Clyde Kluckhohn, and Harry Shapiro into the Association on American Indian Affairs.

Distinguished Native anthropologists of the 1930s include ELLA CARA DELORIA (Lakota), who worked closely with Boas, and ARCHIE PHINNEY (Nez Perce), a student of Boas, and William Morgan (Navajo).

In 1940, together with the University of Chicago's Committee on Human Development, the BIA conducted a systematic study of Indian administration among five tribes. Similar research continued under the National Indian Institute, of which Collier was a director from 1945 to 1950.

Because Boas had encouraged study of the "primitive" side of cultures rather than contemporary issues, culture-change studies were rare before the 1940s. His fear of compromising scientific objectivity ignored the objective fact that BIA policies were affecting the societies under study. Furthermore, anthropology was already politicized prior to Collier, since neither missionaries nor anthropologists could work on reservations without the BIA's permission, as the example of Mooney previously discussed demonstrates. Finally, studies of cultural traditions had always taken priority because these traditions were rapidly disappearing. Yet had anthropologists sought to influence policy, they might have helped save, rather than simply record, traditions and languages.

WORLD WAR II halted further expansion of anthropological studies in the BIA, and after the war these programs were phased out. Under TERMINATION, anthropologists found themselves in the classic professional consultant's dilemma: They knew the policy was bad, but how could they criticize their employers? To be of any benefit, they had to preserve an appearance of neutrality. Be that as it may, anthropologists were never invited to testify in Termination hearings. As Getches and Wilkinson note (in the second edition of *Federal Indian Law: Cases and Materials*): "In more than 1,700 pages of testimony [on the various Termination bills] there is no statement by a sociologist, an anthropologist, a social worker, or anyone else trained in the social sciences." Anthropologists, however, were brought in as expert witnesses before the INDIAN CLAIMS COMMISSION, which began in 1946.

Reacting to Termination, SOL TAX and others developed the concept of "action anthropology." Through his research work, the anthropologist interacts with the community whether he wants to or not, often only for his own benefit and in ways that do not help and may actually harm the community. Through action anthropology, however, the anthropologist learns about the culture precisely by helping the community toward some goal that the community itself defines.

PHILLEO NASH, a former Collier anthropologist, served with James Officer on the Kennedy Task Force on Indian Affairs (1961), which effectively was the beginning of the end of Termination. Nash then became commissioner, with Officer as assistant commissioner. For the first time, anthropologists ran the BIA. Nash worked well with the NATIONAL CONGRESS OF AMERICAN INDIANS. He had an activist style and would often go out to lead initiatives on reservations himself. Leaving office in 1966, he worked as a volunteer with the Menominee in their fight against Termination (see WASHINAWATOK, JAMES A.). Nancy Lurie, one of the action anthropologists who also worked with the Menominee, saw "no rationality" in the Termination policy (as she stated in a 1973 House Indian Affairs Committee hearing). The Cherokee anthropologist ROBERT KNOX THOMAS was an important influence in Indian affairs in the 1960s. BEATRICE MEDICINE and SHIRLEY HILL WITT studied women's issues.

In his 1969 book *Custer Died for Your Sins*, VINE
DELORIA, JR., strongly criticized anthropologists: "... behind
each policy and program with which Indians are plagued, if
traced completely back to its origin, stands the anthropologist.... The fundamental thesis of the anthropologist is that
people are objects for observation, people are then considered
objects for experimentation, for manipulation, and for eventual extinction." Deloria argued that anthropologists work for
themselves and give nothing back to Indians; they represent
themselves as "experts," and even many Indians believe in
their superior knowledge. Wanting Indians to be "primitive,"
they create a false consciousness in Indians.

Another common criticism was that anthropologists
acquire "secret" knowledge, usually from informants who are
hostile to the traditionals (for example, JOSIE BILLY) and therefore willing to make it available to the public and the government. This criticism has especially been leveled against Native
anthropologists (La Flesche, Shotridge, and Tewa ALFONSO
ORTIZ, to name a few). However, in hindsight it is clear that
much of the data they collected on "primitive" culture would
otherwise have been lost, and is now extremely valuable to
Indians themselves.

At the end of the 20th century, two clear trends were
observable: (1) an increasing number of Indians were becoming anthropologists, and (2) anthropologists began taking on
more of an activist role, helping tribes defend their territories and ways of life and helping develop programs for cultural preservation (see INDIGENOUS LANGUAGE USE). In short,
anthropological expertise was being increasingly implemented
for purposes chosen by Indian communities themselves.

Further Reading

Biolsi, Thomas, and Larry Zimmerman, eds. *Indians and
    Anthropologists: Vine Deloria, Jr., and the Critique of
    Anthropology.* Tucson: University of Arizona Press, 1997.
Bonney, Rachel A., and J. Anthony Paredes. *Anthropologists
    and Indians in the New South.* Tuscaloosa: University of
    Alabama Press, 2001.

Aquash, Anna Mae (Anna Mae Pictou)
(1945–1976) *activist*

Anna Mae Aquash was a Micmac Indian rights activist and
member of the AMERICAN INDIAN MOVEMENT (AIM). She
was born on March 27, 1945, in Shubenacadie, Nova Scotia,
the third daughter of Mary Ellen Pictou and Thomas Levi.
Levi abandoned the family before Anna Mae's birth, and in
1949 her mother married Noel Sapir, a poor handyman who
brought them to the Micmac reserve of Pictou Landing.

Anna Mae's youth was hard, and the family's constant
poverty worsened when Sapir died of cancer in 1956. In 1961,
Mary Ellen Pictou abandoned her children, leaving Anna Mae
and her sister Mary to care for their 10-year-old half brother,
Francis. Anna Mae quit school and took the only work she
could find, as a migrant farmworker in Maine, before moving to Boston with fellow tribesman Jake Maloney in 1962. In

1964, she gave birth to the first of two daughters, but by 1969
she had separated from Maloney and had become active in
Boston Indian politics, helping to found the Boston Indian
Council. On Thanksgiving Day 1970, she participated in a
takeover of the *Mayflower II* in Plymouth, Massachusetts, led
by RUSSELL MEANS, and she joined other Boston Indians in
traveling to Washington for the TRAIL OF BROKEN TREATIES
the next year.

By this time, she had met Nogeeshik Aquash, a Chippewa
artist, and together they joined AIM, participating in the
occupation of WOUNDED KNEE in March 1973. Tough and
resourceful, Anna Mae helped dig bunkers and served as a
courier in and out of the besieged encampment. On April 12,
1973, Nogeeshik and Anna Mae were married in Wounded
Knee in a ceremony conducted by WALLACE HOWARD BLACK
ELK. They left the occupation before it ended on May 8, escaping the criminal charges filed against those who remained.

After Wounded Knee, the couple returned to Boston
but, unable to establish an AIM survival school as they had
planned, they moved on to Ottawa. In early 1974, Anna Mae
Aquash organized a successful show at the National Arts
Center in Ottawa before joining AIM in St. Paul, Minnesota.
In August that year, AIM sent Anna Mae, now separated from
Nogeeshik, to Los Angeles to set up a West Coast office and
keep an eye on Douglass Durham, who would later be exposed
as a Federal Bureau of Investigation (FBI) informer. An effective organizer, Aquash was then sent in January 1975 to help
the Menominee who were occupying a church building in
Gresham, Wisconsin. After the occupation ended inconclu-
sively in February, she returned to St. Paul, where she organized a benefit for local AIM schools. Aquash then moved to
the Rosebud Reservation in South Dakota before joining the
growing AIM contingent living in the community of Oglala
on the adjacent Pine Ridge Reservation.

After the occupation of Wounded Knee had ended, AIM
leader DENNIS BANKS married Kamook Nichols, an Oglala
Lakota Sioux from Pine Ridge, and was leading the resistance
to Pine Ridge tribal chairman RICHARD WILSON's increasingly
heavy-handed leadership. AIM had by this time become the
focus of a sophisticated and sometimes violent FBI campaign
to discredit and destroy the organization, and the two sides
were locked in bitter combat over who would control the reservation. The FBI invaded the AIM encampment at Oglala on
June 26, 1975, leading to the death of an Indian man and two
FBI agents (see PELTIER, LEONARD). Although Aquash was not
present at the shoot-out, she aided the fugitive AIM members
in their escape. She was with Dino Butler (see BUTLER, NILAK)
in September when he was caught by the FBI at the camp of
LEONARD CROW DOG in Rosebud. Charged with possession
of weapons, she was released on bail, though in November she
was arrested again in Oregon while helping Leonard Peltier
flee to Canada.

Transported to Pierre, South Dakota, to face the weapons
charges, Aquash was again released on bail. Since the shoot-
out, Pine Ridge had been wracked by violence, largely from
Dick Wilson's paramilitary "goon squads," who went on a

shooting spree in January 1976 that resulted in the death of Byron DeSersa, a great-grandson of BLACK ELK. The death of PEDRO BISSONETTE while in the custody of a BUREAU OF INDIAN AFFAIRS police officer two years earlier had made it frighteningly clear to AIM members that they could not count on the law for protection. To make matters worse, FBI "dirty tricks," which had riddled AIM with informers and provocateurs, had brought increasing paranoia and dissension to the movement—even leading to the wounding of AIM founder CLYDE BELLECOURT by AIM chairman Carter Camp— and some AIM members suspected Aquash of being an FBI informer. It was in this climate of fear and suspicion that she walked out of the courthouse in Pierre on November 24, 1975, and disappeared.

On February 24, 1976, Anna Mae Aquash's body was found on a remote section of the Pine Ridge Reservation. The local pathologist, Dr. W. O. Brown, who was also the pathologist in the controversial case of Bissonette, concluded that Aquash had died of exposure, a finding that was refuted when a second autopsy done at the behest of AIM supporters found a bullet wound in the back of her head. Dr. Brown had also cut off Aquash's hands at the behest of the FBI; they were sent to Washington, ostensibly for identification purposes.

Following a traditional Oglala ceremony led by Billy Good Voice Elk and attended by more than 100 mourners, Anna Mae Aquash was buried at Pine Ridge on March 14, 1976, beside the body of Joe Killsright Stuntz, who had been killed in the June 1975 shoot-out. Aquash's murder, like those of more than 60 Indians on Pine Ridge since the Wounded Knee occupation, was unsolved.

Her death marked the end of AIM as an effective organization. Unable to extricate itself from the increasingly violent character their struggle for Indian rights had taken, the movement quickly disintegrated. What would remain would be the idea of AIM, a vision of warrior men—and women such as Aquash—who would inspire the next generation of activists around the world.

On February 9, 2004, Arlo Looking Cloud, a former member of AIM who had been 22 years old in 1975, was convicted and sentenced to life imprisonment for his role in Aquash's murder. It was established at the trial that after leaving the courtroom in Pierre on November 24, 1975, Aquash traveled to Denver, Colorado, where she found refuge at an AIM safe house. In early December, however, she was again accused of being an informer and was brought back to South Dakota by AIM members Theda Clark, John Boy Graham, and Looking Cloud.

For a few days, Aquash was held at an apartment owned by another AIM member, Thelma Rios, and then on December 12 she was taken to the offices of the Wounded Knee Legal Defense/Offense Committee (WKLDOC) for questioning. From there, she was taken by Clark, Graham, and Looking Cloud to a house on the Rosebud Reservation. While Aquash, guarded by Looking Cloud, remained in the car, Clark and Graham met with senior AIM leaders who decided her fate. Around daybreak on December 13, Theda Clark drove Aquash

and the other two AIM members to a remote location on Pine Ridge. According to Looking Cloud, it was Graham who actually pulled the trigger, though Graham denies this.

On December 6, 2007, Graham, a Southern Tutchone Athabascan from Yukon, Canada, lost his fight to block extradition and was transported to South Dakota to face murder charges in Aquash's death. He was convicted of felony murder on December 10, 2010, and sentenced to life in prison. Theda Clark, an invalid suffering from dementia, was never charged. Despite rampant speculation, the AIM leaders who ordered her death have not been conclusively identified. In 2004, Anna Mae Aquash's remains were returned to her homeland and reburied on the Indian Brook Micmac Reserve in Nova Scotia.

Further Reading

Brand, Johanna. *The Life and Death of Anna Mae Aquash.* Toronto: James Lorimer and Company, 1978.
Hendricks, Steve. *The Unquiet Grave: The FBI and the Struggle for the Soul of Indian Country.* New York: Thunder's Mouth Press, 2006.

art, visual

Prior to 1900, Indian artworks were considered almost exclusively as artifacts of the various Indian cultures, rather than the work of individual artists. Moreover, the development of Indian art was hampered by the 19th-century ultra-assimilationist policies of the American government (see ASSIMILATION), advanced by influential educators such as RICHARD HENRY PRATT, which attempted to erase all facets of Indian culture and which geared any education provided to the Indian toward turning them into laborers or farmers, or to other vocational occupations.

In the early 20th century, a number of recognized Indian painters became established in the Southwest, particularly San Ildefonso artists Alfredo Montoya (ca. 1890–1913), Crescencio Martinez (1879–1918), and Awa Tsireh (1898–1955), who had been contracted by anthropologists to draw Indian ceremonies and Indian life. Foremost among the early artists was the Hopi/Tewa potter NAMPEYO, who by 1910 had achieved an international following. At about the same time, a thawing of the assimilationist policies begun under the administration of Theodore Roosevelt—a change led in part by Indian Commissioner FRANCIS ELLINGTON LEUPP and educator ESTELLE REEL—helped Indian arts and crafts develop further. Organizations such as the INDIAN INDUSTRIES LEAGUE, which was created to help Indians market their crafts and provide an economic base for their communities, began to recognize the beauty of Indian art forms, to call for their preservation, and to provide assistance to individual Indian artists.

In Oklahoma, the return in 1877 of Kiowa, Cheyenne, and other Plains Indian tribesmen from their imprisonment in Fort Marion, near St. Augustine, Florida, also began to transform the Indian artistic landscape. At Fort Marion, many of these new artists had come into contact with Pratt, who had provided prisoners with paper and colored pencils in an attempt to help them pass the time and make the transition to prison life. In light of Pratt's attitude, it is ironic that, on returning to Oklahoma, these prisoners continued to develop their "ledger art" (so called after the ledger books they used as paper). By 1900, Kiowa artists such as James Silverhorn (1861–1941) and Arapaho artists such as Carl Sweezy (1879–1953) had begun to make Anadarko, Oklahoma, a leading center of Indian art. Anadarko's budding art scene directly influenced the KIOWA FIVE, whose works in flat pictograph style of painting and drawing became sought-after collectors' items in the 1920s and 1930s and the first real breakthrough in Indian art.

In the Southwest, meanwhile, another generation of artists had begun to achieve renown. While also commissioned by anthropologists, their art was more distinctive and individual. Among this group were the Hopi Otis Polelonema (1902–81) and FRED KABOTIE, and San Ildefonso potters Julian Martinez and his wife MARIA MONTOYA MARTINEZ.

In 1932, DOROTHY DUNN, an influential art teacher, began working at the Santa Fe Indian School, where she became a proponent of the "Santa Fe," or "Studio," school of Indian painting that would come to dominate 20th-century Indian art. Dunn managed to take advantage of an important reversal in federal Indian policy underway at the time, led by incoming Indian Commissioner JOHN COLLIER, that finally overturned the harsh assimilation policies. Hoping to "establish [Indian painting] as one of the fine arts of the world," as Dunn put it, she asked her students to draw upon their tribal traditions for inspiration and technique. Her amazing crop of students, including PABLITA VELARDE, HARRISON BEGAY, POP CHALEE, and ALLAN HOUSER, became such a force that they effectively defined Indian art for decades to come and helped turn Santa Fe into a mecca of Indian art. Jack Hokeah, one of the Kiowa Five, traveled to the Southwest to study under Dunn, bringing the Studio style back to Oklahoma.

In 1958, the Philbrook Indian Art Annual rejected a painting by Yankton Dakota Sioux artist OSCAR HOWE for not being "traditional Indian art," igniting a controversy that would help transform the Studio style and open the door to less formulaic styles. In 1962, Cherokee LLOYD KIVA NEW founded a new art program at the Institute of American Indian Art. He not only expanded the forms of Indian art to include sculpture, printmaking, and mixed media but also reached out from beyond the Southwest to Indian students from all over the country, helping Iroquois and Northwest Coast Indians join ranks with the established Southwest and Oklahoma artists.

The new atmosphere was bolstered by the addition to the staff of Allan Houser, who taught sculpture and began to experiment in new art forms (such as abstract art) and techniques (such as mixed media), and FRITZ SCHOLDER, who became a faculty member in 1964. The creative ferment at the school, inspired by both teachers and students, led to entirely new forms of Indian art. Continually adding more abstract elements, the institute's artists began moving away from the figurative art form of the Studio school, many of them eventually becoming purely conceptual artists. Scholder himself became the most famous and sought-after Indian artist of the next two decades. Others who helped to break the mold were Caddo/Kiowa/Choctaw painter T. C. Cannon (1946–78), a student of Scholder's, and R. C. GORMAN.

During the 1970s, avant-garde Indian art began to be promoted by Lumbee painter Lloyd E. Oxendine (1942–), who established the first gallery of contemporary Indian art in New York City in 1969. Later the American Indian Community House Gallery in New York became an important force in showcasing new Indian art under a succession of distinguished curators, the Seneca painter Peter Jemison (1945–), Oxendine, and then Joanna Osborn Bigfeather (1952–). Among those modern artists who became prominent during this time were EDGAR HEAP OF BIRDS and JAUNE QUICK-TO-SEE SMITH.

By the end of the 20th century, Indian art, whether painting, sculpture, pottery, or jewelry, was among the most sought-after forms of American art, and Indians such as Allan Houser and R. C. Gorman were among the most prominent American artists. Indian artists helped to turn the Southwest of the United States into one of the most vibrant centers of artistic creation in the country. They also turned Santa Fe itself into the third-largest art market in the United States, after New York City and Los Angeles.

Further Reading

Anthes, Bill. *Native Moderns: American Indian Painting, 1940–1960.* Durham, N.C.: Duke University Press, 2006.
Henke, Robert. *Native American Painters of the 20th Century.* Jefferson, N.C.: McFarland, 1995.
Lester, Patrick D. *The Biographical Directory of Native American Painters.* Norman: University of Oklahoma Press, 1995.
Reno, Dawn E. *Contemporary Native American Artists.* Brooklyn, N.Y.: Alliance Publishing, 1995.
Strickland, Rennard. *Shared Visions: Native American Painters and Sculptors in the Twentieth Century.* New York: New Press, 1991.

arts and crafts, traditional   *See* ART, VISUAL; INDIAN ARTS AND CRAFTS BOARD.

Asah, Spencer   *See* KIOWA FIVE.

assimilation

Assimilation is a sociocultural process whereby people of one ethnic heritage acquire the basic habits, attitudes, and mode of life of a different, dominant culture. It is distinguished from acculturation, in which traits and elements are voluntarily borrowed and grafted into a continuing culture, resulting in new and blended patterns. Assimilation is centered on a single, dominant culture; acculturation emphasizes the choices of the borrowing cultures and is relatively uncentered. The distinction is often a matter of emphasis, however, and may be difficult to make in actual cases. The balance between change and continuity varies greatly among individuals and social groups within a given culture; overall social trends are not necessarily constant or unidirectional; and finally, the observer's cultural perspective may exaggerate one or the other end of the process.

Some degree and some rate of assimilation or acculturation happens normally in contact between peoples and would have happened between Indians and non-Indians in any case. Once all Indians were under federal guardianship, however, official government policy had to be articulated, and assimilation was a main goal. The most important element of the policy in the late 1800s was ALLOTMENT, in which Indian property holding was forced to conform to the dominant mode of property holding (see LAND TENURE). At the same time, the most radical educational theory of assimilation was developed and implemented by RICHARD HENRY PRATT. The spread of Christianity was also a vehicle of assimilation, but missionaries were often criticized for their relative cultural leniency by more radical reformers like Pratt. Increasing intermarriage with other races has always been a powerful factor in introducing dominant cultural values into Indian communities.

Assimilation, or Americanization, had long been a major aspect of U.S. Indian policy. In many cases, Indians wanted the federal government to provide education; but to the government, education was a mechanism of assimilation, whereas to the Indians it was a means of acculturation. Some Indian nations, notably the Five Civilized Tribes (as the Cherokee, Creek, Choctaw, Chickasaw, and Seminole were known), became strongly acculturated in the 19th century, yet they resisted assimilation by developing their own educational systems in their own languages.

By the 1870s, with accelerating shrinkage of the frontier, the goal of assimilation took on real urgency, with liberals urging it as the Indians' only hope for survival. At the opening of the 20th century, almost the only policy makers who did not favor assimilation were those who believed the Indian race was doomed to extinction and should be left to die out in peace.

Attempts to speed and control assimilation took definitive form in the General Allotment Act of 1887 (also known as the Dawes Act). From then until its repeal in 1934, the goal of assimilation permeated through virtually every aspect of government Indian policy, with Allotment as the basic ideology. Allotment was a federal policy in force between 1887 and 1934 which mandated the subdivision of tribally held lands into small "allotments" that were then distributed to individual tribal members. Assimilation involved not only education (broadly interpreted), but also laws and policies that attempted to suppress basic aspects of Indian culture.

Another element came into the picture in the late 19th century. Because of high immigration, mainly from Europe, general concern about assimilation of all ethnic groups was at its height. The United States began to be thought of as a great "melting pot." Assimilation was seen as a matter of survival, and most immigrant children eagerly and rapidly Americanized, at the same time often developing a negative or at best ambivalent attitude toward the culture of their parents. This unsentimentally pragmatic approach influenced attitudes toward Indian assimilation as well, though it overlooked a crucial fact: immigrant children came from cultures that, with few exceptions, were being maintained (albeit undergoing modernization) in their country of origin; Indian children represented the entire future potential for American Indian cultural continuity and survival.

In the 20th century, the period before WORLD WAR I saw a continuation of the intense drive for rapid Indian assimilation. Its leading light was Richard Henry Pratt. Pratt's influence was also strongly felt by the SOCIETY OF AMERICAN INDIANS, an organization of Indian intellectuals and non-Indians founded in 1911.

When traditional culture was strong, assimilation was primarily negative. It meant getting away from what reformers called "the blanket," by which they meant clinging to tradition for security. As a positive concept, Americanization is ambiguous. Reviewing the biographies of the many prominent Indians who as children were the objects of this push to Americanize the Indian, it is clear that their responses varied according to the unique personality and history of each individual and that assimilation meant different things to different people. Among the strongest Native advocates of assimilation were ARTHUR C. PARKER, CARLOS MONTEZUMA, JACOB CASIMERA MORGAN, and Reverend SHERMAN COOLIDGE. Yet Indian assimilationists usually assumed the Indian would somehow remain Indian no matter what changes were made.

Nevertheless, even at this early date, in the face of the heavy push for assimilation, the positive value of traditional Native cultures was already being advocated. Many of these advocates were non-Indians. They included anthropologists (FRANZ BOAS, CONSTANCE GODDARD DU BOIS, FRANK SPECK) and other intellectuals (ERNEST THOMPSON SETON, HAMLIN GARLAND, MELVIN RANDOLPH GILMORE), but also Indians like CHARLES EASTMAN, ANGEL DECORA, and GERTRUDE BONNIN.

During the early 1920s, in the wake of the patriotic fervor stirred up by World War I, with revolution and political instability in Europe and large numbers of as yet unassimilated European immigrants in America, a fear of the "other" swept through the United States. This malaise found expression in attempts by the government and missionaries to suppress traditional Indian ceremonies (see DANCE ORDERS). However, the intense opposition that this campaign aroused among both Indians and non-Indians showed that something was changing. It is noteworthy that JOHN COLLIER, who joined in the defense of Native cultures at just this time, had until then been a social worker among immigrant communities in New York City.

The impressive role of Indians in World War I and the civilian war effort bolstered the drive for assimilation. Not only did many Indians feel a sense of true and equal participation in the general war effort, but the wider public accepted the idea that Indians now deserved CITIZENSHIP. The Indian Citizenship Act of 1924 was the result. This act, also known as the Snyder

Act after its sponsor, Representative Homer P. Snyder of New York, granted full citizenship rights to those Indians who had not already gained citizenship through military service, Allotment, or other means. Completely ignored was a significant segment of the most traditional Indians—including many Hopi, Iroquois, Florida Seminole, and others—who had not wanted U.S. citizenship. These continued to adhere to the sovereignty of their ancient traditional governments.

The 1928 MERIAM REPORT put great emphasis on education but discouraged cultural suppression as a means of assimilation and reflected a more positive attitude toward Native cultures, an attitude held by some of the leading figures of the time, such as HENRY CLARENCE ROE CLOUD, WILL CARSON RYAN, JR., and ERL A. BATES. These educators supported their ideas with findings in the social sciences, criticizing previous government policies as based on religious and ideological grounds. Also during the 1920s, relatively assimilated urban Indians began to take measures to preserve some of their culture.

Between 1934 and WORLD WAR II, federal policy on assimilation was significantly modified. Indian Commissioner John Collier tried to encourage Indian culture. Indeed, one of the best studies of the Collier era is entitled *The Assault on Assimilation: John Collier and the Origins of Indian Policy Reform*, by Lawrence Kelly (1983). Perhaps it would be more accurate to view the Collier approach as a mitigated concept of assimilation, possibly even an idea of federally protected acculturation.

Collier lost influence during World War II, however, and after the war, assimilation became desirable again, even more intensely than was the case after World War I. From this point of view, which corresponds to the period of TERMINATION (1948–63), Indians had now fully "earned the right" to be Americans. In a typical misrepresentation of the problem, SENATOR ARTHUR VIVIAN WATKINS, one of the chief architects of Termination, wrote in a 1957 article of "the questionable merit of treating the Indian of today as an Indian, rather than as a fellow American citizen." There was an effort to portray the Collier years as a deviation from established American policy, necessitated only by the special conditions of the Great Depression.

After the war, Indian culture was no longer officially devalued, although in popular culture, especially in films, some of the most negative portrayals of Native Americans date from this period. The extent to which cultural protection had become associated with government policy under Collier is suggested by the fact that Watkins felt he had to explain that

... doing away with restrictive federal supervision over Indians, as such, does *not* affect the retention of those cultural and racial qualities which people of Indian descent would wish to retain; many of us are proud of our ancestral heritage, but that does not nor should it alter our status as American citizens. . . . I wish to emphasize this point, because a few well-intentioned private organizations [probably Watkins was thinking first and foremost of the ASSOCIATION ON AMERICAN

INDIAN AFFAIRS (AAIA) and the NATIONAL CONGRESS OF AMERICAN INDIANS] repeatedly seek to influence Congress to keep the Indian in a restricted status by urging legislation to retain him as an Indian ward and as a member of a caste with social status apart from others, not basically as what he is—a fellow American citizen.

In reality, Indians had been recognized as American citizens, whether they wanted to be or not, since 1924—and in truth, the vast majority of Indians under federal wardship, as discriminatory a burden as it was, accepted wardship as a trade-off for being able to have their own lands and SOVEREIGNTY.

An important change in thinking about assimilation was signaled by the conference "Institute on American Indian Assimilation," which was held by the AAIA on May 8–10, 1952, in Washington, D.C. It brought together Indian leaders, social scientists, officials, and legislators to discuss assimilation conditions, factors affecting those conditions, and the goals and values involved.

The attempt to wipe out the cultural gains of the 1930s provoked a reaction from Indians, gradually gathering momentum through the RED POWER MOVEMENT and exploding about 1970 with the full-scale militancy of the AMERICAN INDIAN MOVEMENT (AIM). In fact, many of these young people had already lost their Native language and culture as the cumulative result of decades of imposed assimilation, but they were eager to learn from traditional elders.

Overt harsh assimilation effectively petered out in the 1960s. In the 1970s and 1980s, there was a reversal. Through tribal colleges (see HIGHER EDUCATION), Indian community radio, and programs to invigorate indigenous languages, and through new respect for traditional elders and ceremonies, important efforts were made by Native communities to retain traditional culture. But although assimilation was no longer the official policy, it had already caused enough damage to make it an ongoing social force, especially with the education policies of previous years, including much of the mission work; Indian participation in two world wars, Korea, and Vietnam; and exposure to media (especially television), which had left two generations with major language and cultural loss.

All of this now makes it harder to maintain Indian cultural identity and easier to join the mainstream. Aspects of mainstream culture have held the same attraction for most Indians as they have for other ethnic groups. From the vantage point of the start of the 21st century, it can be seen that social factors such as URBANIZATION, education, employment, television, and tribally controlled gaming have propelled the assimilation process forward for Indians as for all other minority cultures. Nevertheless, there are many strongholds of traditional continuity at the start of the 21st century, mainly on the reservations.

In actual practice, the sense of core-group ethnic identity is extremely persistent among Indians. This can be seen especially in some eastern Native communities, which have been under intense assimilation pressure for hundreds of years and still have their own distinct cultural identity. Even among highly assimilated groups, there remains a shared history (even if it amounts to a history of family feuds and intergroup contention) that has no vital meaning to any other people and that persists around a core of the group's identity.

See also ANTHROPOLOGISTS AND AMERICAN INDIANS; AUTOMOBILES, AMERICAN INDIANS AND.

Further Reading

Adams, David Wallace. *Education for Extinction: American Indians and the Boarding School Experience, 1875–1928.* Lawrence: University Press of Kansas, 1995.

Burt, Larry W. *Tribalism in Crisis: Federal Indian Policy, 1953–1961.* Albuquerque: University of New Mexico Press, 1982.

Fixico, Donald L. "*Termination and Relocation: Federal Indian Policies, 1945–1960*". Albuquerque: University of New Mexico Press, 1986.

Hasse, Larry J. "Termination and Assimilation: Federal Indian Policy, 1943–1961." Ph.D. dissertation, Washington State University, 1974.

Hertzberg, Hazel. *The Search for an American Indian Identity: Modern Pan-Indian Movements.* Syracuse, N.Y.: Syracuse University Press, 1971.

Hoxie, Frederick E. *A Final Promise: The Campaign to Assimilate the Indians.* Omaha: University of Nebraska Press, 1984.

Kelly, Lawrence C. *Assault on Assimilation: John Collier and the Origins of Indian Policy Reform.* Albuquerque: University of New Mexico Press, 1983.

Marger, Martin N. *Race and Ethnic Relations: American Global Perspectives.* 7th ed. Belmont, Calif.: Wadsworth, 2007.

Trennert, Robert A. *The Phoenix Indian School: Forced Assimilation in Arizona, 1891–1935.* Norman: University of Oklahoma Press, 1988.

Association on American Indian Affairs (AAIA)

The Association on American Indian Affairs (AAIA) is a membership support organization that has performed important research and legal and public affairs work in addition to lobbying on behalf of Indians, especially during the TERMINATION period. The organization was created in 1937 by the amalgamation of two earlier ones, the Eastern Association on Indian Affairs (EAIA) and the American Indian Defense Association (AIDA).

EAIA was founded in December 1922 by Amelia White, with Herbert J. Spinden, curator of Primitive Art at the Brooklyn Museum, as president. It was closely allied with the New Mexico Association on Indian Affairs (NMAIA), the first organization to publicly oppose the BURSUM BILL. The Bursum bill was an attempt in the early 1920s by Senator Holm O. Bursum of New Mexico to legalize questionable non-Indian claims to Pueblo lands, which led the Pueblo to organize a historic and successful campaign against it. The

NMAIA had been founded earlier that year by a group of artists and writers, including Alice Corbin Henderson, Elizabeth Shepley Sargeant, Witter Bynner, Edgar L. Hewett, and others. Margaret McKittrick was the first chair. In the 1930s, it was aggressively chaired by Margaretta Dietrich and vice chair Charles Minton, who later became executive director himself.

AIDA was founded by John Collier in May 1923, when Stella Atwood, chair of Indian Welfare of the General Federation of Women's Clubs, took the Bursum fight to New York. Collier sought an ethnically and religiously diverse board, although there were no Indians on it. In addition to Atwood, the board included Margaret McKittrick, Amelia White, and Mary Austin, chair of AIDA's publicity council. The objectives of AIDA—articulated in articles by Collier in *Survey* and *Sunset* magazines—were much broader than those of the other organizations. Indeed, AIDA's agenda was the prototype for Collier's New Deal program (see INDIAN NEW DEAL).

From the People's Institute, where he had been treasurer, Fred M. Stein was brought in as treasurer of AIDA. The great constitutional lawyer Louis Marshall provided free legal services for years, and after his death, Nathan R. Margold continued in Marshall's place. (When Collier became commissioner of the BUREAU OF INDIAN AFFAIRS (BIA), he made Margold chief solicitor of the Department of the Interior; Margold hired FELIX SOLOMON COHEN as his assistant for Indian Affairs.)

EAIA and NMAIA, always closely allied, soon grew uneasy with Collier and AIDA. They dissented from Collier on the legitimacy of claims of non-Indians with respect to the Lenroot bill (an alternative bill proposed after the Bursum bill's defeat). The fact that AIDA had Indian support made the other organizations jealous. Amelia White, Carter Harrison, and Fridolin Schuster resigned from AIDA's board, which badly affected the organization's financial support. From 1930 to 1932, OLIVER LA FARGE was director of EAIA. In 1930, EAIA and NMAIA backed the new Republican administration of President Herbert Hoover and Indian commissioners, CHARLES JAMES RHOADS and JOSEPH HENRY SCATTERGOOD, while Collier and AIDA grew cool. The friction intensified with Collier's attacks on Special Indian Commissioner HERBERT JAMES HAGERMAN, which many Indian supporters considered unjustified. In 1932, the name of the organization was changed to the National Association on Indian Affairs (NAIA).

After Collier became commissioner of the BIA in 1934, his relationship with La Farge improved. In 1937, La Farge's NAIA merged with Collier's AIDA to form the American Association on Indian Affairs (AAIA). Margaretta Dietrich and NMAIA bitterly opposed their merger and continued sniping at the new organization.

La Farge served as president of AAIA from 1937 to 1942. In 1946, the name was again changed, from American Association on Indian Affairs to Association on American Indian Affairs. La Farge resumed the presidency from 1948 to his death in 1963. During this period, however, he did less of the actual work and showed a notable lack of judgment in his failure to appreciate the work of Felix Cohen as counsel, especially in the fight against Indian Commissioner DILLON SEYMOUR MYER and his policy of TERMINATION.

Although some of the AAIA staff, particularly Alexander Lesser, did not work well with the NATIONAL CONGRESS OF AMERICAN INDIANS (NCAI), the two organizations soon became strong allies in the fight against TERMINATION. The period of this alliance, the late 1940s through the early 1960s, was AAIA's finest hour. Though perhaps philosophically behind the curve, AAIA boasted some extremely effective fighters, such as LaVerne Madigan and Corinne Locker, and its magazine, *Indian Affairs*, was the best watchdog of Indian affairs of that time.

With the continuing rise of NCAI and then the RED POWER MOVEMENT, the role of AAIA in Indian affairs was inevitably diminished. Nevertheless, as late as the 1980s, it played a significant part in protecting sacred sites and helping with the repatriation of ceremonial objects. In the 1990s, the AAIA became a fully Indian organization and moved its headquarters from New York City to Sisseton, South Dakota.

Further Reading

The records of the Association on American Indian Affairs from 1922 to 1995 are held by the Princeton University Library, Department of Rare Books and Special Collections, Seeley G. Mudd Manuscript Library, Public Policy Papers, Princeton, New Jersey 08544 USA. With some exceptions, records of the AAIA were closed for a period of 20 years following the date of their creation.

The AAIA journal, *Indian Affairs*, was published from 1933 to 1938 and from 1949 to the present.

Ataloa   *See* MCLENDON, MARY STONE.

Auchiah, James   *See* KIOWA FIVE.

automobiles, American Indians and

During the 20th century, the automobile became a dominant force in American life as well as the country's most important industry; it also became a symbol of power and personal expression. Previously, in the 19th century, Western and Great Plains tribes had adopted the horse in relative isolation from European cultures. The car, however, required more contact with the dominant culture, and the transition from horse to car took place while many other aspects of traditional culture—spiritual, political, economic, and geographic—were also changing, often in chaotic and unbalanced ways.

WORLD WAR I, which broke out in Europe in August 1914, soon brought prosperity to America. The Crow had sold ponies to the British during the Boer War and used the profits to buy high-quality breeding stock. By 1915, they were selling the offspring of these horses to the British, French, and Italian governments (see STRONGWOLF, JOSEPH). They used the profits to buy cars, usually expensive ones. As most Crow owned

at least 10–12 horses, they soon had more cars per capita than many American cities.

The war was a windfall for oil-rich tribes as well. By 1915, the price of oil had shot up from 40 cents to $2 a barrel. Wealthiest of all were the Osage, with an average per capita income above $10,000 in 1921. They spent lavishly. Everybody bought cars, as Terry Wilson describes in *Underground Reservation*, and many owned four or five.

In 1915, an invitation from the new Fontenelle Hotel in Omaha, Nebraska, to a banquet in honor of Logan Fontenelle, a famous Omaha chief, brought 50 Omaha tribesmen, some in traditional costume, by car from the reservation, "where almost every man owns an automobile," according to a contemporary news item. It apparently became a custom to invite the Omaha to events in the Nebraska city. In 1920, for example, 150 joined in the Thanksgiving parade, "all in motorcars."

On other reservations, however, the only cash most Indians could get was from selling their allotments (see ALLOTMENT), usually at far below market value. The Indian desire for cars thus became another weapon in the arsenal of land fraud. In one 1915 case on White Earth Reservation, a young woman, on her 18th birthday, signed away 160 acres worth $2,000 for $700 and a team of horses. She sued for fraud a short time later but, after getting married, dropped all charges; when her lawyer went to investigate, he found her riding around the reservation in a crimson secondhand automobile that had formerly belonged to the real estate man.

With the Indian Office's program to develop cattle raising on western reservations came a corresponding reduction of the traditional horse herds. As there was no public transportation on these vast reservations, one consequence was a growing need for cars. By 1922, of the more than 350,000 Indians on reservations, 35,000 owned automobiles. In 1924, the Indian Office superintendent at Klamath complained:

> If I were . . . to name one thing which has tended more than anything else to the squandering of the funds of the Klamath Indians I should mention the purchase of expensive automobiles. The first step was the issuance of a patent in fee for the sale of inherited lands. The second was the turning over of the funds to the Indian. The third step, the purchase of a high-priced automobile, with the subsequent necessity of its upkeep and maintenance. The effect upon the life of the Indian has been demoralizing in that it invites him to take long and expensive trips and to absent himself from his home to the neglect of his farming operations and the building up and improvement of his allotment.

Similarly, the anthropologist Margaret Mead, in *The Changing Nature of an Indian Tribe* (1932), wrote: "The automobile helped greatly to establish a pattern of excessive economic indulgence."

The story of the purchase and rapid deterioration of an individual's first car has become proverbial in Indian country, because few of the Indians knew how to maintain or repair them. A fictional treatment of this theme can be found in *Grandfather and the Popping Machine*, by Henry Tall Bull (Northern Cheyenne) and Tom Weist (1970). Sometimes lack of knowledge about how the new car worked caused Indians a lot of unnecessary trouble. Often as soon as a car broke down, they would sell it for a fraction of its value. Later Indians often showed great ingenuity in fixing broken cars. Navajo (Dineh), among the last Indians to adopt the automobile, became particularly noted for this.

By 1924, the practice of swapping cars had become so widespread on the Chippewa reservations that the Minnesota secretary of state could not collect auto taxes from Indians because no one could trace where any particular car was or who owned it.

While to the dominant culture, young Indians driving cars symbolized the "Americanization" of the red man (see ASSIMILATION), it was really the "Indianization" of the car. The anthropologist Nancy Lurie notes that Indians "did not view the industrial developments of the times with the awe expected of them by those who considered themselves the creators of the modern marvels. Items were examined and adapted to acceptability on Indian terms or rejected. They were not seen as a complex entirety to which only a particular ideology could be attached." The automobile brought increased mobility, but since mobility was part of the traditional culture for many tribes, this preserved and even extended existing Indian social patterns.

According to the anthropologist SOL TAX, writing in the Chicago *Sun-Times*, June 11, 1961, "If a change, no matter how beneficial, is defined as a change from being Indian to being white, it stands a good chance of not being adopted. . . . Precisely because the rifle, the horse and the automobile were never associated with assimilationist interpretations, they were incorporated into Indian cultures." The car made it easier for people to get to ceremonies and other traditional gatherings, so in many ways it actually strengthened tradition. It greatly strengthened pan-Indianism as well. The development of the powwow and the whole powwow circuit owe their existence to the automobile.

The writer VINE DELORIA, JR., complains in *Custer Died for Your Sins* (1969) that these constant trips to POWWOWS and ceremonies (which he blames on anthropologists encouraging Indians to follow the old nomadic ways) led to neglect of home resources—exactly the complaint of the Klamath superintendent in 1924. But the car also brought them to all kinds of conferences and meetings.

The myth of Indians not knowing how to maintain their cars gradually became the basis of another destructive pattern of white-Indian relations. Dealers in reservation border towns would keep special junk cars to be sold only to Indians and would not sell a good car to an Indian even if he or she had money and a job. Meanwhile, the Indian needed a decent car in order to hold a job or to get one in the first place. An informal network developed on the reservation to find parts to keep these old "rez cars" and "one-eyed Fords" going, and many

Indians became extremely resourceful mechanics, as shown in Dowell Harry Smith's classic study of old cars on Pine Ridge in the early 1970s, *Old Cars and Social Productions among the Teton Lakota* (1973).

Further Reading

Adams, William Y. "Navaho Automotive Terminology." *American Anthropologist* 70 (1968): 1181.

Deloria, Philip J. *Indians in Unexpected Places*, 136–182. Lawrence: University Press of Kansas, 2004.

Franz, Kathleen, and Susan Smulyan, eds. *Major Problems in American Popular Culture*, 228, 231–233. Boston: Wadsworth Cengage Learning, 2012.

Smith, Dowell Harry. "Old Cars and Social Productions among the Teton Lakota." Ph.D. dissertation, University of Colorado, 1973.

Vogt, Evon Z. "The Automobile in Contemporary Navaho Culture." In *Selected Papers of the Fifth International Congress of Anthropological and Ethnological Science*, edited by Anthony C. F. Wallace, 359–363. Philadelphia: University of Pennsylvania Press, 1956.

aviation, American Indians in

Like everyone else, American Indians have been attracted to aviation, and even to outer space, throughout the 20th century. The first Indian to fly in an airplane—as a passenger—seems to have been Blackfeet chief JOHN WHITE CALF, of the Glacier Reservation in Montana, in June 1914. WORLD WAR I gave a great number of young Indian men the chance to train as pilots. Other Indians enlisted in the air service of the U.S. Army Signal Corps, including Fred Blythe Bauer (Eastern Cherokee), a Chippewa from the White Earth Reservation, and five Osage. One of these, JOHN JOSEPH MATHEWS, recorded a fictionalized account of his training as a pilot in his autobiographical novel, *Sundown* (1934). Another, CLARENCE LEONARD TINKER, began flying in 1919.

Between the world wars, Indian flyers found commercial employment of various kinds. Chief White Eagle, a Ponca pilot, worked as a flyer in the film industry in southern California; he was killed in 1926 while performing in a parachute-jumping exhibition. Charles E. Parker, a Cherokee, was chief pilot for the Tulsa-based Skelly Oil Company in the 1920s.

Among the notable American Indian aviators who served in WORLD WAR II were Clarence Tinker, Cherokee naval aeronaut JOSEPH CLARK, Crow army ace BARNEY OLD COYOTE, and Wyandot air force pilots LEAFORD BEARSKIN and LELAND S. BEARSKIN. Clarence Tinker's son, also a pilot, was shot down over the Mediterranean in 1943. Dorothy L. Anderson, a Flathead who served in the Women's Air Corps during the war and again from 1949 to 1953, later became an air traffic control specialist with the Federal Aviation Administration (FAA).

Leland and Leaford Bearskin also flew for the United States in the Korean War, as did Choctaw WILLIAM REID POGUE and Shoshone JACK R. RIDLEY. In 1956, Leland Bearskin became the first Indian to land an aircraft in Antarctica. Pogue went on to fly with the air force exhibition team, the Thunderbirds, and to orbit the earth as the first Indian astronaut. Cherokee MARY GOLDA ROSS contributed to aeronautical design, including the design of spacecraft, as the first female engineer employed by Lockheed.

In Alaska, where even at the end of the 20th century most Native communities remained inaccessible by road, there was a special need for Indian and Eskimo pilots. Beginning in 1968, Wien Consolidated Airlines employed several, among them the Native bush pilots William D. English and Thomas Richards, who later flew Boeing 737 jets for the same company.

The FAA runs a Native American Alaska Native Intern Program at various FAA field locations during the summer months.

Further Reading

De Marban, Alex. "Lost in the Wind." *First Alaskans Magazine* 4, no. 2 (April/May 2009): 26–29.

B

Bacon Rind (Wahshehah, "Fat on the Skin")

(1860–1932) *Osage leader*

Bacon Rind was born on January 1, 1860, in Claremore, Indian Territory (now Oklahoma); his Osage name, Wahshehah, is translated as "Fat on the Skin." A tall, statuesque man with striking looks, he was elected assistant chief in 1904 and principal chief of the Osage in 1909 but was removed in 1913 by the Interior Department for illegally approving oil leases on the oil-rich reservation. He was replaced in his position by FRED LOOKOUT but remained a mainstay in Osage politics, and in 1922 he became a member of the Osage tribal council. Bacon Rind was politically progressive and favored the allotment of the Osage reservation and the development of its oil and natural gas resources. He remained a traditionalist in customs, however, and always wore Native dress and an otter-skin cap. He was also a gifted speaker of the Osage language and was one of the most photographed American Indian leaders of his day. Bacon Rind died of cancer on March 28, 1932, in Pawhuska, Oklahoma.

Further Reading

Franks, Kenny A. *The Osage Oil Boom*. Oklahoma City: Oklahoma Heritage Association, 1989.

Wilson, Terry P. *The Underground Reservation: Osage Oil*. Lincoln: University of Nebraska Press, 1985.

Baldwin, Marie Louise Bottineau (1863–1952)

Chippewa ethnologist, genealogist, suffragist, Indian Bureau employee

In the early years of the 20th century, Mary Louise Bottineau Baldwin was one of two Indian women in the United States with a law degree. She was born in Pembina, North Dakota, on December 14, 1863. Her parents, Jean-Baptiste Bottineau and Marie Renville Bottineau, were both three-quarters Chippewa and one-quarter French.

Jean-Baptiste Bottineau, son of Pierre Bottineau, guide and military scout, was a successful fur trader, real estate broker, government timber agent, and justice of the peace in St. Anthony's Falls (later Minneapolis). Around 1880, he moved to Washington, D.C., to work full time for the Turtle Mountain Band of Chippewa. His most important action was his work as an attorney in a claim against the federal government for lands in North Dakota that had been opened to non-Indian settlers without compensation to the Indians. In this effort, he spent thousands of dollars of his own money. The town of Bottineau, North Dakota, was named after him.

Marie Louise Bottineau attended public and private schools in Minneapolis and St. John's School and Ladies College in Winnipeg, Manitoba. In 1887, she married Fred Baldwin, a white man in Minneapolis. In 1911, shortly before her father's death, she enrolled in Washington College of Law in Washington, D.C. In 1914, she became the second Native American woman to receive a law degree. Her master's thesis was entitled "The Need for Change in the Legal Status of the North American Indian." While she did not intend to practice law and never took a bar examination, she believed that legal training would help her be a more effective activist on behalf of Indians. She joined the Indian Bureau (later the BUREAU OF INDIAN AFFAIRS) under Commissioner CATO SELLS and worked for many years as clerk in the purchase division at a time when the procurement of supplies for all reservations was centralized in Washington.

An active member of the SOCIETY OF AMERICAN INDIANS, Baldwin presented a paper entitled "Modern Homemaking and the Indian Woman" at the society's first annual conference in Columbus, Ohio (1911), and published an article on Tuscarora ethnologist JOHN NAPOLEON BRINTON HEWITT in its journal (1914), as well as some comments on art and progress (1917). She was elected treasurer of the society in 1915 and 1916.

A fluent speaker of French, Baldwin volunteered for duty

as an accountant with the U.S. Army in France in 1917. She was a member of the American Anthropological Association and a discerning collector of Indian arts and crafts from reservations throughout the United States. Her collection, assembled over three decades, was for many years on display in the Indian Service Library in the old Department of the Interior Building in Washington. She had a summer cottage in North Beach, Maryland, which became her permanent residence after she was afflicted with arthritis. She died in Los Angeles on May 17, 1952, of a cerebral hemorrhage.

See also CONLEY, LYDA B.

Ballard, Louis Wayne (Honganozhe)

(1931–2007) *Quapaw-Cherokee composer, music educator*
Louis Wayne Ballard was born on July 8, 1931, in Miami, Oklahoma. His mother was of Quapaw and French ancestry, and his father was of Cherokee and Scottish descent. Ballard, also known as Honganozhe (which means "Stands with Eagles"), grew up in a musical environment. His mother was a pianist who composed songs for children; she took her son to many Indian ceremonies, where he learned traditional ceremonial songs. Encouraged by his grandmother to learn piano at a mission chapel near her home, Ballard soon began writing music himself.

After studying music at Bacone College and at Northeast Oklahoma College, Ballard went on to complete a B.A. and a bachelor's degree in music education at the University of Tulsa in 1954. He worked many jobs to help finance his undergraduate education, including performing at a nightclub as a pianist and singer. In 1962, he received a master's degree in music from the University of Tulsa and another one in 1967 from the University of Oklahoma. He later received an honorary doctorate from the College of Santa Fe.

Ballard's creative direction was decisively influenced by his discovery of the music of 20th-century Hungarian composer Bela Bartok while an undergraduate at Tulsa in the early 1950s. Bartok used themes and deeper structures from Hungarian folk music to create a distinctive musical idiom, and Ballard was inspired to develop his own musical style by making use of traditional Indian elements. He was in effect following the trailblazing composers H. W. Loomis (1865–1930), Arthur Farwell (1872–1952), and fellow Quapaw FRED CARDIN (see INDIANIST MUSIC). Ballard explored this approach not only in his compositions but in a whole philosophy and method of ethnic-music education based on American Indian compositions. Though he was at first motivated simply to increase public appreciation of American Indian music, the growing acceptance of his work inspired him to aim for the mainstream of the American musical consciousness.

In the mid-1970s, Ballard was appointed dean of the music department at the Institute of American Indian Arts in Santa Fe, New Mexico, an innovative tribal college operated by the BUREAU OF INDIAN AFFAIRS (BIA). He also became the BIA's music curriculum specialist, with a responsibility for music program development in all federal reservation schools.

In this capacity, he traveled to BIA area offices around the country to establish bicultural music programs from kindergarten to college.

Ballard wrote for many instrumental combinations and in a wide variety of genres. He composed three ballet scores (*Ji-Jo Gweh, Koshare, The Four Moons*); many orchestral pieces, including *Scenes from Indian Life, Incident at Wounded Knee,* and a series of "Fantasies Aborigine"; chamber music for various combinations; choral cantatas (*Portrait of Will Rogers, The Gods Will Hear, Thus Spake Abraham);* numerous works for band; works for percussion ensembles; and others. Many have been recorded and broadcast in North and South America and in Europe.

In the 1960s, Ballard founded First American Indian Films, which produced *Discovering American Indian Music,* a film about the functions of Indian dance and song in traditional ceremony and modern social life, that included one of his own compositions. He also developed *American Indian Music for the Classroom,* an educational kit consisting of a film, four audiocassettes, a teacher's guide, a map of Indian lands, photographs, and a lengthy bibliography.

Ballard frequently lectured on various topics connected with American Indian music and art at universities around the country. He also performed as guest conductor with numerous symphony orchestras. He continued to compose new music into the 1990s, including the opera *Moontide* (1994), which had its premiere in Germany. His educational publication, *Native American Indian Songs,* published in 2004, included two compact discs containing 28 songs from various Native American cultures, photographs, text translations, cultural background, and an accompanying guidebook for music teachers with instructions on how to teach the songs to students.

In 1991 Ballard participated in the Meet the Composer program underwritten by the Lila Wallace Reader's Digest Foundation. He was the first American composer to be honored with a program devoted entirely to his music at the Beethovenhalle concert hall in Bonn, Germany, and became the first classical composer to attain membership in the Oklahoma Music Hall of Fame. In 2000, Ballard served as distinguished visiting professor of music at William Jewell College in Liberty, Missouri, where he received an honorary doctorate in 2001. His wife, Ruth Dore, was a concert pianist. Louis Wayne Ballard died on February 9, 2007, in Santa Fe, New Mexico.

Further Reading

Ballard, Louis, comp. *American Indian Music for the Classroom* (teaching package with four audiocassettes). Santa Fe: New Southwest Music Publications, 2004.

Norrell, Brenda. "Louis W. Ballard: Composer Fuses World with Native Sound." *Indian Country Today* (1 September 2004).

Film

Wilets, Bernard. *Discovering American Indian Music.* Discovering Music Series. St. Louis, Mo.: BFA Educational Media, 1974.

Banks, Dennis James (1937–) *Chippewa cofounder of the American Indian Movement*

A Chippewa, Dennis Banks was born on the Leech Lake Chippewa reservation in Minnesota on April 12, 1937, and was given the name Nowacumig. Taken from his family at the age of five, he grew up in BUREAU OF INDIAN AFFAIRS (BIA) boarding schools in North and South Dakota and Minnesota. In 1953, he joined the U.S. Air Force and was stationed in Japan. Upon his discharge in 1957, he returned to Leech Lake before moving to Minneapolis to find work.

Unable to find employment, Banks turned to alcohol and then to crime. In 1965, he was convicted of burglary, for which he served two and a half years. Jailed again for a parole violation in 1967, he met fellow Chippewa Eddie Benton-Benai and CLYDE HOWARD BELLECOURT. Upon his release, he joined them and the Chippewa community activist George Mitchell in an effort to organize the "red ghetto" in Minneapolis and protest the then-pervasive police brutality in the city. Originally calling themselves Concerned Indian Americans, they soon changed their name to the AMERICAN INDIAN MOVEMENT (AIM).

Dealing mostly with local issues, the group was galvanized by the OCCUPATION OF ALCATRAZ ISLAND in November 1969. In fall 1970, Banks established a small AIM camp on the top of Mount Rushmore in South Dakota. AIM members reoccupied the park in spring 1971, this time with Oglala Lakota Sioux activist RUSSELL MEANS. Means and Banks soon became synonymous with AIM across the country.

In March 1972, Banks and Means led a large demonstration in Gordon, Nebraska, that secured a degree of justice for the family of RAYMOND YELLOW THUNDER, an old man who had been brutally murdered by white assailants. In April that same year, however, their attempts to help the Chippewa at Cass Lake nearly destroyed the fledgling movement. The Chippewa, involved in a fishing-rights dispute with the state of Minnesota, were uncomfortable with the armed, belligerent—and uninvited—AIM supporters, and when AIM was asked to leave and refused, a gun battle nearly ensued.

After the Cass Lake fiasco, Banks lost his leadership position in AIM, and the movement was dormant until the death of RICHARD OAKES led Banks and other AIM members to join the TRAIL OF BROKEN TREATIES march on Washington, D.C., in October–November 1972. The subsequent occupation of the BUREAU OF INDIAN AFFAIRS (BIA) headquarters created a national sensation, and Banks followed it up by organizing a demonstration for murdered Oglala Lakota Sioux Wesley Bad Heart Bull in the town of Custer, South Dakota.

In January 1973, Bad Heart Bull had been found dead with a knife in his chest in the middle of the small town of Buffalo Gap, and local authorities had arrested a young white service station attendant and charged him with only second-degree manslaughter. On February 6, more than 200 Indians, many of them women and children, gathered in front of the courthouse in Custer to demand a first-degree murder charge. As Banks and Means negotiated with the authorities inside, an altercation broke out, leading to a full-scale riot in which the courthouse was set on fire and burned down, two police cars

were destroyed, and 27 Indians were beaten and arrested. The incident led directly to the siege at WOUNDED KNEE, a 71-day standoff that made Banks and Means nationally famous and shed new light on the federal government's treatment of Indian people.

Banks's trusting nature facilitated the Federal Bureau of Investigation (FBI) infiltration of AIM during the Wounded Knee trials, allowing the agency to plant a provocateur named Douglass Durham inside the legal defense team. On March 5, he was exposed as an informant, embarrassing the FBI and damaging the credibility of the prosecution, but also sowing seeds of mistrust and paranoia among AIM members. In 1975, Banks, although acquitted of wrongdoing during the Wounded Knee occupation, was convicted on charges of rioting at Custer. While on trial for the Custer charges, he lived with other AIM members on the Jumping Bull farm at Pine Ridge, where he and his Lakota wife, Kamook Nichols, led the opposition to Pine Ridge tribal chairman RICHARD WILSON. The farm was raided by the FBI on June 26, 1975; but Banks and his wife were in court at the time and escaped the shootout, in which two FBI agents and an Indian were killed (see PELTIER, LEONARD).

Fearing for his life, Banks fled to California, where he was given asylum by Governor Jerry Brown. Between 1976 and 1983, he studied at the University of California, Davis; taught at Stanford University; and, with historian JACK FORBES, founded D-Q University for Indian students. When Brown left office, Banks was forced to move to the Onondaga Reservation in New York State, where he organized the Great Jim Thorpe Run to Los Angeles and the Jim Thorpe Memorial Games (see THORPE, JIM). In 1985, tiring of life on the run, Banks surrendered to South Dakota police; he subsequently served 18 months on the Custer riot charges.

Upon his release from prison, Banks lived for a short time at Pine Ridge before traveling as an advocate for the reburial of Indian remains held by museums and the protection of Indian burial sites (see REPATRIATION). He also continued to organize his national long-distance runs as a way to raise the self-esteem of Indian youth.

Like Means, Banks turned to acting, appearing in *War Party* (1988), *Last of the Mohicans* (1992), *Thunderheart* (1992), and *Older Than America* (2008). A tall, handsome man of considerable charm and thoughtful demeanor, he was the perfect counterpoint to the more flamboyant and impulsive Russell Means. Both were more a product of the militant 1960s than of their respective cultures, but both fought for the traditional values of their people and would inspire a new generation of less confrontational activists. Their leadership of the American Indian Movement, although brief, chaotic, and controversial, revolutionized the political fabric of Indian life.

Further Reading

Banks, Dennis, and Richard Erdoes. *Ojibwa Warrior: Dennis Banks and the Rise of the American Indian Movement.* Norman: University of Oklahoma Press, 2004.
Smith, Paul Chaat, and Robert Allen Warrior. *Like a*

Hopi activist Thomas Banyacya giving one of his frequent lectures on Hopi prophecy in 1986. *(AP/Wideworld)*

Hurricane: The American Indian Movement From Alcatraz to Wounded Knee. New York: New Press, 1996.

Banyacya, Thomas (Thomas Jenkins) (1909–1999)
Hopi activist, political leader

Born on June 2, 1909, in the Hopi pueblo of New Oraibi, Arizona, Thomas Banyacya belonged to the Water Coyote Clan of neighboring Moenkopi. In school, he was given the name Thomas Jenkins by administrators of the Indian Bureau (later the Bureau of Indian Affairs [BIA]), although he subsequently reverted to his original surname. He attended the Sherman Institute in California, and in 1930 he enrolled in Bacone College in Muskogee, Oklahoma, where he was a star long-distance runner. He then returned to the Hopi reservation to become a schoolteacher and even had plans to become a Christian minister.

Banyacya was originally an antitraditionalist, but after his marriage he moved to Hotevilla Pueblo, a center of Hopi resistance, where he became disillusioned with the Indian New Deal (see Indian Reorganization Act) and came under the influence of the Hopi traditional movement, headed by Dan Katchongva. The traditionals, as members of the movement were known, opposed Hopi assimilation into mainstream American culture and advocated continued self-determination

for each Hopi village, in accordance with ancient tradition. Banyacya fought against the 1936 establishment of the Hopi Tribal Council, which would have superseded the leadership of traditional Hopi kikmongwis (chiefs).

The exploding of the atomic bomb in 1945 was seen by Hopi religious leaders as the "gourd of ashes" that legend said would someday fall from the sky and devastate humanity, and when that time came, certain knowledge long held secret by the Hopi was to be delivered to the people of the world. Previously, Katchongva had urged against participation in World War II, and following his advice, Banyacya had gone to prison as a conscientious objector. While there, he became skilled at translating Hopi ideas into English, and in 1948 the Hopi kikmongwis of Shungopavi, Mishongnovi, and Hotevilla pueblos, as well as the leaders of 19 Hopi religious societies, chose Banyacya as one of their interpreters, asking him to help the Hopi articulate their prophetic messages.

Hopi leaders had objected to the 1946 formation of the Indian Claims Commission as well as attempts by the government to arbitrarily settle land claims between the Navajo and the Hopi. Beginning with a letter to President Harry Truman in 1949, the traditional Hopi sought, without success, to meet with U.S. leaders to discuss Hopi prophecies concerning the "purification" of the earth that would be brought about by human destruction of the natural order.

During the 1950s, Banyacya and Katchongva succeeded in convincing the Bureau of Indian Affairs to rescind its policy of requiring the Hopi to get livestock permits for their own lands. The victory was pyrrhic, however, for in 1955, after they met with BIA commissioner GLENN LEONIDAS EMMONS, he decreed that he would recognize only the Hopi Tribal Council as the Hopi's representative, a major setback for the traditional movement. In 1959, traditional Hopi leaders in Hotevilla Pueblo directed Banyacya to communicate with the "House of Mica"—interpreted to mean the United Nations—to present the Hopi perspective, although for decades this effort met with little success.

In the early 1960s, Banyacya became spokesman for the "independent Hopi Nation," a group of traditionals who opposed the revival of the long-dormant Hopi Tribal Council and the attempts of its counsel, JOHN STERLING BOYDEN, to lease Hopi lands for mining. Banyacya began to work with other traditional Indian movements, joining the Unity Caravan, a cross-country tour conceived by WILLIAM RICKARD and led by MAD BEAR ANDERSON, in 1964, as well as working with the AMERICAN INDIAN MOVEMENT.

Banyacya's political activism and growing network of radical connections took him further from the Hopi's traditional policy of passive resistance and more toward the confrontational tactics of the RED POWER movement. This led to strained relationships with many Hopi religious leaders, who objected to the outside supporters, even other Indians, that Banyacya brought to Hopi land. In turn, however, Banyacya brought to his activism a traditional Hopi perspective, which married an uncompromising refusal to bow to American social and political pressure with a spiritual and prophetic mission to preserve the environment in the face of technological exploitation. This perspective was highly influential among many Native activists, including JANET MCCLOUD and OREN LYONS, JR. In 1980, Banyacya joined with McCloud, Lyons, and PHILLIP DEERE to establish the Traditional Circle of Elders and Youth. Banyacya's refusal to cooperate with the Hopi Tribal Council led to a falling out with his protégé, Vernon Masayesva, when Masayesva chose to run for tribal chair in 1990.

Along with Mina Lansa, the kikmongwi of Oraibi Pueblo and daughter of WILSON TEWAQUAPTEWA, and David Monyongwe, Katchongva's successor as the leader of Hotevilla Pueblo, Banyacya supported Navajo threatened with relocation in the BIG MOUNTAIN dispute and traveled across the country to draw support for a less onerous settlement. (See SEKAQUAPTEWA, ABBOTT).

Banyacya also worked with Monyongwe to fulfill his instructions to bring the Hopi prophecies to an international forum. By the time he was finally allowed to speak, all of the former religious leaders who had appointed him had died, but on December 11, 1992, as hurricane-force winds and torrential rains flooded New York City, Banyacya addressed the United Nations, urging its members to follow the right and just path, to search for peace as the Hopi have striven to do, nurture the delicate relationship humans share with nature, and in this way avoid the coming world-ending purification. Banyacya died in Hotevilla Pueblo on February 6, 1999, after a long illness.

Further Reading

Hermequaftewa, Andrew. *The Hopi Way of Life Is the Way of Peace*. Interpreted by Thomas Banyacya. Hotevilla, Ariz.: Dan Katchongva, 1970.

Barfoot, Van T. (1919–2012) *Choctaw Medal of Honor winner*

A Choctaw, Van T. Barfoot was born in Edinburg, Mississippi, on June 15, 1919. He enlisted in the army in 1940 and was assigned to the 1st Infantry Division. After his training, he participated in maneuvers in Louisiana and Puerto Rico. At the outbreak of WORLD WAR II, in December 1941, he was promoted to sergeant and assigned to the newly formed Headquarters Amphibious Force Atlantic Fleet at Quantico, Virginia. When the unit was deactivated in 1943, Barfoot was promoted to technical sergeant and reassigned to the 157th Infantry Regiment of the 45th Infantry Division. Known as the "Thunderbird" Division, some 20 percent of the troops were Indians, and the 45th, which fought in North Africa, Italy, on Anzio Beach, and in the Ardennes forests of France and Germany, produced two other Indian Medal of Honor winners during World War II, ERNEST CHILDERS and JACK CLEVELAND MONTGOMERY.

On May 23, 1949, Sergeant Barfoot's platoon, attempting to assault a fortified German position near the town of Carano, Italy, came under heavy fire. Alone, Barfoot crawled up to a German machine gun nest and threw a grenade into it, killing two of the occupants and wounding the third. Continuing along the German line, he came across another machine gun emplacement, killed two enemy soldiers, and captured three others. The members of another machine gun nest then surrendered to him.

Leaving the prisoners for his squad to pick up, Barfoot continued his actions, singlehandedly capturing a total of 17 German soldiers. He then reorganized his squad's position in time to deflect a German counterattack. Under assault by three Panzer Mark IV tanks, Barfoot fired a bazooka from a distance of 75 yards and hit the lead tank, disabling it and forcing the other two tanks to turn away. He killed three of the crew members as they dismounted the crippled Panzer, then proceeded into enemy territory and destroyed a German howitzer. Upon returning to his platoon, he helped carry two injured soldiers almost a mile back to the safety of U.S. lines.

Not long after this action, Barfoot was promoted to lieutenant. Four months later, his unit was in France's Rhone Valley when he was ordered to division headquarters and informed that he had been awarded the Medal of Honor. Given the choice of returning to the United States for the ceremony or receiving the medal in the field, Barfoot chose the latter so that his men could be present. Lieutenant General Alexander Patch awarded him the medal in Epinal, France, on September 28, 1944. Barfoot also was awarded the Silver

Star, the Bronze Star, and the Purple Heart. After the war he remained with the army, retiring with the rank of full colonel. Barfoot lived in northern Virginia until his death on March 2, 2012.

Barnett, Jackson (1842–1934) *Creek millionaire*

Jackson Barnett was a traditional Creek whose great but accidental wealth, not under his own control, helped draw national attention to Oklahoma's corrupt Indian policies in the 1920s. He was born in 1842 in Indian Territory near Fort Sill, in what is now Oklahoma. Barnett's people, known as Snakes, were followers of traditionalist Creek leader CHITTO HARJO. Barnett grew up an orphan without any known relatives (it was later determined that his father was a man named Siah Barnett). He never learned to read, write, or speak much English. In 1896, he was a laborer living in a tumbledown shack in Henryetta, Oklahoma, and working as a farmhand and as helper on a small ferry near there at 75 cents a day.

In 1906, under the CURTIS ACT, the Department of the Interior allotted to individuals of the Creek Nation 160 acres each in eastern Oklahoma. Like most of the Snakes, Barnett never even went to look at his allotment. This was later interpreted as a sign of idiocy, but in fact it was a principled position, since the Snakes opposed ALLOTMENT. Some time in 1912, the famous Cushing oil pool was discovered near Barnett's land (see OIL, AMERICAN INDIANS AND). The Cushing oil field, discovered in 1912, was one of the richest oil strikes in history. During its peak production from 1915 to 1920, it produced more than 300,000 barrels of oil per day, accounting for 17 percent of U.S. and 3 percent of the world's total output. Though he lived only 40 miles away, Barnett was unaware of this. He was about 70 years old at the time.

An oilman immediately offered Barnett an $800 bonus for a lease on his property, with a one-eighth royalty on all future oil revenues. Barnett fixed his thumbprint to a paper and took the money. Almost immediately, another leasehunter protested the contract on grounds of incompetency. When the matter came to court, Barnett was declared incompetent and a guardian was appointed.

Soon the wells on Barnett's allotment were gushing at 12,000 gallons a day, and he was receiving around $60,000 per month from royalties alone. Yet he continued to live in his shack, spending almost nothing. When the United States entered WORLD WAR I, however, he bought $400,000 worth of Liberty Bonds (see PARKER, GABE EDWARD).

After the war, Indian Commissioner CATO SELLS planned to give several million dollars of Barnett's trust money to charities benefiting Indians. Under the law in force at the time, Barnett's huge estate was held in trust by the Interior Department and managed by the Indian commissioner on the grounds that Barnett was mentally incompetent to manage it himself. Large donations to charity were justified on the grounds that the estate's wealth was far greater than required for any conceivable needs of Barnett himself. On February 20, 1920, however, Barnett, never previously married, became the husband of Anna Laura Lowe, a widow. To evade his guardian, Barnett went with the woman on a long taxi ride to Coffeyville, Kansas, where they were married. Then they got back in the cab and were married a second time in nearby Missouri. Jackson's marriage would inevitably complicate control of his estate; besides, Lowe's motives were suspect. Correctly foreseeing that powerful forces would contest the marriage, Lowe and Barnett had the ceremonies performed in two states to make it ironclad. Years later, in an annulment suit, Barnett's attorney claimed that Lowe had "kidnapped" Barnett and plied him with liquor in order to get him to marry her.

At that period, Barnett's fortune was estimated at $4 million, an astronomical sum for the time. But even if his wife was an adventuress, he was in no danger, for she took good care of him. As the Tulsa *World* wrote of Mrs. Barnett in 1928: "She found him in a hovel, living in filth and dirt without proper food or raiment, and she dressed him up and improved his standard of living. The old Indian says he never had been so happy and had as many comforts of this world in all his life as he now has."

Not everyone was happy, however. Barnett was not a young man, and the county courts of Oklahoma had jurisdiction in probating Indian estates. Lawyers made fortunes by representing phony heirs claiming shares of often substantial oil wealth. From the lawyers' standpoint, it would be unfortunate if the estate were depleted by large donations—or by his wife—before they had a chance to plunder it.

In 1923, the Barnetts went to Washington to ask CHARLES HENRY BURKE, Sells's successor, to put aside half of the $1.1 million in Liberty Bonds for Anna and half for the Baptist Home Mission Society, which would go toward a major expansion of Bacone College. Burke saw this as an opportunity to score a hit against the corrupt Oklahoma probate system. He agreed to set up a trust of $550,000 for the Baptists, which would pay Barnett $20,000 a year for the rest of his life and a trust of $200,000 to Anna Laura, who would pay her husband $7,500 a year; in addition, she would get $435,000 in cash, and her lawyer would collect a fee of $137,500.

In 1923 (undoubtedly with the commissioner's tacit approval), the Barnetts "escaped" to Los Angeles, buying a mansion on Wilshire Boulevard with a barn in back in which they kept a string of Indian ponies. With this, he was safe from his Oklahoma guardian, who soon had to resign. As it turned out, Barnett had also removed his estate from the jurisdiction of the Oklahoma courts.

Before Bacone College could use any of the Liberty Bond money, however, Barnett's guardian brought suit to nullify the donation. After a new guardian was appointed, the latter joined the Justice Department in a similar suit. For the time being, Barnett would get only $2,500 a month for living expenses. Declaring him incompetent, Judge John C. Knox ordered the money returned to the Department of the Interior. The Baptists appealed but lost.

Burke was dogged by a special investigative subcommittee of Congress, and the attorney general also conducted a special investigation, but no one could find any evidence of

Millionaire Creek Jackson Barnett and his wife, Anna Lowe Barnett, leave a courtroom in 1932. *(AP/Wideworld)*

criminal wrongdoing. The attorney general did conclude, however, that in donating Barnett's funds to the Baptists, the secretary of the interior had exceeded his powers. He also recommended that the government, as Barnett's guardian, pursue annulment proceedings against Anna Laura, which they did with eventual success, his lawyers maintaining that Barnett, though he did not realize it, was the victim of "persuasive and seductive wiles."

Barnett was often sensationalized in the press as a "moron." In reality, he was a simple but perfectly normal traditional Indian who knew very well what was in his own best interest, even if he did not know how to secure it on his own. He died at his Los Angeles mansion, aged 92, on May 29, 1934.

Anna, who after the annulment had been allowed to stay on as Barnett's housekeeper, got nothing from Barnett's estate. By 1935, more than 200 "heirs" in at least seven states had appeared; the number ultimately rose to approximately 1,000. The Federal District Court at Muskogee concluded the litigation on December 16, 1939, recognizing 34 claimants, mainly full-bloods, descended from Siah Barnett.

Further Reading

Fixico, Donald. *The Invasion of Indian County in the Twentieth Century: American Capitalism and Tribal Natural Resources.* Niwot: University of Colorado Press, 1998.
Thorne, Tanis C. *The World's Richest Indian: The Scandal over Jackson Barnett's Oil Fortune.* New York: Oxford University Press, 2005.

Barreiro, José (1948–) *journalist, editor, novelist, activist, educator*

Of Guajiro (Cuban mestizo) ancestry, José Barreiro was born on June 19, 1948, in Camaguey, eastern Cuba, the son of Manuel and Isabel (Padron) Barreiro. After the defeat of Cuban dictator Fulgencio Batista in the 1960s, the Catholic Church, fearing that the Marxist revolutionary government of Fidel Castro might send some children to the Soviet Union for schooling, set up a refugee program. Twelve-year-old Barreiro was transferred to a Catholic relocation center in Minneapolis, where he was publicly presented as an example of how communism breaks up families. At first expecting to stay no more than a few months, he ended up living with a foster family for several years.

His first friends in Minneapolis were children of a Chicano father and a mother who was a White Earth Chippewa. Through them he was introduced to both the Native American and Chicano struggles. He attended high school in St. Louis Park, a Minneapolis suburb, and in 1967 enrolled in the University of Minnesota. The following year, Barreiro began writing on Native American and minority issues for the university newspaper, *The Minnesota Daily*. He was involved with Chicano activism and covered local AMERICAN INDIAN MOVEMENT (AIM) events and rallies. In 1971, Barreiro dropped out of college and the following year, as supervisor of a migrant labor camp in Wisconsin, he organized farmworkers. He then returned to Minneapolis, taking more courses at the University of Minnesota in 1973 and 1974.

In 1974, writing on the WOUNDED KNEE trials (see BANKS, DENNIS JAMES, and MEANS, RUSSELL) for the *Minnesota Daily*, Barreiro discovered one of his own articles printed in *Akwesasne Notes*, the leading Native American newspaper of the 1970s and 1980s, published on the Akwesasne Mohawk reservation (see JOURNALISM). After serving as editor of the *Minnesota Monthly*, Barreiro was invited by the staff of *Akwesasne Notes* in 1976 to go to Guatemala with an activist group known as the White Roots of Peace and cover the violent repression of the Maya Indians (see PORTER, TOM). From then on, he was a regular contributor, and in 1976 he became associate editor under JOHN C. MOHAWK, remaining with *Akwesasne Notes* until 1984.

In 1977, Barreiro attended an indigenous human rights conference in Geneva sponsored by the INTERNATIONAL INDIAN TREATY COUNCIL. His language skills and his ability to sort out the different conceptual worlds of the Latin American Indians made him a valued interpreter at the conference. Barreiro also coordinated press coverage for THE LONGEST WALK (1978), a march on Washington, D.C., in 1978 that protested a number of anti-Indian bills pending in Congress at the time. He also oversaw coverage of the Black Hills Alliance (1980), a conference in South Dakota that sought to bring together non-Indian ranchers and Indian leaders. During the early 1980s, Barreiro backed the Miskito Indians of Nicaragua in their struggle against the Sandinista government, a stance that brought charges, particularly from the International Indian Treaty Council and their allies, that he was a tool of the CIA.

In early 1984, Barreiro became the editor of a magazine published by Cornell University's Native American Program, successively known as *Indian Studies, Northeast Indian Quarterly, Akwe:kon,* (pronounced "a-gwey-go") and *Native Americas*. A series of special issues on specific topics, such as *Indian Corn of the Americas, Indigenous Economics,* and *Chiapas: Challenging History,* are important information resources and remain in print.

Although he finished his undergraduate work at the University of Minnesota in 1974, Barreiro did not officially get his B.A. until 1988, when he also received a master's degree from Cornell University. He got his Ph.D. from the State University of New York at Buffalo in 1992. His journalism, meshed with his human rights work, represents the transition from AIM-style confrontational and "media-event" activism to a new style of organizing based on conceptual analysis, accurate information, networking, and coalition building (including alliances with non-Indians). Between 1977 and 1983, Barreiro conducted some 25 human rights campaigns through *Akwesasne Notes* and its Emergency Response International Network (ERIN). His Indigenous Press Network (IPN, 1984–87), a news service produced on an international computer network, was ahead of its time.

In recent years, Barreiro has become known for his work in reinvigorating the Taino nation (the aboriginal inhabitants of Cuba and Puerto Rico) in both the United States and Cuba. In 1992, he published a historical novel, *The Indian Chronicles*, about the Taino response to Christopher Columbus. From 1996 through 2002, Barreiro was associate director of the American Indian Studies Program at Cornell. In 2003, he became senior editor of *Indian Country Today*, leaving in 2006 to become director of the Office for Latin America at the Smithsonian National Museum of the American Indian. He is married to Mohawk traditional midwife and health activist Katsi Cook.

Barsh, Russel Lawrence (1950–) *attorney, legal scholar, economist*

Born May 4, 1950, in New York City, Russel Lawrence Barsh was the son of Dr. Harold Barsh, a dentist, and Jacqueline Gross Barsh, an actress and teacher. He received a B.A. (summa cum laude) from Harvard in 1971, and while working on his doctorate there, he met classmate JAMES YOUNGBLOOD HENDERSON, also a doctoral student. Barsh and Henderson both received the J.D. from Harvard in 1974 and subsequently coauthored *The Road: Indian Tribes and Political Liberty.* Published in 1980, it is a historical study of federal Indian law and Native American sovereignty within the framework of the American constitution. Barsh planned two sequels, respectively titled *The Fire* and *The Chain,* on tribal political culture and tribal political nationalism in the United States and Canada.

From 1974 to 1977, Barsh was assistant professor at the University of Washington; he was subsequently associate professor of business, government, and society (1977–84). He was also editor of the *Journal of Contemporary Business* from 1977 to 1981 and professor of Native American Studies at the University of Lethbridge, Alberta, Canada (1993–2000). Recently, he was appointed adjunct professor of law at the School of Law, New York University.

Barsh is consultant to the Union of Nova Scotia Indians and the Oglala Lakota Sioux tribe. He represents the Mi'kmaq Grand Council at the United Nations and is a fellow of the Society for Applied Anthropology. In addition to his contributions to American Indian and legal journals, Barsh's major publications include *The Washington Fishing Rights Controversy: An Economic Critique* (University of Washington, 1977; rev. ed. 1979); *Understanding Indian Treaties as Law* (Washington State Superintendent of Public Instruction, 1978,

2nd ed. 1986); *Navajo Property Law and Probate, 1940–1972* (self-published 1982); and *Effective Negotiation by Indigenous Peoples: An Action Guide with Special Reference to North America*, prepared for the International Labor Organization of the United Nations (1997). Barsh is currently the director of the Samish Indian Nation's research program in human ecology, archaeology, and marine biology in the San Juan Islands of Washington State.

Further Reading

Blassnig, Roland. "Canada Urged to Shun U.S. Indian System; New Study Outlines Shortcomings in Provisions for Self-Government." *Buffalo News* (Buffalo, N.Y., 11 September 1994), 13.

Juricek, John T. Review of *The Road: Indian Tribes and Political Liberty*, by Russell Lawrence Barsh and James Youngblood Henderson. *Journal of American History* 67, no. 3 (December 1980): 648–649.

Bates, Erl A. (1889–1973) *physician, physical anthropologist, director of Indian Extension at Cornell University, aide to the Six Nations Council*

Erl Augustus Caesar Bates was born in Syracuse, New York, in 1889. Even as a young man he was active in politics, campaigning for women's suffrage and chairing the National Interfraternity Council and the Band of Mercy, a junior animal humane society, as a high school student.

After graduating from Syracuse University, Bates attended Bellevue Hospital Medical School in New York City. He went on to do postgraduate work in medicine in Leipzig, Germany, and in 1914 he received the Simms medal for his contributions to medical research.

The founder of the Indian Welfare movement in New York State, Bates began, as a private citizen, to help the Onondaga in 1910, developing an approach to Indian education known as the Bates Plan. This plan emphasized acceptance of Indian culture rather than stressing assimilation, with special emphasis placed on agriculture. In 1920, Bates won the New England Medal for the Promotion of Education for the Bates Plan.

From 1921 to 1961, Bates was director of the Cornell Indian Extension Service at the New York State College of Agriculture. Known to the Onondaga as Sa-Go-Ye-Watha (he stirs them up to plow and sow), Bates was active in Indian 4-H work and founded the Iroquois Village at the New York State Fair in 1928. Having first become involved with Indians through public health work, he took great satisfaction in the significant decline in infant mortality and death from tuberculosis among the Onondaga, which he attributed to the work of the extension service. He later became known as the "Little White Father" of the Six Nations (Iroquois) in New York.

Bates was not only interested in the health and education of the Iroquois; he was also a supporter of Iroquois sovereignty. During the 1920s, he worked closely with the Six Nations Council in their struggle for international recognition (see GENERAL, LEVI; GENERAL, ALEXANDER). In 1919, Bates spoke eloquently on behalf of the Oneida before the Everett Commission, which eventually found that the Iroquois had valid claims to more than 6 million acres of land within New York State. Bates then clashed with LAURA MIRIAM CORNELIUS KELLOGG over the choice of attorneys to pursue the claim. He preferred Iroquois attorney George Decker over Edward Everett, but Kellogg managed to prevail upon Tadadaho GEORGE E. THOMAS, and Everett was hired.

In June 1925, when Iroquois Jesse Lyons brought eight key historical wampum belts (which represented treaties) down to Washington as evidence that the Iroquois were not U.S. citizens, Bates, with his strong establishment credentials, enhanced their credibility among government officials by publicly announcing that he was initiating a long-term study of the wampum.

While on sabbatical from Cornell, Bates studied at the British Museum from 1929 to 1930, and during his stay in London he received the Tyler medal of the International Archaeological Society for his interpretation of the economic division of Indian clan nomenclature. On June 20, 1929, he married Miriam Jane Bartlett, a home economist with a degree from the University of Chicago, who had also worked for the Cornell Nursery School. A short time later, Bates was elected a fellow of the International Institute of Ethnology of the University of Paris. A world authority on physical characteristics in world populations, Bates was appointed to an advisory committee to the League of Nations on educational approaches to racial problems.

A Quaker, Bates was active in the Republican Party from his youth and eventually became chairman of its Onondaga County chapter. In June 1931, he was appointed by Secretary of the Interior Ray Lyman Wilbur and Indian Commissioner CHARLES JAMES RHOADS to assist in the reorganization of Indian education.

In 1951, after a 30-year search, Bates discovered documentary evidence of the year in which Hiawatha founded the League of the Iroquois, a puzzle that had long eluded scholars. The manuscript of the diary of Dutch historian Jan Wagenaar (1709–73), which had been offered for sale in London, refers to "the Five Nations who founded a powerful united council against their enemies fifty-seven years before our English skipper [i.e., Henry Hudson] anchored his most northern reach in 1609," which would have been 1552. Bates helped plan ceremonies to mark the 400th anniversary in 1952.

He was also a horticulturist, founder of the Syracuse Rose Society, vice president of the State Federation of Horticultural Societies and Floral Clubs, and well known as a lecturer on roses and lilies. A Masonic scholar, Bates was named grand master of the Masonic Quakers of the United States and Canada in October 1931. He died in Hollywood, Florida, on October 5, 1973.

See also POWERS, MABEL; RYAN, WILL CARSON, JR.

Further Reading

The Erl Bates papers (ca. 1920–60) are held by the Division of Rare and Manuscript Collections, Cornell University

Library, Ithaca, N.Y. They include correspondence and memoranda relating to state-sponsored agricultural extension work among the Iroquois in the early 1920s, and correspondence and other materials pertaining to the Cornell Indian Boards, the Six Nations' Agricultural Society, and the Indian Farmers' Schools.

Battle Mountain

Battle Mountain is the site of a long-standing dispute between the Western Shoshone and the Bureau of Land Management (BLM) over the ownership of the traditional Shoshone territory in Nevada. Shoshone lands had been guaranteed to them under the Treaty of Ruby Valley of October 1, 1863. Without the knowledge of the Shoshone, during the first half of the century, the BLM began to issue permits to ranchers to graze on Shoshone lands. The BLM called these lands "public domain," meaning they were uninhabited lands with no previous title, which would then go to the BLM for administration, despite the fact that the lands were protected by treaty and the Shoshone people lived on them.

The issue was brought to the fore by the perseverance of two sisters, Mary and Carrie Dann. Mary (1924–2005) and Carrie (b. 1934) were raised in Crescent Valley, Nevada, by their father, a rancher, and their Western Shoshone mother. After their father's death, the sisters continued to work the family ranch and, maintaining that the "public domain" lands they grazed on legally belonged to the Western Shoshone, stopped taking out permits from the BLM to graze their cattle on those lands. In 1974, the BLM began a lawsuit to force the Danns to take out permits or be evicted from the range.

The Danns argued that the Western Shoshone held title to lands including much of present-day Nevada according to the Treaty of Ruby Valley, and that these rights had never been extinguished by the United States. The U.S. attorneys countered that the title had effectively passed to the federal government through "gradual encroachment," an argument that had no basis in law at the time.

The issue was complicated by a case pending before the controversial INDIAN CLAIMS COMMISSION (ICC). In 1947, the BUREAU OF INDIAN AFFAIRS (BIA) organized a meeting of several Western Shoshone bands to persuade them to bring a case before the ICC to recover moneys from lands allegedly appropriated by the United States, which they finally did in 1951. However, by 1959, some Western Shoshone had begun to doubt the wisdom of pursuing the case and questioned the aims of their law firm, Wilkinson, Cragun, and Barker (see BOYDEN, JOHN STERLING). As the case slowly moved forward, resistance from the Shoshone increased. In 1974, a group of dissenters formed the Western Shoshone Sacred Lands Association in an attempt to block any settlements by the ICC. By this time, most of the Western Shoshone realized that they had been badly misled by the government and their attorneys. Rather than the Shoshone regaining lost lands or being compensated for them, the Claims Commission suit would allow the federal government to assume title to Shoshone lands that

Mary and Carrie Dann, two Western Shoshone sisters, fought to restore Western Shoshone land taken by the Bureau of Land Management in the latter half of the 20th century. *(Ronnie Farley)*

it had appropriated without a legal transfer, along with the remainder of Western Shoshone lands, all in return for a payment based on an assessment of the value of the lands more than 100 years earlier.

That is exactly what the Claims Commission did. In 1977, the ICC awarded the Western Shoshone $26 million for title to the entire land claim. The commission adopted the legal fiction that all the land had been encroached upon by the United States in 1872 and awarded the Western Shoshone the value of the land at that time, or $1 per acre, less than one one-hundredth of its present value. The 1872 date was an arbitrary one agreed on by the government and the Shoshone lawyers; it did not take into account the fact that in 1977 fully one-third of traditional Western Shoshone land was either still in their hands or uninhabited. The Shoshone refused to accept the award, but the BIA accepted it in their stead. The tribe then sued to block the award, but it was upheld by the U.S. Supreme Court in 1979, which ruled that the BIA, acting as trustee, could accept the money and thereby extinguish any Shoshone claims to the land. The next year, the Duckwater

Shoshone Tribe, the Battle Mountain Indian Community, and the Western Shoshone Sacred Lands Association sued their attorneys for fraud and conflict of interest. By this time, the Western Shoshone had begun to attract public support, especially from the antinuclear movement, which rallied behind the tribe's objections to nuclear testing and the proposed siting of MX missiles on the claimed lands.

On April 25, 1980, the trespass case, *United States v. Mary and Carrie Dann*, went before the Federal District Court for Nevada. The court found that up to December 1979, when the Court of Claims judgment became final, the Shoshone had maintained title to their lands under the Treaty of Ruby Valley, but that since that decision, title had passed to the United States, and the Danns would have to get permits in order to graze on them. The Dann sisters, who never accepted the legal sleight of hand that had deprived them of their lands, continued to graze their livestock without a permit. The BLM countered with a campaign of harassment designed to force them to submit to their regulations and began bulldozing the piñon groves that dotted the area, knowing they were sacred to the Shoshone.

In 1991, the Dann sisters helped to start the Western Shoshone Defense Project (WSDP) to raise money and lobby Congress to restore lands to the Shoshone; it garnered wide support among Indians and non-Indians alike. In 1992, the BLM stepped up its campaign by attempting to seize the Danns' livestock. In November of that year, they rounded up 250 of the Danns' horses, killing four of them in the process, and assaulted Clifford Dann, Mary and Carrie Dann's younger brother, who was attempting to halt the roundup. Clifford Dann was arrested and convicted of interfering with federal officers; he served nine months in prison. Since the early 1990s, the BLM has toned down its tactics. For their brave and arduous stand in protecting their lands, the Dann sisters became a symbol of indigenous resistance worldwide, and the BLM and Congress began moving to settle the dispute. A bill sponsored by Senator Harry Reid of Nevada would mandate the distribution of ICC funds held by the BIA to the Shoshone, whether they wanted it or not. They were aided by a growing number of Shoshone who wanted the distribution. The bill died in Congress in 2002, but it is expected to pass sooner or later. Although the Danns and their supporters will undoubtedly continue their resistance, for the United States the appropriation of Western Shoshone lands will be complete. On April 22, 2005, Mary Dann died after an accident with her all-terrain vehicle while repairing fences on the Crescent Valley ranch.

Further Information

Nelson, Cathy, and Thomas E. Luebben. "Update on the Western Shoshone Land Rights Struggle against the U.S. Government." *Indigenous Law Bulletin* 5, no. 19 (August/September 2002): 18–20.

Relph, Daniela. "Native Americans Divided over Land Battle." BBC News Online (July 10, 2004). Available online. URL: http://news.bbc.co.Uk/l/hi/world/americas/3878855.stm. Accessed 22 May 2008.

Film

Broken Treaty at Battle Mountain. Produced and directed by Joel L. Freedman. Cinnamon Productions, 60 min., 1974. Videocassette.

Bearskin, Leaford (1921–2012) *Wyandotte U.S. Air Force pilot, tribal leader*

Leaford Bearskin was born on September 11, 1921, along with his twin brother Leland (see BEARSKIN, LELAND S.), on his parents' allotment (see ALLOTMENT) in Wyandotte, Oklahoma. As soon as Leaford graduated from high school in 1939, he enlisted in the U.S. Army; after basic training he was assigned to Alaska. When the United States entered WORLD WAR II in December 1941, Bearskin was admitted to flying cadet school to train as a heavy-bomber pilot. After completing this course, he was assigned to New Guinea to command a B-24 Liberator bomber, known as "Big Chief," in which he flew 46 combat missions against Japanese forces. Toward the end of the war, Bearskin trained heavy-bomber crews and, after the Japanese surrender, served as a ground-force officer. For his World War II service, he was awarded the Distinguished Flying Cross and the Air Medal.

After the war, Bearskin was reassigned to Europe as a squadron commander, flying 29 missions in the Berlin airlift of 1948, for which he received a presidential unit citation. He was then assigned to a fighter base in Georgia as squadron commander, director of materiel, and deputy commander. He was air base group commander of the first flight of jet fighters across the Pacific Ocean. After attending the staff logistics course at the Air University in Montgomery, Alabama, Bearskin saw service as a squadron commander in the Korean War. After the war, he was squadron commander and assistant headquarters commandant at the Strategic Air Command in Omaha, Nebraska. He retired from the air force in 1960 with the rank of lieutenant colonel.

After his retirement, Bearskin entered the federal civil service as chief of vehicle and aerospace ground equipment at Vandenberg Air Force Base in California, where he worked with ground handling equipment for the Atlas, Titan, and Minuteman missile systems. In 1969, he became executive officer to the director of operations, 15th Air Force Headquarters, where he directed logistical operations of seven major directorates and 19 air bases within the 15th Air Force. He retired to Wyandotte in 1979.

In September 1983, Leaford Bearskin was elected chief of the Wyandotte tribe of Oklahoma. Under his leadership the Oklahoma Wyandotte in 1994 reopened the century-old HURON CEMETERY DISPUTE with the Kansas Wyandot, hoping to win the right to conduct a gambling operation in downtown Kansas City. In 1995, with Bearskin as chief, the Wyandotte were approved for self-governance and no longer had to go through the BUREAU OF INDIAN AFFAIRS (BIA) for funding. This allowed the tribe to select its own priorities, and over the next few years, benefiting from Bearskin's management experience, they rapidly instituted new health, education, and senior citizens' programs. The Turtle Tots Learning Center, which Bearskin helped to start, became the highest-ranked Indian preschool in the United States. Bearskin helped establish cooperative relations with the municipal services of the city of Wyandotte and also revived the tribal powwow (see POW-WOWS). He also supported work on reclaiming the Wendat language, the last native speakers of which died in the 1960s. Bearskin stepped down as chief on May 27, 2011, and died on November 9, 2012.

Bearskin's brothers Leland and Alvin also had distinguished aerospace careers. Alvin W. Bearskin, born January 6, 1919, served in World War II in the Army Engineer Corps. He worked as an aerospace engineer after the war, helping to design experimental craft that became part of NASA's Apollo lunar missions. He died in Paris, Texas, on December 18, 1999.

Further Reading

Bearskin, Leaford. "My Indian World." *Indian Country Today* (18 August 2005).

Witcher, T. R. "Bearskin's Gamble: Introducing the 81-Year-Old Oklahoma Man Who Has Laid Claim to Some of Wyandotte County's Richest Real Estate." *Kansas City, Kansas, Pitch* (12 September 2002).

Bearskin, Leland S. (1921–1993) *Wyandotte U.S. Air Force pilot*

Born in Wyandotte, Oklahoma, on September 11, 1925, with his twin brother, Leaford (see BEARSKIN, LEAFORD), Leland Bearskin enlisted in the U.S. Army field artillery after graduating from high school. He soon transferred to the U.S. Army Air Corps, where he was promoted to second lieutenant. During WORLD WAR II, Bearskin piloted army air corps transports, supplying troops in North Africa and Europe and winning a World War II Victory Medal. After the war, he transferred to the newly formed U.S. Air Force, where he earned a number of medals, including the Air Medal with five Oak Leaf Clusters. A skilled pilot, Bearskin was responsible during the Korean War for flying high-ranking officers safely to their destinations. He also flew numerous missions to the South Pole as part of "Operation Deep Freeze," and in 1956 he led an expedition called "Exercise Arctic Night," which dropped troops onto the Greenland ice cap.

Leland Bearskin took a leading part in setting up the International Polar Year (1957, later called the International Geophysical Year) at the South Pole Station. In recognition of his contribution, the U.S. Geological Survey's Advisory Committee on Antarctic Names named a 9,350-foot peak in the Sentinel Range of the Ellsworth Mountains "Mount Bearskin."

Bearskin retired from the air force in 1961 with the rank of major. He died on October 5, 1993. His brothers, Leaford and Alvin, were also distinguished figures in aviation.

Further Reading

Dufek, G. J. "What We've Accomplished in Antarctica." *National Geographic Magazine* 117, no. 4 (October 1959): 427–557.

Stewart, John. *Antarctica: An Encyclopedia.* Jefferson, N.C.: McFarland, 1990, p. 76.

Beaulieu, Gus H. (1852–1917) *Chippewa Métis real estate speculator, publisher*

Gus Beaulieu was born on June 12, 1852, at Crow Wing, Minnesota, a village founded by his father and other Métis. He was the eldest of six children of Clement H. Beaulieu (1811–93), a Métis agent of the American Fur Company, and Elizabeth Farling Beaulieu (d. 1902). In 1867, when the White Earth Reservation was created by the U.S. government for the Chippewa, Crow Wing had to be abandoned, and its residents were forced to remove to the reservation in 1869.

The Métis, descendants of English, Scottish, or French men and Chippewa women, are unique among mixed-blooded Indians in that they gained a measure of political recognition in Canada as a distinct people. The roots of the Métis go as far back as the early French explorers of the 17th century, and over the centuries they developed their own social organization and even language (Michif). In the United States, the Métis are generally just considered mixed-blood Chippewa and the term Métis is usually not applied. The Métis of Crow Wing were entered in the American government's annuity roll for the Mississippi Band of Chippewa and thus considered part of the tribe. But unlike other mixed-bloods, they were a distinct class of traders who acted as "cultural brokers" between non-Indians and the more traditional Chippewa and exercised a strong political influence. While most outsiders in the United States simply considered them to be Chippewa, on White Earth they were a powerful faction apart from the full-bloods and other mixed-bloods.

The Métis of Crow Wing were determined to maintain their status as traders and power brokers when they moved to White Earth. In August 1868, Clement Beaulieu and Métis trader John Fairbanks were reputed to have ordered the assassination of White Earth head chief Joseph Hole in the Day, who had opposed the influx of, in his words, "French-Canadian mixed-bloods." The death of the influential chief cleared the way for the Métis to seize control of the reservation.

Gus Beaulieu was first educated by a private tutor and then studied at Sinsinewaymound College and St. John's College (Minnesota). Leaving without a degree in 1871, he joined a surveying party and then served as assistant timber agent for the Northern Pacific Railroad. After several years, he returned to White Earth. He married Ella Holmes in 1887.

In 1889, the Minnesota government passed the Nelson Act (1889), which forced residents of the White Earth Reservation to divide up their communal lands. "Surplus" land was to be sold. The reservation was rich in timber, but the federal Indian office (see BUREAU OF INDIAN AFFAIRS) exercised complete control of tribal funds and assets. That year, Beaulieu and his cousin THEODORE H. BEAULIEU bought a printing press and started a newspaper, *The Progress*, in which they continually criticized the federal Indian office. They so vexed Indian Agent Timothy J. Sheehan that he physically destroyed the press. The Beaulieus sued him in federal court and won.

The Métis bitterly resented being treated like ordinary Indians who were considered "wards" and "incompetents" by the state and federal governments. With their experience in the fur trade and land dealings, they were experts in the market economy and well connected with Minnesota politicians. This and a burning hatred of the Indian Office made Gus Beaulieu an ardent assimilationist (see ASSIMILATION) and apparently justified in his mind the use of any means necessary to work the system to his advantage. From the 1890s to about 1910, Beaulieu, his brother Clement, and the son of John Fairbanks, Benjamin L. Fairbanks, controlled the tribal council, holding meetings when and where they pleased, sometimes counting personal meetings as legitimate council meetings, rigging votes, bullying speakers who questioned them, and manipulating rules of order in a way that left the full-bloods bewildered. Beyond this, they acted as go-betweens for lumber magnates to bribe potentially troublesome Indians. Fairbanks, a merchant, threatened to withhold credit for "wrong" votes on election day. Using charisma, political machinations, and pressure to get what they wanted, the three always portrayed their opinions as those of the majority. This became even easier after Gus Beaulieu founded a weekly newspaper, *The Tomahawk*, in 1903 as successor to *The Progress*.

In 1906, the annual U.S. government General Indian Appropriation Bill included a piece of legislation known as the Clapp Rider, which allowed mixed-bloods at White Earth to sell their land allotments (see ALLOTMENT) and opened the way to massive fraud and corruption. Beaulieu was hired by timber concerns as an agent to secure them the best timber lands. Usually he would "reserve" an allotment by paying the owner an advance of $25 on a mortgage, the rest of which was supposed to be paid after the law took effect. The mortgages were to run 10 years and accrue 10 percent interest on the whole amount, to be collected in advance. The largely illiterate and cash-strapped Indians rarely understood this. As the Allotment process had been fraudulent and unfair from the start, the Indians were now often willing victims, since many lived nowhere near their land and had never even seen it. Typically, they would take the advance, spend it on necessities, and have little or nothing left. The lenders would quickly call in the debt, and the property would be foreclosed. During the first three weeks of the Clapp Rider, more than 250 mortgages were arranged in Becker County alone.

In March and April 1909, Warren Moorehead, special agent of the Board of Indian Commissioners, went to White Earth to investigate (see his book *The American Indian* [1914]). Moorehead found the Clapp Rider to be the source of tremendous fraud and corruption. There was also an investigation by the House of Representatives, known as the Graham Commission after Congressman James M. Graham, in 1911 and 1912. Considerable evidence implicated Gus Beaulieu, Benjamin Fairbanks, and John Carl. Documents had been prepared in advance by the timber corporations, and as there was no mechanism to verify tribal status, full-bloods,

sometimes even minors, would be instructed by one of the trio to sign as mixed-bloods of legal age. Beaulieu had even gone to government Indian boarding schools to sign minors. Evidence was presented showing that he had falsified records of a deceased allottee and pretended to be a guardian to orphans. Both mixed-bloods and full-bloods testified that they were unaware of what they were signing. Some stated they had been misled as to the meaning of documents, while others had been plied with liquor. Money promised had never been received, and valuable lands had been signed away for a small fraction of their worth.

In 1916, a council handpicked by the "Beaulieu-Fairbanks Gang" voted to send delegates to Washington to lobby for the liquidation of the reservation's assets and the division of tribal funds and lands among individual members. Moorehead, warned of this by Gus's cousin Theodore Beaulieu, began to wonder why the gang had never been indicted, since many investigations had incontrovertibly established the facts. Noting that the findings had never gone beyond the upper levels of the Department of the Interior, Moorehead concluded that the gang was under the powerful protection of Senator Moses Clapp and the timber and land barons of Minnesota.

In May 1917, Gus Beaulieu moved to Barrows, Minnesota. While on a fishing trip with his family near home on August 8, he suffered a massive stroke and died instantly. His death made little difference to the gang's operations, however, and by the end of the Allotment period, the tribe and its individual members had lost 93 percent of the White Earth Reservation. *The Tomahawk* continued to pretend to represent their interests, viciously attacking Fond du Lac Chippewa James Coffey, the chief whistle-blower, and criticizing the agency at Red Lake, which, through a combination of luck and deft political skills, had managed to avoid allotment. The newspaper survived into 1926.

These frauds gave rise to claims cases that are still pending 90 years later. WINONA LADUKE and other activists founded the White Earth Land Recovery Project in 1985 to deal with some of the consequences of the Allotment period. The White Earth Tribal Council has also recovered small parcels of reservation land.

Further Reading

Meyer, Melissa L. *The White Earth Tragedy: Ethnicity and Dispossession at a Minnesota Anishinabe Reservation.* Lincoln: University of Nebraska Press, 1994.

Beaulieu, Theodore H. (1850–1923) *journalist, orator, farmer, businessman*

Theodore H. Beaulieu, a Métis, was born near Kaukauna, Wisconsin, on September 4, 1850, son of Bazil Beaulieu, a native of Wisconsin, and Mary Saulliard Beaulieu of Michigan. After finishing his education, he spent 12 years in the printing business and then two years with the International Marine Service, sailing between Philadelphia and Liverpool.

In 1879, Beaulieu left Wisconsin to work for the federal

government among the Chippewa. After two years as U.S. land examiner, he took over the land department at the White Earth Reservation. In 1886, he and his cousin Gus Beaulieu established the first English-language Native American newspaper, *The Progress*. Literary work remained a lifelong pursuit, and at his death Beaulieu was a contributor and correspondent to publications in the Twin Cities of Minneapolis and St. Paul.

Beaulieu was active in the SOCIETY OF AMERICAN INDIANS, of which he was elected vice president in October 1919. Though a "progressive," Theodore, unlike his cousin, GUS BEAULIEU, maintained a good reputation with traditional factions at White Earth. In 1916, he criticized Gus for the "steamroller process" by which he had rigged a council meeting to select delegates favorable to the assimilationist faction. In December, when Gus and Benjamin Fairbanks put together a delegation to go to Washington to try to dissolve the reservation and secure the division of tribal funds and lands, Beaulieu warned Indian rights advocate WARREN KING MOOREHEAD of the danger this represented. His criticisms of Gus increased over time.

For the last 15 years of his life, Beaulieu worked in the real estate business, and around 1920 he developed a summer resort on the shores of White Earth Lake. As a township supervisor, he helped establish the road between White Earth and Ogema as a state aid road, saving the township thousands of dollars. After failing to recover from an operation on January 15, 1923, Theodore H. Beaulieu died on May 13, 1923.

Begay, Harrison (Haskay Yah Ne Yah) (1917–2012)
Navajo painter

Harrison Begay was born on November 15, 1917, in White Cone, Arizona, to Black Rock and Zonnie Tachinie Begay—both Navajo (Dineh). They gave him the name *Haskay Yah Ne Yah* (Warrior Who Walked Up to His Enemy). As a young boy, Begay herded his family's sheep around their home near Greasewood, Arizona, until he was sent to school at Fort Wingate in 1927, though after a short time he ran away and returned to herding. His absence from school for four years did not appear to affect his education, as he eventually graduated from Tohatchi Indian School in 1939 as the salutatorian. An excellent athlete, Begay as a youth held the state record for the mile run.

Following his graduation from Tohatchi, Begay attended the Santa Fe Indian School, where he studied art under the influential DOROTHY DUNN. There he learned to paint in the "Santa Fe," or "Studio," style favored at the time, which depicted tribal and ceremonial scenes using soft pastel colors in a flat, two-dimensional manner. While at Santa Fe, Begay was commissioned to paint a mural for Maise's Indian Trading Post. In 1940, he attended Black Mountain College in Blue Ridge, North Carolina, studying architecture, before transferring to Phoenix Junior College in Arizona.

Begay was drafted into the U.S. Army during WORLD WAR II, serving in the signal corps until his discharge in 1945. Resolving to become a full-time artist, he moved back to the Navajo Reservation in 1947. In 1950, Begay was featured in Oscar B. Jacobson's book *American Indian Painters*, and his work appeared in the magazine *Arizona Highways*. In 1954, the French government awarded him its Palmes Académiques, honoring him for his contributions to Native American art. In 1957 he illustrated Ann Nolan Clark's book *Little Indian Basket Maker*.

Begay is known for his delicate lines and clean, cool, softened colors, which give his paintings an ethereal look that is at once serenely still and vitally active. In 1957, he began to study with the artist Don Perceval, who suggested that Begay explore Navajo cosmology in his paintings. In 1967, Begay's book *The Sacred Mountains of the Navajo* featured the legends surrounding the creation of four sacred Navajo landmarks.

Begay became the most influential Navajo painter of his day. His work is held by many important collections, including the Heard Museum, Atlanta; the Museum of the American Indian, New York; and the Museum of New Mexico. He has also won many awards, including first place at the Gallup Intertribal Ceremonies in 1967, 1969, and 1971. In 1990, Begay was invited to Japan to show his work. He took 45 works and sold them within three weeks. In 1995, Begay received the Native American Masters Award from the Heard Museum in Phoenix, Arizona. In 2003, he won the Lifetime Achievement Award from the Southwestern Association for Indian Arts. In his last years he lived in Greasewood, Arizona, near his birthplace. Despite failing eyesight, he still painted a couple of hours a day. He died on August 18, 2012.

Bellecourt, Clyde (1936–) *Chippewa activist, cofounder of the American Indian Movement*

A Chippewa, Clyde Bellecourt was born May 8, 1936, on the White Earth Reservation in Minnesota. His father was a disabled WORLD WAR I veteran. Bellecourt grew up in poverty along with four brothers and seven sisters. At the age of 11, he was arrested for truancy from boarding school and sent to the Minnesota Training School for Boys at Red Wing, an institution of notorious brutality. Three years later, Bellecourt ran away and drifted to Minneapolis. Unable to find employment, he turned to petty crime.

Bellecourt was convicted of burglary and sentenced to the Stillwater State Penitentiary. There, having lost hope, he went on a hunger strike, intending to die. He only ended the hunger strike when fellow Chippewa Eddie Benton-Benai and DENNIS JAMES BANKS convinced him to reform and try to work for his people. In 1968, along with Banks and George Mitchell, Bellecourt founded Concerned Indian American (soon renamed the AMERICAN INDIAN MOVEMENT [AIM]) in Minneapolis as a neighborhood patrol to counter then-pervasive police brutality. With the addition of Sioux activists RUSSELL MEANS and JOHN TRUDELL, AIM soon grew into a national organization. Bellecourt played an active role in the TRAIL OF BROKEN TREATIES, leading a takeover of the Minneapolis BUREAU OF INDIAN AFFAIRS office that anticipated the occupation of the national office in Washington, D.C. Bellecourt also helped lead the occupation at WOUNDED KNEE, though his presence was overshadowed by Banks and Means.

In August 1973, in an atmosphere of paranoia among AIM leaders fueled by the FBI's infiltration of the group, Bellecourt was shot and wounded by AIM chairman Carter Camp. As AIM began to disintegrate under pressure from government prosecutions, FBI "dirty tricks" (see AQUASH, ANNA MAE, and PELTIER, LEONARD), and infighting among various factions, all the early leaders except Bellecourt eventually dropped out. In 1986, Bellecourt and six other men were caught with a large quantity of cocaine; he pled guilty to conspiring to distribute drugs and was sentenced to seven years in prison. After his release, he returned to his position as head of the Minneapolis chapter of AIM. Bellecourt currently directs the Elaine M. Stately Peacemaker Center for Indian youth and the AIM Patrol, which provides security for the Minneapolis Indian community. He is an organizer of the National Coalition on Racism in Sports and the Media and is founder and chairman of the board of American Indian Opportunities Industrialization Center, a program to help Indians get full-time jobs.

Bellecourt's older brother, Vernon Bellecourt (1931–2007), also became an important AIM member. Born on October 17, 1931, his Indian name was Wabun-Inini (Man of Dawn). Vernon Bellecourt lived on the White Earth Indian Reservation until he was 16, when their parents, Charles and Angeline Bellecourt, moved to Minneapolis. When he was 19, he spent time in St. Cloud Prison for robbing a tavern in St. Paul, Minnesota. After his release he became a hairdresser and proceeded to open a series of beauty salons in Saint Paul before moving to Aspen, Colorado. He joined AIM and participated with Clyde in the demonstration in Gordon, Nebraska, in 1972 to bring attention to the murder of RAYMOND YELLOW THUNDER, as well as the Trail of Broken Treaties and the siege of Wounded Knee. Vernon Bellecourt's attempts during the 1980s to curry favor with Libya's Muammar Qaddafi and the controversial Black Muslim leader Louis Farrakhan weakened AIM's credibility among Indians and non-Indians alike. He became a leading advocate in the cause of banning the use of Indian images as mascots and nicknames for professional sports teams. In August 2007, Vernon Bellecourt accepted an invitation from the Venezuelan government to attend the First International Congress of Anti-imperialist Indigenous Peoples of America and visited with President Hugo Chavez in Venezuela. The two discussed the possibility of Chavez providing aid to Native American groups. Soon after the trip he fell ill and was hospitalized. He died of pneumonia on October 13, 2007.

Beltz, William E. (1912–1960) *Inupiat Eskimo politician, first president of Alaska's state senate*

William E. Beltz was born on April 17, 1912, the son of a non-Indian migrant from Pennsylvania and an Eskimo (Inupiat) mother; his father had moved to Alaska in 1897. After growing up in Unalakeet, Beltz became a carpenter and, later, an official of Alaska's carpenter's union. In 1948, he headed a search committee to seek out Alaska Natives to run for the territorial legislature. Unable to find enough candidates, Beltz himself ran as a Democrat for the House of Representatives and won a seat. In 1950, he was elected to the territorial senate. As a legislator, Beltz fought for Native Alaskan rights and sponsored bills to help workers, including a minimum-wage bill and a worker's compensation bill. When Alaska became the 49th state in January 1959, Beltz was elected president of the first Alaska Senate. By then, however, he was already suffering from cancer; he died on November 21, 1960. In 1966, a high school in Nome was named after him.

Further Reading
Wolfe, Ellen R. *William Beltz: The Story of a Native American.* Minneapolis, Minn.: Dillon Press, 1975.

Bender, Charles Albert (Chief Bender) (1883–1954) *Chippewa baseball pitcher*

Charles Bender was born in Brainerd, Minnesota, on May 5, 1883, the fourth of 13 children of Albertus Bliss Bender, a German-American homesteader, and Mary Razor Bender, a full-blood Chippewa. There is some confusion as to Charles Bender's actual birth date, and many sources give the year as 1884; however, according to his birth certificate it was 1883. Furthermore, his WORLD WAR I and WORLD WAR II draft registration forms, which Bender himself filled out, state that he was born on May 5, 1883, in Brainerd. At the time of Bender's birth, the family lived about 20 miles east of Brainerd on Partridge Lake, which was then an undesignated area of Brainerd township but now lies within the village of Deerwood. Soon after his birth, they moved to his mother's 160-acre allotment on the White Earth Reservation. His sister Elizabeth later married the Winnebago educator HENRY CLARENCE ROE CLOUD, and his brother Fred also became an influential educator (see CLOUD, ELIZABETH BENDER).

At the age of eight, Bender was sent to the Lincoln Institute in Philadelphia, a boarding school for Indian students. He returned to White Earth for a few months in the summer of 1896 before leaving to attend the Carlisle Indian School in Pennsylvania. Bender played baseball for POP WARNER at Carlisle, and after graduating in 1902 he played semiprofessionally in Harrison, Pennsylvania. Connie Mack, famed coach of the Philadelphia Athletics, saw Bender beat the Chicago Cubs in an exhibition game in 1902 and promptly signed him to a contract worth $1,800, a large sum at the time.

Between 1903 and 1914, Bender won 206 games and threw 36 shutouts for the Philadelphia Athletics; he also became the first pitcher in major league history to win six World Series games. In a memorable game in 1906 against the Boston Red Sox, Bender, an equally good fielder and hitter, was called in the sixth inning to replace an outfielder and ended up hitting two home runs. As a pitcher, the right-hander was a major force behind one of the greatest baseball teams of all times, the 1910–14 Athletics, which won the American League pennant four of those five years and featured the $100,000 infield

Chippewa athlete Charles Albert "Chief" Bender, star pitcher for the Philadelphia Athletics from 1902 to 1914, plays an exhibition game in 1930. *(AP/Wideworld)*

of Frank (Home Run) Baker, Jack Barry, Eddie Collins, and Stuffy McInnes. In a stable that included three other Hall of Fame pitchers—Rube Waddell, Eddie Plank, and Herb Pennock—as well as the fearsome Jack Coombs, Connie Mack still considered Bender the best money pitcher of all time. "If everything depended on one game," he was quoted as saying, "I just used Albert."

Bender's greatest year was 1910, when he pitched a no-hitter against the Cleveland Indians on the way to a 23-5 record, helping to lead the Athletics to the world championship. In 1911, he sported the league's best mark, 17 wins to only 5 losses, when he faced Hall of Fame pitcher Christy Mathewson of the New York Giants in the World Series. Mathewson, who had JOHN TORTES MEYERS catching for him, outdueled Bender in the first game, 2-1, even though Bender struck out 11. Bender rebounded to beat Mathewson in the fourth game and then threw a four-hitter to take game six and the title.

In 1913, Bender went 21-10 and won two World Series games to lead the Athletics to their third world championship. In 1914, he won 14 straight games to give the A's the pennant, though they were then swept in the World Series by the Boston Braves. In 1915, Bender moved to the Baltimore Terrapins as part of the short-lived Federal League, and he ended his career

in 1917 with the Philadelphia Phillies. In 1918, with the United States at war, Bender worked as a bolter and foreman at the American International Shipbuilding yard at Hog Island, near Philadelphia.

In 1925, he tried to make a comeback with the Chicago White Sox, but that lasted only one inning. He ended his career with 212 wins and 127 losses, 1,711 strikeouts, and an earned run average of 2.46.

A rare gentleman in the rough-and-tumble world of turn-of-the-century baseball, Bender was widely admired by fans and players alike. He quietly suffered the nickname "Chief" as well as the taunts and war whoops from rude fans. Bender would occasionally reply "Foreigners! Foreigners!" back to the loudest and most obnoxious, but always in good-humored fashion. After his playing days ended, he became a successful minor- and major-league coach, winning four pennants with the Athletics' minor league teams. He was also a standout as a billiard player and a marksman, hobbies he pursued in later life. In September 1953, Bender was elected to the Baseball Hall of Fame. He died on May 22, 1954, in Philadelphia.

Further Reading

Kashatus, William C. *Money Pitcher: Chief Bender and the Tragedy of Indian Assimilation.* University Park: Pennsylvania State University Press, 2006.

Swift, Tom. *Chief Bender's Burden: The Silent Struggle of a Baseball Star.* Lincoln: University of Nebraska Press, 2008.

Bennett, Robert LaFollette (1912–2002)

commissioner of Indian affairs

An Oneida, Robert LaFollette Bennett was born on the Oneida reservation near Green Bay, Wisconsin, on November 16, 1912. His father was a white farmer, his mother, Lydia Doxtater Bennett, was a full-blooded Oneida, and his grandmother was a traditional who did not speak English. Bennett attended public and parochial schools before graduating from Haskell Institute in 1931. (The Haskell Indian Institute, now Haskell Indian Nations University, was founded in 1884 as a vocational training school for young Indians.)

At 21, Bennett took a job with the Indian Office (later the BUREAU OF INDIAN AFFAIRS [BIA]). A career BIA officer, he served at the Ute Agency and at the Washington, D.C., headquarters. He received his law degree from Southeastern University School of Law (Washington, D.C.) in 1941. He then served on the Navajo reservation in Arizona before joining the U.S. Marines during WORLD WAR II (October 1944). After the war, he briefly worked in the Veterans Administration, helping Indian veterans obtain benefits under the G.I. Bill. He then returned to the BIA and became a placement officer in South Dakota for their controversial employment program known as Relocation (see URBANIZATION, AMERICAN INDIANS AND). Bennett pursued the innovative strategy of finding opportunities for Indians close to their reservations instead of relocating them to urban areas such as Los Angeles.

Thus began his low-key approach of creatively altering misguided BIA programs rather than directly challenging them.

In 1962, Bennett was promoted to director of the Juneau Area Office in Alaska, where he worked to protect Indian land claims and gained the respect of national Indian leaders. On April 27, 1966, after being handpicked by Secretary of the Interior Stewart Udall, Bennett replaced PHILLEO NASH as commissioner of the BIA. He was the first Native American commissioner since Ely Parker almost a century earlier. Under pressure from the rising expectations spawned by President Lyndon Johnson's "Great Society" agenda, which sought to improve the living standards of poor Americans, Udall was anxious for radical reform and needed a man who could work well with tribal leaders without antagonizing Congress. In Robert Bennett, Udall found a commissioner with solid credibility among Native Americans and a high level of bureaucratic expertise.

Bennett knew better than to try to shake up an entrenched bureaucracy. Instead, he set up a coalition (later formalized as the National Council on Indian Opportunity) of all the federal groups that rendered services to Indian people, thus streamlining the decision making and lessening the conflicts and duplication that had previously characterized federal aid to Indians. Bennett expanded the controversial Relocation program but, following his practice in South Dakota, dramatically reduced the displacement of Indians outside their home states.

Under pressure from Senator Robert Kennedy and the Senate's scathing report on Indian education (see ADAMS, HANK), Bennett moved to expand the BIA's educational efforts, doubling the funding for higher education, establishing a kindergarten program, and setting up local school boards. Bennett was opposed to TERMINATION, the federal policy at the time; through his deft handling of the issue, he kept Congress from terminating several tribes. He attempted to eradicate what he called the "occupational disease of paternalism" that characterized BIA philosophy and instead promoted Indian self-determination. He instituted a policy in which individual tribes set their own goals and would have the BIA help to carry them out, beginning a fundamental shift that would bear fruit under President Richard Nixon.

Bennett was not without his critics, such as the NATIONAL CONGRESS OF AMERICAN INDIANS and the growing RED POWER MOVEMENT, who felt he was not moving fast enough. His promotion of Indian self-determination and economic development led in many cases to the controversial leasing of tribal land for extraction of natural resources. These leases would become the focus of protests by the AMERICAN INDIAN MOVEMENT in the 1970s and 1980s. His 1966 administrative order, known as the "Bennett Freeze," restricted development on parts of the Navajo and Hopi reservations that were contested by both tribes (see BIG MOUNTAIN).

On the whole, however, Bennett's administration is generally characterized by concrete results carried out in a non-confrontational, behind-the-scenes manner. His long tenure with the agency allowed him to avoid the treacherous political infighting that generally derailed any attempts at reform.

After helping the transition of the new Nixon administration, Bennett resigned on May 31, 1969, in favor of LOUIS ROOK BRUCE, JR. Bennett remained active in Indian affairs, founding the American Indian Athletic Hall of Fame and the American Indian Graduate Center later that year. In 1970, he became the director of the American Indian Law Center at the University of New Mexico. He retired in 1975 but continued to lecture on Indian affairs. In 1988, he was honored by the Oneida of Wisconsin, who named him their most outstanding member for his contributions to Native American rights. Bennett died on July 11, 2002, in Albuquerque, New Mexico.

Further Reading

Castile, George Pierre. *To Show Heart: Native American Self-Determination and Federal Indian Policy, 1960–1975.* Tucson: University of Arizona Press, 1998.

Nelson, Mary Carroll. *Robert Bennett, The Story of an American Indian.* Minneapolis, Minn.: Dillon Press, 1976.

Big Mountain

During the 1980s and 1990s, a long-simmering land dispute between the Hopi and Navajo tribal governments resulted in the forced relocation of thousands of traditional Navajo (Dineh). This bitter episode occurred in the Big Mountain area of the Hopi Reservation in the Four Corners region of the Southwest. The dispute had its roots partly in the rapid increase in population of Navajo in that area, strongly traditional Indians who at the beginning of the 20th century were primarily sheepherders.

During the late 19th and early 20th centuries, as the Navajo migrated from their traditional territory westward into northwestern Arizona, they gradually encroached on Hopi lands. This created problems for the Hopi, but the problems might have been dealt with in various ways. The fact that relocation was chosen as the solution was largely due to a need by powerful interests to clear title to lands claimed by both the Navajo and the Hopi, in order to allow for the prospecting of the lucrative oil, gas, and coal deposits that underlay the disputed lands.

In 1882, the federal government established the Hopi Reservation, though they did little to prevent the Navajo from moving closer to Hopi lands. Due to rapidly increasing population, the government made several additions to the Navajo Reservation, until it completely surrounded the Hopi Reservation. Even with that, the Navajo continued to settle on the Hopi side of the boundary, leaving the Hopi with little more than the mesas on which their villages were located.

Federal officials had little sympathy for the Hopi complaints of Navajo intrusion, as they were locked in a bitter struggle with Hopi traditional leaders over government attempts to gain more control of the Hopi. As early as 1891, federal troops began arresting and imprisoning Hopi who refused to send their children to school (see ASSIMILATION and EDUCATIONAL POLICY, AMERICAN INDIANS AND). Hopi

During the Navajo-Hopi dispute, Navajo activist Katherine Smith holds a flag bearing a message in front of her home near Big Mountain, Arizona, where she fought to remain on her land. *(AP/Wideworld)*

traditionalists such as YOUKIOMA were repeatedly imprisoned for their staunch resistance to assimilation. Attempts by government officials to encourage the Hopi to move off the high mesas and live on the more open lands below them were also largely unsuccessful. The Hopi preferred to be close to their village communities, where they could participate in their complex ceremonial life. Many Hopi used the open lands only during the summer, spending the winter in the villages. By 1920, Navajo pressure had confined the Hopi to 384,000 acres, less than one-sixth the area of the original Hopi Reservation.

During the 1930s, the federal government began efforts to bring together into a political faction those "progressive" Hopi who were not necessarily inclined to live on the mesas. Since these Hopi had become uncomfortable living in strongly traditional Hopi villages such as Oraibi, Hotevilla, or Shungopovi, the government efforts met with success. As the new progressives, such as cattle rancher EMORY SEKAQUAPTEWA and his family, moved onto their traditional clan lands, they began to come into conflict with the Navajo.

The political balance of power began to shift in favor of the Hopi progressives when a "tribal" government was created by OLIVER LA FARGE in 1937 under the INDIAN REORGANIZATION ACT. The new Hopi government usurped the authority of each of the eight Hopi villages, which were traditionally independent of each other, and although the new constitution gave the village heads (kikmongwis) some say in the process of electing the tribal council, the manner by which Hopi leadership was selected was totally alien to Hopi traditions (see COLTON, HAROLD SELLERS). The Navajo Tribal Council, having been founded by the notorious ALBERT BACON FALL in 1924 to negotiate oil leases, likewise bore little relation to traditional Navajo leadership (see HAGERMAN, HERBERT JAMES; OIL, AMERICAN INDIANS AND).

Opposition from traditional Hopi kept the newly formed Hopi Tribal Council from functioning, and it quickly became dormant. The situation between the Navajo and the Hopi also remained tense but uneventful until the early 1950s, when the potential mineral wealth of Black Mesa, one of the richest geological deposits in the United States, attracted the attention of the Salt Lake City lawyer JOHN STERLING BOYDEN. Over the objections of the traditional Hopi, Boyden reconstituted the Hopi Tribal Council and began to pursue the eviction of the Navajo from the Hopi Reservation. In 1960, Boyden brought suit on behalf of the Hopi Tribal Council, and the court case, *Healing v. Jones*, was decided on September 28, 1962. The federal district court in Prescott, Arizona, ruled that a portion of the Hopi Reservation where the Hopi villages were located, known as District 6, was owned exclusively by the Hopi. The rest of the reservation, the court ruled, belonged jointly to both tribes, although the court said only Congress had the power to determine how the land should be shared. The position of Boyden and the Hopi Tribal Council was that the ruling meant the Hopi were entitled to half of the Joint-Use Area (JUA), as the land outside of District 6 came to be known. The problem was that this area was almost exclusively settled by Navajo.

In 1966, Indian Commissioner Robert Bennett, through an administrative order known as the "Bennett Freeze," restricted all new construction and even repair of existing dwellings on 1.5 million acres, covering 10 chapters (districts) of the Navajo Reservation. The court decision led to a boom in oil, gas, and coal exploration on the undisputed lands—District 6 on the Hopi Reservation and the Navajo Reservation adjacent to the JUA. Boyden, who while working for the Hopi tribe also represented Peabody Coal, began to negotiate mineral leases for the Hopi Tribal Council for District 6 while pursuing legislation to partition the JUA. After a fierce lobbying effort led by Hopi tribal chairman Abbott Sekaquaptewa, and despite the efforts of Navajo leader Peter MacDonald, President Gerald Ford signed Public Law 93-531 on December 22, 1974, mandating the partition of the JUA between the tribes and, under section 10(f), cemented into law the ban on construction and repair initiated by the Bennett Freeze eight years earlier.

Soon after, a number of government officials who worked for the bill's passage left government employ to work for energy companies or firms with an interest in the JUA. These included Harrison Loesch, former head of the Bureau of Land Management and minority counsel for the Senate and Interior Affairs Committee, who became the vice president of public relations for Peabody Coal; Congressman Wayne Owens, sponsor of the bill, who went to work for John Boyden's Salt Lake City firm; and Jerry Verkler, staff director of the Senate Interior and Insular Affairs Committees, who became the chief lobbyist for Texas Transmission Corporation. (See Presidential Commission on Indian Reservation Economies.)

Public Law 93-531 was opposed by traditional Hopi such as Mina Lansa, kikmongwi of Oraibi and daughter of Wilson Tewaquaptewa; David Monyongwe, leader of Hotevilla; and Thomas Banyacya, who considered the actions of the Hopi Tribal Council illegal and feared the real purpose of the relocation was to open up the land around the mesas to energy development. Banyacya and other traditional Hopi actively worked with the Navajo to try to overturn the bill and stop the relocation.

The law ordered that the JUA be evenly split and boundary lines drawn. The Navajo in the JUA were forced to accept 90 percent reduction in their livestock and were restrained from any new construction or improvements to their dwellings. The law also established a relocation commission whose function was to plan for the removal of what was at first believed to be 3,300 Navajo, although the actual number turned out to be at least twice that many. The Navajo tribe was entitled under the law to acquire 400,000 acres to accommodate the

relocatees, but New Mexico and Arizona were reluctant to give up any lands within their states to accommodate the tribe. The boundaries were finalized in 1977, and construction of a 300-mile-long fence was begun to partition the land. The fence and the livestock reduction, implemented in 1981, met with fierce resistance from the Navajo, led by elders Pauline Whitesinger, Katherine Smith, sisters Ruth and Alice Benally, and Roberta Blackgoat.

Although the relocation was supposed to have begun in 1981 and to have been finished by 1986, by the beginning of 1986 little had been done. Resistance from the Navajo and increasingly bad publicity stymied the relocation commissions. Those Navajo who had relocated, mostly to towns and cities outside the reservation, had fared poorly. Those remaining in the JUA were suffering severe deprivation from the effects of stock reductions that hampered their traditional way of life and their ability to earn an income. The dispute became a national issue through the efforts of the lead lawyers for the resisters, Lew Gurwitz, a veteran of the Wounded Knee trials, and Lee Phillips. The Big Mountain Legal Defense-Offense Committee (BMLDOC), as the legal office was known, along with militant remnants of the American Indian Movement (AIM), raised the specter of a massive forcible removal of the thousands of resisters by the American military in July 1986, the deadline for relocation, effectively mobilizing concerned individuals around the country who were prepared to go to Arizona in an attempt to prevent bloodshed. The flames were fanned by the emotional appeal of the documentary *Broken Rainbow*, by Victoria Mudd and Maria Florida, which vividly portrayed the dispute, albeit very much from the perspective of the Navajo tribal council.

The result was a massive groundswell of support in winter 1985 and spring 1986. Legislators were bombarded with calls to repeal Public Law 93-531. The movement to stop the relocation was powerful, but the lack of a political strategy and legislative alternatives to counter the well-funded Hopi effort or of a qualified political lobbyist in Washington, D.C., caused support to dissipate. Moreover, BMLDOC's unwillingness to allow the participation of the environmental movement, which might have countered the powerful natural resource interests behind the bill, hamstrung their efforts.

The movement BMLDOC unleashed was fleeting, lasting a few short months. Although *Broken Rainbow* won an Academy Award, most members of Congress dismissed it as propaganda, and the film ultimately caused a backlash. When the July 1986 deadline came and went without the anticipated military roundup, grassroots support for the Navajo evaporated. The policy adopted by the federal government and the Hopi Tribal Council was to concentrate on selected Navajo resisters, forcing them to abandon the JUA one by one. In return for being allowed to stay on their lands, elder Navajo were encouraged to sign life estates that would turn their land over to the Hopi tribe after their deaths.

Although there have been attempts to revive the Big Mountain issue, the interests behind the relocation were simply too powerful to be stopped. In addition, the militant tactics pioneered by AIM, like AIM itself, had lost their effectiveness by the 1980s. With more than 8,000 Navajo and 100 Hopi forced to move, Big Mountain became the largest relocation of Indians in the 20th century. To date, there remain only a handful of Navajo resisters who have not come to terms with the Hopi tribe or who have not left the JUA. The Bennett Freeze was repealed in 2006, after 40 years.

See also JONES, PAUL.

Further Reading

Benedek, Emily. *The Wind Won't Know Me: A History of the Navajo-Hopi Land Dispute.* Norman: University of Oklahoma Press, 1999.

Nies, Judith. *Unreal City: Las Vegas, Black Mesa, and the Fate of the West.* New York: Nations Books, 2014.

Parlow, Anita. *Cry Sacred Ground: Big Mountain, U.S.A.* Washington, D.C.: Christic Institute Press, 1988.

Sills, Mark. "Sovereignty and Legitimacy in Hopi Country." *Fourth World Bulletin* 3, no. 2 (April 1994).

Wilkinson, Charles F. *Fire on the Plateau: Conflict and Endurance in the American Southwest.* Washington, D.C.: Island Press, Shearwater Books, 1999.

Big Tree, John (Isaac Johnny John) (1875–1967)
Seneca actor, reputed model for the Indian-head nickel

Born Isaac Johnny John in 1875 on the Cattaraugus Reservation in New York, John Big Tree was the grandson of Steve Jameson, a full-blood Seneca who had fought in the Civil War. With little formal education, he left home at 13 and joined a wagon show. For the next 60 years, he worked in circuses, Buffalo Bill's Wild West Show, and especially Hollywood.

Big Tree was working in a Coney Island sideshow in 1912 when he was reputedly asked by sculptor James Earle Fraser to pose for a new five-cent piece. According to Big Tree, he sat for three hours and was paid $1.50 an hour. Some sources report that the final design used his face down to the mouth. Other reported models include Chief Iron Tail, a Cheyenne (the chin), and Chief John Wolf Robe, a Sioux (hair and feathers).

However, in a June 10, 1931, letter to Indian Commissioner CHARLES JAMES RHOADS, Fraser stated: "I used three different heads: I remember two of the men, one was Irontail, the best Indian head I can remember; the other one was Two Moons [a Cheyenne chief who fought against Custer at Little Big Horn], and the third I cannot recall." Whether it was really Wolf Robe or Big Tree is not known. (For still another claimant, see WHITE CALF, JOHN.)

Between 1913 and 1938, when the Jefferson nickel design was introduced, more than a billion of the Indian Head coins were minted. "They're getting those nickels out of circulation fast," Big Tree quipped in 1966. "They must be sick and tired of my face."

Big Tree, who described himself as "the best bareback rider in Hollywood," acted in more than 100 films. Though he never had a starring role, many of his parts were substantial, with some of his best work being done for director John

John Big Tree poses with a model of the nickel coin on May 9, 1966, in ceremonies commemorating the 100th anniversary of the nickel piece that were held at the money museum of the Chase Manhattan Bank in New York City. *(AP/Wideworld)*

Ford. His first film with Ford was *A Fight for Love* (1919), starring Harry Carey. Among his most notable films were *Custer's Last Stand* (1936), *Destry Rides Again* (1939), *Drums along the Mohawk* (1939), and *Stagecoach* (1939).

In retirement, Big Tree lived with his Onondaga wife on the Onondaga Reservation in New York, surviving on a meager social security check, the vegetables they grew in their garden, and, as he put it in one of his last interviews in May 1966, "75 cents a year" from the federal government.

Big Tree died on July 5, 1967, at Onondaga, survived by his wife. A son from a previous marriage, Cleveland Big Tree, had died in action in WORLD WAR I.

Further Reading

Van Ryzin, Robert R. *Twisted Tails, Sifted Fact, Fantasy, and Fiction from U.S. Coin History.* Iola, Wis.: Krause Publications, 1995.

Billie, James (1944–   ) *Seminole Tribal Council chair, gaming industry advocate*

James Billie was born in Dania, Broward County, Florida, on March 20, 1944, the son of Agnes Billie, a full-blooded Seminole who made crafts for tourists. His father was an Irish-American pilot who deserted his mother before James was born. Billie attended local schools in Broward, Henry, and Palm Beach Counties. While living on the Big Cypress and the Dania (now Hollywood) Seminole reservations, he also worked with his grandmother, Tommie Billie, as a migrant laborer, picking vegetables on farms. After high school, Billie attended the Haskell Institute, graduating in 1964.

The next year, Billie joined the army, serving two tours of duty in Vietnam before being discharged in 1968 with the rank of staff sergeant. He held a number of odd jobs, from alligator wrestler (losing a finger in the process) to tourist attraction manager and, later, cattle rancher. Then, in the mid-1970s, he took a job with the Seminole tribe and was elected to the tribal council in 1977. In 1979, Billie was elected tribal council chair, a post he continued to hold until March 2003.

In 1987, Billie came to national attention over his 1983 shooting of a Florida panther, a rare subspecies of the puma or mountain lion, on the Seminole's Big Cypress Reservation. After this incident, the Department of Justice began a costly effort to prosecute him for violation of the Endangered Species Act. Because Billie claimed to have killed the panther as part of a tribal ritual, the case pitted the efforts of the federal government to protect endangered animals over the rights of Indians to hunt and observe their religious beliefs on their own lands. The state of Florida also began prosecution of Billie, but he was acquitted in the state trial in October 1987. The federal case ended in a mistrial, with all charges being dropped.

The federal and Florida governments also locked horns with Billie in a bitter court case over the right to bring gaming onto the Seminole reservation. Following the lead of his predecessor, Howard Tommie, who had pioneered the opening of "smoke shops" (stores that sell cigarettes without charging state taxes), Billie encouraged the growth of the small high-stakes bingo parlor that Tommie had established on the reservation, in the hope of providing reservation residents with much-needed jobs and income.

Local law enforcement, including Broward County sheriff Robert Butterworth, attempted to block the effort under the strict state and county antigambling laws. Other tribal governments, including the Puyallup of Washington State, had already run afoul of state antigambling ordinances when they attempted to open casinos. But Billie staked his case on a unique interpretation of federal and state law: rather than open a casino, the Seminole opened a bingo parlor. They argued that federal laws granting states jurisdiction over Indian reservations, such as Public Law 280, enacted during the TERMINATION era, granted the state criminal jurisdiction, not civil jurisdiction.

The distinction was important. Bingo, unlike other forms of gambling, was not against the law in Florida, although it was strictly regulated. In Florida, bingo parlors were allowed to be run only by charitable nonprofit organizations such as churches and veterans' clubs. Jackpots were limited to just $100 and could be held only once a night; only unpaid members of the charity could operate the game, and all the bingo profits had to go to the charity. The Seminole argued before the court that, despite the severe penalties for defying the regulations, bingo was actually a civil, not a criminal matter. After opening their bingo hall, they were immediately granted an injunction preventing Sheriff Robert Butterworth from enforcing Florida's bingo laws on the reservation or making any arrests.

The sheriff appealed the injunction, and the state tried to argue that high-stakes bingo, such as the Seminoles', was illegal, and therefore that the Seminole were committing a crime. Since Florida's criminal laws applied to the reservation under Public Law 280, the state could make arrests. They repeatedly raided the reservation and broke up the bingo games.

The landmark case *Seminole Tribe of Florida v. Butterworth* went all the way to the Fifth Circuit Court of Appeals, where the court ruled that if the state of Florida allowed bingo, in however limited a manner, then bingo laws must be considered regulatory, not criminal. Therefore Public Law 280 did not authorize a state to extend its regulatory jurisdiction over the reservations. The ruling was a tremendous victory for Indian sovereignty, and the precedent it set, known as the "prohibitory/regulatory distinction," would become the test applied to all future Indian gambling ventures. Indians at the time could still not open casinos or install slot machines (which are banned in most states), but since almost every state allows some form of charity bingo or lottery, the way was open for Indians to raise the stakes.

The victory paved the way for the establishment of gaming on Indian reservations across the country. However, it proved costly to the Seminole Tribe. The state of Florida never admitted defeat, and through lawsuits and delaying tactics, it successfully blocked attempts by the Seminole to open a full-fledged casino in the manner of RICHARD ARTHUR HAYWARD and the Pequot in Connecticut. Under Billie, however, the Seminole branched out into a number of enterprises and have become one of the most economically successful tribes in the United States.

In May 2001, the Seminole tribal council suspended Billie after allegations of sexual harassment and financial mismanagement were raised against him. In 2002, Billie was indicted on charges of embezzling $2.7 million and funneling the cash to an offshore corporation, although the charges were later dropped. That same year, the tribe broke ground on a new $300 million Hard Rock Hotel and Casino complex in Hollywood and in Tampa. On March 18, 2003, the tribal council removed Billie from office for insubordination and refusing to adhere to the tribal constitution, ending his 24-year tenure. Since then, the Seminole casino complex has become one of the most profitable in the country, and in 2006 the tribe purchased the Hard Rock Cafe chain for $965 million. On May 10, 2011, Billie was elected chair of the tribe, defeating his successor and two-term incumbent Mitchell Cypress.

See also GAMING ON AMERICAN INDIAN RESERVATIONS; SOVEREIGNTY, INDIGENOUS AND TRIBAL.

Further Reading

Oeffner, Barbara. *Chief-Champion of the Everglades: A Biography of Seminole Chief James Billie*. Palm Beach, Fla.: Cape Cod Writers, Inc., 1995.

Billings, Robert J. (1926–1995) *Mohawk religious activist, cofounder of the Moral Majority*

Robert J. Billings was born on September 3, 1926, near the Akwesasne Mohawk (St. Regis) Reservation in upstate New York. His family was so poor that, as was not uncommon for Mohawk children during this time, he was raised in an orphanage.

In his early teens, Billings attended a revival meeting and became a devout Christian. After graduating from the Allentown Bible Institute in Pennsylvania and Bob Jones University in Greenville, South Carolina, he became a missionary in the British West Indies. Preaching throughout the South and Midwest, Billings finally settled in Hammond, Indiana, where he founded the Christian-oriented Hyles-Anderson College in 1971. Billings was heavily influenced by Rousas John Rushdoony, founder of the Christian Reconstructionist movement, who advocated that governments must adhere to biblical law. Billings began mixing religion and politics in the early 1970s; he unsuccessfully ran for election to the U.S. House of Representatives in 1976, and in 1978 formed the National Christian Action Coalition.

With the election of Jimmy Carter to the presidency in 1976, Billings decided to raise his level of political activity. Angered by what he called an increase in immorality in popular culture and the "Godless humanism" of new educational policies, he began to plan a new political-religious movement. In May 1979, Billings invited Christian activists Jerry Falwell and Ed McAteer, along with conservative political strategists Howard Phillips (a former aide to President Richard Nixon), Richard Viguerie (a master direct-mail organizer), and far-right tactician Paul Weyrich to a meeting to "draw up a game plan to save America." The new movement would hinge on the issue of abortion, a tactic designed to turn the powerful Catholic vote away from its solid support for the Democratic Party.

Choosing Jerry Falwell as its public spokesperson, and with Billings serving as the executive director, the group formed the Moral Majority. The organization helped transform the religious right into a political force not seen in American politics since the 1920s, and is widely credited with winning Ronald Reagan the 1980 presidential election. Billings joined the Reagan administration, serving for six years as the coordinator for the Department of Education. After his tenure in the executive branch, he retired to Haines City, Florida, where he died of cancer on May 28, 1995.

Further Reading

Diamond, Sara. *Spiritual Warfare: The Politics of the Christian Right*, 43, 60, 63–64. Boston: South End Press, 1989.
Utter, Glenn H., and John W. Storey. *The Religious Right: A Reference Handbook*. Santa Barbara, Calif.: ABC–CLIO, 2001.

Billy, Josie (Ayo:posayki, "Crazy Spherical Panther") (ca. 1885–1980) *Mikasuki Seminole medicine man, traditional healer*

Born near the Big Cypress Swamp in Florida during the 1880s, Josie Billy was a member of the Tiger clan of the Mikasuki Seminole through his mother. He learned many very old Seminole customs and traditions from his maternal grandmother, Nancy Osceola (ca. 1815–ca. 1910), who had lived through most of the Seminole Wars.

Billy's father (ca. 1860–1926), a Mikasuki of the Wind Clan known as Little Billie Fewell, Billie Conepatchie, or Koniphadjo, lived with Capt. F. A. Hendry at Fort Myers (1879–82), where he worked as a cowboy. Conepatchie had attended a non-Indian school, which at the time violated Seminole law. The anthropologist Clay MacCauley, who met him in 1881, reported that he was "the one Seminole with whom I could hold even the semblance of an English conversation." He was greatly disliked by the other Seminole for separating himself from his people and casting in his lot with whites. His older brother, Billy Fewell (b. ca. 1846), also lived for a while among whites in Key West, something then almost unheard of.

In 1917, the acting Seminole agent described Billie Conepatchie as "about the most progressive and intelligent member of the Big Cypress bands." As the only Seminole who could speak English, he became an unofficial contact person. Whites considered him "chief," though in reality the traditional Seminole have no chiefs, and he did not even hold an important ceremonial or political position. He died in a drunken brawl in October 1926.

As a boy, Josie Billy lived near Fort Shackleford. Though he never attended school, he often visited the home of his friend Frank Brown, whose father ran the trading post near Big Cypress, and one of the women there taught him English. Billy received his adult name, Crazy Spherical Panther, at about age 15. He then began visiting traditional doctors, asking questions about healing, and he was taught some songs and remedies. At about 18, he apprenticed himself for two years to an *ayikcomí* (traditional medicine maker) named Old Motlow, then to Tommy Doctor for four years, accompanying him on medical visits to Mikasuki and Cow Creek Seminole camps and learning to speak the latter's Muskogee (Creek) language. By about 1917, he was qualified by the traditional authorities and at Tommy Doctor's death in 1920, took over his practice. By then Billy was probably the best trained traditional healer among the Seminole.

Billy spoke English, not well, but better than his father did. Like his father, he became a contact with the non-Indian world, and locals thought of him as a "chief" of the Seminole. In 1928, the Tamiami Trail was built from Tampa to Miami, skirting the southern boundary of Seminole territory and making the Seminole accessible to outsiders for the first time. Josie settled in a camp on the trail near Ochopee. He respected non-Indian mainstream medicine and had begun trying to get government and social agencies to help procure medical services, especially dentistry, for the Seminole. In the 1930s, he accompanied ill Seminole to a Dr. Pender in Everglades City, Florida, particularly during the 1934 malaria epidemic.

In addition to being a traditional healer, Billy trained as a medicine man, a position that also afforded him custody of one of the six Seminole medicine bundles. The Seminole believe that each member is under the protection of the medicine man who holds the bundle of his clan group and attends their medicine man's Green Corn Dance in the spring. The bundle has to be properly cared for, as it affects the lives of all who are under the medicine man's charge. Since boyhood, Billy had assisted at Green Corn dances, working his way up through various ceremonial functions. For about four years starting in 1920, he assisted medicine man Jimmy Doctor, at the end of which time he received from him a second adult name ("war name"). Upon Jimmy Doctor's retirement, Billy took custody of his medicine bundle for four years. After Jimmy Doctor's death, he gave the bundle to its rightful custodian and received a second war name. About 1930, Billy became one of three men in Billie Motlow's busk council and a headman of the council that meets on the fourth day of the Green Corn ceremony to deal with political and judicial matters. When Billie Motlow died about 1937, Josie Billy took custody of his bundle, associated with the Tiger clan. Now a full medicine man, Billy had the responsibility of carrying out very extensive duties for the people under his care.

In the 1920s, Billy developed a drinking problem. In December 1928, while drunk, he stabbed and killed a female relative and member of his clan. In those days, Seminole police handled their own homicide cases. Such perpetrators would normally have been condemned to death, but Billy was let off. Nevertheless, he continued to drink heavily.

In 1929, Billy headed a group of 30–40 Seminole who performed for tourists in St. Petersburg, Florida. In 1933, he spent several months at the Chicago World's Fair with a performing Seminole group. He traveled to New York in 1938, and in 1940 he was part of the Seminole Village at the New York World's Fair.

In the mid-1930s, the Cow Creek Seminole approved the INDIAN REORGANIZATION ACT, swore allegiance to the United States, and laid claim to Mikasuki hunting grounds in Big Cypress Swamp. Billy, however, sided with the resisters, led by Cory Osceola. (He would stand with the same group in 1950 when they dissociated the Mikasuki from the Seminole claim filed with the INDIAN CLAIMS COMMISSION.)

Because of drinking and other behavior considered inappropriate for a medicine man, Billy left his very conservative community around 1943 and went to the Big Cypress Reservation, considered one of the most "progressive." He came back to run the Green Corn Dance in 1944, but at its conclusion he was told to hand the medicine bundle over to his brother, Ingraham. That was the last Green Corn Dance he attended.

In 1943, a Creek missionary from Oklahoma, Reverend Stanley Smith, was sent to Florida by the Muskogee, Wichita, and Seminole Baptist Association. There were as yet practically no Christian Mikasuki, although the Cow Creek Seminole had long been in contact with Seminole missionaries from Oklahoma. Josie Billy was baptized by Smith on January 2, 1945, at a revival at Big Cypress, along with many other Big Cypress Mikasuki members. This was the first missionizing breakthrough among the Seminole. In 1947, Smith baptized 197. From the time of his conversion, Billy never drank again. In 1946, he began a training course at the Florida Baptist Institute. Upon completing his studies, he became assistant pastor of a new church at Big Cypress in July 1948. Except for one older sister, his family did not follow. His children stayed with the non-Christian group, his brother Ingraham was the head medicine man of the Tamiami Trail Seminole, and the latter's son was extremely traditional, as were his wife's immediate relatives.

Beginning in 1945, Billy traveled every fall to the Creek and Seminole reservations in Oklahoma, where he was much in demand as a traditional doctor. Although Billy was not personally popular, he had a vast amount of traditional knowledge, and even very conservative Seminole came to him regularly for treatment. By the early 1950s, he was the last of the old healers. In 1953, a boy from a very conservative family came to him and asked to be taught traditional medicine. By 1970, Josie Billy had stopped practicing and began running a small grocery store on the Big Cypress Reservation. He died in 1980.

Further Reading

Snow, Alice Micco, and Susan Enns Stans. *Healing Plants: Medicine of the Florida Seminole Indians*. Gainesville: University Press of Florida, 2001.

Bissonette, Pedro (1944–1973) *Oglala Lakota Sioux activist, leader of the 1973 Wounded Knee occupation*

Pedro Bissonette was born on April 20, 1944, and raised by his aunt Gladys Bissonette after his parents died when he was young. He grew up in a traditional household amid the desperate poverty of the Pine Ridge Reservation and learned to speak Lakota fluently. Like many Oglala Lakota Sioux traditionals, he was also a Catholic, and he attended the Holy Rosary Catholic Church's Red Cloud Mission School. After graduating, he became a boxer, winning the Golden Gloves award, and then became a steelworker.

In 1972, Bissonette founded the Oglala Sioux Civil Rights Organization (OSCRO) with his aunt Gladys, Vern Long, Severt Young Bear, and Edgar Bear Runner to combat the low rents Pine Ridge land earned under the BUREAU OF INDIAN AFFAIRS' (BIA) leasing policy, which encouraged the leasing of Indian land to non-Indian farmers and ranchers. The group also sought the removal of newly elected tribal chair RICHARD WILSON.

The traditional camp in Pine Ridge had long been shut out of the electoral politics of the reservation, which was dominated by the assimilated "progressives," and as a consequence the traditionals received few benefits from the entrenched patronage system. The new tribal chairman, a stock raiser and owner of a trucking business, proved to be even more corrupt than his predecessors. Wilson, who had once made the statement "There's nothing in tribal law against nepotism," placed his brother in the lucrative post of head of the planning committee of the tribe and his wife as director of the Head Start Program, and he hired his sons, nephews, and cousins for other posts. In order to accommodate his family, friends, and supporters on the government payroll, Wilson dismissed dozens of tribal employees, among them Ellen Moves Camp, who joined the disaffected traditionals in seeking his ouster.

Although OSCRO managed to get the tribal council to impeach Wilson, on February 23, 1973, the tribal chair summarily ended the trial, dismissed the council, and refused to step down from his post, leading to a public outcry. The next day, Pedro Bissonette led a march on the tribal council building, only to find it blocked by federal marshals, sandbags, and machine guns. Wilson had been concerned that the traditionals would turn to the AMERICAN INDIAN MOVEMENT (AIM) for help and had prepared accordingly. OSCRO, which had taken part in the AIM demonstration in Custer, South Dakota, on February 6 to seek justice for the murder of Wesley Bad Heart Bull, did call on the activist organization for help a few days later. A meeting was held at the Calico Hall community building, near Pine Ridge Village, on February 27, and more than 600 Oglala, including five traditional chiefs—FRANK FOOLS CROW, Edgar Red Cloud, Tom Bad Cob, Iron Cloud, and Jake Kills Enemy—as well as respected holy men PETER CATCHES, WALLACE HOWARD BLACK ELK, Everette Catches, Ellis Chips, and Morris Wounded, met with AIM leaders RUSSELL MEANS, DENNIS JAMES BANKS, and CLYDE BELLECOURT.

At the meeting, it was decided that only a symbolic confrontation would draw attention to the long-standing problems on the reservation, and the next day a caravan of more than 200 Indians traveled to Wounded Knee village and occupied it. On March 11, the traditional leaders renounced the Pine Ridge Tribal Council and proclaimed the revival of the Independent Oglala Nation.

The occupation drew a massive response by federal, state, and tribal police, as well as "goons" deputized by Wilson. During the ensuing siege, Pedro Bissonette became an important part of the Wounded Knee negotiating team, and his ties with the traditional Lakota leaders ensured continuing community support for the encampment. Gladys Bissonette and Ellen Moves Camp were among the local Oglala women who stayed at Wounded Knee through the entire siege and helped keep the camp functioning.

Despite his status as a negotiator, on April 27, 1973, Bissonette was arrested in Rapid City and charged with interfering with a federal officer. Bissonette refused to provide information about AIM and was threatened with jail, but he was set free after evidence of police misconduct during his arrest surfaced.

Bissonette was among those charged and arrested when the occupation ended on May 9, but he never went to trial. Freed on $25,000 bail, he was arrested again on September 6, this time for assaulting a man in White City, Nebraska, although many regarded the arrest as another political move.

On October 17, 1973, Bissonette was shot to death by BIA police for resisting arrest. The police claimed that after being stopped for a routine check he stepped out of the car, then got back in the car and emerged with a rifle, provoking police fire. Bissonette's gun, however, was never found. Dr. W. O. Brown, resident pathologist of Scottsbluff, Nebraska, performed the autopsy and exonerated the police, although it was later determined that Bissonette was killed at extreme short range with a shotgun blast. Brown was the same pathologist who later performed a misleading autopsy on ANNA MAE AQUASH.

The killing of Bissonette shocked Pine Ridge. Despite Dick Wilson's attempt to bar AIM leaders from attending, Bissonette's four-day funeral became an important rallying point for traditionals.

Rather than remove the heavy-handed Wilson administration, the occupation of Wounded Knee unleashed a wave of violence on the reservation that lasted more than two years and was directed mostly against the traditionals and sympathizers of AIM. Among the more than 60 people killed in the ensuing clashes were Bissonette's sister-in-law, Jeanette Bissonette, who was shot by a sniper in March 1975.

See also PELTIER, LEONARD; WOUNDED KNEE, OCCUPATION OF.

Further Reading

Akwesasne Notes. *Voices from Wounded Knee, 1973.* Roosevelt Town, N.Y.: Akwesasne Notes, 1974.

Black Elk (Nicholas Black Elk, Hehaka Sapa)
(1863–1950) *Oglala Lakota Sioux holy man*

Black Elk, an Oglala Lakota Sioux, was born in December 1863 on the Little Powder River in northeastern Wyoming. His father was also named Black Elk, or Hehaka Sapa, and his mother was White Cow Sees Woman. Black Elk was raised during the U.S. Army's wars against the Sioux Nation (Dakota, Lakota, Nakota), and when he was only three, his father was wounded in what became known as the Fetterman Fight. Black Elk had his first vision at age five and his second at age nine, which led him to his spiritual calling. The vision, which Black Elk struggled most of his life to try to understand and carry out, instructed him to help lead his people down the road of life, peace, and prosperity by "nurturing the sacred tree and keeping the nation's hoop intact," a reference he took to mean the preservation of traditional Lakota religion.

In 1876, at age 12, Black Elk participated in the Battle of Little Bighorn, in which George Armstrong Custer's Seventh Cavalry was destroyed. Black Elk's family followed Crazy Horse's "hostiles" until the war chief's death the next year. They then joined Hunkpapa Lakota chief Sitting Bull, who had fled from the unrelenting U.S. military attacks to the safety of Canada. There the young mystic's reputation grew. When Black Elk's family returned to the United States and settled on the Pine Ridge Reservation, Black Elk revealed his early vision to the medicine men of the tribe. In 1881, they allowed Black Elk to lead the Horse Dance ceremony, beginning his long tenure as a spiritual leader.

In 1886, Black Elk joined Buffalo Bill's Wild West Show for a European tour, leaving it in England to join Mexican Joe's Wild West Show. While in Paris in 1889, he became sick, fainted, and dreamed that his people were in turmoil. The dream prompted him to return to Pine Ridge in time to witness the Ghost Dance religion spreading across the plains. Although at first skeptical of the messianic movement, Black Elk later became an adherent after a Lakota Sioux delegation met with the Ghost Dance's Northern Paiute founder, Wovoka, and brought their version of his teachings back to Pine Ridge. Black Elk then had a vision in which he was shown how to make and paint Ghost Dance shirts—which the Lakota believed would protect them from harm, including bullets.

The Ghost Dance movement caused a military backlash against the Lakota Sioux, leading to the murder of Sitting Bull and the massacre at Wounded Knee in 1890 (which occurred only a few miles from Black Elk's home). The deaths of more than 150 men, women, and children had a profound affect on the spiritual man, and as he said in *Black Elk Speaks*, "Something else died in the bloody mud and was covered up by the blizzard. A people's dream died there. It was a beautiful dream."

In 1892, Black Elk married Katie War Bonnett. She converted to Catholicism, and all three of their children were baptized in the Catholic faith. After her death in 1903, Black Elk decided to convert. On December 6, 1904, the feast day of St. Nicholas, Black Elk was baptized into the Catholic faith as Nicholas Black Elk. He spent the rest of his life as a catechist under the Society of St. Joseph, bringing many of his people into the Catholic fold. While it appears that Black Elk, like many Indians, did not see traditional Native and Catholic religions as incompatible, he also recognized that, in his words, his "children have to live in this world." Unlike other Lakota spiritual leaders who were also Catholic, such as FRANK FOOLS CROW and PETER CATCHES, Black Elk relinquished his leadership of Lakota ceremonies, and his children grew up in the Catholic Church. In 1905, he married Anna Brings White, a widow with two daughters. She bore him three more children and remained his wife until her death in 1941.

In 1931, John G. Neihardt—poet laureate of Nebraska—recorded Black Elk's oral history, and the next year this account was published as *Black Elk Speaks: Being the Life Story of a Holy Man of the Oglala Sioux*. In 1944, Neihardt again interviewed Black Elk about the period before contact with non-Indians and published these stories as *When the Tree Flowers* (1951). Black Elk also provided Joseph Epes Brown with the material for his book on the Lakota Sioux religion, *The Sacred Pipe*, published in 1953. *Black Elk Speaks* and *The Sacred Pipe*, which detailed the philosophy and cosmology of the Lakota people, while well regarded, attracted little attention during their first years and quickly went out of print.

In 1961, a paperback reprint of *Black Elk Speaks* appeared. It resonated with the alternative attitudes of the 1960s and became a popular success, playing an influential role in the acceptance among non-Indian people of the legitimacy of Indian beliefs and helping to inspire a revival in Indian traditional practices. Black Elk, a profoundly spiritual man whose thinking spanned many religious outlooks, died on August 17 or 19, 1950. His vision to preserve and help restore the Lakota Sioux religion came to fulfillment in the decades after his death.

Further Reading

Brown, Joseph Epes. *The Sacred Pipe: Black Elk's Account of the Seven Rites of the Oglala Sioux*. Norman: University of Oklahoma Press, 1989.
———. *The Spiritual Legacy of the American Indian*. Commemorative ed. with letters. Bloomington, Ind.: World Wisdom Books, 2007.
Neihardt, John G. *Black Elk Speaks: Being the Life Story of a Holy Man of the Oglala Sioux*. Lincoln: University of Nebraska Press, 1988.
Steltenkamp, Michael. *Black Elk: Holy Man of the Oglala*. Norman: University of Oklahoma Press, 1993.

Black Elk, Wallace Howard (1921–2004) *Lakota Sioux spiritual leader*

A Lakota Sioux born on July 18, 1921, on the Rosebud Reservation in South Dakota, Wallace Howard Black Elk—who was not related to BLACK ELK—was trained from an early age as a traditional medicine man. After serving in WORLD WAR II, he was committed for a short time to an insane asylum for practicing his traditional beliefs. Black Elk, along with Lakota Sioux holy men FRANK FOOLS CROW and PETER CATCHES, supported the AMERICAN INDIAN MOVEMENT's (AIM) occupation of WOUNDED KNEE in 1973, and Black Elk performed the marriage ceremony between Nookik Aquash and ANNA MAE AQUASH inside the encampment. He became an influential spiritual leader of the movement. After AIM's demise, Black Elk joined SUN BEAR and his largely non-Indian Bear Tribe in their Medicine Wheel gatherings that were held throughout the country. Black Elk's status lent the controversial New Age leader important credibility. Wallace Black Elk died on January 25, 2004, at his home in Denver, Colorado.

See also NEW AGE MOVEMENT.

Further Reading

Black Elk, Wallace H. *The Sacred Ways of a Lakota*. San Francisco: Harper, 1991.

Blackgoat, Roberta (1919?–2002) *Navajo (Dineh) weaver, relocation resistance leader*

Born into the Bitter Water Clan on the Navajo Reservation, Roberta Blackgoat was raised in the traditional Navajo culture, herding sheep and goats and learning to weave rugs as a child. All sources give her birthday as October 15, but the year ranges between 1916 and 1919. She lived through the sheep stock reduction plans under the INDIAN NEW DEAL (see INDIAN REORGANIZATION ACT). In 1941 she married Benny Blackgoat.

When, in 1974, the federal government ordered the partition of a disputed part of the Navajo and Hopi reservation (see Big Mountain), Blackgoat, along with Pauline Whitesinger, began to organize resistance to the attempts to forcibly relocate Navajo living in the area awarded to the Hopi. She fought efforts to relocate her and other Navajo, leading a national campaign that reached its peak of effectiveness in 1986. However, after that time, the issue faded from the public eye, and most of the resisters reluctantly came to an agreement with the Hopi tribe.

Roberta Blackgoat died of a heart attack on April 23, 2002.

Further Reading

LaDuke, Winona. "Interview with Roberta Blackgoat, a Dine Elder." *Woman of Power* 4 (Fall 1986): 29–31.

Blackstone, Tsianina Evans (Tsianina Redfeather)

(1882–1985)   *Cherokee-Creek mezzosoprano*

Tsianina Evans Blackstone was born on December 13, 1882, in Oktaho, Oklahoma, to Alec and Winona Evans. Her parents were both Cherokee, with some Creek blood on her mother's side. Tsianina began piano lessons at the Creek Nation Boarding School at Eufaula, Oklahoma. Congresswoman Alice Robertson noticed the young girl's musical aptitude during her frequent visits to the school.

When Tsianina was in her teens, her mother died. Robertson took her in, and she traveled with the congresswoman around the United States and saw something of the world abroad. Eventually, Robertson and her husband brought Tsianina to Denver, where she resumed the study of piano with Arthur B. Fleck. One day he asked her to sing and was so impressed that he immediately took her to his friend John C. Wilcox, a voice teacher originally from Detroit. She sang "Just A-weeping for You," and Wilcox agreed to take her on as a student. Her progress was so remarkable that she never felt the need to study with any other teacher. After three weeks of lessons, Wilcox recommended her to composer Charles Wakefield Cadman, then visiting Denver, as ideal to sing his songs, which made use of Native American elements and themes. Though Cadman was not immediately impressed, Wilcox eventually won him over.

Tsianina married Albert Blackstone on December 13, 1910. She first took part in what became known as the "Cadman-Redfeather Indian Music-Talk" on April 24, 1913. For several years thereafter, she toured the country with Cadman and received enthusiastic reviews everywhere. A publicity brochure described the Music-Talk as "not a dry lecture recital. Mr Cadman, seated at the piano, speaks informally and delightfully of the peculiar characteristics of Indian song and rhythm. The program is vocally illustrated by the Princess Tsianina Redfeather . . ."

When the Music-Talk had its New York debut at Aeolian Hall on October 17, 1916, some of the greatest performers of the day were in the audience, including Alice Nielsen, Maude Powell, John McCormack, and Frank Damrosch. The ethnomusicologists Francis La Flesche (Omaha) and Alice Fletcher, and IRENE EASTMAN, a promising Dakota Sioux singer whose stage name was Taluta, also attended.

In 1919–20, Tsianina entertained troops of the American Expeditionary Forces in France and Germany. During her concert career, she always dressed in sumptuous Indian clothing—offstage as well as on—which she designed and made herself. She did so to make a point, as she said in a 1916 interview: ". . . all things are idealized by progress. Why shouldn't the Indians advance as well as all other peoples taking the line of their own art in music, costuming, bead work, etc?"

In 1920, Reverend SHERMAN COOLIDGE (Arapaho), who also lived in Denver, engaged her to play the lead in a "great Indian drama" to be produced by the American Indian Film Company, which he had recently organized, Cadman composing the music. However, the project never got off the ground.

The libretto to Cadman's "Indian" opera *Shanewis*, written by Nelle Eberhart, was said to have been suggested by Tsianina's life. It premiered at the New York Metropolitan Opera on March 23, 1918. Tsianina was much involved when Cadman was writing and rehearsing it, but she did not sing the lead herself until its performance at the Hollywood Bowl in 1926. This proved to be her swan song. Immediately thereafter, she gave up performing.

In 1930, Tsianina joined the Mother Church of Christian Science in Boston and became a full-time Christian Science practitioner in 1935. She was active in the Republican Party. In 1956, she established the Foundation for American Indian Education. Her autobiography, *Where Trails Have Led Me*, appeared in 1970. A third edition was published in 1982. In later life, Tsianina Evans Blackstone lived in Burbank, California. She died on January 10, 1985, in San Diego at the age of 102. The distinguished Creek historian K. Tsianina Lomawaima is her grand-niece.

Blatchford, Herbert Charles

(1928–1996)   *Navajo (Dineh) founder and first executive officer of the National Indian Youth Council, editor of* The Aborigine

Herbert Blatchford was born March 16, 1928, on the Navajo (Dineh) Reservation near Fort Defiance, Arizona. Son of Walter and Pauline (Manuelito) Blatchford, Herb Blatchford was the grand-nephew of Navajo chief Manuelito. As a boy, Blatchford herded sheep like other traditional Navajo children on the reservation. He was sent to mission schools, first a Methodist school and then the Reformed Church school, before entering the University of New Mexico. In 1954, he organized a meeting of tribal leaders from the Pueblo, Navajo, and Apache nations together with young university-educated Indians in Santa Fe, leading to the establishment of a number of Indian clubs in different universities, which evolved into the Southwest Regional Youth Council in 1957. Blatchford became president of the Regional Youth Council and helped to organize a regional gathering in 1960 that included 350 Indian students from 57 tribes.

After graduation from the University of New Mexico in 1956, Blatchford became counselor for Kinley County Public Schools at Gallup, New Mexico, where he helped keep students from dropping out. In 1963, he was appointed manager of the Gallup Indian Community Center by Kinley County, the City of Gallup, and the Navajo Tribe. Highly effective in his work with youth, Blatchford also worked with the New Mexico Commission on Alcoholism to develop programs for the Navajo.

In 1961, at the AMERICAN INDIAN CHICAGO CONFERENCE, Blatchford chaired the youth caucus that formulated a statement of purpose proposing an entirely new concept of Indian activism. The statement argued that Indians have "the inherent right of self-government" that any small nation would have, and they were "earnestly determined to hold on to identity and survival." After the conference, Blatchford suggested to the other young attendees that they meet again at the Inter-Tribal Ceremonial held in Gallup, New Mexico. There the NATIONAL INDIAN YOUTH COUNCIL (NIYC) was created.

Blatchford became the editor of NIYC's journal, *The Aborigine* (also titled at various times *American Aborigine* and later *Americans Before Columbus*). Reflecting the group's scholarly bent, he wrote a number of articles that helped give the NIYC a coherent political perspective. (Another important contributor was the Cherokee anthropologist ROBERT KNOX THOMAS.) Blatchford's "Historical Survey of American Indians," written in 1963 for *American Aborigine*, is one of the first in-depth analyses of non-Indian–Indian relations from an Indian perspective, and it foreshadowed the later work of legal scholars such as VINE DELORIA, JR., and JAMES YOUNGBLOOD HENDERSON. Blatchford continued to work with Indian youth until his death on December 1, 1996.

Further Reading

Gilpin, Laura. *The Enduring Navaho.* Austin: University of Texas Press, 1968.

Blue Eagle, Acee (Alex C. McIntosh, Chebona Bula, Laughing Boy) (1907–1959) *Creek-Pawnee artist, educator*

The Creek name of Acee Blue Eagle—born Alex C. McIntosh on August 17, 1907, north of Anadarko, Oklahoma, on the Wichita Reservation—was Chebona Bula (Laughing Boy), though his family preferred to call him Acee, after his initials A. C. His mother was Mattie Odom McIntosh, and his father, Solomon McIntosh, was the son of Creek chief William McIntosh, also known as Blue Eagle. After studying at the Chilocco Indian School, Acee McIntosh adopted the name Blue Eagle and began to paint. He studied at Bacone College in Muskogee, Oklahoma, and with Oscar Jacobson at the University of Oklahoma.

In 1935, Blue Eagle lectured on Indian art, dance, and song at Oxford University, as well as other European universities. He even gave a command performance in full Indian regalia at Buckingham Palace, greatly impressing the queen and her two daughters, Margaret and Elizabeth (Queen Elizabeth II). When he returned from his continental tour, he founded the art department at Bacone, which would subsequently become important in the development of Indian art. A gregarious,

Acee Blue Eagle, Creek-Pawnee artist and educator, in 1936. *(AP/Wideworld)*

outgoing man, Blue Eagle did much to promote Indian art throughout the world. The college gave birth to a style known as the "Bacone school," which drew on tribal traditions. Blue Eagle was succeeded at Bacone by WOODY CRUMBO in 1938 and by WALTER RICHARD WEST, SR., in 1947.

During the 1930s, Blue Eagle became known for his murals, which adorned various schools and federal buildings in Oklahoma. His mural *The Buffalo Hunt*, commissioned for USS *Oklahoma*, was destroyed when the ship was badly damaged in the Japanese attack on Pearl Harbor. Blue Eagle then enlisted in the U.S. Air Force, although he was already 33 years old. In 1946, he joined the staff of the Oklahoma State University Technical School, and in the early 1950s he hosted a children's television show in Tulsa. From 1946 to 1952, Blue Eagle was married to the famous Balinese dancer and actress Devi Dja.

In 1958, Blue Eagle was voted America's Outstanding Indian and was elected to the Indian Hall of Fame at Anadarko, Oklahoma. He died on June 18, 1959, in Muskogee, Oklahoma, of a liver infection.

Further Reading

Elder, Tamara L. *Lumhee Holot-tee: The Art and Life of Acee Blue Eagle.* Edmond, Okla.: Medicine Wheel Press, 2006.

Kelly, Michael. "Acee Blue Eagle: Native American Artist and Much More." *Collector Glass News*, no. 13 (April 1991).

Petete, Timothy, and Craig S. Womack. "Thomas E. Moore's Sour Sofkee in the Tradition of Muskogee Dialect Writers." *Studies in American Indian Literatures* 18, no. 4 (Winter 2006): 1–37.

Blue Lake

This lake in northern New Mexico, sacred to the Tiwa people of Taos Pueblo, was the center of a land dispute between the pueblo and the U.S. government. Lying 11,800 feet above sea level in the Sangre de Cristo Mountains in New Mexico, Blue Lake is the source of the Pueblo River, which flows through Taos Pueblo and is an important ceremonial site.

In 1906, the lake and 50,000 acres of Taos land were seized by the federal government and included in the newly formed Carson National Forest. Although Taos Pueblo's original homeland comprised more than 300,000 acres, only 17,000 acres were recognized by the United States upon the transfer of the Southwest from Mexico after the Mexican War. The rest of Taos land, including Blue Lake, was considered part of the public domain. Taos leaders were at first not opposed to the formation of Carson National Forest, believing that such a designation would protect the lake and its surrounding areas from settlement and exploitation, and they asked the head of the Agriculture Department, Gifford Pinchot, who supervised the Forest Service, to allow the Tiwa to continue using the lake as a sacred site. In 1916, the new supervisor of Carson National Forest decided the lake should be opened up to outsiders. It was stocked with trout, allowing sports fishing to begin on the sacred waters, the watershed was opened to cattlemen, and the surrounding pine forest was subjected to logging.

The need for the Tiwa to hold their sacred ceremonies at Blue Lake undisturbed by outsiders was a concept foreign to the federal government of the time, which was attempting to stamp out Indian cultural practices (see DANCE ORDERS). In 1921, Indian Commissioner CHARLES HENRY BURKE personally led the campaign to have Taos leaders imprisoned for practicing their ceremonies, which had been outlawed under the Religious Crimes Act.

Although, through a 1927 agreement with the forest service, Taos Pueblo managed to halt the threat of mining around the lake, the increasing hordes of tourists and a cabin built in 1928 on the shores of Blue Lake had seriously diminished the pueblo's ability to use the area. In 1940, BUREAU OF INDIAN AFFAIRS (BIA) commissioner JOHN COLLIER managed to forge an agreement with the Department of Agriculture that cut down the number of tourists somewhat, but cattle grazing and logging continued unabated.

Frustrated by the lack of government action, the Taos community mounted a campaign to have the lake restored to them. Led by the spiritual leader of Taos, JUAN DE JESÚS ROMERO (Deer Bird), town governor and councilman Seferino Martinez, and secretary Paul Bernal, the Tiwa slowly gathered support, first enlisting Collier and OLIVER LA FARGE

and, after their deaths, New York senator Robert Kennedy and Interior Secretary Stewart Udall. In 1965, the INDIAN CLAIMS COMMISSION ruled that the Taos people were entitled to compensation for the loss of 130,000 acres of land, including the area around Blue Lake, that had been unjustly taken by the United States. However, the commission did not have the power to return the land to the pueblo. Only Congress could do so. Despite recruiting an impressive array of Indian and non-Indian support, the pueblo could not overcome the formidable opposition of the Agriculture Department, loggers, cattlemen, and their main legislative champion, New Mexico senator Clinton Anderson. Moreover, the federal government was unwilling to establish a precedent whereby claims by Indian people for land, particularly for religious purposes, would be honored.

It was not until the 1968 election of President Richard Nixon, who was open to ending the federal policy of TERMINATION and was looking for a highly visible way to publicize his new self-determination policy, that Taos Pueblo broke through the legislative logjam. Nixon was also motivated by a concern that the Democratic Party, led by Senators Ted Kennedy and Fred Harris, husband of LADONNA HARRIS, was moving in favor of the restoration.

In a dramatic speech on July 1, 1970, Nixon announced his new self-determination policy and threw his support behind legislation that would return Blue Lake to the Taos people. On December 15, 1970, the president signed a bill that granted Taos Pueblo trust title to the lake and 48,000 acres of surrounding land, ending more than 60 years of struggle and marking one of the few times that land taken from Indians has been returned to them.

See also BRUCE, LOUIS ROOK, JR.; LAND TENURE; RELIGIOUS FREEDOM, AMERICAN INDIAN; THOMPSON, MORRIS.

Further Reading

Gordon-McCutchan, R. C., and Frank Waters. *Taos Indians and the Battle for Blue Lake*. Santa Fe, N.Mex.: Red Crane Books, 1990.

Waters, Frank. *The Man Who Killed the Deer*. Athens: Ohio University Press, 1970.

Wilkinson, Charles F. *Blood Struggle: The Rise of Modern Indian Nations*, 208–220. New York: W. W. Norton, 2005.

Boas, Franz (1858–1942) *founder of modern American anthropology*

Franz Boas was born into a Jewish family on July 9, 1858, in Minden, Westphalia, Germany, the son of Meier and Sophie Meyer Boas. From 1877 to 1881, he studied physics, chemistry, and mathematics at the universities of Heidelberg, Bonn, and Kiel. Although he had no university training in either anthropology or linguistics, Boas became interested in the historical and ethnographic influences of physical geography while still a student. He received his Ph.D. from the University of Kiel in 1881.

In Berlin the following year, Boas supplemented his interest in psychophysics and ethnic psychology with library research on the Eskimo, also frequently attending meetings of the Berlin Anthropological Society. After a year (1883–84) in an Inuit (eastern Eskimo) settlement on Baffin Island, he concluded that physical geography did not determine the culture as strongly as he had expected. What emerged as more interesting was the question of the relation between a people's physical constitution and its cultural traditions.

Boas went to the United States in 1886. Two years later, at the invitation of the psychologist G. Stanley Hall, president of Clark University, he was appointed docent in anthropology, teaching there until 1892. In 1896, Boas received an appointment at Columbia University, becoming a full professor in 1899. He was named assistant curator of the American Museum of Natural History the same year and served as curator from 1901 to 1905.

Boas carried out most of his ethnographic fieldwork among the Kwakiutl of Vancouver Island and other Northwest Coast peoples, mainly between 1886 and 1900. In 1911, he published two seminal works, *Handbook of American Indian Languages* and *The Mind of Primitive Man*. He made further ethnographic field trips to the Northwest Coast in the 1920s and, on his last expedition to the Kwakiutl in 1930, made research films and audio transcriptions.

Boas had his greatest influence in the area of race and cultural evolution. While recognizing certain broad universals of cultural evolution, he rejected the linear "stages of civilization" theory popularized by such earlier writers as Lewis Henry Morgan (which was still a big influence on ARTHUR C. PARKER, for example). His finding that physical differences between the races were small cast doubt on prevailing doctrines of racial superiority and inferiority. He was equally opposed to the implication that culture was a disposable item, that simply through imposed culture change one could (in the words of RICHARD HENRY PRATT) "kill the Indian and save the man." Observation of a wide range of cultures revealed great diversity in patterns of development. Boas concluded that all cultures are equally capable of development but that under normal conditions each would develop its own inherent potentials along its own unique path. This finding, however, as he wrote in an early paper, "Human Faculty as Determined by Race" (1894), was complicated by the fact that "rapid dissemination of Europeans over the whole world cut short all promising beginnings which had arisen in various regions." There was, however, an alternative to pure assimilation: He believed a culture could continue to develop in a self-determined way, choosing for itself what to adapt and what to retain.

A later paper, "The Ethnological Significance of Esoteric Doctrines" (1902), written after he had done a good deal of work on Northwest Coast texts and rituals, shows a marked development in Boas's thinking. He wrote of positive value not merely in the "racial capacities" of Native peoples but in the cultures they already have. "The symbolic significance of complex rites and the philosophic view of nature which they reveal," he writes, "have come to us as a surprise, suggesting a higher development of Indian culture than is ordinarily assumed." His new perspective went against the views of the "ultra-assimilationists" who sought to stamp out Indian culture completely (see ASSIMILATION). The loosening of harsh restrictions on Indian religions and ceremonies that occurred under Indian Commissioner FRANCIS LEUPP owed much to Boas's influence.

Though his ideas were highly influential, especially in the area of Indian education, Boas, like most other anthropologists of the time, was not an activist and avoided direct involvement in policy issues. JOHN COLLIER sought his aid in 1922 in the struggle to end repression of traditional Native ceremonies (see DANCE ORDERS), but although Boas was sympathetic, he did not actively assist until years later, when in 1938 he provided expert testimony during the New Mexico peyote controversy (see NATIVE AMERICAN CHURCH).

In summer 1931, in a speech to the American Association for the Advancement of Science, Boas said: "None of the civilizations was the product of the genius of a single people. . . . As all have worked together in the development of the ancient civilizations, we must bow to the genius of all . . ."

Boas's legacy in his scientific research and his great influence on the development of academic anthropology helped to undermine the intellectual respectability of long-standing racial and cultural prejudices about American Indians and other nonwhite peoples. He also made a huge contribution to the collection of American Indian folklore and tales. He and virtually all his students amassed an enormous quantity of texts, many of which remain unpublished.

Boas died in New York City on December 21, 1942. Of his many illustrious students or research associates, five are of particular interest for the history of Indians in the 20th century: WILLIAM JONES (Fox), ELLA CARA DELORIA (Oglala Lakota), ARCHIE PHINNEY (Nez Perce), FRANK GOULDSMITH SPECK, and Lucy Kramer Cohen, the wife of FELIX COHEN.

See also ANTHROPOLOGISTS AND AMERICAN INDIANS.

Further Reading

Boas, Franz. "Anthropology. A lecture delivered at Columbia University . . . December 18, 1907." New York: Columbia University Press, 1908. Reprinted in *The Shaping of American Anthropology, 1883–1911, a Franz Boas Reader*, edited by George W. Stocking, Jr., 267–281. New York, Basic Books, 1974.

Boas, Norman Francis. *Franz Boas, 1858–1942: An Illustrated Biography*. Mystic, Conn.: Seaport Autographs Press, 2004.

Goldschmidt, Walter, ed. *The Anthropology of Franz Boas: Essays on the Centennial of His Birth*. Memoir no. 89. San Francisco, Calif.: American Anthropological Association, 1959.

Williams, Vernon. *Rethinking Race: Franz Boas and his Contemporaries*. Lexington: University Press of Kentucky, 1996.

Bomberry, Daniel R. (1945–1985) *Salish-Cayuga community activist, magazine editor, publisher*

Daniel Richard Bomberry was born on March 24, 1945,

near Vancouver, British Columbia, Canada, to a Coastal Salish mother and a Cayuga father; his grandfather, Daniel Bomberry, was a "condoled" chief of the Cayuga. (A "condoled" chief is one who has been raised through a condolence ceremony, at which all Six Nations of the Iroquois are represented, to the rank of one of the 50 chiefs of the Iroquois Confederacy, thus becoming a voting member of the Grand Council for life.) Known for his advocacy of low-cost, environmentally appropriate technology for reservation self-sufficiency projects, Daniel Bomberry was a skilled fund-raiser and actively supported economic self-sufficiency projects among Indian communities in Canada, the United States, and Latin America.

In November 1969, Bomberry was one of the contingent of Indians who occupied Alcatraz Island in San Francisco Bay (see ALCATRAZ ISLAND, OCCUPATION OF), where he came in contact with the burgeoning RED POWER MOVEMENT. He graduated from California State University in 1970 with a B.A. in political science. Shortly thereafter, Bomberry became director of the Owens Valley Indian Education Center in Bishop, California, an agency serving the local Paiute-Shoshone community. In 1971, he urged Congress to support a bill to reform Indian education policy, which eventually became law as the Indian Education Act of 1972. The next year he protested against an attempt by the BUREAU OF INDIAN AFFAIRS (BIA) to bypass the Johnson-O'Malley Act and reduce funding to off-reservation Indian schoolchildren in California (see EDUCATIONAL POLICY, AMERICAN INDIANS AND). In addition to being director, Bomberry edited the Owens Valley Center's monthly newsletter; he was still listed as the editor in 1979.

In 1972, Bomberry cofounded the Native American Training Associates Institute of Sacramento, California, a research and advocacy organization directed by Dennis Magee (Luiseno Band of Mission Indians) that defended the land rights of California Indians. In 1978, Bomberry was asked by ROBERT COULTER to join the board of the newly formed Indian Law Resource Center. A short time later, Bomberry became director of Native American Studies at California State University's Sonoma Campus, at Rohnert Park, California.

In 1977, as a member of the INTERNATIONAL INDIAN TREATY COUNCIL, Bomberry helped organize the International Non-Governmental Organizations Conference on the Indigenous Peoples of the Americas in Geneva, Switzerland. The conference was a success, but after clashes with Treaty Council director JIMMIE DURHAM, who favored the militant stance of the AMERICAN INDIAN MOVEMENT (AIM), Bomberry left the Treaty Council. By this time he had come to the conclusion that community building was more important than protests. In the words of his wife, Victoria Bomberry (Muskogee-Lenape), he saw "the need for Indian nations to develop economic independence in order to achieve tribal sovereignty or any form of political independence." This new perspective, based on the developing concepts of INDIGENOUS ECONOMICS, came just as AIM was breaking up and its influence waning.

In 1977, Bomberry became one of the founders of the Native American Tribal Sovereignty Program. Operating with a staff of three, based in Guerneville, California, and later in Forestville, the Tribal Sovereignty Program began as one of several "special programs" of the Youth Project, a foundation in Washington, D.C., affiliated with the Center for Community Change, that provided local community organizations with technical assistance, workshops, and access to other funding sources. The Tribal Sovereignty Program, of which Bomberry was program coordinator, acted as a funding source and advocacy group to help Indian communities retain their traditions through culturally appropriate economic development. One year later, Bomberry founded the magazine *Native Self-Sufficiency*, which was edited first by Paula Hammett (then a staff member at the Tribal Sovereignty Program, later a librarian at Sonoma State University), and subsequently by Victoria Bomberry, who kept it going until 1988. The magazine was an outstanding vehicle for presenting modern applications of traditional Native philosophy in such areas as tribal sovereignty, women and families, housing, alternative technology, ecological agriculture, and indigenous economics.

Bomberry worked closely with *Akwesasne Notes*, the influential Mohawk newspaper edited by JOHN C. MOHAWK and JOSÉ BARREIRO, which was congenial to his thinking and had an international focus. In 1983, Bomberry supported projects among the Maya in Guatemala and worked on a campaign to publicize the persecution of the Native peoples of that country.

In 1984, the Tribal Sovereignty Program was reorganized as an independent foundation, the Seventh Generation Fund—the first Indian-controlled nonprofit foundation in North America. Seventh Generation, headed since 1986 by Chris Peters (Yorok/Karok) and now based at Arcata, California, still provides small grants and technical assistance in such areas as the arts, environment, sustainable development, and Native leadership.

Also in 1984, Bomberry wrote the foreword to the second edition of Joseph Jorgensen and Sally Swenson's seminal book, *Native Americans and Energy Development*. That year Bomberry became ill with cancer, as did his spiritual teacher, PHILLIP DEERE. Extraordinary as it may seem, both Bomberry and Deere died in the early morning hours of the same day, August 16, 1985. Victoria Bomberry, currently professor of Native American Studies in the Department of Ethnic Studies at the University of California at Riverside, raised their three sons.

Though his life was short, Bomberry's impact was far-reaching. His wife noted that his unique "approach was centered on people, taking a step at a time to develop healthy individual self-sufficiency and rebuild healthy, viable communities. It came from within the community, it wasn't imposed or planned by a faraway bureaucracy." The technology critic Jerry Mander, a close friend, acknowledged Bomberry's great influence on his own thought. Mander's well-known book, *In the Absence of the Sacred*, is dedicated to his memory.

Further Reading

Bomberry, Dan. "California Indian Education, Past, Present and Future." In *Perspectives on Contemporary Native*

American and Chicano Educational Thought, edited by Miguel Trujillo and Joshua Reichert. Davis, Calif.: D-Q University Press, 1974.

Johnson, Troy R. "Interview with Daniel Bomberry." In *The Occupation of Alcatraz Island: Indian Self-Determination and the Rise of Indian Activism*, edited by Troy R. Johnson, 106–108. Urbana: University of Illinois Press, 1996.

Jorgensen, Joseph G., and Sally Swenson. *Native Americans and Energy Development II*. Boston: Anthropology Resource Center and Seventh Generation Fund, 1984.

Mander, Jerry. *In the Absence of the Sacred: The Failure of Technology and the Survival of the Indian Nations*. San Francisco: Sierra Club Books, 1991.

Bonnin, Gertrude (Gertrude Simmons, Zitkala-Sa, Red Bird) (1876–1938) *Yankton Nakota Sioux writer, musician, political activist, reformer*

Gertrude Bonnin was born on February 22, 1876, on the Yankton Reservation. Her mother, Tate I Yohin Win (Reaches for the Wind) was a traditional Nakota who never learned English; her father, a white man named Felker, deserted the family before she was born. She was given the surname Simmons from her mother's second husband, also a white man, but she later named herself Zitkala-Sa (Red Bird) following a dispute with her sister-in-law.

Over the objections of her mother, at age eight, missionaries took Gertrude to a Quaker school, White's Manual Labor Institute at Wabash, Indiana, where she remained for three years. After a stay at the Santee Normal Training School in Flandreau, Nebraska (1888–89), she returned to White's in 1895. In that year, she began attending another Quaker institution, Earlham College in Richmond, Indiana, where she developed her remarkable talent for music. She studied violin at the Boston Conservatory for some years and later at Otterbein University in Ohio. She also competed in oratorical contests, winning a statewide competition in 1896.

In 1898, Gertrude was hired by RICHARD HENRY PRATT to teach at the Carlisle Industrial School in Carlisle, Pennsylvania. Aside from teaching, she frequently performed with the Carlisle Indian Band. There she met CARLOS MONTEZUMA, to whom she subsequently became engaged. Around this time, with her excellent command of both Nakota and English, she began to write down Nakota legends, many of which she knew from childhood. Some of her autobiographical sketches and stories appeared in *Harper's* and *Atlantic Monthly* in 1900 and 1901, and she published 14 of the stories in 1901 as *Old Indian Legends*. These are some of the earliest publications by a Sioux writing in English and are among the earliest literary works by a Native American writer. Through her writings under the name Zitkala-Sa, she became a well-known personality among New England intellectuals and reformers. An article written for *Atlantic Monthly* in 1900, "Impressions of an Indian Childhood," was particularly influential. In part a defense of traditional Indian culture, the chapter, "The Big Red Apples,"

alludes to the biblical story of Adam and Eve's fall as a metaphor for the seduction of Indians by mainstream society. Bucking the trend toward ASSIMILATION, her article, "Why I Am a Pagan," in *Atlantic Monthly* two years later promoted traditional Indian religion at a time when most non-Indians believed that these religions should be stamped out in favor of Christianity.

After breaking off her engagement to Montezuma in 1902, Gertrude Simmons married Captain Raymond T. Bonnin of the U.S. Army, also a Yankton Nakota. Their son Ohiya (Raymond) was born in 1903. Over the ensuing years, Captain Bonnin worked for the Indian Service (as the BUREAU OF INDIAN AFFAIRS [BIA] was then known) at several reservations. Zitkala-Sa did important volunteer work, helping Indians in various ways to work with non-Indian culture, but the constraints of marriage and raising a child made it difficult for her to write. In 1913, she collaborated with the composer William Hanson on *Sun Dance*, an opera that gives a sympathetic and accurate portrayal of Indian life. This work, incorporating traditional melodies that Bonnin had played to Hanson on the violin, met with success and was revived several times.

In 1916, after many years of working on various reservations, Bonnin was elected secretary of the SOCIETY OF AMERICAN INDIANS (SAI), and she and her family moved to Washington, D.C. During 1918–19, she was acting editor of the society's publication, the *American Indian Magazine*, replacing ARTHUR C. PARKER. The deep split in SAI over the manner in which the assimilation policy should be carried out found her siding with the moderate faction and against the ultra-assimilationists led by her former fiancé Carlos Montezuma. Bonnin also opposed the spread of the use of peyote among Indians, in part because of what she perceived as its harmful physical effects and also because she felt it was not a true traditional Native practice that needed to be protected (see NATIVE AMERICAN CHURCH). The issue was deeply contentious among SAI members and ultimately led to the breakup of the organization. In 1920, Bonnin moved to the GENERAL FEDERATION OF WOMEN'S CLUBS, where she was largely responsible for the establishment of an Indian Welfare Committee in 1921. One result of her work with this committee was the launching of an investigation by the INDIAN RIGHTS ASSOCIATION into the treatment of some of the tribes in Oklahoma (see CURTIS ACT).

In 1921, again under the name Zitkala-Sa, Bonnin published her second book, *American Indian Stories*, a collection of biographical and autobiographical essays illustrating the problems of contemporary Indians trying to adjust to mainstream American culture. Included were some of her early pieces from *Harper's* and *Atlantic Monthly*.

After completing its Oklahoma investigation, the Indian Rights Association published a report (1924), with sections by Gertrude Bonnin and others, under the title *Oklahoma's Poor Rich Indians: An Orgy of Graft and Exploitation of the Five Civilized Tribes—Legalized Robbery*. The ensuing outcry led to the appointment by President Herbert Hoover of two members of the Indian Rights Association to top positions in the Indian

Service in 1928 (see RHOADS, CHARLES JAMES; SCATTERGOOD, JOSEPH HENRY), and to the release of Lewis B. Meriam's famous report of the same year (see MERIAM REPORT), which was in many ways the prelude to the INDIAN REORGANIZATION ACT of 1934.

In 1926, Gertrude and Raymond Bonnin founded the National Council of American Indians in Washington, D.C. She invited MARY CHINQUILLA to join the council, but rescinded the offer on discovering Chinquilla was associated with suspected impostor RED FOX ST. JAMES. The aim of the council was to help Indians participate in politics and serve as a national intertribal advocacy group, but it had only limited success. Bonnin served as president until her death on January 26, 1938. She is buried in Arlington National Cemetery beside her husband.

Gertrude Bonnin worked in many ways for the survival of Indians and their cultures. Despite her training at schools that promoted a philosophy of assimilation, her Indian identity remained the driving force of her life, and she was openly critical of the educational ideals of Carlisle even while she taught there. Although her education allowed her to become a champion of Indian rights, it also left her estranged from her culture and family on the reservation. Bonnin challenged the simplistic views of assimilation that prevailed at the time and in her writings grappled with its complexities. Her far-reaching activities were directed toward helping Native Americans not only survive under very difficult circumstances, but be better understood, obtain justice, and exert a positive influence on American society.

Further Reading
Johnson, David L., and Raymond Wilson. "Gertrude Simmons Bonnin, 1876–1938: 'Americanize the First Americans.'" *American Indian Quarterly* 12 (Winter 1988): 27–40.
Lisa, Laurie. "The Life Story of Zitkala-Sa/ Gertrude Simmons Bonnin: Writing and Creating a Public Image." Ph.D. dissertation, Arizona State University, 1996.
Tibbitts, Tim. "Into Personal and Political Power: The Rhetoric of Gertrude Simmons Bonnin (Zitkala-Sa), 1876–1938." M.A. dissertation, George Washington University, 1996.
Udall, Catherine. "Bonnin, Gertrude." In *Native American Women: A Biographical Dictionary*, edited by Gretchen M. Bataille and Laurie Lisa. 2nd ed., 42–44. New York: Routledge, 2001.
Welch, Deborah. "Zitkala Sa: An American Indian Leader, 1876–1938." Ph.D. dissertation, University of Wyoming, 1985.
Williard, William. "Zitkala Sa: A Woman Who Would Be Heard." *Wicazo Sa Review* 1 (Spring 1985): 11–16.

Boucha, Henry Charles (1951–) *Chippewa Olympic silver medalist in hockey, professional hockey player*

Henry Charles Boucha was born on June 1, 1951, in Warroad, Minnesota, on the Red Lake Reservation, known as "Hockey Town, U.S.A." Boucha played hockey for Warroad High School, leading his team to the 1969 state tournament. He joined the U.S. Army after graduating from high school in 1970. That same year, he was chosen for the U.S. national ice hockey team. With Team USA he played in the 1971 Ice Hockey World Championships in Berne, Switzerland, where he scored seven goals in 10 games. He was also a star of the Olympic team that won the silver medal in Japan in 1972. Boucha then left the army and joined the Detroit Red Wings in 1973, subsequently winning Rookie of the Year honors. The next year he was traded to the Minnesota North Stars, but his promising career was cut short by injury, and he had to retire after the 1976–77 season. He was the first NHL player to wear a headband, which was his trademark. Boucha later returned to Warroad to become the high school's hockey coach. Since 1987, he has been active in real estate as well as in Native causes and charities. He was inducted into the U.S. Hockey Hall of Fame in 1995. His cousin Gary Sargent, also a Chippewa from Red Lake, was an NHL player from 1975 to 1983.

Further Reading
Schofield, Mary Halverson. *Henry Boucha: Star of the North*. Edina, Minn.: Snowshoe Press, 1999.

Box Canyon murder (1974)

On October 10, 1974, a non-Indian was murdered at an AMERICAN INDIAN MOVEMENT (AIM) camp in Box Canyon, north of Los Angeles, California. The camp was located in Ventura County near the Los Angeles County line, in Box Canyon in the Santa Susanna Mountains near Simi Valley. The land had been owned since 1948 by WKFL (Wisdom, Knowledge, Faith, Love) Fountain of the World, a cult group founded in 1948 by "Krishna Venta" (born Francis H. Pencovic, 1911–58), who had been blown up in a dynamite explosion set by two of his followers who accused him of improprieties. However, the organization continued to exist and still owned the land. A few followers who still lived there in 1972 invited Chumash religious leader Semu Huaute and the Red Wind Foundation, who hoped to establish a traditional community as a "living museum," to occupy a part of the land. Despite a favorable reception from the local residents and the county authorities, however, the Indians found the bureaucratic hurdles too daunting and had to abandon the plan in January 1973.

In January 1974, the WKFL property was taken over by AIM, under the leadership of the organization's California coordinator, a Yaqui who gave his name as Nacho. The opening of the camp was directly linked with the Wounded Knee trials that followed the armed standoff between AIM members and federal law enforcement agents the previous year (see WOUNDED KNEE, OCCUPATION OF). AIM said the camp was intended as a way station for Indians traveling through California in support of the Wounded Knee defendants, DENNIS JAMES BANKS, RUSSELL MEANS, and others, being tried in South Dakota.

Instead, it quickly turned into a hangout for dissolute characters, both Indian and non-Indian. Its increasingly bad reputation led AIM to withdraw financial support, but the camp continued to be maintained covertly through the Federal Bureau of Investigation's secret COINTELPRO program (see PELTIER, LEONARD). The government, concerned about the fact that the Hollywood film community was a significant source of financial support and media exposure for AIM, hoped to use the rowdy camp as a means to discredit the Indian organization. The FBI assigned two operatives and AIM infiltrators to raise money to keep the camp going—Virginia De Luce, a former actress who used the name Blue Dove, and Douglass Durham, later exposed as an FBI informer during the trials following the occupation of Wounded Knee.

It was simply a matter of time before trouble arose, but no one could have predicted how grisly it would be. In the first incident, on October 8, 1974, there was no fatality: The victim was a 49-year-old unemployed laborer, Herrell A. Wood, who lived alone in a cabin on Box Canyon Road. At about 7:30 P.M., two young Indians carrying deadly weapons, Leonard Rising Sun and Robin Louis Black Cloud (the latter only 17 years of age), forced their way into Wood's cabin, assaulted him, took his money, drank his beer, and repeatedly tormented and hit him for several hours until a neighbor alerted the county sheriff's office. The two were apprehended.

The actual murder occurred at the camp itself two days later. On the evening of October 10, five people who had been staying there decided to go to the house of David Carradine, star of the popular television series *Kung Fu*, thinking that there was a party that night. Marvin Redshirt (a Lakota from Pine Ridge); his girlfriend Holly Broussard, daughter of a wealthy Long Beach businessman; Marcella Makes Noise Eaglestaff (also known as Marcella McNoise and a woman of dubious Indian ancestry with a serious criminal record in her hometown of Seattle); Roland Knox, who claimed to be from Alaska; and Carradine's friend Lee War Lance, another Pine Ridge Lakota with a history of alcoholism, all took off in Broussard's car. When they arrived at Carradine's, however, they found no one home. Knox left with Broussard's car, but since War Lance had the key to Carradine's house, the rest stayed and spent the evening drinking. At 10 P.M., Redshirt, Broussard, and Eaglestaff phoned the Red and White Cab Company for a ride back to the AIM camp. Soon George Aird, a 27-year-old white cabdriver, arrived, and they headed back toward Box Canyon.

From here on accounts differ, but there was evidently an altercation in the cab, since the meter was found to have been pulled out when it reached $6, and Redshirt drove the cab the latter part of the journey. After the cab had crossed the gate into the camp, Aird either got out or was pulled out and was stabbed 17 times. His dead body was stuffed into a drainpipe. Redshirt's fingerprints were found not only on Aird's body but also on cab company papers that had been jammed into an incinerator but not burned.

The police lost no time in apprehending the three occupants of the cab, finding Redshirt and Eaglestaff (neither of whom were AIM members), as well as Broussard, drunk, blood-splattered, and passed out near the scene of the crime. However, the suspects were released from jail after they accused two young AIM members—Paul "Skyhorse" Durant (Chippewa) and Richard "Mohawk" Billings (Tuscarora-Mohawk), usually referred to as Richard Mohawk—of killing the cabdriver.

AIM disowned Skyhorse and Mohawk, who were well known for their drunken binges and who admitted they had been drunk the night of the murder and could not remember what had happened. However, AIM could not escape the bad publicity of the investigation and trial, which the federal government prolonged as much as possible. After two and a half years of pretrial deliberations (the longest in California history), the venue, due to prejudicial pretrial publicity, was moved from Ventura to Los Angeles County.

The trial itself took another year. The government's case against Skyhorse and Mohawk collapsed when star government witness Marvin Redshirt showed up in court drunk and then admitted on the stand that he had stabbed the cabdriver first. The other government witnesses did little better; Broussard was unable to remember if Skyhorse and Mohawk were even at the scene and Marcella McNoise refused to answer the defense attorney's questions during cross-examination and was jailed for contempt of court. Skyhorse and Mohawk, having spent three and a half years in prison, were acquitted of murder charges on May 24, 1978. However, by then, AIM's reputation in California was in tatters and its formerly close relationship with the Hollywood elite had been destroyed. Redshirt, Broussard, and McNoise were never charged with the murder of Aird. In 1978, Marvin Redshirt was rearrested and charged with the near-fatal stabbing of his girlfriend Holly Broussard.

Further Reading

Hendricks, Steve. *The Unquiet Grave: The FBI and the Struggle for the Soul of Indian Country*, 249–252, 256. New York: Thunder's Mouth Press, 2006.

Boyden, John Sterling (1906–1980) *Mormon attorney in Navajo-Hopi land conflict*

John Sterling Boyden was born in Coalville, Utah, on April 14, 1906. After passing the bar, he worked as a U.S. attorney in Salt Lake City, Utah. He then became a partner of the Mormon attorney Ernest Wilkinson, an architect of the INDIAN CLAIMS COMMISSION Act (1946), which did not allow tribes to recover lost land and awarded claims strictly in cash payments valued as per the time of loss (usually some 50–100 years earlier). Critics called it the "Indian Lawyers Welfare Act," because at fees ranging from 7 to 10 percent of all awards, the more land that was proved "lost," the more money the lawyers made. After the act's passage, Wilkinson's firm contracted to pursue claims for several tribes, including the Ute and the Hopi, with Boyden and Wilkinson later sharing a $50 million claims settlement for the Ute.

Boyden eventually set up his own firm: Boyden, Kennedy,

Romney. As Ute general counsel, he negotiated a deferral of Ute water rights to divert water to Salt Lake City. For this, the Ute tried to fire him but were overruled by William McConkey, an attorney with the Department of the Interior. Boyden also negotiated gas leases with Mountain Fuel and Gas Supply, Utah's largest gas company. The Mormon church had a large financial stake in Mountain, and prominent Mormons sat on its board.

In 1949, Boyden was a candidate for the federal judgeship in Salt Lake City. Backed by the Mormons, he would have been the first member of the Church of Latter-day Saints to hold that position (due to long-standing tensions between the church and the federal government going back to the 1850s). After a bitter fight, however, Boyden lost to Willis W. Ritter, a law professor at the University of Utah.

Having handled many tribal cases as a U.S. attorney, Boyden had both experience and contacts. In 1951, as the land claims deadline loomed, he wanted to file for the Hopi to regain land lost to the neighboring Navajo (Dineh). This required authorization from the tribal council and the secretary of the interior, but the tribal council system, imposed on the Hopi in 1935 by BUREAU OF INDIAN AFFAIRS (BIA) OLIVER LA FARGE and BIA Commissioner JOHN COLLIER under the INDIAN REORGANIZATION ACT, was defunct. Each Hopi village governed itself, as it had for the last 1,000 years or more.

With BIA authorization, Boyden and a BIA superintendent visited the villages to explain the proposed land claim. The five traditionalist villages refused their offer. In others, Boyden led villagers to believe they might get some land back or that more land might be bought with revenues from oil that might be found on the reservation. Votes were held in those villages, though few participated. In the end, Boyden negotiated a contract as attorney for seven Hopi villages, in his words "a majority of the villages representing a majority of the people." The federal government approved his claim on July 27, 1951, and it was filed as Docket 196.

The Navajo-Hopi Rehabilitation Act of 1950 awarded $90 million to the tribes, but the Hopi, with no tribal council, got little of it. Boyden determined to reconstitute a council. A confidential memo in the BIA files states: "When he has obtained the trust of a solid majority, he believes that he can then develop a representative tribal council with whom the BIA and outside interests may deal." A BIA official wrote in 1952: "Remuneration for his services will depend largely on working out a solution to many of the Hopi problems to such a point that oil leases will provide funds."

By late 1955, the BIA office in Keams County, Arizona, had its council of nine "progressive" Hopi. According to the 1935 constitution, however, there should have been 17 councilors. Eight seats remained unfilled because the traditionals refused to participate (see KATCHONGVA, DAN). This unofficial council retained Boyden as general attorney. Lacking funds, the council agreed to come to terms at a later date.

In the mid-1950s, Boyden lobbied Congress to authorize the Hopi to sue the Navajo in federal court for former Hopi lands now located outside their present reservation boundary.

These included Black Mesa, a sacred site extremely rich in coal and other minerals. Boyden did not intend to seek surface rights on the lost lands, only an interest in subsurface minerals. His handpicked tribal council would take care of the rest. By 1960, the council had passed regulations opening the reservation for prospecting. At Boyden's request, Interior Secretary Stewart Udall issued a decision on March 30, 1961, giving the tribal council power to sign leases. They signed their first mineral lease later that year.

Public Law 85-547, introduced by Senators Carl T. Hayden and Barry Goldwater and passed July 23, 1958, authorized the chairmen of the Navajo and Hopi tribal councils to sue each other to determine their respective rights within the boundaries of the former 1882 Hopi reservation. In 1962, a special three-judge federal court in Arizona decided the case, *Healing v. Jones*, confirming the present Hopi boundaries and assigning them "joint use" with the Navajo of their former lands. This was affirmed by the Supreme Court in 1963.

In 1964, the Hopi signed their first big oil lease with Aztec Oil and Gas. At the time, Boyden was lawyer for Aztec as well as for the Hopi tribe, but this did not trouble him. On December 5, 1964, with Hopi now holding oil leases worth $3 million, the tribal council settled as per their 1955 agreement, paying Boyden $1 million for services rendered between 1938 and 1965.

In June 1966, the Hopi Tribal Council leased to Peabody Coal subsurface rights to 58,000 acres on Black Mesa, soon to become the world's largest strip mine. The coal was conveyed by slurry pipeline to a huge power plant at Page, Arizona, that provided electricity for the southwest grid, represented by WEST (Western Energy Supply and Transmission) Associates, an association of 23 utilities from Texas to California. The traditionals protested that the council probably did not have a quorum when it issued the lease. Boyden therefore persuaded the Hopi Tribal Council to hire Evans and Associates, the same Salt Lake City public relations firm that represented WEST. The "interests" of the tribe and the utility association were now perfectly synchronized. Evans and Associates even wrote speeches for tribal chair Clarence Hamilton and his successor, ABBOTT SEKAQUAPTEWA.

More legislation resulted from the 1962 judgment upholding the Hopi's right to joint use of their former lands. Officials quickly realized that the ruling was unenforceable without partitioning the land: There were just too many Navajo. In 1971, Boyden, assisted by Harrison Loesch, assistant secretary of the House Interior Committee, and Republican congressman Sam Steiger of Arizona, drafted a bill authorizing partition. A second version was prepared by Arizona's Republican senators Barry Goldwater and Paul Fannin. The final version, prepared by Boyden and introduced by Utah congressman Wayne Owens, authorized the federal district court of Arizona to determine the partition boundary. It was signed by President Gerald Ford on December 22, 1974, as PL 93-531. This law would result in the forced relocation of thousands of Navajo from the former Joint-Use Area (see BIG MOUNTAIN).

Many years later, in 1996, the University of Colorado law

professor Charles Wilkinson was able to document for the first time the shocking fact that in the mid-1960s, Boyden, at the same time that he was counsel for the Hopi, was secretly on the payroll of Peabody Coal, a situation contrary to all canons of legal ethics.

An official at Interior characterized Boyden in a memorandum as "first of all a Mormon, secondly a very strong state's advocate, and, thirdly, an advocate for Indian people." Parker Nielson, a Salt Lake City attorney, described him as "not intentionally devious, but he had a very myopic view of Indians and their problems. He saw it as a problem of converting them to round-eyed Caucasians and particularly Mormon round-eyed Caucasians. That was the intention of [Watkins's] termination policy, which [Boyden] helped to design. It forced the Indians off the reservation and into the cities."

Boyden died on July 17, 1980.

See also TERMINATION; WATKINS, ARTHUR VIVIAN.

Further Reading

Boyden, Ophe Sweeten. *John S. Boyden: Three Score and Ten in Retrospect*. Cedar City, Utah: Southern Utah State College Press, 1986.

Dougherty, John. "Dark Days on Black Mesa." *Phoenix New Times*, 24 April 1997.

———. "A People Betrayed." *Phoenix New Times*, 1 May 1997.

Nies, Judith. "The Black Mesa Syndrome: Indian Land, Black Gold." *Orion* (Summer 1998): 18–29.

———. "The Indian Lawyer and a Brief History of Coal." In *Unreal City: Las Vegas, Black Mesa, and the Fate of the West*, by Judith Nies, 69-92. New York: Nations Books, 2014.

Wilkinson, Charles F. *Fire on the Plateau: Conflict and Endurance in the American Southwest*. Washington, D.C.: Island Press, 1999.

Brave, Benjamin (Ohitika) (1865–1948) *Lakota Sioux minister, politician, activist*

Benjamin Brave was a Lakota Sioux born near the Cheyenne River in South Dakota in 1865. Both of his parents were Lakota Sioux. His father, a cousin of Lakota Sioux chief Sitting Bull, took part in the Black Hills War, while his mother fled southward with the boy when he was six years old. His mother named him Ohitika (brave), and he learned much about Lakota spiritual ways from her, though she died when he was still young.

In 1878, Brave moved to the Lower Brulé Agency, where his sister lived. Soon after his arrival, he went to live with Reverend Luke C. Walker, an Indian clergyman. When Brave was 15, General Samuel Chapman Armstrong, the founder and director of the Hampton Institute in Virginia, came to Lower Brulé looking for prospective students. Armstrong brought Brave and several other Indian children to Hampton in October 1881. At his enrollment, Brave's age was given as 16.

Armstrong had set up Hampton as a school to provide technical training to freed slaves and their children. The idea of admitting Indians was a new experiment. At the time Brave entered, the man in charge of Indian students was African-American educator Booker T. Washington. At Hampton, Brave became friendly with fellow student Robert R. Moton, later head of the Tuskegee Institute. Both were members of teams sent out to raise interest in the work of Hampton, and after their days at the school, their friendship continued.

Brave graduated in July 1885. After leaving Hampton, he went back to South Dakota where he became a teacher and organized a Sunday school. Also in 1885, he married Ida Rencontre, a Lakota who had also recently graduated from Hampton. For a while he worked as a shoemaker at the government Indian school, where he was later appointed disciplinarian. He organized the Returned Student and Progressive Indian Association at Lower Brulé.

Strongly desiring to do missionary work, Brave became a minister at Eagle Butte. After his ordination in the Congregational Church, Brave became pastor at the Rosebud Reservation and pastor-at-large at the Standing Rock Reservation in charge of Congregational fieldwork, a position he held until his retirement. As head of the Standing Rock tribal council in 1916, Brave was sent to Washington as a delegate to press the Sioux claims to the Black Hills.

Brave was a board member of the SOCIETY OF AMERICAN INDIANS after Dakota Sioux CHARLES ALEXANDER EASTMAN took over as president in 1917. He was a powerful orator and often spoke at important gatherings. At the unveiling of a monument commemorating the return of Sitting Bull and his band from Canada in 1882, Brave delivered the invocation. In 1931, invited by his old friend Moton, he delivered an address on Booker T. Washington at the 50th anniversary celebration of the Tuskegee Institute in Alabama. On his way home, he stopped at Hampton Institute to visit his alma mater, went to Washington, where he spoke with President Herbert Hoover, and continued on to Philadelphia where he saw Herbert Welsh and Matthew K. Sniffen, his old friends from the INDIAN RIGHTS ASSOCIATION.

In 1941, he said a prayer at the Pierre state capitol exercises in South Dakota. Brave died in December 1948.

Further Reading

Lindsay, Donal F. *Indians of Hampton Institute, 1877–1923*. Urbana: University of Illinois Press, 1995.

Brave Bird, Mary (Mary Crow Dog, Ohitika Win, Mary Ellen Moore) (1954–2013) *Lakota Sioux activist, author*

A Lakota Sioux born on the Rosebud Reservation in South Dakota, Mary Brave Bird became a political activist whose subsequent autobiographies are now well-known testaments of personal and political development. Mary Ellen Moore was born on September 26, 1954; her father, Bill Moore, was white and her mother, Emily Brave Bird, was Lakota Sioux. Mary Brave Bird was thus an *iveska*, or half-blood, and was raised in an environment dominated by poverty, where she found herself caught between two worlds.

Shortly after Mary Brave Bird's birth, her father abandoned the family, and the girl was brought up largely by her grandparents. Together with members of her extended family, they acquainted her with the oral traditions of her people. Brave Bird became the third generation of her family to be taken from home to the St. Francis Mission boarding school, where hostility to her tribe's culture and language was enforced through brutal discipline. Her subsequent adolescent confusion was mired in battles with alcoholism, poverty, and domestic violence.

In the early 1970s, Brave Bird became involved with the AMERICAN INDIAN MOVEMENT (AIM). This had a profound effect, enabling her to understand and focus her rebellious energies and to reclaim her cultural inheritance. As she described it, "AIM made medicine men radical activists, and made radical activists into sundancers and vision seekers." Brave Bird joined the TRAIL OF BROKEN TREATIES protest march, and she was among the group that took over the BUREAU OF INDIAN AFFAIRS (BIA) building in Washington, D.C., in 1972. At the OCCUPATION OF WOUNDED KNEE in South Dakota in 1973, she gave birth to her first child. In the aftermath of Wounded Knee, she met and married Brulé Lakota Sioux medicine man LEONARD CROW DOG. When he was jailed for his activities with AIM, she campaigned relentlessly—and successfully—for his release.

The siege itself was the focal point of Brave Bird's autobiography, *Lakota Woman*, which pulled together both present and past injustices experienced by Native Americans and described them from the vivid perspective of a young participant in the contemporary struggle. Brave Bird dictated her life story to Richard Erdoes, a photographer and illustrator, who also cowrote Leonard Crow Dog's biography. The book was initially issued using her married name, Mary Crow Dog, and was published in two volumes. The first volume, released in 1990 under the title *Ohitika Woman*, was printed by Grove Press. Reissued the next year by HarperCollins as *Lakota Woman*, it became a popular best seller.

In 1993, HarperCollins released the second volume, *Ohitika Woman*, this time using the author's family name, Mary Brave Bird. *Ohitika Woman* took up the story of her later life, while also recapitulating her earlier experiences from the viewpoint of her older self. Darker in tone, dealing with life after the downfall of the RED POWER MOVEMENT rather than during the heady days of its prime, the book chronicles Brave Bird's deteriorating relationship with her husband, her participation in the NATIVE AMERICAN CHURCH, and her recurring struggles with poverty and alcoholism. The traditions, the rituals, and the medicine that were equally part of her cultural inheritance were woven into her narrative as the constants that enabled her to survive. It is this combination of Brave Bird's unflinching realism together with her commitment to tradition that give both her books their power as records of contemporary Native experience.

In 1994, *Lakota Woman—Siege at Wounded Knee* was made into a TV movie by Turner Home Entertainment, starring Irene Bedard as Mary Crow Dog.

Despite her fame, Mary Brave Bird continued to struggle with alcoholism and poverty, and her publishing royalties were garnished by the IRS to pay back taxes. Mary Ellen Moore-Richard died on February 14, 2013, in Crystal Lake, Nevada.

Further Reading

Brave Bird, Mary, with Richard Erdoes. *Ohitika Woman.* New York: Grove Press, 1993.

Crow Dog, Mary, and Richard Erdoes. *Lakota Woman.* New York: G. Weidenfeld, 1990.

Bresette, Walt (1947–1999) *Chippewa environmental and community activist, writer, researcher, artist, news director, radio commentator*

One of seven sons of a freelance lumberjack, Walt Bresette was born on July 4, 1947, on the Red Cliff Indian Reservation in northern Wisconsin. When he was 12, he attended a summer school for Indian youth organized by noted educator and supporter of Indian causes Veda Stone at the University of Wisconsin–Eau Claire. Later his maternal aunt, Victoria Gokee, the first woman to serve as tribal chair of the Red Cliff Band of Lake Superior Chippewa, involved Bresette and his brothers in research on Indian issues.

Bresette did four years of military service during the Vietnam War, mostly in Japan doing electronic monitoring with a U.S. Army intelligence unit. After his discharge from the army, a grant from the BUREAU OF INDIAN AFFAIRS (BIA) enabled Bresette to study commercial art in Chicago, where he took part in some antiwar protests and Indian demonstrations led by Mike Chosa and Betty Jack of the Lac du Flambeau Reservation. In Chicago, he lived with his maternal uncle, Leo La Fernier, who later became a tribal officer at Red Cliff.

In the late 1970s, Bresette began working for the Great Lakes Intertribal Council (GLIC). In 1978, he took over as the council's public information officer. At the same time, he published a small monthly magazine at Red Cliff. He also worked as a reporter for WOJB Radio, the Public Broadcasting Service station of the Lac Court Oreilles reservation (see RADIO, AMERICAN INDIANS AND). In 1979, he organized an event to commemorate the 125th anniversary of the 1854 La Pointe treaty at Red Cliff, with ceremonies on Madeleine Island, sacred ground for the Chippewa. The celebration spontaneously became the focus for political education of the local people.

Bresette was still a reporter in 1983 when *Lac Court Oreilles Band of Chippewa v. The State of Wisconsin* (better known as the Voigt Decision) reaffirmed Chippewa treaty rights to hunt and fish on ceded lands (see HUNTING AND FISHING RIGHTS). When the GREAT LAKES INDIAN FISH AND WILDLIFE COMMISSION (GLIFWC) was established in 1984, Bresette was hired to edit its newspaper, *Masinaigan*, and also designed the GLIFWC logo. He became increasingly active as a speaker in support of treaty rights; in particular, rights to spearfishing on off-reservation ceded territories.

In the 1980s, Bresette served as media consultant to the NATIONAL CONGRESS OF AMERICAN INDIANS (NCAI). Though he considered running for tribal office himself, he became disenchanted when he learned of the experiences of some of his contemporaries who had become tribal officers. In 1986, while attending an NCAI conference in Tampa, Florida, Bresette was contacted by a complete stranger, a 90-year-old white woman, who gave him a war club that had been passed down through her late husband's family. It had belonged to Black Hawk, war chief of the Sac and Fox who died nearly 150 years earlier. For some time, Black Hawk heroically resisted U.S. Army attempts to remove him and his people from their homelands at Rock Island, Illinois. A medicine man advised Bresette to keep the war club, as it had been given to him for a reason. For the rest of his life, he carried it with him to all ceremonies, protests, and public gatherings.

Bresette was concerned about threats not only to Native SOVEREIGNTY, INDIGENOUS AND TRIBAL, but to rural America in general. From the mid-1980s, he was active as a "multi-cultural networker," founding several groups in which people of diverse cultures worked together on environmental and Indian treaty issues, two aspects of the same thing as far as he was concerned. He was active in the Green Party, founded the Lake Superior Greens, and was a founding member of the Wisconsin Greens. From 1988, he was involved in anti-mining efforts in northern Wisconsin that threatened to contaminate nearby lakes and rivers with metallic sulfides, and he was active in the INDIGENOUS ENVIRONMENTAL NETWORK. He was also a cofounder of the Milwaukee Witness for Non-violence program (1988–92), which documented and defused racial violence against Indian spearfishers, and of the Midwest Treaty Network (1989).

During the 1980s, Wisconsin Indians were especially concerned about mineral exploration and government projects for a nuclear depository and underground antennae to guide nuclear submarines, to be built in northern Wisconsin. One of Bresette's goals was to bring together midwestern tribes to take a unified political stand on threats to the environment. At a meeting in Eau Claire, 25 tribes passed resolutions against these and other environmentally questionable programs.

Bresette organized a Woodland Indian Arts Collective and became a partner, with his wife, Cass Joy, in the Buffalo Bay Trading Company, an Indian arts and crafts business in Bayfield, Wisconsin, which they ran until the mid-1990s. Walt Bresette died of a heart attack on February 21, 1999, while visiting friends in Duluth, Minnesota. He was buried on the Red Cliff Reservation.

Further Reading

Bresette, Walt, and Rick Whaley. *Walleye Warriors: An Effective Alliance against Racism and for the Earth.* Philadelphia: New Society Publishers, 1994.
Gedicks, Al. *The New Resource Wars: Native and Environmental Struggles against Multinational Corporations.* Montreal and Cheektowaga, N.Y.: Black Rose Books, 1994.
Whaley, Rick. "The Centrality of Native Americans to Green Philosophy and Practice." *Synthesis/Regeneration*, no. 29 (Fall 2002): 32–33.

Bronson, Ruth Muskrat (1897–1982) *Cherokee educator, administrator, community development activist*

The daughter of a Cherokee father, James Ezekiel Muskrat, and an Irish-English mother, Ida Lenore (Kelly) Muskrat, Ruth Muskrat Bronson was born on October 3, 1897, and raised on a farm in Grove, Oklahoma, in the Delaware District of the Cherokee Nation. As a young girl, she experienced the dissolution of the Cherokee Nation under the CURTIS ACT and saw the damage it inflicted on the community.

Muskrat began preparatory school at Tonkawa, Oklahoma, in 1912 and later attended the University of Oklahoma, University of Kansas, and Mount Holyoke College in Massachusetts, where she received her B.A. in 1925. In 1921, she ran a summer program for girls on the Mescalero Apache reservation in Arizona and the following year she visited China with the World Student Christian Federation. In those years (not unlike her contemporary, MARY STONE MCLENDON [Ataloa]), she was already campaigning for improved education for Indians. The type of education that she sought was not strongly assimilationist (see ASSIMILATION) and would allow the preservation of many aspects of tribal cultures.

In 1925, Ruth Muskrat began teaching eighth grade at the Haskell Institute in Kansas. (The Haskell Institute, now Haskell Indian Nations University, was founded in 1884 as a vocational training school for young Indians.) In 1928, she married John F. Bronson of Connecticut, who worked at the U.S. Naval Medical Research Unit. Two years later, she took a position with the new guidance office in the BUREAU OF INDIAN AFFAIRS's (BIA) Office of Education. In 1932, one year before JOHN COLLIER became BIA commissioner, Ruth Bronson began running a new program that provided loans for HIGHER EDUCATION or training. In 1935, she and her husband moved to Washington, D.C., and three years later, the Bronsons adopted a baby girl, the orphan of a close friend from Laguna Pueblo.

Bronson retired from government service in 1943, but she continued her work on behalf of Indians. She was one of the founders of the NATIONAL CONGRESS OF AMERICAN INDIANS (NCAI) in 1944 and ran the organization's legislative review service in the earliest years of its existence. Between 1946 and 1949, a period of renewed pressure on Indians to assimilate, she served as NCAI's executive director. Even after stepping down from the leadership of NCAI, Bronson remained a powerful lobbyist against the federal government's prevailing TERMINATION policy and played a leading role in the ouster of BIA commissioner DILLON SEYMOUR MYER in 1953.

Bronson was active in the first community development workshop of D'ARCY MCNICKLE's American Indian Development (AID), an adjunct organization of NCAI, and was a member of the Council on Indian Affairs. In 1957, she took a position as community health educator with the Indian Health Service at San Carlos Apache Reservation in Arizona, where she helped local women build leadership skills. A core from this group formed an outreach program for the local Indian hospital and by 1960 was designing and running a range of community programs.

In 1962, Bronson moved to Tucson, Arizona, where she was a consultant for Save the Children Federation programs on the Yaqui and Tohono O'odham (Papago) reservations. In the early 1970s, she suffered a stroke that left her partially paralyzed. Ruth Bronson died on June 12, 1982.

Further Reading

Harvey, Gretchen G. *Cherokee and American: Ruth Muskrat Bronson. 1897–1982.* Ph.D. thesis, Arizona State University, 1996.

Brophy, William Aloysius (1903–1962) *commissioner of Indian affairs*

Born on February 7, 1903, in New York City, William A. Brophy attended public schools in New York and Chicago and later moved to New Mexico, where he attended the University of New Mexico. After earning his LL.B. from the University of Colorado in 1931, Brophy returned to New Mexico to work for the law firm of Hanna and Wilson in Albuquerque. With the firm, Brophy represented the Pueblo Indians of the area, developing a lifelong commitment to Indian issues.

In 1934, Brophy was appointed special attorney for the Pueblo Indians, under the Department of the Interior's Office of the Solicitor, serving until 1942. His future wife, Sophia D. Aberle, was named superintendent of the newly consolidated Pueblo agency the following year. (They were married in 1944.) As special attorney, Brophy developed his view of the relationship of the U.S. government to the Pueblo, which he modeled after the "protector of the Indians" philosophy of Spanish law. In 1940, Brophy presented a paper at the historic First International Conference on Indian Life, held in Pátzcuaro, Mexico, in which he argued that the United States had misunderstood the status of Pueblo Indians under Spanish and Mexican law and had therefore mistakenly allowed non-Indians to settle on their lands in violation of the 1848 Treaty of Guadalupe Hidalgo, which guaranteed Indians the rights to their homelands. As special attorney to the Pueblo, Brophy maintained that he was simply fulfilling the role of "protector of the Indians" under Spanish law, a role that required him to look after Indian land and water rights.

Brophy fought for Indian rights at every turn, successfully winning the right of the Walapai Indians to the water of Peach Springs (*United States v. Santa Fe Pacific Railroad Company*), as well as fighting for the right of Indians to vote and supporting religious freedom under *Toledo v. Pueblo de Jemez* in 1954.

In 1942, Brophy was assigned to work on Puerto Rican issues for the Department of the Interior. He returned briefly to his law firm—now Hanna, Wilson, and Brophy—in 1943, leaving after a few months to rejoin the government as head of the Puerto Rican section of the Division of Territories and Island Possessions in the Interior.

After a bruising confirmation, Brophy was named as commissioner of the BUREAU OF INDIAN AFFAIRS (BIA) on March 6, 1945, succeeding JOHN COLLIER. By this time the mood in Congress had shifted away from the INDIAN NEW DEAL (see INDIAN REORGANIZATION ACT), partly as a result of Indian accomplishments during WORLD WAR II. Moreover, the political climate had shifted away from Franklin Roosevelt's social policies, and in Congress the critics of Collier's culture-based programs began to call for a return to the policies of ASSIMILATION, known by the new name of TERMINATION.

With the war winding down, Brophy's immediate concern was to replace the income generated by Indian soldiers and workers in the war industries, and he set up a program with the U.S. Employment Service to help Indians find jobs in other fields. Brophy did not fight Congress's attempts to reorganize the BIA, and in May 1946, the bureau was split into five geographical districts, based in Billings, Minneapolis, Oklahoma City, Portland, and Phoenix. Brophy also acquiesced to the establishment of the controversial INDIAN CLAIMS COMMISSION, which was created to resolve outstanding Indian land claims.

Brophy became ill in 1946 and had to take an extended leave of absence. During this time William Zimmerman, assistant commissioner, acted in his stead. By this time, the Termination mood in Congress had reached the point of action, and in 1947 Congress contemplated various means of dissolving the BIA. The Truman administration also favored Termination, and Assistant Secretary of the Interior William Warne stated in January 1948 that the BIA's task was to "work itself out of a job." The bureau's budget, badly cut during the war years, was trimmed further. Zimmerman was helpless to stop the tide, and when asked to present a list of Indian tribes that were ready to be severed from the bureau's control, a list that would be used to determine those tribes to be terminated, Zimmerman complied. In the meantime, Brophy, unable to fulfill his obligations, resigned on June 3, 1948, and was succeeded by JOHN RALPH NICHOLS.

Brophy returned to New Mexico and again became special attorney for the Pueblo, serving until 1955. He contributed to the Commission on the Rights, Liberties, and Responsibilities of the American Indians, helping to draft its influential report *The Indian: America's Unfinished Business*. The report, however, was not published until 1966, four years after Brophy's death on March 24, 1962. The William A. Brophy and Sophia Aberle Brophy Papers (1923–73) are at the Harry S. Truman Library, Independence, Missouri.

Further Reading

Fixico, Donald L. *Termination and Relocation: Federal Indian Policies 1945–1960.* Albuquerque: University of New Mexico Press, 1974.

Hasse, Larry J. "Termination and Assimilation: Federal Indian

Policy 1943–1961." Ph.D. dissertation, Washington State University, 1974.

Tyler, S. Lyman. "William Brophy." In *The Commissioners of Indian Affairs, 1824–1977*, edited by Robert M. Kvasnicka and Herman Viola. Lincoln: University of Nebraska Press, 1979.

Brown, Dee (Dorris Alexander Brown)

(1908–2002) *author*

Dee Brown was born Dorris Alexander Brown in Alberta, Bienville Parish, Louisiana, on February 28, 1908. His father died when he was five. About 1914, the family moved to the small town of Stephens, Arkansas, where his mother became the town postmaster. In the early 1920s, when Brown was a young teenager, oil was discovered, and Stephens became a boomtown. Among the many laborers flooding into Stephens were Indian oilfield workers from Oklahoma. A number of the Indian boys became Brown's friends, and when they went to the movies and saw Westerns together, he cheered for the Indians along with them. In 1924, the Browns moved to the city of Little Rock, Arkansas, where Dee attended high school. The Indian baseball player Bill "Chief" Wano, superlative first baseman for Little Rock's team, the Arkansas Travelers, became Dee's hero.

He attended Arkansas State Teachers College at Conway (now University of Central Arkansas), graduating in 1927. Later he attended the University of Illinois and, after graduating in 1937, settled into his long career as a librarian. Brown's first book, *Wave High the Banner*, was published in 1942, and he would go on to author more than 25 books on the American West, including *Folktales of the Native American*, featuring illustrations by LOUIS MOFSIE, published in 1979 and rereleased in 1993.

Bury My Heart at Wounded Knee, published in 1971, became far and away Brown's most successful book and has sold more than 5 million copies worldwide. Published at the same time that the growing RED POWER MOVEMENT was galvanizing Indians across the country, the book, a heroic but ultimately tragic account of the Indians wars of the 19th century, was profoundly sympathetic to the Indian point of view and helped provide an important historical context to the growing demands of Indian people. Released the same year as the bitterly indicting movie about the Sand Creek massacre of 1864, *Soldier Blue*, and one year after *Little Big Man*, starring Dustin Hoffman and DAN GEORGE, revolutionized the perception of the Indian in films, *Bury My Heart at Wounded Knee* helped to create a climate of sympathy and respect for Indian people and their cultures in the early 1970s, and contributed to the end of the TERMINATION era.

Dee Brown died in Little Rock, Arkansas, on December 12, 2002. He was 94 years old.

Further Reading

Courtemanche-Ellis, Anne. "Dee Brown, a.k.a. Dorris Alexander Brown." *Encyclopedia of Arkansas History and Culture*. Available online. URL: http://www.encyclopediaofarkansas.net/encyclopedia/entry-detail.aspx?search=1&entr yID=1086. Accessed 7 October 2011.

Brown, Ellison Myers (Tarzan Brown, Deerfoot) (1914–1975) *Narragansett athlete*

Born on September 22, 1914, in Potter's Hill, Rhode Island, Ellison Brown was a Narragansett whose tribal name was Deerfoot. He got the nickname "Tarzan" from his childhood ability to climb trees and swing from branch to branch. As he grew older, his formidable physique only made his nickname more appropriate. Tarzan Brown's uncle, Horatio Stanton, was a noted long-distance runner, and as a child Brown would run along when his uncle was training. Stanton introduced young Tarzan to the Westerly High School track coach, Thomas "Tippy" Salerno, who took the child under his wing.

In 1935, Brown, extremely poor and wearing homemade clothes, entered the Boston Marathon, at the time the premier long-distance race in the world. Near the end of the race, his shoes fell apart, and Brown ran the last five miles barefoot yet still finished 13th. In 1936, armed with some support from a running club in Providence, he returned to the Boston Marathon and shattered course records over the first 20 miles. At the hills near the end of the race, Brown slowed and was caught by John Kelly, the defending champion, in a furious sprint. As Kelly passed Brown, he patted him on the back and

Ellison "Tarzan" Brown after winning the Boston Marathon on April 19, 1939. (*AP/Wideworld*)

said, "Nice try." Kelly, however, had spent himself trying to catch Brown, who had not even broken a sweat. Kelly had to walk the last mile and Brown easily cruised past him for the victory in a time of 2 hours, 33 minutes, and 40 seconds.

Also that year, Brown qualified for the 1936 Olympics in Berlin, where he was arrested and spent the night before the marathon in jail after brawling with a group of Adolf Hitler's Blackshirts at a bar. Even though he had suffered a hernia, he entered the event and was in the lead when he was forced to quit after 16 miles.

He then entered the 1937 Boston Marathon as the favorite, only to finish a disappointing 31st. The next year his record was even worse, a distant 51st. In 1938, Brown was not expected to do much, but he ran his fastest race, setting a new course record and grabbing his second victory with a time of 2:28:51.

In 1940, Brown finished 13th in the Boston Marathon. He was scheduled to participate in the Summer Olympics that year in Helsinki, but it was canceled due to the outbreak of WORLD WAR II. During the war, he worked at a defense plant. After the war, he was laid off and worked variously as a stonemason, woodchopper, and handyman in Westerly, Rhode Island. He was accidentally run over in the parking lot of a bar on August 23, 1975.

Further Reading
Ward, Michael. *Ellison "Tarzan" Brown: The Narragansett Indian Who Twice Won the Boston Marathon.* Jefferson, N.C.: McFarland, 2006.

Brown, Samuel William, Jr. (1879–1957) *Yuchi chief*
Samuel William Brown, Jr., was born in Bixby, Oklahoma, on June 9, 1879. His father, Samuel William Brown, Sr., was chief of the Yuchi tribe from 1867 until his retirement in 1916. The Yuchi traditionally lived near the Creek Nation in Alabama, Georgia, and Mississippi, but they spoke their own language and observed their own rituals. Upon their removal west, they were listed in the rolls of the Creek Nation and took part in its government.

Young Brown was sent to school at Eufaula but fought with the Creek students, who were the majority in the school, and ran away. After his mother, Neosho Parthenia Porter Brown, died in 1897, he lived with two great-uncles, Sakasenney (Little Bear) and Sincohah (Fus Hudge). They were cattle ranch operators and Brown worked for them as a cowboy. Brown then became a successful rancher himself. In 1904, he married Mattie May Payne, whom he met after stopping at a ranch for a meal during one of his cattle drives through Indian Territory (as Oklahoma was known at the time).

Brown assisted his father in handling tribal affairs and his fluency in Yuchi and four other Indian languages made him invaluable as an interpreter. Brown became the last chief *(zopathla)* of the Yuchi in 1916, when his father stepped down, and continued his father's policy of trying to preserve Yuchi traditions. Shortly before his death, Brown revisited the

ancient Yuchi homelands in Georgia and Alabama, searching for sites his father had described to him. In October 1957, he found the ancient Yuchi campgrounds, where he and other Yuchi religious leaders performed their ancient dances. Brown died on December 31, 1957, in Mathis, Texas.

See also SPECK, FRANK GOULDSMITH.

Further Reading
Abley, Mark. *Spoken Here: Travels among Threatened Languages,* 53–82. New York: Mariner Books, 2005.
Foreman, Carolyn Thomas. "The Yuchi: Children of the Sun." *Chronicles of Oklahoma* 37 (Winter, 1959–60): 51.
———. "Samuel W. Brown Sr., Chief of the Yuchi Tribe." *Chronicles of Oklahoma* 37 (1959–60): 485–495.
Jackson, Jason Baird. *Yuchi Ceremonial Life: Performance, Meaning and Tradition in a Contemporary American Indian Community.* Lincoln: University of Nebraska Press, 2003.
Russell, Orpha B. "Notes on Samuel William Brown Jr., Yuchi Chief." *Chronicles of Oklahoma* 37 (1959–60): 497–501.

Bruce, Louis Rook, Jr. (1906–1989) *Lakota-Mohawk commissioner of Indian affairs*
Louis Rook Bruce, Jr., was born on December 30, 1906, on the Onondaga Reservation in New York State. His father, Louis Bruce, Sr., was a Mohawk from Akwesasne (St. Regis Reservation) in New York, and his mother, Nellie Rook, was an Oglala Lakota Sioux. Louis Bruce, Sr., was a professional baseball player who studied dentistry before finally becoming a Methodist pastor and settling on the Onondaga Reservation in upstate New York. Bruce, Sr., had been a leader in the efforts to overturn the Everett Report of 1922, which had affirmed Iroquois rights to their lands; he advocated state jurisdiction over Indian reservations. (see THOMAS, GEORGE E.).

Louis Jr. grew up on the Onondaga Reservation and, following his father's religious example, enrolled in the Cazenovia Seminary at age 17. He graduated from Syracuse University in 1930 and took a job as a clerk in a department store, where his managerial skills quickly won him a promotion to department manager. During the Great Depression, Bruce, who was active in the Boy Scouts, created a program to send Indian youths to summer camps that taught Indian lore and crafts. In 1935, he was appointed to oversee New York's Works Progress Administration (WPA) programs for Indians, thus beginning a long political career that would include a stint as special commissioner for the Federal Housing Administration from 1959 to 1961. He was also a successful dairy farmer and taught part-time at Columbia University, Pennsylvania State University, and Cornell University. Bruce was active in a wide range of youth groups and farmers' associations, as well as Indian activities, and was one of the founders of the NATIONAL CONGRESS OF AMERICAN INDIANS (NCAI).

When Richard Nixon was elected president in 1968, he was anxious to replace Commissioner of Indian Affairs ROBERT

LA FOLLETTE BENNETT with an Indian who was a member of the Republican Party. Bruce was only the third Indian in U.S. history to be named commissioner. However, the announcement of his appointment drew almost unanimous criticism from Indian groups. A new militancy had begun to characterize Indian politics, and Bruce was not considered activist enough, even by moderate groups such as the NCAI.

Bruce, however, quickly proved his detractors wrong, and in July 1970, Nixon shocked the Indian establishment by calling for the repeal of TERMINATION, effectively ending the feared policy of eliminating reservations which had been in place for more than two decades. Later that year, Nixon also restored the sacred BLUE LAKE to the Taos Pueblo six decades after it had been seized by the federal government, and he restored Mount Adams to the Yakima. As for the BUREAU OF INDIAN AFFAIRS (BIA), Bruce began to formalize the self-determination policy that his predecessor Bennett had tried to implement through political skill. Bruce also established programs to help off-reservation Indians who had suffered under the Relocation policies of the past (see URBANIZATION, AMERICAN INDIANS AND).

In May 1970, the Zuni tribe was given the right to administer all BIA activities in their pueblo, a right extended soon after to the Miccosukee in Florida. However, Bruce's goal of turning the BIA from a paternalistic management organization into a service agency met with bitter opposition from career bureaucrats and led to a power struggle between Bruce and Deputy Commissioner JOHN ORIEN CROW, a longtime BIA functionary who had just completed a stint in the Bureau of Land Management.

Bruce had the fortune or misfortune to become commissioner at precisely the time when the Indian political landscape was undergoing a revolution. The OCCUPATION OF ALCATRAZ ISLAND in late 1969, although eventually resolved by the administration in a satisfactory manner, foreshadowed a rising discontent among young Indians that would lead to greater protests and even violence. Bruce attempted to accommodate this rising tide by bringing in a group of young radical BIA staffers, known as "the Young Turks," as his advisers, but this did little to quell growing Indian militancy and only further antagonized entrenched BIA bureaucrats. In 1970, the AMERICAN INDIAN MOVEMENT (AIM) occupied the BIA office in Denver, though Bruce managed to negotiate a peaceful settlement. Later that year, RUSSELL MEANS began his highly publicized string of protests, beginning with the seizure of the *Mayflower* on Thanksgiving Day and including an attempt to seize the BIA headquarters in September 1971 with the object of arresting John Crow, WILMA L. VICTOR, and other disliked BIA employees.

Bruce weathered these storms, but his political hold on the bureau worsened with the resignation of Interior Secretary Walter Hickel, who favored Bruce's reforms, and his replacement by Rogers B. Morton, who backed John Crow. When the TRAIL OF BROKEN TREATIES began its march across the country in November 1972, the Interior Department, under the direction of Assistant Secretary Harrison Loesch, decided to take a strong stand against the activists and ordered the BIA not to lend the caravans any assistance for their journey to Washington, D.C. Finding no place to stay in the nation's capital, the protesters stormed the BIA building and occupied it, leading to a political crisis for the administration just before the national elections. Bruce, who had opposed the Interior Department's hard line, met with the occupiers in an attempt to negotiate a peaceful settlement. His obvious sympathy for the militants led to a rift between him and Loesch and Crow, who wanted to have the police retake the building, by force if necessary.

The occupation ended a week later with the building ransacked and the administration's formerly glowing reputation for dealing with Indians badly tarnished. On December 6, Nixon fired Loesch, Crow, and Bruce, whom he blamed for the occupation. Despite this ignominious end to his tenure, Bruce left knowing that he had garnered the respect of the Indian people, and none other than Russell Means called him the "greatest Indian commissioner since JOHN COLLIER." Bruce continued to work on Indian issues, forming Native American Consultants, Inc., and serving on the influential AMERICAN INDIAN POLICY REVIEW COMMISSION from 1975 to 1977. He died of cancer and heart failure on May 20, 1989, in Arlington, Virginia.

Further Reading

Cash, Joseph H. "Louis Rook Bruce (1969–73)." In *The Commissioners of Indian Affairs, 1824–1977*, edited by Robert M. Kvasnicka and Herman J. Viola, 333–340. Lincoln: University of Nebraska Press, 1977.

Castile, George Pierre. *To Show Heart: Native American Self-determination and Federal Indian Policy, 1960–1975.* Tucson: University of Arizona Press, 1998.

Forbes, Jack D. *Native Americans and Nixon: Presidential Politics and Minority Self-determination, 1969–1972.* Los Angeles: American Indian Studies Center, UCLA, 1981.

Kotlowski, Dean J. "Alcatraz, Wounded Knee, and Beyond: The Nixon and Ford Administrations Respond to Native American Protest." *Pacific Historical Review* 72, no. 2 (2003): 201–227.

Bruce, Robert Emil (1893–1968) *Turtle Mountain Chippewa musician*

Robert Emil Bruce was born on September 15, 1893, in Belcourt, North Dakota, on the Turtle Mountain Reservation. His parents, Joseph and Rosalie Bruce, were Canadian-American Métis of Scottish, French, and Chippewa ancestry. The family was Catholic and spoke French and Métis-Cree (Michif). Robert went to school at Fort Totten, North Dakota, and Flandreau, then to Haskell Institute in Lawrence, Kansas. Although trained as a tailor, he was more interested in music. On July 9, 1917, he joined the band of the Headquarters Company, Second Infantry, North Dakota National Guard as a cornetist. This band, under the direction of Harold Burton Bachman, was incorporated into the 116th Engineers when that regiment was organized later in 1917 to go overseas as part of the 41st "Sunset" Division. Comprised of 35 midwestern musicians, it was destined to become one of the most famous musical units of America's fighting forces, under the name the Million Dollar Band. The band served overseas from November 26, 1917, to February 23, 1919. (See WORLD WAR I, AMERICAN INDIANS AND.)

Robert and his older brother, Fred Bruce, a Carlisle Indian School graduate and electrician, were among the first to join the reorganized band. Robert entered Company B, 116th Engineers, with the rank of musician first class, Fred with the rank of musician second class. The Bruces were featured in solo numbers. Robert won several medals for his talent as a cornetist, and Fred had an equal reputation on clarinet. They were discharged at Camp Dodge, Iowa, on March 11, 1919, Robert with the rank of master engineer and Fred with the rank of sergeant first class.

After the war, the band continued for some years as a professional concert organization under the name Bachman's Million Dollar Band, touring the country on its own special train. The Bruces played with them a total of five years (1917–21). Robert Bruce also played with the James Wheelock Indian Band at the Philadelphia sesquicentennial (1926). Later he worked four years with the C. G. Conn Instrument Company as a tester, soloist, and representative, and another four years with the Martin Band Instrument Company in the same capacity. He toured North Dakota with the Lawrence Welk Band before it became known nationally.

For a time, Bruce was director of the band and orchestra at Haskell Institute. He became band director at the Notre Dame Academy in Willow City, North Dakota, in the early 1960s. Near the end of his life, he lived for a couple of years at Rolla, North Dakota. From there he went to the veterans' home at Hot Springs, South Dakota, where he died on November 25, 1968. He was buried in the military cemetery in Sturgis, South Dakota.

Robert Bruce should not be confused with the Sioux trombonist and bandleader Robert Bruce (Indian name, Nagiyanpe, 1879–ca. 1920), a full-blood Yanktonai Nakota from the Fort Peck Reservation in Montana. As a boy, he played trombone in theater orchestras in Salt Lake City and Cheyenne, then attended Carlisle, where he was a contemporary of the Quapaw violinist FRED CARDIN. This Robert Bruce toured the country with the Carlisle Indian Band under DENNISON WHEELOCK, and was named director of the (non-Indian) Municipal Band of Carlisle, Pennsylvania in 1902.

Bruchac, Joseph (1942–) *Abenaki short story writer, poet, novelist*

Joseph Bruchac was born on October 16, 1942, in Saratoga Springs, New York. His father, Joseph E. Bruchac, was a taxidermist, and his mother, Flora Bowman Bruchac, was part Abenaki. Bruchac was raised by his Abenaki grandfather and his grandmother near the Adirondack Mountains in upstate New York. He attended Cornell University, earning his degree in 1965, before receiving a creative writing fellowship at Syracuse University. Between 1966 and 1969, Bruchac taught in Ghana, returning to the United States to pursue graduate studies at the State University of New York, Albany, and to teach creative writing at the Great Meadows Institute, Comstock Prison, New York. He received his doctorate from the Union Graduate School (now Union Institute and University), Cincinnati, Ohio, in 1975.

By this time, Bruchac had already begun his prolific writing career, publishing three books of poetry—*Indian Mountain and Other Poems* (1971), *The Buffalo in the Syracuse Zoo* (1972), and *Flow* (1975); a book of essays, *The Poetry of Pop* (1973); and a collection of Iroquois stories, *Turkey Brother and Other Tales* (1975). He published his first novel, *The Dreams of Jesse Brown*, in 1977. He also edited two anthologies of prison writings.

As an editor and publisher, Bruchac has made an important contribution to the popularization of contemporary Native American poetry. In 1969, he founded the *Greenfield Review*, which debuted the works of writers such as Coeur d'Alene novelist and poet Janet Campbell Hale, Shawnee-Cayuga writer and poet Barney Bush, and Chickasaw novelist LINDA HOGAN. In 1983, Bruchac edited *Songs from This Earth on Turtle's Back*, an anthology featuring more than 50 contemporary Indian poets that remains one of the most outstanding collections available.

Bruchac won wide acclaim for his 1993 novel *Dawn Land*, which recounts in poetic prose the idyllic existence of the Abenaki 10,000 years ago in New England. It is his storytelling, however—as collected in such works as *Stone Giants and Flying Heads* (1978), *Turtle Meat and Other Stories* (1992), and *The Great Ballgame: A Muskogee Story* (1994)—that has brought him the greatest critical praise. Bruchac performs widely, telling his stories in Europe and throughout the United States.

Further Reading
Bruchac, Joseph. *Bowman's Store: A Journey to Myself.* New York: Dial Books, 1997.

Bureau of Indian Affairs (BIA) (Office of Indian Affairs, Indian Service, Indian Office, Indian Bureau)

The Bureau of Indian Affairs (BIA) is the federal agency responsible for the administration and management of 56 million acres of land held in trust by the United States for American Indians and Alaska Natives. The BIA administers 43,450,266.97 acres of tribally owned land, 10 million acres of individually owned land, and 309,000 acres of federally owned land held in trust status. The BIA also currently provides a variety of federal services to approximately 1.5 million American Indians and Alaska Natives who are members of more than 562 federally recognized Indian tribes.

The BIA was founded on March 11, 1824, under the Department of War (now known as the Department of Defense). At that time, it was known as the Office of Indian Affairs. Until

1934, the Bureau of Indian Affairs was generally referred to as the Indian Service, Indian Office, or, to a lesser extent, the Indian Bureau. It was not until 1934 that it became known by its present name, the Bureau of Indian Affairs. For most of the 20th century, the BIA reported directly or indirectly to the secretary of the Department of the Interior, which has jurisdiction over the vast majority of federal lands, generally under its Bureau of Land Management (BLM). In 1977, it was separated from the BLM, and since then it has existed as a separate agency within the Department of the Interior. For most of the 20th century, the BIA was headed by a commissioner of Indian affairs. In 1977, the office of assistant secretary for Indian affairs was created within the Interior Department. This superseded the commissioner's office, which was abolished in 1981.

The first commissioner of the 20th century was WILLIAM ARTHUR JONES, who served under Presidents William McKinley and Theodore Roosevelt from 1897 to 1904. Jones efficiently carried out the federal policies of the day, aimed at the complete ASSIMILATION of Indian people into the American mainstream. At that time, the BIA and the individual reservation superintendents had absolute control over every aspect of Indian life, and under the assimilation policy Indian religions were banned, most customs were outlawed, and Indian governments were dissolved. Children were sent to boarding schools where the use of Native languages was prohibited, and all efforts were made to stamp out Native customs and religion.

The policy also sought the breakup of INDIAN RESERVATIONS, which were seen as holding Indians back from becoming workers or farmers, through the system of ALLOTMENT, begun in 1887. On reservations that were allotted, communal Indian ownership of lands was abolished, and in return individual Indians received a small parcel of land, usually 160 acres. The remaining land on the reservation was then sold off.

At this time, the BIA controlled a vast network of schools, hospitals, police, and administrative forces, all of which were considered substandard, corrupt, and inept. Moreover, the Allotment process and the leasing of valuable mineral rights on Indian lands led to numerous frauds against Indians. Commissioner Jones attempted to reform the BIA; however, the agency's ability to resist reform remained a constant throughout the 20th century.

Jones stepped down in 1905, to be followed by the Progressive Era commissioners: FRANCIS ELLINGTON LEUPP (1905–09), ROBERT GROSVENOR VALENTINE (1909–12), and CATO SELLS (1913–21). Under these commissioners, the harsher aspects of the assimilation policy, particularly in the realm of education, were toned down somewhat. The Allotment policy, however, continued unabated, leading to the breakup of many reservations and the despoliation of Indian Territory (now Oklahoma) under the CURTIS ACT.

In 1921, with the ascension of CHARLES HENRY BURKE to the commissioner's office under President Warren Harding, the harsh assimilationist policies returned, including a clampdown on Indian religions under the DANCE ORDERS. The corruption in the Indian Office, always endemic, reached

new heights under Burke and his superior in the Interior Department, ALBERT BACON FALL The subsequent scandals, many of them over the allotment of Indian lands in Oklahoma, as well as the desperate conditions on Indian reservations (see HEALTH, AMERICAN INDIAN), led to the formation of a panel to study Indian policy, the COMMITTEE OF ONE HUNDRED. A growing reform movement sparked in a large part by the BURSUM BILL, an attempt to legalize the status of non-Indian squatters on Pueblo Indian lands, led in 1928 to the MERIAM REPORT, a stunning rebuke of federal Indian policy and the BIA's handling of Indian affairs.

A policy of reform began in 1929 under Commissioner CHARLES JAMES RHOADS and his assistant, JOSEPH HENRY SCATTERGOOD. This policy reached its fruition under JOHN COLLIER, who was appointed commissioner in 1933 by Franklin Delano Roosevelt. Under Collier, the BIA and federal Indian policy was changed from a system designed to destroy the Native land base and culture into one that tried to promote them. The disastrous Allotment policy was ended, and with the help of legal paradigms designed by FELIX SOLOMON COHEN, a new relationship between Indian tribes and the federal government emerged that vastly curtailed the dictatorial powers of the BIA-appointed reservation superintendents. Important initiatives under Collier include the INDIAN CIVILIAN CONSERVATION CORPS (1933); the INDIAN REORGANIZATION ACT (1934), which reorganized tribal governance; the JOHNSON-O'MALLEY ACT (1934) to improve Indian education; and the INDIAN ARTS AND CRAFTS BOARD (1936). During WORLD WAR II, the BIA actively encouraged Indians to join the armed forces, in which they participated heroically, as well as to help out on the home front. However, Collier's ambitious attempts to transform Indian policy led to a backlash, and by 1945 the mood in Congress began to shift back to the old policies of assimilation and the breakup of Indian lands, this time under the name TERMINATION.

Commissioner WILLIAM ALOYSIUS BROPHY succeeded Collier in 1945, but due to illness he was unable to effectively run the BIA as the tide turned toward Termination. In 1949, JOHN RALPH NICHOLS was appointed by President Harry S. Truman to succeed Brophy, but Nichols's attempt to forge an effective and humane assimilation policy was prohibitively expensive, and he did not last long. The next year, the terminationists found their champion in Commissioner DILLON SEYMOUR MYER, the former head of the Japanese-American internment camps during World War II. Myer quickly set out to dissolve Indian reservations and assimilate Indians through policies such as Relocation (see URBANIZATION, AMERICAN INDIANS AND), but his unsympathetic determination and brusque style also gave rise to a vigorous Indian rights movement under the leadership of a new organization, the NATIONAL CONGRESS OF AMERICAN INDIANS. President Dwight D. Eisenhower replaced Myer with GLENN LEONIDAS EMMONS in 1954, but the Termination policy continued. It led to severe loss of Indian lands through massive dam projects such as the PICK-SLOAN PLAN and uncontrolled mineral development (see MINING, AMERICAN INDIANS AND). These policies led to the increasing politicization of Indian people, and in particular Indian youth, which came to a head at the AMERICAN INDIAN CHICAGO CONFERENCE in 1961 and the formation of the NATIONAL INDIAN YOUTH COUNCIL.

Commissioner PHILLEO NASH, President John F. Kennedy's choice to succeed Emmons in 1961, was a member of the board of directors of the ASSOCIATION ON AMERICAN INDIAN AFFAIRS and one of many anthropologists who had worked on behalf of Indian rights (see ANTHROPOLOGISTS AND AMERICAN INDIANS). However, the mood in Congress, led by Utah senator ARTHUR VIVIAN WATKINS, was still in favor of Termination. Nash fought repeatedly with Congress until President Lyndon B. Johnson replaced him in 1966 with ROBERT LaFOLLETTE BENNETT, whose diplomatic skills would go a long way in mitigating the effects of the Termination policy. Bennett, the first American Indian commissioner of the 20th century, accelerated the integration of Indians into the "Great Society" programs of the 1960s, which brought increased funding for Indian health care, job training, and education. Yet the growing RED POWER MOVEMENT demanded even greater change and became increasingly militant as the 1960s drew to a close.

President Richard M. Nixon made solving Indian problems a top priority of his administration, and under LOUIS ROOK BRUCE, JR., the Termination era was officially ended. However, Bruce's attempts to reform the BIA, coupled with the rise of the AMERICAN INDIAN MOVEMENT (AIM), led to increasing schisms within the agency. Bruce was fired in 1972 after the TRAIL OF BROKEN TREATIES demonstration in Washington went awry and AIM demonstrators took over the BIA headquarters and ransacked it. The BIA went through a period of upheaval and low morale, and Nixon appointed MORRIS THOMPSON in 1973 to stabilize the agency. Thompson accelerated the policy toward Indian self-determination, helping to pass the Indian Self-Determination and Education Act of 1975. Thompson's successor, BENJAMIN REIFEL, served for only a year. In 1979 Reifel was replaced in turn by WILLIAM E. HALLET, the last commissioner. By this time the position had been made obsolete by the creation of a new office of assistant secretary for Indian affairs, first occupied by FORREST J. GERARD.

Gerard, appointed by President Jimmy Carter in 1977, led the BIA to its most productive period as spending for services reached its apex and poverty levels for Indian people fell to their lowest point in the 20th century. Gerard was replaced in 1981 by KENNETH L. SMITH, who oversaw huge domestic budget cuts under President Ronald Reagan. Indian poverty levels once again began to climb under Smith and his successor, ROSS O. SWIMMER, who was appointed by Reagan in 1985. The BIA was rocked by scandals during this period, particularly over the mismanagement of Indian oil and mineral royalties. The PRESIDENTIAL COMMISSION ON INDIAN RESERVATION ECONOMICS drew up a new agenda for Indian affairs. Under Swimmer and his successor, Ed Brown, tribes began to establish casinos and other betting establishments, leading to the rise of GAMING ON INDIAN RESERVATIONS.

In 1993, President Bill Clinton appointed ADA ELIZABETH DEER as assistant secretary for Indian affairs, the first woman ever to head the BIA. She was unable to reverse the decline in federal funding for Indians, and as these funds were not offset by profits from the growing gaming industry, this led to further poverty on Indian reservations. In 1997, Deer was replaced by KEVIN GOVER, the last head of the BIA in the 20th century. Under Gover, the BIA was again attacked for failing to account for royalty moneys due to individual Indians, a chronic problem that dogged the BIA for much of the 20th century.

At the end of the 20th century, the BIA was a vastly different agency from what it had been at the start. Whereas at the beginning of the century, at best only a handful of Indians worked at the agency, by the end, more than three-quarters of its workforce of 12,000 were Indians. Yet the BIA had lost its tremendous power over everyday Indian life. Gone were the days when it could force Indians to cut their traditionally long hair or prevent them from performing their religious ceremonies. Control over education and health had also been shifted to other agencies or to the reservations themselves. Rather than appointing superintendents with absolute powers over Indian reservations, the BIA now works with tribal governments that have legislative and executive authority over their own reservations. In 2000, the BIA's budget was $1.9 billion, much of which was in turn regranted to Indian reservations for education, resource management, police, and other duties.

See also EDUCATION, AMERICAN INDIANS AND; PRATT, RICHARD HENRY; OIL, AMERICAN INDIANS AND; RELIGIOUS FREEDOM, AMERICAN INDIAN.

Further Reading

Deloria, Vine, ed. *American Indian Policy in the Twentieth Century.* Norman: University of Oklahoma Press, 1985.
Kvasnicka, Robert M., and Herman J. Viola, eds. *The Commissioners of Indian Affairs, 1824–1977.* Lincoln: University of Nebraska Press, 1979.
Parman, Donald L. *Indians and the American West in the Twentieth Century.* Bloomington: Indiana University Press, 1994.
Prucha, Francis Paul. *The Great Father: The United States Government and the American Indians.* Lincoln: University of Nebraska Press, 1984.

Burke, Charles Henry (1861–1944) *South Dakota congressman, commissioner of Indian affairs*

Born near Batavia, New York, on April 1, 1861, Charles Henry Burke moved to Dakota territory at age 21 and was admitted to the bar in 1886. He settled in Pierre, where he established a real estate company. Burke was elected to the South Dakota House of Representatives in 1895. In 1898, he ran successfully for the U.S. House of Representatives and joined the House Committee on Indian Affairs. In 1906, he authored an important amendment to the Dawes Act known as the Burke Act, which, while extending some federal protections accorded to Indians whose lands had been allotted, also gave the commissioner of Indian affairs broad discretion to remove Indians from federal supervision (see ALLOTMENT).

Burke fought to place district agents in charge of the affairs of the Five Civilized Tribes (as the Creek, Cherokee, Seminole, Chickasaw, and Choctaw were collectively known at that time), who had been plagued by carpetbaggers since passage of the CURTIS ACT. In 1912, he supported a report to Congress by M. L. Mott, a Creek attorney who had found systematic abuses in the Oklahoma guardianship system, which led to significant, albeit short-lived, reforms. In South Dakota, however, Burke's attempts to have 1 million acres of the Rosebud Reservation sold to friends ran afoul of the INDIAN RIGHTS ASSOCIATION (IRA), badly tainting the tenure of Indian Office (see BUREAU OF INDIANS AFFAIRS [BIA]) commissioner FRANCIS ELLINGTON LEUPP. Burke lost his seat in Congress in 1907 but won it back two years later and served until 1915, after which he returned to real estate.

Burke's appointment as Indian commissioner on March 21, 1921, was a political compromise by President Warren G. Harding, who had trouble finding a replacement for CATO SELLS. Burke had the great misfortune of serving under Interior Secretary ALBERT BACON FALL, a New Mexico attorney and rancher who was an archfoe of conservationists and Indians and whose tenure in public service was noteworthy for his attempts at self-aggrandizement. Burke also found his powers curtailed by Assistant Commissioner Edgar B. Meritt, a Sells holdover and brother-in-law of Senate minority leader Joseph Robinson. Moreover, as soon as he entered office, Burke found himself immediately embroiled in the controversy over the BURSUM BILL. Sponsored by Senator Holm O. Bursum of New Mexico at Fall's request, the bill introduced Burke to a formidable opponent, JOHN COLLIER, who mobilized Indian and non-Indian support against Fall and Burke's policies.

Fall also mounted an extensive and tempestuous campaign to open Indian reservations to oil and gas development, which he then used to enrich his close friends in the oil business and which Burke was unable to oppose (see OIL, AMERICAN INDIANS AND). Burke first attempted to improve Indian education, and also to comply with a 1920 bill mandating the compulsory education of reservation youngsters, reorganizing the bureau's education department and transferring as many Indian children as possible from reservation schools to local public schools (see EDUCATIONAL POLICY, AMERICAN INDIANS AND). However, he was unable to secure the necessary appropriations to build new schools and hire qualified teachers, and by 1924 his education initiative was a shambles, with overcrowded conditions and malnutrition among Indian students commonplace. His attempts to improve Indians' HEALTH met a similar fate, and despite the establishment of a position of chief medical director overseeing a new health department—for the first time in the Indian office—the overall health of Indians declined precipitously under his tenure.

Burke revoked Sells's disastrous Allotment policy, an unintended consequence of the Burke Act, by which Indians with less than one-half Indian blood were automatically released from the government protections that prevented the alienation of their allotments, and he tightened the procedures for determining "competence." Like Sells before him, Burke moved to halt the most egregious abuses of the guardianship system in Oklahoma (see BARNETT, JACKSON), which was a national scandal, ordering a study of the probate system in fall 1923. The report, written by Shade Wallen, found numerous instances of fraud.

Buoyed by the outcry surrounding the IRA's pamphlet *Oklahoma's Poor Rich Indians: An Orgy of Graft and Exploitation of the Five Civilized Tribes—Legalized Robbery*, written by reformers Mathew K. Sniffen, Charles H. Fabens, and GERTRUDE BONNIN, Burke sought legislation transferring the probate process to the Indian Office and away from the state. The Oklahoma delegation, led by powerful oilman W. B. Pine, managed to derail the legislation by forming the Hastings Committee, ostensibly to investigate the abuses. Led by Cherokee mixed-blood congressman WILLIAM WIRT HASTINGS, the committee suppressed the Wallen report, accused Bonnin and the others of publishing unsubstantiated rumors, and managed to cover up the abuses until the outcry had passed. Moreover, Pine in turn accused Burke of mishandling the Five Civilized Tribes' money, leading to another congressional investigation.

Albert Fall left under a cloud of suspicion and was replaced by Hubert Work, whose reputation for honesty did not preclude negotiating unfavorable deals for Indians. In 1927, with Work's approval, Burke negotiated a deal with the Montana Power Company and the Flathead irrigation district to create a dam on Flathead land, from which the Indians would receive only one-third of any revenues generated by electricity and none of the water. Burke did successfully fight for the water rights of the Paiute Indians at Walker River, Nevada. Nevertheless, irrigation on Indian lands continued to be a major problem as Indians were unable to recoup the moneys they had spent on reclamation projects, most of which ended up benefiting non-Indian farmers (see WINTERS DOCTRINE). Burke favored the Citizenship Act of 1924, but although he encouraged Indians to vote, did little to prevent the practice of some states of barring Indians from the polls.

From 1921 to 1926, Burke zealously promoted a series of DANCE ORDERS that sought to curb Indian religions, going so far as to personally lead raids in Taos and other pueblos in an attempt to shut down "heathenish" Indian dances. Again Burke had to contend with John Collier—and again he lost.

Burke's attempt to untangle the affairs of Jackson Barnett, the richest Indian in the country, who was plagued by grifters, only created further controversy and ultimately led to an attack on him by the Senate Indian Affairs Committee.

The controversies between Collier and Burke, as well as Fall's complicity in the emerging Teapot Dome Scandal, forced Work to form the COMMITTEE OF ONE HUNDRED to review Indian policy. This eventually led to the publication of the MERIAM REPORT in 1928. The report, a scathing indictment of the Indian Office, along with the personal attacks led by Collier and Pine, forced Burke to submit his resignation, which was accepted by incoming president Herbert Hoover on March 7, 1929. Replaced by CHARLES JAMES RHOADS, Burke retired from public life. He died in Washington, D.C., on April 7, 1944.

Further Reading

Kelly, Lawrence C. "Charles Henry Burke." In *The Commissioners of Indian Affairs, 1824–1977*, 251–262, edited by Robert M. Kvasnicka and Herman J. Viola. Lincoln: University of Nebraska Press, 1979.

Philp, Kenneth R. *John Collier's Crusade for Indian Reform, 1920–1954.* Tucson: University of Arizona Press, 1977.

Stratton, David H. *Tempest over Teapot Dome: The Story of Albert B. Fall.* Norman: University of Oklahoma Press, 1998.

Burke Act (1906)   *See* ALLOTMENT; BURKE, CHARLES HENRY.

Burnette, Robert Phillip (1926–1984) *Brulé Lakota Sioux author, political leader*

Born to Grover and Winnie (Rogers) Burnette on the Rosebud Reservation in South Dakota on January 26, 1926, Robert Phillip Burnette, a Brulé Lakota Sioux, attended the local boarding school until he was 17, when he enlisted in the U.S. Marines. With WORLD WAR II underway, he was sent to the South Pacific, where he served as an antiaircraft gunner. Burnette returned from the war to work on his father's ranch, but his interest in politics led him to run for a position on the Rosebud Tribal Council in 1952. In 1954, he was elected tribal president, in which post he served until 1961, when he resigned to become executive director of the NATIONAL CONGRESS OF AMERICAN INDIANS (NCAI) in Washington, D.C. There he became part of a national movement to reform the corrupt BUREAU OF INDIANS AFFAIRS (BIA) and end the TERMINATION policy of the day. Returning to Rosebud in 1964, Burnette ran unsuccessfully for tribal president.

In 1967, he led a delegation of Rosebud Sioux, including Henry Crow Dog, his son LEONARD CROW DOG, and JOHN FIRE LAME DEER, to join Martin Luther King, Jr.'s Peace March on Washington, D.C. Burnette by then had become the director of the American Indian Civil Rights Council, an organization that worked with the growing Civil Rights movement of the day. His book *The Tortured Americans* (1971) put him at the forefront of moderate leaders fighting for greater self-determination for Indian tribes. Although not a member of the AMERICAN INDIAN MOVEMENT (AIM) or other RED POWER MOVEMENT organizations, Burnette was one of the organizers of the TRAIL OF BROKEN TREATIES in 1972. As the point man for the demonstration in Washington, D.C., he was hamstrung by the lack of support from the BIA, and he was held responsible for the poor planning that resulted in hundreds of demonstrators occupying the BIA headquarters to find some place to sleep.

Burnette also helped mediate an end to the siege of WOUNDED KNEE in 1973 and coauthored an important book on the subject, *The Road to Wounded Knee* (1974). In 1974, he regained the tribal presidency, but in the last decade of his life he was caught up in bitter political fights on the reservation. He was accused of misconduct and forced to step down, although eventually cleared of all charges. A rarity among tribal presidents of his day, he favored the traditional elements of his community and became a national leader and advocate for Indian rights. Robert Phillip Burnette died of a heart attack on September 12, 1984.

See also AMERICAN INDIAN CHICAGO CONFERENCE.

Further Reading

Burnette, Robert. *The Tortured Americans.* Englewood Cliffs, N.J.: Prentice Hall, 1971.

Burnette, Robert, and John Koster. *The Road to Wounded Knee.* New York: Bantam Books, 1974.

Washington Daily News, 28, 29, 30 October 1963.

Burns, Mark L. (1879–1947) *Chippewa political figure, lumberman*

Mark L. Burns was born on September 24, 1879, in Grand Rapids, Minnesota, the son of Christopher and Julia Burns. His mother was a full-blooded Chippewa and a member of the White Oak Point Band. His father came to America from Ireland at age 15 and was successful in the lumber business; he also spent several years mining in Montana.

Burns attended school in Grand Rapids and at the Educational Institute, a school for Indian boys in Philadelphia, then worked with his father as a lumberman in northern Minnesota from 1898 to 1903. In 1903, he joined the U.S. Forestry Service at Cass Lake, and in 1908, he joined the Indian Forest Service, building a sawmill at Menominee and salvaging burned timber on the Bad River Reservation in Wisconsin. In 1910, he surveyed timber at Nett Lake. A skilled and experienced civil engineer, he held the position of lumberman-at-large for the Indian Bureau (later the BUREAU OF INDIAN AFFAIRS [BIA]).

In 1925, Burns became superintendent of the Red Lake Reservation, a position rarely held by an Indian in those times (see YELLOWTAIL, ROBERT SUMMERS). His policy goals, however, were in tune with only a small minority of the band. According to a contemporary account, Burns intended to "remove the last vestige of aboriginal customs still existing in this isolated section—the 'medicine man' and the self-torture to appease the anger of traditional 'evil spirits.'" The Indian Bureau, "acting at the request of younger tribesmen and the demands of Chippewas in general . . . has taken steps toward breaking up the great reservation, [proposing] to allot the rich timber lands according to the rule which has permitted virtually all American Indians to assume control of their own property" (see ALLOTMENT; BEAULIEU, GUS H.). Supported by the 1863 treaty, the traditionals, always very strong at Red Lake, fought Allotment as successfully as they had in the past (see GRAVES, PETER).

Burns stayed at Red Lake less than five years. He was appointed superintendent of the Consolidated Chippewa

Agency at Cass Lake in 1930. In 1936, he became coordinator for the Indian Service in the Lake States Area, working out of Minneapolis as a liaison between superintendents, medical directors, and the BIA. He worked with the Indians; the state governments of Minnesota, Michigan, and Wisconsin; and medical directors to implement a plan based on the recommendations of a study of the Chippewa situation (1930) spearheaded by the Indian Rights Association. In 1938, Burns and ARCHIE PHINNEY helped the various Chippewa reservations organize themselves into bands integrated within the tribal system of the INDIAN REORGANIZATION ACT, with the exception of Red Lake, which had withdrawn from the Indian Reorganization Act in 1936.

Burns was responsible for building an Indian hospital at Cass Lake and for bringing the Indian Service Department of Roads to that town. Shortly after his retirement from the BIA in 1942, he became one of the first people to get involved in the planning of the future NATIONAL CONGRESS OF AMERICAN INDIANS. An Episcopalian and a Mason, Burns spent his later years on a 300-acre farm near Cass Lake, where he bred Guernsey cattle. He died on July 26, 1947.

Bursum bill (1922)

This controversial bill, introduced during the Warren G. Harding administration, affected the land rights of the New Mexican Pueblo Indians. The successful campaign against it proved to be one of the defining moments of American Indian history in the 20th century.

The status of the Rio Grande Pueblo Indians differs from that of other Indians in that they hold Spanish land grants that were guaranteed by the Treaty of Guadalupe Hidalgo (1848), which transferred a large portion of Mexico to what is now the southwestern United States.

Since *United States v. Joseph* (1876), which found the Pueblo "unusually civilized," they had not been considered wards of the government like other Indians. In 1912, New Mexico became a state, and in the *Sandoval* decision of 1913 (*United States v. Sandoval*), a Hispanic man charged with selling liquor at Santa Clara Pueblo argued on the grounds of the 1876 decision that federal jurisdiction over the Pueblo was unconstitutional. On appeal, the U.S. Supreme Court reversed itself, saying that the Pueblo were "simple, uninformed and inferior people" who were "largely influenced by superstition and fetishism." The Court found that the Pueblo Indians were federal wards and had been since 1848. This meant, in addition, that their landholdings were perfect and unimpaired, and all encroachments illegal. This was because, being wards, the Pueblo would not have had the right to alienate land, and the federal government (as their trustee) would now have to regard any Pueblo lands that non-Indians claimed as being illegally encroached upon.

There were 3,000 non-Indians—both Anglos and Hispanics—occupying Pueblo lands, with or without permission of the Indians. The court decision threw them into turmoil. Although the dispute affected only around 10 percent of

Pueblo land, much of it was the best of the irrigated territory. By 1921 the situation was chaotic, with the Indians caught in the middle. They needed the U.S. government's legal protection but not its interference with the traditional authority of the Pueblo governors.

Into this chaos, on July 19, 1921, Senator Holm O. Bursum of New Mexico introduced S.R. 2274, which effectively legalized almost all non-Indian claims on Pueblo lands. One section called on state courts (which would certainly favor non-Indians) to adjudicate Pueblo water rights and contested land. The Pueblo would be compensated in the form of "public agricultural land" (which was virtually nonexistent) or cash (which could in no way help them continue their way of life).

Drafted in large part by Interior Secretary ALBERT BACON FALL, the Bursum bill did not consider the option of compensating the squatters, for the underlying philosophy of the bill's framers was to dissolve the reservations and develop New Mexico's public domain lands. (The idea of compensating the squatters was later introduced in hearings by Pueblo leader PABLO ABEITA in 1923.)

The Bursum bill passed the Senate in 1922 with no public hearings. In the House of Representatives, however, Congressman William E. Borah of Idaho called for public hearings, so the bill was referred back to the Senate Committee on Public Lands.

The fight against the Bursum bill was one of the first modern Indian rights campaigns (see also, GENERAL, LEVI and the fight for Iroquois sovereignty in the early 1920s) as well as the prototype of many Indian legal battles of the 20th century. What made it modern was the relative absence of Christian organizations and specifically Christian priorities, and its embodiment of a critique of American culture—the insistence that the United States did not benefit by destroying traditional Native cultures, but that, on the contrary, the survival of Native cultures was of great importance to all Americans. The public education effort was very sophisticated, especially with JOHN COLLIER's impassioned articles and the writer and art patron Mabel Dodge Luhan's publicity campaign, which first enlisted the support of well-known artists.

The All-Pueblo Council, last convened in 1680, was reconstituted in a meeting on November 5, 1922. Luhan's husband, Antonio Luhan, brought Collier in, and with linguistic assistance from Luhan and Father Fridolin Schuster, Franciscan missionary to the Pueblo, Collier heard the bill read and discussed far into the night, in English, Tiwa, Tewa, Keres, and Zuni.

An appeal and petition was signed by 114 representatives of the All-Pueblo Council. For the rest of his life, Collier would point to "Pueblo democracy" as a model of communitarian democracy. Although in fact many elements of traditional Pueblo society are not democratic at all, it was at the meetings of the All-Pueblo Council that Collier experienced the democracy to which he so often referred.

In November 1922, Congressman Borah recalled the Bursum bill, and on January 3, 1923, President Harding announced Fall's resignation as interior secretary, effective

March 4. The bill was still alive in committee, however, where hearings were set for mid-January. John Collier and Antonio Luhan urged the Pueblo to send their own representatives to testify, and 17 went to Washington to plead for rejection of the Bursum bill and to support an alternative (known as Jones-Leatherwood), drafted by the GENERAL FEDERATION OF WOMEN'S CLUBS (GFWC), that would establish a three-person commission to adjudicate contested claims and authorize almost a million dollars for irrigation and drainage projects beneficial to the Pueblo.

Collier and Luhan, aiming to launch a national movement to raise America's consciousness about Indians, planned an extensive publicity tour in Chicago and New York, ending with appearances in Washington. Drumming and dancing at the New York Stock Exchange brought business to a halt. On January 17, 1923, the author Mary Austin, who had written about the Pueblo, made a public appearance with Pueblo representatives in Washington, D.C. At the hearing, Paul Twitchell, attorney for the claimants, finally admitted that the Bursum bill had few equities for the Pueblos, that it was not viable, and that it needed to be substantially rewritten.

The Bursum bill not only revived the All-Pueblo Council, it also gave rise to four important support organizations: the Eastern Association on Indian Affairs; Collier's American Indian Defense Association; the New Mexico Association on Indian Affairs; and Mary Austin's Indian Arts Fund, founded in fall 1923 to promote political activism, with a focus on protecting and encouraging traditional Indian arts—really the issue of Indian cultural integrity. A fifth organization, the Committee on Indian Welfare of the GFWC, though founded slightly earlier, took the Bursum bill on as its first important issue, hiring John Collier as a research specialist and becoming principal financial supporter of the campaign.

After the bill's defeat and the proposal of the Jones-Leatherwood alternative, important differences in goals and attitudes quickly emerged among these organizations. The Lenroot bill was advocated by GFWC's attorney Francis C. Wilson, but it was too weak for Collier because it recognized some non-Indian interests as legitimate. By August 1923, the debate over this bill led to a split in the GFWC, already divided over the DANCE ORDERS of 1923. It narrowly missed passage.

Many campaigners considered Collier too radical, but his position was actually based on what the Indians said they wanted. Earlier they had tried to object to the Lenroot bill, as they were unwilling to lose any land, except for a few small parcels such as churches and cemeteries for which they should be compensated. Thus they supported Collier's American Indian Defense Association (AIDA), which only increased the jealousy of the other organizations. AIDA board members Amelia White, Carter Harrison, and Fridolin Schuster resigned, badly affecting the organization's financial support.

When Senator Bursum introduced another bill modeled on Lenroot, a delegation of Pueblo representatives once again traveled to New York and then to Washington, where a compromise bill, the Pueblo Lands Act, was hammered out and

presented to Congress; President Calvin Coolidge signed it into law on June 7, 1924. The act set up a Pueblo Lands Board consisting of three people in Santa Fe who would rule on all claims and determine boundaries. Two would be appointed by the secretary of the interior and the attorney general, the third by the president. Some non-Indian claims would be allowed, but the Indians had the right to hire their own attorneys and contest such claims. The Pueblo would be compensated for land and water lost through the process, and further land transfer would be prohibited (unless with advance approval from the interior secretary). HERBERT J. HAGERMAN was appointed commissioner of the board. While he proved not as sympathetic to the Indians as Collier had hoped, they at least had a fighting chance under the new system.

The battle over the Bursum bill was of great historical importance. The 1920s promised to be an era of particularly harsh Indian policy. Promotion of ALLOTMENT and ASSIMILATION was the order of the day. Nonetheless, only a few years into the decade, a group of traditional Native American communities, with the help of a multifaceted support strategy, stopped the attempt to destroy their way of life. The Bursum bill backfired: It galvanized Indians and the mainstream public, and it introduced John Collier and other tireless fighters to the Indian issue. Increased public attention to injustice against Indians necessitated the creation of the COMMITTEE OF ONE HUNDRED (1923) and, more important, the MERIAM REPORT (1928). Within little more than a decade, Collier, as President Franklin D. Roosevelt's Indian commissioner, would make the most far-reaching changes in Indian policy, largely based on what he had learned from the fight against the Bursum bill and the dance orders.

Further Reading
Collier, John. *Indians of the Americas*, 146–152. New York: New American Library, 1947.
Dauber, Kenneth. "Pueblo Pottery and the Politics of Regional Identity." *Journal of the Southwest* 32 (1990): 576–596.
Hurtado, Alberto, and Peter Iverson. *Major Problems in American Indian History*. Lexington, Mass.: D.C. Heath, 1994.
Thompson, Mark. *American Character: The Curious Life of Charles Fletcher Lummis and the Rediscovery of the Southwest*, 252–253, 287, 311–312. New York: Arcade Publishing, 2001.
Wenger, Tisa. "Land, Culture, and Sovereignty in the Pueblo Dance Controversy." *Journal of the Southwest* 16, no. 2 (Fall 2004): 381–412.
Willard, William. "The Plumed Serpent and the Red Atlantis." *Wicazo Sa Review* 4, no. 2 (Autumn 1988): 17–30.

Butler, Nilak (Kelly Jean McCormick)

(1953–2002) *Inupiat Eskimo activist*
Born on September 3, 1953, to an Inupiat Eskimo family in Alaska, Nilak Butler was given up for adoption as an infant. She was adopted by Archie and Alma McCormick, who gave

her the name Kelly Jean McCormick. Her parents were psychologists who lived in Tacoma, Washington. She attended Adastra School for Gifted Children in Seattle and graduated at the young age of 13, and she began college at age 14. In her late teens she ran away to Los Angeles, where she became an actress. Under the name Neelak, she appeared in the movie *White Dawn* (1974), based on a true story of explorers marooned in the Arctic in 1900 who are befriended by an Eskimo community. During the filming on location in Alaska, she was drawn to her own heritage, and when she returned to Los Angeles, she began to work with the local Native American artistic community there. In 1974, McCormick appeared in the play *Savages*, by Christopher Hampton. In the audience were members of the AMERICAN INDIAN MOVEMENT (AIM), who encouraged her to join the group.

In January 1975, McCormick participated in the takeover by AIM and the Menominee Warrior Society of an unused abbey belonging to the Alexian Brothers Novitiate in Gresham, Wisconsin. There McCormick met Dino Butler, a Rogue River Tututni and AIM activist, and they married. In February, Nilak Butler and her husband joined the AIM camp at the Jumping Bull farm on the Lakota Sioux Pine Ridge Reservation in South Dakota. In early June, the Butlers attended the AIM National Convention in Farmington, New Mexico. They returned to Pine Ridge around June 20. By that time, the reservation was in a virtual state of civil war, as supporters of tribal chairman RICHARD WILSON were locked in a violent confrontation with traditional Lakota leaders and AIM members led by DENNIS JAMES BANKS. Nilak Butler was in the AIM camp at the Jumping Bull farm on June 26, 1975, when it was raided by two FBI agents. The ensuing shootout left one Indian and two FBI agents dead (see PELTIER, LEONARD), and Nilak Butler and her husband became fugitives.

On September 5, Dino Butler was captured by police on LEONARD CROW DOG's farm on the Rosebud Reservation in South Dakota and was charged with the murders of the FBI agents. Nilak Butler was picked up by the police on September 13, but she was not charged with a crime and was released. After a long trial, Dino Butler and codefendant Bob Robideau were acquitted of all charges on July 16, 1976. Leonard Peltier was less fortunate, and he was convicted of the murders in a separate trial on April 18, 1977. Afterward, Nilak Butler worked unsuccessfully for Peltier's release. She also began to campaign for the release of other Indian prisoners, notably Norma Jean Croy, a Shasta woman who, along with her brother and three other relatives, was involved in a shootout with police in 1978.

Nilak Butler eventually separated from Dino Butler and turned her activities to community organizing. She worked in Point Hope, Alaska, where during the 1950s the Department of Defense had conducted low-level nuclear testing as part of its unsuccessful bid to use nuclear warheads to blast out a port (see ROCK, HOWARD). With WINONA LADUKE and INGRID WASHINAWATOK, she helped to found the Indigenous Women's Network as well as the INDIGENOUS ENVIRONMENTAL NETWORK. In 1991, she joined the environmental organization Greenpeace to head their efforts to prevent the siting of nuclear wastes on indigenous people's lands.

After a long battle with ovarian cancer, Nilak Butler died on December 26, 2002, in Laytonville, California.

Cajete, Gregory (Greg Cajete) (1952–)
Tewa educator, educational consultant, artist, philosopher

A Tewa, Gregory Cajete was born in 1952 at Santa Clara Pueblo, New Mexico, and grew up there. As a young man, Cajete taught at the Institute of American Indian Arts at Santa Fe, New Mexico, where he chaired the department of cultural studies. There he also founded and directed the Center for Research and Cultural Exchange. He received a doctorate in education from International College, Los Angeles, in 1986.

Cajete is a prolific writer. Among his publications are: *Educating American Indian/Alaska Native Elementary and Secondary Students: Guidelines for Mathematics, Science and Technology Programs* (1995); *Look to the Mountain* (1997), which deals with general educational issues; *Health, Nutrition and Traditional Foods* (1998); *Igniting the Sparkle: An Indigenous Education Model* (1999); and *Native Science: Natural Laws of Interdependence* (2000). He also edited the collection *A People's Ecology: Explorations in Sustainable Living* (1999), which contains his own "Look to the Mountain" and "Indigenous Foods, Indigenous Health: a Pueblo Perspective."

In 1993, under the auspices of the American Herbalists Guild, Cajete produced the lecture tape "Herbal Traditions of Northern New Mexico" and "Southwestern Native American Herbal Traditions" (with David Winston). He also appears with Tewa anthropologist ALFONSO ORTIZ and anthropologist Edward T. Hall in *K'uu T'áhn*, an educational video about the Pueblo petroglyphs (ancient rock paintings) and their meaning, which won the 1997 Silver Telly Award for outstanding video productions.

Greg Cajete is an associate professor at the College of Education, University of New Mexico. He also directs UNM's Native American Studies Program. Although the university introduced Native American Studies as early as 1970, largely as a support for Indian students, it was not until 2004, under Cajete's leadership, that the regents approved a B.A. degree in this field. A master's degree was introduced in 2007.

Cajete continues to live at Santa Clara Pueblo.

Further Reading

Simonelli, Richard. "Native Science Assists a Science Major or Graduate Program: An Interview with Dr. Gregory Cajete." *APA Newsletters (American Philosophical Association): Newsletter on American Indians in Philosophy.* (Spring 2001). Available online. URL: http://www .apa.udel.edu/apa/publications/newsletters/v00n2 /amindians/09.asp. Accessed 17 October 2007.

Calac, Pete (1892–1968) *Luiseño athlete*

One of the premier running backs in the early days of professional football, Pete Calac was born on May 13, 1892, in Valley Center, California, the son of Francisco and Felicidad Calac. A Luiseño from the Rincon Band of Mission Indians, he attended the Rincon Day School and nearby Fallbrook District School before entering Carlisle Indian School in Pennsylvania in 1908. Playing football under Carlisle coach POP WARNER, he was named to the All-American team in 1912 as a lineman. Calac then transferred to West Virginia Wesleyan College, where he played halfback from 1913 to 1915. He left West Virginia Wesleyan to join the Canton Bulldogs, a professional football powerhouse that boasted Native American players such as JIM THORPE and GUSTAVUS WELCH. In the final game of the 1916 season, Calac scored a touchdown to secure a victory over the Massillon Tigers and give the Bulldogs the world championship. In 1917, he helped the Bulldogs repeat as world champions. Calac enlisted in the army during WORLD WAR I, serving in France and Belgium. Rejoining the Bulldogs in 1919, Calac, with Thorpe and JOE GUYON, formed an all-Indian backfield that led Canton to an undefeated season and another title. In 1920, even while sharing the ball with both Guyon and Thorpe, Calac managed to finish second in the league in rushing yards and fifth in total points scored. Calac went with Guyon to the Washington Senators in 1921, but midway through the season they both defected to the Cleveland Tigers, where Thorpe had become head coach.

Like Guyon and Thorpe, Calac, who was 5 feet 10 inches tall and weighed 200 pounds, combined size and strength with tremendous speed. He was the main running and scoring threat of the OORANG INDIANS in 1922 and 1923, as both Thorpe and Guyon were often injured. When the Indians folded, Calac joined the Buffalo Bisons before going back to the Canton Bulldogs in 1925. He retired in 1927. For the next 25 years he was a popular and well-respected Canton policeman. Despite spending most of his career under the shadow of his two great teammates, he was nominated for the Pro Football Hall of Fame in 1968. Pete Calac died on January 13, 1968, in Canton, Ohio.

Further Reading

Adams, David Wallace. "More than a Game: The Carlisle Indians Take to the Gridiron, 1893–1917." *Western Historical Quarterly* 32, no. 1 (Spring 2001): 22–53.
Oxendine, Joseph B. *American Indian Sports Heritage.* Lincoln: University of Nebraska Press, 1995.
Whitman, Robert L. *Jim Thorpe and the Oorang Indians: The N.F.L.'s Most Colorful Franchise.* Mount Gilead, Ohio: Marian County Historical Society, 1984.

Campbell, Ben Nighthorse (1933–   )
Northern Cheyenne politician, U.S. senator, artist

Ben Nighthorse Campbell was born in Auburn, California, on April 13, 1933. His mother, Mary Vierra, was Portuguese. The ancestry of his father, Albert Campbell, who was orphaned at an early age, is difficult to determine, but he is known to have been of white as well as possibly Apache, Pueblo, and Northern Cheyenne ancestry. Ben Campbell himself had to spend much of his youth in St. Patrick's Catholic Orphanage in Sacramento, California, because his father was an alcoholic and his mother was frequently hospitalized for tuberculosis.

After his junior year, Campbell dropped out of high school and became a fruit picker in the Sacramento Valley. There he befriended some Japanese boys who taught him judo. According to Campbell, the sport "kept me off the streets and out of jail." He joined the U.S. Air Force in 1951, serving as a military policeman during the Korean War while keeping up his judo training. After he was discharged in 1953, Campbell worked variously as a fruit picker and a truck driver. He then enrolled in San Jose State University, graduating in 1957 with a degree in physical education and fine arts.

In 1960, Campbell studied judo at Meiji University in Tokyo, a world center for the sport. A four-time Pacific Coast Judo Champion, he won a gold medal in the Pan-American games in Brazil in 1963, then competed in the Tokyo Olympics of 1964, the same Olympics in which BILLY MILLS scored his famous triumph by capturing the gold medal in the 10,000-meter run. Campbell later taught judo, training three members of the 1972 U.S. Olympic team and writing a training manual *Championship Judo: Drill Training* in 1974. By this time he had married (in 1966) Linda Price, with whom he had two children.

While in Japan, Campbell became interested in his Native heritage, and when he returned to the United States, he began to search out his roots. His father believed he had Cheyenne ancestry and was somehow related to a family called Night Horse or Black Horse. In 1966, Campbell began visiting the Northern Cheyenne Reservation, where he found and was adopted by the Black Horse family and given the name Nighthorse. He was enrolled in the Cheyenne tribe in 1980 and inducted into the Cheyenne Council of Forty-Four Chiefs in 1985.

Also while in Japan, Campbell was influenced by Japanese jewelry-making techniques, and after his career in judo, he began teaching jewelry-making classes in San Jose, California. Many of his students there were Native American. He moved to Sacramento, where his career as a jewelry maker took off, and he was featured in a 1979 article in *Arizona Highways.* That year, Campbell moved to Colorado, his wife Linda's home state, where they began raising champion quarter horses.

Campbell's entry into politics was accidental. In late 1981, bad weather made it impossible for him to fly from Colorado to the West Coast to deliver some jewelry. He ended up attending a meeting of Colorado Democrats seeking a candidate for the state's 59th house district. At that meeting, Democratic leaders persuaded him to run for office. In 1982, he was elected to the Colorado state legislature, where he served two terms. In 1986, he defeated a Republican incumbent to win the right to represent Colorado's third congressional district in the U.S. House of Representatives, becoming the first Native American congressman since BENJAMIN REIFEL.

As a congressman, Campbell served on the House Committee on Agriculture and the House Committee on Interior and Insular Affairs, playing an important role in securing legislation to settle American Indian water rights. He helped the Smithsonian Institution acquire the Museum of the American Indian (Heye Foundation) in New York City and also sponsored the legislation that changed the name of the Custer National Battlefield Monument to Little Bighorn Battlefield Monument.

Campbell was elected to the Senate in 1992, becoming the first Native American senator since ROBERT LATHAM OWEN, JR. and CHARLES CURTIS. In the midterm elections of 1994, following the disastrous defeat of the Democrats, Campbell switched his allegiance to the Republican Party. While his conservative political views, especially those on the environment, were not necessarily representative of Indians—who are overwhelmingly inclined to the Democrats—Campbell was a defender of Indian SOVEREIGNTY rights. In 1997, he killed a bill by Washington senator Slade Gorton that would have ended the sovereign immunity of Indian tribal governments.

In 2002, when the Republicans took control of the Senate,

Campbell replaced the longtime chairman of the Committee on Indian Affairs, Daniel K. Inouye of Hawaii, becoming the first American Indian since Charles Curtis to head the committee. Campbell was also a member of three other important Senate Committees: the Appropriations Committee, the Energy and Natural Resources Committee, and the Veterans Affairs Committee. He chose not to run for reelection in 2004, and his seat was won by Democrat Ken Salazar. Campbell subsequently turned down an opportunity to run for governor of Colorado, where he still lives.

Further Reading

Viola, Herman J. *Ben Nighthorse Campbell, an American Warrior*. New York: Orion Books, 1993.

Cardin, Fred (Pejawah) (1895–1960) *Miami-Quapaw violinist, conductor, composer*

A Miami-Quapaw, William Frederick "Pejawah" Cardin was born on April 18, 1895, near Quapaw, Oklahoma, the eldest of two children of John Alexander Cardin and Martha Ella (Kenoyer) Cardin. His grandfather, Thomas Jefferson Cardin, a Miami adopted by the Quapaw, was descended from Miami chief J. B. Richardville. Cardin was educated at St. Mary's School on Quapaw territory, where one of the nuns started him on the violin. He then attended the Carlisle Indian School in Pennsylvania, graduating in 1912. After that he worked at Carlisle in the business department so that he could continue to study under Fred Stauffer, the school's music director. Cardin attended the Dana Musical Institute in Warren, Ohio, on scholarship (1914–15), then played first violin in the Indian String Quartet, which, in addition to Cardin, featured Alex Melovidov (Aleut) from St. Paul of the Pribilov Islands in the Bering Sea as second violin; William Palin (Kootenai), a Carlisle graduate, on viola; and Willie Reddie (Haida) from Alaska on cello. The quartet toured on the Chautauqua circuit in 1916 and 1917 to critical and popular acclaim.

During WORLD WAR I, Cardin served in the U.S. Army in the 315th Cavalry and the 69th Field Artillery of the 95th Division. Resuming his music career after the war, Cardin joined the Kansas City Symphony, then taught violin at the School of Music, University of Nebraska, where he was "discovered" and sponsored by Indianist composer Thurlow Lieurance. (INDIANIST MUSIC, popular in the early 20th century, was a form of modern classical music influenced by traditional American Indian scales, rhythms, and motifs.) The two men organized the Cardin-Lieurance piano quintet, which had several successful concert seasons. After a number of seasons in which he conducted the Standard Symphony of the Standard Lyceum and Chautauqua Bureau, a popular traveling lecture and concert circuit that operated in the Midwest, Cardin won a scholarship to the Curtis School of Music in Philadelphia. In 1926, he was awarded a scholarship to the Conservatoire Americaine at Fontainebleu, France.

In a brief article in *Indian Tepee* (May–June 1928), Cardin wrote: "The music of the American Indian is more than folk music. Its unique melodic line and rhythmic background combined with the tradition of its use, makes it a real heritage to the patron of American music, especially the composer. I sincerely believe that when the white man has been here long enough, natural environment will make him regard the Indian arts as the true expression of American life."

In 1930, Cardin secured a position as conductor and music director of Reading High School, Reading, Pennsylvania, where he remained through 1957. There he composed numerous works for violin, chorus, and orchestra, as well as music for 10 historical pageants. He directed the Reading Civic Opera Society for a time, led the Ringgold Band of Reading from 1936 to 1960, and lectured around the country on Indian life and music. He was one of the few composers of the Indianist school who was actually an Indian.

Cardin's single best-known composition is the *Cree War Dance*, which was recorded by Thurlow Lieurance. *Ghost Pipes* for violin and piano was published by Theodore Presser. Cardin coauthored and composed *Thunder Mountain*, an educational pageant based on Indian cultures. His *Great Drum*, which premiered at Town Hall in New York City in 1930, was given the unusual honor of a repeat performance the following winter. Cardin wrote the libretto and music for *A Mountain Madrigal*, which had its premier at Reading in 1947.

Fred Cardin died of a heart attack on August 29, 1960, in Reading, Pennsylvania.

Further Reading

Troutman, John William. "Indian Blues: American Indians and the Politics of Music, 1890–1935." Ph.D. dissertation, University of Texas at Austin, 2004.

Carewe, Edwin (Jay Fox, Chulla) (1883–1940) *Chickasaw actor, film director*

Born Jay Fox on March 5, 1883, in Gainesville, Texas (his nickname Chulla means "fox" in Chickasaw), Edwin Carewe was the son of a lawyer in Purcell and Ardmore, Indian Territory (now Oklahoma). His grandmother on his mother's side was the daughter of Chief Tabuscabano of the Chickasaw. Carewe had two younger brothers also involved in film, the screenwriter FINIS FOX and the director WALLACE W. FOX.

In 1898, Jay Fox ran away from home and joined the Dearborn Stock Company, a small repertory group doing one-night stands in Missouri. He pursued an education at Arkadelphia Methodist College (Arkansas), Polytechnic College (Fort Worth, Texas), and Missouri State University, but also traveled around the country with various stock companies. He made his Broadway debut with Chauncey Olcott, the well-known composer and singer of Irish ballads, and appeared in New York, Philadelphia, Washington, Chicago, and Los Angeles with famous contemporary stage personalities such as Otis Skinner, Rose Coghlan, and Laurette Taylor. He also directed for the stage and produced several of his own plays.

In August 1906, while playing with a New York stock company, Fox was vacationing with friends at the Staten

Chickasaw actor and film director Edwin Carewe posed for this photograph in 1932. *(AP/Wideworld)*

Island shore when a fellow actor suggested that Jay Fox was not a good professional name. Then and there, Fox changed it to Edwin Carewe, taking the first name from his favorite actor, Edwin Booth, and the last from the character he was then playing.

Carewe ended his connection with the stage when he joined the Lubin Film Company in 1914. In that year, he starred in *The Three of Us* (Rolfe photoplays), directed by John W. Noble. In 1915, he began directing at Metro with *The Final Judgement*, followed by *The House of Gold* (Metro, 1918), *Isobel* (David Distributing, 1920), *Habit* (Associated First National, 1921), and more than 25 other silent features, including *Mighty Lak' a Rose* (1922), *The Girl of the Golden West* (1923), *A Son of the Sahara* (1924), and *Ramona* and *Revenge* (1928).

Carewe made a successful transition to talkies, directing *Evangeline* (United Artists, 1929), which he also coproduced; *The Spoilers* (Paramount, 1930), which he also produced; and *Resurrection* (Universal, 1931). *Are We Civilized?* (Raspin, 1934), a 16-mm educational film, dramatized threats to freedom of the press and speech and the basic liberties of humanity from the rise of totalitarian dictatorships around the world. In 1935, he sailed to Palestine to shoot background scenes for *The Life of Christ*, but the film was never completed.

As a producer, Carewe's most memorable films were the silent version of Tolstoy's *Resurrection* in 1927 and the talking transcription of the same story in 1931. As a sound director, he is remembered chiefly for his version of *The Spoilers*, featuring one of the greatest fight scenes in early cinema history. Of all his films, Carewe's own personal favorite was *Ramona* (1928), the third of four screen versions of Helen Hunt Jackson's "story of the white man's Injustice to the Indian." At the peak of his career in the late 1920s, Carewe was reputed to be a millionaire. A friend disclosed that his percentage from the gross of *Ramona* in one year was $380,000 and his cut on *Resurrection* was $320,000, a princely sum in those days.

Carewe was married three times, twice to the former actress Mary Akin of Lake Forest, Illinois, in 1926 and again in 1929. She bore him three children: Sally Ann, Carol Lee, and William. By his first wife, a nonprofessional, he had two daughters, Rita and Mary Jane. Rita Carewe became a prominent screen actress, playing an important role in her father's 1926 film *Joanna*.

Carewe was largely responsible for the rise to fame of a number of Hollywood stars, such as Francis X. Bushman, Gary Cooper, Wallace Beery, and Mary Akin, but his most important "discovery" was Dolores Del Rio. When he and Mary Akin eloped to Mexico in 1926 and were married there, they met Jaime Del Rio and his beautiful wife, Dolores. Carewe suggested to Jaime that he be permitted to bring Del Rio to Hollywood for a screen test. He subsequently built her into one of the biggest stars of the silent era.

Carewe viewed life as a dramatist: "Show me a man with strong opinions, and I'll show you a man with good ideas. Of course, the ideas may not always be right, but anything forceful is bound to be dramatic, right or wrong, and some good can usually be extracted from it. Conflict is the essence of drama, and a difference of opinion makes conflict. If two individuals who differ in viewpoint can, at the same time, maintain an open mind, both are bound to benefit from the exchange."

Edwin Carewe died in his bed in Hollywood of a heart attack on the night of January 21/22, 1940.

Carlisle Indian School   *See* PRATT, RICHARD HENRY; WARNER, POP.

Carter, Charles David (1868–1929) *Chickasaw U.S. congressman*
Born on August 16, 1868, near Boggy Depot, Indian Territory (now Oklahoma), Charles David Carter was descended from a white man captured in childhood at the Wyoming Valley Massacre in 1757 and adopted by the Cherokee. Although one-quarter Cherokee and only one-eighth Chickasaw, Carter was an enrolled Chickasaw citizen and was educated in the excellent Chickasaw tribal schools in Indian Territory. He became a fire insurance salesman in Ardmore, where he favored the protections for full-blood ALLOTMENTS under the CURTIS ACT. He was concerned that as Indian Territory was broken up into individual parcels, the traditional Indians would be subject to fraud and violence. Carter was appointed in 1900 to oversee the mining industry of Indian Territory and served as

secretary-treasurer of the Democratic Executive Committee of the proposed state of Oklahoma.

When Oklahoma became a state in 1907, Carter was one of its first five representatives in Congress, joining mixed-blood Cherokee ROBERT LATHAM OWEN, JR., one of the state's two senators, as the only two Indians in the Oklahoma delegation. By this time, Carter favored removing all restrictions on the alienability of Indian allotments. Carter no longer sided with the traditionals, who wanted to protect Indian lands from being sold. A Democrat, Carter fought South Dakota Republican CHARLES H. BURKE's attempts to appoint district agents to oversee the Allotment process among the Five Civilized Tribes (as the Creek, Cherokee, Seminole, Chickasaw, and Choctaw were known at that time), a largely partisan dispute over who would control the vast spoils made available by the CURTIS ACT.

The district agents would appoint guardians for traditional Indians and settle disputes over land ownership, a powerful position that invited corruption. Carter introduced a bill in Congress in 1912 that would codify Indian tribal law, but despite the support of the SOCIETY OF AMERICAN INDIANS, of which he was a member, the bill failed.

With the addition of Cherokee congressman WILLIAM WIRT HASTINGS in 1915, the mixed-blood members of the Oklahoma delegation joined with their colleagues to successfully fend off attempts by BUREAU OF INDIAN AFFAIRS commissioner CATO SELLS to reform the Allotment process for the Five Civilized Tribes under the onerous provisions of the Curtis Act. Carter held his seat until his retirement in 1927. He died on April 9, 1929.

Further Reading

Debo, Angie. *And Still the Waters Run: The Betrayal of the Five Civilized Tribes.* Norman: University of Oklahoma Press, 1934.

McDonell, Janet A. *The Dispossession of the American Indian, 1887–1934.* Bloomington: Indiana University Press, 1991.

Castañeda, Carlos (Carlos César Salvador Arana)
(1925–1998) *anthropologist, author*

Though he publicly claimed he was born on December 25, 1931, in São Paolo, Brazil, Carlos Castañeda was actually born on December 25, 1925, in Cajamarca, Peru. He was the son of César Arana Burungary, a watchmaker and goldsmith, and Susana Castañeda Navoa, and his full name was Carlos César Salvador Arana. He took his surname from his mother.

In northern Peru, *curanderos* (Native folk healers) were part of everyday life. As a boy, Castañeda often heard them talking in the marketplace, but he had no special involvement with them. In 1948, the family moved to Lima. There, after graduating from the Colegio Nacional de Nuestra Señora de Guadalupe, Castañeda studied sculpture and painting at the National School of Fine Arts, and in his spare time he pored over the collections of indigenous ceramics in the city's museums and galleries.

Castañeda's mother died in 1949, and in 1951 he emigrated to the United States, intending to become an artist. He settled in Los Angeles, attending Los Angeles Community College from 1955 to 1959. During that period, he became one of a small circle of friends interested in mysticism, including his future wife, Margaret Runyan, a follower of New Age guru Neville Goddard. But it was his 1956 reading of Aldous Huxley's *The Doors of Perception*, which recounted the author's experiences with mescaline, that really sparked Castañeda's interest in altered states of perception and psychic phenomena. Later, Andrija Puharich's *The Sacred Mushroom* introduced him to the writings of Gordon Wasson on the mushroom *Amanita muscaria* and of James Sydney Slotkin on peyote.

Castañeda enrolled in the University of California, Los Angeles (UCLA), in fall 1959. In 1960, he took an undergraduate course on California ethnography taught by archaeologist Clement Meighan and interviewed several California Native informants on the ritual use of Jimson weed *(Datura stramonium)*. The data obtained from one of these informants, identified as part Yuma and part Yaqui, represented a kind of knowledge thought to have died out decades earlier, and apparently not previously recorded. The paper so impressed Meighan that Castañeda was persuaded to become an anthropologist. He continued with graduate study at UCLA, receiving a Ph.D. in 1972.

Castañeda's first book, *The Teachings of Don Juan: A Yaqui Way of Knowledge*—ostensibly based on field research in Sonora, Mexico, with a Yaqui shaman—was originally his master's thesis. Though published by the University of California Press in 1968, it was not widely read until a paperback edition appeared in 1970, coinciding with a thirst among American youth for spiritual knowledge, experimentation with mind-expanding drugs, and resurgent interest in American Indians, all of which are major elements of the book.

Castañeda followed this with *A Separate Reality: Further Conversations with Don Juan* (1971), *Journey to Ixtlan: The Lessons of Don Juan* (1972, his doctoral dissertation), *Tales of Power* (1974), *The Second Ring of Power* (1977), *The Eagle's Gift* (1981), *The Fire from Within* (1984), and *The Power of Silence: Further Lessons of Don Juan* (1987). The books were translated into 17 languages and sold millions of copies.

There has been much debate about whether Don Juan really existed or was a fictional creation. The question is of both scientific and literary importance, for the books claim to be accounts of actual events and phenomenological experiences and, if not true, would in the opinion of some represent one of the greatest intellectual hoaxes of modern times. But for the majority of readers, the question is ultimately academic. The books led them along paths of inner discovery, and if Don Juan did not exist as an actual person, then at least the wisdom attributed to him does. It had to have come from somewhere, no doubt a multitude of sources, and was obviously acquired by Castañeda. At least this is so for the first three books, which are the real classics; the remainder show a falling-off in quality.

Castañeda's interest had been nurtured in the California

"human potential" movement of the late 1950s and early 1960s, one of the sources of the NEW AGE MOVEMENT of the 1980s and 1990s, and his books were the greatest single stimulus to the interest in shamanism that emerged among the New Agers. But Castañeda himself was not part of the movement. For most of his life, he did not make public appearances and would not even allow himself to be photographed or tape-recorded. In his last years, however, he began giving expensive seminars and selling videos on a movement system called "Tensegrity," described in the literature of Cleargreen, Inc., the firm that markets it, as "the modernized version of some movements . . . developed by Indian shamans who lived in Mexico in times prior to the Spanish conquest." Why Castañeda's life took this turn at the end is just one more mystery and, to many of his admirers, a disappointing one. Barry Klein, a Castañeda admirer, stated, "It really seemed to me that the Carlos Castañeda that I met and who was giving these workshops was not even the same person who had written the truly fine books on the teachings of Don Juan."

Castañeda continued to write up to the time of his death. He died at his home in Los Angeles on April 27, 1998, of liver cancer.

Further Reading

Castañeda, Margaret Runyan. *A Magical Journey with Carlos Castañeda*. Victoria, B.C., Canada: Millennia Press, 1996.
De Mille, Richard, ed. *The Don Juan Papers: Further Castañeda Controversies*. Belmont, Calif.: Wadsworth, 1990.
Fikes, Jay Courtney. *Carlos Castañeda, Academic Opportunism and the Psychedelic Sixties*. Victoria, B.C., Canada: Millennia Press, 1996.

Catches, Peter (Petaga Yuka Mani, "Walks with Hot Coals") (1912–1993) *Oglala Lakota Sioux holy man, traditional leader*

Peter Catches was born on the Lakota Pine Ridge Reservation on March 17, 1912. His Lakota name was Petaga Yuka Mani (Walks with Hot Coals). He was orphaned at an early age and raised at the Holy Rosary Mission in Pine Ridge, eventually becoming a teacher of catechism. During the 1950s, while continuing to practice Catholicism, he began to turn to traditional Lakota ways, becoming a leader in the Sun Dance ceremonies after the ban on Sun Dances was lifted (see RELIGIOUS FREEDOM, AMERICAN INDIAN). In 1964, the Oglala Sioux Tribal Council named Catches as the official Sun Dance chief on the Pine Ridge Reservation. In 1973, during the WOUNDED KNEE occupation, Catches was one of many traditional Lakota spiritual leaders, along with FRANK FOOLS CROW and WALLACE HOWARD BLACK ELK, who sided with militants of the AMERICAN INDIAN MOVEMENT (AIM), lending the movement important credibility in its struggle against the federal government.

Catches eventually abandoned the Catholic faith completely and immersed himself in Lakota traditions. He rejected non-Indian influences such as mainstream American material possessions and even refused to travel in automobiles. After his death on December 3, 1993, his son Peter V. Catches, also a respected holy man, compiled his father's teachings into a book, *Oceti Wakan–Sacred Fireplace* (1997), which was republished in 1999 by Clear Light Publishers.

Further Reading

Catches, Pete. *Sacred Fireplace (Oceti Waken): Life and Teachings of a Lakota Medicine Man*, edited by Peter V. Catches. Santa Fe, N.Mex.: Clear Light Publishers, 1999.

Charles, Wilson D. (Buster Charles) (1908–2006) *Oneida athlete*

An Oneida, Wilson D. "Buster" Charles was born on April 4, 1908, in Green Bay, Wisconsin. At Flandreau High School in South Dakota, he was the state high-jump and long-jump champion. Charles attended the Haskell Indian School in Lawrence, Kansas, from 1928 to 1932. There, in 1930, he won the decathlon at the Kansas relays and then the National Amateur Athletic Union (NAAU) competition, the premier American track-and-field event of the day. In 1931, he repeated as NAAU decathlon champion, defeating Jim Stewart of the Los Angeles Athletic Club in the final event, the 1,500-meter race, to win a closely fought contest.

While at Haskell, Charles also played football and suffered a broken back in 1931. He was in a body cast for six weeks. Despite this, he was a member of the 1932 U.S. team in the Los Angeles Olympic Games, placing fourth in the decathlon. He is enshrined in the South Dakota Hall of Fame and the American Indian Athletic Hall of Fame. Buster Charles died on June 6, 2006, at his home in Camp Verde, Arizona.

Childers, Ernest (1918–2005) *Creek war hero*

A Creek, Ernest Childers was born in Broken Arrow, Oklahoma, on February 1, 1918. He attended Chilocco Indian Agricultural School in 1937 and joined the school's National Guard Unit. Upon the outbreak of WORLD WAR II, Childers was assigned to the 45th Infantry Division, the same division as VAN T. BARFOOT, another Native American Medal of Honor winner.

On September 22, 1944, Second Lieutenant Childers, although suffering from a broken foot, advanced with eight enlisted men toward an enemy position in the town of Oliveto, Italy. With his men laying down a suppressing fire to cover him, Childers crawled toward a house that contained two snipers, killing both of them. He then killed all of the occupants of one German machine-gun nest and one member of another nest. He continued to another house, where he captured a German artillery observer. Childers was awarded the Medal of Honor on April 8, 1944. After the war, he remained with the army, eventually rising to the rank of lieutenant colonel. After his retirement, he lived in Coweta, Oklahoma, near Tulsa. Ernest Childers died in Tulsa on March 17, 2005, as the result of a stroke.

Cherokee lieutenant Ernest Childers is awarded the Medal of Honor by Lieutenant General Jacob L. Devers in a ceremony in Italy in 1944. *(AP/Wideworld)*

Wendell Chino, shown seated next to presidential candidate Jimmy Carter in Albuquerque, New Mexico, on October 8, 1976. *(AP/Wideworld)*

Chino, Wendell (1923–1998) *Mescalero Apache leader, activist*

Wendell Chino was born on the Mescalero Apache Reservation in New Mexico on December 27, 1923. After learning English at the reservation school, Chino was sent to a Dutch Reform college in Michigan; he graduated and was ordained a minister in 1954.

At the beginning of the 20th century, the Mescalero had just finished undergoing a period of harsh ASSIMILATION, mitigated only slightly by the assignment of Indian agent James A. Carroll in 1902. During his 10-year tenure, Carroll fought attempts by powerful New Mexican families, in particular the rapacious ALBERT BACON FALL, to encroach on Apache lands. During this time, the reservation was settled with Lipan Apache, as well as Chiricahua who had formerly been interned in Fort Sill, including Chino's parents, who were released from captivity in 1913, (see also CLEGHORN, MILDRED). In 1915, the headmen of the various Apache bands on the reservation began to form a tribal government to express their demands to the Indian agent. Under the INDIAN REORGANIZATION ACT of 1934, a tribal council was established, led by William Magoosh and later Asa Daklugie. Wendell Chino, who had only recently returned to the reservation, was elected tribal chairman in 1955. He subsequently assumed the new post of tribal president when it was created in 1965 under a new constitution; Chino held this position for the rest of his life.

Chino was well known for his advocacy for Indian rights. He fought attempts by the state of New Mexico to assert its jurisdiction over non-Indians on the reservation, successfully defending Apache reservation-based HUNTING AND FISHING RIGHTS in the landmark Supreme Court decision *New Mexico v. the Mescalero Apache Tribe* (1983). Chino lost an important tax case in 1973 when the state of New Mexico successfully argued that the tribe must pay state taxes on off-reservation property, including its ski resort; the tribe was allowed tax immunity on any capital purchases for the resort itself.

Chino believed Indian people should make decisions about Indian land, a notion he described as "red capitalism." Before Chino took office, the BUREAU OF INDIAN AFFAIRS (BIA) had significant control over the Mescalero reservation, overseeing everything from mining to lumber to grazing contracts on the reservation. As those contracts expired, Chino did not renew them and instead created lumber and cattle companies controlled by the tribe. Chino fostered the successful development of tribal industries, including a metal fabrication plant, a sawmill, and tourism centered around the Inn of the Mountain Gods resort hotel. Chino was fond of saying, "Zunis make jewelry, Navajos make rugs, Apaches make money." He joined his longtime friend ROGER JOURDAIN in opposing the Indian Gaming Regulatory Act of 1988, arguing that it transferred regulatory powers to the states. But Chino was not opposed to gaming per se, and in the 1980s, he established a gaming operation, Apache Casino, which the state of New Mexico unsuccessfully attempted to shut down.

Chino split with other New Mexico Indian leaders in 1997, refusing to honor a gaming revenue-sharing agreement with the state because he "did not recognize the state as a legitimate entity" and would only deal with the federal government, nation to nation (see SOVEREIGNTY, INDIGENOUS AND TRIBAL).

In the early 1990s, Chino conceived of the idea of turning a part of the reservation into a "private depository" of nuclear waste. Congress had passed the Nuclear Waste Policy Act in 1982 to locate and develop monitored, removable, and retrievable storage sites for nuclear wastes. Chino was the first to sign up for this program, and in February 1994 the Mescalero reached a deal with Northern States Power Company. Under this agreement, 400,000 metric tons of nuclear waste from commercial power plants would be shipped to the reservation. In return, the tribe would profit by more than $250 million. The proposal, however, drew fire from New Mexico officials, environmentalists, and a large portion of the Apache as well. A community-based campaign, led by the grandson of Geronimo, Joseph Geronimo, and Rufina Marie Laws, forced a tribal referendum on the depository, which the Apache overwhelmingly rejected on January 31, 1995, in a stunning upset of the tribe's political order. Chino then called a new referendum less than two months later, and through the use of strong-arm tactics—another well-known aspect of Chino's rule—the Apache people gave their approval for the site on March 10, 1995. Despite the yes vote, the project requires federal approval, which it is unlikely to receive (see NUCLEAR INDUSTRY, AMERICAN INDIANS AND THE).

Chino, who suffered from a heart ailment, collapsed while walking on a treadmill at a health clinic in Santa Monica on November 2, 1998. Although he revived briefly, he suffered a second heart attack at the Santa Monica-UCLA Medical Center in California and died on November 3.

Despite the many critics of Chino's dictatorial style of governing, few could deny his tremendous economic success. By the time of Chino's death, the per-capita income on the Mescalero reservation had risen to $16,536, double or triple that of neighboring reservations. Wendell Chino's son, Mark Chino, became tribal president in 2004.

Further Reading

Vincent, Myla, and Peter Iverson. "The Inalienable Right to Govern Ourselves: Wendell Chino and the Struggle for Indian Self-determination in Modern New Mexico." *New Mexican Lives: Profiles and Historical Stories*, edited by Richard Etulain, 265–284. Albuquerque: University of New Mexico Press, 2002.

Chinquilla, Mary (Princess Chinquilla)

(ca. 1865–1938) *performer, lecturer, writer, organizer*
Known professionally as Princess Chinquilla, Mary Chinquilla constructed an identity so successfully that to this day many key facts of her life remain unknown, though no one any longer believes her claim to be a Cheyenne. It is not even known if Chinquilla (a variant of the Spanish name Chinchilla) was her actual family name—or, if not, why she chose it.

Chinquilla was born about 1865, perhaps a few years earlier, allegedly near Camp Supply, Indian Territory (later Oklahoma). She represented herself, as reported in the *Duluth News Tribune*, July 22, 1905, as the "daughter of the great chieftain, the late Lone Star, who journeyed to Washington and made a famous address in favor of his people from the steps of the capitol"— but there was no such person. Later she claimed to have been raised by white parents, then adopted by the Blackhorse family on the Tongue River Reservation in Montana. She also claimed to have studied at the Carlisle Indian School, but there is no record of her attendance.

Apparently in the 1880s, she married a white man named Cole. The only thing known of this is that a son, Harry K. Cole, was born in 1888. About that time, according to her story, she performed with the Buffalo Bill Wild West show as an Indian tight-wire walker. Around 1890, while in Canada with the Howe's London Shows, a traveling circus well known at the time, she met Abraham Bliss ("Major Ed") Newell, a juggler (born in Rhode Island in 1867), and formed a business partnership with him.

For the next six years, Newell and Chinquilla did one-night stints through New England and the Maritime Provinces of Canada. Beginning in 1897, they toured on the famous Proctor vaudeville circuit as a banjo duet and juggling act, in which Chinquilla also sang. According to her publicity, she was "the only genuine Indian lady upon the vaudeville stage" and that "her act is at once original and aboriginal . . ." Adding a young Italian, Salvatore Dinufrio, to their act, they toured as "Newell, Chinquilla, and Dinufrio."

On April 26, 1905, at Ogden, Utah, Chinquilla and Ernest L. Barbour, the manager of the Grand Opera House in Butte, Montana, obtained a marriage license. Barbour— at least six years her junior, freshly divorced, and the father of daughters aged 10 and 13—was the son of Baptist minister Reverend Herman Humphrey Barbour of Newark, New Jersey, and grandson of a prominent judge of the same name from Hartford, Connecticut. The actual wedding took place the following day aboard a fast Pullman train of the Oregon Short Line a few miles south of Pocatello, Idaho. The marriage was the source of much mawkishly romantic publicity at the time.

Chinquilla went on to San Francisco to resume her vaudeville act with Newell. Joined by Barbour in mid-May 1905, they formed a trio and were signed by M. B. Curtis for a Pacific tour with his American Novelty Company, playing Honolulu in June, Samoa and Fiji in July, New Zealand in July and August, and finally returning to San Francisco by way of Vancouver at the end of September 1905. Though their act was well received, they returned from this grueling circuit with empty pockets. By October, Barbour and Chinquilla had gone their separate ways; they were divorced in Montana on October 27, 1907.

Newell eventually divorced his first wife and married Chinquilla in Corning, New York, in 1912. They bought a pigeon and poultry farm on Idlewild Street (now 157th Street) in the Springfield section of Jamaica, Queens. Meanwhile her son, Harry Cole, had become a successful vaudeville performer under the name "Red Cloud," playing both cowboy and Indian roles with Captain Brunswick's Wild West Company and Matt Kennedy's Tiger Lilies Company. His stage partner was the soprano Anna Hastings, known as "Red Flower," who became his wife. He died at the age of 27, of cancer, at his mother's home in South Jamaica, on January 14, 1915.

In the 1920s, Chinquilla ran a lecture bureau. According to her obituary in the *New York Times*, "She glorified the out-of-doors in talks in New York schools and museums. She herself was a runner, archer, marksman, swimmer, and canoeist. In 1921 she and a companion traveled by canoe from Lake Sebago, Maine to the mouth of the Connecticut river by inland streams."

Exactly when Chinquilla first met the activist Red Fox St. James is not known, but in 1926, under the auspices of the American Indian Association (AIA), the two of them rented a house at 72 Grove Street, just south of Sheridan Square in New York City's Greenwich Village (see Tipi Order of America). This functioned as a social club for Indian residents in New York and a port of call for transient and newly arrived Indians unfamiliar with the city. It was one of the first urban Indian centers (see Urbanization, American Indians and). Chinquilla led the Daughters of Sacajawea, an auxiliary of the AIA dedicated to Indian history and folklore.

Chinquilla was ubiquitous at New York–area Indian events, and her speeches were a feature of the American Indian Day celebrations held at Central Park through 1925, and then, beginning in September 1926, at Manhattan's new Inwood Hill Park on the site of an ancient Indian camp. The custom of holding an Indian festival in Inwood Hill Park in September was revived in the 1980s under the auspices of the Native American Heritage Committee and the Urban Park Rangers. One of the park's footpaths is designated on older maps as Chinquilla Trail.

In the 1920s, a number of pan-Indian organizations were founded, after the example of the Society of American Indians, to work toward the betterment of conditions among Indians. When Gertrude Bonnin formed the National Council of American Indians in 1926, she intended to invite Chinquilla to join, but upon discovering that Chinquilla worked closely with Red Fox St. James, who was suspected of being an Indian imposter, Bonnin grew suspicious. The following year, she recruited an assistant to investigate Chinquilla. Years later, Mari Sandoz, historian of the Northern Cheyenne, did the same. (Sandoz's correspondence on the subject, January–March 1954, is in the University of Nebraska Library at Lincoln.) Both investigations found that Chinquilla was not who she said she was but failed to discover her real origin.

Like her colleagues Red Fox and Joseph Strongwolf, Chinquilla was active in Republican politics, especially the presidential campaign of Herbert Hoover in 1928. Chinquilla and Newell converted the poultry farm into an Indian crafts museum, later demolished to build the Nassau Expressway

and Idlewild (now JFK) International Airport. The museum also housed a printing press, on which were produced a number of pamphlets such as *Old Indian's Almanac; being a cronological [sic] account of land cessions, treaties, etc., and the various quarrels . . . between the N.A. Indians and the U.S. Gov't., from . . . 1550 to 1938.*

Chinquilla was a classic example of the self-made Indian. She never had a credible connection to any known Native community except the one she created around herself. In reality she was a performer with many talents, a quick intelligence, and breathtaking audacity. She had the gift of blarney and the ability to get herself quoted in the newspapers. Throughout her life, she learned, lectured, and wrote on Indian lore, history, and crafts. Although she dealt in stereotypes, she used them in creative ways to advance a more enlightened concept of acculturation for Indians in the context of the 1920s.

Chinquilla died at her home on the night of October 27, 1938—the same year as Gertrude Bonnin. After her death, her husband, A. B. Newell, published *Town Hall Tonight: a night with the spirits; twenty-five hundred and fifty one night stands, experienced by Princess Chinquilla & A. B. Newell thru New England and Maritime Provinces, 1888–1896, and a different performance each night* (1951) at their museum press.

Further Reading

Carpenter, Cari. "Detecting Indianness: Gertrude Bonnin's Investigation of Native American Identity." *Wicazo Sa Review* (Spring 2005): 139–159.

Chinquilla. *Natives of North America.* Lame Deer, Mont.: Tongue River Agency, 1932.

———. *Old Indian's Almanac; being a cronological [sic] account of land cessions, treaties, etc., and the various quarrels . . . between the N.A. Indians and the U.S. Gov't., from . . . 1550 to 1938.* Jamaica, N.Y.: Indian Craft Museum, 1937.

Hertzberg, Hazel. *The Search for an American Indian Identity: Modern Pan-Indian Movements.* Syracuse, N.Y.: Syracuse University Press, 1971.

Newell, A. B. *Town Hall Tonight: A night with the spirits; twenty-five hundred and fifty one night stands, experienced by Princess Chinquilla & A.B. Newell thru New England and Maritime Provinces, 1888–1896, and a different performance each night.* Jamaica, N.Y.: Chinquilla Publications, 1951.

Red Jacket. *A Speech by Red Jacket, Eloquent Seneca Chief, and Done into a Little Book.* Jamaica, N.Y.: Chinquilla's Indian Craft Museum, 1935.

Chouteau, Yvonne (Myra Yvonne Chouteau Terekhov) (1929–) *Shawnee dancer*

Yvonne Chouteau was born on March 7, 1929, the only child of Corbett Edward (an oilman who was part Anglo-French and part Shawnee) and Lucy Arnett Chouteau. She is a direct descendant of Major Jean Pierre Chouteau, who established Oklahoma's oldest white settlement, at the present site of Salina, in 1796. Profoundly impressed by her first experience of a powwow (see POWWOWS) she became a noted performer of Indian traditional dance while still a child. She studied ballet from age five and at age 12 won a scholarship to the School of American Ballet. At 14, Chouteau joined the Ballet Russe de Monte Carlo, making her debut as a soloist in 1945. Promoted from the corps de ballet to ballerina in 1950, she remained with the company until 1957. She married another member of the company, Miguel Terekhov, in 1956.

In 1959, after working with the Montevideo State Opera as a guest ballerina, Chouteau returned to the United States and opened the Chouteau-Terekhov Academy of Ballet with her husband. She and Terekhov established the University of Oklahoma's School of Dance in 1961, and that same year, they founded the Oklahoma City Civic Ballet. At the Civic Ballet in 1963, Chouteau and Terekhov directed MARIA TALLCHIEF in a performance of her legendary leading role in choreographer George Balanchine's *Nutcracker*. Chouteau built up the company throughout the next decade, and it was well established when, in 1971, she withdrew to concentrate on her work at the Chouteau-Terekhov Academy. The company, whose name eventually changed to Ballet Oklahoma, continued to flourish, and in 1986 former New York City Ballet soloist Bryan Pitts took over as artistic director.

Yvonne Chouteau was inducted into the Oklahoma Hall of Fame and holds honorary degrees from both the University of Oklahoma and Phillips University. She was awarded both the Distinguished Merit Award by the University of Oklahoma and the Governor's Arts Award by the state of Oklahoma.

Further Reading

Livingston, Lili Cockerille. *American Indian Ballerinas.* Norman: University of Oklahoma Press, 1997.

Churchill, Ward (1947–) *Cherokee essayist, member of the American Indian Movement*

Little is known of Ward Churchill's early life, and although he claims to be of Creek, Cherokee, and Métis descent, others have disputed this, and even questioned whether he is Indian at all. Churchill was born on October 2, 1947, in Elmwood, Illinois. He attended Elmwood High School and in 1966 was drafted into the U.S. Army. He subsequently attended Sangamon State University, now the University of Illinois at Springfield, where he earned his B.A. in technological communications in 1974 and M.A. in communication theory in 1975. He is an associate member of the United Keetoowah Band of Cherokee, an affiliation that does not necessarily connote Indian blood.

Churchill is the author of more than 100 essays and a number of books on contemporary Native American issues, including *Fantasies of the Master Race: Literature, Cinema and the Colonization of American Indians* (1992); *Struggle for the Land: Indigenous Resistance to Genocide, Ecocide, and Expropriation in North America* (1993); *Indians Are Us? Culture and Genocide in Native North America* (1994); *Since the Predator Came: Notes from the Struggle for American Indian Liberation*

(1995); and *A Little Matter of Genocide* (1997). He has also edited a number of important anthologies, including *Marxism and Native Americans* (1983) and *Cages of Steel: The Politics of Imprisonment in the United States* (1992). With WINONA LADUKE, he authored an important article on the nuclear industry, "Native North America: The Political Economy of Radioactive Colonialism" (1983).

An admirer of Cherokee anthropologist ROBERT K. THOMAS, Churchill generally refers to himself as an "indigenist," meaning one who believes in the rights of indigenous peoples as being paramount and who draws upon the traditions of indigenous peoples to criticize Western thought, in particular its attempts to colonize the indigenous world. Churchill borrows the term from the Latin American concept of *indigenismo* as articulated by the prominent Mexican anthropologist Bonfil Batalla. *Indigenismo* is itself a product of the Mexican leftist movements of the 1930s and Churchill's works more accurately reflect the perspectives of the modern American Left than traditional Indian thought. His most important work, *Agents of Repression* (1988), with Jim Vander Wall, is a detailed criticism of the FBI's policy of targeting and harassing American Indians and African-American activists during the Civil Rights era.

Churchill, along with Shawnee academic Glenn T. Morris, is a leader of the Colorado chapter of the AMERICAN INDIAN MOVEMENT (AIM), one of the few chapters still in existence and the only one that continues AIM's original militant bent. He also served as coordinator of American Indian Studies for the University of Colorado at Boulder.

In 2001, Churchill wrote "On the Justice of Roosting Chickens," an essay which argued that the September 11, 2001, attacks on the World Trade Center in New York and the Pentagon in Washington, D.C., were provoked by U.S. foreign policies. In the essay, Churchill questioned the innocence of some of the 9/11 victims, labeled some of them as "little Eichmanns," and made other inflammatory remarks. Further controversy arose in 2005 when Churchill was invited to speak at Hamilton College—an invitation that was rescinded after a widespread outcry. In response to the many complaints against him, the University of Colorado ordered an investigation of Churchill's writings, which found him to have engaged in "serious research misconduct," including falsifying and fabricating information and plagiarizing others. The university fired Churchill on July 24, 2007.

Further Reading

Churchill, Ward. *A Little Matter of Genocide: Holocaust and Denial in the Americas, 1492 to the Present.* San Francisco: City Lights Books, 1997.
———. *Marxism and Native Americans.* Boston: South End Press, 1983.
Churchill, Ward, and Jim Vander Wall. *Agents of Repression: The FBI's Secret War against the Black Panther Party and the American Indian Movement.* Boston: South End Press, 1988.
———. *The COINTELPRO Papers: Documents from the FBI's*

Secret Wars Against Domestic Dissent. Boston: South
   End Press, 1990.
Harjo, Suzan Shown. "Why Native Identity Matters: A
   Cautionary Tale." *Indian Country Today*, 16 February
   2006, Editorial page.

citizen bands

The designation *citizen bands* was applied to a number of tribes
that had been relocated, mainly from Ohio and Michigan, to
the territory of Kansas in the early 19th century. A few decades
after arriving in Kansas, many members of the Wyandot, Kaw,
Potawatomi, Piankashaw, Wea, Kaskaskia, Miami, and Peoria
accepted ALLOTMENT and U.S. CITIZENSHIP. (The majority of
American Indians did not become U.S. citizens until passage
of the Indian Citizenship Act of 1924.) A portion, however,
either at the time or somewhat later, opted to retain or recover
tribal status and moved to Indian Territory (later Oklahoma).
Most of the groups who stayed in Kansas were referred to as
citizen bands. Among the Kaw and the Potawatomi, however,
the citizen bands relocated to Oklahoma.

These splits were not only geographic, they represented
clashes between traditionals and acculturationists, and out of
them would grow conflicts over claims and other rights that
had belonged to the tribe as a whole prior to the splits (see, for
example, HURON CEMETERY DISPUTE). The most important of
those allotment treaties was that of February 23, 1867, but the
Wyandot had U.S. citizenship from 1855 and the Potawatomi
from 1861. The Kaw were removed to Oklahoma in 1873 without a treaty.

See also CONLEY, LYDA; CURTIS, CHARLES.

citizenship

At the start of the 20th century, only a small proportion of
Indians in the United States were citizens, these owing largely
to special agreements whereby certain tribes had accepted
allotted lands (see CITIZEN BANDS) or because they were not
full-blood wards and were certified "competent." ALLOTMENT
was a necessary but not sufficient condition for eligibility. The
BUREAU OF INDIAN AFFAIRS (BIA) decided which were "fit"
for citizenship, and through a special and somewhat absurd
ceremony, (including the shooting of "the last arrow" and
receiving a flag and a badge), inducted them into U.S. citizenship. By the time of America's entry into WORLD WAR I (1917),
approximately half of all Indians were citizens.

Because the major thrust of Indian policy in the Allotment
period was ASSIMILATION (see PRATT, RICHARD HENRY), and
because it was those Indians most successfully assimilated
who formed the nucleus of Indian organizations at the time,
it seemed to them a glaring discrepancy that half the nation's
Indians were denied the basic rights of all citizens. The millions of immigrants then joining the U.S. "melting pot" added
to their frustration. In truth, many Indians did not seek citizenship, either equating it with the forced breakup of the tribe
or rejecting it as a violation of their traditional SOVEREIGNTY.

An article in the SOCIETY OF AMERICAN INDIANS' (SAI)
American Indian Magazine (1918) asks: "Why, when a bill for
conferring citizenship upon Indians is introduced, do Congressmen immediately commence to make exceptions of the
Osage, the Five Civilized Tribes and the New York [Iroquois]
Indians?" The answer was that those Indians who maintained
a strong position of traditional sovereignty considered the
unilateral conferral of citizenship on the citizens of their own
nation a violation of their own sovereignty. (See GENERAL,
LEVI, and LYONS, OREN, JR.) Some to this day do not acknowledge U.S. citizenship.

After World War I, in which so many Indians (mainly
volunteers) had served so gallantly for a country in which they
did not enjoy the most basic rights, furor over this issue only
increased. Bills introduced by Congressman Carl Hayden and
CHARLES DAVID CARTER in 1918 would have granted citizenship to all allotted Indians. A bill introduced by Carter in 1919
granted citizenship, *if wanted*, to Indians who had served in
the war.

The SAI effectively dissolved after 1923, but its campaign
for citizenship was continued by a related organization, the
American Indian Association (see STRONGWOLF, JOSEPH),
and in the following year this goal was achieved. By an act
of Congress (43 Stat. 253) of June 2, 1924, originally drafted
by Samuel L. Brosius of the INDIAN RIGHTS ASSOCIATION,
all Indians born within the country's territorial limits were
declared citizens of the United States.

Though the drive for Indian citizenship was led by an
elite group of assimilationists and their supporters, who had
no faith in the doctrine of tribal sovereignty and of whom
many were actively antitribal, it is probable that a majority
of Indians desired it, as it was seen as the primary means of
advancement.

However, conferral of citizenship was a unilateral act
of Congress, not an agreement with tribes. It implied a
view of the Indian nations as national minorities denied
civil rights rather than nations exercising sovereignty in a
government-to-government relationship. Subsequent to the
1924 Indian Citizenship Act, it was gradually established in
law that the citizenship of individual Indians in no way altered
the government-to-government relationship with the United
States founded on the sovereignty of the tribes, which long pre-
dates that of the United States; and indeed that in matters of
civil rights, tribal jurisdiction should take precedence over the
federal. The majority of Indians today accept the idea of dual
citizenship.

See also INDIAN CIVIL RIGHTS ACT OF 1968.

Further Reading

Kawashima, Yasuhide. "Strangers in Their Own Land:
   American Indian Citizenship in the United States." *Alizes*
   (French publication), special issue (April 2001): 105–113.
Porter, Robert B. "The Demise of Ongwehoweh and the Rise
   of the Native Americans: Redressing the Genocidal Act of
   Forcing American Citizenship upon Indigenous Peoples."
   Harvard Black Letter Law Journal 15 (1999): 107–183.

Clark, Joseph (Jocko Clark) (1893–1971) *Cherokee U.S. naval officer*

A Cherokee, Joseph Clark was born in a log cabin in Chelsea, Indian Territory (now Oklahoma) on November 12, 1893. His father, William A. Clark, was raised and educated in the Cherokee Indian Orphan Asylum in Salina, Indian Territory. Jocko Clark's mother, Mary Polly Ward Clark, died during childbirth a few years after he was born. After graduating from the U.S. Naval Academy at Annapolis in 1917, the first Native American to achieve this, Clark saw convoy duty in WORLD WAR I aboard the armored cruiser USS *North Carolina*. In 1921, Clark was assigned his first command, the destroyer USS *Brooks*. He became an aviator in 1925, one of the few officers to specialize in naval aviation at the time. In 1931, he was appointed to command the fighter squadron on the navy's first modern aircraft carrier, the *Lexington*.

During the first year of WORLD WAR II, Clark was the air officer of the *Lexington* and then the *Yorktown*. In September 1942, now a captain, he fitted out the new escort carrier *Suwannee* and commanded it during Operation Torch, the attack on North Africa. In April 1943, he was given command of the brand-new *Yorktown* and participated in the assaults of Marcus Island in August, Wake Island in October, and the Gilbert Islands in November 1943.

On January 26, 1944, Clark was appointed rear admiral and took command of a task force of fast aircraft carriers. From his flagship, the *Hornet*, he participated in virtually every major naval engagement in the Pacific, from the liberation of the Marianas to the end of the war. Commanding Task Force 58.1, Clark led the bombardment of the islands of Tinian, Saipan, Guam, and Rota in June 1944. On June 19, his task force participated in the Battle of the Philippine Sea, one of the decisive battles of the war, and destroyed what was left of Japanese naval airpower in the "Marianas Turkey Shoot," as the air combat was commonly known. The next day his task force found the Japanese fleet and sank the carrier *Hiyo* and two tankers, but the encounter ended while the sun was setting and the American planes were forced to try to return to the carriers in the dark—an almost impossible task at that time. Clark achieved fame by ignoring the potential danger to the fleet and brazenly ordering his task force to light up the skies with search beams, ensuring that his pilots got back safely.

When his superior officer, Vice Admiral Marc "Pete" Mitscher was rotated out of combat duty, Clark chose not to serve under his replacement, Vice Admiral John Sidney McCain, Sr., and was given shore duty in September 1944. During his time in the United States, Clark was an adviser to the film *The Fighting Lady*, about carrier warfare. Clark returned to action in February 1944 and led a strike on Tokyo. His task force then provided air and gunnery support for the bloody assault on Iwo Jima (see HAYES, IRA) in late February and early March. After more strikes on Tokyo, Clark's forces provided support for the amphibious assault on Okinawa in April. On April 6, his task force participated in the sinking of the battleship *Yamato* and its accompanying fleet, finishing off the Japanese Navy as an effective fighting force. His fighting spirit earned him the Navy Cross, the Distinguished Service Medal, the Silver Star, and the Legion of Merit Medal.

After the war ended, Clark commanded a number of carrier groups and naval air bases, finally becoming commander of the Seventh Fleet during the Korean War. A blunt, energetic officer and an outspoken proponent of air power, he wrote *Sea Power and Its Meaning* (1966) and an autobiography, *Carrier Admiral* (1967).

Clark retired from the navy in 1953 with the rank of full admiral, the highest-ranking military official of Indian descent in the 20th century. He then became head of a construction and investment firm in New York City and was made an honorary chief of the Cherokee nation. He died on July 13, 1971, in New York City and is buried in Arlington National Cemetery. On May 9, 1980, the navy commissioned a guided missile frigate, named the USS *Clark* in his honor.

Further Reading

Reynolds, Clark G. *On the Warpath in the Pacific: Admiral Jocko Clark and the Fast Carriers.* Annapolis, Md.: Naval Institute Press, 2005.

Cleghorn, Mildred (Mildred Imoch) (1910–1997) *Chiricahua Apache leader*

A Chiricahua Apache, Mildred Imoch, later Cleghorn, was born to Richard Imoch and Amy Warren on December 11, 1910, at Fort Sill, Oklahoma, where her parents were confined as prisoners of war. After the capture of Chiricahua leader Geronimo, he and nearly 400 of his people were imprisoned in Florida in September 1886. In 1894, they were transferred to Fort Sill. The Department of War was originally supposed to turn Fort Sill, which was slated for abandonment, over to the Chiricahua under an 1897 executive order that also procured an additional 27,000 acres for the fort, for the benefit of the Apache. The entire post, comprising more than 50,000 acres, was itself carved out of the Kiowa, Comanche, and Apache reservation, and it had therefore been assumed that it would revert back to Indian use once it was no longer needed. But in 1903, the military decided to keep the post for themselves, and so the Fort Sill Apache, as they became known, were kept on the post in military confinement and not set free until 1913. Those Chiricahua so desiring were removed to New Mexico, but those who chose to remain in Oklahoma were placed on allotments of deceased Kiowa and Comanche.

Cleghorn later remembered her first moments of freedom, when she and her family left Fort Sill in a horse-drawn wagon. She was three years old when her family settled on a 40-acre plot near Apache, Oklahoma. "The families weren't allowed to live together," Cleghorn said. "So they scattered us all over. If we wanted to go visit someone, it would be an all-day trip. I guess they were afraid of another uprising." After having established a thriving cattle industry on the post, the Chiricahua were spread apart and the herd sold off. They quickly became destitute and also began to lose their cultural and social identity, as they were unable to practice their traditions and had no recognized government.

Mildred Imoch, as she was then known, went to public school in Apache, Oklahoma, before attending the Haskell Indian Institute in Lawrence, Kansas. She then took a position at the Kansas office of the Bureau of Indian Affairs (BIA). While working for the Pawnee tribe, she met Bill Cleghorn, a Mescalero Apache, and married him on the Mescalero reservation in New Mexico. She left the BIA in 1937 to continue her education, enrolling at Oklahoma State University and graduating in 1941. She then taught home economics at the Fort Sill Indian School and at the Riverside Indian School in Anadarko, Oklahoma. In the meantime, the Fort Sill Apache began to meet informally to try to put the tribe back together. During the 1950s, an attempt to terminate the tribe galvanized them into action. Cleghorn participated in the Fort Sill Apache Tribal Committee, as the informal tribal government was known, and helped to fend off Termination. She also began to advocate a cultural revival of Apache traditions. Overcoming their distrust of the BIA, the Apache began to work with the agency to establish a formal tribal government.

During 1972–74, Cleghorn served as the national director of education for the North American Indian Women's Association. By then she was the de facto head of the tribe. On October 30, 1976, a constitution and bylaws were finally ratified, and Cleghorn was elected chair of the Fort Sill Chiricahua/Warm Springs Apache Tribe. She served for 18 years, retiring in 1995. During her tenure, the Apache embarked on a successful program of cultural preservation, including the reacquisition of sacred sites.

After her retirement, Cleghorn was appointed to the Oklahoma Indian Affairs Commission. In 1996, she became one of the lead plaintiffs in a class-action suit against the U.S. government for mismanagement of Indian money held in trust. The suit, filed on behalf of more than 300,000 Indians who had trust fund accounts with the BIA, charged that the federal government had mismanaged Indian money and destroyed important documents. Also in 1996, on the anniversary of the terrorist bombing of the Murraugh federal office building in Oklahoma City, Cleghorn helped to read the 168 names of the bombing victims in the company of Governor Bill Anoatubby of the Chickasaw Nation and other tribal leaders.

Mildred Cleghorn died on April 15, 1997, from injuries suffered in a car accident not far from her home in Apache, Oklahoma.

Further Reading

Stockel, H. Henrietta. *Chiricahua Apache Women and Children: Safekeepers of the Heritage*. College Station: Texas A & M University Press, 2000.

———. *Women of the Apache Nation: Voices of Truth*. Reno: University of Nevada Press, 1991.

Chippewa educator and social worker Elizabeth Bender Cloud holds her granddaughter in 1950, when she was chosen "American Mother of the Year" by the American Mothers Committee. *(AP/Wideworld)*

Cloud, Elizabeth Bender (Elizabeth Georgian Bender) (1888–1965) *Chippewa educator, social worker*

Elizabeth Georgian Bender was born on April 2, 1887, at Fosston, Minnesota, on the White Earth Reservation, the daughter of a Chippewa woman and a German homesteader. Her sister, Anna Bender, was the first Chippewa woman to graduate from Hampton Institute, and her brother, "Chief" Charles Albert Bender, became a famous baseball player.

Beginning her education at the Philadelphia Home School, an Episcopal school for Indians, Bender later attended the Hampton Institute in Virginia. After graduation she worked as a teacher among the Blackfeet in Montana and at Carlisle. Afterward, she attended the University of Wichita and the University of Kansas. Active in the Society of American Indians, Bender met Winnebago Henry Clarence Roe Cloud at the organization's 1914 conference. The following year, she helped him set up the American Indian Institute in Wichita, and she would later assist in running it. They were married on June 12, 1916.

Elizabeth Bender Cloud raised five children in Wichita and Lawrence, Kansas, during the 1920s and 1930s; she lived at the Umatilla Agency in Oregon from 1939 to 1948, and thereafter in West Linn, a suburb of Portland, Oregon. In 1940, President Roosevelt appointed her a delegate to the White House Conference on Youth and Children. She was one of the very few veterans of the old Society of American Indians to become involved with the new NATIONAL CONGRESS OF AMERICAN INDIANS (NCAI), founded in 1944. After the sudden death of her husband in February 1950, she came to play an increasingly important role in the Indian politics of the day, including the ultimately successful fight against TERMINATION.

Named "Mother of the Year" at the 1950 Washington Conference on Women and Children, Elizabeth Bender Cloud enjoyed the benefit of a prominent national spotlight. After the conference, she, fellow NCAI member RUTH MUSKRAT BRONSON, and D'ARCY MCNICKLE, founder of American Indian Development (AID), began devising an action program on community development to be administered through AID. In order to collect funds for AID, McNickle got the NCAI to create a tax-exempt branch, Arrow, Inc. (see ROGERS, WILLIAM VANN). As one of the initiators of the idea and director of AID for several years herself, Cloud played a key role in launching the kind of community development work that offered Indians the ability to make decisions affecting their own lives and to extricate themselves from the straitjacket of BUREAU OF INDIAN AFFAIRS paternalism.

By no means a radical, Cloud, in a speech at the 1951 NCAI conference, urged Indians to be individually responsible "partners in democracy" to solve some of the problems confronting them as a group. "We are American Indians but, even more, we are Americans."

Cloud founded the Oregon Trails Club in Pendleton, one of two Indian women's clubs in the nation. It was affiliated with the Oregon Federation of Women's Clubs. After serving as chair of Indian welfare for the Oregon Federation, she was national chair of Indian affairs for the GENERAL FEDERATION OF WOMEN'S CLUBS (GFWC) from about 1950 to 1958. Much in demand as a speaker at women's clubs around the country, Cloud used her position to act as a kind of low-profile liaison between the NCAI and the general public. In 1952, for example, the Indian Affairs committee's agenda expressed concern for public education about Indian needs and culture, and focused on lobbying. "Keep your congressmen alert and responsive to legislation regarding the Indian," she urged state federations of women's clubs. In 1954, during the worst days of Termination, she explained her activities in more detail: "We have stressed legislation and kept 29 [GFWC] state chairmen informed of the major issues affecting the Indians." In addition, the state GFWC organizations collected and distributed money for college scholarships for Indian students.

During the mid-1950s, Cloud worked for the Field Foundation on a project to aid Indian people in the Southwest. She was a member of the National Grange and the National Conference of Social Workers. Elizabeth Bender Cloud died on September 16, 1965, after a long illness.

Cloud, Henry Clarence Roe (Wo-Na-Xi-Lay Hunkah) (1884–1950) *Winnebago educator, minister*

Henry Clarence Cloud, or Wo-Na-Xi-Lay Hunkah ("War Chief"), was born in a tipi on the Winnebago Reservation in Nebraska on December 28, 1884. He began his education at the Indian School at Genoa, Nebraska, then transferred to Santee Normal Training School at Santee, Nebraska, where he learned printing and blacksmithing and became a Christian. From there, he went to Mount Hermon, a college preparatory school at Northfield, Massachusetts. He graduated in 1906 and was accepted at Yale University.

Cloud met Walter and Mary Roe, nationally respected workers in Indian affairs, when they came to speak at Yale. They were Reformed missionaries at John Seger's Colony in Oklahoma, a subagency, boarding school, and farm for the Cheyenne and Arapaho. The Roes took Cloud under their wing, and he spent the summers with them at Colony and later at Winnebago, adopting the name Roe as a sign of admiration.

Henry Roe Cloud went on to become the most educated Indian of his time. He received a B.A. in psychology and philosophy in 1910 as the first Indian ever graduated from Yale. That same year, he was a keynote speaker at the Lake Mohonk Conference, an annual gathering of non-Indian religious and social organizations interested in the reform of Indian affairs, held on Lake Mohonk in upstate New York. Interested in social science, Cloud went on to study sociology and anthropology at Oberlin College in Ohio, then attended the Auburn Theological Seminary in Auburn, New York. While studying there, he simultaneously did graduate work in anthropology at Yale, receiving an M.A. in 1912. In 1913, he graduated from Auburn and was ordained a Presbyterian minister.

In 1911, Cloud became the youngest of the Native leaders to emerge at the founding convention of the SOCIETY OF AMERICAN INDIANS (SAI). He met Elizabeth Bender (Chippewa [Ojibway]), sister of famous baseball player CHARLES BENDER, at the 1914 SAI conference. They were married on June 12, 1916 (see CLOUD, ELIZABETH BENDER). Cloud was the society's vice president for education in 1915 and 1916. Unlike many other SAI members, Cloud was active in the affairs of his own tribe. The use of peyote in the services of the NATIVE AMERICAN CHURCH, a divisive issue in the society, was widespread on the Winnebago reservation. Though against peyote use himself, Cloud was relatively tolerant, an approach reflecting his even-tempered, balanced personality. He did not ignore the fact that peyote eliminated the desire for alcohol and that some of the most capable and educated people at Winnebago were members of the NATIVE AMERICAN CHURCH.

Of all the SAI's leading figures, Cloud was one of the few who played a significant role in the reformulation of federal Indian policy in the 1920s, and he and his wife were perhaps the only ones to make the transition to the new thinking of the 1930s (see INDIAN REORGANIZATION ACT). His greatest contribution would be in the area of Indian education.

In 1914, Cloud was member of a federal commission surveying government Indian schools. In 1915, with the support of philanthropists such as Denver's William E. Sweet, he founded the Roe Indian Institute at Wichita, Kansas, a preparatory school for Indian boys, operated in conjunction with Fairmount College. The idea went back to 1908, when Cloud had first discussed it with the Roes. It was named in memory of Walter Roe, though later the name was changed to the American Indian Institute. The only Indian high school in the country, it survived to 1931. Its first graduate (1919) was Harry Coons, later president of the Pawnee Tribal Council (1927).

Cloud was also a member of the standing COMMITTEE OF ONE HUNDRED on Indian affairs (1923). As sociologist FAYETTE AVERY MCKENZIE pointed out, the committee's resolutions generally resembled those of the old SAI. However, they set in motion a reform process that resulted in something quite different. This difference could already be seen in the 1928 MERIAM REPORT. Cloud was a staff member on a survey of Indian affairs conducted by the Institute for Government Research (1926–27), which provided the data for the Meriam Report. In addition, he was the only Indian on the Brookings Institution research panel that prepared this famous report.

In 1931, Cloud discontinued the American Indian Institute to work for the BUREAU OF INDIAN AFFAIRS (BIA) under CHARLES JAMES RHOADS as field representative-at-large for Indian education. In June 1932, Cloud received the degree of Doctor of Divinity from the College of Emporia (Illinois). In 1933, he was appointed superintendent of the Indian school at Haskell, Kansas, but left in 1934 when Commissioner of Indian Affairs JOHN COLLIER gave him the special assignment of meeting with tribal leaders, mainly in North and South Dakota, about the new Indian Reorganization Act.

In 1935, Cloud received the third Annual Achievement Award of the Indian Council Fire in Chicago. The following year, he was appointed supervisor of Indian education for the BIA. In 1939, he went to Pendleton, Oregon, to serve as superintendent of the Umatilla Agency. This was the period of construction of hydroelectric dams on the Columbia River, a time of great hardship for the Umatilla and other local tribes, whose culture and traditions were based on fishing for salmon in the Columbia River.

During the 1930s, Cloud played a very active role on the Committee on the American Indian of the National Conference on Social Work, which after 1936 was no longer a committee but a distinct organization known as the Forum on the American Indian, open to Indians and non-Indians.

For the last few years of his life, Roe worked at the Portland Area Office of the BIA, tracing family histories to determine who among Oregon coastal Indians were eligible for payments from a court award of some $16 million in compensation for land taken by the government. He died of a heart attack on February 9, 1950, at Siletz, Oregon.

See also EDUCATIONAL POLICY, AMERICAN INDIANS AND.

Further Reading

Crum, Steven J. "Henry Roe Cloud, a Winnebago Indian Reformer: His Quest for American Indian Higher Education." *Kansas History* 11, no. 3 (1988): 171–184.
Pfister, Joel. *The Yale Indian: The Education of Henry Roe Cloud.* Raleigh, N.C.: Duke University Press, 2009.
Ramirez, Renya K. "Henry Roe Cloud: A Granddaughter's Native Feminist Biographical Account." *Wicazo Sa Review* 24, no. 2 (Fall 2009): 77–103.
Tetzloff, Jason M. "*To do some good among the Indians*": *Henry Roe Cloud and Twentieth Century Native American Advocacy.* Ph.D. diss., Purdue University, 1996.

code talkers

Code talkers were special U.S. military units made up of American Indians whose mission was to transmit secret messages in codes created using their own Indian languages. The first known use of Indian code talkers was in WORLD WAR I. Choctaw soldiers transmitted telephone messages, in Choctaw, for the 142nd Infantry Regiment, 36th Division, on October 26, 1918, ordering the withdrawal of two brigades from the German-held Vaux-Champagne region of France. Two days later, Choctaw code talkers coordinated an assault that overwhelmed the German troops at Forest Ferme. Eighteen Choctaw code talkers served with the 36th Division and helped the U.S. Expeditionary Force win several key battles in the Meuse-Argonne Campaign. The success of the 142nd led other regiments to enlist the aid of Indians, and Comanche, Osage, Cheyenne, Cherokee, and Sioux worked as secure telephone operators and messengers.

In 1940, as the U.S. entry into WORLD WAR II appeared imminent, the army began to reestablish Indian code-talking units. The units, generally consisting of between 15 and 20 men, were usually trained at Fort Benning, Georgia, developing a code based around indigenous languages. Since many military terms did not exist in these languages, substitutes had to be devised. In Comanche, for example, *turtle* was the word for *tank*, *stovepipe* for *bazooka*, and the name for Hitler was *posah-tai-vo*, or "crazy white man." Initially Chippewa, Oneida, Comanche, and Sac and Fox code-talking units were formed. After the Japanese bombing of Pearl Harbor in 1941, new units of Hopi, Assiniboine, Cherokee, Choctaw, Kiowa, Pawnee, Sioux (both Dakota and Lakota), Menominee, Creek, and Seminole code talkers were created. These units served in both the European and Pacific theaters of the war. Among the most successful of the army units was the Comanche Signal Corps, which took part in the D-day assault on northern France in 1944 and coordinated the landing on Utah Beach.

The largest and most celebrated code-talking unit of all was the Navajo Code Talkers. The idea originated with a non-Indian engineer, Phillip Johnston, who had been raised on the Navajo (Dineh) Reservation and was fluent in Navajo. Johnston was aware that Native languages had been successfully used in World War I by the U.S. Army, and he believed that the Navajo could perform the same service for the U.S. Marines. Early in 1942, Johnston met with Major General Clayton B. Vogel, the commanding general of Amphibious Corps, Pacific Fleet, and his staff in an attempt to convince them of the Navajo language's value as code. On February 28, 1942, Johnston staged a demonstration in which two pairs of Navajo encoded, transmitted, and then decoded a three-line

English message in 20 seconds. Machines of the time would have required 30 minutes to perform the same job. Convinced, General Vogel recommended to the commandant of the Marine Corps that the marines begin a code-talking unit. By April 1942, the Marines had selected 29 Navajo, some as young as 15, to train at Camp Pendleton in Oceanside, California.

The first group, fluent in both Navajo and English, developed the code among themselves using Navajo words, such as *wollachee* (ant) for the letter A and *shush* (bear) for the letter B. The code was complex, with Code Talkers alternating words for letters as well as substituting similar Navajo words to stand for objects, airplanes, or warships for which there was no word in Navajo. The men underwent extensive training in receiving and transmitting messages. Two of them became instructors and another two recruiters. The remainder were sent to Australia to join the 1st Marine Division for the assault on the Pacific island of Guadalcanal on August 7, 1942. In December, when the 1st Marine Division was finally withdrawn from Guadalcanal, the division's commander, Major General Alexander A. Vandegrift, was so impressed by the Code Talkers' performance that he requisitioned the Marine Corps for 83 additional Navajo to be assigned to his division. Another 200 Navajo were recruited over the next year to become Code Talkers, all of them training at Camp Pendleton.

Navajo Code Talkers served in all six Marine divisions assigned to the Pacific and participated in every major Marine operation, including the invasions of the Solomons, the Marianas, and Peleliu. They distinguished themselves in the ferocious assault on Iwo Jima (now Iwo To), where the entire military operation (see HAYES, IRA) was directed through the Navajo. Major Howard Connor, 5th Marine Division signal officer, declared, "Were it not for the Navajos, the Marines would never have taken Iwo Jima." Connor had six Navajo Code Talkers working around the clock during the first two days of the battle, and they sent and received more than 800 messages without fail.

A total of 421 Navajo served in the code-talking unit, including the artist Carl Gorman, father of R. C. GORMAN, and future Navajo tribal chairman PETER MACDONALD. Not one of the 17 Indian code-talking units in the U.S. Army and the U.S. Marines ever had their codes broken, and their success in World War II led their important role to be kept a military secret until it was declassified in 1969.

Further Reading

Aaseng, Nathan. *Navajo Code Talkers: America's Secret Weapon in World War II.* New York: Walker & Company, 1992.
Durrett, Deanne. *Unsung Heroes of World War II: The Story of the Navajo Code Talkers.* New York: Facts On File, 1998.
McClain, Sally. *Navajo Weapon: The Navajo Code Talkers.* Tucson, Ariz.: Rio Nuevo Publishers, 2002.
Meadows, William C. *The Comanche Code Talkers of World War II.* Austin: University of Texas Press, 2003.
Paul, Doris Atkinson. *The Navajo Code Talkers.* Philadelphia: Dorrance, 1973.

Cody, Iron Eyes (Oscar Cody, Oscar DeCorti, Espera DeCorti) (1904–1999) *Screen actor, stuntman*

Although for some 70 years, Iron Eyes Cody claimed to be of Cherokee and Cree descent, the son of Oklahoma Cherokee Thomas Long Plume, rumors surfaced around 1985 that he was not an Indian at all. In the 1990s, it was discovered that his real parents were Sicilian immigrants: Francesca Salpietra, who arrived in New Orleans in 1902, and Antonio DeCorti, who had come shortly before that. They soon left New Orleans to work in the Louisiana sugarcane fields, and Cody was born on April 3, 1904, in the small town of Kaplan in the parish of Vermilion, the second of their four children. His real name was Espera DeCorti, but he was usually called Oscar.

The family, though very poor, started a small grocery in Gueydan, Louisiana. In 1909, persecuted by an organized crime ring known as the Black Hand, Antonio DeCorti ran away to Orange, Texas. A short time later, Francesca married Alton Abshire, with whom she had five more children. Several years later, the couple came to Orange to work briefly in the oil refineries. Returning to Gueydan less than a year later, they left the three DeCorti boys with their natural father, who, under the name Tony Corti, later managed a poolroom in Houston. He died in 1924 at age 45.

Oscar, now about 15, went with his brothers to California. There they changed their last name to Cody, and Oscar, who had been fascinated with all things Indian since boyhood, now "turned 100 percent Indian," in the words of his half sister May Abshire. He began working in films, as did his brothers until they went into other lines of work. (Frank Cody was killed in a hit-and-run accident in 1949; Joe Cody died in 1978.)

Although Cody appeared as an extra as early as 1919 in the silent *Back to God's Country*, one of his earliest credited roles was in Cecil B. DeMille's *The Road to Yesterday* (1925). In all, Cody performed in more than 100 Hollywood films, including *Fort Osage* and *Montana Belle* (both 1952), *Sitting Bull* (1954), *The Great Sioux Massacre* (1965), *Nevada Smith* (1966), *A Man Called Horse* (1970), *Grayeagle* (1978), and (his last role) *Ernest Goes to Camp* (1987). He also made guest appearances in television Westerns such as *Bonanza*, *Gunsmoke*, and *Rawhide*.

In 1936, Cody married Ga Yeawas (Bertha "Birdie" Parker, Seneca), daughter of ARTHUR C. PARKER and granddaughter of scenario writer and silent-screen actress Dove Eye Dark Cloud. They adopted two Cherokee boys. Iron Eyes appeared regularly with Ga Yeawas on the *Iron Eyes Tipi* television show out of Los Angeles. She died in 1978.

Cody created his most powerful public image in a public-service television spot for Keep America Beautiful, Inc., first broadcast on Earth Day 1971 (see ENVIRONMENTAL MOVEMENT, AMERICAN INDIANS AND THE). Paddling a canoe in one scene, walking down a road in another, he played a traditional Indian of bygone days who returns to once-pristine environments only to find them fouled with garbage, litter, and pollution. In a final closeup, a tear is seen in his eyes. Though there is a voice-over by actor William Conrad, Cody has no speaking part—as in the old days of silent films, the message is carried entirely by his face. Though sentimental, the appeal

Actors Iron Eyes Cody and George Montgomery at an award ceremony in Los Angeles in 1986. *(AP/Wideworld)*

was so effective that Cody became identified with the campaign, and for the rest of his life he continued to give public appearances and talks to schoolchildren on its behalf. Sequels appeared in 1975 and 1998.

Cody was an expert practitioner of all the skills needed by a specialist in Indian roles. He was a fluent communicator in Plains Indian sign language, a champion archer, and an expert Indian dancer. He was also an avid photographer and photographed many Indian ceremonials, "where allowed" (as he noted) throughout the United States, developing and printing the pictures in his basement darkroom.

Cody's Moosehead Museum, which was open to the public, was housed in his basement and featured his collection of artifacts, costumes, books, paintings, one of the best private Indian collections in the United States. He wrote several newspaper and magazine articles on the American Indian, as well as the book *Indian Sign Talk in Pictures* (1970).

For an astonishing period of 80 years, Cody loved, respected, and portrayed American Indians and actively participated in the development of the Hollywood Native American community. Thus, he lost neither their respect nor their friendship when his true identity became known. In fact, he was honored on February 11, 1995, at the third annual awards of First Americans in the Arts, an organization that promotes the participation and recognizes the achievements

of American Indians in the entertainment industry with their Trustee Award. During the presentation, it was emphasized several times that the award was being given to Cody as a "non-Native," even though Cody himself always maintained that he was an Indian.

In his last years, Cody suffered a stroke that left him paralyzed. He died of natural causes at his home in Los Angeles on January 4, 1999.

Further Reading

Aleiss, Angela. "Native Son." *Times Picayune* (New Orleans), 26 May 1996, D1.

Russell, Ron. "Make-Believe Indian." *New Times* (Los Angeles), 8 April 1999, 14–21.

Cohen, Felix Solomon (1907–1953) *attorney, philosopher, authority on federal Indian law*

Born in New York City on July 3, 1907, Felix S. Cohen was the son of the philosopher Morris R. Cohen, at that time professor of mathematics at the City College of New York, and Mary Ryshpan Cohen, a former schoolteacher also trained in philosophy. Felix grew up in an unusually stimulating intellectual environment. His father, who later became one of the best-known American philosophers, counted among his friends jurist Roscoe Pound, philosopher Bertrand Russell, and physicist Albert Einstein.

After attending schools in Yonkers and New York City, Cohen did his undergraduate work at City College and graduate work in philosophy at Harvard University. He entered Columbia Law School in 1928, received his Ph.D. from Harvard in 1929, and earned his LL.B. from Columbia in 1931. That same year, after being accepted as research assistant to a New York Supreme Court judge, he married Lucy M. Kramer.

In 1933, Harold Ickes became secretary of the interior in Franklin D. Roosevelt's new administration and chose Nathan Margold as his solicitor. Margold asked Cohen to come to Washington to help draft legislation giving Indian tribes greater authority over their own affairs. This eventually became the INDIAN REORGANIZATION ACT of 1934. Cohen also helped draft a model tribal constitution. (See INDIAN NEW DEAL; COLLIER, JOHN.)

Originally hired as assistant solicitor, Cohen was soon promoted to associate solicitor. He administered a staff of approximately 250 lawyers, his duties covering not only Indian affairs but the entire range of Interior Department responsibilities.

Cohen's first book, *Ethical Systems and Legal Ideals*, his Harvard dissertation, was published in 1933. In it, he argued that a legal system must be based on a system of ethical norms, a principle he would soon put into practice in the drafting and administration of federal Indian law.

In 1939, Cohen was "loaned" to the Department of Justice for one year to head a survey of federal Indian law. With the help of Theodore Haas, he compiled a collection of federal laws and treaties relating to Indians, totaling 46 volumes, which became the basis of his classic *Handbook of Federal Indian Law*, published in 1942. He also helped set up the INDIAN CLAIMS COMMISSION in 1946.

In 1947, the federal government officially embarked on its TERMINATION policy, with the aim of ending the legal existence of all tribes and ending federal services to Indians. An opponent of the policy, Cohen resigned from the Interior Department on January 2, 1948, and turned to private practice.

In July 1948, in one of his first cases, Cohen secured for Indians the right to vote in two of the last states that had denied it to them, Arizona and New Mexico. He successfully defended the right of Indians to Social Security benefits (*Arizona v. Hobby*, D.C. Cir.) and to attend public schools in southern California (*Acosta v. County of San Diego*). He was made a member of the Blackfeet tribe and named Double Runner for the speed with which he secured civil rights for Indians. Cohen was such a formidable opponent of Termination that, in the early 1950s, Indian Commissioner DILLON SEYMOUR MYER attempted to destroy his career. Instead, Myer himself was removed in March 1953.

During the last seven years of his life, Cohen kept up an extremely demanding schedule. He not only maintained an active legal practice in Washington and served as counsel to the ASSOCIATION ON AMERICAN INDIAN AFFAIRS, but was also a visiting professor at Harvard and City College.

Cohen died of lung cancer on October 19, 1953, in Washington. His *Federal Handbook* met a strange fate. Though already considered the standard work on the subject, in the new context of Termination it was an embarrassment to the government. The Interior Department therefore had it "revised," under the pretext that it was outdated. In reality, it was rewritten. The new version, which appeared in 1958 and was later reissued by two other publishers, was still called Felix Cohen's *Handbook of Federal Indian Law* and enjoyed the authority of Cohen's actual work, but it was quite different. Cohen's original handbook emphasized tribal sovereignty, but the new work emphasized the idea that federal plenary power could always overrule tribal sovereignty (see SOVEREIGNTY, INDIGENOUS AND TRIBAL). After the failure of Termination and its revocation by President Richard Nixon in July 1970, the genuine text of Cohen's *Handbook* was reprinted in 1971 by the American Indian Law Center at the University of New Mexico.

No one can deny the high intellectual caliber of Felix Cohen's contribution to federal Indian law or the passion for justice that motivated him. He found Indian law, in the words of former Supreme Court justice Felix Frankfurter, "a vast hodgepodge of treaties, statutes, judicial and administrative rulings, and unrecorded practice in which the intricacies and complexities, confusion and injustices of the law governing Indians lay concealed," and left it a unified body of law with consistent doctrines and clear constitutional foundations. Cohen's work represents a monumental step in the recognition of Indian rights as integrated into and supported by the legal traditions of the United States.

Further Reading

Kehoe, Alice. *A Passion for the True and Just: Felix and Lucy Kramer Cohen and the Indian New Deal.* Tucson: University of Arizona Press, 2014.

Martin, Jill E. "The Miner's Canary: Felix S. Cohen's Philosophy of Indian Rights." *American Indian Law Review* 23 (1998–99): 165.

Soifer, Aviam. "Descent." *Florida State University Law Review* 29 (2001): 269–276.

Tsuk Mitchell, Dalia. *Architect of Justice: Felix S. Cohen and the Founding of American Legal Pluralism.* Ithaca, N.Y.: Cornell University Press, 2007.

Tsuk, Dalia. "'A Double Runner': Felix S. Cohen and the Indian New Deal." *Political and Legal Anthropology Review* 25, no. 1 (2002): 48–68.

Collier, John (1884–1968) *sociologist, Indian rights advocate, commissioner of the Bureau of Indian Affairs*

John Collier was born in Atlanta, Georgia, on May 4, 1884, the son of Charles A. Collier, a banker and later mayor of the city, and Susie Rawson Collier. After attending public school in Atlanta, he studied literature and drama at Columbia University (1902), marine zoology at Woods Hole (1902–05) in Massachusetts, and psychology at the College de France in Paris (1906–07).

Collier passed his formative years in Progressive-era New

In 1938, Commissioner of Indian Affairs John Collier *(center)* with two survivors of the Wounded Knee Massacre of 1890, Dewey Beard *(left)* and James Pipe-on-Head. *(AP/Wideworld)*

York City, as a social worker among the city's European immigrants. He was greatly influenced by the communitarian, cooperative ideas of William Morris, Peter Kropotkin, sociologist Lester Frank Ward, and James Peter Warbasse, leader of the cooperative movement (which sought to develop consumer, producer, and residential cooperatives). He knew Warbasse from the People's Institute in New York City, a "school without walls" that provided college-level lectures, mainly to the working poor, where Collier was civic secretary from 1909 to 1919. In his memoirs, Collier mentions "the technics [*sic*] and inspiration of the distributive cooperative movement" for which Warbasse is best known, as but "one of a hundred items" that he thought contributed to the INDIAN NEW DEAL. Between 1913 and 1915, Collier became a regular at Mabel Dodge's Greenwich Village salon where he met the writer Mary Austin and where his own topic of discussion was always "some phase of the problem of community."

In 1919–20, Collier directed California's adult education program. In late 1920, he traveled to Taos, New Mexico,

to visit Dodge (now Dodge Luhan—she had married Taos Pueblo Indian Tony Luhan in 1918), and Austin, who had relocated there. Like them, Collier became fascinated by traditional Pueblo Indian culture. At first, he shared the usual assumption that this communal, ceremonial, ecologically based culture was disappearing, but soon realized that it was very much alive. Indeed, he became convinced that this culture held the secret to what was missing in American society—a strong sense of community. These ideas, along with a realization of the need for radical changes in Indian policy, took form during 1921–22, a year that Collier spent teaching social science at San Francisco State Teachers' College, and were first publicized in an article in *Survey* magazine in October 1922 at the start of the BURSUM BILL land-rights controversy.

In May 1922, the GENERAL FEDERATION OF WOMEN'S CLUBS sent Collier to New Mexico to investigate the Pueblo situation, with regard to the Bursum bill. To aid the pueblos in their struggle to regain their lands, he founded the American

Indian Defense Association (AIDA) on March 2, 1923. Collier served as executive secretary, with the young Adolph Berle, Jr., as legal counsel (Berle was later replaced by Lewis Marshall and then Nathan Margold). Collier held this position until his appointment as commissioner of the BUREAU OF INDIAN AFFAIRS (BIA) in 1933.

In 1923, through AIDA and with the help of Judge Richard H. Hanna, Collier began a campaign for legislation on TAOS BLUE LAKE (a sacred site), demanding exclusive use of the 30,000-acre Blue Lake mountain area for the Taos people, a struggle that would continue for the rest of his life. He became a leading opponent of the DANCE ORDERS of 1923, promulgated by Indian Commissioner CHARLES HENRY BURKE, which attacked Native ceremonies and dances. In April and May 1924, he and Matthew Sniffen of the INDIAN RIGHTS ASSOCIATION helped to mediate disputes between "progressive" Pueblo Indians and their tribal governors. In 1931, Collier led an attack on Special Navajo Commissioner HERBERT JAMES HAGERMAN. Between 1926 and 1933, he edited the AIDA magazine *American Indian Life*.

In April 1933, John Collier was appointed by President Franklin D. Roosevelt to replace BIA commissioner CHARLES JAMES RHOADS. Though Rhoads had to some extent prepared the way, it was Collier who brought about lasting and fundamental change in U.S. Indian policy by transforming a system designed to deprive Indians of their land and destroy their culture into a policy that promoted Indian culture and tried to preserve their lands. Collier believed that Indian cultures, if encouraged to show their potential, could become a model for progressive social policy in America as a whole, and even the world.

As BIA commissioner, Collier's main achievements were ending the policy of ALLOTMENT, which in 45 years had reduced the post-treaty Indian land base by two-thirds; the inauguration and administration of the Indian Emergency Work Program, popularly known as the INDIAN CIVILIAN CONSERVATION CORPS (1933–42); passage and implementation of the JOHNSON-O'MALLEY ACT (1934) to improve Indian education; passage and implementation of the Wheeler-Howard bill, later known as the INDIAN REORGANIZATION ACT (1934), including the chartering of some 180 tribal governments; and the establishment of the INDIAN ARTS AND CRAFTS BOARD in 1936 (on which he served as a board member from 1936 to 1945). Collier also presided over the repeal of the "espionage acts" (legislation enacted in the 19th century that restricted the movement of Indians), and he scrapped the regulations limiting traditional religious ceremonies. He established and wrote regularly for *Indians at Work*, the magazine of the Roosevelt BIA. Finally, between 1935 and 1945, his preferential hiring system brought many more Indians into the BIA.

Collier was a brilliant thinker who possessed a rare ability to translate far-ranging theoretical insights into political and administrative action. Pueblo culture was his inspiration, but his understanding of that culture was colored by his own conception of the common good for America and for humankind. He relied too heavily on an idealistic and not completely accurate idea of the Pueblo culture as a model for all Indian cultures throughout the hemisphere. His insights were comprehensive but not well adapted to specific local conditions. His son later wrote that Collier "only focused sharply on distant circumstances . . . as if he could not comprehend or directly involve himself with life directly before him."

Collier's attempts to create some kind of unified national system for hundreds of separate communities, each with its own history, culture, and specific problems, was bound to run into difficulties on a local level. Although he understood the need for flexibility, there was rarely sufficient time, funding, or personnel to carry out these programs. Under the repressive policies of the past, the indigenous institutions of most Indian cultures had been destroyed, yet they had not been allowed to develop new systems of their own—as the Pueblo, the Iroquois, the Cherokee, and some other eastern communities had been able to do. The old federal mandate had been one of ASSIMILATION, and many of the more successfully assimilated Indians resented Collier's programs. Finally, even with the best and most progressive intent, the Indian administration was still a colonial system.

During WORLD WAR II, BIA resources were increasingly used for the internment of Japanese Americans on Indian reservations, while funds for Indian programs were cut. Collier clashed with DILLON SEYMOUR MYER, who oversaw the Japanese-American internment camps, and sought to mitigate Myer's heavy-handed policies. Finding his ability to run the bureau compromised, Collier resigned on January 19, 1945. Almost immediately, his old enemies and their new allies began laying plans to either dismantle his reforms or find ways to use them, especially the tribal-council system, to their advantage. The changes Collier introduced, however, despite their faults and limits, were so far-reaching and so much in tune with the goals of most Indians themselves, that even the most concerted and damaging actions of his opponents (see TERMINATION) were unable to completely reverse them. Thus, the Collier administration represents a fundamental turning point and the beginning of a new era for Indians in the United States. Indians became politically active on their own behalf; the founders of the NATIONAL CONGRESS OF AMERICAN INDIANS (1944) were nearly all Native employees of the Collier BIA.

After leaving office, Collier directed the National Indian Institute from 1945 to 1950. From 1942 to 1951, he worked under the U.S. coordinator of inter-American affairs as the U.S. delegate to the governing board of the Inter-American Institute of the Indian in Mexico City. This was an organization founded by Indian rights champion Lázaro Cárdenas. Cárdenas, president of Mexico from 1934 to 1940, shared with Collier a vision of broadening Indian rights across the hemisphere. At that time, Collier had been keenly interested in Moises Sáenz's revival of the old Spanish *ejido*, a common-land system in Mexico similar to the pueblos of the American Southwest. Like so many other Collier policies, this early impulse for indigenous rights fell victim to the cold war. Collier also went into academia, becoming a professor of sociology and anthropology at the City University of New York from 1947 to 1954, and then professor emeritus from 1954 to 1968. For the last 10 years of his life, he lived near Taos, New Mexico, where he died on May 8, 1968.

Further Reading

Collier, John. *Indians of the Americas.* New York: W. W. Norton & Company, 1947.

Daily, David W. *Battle for the BIA: G. E. E. Lindquist and the Missionary Crusade against John Collier.* Tucson: University of Arizona Press, 2004.

Kelly, Lawrence C. *The Assault on Assimilation: John Collier and the Origins of Indian Policy Reform.* Manchester, N.H.: Olympic Marketing Corp., 1983.

Philp, Kenneth R. *John Collier's Crusade for Indian Reform, 1920–1954.* Tucson: University of Arizona Press, 1981.

Rusco, Elmer R. "John Collier: Architect of Sovereignty or Assimilation?" *American Indian Quarterly* 15, no. 1 (1991): 49–54.

United States National Archives and Records Administration. *Native Americans and the New Deal: The Office Files of John Collier, 1933–1945,* edited by Robert Lester. Bethesda, Md.: University Publications of America, 1993.

John Collier's papers are in the Yale University Library.

Colton, Harold Sellers (1881–1970) *zoologist, museum director, Indian rights advocate*

Harold Sellers Colton was born in Philadelphia on August 29, 1881, the son of Sabin Woolworth and Jessie Sellers Colton, and educated at the Ethical Culture School, Forsyth School, and DeLancey Street School. From 1900 to 1904, he studied zoology at the University of Pennsylvania and, like his younger contemporary JOHN COLLIER, was at Woods Hole in Massachusetts during the summers for study in marine biology. He received his Ph.D. from Pennsylvania in 1908 and taught zoology there from 1912 to 1926.

In the summers of 1910 and 1911, Colton toured the Southwest, and in 1913, with the help of trader Lorenzo Hubbell, he took his first trip through the lands of the Navajo (Dineh) and Hopi. From then on, Colton and his wife, Mary Russell Ferrell Colton, made every effort to learn more about these two cultures through research in Philadelphia and summer trips to the Flagstaff, Arizona, area. In 1922, Colton joined the INDIAN RIGHTS ASSOCIATION (IRA). The founder's son had been his classmate at DeLancey, and JOSEPH HENRY SCATTERGOOD, one of the most active members, was Colton's cousin. In the early 1920s, when the IRA joined Indian Commissioner CHARLES HENRY BURKE's campaign against traditional Native American dances and ceremonies, particularly those of the Hopi and Navajo, Colton dissented, urging toleration (see DANCE ORDERS; RELIGIOUS FREEDOM, AMERICAN INDIAN).

Though only recently appointed full professor, Colton retired from the University of Pennsylvania in 1926 and moved permanently to Flagstaff, where he became director of the new Museum of Northern Arizona. For much of the 1930s and early 1940s, he was also on the board of directors of

the laboratory of anthropology at the Museum of Indian Arts and Culture in Santa Fe. In 1928, the Coltons, with the help of Hopi author Edmund Nequatewa, began organizing the Hopi Craftsman Exhibition, which was held in Flagstaff in 1930. It was so successful in improving the local economy and the quality of arts that, except for a suspension during WORLD WAR II, it has been held annually ever since.

Colton had been interested in Navajo-Hopi land conflicts since his arrival in Flagstaff. By 1930, twice as many Navajo as Hopi were living on the Hopi reservation. Burke's successor as Indian commissioner, CHARLES JAMES RHOADS, asked Colton to present the Hopi case and OLIVER LA FARGE that of the Navajo. After hearing their reports, Rhoads called a meeting of Hopi and Navajo leaders. Chaired by Navajo Special Commissioner HERBERT JAMES HAGERMAN, the meeting was held at the Museum of Northern Arizona on November 6, 1930. It went on for half a day but was canceled when Hagerman discovered that the Hopi delegation were merely observers with no power to act. Hagerman eventually proposed a partition plan embodying Colton's suggestion that the Hopi retain rights to their sacred sites and the gathering of wood in the Navajo area (see BIG MOUNTAIN).

In 1931, Colton defended Hagerman from attacks by the Senate Indian Affairs Committee and JOHN COLLIER. He even blamed Collier's "bitter attacks" for hastening Hagerman's death a few years later. Colton also felt Collier was impatient and unfair in accusing Rhoads and Assistant Commissioner Scattergood of not moving fast or far enough.

In spring 1932, Colton helped Scattergood interpret several letters he had received from traditional Hopi leader DAN KATCHONGVA over the previous few months. With Collier due to become the new commissioner of Indian affairs and some form of reorganization act soon to come, Colton knew that the Hopi governing and land-tenure systems would be an issue. In December 1934, he published an article in the museum's journal *Museum Notes,* entitled "A Brief Survey of Hopi Common Law," in which he wrote: "The Hopi people do not form a tribe in the ordinary sense of the word. They are a group of independent and semi-independent towns with little but common customs and in most cases a common language, to hold them together. They are as independent as the Greek cities at the time of the Trojan war."

In 1936, Collier, by then commissioner of the BUREAU OF INDIAN AFFAIRS, hired Oliver La Farge to try to create a "Hopi" government under the framework of the new INDIAN REORGANIZATION ACT, and La Farge made some concessions to the village chiefs, or kikmongwis. Yet in the very attempt to write a constitution for a "tribe" that did not exist, Collier and La Farge ignored Colton's main point—that the Hopi towns were autonomous and self-governing. The 1936 constitution would cause many problems in the years ahead (see, for example, BOYDEN, JOHN STERLING).

Colton was an important figure in the Indian reform movement associated with the MERIAM REPORT (1928) that had led to the appointments of Rhoads and Scattergood. Many of Colton's observations, particularly in regard to Hopi-Navajo issues, showed a greater understanding of these complex Indian cultures, an understanding the Collier administration would too often ignore in its haste to implement new reforms.

Harold Colton died in Flagstaff on December 29, 1970.

Further Reading
Miller, Simon H. *The Life of Harold Sellers Colton: A Philadelphia Brahmin in Flagstaff.* Tsaile, Ariz.: Navajo Community College Press, 1991.

Committee of One Hundred (Advisory Council on Indian Affairs) (1923)
In 1923, the Department of the Interior was reeling from the scandals of Secretary ALBERT BACON FALL and much ill feeling about the BURSUM BILL and the DANCE ORDERS of Indian Commissioner CHARLES HENRY BURKE. In response, President Warren G. Harding asked newly appointed interior secretary Hubert Work to create a panel of respected public figures to discuss government Indian policy. Known officially as the Advisory Council on Indian Affairs, but popularly as the Committee of One Hundred, it was chaired by Seneca archaeologist ARTHUR C. PARKER, with his longtime colleague FAYETTE AVERY MCKENZIE as chairman of the resolutions subcommittee and Matthew Sniffen of the INDIAN RIGHTS ASSOCIATION as secretary.

The committee members represented a wide political spectrum, from Oswald Villard, the radical editor of the *Nation*, to fundamentalist lawyer William Jennings Bryan. Several members of writer and artist ERNEST THOMPSON SETON's circle, such as David Starr Jordan, ethnologist Frederic Webb Hodge, and Dakota physician and writer CHARLES EASTMAN, served on it. Other Native American leaders on the committee were Reverend HENRY CLARENCE ROE CLOUD, Reverend SHERMAN COOLIDGE, Reverend PHILIP B. GORDON, and attorneys THOMAS L. SLOAN and DENNISON WHEELOCK.

The committee held its only conference on December 12 and 13, 1923, in Washington, D.C. Its report was published as *Indian Policies: Comments on the Resolutions of the Advisory Council on Indian Affairs.*

While the Committee of One Hundred helped in some measure to defeat the DANCE ORDERS of 1923 and brought pressure to pass the Indian Citizenship Act of 1924 (see CITIZENSHIP) and other legislation, its conclusions were basically conservative, and the changes it called for had long been advocated and were widely supported. Thus, while the committee recommended surveying reservation health conditions and improving medical care, establishing a court of Indian claims, and protecting Indians' mineral rights, it made no recommendations on the controversial issue of Pueblo land claims (see Bursum bill).

Further Reading
Work, Hubert, ed. *Indian Policies: Comments on the Resolutions of the Advisory Council on Indian Affairs.* Washington, D.C.: Government Printing Office, 1924.

Conepatchie, Billie (Little Billie Fewell, Koniphadjo)   *See* BILLY, JOSIE.

Conley, Helena   *See* CONLEY, LYDA B.

Conley, Ida   *See* CONLEY, LYDA B.

Conley, Lyda B.   (1874–1946)   *Wyandot lawyer*
Eliza Burton Conley was born in Kansas City, Kansas, the daughter of Andrew S. Conley (d. 1885), an Englishman, and Eliza Zane Conley (d. 1879), the granddaughter of Isaac Zane, a white captive who later married a Wyandot chief's daughter. Known as Lyda, Conley was the first American Indian woman lawyer to plead before the U.S. Supreme Court. She and her two older sisters, Ida and Helena (Helene) Gros Conley (Floating Voice), dedicated their lives to protecting the Wyandot burial ground that held the graves of their parents and ancestors. Without the Conleys' heroic efforts, it would not exist today.

In 1842, the Wyandot, formerly living in Ohio, ceded their lands in exchange for a parcel that later became downtown Kansas City, Kansas. After a terrible epidemic in 1843, the Kansas Wyandot set aside two acres of this land as a burial ground. Twelve years later, when they signed a treaty agreeing to the conversion of their tribal land to individual ownership, or ALLOTMENT, they legally terminated the tribe and became U.S. citizens. This same treaty stipulated, however, that the burial ground would be "permanently reserved and appropriated for that purpose."

By a treaty of February 23, 1867, about 200 of 700, mainly poor and more traditional, Kansas Wyandot voluntarily removed to Indian Territory (near present-day Miami, Oklahoma). Meanwhile, the old cemetery had become a highly desirable property in the downtown district and was being eyed as the site for a new city hall. In 1895, it was surveyed by a lawyer named William E. Connelly, and four years later he traveled to Indian Territory on behalf of Kansas City speculators to negotiate with the Indians there (who use the spelling Wyandotte), promising to help them regain tribal status. On March 22, 1899, this Wyandotte council gave Connelly power of attorney to have the graves moved and sell the old cemetery, for which he would receive a 15 percent commission.

The Kansas Wyandot were absolutely opposed to this. Lyda Conley, who in the late 1890s had been teaching telegraphy at the Spaulding Business College and bible classes at the Seventh Street Methodist Church, felt so strongly about it that she took up the study of law expressly to protect the burial ground. Graduating with honors from the Kansas City School of Law in 1902 and admitted to the Missouri bar the same year, she became the first, and for several years remained the only, American Indian woman lawyer.

When the city government approved the removal of the bodies to another cemetery in 1905 and Congress authorized the property's sale in 1906, the Conley sisters occupied

Lyda Conley, 1902.

the cemetery as their own property, padlocked the gates, and built a shack, dubbed "Fort Conley," over their parents' graves, threatening to shoot any trespassers. They were arrested, but Lyda immediately filed suit in federal court against the secretary of the interior. Meanwhile, the sisters made Fort Conley their legal residence. Armed with shotguns, they remained even through the winters. When they were briefly absent one night, the U.S. marshal demolished the shack, but the sisters immediately rebuilt it. Their courage and persistence soon won the support of nearly everyone in Kansas City.

As the case wound through the courts, Lyda Conley argued her Fifth Amendment property rights as a citizen. In the October 1909 term, Lyda Conley became the first Indian woman to plead before the U.S. Supreme Court (*Conley v. Ballinger*). On January 31, 1910, the Court found against her, but the justices were sympathetic and did not impose costs. There was now at least a temporary reprieve, since the stipulated period of sale had expired. Pressure immediately resumed, but Kansas senator CHARLES CURTIS, won over to the cause, got the law authorizing sale of the land repealed in the Senate and in June 1913 obtained $10,000 from the

federal government for maintenance work. After that, the city agreed—on March 20, 1918—to care for the plot in perpetuity. On February 3, 1921, the House of Representatives ratified the repeal.

On several other occasions (1918, 1922, 1929, 1937), Lyda and her sisters resumed their defense of the grounds over various incursions. Thanks to their lifelong efforts, the cemetery continues in active use as an exclusive Wyandot burial ground. Lyda Conley died on May 28, 1946; Ida on October 6, 1948; and Helena on September 15, 1958; all were buried there.

See also BALDWIN, MARIE LOUISE BOTTINEAU; HURON CEMETERY DISPUTE.

Further Reading
Conley, Lyda. "Lyda Conley's Legal Argument to Preserve the Huron Indian Cemetery." Available online. URL: http://www.wyandot.org/consis.htm. Accessed on 15 March 2007.

Coolidge, Sherman (Runs-on-Top, Des-che-wa-ah)
(1862–1932) *Arapaho Episcopal priest, member of the Society of American Indians*
An Arapaho, Sherman Coolidge was born on February 22, 1862, to Big Heart and Turtle Woman near Goose Creek, Wyoming, and named Runs-on-Top (Des-che-wa-ah) after his Arapaho great-grandfather. When he was seven, his father was killed by Bannock warriors. That same year, the U.S. Army's cavalry made an unprovoked attack on his band and killed many of his family members. In 1870, he and two younger brothers were captured by a group of Shoshone and Bannock, who turned them over to soldiers at Camp Brown, Wyoming. Runs-on-Top was adopted by the family of Lieutenant Charles A. Coolidge and renamed Sherman Coolidge.

When Lieutenant Coolidge was sent on recruiting duty to Cleveland, Ohio, in 1870, Mrs. Coolidge took the boy to her home in New York City, where he was baptized into the Episcopal faith at age nine. She sent him to school, and he decided while still a boy to become a missionary to Indians. In 1877, he entered Shattuck Military Academy in Faribault, Minnesota. In 1880, he went to Seabury Divinity School, graduating with a bachelor of divinity degree in 1884. Ordained a deacon by Bishop Henry B. Whipple at Faribault that year, Coolidge left to preach at the Wind River Reservation in Wyoming for two years; he was ordained into the priesthood by Bishop John Franklin Spalding of the Diocese of Colorado at Cheyenne, Wyoming, in 1885.

Coolidge took a special course at Hobart College in New York from 1887 to 1890. In 1902, he married Grace Darling Wetherbee, daughter of the owner of the Manhattan Hotel in New York, who later authored a book, *Teepee Neighbors* (1917), on their experiences among the Shoshone and Arapaho. In 1911, Coolidge became one of the founding members of the SOCIETY OF AMERICAN INDIANS. For several years, he was an Episcopal missionary among the Arapaho. Afterward, he became canon of the cathedral at Laramie, Wyoming, then canon of St. Johns Cathedral in Denver, Colorado, later serving as rector of the Church of the Good Shepherd in Colorado Springs.

Having been raised in a non-Indian environment from age eight, Coolidge was a committed assimilationist. ASSIMILATION, or "Americanization"—that is, the process of eliminating the traditional cultural, religious, economic, and social norms of American Indians and replacing them with Western ones, was a central aspect of U.S. Indian policy for much of the 19th and 20th centuries. Generally, those Indians who resisted this process and attempted to maintain the old ways were labeled *traditionals*, whereas those who favored Americanization were often called *assimilationists* or *progressives*. But there were varying degrees of both tendencies, and assimilationists did not necessarily reject some kind of Indian cultural distinctiveness.

As a missionary for 46 years, mainly in Wyoming, Minnesota, Oklahoma, Nevada, and Colorado, Coolidge was a leader in Indian affairs and tried to "uplift the race" according to his own philosophy. In an address to the Society of American Indians in 1919, he stated.

My wife is a full-blooded white woman. I am a full-blooded Arapahoe. My children are half-breeds. In a short time there will not be such a thing as an Indian, a pure-blooded Indian. We are being overwhelmed by the vast majority of other races. So I am anxious that this Society shall be a model to all other organizations who want to help their nation and their race in other countries.

In 1920, Coolidge established the American Indian Film Company in Denver, intending to produce a "master film of Indian life," with TSIANINA EVANS BLACKSTONE in the lead role and an all-Indian cast. "Ideas, suggestions and data" were sought as a basis on which to build a scenario that, according to Coolidge, would "to the fullest possible extent reveal both the primitive and modern life of the American Indian." The first part was supposed to be based on "picturesque and poetic elements in early tribal life," while the second would show "the Indian's part in American civilization, culminating with his splendid achievements in the late world war . . ." Though the project never materialized, it reflected the proud but assimilative spirit in which Coolidge viewed the place of the Indian in modern America, comparable to contemporaries such as CHARLES EDWIN DAGENETT or ARTHUR C. PARKER. Coolidge died suddenly on January 24, 1932, in Los Angeles.

See also TIPI ORDER OF AMERICA; URBANIZATION, AMERICAN INDIANS AND.

Further Reading
Coolidge, Sherman, D.D. "The Indians of To-day." *Colorado Magazine* 1, no. 2 (May 1893).
Parker, Arthur S. "Sherman Coolidge." *Society of American Indians Quarterly Journal* 3 (1915): 124–127.

Cornelius, Chester Poe (Geyna) (1869–1933)
Oneida lawyer, economic reformer

Chester Poe Cornelius was born on the Oneida Reservation at Green Bay, Wisconsin, on September 7, 1869, the eldest of five children of Adam Poe and Celicia Bread Cornelius. His sister, LAURA MIRIAM CORNELIUS KELLOGG, was a noted writer, political thinker, and claims advocate. Chester Poe Cornelius came from a distinguished lineage. His paternal grandfather was John Cornelius, Oneida chief and brother of Jacob Cornelius, also a chief, and his great-grandfather was the chief Dagoawi. His maternal grandfather was Chief Daniel Bread, known as Dehowyadilou (1800–73), who played a central part in acquiring land in Wisconsin for the Oneida, thus averting their removal west of the Mississippi.

Cornelius attended the Carlisle Indian Academy at Carlisle, Pennsylvania. Beginning his higher education at Dickinson College in Carlisle, he later transferred to the University of Pennsylvania. He attended summer sessions at Harvard University and finally enrolled in the Eastman Business College in Poughkeepsie, New York, from which he received a diploma. After some unsuccessful business ventures in the west, Cornelius returned to Wisconsin, where he studied law and was admitted to the bar. He worked on the long-standing claim to moneys due the Oneida for land granted to them in Kansas in the early 19th century on which the government later allowed whites to settle.

Near the end of the 19th century, Cornelius moved to Indian Territory (now the state of Oklahoma), where he worked on a $5 million Cherokee claim. On June 7, 1899, in El Reno, Indian Territory, he married Laura Gertrude Smith, described by the *Oneida Tribune* as "an accomplished white girl of Darlington." The writer HAMLIN GARLAND, who met Cornelius in April 1900 in Darlington, Indian Territory, describes him in *Companions on the Trail* (1931) as "a giant in size and a man of ability. . . . [He] had located here, after a most astonishing educational career in New York," of which Garland reveals nothing further. "'I intend to grow up with the law business of this country,' he said. 'Lawyers here will always be concerned largely with Indian lands, inheritance, and titles.'" Cornelius explained to Garland that because tribal rolls did not show family relationships and there was no system of surnames through which titles could be traced, allotment of lands to individuals would cause ample litigation in the future. The federal policy of ALLOTMENT, in force between 1887 and 1934, mandated the subdivision of tribally held lands into small "allotments" that were then distributed to individual tribal members. Cornelius suggested that Indians be given standard surnames to protect their property rights. After appealing to the Indian Office, as the BUREAU OF INDIAN AFFAIRS was then known, Garland was hired to manage the project for several years.

A biographical account published in Thomas Henry Ryan's *History of Outagamie County, Wisconsin* around 1911 tells of Cornelius's dream of installing "the most highly organized system of scientific agriculture" on Oneida lands in Wisconsin.

. . . it is his intention to forsake his profession and

devote his whole life to making Oneida a garden spot of the country. The Oneida Stock Farm, with its most modern barn in the county and its acres presaging such wonderful possibilities, is an example of his idea of bringing beautiful culture out of the wilderness. In cooperation with his sister, Laura M. Cornelius, who has originated a scheme for industrial organization for all Indians and who hopes to establish a Cherry Garden City for the Oneidas, C.P. Cornelius stands in a position to demonstrate to the world the large abilities and possibilities of the Indian race.

While on a trip to Washington, D.C., in July 1914, Cornelius and his sister Laura met REDBIRD SMITH, spiritual leader of the Nighthawk Keetoowah (Cherokee), who lived in isolated communities in the Wild Horse Mountains of northeastern Oklahoma. For reasons not entirely clear, the siblings came to exert an extraordinary influence on Smith and his followers. From their biographies, it can be seen that both Chester and Laura had great personal magnetism and ideas for wonderful projects. Smith and his followers placed great trust in Chester Cornelius, not only in business matters but, even more extraordinary, in matters of ritual and religion. The Oneida are part of the Iroquois culture, to which the Cherokee are distantly related, but over a long period of time, Cherokee traditions were strongly influenced by their neighbors and close allies, the Natchez. Redbird Smith was very interested in bringing the Keetoowah ceremonies closer to the Iroquois traditions, and thus he adopted a number of major ritual changes suggested by Cornelius.

Cornelius, in fact, was descended from families that had been Christian for several generations, but he was undoubtedly familiar with much Iroquois lore, as well as being "a thirty-second degree Scottish Rite and a Knight Templar of the Masonic fraternity," and a member of "the Ancient Arabic Order of Nobles of the Mystic Shrine," as Thomas Henry Ryan notes in his *History of Outagamie County*.

After Smith's death in November 1918, Cornelius was with Smith's son John at the Keetoowah dancing ground (or "stomp ground"). Pointing to a crane in a tree, Cornelius said, "You watch and see if that crane isn't down by the graveyard when we bury your father." As John Smith told the story later, "Pretty soon the crane flew off and lit in a tree just west of the graveyard. When we carried my father's coffin down to the graveyard, the crane sat there in that tree and hollered. After we buried my father, the crane sat there until sundown and then flew off to the west."

Cornelius had interested Redbird Smith and the Keetoowah in a project for community economic development. Though it began well, some time after Smith's death it failed badly. Cornelius had advised the Keetoowah to make several large capital investments, the first of which was the purchase of 200 head of Aberdeen cattle in 1917. A large portion of this capital came from mortgages which individual members took out on their own property. Though a lawyer, Cornelius had never had the society legally incorporated. When financial disaster struck later, these individuals were personally liable and suffered heavy losses.

In the 1920s, Cornelius worked with his sister Laura and her husband on the Oneida land claims in New York. In 1927, the three were arrested in Canada for fraud. They had collected $15,000 from Iroquois in Ontario and Quebec to support their legal work; however, the land claims foundered. All three were later tried and acquitted. It should be noted that at that period tensions were particularly high between the Canadian government—which had passed a series of laws that encroached on Iroquois rights—and the supporters of Iroquois sovereignty (see GENERAL, LEVI).

In 1927, Cornelius was a member of the Resolution Committee of the Society of Oklahoma Indians, an organization representing 26 tribes. At that time, he resided in Gore, Oklahoma (Sequoiah County).

Cornelius told a reporter for the *Daily Oklahoman* in 1923 that he wanted the Keetoowah some day to be "in a position where they can work for the common good and build up a surplus for the good of the community." As with Laura's project to unite the Oneida, however, there is controversy to this day among the Keetoowah as to whether Cornelius was altruistically motivated or simply a con artist. There is no question that the failure of his development schemes brought considerable hardship to the Keetoowah, but it is not clear that he derived any personal benefit from their misfortune. Perhaps it would be more accurate to say that he, like his sister Laura, was a sincere reformer whose business skills were not equal to his visions.

Chester Poe Cornelius died on November 30, 1933. He was survived by a daughter, Mildred Cornelius.

Further Reading

"Communism among the Cherokees Is Means to End to Equal Whites." *Dallas Morning News*, 12 February, 1922.

Cornplanter, Edward (Sosondowah, Deep or Great Night) (1856–1918) *Seneca traditional chief, principal singer*

A Seneca, Edward Cornplanter, the son of Moses and Sarah (Phillips) Cornplanter, was born in November 1856 on the Cattaraugus Reservation in northern New York state. Moses Cornplanter was the great-grandson of the celebrated Iroquois chief Cornplanter (ca. 1750–1836), for whom Congress established a reservation near Erie, Pennsylvania. Sosondowah (Deep or Great Night), as Edward Cornplanter was known in the Seneca language, was one of the few Iroquois chiefs authorized to hold the Gaiwiio, or Code of Handsome Lake (teachings of the Seneca prophet Handsome Lake). Normally transmitted orally and memorized by these leading chiefs, beginning in 1903 Cornplanter, fearing that the Gaiwiio might become lost, wrote it down for posterity. He was also the source of much of the Seneca history and lore in the books of ARTHUR C. PARKER and Harriet Maxwell Converse.

Cornplanter was the captain of the Newtown, New York, LACROSSE team and often toured to play other teams. He also toured as an actor with theatrical troupes. In 1882, he married Nancy Jack. Considered the last of the great preachers of the Gaiwiio, Cornplanter regularly traveled from reservation to reservation, admonishing the Iroquois to refrain from alcohol and other vices.

Edward Cornplanter died at the Cattaraugus Reservation on June 16, 1918, just before his son, JESSE CORNPLANTER, was sent overseas with the U.S. Army to fight in WORLD WAR I. A brief obituary in the *New York Times* noted: "Edward Cornplanter was one of the leading Indian chiefs of surviving Iroquois, and although educated, believed in a restoration of pagan customs." For his efforts to maintain these customs, he was buried next to Handsome Lake on the Onondaga Reservation.

Cornplanter, Jesse (Hayónwan'i:s, "He Strikes the Rushes," "Canoe Gatherer") (1889–1957) *Seneca artist, actor, storyteller, chief of the Snipe Clan*

Jesse Cornplanter, a Seneca, was born at Newtown on the Cattaraugus Reservation in New York on September 16, 1889, the son of EDWARD CORNPLANTER, chief of the Wolf Clan, and Nancy Jack Cornplanter (Snipe Clan). His Seneca name was Hayónwan'i:s (He Strikes the Rushes, or Canoe Gatherer).

Jesse won fame at a very early age as "the boy Indian artist." He began at age nine to sketch the life, dances, and ceremonies of the Longhouse Religion of the Iroquois. Some of these drawings were issued in 1903 under the title *Iroquois Indian Games and Dances*. Completing fifth grade in the local school, young Cornplanter later toured Europe with his father in a theatrical troupe (1904–05). In 1912, Jesse Cornplanter began touring the country with other Indian players in a production of *Hiawatha*, performing weeklong stints through the South and the Northeast. He starred in a silent film version made later that year, produced by Frank E. Moore. An item in *Moving Picture News* of March 15, 1913, called the 6-foot 2-inch Cornplanter ". . . one of the handsomest men ever shown in moving pictures. . . . [A] mute poet, the expression of his eyes revealing the unspoken yearnings of his nature."

The troupe played in Baltimore in summer 1913 and toured Ohio in 1915. At the end of that season, Cornplanter remained in Ohio, taking a job with the Willys-Overland Automobile Company in Toledo. When the United States entered WORLD WAR I in April 1917, he enlisted in the army and was assigned in June 1917 to the machine-gun company of the old 6th Ohio Regiment, where he rapidly reached the rank of corporal. After 10 months' training, his company went overseas as part of the 147th Infantry, 37th Division. His father, a traditional who did not believe Iroquois should serve in the U.S. military, was very unhappy that Jesse had enlisted. After predicting that they would never see each other again, he died a day or two before Jesse went overseas.

Jesse Cornplanter saw nine months of active service through the campaigns at Beaumont, Baccarat, Avoncourt,

Seneca Jesse Cornplanter was a craftsman as well as an actor, storyteller, and traditional chief of his people. *(AP/Wideworld)*

and the big drive at Argonne Forest. He was gassed severely and at the hospital developed shell shock. He left Brest, France, with his original contingent on March 15, 1919, arriving in New York on March 23. He was mustered out at Camp Sherman on April 19 after receiving the tragic news that his mother, sister, brother-in-law, and two of his children had died in the recent influenza epidemic. In 1920, he left Newtown for Quaker Bridge on the Allegany Reservation. In 1925, he left Allegany to live first in Buffalo, then in Tonawanda, New York.

A master carver of false-face masks, Cornplanter was an instructor in the Works Progress Administration (WPA) Indian Arts and Crafts Project run by ARTHUR C. PARKER during the 1930s. In that period, Cornplanter was frequently heard on radio stations in Rochester and Buffalo. He supplied the Seneca stories and legends for Carl Carmer's *Listen for a Lonesome Drum* (1936), and in 1938 he published his own book *Legends of the Long House*, which he illustrated himself. In his later years, he worked on a book on the early life and current situation of the Seneca but never completed it. From 1933 until his death, he was the chief informant for anthropologist William N. Fenton.

Though he continued living at Tonawanda, N.Y., with his Seneca wife, Elsina Billy, Cornplanter, a chief of the Snipe clan, frequently returned to Newtown for ceremonies. In his 50s, Cornplanter suffered two strokes, and though he recovered, he was in delicate health the last decade of his life. He died on March 18, 1957, from injuries suffered in an automobile accident.

Further Reading
Liberty, Margot. *American Indian Intellectuals*. St. Paul, Minn.: West Publishing Company, 1978.

Cornwall Bridge Blockade (1968)

This important event in the history of Indian activism opened a new era of militant Indian confrontation. The blockade of the Seaway International Bridge—linking New York State and Cornwall Island in Ontario, Canada, and spanning the St. Lawrence River—was begun by approximately 100 unarmed Mohawk on December 18, 1968. The Mohawk were protesting Canada's failure to live up to the Jay Treaty of 1794, which guaranteed Indians the right to cross the U.S.-Canadian border without restrictions. Earlier attempts by Canada to restrict free passage had been defeated by the Iroquois, led by Tuscarora chief CLINTON RICKARD, during the 1920s. The Canadian government began imposing custom duties on the Mohawk of the Akwesasne (St. Regis) Reservation in November 1968. The reservation is bisected by the border, and residents use the Cornwall Bridge to travel from one part of their reservation to another.

The Mohawk of Akwesasne had become more militant after a boycott of state schools in April 1968. Led by Chief John A. Cook and Minerva White, the Mohawk had demanded more participation in the way the schools were run and in the planning of a new school near their reservation.

The bridge blockade was led by Ernie Benedict, Mike Mitchell, and other Mohawk, all of whom would become prominent 10 years later in the two-year police siege of Akwesasne (see AKWESASNE, SIEGE OF). One hundred Mohawk men, women, and children, in 25 cars, blocked the bridge and then formed a human chain to prevent the cars from being towed away. Forty-seven Indians were arrested by Canadian police. The Mohawk called off further demonstrations after Canada acceded to their demand that they not impose the duties.

The successful result of the blockade led to the creation of *Akwesasne Notes*, the most influential Indian newspaper of the latter part of the 20th century, and the White Roots of Peace, a traveling lecture group that spread the Iroquois tradition of sovereignty and militancy across the country. The blockade inspired Richard Oaks, a Mohawk living in California, to organize Indians in the San Francisco Bay area, eventually leading to the OCCUPATION OF ALCATRAZ ISLAND (see also PORTER, TOM).

Costo, Rupert (1906–1989) *Cahuilla scholar, activist, founder of the American Indian Historical Society*

A Cahuilla born on May 10, 1906, in Hemet, California, Rupert Costo attended Haskell College in Lawrence, Kansas, where he was a star athlete. He then attended Whittier College in California, where he played football alongside fellow student Richard M. Nixon under their Indian coach Wallace "Chief" Newman. After graduation, he became an engineer with the California State Highway Department. In the 1930s, he became a vocal critic of the INDIAN NEW DEAL (see INDIAN REORGANIZATION ACT), and during the 1950s, he was the tribal chair of the Cahuilla.

In the early 1960s, after retiring from the Highway Department, Costo, together with his wife, Jeanette Henry Costo (Eastern Cherokee), founded the American Indian Historical Society (AIHS) in San Francisco. The AIHS developed a number of important publications, including *Wassaja*, a magazine that focused on Indian current events, and *The Indian Historian*, which attempted to render an accurate historical portrayal of Indian people. Both magazines exercised an important influence on the growing West Coast RED POWER MOVEMENT that later manifested itself in the OCCUPATION OF ALCATRAZ ISLAND in 1969.

In 1970, the AIHS founded the American Indian Historical Society Press, which published more than 50 works. Near the end of his life, Costo endowed the Rupert Costo Chair in American Indian History at the University of California, Riverside. He and his wife also established the Costo Library of the American Indian at the University of California, Riverside, which contains one of the most comprehensive collections of American Indian materials in the United States. Rupert Costo died on October 20, 1989. In 1994, the University of California, Riverside, renamed its student service building Costo Hall in his memory.

Further Reading
"Library Is Dedicated to Costo." *Indian Country Today*, 4 December 1985, 3.

Coulter, Robert (Tim Coulter) (1945–)
citizen band Potawatomi attorney, founder of the Indian Law Resource Center

Born in Rapid City, South Dakota, on September 19, 1945, Robert "Tim" Coulter received his bachelor's degree from Williams College in Williamstown, Massachusetts, in 1966. He earned his J.D. from Columbia University in 1969. For many years thereafter, he served as the attorney for the traditional Iroquois government in New York State.

During his career, Coulter became influential in international Indian affairs. In 1977, he helped to organize a conference in Geneva under the auspices of the United Nations, entitled "Discrimination against the Indigenous Populations in the Americas." In 1978, he founded the Indian Law Resource Center (ILRC) in Washington, D.C., along with attorney Steve Tolberg. In 1979, Coulter and Tolberg compiled a report for the traditional Hopi leaders that was an important statement of their rights as an independent and autonomous government. The ILRC also aided the Miskito Indians of Nicaragua in their attempts to defend themselves from attacks by the Sandinista government during the early 1980s, an action that brought charges, particularly from the INTERNATIONAL

Indian Treaty Council, that the ILRC was a tool of the CIA. Although the accusations were false, the center did successfully lobby the administration of Ronald Reagan for American funds for the Miskito to fight the Sandinistas, an effort that cost the center considerable Indian as well as leftist support (see also Bomberry, Daniel R.).

The center has also been active in the United Nations Working Group on Indigenous Populations, and Coulter played an important role in drafting the Declaration on the Rights of Indigenous Peoples, which was adopted by the United Nations on September 13, 2007. He has published a number of works, including *Indian Rights—Human Rights*, an ILRC handbook released in 1984. In addition to serving as executive director of the ILRC, Coulter is active in a number of environmental organizations such as the River Network, which helps protect rivers and watersheds.

See also sovereignty, indigenous and tribal.

Further Reading

Coulter, Robert T. "The Draft UN Declaration on the Rights of Indigenous Peoples: What is it? What does it mean?" *Netherlands Quarterly of Human Rights* 13 (1995): 123–138.

Indian Law Resource Center. *Indian Rights—Human Rights: Handbook for Indians on International Human Rights Complaint Procedures*. Washington, D.C.: Indian Law Resource Center, 1984.

Council of Energy Resource Tribes (CERT)

This coalition of 22 energy-rich tribes was formed in 1975 in an attempt to maximize the value of Indian energy resources. With the oil shortages of the early 1970s and the formation of OPEC (Organization of Petroleum Exporting Countries) by the large oil-producing nations, energy prices skyrocketed. Savvy Indian leaders such as Navajo tribal chairman Peter MacDonald decided that an "Indian OPEC" would help tribes in their negotiations with the Bureau of Indian Affairs (BIA) and the energy companies, negotiations that in the past had left Indians shortchanged. Indians were now in an enviable position, it seemed, because in 1975, 15 percent of the nation's known coal reserves, including 30 percent of the strippable low-sulfur coal, 4 percent of the nation's oil and gas reserves, and 50 percent of the nation's uranium reserves, lay beneath Indian lands.

With the help of the Comanche political activist LaDonna Harris, and under the leadership of MacDonald, the Council of Energy Resource Tribes (CERT) opened its offices in Washington, D.C., in 1977. CERT worked particularly closely with the Department of Energy (DOE), which allowed them some leverage in dealings with the BIA and other branches of the Department of Interior. The organization was also advantageous to energy companies, which found DOE easier to work with than the Department of the Interior.

The formation of CERT soon caused a backlash against Indian tribes, who were seen as profiteering from the energy crisis of the late 1970s. Moreover, traditional Indian leaders

and militant organizations, such as the American Indian Movement, who objected to energy development and mining of any kind on Indian reservations, attacked CERT as being destructive to the environment and against Indian culture. Rather than becoming independent of the energy corporations and the federal government, as professed, CERT's large staff was drawn from the very same energy corporations, while its funding came almost exclusively through government or corporate grants.

The organization was also affected by the political problems of MacDonald, who at the time was engaged in a running battle with the Republican Party. But CERT found a friend in the Reagan administration's new BIA director, Kenneth L. Smith, winning a political victory with the 1982 passage of the Indian Mineral Development Act and the Federal Oil and Gas Management Act, which gave the tribes more control over mining on their lands, albeit at the expense of environmental regulations. Despite this small political victory, CERT's primary task became to supply technical assistance to tribes as well as provide scholarships for young Indians interested in careers in the energy fields. By 1984, the organization had grown to include 39 tribes. However, the collapse of energy prices that year ended any hope of further political gains. With 48 members in the United States as of 2002, CERT began to admit Canadian tribes as well.

See also mining, American Indians and; oil, American Indians and; Presidential Commission on Indian Reservation Economies.

Further Reading

Ambler, Marjane. *Breaking the Iron Bonds: Indian Control of Energy Development*. Lawrence: University Press of Kansas, 1991.

Jorgensen, Joseph G., ed. *Native Americans and Energy Development*. Cambridge, Mass.: Anthropology Resource Center, 1978.

———. *Native Americans and Energy Development II*. Boston: Anthropology Resource Center; Forestville, Calif.: Seventh Generation Fund, 1984.

crime and criminality among American Indians

One of the first systematic attempts to analyze 20th-century intertribal crime patterns among Native Americans was Norman S. Hayner's "Variability in the Criminal Behavior of American Indians," published in 1942 in the *American Journal of Sociology*. Using the findings of the 1928 Meriam Report, as well as individual interviews and investigations, Hayner found that the rate of arrest and "demoralization" of Indians was highest where the degree of contact with non-Indians was the greatest. The criminality of Indians increased proportionately with the wealth of the reservations and the value of the reservation's resources, a fact that the study attributed to the increase in the presence of criminal non-Indians on those reservations with more wealth and greater access to alcohol (see alcoholism, American Indians and).

A second important study, "The Delinquency of the American Indian," by Hans Von Hentig, published in the *Journal of Criminal Law, Criminology, and Police Science* in 1945, examined the types of crimes Indians committed and the circumstances of their arrests, using the FBI's Uniform Crime Reports and census information. The study found that during the 1920s, more than half of all Indian offenses were for public drunkenness. Von Hentig further found that Indian agents or superintendents had enormous discretionary power over Indian courts and Indian police on reservations, and that Indian courts were much more likely to hand down jail sentences for crimes for which a federal court would tend to apply fines. In the decade from 1935 to 1944, Indian arrests and imprisonment increased, becoming proportionately higher than the rates for whites.

Contributing to Indian criminality was the fact that Native American legal norms were not incorporated into American criminal law. On the contrary, as pointed out by Sidney Harring in his 1982 article "Native American Crime in the United States," for much of the century, "the BIA-imposed tribal legal codes were nothing less than naked attempts to enforce the dominant moral standards by force, an important aspect of the overall assimilationist design. The first Indian penal code prohibited dancing, polygamy, practicing as a medicine man, prostitution and drunkenness." Other offenses for which Indians were charged, such as fishing- and hunting-law violations, trespass offenses, and "moral" crimes such as adultery were not necessarily crimes in the Indians' particular traditional cultures (see ASSIMILATION).

The criminality rate among Indians grew rapidly during the 1950s and the 1960s, in part owing to the Relocation programs of the TERMINATION era, which rapidly accelerated the URBANIZATION of Indians. Relocation, critics charged, was little more than a one-way bus ticket from the reservation to an urban area, where Indians with few skills and no money would invariably drift into poverty and often into crime. During the 1960s, when statistical data on crime patterns in the United States began to be systematically collected and organized, the data, though still not comprehensive, made it clear that crime in Indian communities was a serious problem. The arrest rate for Indians in 1960 was found to be 14,364 per 100,000, or almost 10 times the white rate (1,655 per 100,000) and more than twice the rate of blacks (5,908 per 100,000). However, the bulk of the arrests were still for alcohol-related crimes, such as public drunkenness and disturbing the peace.

In 1970, the Indian arrest rate hit its peak, at 15,883 per 100,000. Since then, however, crime among American Indians has been declining, in marked contrast to the general population, where it continued to increase well into the 1990s before also going into decline. The arrest rate for Indians declined to 7,707 per 100,000 in 1980 and to 6,256 per 100,000 in 1990. This is still almost twice as high as the white rate (3,862 per 100,000), but much less than that among blacks (10,751 per 100,000) in 1990. It is likely that declining use of alcohol has been a factor in these trends.

Between 1980 and 1984, homicides among Indians were 9.6 per 100,000, more than twice the white rate (4.6 per 100,000), but far less than among blacks (33.1 per 100,000). Most homicides were committed by family members or acquaintances, with 17 percent by strangers, less than among whites (28 percent) or blacks (21 percent). The rate fell slightly over the middle of the century, but throughout most of the century the homicide rate remained constant at between 10 and 13 per 100,000. The Indian arrest rate for homicides (5 per 100,000) was slightly lower than that of the general population (7.5 per 100,000), higher than whites (4 per 100,000) and lower than blacks (34 per 100,000).

Suicide rates among American Indians have generally been the highest of any ethnic group, though in some years they have been surpassed by whites. In 1965, the suicide rate among Indians was 10 per 100,000, less than whites (13 per 100,000), but greater than blacks (5 per 100,000). By 1972, Indian suicides had shot up to 17 per 100,000, but in the 1980s the Indian rate was comparable to whites, at 13 per 100,000. But the degree varies among tribes with some tribes having a rate as high as 150 per 100,000. Moreover, the rate is much higher among Indian youth. In 1992, among male youths between the ages of 15 and 24, it was 64 per 100,000, more than four times the comparable white rate (21.9 per 100,000). High rates of homicide and suicide are directly related to the use of alcohol. A lack of jobs and opportunities on most reservations may also be a factor. Alcohol-related offenses, such as public drunkenness and driving while intoxicated, average between four and five times that of the remainder of the population.

In the 20th century, Indians had the lowest arrest rate of any group, including whites, for drug abuse. Declining since its peak in 1980, the Native American arrest rate for drug offenses in 1992 (170 arrests per 100,000) was less than the white rate (230 per 100,000) and far less than the black rate (1,501 per 100,000). But methamphetamine abuse has skyrocketed on many reservations since then.

A recent phenomenon among Indian youths has been the growth of Indian gangs. Unheard of before the 1990s, they established themselves in Oklahoma, on the Navajo Reservation, and elsewhere. In many areas, police attribute the spread of gangs to television and movies, as well as the return of urban Indians to reservations.

A study released by the Justice Department in February 1999, the first of its kind by the department, found that Indians are victims of violent crime at a rate more than twice the national average, but that in 70 percent of these cases, the perpetrators were from another race. Whereas 69 percent of the violent crimes committed against whites were by other whites, and 81 percent of those committing crimes against blacks were black, 60 percent of those who committed violent crimes against Indian were white, 10 percent were black, and only 29 percent were Indians. Indian women were the most prone of any group to be the victim of a violent crime, with a rate more than 50 percent higher than that of black men, the next highest group. Experts attribute these results largely to lingering racism and alcohol use among poor whites near Indian reservations.

In the first decade of the 21st century, rates of violent crime began rising on Indian reservations, due in part to drug traffickers taking advantage of gaps in law enforcement. In 2010, President Barack Obama signed the Tribal Law and Order Act, which provides greater law enforcement powers for tribal authorities on reservations.

Further Reading

Bachman, Ronet. *Death and Violence on the Reservation: Homicide, Family Violence, and Suicide in American Indian Populations.* New York: Auburn House, 1992.

French, Laurence, ed. *Indians and Criminal Justice.* Totowa, N.J.: Rowman & Littlefield, 1982.

Greenfeld, Lawrence A., and Steven K. Smith. *American Indians and Crime.* Washington, D.C.: U.S. Department of Justice, Office of Justice Programs, Bureau of Justice Statistics, 1999.

Lester, David. *Crime and the Native American.* Springfield, Ill.: Charles C. Thomas, 1999.

Nielsen, Marianne O., and Robert A. Silverman, eds. *Native Americans, Crime, and Justice.* Boulder, Colo.: Westview Press, 1996.

Crow, John Orien (1912–1994) *Cherokee Bureau of Indian Affairs official*

Born on a farm in Salem, Missouri, on September 7, 1912, John Orien Crow was one-quarter Cherokee. He grew up in Commerce, Oklahoma, and then attended the Haskell Indian Institute in Lawrence, Kansas. After graduating in 1933, he played two years of professional football with the Boston Redskins. Crow began working for the Bureau of Indian Affairs (BIA) as a junior clerk in Valentine, Arizona in 1935 and was appointed superintendent of that agency in 1942. He became superintendent of the Mescalero Apache Agency in 1946, but was transferred shortly thereafter at the request of the Mescalero. In 1949, he was removed from his post at the Colorado River Agency after the Indians there accused him of being a "dictator." An assimilationist (see ASSIMILATION), he pushed for the TERMINATION of the Ute tribe while he was their agency superintendent during the 1950s.

Crow gradually rose through the ranks of the BIA, finally becoming acting commissioner from January to July 1961, replacing GLENN LEONIDAS EMMONS. He then stepped down to the position of deputy commissioner under commissioners PHILLEO NASH and ROBERT LAFOLLETTE BENNETT. In 1966, Crow left to become assistant director of the Bureau of Land Management (BLM). He returned to the BIA as deputy commissioner in 1971 under LOUIS ROOK BRUCE, JR. While there, he engaged in a power struggle with the reform-minded Bruce, who was attempting to mollify the growing militancy of the RED POWER MOVEMENT. Many viewed Crow's transfer from the BLM back to the BIA as an effort by Assistant Secretary of the Interior Harrison Loesch to block the reforms Bruce was contemplating, provoking AMERICAN INDIAN MOVEMENT (AIM) leader RUSSELL MEANS in September 1971 to attempt

a takeover of BIA headquarters and "arrest" Crow, WILMA VICTOR, and other members of the BIA old guard.

The tense situation in the bureau rose to a boiling point in November 1972, when Indians occupied BIA headquarters in Washington, D.C., during the TRAIL OF BROKEN TREATIES protest march. Crow, who along with Loesch had helped to sabotage what was intended to be a peaceful demonstration by a wide variety of Indian organizations, pressed for the Nixon administration to take a hard line against the militants, calling for police to storm the building and forcibly evict the occupiers. Bruce, on the other hand, advocated a compromise and attempted to negotiate, even joining the militants in their occupation until ordered out by Loesch.

When the occupation ended in a disastrous ransacking of the building, embarrassing the Nixon administration on the eve of the national elections, Nixon fired Crow, Loesch, and Bruce.

John O. Crow died on June 21, 1994, in Phoenix, Arizona.

Further Reading

Kotlowski, Dean J. "Alcatraz, Wounded Knee, and Beyond: The Nixon and Ford Administrations Respond to Native American Protest." *Pacific Historical Review* 72, no. 2 (2003): 201–227.

Crow Dog, Leonard (1942–) *Brulé Lakota Sioux activist, spiritual leader*

A Brulé Lakota Sioux, Leonard Crow Dog was born on August 18, 1942, on the Rosebud Reservation in South Dakota. His father, Henry Crow Dog, and his mother, Mary Gertrude Crow Dog, were both raised in the traditional Sioux-Catholic mixture of religion common among the Lakota Sioux of Rosebud and Pine Ridge, and both became members of the NATIVE AMERICAN CHURCH.

Leonard Crow Dog did not attend school, having been raised to become a *pejuta wichasha*, or spiritual man. He studied under Good Lance, Dick Fool Bull, and other Lakota Sioux traditionals, and also became versed in the peyote rituals of the Native American Church. At age 14, he was caught by police in a car his friends had stolen and was sent to reform school. Two years later, he was arrested for helping some of his friends attempt to escape from the police after they had been locked up for public drunkenness. He was sent to prison for a short period. Upon his release, Crow Dog began working as a ranch hand in South Dakota and Nebraska. He later worked as a glass cutter and fitter in an automobile repair shop.

Crow Dog joined his father Henry, JOHN EIRE LAME DEER, and other Sioux in a delegation led by ROBERT PHILLIP BURNETTE to Martin Luther King, Jr.'s 1967 Peace March in Washington, D.C. In 1970, DENNIS JAMES BANKS visited Henry Crow Dog, seeking a spiritual leader for the newly formed AMERICAN INDIAN MOVEMENT (AIM), and eventually recruited Leonard Crow Dog to the cause. Crow Dog invited AIM leaders to the Sun Dance Ceremony held in Pine Ridge the next year. He participated in the demonstration in

CROW DOG, MARY 111

Gordon, Nebraska, in 1972 that resulted in the arrest of the killers of RAYMOND YELLOW THUNDER. That same year, Crow Dog invited AIM leaders, as well as other prominent Indians, to the Sun Dance held on his family's Rosebud allotment, known as Crow Dog's Paradise, where the TRAIL OF BROKEN TREATIES was conceived.

Crow Dog served as doctor for the besieged encampment at WOUNDED KNEE in 1973 and, along with WALLACE HOWARD BLACK ELK, led a revival of the Ghost Dance Ceremony, not performed since its ban in the late 19th century. He also offered his land for the burial plot of Frank Clearwater, a Cherokee AIM member killed during the Wounded Knee siege, and performed the funeral ceremony. He chose not to escape before the end of the occupation and was one of 146 members of the encampment arrested when the siege ended on May 8.

Crow Dog married MARY BRAVE BIRD, who had been at the siege, and she moved with him to Crow Dog's Paradise. On September 15, 1975, more than 100 federal officers invaded the couple's encampment searching for LEONARD PELTIER and, not finding him, subsequently attempted to prosecute Crow Dog.

By this time, the Federal Bureau of Investigation (FBI) was using its infamous COINTEL program to selectively harass, intimidate, and otherwise destroy AIM, and as its spiritual leader, Crow Dog was one person the FBI wanted behind bars. In the first trial, the government contended that Crow Dog had participated in the kidnapping of four postal inspectors who had been sent to spy on the encampment at Wounded Knee, although the "kidnapping" was simply their detention for less than one hour by AIM's security force. Although the all-white jury found Crow Dog guilty, the presiding judge, Edward McManus, suspended his sentence, giving him only five years' probation. The second trial revolved around a small altercation at Crow Dog's camp, begun by a lifelong criminal and FBI provocateur named Robert Beck, who had trespassed on Crow Dog's land in July 1975 and had briefly scuffled with some of his relatives. Despite Crow Dog's lack of involvement in that incident, an all-white jury found him guilty of assault, and this time the judge sentenced him to five years in prison. The government was still not finished, however, and prosecuted Crow Dog for assaulting a non-Indian who had come to his home uninvited and grabbed Mary Crow Dog. Again an all-white jury found Crow Dog guilty, and he was sentenced to five more years in prison. In each trial, the government prosecutor was R. D. Hurd. Unlike some of the more prominent AIM leaders, who could count on the likes of William Kunstler or Mark Lane, Crow Dog was forced to use either a court-appointed attorney or a local, inexperienced lawyer.

Crow Dog was imprisoned on November 30, 1975, and sent first to Leavenworth, Kansas, and then to Lewisburg, Pennsylvania, one of the most notorious and violent prisons in the country. In his first day at Lewisburg, Crow Dog witnessed the murder of one inmate by a group of other prisoners. With the aid of the author Richard Erdoes, a campaign was launched by the National Council of Churches to address the injustice of Crow Dog's trials and his incarceration in Lewisburg. With the legal expertise of Kunstler, Sandy Rosen, Ken Tilsen, and VINE DELORIA, JR., Crow Dog won a release on appeal on March 10, 1976. The government fought his release, however, and managed to have him reincarcerated two months later. He was held in Deadwood, South Dakota. In September, over the strenuous objection of government prosecutor Hurd, Judge Robert Merhidge, citing the thousands of letters from all over the world he had received asking for leniency, ordered Crow Dog's sentence reduced to time served.

Crow Dog returned to Rosebud, where a feast and giveaway were held by his tribe to honor his return. He later performed in Oliver Stone's film *The Doors*. Although himself a product of the American Indian Movement, and therefore imbued with many of the character flaws that limited the movement's appeal—Crow Dog helped bring to the movement one of the keys to its success, a spiritual focus that gave it a strength and determination lacking in earlier pan-Indian movements. Crow Dog continues to host Sun Dances and is an important religious leader in his community.

Further Reading
Crow Dog, Leonard, and Richard Erdoes. *Crow Dog: Four Generations of Sioux Medicine Men.* New York: HarperCollins, 1995.

Crow Dog, Mary *See* BRAVE BIRD, MARY.

Crumbo, Woody (Woodrow Wilson Crumbo)
(1912–1989) *Potawatomi painter, sculptor*
Woody Crumbo was a Potawatomi born on January 21, 1912, in Lexington, Oklahoma; his parents, Alex and Mary Crumbo, named him Woodrow Wilson after the president. Woody's father, a horse trader, died when he was only four, and his mother passed away three years later. He left school in the third grade, having been encouraged by Susie Peters, discoverer of the KIOWA FIVE painters, to become an artist. He was so small that he would sit on a gallon paint bucket and use the back of a chair for an easel.

Ten years later, at 17, Crumbo returned to school to finish his education, transferring to the Chilocco Indian School in Oklahoma in 1931. Two years later, he entered the University of Wichita, graduating in 1936, after which he attended the University of Oklahoma for two years. Like many Indian painters of the day, he studied mural making under Pine Ridge artist-in-residence Olaf Nordmark. In addition, Crumbo studied watercolor painting under Kansas artist Clayton Henri Staples, and painting and drawing under Swedish-American artist Oscar Brousse Jacobson. Besides being a visual artist, Crumbo was also a musician and dancer.

In 1939, Crumbo's *Deer and Birds* was the first American Indian painting acquired by the Philbrook Art Center in Tulsa, Oklahoma, for its collection. Crumbo then succeeded ACEE BLUE EAGLE as the director of the Art Department at

Bacone College in Oklahoma. The college became famous for its influence on Indian art, giving rise to an entire style known as the Bacone School. Crumbo himself was succeeded as art director by WALTER RICHARD WEST, SR., in 1947.

During WORLD WAR II, Crumbo worked for the defense industry, helping to build aircraft. After the war, he moved to Taos, New Mexico, where he continued to develop his art. In 1960, he was named assistant director at the El Paso Museum of Art in Texas, and in 1968 he became the museum's director. While in El Paso, he helped the Tigua Ysleta del Sur Pueblo gain state and federal recognition as a tribe. He left the museum in 1974 to move back to Oklahoma where he served on the Oklahoma State Arts Council from 1978 to 1984 before returning to New Mexico.

Crumbo was also a successful mineral prospector. Starting in the 1950s with a mail-order mineral identification kit he bought for three dollars, he went on to find ore deposits worth millions of dollars, which allowed him all the time and resources he needed to work on his art. Crumbo died on April 4, 1989, in his home in Cimarron, New Mexico.

Further Reading

Curtis, Gene. "Only in Oklahoma: Indian Artist's Prospects Panned Out." *Tulsa World*, 31 August 2007.

Curtis, Charles (1860–1936) *Kaw attorney, congressman, U.S. senator, vice president of the United States*

Charles Curtis was born in North Topeka, Kansas, on January 25, 1860, to Orren Armes Curtis, a white man, and Ellen Curtis, who was one-quarter Kaw and one-quarter Osage. After his mother died of cholera in 1864, Curtis lived with his maternal grandmother, a descendant of Kaw leader White Plume, on the Kaw reservation near Council Grove, Kansas. Curtis attended the Friends Mission School until 1868, when the removal of the Kaw to Indian Territory (now Oklahoma) and unrest among the Cheyenne forced him to return to North Topeka and live with his paternal grandmother, who raised him as a strict Methodist and Republican.

After graduating from Topeka High School in 1879, Curtis apprenticed to a local attorney and was admitted to the bar in 1881 at age 21. He was removed from the Kaw annuity rolls in 1878 for not moving to the Kaw reservation or being present at an annuity distribution. (An annuity roll is the roster of tribal members eligible for money, food, or items from the federal government. They were usually required to live on a reservation. In many cases, the annuity roll was used as the official record of a tribe's members.) However, upon the death of his maternal grandmother, Curtis and his sister inherited a 40-acre allotment on ceded Kaw lands. Curtis turned those acres into a profitable enterprise, afterward using his example as an argument in favor of the federal policy of ALLOTMENT.

In 1885, Curtis was elected attorney of Shawnee County, Kansas, where he established his reputation as a zealous prosecutor of bootleggers and other petty criminals. His success at this job led to his election to Congress in 1892. In the House

of Representatives, Curtis became active in Indian affairs and authored the CURTIS ACT of 1898, which dissolved the governments of the Five Civilized Tribes (as the Creek, Chickasaw, Cherokee, Choctaw, and Seminole were known) and extended the Allotment policy to their reservations, paving the way for Oklahoma statehood. Curtis became chair of the House Committee on Indian Affairs in 1903, helping in 1906 to pass the controversial Burke Act, which removed the few protections Indians had been accorded under the Allotment policy. An avowed assimilationist, Curtis sought at every turn to diminish the role of reservations, end the communal ownership of property, and detribalize Indians, believing, like most progressives of his day, that these aspects of Indian culture were hindering Indians from becoming a part of American society. (See ASSIMILATION.)

Curtis was also an ardent supporter of free enterprise, particularly big business, and while publicly championing the rights of Indians, he was a major force in opening up INDIAN RESERVATIONS to the interests of railroads, oil companies, and mining companies. Curtis's close relationships with railroad tycoons and oilmen—his son worked for oil baron Harry Sinclair—led to numerous frauds against Indians, particularly in oil-rich Oklahoma, and ultimately led to his being "singed" in the Teapot Dome Scandal of the 1920s (see FALL, ALBERT BACON). Curtis personally played a role in the allotment of his tribe and was not above returning to the tribal rolls in time to share in the liquidation of tribal assets, in the end pocketing $22,136 and 1,676 acres of former Kaw land.

In 1907, Curtis was appointed to fill the unexpired term of recently deceased Kansas senator Joseph R. Burton, joining Cherokee ROBERT LATHAM OWEN, JR., from Oklahoma as one of two Indians in the Senate. Curtis was then elected to the seat in 1914. In 1924, Curtis and Senator Henry Cabot Lodge got the U.S. attorney general to rule against Secretary of the Interior Henry Work's interpretation of an administrative ruling by Work's predecessor Albert Fall that passed 22 million acres of federally mandated Indian land to the public domain, thereby opening it to oil and mineral prospecting (see OIL, AMERICAN INDIANS AND). That same year, he succeeded Lodge as Senate majority leader and gradually became detached from Indian affairs. A consummate insider in an age when national policy was made in smoke-filled rooms, Curtis was known as "the whisperer" for his power brokering and reticence to give speeches. His colleagues and opponents often called him "the Injun," though he was quite astute at turning his background to political advantage.

In 1929, Curtis sought the Republican nomination for the presidency but had to settle for second place on the ticket in favor of Herbert Hoover. His four-year tenure as the 31st vice president was unhappy, and he grew tired of his mostly symbolic duties. As the country began its plunge into the Great Depression, the defeat of Hoover in 1932 ended Curtis's career and brought an era in Indian policy to a close. Curtis, in his four decades in Congress as chair first of the House and then the Senate committees on Indian affairs, was a major force behind the disastrous assimilation policies of the day—which attempted to stamp out Indian culture and resulted in the loss of some two-thirds of the Indian land base. The subsequent election of Franklin Delano Roosevelt brought the INDIAN NEW DEAL (see INDIAN REORGANIZATION ACT) and an abrupt change in federal Indian policy. After the 1932 election, Curtis returned to private law practice in Washington, D.C., where he died on February 8, 1936, of a heart attack.

Further Reading

Unrau, William E. *Mixed-bloods and Tribal Dissolution: Charles Curtis and the Quest for Indian Identity.* Lawrence: University Press of Kansas, 1989.

Curtis Act (1898)

This legislation, named for its sponsor, CHARLES CURTIS, led to the dissolution of the Cherokee, Choctaw, Chickasaw, Creek, and Seminole tribes, who lost their considerable land base and natural wealth, and to the end of their powerful independent governments.

The nations, known as the Five Civilized Tribes (ironically because of their relatively high degree of acculturation to Euro-American cultural forms), held title to the eastern and southern half of Indian Territory (now Oklahoma). They had recovered dramatically from the Trail of Tears (the forced march from their southeastern homelands) and the Civil War, and by the late 19th century were relatively prosperous, even by mainstream American standards. Their lands, mostly held in common, were agriculturally and minerally rich, and the territory was dotted with fine towns, good schools, churches, and industries of every kind. However, pioneers and land speculators were clamoring for the opening of these lands to non-Indian settlement. An added factor, as stated in 1872 by the minority report of the House Committee on Territories, was "that Congress, in an unwise moment, granted many millions of acres belonging to the Indians to railroad corporations, contingent upon the extinction of Indian title." The railroads had carefully chosen routes that coincided with valuable Indian coal deposits and had sold millions of dollars' worth of bonds to investors on the assumption that Congress would validate the contingent land grants.

The first railroad was permitted through Indian lands in 1870. Within two years, railroads bisected both the Creek and Cherokee nations, bringing in their wake thousands of non-Indian squatters, fortune seekers, and criminals, many of them former soldiers of the Civil War. Organized invasions of Indian lands by "boomers" such as Colonel C. C. Carpenter, who began the boomer movement in 1879, and Captain David L. Payne (known as the "Father of Oklahoma") put added pressure on the Five Civilized Tribes, forcing them in 1893 to cede the Cherokee Strip, also known as the Cherokee Outlet, an 8,144,693-acre tract of land in northwestern Indian Territory, along with other lands.

By 1890, intruders had become so numerous that they outnumbered the 50,055 Indians in Indian Territory by more than two to one, and with the tacit consent of the federal government, they were pouring onto Indian lands at a rate of 2,000 a month. Crime was so rampant that, between 1875 and 1896, one judge presiding in Fort Smith, Isaac C. Parker, had alone sentenced 172 men to death, almost exclusively non-Indians (see OSKISON, JOHN MILTON). The tribes fought to preserve their territory through every legal means possible. They scored a victory when they were exempted by the Dawes Act of 1887, which was intended to divide all commonly held Indian land into individual allotments, but that same year they lost their jurisdiction to try capital cases to the federal courts.

The pressure on Indian landholdings increased in 1893, when the Commission to the Five Civilized Tribes, better known as the Dawes Commission, headed by former senator Henry Dawes, was established to negotiate the cessions of land necessary to lay the foundations for the creation of a new state. The commission met with considerable resistance, leading the United States to threaten to dissolve the tribes without their consent. Eventually three of the tribes, beginning with the Seminole, reached agreements with the federal government.

The Choctaw came to an accord, known as the Atoka Agreement, on April 23, 1897. It dictated the terms for the division of Choctaw lands and assets, protecting their considerable coal and asphalt holdings as a communal resource, but it also limited the authority of the tribal government, which could now only pass legislation with the approval of the president of the United States. However, Chickasaw voters rejected the Atoka Agreement negotiated by their leaders (see FOX, FINIS). Meanwhile, the Creek, under Chief Pleasant Porter, and especially the Cherokee, under C. J. Harris and S. H. Mayes, remained intransigent, refusing even to negotiate with the Dawes Commission. The federal government carried through on its threat and passed the Curtis Act on June 28, 1898.

The bill, disingenuously called "An act for the protection of the people of Indian territory and for other purposes," mandated the termination of Indian governments by April 26, 1906. It immediately abolished Indian tribal courts, invalidated all tribal laws, and authorized an inspector, a post held from 1898 to 1907 by J. George Wright, to assume complete control over the tribes' governance and legal matters. The bill also prescribed the procedures for allotting Indian lands and otherwise distributing or selling off all tribal assets. With few remaining options, the Creek came to an agreement with the federal government on May 25, 1901, and the Cherokee on July 1, 1902. Full-bloods and other traditionals continued to oppose any settlement. Among the Cherokee the Keetoowah, and among the Creek the Crazy Snakes, stubbornly advocated noncooperation and resistance, armed if necessary. Attempts by moderate Cherokee, Creek, and Choctaw leaders to create the separate state of "Sequoyah" were rejected by the federal government (see STARR, EMMET). In 1901, all the members of the Five Civilized Tribes officially became citizens of the United States, whether they wanted to or not.

After the agreements were signed, a bitter fight resulted over tribal membership and who would share the consequent distribution of assets. Inspector Wright accepted the membership rolls compiled by the Dawes Commission over those proffered by the tribes themselves, causing many non-Indians to be included in the distribution of land and many Indians to be left out. Moreover, since the inspector's office could add names or strike them from the rolls, thousands of non-Indians, aided by unscrupulous attorneys, clamored to be admitted to the tribes on spurious claims of having Indian blood. The tribes were forced to hire law firms to protect their interests, and the litigation and controversy continued for years.

In all, 15.9 million acres were allotted to 101,506 tribal members, which included 2,582 whites and 23,405 black former slaves. However, the Dawes Commission had appraised the Indian lands at values far below the market. This created pressure from non-Indian "boosters" who wished to buy the allotments, many of them sited over valuable oil and mineral deposits, at the low appraisal figures and then sell them for a substantial profit. The pressure led to legislation in 1904 and 1906 that authorized the Department of the Interior to remove certain allotted Indian lands from trust protection and resulted in a frenzy of carpetbagging. In the years to come, thousands of non-Indians would swoop down to seize the valuable Indian allotments, often using any means possible, including kidnapping and murder (see OSAGE REIGN OF TERROR).

The first major scandal erupted in 1903, when an investigation prompted by the INDIAN RIGHTS ASSOCIATION found that employees of the Dawes Commission and the federal courts had engaged in land speculation. The culprits were never prosecuted, however. In 1908, the federal government moved to stop the transfer of 3,842,553 acres of Indian land that investigations had determined to have been fraudulently acquired by non-Indians, but the suits were derailed by Congress and the local courts, neither of whom had any interest in protecting Indian lands. That same year, an attempt to prosecute Oklahoma governor Charles Haskell and other influential "boosters," for illegally acquiring valuable town lots, was effectively stalled by sympathetic judges until the statute of limitations expired. In addition, a class of professional "guardians" was established to oversee allotments made to Indian children, only to fleece them.

The abuses became so egregious that Indian Commissioner CATO SELLS managed to enact some reforms in 1914. Sells also managed to increase funding for probate attorneys for Indian plaintiffs, but by 1918 all his reforms had been overturned by Congress, which at the time included three Indian mixed-bloods from Oklahoma, ROBERT LATHAM OWEN, JR., in the Senate and CHARLES DAVID CARTER and WILLIAM WIRT HASTINGS in the House, all of whom actively sided with the "booster" movement.

The illegal dealings continued throughout the early 1920s, when the abuses in Oklahoma again came to national attention, in part through a pamphlet, written by Yankton Nakota writer and political reformer GERTRUDE BONNIN, called *Oklahoma's Poor Rich Indians: An Orgy of Graft and Exploitation of the Five Civilized Tribes—Legalized Robbery*. Once again, however, attempts by the Indian commissioner—in this case CHARLES HENRY BURKE—to institute reforms

were stalled by Congress until the outcry had passed. As the decade wound down, the despoliation of the former Indian Territory became complete, and the formerly powerful Five Civilized Tribes had all but ceased to exist as nations. They had no governments and no tribal land, and what little of their governmental affairs remained were administered by a "chief" appointed by the president of the United States. Ultimately, the Curtis Act had resulted in a frenzy of organized thievery and violence that was, in the words of the historian Angie Debo, "almost beyond belief."

See also HARJO, CHITTO; INDIAN RESERVATIONS; OIL, AMERICAN INDIANS AND; SMITH, REDBIRD.

Further Reading
Carter, Kent. *The Dawes Commission and the Allotment of the Five Civilized Tribes, 1893–1914*. Orem, Utah: Ancestry, 1999.
Debo, Angie. *And Still the Waters Run: The Betrayal of the Five Civilized Tribes*. Princeton, N.J.: Princeton University Press, 1991.
———. *The Road to Disappearance*. Norman: University of Oklahoma Press, 1941.

Custer riot (1973)

On January 21, 1973, a young Lakota Sioux Indian named Wesley Bad Heart Bull was stabbed to death in Buffalo Gap, South Dakota, by a white man named Darold Schmidt, who was charged, as in the case of another murdered Indian, RAYMOND YELLOW THUNDER, with involuntary manslaughter.

On February 6, 1973, more than 200 Indians, brought by leaders of the AMERICAN INDIAN MOVEMENT (AIM), traveled to Custer, South Dakota, to support Sarah Bad Heart Bull, Wesley's mother, in her search for justice. State and county authorities, nervous at such a large Indian presence, called for police backup and agreed to meet only with AIM spokesmen DENNIS JAMES BANKS, RUSSELL MEANS, LEONARD CROW DOG, and David Hill, a Choctaw. While they were inside the county courthouse, Sarah Bad Heart Bull attempted to join the proceedings but was prevented from doing so by two police officers, who seized her and beat her. Other protesters then came to her rescue, and the steps of the courthouse turned into a giant melee. Two police cars were overturned, and the building next to the courthouse was set on fire before the riot was quelled about an hour after it started.

Thirty-five Indians were arrested, including Sarah Bad Heart Bull. Charges of rioting were later filed against the AIM leaders, even though they had nothing to do with it, and Dennis Banks was forced to go into hiding after his conviction on those charges. The riot helped to trigger the occupation of WOUNDED KNEE two weeks later.

Further Reading
Hendricks, Steve. *The Unquiet Grave: The FBI and the Struggle for the Soul of Indian Country*, 51–57. New York: Thunder's Mouth Press.

Dagenett, Charles Edwin (1873–1941)

Peoria Indian Service agent, supervisor

A Peoria born in Wea, Kansas, on September 17, 1873, Charles Edwin Dagenet was the son of Edward R. and Elizabeth Dagenet. His grandfather Christmas Dagenet had been the agent on the Miami-Peoria Reservation. In 1887, Charles entered Carlisle Indian School in Pennsylvania, where he learned the printing trade and edited the Carlisle *Red Man.* After graduating as salutatorian in 1891, Dagenett (as he now spelled his name) spent a year at Dickinson College preparatory school, also in Pennsylvania, and then went to Eastman Business College in Poughkeepsie, New York. On his return home, he married Carlisle graduate Esther Miller (Miami), and together they started a weekly newspaper, *The Miami Chief,* which they printed on a small handpress.

Dagenett joined the Indian Service (later the Bureau of Indian Affairs) in 1894, working first with the Lower Yanktonai (Nakota) at the Crow Creek Reservation, Fort Thompson, South Dakota, and then with Apache prisoners of war at Fort Apache, Arizona. Around 1896–98, he was at the Chilocco Indian School in Oklahoma, where he worked his way up from teacher to disciplinarian to clerk. He was offered a reservation superintendency but turned it down.

Since his student days, Dagenett had been developing a plan that applied the principle of Carlisle's "outing system" (see Pratt, Richard Henry) on a national scale. With the help of Indian Commissioner Francis Leupp, he prevailed on Congress to create an Office of Indian Employment, of which he was appointed supervisor in spring 1905, with his headquarters first in Albuquerque, then Denver (with a larger office staff and more field assistants), and finally Washington, D.C. His task was to track down labor-intensive projects, such as railroad or dam construction or large-scale agricultural ventures, bargain with the employer to accept a certain number of Indian workmen, and then notify every agency superintendent in the area as to the number of men wanted, the kind of work, and the wages. The superintendents would get the word out on the reservations, "at the same time drawing the lines a little tighter on the ration distribution, if any were in use there," as Leupp put it. Dagenett's favorite motto was, "No work, no eat."

Dagenett placed 600 men in his first season, and by summer 1906 he had placed 1,100 on the Salton Sea flood control project in Southern California; some 200 on the construction of the Saint Mary's Canal on the Blackfeet Reservation in Montana; more than 200 ballasting on the Santa Fe Railroad; 600 in the sugar-beet fields at Rocky Ford, Colorado; and about 3,000 in other activities, including sheepherding, lumbering, cantaloupe growing, road construction, and irrigation projects. The Zuni Dam at Blackrock, New Mexico, was also built by Indian labor. A white overseer with each crew acted as liaison to the employer and was responsible for scheduling, helping the men with problems, and overseeing their health. Though the Indians had to pay for food, clothing, and supplies out of their wages, it was reported that they still took home between 60 percent and 93 percent of the proceeds. Many Indians who showed aptitudes for special kinds of work received training and became skilled workers.

In 1907, with winter approaching, President Theodore Roosevelt sent Dagenett out to Thunder Butte, South Dakota, to deal with a band of starving White River Ute who had left their reservation in protest against Allotment and Mormon encroachments on their land. They asked the government to take them home, but Dagenett helped them set up a winter camp and made them work for their passage. He got them hired on the construction of a railroad in the Black Hills, and as the wages were good, many stayed on until summer.

During his career, Dagenett made official trips to Canada, Mexico, Puerto Rico, and South America. During the winter of 1910–11, he spent three weeks in the Florida Everglades investigating conditions among isolated Seminole there.

In 1911, Dagenett was one of six Indians who formed the SOCIETY OF AMERICAN INDIANS (SAI). For the first several years, he was very active, serving first as secretary and later as vice president for membership. In September 1912, in the waning days of the Taft administration, the president consulted with Dagenett in regard to the post of Indian Commissioner, recently vacated by ROBERT VALENTINE. By 1913, there were some 2,300 Indians working for the Indian Service, and as Dagenett held the highest office of any, he was an important figure. His friend and associate, the Seneca ARTHUR C. PARKER, writing in 1914, described Dagenett's position as "one of the most vital . . . that a man can hold in the Indian Service," adding that "Mr. Dagenett is fearless in his recommendations to the [Indian] Bureau, and [I have] more than once witnessed his struggle to obtain justice for his brother Indian." However, a large faction of the SAI, led by Yavapai physician and author CARLOS MONTEZUMA, wanted the Indian Bureau eliminated and opposed its influence within the society. The pressure proved too great for Dagenett, and after 1915 he withdrew from active participation in the organization.

With the outbreak of WORLD WAR I, Dagenett was able to place many Indian mechanics in the expanding American auto industry. By 1917, the Willys-Overland Company in Toledo, Ohio, employed a score of Indians from various tribes, including Seneca JESSE CORNPLANTER. Charles Doxon, a skilled Onondaga mechanic, was at the Franklin Motor Works. One account states that by 1922, "a dozen of the leading manufacturers of automobiles . . . [had] constant orders in with the Indian Service and the trade schools for young redskins to serve as apprentices in their factories and to learn the automobile business. They report that the Indians rank among the best mechanics that they employ. . . . They do not talk during working hours and do not waste as much time as some of the other motor mechanics."

At the outset of his appointment, Francis Leupp had told Dagenett that "his future career in the Service [was] dependent on his carrying the experiment to success." Evidently he was valued, as he was kept on under commissioners Robert Valentine, CATO SELLS, and CHARLES H. BURKE, retiring for reasons of health only in 1927. Thereafter, he spent most of the year in a log cabin in the Ouachita Mountains near Mena, Arkansas, returning home to Tulsa only for the winter. Charles Dagenett died on March 16, 1941, in Tulsa, Oklahoma.

Further Reading

Hertzberg, Hazel W. *The Search for an American Indian Identity: Modern Pan-Indian Movements.* Syracuse, N.Y.: Syracuse University Press, 1971.

Houghton, Louise Seymour. *Our Debt to the Red Man: The French-Indians in the Development of the United States,* 154–156. Boston: Stratford Company, 1918.

dams on American Indian lands

In the 20th century, the federal government instituted a large number of major hydrological engineering projects throughout the United States, with the primary objects of flood control and hydroelectric power generation. Many of these projects affected Indian reservations, sometimes for the better, but usually for the worse. In many cases, dams have severely harmed tribes by flooding important bottomlands, not only destroying their most important natural resources but creating new forms of pollution and physical barriers to the cohesiveness of the reservation.

The damming of the Truckee River by the Derby Dam in the early 1900s seriously affected the Pyramid Lake Reservation of the Northern Paiute (Numu) in western Nevada (see PYRAMID LAKE). Beginning in the 1930s, a series of dams on the Columbia River devastated the largest Native American salmon fishery in North America and effectively destroyed the fishing economy there. In 1957, the Bonneville Dam, also on the Columbia River in the state of Oregon, flooded Celilo Falls, the most important Indian fishing ground on the continent. This was the last blow to the Indian fishing economy, with the exception of a few diehards who for spiritual reasons refused to give up their traditional way of life despite a greatly depleted salmon run (see SOHAPPY, DAVID).

Of dam projects that badly affected Indians, one of the most notorious was the gigantic PICK-SLOAN PLAN for the Missouri River and its tributaries in the Dakotas, built after WORLD WAR II. Many other huge dam projects were built on Indian lands in the 1950s under the aegis of Indian Commissioner GLENN LEONIDAS EMMONS.

The KINZUA DAM, built in 1964 by the Army Corps of Engineers for flood control on the Allegheny and Ohio Rivers, destroyed more than 9,000 acres of Seneca lands, including the last remaining tribal lands in Pennsylvania and some of the Allegheny Reservation in New York.

In some cases, tribes have successfully fought off harmful projects. A proposed dam that would have flooded 23 acres of the Courts d'Oreille Reservation in Wisconsin was defeated by the Chippewa in 1916. In 1958, the Tuscarora defeated the New York Power Authority's plan to convert one-fifth of the Tuscarora reservation into a storage reservoir for the giant St. Lawrence Seaway project, although some portions of the reservation were submerged (see ANDERSON, MAD BEAR).

Proponents of large-scale damming cite benefits to tribes from such reclamation programs as the San Carlos Indian Irrigation Project in Arizona and the Navajo Indian Irrigation Project in Nevada. But even these have come with many strings attached (see WATKINS, ARTHUR VIVIAN).

The 1907 WINTERS DOCTRINE legally protects the prior and superior water rights of Indian tribes, but in practice this doctrine has been ignored by the relevant government agencies. Among the tribes whose water rights have been affected are the Akimel O'odham (Pima) (Arizona), Mission Indians (California), Coastal Salish, Kootenai, and Yakama in the Pacific Northwest, as well as the Seneca (Pennsylvania/New York).

See also GARRISON DAM; PIMA-MARICOPA WATER RIGHTS.

dance orders (1921–1926)

This series of Indian Office (see BUREAU OF INDIAN AFFAIRS) orders and congressional bills, issued or submitted between

1921 and 1926, attempted to curtail traditional Native American ceremonies and dances. Though ultimately unsuccessful, they had the additional effect of temporarily splitting some of the opposition to the BURSUM BILL and other anti-Indian legislation.

The Progressive Era saw "good government" as a moral and scientific ideal and showed genuine interest in cultural diversity. The administrations of Indian commissioners FRANCIS ELLINGTON LEUPP, ROBERT GROSVENOR VALENTINE, and CATO SELLS reflected these values to varying degrees. But U.S. entry into WORLD WAR I on April 6, 1917, changed this outlook. Almost overnight, a barrage of war propaganda put an America of ethnic diversity into a mood of resurgent nationalism and conformity.

After the armistice of November 11, 1918, the wartime profiteering that had so greatly expanded the nation's industrial capacity was transformed into a spirit of smug boosterism. The ensuing drive for resource exploitation, accompanied by reduction of federal services on Indian reservations, clashed head-on with the burgeoning modernism of artists and intellectuals for whom the war, with its unprecedented brutality, had raised serious questions about the viability of Western civilization itself.

New ideas in science, such as Sigmund Freud's theory of the unconscious and Albert Einstein's theory of relativity, as well as rapidly changing social mores regarding gender and race, further unsettled the status quo. The cultural historian Roderick Nash describes how the prospect of an irrational world led to "cultural nervousness," which fueled "scientific racism" and the resurgence of evangelism, the Klu Klux Klan, and the 1924 restrictions on immigration. In 1920, laws banning the manufacture, sale, and consumption of alcohol (known as Prohibition) were implemented as the result of the powerful, largely Christian-based, Temperance movement.

For many years, it had been a goal of federal policy makers to destroy tribal culture and identity, but the new mood of insecurity and anxiety in America led the government to take an especially hard line against Indian traditions. The new administration of President Warren G. Harding was particularly unsympathetic. The early 1920s saw a strong renewal of attacks on ceremonial dances on the grounds that some, such as the Hopi snake dance, were sexually explicit. Herbert Welsh, president of the INDIAN RIGHTS ASSOCIATION, led the charge, basing his complaints on a report by Interior Department inspector Reverend E. M. Sweet, whose information came solely from the gossip of non-Indians and Christianized Indians. Father W. H. Ketcham, in a report of 1918, had made similar charges, and the Indian Rights Association's correspondence for 1920 includes several affidavits of this kind.

Soon after taking office on March 21, 1921, Indian Commissioner CHARLES HENRY BURKE responded. In Circular 1665 of April 26, 1921, addressed to all Indian superintendents (agents), he urged that missionaries redouble their efforts to "civilize" the Indians and prepare them for CITIZENSHIP. He particularly targeted ceremonies involving self-torture, the use of drugs (especially peyote) or alcohol, what he called "immoral relations between sexes," and giving away property (potlach)—with penalties of fines and imprisonment for offenders.

Burke's circular to the Indians of February 24, 1923, came next. In this, as well as in a follow-up letter to leaders of all tribes, dated March 28, he urged that "questionable" ritualistic dances be stopped by the Indians themselves, without definite orders from the BUREAU OF INDIAN AFFAIRS (BIA).

The main reason for the orders was that the dances made it more difficult for the missionaries to make and keep converts. According to activist JOHN COLLIER in *Indians of the Americas*, Native American religions "made the tribes strong, and made the individuals of the tribes immune to intimidation and corruption. The Bureau's new onslaught fell upon all the Pueblo Native religions and upon the expanding, intertribal Native American Church." Collier continued: "The Bureau sent out inspectors. These men collected pornographic gossip about the tribes. . . . The Bureau submitted it . . . to no Indian and no ethnologist. The foul pages, numbering 193, were photostated and turned over to . . . leading editors, churchmen, and heads of women's organizations."

One report, written by William E. (Pussyfoot) Johnson, director of the World League against Alcoholism and former chief officer of the Indian Service, describes two Zuni dances in unflattering but realistic terms. His argument was answered by the anthropologist Ruth Benedict, who in reply proposed a kind of theory of cultural relativism.

A letter from Edith Dabb, secretary of the YWCA's Committee on Indian Affairs (*New York Times*, 2 December 1923), represented the views of religious conservatives. In the letter, she stated that at dances young girls frequently became pregnant and that dances were "degrading and demoralizing" to participants and to Indian family life. She maintained that the government regulations were meant only to protect Indian youth and give them the same opportunities as everyone else.

Reformers such as Mabel Dodge Luhan, Mary Austin, John Collier, Charles Lummis, HAMLIN GARLAND, ERNEST THOMPSON SETON, and Frederick Webb Hodge defended the ceremonies. Not even all members of the Indian Rights Association supported the policy. HAROLD SELLERS COLTON wrote to Jesse W. Fewkes, director of the Bureau of American Ethnologists, urging tolerance; Fewkes agreed.

The dance orders and the Bursum bill, coinciding with the scandals of recently fired Interior Secretary ALBERT BACON FALL, brought the BIA much bad publicity. To counter this, the new interior secretary, Herbert Work, put together the COMMITTEE OF ONE HUNDRED. Among many recommendations for improvements in Indian administration, the committee's report addressed the problem of the dance orders with a toothless resolution stating that "all lawful ancient ceremonies, rites and customs of the Indian race" were the "privilege and liberty of the Indians, not to be curtailed or infringed." But if contrary to law or against "the interests of morality," they should be "discontinued and discouraged."

In no way satisfied by this, traditional Indians began to protest to the BIA. By spring 1924, the protest movement was broadening into a general defense of Indian religious practices. In April, Commissioner Burke went out to Taos, New Mexico, to deal with a controversy over two Indian boys temporarily taken out of school for traditional religious training. This proved a dramatic turning point. Burke's order requiring them to attend school was seen by Indians as unreasonable and dictatorial, while the Pueblo's Native governors saw it as meddling in their affairs. At a meeting called at Santo Domingo (Taos, New Mexico) on May 5, 1924, the All-Pueblo Council drafted a statement condemning religious persecution and refusing to follow Burke's order.

With the exception of the Indian Rights Association, all the support organizations opposed to the Bursum bill also fought the dance orders. The American Indian Association (see TIPI ORDER OF AMERICA), the nearest thing to a national pan-Indian organization that existed at the time, also opposed it. In 1924, however, the GENERAL FEDERATION OF WOMEN'S CLUBS (GFWC) split on the issue.

John Collier, who had been contracted by the GFWC to investigate Indian affairs, defended Indian religious freedom at the organization's convention in June 1924, reading a letter that Charles Lummis had written to Interior Secretary Work. However, members of the Indian Rights Association brought some members of the "General Council of Progressive Christian Indians" to the same convention. In their view, it was the good Christian Indians who were being persecuted by the bad pagan chiefs. Although Stella Atwood, GFWC chair of the Indian Welfare Committee, held firm, the Christian side sowed confusion and created a split. No decisive action was taken, and five months later, Collier's contract was terminated.

Collier bounced back, however, finding support from several wealthy Californians. His passionate and effective writings in defense of Indian RELIGIOUS FREEDOM attracted political support. In fact, the dance orders proved to be the swan song of the old-fashioned Protestant Indian welfare organizations as a major influence in Indian affairs.

In summer 1925, two members of the NATIVE AMERICAN CHURCH were publicly whipped at Taos for appearing at a ceremony in improper dress. The BIA agent arrested nearly all the Pueblo council members. At their trial in Santa Fe, New Mexico, the judge dismissed the case, stating that he had "no jurisdiction in the Pueblos' internal affairs."

At a meeting of the All-Pueblo Council, tribal leaders publicly attacked the BIA for slandering them in documents about ceremonies and for meddling in their internal affairs (resolution of August 31, 1925). They voted to send Collier and 12 Pueblo representatives on a fund-raising tour of the West. With dances, songs, and lectures on Pueblo religion, presented mainly at well-to-do homes, theaters, and clubs, this tour was highly successful.

Meanwhile, Burke and his assistant commissioner Edgar B. Meritt drafted the Leavitt bill (1926) as a "final mighty effort" to impose morals, as they saw it, including a ban on traditional Indian marriage and divorce. This just called forth more protests from prominent citizens, such as journalist Elizabeth Shepley Sergeant, GFWC leader Stella Atwood, and anthropologist Alfred Kroeber. Sotero Ortiz, chair of the All-Pueblo Council, testified against the bill at a hearing before the House Indian Affairs Committee in February 1926. Collier argued that it deprived Indians of due process and the constitutional right to govern their own affairs.

On behalf of Burke, who was ill, Meritt answered Collier's charges. Now that Indians were citizens, he said, a transition had to take place between Indian laws and federal and state laws. The ban on traditional marriage and divorce would help stem the tide of "immorality and irreligion." Representative George Brummel of Pennsylvania noted that Indian weddings were already recognized by state common law. But the bill did not pass. Collier had successfully framed the issue. With Indian citizenship, self-determination in civil and religious matters took precedence over ASSIMILATION.

Coming on the heels of the Indian Citizenship Act (1924), the campaign against the dance orders represents one of the first attempts to use citizenship as an argument for rather than against tribalism. It was successful and continued to be used for many years, until challenged in 1961 by Tuscarora an activist WILLIAM RICKARD, who insisted that tribal sovereignty, rather than U.S. citizenship, was the more fundamental legal basis for Native rights.

Further Reading
Collier, John. *Indians of the Americas*. New York: New American Library, 1947.

Jacobs, Margaret D. *Engendered Encounters: Feminism and Pueblo Cultures, 1879–1934*. Lincoln: University of Nebraska Press, 1999.

Jones, Carter. "Hope for the Race of Man: Indians, Intellectuals and the Regeneration of Modern America, 1917–1934." Ph.D. dissertation, Brown University, 1991.

Kelly, Lawrence C. *The Assault on Assimilation: John Collier and the Origins of Indian Policy Reform*. Albuquerque: University of New Mexico Press, 1983.

Philp, Kenneth R. *John Collier's Crusade for Indian Reform, 1920–1954*. Tucson: University of Arizona Press, 1977.

Thompson, Mark. *American Character: The Curious Life of Charles Fletcher Lummis and the Rediscovery of the Southwest*, 252–253, 287, 311–312. New York: Arcade Publishing, 2001.

Wenger, Tisa. *The Pueblo Indian Dance Controversy and the Cultural Invention of Religion in America*. Chapel Hill: University of North Carolina Press, 2008.

Daniels, Victor (Victor Daniel, Chief Thunder Cloud) (1899–1955) *Tohono O'odham(?), film actor*

Victor Daniels was an American Indian actor who appeared in more than 100 motion pictures under the name Chief Thunder Cloud (also spelled Thunder-Cloud or Thundercloud). Biographical information about him is both scanty and contradictory. According to his publicity, he was born in Muskogee, Oklahoma, on April 12, 1899, the eldest of nine children of Dark Cloud and Morning Star (usually identified as Cherokee), but raised on a ranch in Arizona. He attended the

University of Arizona at Tucson, where he was an excellent student and athlete (especially in football and boxing), and subsequently worked as an unskilled laborer on cattle ranches and at rodeos. He also worked as a mining foreman, boxer, and guide. Migrating to Hollywood in the late 1920s, he trained to become a singer of tribal folk songs but soon found work as a stuntman in Westerns.

Daniels gives quite different information on his 1937 Social Security application, unearthed by B-Western film buff Chuck Anderson. While the birthdate is the same, April 12, 1899, he names his parents as Jesus F. Daniels and Tomaca [sic] Daniels, and his birthplace as "Santa Rita Mountains, San Cruse [sic] County, 75 miles SE of Tucson, Arizona." Santa Cruz County was created by the Arizona territorial legislature on March 15, 1899, out of parts of Pima and Cochise Counties. The only part of the Santa Rita Mountains that fits these specifications is in the general vicinity of Patagonia, Arizona, which at the time of Daniels's birth was a profitable mining district rich in gold, silver, copper, and lead.

The federal census of 1900 confirms that a Jesus and Tomasa Daniel (not Daniels), aged 40 and 20, respectively, both born in Mexico, were living in what is there designated Pima County, Precinct One, "Papago Town," to the southeast of Tucson—not on the Papago (Tohono O'odham) reservation to the city's west. They had a son Leonardo, two years old, and daughter, Guadalupe, three months. The 1910 census finds them in Oracle, Arizona, about 30 miles north of Tucson, with two more children, Maria (four) and Pascual (10 months), and the wife's name is here given more fully as Tomasa Arana Daniel. The son Leonardo is about the same age as Victor, and it is possible that Victor was part of his given name—or perhaps he simply changed it later on.

Other details of Daniels's stage biography may well be true, but there is no evidence of any Cherokee named Dark Cloud or Morning Star, and the names Jesus and Tomasa Arana, as well as their place of residence, are unlikely for Cherokee. The documentation suggests, rather, that the Daniel family was actually Papago (Tohono O'odham), a tribe whose territory straddles the Mexican border. The area of Patagonia definitely lies within Papago country. This would also explain the references to Arizona and mining in his biography. It is hard to say why Daniels preferred to be known as a Cherokee rather than a Papago in Hollywood; it might have started as a matter of circumstance, which he later found difficult to change.

More is known about Daniels's Hollywood career. He began about 1928 as a stuntman, just when sound films were taking over. Soon he took acting parts. His earliest credited roles (as Chief Thunder Cloud) date from 1935. He most famous role was as Tonto in the 15-chapter Republic film serial Hi-Yo Silver (1938), the very first Lone Ranger film (also known by the title The Lone Ranger). Directed by William Witney and John English with Lee Powell in the title role, it is considered by B movie aficionados to be, in the words of Michael R. Pitts in Western Movies (1986), "one of the all-time great sound serials." Another, less successful Republic serial, The Lone Ranger Rides Again (1939), this time with Bob Livingston in the title role, is remarkable for long scenes in which the Lone Ranger appears without his trademark mask.

Among Daniels's other credits were Ramona, Custer's Last Stand, For the Service, Ride Ranger Ride (all 1936); The Plainsman, Renfrew of the Royal Mounted (both 1937); Murder on the Yukon, Northwest Mounted Police, Wyoming, Young Buffalo Bill (all 1938); The Cat and the Canary, Union Pacific (both 1939); Typhoon (1940); Traveling Saleswoman, Colt .45, Davy Crockett, Indian Scout, and Ambush (all 1950). He appeared in many other low-budget B films, mainly Westerns, and had a leading role, along with CHIEF YOWLACHIE, in the 1942 Monogram B feature, King of the Stallions.

In the early 1950s, Daniels was one of a number of Hollywood screen veterans who worked at Western film star Crash Corrigan's Corriganville Movie Ranch in Chatsworth, California, when it was open to the public as a kind of Western theme park. There he operated a photo shop selling Indian memorabilia and photographs, including autographed photos of himself. He also made publicity appearances for Transcontinental and Western Airways.

In his last years, Daniels worked less because of heart problems. His final appearance, uncredited, was in the Warner Brothers production The Searchers, filmed in 1955 and released the following year. He died in Ventura, California, on December 1, 1955, shortly after undergoing surgery for cancer, survived by his wife, Frances, a former singer, and two children.

Daniels is often confused with his contemporary, Scott T. Williams, an Ottawa who claimed to have played Tonto on radio in the early 1930s and who also used the stage name Chief Thundercloud (usually spelled as one word).

Dann, Mary, and Dann, Carrie
See BATTLE MOUNTAIN.

Davis, Alice Brown (1852–1935) Seminole missionary, chief
Alice Brown Davis was a Seminole born at the Cherokee mission town of Park Hill, Indian Territory (now Oklahoma), on September 10, 1852. Her father, John Frippo Brown, was a Scottish physician who had chosen to accompany the Seminole on the 1832 forced march to Indian Territory (now Oklahoma) known as the Trail of Tears. Her mother was Lucy Greybeard, a member of the influential Tiger Clan. Alice was one of eight children; her older brothers became important in Seminole politics: John Frippo Brown, Jr., became principal chief, and Andrew Jackson Brown served as tribal treasurer.

Alice Brown attended Cherokee and Seminole mission schools. In 1874, she married a white man, George Rollins Davis, and moved to the Cherokee Nation. In 1882, they returned to Seminole territory, where they established a trading post and a ranch. After her husband's death, Davis ran both the post and the ranch and eventually became superintendent of the Seminole's Girl School, Emahaka, until its takeover by federal authorities after Oklahoma became a state. In 1905, she served as an interpreter for a Seminole man charged with murder in Palm Beach, Florida. In that same year, she traveled to Mexico City to research claims of a Spanish land grant awarded to the Seminole.

A devout Christian who read a chapter of the Bible every morning, Davis was sent by Christian Seminole in 1909 to convert the Florida Seminole, who were bitterly resisting any non-Indian encroachment. After several months, she succeeded in forging ties between the two estranged communities. In 1922, she was appointed chief of the Seminole by President Warren G. Harding, succeeding her brother John and making her the first woman chief of the tribe. After the CURTIS ACT effectively dissolved the Seminole government in 1906, the tribal chiefs who were subsequently appointed mostly oversaw the disbursement of tribal assets. By the time Davis became chief, there was little left to disburse and little to do, as the position had become one of merely signing off on the conveyance of Seminole property. Despite her limited power, she refused in 1923 to sign a deed awarding Seminole property to a white man; the federal government then appointed two other chiefs in quick succession, George Jonas and Harry Tiger, who also refused to sign. Finally the federal government allowed the transaction to go ahead without the signature of any Seminole chief.

Davis also fought attempts to have Seminole lands transferred to the Creek, serving as chief as the need arose until her death on June 21, 1935. Alice Brown Davis was inducted into the Oklahoma Hall of Fame in 1930. In 1951, the University of Oklahoma dedicated Davis House in her honor.

Further Reading

Trimble, Vance H. *Alice and J.F.B.: The Hundred-Year Saga of Two Seminole Chiefs*. Wilmington, Del.: Market Tech Books/Poets of America Press, 2007.

Waldowski, Paula. "Alice Brown Davis: A Leader of Her People." *Chronicles of Oklahoma* 58 (Winter 1980–81): 455–463.

Davis, Jesse Ed (1944–1988) *Kiowa guitarist*

Jesse Edwin Davis III, a Kiowa, was born in Norman, Oklahoma, on September 21, 1944. His mother, Vivian Mae (Saunkeah) Davis, was Kiowa and taught piano. His father, Jesse Ed Davis II, a mural painter who also played drums for a Dixieland jazz band, was Cherokee and Kiowa. Jesse Ed's early life was filled with music, as the household members were continually holding jam sessions with their friends. He played guitar while in high school with other young talented musicians such as drummer John Ware, bass player John Selk, and vocalist Jerry Fisher. He graduated from Northeast High School in 1962 along with Mike Brewer, of Brewer and Shipley fame.

Davis attended the University of Oklahoma, majoring in literature. Strongly drawn to music, however, he quit Oklahoma and began playing guitar for country music great Conway Twitty. Davis then moved to Los Angeles, where he met fellow Oklahoman Leon Russell and bluesman Taj Mahal. His distinct, full-bodied sound soon made him a sought-after session guitarist. His guitar playing was featured on Taj Mahal's self-titled debut album, released in 1968, and he later played on three other Taj Mahal albums. He also played on Eric Clapton's *No Reason to Cry* (1976), B. B. King's *L.A. Midnight* (1972), Jackson Brown's *Doctor My Eyes* (1972), BUFFY SAINTE-MARIE's *She Used to Wanna Be a Ballerina* (1977), and Leon Russell's classic album *Shelter People* (1971).

During this time, Davis also released a number of solo albums, including *Jesse Davis* (1971), *Ululu* (1972), and *Keep Me Comin'* (1973), on which were featured the talents of Leon Russell, Eric Clapton, Jim Keltner, Donald "Duck" Dunn, and Gram Parsons. In 1969, while working with Taj Mahal in the Rolling Stones' film *A Rock and Roll Circus* (not released until 1996), Davis found himself playing with John Lennon, and the two became good friends. Davis played with Lennon and Harry Nilsson on their album *Pussycats*, released in 1974, and was Lennon's lead guitarist for his solo albums *Rock 'N' Roll* and *Walls and Bridges*, both released in 1975.

Davis joined George Harrison for his landmark concert and film, *Concert for Bangladesh*, in 1971, and played on Harrison's album *Extra Texture*, released in 1975. Davis also played on Ringo Starr's albums *Goodnight Vienna* (1974), and *Ringo's Rotogravure* (1976). Sporting a soulful lead guitar that could be happy and vibrant one minute and wistful and weepy the next, Davis was a welcome addition to touring bands, and he was on the road regularly with top acts, including the Monkees, B. B. King, Rod Stewart, Linda Ronstadt, and Bob Dylan. By 1976, Davis was among rock and roll's most sought-after session guitarists, playing on more than a dozen albums a year.

For most of his career, Davis struggled with alcohol and heroin addiction, and after 1977 he spent much of his time in drug rehabilitation centers. In 1985, he went into rehabilitation at the Eagle Lodge Center in Long Beach, California. There he heard the poetry of JOHN TRUDELL and, after one of Trudell's readings, offered to set the poetry to music. In 1986, they released their first album, *AKA: Grafitti Man*, on their own record label, the Peace Company. The album was critically acclaimed, won a Grammy nomination, and was proclaimed by Bob Dylan as the "album of the year." In 1987, when they released *Heart Jump Bouquet* and the band was on the verge of breaking out, Davis suffered a stroke that caused him to lose some feeling in his right hand. He also had not fully recovered from his debilitating bouts with alcohol and drugs.

On June 22, 1988, Jesse Ed Davis was found dead in the laundry room of an apartment building in Venice, California, apparently of a drug overdose. In 1992, a new version of *AKA: Grafitti Man* was released, this time by a major record label; it received critical acclaim.

Dawes Commission *See* CURTIS ACT.

DeCora, Angel (Henook Makhewe Kelenaka, "Queen of the Clouds") (1871–1919) *Winnebago artist, educator*

Angel DeCora was born on the Winnebago reservation in

Nebraska on May 3, 1871. Her father, David DeCora, was the son of Winnebago hereditary chief Little DeCora, and her mother was from another prominent Winnebago family, the LaMeres. Her Winnebago name, Henook Makhewe Kelenaka ("Queen of the Clouds" or "Woman Coming on the Clouds in Glory") was translated "Angel." Angel DeCora was born in a wigwam and grew up in the traditional Winnebago lifestyle of hunting and farming, learning from her grandfather and father the laws and customs of her people.

In 1883, after being enrolled in her reservation school for only a few weeks, she was sent to Hampton Institute in Virginia without her parents' consent. After five years, she was allowed to return home for a visit, only to find that her father and grandfather had died and that the traditional lifestyle the family had led had ended. She decided to return to Hampton, graduating in 1891.

From there, she went to the Burnham School in Northampton, Massachusetts, and in 1892 enrolled in a four-year art course at Smith College, also in Massachusetts, where she was particularly influenced by painter Dwight Tryon. In 1896, she went to the Drexel Institute in Philadelphia, where she was a student of the famous illustrator Howard Pyle, and in 1900 entered the Boston Museum of Fine Arts, studying there for two years with leading artists Frank W. Benson and Edmund Charles Tarbell. After that, she ran studios in Boston (1899–1903) and New York City (1903–06).

DeCora opposed ASSIMILATION in Indian education and keenly supported the survival of traditional Indian crafts. An article of hers promoting traditional crafts education was published in the *Journal of Addresses and Proceedings of the National Education Association* for 1907. That same year, Indian Commissioner FRANCIS ELLINGTON LEUPP asked her to set up a school of design at the Carlisle Indian School in Pennsylvania. DeCora's own work was eclectic and much influenced by her formal training; she was also interested in the traditional crafts of other cultures. While at Carlisle, for example, she learned and then taught oriental rug weaving, to which she adapted Native American figures and coloring.

One of DeCora's students at Carlisle was WILLIAM DIETZ (Oglala Lakota Sioux), later a celebrated football coach. They fell in love and were married in summer 1908. After that, he assisted her in her art classes. Dietz remained at Carlisle until 1915, and during this period the couple worked on a number of projects together, including the illustrations for *Yellow Star: A Story of East and West* (1911) by DeCora's lifelong friend Elaine Goodale Eastman, whom she had known since her student days at Hampton.

From about 1914, Dietz and DeCora began to grow apart. The following year, he left Carlisle to coach at the University of Washington. She gave up her position at Carlisle to go with him but wound up staying in the town of Carlisle, where she opened a studio. They were divorced in Spokane, Washington, on November 30, 1918.

In summer 1918, DeCora taught arts and crafts to the girls at Camp Oahe in New Hampshire, run by her friends Elaine and CHARLES EASTMAN, the latter a Lakota physician and educator. In 1918, she was hired by the New York State Museum in Albany as a substitute for an artist serving in the military. Experts rated her drawings of fossils for a memoir on Devonian fauna as "equal to the best." When the draftsman returned, she went to Northampton to stay with an old college friend and formulated a plan to provide handicrafts therapy to disabled soldiers. She was also planning at least one book on Indian life and culture. At the time, however, the great influenza pandemic of 1918, which had already taken the life of the Eastmans' daughter, IRENE EASTMAN, was raging. DeCora contracted the disease and succumbed to pneumonia on February 6, 1919.

DeCora's work includes illustrations for *Old Indian Legends* by Zitkala-Sa (GERTRUDE BONNIN), *The Middle Five* by FRANCIS LA FLESCHE, and *The Indians' Book* by Natalie Curtis. Her stories and pictures appeared in *Harper's* magazine. She was a charter member of the SOCIETY OF AMERICAN INDIANS at its foundation in 1911 and bequeathed $3,000 to the society in her will.

Further Reading

Gere, Anne Ruggles. "An Art of Survivance: Angel DeCora of Carlisle." *American Indian Quarterly* 28, nos. 3, 4 (Summer/Fall 2004): 649–684.

McAnulty, Sarah. "Angel DeCora: American Artist and Educator." *Nebraska History* (Summer 1976): 143–199.

Quilter, Sarah McAnulty. "Angel DeCora Dietz—The Art Career of a Winnebago Woman." In *Perspectives: Women in Nebraska History*, 98–115. Lincoln: Nebraska State Department of Education and Nebraska State Council for the Social Studies, 1984.

Deer, Ada Elizabeth (1935–) *Menominee activist, assistant secretary for Indian affairs*

The first woman to head the BUREAU OF INDIAN AFFAIRS (BIA), Ada Elizabeth Deer was born on August 7, 1935, in Keshena on the Menominee reservation in Northern Wisconsin. Her father, Joseph Deer, was a Menominee lumberman, and her mother, Constance Stockton (Wood) Deer, a white woman from Philadelphia, had worked as a nurse for the BIA. The eldest of five children, Deer grew up in a log cabin without running water or electricity. After high school, she enrolled in the University of Wisconsin at Madison, earning a B.A. in social work in 1957. In 1961, she became the first Indian to earn a master's degree in social work from Columbia University.

After a stint in the Peace Corps and social work in New York City, Deer joined the BIA in 1964 as a community service coordinator in Minnesota. After three years, she left the post to work for the University of Minnesota's Training Center for Community Programs. She briefly attended law school before joining with Menominee activist JAMES A. WASHINAWATOK to form Determination of the Rights and Unity for Menominee Shareholders (DRUMS) in 1970. The group began to press the federal government to restore the Menominee nation, which had been terminated in 1961 (see TERMINATION). From 1972 to 1973, Deer was the vice president and lobbyist for the National Committee to Save the Menominee People and Forest, Inc., which expanded on the work of DRUMS and helped persuade President Richard M. Nixon to sign the Menominee Restoration Act on December 23, 1973.

Deer became the chair of the Menominee Restoration Committee, which planned the transition back to a reservation life. On January 1, 1975, a group called the Menominee Warrior Society occupied an unused abbey belonging to the Alexian Brothers Novitiate in Gresham, Wisconsin, with the aim of converting it into a health center. Deer tried to negotiate a peaceful settlement, but the takeover turned into a violent confrontation when local and federal police attempted to force the militants out.

After a new Menominee government was established, Deer resigned from the Restoration Committee to teach at the University of Wisconsin-Madison. She then served as legislative liaison for the NATIVE AMERICAN RIGHTS FUND. In 1982, she entered Wisconsin politics. Though she lost her bid to become secretary of state, Deer became an important figure in the Wisconsin Democratic Party, serving in Walter Mondale's campaign for the presidency in 1984 and running unsuccessfully in 1992 for a seat in Congress. In 1993, she was nominated by President Bill Clinton to become assistant secretary for Indian affairs in the Department of the Interior, replacing Ed Brown.

Deer quickly became enmeshed in the disputes over GAMING ON INDIAN RESERVATIONS that were flaring up across the country. When Oneida representative Ray Halbritter broke away from the Iroquois Confederacy and independently negotiated a gaming agreement with New York State, dealing the ancient traditional government a serious setback, Deer at first supported the traditional government, but under pressure from gaming interests was forced to side with Halbritter. She also settled leadership disputes among the Cherokee and Winnebago. Although Deer sought to reorganize the BIA after 12 years of Republican neglect, she was unable to halt the decline in federal funding that began under President Ronald Reagan. Moreover, she was unable to reform the bureau's chronic mismanagement. During her administration, more than 10 percent of the budget went unaccounted for. Deer was an effective advocate for Indian self-determination, however, and under her tenure the Clinton administration was largely protective of Indian rights. In addition, she gave greater responsibilities to the tribal governments for the management of their trust funds, a program they had viewed with suspicion under previous administrations. Shortly after Clinton's reelection in 1996, Deer resigned and was replaced by KEVIN GOVER.

She currently directs the American Indian Studies program at the University of Wisconsin-Madison, where she also is a distinguished lecturer in the School of Social Work.

Further Reading

Deer, Ada. *Speaking Out*. Danbury, Conn.: Children's Press, 1970.

Marsh, Carole. *Ada Deer: Notable Native American*. Decator, Ga.: Gallopade Publishing Group, 1988.

Deere, Phillip (1929–1985) *Creek spiritual leader, activist*
Phillip Deere, a Creek, was born on February 8, 1929, on his mother's 160-acre allotment in Okemah, Oklahoma. He was raised speaking Muskogee and steeped in Creek lore. The area where he grew up was also known as Nuyaka (a variant of New York) Tribal Town, a traditional Creek stronghold so steadfast in their old ways that they refused to acknowledge the Creek National Government formed under the constitution of 1867. Deere's family had been followers of CHITTO HARJO, the leader of the Crazy Snake Rebellion of 1900–1909, in his unsuccessful attempts to preserve Creek autonomy. From the older traditional healers who lived nearby, Deere learned Creek healing chants in Old Muskogee, according to Deere "an old language even Muskogee speakers did not know." He also became skilled in using herbal medicines.

Deere attended the local elementary school but dropped out before high school to work as a carpenter to support his family. While working construction, he also became a Methodist pastor, preaching for almost 20 years. Influenced by the activism of the nascent RED POWER era, however, Deere returned to Creek ways in the 1960s. He then began to lead Creek ceremonies and organized stickball camps and other youth leadership activities in an effort to encourage younger Creek to maintain traditional ways.

During the 1970s, Deere became involved with the AMERICAN INDIAN MOVEMENT (AIM) and served as its spiritual adviser. In 1978, Deere, an accomplished orator, gave the opening address at the large demonstration in Washington, D.C., that marked the end of the LONGEST WALK. Combining his spiritual outlook with a frank discussion of the injustices Indians had endured, Deere argued that Indians should follow the "law of love, peace, and respect," which "no man-made laws will ever take the place of." During the Longest Walk, he was filmed for the documentary *Raoni*, in which he appears at the beginning in conversation with the actor Marlon Brando.

Deere's stature as a religious leader and as an activist was instrumental in uniting the various Indian political factions in the United States as well as bringing together indigenous peoples from around the world in a common front to argue for indigenous rights in international forums such as the United Nations. In 1975, he was sent by AIM to try to mend the organization's relationship with the Navajo Tribal Council. AIM and the Navajo, led by Peter MacDonald, had fallen out after AIM's occupation of the Fairchild Semiconductor plant on the Navajo reservation backfired, causing the plant to be shut down and putting hundreds of Navajo out of work. Deere appeared before the Navajo Tribal Council in June 1975, a few months after the shutdown. AIM had hoped that Deere could get the Navajo to allow AIM to hold its national convention on their reservation. Not even his eloquence could mollify the bitter feelings, however, and the Navajo Tribal Council voted

Creek Phillip Deere, spiritual leader of the American Indian Movement at their 1973 convention in White Oak, Oklahoma. *(AP/Wideworld)*

gathering of indigenous spiritual leaders held at the United Nations. Deere's international organizing eventually bore fruit in May 2002, when the United Nations established the Permanent Forum for Indigenous Peoples (see SOVEREIGNTY, INDIGENOUS AND TRIBAL), but he did not live to see this important achievement. Among the most widely respected and admired Indian religious figures of the late 20th century, Phillip Deere died of a brain tumor on August 16, 1985.

See also BOMBERRY, DANIEL R.

Further Reading

Hart, John. *Sacramental Commons: Christian Ecological Ethics*, ch. 3. Lanham, Md.: Rowman & Littlefield, 2006.

Vecsey, Christopher. "The Genesis of Phillip Deere's Sweat Lodge." In *Imagine Ourselves Richly: Narratives of North American Indians*, ch. 7. New York: Crossroad, 1988.

DeLaCruz, Joseph Burton (1937–2000) *tribal chair of the Quinault Nation*

Joseph Burton DeLaCruz was born in Washington State on July 16, 1937; his father was Filipino and his mother Quinault. After attending high school, "Skinny," as he was known to his friends, worked in a federal job until 1967, when the Quinault asked him to return to help lead the tribe. Serving first as the tribe's business manager, DeLaCruz began to help the Quinault reassert authority over their own reservation, which had become overrun with non-Indians. In 1969, he gained national attention when the tribe closed the 23-mile-long Quinault beachfront to outsiders.

In 1971, DeLaCruz was elected tribal president and joined the wave of younger, more militant tribal leaders, such as WENDELL CHINO of the Apache and PETER MACDONALD of the Navajo (Dineh), who were coming to power in the late 1960s and early 1970s. Fed up with the chronic mismanagement of Indian resources by the BUREAU OF INDIAN AFFAIRS (BIA), DeLaCruz set his sights on regaining control of the tribe's vast timber reserves. Non-Indian logging concerns controlled the 211,000-acre reservation and were rapidly deforesting the rich temperate rain forest. Not one to refrain from confrontation, DeLaCruz once drove his pickup truck onto a bridge and blocked loggers from gaining access to the reservation. After establishing the Quinault Forest Management Program and a land-restoration program, DeLaCruz managed to wrest control of fishing and shellfishing from the BIA.

While continuing to serve as president of the Quinault tribe, DeLaCruz from 1977 through 1981 headed the NATIONAL TRIBAL CHAIRMAN'S ASSOCIATION, where he was instrumental in securing the passage of the INDIAN CHILD WELFARE ACT. In 1981, he was elected president of the NATIONAL CONGRESS OF AMERICAN INDIANS (NCAI). DeLaCruz revived the organization and successfully fought attempts under President Ronald Reagan and his commissioner of Indian affairs, KENNETH L. SMITH to curtail Indian rights.

From 1985 until 1988, DeLaCruz mediated the negotiations that ultimately led to the Pacific Salmon Fisheries Treaty

48-0 to reject AIM's application, dealing the organization a serious blow.

Deere was one of the founders of the INTERNATIONAL INDIAN TREATY COUNCIL, the first international pan-Indian organization, and was active in promoting American Indian rights internationally. He was also one of the leaders of the North American delegation at the International Non-Governmental Organizations Conference on the Indigenous Peoples of the Americas, held in Geneva in 1977. He gave the closing address at the Fourth Russell Tribunal, a landmark international forum devoted to indigenous issues, held in Geneva, in November 1980. In the international arena, he championed the rights of indigenous peoples through his forceful but soft-spoken message, saying, "The people of the red clay of the Americas will continue to go on. . . . [T]hrough many years of struggle and sufferings, we refuse to die."

In 1980, along with philanthropist Robert Stafferson, Hopi elder THOMAS BANYACYA, Iroquois chief OREN LYONS, JR., and others, Deere helped to found the Traditional Circle of Elders and Youth, and in 1982 he participated in an international between the United States, Canada, and regional Indian tribes. Beginning in 1985, DeLaCruz served as a member of the Northwest Indian Fish Commission, which regulates fishing in the region (see also HUNTING AND FISHING RIGHTS).

After his retirement as president of the Quinault tribe in 1994, DeLaCruz founded the First American Education Project, a political education and fund-raising organization, which helped oust Senator Slade Gorton of Washington State, an archenemy of Indian rights, in the 2000 elections. Sadly, DeLaCruz did not live to witness his last triumph. One of the most important tribal leaders of the 20th century and a tireless organizer, he died of a heart attack in Seattle on April 16, 2000, while en route to a health conference.

Deloria, Ella Cara (Apatu Waste Win, "Beautiful Day Woman") (1889–1971)
Yankton Nakota Sioux anthropologist, linguist, novelist

Ella Cara Deloria was born on January 31, 1889, in South Dakota in the White Swan district of the Yankton Nakota Sioux Reservation. Her father, Phillip Joseph Deloria, was a Yankton Episcopal priest and her mother, Mary Sully, was the daughter of U.S. Army general Alfred Sully and a Yankton woman. Her brother, VINE DELORIA, SR., followed in their father's footsteps into the ministry, and her nephew, VINE DELORIA, JR., became a prominent Indian intellectual.

Shortly after Ella Deloria's birth, the family moved to the Standing Rock Reservation, home of the Hunkpapa and Blackfeet bands of the Lakota Nation and the Hunkpatinas and Cuthead bands of the Dakota Nation. Her father's frequent travels throughout the state allowed her to learn all three Sioux dialects: Lakota, Nakota, and Dakota.

Ella Deloria attended St. Elizabeth's Mission School in Wakpala before transferring to All Saint's School in Sioux Falls, South Dakota, in 1906. After her graduation in 1910, she attended the University of Chicago, Oberlin College in Ohio, and Columbia University Teachers College, New York, where she received a B.S. in education in 1915. At Columbia, while she did not formally study anthropology, she was hired by anthropologist FRANZ BOAS to translate the manuscripts of George Bushotter, a Sioux who had collaborated with the anthropologist James Dorsey in the 1880s.

Deloria returned to South Dakota in 1915 to teach at All Saint's School until 1919, when she took a position with the Young Women's Christian Association (YWCA) as health education secretary for Indian schools. In 1923, she became a physical education teacher and dance instructor at the Haskell Institute in Lawrence, Kansas, remaining there until 1927, when she again began to collaborate with Boas. Moving back to New York, Deloria published her first work, an article on the Sun Dance, in the *Journal of American Folk-Lore* in 1929. In 1932, her first book, *Dakota Texts*, a bilingual collection of Sioux oral narratives appeared, followed by *Dakota Grammar*, in collaboration with Boas, in 1941. While in New York she also met the anthropologist Ruth Benedict, another former student of Boas. Benedict encouraged Deloria to focus

her study on kinship patterns, tribal structure, and the role of women among the Sioux, and the two corresponded until Benedict's death in 1948.

While intellectually rewarding, her work with Boas brought financial difficulties and forced her to seek various forms of employment. In 1943, she received a research grant from the American Philosophical Society that allowed her to begin an ethnographic study of the Sioux, and in 1944 she published a popular look at Indian culture, *Speaking of Indians*. During this time, she also wrote a novel *Waterlily*, a historical and ethnographic work that details the life of a fictional 19th-century Lakota Sioux woman. It was not published until 1988.

Deloria returned to St. Elizabeth's Mission School in 1955 to serve as its director. She left the school in 1958 and spent the rest of her life alternately teaching, lecturing, and writing about Indian culture. A leading authority on Sioux culture in the 20th century, Deloria was working on a Dakota dictionary when she died on February 12, 1971, in Vermillion, South Dakota.

She left a vast body of unpublished manuscripts, notes, interviews with Native subjects, and other research materials, some of which has begun to see the light of day in recent times. Three of her posthumously published works, *Deer Women and Elk Men: The Lakota Narrative of Ella Deloria* (1992), *Ella Deloria's Iron Hawk* (1993), and *Ella Deloria's The Buffalo People* (1994), were edited by Julian Rice, an author on Sioux subjects. The Dakota Indian Foundation, located in Chamberlain, South Dakota, has custody of Deloria's papers and has placed much of her correspondence and notes online. The foundation also aided in publishing her ethnographic manuscript, *Dakota Way of Life*, in 2007. A new edition of *Waterlily* was published in 2009.

Further Reading

Bucko, Raymond A. "Ella Cara Deloria." In *Encyclopedia of Anthropology*, edited by H. James Birx. Thousand Oaks, Calif.: SAGE Publication, 2006.

Deloria, Ella Cara. *Dakota Way of Life*. Sioux Falls, S.Dak.: Mariah Press, 2007.

———. *Waterlily*. Lincoln: University of Nebraska Press, 1998.

Gardner, Susan. "Speaking of Ella Deloria: Conversations with Joyzelle Gingway Godfrey, 1998–2000, Lower Brule Community College, South Dakota." *American Indian Quarterly* 24, no. 3 (2000): 456–475.

Murray, Janette K. "Ella Deloria: A Biographical Sketch and Literary Analysis." Ph.D. dissertation, University of North Dakota, 1974.

Rice, Julian. *Deer Women and Elk Men: The Lakota Narratives of Ella Deloria*. Albuquerque: University of New Mexico Press, 1992.

Deloria, Vine, Jr. (1933–2005) *Yankton Nakota Sioux writer, theologian, philosopher, Indian rights advocate*

Vine Deloria, Jr., was born on March 26, 1933, in Martin, South Dakota, to a distinguished Yankton Sioux family. His father was VINE DELORIA, SR., and his mother was Barbara Eastburn Deloria; anthropologist ELLA CARA DELORIA was his aunt. Young Deloria attended grade school in Martin, then went to the Kent School in Kent, Connecticut. After graduation in 1954, he joined the U.S. Marine Corps. Discharged in 1956, Deloria enrolled in Iowa State University, where he received his B.S. degree in 1958. He then worked as a welder while attending the Augustana Lutheran Seminary in Rock Island, Illinois, where he earned a master's degree in theology in 1963.

Deloria worked for the United Scholarship Service for a year, helping to place Indian students in Ivy League colleges. In 1963, he was named executive director of the NATIONAL CONGRESS OF AMERICAN INDIANS (NCAI) on the crest of a new wave of Indian activism emanating from the influential AMERICAN INDIAN CHICAGO CONFERENCE of 1961. Shunning the confrontational tactics of activists CLYDE WARRIOR and HANK ADAMS, Deloria preferred to create coalitions to address Indian issues, in particular to counter ongoing attempts by Congress to revive the TERMINATION policy. He also served on the board of directors of the Citizens' Crusade against Poverty and of the Council of Indian Affairs in Washington, D.C. Though he stepped down from the directorship of NCAI after one year, Deloria remained with the group as a consultant on special programs until 1967, when he entered law school at the University of Colorado. After earning his law degree in 1970, he became a lecturer, first at Western Washington State College, and then at the University of California, Los Angeles (UCLA).

In 1969, Deloria published his first book, *Custer Died for Your Sins: An Indian Manifesto*, to instant acclaim. Deconstructing the numerous myths surrounding Indians, he wryly lambasted do-gooders, anthropologists, missionaries, and government officials, while arguing against the policy of Termination and in favor of a new policy based on upholding Indian treaties. He challenged the prevailing tendency to portray Indians as a part of America's past "heritage," rather than of the present day, which effectively rendered them invisible as a people. The next year, his article "This Country Was a Lot Better Off When the Indians Were Running It" appeared in the *New York Times Magazine*, followed in the same year by his book *We Talk, You Listen*. In these works, Deloria expanded on the themes he formulated in *Custer Died for Your Sins*: Not only should Indians be the masters of their own destinies, but non-Indians would benefit from learning about Indian society and Indian thought. Deloria argued that Indians, with their "tribal" societies, fostered a more stable and mature community than that which resulted from the individualism, institutional corporatism, and bureaucracy fostered by Western societies.

Although criticized by some for overgeneralization, a complaint that would follow him throughout his career, Deloria in his early works provided intellectual ammunition to the nascent RED POWER MOVEMENT, helping to focus activist demands on fundamental Indian issues such as sovereignty and directing the movement away from the civil rights orientation that characterized other social justice movements of the time.

In the early 1970s, Deloria tried to build a national coalition between NCAI, the NATIONAL INDIAN YOUTH COUNCIL, the newly formed AMERICAN INDIAN MOVEMENT (AIM), and the NATIONAL TRIBAL CHAIRMAN'S ASSOCIATION to fight for Indian rights. His hopes for a unified approach to solving Indian problems were dashed by the TRAIL OF BROKEN TREATIES protest march, culminating in the takeover of the BUREAU OF INDIAN AFFAIRS (BIA) headquarters in November 1972, which split the groups.

In 1971, Deloria edited an anthology of historical documents chronicling relations between Indians and the American government, *Of Utmost Good Faith*, before turning to theological issues in 1973 with the release of *God Is Red*. For Deloria, modern society was in danger of being overcome by its incessant pollution and plunder of the Earth, an imperative stemming in part from a Christianity that had lost sight of humanity's relationship to the natural world. Deloria traced this failure of Christian theology to the notion that "with the Fall of Adam the rest of nature also falls out of grace with God." In contrast, with Indian religions, the "whole of the creation was good, because the creation event did not include a 'fall,' the meaning of creation was that all parts of it functioned together to sustain it." Rather than the "brotherhood of man" under a Christian identity, Deloria advocated a "brotherhood of life," where humans must stand within, not without, the great natural ecosystems.

Deloria returned to political matters with *Behind the Trail of Broken Treaties* (1974), in which he provided a historical and political background to the 1972 demonstration. In the same year, he published *The Indian Affair*, a historical account of the legal devices used by the United States in the 20th century to deprive Indians of their rights. Also in 1974, in four trials growing out of the 1973 WOUNDED KNEE occupation, Deloria served as an expert witness on the 1868 Fort Laramie Treaty and Sioux history, providing the defense team with a historical motive for the three-month-long occupation.

After *Indians of the Pacific Northwest* (1977), Deloria returned to philosophy in 1979 with the *Metaphysics of Modern Existence*, in which he attempted to analyze the differing concepts of reality embodied in Indian and Western thought. Surveying the divergent views of reality presented by Western religion, philosophy, and science, Deloria argued that these separate disciplines must unite for "a general quest for reality on the part of everyone." In searching for "a more mature understanding of the universe," Western thought must "come to reflect what people are rather than what they believe to be true."

With Clifford Little, Deloria wrote *American Indians, American Justice* (1983) and *The Nations Within* (1984). An examination of the INDIAN NEW DEAL policies of former BIA superintendent JOHN COLLIER, *The Nations Within* provides the clearest picture of Deloria's belief in Indian culture as the anchor of Indian identity and a central element in Indian governments and economics, with the capacity of fostering a relationship of mutual respect between tribal governments and state and federal governments. Deloria also argues that the title to Indian land is intertwined with a sovereignty that is inherent in Indian tribes (see SOVEREIGNTY, INDIGENOUS AND TRIBAL). Rather than take the view that Indian treaties "gave" Indians land, Deloria points out that under the treaties it was the Indians who gave the land to the United States. The treaties simply confirm Indian title to those lands they did not cede (see COHEN, FELIX SOLOMON; LAND TENURE).

In 1995, Deloria issued another ambitious work, *Red Earth, White Lies: Native Americans and the Myth of Scientific Fact*. The book originated as an attempt to debunk the established scientific view that Indians migrated from Asia less than 14,000 years ago, but it ended up as a wholesale assault on the kind of "truth" that science is capable of determining. The book was savagely attacked by members of the scientific establishment who felt that among other things it was not scientific enough and that the evidence Deloria used to prove his case was selective. Deloria only fanned the flames of animosity further by using pariahs of the scientific community, such as psychiatrist Dr. Immanuel Velikovsky, to make his points about scientific bias. Deloria argued that scientists would gain a better understanding of the Earth and its natural processes if they gave serious consideration to non-Western beliefs and traditions. In the end, Deloria may have the last laugh, as recent archaeology appears to prove that humans have been in this hemisphere far longer than previously thought.

Shortly before *Red Earth, White Lies* was released, Deloria suffered a blow when a fire in his house destroyed his extensive library as well as several incomplete manuscripts, halting his normally prolific literary output.

Deloria served on the board of directors of the Museum of the American Indian Heye Foundation, before becoming vice chairman of its successor, the National Museum of the American Indian of the Smithsonian Institution in 1989. A tireless activist, he served on the boards of more than 50 organizations, many of which, including Save the Children and Disability Rights and Education Fund, aid non-Indian causes.

Deloria was also a distinguished educator. He joined the University of Arizona as a visiting professor in 1978, then stayed to direct its American Indian Studies Program from 1979 to 1982. He was also professor of law and political science at Arizona from 1979 until 1990, moving from there to the Center for Studies in Ethnicity and Race at the University of Colorado in Boulder, where he taught law, history, political science, and religious studies.

As a thinker on contemporary Indian issues, Deloria was outstanding for his attempts to seek dimensions far beneath the surface—dimensions that few other writers on Native American issues have dared to explore. His work to reformulate Indian law, in particular his emphasis on the inherent sovereign powers of Indian tribes and their right to self-government, has influenced Indian legal scholars such as K. KIRKE KICKINGBIRD, with whom he founded the Institute for the Development of Indian Law, and JAMES YOUNGBLOOD HENDERSON. Much like his contemporaries N. SCOTT MOMADAY and JOHN MOHAWK, Deloria sought as a philosopher to find in Indian culture answers to the problems faced by Western civilization. Although not without his critics, his

unique fusion of Christian and traditional Indian thought and the immense scope of his work made him one of the most important and influential Indian figures of the 20th century.

Vine Deloria, Jr., died on November 13, 2005, in Tucson, Arizona.

Further Reading
Biolsi, Thomas, and Larry J. Zimmerman, eds. *Indians and Anthropologists: Vine Deloria, Jr., and the Critique of Anthropology.* Tucson: University of Arizona Press, 1997.

De Maillie, Raymond J. "Vine Deloria Jr. (1933–2005)." *American Anthropologist* 100, no. 4 (2006): 932–935.

Deloria, Vine, Jr. *Behind the Trail of Broken Treaties: An Indian Declaration of Independence.* New York: Delacorte Press, 1974.

———. *Custer Died for Your Sins: An Indian Manifesto.* New York: Macmillan, 1969.

———. *God Is Red.* New York: Grosset & Dunlap, 1973.

———. *The Metaphysics of Modern Existence.* San Francisco: Harper & Row, 1979.

———. *Red Earth, White Lies: Native Americans and the Myth of Scientific Fact.* New York: Scribner, 1995.

———. *Singing for a Spirit: A Portrait of the Dakota Sioux.* Santa Fe, N.Mex.: Clear Light Publishers, 1999.

———. *We Talk, You Listen: New Tribes, New Turf.* New York: Macmillan, 1970.

Deloria, Vine, Jr., and Clifford M. Lytle. *The Nations Within: The Past and Future of American Indian Sovereignty.* New York: Pantheon Books, 1984.

Deloria, Vine, Jr., ed. *American Indian Policy in the Twentieth Century.* Norman and London: University of Oklahoma Press, 1985.

Pavlik, Steve, and Daniel P. Wildcat, eds. *Destroying Dogma: Vine Deloria, Jr., and His Influence on American Society.* Golden, Colo.: Fulcrum Publishing, 2006.

Deloria, Vine, Sr. (1901–1990) *Yankton Nakota Sioux Episcopal priest*

A Yankton Nakota Sioux, Vine Deloria, Sr., was born on October 6, 1901, in Wakpala, on the Standing Rock Reservation in South Dakota. His father, Phillip Joseph Deloria, was a distinguished Episcopal priest and the son of François Des Lauriers, a Yankton leader and medicine man who converted to Christianity a few years before his death in 1876. Vine Deloria's sister, ELLA CARA DELORIA, was a prominent anthropologist.

Deloria attended Kearney Military Academy in Nebraska before going to St. Stephens College, now Bard College, in New York, where he excelled in athletics. After graduating in liberal arts in 1926, he worked as a coal miner in Colorado and coached sports at the Fort Sill Indian School in Oklahoma. In 1928, bowing to his father's wishes, Deloria entered the General Theological Seminary in New York City. He returned to Wakpala to be ordained an Episcopal deacon shortly before Phillip Deloria's death in 1931.

Ordained a priest in 1932, Deloria pursued his ministry on all the Indian reservations in South Dakota. In 1954, he was appointed to the Episcopal National Council, heading the church's Indian missions and becoming the first American Indian to hold a major post in a national church. He served as archdeacon of Niobrara Deanery and then as archdeacon of Pierre before retiring in 1968, though he continued to serve as a priest at St. Paul's Episcopal mission in Vermillion, South Dakota, for another two years. He moved to Tucson, Arizona, in 1986 and died there on February 26, 1990.

Deloria attempted to bridge the gap between Christianity and Native traditions, arguing that Indians should maintain their cultural identity while acculturating and accepting Christianity. Along with his father and grandfather, Vine Deloria, Sr., was responsible for bringing thousands of Sioux (Dakota, Lakota, Nakota) into the Episcopal fold. Later in life, he became somewhat disillusioned with the way Christianity was taught, believing that the emphasis on the spiritual nature of Christ as opposed to his humanity, and faith as opposed to good works, was failing to alleviate the problems of Indian people. His son, VINE DELORIA, JR., became an influential theologian in his own right.

Further Reading

Bruquier, Leonard Rufus. "A Legacy in Sioux Leadership: The Deloria Family." In *South Dakota Leaders*, edited by Herbert T. Hoover and Larry J. Zimmerman, 367–381. Vermillion: University of South Dakota Press, 1989.

Deloria, Phillip J. *Indians in Unexpected Places*, 109–135. Lawrence: University of Kansas Press, 2004.

Deloria, Vine, Jr. *Singing for a Spirit: A Portrait of the Dakota Sioux.* Santa Fe, N.Mex.: Clear Light Books, 2000.

DeMain, Paul (1955–)

White Earth Chippewa journalist, publisher

A Chippewa born on October 8, 1955, in Hayward, Wisconsin, Paul DeMain attended the University of Wisconsin in Eau Clair. After leaving in 1977, DeMain became acting director of the Great Lakes Indian News Association and also managed a design company, Lac Courte Oreilles Graphic Arts, Inc. In 1981, he began working for the Lac Courte Oreilles Band of Lake Superior Chippewa.

From 1977 until 1982, DeMain was the managing editor of the *Lac Courte Oreilles Journal*. In 1982, he established *News from Indian Country*, which became one of the leading Indian newspapers in the United States. DeMain also became a major force in establishing and helping to direct the Native American Journalism Association (NAJA). In 1994, while president of NAJA, DeMain successfully helped coordinate a national conference of Native American, African-American, Hispanic, and Asian-American press associations, known as the UNITY conference. He has also served as a political adviser on Chippewa affairs, acting as a liaison between the Wisconsin governor's office and 11 Chippewa bands located in the state.

DeMain's investigative work helped lead to the discovery of ANNA MAE AQUASH's killers and the role of the AMERICAN INDIAN MOVEMENT (AIM) leadership in her death. He has also led the search to determine the fate of African-American activist Perry Ray Robinson after the OCCUPATION OF WOUNDED KNEE in 1973. Robinson, who disappeared a short time after joining the occupation, may have been shot by AIM members and buried near Wounded Knee. DeMain's anti-AIM crusade, while revealing much about the seamy side of the organization, also led to a countersuit by political prisoner and AIM member LEONARD PELTIER, who accused DeMain of falsely implicating Peltier in Aquash's murder. DeMain lost the suit and was forced to write a declaration that he did not believe Peltier had a role in her death.

See also JOURNALISM.

Further Reading

Adams, Jim. "Peltier Accepts Settlement over Aquash Murder." *Indian Country Today*, 16 June 2004.

demographics

At the start of the 20th century, the American Indian population had reached historic lows. Decreasing quickly throughout the 19th century, it had, according to the U.S. Census, declined to only 248,253 persons by 1890. In 1900, it bottomed out at 237,196, only 0.3 percent of the total U.S. population. From that point on, the Indian population began to increase, reaching 265,683 by 1910. In that year, the state with the largest Indian population was Oklahoma, which with 74,825 resident Indians represented more than one-quarter of the total. The next largest Indian populations were in Arizona (29,201), New Mexico (20,573), South Dakota (19,137), California (16,371), and Washington (10,997). The Indian population in 1910 was almost exclusively rural, with only 11,925 Indians, or 4.5 percent of the total, living in urban areas. The largest Indian group in 1910 was the Cherokee, with 31,489 members. The next largest were the Sioux (Dakota, Lakota, Nakota) with 22,748 members, the Navajo (22,455), the Chippewa (20,214), the Choctaw (15,917), the Iroquois (7,837), and the Creek (7,341). According to the census, 60.7 percent of the American Indian population was full-blood, and 37.8 percent was mixed-blood. In 1910, 27.6 percent of all Indian males over the age of 10 spoke only their tribal language, and 35 percent of all Indian females were also unable to speak English. In that same year, 50.8 percent of all Indian males over 21 and 61.4 percent of all females were unable to read or write.

In 1920, the census found that the population had suffered a slight decline again, down to only 244,437, probably due in large measure to mortality from the influenza epidemic of 1918. The Indian birthrate, however, remained very high. In 1920, fully half of the Indian population was under 20 years of age, and the median age was only 19.7, compared with a median age of 25.6 for whites.

By 1930, the Indian population had increased to 332,397. It grew slightly, to 345,252, by 1940. In 1938, the death rate of

Indians was still a very high 14.9 per 1,000, but the birthrate was even higher, 22.9 per 1,000. During the war years and immediately afterward, the American Indian population increased only slightly, to 357,499 by 1950. By 1960, however, it had jumped to 523,591, and in 1970 it stood at 792,730. The large increases were due in part to the discovery of medical treatments for the infectious diseases that had most contributed to Indians' high mortality rate (see HEALTH, AMERICAN INDIAN) and in part to a high rate of intermarriage between Indians and non-Indians. (The progeny, though of mixed blood, were generally counted as Indians until the 2000 census, when mixed-race tabulations were first introduced.) Scholars also believe that more nonfederally recognized Indians were beginning to identify themselves as Indians in the census returns as racism against Indians began to subside. By 1980, the Indian population stood at 1,366,676.

By 1990, the census counted the total American Indian population in the United States at 1,959,000, approximately 0.8 percent of the total American population. The Cherokee were the largest group in the United States in 1990, with 308,132. Of these, 122,000 were enrolled members of the Cherokee Tribe of Oklahoma, and 9,800 were members of the Eastern Band of Cherokees. The Navajo were second with a population of 219,000, followed by the Chippewa (103,826), Sioux (Dakota, Lakota, Nakota) (103,255), Choctaw (82,299), Pueblo (52,939), Apache (50,051), Iroquois (49,038), Lumbee (48,444), and Creek (43,550). The median population of American Indians in 1990 was younger than the national average. In 1990, the median age of the Indian population was only 26, compared with the national median age of 33, with 39 percent of the Indian population under the age of 20, compared with only 29 percent nationally.

According to the 1990 census, the states with the largest Indian populations were Oklahoma (252,089), California (236,078), Arizona (203,009), New Mexico (134,097), and North Carolina (79,825). Alaska's Native American population was 86,000, which included 31,000 American Indians, 44,000 Eskimos, and 10,000 Aleut. The metropolitan areas with the largest Indian populations were Los Angeles (87,487), Phoenix (48,802), New York City (48,758), Tulsa, Oklahoma (48,196), and Oklahoma City (45,720).

The U.S. Indian population, though larger than Canada's (892,000), was far smaller than that of Mexico (10,537,000, the largest of any country in the hemisphere), Peru (8,097,000), Guatemala (5,423,000), Bolivia (4,985,000), or Ecuador (3,753,000).

In the census of 2000, rules were changed to allow for a broader reporting of heritage, making it possible to include more than one category of descent in the census form. The number of U.S. residents who reported themselves as American Indian and Alaska Native either alone or in combination with one or more other races shot up to 4.1 million, amounting to 1.5 percent of the total population. The 2.5 million that reported themselves as American Indian and Alaska Native alone represented 0.9 percent of the total U.S. population.

According to the 2000 census, the largest groups were the Cherokee with 302,569 members, followed by the Navajo

(276,775), Sioux (Lakota, Nakota, and Dakota, 113,713), Chippewa (110,857), Choctaw (88,192), Pueblo (59,621), Apache (57,199), Lumbee (52,614), Iroquois Confederacy (47,746), Creek (40,487), Blackfeet (28,731), Chickasaw (21,098), Tohono O'odham (17,223), Potawatomi (16,164), Yaqui (15,632), Tlingit-Haida (15,212), Alaska Athabascan (14,700), and Seminole (12,790). The 10 states with the largest American Indian populations in 2000 (using the "Indian Alone" figures) were Oklahoma (252,420), California (242,164), Arizona (203,527), New Mexico (134,355), Alaska (85,698), Washington (81,483), North Carolina (80,155), Texas (65,877), New York (62,651), Michigan (55,638), South Dakota (50,575), and Minnesota (49,909).

New York City (41,289) and Los Angeles (29,412) were the cities with the largest American Indian populations, followed by Phoenix (26,696), Anchorage (18,941), Tulsa (18,551), Oklahoma City (17,743), and Albuquerque (17,444).

Reliance on census figures to determine Indian populations is approximate at best, owing to inconsistencies of methodology in different years and undercounting as a result of the unwillingness of some individuals and communities to be enumerated, as well as budgetary constraints within the Census Bureau. In 1990, the use of sampling, an attempt to estimate those who were missed in the actual count, led to some controversy when it was discovered that more than 8 million people, mostly young blacks and Hispanics in urban areas, had been missed. Although in 2000 attempts were made to rectify this, the new changes in methodology made the 2000 census, if anything, less accurate than previous censuses when it comes to counting American Indians.

Further Reading

Dobyns, Henry F. *Native American Historical Demography: A Critical Bibliography*. Bloomington: Indiana University Press, 1976.

Ogunwole, Stella U. *We the People: American Indians and Alaska Natives in the United States*. Washington, D.C.: U.S. Dept. of Commerce, Economics and Statistics Administration, U.S. Census Bureau, 2006.

Shoemaker, Nancy. *American Indian Population Recovery in the Twentieth Century*. Albuquerque: University of New Mexico Press, 1999.

Snipp, C. Matthew. "The Size and Distribution of the American Indian Population: Fertility, Mortality, Residence, and Migration." In *Changing Numbers, Changing Needs: American Indian Demography and Public Health*, edited by Gary D. Sandefur, Ronald R. Rindfuss, and Barney Cohen, 17–53. Washington, D.C.: National Academy Press, 1996.

Thornton, Russell. *American Indian Holocaust and Survival: A Population History since 1492*. Norman: University of Oklahoma Press, 1987.

U.S. Bureau of Indian Affairs. *Statistics of Indian Tribes, Agencies, and Schools. Compiled to July 1, 1903*. Washington, D.C.: Government Printing Office, 1903.

U.S. Bureau of the Census. *1980 Census of Population. Volume 2, Subject reports. American Indians, Eskimos, and*

Aleuts on Identified Reservations and in the Historic areas of Oklahoma (excluding urbanized areas). Washington, D.C.: U.S. Dept. of Commerce, 1986.

U.S. Bureau of the Census Economics and Statistics Administration. *American Indians & Alaska Natives in the United States*. Washington, D.C.: U.S. Department of Commerce, Economics and Statistics Administration, Bureau of the Census, 1999.

U.S. Office of Indian Affairs. *Annual Report of the Commissioner of Indian Affairs*. Washington, D.C.: Office of Indian Affairs, 1871/72–1946/47.

Deskaheh   *See* GENERAL, ALEXANDER; GENERAL, LEVI.

Diabo, Paul   *See* IRONWORKERS, AMERICAN INDIAN.

Dietz, William Henry (Wicatopi Isnata, "Lone Star" Dietz) (1884–1964) *Oglala Lakota Sioux football coach, artist, illustrator, writer*

According to his own account, William Henry "Lone Star" Dietz was born in a tipi on August 16, 1885, on the Rosebud Reservation in South Dakota. His father, William W. Dietz, supposedly a German railroad engineer captured by famed Sioux Chief Red Cloud, married Julia One Star, an Oglala woman from Red Cloud's band. Shortly after William Henry was born, his father left Rosebud, taking the infant boy to Rice Lake, Wisconsin, where he remarried and raised him as white. Young William was sent to a prep school but, discovering his real identity, ran back to his mother's people and lived there with his uncle One Star, who taught him Oglala customs, religion, and lore. Later he supposedly went to the federal Indian school at Chilocco, Oklahoma. This account of his life has been disputed in recent times, and many of Dietz's claims about his upbringing have been found to be untrue.

What is certain is that Dietz's father, the sheriff for Rice Lake, had not been captured by Red Cloud and was in fact living in Rice Lake, married to a white woman, Leanna Ginder Dietz, at the time William was supposedly born in a tipi. According to the testimony of both Leanna Dietz and her mother, Leanna M. Barry, in August 1884, Leanna Dietz had a stillborn child, and her husband, anxious for a son, left the house and returned about a week later with a new baby wrapped in a red Indian shawl. Both were then sworn to secrecy, and the new child was passed off as having been born to Dietz. It was observed by other family members that the baby was unusually dark, but they and the rest of the town believed that Leanna Dietz was William's natural mother. Dietz was raised in Rice Lake and attended Rice Lake public schools, completing his high school studies at Macalester College in St. Paul, Minnesota, in 1903. At school, his classmates taunted him incessantly over his distinctly Indian features, and although he confronted his parents regarding his true ancestry, his father never publicly acknowledged that

his son was Indian. It is also certain that William did not attend Chilocco Indian school, although he appears to have had some relationship with the school in the fall of 1904. He attended the Friends University in Wichita, Kansas, in 1904–05. If Dietz did travel to South Dakota to live among his Sioux relatives as he claimed, it was only for a very short period of time.

By the time he was in high school, he had discovered, ostensibly from information gleaned from his father, that he was Sioux and that his mother had been named One Star. In 1904, Dietz was hired to work as a Sioux artist for the Model Indian Exhibit at the St. Louis World's Fair. There he met other Indians, including celebrated Brulé Sioux Chief Yellow Hair, a participant in the Battle of Little Bighorn. Dietz asked him if he knew of a woman named One Star, who might have given a baby up for adoption. Yellow Hair suggested to Dietz that his mother was likely Julia One Star. It was also at the World's Fair where Dietz met his future wife, ANGEL DeCORA, an artist 12 years his senior.

In 1907, DeCora was hired to teach art and design at the Carlisle Indian School in Pennsylvania, where Dietz enrolled on September 17, 1907, and became her student. Soon he joined her as assistant art instructor, and in July 1908 they married.

From 1909 through 1915, Dietz drew the covers and interior logos for Carlisle's monthly publications, *The Indian Craftsman* and *The Red Man*. In 1911, the couple jointly prepared the illustrations for Elaine Goodale Eastman's book *Yellow Star: A Story of East and West*. That same year, they joined the newly formed SOCIETY OF AMERICAN INDIANS.

In addition to being an artist, Dietz was a superb athlete. A member of the famous 1909–11 Carlisle football teams that featured Olympian JIM THORPE, he played tackle and was captain during the great 1911 season (see WARNER, POP). After completing an art course at the Pennsylvania School of Industrial Art on a scholarship he received under Carlisle's "outing system" (see PRATT, RICHARD HENRY), Dietz returned to Carlisle as Warner's assistant coach. He was also appointed art instructor and taught illustration, arts and crafts, and mechanical drawing. Meanwhile, he raised Russian wolfhounds at his home in Carlisle. At one time, he owned five champions, and in 1917 he won the Breeder's Trophy at Madison Square Garden for the best wolfhound.

Dietz left Carlisle in 1915 to become head football coach at Washington State College. During his three years there, his teams won two Pacific Coast championships while compiling an 18-2-1 record and scoring 497 points while surrendering only 38. On January 1, 1916, he coached Washington to an undefeated season and his first postseason tournament game where Washington defeated Brown University 14-0 in the Rose Bowl in Pasadena, California.

Dietz's marriage to DeCora ended in divorce on November 30, 1918, and tragically, she died just a few months later in the influenza epidemic that ravaged the country.

In the 1918–19 football season, while WORLD WAR I was under way, Dietz coached the U.S. Marines football team at Mare Island, California, leading them to the Service

Oglala Lakota Sioux artist, illustrator, writer, and one of the United States' finest collegiate football coaches, William "Lone Star" Dietz was the head coach of the Haskell Institute until 1932. *(AP/Wideworld)*

Championship of the Pacific Coast and making his second appearance in the Rose Bowl.

After World War I ended, Dietz was accused of draft evasion, a charge some Washington State fans felt had been trumped up in order to derail his return to coaching at the school. Because of failed motion picture investments, Dietz was unable to pay for his defense; he pleaded nolo contendere and was sentenced to 30 days in jail. A major part of the trial hinged on whether or not Dietz was an Indian and thus not subject to the draft, and although the evidence presented provided new details regarding Dietz's background, it could not be determined whether or not he was the son of Julia One Star. The trial, which was widely publicized, damaged Dietz's image and forced him to look elsewhere for coaching opportunities. In 1921, he became head coach at Purdue University. He also coached at Louisiana Tech (1922–23) and the University of Wyoming (1924–26).

In the mid-1920s, unhappy with the portrayal of Native Americans in Westerns, Dietz briefly interrupted his football career to act in films and provide technical assistance to Hollywood directors. In 1926, he contributed 40 pen-and-ink drawings for Pop Warner's classic *Football for Coaches and Players*. In 1927, he returned to football when Warner invited him to Stanford University as freshman coach. From 1929 to 1932, when the Haskell Indian School in Lawrence, Kansas, enjoyed the addition of a junior college division, Dietz coached there. After that, he went to Boston to become the first coach of the new Boston Redskins, a professional team, for two years (1933–34), leading them to an 11-11-2 record. In 1935, Dietz rejoined Warner as an assistant at Temple University, and from 1937 to 1942 he was head coach at Albright College.

Dietz was the most successful Indian football coach in the profession. In 27 years of coaching, he had 185 wins, two teams in the Rose Bowl, and seven undefeated teams. Pop Warner called him the best of all the coaches he had ever turned out and one of the 10 best in America.

Dietz was also a writer. In addition to poems and stories, he wrote on Indian art, and after his football career he entered the field of advertising. In 1942, he became production manager and director of Jackson and Company, New York City, and later Frank Best & Company. In 1946, he and advertising artist Montgomery Welbourne opened the short-lived Melbourne School of Advertising Art in Pittsburgh.

In the 1950s, Dietz appeared in programs sponsored by the Redpath Lecture Bureau. (Redpath Lyceum Bureau [Chatauqua] was founded by James C. Redpath in 1868.) He had to give it up, however, because of a rapid increase in art commissions, particularly portrait painting. He struggled in his later years, living in poverty much of the time. In 1957, he returned to Reading, Pennsylvania, where he worked as an independent artist.

"Lone Star" Dietz died in Reading on July 20, 1964. Years after his death, Dietz's name would be dragged into the controversy surrounding the use of Indian stereotypes by sports teams (see HARJO, SUZAN SHOWN). The Boston Redskin owner George Preston Marshall is reputed by Redskin fans to have named the team (now the Washington Redskins) in honor of Dietz, though that is unlikely given that the team was called the Boston Braves (as was the local baseball team where they shared a stadium) even before Dietz coached it. Marshall was forced to change the name when he moved from the Boston Braves' stadium to Fenway Park in 1932, and it would appear that rather than honoring Dietz, he was merely trying to maintain continuity with the old name. Conversely, critics of the Redskins have been trying to disprove Dietz's Indianness. There is no question that Dietz was an Indian, and that he embraced his Indian identity, at a time when there was little advantage to it. Having been subjected to the racism and abuse that Indian children at that time experienced growing up in a non-Indian environment, he still cast his lot with Indian people and, despite the obstacles, became a celebrated artist and sports figure. Dietz was posthumously inducted into the Pennsylvania Sports Hall of Fame on August 23, 1997.

Further Reading

Benjey, Tom. *Keep A-goin': The Life of Lone Star Dietz.* Carlisle, Pa.: Tuxedo Press, 2006.

Dillon, Patti (Patti Lyons, Patti Catalano) (1953–)

marathoner, long-distance runner

Patti Lyons was born on April 6, 1953, on a U.S. Navy ship docked in Chelsea, Massachusetts. Her second-generation Irish father, John Lyons, was a champion all-navy boxer who later worked in the boiler room of the U.S. Appraiser's Stores (Food and Drug Administration Building) on the Boston waterfront and cared for stray animals at the Boston Animal Rescue League. Her mother, Freda, was a Micmac from Antigonish, Nova Scotia, who, during WORLD WAR II, at the age of 11, left the reserve and wound up in Quincy, Massachusetts, where she got work as a babysitter by lying about her age.

At St. Ann's parochial school in Quincy, Patti Lyons was so quiet that she acquired the nickname Still-Mouth. The only sport she took part in was swimming. She was on the school team for a couple of years and at age 12 actually held the New England record for her age group in the 100-yard breast stroke, but lost interest in her final year. Entering Sacred Heart High School in Weymouth, on Boston's south shore, she got an evening job at the age of 14 (claiming she was older) in the Quincy shipyard commissary, and from age 16 until graduation she was an aide in a nursing home. Her mother discouraged her aspirations to be a cheerleader and to take the College Board examinations.

When she was 18, her father died. As the next youngest child was 13 and the youngest only two, Patti helped raise her siblings. But friction developed over the children (Patti was stricter with them but also more popular), and her mother threw her out. She moved to Sandwich on Cape Cod, where she worked in a nursing home. Lonely and unhappy, she lived on junk food and spent evenings in bars drinking beer, to the point where, at 5'4" in height, she weighed 148 pounds.

After 18 months, Patti returned to Quincy and enrolled in junior college but dropped out after a month to work as nurse's aide at Quincy Hospital. One day, a month before her 23rd birthday, she happened to see a high-school classmate at the hospital and was shocked at how trim and healthy she looked. Patti vowed to lose weight. She read in Kenneth Cooper's popular book *Aerobics* that running was the fastest and most effective way to burn calories. "I didn't know what I was doing. I read to wear comfortable shoes, and my Earth shoes were the most comfortable I knew of, so that's what I wore." Earth shoes, with heels lower than the toe, are not designed for running and are probably among the worst footwear for a beginning runner. She found a mile path around Mount Wollaston Cemetery near her apartment and proceeded to run seven laps. The next day she was so sore she could not get out of bed, and she could not walk for two weeks. But the intense pain convinced her she was doing something right, so she kept it up. Still smoking two packs a day, she was coughing up brown phlegm for an entire year.

The Boston Marathon, at the time the premier long-distance race in the world, had seen a number of Indian champions, including the Canadian-born Tom Longboat and Narragansett "Tarzan" Brown (see BROWN, ELLISON). It was an exciting time for a woman to get involved in long-distance running, with both the women's movement and the running boom at their high point. Until 1971, women had been restricted from running races longer than a mile and a half. A marathon, at 26.2 miles, is the longest of all.

A month after Lyon's first run she fell in with a group of male runners at the Quincy YMCA who were training for the Boston Marathon. In June, she learned that in order to qualify, one had to have run in at least one previous marathon. There was one coming up in four months, the Ocean State Marathon in Newport, Rhode Island. She decided to train for it.

In August 1976, she married one of the runners from the YMCA, Boston transit worker John LaTora, 10 years her senior, who was training for the same race. In September, she quit smoking (temporarily, as it turned out) and acquired her first pair of real running shoes. In October, less than six months after she started training, she won the woman's title in the Ocean State Marathon in an excellent 2 hours, 53 minutes, and 40 seconds—only 40 seconds slower than her husband in the same race. The attention and admiration she received—the first in her life—gave her a fierce determination to continue. A short time after Ocean State, she and LaTora separated. She went back to smoking two packs a day and gorging on junk food. She would not quit smoking for good until 1978.

Joe Catalano, a 28-year-old track-and-field coach at Quincy High School, who also worked out at the Y, had already heard about her when, one day in fall 1976, she showed up and someone introduced them. He offered to help her train, but they did not see each other again for another year.

She did not enter the Boston Marathon in 1977 because of a cyst on her leg, which required an operation and grounded her for seven months. In June 1977, she started training again and in October remembered Catalano and asked him to help her prepare for a 10-km race coming up in two weeks. He gave her intensive training, mainly for speed. She won the race with a time of 34:50, beating Boston 1976 marathon winner Kim Merritt.

In winter 1977, she was unhappy, going through a divorce from LaTora and back living with her mother. Joe Catalano meanwhile was living alone in a big empty house. In late 1977, Patti decided to rent a room on the third floor. Inspired by Gayle Barron's victory in the 1978 Boston marathon, and at Catalano's constant urging, Patti finally decided to stop smoking and get serious about her diet. Starting as her coach, he also became friend and confidant. She qualified for Boston again in 1978, but a hip injury kept her out. She went back to smoking and gaining weight, going up to 135. But later in 1978, by placing in the top five at the Nike Marathon in Eugene, Oregon, she won a free trip to the Honolulu marathon. In Honolulu, she not only won the race, but set a course record. Catalano quit his job in 1979 to coach her full time. They lived on food stamps. Later they supported themselves by appearing as consultants for Nike shoes.

She finally ran her first Boston Marathon in 1979. Due to bursitis in her foot, she could not stay with Joan Benoit's record-setting pace and was passed by Benoit at Heartbreak Hill, 16 miles into the course. Still, Lyons came in a close second to Benoit's record-breaking time.

In 1980, she won 12 of 16 races, including the Bermuda International Marathon and her third consecutive Honolulu Marathon, as well as the Montreal Marathon and the Bonne Belle 10 km. She also set the world record for 20 km on a very tough course in Wheeling, West Virginia.

The 1980 Boston Marathon was a messy affair, marred by the disqualification of Rosie Ruiz—the apparent winner—for cheating. Lyons, who was favored to win, thought she was in the lead and did not realize that Jacqueline Gareau of Montreal was far ahead until told by a male runner. It was too late to catch up, but she clocked in second at 2:35:08.

Lyons married Joe Catalano on May 17, 1980, and began running professionally under the name Patti Catalano. She got down to 104 pounds, and by October 1980 was running well over 100 miles a week, working with weights and using massage, and every Friday running the 600 yards up Boston's Heartbreak Hill 10 times.

With her husband constantly after her to keep her weight down, she became bulimic. (Bulimia is an eating disorder in which secretive episodes of binge-eating are followed by inappropriate methods of weight control, such as self-induced vomiting.) Without telling her husband, she went to the eating-disorder unit at Massachusetts General Hospital, but she was recognized. She tried once more but was too self-conscious to continue.

She entered the marathon for the third time in 1981. The duel was expected to be between Catalano, Joan Benoit, and Jacqueline Gareau of Canada, the 1980 winner. Catalano, setting a record-breaking pace, easily outdistanced her rivals, with Allison Roe running to catch up, but at Cleveland Circle Patti was involved in a bizarre accident. As she told interviewer Bob Kopac in 2006:

> The crowd control is poor, there is only enough room for one runner to get through. As you come over the hills and go down by Boston College, and just after B.C., by the reservoir, coming around that turn there before you pass Billy's old store at Cleveland Circle to take the left hand turn down to go down Beacon Street, only one runner can go through. And you are running and you are pumping your arms, and you say, "Excuse me! Excuse me, please!" Get these people out of your face! And I am leading, I am absolutely leading!

What happened next is detailed by Tom Derderian, college track coach and historian of the Boston Marathon, who was running right behind her (as quoted by Douglas Perry in 2002).

> The fans were lining each side, the road getting ever narrower, with each [person] leaning out to get a look, to the point where spectators were almost banging heads with those on the other side. . . . People would lean forward, and then pull back as the runners came through.

So you had this narrowing canyon of spectators, and there's this [police officer] on a horse, and there are trolley tracks . . . The horse is sliding around and getting agitated because it can't get its footing on the tracks, and, of course, runners are coming through very fast. And between the crowd and the runners and the noise, Patti runs into this horse's ass—boom!— and bounces into me. I caught her, as anybody would, and after a moment she got her feet under her.

But the impact had knocked the wind out of her, and Roe, who had been just a few steps behind Dillon, ran around the pileup and took the lead. Patti was never able to catch her.

New Zealander Roe broke the course record by an amazing seven minutes and 42 seconds. Yet even with the mishap, Patti's second place time of 2:27:51 set a new American record. Nevertheless, she had finished a disappointing second in the Boston Marathon for the third straight year. It was the last time she would run it.

Her husband was angry. As she recalled to Lia Grimanis of the web page "Up with Women" in 2007,

> It was one thing for him to be disappointed as my coach, but for him to be disappointed as my husband . . . it just took its toll. . . . and then I thought "you know, if I don't leave this, I'm going to die." . . . I was throwing up nine, 12 times a day, I was a complete mess. My hair was already falling out, my teeth were bleeding, my throat was swollen. . . . I was going to die.

During this crisis, she became active in the movement to legitimatize payment for amateur runners. In fall 1981, she was suspended by the AAU for talking publicly about "under-the table payments that race promoters used to lure top runners to their races." This practice had been going on for years, but the money was getting bigger.

In December 1981, she ran in Honolulu Marathon and won for a fourth consecutive year in 2:33:24—as in the three previous years, a new course record.

The year 1982 was a difficult one. A string of injuries prevented her from competing. Shortly after the Honolulu victory, while she was body surfing, a powerful wave threw her against a rock, breaking her coccyx. She was bedridden for three months. It was made worse because she did not go to the doctor right away and these were complications from anemia and hypoglycemia (fatigue due to low blood sugar). She became severely depressed, could not sleep, and considered quitting running. Her weight went from 102 to 128. She suffered from low self-esteem and began to grow away from her husband. After that she injured her hip and hamstring, then ruptured a tendon in her foot, and then got a stress fracture in the same foot. She missed the 1982 Boston Marathon.

Despite the difficulties with their marriage, she and Joe bought a new house in Dedham, just southwest of Boston. In late 1982, she began to train again, working on endurance, speed, weight training, with weekly chiropractic treatments and frequent rubdowns by a masseuse. On Thanksgiving Day, she ran a five mile race in Boston, not to win, merely keeping up a steady seven minute pace. She finished in 35 minutes 40 seconds. She and Joe set targets for 1983: the Boston Marathon and the World Games in Helsinki. As it turned out, she needed a foot operation and did not compete in either event.

However, when she found out that the Olympics would for the first time have a women's marathon in the 1984 games in Los Angeles, she resumed training, trying to conquer her eating disorder. The training was going well, but at a difficult moment her husband said to her, "If I knew you were like this, I never would have married you." As she later told interviewer Douglas Perry, "I was crushed, absolutely crushed." That spring she finished far back in the Olympic trials and did not qualify. She left her husband that same week, and divorce soon followed.

Later in 1984, she moved to Vermont, where she decided to open a health food store, though she had no business experience. The store opened on June 4, 1985. Meanwhile she had continued training, and on June 15, 1985, ran in the marathon at Rio de Janeiro, winning in 2:38:44. But this was her last marathon. Later she sold the store, got lonely, and returned to Boston.

In 1988, she was working as a job-training specialist at the North American Indian Center at Jamaica Plain. That year she married again—a childhood sweetheart—but the marriage was a mistake from the start and quickly turned abusive. In winter 1989, she lost her job and left her husband. She was homeless for several months, living in her car, but felt safe parking in her own neighborhood and was happy to be independent and have a chance to think. She ate healthy food at a friend's restaurant, showered at various Boston universities where she was known, and did rather well for a homeless person.

In 1992, she met Dan Dillon, a former cross-country runner and freelance sound engineer. They fell in love on their first date and married a week later. After their children, Aaron and Raven, were born, Patti gave up running. They settled in New London, Connecticut, where they still live.

In 2002, she was invited to Honolulu for induction into the Honolulu Marathon Hall of Fame. For old time's sake, she and her husband ran part of the course, and this inspired her to train for it the following year. She got back into shape with Bill Squires, founding coach of the Greater Boston Track Club, as her coach. Although she did not end up competing in Honolulu, she continued training, still aspiring to run both the Honolulu and Olympic marathons. As of this writing she has yet to do so, but on June 2, 2007, she won her first race in 22 years, the 10-km Duathlon and Road Race at Rye, New Hampshire, in 7:48, beating 28-year old Nicole Hedgecock by one second. Patti Dillon recounted: "I was in the lead against this young lass . . . and I realized that I was ahead. I just thought 'try to pass me, baby.' In the end I won, but I was a wreck!"

During her career, Dillon held the American record for almost every distance from the five mile to the marathon and held world records in the half marathon, 20 kilometers, 30 kilometers, and five mile. She was ranked as the number one female distance runner in the world in 1980 and 1981. From April 1980 to April 1981, she won 44 of the 48 distance races she ran—everything from the indoor mile (4:51) to the marathon (2:27). She also was the first American woman, and the second woman in the world, to run the marathon in under 2:30. She set the American marathon record three times (1980 Montreal 2:30:57, 1980 New York City 2:29:33, and 1981 Boston 2:27:51). She took second place in the Boston Marathon three years in a row (1979–81) and won the Honolulu Marathon four years in a row (1978–81). In hindsight, it is only fair to note that as difficult as her marriage to Catalano was, she achieved almost all of her triumphs on the track during the six years she worked with him.

In 2002, she was inducted into the Honolulu Marathon Hall of Fame and the Road Runners Club of America Hall of Fame. She was also inducted into the National Distance Running Hall of Fame in 2006.

Patti Dillon currently travels and lectures as a motivational speaker. (See also SPORTS, AMERICAN INDIANS AND.)

Further Reading

Jennes, Gail. "In the Long Run, Patti Catalano Aims to Be the Best in the World." *People* 15, no. 15 (April 20, 1981).

Kopac, Bob. "Chat: Patti Catalano Dillon." *Runner's World*, 5 November 2006.

Luis, Cindy. "Legendary Lessons: Patti Dillon Has Gone from Dominating Races to Learning about Life the Hard Way. *Honolulu Star Bulletin*, 8 December 2002.

Perry, Douglas. "The Girl Who Could Fly." *Fort Worth Star Telegram*, 14 April 2002.

Pileggi, Sarah. "No. 1 is No. 2 . . . and Closing." *Sports Illustrated*, 27 October 1980.

Preer, Robert. "Running for Her Life." *Boston Globe*, 30 November 2003.

Rogers, Kim Steutermann. "Dancing through Life. Patti Dillon Today: Looking Forward, Looking Back." *Running Times*, October 2003.

Dodge Wauneka, Annie   *See* WAUNEKA, ANNIE DODGE.

Dodge, Henry Chee (Kitchii) (1857–1947) *Navajo (Dineh) tribal chairman*

Henry Chee Dodge, or Kitchii, was born at Fort Defiance, Arizona, in the late winter or early spring 1857. His father was a white army officer, Colonel Henry L. Dodge, who was killed in a battle with Apache a few months before Henry was born. His mother, Bisnayanchi, a Navajo (Dineh) of the Coyote-Pass Clan, was killed in 1864 during Kit Carson's campaign against the Navajo. Young Henry Dodge was adopted by a Navajo family and accompanied them on the forced march to Bosque Redondo, the infamous camp where Indians were held under harsh conditions.

After enduring Bosque Redondo for four years, during which many Navajo died, Dodge returned to Fort Defiance

Henry Chee Dodge in Denver in December 1946. (AP/Wideworld)

and was reunited with members of his family, learning English from an Indian Office employee and trader, Perry H. Williams, who had married his aunt. He then went to live with Indian agent William F. N. Army, who sent him to Fort Defiance Indian School. Dodge also learned Spanish and was soon employed as the official interpreter on the Navajo reservation, serving as translator for the assistant army surgeon at Fort Defiance, Dr. Washington Matthews. Matthews arranged for Dodge's trip to Washington in 1884 in company with a delegation of medicine men. He was later chosen by Indian agent Lieutenant Edward Hinkley Plummer as one of two Navajo taken to the Chicago World's Fair in 1893. Dr. Matthews would become a well-known ethnographer, and Dodge helped him collect the Navajo legends and chants that would later be published as *Navajo Legends* (1897) and *The Night Chant* (1901).

In the first few decades after Bosque Redondo, tensions were high between the Navajo and their non-Indian neighbors. There were boundary problems and disputes over water, grazing, and prospecting on Navajo lands. Dodge, with his diplomatic skills and ability as an interpreter, was often called on to mediate disputes. In 1884, the Indian agent Dennis M. Riordan appointed him chief of the Navajo Police and, later that year, head chief. While not immediately accepted as a leader, he gradually won the people over. Although a mixed-blood, he lived in a traditional manner, marrying several women (as was considered fitting for a man of his prominence),

and his familiarity with the non-Indian world was an important advantage to the tribe.

For more than a decade, beginning in 1890, Dodge ran a trading post at Round Rock, Arizona, in partnership with Stephen E. Aldrich, a white trader. This trading post played a significant part in the promotion of Navajo arts and crafts, though it was not especially profitable.

Dodge had greater success with stock raising. His sheep herd, the result of careful selective breeding for wool and meat, made him rich. He eventually ran two ranches, raising cattle as well. In 1922, he formed a company with Navajos Dugal Chee Bekiss and Charley Mitchell to handle potential oil leases on the Navajo Reservation (see OIL, AMERICAN INDIANS AND). With his good looks, fine clothes, and winning personality, he was the acknowledged leader of the tribe, and when a tribal council was formed by Special Commissioner HERBERT JAMES HAGERMAN in 1923, Dodge became its first chairman. Though he held this position for only five years, he remained the leading Navajo politician for the rest of his life. Despite his financial success and knowledge of mainstream American culture, Dodge remained traditional, and his rivalry with Navajo leader JACOB C. MORGAN would come to epitomize the factional struggle between traditionalists and progressives. In 1928, he stepped down as tribal chair to tend to his sheep ranches. By this time, raising sheep was the most important industry on the reservation and had led to severe overgrazing.

The INDIAN NEW DEAL of the 1930s (see also INDIAN RE-ORGANIZATION ACT), a constructive period for most tribes, was difficult for the Navajo. The high rate of grazing on mostly marginal land had severely deteriorated the range, but Indian Commissioner JOHN COLLIER's attempts to deal with this problem through a stock-reduction program was heavy-handed and made for bad relations between the Navajo and the BUREAU OF INDIAN AFFAIRS. Dodge himself lost three-quarters of his own herd, and he pleaded with Collier to stop the reduction, to no avail. During the height of this period, 1933–35, Dodge's son THOMAS H. DODGE served as tribal chairman; the elder Dodge, who under other circumstances might have been an important link with Washington, could do little, because his traditionalist constituency felt betrayed by the federal government.

In 1942, Dodge, already well over 80, was reelected chairman of the tribal council. He was reelected again in 1946 but died of pneumonia on January 7, 1947, before he could take office. He was succeeded by Sam Ahkeah.

In addition to his son, Thomas Dodge, his daughter, ANNIE DODGE WAUNEKA, was an important tribal figure in her own right.

Further Reading

Bailey, Garrick, and Roberta Glenn Bailey. *A History of the Navajos: The Reservation Years.* Santa Fe, N.Mex.: SAR Press (School of American Research), 1986.

Blue, Martha. *Indian Trader: The Life and Times of J. L. Hubbell.* Walnut, Calif.: Kiva Publishing, 2000.

Brugge, David M. "Henry Chee Dodge: From the Long Walk to Self-Determination." In *Indian Lives: Essays* on *Nineteenth- and Twentieth-Century Native American Leaders*, 91–112. Albuquerque: University of New Mexico Press, 1985.

Chamberlain, Kathleen P. *Under Sacred Ground: A History of Navajo Oil, 1922–1982*. Albuquerque: University of New Mexico Press, 2000.

Iverson, Peter. *Diné: A History of the Navajos*. Albuquerque: University of New Mexico Press, 2002.

———, ed. *"For Our Navajo People": Diné Letters, Speeches, and Petitions, 1900–1960*. Albuquerque: University of New Mexico Press, 2002.

Dodge, Thomas H. (1900–1987) *Navajo (Dineh) lawyer, tribal leader, Indian office official*

The son of Navajo (Dineh) leader HENRY CHEE DODGE and his third wife, Asza Yaze, Thomas H. Dodge was born in 1900 in a hogan on the Navajo reservation and raised in the traditional way until he went to school at St. Michael's Franciscan Mission in Fort Defiance, Arizona. He graduated from St. Regis College in Denver and received an LL.B. from St. Louis University in 1924, the first Navajo to earn a law degree. He was admitted to the bar in Missouri in 1924 and in New Mexico two years later.

Dodge first practiced corporate law in Santa Fe but left to serve as chairman of the Navajo Tribal Council from 1933 until 1935. In this position, he consolidated the six Navajo agencies into one (1935) and inaugurated programs for day schools, conservation, water, and the INDIAN CIVILIAN CONSERVATION CORPS. He also attempted to implement the U.S. government's livestock-reduction program. The government had found the number of Navajo sheep and goats to be double the carrying capacity of their rangeland, and Dodge believed the program, though painful, was needed to preserve the fertility of the land—and the Navajo livelihood. The first reduction in 1933 was fairly successful, but the second in 1934 was badly handled and extremely unpopular (see COLLIER, JOHN). At a meeting called to explain it, Dodge had to wait for two hours before the crowd of 3,000 would even listen to him.

Dodge found the experience so draining that he resigned to become assistant superintendent of the Navajo agency, serving until 1939. Later, he helped oversee his father's business interests. At the outbreak of WORLD WAR II, he was appointed Navajo district supervisor, the first Navajo to hold that position; he left in 1946 to become superintendent of the Truxton Canyon Agency, administering several tribes in Nevada and Arizona.

In 1951, Dodge was superintendent at the San Carlos Apache Reservation, where he launched programs for cattle and range management and independent fund management. He also acted as liaison to educational institutions, consultants, and business firms. In 1958, he became superintendent of the Osage Agency at Pawhuska, Oklahoma.

After his retirement, Dodge and his wife, Vivien, lived in Scottsdale, Arizona. In 1965, he received the Distinguished Service Award from the Department of the Interior. In 1984, he

sold at a Sotheby's auction some very valuable old Navajo craft objects—textiles, jewelry and belts—that had belonged to his father. He said he needed the money for medical expenses. Dodge died on August, 15, 1987, at Paradise Valley, Arizona, where he had lived since 1965. His papers are at the Labriola Center, Arizona State University.

Further Reading

Iverson, Peter, ed. *"For Our Navajo People": Diné Letters, Speeches, and Petitions, 1900–1960*. Albuquerque: University of New Mexico Press, 2002.

Dorris, Michael (1945–1997) *Modoc author, educator*

Born on January 30, 1945, in Dayton, Washington, Michael Dorris was the son of Jim Dorris, who was part Modoc, and Mary Betsy Burckhardt Dorris, who was of European descent. Dorris's father died when he was very young, and he grew up in a household filled with women, including his aunts and grandmother. He earned degrees in English from Georgetown University and in anthropology from Yale University. In 1972, he was hired by Dartmouth College to found a Native American studies program. While there, he met his future collaborator and wife, Chippewa LOUISE ERDRICH. By then, Dorris had already adopted a son and two daughters of Native American descent—he was the first single male in the United States to legally adopt a child. After he married Erdrich in 1981, she adopted them as well.

Dorris collaborated with Erdrich on a series of short stories published under the pseudonym Milou North and published, with Arlene Hirschfelder and Mary Lou Byler, *A Guide to Research on North American Indians* in 1983. In 1987, Dorris scored his first success with the publication of the novel *A Yellow Raft in Blue Water*. Highly acclaimed, this was an intergenerational narrative woven from the stories of three Native American women—daughter, mother, and grandmother—who live on a reservation in Montana.

Two years later, Dorris published *The Broken Cord*, which chronicled the problems suffered by his adopted son, Abel, who suffered from fetal alcohol syndrome (FAS). It won the National Book Award, the Christopher Award, and the Heartland Prize, bringing national attention to the problem of FAS and spurring legislation that mandated warnings for women of the dangers of drinking while pregnant. In 1992, when he was 23, Abel Dorris was struck by a car and killed. After Abel's death, Dorris and Erdrich experienced more trouble with another adopted son, Jeffrey, who spent time in institutions as a result of fetal alcohol effect (a milder form of FAS) and had been incarcerated as well. (See ALCOHOLISM, AMERICAN INDIANS AND.)

In 1991, Dorris and Erdrich coauthored *The Crown of Columbus*, a novel about Christopher Columbus. Dorris released a travel memoir, *Route Two and Back*, the same year. A collection of short stories, *Working Men*, was published in 1993, and a collection of essays, *Paper Trail*, the next year. Dorris also wrote a number of children's books, including

The Window, released in 1997. One of the most acclaimed and highly regarded Indian novelists of his generation, his works won wide praise for their evocative settings and distinctive characters.

In 1995, after a series of court cases, Jeffrey Dorris was unsuccessfully prosecuted after he threatened his adoptive parents with physical harm unless they gave him $15,000 and published a manuscript he wrote. Fearful of the threats, Dorris and Erdrich left Dartmouth for Montana and eventually settled in Minneapolis. Dorris, however, suffered from chronic depression, a "suicidal" condition as Erdrich described it in an interview in *Newsweek*, "that he'd had from the second year of our marriage." The depression grew worse when he and Erdrich separated in 1997. His last novel, *The Cloud Chamber*, was well received when it came out that year, but by that time he was determined to commit suicide.

During the last months of his life, rumors began surfacing alleging that Dorris was under investigation in Minneapolis for sexually abusing one of his young daughters. Although there was no confirmation of these reports, they only made his mental state worse. On March 29, 1997, Dorris attempted suicide in his home in Cornish, New Hampshire, but a friend alerted the police, and he was hospitalized and released, later entering a Vermont mental health and rehabilitation center. On April 10, he checked out of the center on a one-day pass, rented a car, bought three bottles of Nytol and a bottle of vodka, and checked into the Brick Tower Motor Inn in Concord, New Hampshire, using a fake name, address, and license plate number. Michael Dorris was found dead in his hotel room on Friday, April 11, 1997, the cause of death an overdose of drugs and alcohol.

Further Reading

Chavkin, Allan, and Nancy Feyl Chavkin, eds. *Conversations with Louise Erdrich and Michael Dorris*. Oxford: University Press of Mississippi, 1994.

MeuNab, David T. "Of Beads and Crystal Vase: An Exploration of Language into Darkness, of Michael Dorris's *The Broken Cord* and *The Cloud Chamber*." *West Virginia University Philological Papers* 47 (2001): 109–119.

Dozier, Edward P. (1916–1971) *Tewa anthropologist, author*

Edward Pasqual Dozier was born in Santa Clara Pueblo, New Mexico, on April 23, 1916, to Thomas Sublette and Leocadia Gutierrez Dozier. Both his parents were Tewa, and his mother spoke no English. His older brothers worked so that he could attend a Catholic high school in Santa Fe, and although hampered by a lack of funds, he attended the University of New Mexico and Georgetown University before serving in WORLD WAR II.

Dozier returned from the war better able to pursue his interests in anthropology and ethnography thanks to the G.I. Bill. He received his B.A. and master's degree in linguistics from the University of New Mexico in 1951, and he became the first person to receive a Ph.D. in anthropology from the University of California, Los Angeles (UCLA). Dozier then taught at the University of Oregon and Northwestern University before moving to Stanford University in 1958. In 1960, he became professor of anthropology at the University of Arizona, where he founded the university's American Indian Studies Program. Dozier studied the tribal people of the Philippines and wrote two books: *Mountain Arbiters: The Changing Life of a Philippine Hill People* (1966) and *The Kalinga of Northern Luzon* (1967). In addition, he wrote two books on American Indians—*Hano, A Tewa Community in Arizona* (1966) and *The Pueblo Indians of North America* (1970), as well as numerous scholarly articles. He died on May 2, 1971.

Further Reading

Enos, Anya Dozier. "Dozier, Edward P." In *Encyclopedia of North American Indians*, edited by Frederick E. Hoxie, 167–168. New York: Houghton Mifflin, 1996.

Norciai, Marilyn. *Edward P. Dozier: The Paradox of the American Indian Anthropologist*. Tuscon: University of Arizona Press, 2007.

D-Q University   *See* FORBES, JACK D.

Du Bois, Constance Goddard (ca. 1857–1934) *novelist, ethnologist, Indian rights advocate*

Of Huguenot, Puritan, and Scottish descent, Constance Goddard Du Bois was born in Zanesville, Ohio, about 1857, the daughter of John Delafield Du Bois, an attorney, and Alice Cogswell Goddard Du Bois. Like her mother, she was educated at the Putnam Female Seminary near Zanesville, graduating in 1874. She subsequently lived in Charleston, West Virginia, and Watertown, New York, before settling in Waterbury, Connecticut.

Du Bois wrote several novels, contributed to many magazines, was a staff writer for *Out West* magazine (Los Angeles), and was editor of the *Asa Grey Bulletin* (1893–1900). Her one Indian-related novel, *A Soul in Bronze: A Novel of Southern California*, was completed in 1898. First published serially in the pages of her friend Charles F. Lummis's magazine *Land of Sunshine*, it appeared in book form in 1900.

Du Bois was a member of the INDIAN RIGHTS ASSOCIATION, a board member of the INDIAN INDUSTRIES LEAGUE, and president of the Waterbury branch of the Women's National Indian Association. As an ethnologist and reformer, she is most significant for her work with the Luiseño and Diegueño Mission Indians of Southern California.

Like nearly all reformers of the time, Du Bois was first drawn toward Indians as objects of charity, as they were conceived at the time. Invited to visit the Mesa Grande Mission Indian community (some 60 miles from San Diego) by her friend Mary Brier Watkins, she spent summer 1897 there. Her visit became an annual summer trip.

Perhaps influenced by the fact that her father's family had been in the pottery manufacturing business in Zanesville, Du Bois was strongly interested in the possibility of developing a traditional crafts industry to improve economic conditions in the Mission community, particularly among the women. She became a member of the executive committee of the Indian Industries League in 1901. By 1903, at her urging, the league was supporting the mission basket industry.

Du Bois experienced a gradual transformation in attitude as she developed personal relationships with the Indians. At first critical of the older people who kept up their traditional religion, she was soon defending their dances and ceremonies. She spent long periods in the field, learning about the myths, traditions, and ceremonies, and she and Watkins were drawn into the spiritual world of their Indian informants.

The more Du Bois came to respect Indian traditions, the more skeptical she grew of prevalent assimilationist views (see ASSIMILATION). She found Indians to be industrious, not lazy, and their family life not "degraded" but exemplary, with women greatly respected. Furthermore, these admirable qualities rested on deeply rooted cultural values: ". . . no one could live among them for a time as I have done without seeing many evidences of superiority, and this chiefly among the old men who are typical of the past," she wrote in an unpublished paper, "The Religion of the Luiseño and Diegueño Indians of Southern California."

Well known in Indian reform circles, Du Bois was as advanced in her thought as anyone at the time. As a member of the Indian Industries League, her arguments, often delivered in lectures to women's clubs, went beyond philanthropy to actively oppose assimilationist dogmas, including ALLOTMENT. Du Bois was among the first ethnologists to see traditional Native cultures as highly developed, not "primitive." In this respect, she was perhaps ahead of even the famous anthropologist FRANZ BOAS, and she was certainly more outspoken.

Du Bois was in close contact with anthropologists such as Ed H. Davis, Pliny Earle Goddard, and Alfred L. Kroeber. In 1905 and 1906, as a project for the University of California Ethnological and Archaeological Survey, she recorded numerous cylinders of Luiseño songs at La Jolla and Campo and Diegueño songs at Warner's ranch in San José. They are preserved in the archives of traditional music at Indiana University.

Du Bois's ethnological publications include *The Condition of the Mission Indians of Southern California* (1901); *The Mythology of the Diegueños; Mission Indians of San Diego County, California, as proving their status to be higher than is generally believed* (ca. 1905); and *The Religion of the Luiseño Indians of Southern California* (1908). Her papers are at the Cornell University Library in Ithaca, New York.

Further Reading

Laylander, Don, ed. *Listening to the Raven: The Southern California Ethnography of Constance Goddard Du Bois.* Salinas, Calif.: Coyote Press, 2004.
Trump, Eric Krenzen. "'The Idea of Help': White Women Reformers and the Commercialization of Native American Women's Arts." In *Selling the Indian: Commercializing and Appropriating American Indian Cultures*, edited by Carter Jones Meyer and Diana Royer, 159–189. Tucson: University of Arizona Press, 2001.
———. "The Indian Industries League and Its Support of American Indian Arts, 1893–1922: A Study of Changing Attitudes toward Indian Women and Assimilationist Policy." Ph.D. dissertation, Boston University, 1996.

Dukepoo, Frank Charles (Pumatuhye Tsi Dukpuh, "First Crop Snake Sack") (1943–1999) *Hopi-Laguna geneticist*

Frank Dukepoo was born on the Mojave reservation in Parker, Arizona, on January 29, 1943, the fourth of 11 children of Anthony Dukepoo (Hopi) and Eunice Martin Dukepoo (Laguna Pueblo). He became interested in science as a first-grade schoolboy, went to elementary and high school in the Phoenix area, and then went on to Arizona State University, graduating with a B.S. He continued there through graduate school, publishing his research on albinism among the Hopi in *Science* (1969) and receiving his Ph.D. in zoology (genetics) in 1973, the first Hopi to obtain a doctorate and one of the first American Indians to earn a doctorate in the sciences.

After teaching biology at San Diego State University from 1973 to 1977, while also serving as secretary of the BUREAU OF INDIAN AFFAIRS (BIA) science program (1973–75), Dukepoo taught briefly at Palomar Junior College, then at Northern Arizona University at Flagstaff. In 1980, he joined the faculty of Northern Arizona University, Flagstaff, as a biology teacher and special assistant to the academic vice president. There he also directed the Indian education program and a highly successful National Science Foundation support program.

Dukepoo was one of the founders of the AMERICAN INDIAN SCIENCE AND ENGINEERING SOCIETY (AISES) in 1977. In 1982, he founded the National Native American Honor Society for students. He was also a founding member of the Society for the Advance of Chicanos and Native Americans in Science (SACNAS) and a founding board member of the Indigenous Peoples' Council on Biocolonialism, as well as an active member of the Indigenous Peoples' Coalition against Biopiracy. He served as a consultant to many government agencies, such as the BIA, the National Science Foundation, and the National Institutes of Health.

Dukepoo published studies of biological responses to alcohol differentiated by race and conducted research on the minority aged. His research interests also included the effects of uranium on Indians; birth defects; Indian biomedical problems; and the relationship between religion, Indian values, and science. His sociomedical study, *The Elder American Indian* (1980), was based on research carried out at San Diego State University.

One of only two American Indian geneticists in the country, Dukepoo was also much concerned with scientific ethics and the rights of indigenous subjects in scientific experiments.

Although he worked with the Human Genome Diversity Project, he spoke out about any attempts to simplify cultural diversity to a mere genetic entry in a database. He was quoted in the *San Francisco Chronicle* (1998) as saying, "Scientists say it's just DNA. For an Indian, it is not just DNA, it is part of a person, it is sacred, with deep religious significance. It is part of the essence of a person."

Frank Dukepoo was also a talented saxophonist and an amateur magician. He died unexpectedly of natural causes at his home in Flagstaff on April 18, 1999.

Further Reading

Harry, Debra. *Indians, Genes and Genetics: What Indians Should Know about the New Biotechnology*. Nixon, Nev.: Indigenous Peoples Coalition Against Biopiracy, 1998.

Dunn, Dorothy (1903–1992) *art teacher, founder of the Santa Fe (Studio) school of Indian painting*

Born on December 2, 1903, at St. Mary's, Kansas, Dorothy Dunn was the daughter of a general store owner. After graduating from Decatur County High School in 1921, she completed a year of teacher's training and then moved to Iowa, where she taught elementary school. She subsequently trained at the Art Institute of Chicago before being hired by the Indian Field Service of the BUREAU OF INDIAN AFFAIRS (BIA) to teach at the Santo Domingo Pueblo Day School.

After taking a year's leave of absence in 1931, Dunn was hired to begin an art program at the Santa Fe Indian School. The school, opened in 1890 and modeled after the Carlisle Indian School and other military-style schools of the period, was geared toward the ASSIMILATION of young Indians into mainstream American culture (see EDUCATIONAL POLICY, AMERICAN INDIANS AND). Santa Fe in the early 20th century was a mecca for American artists, and despite the government's attempts to stamp out Indian culture, many of these artists, such as Robert Henri, Frank Applegate, and John Sloan, began to champion traditional Indian art. Kenneth Chapman, who had moved to Santa Fe in 1899, was particularly influential, encouraging the careers of many Pueblo and Navajo artists, including Navajo painter Apie Begay. Chapman urged anthropologist Edgar Hewett, who had worked with San Ildefonso potter MARIA MARTINEZ, to enroll Indian painters in the School of American Archaeology in Santa Fe (later the School of American Research and now the School of Advanced Research), where Hewett was the director. Among the early students at the school were San Ildefonso painters Awa Tsireh and Crescencio Martinez.

The success of the early Indian painters and potters led many artists and writers to advocate for a loosening of government restrictions against Indian traditions. The author Mary Austin pressed officials in the BIA to allow Native art to be taught in BIA schools, finally convincing WILL CARSON RYAN, JR., director of education for the BIA, in 1930 to create a plan to add Native art to the curriculum. By this time, a major shift in Indian policy was under way. In the 1930s, a policy of cultural pluralism led by commissioner JOHN COLLIER began to counter the notion of stamping out Indian culture and influenced Dunn to experiment in multicultural education.

Dunn was familiar with the Kiowa school of Indian painting popularized by the KIOWA FIVE and based in part on the flat art, pictographic style of the Pueblo artists that originated at San Ildefonso around 1908. Riding the anti-assimilationist backlash, she discouraged any non-Indian influences for the training of her students and encouraged them to seek inspiration in their traditions, ceremonies, and lives. She institutionalized the two-dimensional (lacking in visual perspective and depth) watercolors then in vogue on the Plains and in the Southwest, a style that emphasized simple rhythmic linearity and pastel colors in themes that almost always depicted cultural activities, such as dancing or hunting. Her unmatched crop of students, which included OSCAR HOWE, PABLITA VELARDE, HARRISON BEGAY, POP CHALEE, and ALLAN HOUSER, came to dominate Indian art to such an extent that this style became known by Indians and non-Indians as "traditional Indian painting." One of the Kiowa Five, Jack Hokeah, traveled to Santa Fe to take classes under Dunn, then brought the "Studio" technique (as Dunn's teachings came to be called) back to Oklahoma.

Other well-known artists who studied in the studio under Dunn included Andy Tsihnahjinnie (Navajo); Wilson Dewey (Apache); Joe Hilario Herrera (Cochiti Pueblo); and Ben Quintana (Cochiti Pueblo), whose promising career was cut short by his death in the battle of Leyte Gulf during WORLD WAR II. Until the late 1950s, when Howe and Houser rebelled against the style, adding abstract elements, Indian painting was dominated by the influence of the Studio, or Santa Fe, school.

In 1937, feeling hamstrung by the BIA, which did not recognize the talents of her students, Dunn left the school to Geronima Cruz Montoya, a San Juan Pueblo student who continued to teach the Santa Fe tradition until 1962, when the school was replaced by the Institute of American Indian Arts. Dunn, who was married to Max Kramer, a mathematics teacher and principal of a school in Taos, retired to spend more time with her husband and daughter, although she continued to champion Indian art and organize exhibitions, including one at the National Gallery of Art in Washington, D.C., in 1953. In 1968, she published her life's work, *American Indian Painting of the Southwest and Plains Areas*. By then, however, the style she had so bravely championed was largely out of fashion, replaced by the abstract paintings of such artists as R. C. GORMAN and FRITZ SCHOLDER. Dorothy Dunn died on July 5, 1992, in Mountain View, California, after a long battle with Alzheimer's disease.

Further Reading

Dunn, Dorothy. *American Indian Painting of the Southwest and Plains Areas*. Albuquerque: University of New Mexico Press, 1968.

Eldridge, Laurice. "Dorothy Dunn and the Art Education of Native Americans: Continuing the Dialogue." *Studies in Art Education* 42, no. 4 (Summer 2001): 318–332.

Smith, Peter. "The Unexplored: Art Education Historians' Failure to Consider the Southwest." *Studies in Art Education* 40, no. 2 (Winter 1999): 114–127.

Durant, William Alexander (1866–1948)
Choctaw tribal leader, politician

A Choctaw, William Alexander Durant was born on March 18, 1866, in Bennington, Indian Territory. His father, Sylvester Durant, after whom the town of Durant, Indian Territory, was named, was a prominent Presbyterian minister and a member of the Choctaw House of Representatives. His mother, Martha Robinson, was white. Durant attended Indian schools in Durant and Bennington and graduated in 1886 from Arkansas Presbyterian College in Batesville, Arkansas, with a master's of art degree. He practiced law in the town of Durant and then served as superintendent of the Jones Male Academy, a Choctaw boarding school and one of the top schools in Indian Territory. He also served as a district judge for the Choctaw and was a successful farmer.

In 1890, he was elected to the Choctaw house of representatives, becoming speaker in 1891. Durant was its presiding official when the council and the entire Choctaw government were abolished under the CURTIS ACT in 1906. The following year, he served as sergeant at arms at the Oklahoma Constitutional Convention, which incorporated what had been called Indian Territory as the eastern part of the state of Oklahoma. He then served as a member of the Oklahoma House of Representatives between 1907 and 1912, again rising to speaker, a position that made good use of his skills as an orator. After an unsuccessful run for governor in 1918, he held various posts in the Oklahoma school system.

In 1937, President Franklin D. Roosevelt appointed Durant principal chief of the Choctaw, succeeding BEN DWIGHT. Although the Thomas-Rogers Act of 1936 had extended some provisions of the INDIAN REORGANIZATION ACT to most Oklahoma tribes, it did not apply to the former Five Civilized Tribes (as the Cherokee, Choctaw, Chickasaw, Creek, and Seminole were known).

In 1944, a group of Choctaw led by Harry J. W. "Jimmy" Belvin (1900–86) wrote to members of Oklahoma's U.S. congressional delegation requesting that Durant not be reappointed to a fifth term. They wanted the right to elect their principal chief and were advised to petition the BUREAU OF INDIAN AFFAIRS (BIA). The congressmen, however, were partial to Durant, and the solicitors of the Interior Department ruled in 1946 that under the terms of the Curtis Act, the appointment of the Choctaw principal chief was solely at the discretion of the president.

In 1948, Durant signed a controversial agreement with the federal government transferring the mineral rights of the remaining unallotted Choctaw lands to the United States for $8.5 million. Durant continued as chief until his death on August 1, 1948, in Tushka Homma, Oklahoma. Later that year, Secretary of the Interior Carl Albert acceded to the democratic movement, and the Choctaw were granted the right to elect their own principal chief. The election was won easily by Jimmy Belvin, who served until 1975.

Further Reading
Green, Richard. "Jimmy Belvin and the Rise of Tribal Sovereignty, 1944–48." *Chickasaw Times* (February 2009), 27, 30.

Durham, Jimmie (1940–) *Cherokee journalist, sculptor, poet*

Jimmie Durham was a Cherokee born in Washington, Arkansas, in 1940. In the 1960s, he was one of the founders of Adept, a minority artists' center in Houston, Texas. He showed his first performance piece in 1964 and mounted his first solo exhibition in 1966 at the University of Texas in Austin. He continued his art education at the École des Beaux-Arts in Geneva, Switzerland, receiving his B.F.A. in 1973.

During the 1970s, Durham joined the AMERICAN INDIAN MOVEMENT (AIM) and was a founder in 1974 of its international offshoot, the INTERNATIONAL INDIAN TREATY COUNCIL (IITC). He was the council's director through 1979, when he resigned after clashing with Cayuga-Salish activist DANIEL R. BOMBERRY and becoming disenchanted with the continual infighting among the various IITC factions. By then, he was already known for his humorous mixed-media sculptures, which poked fun at various stereotypes of Indians. From 1981 to 1983, he was the director of the Foundation for the Community of Artists in New York City.

WINONA LADUKE, as a Harvard freshman in the late 1970s, heard Durham give a speech that, she later recalled, marked the beginning of her political awareness. "It was like a curtain getting lifted. In white public schools, we were taught about 'Indian problems.' Then here was this guy saying that it wasn't an Indian problem, it had to do with U.S. policy. It was an historic problem, with an association to colonialism, that affected Asians, Indians, and Aboriginals." Through Durham, she began her career as an activist with the IITC.

In 1983, Durham released a book of poetry *Columbus Day* and in 1993 he published *A Certain Lack of Coherence*, a book of political essays. In the late 1980s, Durham left the United States to live in Cuernavaca, Mexico, in response to federal efforts to criminalize any artist who identified himself or herself as an Indian without being an enrolled member of a federally recognized tribe. The effort culminated in the passage of the Act to Promote Development of Indian Arts and Crafts in 1990 (see INDIAN ARTS AND CRAFTS BOARD). Not deigning to allow the federal government to determine whether or not he is an Indian, Durham now calls himself a "full-blood contemporary artist." He currently resides in Brussels, Belgium, where he continues to work on his art.

Further Reading
Editors of Phaidon Press. *Jimmie Durham*. London: Phaidon Press, 1995.
Pietroiusti, Cesale, Anna Dameri, and Robert Pinto, eds.

Jimmie Durham. Milan: Charta/Fondazione Antonio Ratti, 2005.

Dwight, Ben (1890–1953) *Choctaw chief, politician*

Ben Dwight was a Choctaw, born on November 24, 1890, in Mayhew, Indian Territory (now Boswell, Oklahoma). His father, Simon Timothy Dwight, was supervisor of Indian education of the Choctaw Nation and superintendent of the Jones Academy, the Choctaw school for elementary- and secondary-age children. A leader of great promise, he died tragically at the age of 28 in 1893. Ben Dwight's mother, Mary Jane Hunter Dwight, was also Choctaw, though her mother was white. In a 1938 interview, Dwight characterized his cultural background: "My people were not very superstitious, and if there were any legends in the family they never told them. I never attended an Indian dance or Indian cry [A yearly ceremony where Choctaws mourn their deceased], but I did attend an Indian ball game . . . a hard fought game and the players were very rough with their ball sticks." (See LACROSSE).

Ben Dwight spent four years at the Armstrong Academy in Indian Territory; went on to high school in Honey Grove, Texas, graduating in 1908; he then studied at the University of Michigan (1908–09) and Columbia University, where he received a B.A. in 1912. He studied law at the University of Oklahoma (1912–13) and then went to Stanford University, where he received a law degree in 1915. Denied enlistment in the U.S. Marines on the U.S. entry into WORLD WAR I due to poor eyesight, he was accepted by the army and assigned to army intelligence at Fort Sam Houston, Texas, where he focused on anti-American propaganda and spy activity. After the war, he worked as an attorney in Durant, Oklahoma. In 1930, President Herbert Hoover appointed him principal chief of the 25,000-member Choctaw tribe.

Dwight's appointment was significant, coming at a time when Indian Commissioner CHARLES JAMES RHOADS was attempting to reform the BUREAU OF INDIAN AFFAIRS (BIA) after years of corruption and mismanagement. It was still rare for an Indian to be appointed chief of his own people, and there were few Indians with a level of educational achievement comparable to Dwight's. Commenting on the appointment,

the *New York Times* noted that "the Indians in Oklahoma have suffered more than anywhere else at the hands of unscrupulous white men. . . . Owing to the wealth, both real and latent, of many Indians whose lands are in the oil belt they are especially in need of wise and sympathetic guidance. . . . The new Choctaw chief . . . can meet the predatory whites with full knowledge of their methods."

After Dwight completed his second term as chief in 1934, he was reappointed by President Franklin Delano Roosevelt for six months. When the choice was given to the Choctaw voters, he was reelected, continuing as chief until 1936. He left to become a regional director in the Organization Division of the Office of Indian Affairs, serving until 1939. He was succeeded as chief of the Choctaw by WILLIAM ALEXANDER DURANT.

From March 1935 to March 1936, Dwight published the biweekly *Tushkahomman* (The Red Warrior) at Stroud, Oklahoma, one of the earliest attempts at a national Indian newspaper (see JOURNALISM). Against the opposition of many conservative businessmen and politicians, as well as the right-wing AMERICAN INDIAN FEDERATION, he strongly supported the Thomas-Rogers Act, which with some modifications extended the provisions of the INDIAN REORGANIZATION ACT to Oklahoma; the bill became law in June 1936.

For eight years, Dwight was president of the Oklahoma Inter-Tribal Council. In 1943, he was appointed special assistant to Governor Robert S. Kerr of Oklahoma. In 1944, he became national attorney for the Choctaw Nation. He was one of the most active founders of the provisional NATIONAL CONGRESS OF AMERICAN INDIANS (NCAI), which met for the first time in Denver, Colorado, in November 1944 under his chairmanship. At this historic convention, the delegates drafted a constitution, determined membership qualifications, elected an executive council, and developed a program of action for the NCAI. Ben Dwight died on July 18, 1953, in Oklahoma City.

Further Reading

Cowger, Thomas W. *The National Congress of American Indians: The Founding Years*. Lincoln: University of Nebraska Press, 1999.

Dwight, Ben. *Choctaw Social Welfare*. Washington, D.C.: Board of Indian Commissioners, 1931.

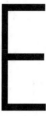

Eagle Shirt, William (William Good Lance Eagle Shirt) (1873–1938) *Oglala Lakota film actor*

One of the first Indian actors in Hollywood, William Good Lance Eagle Shirt was born in 1873 on a portion of the Great Sioux Reservation in South Dakota that would later become known as Pine Ridge. Eagle Shirt (written as two words on all contemporary documents, including the Bureau of Indian Affairs census) spent his early life on the Great Plains until his family was forced to settle on the reservation in 1889. While living there, he married a woman named Mottie; they had a daughter, Bessie.

In 1909, the cowboy performer Vern Tantlinger began recruiting Oglala from Pine Ridge for the Miller Brothers 101 Ranch Wild West Show. The 101 Ranch was located near Bliss, Oklahoma, and, starting in 1905, the three Miller Brothers, Joseph, George, Jr., and Zack began staging Wild West shows in the manner of showman Buffalo Bill Cody. Among their famous performers were future motion picture stars Tom Mix and Ken Maynard, trick roper Bee Ho Grey, legendary black cowboy Bill Pickett, and rodeo champion Hoot Gibson. Eagle Shirt joined the Miller Brothers Wild West Show some time around 1910.

In late November 1911, the 101 Ranch Wild West show was at its winter quarters in Venice, California, only a few miles from where the New York Motion Picture Company (NYMP) filmed their Westerns under the Bison trademark. Bison Films, although successful under their two Indian stars, James Young Deer and Lilian St. Cyr, was seeking to expand its production capabilities. NYMP executives Fred Balshofer and Charles Bauman went to see the 101 show and afterward contracted with the show's director, Joe Miller, for, in Balshofer's words, "the use of about seventy-five cowboys, twenty-five cowgirls, and about thirty-five Indians. . . ." The Indians were all Oglala from Pine Ridge, and among them was Eagle Shirt.

With the addition of the 101 Ranch performers, Bison Films was renamed Bison 101 Films. The studio was further transformed with the recruitment of groundbreaking director Thomas H. Ince (1882–1924) who, in the words of film historian Georges Sadoul, "between 1912–1924, turned the Western into an art." Ince, who had only recently arrived in California, set up his studio on the Pacific coast but did most of his filming in Santa Ynez Canyon in the nearby Santa Monica Mountains. The Oglala were given their own quarters at "Inceville" (as the studio came to be called). The Indian Bureau, as the Bureau of Indian Affairs was then known, required Ince to sign an agreement to provide the Indians with a certain number of hours of schooling each week and to take full responsibility for their care and well-being. In 1912, Oglala Lakota Luther Standing Bear, another 101 Ranch veteran, joined the studio.

Ince immediately began to give important parts to Indian actors but still entrusted the starring roles, even the Indian ones, almost always to non-Indians. Despite this, Ince took a particular liking to Eagle Shirt and used him in prominent parts in most of his early films at Inceville. Ince's attempts to provide a more realistic perspective did much to advance the Western genre. As Michael Wallis notes in his book, *The Real Wild West* (1999), "By using real Indians such as Eagleshirt [*sic*]—an imposing figure in flowing warbonnet and authentic Sioux costume—Ince won much critical acclaim."

Eagle Shirt's filmography is not completely known. He may have played in *An Indian Martyr* (Bison, 1911), which won critical acclaim for its restraint and visual beauty, but the credits for this film have not been established. The first film in which Eagle Shirt was credited as an actor was *War on the Plains*, an epic two-reeler directed by Ince and released by Bison on February 23, 1912. A milestone in Western film history, its scenario was actually written by Eagle Shirt. According to Larry Langman in his *A Guide to Silent Westerns* (1992), the film ". . . attempted to present a more well-rounded characterization of the Indian [and] . . . a more realistic picture of Indian culture, and put forth a more even-handed description of the Indian-white conflicts." *War on the Plains* also starred Francis Ford, the brother of director John Ford, and famed cowpuncher Art Acord, both regulars in Ince's early films.

Eagle Shirt next appeared in *Indian Massacre* (Bison, 1912, reissued 1913 as *The Heart of an Indian*), another early Ince two-reeler, and then acted in and wrote the scenario for *Battle of the Red Men* (Bison, 1912). Other Bison films from 1912 featuring Eagle Shirt are *Custer's Last Fight*, *His Squaw*, *The Lieutenant's Last Fight*, and *The Outcast*. He also starred in *The Invaders*, made in 1912 for Ince's Kay-Bee film company and directed by Ince and Francis Ford. In 1914, Eagle Shirt appeared in Jay Hunt's *The Arrow Maker's Daughter*, another Kay-Bee release. In *Last of the Line* (Domino, 1914), Eagle Shirt co-starred with Japanese-American film idol Sessue Hayakawa and his wife, pioneering Japanese-American film actress Tsuru Aoki. Eagle Shirt's last two films were *The Silent Lie* and *The Conqueror*, both directed by Raoul Walsh and released in 1917.

Sometime during his years in California, Eagle Shirt left Mottie and married fellow Bison personality and legendary Indian sharpshooter Princess Wenona (1871–1930). Wenona, whose real name was Lillian Frances Smith, was born in Coleville, California, and became a crack shot with the rifle by the age of nine. She likely met Eagle Shirt when they were both working for the Miller Brother's Wild West Show. The marriage did not last very long. Mottie and Bessie Eagle Shirt eventually moved to Buffalo, New York, where they were still living as late as 1956.

In 1913, Eagle Shirt received title to 480 acres on Pine Ridge, part of which was his family's allotment. Studio publicity incorporated in a review of *The Conqueror* in the *Atlanta Constitution* (April 7, 1918) gives an idea of his life at this period: "Another of the Indians in the group is William Eagle Shirt, descendant of a long line of chiefs. . . . William is at present about 37 years old. He owns a large ranch on the Dakota reservation, and he has several hundred head of cattle on the lot. Every fall William manages to get into communication with one of the film producers and comes to Los Angeles for the winter. Then, when summer returns and the winds are warm again on the northern plains, William Eagle Shirt returns to take count of his steers and to see his aged mother."

By 1918, Eagle Shirt had married for the third time, to a woman named Emma, and had returned to the reservation for good. On his draft registration of June 18, 1918, he lists his occupation as farmer and builder of log houses, and explains that he filed late because he was "working alone in the country and didn't know he was expected to register in September." From then on, he and Emma appear regularly in the BIA census for Pine Ridge, with the last entry, giving his full name as William Good Lance Eagle Shirt, dated January 1, 1937. He died in 1938.

Further Reading

Wallis, Michael. *The Real Wild West: The 101 Ranch and the Creation of the American West.* New York: St. Martin's Griffin, 1999.

Eastman, Charles Alexander (Ohiyesa, the Winner, Hakadah, Pitiful Last One) (1858–1939)

Wahpeton-Mdewakanton Santee Dakota Sioux physician, government employee, writer, lecturer, philosopher

Charles Alexander Eastman was born in Redwood Falls, Minnesota, in February 1858. He was the son of Jacob Eastman (Many Lightnings) and Mary Nancy Eastman, who was the daughter of Dakota Wakan Tankawin and Captain Seth Eastman, a white soldier and artist at Fort Snelling, Minnesota. Mary Nancy Eastman died shortly after her son's birth, and so he was named Hakadah (Pitiful Last One). At age four, he was renamed Ohiyesa (the Winner), in honor of his village's victory in a LACROSSE game.

In 1862, after years of abuse by encroaching whites, the Santee Dakota launched a series of attacks that became known as the Minnesota Uprising. To avoid the warfare, Ohiyesa was taken by his grandmother, Wakan Tankawin, and his uncle, White Foot Print, to what is now North Dakota. By 1864, they had moved to Manitoba.

Until his 15th year, Ohiyesa lived the traditional life of a Dakota Sioux boy. Then, in 1872, he was amazed when his father, Jacob Eastman, showed up. He had thought his father had been executed with other members of the Minnesota Uprising years before. In fact, Jacob Eastman and his two older sons had been captured but not killed. During their incarceration in Davenport, Iowa, they had become familiar with mainstream American culture. Many Lightnings had changed his name to Jacob Eastman in honor of his first wife's father. Released in 1866, he had remarried and now had a homestead in Flandreau, Dakota Territory. Ohiyesa went to live with his father and was baptized and given the name Charles Alexander Eastman.

Knowing no English and nothing but life among the Dakota, Eastman went through a tremendous transformation over the next 17 years. Later, he would say that his father, more than any other person, had "made it possible for me to grasp the true principles of civilization." In 1874, he entered the Santee Normal Training School (Nebraska), whose founder and director, Dr. Alfred Riggs, was his mentor. In 1876, he went to the Beloit College Preparatory School (Wisconsin), and in 1879 to the Knox College Preparatory School (Galesburg, Illinois), from which he graduated in 1881. In 1883, he entered Dartmouth College, New Hampshire, receiving his B.A. in 1886. He then entered Boston University Medical School and earned an M.D. in June 1890 at the age of 32.

Appointed agency physician to the Sioux at the Pine Ridge Reservation in South Dakota in fall 1890, Eastman saw firsthand the deplorable state of Indian health (see HEALTH, AMERICAN INDIAN). He was at Pine Ridge at the time of the Wounded Knee massacre in December 1890 and was the first physician to reach the scene of carnage and treat survivors at the makeshift agency hospital. During this crisis, he met Elaine Goodale, a young reformer from Massachusetts who, after teaching for several years on the Great Sioux Reservation, had been appointed superintendent of Indian education for Dakota Territory. They married in New York City on June 18, 1891.

Charles Eastman, 1906. *(Beinecke Rare Book and Manuscript Library)*

Tensions continued at Pine Ridge under a severe military regime, and in attempting to mediate for the Indians, the East-mans ran into trouble with the agent, Captain George Leroy Brown. Forced to resign their positions in 1892, they moved to St. Paul, Minnesota, where Eastman started a private medical practice. About 1893, he began to write, at his wife's urging, about his Indian past and outlook on the present. Never comfortable with the writing process, he was helped at every step by his wife's great literary and poetic skills. Eastman expressed not only his views on contemporary Indian problems but also the traditional values he had been raised with, including reverence toward nature, thus becoming one of the first to communicate a Native American environmental philosophy (see ENVIRON-MENTAL MOVEMENT, AMERICAN INDIANS AND THE).

In 1894, Eastman helped set up Young Men's Christian Association (YMCA) chapters for American Indians; he continued in this endeavor, with increasing disillusionment, until 1897, when he went to Washington, D.C., to lobby for restoration of Santee treaty rights, which had been revoked after the Minnesota Uprising. After a year, frustrated and facing financial difficulties, he reapplied to the Indian Health Service. In the meantime, he worked in Pennsylvania for Captain RICH-ARD HENRY PRATT in 1899 as outing agent at the Carlisle

Indian School. (An outing agent supervised the placement and progress of Indian students living with white families, as part of the system Pratt had developed.)

In fall 1900, Eastman was appointed agency physician at the Crow Creek Reservation in South Dakota. By this time, he had published some of his writings in magazines and was beginning to enjoy a literary reputation. His first book, *Indian Boyhood*, a collection of essays and stories, appeared in 1902. With politics once again creating problems for him at the agency, he remained in the Indian Service only with the help of writer HAMLIN GARLAND, who had been appointed by President Theodore Roosevelt to assign Indians standard surnames to avoid future problems in proving inheritance rights. As renaming clerk (1903–09), Eastman officially translated and registered Sioux names. More important, this job provided the opportunity to speak with many Sioux elders. He also continued to write and lecture.

In 1910, with some financial help from the University of Pennsylvania Museum, Eastman revisited his boyhood home in the forests of northern Minnesota. The Dakota no longer lived there, but their traditional enemy, the Ojibwa, still made it their home. The country was still pristine, and Eastman emerged with renewed spirits and a strengthened sense of identity. It was at this time that he wrote what Eastman scholar David Reed Miller calls "his most expressive and articulate essay," *The Soul of the Indian* (1911). From this time on, his writings would become more philosophical.

Eastman's return to nature fitted the mood of the country, and from 1910 his interest in the outdoor youth movement continued to grow. He was friendly with ERNEST THOMPSON SETON, founder of the Boy Scouts, and during summer 1914, as counselor at a scout camp in Maryland, he developed numerous ideas later published in *Indian Scout Talks: A Guide for Boy Scouts and Camp Fire Girls*. The Eastmans then decided to open their own camp for girls. Lured by his memories of Dartmouth, Eastman moved the family, which now included five children, to a place on Granite Lake near Keene, New Hampshire. At first called the School of the Woods, it was renamed Camp Oahe (Hill of Vision) the next year.

Eastman's psychological return to his origins and the skepticism toward modern "civilization" that had first overwhelmed him in 1910 continued. In his last significant work, *From the Deep Woods to Civilization* (1916), he expressed his belief that his traditional Sioux culture was closer to Christianity than was modern society.

Eastman had been a founding member of the SOCIETY OF AMERICAN INDIANS in 1911, but he was not active until 1917; in 1919, he was elected president. In 1920, he was part of the faction, also including GERTRUDE BONNIN, that left the organization over the controversy regarding the use of peyote (see NATIVE AMERICAN CHURCH).

Though the summer camp had gone well, the period of 1918–21 brought personal crisis. His daughter, IRENE EASTMAN, died in 1918 and was buried at Oahe, which consequently became a place of sadness to him. WORLD WAR I, which the United States entered in 1917, had put the camp under financial strain, which by 1921 had plunged the Eastmans into debt. Their marriage had been faltering for some time, and with the loss of Irene and the other children now grown, they separated in summer 1921. Eastman turned the camp over to his wife and daughters, and it survived through the 1926 season.

He moved to Detroit, where his son lived. In 1922, the Santee compensations, for which he had lobbied back in 1898, were settled, and he received a badly needed $5,000 as his share of legal fees. In 1923, he was rehired by the Indian Office (later the BUREAU OF INDIAN AFFAIRS [BIA]) as an inspector, and that summer he organized a reception and naming ceremony for visiting former British prime minister David Lloyd George. In December 1923, he took part in the COMMITTEE OF ONE HUNDRED reform panel.

By this time, Eastman was perhaps the best-known Indian in the United States, and he was treated as a spokesman. As with other people in this position, his knowledge and abilities were sometimes exaggerated and overextended beyond his competence. For example, in 1925 Indian Commissioner CHARLES HENRY BURKE put him in charge of a highly publicized historical research project aimed at determining the time and place of the death of Sacajawea, the Shoshone guide of the Louis and Clark expedition.

In addition to numerous stories and articles in magazines, Eastman had published *Indian Boyhood* (1902), *Red Hunters and Animal People* (1904), *Old Indian Days* (1907), *Smoky Day's Wigwam Evenings: Indian Tales Retold* (1910), *The Soul of the Indian* (1911), and *From the Deep Woods to Civilization* (1916). The importance of Elaine Goodale Eastman to Eastman's writing is suggested by the fact that he never published anything after their breakup in 1921. In 1925, he resigned from the Indian Office for health reasons. He then bought a wooded lot on the north shore of Wilson's Channel in Desbarats, Ontario, and erected a cabin he named Matotee Lodge.

Eastman lived his last decade as a revered figure among youths, hobbyists, and Indian enthusiasts. Now old, he rarely traveled, only making one last trip to his daughter's grave in 1938. He spent his summers camping out on the land of his friend Milford Chandler. After a 1938 campout, Chandler let him keep his tipi up a few more months, and they spent much time in conversation there. One day, as the weather was growing cooler, they built a fire. It went out of control, and Eastman, who already had problems with his lungs, was overcome by smoke. He never recovered his health and died of pneumonia and cardiac problems on January 8, 1939.

Throughout his life, Eastman sought opportunities to talk with elders of the Sioux, Ojibwa, and other tribes. His writings still provide one of the richest sources of Sioux folklore. His article "The Story of Little Big Horn" (1900), in particular, incorporates material from discussions with Sioux veterans of that battle. Yet Eastman was never an ethnographer or a historian in the academic sense. He was really a moral and religious teacher, the first in a line of Sioux scholars and philosophers, including Gertrude Bonnin, CHAUNCEY YELLOW ROBE, LUTHER STANDING BEAR, and (through John G. Neihardt) BLACK ELK, who wanted to instill a positive image of Indian cultures in the American consciousness and who believed their traditional values were of universal importance.

Eastman has been criticized for making changes or omissions in some of his material to make it more palatable or comprehensible to the American public. These criticisms are beside the point, however, if one considers him not as a scientist recording data but as a translator of one culture to another. By opening the American mind to Native American moral values, Charles Eastman helped nurture a trend in public opinion that would become increasingly visible through the 1920s.

Further Reading

Bess, Jennifer. "'Kill the Indian and Save the Man!' Charles Eastman Surveys his Past." *Wicazo Sa Review* 15, no. 1 (Spring 2000): 7–28.

Eastman, Charles A. *Light on the Indian World: The Essential Writings of Charles Eastman (Ohiyesa)*. Introduction by Janine Pease-Pretty on Top. Edited by Michael O. Fitzgerald. Bloomington, Ind.: World Wisdom Books, 2007.

Martinez, David. *Dakota Philosopher: Charles Eastman and American Indian Thought*. St. Paul: Minnesota Historical Society Press, 2009.

Wilson, Raymond. *Ohiyesa: Charles Eastman. Santee Sioux*. Chicago: University of Illinois Press, 1983.

Eastman, Irene (Taluta, Bright One) (1894–1918)
mixed-blood Dakota Sioux singer

Dakota Sioux singer Irene Eastman was the second daughter and one of six children of physician and author CHARLES ALEXANDER EASTMAN and poet Elaine Goodale Eastman. Irene was born in St. Paul, Minnesota, on February 24, 1894; her Dakota name was Taluta (Bright One). Throughout her youth, Irene pursued musical studies, and after she turned 18, she began taking singing lessons, first for three years in Springfield, Massachusetts, and then for two more years in New York. Endowed with a beautiful soprano voice of unusual quality, she began getting concert offers after only one year of professional training. Then, according to publicity material, "as the critics heard her voice more demands came, but even with this encouragement and with the large remuneration that came with it she did not abandon her studies." She was tempted by an offer from "a famous Broadway opera company but preferred to cling to her ideals of what vocal music should be. And yet Mr. Richard Hageman, the conductor of the Metropolitan Opera House in New York, insists that Miss Eastman has all the natural qualifications and material necessary for concert or opera singing."

Taluta, as she was known when she performed, appeared in many cities in the United States, often accompanying her father on his lecture tours. Her repertoire included songs by Indianist composers Carlos Troyer, Thurlow Lieurance, Frederick Russell Burton, Harold Amasa Loring, and Charles Wakefield Cadman (see INDIANIST MUSIC). Writer HAMLIN GARLAND stated in a letter to Eastman's mother, "Your

Irene Eastman, around 1915. *(Private collection)*

daughter's charming presence and sweet and sympathetic voice gave even the dullest of her hearers a realizing sense of the wild beauty which had its place in the world that is almost gone." Taluta's sights, however, were set on the future.

Eastman's singing and Indian recitations were an inspiration to Boy Scouts cofounder ERNEST THOMPSON SETON and other youth workers. During the summers, she worked as a counselor at the Eastman family's summer camp for girls, School of the Woods, later known as Oahe, at Granite Lake near Munsonville, New Hampshire, which first opened in July 1915. Her promising career came to a tragic end, however, when she died of Spanish influenza in Keene, New Hampshire, on October 23, 1918. She was buried in an unmarked grave under a tree at Oahe.

Echohawk, Brummett (1922–2006) *Pawnee illustrator, commercial artist, comic strip artist*

Brummett Echohawk was born on March 3, 1922, in Pawnee, Oklahoma, to Elmer Price and Alice Jake Echohawk. Elmer Echohawk was a former Wild West show actor. After attending Chilocco Indian School in Oklahoma, he studied at the Art Institute of Chicago and the Detroit Art Institute.

Echohawk served in the U.S. Army in WORLD WAR II, first training soldiers in hand-to-hand combat and then working as a sketch artist in the 45th Infantry Division, famously known as the Thunderbird Division. This unit was from Oklahoma and had a high percentage of Indians in its ranks. At the Anzio beachhead on the coastline of Italy, Echohawk and Potawatomi William Lasley led the Thunderbird charge to take "the factory," as the town of Aprilia was called. Lasley was killed in the assault, and Echohawk was wounded three times. He received three Bronze Stars and three Purple Hearts during the war.

Echohawk's war sketches were syndicated in more than 88 newspapers across the country. After the war, he became staff artist of the *Daily Times* and, later, the *Chicago Sun Times*. Inspired by realist painters such as Winslow Homer, George Catlin, and Frederic Remington, he became an authority on American Indians and the West. Echohawk worked with renowned painter Thomas Hart Benton on the Western mural for the Truman Library in Independence, Missouri. His comic strip *Little Chief*, which appeared in the *Tulsa World*, made him well known to most Oklahomans.

Brummett Echohawk was a sought-after commercial painter whose commissions included a painting of the guided missile cruiser USS *Anzio*. His works have been shown throughout the world, including at the Imperial War Museum in London and museums in Germany, Pakistan, and India. In his later years, he worked as an actor, appearing in the television miniseries *Oklahoma Passage* (1989) and the TV show *Walker, Texas Ranger*. He died on February 13, 2006.

Echohawk, John Ernest (1945–) *Pawnee attorney, director of the Native American Rights Fund*

John Echohawk was born on August 11, 1945, in Albuquerque, New Mexico, to Ernest Echohawk (brother of Pawnee artist BRUMMETT ECHOHAWK) and a non-Indian woman, Jane Conrad. He attended the University of New Mexico, where he received his law degree in 1970. Upon graduation, Echohawk received the Reginald Heber Smith Community Lawyer fellowship, and he worked with the California Indian Legal Services program in Sacramento, California. He then joined the NATIVE AMERICAN RIGHTS FUND (NARF) in 1970 as a staff attorney. Two of his four brothers are also prominent lawyers: Walter Echohawk is a staff attorney at NARF, and Larry Echohawk ran unsuccessfully for the Idaho governor's office in 1994.

As deputy director of NARF from 1972 to 1973, Echohawk helped investigate the murder of RAYMOND YELLOW THUNDER on behalf of the AMERICAN INDIAN MOVEMENT (AIM) and aided AIM chairman REUBEN SNAKE's efforts to protect Winnebago land from annexation by the Army Corps of Engineers. After assuming the directorship of NARF in 1973, Echohawk turned the legal aid organization into one of the most influential and financially well-endowed Indian organizations in the country, working to force the federal government to recognize the validity of Indian treaties, as well helping to author an important bill on REPATRIATION.

In 1989, he won a case for the Catawba of South Carolina, which enabled the tribe to recover 144,000 acres of land

John Echohawk is shown looking through files in the Native American Rights Fund headquarters on March 25, 1976. *(AP/Wideworld)*

around Rock Hill. In 1993, Congress passed a Catawba tribal land claim settlement allowing restoration of the tribe and more than $80 million for land acquisition, economic development, and education.

In 1992, Echohawk won a federal district court decision in North Dakota to uphold the civil jurisdiction of tribal courts on tribal lands. That same year, he won a settlement with the state of Montana recognizing rights to 90,000 acre-feet of water for the Northern Cheyenne tribe and also won recognition for the tribal status of the San Juan Southern Paiute tribe.

Named one of the 100 most influential attorneys in the United States by the *National Law Journal*, Echohawk serves on the boards of numerous organizations, including the Association on American Indian Affairs.

Further Reading
Echohawk, John E. "Using Their Law and Their History to Protect Our Rights." *Indian Country Today*, 11 January 2006.

educational policy, American Indians and
Education—that is, the formal, institutionalized system identified with Western culture—was the chief vehicle for

assimilation during the first third of the 20th century, with the central purpose of supplanting traditional forms of learning in order to rapidly acculturate Indians to the dominant society. In the late 19th and early 20th centuries, Indian children and young adults were taken from their families and tribal homes and sent to boarding schools, where it was hoped that strict discipline would eradicate all trace of their Indian culture. The architect of the boarding school system was Richard Henry Pratt, whose flagship Carlisle Indian School was founded in Pennsylvania in 1879. By 1900, there were 26 federal Indian boarding schools, all of them oriented toward vocational training rather than college preparation. Pratt also developed the "outing system," in which Indians were placed with non-Indian families, for whom they worked as servants or laborers in order to learn non-Indian culture.

Also available to Indian children at the turn of the century were the mission schools, which were run by various Christian denominations. Pratt disliked these schools, considering them too tolerant of traditional cultures. These mission schools, most of which were Roman Catholic and run by the Bureau of Catholic Indian Missions, were a source of contention among the various Christian denominations, who all vied for the lucrative federal funding.

With the election of Theodore Roosevelt as U.S. president and the inauguration of the Progressive Era of government policy, Indian commissioners William Arthur Jones, Francis Ellington Leupp, Robert Grosvenor Valentine, and Cato Sells began to steer education policies away from boarding schools and their arch-assimilationist approaches and to focus instead on the creation of reservation day schools, which were seen as less disruptive to Indian culture and family life. Assimilation was still the goal, but it was to take place in a more gradual way and would allow for some retention of tribal culture. These commissioners also began reducing the role of mission schools, preferring to enroll Indian children in the new government schools. Guided by the longtime superintendent of Indian schools, Estelle Reel, who served under Jones, Leupp, and Valentine, Indian education was given an even more practical emphasis. Reel also recognized the educational value of traditional cultures, encouraging pupils, for example, to use Native cultural subjects in English compositions. Angel DeCora, an Indian art teacher, enthusiastically supported this policy. Under Commissioner Leupp, the battle between Catholic and Protestant control over mission school funding came to a head when Leupp attempted to enact regulations that would severely restrict the Catholic Church's ability to receive funding for its schools and to place teachers in government schools.

Carlisle, the most prestigious of the federal boarding schools (largely because of its reputation in sports), was closed in 1918 after an investigation prompted by prominent students such as Gustavus Welch, but strong congressional support for the boarding schools and their assimilationist policies kept the system going, albeit in a declining fashion, throughout the first three-quarters of the 20th century.

With the appointment of Charles Henry Burke as Indian commissioner in 1920, harsh assimilation once again became the educational policy. Burke encouraged the expansion of mission schools and placed Christian educators in charge of many federal schools. In the late 1920s, responding to attacks on his new policies from the American Indian Defense Association, Burke requested that each superintendent name a committee of local citizens to report on conditions on his or her reservation. In 1929, HAROLD SELLERS COLTON and his wife served on the committee investigating the western Navajo (Dineh) reservation. At the Indian Bureau school in Tuba City, they were struck by the military discipline and an assimilationist policy so strong that the children were taught the song "Ten Little Indians," ending with the words "and then there were none."

From 1928 until 1932, during the commissionership of CHARLES JAMES RHOADS, a major issue at the bureau schools was insufficient food. Although President Herbert Hoover had appointed a group to study the nutrition of these children, which reported in 1930 that inadequate diet made them vulnerable to disease, Michigan congressman Louis C. Cramton continually reduced the appropriations requested by Hoover himself to provide adequate food (see HEALTH, AMERICAN INDIAN). In 1930, Rhoads also commissioned ERL A. BATES, already known for his approach to Indian education, the "Bates Plan," to formulate an extensive national education agenda for Indians. In 1931, Rhoads appointed WILL CARSON RYAN, JR., as superintendent of Indian education. Ryan was an internationally known educator who had written the education section of the 1928 MERIAM REPORT, the most extensive and influential critique of federal Indian policy up to that time.

Conceived by Ryan under the previous administration, the JOHNSON-O'MALLEY ACT, passed in 1934, was the educational keystone of Indian Commissioner JOHN COLLIER's culturally based Indian policy, known as the INDIAN NEW DEAL (see also INDIAN REORGANIZATION ACT). The Johnson-O'Malley Act was the single most important piece of legislation on Indian education and would shape educational policy for the remainder of the 20th century.

Collier's commitment to traditional Indian cultures went far beyond that of any previous commissioner. He even hired anthropologists such as OLIVER LA FARGE and Edward Sapir to work in the education branch. In 1936, Collier appointed HENRY CLARENCE ROE CLOUD supervisor of Indian education in the BUREAU OF INDIAN AFFAIRS (BIA). Since 1914, when he served on a federal commission surveying government Indian schools, and 1915, when he opened the first college preparatory high school for Indians, Cloud had been the most influential Indian educator in the country.

Although the Johnson-O'Malley Act was based on the theory that the states and the federal government could work together to administer Indian education, it largely failed to improve education for Indian students. Johnson-O'Malley funds were supposed to be specifically earmarked for Indian education, but most states used them for other purposes and continued to neglect the needs of Indian students. During the TERMINATION era, commissioners DILLON SEYMOUR MYER and GLENN LEONIDAS EMMONS increased the transfer of Indian students from BIA schools to state schools, but funding for the students was considered far too low until bolstered during the 1960s by commissioners PHILLEO NASH and ROBERT LAFOLLETTE BENNETT. Also during the Termination era, boardings schools made a comeback, notably, the Intermountain Indian School built in Brigham City, Utah (see VICTOR, WILMA L.).

With the advent of the RED POWER MOVEMENT of the late 1960s and early 1970s, private "freedom schools" were established to encourage the teaching of traditional culture and languages. The most successful, the Akwesasne Freedom School on the Akwesasne Mohawk Reservation and the Heart of the Earth Survival School (now Heart of the Earth Charter School) in Minneapolis, Minnesota, continue to operate.

In 1969, a report of the Special Senate Subcommittee on Indian Education, entitled "Indian Education—A National Tragedy, A National Challenge" (commonly known as the Kennedy Report, after committee chair Senator Edward Kennedy), delineated severe shortcomings in the Indian educational system, finding that dropout rates among Indian students were twice the national average—with some districts approaching a rate of 100 percent—and that achievement levels of Indian students tended to be two or three years below those of their white counterparts. The report led to the passage of the Indian Education Act of 1972, which provided special programs for Indian children in reservation schools and, for the first time, special programs for urban Indian students as well.

In 1975, the Johnson-O'Malley Act was amended by the Indian Self-Determination and Education Assistance Act, which allowed tribes to contract for education funds. As a result, many Native communities have successfully established their own local educational systems. However, the BIA came to see the act as undermining its authority as well as siphoning badly needed funds outside of its mandated areas, the reservations. During the administration of President Ronald Reagan, BIA commissioner Ross O. SWIMMER attempted to have the act defunded. Despite these attempts, of all items on the Indian agenda in the second half of the 20th century, education had made the greatest substantial gains, and in reservation schools at least, true Indian control and content would be achieved.

See also HIGHER EDUCATION; RELIGIOUS FREEDOM, AMERICAN INDIAN.

Further Reading

Faircloth, Dr. Susan C., and John W. Tippeconnic, III. "Resource Guide: Utilizing Research Methods That Respect and Empower Indigenous Knowledge." *Tribal College Journal of American Indian Higher Education* 16, no. 2 (Winter 2004): 24–27.

Lomawaima, K. Tsianina. "American Indian Education: *by* Indians versus *for* Indians." In *A Companion to American Indian History*, edited by Philip Joseph Deloria and Neal Salisbury, 422–440. Malden, Mass.: Blackwell Publishing, 2004.

Pewewardy, Cornel. "Learning Styles of American Indian/

Alaska Native Students: A Review of the Literature and Implications for Practice." *Journal of American Indian Education* 41, no. 3 (2002): 22–56.

Szasz, Margaret Connell. *Education and the American Indian: The Road to Self-Determination Since 1928*. 3rd. ed. Albuquerque: University of New Mexico Press, 1999.

Tippeconnic, III, John W. "The Education of American Indians: Policy, Practice, and Future Directions." In *American Indians: Social Justice and Public Policy*, edited by Donald E. Green and Thomas V. Tonneson, 180–207. Milwaukee: University of Wisconsin System Institute on Race and Ethnicity, 1991.

Edwards, Bronwen Elizabeth   *See* ROSE, WENDY.

El-Issa, Ingrid Washinawatok   *See* WASHINAWATOK, INGRID.

Emmons, Glenn Leonidas (1895–1980) *commissioner of Indian affairs*

Born in Atmore, Alabama, on August 15, 1895, Glenn L. Emmons moved with his family to Albuquerque, New Mexico, in 1904. He enrolled in the University of New Mexico in 1914, leaving in 1917 to enlist in the U.S. Army Air Corps. He was discharged in 1919 with the rank of first lieutenant and entered the banking business in Gallup, New Mexico, rising to the position of president and chair of the board of the First State Bank of Gallup. The bank's strong financial relationship with the Navajo (Dineh) Tribe gave Emmons some experience with Indians.

Emmons was also active in the state's Republican Party, serving as an alternate delegate to the 1952 Republican Convention. He was appointed to succeed the embattled DILLON SEYMOUR MYER as head of the BUREAU OF INDIAN AFFAIRS (BIA) on August 10, 1953, inheriting Myer's plan to drastically reduce the government's role in managing Indian affairs. The policy, known as TERMINATION, had strong support in Congress, in particular in the Senate Subcommittee on Indian Affairs, chaired by ARTHUR VIVIAN WATKINS. Nine days before Emmons took office, Congress passed Concurrent Resolution 108, which called for the rapid ASSIMILATION of Indians and their transformation into private citizens. The resolution designated nine tribes for immediate Termination, meaning the dissolution of their reservations and an end to all government services. Emmons speedily complied with the resolution, which directed the BIA to prepare the Termination legislation, and by early 1954 he submitted to Congress recommendations for terminating tribes in California, Florida, New York, and Texas, as well as the Menominee of Wisconsin, the Klamath of Oregon, the Flathead of Montana, and the Turtle Mountain Chippewa (Ojibway) of North Dakota.

In June 1954, Public Law 399 was passed, with the Menominee being the first tribe scheduled for Termination in 1957 (later extended to 1961). The next year, Congress passed Termination bills for the Klamath, the Uintah and Ouray Paiute, and the Alabama-Coushatta of Texas. The Paiute bands were terminated first on February 28, 1957. Lacking in educational resources, financial stability, or a modern standard of living, the bands were scattered and virtually destroyed within four years. In 1959, the Klamath were terminated, and more than 78 percent of their reservation was sold outright, with rich timberlands going largely to the U.S. government and the Crown Zellerbach Corporation.

In addition to selling off Indian reservations and breaking up tribes, Termination involved the transfer of jurisdiction over Indian lands from the federal government to the states. On August 15, 1953, Congress passed Public Law 280, which shifted responsibility for law enforcement on reservations in California, Nebraska, Minnesota (except the Red Lake Reservation), Oregon (except Warm Lake), and Wisconsin (except the Menominee) from the BIA to the respective states. In 1957, South Dakota and Washington were added. Emmons also supported Public Law 568, passed on August 5, 1954, which mandated the transfer of Indian health services from the BIA to the U.S. Public Health Service. The transfer took place on July 1, 1955, when the Public Health Service took control over 58 Indian hospitals and other BIA health care facilities.

Emmons also expanded Myer's Relocation program. During his first two years, he managed to relocate more than 5,000 Indians off their reservations and into large cities. The program, although designed to provide training, education, and employment opportunities in cities such as Denver, Chicago, Los Angeles, and San Francisco, was in actuality simply a one-way bus ticket from the reservation to the city. Without any employment or housing opportunities, most people fell victim to poverty or crime, and more than 20 percent of them returned home after a year (see URBANIZATION, AMERICAN INDIANS AND).

Emmons did attempt to address education problems among Indians, in particular the lack of schools on many reservations. In 1954, he inaugurated the Navajo Emergency Education Program, which included using mobile schools that followed Navajo sheep camps. By 1957, the commissioner reported a record 132,000 Indian children enrolled in school. Emmons also shifted more responsibility for Indian education from the BIA to the states under the JOHNSON-O'MALLEY ACT. (See EDUCATIONAL POLICY, AMERICAN INDIANS AND.)

Under Interior Secretary Douglas McKay, dubbed "Giveaway McKay" for his policies toward public lands and natural resources, and then his successor, former Nebraska senator Fred Seaton, Emmons allowed Indian lands to be taken for massive public works projects. Along with assistant interior secretaries Ralph Tudor, a construction executive and former colonel for the Army Corps of Engineers, and Wesley D'Ewart, a former congressman and advocate of Termination, the Interior Department, through the Bureau of Reclamation, seized lands from the Fort Mohave, Chemehuevi, Colorado River, Yuma, and Gila Bend Reservations for giant dam projects on the Colorado River. The PICK-SLOAN PLAN, on the

Missouri River system, flooded Chippewa, Mandan, Crow, Cree, Blackfeet, and Assiniboine lands. More than 200,000 acres of Sioux (Dakota, Lakota, Nakota) land in North and South Dakota were also flooded for the Fort Randall, Oahe, and Big Bend Dams. Along with a compliant Justice Department, which had previously defended Indian lands under Commissioner JOHN COLLIER, the Interior Department fought fierce efforts by Indians, such as in the case of the Seneca and KINZUA DAM, to stop the massive projects. (See DAMS ON AMERICAN INDIAN LANDS.)

Emmons also encouraged oil, uranium, and coal leasing on Indian lands. He inaugurated a massive road-building project, constructing more roads and bridges than all the previous commissioners combined. In 1957, he received the Distinguished Service Award from the Department of the Interior. (See also MINING, AMERICAN INDIANS AND; NUCLEAR INDUSTRY, AMERICAN INDIANS AND THE; OIL, AMERICAN INDIANS AND.) Termination resulted in increasing Indian dissatisfaction with Emmons and the BIA, and Indians mobilized under organizations such as the NATIONAL CONGRESS OF AMERICAN INDIANS (NCAI) to put an end to the policy. On September 18, 1958, Secretary Seaton attempted to allay Indian fears by announcing that Indians would not be terminated without their consent, but by then a growing militancy among Indians had begun to take hold, leading to MAD BEAR ANDERSON's attempt to make a citizen's arrest on Emmons on March 29, 1959, and climaxing with the AMERICAN INDIAN CHICAGO CONFERENCE of 1961 and the formation of the NATIONAL INDIAN YOUTH COUNCIL.

With incoming president John F. Kennedy intent on changing Indian policy, Emmons left office on January 7, 1961, to be succeeded by PHILLEO NASH. Emmons remained in Washington until 1964, then returned to Albuquerque, New Mexico, and retired from public life and from the banking industry, although he continued to serve as a director to a number of charitable and banking organizations. He died in Albuquerque on March 14, 1980.

Further Reading
Burt, Larry W. *Tribalism in Crisis: Federal Indian Policy, 1953–1961.* Albuquerque: University of New Mexico Press, 1982.

environmental movement, American Indians and the
The environmental movement in the United States, also known in its early days as the conservation movement and now often referred to as the green movement, is a widely diverse political and social movement that seeks in general to mitigate or eliminate the destruction of natural ecosystems caused by industrialization and urbanization. Although the concept of stewardship of the Earth and protection of the natural order is ancient in many cultures, including Western ones, the political movement now called environmentalism is a comparatively recent phenomenon resulting from the gradual recognition

that human activity over the last two centuries has seriously compromised the Earth's natural environment.

This activity, which includes deforestation, desertification, pollution, and species extinction, stands in marked contrast to the manner in which American Indians had lived in North America. It became clear to many Western observers that, despite wide diversity in Native cultures, Native Americans generally held the natural world in great regard and had developed economic and social systems that usually coexisted in balance with the environment.

As the modern conservation and environmental movement began to take shape in the United States, Indians, while not its only source, became a major influence. Santee Dakota Sioux CHARLES ALEXANDER EASTMAN was probably the first Indian to articulate an indigenous environmental world view in the English language. His earliest articles, published in *St. Nicholas* magazine in 1893–94 and later collected in *Indian Boyhood* (1902), contain much environmental philosophy and discussion. Eastman's friendship and collaboration with GEORGE BIRD GRINNELL, ERNEST THOMPSON SETON, and HAMLIN GARLAND were important factors in the development of the conservation movement. In 1914, with Seton's encouragement, Eastman published *Indian Scout Talks: A Guide for Boy Scouts and Campfire Girls.* The first *Official Boy Scout Handbook* (1917), which Seton compiled, was based on his woodcraft philosophy, itself heavily influenced by his interactions with Indians. (The woodcraft philosophy stressed the value of outdoor recreation and conservation for the education of children and young adults.) The section on conservation was written by Seton's old friend William Temple Hornaday, zoologist, president of the American Bison Society, and founder of an early conservation organization, the Camp Fire Club of America (1897). Seton was an active member in both organizations.

In detailed communications published in the *Oregonian*, a Portland newspaper, Ashland timberlands owner Norman F. Throne (July 25 and August 28, 1910, January 18, 1911), poet and forester Joaquin Miller (Sept. 12, 1910), and an anonymous "Pioneer of '47" (January 26, 1911) advocated the Indian method of controlled burning of underbrush to prevent major forest fires, noting that the condition of the Pacific forests had greatly deteriorated since the coming of the white man. Miller had been promoting the practice of controlled burning since as far back as 1882 (in a letter to the *New York Independent*).

In several articles in *The Red Man* and *The Southern Workman* in 1912–14, the anthropologist FRANK GOULDSMITH SPECK presented conservation as a traditional American Indian value. Speck's views were endorsed by forester and conservationist Gifford Pinchot in an article, "American Indian as Conservationist," published in the *Christian Science Monitor* of May 15, 1919. ARTHUR C. PARKER, writing under his Seneca name Gawasa Wanneh in *American Indian Magazine* (1917), emphasized the environmental orientation of Native cultures. Outdoorsman Jack Snetsinger wrote a defense of Indian hunting practices, published in *Rod and Gun* in December 1926, calling Indians "the greatest outdoor lovers and outdoor conservationists of all" and recommending that they be employed as game wardens. Teton Lakota Sioux LUTHER STANDING BEAR, in *Land of the Spotted Eagle* (1933), gave an eloquent statement of the Lakota philosophy of the environment, stating the "Lakota was a true naturist—a lover of Nature." WILLIAM CHRISTIE MACLEOD, Speck's former graduate student at the University of Pennsylvania, published perhaps the first attempt to analyze the issue, "Conservation among Primitive Hunting Peoples," in *Scientific Monthly* in 1936. Speck published another brief article on the subject, "Aboriginal Conservators," in *Bird-Lore* (1938). Traditional Mohawk leader RAY FADDEN, writing under the name Aren Akweks, published the pamphlet *Conservation as the Indian Saw It* in 1948.

An early instance of environmental cooperation between Indians and non-Indians occurred in the 1920s, when mechanical harvesters were first used to collect wild rice in Minnesota on lakes legally reserved for Chippewa rice harvesting. The machines destroyed the rice beds, fouled the shallow lakes by stirring up silt and decayed vegetation, and ruined the environment for fish and waterfowl. The practice was decried equally by Indian and non-Indian residents. Non-Indian protesters acknowledged that the only legal protection available was the U.S. treaty of 1837 with the Chippewa at St. Peters, Wisconsin (see GREAT LAKES INDIAN FISH AND WILDLIFE COMMISSION).

The Indian role in the environmental movement remained limited, however, until environmentalism itself became a major trend and more Americans began to listen to Indians, neither of which happened until around 1970. The new atmosphere is symbolized by the famous 1971 public service television announcement for Keep America Beautiful, Inc., featuring actor IRON EYES CODY. At the same time, a speech attributed to Chief Seattle but actually written by dramatist TED PERRY, was widely circulated by environmentalists. The hugely popular paperback editions of CARLOS CASTAÑEDA's first three books also appeared at this time; while not specifically about Indian environmentalism, they demonstrated the increasing interest in Indian world views. VINE DELORIA, JR.'s most important critique of the Western attitude toward the environment appeared in 1973 in his *God Is Red*.

A countereffort has also arisen that denies that Indians practiced conservationist philosophy. Its proponents suggest that drastic changes in the environment are "natural" activities for humankind in general (thus avoiding any responsibility or need to rethink long-entrenched values). The backlash was inaugurated in 1972 by frontier historian W. H. Hutchinson, who condemned what he saw as a "resurrection of the myth of the noble savage." The historians Charles Bishop, Calvin Martin, and Robert Brightman have also debunked the role of Indians as conservationists, though their methodologies have been seriously challenged by other historians. A preponderance of evidence shows that conservation has been central to many indigenous cultures and has been followed with great knowledge and skill. Examples of Indians engaging in counterecological practices, assuming they are true, only confirm that harmful results ensue when people fail to follow their own traditional ecological wisdom. Until recently, however, modern European thought has not even pretended to hold such values paramount and, when faced with countless examples of negative social impacts from destructive environmental practices, more commonly reacts with denial rather than giving central place to the environmental perspective. The attack on Indian traditional environmentalism is one example of this.

While an ecological outlook tends to promote unity, cultural differences have sometimes impeded cooperation. Non-Indian environmentalists have often been reluctant to work with Indians and have scapegoated them for problems they did not cause; made deals with governments over their heads; been unwilling to trust tribal governments to uphold sound environmental standards; and been generally uninterested in, or even suspicious of, an issue of central importance to Indians, SOVEREIGNTY.

For their part, Indian governments have indeed sometimes adopted destructive practices from the larger society (for example, yellow pine cutting on the Navajo Reservation, waste dumping at Campo Rancheria, clear-cutting forests on the Eyak Corporation in Alaska). They have sometimes viewed sovereignty from an "I want my piece of the American pie" perspective, in contrast to the traditional understanding of sovereignty, that is, a covenant with the Creator to maintain natural balance.

A major step forward for Indians was the founding of the INDIGENOUS ENVIRONMENTAL NETWORK in 1991, a coalition of local Native environmental groups that has coordinated with Greenpeace and other mainstream environmental organizations, many of which now have Indians on their boards of directors.

Despite all differences, practical links grew between Indian and non-Indian environmentalists, especially during the final decade of the 20th century. Many began to see that there was much overall agreement and a need for coalitions. Contemporary Indian activists, such as WALT BRESETTE, NILAK BUTLER, WINONA LADUKE, OREN LYONS, JR., and GRACE THORPE have made it a point to work with the larger environmental movement. Force of circumstance makes this trend likely to continue.

Further Reading

Gedicks, Al. *The New Resource Wars: Native and Environmental Struggles against Multinational Corporations.* Boston: South End Press, 1993.

LaDuke, Winona. "The Dilemma of Indian Forestry." *Earth Island Journal* (Summer 1994).

———. "Native Environmentalism." *Cultural Survival Quarterly* 17, no. 4 (1994): 46–48.

———. *All Our Relations: Native Struggles for Land and Life.* Boston: South End Press, 1999.

Martin, Calvin. "Epilogue: The Indian and the Ecology Movement." In *Keepers of the Game: Indian-Animal Relationships and the Fur Trade.* Berkeley: University of California Press, 1982.

Nadasdy, Paul. "Transcending the Debate over the

Ecologically Noble Indian: Indigenous Peoples and Environmentalism." *Ethnohistory* 52, no. 2 (Spring 2005): 291–331.

Zimmerman, David R. "Can Indians and Environmentalists Find Common Ground?" *The Progressive* 40, no. 12 (December 1976): 27–29.

Erdrich, Louise (Karen Louise Erdrich) (1954–)

Turtle Mountain Chippewa novelist, poet

Louise Erdrich was born Karen Louise Erdrich on July 6, 1954 (some sources give June 7, 1954), in Little Falls, Minnesota. Her mother, Rita Joanne Gourneau, was Chippewa, and her father, Ralph Louis Erdrich, was of German descent. Louise Erdrich's parents both worked for the Bureau of Indian Affairs (BIA) as teachers at the Wahpeton Indian school. The first of seven children, Louise Erdrich was encouraged to write by her father, who paid her a nickel per story, and her mother, who stapled construction paper together for book covers. Erdrich often visited her relatives on the Turtle Mountain Chippewa Reservation when she was growing up, and both her grandfather Pat Gourneau, who served for a time as tribal chairman, and her father, who, according to Erdrich, was "a terrific storyteller," were among her many formative influences.

Erdrich attended public schools as well as a local Catholic school, St. Johns, before applying to Dartmouth College, New Hampshire, in 1972. One of the first women to be admitted to the previously all-male institution, she quickly established herself as a promising writer, winning the Cox Prize for fiction as well as a prize from the American Academy of Poets. While taking a course in the newly founded Native American Studies Program, Erdrich was encouraged by Michael Dorris, the program's founder, to draw upon her Chippewa heritage for her stories.

After receiving her B.A. in 1976, Erdrich taught for the Poetry in the Schools program sponsored by the National Endowment for the Arts and was a visiting poet and teacher for the North Dakota State Arts Council. In 1978, she received a fellowship to teach composition and creative writing at Johns Hopkins University. After completing her M.A. at Johns Hopkins in 1979, she moved to Boston to serve as editor of the Boston Indian Council's newspaper, the *Circle*. In 1980, while writer in residence at Dartmouth, she gave a poetry reading that Dorris attended. They began dating and were married in 1981, beginning a fruitful literary collaboration. Erdrich found employment as a textbook writer for the Charles Merrill Company, which published her first book, *Imagination*, in 1981.

During this time, Erdrich won numerous awards, including being named a MacDowell Colony Fellow in 1980 and Yaddo Colony Fellow in 1981, and receiving a National Endowment for the Arts Fellowship in 1982. In 1982, her short story "The World's Greatest Fisherman" won the Nelson Algren fiction award. The next year, "Scales" won the National Magazine Award for fiction and was included in *The Best*

American Short Stories, 1983. Also in 1983, Erdrich received the Pushcart Prize for her poem "Indian Boarding School," and the next year she published her first collection of poems, *Jacklight*. Here the themes that would come to dominate her later work emerged: the confusion of her generation, unable to escape its heritage or its past, and the strength and character of her German-American and especially her Chippewa upbringing.

Erdrich's first novel, *Love Medicine*, released in 1984, won instant acclaim and garnered the National Book Critics' Circle Award and the Sue Kaufman Prize for Best Novel from the American Academy and Institute of Arts and Letters. The novel, a complex and intimate set of stories revolving around several Chippewa families in North Dakota, was widely praised for its poetic storytelling and vivid characters. Her striking evocation of an American landscape drew comparisons to William Faulkner's *Go Down Moses*, while her characters moved beyond the stereotype of the "vanishing Indian," finding strength and affirmation in the tribal lore that remains.

Beet Queen, released in 1986, paralleled the story of *Love Medicine*, focusing this time on a small midwestern town and the activities of mostly German- and Scandinavian-descended families whose lives intersect with some of the characters from *Love Medicine*. Also a critical and popular success, *Beet Queen* was followed by *Tracks* in 1988. In *Tracks*, the clash of the two cultures presented in Erdrich's previous works comes to the fore. In this brooding, darker work, lacking the multiple voices of the author's prior novels, the two narrators hearken back to the time in the mid-20th century when the Chippewa land, culture, and spirituality were replaced by towns, Western habits, and the Catholic Church. Erdrich continued the series in the *Bingo Palace* (1994), which—although it received mixed reviews—confirmed her standing as one of America's best-selling authors.

Erdrich published a volume of poetry in 1989, *Baptism of Desire*. In 1991, she and Dorris coauthored *The Crown of Columbus*, a popular novel that coincided with the Columbus quincentenary the next year. Although it was the first work that they had officially coauthored, they had long had an unusual working relationship in which they contributed extensively to each other's works. A prolific writer, Erdrich released *The Blue Jay's Dance: A Birth Year* in 1995 and *Tales of Burning Love* and *Grandmother's Pigeon*, a children's book, in 1996. By this time, her relationship with Dorris had become deeply troubled, and the family had undergone a series of upheavals. In 1992, their son Abel was killed in a car accident, and the next year their son Jeffrey was jailed for trying to extort money from them. In 1996, they separated, and the following year Dorris took his own life.

Erdrich continues to write, and in 1998 she released *The Antelope Wife: A Novel*, which was well received. In 1999, her children's book *The Birchbark House* was a National Book Award finalist. The next year, she opened a bookstore in Minneapolis, Birch Bark Books, as a showplace for American Indian culture. In 2001, she was again the focus of critical acclaim when her novel *The Last Report of the Miracles at Little*

No Horse was a finalist for the National Book Award. (Her recent novels include *The Master Butcher Singing Club* (2003), *Four Souls* (2004), *The Painted Drum* (2005), *The Plague of Doves* (2008), and *Shadow Tag* (2010).

One of America's most popular women novelists, Erdrich is also a highly regarded poet. Her work has been praised for "infusing the commonplace and the mundane with the richness of myth."

Further Reading

Beidler, Peter G., and Gay Barton. *A Reader's Guide to the Novels of Louise Erdrich.* Columbia: University of Missouri Press, 1999.

Chavkin, Allan, ed. *The Chippewa Landscape of Louise Erdrich.* Tuscaloosa: University of Alabama Press, 1999.

Jacobs, Connie A. *The Novels of Louise Erdrich: Stories of Her People.* New York: Peter Lang, 2001.

Wong, Hertha Dawn, ed. *Louise Erdrich's Love Medicine: A Casebook.* Oxford: Oxford University Press, 1999.

Evans, Ernest Edwin (1908–1944) *Cherokee decorated U.S. naval officer*

Ernest Edwin Evans, a Cherokee, was born on August 13, 1908, in Pawnee, Oklahoma, and attended Central High School in Muskogee. On May 29, 1926, he enlisted in the U.S. Navy. After a year's service as an enlisted man, he was appointed to the U.S. Naval Academy in Annapolis, Maryland, entering as a midshipman on June 29, 1927. He graduated in 1931 with a bachelor of science degree.

Following the outbreak of WORLD WAR II, Evans participated in the battle of Java Sea, where on February 28, 1942, U.S., British, and Dutch forces were routed by the Japanese navy. Afterward, Evans swore that if he were ever again given command of a ship, he would never retreat from the enemy. In March 1942, he was named commander of the USS *Alden.* However, the old World War I–vintage destroyer was only fit for escorting convoys between Hawaii and the mainland.

In October 1943, Evans took command of the USS *Johnston,* a destroyer, right after its commissioning. The new ship was nicknamed "General Quarters (GQ) Johnny" because Evans, a hard taskmaster, put the crew on a relentless training schedule. In its first year, the *Johnston* participated in the bombardment of Kwajalein and the invasion of Guam, for which Evans was awarded the Bronze Star for action against a Japanese submarine. When U.S. forces began the reconquest of the Philippines on October 17, 1944, the *Johnston* guarded a group of escort carriers that bombarded the island of Mindanao, the opening salvo in the seven-day battle of Leyte Gulf.

On the morning of October 25, a powerful Japanese force consisting of four battleships (including the super-battleship *Yamato*), seven cruisers, and nine destroyers slipped unnoticed through the San Bernadino Strait and stumbled onto a small group of American escort carriers providing cover for troops landing on the island of Samar. The six escort carriers, slow and defenseless, were guarded by only three destroyers, one of which was the *Johnston,* and three even smaller destroyer escorts.

When the Japanese fleet was spotted, Commander Evans reacted instantly, laying a smoke screen so the carriers could try to get away. He ordered the *Johnston* to attack the lead Japanese ship, the heavy cruiser *Kumano,* which he disabled with a torpedo strike. A battleship and cruiser then fired on the tiny destroyer, hitting it six times and jamming the steering, flooding the engine room, and killing all of the officers on the bridge except Evans, who was seriously wounded. The little ship was saved by a rain squall, which provided cover for a few minutes while repairs could be made.

After restoring partial power, the *Johnston* emerged from the rain squall and made directly for the enemy, providing covering fire for torpedo strikes by the other two U.S. destroyers and the destroyer escorts. The *Johnston* attacked the heavy cruisers *Haguro* and *Tone,* exchanging gunfire with them before taking on the battleship *Kongo,* which had just finished sinking the *Johnston*'s companion destroyer, the USS *Holm.* Dancing in and out of its own smoke, the *Johnston* harried the bigger ships, buying the carriers time to launch a counterstrike.

Evans tried to stop the heavy cruiser *Chokai* from sinking the carrier *Gambier Bay* but had to disengage when he observed a Japanese light cruiser and four destroyers attempting to make a torpedo run at the remaining carriers. He immediately ordered the *Johnston* to attack them, forcing the ships to fire their torpedoes prematurely and turn away.

As the battered carriers began to make their escape, the Japanese fleet took out their frustrations on the *Johnston,* which was now sandwiched between a battleship, two heavy cruisers, and several destroyers. The ship was virtually shot to pieces. In its last minutes, Evans was seen commanding the burning ship from the fantail, yelling orders through an open hatch to men turning the rudder by hand and directing the fire of the lone working gun. When the ship was finally reduced to a burning hulk, a Japanese destroyer delivered the coup de grâce.

As the *Johnston* rolled over and sank, the Japanese commander saluted the men who had helped hold off an entire fleet. In his epic *History of United States Naval Operations in World War II* (1947), Samuel Elliot Morrison wrote: "In no engagement of its entire history has the United States Navy shown more gallantry, guts, and gumption than in those two morning hours between 0730 and 0930 off Samar." Only 141 crewmen of the *Johnston* were rescued; Commander Evans and 185 men went down with the ship. He was posthumously awarded the Medal of Honor on November 24, 1945. On June 14, 1952, the U.S. Navy commissioned the USS *Evans,* a destroyer escort, in honor of Ernest Evans.

Further Reading

Thomas, Evan. *Sea of Thunder: Four Commanders and the Last Great Naval Campaign 1941–1945.* New York: Simon & Schuster, 2006.

Exendine, Albert Andrew (1884–1973) *Delaware
football player, coach*

Albert Andrew Exendine, a Delaware (Lenape), was born in Bartlesville, Indian Territory (now Oklahoma), on January 27, 1884, the son of Jasper and Amaline Exendine. Jasper Exendine was a chief of the Delaware and a prosperous merchant and rancher who had begun his career as a deputy U.S. marshal appointed by the infamous "Hanging" judge Isaac Parker (see the CURTIS ACT). In 1875, Exendine was riding with George B. Keeler near Bartlesville, when they came across a pond covered with oil, becoming the first to discover oil in Oklahoma (see OIL, AMERICAN INDIANS AND). Young Albert Exendine attended the Mautame Boarding School in Anadarko, Indian Territory. He later attended the Carlisle Indian School in Pennsylvania, where he played football under Carlisle's famed coach, POP WARNER. Beginning in 1901, Exendine played six years of varsity football at Carlisle, becoming the team captain in 1906 and making second-team All-American the next year, when Carlisle fielded one of the finest college football teams of all time. Under Exendine, Carlisle's football team became the first to use the forward pass as a deliberate part of its offense; they unveiled it in 1907 during their upset win over Amos Alonzo Stagg's mighty "Chicago Eleven," the reigning Big Ten champions.

The next year, Exendine became Warner's assistant. He continued to develop the forward passing game with upcoming Carlisle stars JIM THORPE—whom Exendine had recruited—and GUSTAVUS WELCH. Exendine left Carlisle in 1909 to coach Otterbein College (Ohio) for three years, working on his law degree during the off seasons. After graduating from Dickinson Law School (Carlisle, Pennsylvania) in 1912, he began practicing law in Anadarko, Oklahoma, though he continued to coach football at a local high school. In 1913, Warner asked Exendine to assist him at Carlisle again, and then lent Exendine to Georgetown University for their game against the University of Virginia. Georgetown won the game, and they were so impressed with Exendine that they asked him to stay on as head coach, a position he filled until 1922. In 1916, his Georgetown squad compiled one of the highest-scoring totals of any college football team.

In 1923, Exendine left Georgetown for Washington State University, where another Warner protégé WILLIAM HENRY DIETZ had coached four years before. In 1926, he took over the helm at Occidental College (California), leaving it two years later to coach at Northeastern Oklahoma State Teachers College for one year. From 1929 until 1933, he served as the baseball coach at Oklahoma State University, and he became its head football coach for the 1934 and 1935 seasons.

Exendine retired from college football in 1935 and began working for the BUREAU OF INDIAN AFFAIRS as a lawyer, although he continued to coach high school football in his spare time. He was elected to the National Football Foundation's Hall of Fame in 1970. Albert Exendine died on January 4, 1973, in Tulsa, Oklahoma.

Fadden, Ray (Aren Akweks, Tehanetorens)

(1910–2008) *Mohawk teacher, historian, museum curator*

Ray Fadden was born on August 23, 1910, in Onchiota, New York. His parents, Carroll and Matilida Fadden, were mainly of Scottish descent. Ray attended the Fredonia Normal School and then the State University of New York at Plattsburgh. He then taught at the Indian school on the Tuscarora Reservation near Niagara Falls, where he met his wife, Christine Chubb, a Mohawk from the St. Regis (Akwesasne) Reservation. After their marriage in 1935, they moved to the St. Regis Reservation, where Fadden taught at the Mohawk School in Hogansburg. Fadden was adopted by the Akwesasne Mohawks, who made him a member of the Wolf Clan and gave him the name Tehanetorens (He Peers Through the Trees).

Fadden was influenced by the youth programs inaugurated on New York INDIAN RESERVATIONS by LOUIS ROOK BRUCE, JR., during the Great Depression. During the late 1930s, Fadden founded the Akwesasne Mohawk Counsellor Organization, which taught Mohawk language and culture to the reservation's youths. He became an important figure in reviving Mohawk culture and the traditional Longhouse Religion, which by the turn of the century had dwindled to fewer than 30 adherents on the Akwesasne Reservation. (The remainder of the reservation was Roman Catholic.) Under the name Aren Akweks, he wrote more than 20 pamphlets chronicling the history of the Iroquois, their culture, and traditions. Among these pamphlets are *Conservation as the Indian Saw It*; *The Formation of the Ho-de-no-sau-ne or League of the Five Nations*; *The History of the St. Regis Mohawks*; and *The Great Gift, Tobacco*. Written during the 1940s, the pamphlets were published by the Akwesasne Counsellor Organization, Hogansburg, in 1948.

In 1954, Fadden founded the Six Nations Indian Museum at Onchiota, New York. In the heart of the Adirondack Mountains on land he inherited from his parents, Fadden built the museum out of logs he cut by hand. At the same time that he founded the museum, Fadden also began to teach science to seventh graders in the Saranac Central School District. He retired as a teacher in 1967.

Fadden worked to protect the Adirondacks from acid rain and clear-cutting and was known for looking after local bears and other wild animals that were having trouble finding food. The cultural revival he had worked for started to bear fruit in the late 1960s and early 1970s, when a number of younger Mohawk, such as TOM PORTER and JAKE SWAMP, began to take their places on the Mohawk Chief's Council. His own son, John Kahionhes Fadden (born 1938), is a noted artist and teacher. Recently, many of Ray Fadden's works have been republished under his Mohawk name Tehanetorens. These include *Tales of the Iroquois* (1990), *Legends of the Iroquois* (1998), and *Roots of the Iroquois* (2000). Ray Fadden died on November 14, 2008, at a nursing home in Akwesasne.

Further Reading

"An Appreciation of Ray Fadden-Tehanetorens." *Indian Country Today*, 26 May 2004.

George-Kanentiio, Douglas M. *Iroquois on Fire: A Voice From the Mohawk Nation*. Lincoln: University of Nebraska Press, 2008.

Fall, Albert Bacon (1861–1944) *secretary of the Department of the Interior*

Albert Bacon Fall was born in Frankfort, Kentucky, on November 26, 1861, to Williamson Ware Robertson Fall, a schoolteacher, and Edmonia Taylor Fall, daughter of a distinguished Kentucky family. He had little formal education but was tutored by his paternal grandfather, Philip Slater Fall, a Campbellite minister and one of the founders of the Church of the Disciples of Christ in the South. At 18, Fall moved to

Texas to seek his fortune. Working as a miner, he drifted to New Mexico Territory, where he began a lifelong association with oilmen such as Edward L. Doheny, later known as the "Oil King of Mexico," and Harry Sinclair. In 1892, Fall gave up mining for the lucrative opportunities offered by the politics of the day. Working as a reformer against the Republican Party machine known as the "Santa Fe Ring," Fall became attorney general and served on the territory's Supreme Court. By 1912, however, as one of the newly established state of New Mexico's first two senators, he had joined the Republicans.

In his maiden speech to Congress, Fall criticized the federal government's new conservation programs, arguing that they were "a restriction on the individual." He favored a "states' rights" approach to resource exploitation, arguing for the transfer of all public domain lands from the federal government to the states and calling for the abolition of the BUREAU OF INDIAN AFFAIRS (BIA) and INDIAN RESERVATIONS. Fall had a personal stake in the elimination of Indian reservations. Since acquiring a property he called Three Rivers Ranch, adjacent to the Mescalero Apache Reservation in New Mexico, in 1906, he had fixed his sights on Apache lands and water. His attempts to graze cattle on Mescalero lands and to take their valuable timber were fought by Mescalero Indian agents James A. Carroll and Ernest Stecker, but in 1910 Fall managed to acquire part of the Mescalero water supply through a shady deal with the BIA. He also secured valuable grazing leases on the reservation for his son-in-law. As senator, hoping to build a tourism industry for his ranch, Fall unsuccessfully sponsored legislation to turn part of the reservation into a national park.

Fall and other Western politicians were largely unsuccessful in their attempts to turn public domain lands and Indian reservations over to state control, because the Progressive Era political atmosphere under Woodrow Wilson espoused scientific management of natural resources and more efficient management of agencies such as the BIA. Fall's legislation to prevent landless Indians from acquiring ALLOTMENTS on the public domain of New Mexico and Arizona failed in 1913, and his attempts to end executive-order expansions of Indian lands and the patenting of public domain lands to Indians died in 1918. Fall suffered a major defeat when the General Leasing Act of 1920 made the federal government responsible for leasing and resource extraction on public domain lands.

With the new political climate brought on by the election of Warren G. Harding in 1920, Fall was appointed Secretary of the Interior. He was determined to see his political views written into law, but his first order of business was to enlarge his own ranch. Transferring his foe Stecker from the Mescalero Agency, he was able to renege on a deal to build a dam and water-supply system for the Mescalero in return for some of their water. His old friends Edward L. Doheny and Harry Sinclair then gave Fall money to buy out other ranches near the reservation that competed for Mescalero water and grazing lands.

Chief Forester Gifford Pinchot successfully stopped Fall from selling off the national forest system, but the new secretary was able to wrest the reins of Indian policy away from

Commissioner CHARLES HENRY BURKE. Fall lobbied for the Omnibus Bill of 1922, which extended CATO SELL's disastrous "competency commissions," which were set up ostensibly to allow "competent" Indians to sell their allotments, otherwise protected by law, but ended up facilitating the theft of Indian allotments. Fall personally supervised the drafting of the controversial BURSUM BILL, sponsored by his successor in the Senate, Holm O. Bursum. A protégé of Fall, Bursum himself had once been charged with embezzling money when he was New Mexico's territorial warden, but the attorney general at the time—none other than Albert Fall—did not mount a case. Although not inclined to religion himself, Fall supported efforts by Protestant missionaries to ban Indian religions through Burke's DANCE ORDERS. However, his attempt through the Omnibus Bill of 1923 to dissolve Indian reservations and divide tribal assets among individual tribal members, was narrowly defeated in Congress.

Fall's sympathy for "Big Oil" found a warm reception in the Harding cabinet, which was filled with oil company representatives, including Secretary of State Charles Evans Hughes, former counsel for Standard Oil of New Jersey; Secretary of the Treasury Andrew Mellon, majority owner of Gulf Oil; and Assistant Secretary of the Navy Theodore Roosevelt, Jr., a former director of Sinclair Oil. The discovery of oil on Navajo lands led Fall to have Burke attempt to organize an informal Navajo council in May 1922 to approve exploratory leases, but the ad hoc council turned them down. A second council organized in March and a third in April also refused all but one exploratory lease. Fall then secured the passage of a bill permitting oil and gas leasing on Navajo lands, and in 1923 he placed HERBERT JAMES HAGERMAN in charge of leasing the Navajo reservation to oil interests and of forming a Navajo tribal council to approve the leases (see DODGE, HENRY CHEE; OIL, AMERICAN INDIANS AND).

Using his powers of approval, Fall refused to permit foreign oil companies, in particular Royal Dutch Shell, at that time engaged in a worldwide feud with Standard Oil, to drill on Indian lands. Fall also threw himself into opening executive-order reservations—that is, those reservations created by an order of the president rather than by treaty—to oil and gas development. Ruling that executive order reservations were actually part of the public domain and not truly Indian lands, Fall issued a controversial administrative order opening the executive order reservations to prospecting under the General Leasing Act. As this act made no provision for sharing the proceeds with Indians, Fall came under fire from the INDIAN RIGHTS ASSOCIATION.

After two tumultuous years in the Department of the Interior, Fall was replaced by Hubert Work, whose reputation for honesty was doubtless a reason for his appointment. Under pressure from Senator CHARLES CURTIS, the new secretary of the Interior froze all exploratory leases granted under Fall's tenure.

While interior secretary, Fall rewarded Harry L. Sinclair and Edward Doheny by leasing the Teapot Dome Naval Oil Reserve to Sinclair and the Elks Hills Reserve to Doheny. Fall's role in the infamous Teapot Dome scandal, first made public in 1924, finally landed him in prison in 1931. Saddled with large debts, he was forced to sell his Three Rivers Ranch in 1935 and spent most of the last decade of his life in poverty and ill health. He died on November 30, 1944, in El Paso while recuperating from gallbladder surgery. His scandalous reputation as interior secretary gave impetus to the powerful new Indian reform movement launched by future Indian commissioner JOHN COLLIER and others in the wake of the Bursum bill, and forced the Harding administration to establish the COMMITTEE OF ONE HUNDRED to review Indian policy.

Further Reading

Keleher, William Aloysius. *The Fabulous Frontier: Twelve New Mexico Items*. Albuquerque: University of New Mexico Press, 1982.

Stratton, David H. *Tempest over Teapot Dome: The Story of Albert B. Fall*. Norman: University of Oklahoma Press, 1998.

Farmer, Gary Dale (1953–   ) *Cayuga actor, producer, publisher*

Born on June 12, 1953, on the Six Nations Reserve in Ontario, Canada, Gary Dale Farmer attended Genesee Community College and Syracuse University in New York State. A Cayuga, he once aspired to be a policeman and an FBI agent but ended up studying acting and motion picture production at Ryerson Polytechnical Institute in Toronto. Farmer appeared in a number of stage revivals in Toronto, as well as in Tomson Highway's play *Dry Lips Oughta Move to Kapuskasing*, and he also had roles in films such as *Blue City Slammers* and *The Believers*.

In 1987, Farmer was chosen to appear in the landmark independent film *Powwow Highway*, based on the novel by Abenaki writer David Seals. His portrayal of the slow-witted but ever-cheerful Cheyenne Philbert Bono, who eventually finds strength and wisdom on a mystical journey to rescue a childhood friend, won him wide praise. Farmer has also appeared in numerous Hollywood films, including *Friday the Thirteenth*, *Police Academy*, and *The Dark Wind*, and on television in the series *Miami Vice* and *China Beach*.

Farmer produced documentaries "Our Native Land" and "Powwow" for Canadian television, and in 1995 he founded *Aboriginal Voices*, an award-winning magazine about Native American arts and media. In 1998, he starred with Irene Bedard, Tantoo Cardinal, and Adam Beach in the film *Smoke Signals*, directed by Cheyenne-Arapaho filmmaker Chris Eyre and written by SHERMAN ALEXIE. In 2002, he appeared along with GRAHAM GREENE and Eric Schweig in Chris Eyre's film *Skins*. A prolific actor, Farmer's recent films include *Disappearances* (2006), *One Night with You* (2006), and *California Indian* (2007). Farmer also tours extensively with his Rockabilly/Blues band Gary Farmer and the Troublemakers.

Further Reading

Isaacs, Cheryl. "Aboriginal Voices: Canada's Aboriginal Peoples in Their Own Words." In *Hidden in Plain Sight:*

Contributions of Aboriginal Peoples to Canadian Identity and Culture, edited by David Newhouse, Cora Jane Voyageur, and Daniel J. K. Beavon, Vol. 1. Toronto: University of Toronto Press, 2005.

Farver, Peru (1888–1967) *Choctaw educator, career Indian Service employee*

Peru Farver was born on February 8, 1888, in Eagletown, Indian Territory (now Oklahoma), to Sim and Helen (Bails) Farver. Sim Farver was a full-blooded Choctaw, and Helen Farver was the daughter of a white merchant from Kansas. Peru Farver was named after his grandfather, a relatively prosperous Choctaw plantation owner. In 1902, Peru Farver entered Armstrong Academy, one of four schools—two for girls, two for boys—established by the Choctaw soon after their removal to Indian Territory. He graduated in 1909 and then briefly attended the University of Chicago before returning to Armstrong as an assistant teacher. In 1911, he attended the Oklahoma Agricultural and Mechanical College (now Oklahoma State University at Stillwell) but returned to Armstrong in 1913 to replace GABE EDWARD PARKER as superintendent of the school. Leaving in 1917 for military service, Farver entered the Indian Service (later the BUREAU OF INDIAN AFFAIRS [BIA]) shortly after the war. He then served as superintendent of another of the old Choctaw schools, the Tushkahoma Academy.

In 1935, Farver was appointed field agent for the Great Lakes Region, working with ARCHIE PHINNEY and MARK BURNS to assist 26 bands and tribes to draft constitutions and charters under the INDIAN REORGANIZATION ACT. Farver supported the creation of the NATIONAL CONGRESS OF AMERICAN INDIANS (NCAI) in 1944 and was one of many BIA employees who lent their skills to the fledgling organization.

From 1947 to 1952, he was superintendent of the Red Lake Agency in Minnesota. He then served as superintendent of the Tomah Agency (comprising the Wisconsin Winnebago, Stockbridge and Oneida, Michigan Ottawa and Chippewa, and the Sac and Fox of Iowa). Later, he worked for the Indian Health Program. When this responsibility was turned over to the Public Health Service in 1955, Farver was named adviser on relations with Indian and Native Alaskan peoples. He received the Interior Department's Superior Service Award in 1956. As a career employee in the postwar BIA, Farver supported TERMINATION. He retired as a tribal relations officer in 1957 and was succeeded by FORREST J. GERARD. In 1960, he stated: "Most Indians could be integrated into the general community now, and successfully." Peru Farver died in 1967.

Further Reading

Gabbett, Harry. "Indian Aide Retires from HEW at 70." *Washington Post and Times Herald*, 28 February 1957; B8 (with photo).

film, American Indians and

Western themes were popular in American films from the very

beginning of the silent era. Usually Indians were involved, whether as mass extras, as minor characters, or occasionally even as major ones. Films were a popular product, and in the earlier days of American movie production, had little pretention to high "art." There was great emphasis, especially considering the nonverbal nature of the silent film medium, on "types" of all kinds, including ethnic types. Stereotypes were thus part of the very language of silent film, and this was certainly true of the portrayal of Indians. Like all cultural expression, this silent "language" of film both mirrored the culture that produced it and recycled that culture back to the mainstream audience by way of its powerful visual images.

American culture had both negative and positive stereotypes of the American Indian. Negative was the cruel, ignorant savage; positive was the noble, faithful red man. Another stock image was the Indian maiden who falls in love with a white man and either rescues him, runs away with him, or dies—or all three. There were also sympathetic images of a people wronged by the dominant society. Indians were, like the frontier itself, "standing in the way of progress." Much of this cultural imagery was prefigured by the Wild West shows of the late 19th century, which were in fact the training ground for most of the Indian actors in early film.

Around 1910, at the very time that the precursors of today's American movie industry were getting established in Southern California, Indian intellectuals were coming together in the SOCIETY OF AMERICAN INDIANS (SAI), the first pan-Indian organization. One of their concerns was the public image of American Indians. Thus, a movie based on the celebrated case of WILLIE BOY brought numerous protests from prominent Indians as early as 1911, as did one about the 1890 massacre at Wounded Knee, made in 1913 (see GILMORE, MELVIN RANDOLPH). These films went beyond mere negative stereotypes to gross distortions of historical fact. Arapaho SHERMAN COOLIDGE, one of the leaders of the SAI, even tried to start his own film production company in 1920 to project what he considered a positive image of the American Indian. Another leading SAI figure, CHAUNCEY YELLOW ROBE, who was particularly known for his opposition to the Wild West show image of the Indian, starred with SYLVESTER LONG LANCE in The Silent Enemy, a 1930 film with an all-Indian cast, which tried to present an accurate portrayal of traditional Ojibwa life.

While most of what has been written about Indians in Hollywood focuses on the question of stereotypes, there is another aspect to the story, no less interesting. The new industry was a field of open opportunities. While many Indian parts were played by whites in makeup, a large number of real Indians built careers in the new world of films. Major Indian actors of the silent era included WILLIAM EAGLE SHIRT and LUTHER STANDING BEAR (both Lakota), JAMES YOUNG DEER (Lenni Lenape), and LILIAN RED WING ST. CYR (Winnebago). In the decade of the 1910s, Young Deer was also an important director of Westerns who always tried to portray Indians in a positive and sympathetic light. EDWIN CAREWE (Chickasaw) was one of Hollywood's major directors in the 1920s. WALLACE

Fox (Chickasaw) directed B movies for many years, and FINIS Fox (Chickasaw) was a busy scenario writer for silent films. MOLLY SPOTTED ELK (Penobscot) began her career as an actress in the silents. JOHN WHITE CALF starred as Sitting Bull in Bob Hampton of Placer (1921), a film about the Battle of Little Bighorn that, unusual for the time, was sympathetic to Indians as defenders of their homeland. Luther Standing Bear founded the Indian Actors' Association. In 1928, Pawnee-Otoe entertainer JOSEPH SHUNATONA starred in one of the first sound films, the Paramount short The Moon Bride's Daughter. NIPO STRONGHEART (Yakama) was practically a one-man institution for historical and cultural accuracy in Indian scenes.

Indians active in the period of big feature Westerns, B Westerns, and serials, which spanned the silent era into WORLD WAR II, included Edwin Carewe, JOHN BIG TREE (Seneca), VICTOR DANIELS (Tohono O'odham), SCOTT T. WILLIAMS (Ottawa), RODERIC REDWING (Chickasaw), Molly Spotted Elk, Nipo Strongheart, and CHIEF YOWLACHIE (Daniel Simmons, Puyallup). After the war, new stars emerged, including Mohawk actor JAY SILVERHEELS, who first achieved fame with his portrayal of Tonto in the Lone Ranger television series and starred in a number of Westerns during the 1960s.

During the 1950s and early 1960s, the period of the cold war—concurrent with the TERMINATION era, which sought to stamp out Indian culture—and of the dominance of large studios in Hollywood, Indians had no opportunity to make their own films or shape their own characters. However, non-Indian director Kent Mackenzie created a vivid picture of Indian dislocation in the Bunker Hill section of Los Angeles in The Exiles (1961), with an all-Indian cast. The prevailing attitude of the period was summed up by one of the icons of the Hollywood Western, John Wayne, in an interview in the magazine Playboy in May 1971: "I don't feel we did wrong in taking this great country away from them. . . . There were great number of people who needed new land, and the Indians were selfishly trying to keep it for themselves."

In the late 1960s, however, as Westerns became more complex and incorporated more modern themes, a greater diversity of roles emerged for Indian actors. Little Big Man, made in 1971, was a landmark film in its attempt to demystify and deromanticize the Wild West. It ended up presenting a complex and sympathetic portrayal of Indian people. Chief DAN GEORGE (Salish) was nominated for an Academy Award for his portrayal of a Cheyenne elder in the film, the first Native American actor to be so honored. Three years later, WILL SAMPSON, JR., was also nominated for an Academy Award for his role in One Flew Over the Cuckoo's Nest.

In the 1980s, as independent filmmaking began to emerge, Indians once again began to have a hand in the making of films. In 1984, Harold of Orange, written by Chippewa author GERALD VIZENOR and starring Seneca comedian CHARLIE HILL, became the first modern movie with an Indian perspective. It was followed in 1987 by the cult classic Powwow Highway, based on the novel by Abenaki writer David Seals and starring GARY DALE FARMER. In 1990, GRAHAM GREENE and FLOYD WESTERMAN won critical acclaim for their roles in

Dances with Wolves, an epic Hollywood movie with an Indian focus, including much dialogue in Lakota Sioux.

By the 1990s, new Native filmmakers were emerging, such as Cheyenne director Chris Eyre and Spokane-Coeur d'Alene screenwriter SHERMAN ALEXIE, heralding a new revival of Indian filmmaking. Noted Indian scholars who have tackled the issue of Indian stereotypes in Hollywood include Seneca artist and professor Rick Hill and Cherokee historian RENNARD STRICKLAND.

Further Reading

Aleiss, Angela. "Native Americans: The Surprising Silents." *Cineaste* 21, no. 3 (Summer 1995): 34–35.

Battaille, Gretchen M., and Charles L. P. Silet. *Images of American Indians on Film: An Annotated Bibliography.* New York and London: Garland, 1985.

Deloria, Philip J. *Indians in Unexpected Places*, 52–108. Lawrence: University Press of Kansas, 2004.

Friar, Ralph, and Natasha Friar. *The Only Good Indian: The Hollywood Gospel.* New York: Drama Book Specialists, 1972.

Grab, Jacqueline K. "Will the Real Indians Please Stand Up?" In *Back in the Saddle: Essays on Western Film and Television Actors.* Edited by Gary A. Yuggy. Jefferson, N.C.: McFarland, 1998.

Keshena, Rita. "The Role of American Indians in Motion Pictures." *American Indian Culture and Research Journal* 1, no. 2 (1974): 25–28.

Kilpatrick, Jacquelyn. *Celluloid Indians: Native Americans and Film.* Lincoln: University of Nebraska Press, 1999.

Langman, Larry. *A Guide to Silent Westerns.* Westport, Conn.: Greenwood Press, 1992.

Rosenthal, Nicholas G. "Representing Indians: Native American Actors on Hollywood's Frontier." *Western Historical Quarterly* 36 (Autumn 2005): 329–352.

Strickland, Rennard. "Tonto's Revenge, or, Who Is That Seminole in the Sioux Warbonnet?" In *Tonto's Revenge: Reflections on American Indian Culture and Policy.* Albuquerque: University of New Mexico Press, 1997.

Verhoeff, Nanna. *The West in Early Cinema: After the Beginning.* Amsterdam: Amsterdam University Press, 2006.

Fire, Archie   *See* LAME DEER, JOHN FIRE.

fishing rights, Indian   *See* HUNTING AND FISHING RIGHTS.

Fonseca, Harry (1946–2006) *Maidu painter*

The youngest of seven children, Harry Fonseca was born in Sacramento, California, on January 5, 1946, to a father of Portuguese descent and a mother who was half-Hawaiian and half-Maidu. Fonesca attended Christian Brothers High School, then entered California State University in Sacramento but left to join the U.S. Navy. After a four-year stint in the service, Fonseca returned to California State and began to study painting. In 1977, he completed his first major piece, *The Creation Story*, which focused on the traditional culture of the Maidu people.

In 1980, Fonseca moved to New Mexico, where his playful and colorful renditions of hip, humanlike coyotes began to attract national attention. Beginning with *Coyote Leaves the Reservation, N.Y., N.Y.* (1982) and *Coyote in Front of Studio*, (1983) Fonseca's "flat-art" coyote paintings became recognizable and sought-after images. Their very popularity led Fonseca to abandon the series in the late 1980s. He then began to concentrate on abstract, mixed-media pieces that received widespread acclaim. His work began to turn more political with his *Discovery of Gold and Souls in California* (1992) series. The 160-piece mixed-media series focuses on the genocide of the California Indians during the gold rush of the 19th century.

In 1993, Fonseca opened the Fonseca Gallery in Santa Fe, New Mexico, to exhibit his works. His later work shows him returning to his Maidu roots, centering on the spiritual meaning of the Maidu deer dancer, and his similarities to mainstream cultural icons, such as Icarus and Saint Francis. Harry Fonseca died on December 26, 2006, in Albuquerque, New Mexico, of a brain tumor.

Further Reading

Fonseca, Harry. "The Strength That Continues to Go on for All of Us." *Museum Anthropology* 24, nos. 2, 3 (Fall 2000/Winter 2001): 36–40.

Fools Crow, Frank (1897–1989) *Teton Lakota Sioux holy man, traditional chief*

Frank Fools Crow was a Teton Lakota Sioux born in Porcupine on the Pine Ridge Reservation in South Dakota on June 27, 1897. Raised by a traditional family who kept him from enrolling in school, Fools Crow was sent to study at age 13 with Stirrup, a well-known Lakota holy man, and became a healer and ceremonial leader.

In 1917, Fools Crow became a Roman Catholic, following in the footsteps of his famous uncle and renowned medicine man, BLACK ELK. Unlike Black Elk, however, he did not give up leading traditional ceremonies.

During the 1920s, Fools Crow participated in many Wild West shows, including one tour of Europe. In 1925, he became the leader of the Porcupine District on the Pine Ridge Reservation, a position that had been held by his father.

Traditional Indian religious practices were largely forbidden in the United States in the first half of the 20th century, and many of the most sacred Lakota ceremonies, such as the Sun Dance, had to be conducted surreptitiously (see RELIGIOUS FREEDOM, AMERICAN INDIAN). In 1929, Fools Crow was given permission to conduct a Sun Dance on the Pine Ridge Reservation, although no traditional body piercing was allowed. Not until 1952 could Fools Crow conduct a Sun Dance in the fully traditional way.

Teton Lakota Sioux holy man Frank Fools Crow poses in front of the U.S. Capitol building after delivering the opening prayer in the Senate as guest chaplain in 1975. *(AP/Wideworld)*

Fools Crow sided with AMERICAN INDIAN MOVEMENT (AIM) leaders when they occupied WOUNDED KNEE in 1973, lending the militants important credibility in their struggle against Pine Ridge's tribal chairman RICHARD WILSON and the federal government. He was an important member of the Lakota delegation that negotiated an end to the 71-day occupation. On September 5, 1975, while leading a delegation of Sioux leaders to discuss Indian treaty rights, Fools Crow became the first traditional Indian spiritual leader to give an opening prayer for a session of the U.S. Senate. He died on November 27, 1989, near Kyle, South Dakota, on the Pine Ridge Reservation.

Further Reading

Fools Crow, Frank, and Thomas E. Mails. *Fools Crow.* Lincoln: University of Nebraska Press, 1979.

Forbes, Jack D. (1934–2011) *Powhatan–Lenni Lenape writer, cofounder of D-Q University*
Jack D. Forbes, a Powhatan–Lenni Lenape, was born in Long Beach, California, on January 7, 1934. He grew up on a half-acre farm in El Monte and went to high school in Eagle Rock, where he wrote for the school newspaper. After receiving an Associate degree from Glendale College in 1953, he earned his B.A. (1955), M.A. (1956), and Ph.D. in history (1959) at the University of Southern California. In the mid-1960s, he taught at the University of Nevada at Reno.

A prolific writer and essayist, Forbes published his first work, *Apache, Navajo, and Spaniard*, in 1960. Some of his most important books on Indians include *The Indian in America's Past* (1964), *Warriors of the Colorado* (1965), and *Native Americans of California and Nevada* (1982). In addition, Forbes wrote extensively on non-Indian issues, including *Afro-Americans in the Far West* (1967) and *Aztecas del Norte: The Chicanos of Aztlan* (1973).

Known for his pan-Indian nationalist perspective, Forbes founded two short-lived pan-Indian organizations during the early 1960s, and his essays on treaty rights had a major influence on national groups such as the AMERICAN INDIAN MOVEMENT. Forbes provided historical research on a number of Indian issues, notably the case of the Western Shoshone and their quest to have the United States uphold the Treaty of Ruby Valley of 1868 (see BATTLE MOUNTAIN).

Like ARTHUR C. PARKER years earlier, Forbes was interested in the possibility of an Indian university. In 1960, he formed the American Indian College Committee with Navajo artist Carl Gorman and others. In the same year, he developed a proposal for an American Indian studies program at California State University, Northridge. By 1961, Forbes had already put together a proposal for a university, and in 1971, with David Risling, Jr. (Hoopa) and Kenneth R. Martin (Assiniboine), he founded D-Q University at Davis, California, the first Indian-run institution of HIGHER EDUCATION in the United States not affiliated with a reservation. The name stands for Deganawida-Quetzalcoatl, the former being the 16th-century founder of the Iroquois Confederacy and the latter the legendary Aztec serpent god. The university occupies 643 acres on the site of a former army communications relay station in Davis, California.

Forbes was the leading Native American critic of the 1993 North American Free Trade Agreement (NAFTA) and wrote extensively on the effects of globalization on Indian communities. In 1997, he published a novel *Red Blood* and in later years, he turned to writing poetry. Forbes chaired the Native American Studies Program at the University of California, Davis, founded by Risling in 1970, and served as a trustee of D-Q University. He retired from Davis in 1992, continuing as professor emeritus in Native American studies and anthropology and as a frequent contributor to *Indian Country Today* and *Wind Speaker*, Canada's national online newspaper. In recent times, D-Q University struggled to stay open, and in 2005 it lost its accreditation and closed the next year. In 2007, the campus was occupied by former students and community activists. A new board of directors tried to have the occupiers evicted, at times using the police, but was unable to find the funding to reopen the school. On March 31, 2008, the Yolo County Sheriff's Department raided the campus and arrested the 18 occupiers.

Although D-Q no longer functioned as a university, the campus continued in use for community events, educational workshops, and ceremonies. On September 3, 2010, Mohawk spiritual leader JAKE SWAMP participated in a peacemaking and permaculture course. The Tree of Peace he brought with him was the last one he would plant before his death. Swamp's visit inspired a movement to revive the school as a learning center with sustainable gardens, farm animals, and alternative energy. The D-Q Web site in 2011 stated that they were working toward regaining accreditation for academic programs, with the goal of providing higher education to Native and non-Native people in an environment connected to Native American cultural roots and dedicated to the preservation and development of indigenous languages, ethics, sustainable technologies, and an intimate relationship with the natural world. (See INDIGENOUS ECONOMICS.)

Jack Forbes died in Davis on February 9, 2011.

Further Reading

Anon. "Native American Scholar Forbes Dies." *Davis Enterprise*, 25 February, 2011.

Forbes, Jack D., Kenneth R. Martin, and David Risling. *The Establishment of D-Q University: An Example of Successful Indian-Chicano Community Development.* Davis, Calif.: D-Q University, 1972 (pamphlet).

Greenberg, Henry, and Georgia Greenberg. *Carl Gorman's World*, 139–144. Albuquerque: University of New Mexico Press, 1984.

Fortunate Eagle, Adam (Adam Nordwall)

(1929–) *Chippewa activist, artist, spiritual leader*
Adam Fortunate Eagle was born Adam Waldemar Nordwall in Red Lake, Minnesota, on July 18, 1929, to Anton Nordwall, a Swedish immigrant, mechanic at the Indian school, and Rose Nordwall, a Chippewa. He lived on the Red Lake Reservation before attending the Pipestone Indian Boarding School in southwestern Minnesota for 10 years. While at Pipestone, Nordwall learned how to craft pipes from the Chippewa and Dakota Sioux pipe makers who worked the sacred catlinite (pipestone) quarries located only a half mile from the school. He attended Haskell Indian Institute in Lawrence, Kansas, from 1945 until 1950.

Under the Relocation program connected with the TERMINATION policies of the 1950s (see URBANIZATION, AMERICAN INDIANS AND), Nordwall migrated to California's San Francisco Bay area, where he became a prominent leader of the region's large Indian community.

After finding work with a local exterminator, he founded his own company, the First Americans' Exterminating Company, and became a successful entrepreneur. Nordwall chaired the Council of Bay Area Indian Affairs for more than 10 years and also taught sociology at the University of California, Hayward. A practical joker with a flair for publicity, he caused a stir when, during San Francisco's Columbus Day pageant in 1968, he attempted to "scalp" the man portraying Columbus.

The next year, he placed a curse on the town of Livermore's sewer system when the town's workers damaged a totem pole Nordwall had carved for them. As fate would have it, Livermore's sewers backed up two weeks later, and the town repaired Nordwall's sculpture.

Nordwall participated in the first takeover of Alcatraz Island by Indian activists in 1964. He led the planning of the second occupation in 1969 and recruited the Mohawk activist RICHARD OAKES to lead the actual takeover. (See ALCATRAZ ISLAND, OCCUPATION OF.) Nordwall led efforts on the mainland to enlist support for the occupiers, but their youthful perspective and militant stance eventually alienated him and other mainland Indians.

Continuing his activism, Nordwall changed his name to Fortunate Eagle in 1971. In 1973, he caused a sensation in Europe when, as a delegate to the International Conference on World Futures Research, he plunged a lance into the ground at Rome's airport and claimed Italy for Indians under the doctrine of discovery. The federal government took notice of Fortunate Eagle's activism and began a campaign of harassment that eventually led to the closing of his exterminating company in 1974. An audit by the Internal Revenue Service in 1975 then drove him to bankruptcy. He was forced to move to Fallon, Nevada, where his wife, Bobbie, a Shoshone, had a home on the Paiute-Shoshone reservation.

In Fallon, Fortunate Eagle began to sell his sculptures full time and opened a gallery, the Round House Art Gallery. He also became a pipe maker and ceremonial leader, though not without controversy. Priced from $170 to $1,500, the sale of his pipes, considered sacred objects by many Indian spiritual leaders, led some to accuse him of selling out.

In 1991, Fortunate Eagle published an account of his experience on Alcatraz, entitled *Alcatraz! Alcatraz!: The Indian Occupation 1969–1971*. In 2001, he was awarded an honorary doctorate in Humane Letters by the State University of New York at New Paltz. In 2002, a new account of his Alcatraz experience, *Heart of the Rock*, was published, with a foreword by VINE DELORIA, JR. Fortunate Eagle was the voice of Sitting Bull in the movie *Sitting Bull: A Stone in My Heart* (2007).

Further Reading

Fortunate Eagle, Adam, with Tim Findley. *Heart of the Rock: The Indian Invasion of Alcatraz*. Foreword by Vine Deloria, Jr. Norman: University of Oklahoma Press, 2002.

Fox, Finis (Frank Finis Fox)

(1882–1949) *Chickasaw newspaperman, legislator, Hollywood scenario writer*
A Chickasaw, born in Caddo, Indian Territory (now Oklahoma), on October 8, 1882, Frank Finis Fox, like his younger brothers, directors EDWIN CAREWE and WALLACE WARE FOX, worked in the Hollywood film industry. As a young man in his early 20s, however, Finis seemed destined for a career in politics. His father, a lawyer and businessman, was Franklin Marion Fox (1843–1925), a white man born in Indiana, who is said to have driven a wagon from Abilene, Kansas, to Fort

Worth, Texas, before the coming of the railroads. His mother, Sallie J. (Priddy) Fox (1855–1899) was one-eighth Chickasaw, the granddaughter of Chief Tabuscabano on her mother's side. As a girl she attended the Lamar Female Seminary at Paris, Texas.

Finis Fox grew up in Purcell, Chickasaw Nation, Indian Territory, a region where tensions among Chickasaw political factions had been simmering for many years. After the Civil War, many whites had settled on the lands of the Five Civilized Tribes (as the Cherokee, Creek, Choctaw, Chickasaw, and Seminole were known at the time) without permission, and many married Native citizens. The problem was particularly severe for the Chickasaw. Many of the whites who intermarried were rich and influential, and buckling to pressure, the Chickasaw government offered them citizenship. However, intruders continued to arrive in ever-growing numbers, increasingly polarizing Chickasaw politics. A "Progressive" Party arose that pushed for the ALLOTMENT of tribal lands, the ASSIMILATION of the Chickasaw in culture, language, and law, and the full participation of intermarried whites in Chickasaw national affairs.

By contrast, the full-blood, or "Pullback," Party hoped to preserve Chickasaw nationality and moved to disenfranchise the whites. The conflict came to a head in August 1886 over the disputed election for governor of the Chickasaw Nation, when William Leander Byrd, leader of the Pullbacks, ran against William M. Guy, leader of the Progressives. Although Guy was eventually seated, the legislature passed an act on April 8, 1887, disenfranchising adopted and intermarried citizens. In August 1888, Byrd again ran against Guy, and again it was disputed, but this time Byrd was declared the winner. After serving a second term from 1890 to 1892, Byrd was succeeded as governor by Jonas Wolf, a full-blood who spoke only Chickasaw.

Wolf faced a dire situation. As the *Purcell Register* stated on January 19, 1893, "This fair land is held by a nation of about 6,800 citizens. These dwell amidst a population of over 40,000 non-citizens." At this time, the federal government was moving to end the autonomy enjoyed by the Five Civilized Tribes, and on March 3, 1893, Congress passed the act creating the Dawes Commission (see CURTIS ACT). In February 1894, the commission arrived in Tishomingo, the Chickasaw capital, to meet with a delegation of 20 full-blood Chickasaw appointed by Governor Wolf. After explaining the Allotment Act and urging the Chickasaw to accept it, the commission adjourned for lunch, expecting to hear the Indians' response in the afternoon. The Chickasaw were so uninterested, however, that they simply went home.

In an interview published on June 28, 1894, in the *Marlow Magnet* (a newspaper in Marlow, Chickasaw Nation), Governor Wolf stated that the encroachments on the public domain made him fear for the safety and integrity of the Chickasaw government. In one county, Pickens (now Carter), intruders were so dominant that the situation was practically out of control: They defied the law, obstructed government officers, and held the governor's authority in such contempt that the county might as well be called, as the governor put it,

the "Free State of Pickens." He suggested it might be time to ask the Indian Agency to call in the military, because "the men thus entrenched upon Chickasaw soil are strong in numbers, fruitful in resources and resolute in character and are not to be dislodged by any 'rosewater or milk and cider policy,'"

Pickens County was where the Fox family lived, but unlike most intermarried whites, F. M. Fox supported the full-bloods. In 1895, shortly after Wolf had been succeeded as governor by his interpreter Palmer S. Mosely, a full-blood Choctaw-Chickasaw, F. M. Fox held the post of permit collector at Purcell. In line with full-blood policy, Fox petitioned Commissioner of Indian Affairs D. M. Browning for help because white traders at Chickasha were refusing to pay their license taxes to the Chickasaw government.

On April 23, 1897, the Choctaw and Chickasaw came to terms with the Dawes Commission and signed the Atoka Agreement, which called for the division of their lands and assets, including their considerable coal and asphalt holdings, and limited the authority of the tribal government, which could henceforth legislate only with the approval of the president of the United States. However, the Chickasaw electorate voted to reject the pact, triggering a harsh response from Congress. On June 28, 1898, Congress adopted the Curtis Act, which incorporated the Atoka Agreement, abolished tribal courts and enforcement of tribal laws, and scheduled the termination of all governments of the Five Civilized Tribes by March 4, 1906. In response, the Chickasaw joined the Choctaw, Cherokee, Seminole, and Creek in a movement for statehood for the Indian Territory. The Sequoyah Convention, held in Muskogee in August 1905, adopted a constitution and plan for an Indian state. But the U.S. government rejected their petition for statehood.

In the 1890s, Finis Fox had attended Arkadelphia Methodist College in Arkansas (now Henderson State University) for two years, then entered the Polytechnic College at Fort Worth, Texas (now Texas Wesleyan University), and finally Fort Worth University. He broke off his studies to enlist in the First Texas Cavalry as soon as President McKinley called for volunteers to fight the war with Spain (April 23, 1898).

Fox returned to Chickasaw as the political turmoil was coming to a climax. Though only 18 years old, he decided to start a newspaper with the financial backing of his father. The daily and weekly *Ardmore Appeal* first saw the light on July 5, 1901, with Fox as editor and A. Charles Owens as publisher. It continued into 1903.

Fox also sought political office. In August 1901, he was elected one of five representatives from Pickens County to the 20-member lower house of the Chickasaw national legislature. As the gubernatorial election of August 1902 loomed, the big issue was the Supplemental Choctaw-Chickasaw Agreement, which provided for the final allotment of the tribal domain among its individual members. While the Atoka Agreement had protected the tribal coal lands from sale and reserved coal revenues for school financing, the supplemental treaty would put about a half-million acres of these coal lands up for sale at public auction.

The agreement was embodied in an act of Congress that stipulated a plebiscite would be called by the new governor a month after the August elections. Choctaw and Chickasaw representatives, of which Finis Fox was one, held a convention at Tishomingo on May 9, 1902, to take steps to ensure the rejection of the agreement by the Chickasaw voters. The side advocating approval was led by mixed-bloods Douglas H. Johnston, a former governor, and U.S. Marshal Benjamin H. Colbert, a Rough Rider friend of President Theodore Roosevelt. He was also an operative in a massive land-fraud operation based in Tishomingo known as the Tribal Development Company, of which Governor Mosely and Pliny L. Soper, U.S. attorney for the Northern District of Indian Territory, were directors. Mosely had switched sides and was now Progressive candidate for governor. William Byrd came out of retirement to run against him. The federal government, knowing that a Byrd victory would doom the Supplemental Agreement, used its local officials to promote Mosely's election. Mosely won, and on September 25 the Chickasaw electorate ratified the Supplemental Agreement. The full-bloods refused to accept defeat, and on November 11, 1902, at Ardmore, Finis Fox was elected secretary of an organization aimed at forming a separate Chickasaw state, rejecting the idea of union with Oklahoma.

On August 24, 1903, Finis Fox filed charges against Marshal Ben Colbert, accusing him of using intimidation to further the ambitions of his political cronies; taking prisoners out of jail to vote as he directed them; threatening to throw an Indian in prison if he did not vote as directed; and neglecting his duties as federal marshal. Fox also charged that Colbert's stock in the Tribal Development Company, which stood to benefit from the political machinations, had been given to him by proponents of the breakup of the Chickasaw Nation.

Fox's assertions were backed up by the INDIAN RIGHTS ASSOCIATION'S (IRA) Washington agent, S. M. Brosius. In a report Brosius had written accusing government officials of holding stock in companies designed to cheat Indians, he mentioned Governor Mosely as a stockholder in the Tribal Development Company and noted that a U.S. Internal Revenue inspector, Guy P. Cobb, had resigned his office to become the development company's principal stockholder. Fox's accusations were covered by newspapers across the country, and on September 5, 1903, Inspector Taylor of the U.S. Justice Department arrived at Ardmore to begin a complete investigation of the marshal's office.

In the legislative election on August 12, 1903, Finis Fox was reelected as a representative from Pickens County. When the lower house convened on September 7, each side attempted to disqualify representatives of the other. Fox was one of the Byrd supporters whose election was challenged; as Colbert's accuser, he was a particular target of the Mosely faction. On September 8, 1903, the lower house was organized with the Mosely party in control. The expected contest over the seating of the Pickens County delegation did not materialize, but the first test of the relative strength of the two parties was the election of the speaker of the House. The Pullback Party picked

Fox as their candidate, but he lost to the Mosely candidate, C. H. Brown, by three votes.

On March 29, 1904, Fox's first wife (her name is not known) died at Tishomingo. She was buried in Kansas City. Fox went to Oklahoma City, where for a short time he was on the editorial staff of the *Daily Oklahoman*. Between 1905 and 1917, he held a number of jobs, including working as traveling salesman selling various lines of merchandise from Cuba to Alaska. He also became involved in copper mining in Alaska and developing fruit orchards in Washington State.

Fox first got involved in the motion picture business in 1917 when he was in New York. He began film work as feature writer for Metro Pictures, where his brother Edwin Carewe had been directing features since 1915. Fox wrote his first photoplay, *The Jury of Fate*, in 40 minutes. He continued writing for Metro and even directed a few Westerns. The brothers' first collaboration was on the Metro film *The Voice of Conscience* (1917), starring Francis X. Bushman.

Among Fox's most important scenarios were: *Blackie's Redemption*, directed by John Ince (1919); *Merry-Go-Round*, directed by Erich von Stroheim (1922–23); *My Son*, produced and directed by Edwin Carewe, with Wallace Fox as assistant director (1925); *The Flame of the Yukon* (1926); and *Resurrection*, directed by Carewe (1927), as well as Carewe's sound remake of the same story in 1931. Fox adapted the photoplay for Carewe's Indian classic *Ramona* (1928), which included Wallace's brother-in-law Richard Easton as assistant director and starred Dolores del Rio. Fox also adapted *Evangeline* (1929), based on the poem by Henry Wadsworth Longfellow and starring del Rio. One of a number of films the three brothers made together, it was produced and directed by Edwin Carewe, with Wallace Fox as chief production aide. Finis also published a novelization of this film.

His few efforts as a director date mostly from in 1922–24. The remake of *Ramona* in 1931, his only "talkie," was not a great success. Writing a script for a talking picture requires different skills from writing a silent "scenario" or "photoplay." Unable to make the transition, Fox retired. After Carewe's death in 1940, he left Hollywood and went to Mexico. He later lived in Arizona, then Texas. Fox was married four times; his second wife was named Leona and his third Loris. He died in San Antonio, Texas, on November 7, 1949, survived by his last wife, Conchita, and stepson, Joaquin.

Further Reading

Carter, Kent. *The Dawes Commission and the Allotment of the Five Civilized Tribes, 1893–1914*, 78–80. Provo, Utah: Ancestry Publishing, 1992.

Champagne, Duane. *Social Order and Political Change: Constitutional Governments among the Cherokee, the Choctaw, the Chickasaw, and the Creek*, 224–228. Palo Alto, Calif.: Stanford University Press, 1992.

Meserve, John Bartlett. "Governor Jonas Wolf and Governor Palmer Simeon Mosely." *Chronicles of Oklahoma* 18, no. 3 (September 1940): 243–251.

O'Beirne, Harry F. *Leaders and Learning Men of the Indian*

Territory: With Interesting Biographical Sketches. Vol. I. Chicago: American Publishers' Association, 1891.

Fox, Wallace Ware (1895–1958) *Chickasaw film director, producer*

Wallace Fox was born on March 9, 1895, in Purcell, Indian Territory (now Oklahoma), youngest son of Franklin Marion Fox, a lawyer and businessman born in Indiana, and Sallie J. (Priddy) Fox, a Chickasaw. His mother died when he was four, and about 1904 his father married a much younger woman of Louisiana French extraction named Nellie. The Foxes moved to Corpus Christi, Texas, where they built a beautiful residence on Water Street, known as one of the showplaces of the city, along with six rental cottages along the waterfront from Power to Palo Alto Streets and a recreational pier. In the hurricane that struck Corpus Christi on August 20, 1916, the house was badly damaged and the Fox cottages and Fox pier were totally destroyed.

Wallace enlisted in the U.S. Navy about 1911 and was stationed overseas. He remained in service until the Armistice ended WORLD WAR I in 1918. Later that year, he moved to California, where his brothers, EDWIN CAREWE and FINIS FOX, were working in the film industry. They were joined by their father and stepmother, who by 1920 had a home in Redlands, near Los Angeles. F. M. Fox remained in good health until shortly before his death on July 8, 1925.

On September 6, 1919, Wallace Fox married Cleo Inez Easton (not an Indian) in Indianapolis. The Eastons, originally from Indiana, had lived in Purcell from about 1883 to 1900 and were close friends and possibly relations of the Foxes. Wallace's brother-in-law, Richard Easton, joined them in California, where he first worked as a prop man in the film industry. In 1928, Easton was assistant director to Edwin Carewe on two Dolores del Rio films, *Revenge* and *Ramona*, for which Finis Fox wrote the screenplays. Easton was also assistant to Wallace Fox on *Come and Get It!* (1929), but he contracted pneumonia before the movie was released and died on December 19, 1928, at the age of 29.

Wallace Fox began directing as chief assistant to his brother Edwin Carewe. His first credit was as Carewe's assistant director on the Louis B. Mayer–Anita Stewart production *The Invisible Fear* (1921). For the next several years, all his credits were as Carewe's assistant, including *My Son* (1925), starring Nazimova and Jack Pickford, with screenplay by Finis Fox. Starting with *Breed of the Sea* (directed by Ralph Ince, 1926), he assisted a few other directors, and with the FBO production *The Bandit's Son* (1927) inaugurated a long line of his own features.

Probably the most important film of his career was the 1936 production of *The Last of the Mohicans*, starring Randolph Scott as Hawkeye, on which Fox was associate director under George B. Seitz. Fox directed a second crew at locations in northern California, the San Bernardino National Forest, and at Kern River near Bakersfield. Although none of the major roles in this Indian story were played by Indians, Yurok, Hoopa, and Tolowa extras were employed. Fox also directed two films of his own with Indian themes: *The Riding Renegade* (1928) and *Wild Beauty* (1946), but used no credited Indian actors.

Unlike his brothers, Wallace Fox continued to work long into the sound era, directing a large number of low-budget B films, including many Westerns, several Bowery Boys comedies, and horror films, including two with Bela Lugosi, *Bowery at Midnight* and *The Corpse Vanishes* (both Monogram, 1942). His last feature was *Blazing Bullets* (Monogram, 1951). Between 1945 and 1950, he also produced 12 B westerns.

From 1951 on, Fox made television films, directing five episodes of *The Gene Autry Show* (1951–53), nine episodes of *Ramar of the Jungle* (1953–54), and others. He died on June 30, 1958.

Frank, Billy, Jr. (1931–2014) *Nisqually fishing rights activist*

The son of Willy Frank—the last full-blooded Nisqually, who died in 1983 at the age of 104—Billy Frank, Jr., was born on March 9, 1931, on the Nisqually reservation on the banks of the Nisqually River in Washington State. His father was active in the fishing-rights struggle, and young Billy was first arrested at the age of 14 for fishing in a restricted area with his father.

Along with JANET MCCLOUD, DAVID SOHAPPY, and HANK ADAMS, Billy Frank, Jr., helped to uphold the rights of Indians of the Northwest to fish in their traditional manner unmolested by state game laws. Beginning in the early 1960s, Frank helped lead the "fish-ins" that inaugurated the era of the RED POWER MOVEMENT. As confrontations between Indians, state regulators, and sports fishers grew more violent, Frank was frequently arrested and jailed for his efforts. His perseverance paid off in the Boldt Decision of 1974, which upheld the Indians' right to catch up to 50 percent of the fish in the rivers of the Northwest (see HUNTING AND FISHING RIGHTS). After the victory, Frank became less confrontational in his activism, and he subsequently led efforts to establish guidelines for a fishing-rights policy in the Northwest. He later became chair of the Northwest Indian Fisheries Commission, which represents 20 tribes in negotiations with the state of Washington over the management of fish stocks in the state's rivers. In 1992, Frank was presented with the Albert Schweitzer Award for his role as a mediator between Indians and non-Indian fishermen. He died on May 5, 2014.

Further Reading

Wilkinson, Charles. *Messages from Frank's Landing: A Story of Salmon, Treaties, and the Indian Way.* Seattle: University of Washington Press, 2000.

Frechette, Evelyn (Billie Frechette) (1907–1969) *Menominee gun moll*

Billie Frechette was the notorious moll of famed gangster and Public Enemy Number 1, John Dillinger. She was born on the Menominee reservation in Neopit, Wisconsin, on September 15, 1907, to a French father and Menominee mother.

Evelyn "Billie" Frechette, Menominee girlfriend of Public Enemy Number 1 John Dillinger, waited for her imminent release from prison in 1936. *(AP/Wideworld)*

When Frechette was eight, her father died. She attended St. Anthony's Catholic mission school on the reservation until the age of 13, when she left to attend the Riggs Indian Vocational High School in Flandreau, South Dakota, for four years. She then moved to Milwaukee and later Chicago, working as a nursemaid and a waitress. While in Chicago, she married a minor hoodlum named Welton Sparks, who eventually wound up in prison for mail fraud.

Frechette was working as a hatcheck girl in a Chicago nightclub when she met Dillinger in fall 1933, a few months after the gangster had been released from serving seven years in the Indiana State Penitentiary for a botched robbery committed during his youth. While in prison, Dillinger had recruited a number of hoodlums to become part of his gang, and he helped them break out of prison in a daring escape in September 1933. The gang then fled to Cincinnati, where Dillinger sent for Frechette to join him. Captured and imprisoned in a small town in Ohio, Dillinger broke out of jail in time to meet her in Cincinnati, and the two of them, along with gang member Harry Pierpont and his girlfriend, Mary Kinder, decided to return to Chicago. Along the way, Dillinger and Pierpont brazenly attacked police stations in Auburn and Peru, Indiana, making off with tommy guns and bulletproof vests.

Frechette and Dillinger laid low in Chicago, moving from apartment to apartment, although Dillinger took time off to rob $75,000 from a bank in Greencastle, Indiana. Frechette and Dillinger were caught in a police ambush on November 15, 1933, but escaped after a high-speed chase and running gun battle through the streets of Chicago.

A short time later, the Dillinger Gang held up a bank in Wisconsin and broke into the safe-deposit vaults of Chicago's Unity Trust and Savings Bank before traveling to Florida for a vacation. There Dillinger, who was violently jealous, accused Frechette of being unfaithful. After he beat her severely, she returned to the Menominee reservation. The separation did not last long, however, and in January 1934 Dillinger picked her up in Wisconsin after robbing a bank in Chicago. The two of them then traveled to Arizona, where they were captured in Tucson by the local police. Dillinger was extradited to Indiana, but Frechette, using the name Anne Martin, went unrecognized and was released.

During Dillinger's imprisonment, Frechette acted as a courier between him and the gang, but the gang was unwilling to dynamite the jail as Dillinger had hoped. Dillinger nevertheless managed to escape by carving a fake tommy gun out of a washboard and making off in the warden's car. Joining up with Billie, he hid out with her in the apartment of her half sister, Frances "Patsy" Frechette. After Dillinger robbed two more banks, the couple were raided by the police in the middle of the night of March 31 while staying in a room in St. Paul, Minnesota. While Frechette stalled the police at the door, Dillinger dressed, packed, and armed himself with a custom-made machine pistol. He then raked the closed door with bullets, causing the police to scatter down the hallway. With Dillinger covering their retreat, the couple emerged from their room amid a blaze of gunfire and made for the back stairway. Frechette carried their bags to the alley and pulled out their car, driving the wounded Dillinger to a hideout where he could be treated by a doctor.

With the greatest manhunt in police history under way, the couple went on to Mooresville, Indiana, where Dillinger visited his father, to whom he introduced Billie as his wife. On April 9, 1934, the couple returned to Chicago to meet an associate in a bar, unaware that they were walking into a police trap. Frechette went into the club first to make sure all was clear and was immediately surrounded by lawmen. Dillinger, still in the car, drove off when Frechette did not reappear.

Despite being roughed up by the police, Frechette refused to talk and was arraigned four days later on charges of harboring a criminal. Bail was more than the Dillinger Gang could afford at the time, and although Dillinger desperately considered attempting to break her out of jail, Frechette convinced him not to try. She was convicted on May 23, 1934, and sentenced to two years in prison.

Dillinger anxiously followed the case and raised the money to have the conviction appealed. The gangster had less than two months to live, however. He died on July 22, betrayed by another woman. Billie completed her sentence and was released in 1936. She toured the country for a time with Dillinger's father in a "crime does not pay" carnival sideshow. Eventually, Frechette moved back to Wisconsin, where she remarried. She died of cancer in Shawano, Wisconsin, on January 13, 1969.

Further Reading
Poulsen, Ellen. *Don't Call Us Molls: Women of the John Dillinger Gang*. New York: Clinton Cook Publishing, 2002.

French, Richard E. (1939–1998) *Yakama forester*
Richard E. "Dick" French was born on June 22, 1939, in Toppenish, Washington, on the Yakima (now Yakama) reservation. He studied at Yakima Valley Junior College and went on to earn a B.A. in forestry from Washington State University on a Yakima Tribal Scholarship, becoming the first Indian to earn a degree in forestry. He later received a master's degree in public administration from Lewis and Clark College in Portland, Oregon.

From 1963 to 1965, French served in the U.S. Army, where he held the rank of staff sergeant. For the rest of his life, he was active in veterans' affairs and was one of the most prominent members of the Northwest Indian Veterans Association and its parent group, the Veterans Affairs Committee of the Affiliated Tribes of Northwest Indians, which represents 43 tribes in six states.

Like LUTHER BURBANK GRASS, French was involved in the American Indian component of the U.S. Agricultural Research Service's Equal Employment Opportunity Committees. He worked for the U.S. Forest Service for 35 years, managing forests on the Fort Apache Reservation in Arizona; the Blackfoot Reservation in Montana; and other reservations in Montana, Idaho, Washington, and Oregon. French was a president of the Portland chapter of the AMERICAN INDIAN SCIENCE AND ENGINEERING SOCIETY and served for a time on the national board. He was also a member of the Society of American Foresters and the American Forest Association.

French retired in 1994. He succumbed to a heart attack while playing golf on July 21, 1998, in Portland, where he had made his home since 1976. Interviewed not long before his death for the Portland newspaper *Senior Lifestyles*, French was asked how he would like to be remembered. His answer: "I tried to open a door for Indian people."

gaming on Indian reservations

The gaming industry on Indian reservations became, in the last part of the 20th century, one of the few economic success stories for Indian people—though the effects on Indian communities are quite complex and have yet to be fully determined.

The relationship between the legalized gambling industry and Indian reservations began in 1981, after Florida's Fifth Circuit Court of Appeals, in *Seminole Tribe of Florida v. Butterworth*, ruled in favor of the Seminole tribe, which had opened a high-stakes bingo hall. The ruling upheld the sovereignty of Indian reservations. The state of Florida had argued that it had the right to control or suppress gambling within its borders, but the court found that states do not have civil jurisdiction over federal Indian reservations (see BILLIE, JAMES; SOVEREIGNTY, INDIGENOUS AND TRIBAL).

At first, gambling was limited to high-stakes bingo. By 1986, 80 Indian tribes in 16 states had built bingo halls on their reservations—some of which awarded jackpots of $100,000 or more—and together they were generating a total of $100 million per year. The states fought these establishments at every turn until 1987, when the U.S. Supreme Court, in the landmark decision *California v. Cabazon Band of Mission Indians*, affirmed and expanded the right of Indians to conduct gambling on their reservations. In order to maintain some semblance of control over the reservations, which were beginning to open full-fledged casinos, the federal government passed the Indian Gaming Regulatory Act in 1989, establishing a mechanism for opening and overseeing these operations.

The act was controversial among tribal leaders. ROGER JOURDAIN and WENDELL CHINO charged that it violated federal trust responsibility by shifting jurisdiction to states to regulate Indian ordinances and the industry. They also protested that no hearings were held on the final draft of the bill. Many states also opposed the bill, but in the end they were unable to prevent gaming from becoming a legitimate industry on

Indian reservations. By the end of 1997, 142 Indian tribes in 24 states operated 281 casinos or bingo halls where a total of $65 billion annually was wagered.

For a few reservations, gaming proved to be a cure for poverty. On the Wisconsin Oneida reservation, unemployment dropped from more than 30 percent in 1980 to almost zero in 1990. On the Prairie Island Dakota Reservation in Minnesota, unemployment plunged dramatically from 77 percent to 7 percent in the same period. The members of the tribes with the two most successful casino operations, the Mashantucket Pequot in Connecticut and the Shakopee Sioux in Minnesota, have become very wealthy. In fact, the Pequot opened the single most profitable casino in the world. By the end of 1995, their Foxwoods Casino had become Connecticut's largest employer, netting more than $1.6 billion per year. The $140 million that Connecticut receives every year from the Pequot in lieu of taxes has become essential to the local economy (see HAYWARD, RICHARD ARTHUR).

The big success stories in gaming, however, are actually the exceptions rather than the rule; gaming has altered perceptions of Indian wealth much more than it has improved conditions for most Indian people. In 1994, a mere 10 tribes accounted for almost half of all the gaming revenue in the country. Most of these tribes are among the country's smallest and located nearest to large urban areas.

Many Indian tribes are opposed to gaming on moral grounds. The Hopi tribe rejected a proposed casino on their lands in 1995, and for many traditional Iroquois, gaming is specifically prohibited by the religious code of Handsome Lake. Other Native opponents to gaming have drawn attention to the increasing regulation of the industry that has led to the erosion of Indian sovereignty and self-determination. For many tribes, gaming is not a viable option. In areas such as Alaska, 80 percent of the Native villages cannot even be reached by road, and many other reservations such as the Navajo Reservation, the largest in the country, are located in remote, isolated parts of the country. Moreover, some states with large Indian populations, such as Montana and South Dakota, have legalized gambling, weakening the competitive advantage for reservations.

Thus, despite the promise of gaming, life became worse for most Indians on reservations, not better, during the gaming boom of the 1980s and 1990s. None of the 10 largest reservations, where fully half of all reservation Indians live, is expected to be able to build a casino that would significantly improve their economy. Poverty levels, with one exception, rose on these reservations during the 1980s, despite the fact that five of them have gaming. By 1990, the percentage of reservation Indians in the United States who were living below the poverty level had risen to 51 percent.

Different tribes came up with varying economic development approaches to the use of gaming money. Many, such as the Mdewakanton Sioux of the Prairie Island Reservation, distributed profits to their enrolled members on a per-capita basis. In the case of Prairie Island, a relatively small community, the "per-caps" could be considerable, averaging $2,000 per month for each tribal member—a far cry from just a few years before, when the entire annual median income on the reservation was under $4,000. Distributing bingo money through per-caps was the popular political move for the tribal leadership, and in many cases it was the means by which the tribal councils secured the local support to develop the gaming industry.

The Wisconsin Oneida, on the other hand, eschewed the per-caps in order to focus funds on long-term economic development and tribal renewal. They built a vacation resort complete with a first-class hotel, and they regained, through purchase, a considerable portion of lands lost over the previous 100 years. They established a highly regarded national newspaper and also inaugurated successful language and cultural programs for their children.

The rush of newfound wealth, and sometimes the mere promise of it, often exacerbated factionalism within tribes. Conflicts over how to distribute gaming funds erupted on some reservations, leading to a virtual paralysis of nonessential government functions. In three separate cases, the BUREAU OF INDIAN AFFAIRS had to intervene in leadership disputes that arose on reservations as a result of differences over the management of gaming funds. Moreover, while most operations were generally considered free from criminal activity, some of the management companies hired by the tribes were accused of fraud, and a few tribal officials became implicated in gaming scandals. Thus, the results of the gaming industry in the 20th century were largely mixed, with some winners, some losers, and, in most areas, little change. As of 2007, there were 423 Indian gaming operations in the United States operated by 225 tribes in 28 states, generating $26 billion in revenue.

See also SHENANDOAH, LEON.

Further Reading

Lane, Ambrose I. *Return of the Buffalo: The Story behind America's Indian Gaming Explosion.* Westport, Conn.: Bergin & Garvey, 1995.
Light, Steven Andrew, and Kathryn R. L. Rand. *Indian Gaming and Tribal Sovereignty: The Casino Compromise.* Lawrence: University Press of Kansas, 2007.
Mason, W. Dale. *Indian Gaming: Tribal Sovereignty and American Politics.* Norman: University of Oklahoma Press, 2000.
Mullis, Angela, and David Kamper, eds. *Indian Gaming: Who Wins?* Los Angeles: UCLA American Indian Studies Center, 2000.

Ganienkeh

On May 13, 1974, a group of militant Mohawk began an armed standoff in upper New York State at an abandoned Girl Scout camp near Moss Lake in Herkimer County. Earlier seizures of property in 1957 and 1958 near Fort Hunter by Mohawk led by Standing Arrow had not achieved much. In the 1974 attempt, the Mohawk, largely from the Caughnawaga Reserve in Canada, took the property in the Adirondack Mountains, claiming that it was Mohawk land according to the 1783 Treaty of Fort Stanwix. The 612 acres at Moss Lake had been purchased by New York State in 1973 in order to turn it into a wilderness site. State police and local vigilantes engaged the Indians in several gun battles until two of the vigilantes were wounded. Although the state sought to evict the Indians, a negotiating team led by future governor Mario Cuomo settled with the Mohawk in 1977 by exchanging the Moss Lake land for two parcels, one near Altona, New York, and other near the McComb reforestation area. However, the Mohawk were only given use of, not title to, this land.

Renaming the Altona land Ganienkeh, "Land of the Flint," Mohawk began to establish a community there, many of them moving in after the two-year siege at the Akwesasne Mohawk reservation (see AKWESASNE, SIEGE OF). The community was short-lived, however, and by the mid-1980s, Thomas Delaronde and his family had usurped control of Ganienkeh in an attempt to turn it into their personal enclave, evicting the activist Loraine Canoe, clan mother Loraine Montour, and members of other prominent Mohawk families in the process. The disintegration of Ganienkeh foreshadowed a greater disintegration of the Iroquois Confederacy after the Akwesasne siege, as the confederacy struggled to keep the loyalty of its various factions.

Further Reading

Doran, Kwinn H. "Ganienkeh: Haudenosaunee Labor-Culture and Conflict Resolution." *American Indian Quarterly* 26, no. 1 (Winter 2002): 1–23.
Landsman, Gail. *Sovereignty and Symbol: Indian-White Conflict at Ganienkeh.* Albuquerque: University of New Mexico Press, 1988.

Gansworth, Howard Edwards (1876–1956) *Tuscarora-Seneca historian, business executive*

The son of a Tuscarora father, John Andrew Gansworth, and a Tonawanda Seneca mother, Carrie Griffin, Howard Edwards

Gansworth was the grandnephew of Tuscarora chief Mount Pleasant, a descendant of Red Jacket, and a relative of General Eli S. Parker. He was born on April 12, 1876, on the Tuscarora reservation near Lewiston, New York. Along with his brother, Leander, and sister, Alberta, Howard was educated at the Carlisle Indian School in Pennsylvania, where he was one of a group of unusually gifted students whom RICHARD HENRY PRATT helped go on to HIGHER EDUCATION during the 1880s and 1890s. Few were successful, however. Gansworth, after graduation from Carlisle in 1894, attended Dickinson Preparatory School in Pennsylvania and then became the first Indian student to enter Princeton University, where he achieved an excellent record. At Princeton, he attended classes taught by future president Woodrow Wilson. Gansworth was one of the first Carlisle students, possibly the first, to get a university degree, receiving his B.A. in 1901.

In 1903, Gansworth was employed at Carlisle as assistant disciplinarian. He resigned in 1905 to work for the Baldwin Locomotive Works, at the same time pursuing graduate studies at Princeton, where he received an M.A. in 1906 for his thesis, "The Iroquois Confederacy." In 1906, Gansworth moved to Buffalo, New York, where he worked as an advertising manager for the W. B. Pierce Company. In 1916, he was hired as general manager of the General Specialty Company, a manufacturer of boiler-tube cleaning equipment. In 1929, he was elected president of the company. After his retirement, he moved to Waterbury, Connecticut, where he died on May 12, 1956.

Gansworth was an avid collector of books on the Iroquois. He was active in the Indian Welfare Society, the Buffalo and Erie County Historical Society, and the All Saints Episcopal Church, and he had been a president of the Buffalo Princeton Club. His papers are in the library of the Buffalo and Erie County Historical Society.

Further Reading

Boyd, Douglas Power. "The Irony of Assimilation: Howard Edwards Gansworth and the Burden of Iroquois History." *New York History* 72, no. 1 (January 1991): 4–44.

Gardipe, Carol Metcalf (1929–)
Penobscot-Passamaquoddy geologist
Born in 1929 in New England, Carol Metcalf Gardipe, a Penobscot-Passamaquoddy, grew up on the coast of Maine in a family of teachers. Her grandfather was one of the first civil engineers in Maine. Gardipe's high school interests included music, drama, and art; she won a national drawing competition. She first attended the University of Wyoming at Laramie, then took a B.A. in geology and taught at Colby College in Maine. In subsequent years, she worked in Washington, D.C., and on field-mapping teams in the Southwest for the U.S. Geological Survey.

Gardipe entered graduate studies in geography and natural resources at the University of New Mexico, where she directed the American Indian Engineering Program for two years, the first program in the country for American Indian engineers, supported by the Sloane Foundation. At this time, she also worked with the National Research Council Committee on Minorities in Engineering. In 1977, she was one of the seven founders of the AMERICAN INDIAN SCIENCE AND ENGINEERING SOCIETY (AISES) and the only woman.

Following her husband's transfer to the BUREAU OF INDIAN AFFAIRS (BIA), Gardipe joined the National Oceanic and Atmospheric Administration (NOAA) in Washington, D.C., for which she traveled and spoke extensively as an assistant for university and minority outreach. She later worked for the Cooperative Institute for Research in Environmental Sciences at the University of Colorado, retiring in 1983. She was elected a fellow of the Geological Society of America in 1983–84. In the early 1990s, Gardipe resettled in southeastern Maine. She received AISES's Ely S. Parker Award in 2003.

Garland, Hamlin (1860–1940) *writer, Indian rights advocate*
As a boy, Hamlin Garland, born into a farming family in West Salem, Wisconsin, on September 14, 1860, had been fascinated by the local Indians. In 1869, the family moved to Osage, Iowa, and later to South Dakota. Garland acquired his own homestead in Ordway, South Dakota, in 1883 but moved to Boston a year later, where he enrolled in the Boston School of Oratory, intending to embark on a literary career. After he published his first article in 1885, his reputation grew rapidly, and his first book, *Main-Travelled Roads*, appeared in 1891. Many other articles and books followed over the next several years.

Garland toured the West in summer 1895, and in 1896 he met Ute, Hopi, Navajo, and Pueblo Indians on a trip through Colorado, New Mexico, and Arizona. He first became known as an Indian advocate through numerous stories published in 1896 and 1897. At a luncheon in New York City in October 1896, Garland began two lifelong friendships, with writer ERNEST THOMPSON SETON and with future president Theodore Roosevelt. In the years to come, Garland and Seton would go on many camping trips together. In 1897, visiting the Blackfeet Reservation, Garland was asked to take messages from several tribal members to a friend of theirs in New York City. This was Garland's introduction to GEORGE BIRD GRINNELL, who was to become another close friend.

In 1900, the agent at the Cheyenne and Arapaho Agency in Darlington, Indian Territory, invited Garland and his new bride to come for a visit. While there, Garland met lawyer CHESTER POE CORNELIUS, who pointed out that the lack of standardized Indian family names among many tribes was sure to cause legal chaos in the future, especially in determining inheritance. This gave Garland, who had been interested in Indian languages and Indian naming systems since his visit to the Ute in 1895, the idea for a project to standardize Indian personal names.

Garland also visited John Homer Seger's nearby "colony" of Cheyenne and Arapaho, which he ever after would take as a model of how Indians could learn and adjust to mainstream

American culture in the right way—very gradually. Seger, after 12 years as superintendent of the Federal Indian School at Colony, Indian Territory (1872–84), founded his own Seger Training School ("Seger Colony") in Washita County in 1885. The school emphasized the preservation of Indian arts and crafts, a very unusual policy for the time.

Returning to the Cheyenne in 1901, Garland gathered material for a new novel, which would become *The Captain of the Grey-Horse Troop*. This time he had much opportunity for conversation with Seger. The novel, which includes many Indian characters and subjects, appeared in March 1902. Calling at the White House to leave a copy of the book for President Roosevelt, Garland was invited to attend a cabinet meeting the next day. There he advocated his principles of gradualism for Indian administration. Major changes also were needed in the ALLOTMENT policy. According to Garland, the Indians should not be expected to live as solitary homesteaders but rather "as French peasants do, in villages, and farm their outlying lands. Others . . . like the Navajo, are natural herders and should be allowed to continue as such." Garland also presented his plan for the standardization of Indian surnames, and Roosevelt gave him an introduction to the secretary of the interior.

In 1902, Garland was hired by the government to implement his naming plan. He was assisted by the Dakota physician CHARLES ALEXANDER EASTMAN, Seger, W. J. McGee of the U.S. Bureau of Ethnology, and C. Hart Merriam of the Department of Agriculture. Garland preferred a modified form of the name the family used in their own language rather than English translations such as "Side Hill Calf" or "Boss Ribs Hunter." The official name did not need to mean anything to non-Indians. The project went on until 1909 but was eventually devolved back to reservation agents. One result of the work on this six-year project was that Garland and Eastman became close friends.

Garland opposed the reigning policy of Allotment. In the 1897 story "The Stony Knoll," he lamented "that the beautiful sentiment which had considered the earth as common property should give way to the system of the white man." Some of the ideas Garland expressed at the 1902 cabinet meeting reappeared later that year in "The Red Man's Present Needs," an article in *Atlantic Monthly* in which he complained that the system of Allotment was based on a theory of LAND TENURE sociologically unsuited to Indian cultures. Although most tribes recognized ownership of personal property, tools, and clothing, "the red man's feeling, that the earth is for the use of all men, is right; he always distinguished between the ownership of things and the ownership of land and water."

Recognizing Indians as sociable, gregarious people, Garland pleaded in "The Red Man's Present Needs" that allotment should be communal rather than individual. Families of each tribe should be grouped along water courses in settlements of four to five families, with their lands outlying, instead of isolating them on individual plots in bleak uplands—a communitarian approach foreshadowing such later ideas as the restoration of the *ejido* advocated for Mexican Indians by Moises Saenz (see COLLIER, JOHN) and the Lolomi Plan of LAURA MIRIAM CORNELIUS KELLOG).

Garland went on to recommend that each reservation should be divided into farming districts where Indians would be taught to farm by excellent teachers. In each district, a really dedicated matron would teach the women how to keep house. (See INDIAN INDUSTRIES LEAGUE.) Traditional crafts should be revived and encouraged in every way, and an industrial school should be established in each farm district.

"The theory" railed Garland, "that to civilize the red man it is necessary to disrupt families and to smother natural emotions by teaching the child to abhor his parents, is so monstrous and so unchristian that its failure was foretold by every teacher who understands the law of heredity." He cautioned that missionaries ought to have no more rights than any other visitors to the reservation, and should have no authority to define what kind of recreation is proper and improper. The allottee should automatically become a citizen, free to come and go as he likes; the agent should be a friend and adviser, not a commander. Finally, reservations should be protected from predatory cattlemen, etc., although in some cases, where conditions are different (for example, Indian Territory) the borders can be dissolved.

In the same article, Garland stated that bad Indian policy stemmed ultimately from false religious conceptions, but science could supply the corrective. He wrote: "Science has come to our aid: we understand as never before the constitution of a red man's mind. The philosophy of evolution has broadened our conception of the universe, and in our dealings with primitive men, religious bigotry and race hatred should no longer enter."

There was a gap in Garland's published writings on Indians from 1907 to the 1923 publication of *The Book of the American Indian*, a collection of stories of Indian life. Hamlin Garland died in Hollywood, California, on March 4, 1940.

Further Reading

Folsom, James K. *The American Western Novel*, 149–155, 180–184. New Haven, Conn.: College and University Press, 1966.

Newlin, Keith. Introduction to *The Book of the Indian*, xi–xliii. Acton, Mass.: Copley, 2002.

Underhill, Lonnie E., and Daniel F. Littlefield, Jr., eds. *Hamlin Garland's Observations on the American Indian, 1895–1905*. Tucson: University of Arizona Press, 1974.

Garrison Dam

The Garrison Dam was the first of the dams constructed by the Army Corps of Engineers as part of the PICK-SLOAN PLAN for flood control on the Missouri River. The dam flooded the 153,000 most valuable acres of the Fort Berthold Reservation of the Three Affiliated Tribes (Mandan, Hidatsa, and Arikara) in North Dakota. These rich bottomlands were the home of 90 percent of the tribal population and the site of their agricultural productivity, religious ceremonies, and ancestral burials.

George Gillette *(left)*, chair of the Fort Berthold tribal council, weeps as Secretary of the Interior J. A. Krug signs a contract condemning 155,000 acres of the Fort Berthold Indian Reservation for the Garrison Dam project in 1948. *(AP/Wideworld)*

Colonel Lewis A. Pick of the Army Corps of Engineers had envisioned the dam during 90 days of planning. His rival, W. Glenn Sloan of the U.S. Bureau of Reclamation, suggested that it was unnecessary, and the BUREAU OF INDIAN AFFAIRS (BIA) commented during congressional debates that the site seemed to have been chosen because most of the affected land would be Indian property, which the Corps of Engineers could claim by right of eminent domain. In spite of tribal testimony, memorials, and petitions to Congress that this act violated the Treaty of 1851, in 1944 the Pick-Sloan Plan was funded. Replacement lands were offered by the army but rejected by the Indians, who refused to sell their homeland. The council wrote: "We have permanently located on these lands. Our forefathers also have lived on these grounds and it is the hopes and plans to have our children and their children to occupy

this land continually forever; and money or exchange for other land will not compensate us." The alternative dam site they proposed was rejected by the army.

Construction began in 1946. In 1948, the Corps of Engineers offered the tribes $5,105,625, as a compensatory contract; however, the dam could not be stopped, and the tribe had no choice but to accept the money. The contract was ratified by a vote of adults, with 65 percent in favor, and was signed by Secretary of the Interior Julius A. Krug, as George Gillette, chairman of the Fort Berthold Tribal Business Council, watched with tears in his eyes. His words at the time were: "Our Treaty of Fort Laramie, made in 1851, and our tribal constitution are being torn to shreds by this contract." Between 1951 and 1954, as the dam went up, the Fort Berthold Indians were forced to move to the barren uplands of the reservation, a treeless, farmless, waterless area. Many older Indians said they would prefer to stay and be drowned.

The rising waters split the reservation into five segments, destroying the cohesiveness of the community. Congress later appropriated an additional $7 million, but this, too, did not begin to compensate the tribe for a lost way of life. Dani Sue Deane testified to Congress that the flooding of the reservation had shattered their self-confidence and deprived a self-sufficient people of its economic heartland; it produced a "breakdown of families, communities, clan culture, tribal government, and left many feeling totally defeated." Carl Whitman, tribal chair during part of this period, said, "We should really be used to these broken promises, but it seems like each broken promise never loses its punch." By 1966, Robert Fox, chair of the tribal council, reported that half the tribal enrollment had left the reservation to find work. By 1970, there were no traditional villages left on the reservation.

Following the relocation of the villages, there was a dramatic rise in welfare and unemployment rates among the reservation's population. In 1986, an Interior Department study of the effects of the Garrison Dam estimated that fair compensation for the economic, social, and cultural damages to the Three Affiliated Tribes should be set between $178.5 and $411.8 million. The commission also called for the government to keep its promises to provide low-cost hydroelectric power for the reservation; grant tribal members hunting, fishing, and recreation rights at the reservoirs; and replace roads and hospitals destroyed by the dams. It also recommended the return of excess lands to the tribes, but the army retorted that no such lands existed. These proposals were not given a high priority by the Reagan administration. Up to the present day, the Three Affiliated Tribes are still struggling to recover from the losses inflicted upon them by the Garrison Dam.

See also DAMS ON INDIAN LANDS.

Further Reading

Springer, Patrick. "A Flood of Tears: Five Decades Later, Tribes Still Recovering from Dam Losses." *The Forum* (Fargo, N.Dak.), 8 June 2003.

Garry, Joseph Richard (1910–1975) *Coeur d'Alene political leader*

Joseph Garry was born on March 8, 1910, on the Coeur d'Alene Reservation in northern Idaho. His mother was Susette Revais, and his father, Ignace H. Garry, was a traditional chief. Garry attended the Haskell Indian Institute in Lawrence, Kansas, before transferring to Butler University in Indiana. In 1936, he joined the BUREAU OF INDIAN AFFAIRS (BIA) as a clerk in the Northern Idaho agency, then worked for the U.S. Navy until WORLD WAR II, when he was drafted into the U.S. Army.

After the war, Garry became embroiled in a dispute with the Internal Revenue Service (IRS), which attempted to arrest him and 17 other members of the Coeur d'Alene tribe for failing to pay taxes on income derived from allotted Indian lands. Garry organized tribes across the West to fight this new IRS

policy, which encroached on Indian rights. Eventually, the policy was overturned by federal courts.

Garry's organizing skills helped him to become president of the Affiliated Tribes of the Northwest before being elected president of the NATIONAL CONGRESS OF AMERICAN INDIANS (NCAI) in 1953. He convened an emergency session to challenge the TERMINATION policy proposed by BIA commissioner DILLON SEYMOUR MYER, which sought to end the federal trust relationship with Indians and break up their reservations, in effect rolling back the achievements of the INDIAN NEW DEAL (see INDIAN REORGANIZATION ACT). Garry's intensive lobbying as head of NCAI from 1953 until 1959 helped to minimize the damage to Indian people from the policy, though he was not able to prevent the termination of tribes such as the Menominee and the Klamath. With the election of John F. Kennedy in 1960, and the replacement of GLENN LEONIDAS EMMONS by PHILLEO NASH as commissioner of Indian affairs, the federal policy was scaled back, saving many tribes that had been slated for termination. Termination was officially ended in 1970.

Garry was also chair of the Coeur d'Alene tribe during this time, but he left the post to run successfully for the Idaho House of Representatives in 1957. In 1959, he ran unsuccessfully for the U.S. Senate, after which he returned to the Coeur d'Alene to develop a constitution and legal code for the tribe. In 1967, he served in the Idaho Senate, then returned once more to the tribal council. One of the most active Indian leaders in the 1950s and 1960s, Joseph Garry died on January 31, 1975.

Further Reading

Fahey, John. *Saving the Reservation: Joe Garry and the Battle to Be Indian*. Seattle: University of Washington Press, 2001.

Geiogamah, Hanay (1945–) *Kiowa–Lenni Lenape choreographer, playwright, Native American Dance Theater founder*

A Kiowa–Lenni Lenape born in Lawton, Oklahoma, Hanay Geiogamah studied journalism at the University of Oklahoma before receiving his B.A. in drama and theater from Indiana University. He then went to work for the BUREAU OF INDIAN AFFAIRS (BIA) under Commissioner LOUIS ROOK BRUCE, JR. While working for the BIA, he wrote his first play, *Body Indian*. It was premiered in 1972 at the La Mama Theater in New York City by the Native American Theater Ensemble, a group he had founded earlier that year. *Body Indian* won high praise for its bold and realistic treatment of the alcohol problem among Native people. The following year, Geiogamah's play *Foghorn*, a series of vignettes presenting a historical overview of Indians since the arrival of Columbus, opened in Berlin, Germany. In 1975, his *49* premiered in Oklahoma City, making dramatic use of sound and ethereal lighting to highlight the ceremonial grounds where the action of the play takes place. Geiogamah later used these same techniques in his work with the Native American Dance Theater.

While in New York City, Geiogamah helped choreograph

dances for the Thunderbird American Indian Dancers and worked for the theater department of the American Indian Community House (see MOFSIE, LOUIS). In 1987, he formed the Native American Dance Theater in Los Angeles with New York producer Barbara Schwei. Featuring some of the finest Native dancers from across the country, the troupe performed stylized versions of traditional dances, including the Pueblo Eagle Dance, the Zuni Buffalo Dance, and the Northwest Coast Whale Dances, with a modern, dramatically lit backgrounds. The Native American Dance Theater has become the most popular and successful Indian dance troupe of all time, with appearances on public television and regular, sold-out performances at New York's Joyce Theater.

Geiogamah is currently a professor in the UCLA Department of Theater and is the managing editor of the *American Indian Culture and Research Journal*.

Further Reading

Geiogamah, Hanay, and Jaye T. Darby. *American Indian Theater in Performance: A Reader*. Los Angeles: UCLA American Indian Studies Center, 2000.

General, Alexander (Deskaheh) (1889–1965)
Cayuga-Oneida religious and political leader

Alexander General, a Cayuga-Oneida, was born in 1889 on the Grand River (now Six Nations) Reserve near Hamilton, Ontario, the youngest of eight children of Lydia and William General, subsistence farmers and agricultural laborers. His mother was Oneida and his father Cayuga, and though technically an Oneida of the Young Bear Clan, Alexander grew up as a Cayuga. When he was 10 years old, he was involved in a terrible tragedy: He was holding his father's hunting rifle when it went off by accident, killing his father instantly. To support themselves, the family then had to rent out the farm and work most of the year as hired help among the whites.

As a teenager, General attended school at Ohsweken on the Grand River (Six Nations) reserve near Brantford, Ontario, during the winters. He had a good teacher and learned quickly but never went beyond grade four or five. When he was old enough to work, he had to help support his mother. He worked in Hamilton, on the railroads, and in a foundry during WORLD WAR I. After the war, he worked as a farmhand and managed to save enough money to start a farm with his brother Timothy, which did well. At his mother's death, he inherited the family farm and became successful in dairy and wheat.

From about 1907 on, General began secretly to memorize the ritual speeches he heard in the Sour Springs Longhouse. Gradually he caught the attention of the elders and was slowly groomed for a role as Longhouse speaker. In 1917, he was installed as deputy, or "runner," to his brother LEVI GENERAL, known by his title Deskaheh, the Cayuga name traditionally given to the chief of the Snipe Clan. From then on, he was deeply involved in the political struggles led by his brother.

Despite his devotion to the Longhouse Religion, General became engaged to a Christian. They discussed the subject of religion a great deal and agreed never to interfere with each other's religious beliefs. Both were stricken by the terrible influenza epidemic of 1918; he recovered, but she died. It has been suggested that General's lifelong tendency to explain Iroquois Longhouse beliefs to the non-Indian public within a Christian frame of reference reflects her influence.

General's brother Levi died in June 1925, and Alexander was installed as the new Deskaheh in December. In 1930, he traveled to England to persuade the king that the Iroquois were not under Canadian jurisdiction, but he met with no more success than his brother had in 1921. Completely out of funds, the Iroquois delegation, with the assistance of the Salvation Army, returned home after two months.

Alexander General was active in the Indian Defense League (see RICKARD, CLINTON), supporting the enforcement of the Jay Treaty of 1794. He was also a close friend of anthropologist FRANK GOULDSMITH SPECK, whom he first met around 1924 or 1925 and with whom he collaborated on one of Speck's last published works, *The Midwinter Rites of the Cayuga Long House* (1949). From about 1932 to 1952, General was known as the leading ritualist of the Upper Cayuga. In addition to Speck, he worked with anthropologists William Fenton, Charles-Marius Barbeau, John A. Noon, Marcel Rioux, John Witthoft, Floyd Lounsbury, Martha C. H. Randle, Fred W. Voget, Ernest Stanley Dodge, Gertrude Kurath, Sally Weaver, and Annemarie Shimony.

Alexander General died of tuberculosis at Brantford General Hospital in Brantford, Ontario, in September 1965. His political work, addressing matters of importance to all Iroquois people, including the sovereignty of the Six Nations and the applicability of the Canada-U.S. border for the Iroquois, made him one of the most important 20th-century Iroquois leaders on both sides of the border.

See also SOVEREIGNTY, INDIGENOUS AND TRIBAL.

Further Reading

Shimony, Annemarie. "Alexander General, Deskaheh." In *American Indian Intellectuals: Proceedings of the American Ethnological Society*, edited by Margot Liberty, 177–98. St. Paul, Minn.: West Publishing, 1978.

General, Levi (Deskaheh) (1873–1925) *Cayuga-Oneida leader, political activist*

A Cayuga-Oneida, Levi General was one of eight children of Lydia and William General. He was born in 1873 on the Grand River (now Six Nations) Reserve near Hamilton, Ontario, Canada. Lydia was a clan mother of Oneida descent; William, a subsistence farmer, was Cayuga.

After completing a few years of grammar school, Levi moved to the United States and worked as a lumberjack in the Allegheny Mountains. After an accident, however, he returned to Grand River and became a farmer. He married a mixed-blood Cayuga woman, and they raised a family of five sons and four daughters. Although General's main language was Cayuga and he was a ritualist in the Cayuga Longhouse, he was technically an Oneida. However, he identified himself as Cayuga or Cayuga-Oneida.

With the outbreak of WORLD WAR I in 1914, many Iroquois youths volunteered for military service in the Canadian and British armed forces, in higher proportion than the Canadians themselves did. Canada had generally treated the Iroquois as a sovereign nation, and the Iroquois felt a strong loyalty to the British Crown. The text of a memorial address to the Grand River Iroquois, dated as recently as December 4, 1912, and filed by Great Britain, states, "The documents, records, and treaties between the British governors in former times, and your wise forefathers, of which, in consequence of your request, authentic copies are now transmitted to you, all establish the freedom and independency of your nations." Despite this, Canada decided to enforce its draft laws on the Iroquois. Levi General went to Ottawa to explain to the Canadian government that they had no jurisdiction to do so. His arguments were persuasive, and the Canadians relented for the time being.

Levi General had a high reputation at Grand River, based on his character as well as his oratorical prowess in the Cayuga language. In 1917, he was installed as the new Deskaheh at Ohsweken, capital of Six Nations Reserve, and his youngest brother, ALEXANDER GENERAL, was made deputy ("runner"). Traditionally, the Cayuga title Deskaheh was given to a chief of the Snipe Clan (one of the 50 hereditary positions of the Iroquois Grand Council). General belonged not to the Snipe clan, however, but to the Oneida Young Bear clan. Because the Snipe Clan had lacked an eligible male heir, the title had been transferred to the Young Bear clan during the time of their maternal grandmother. In 1918, General was appointed deputy speaker of the Six Nations Council and in 1921 official speaker. He worked closely with DAVID RUSSELL HILL (Mohawk).

In 1920, an amendment to Canada's Indian Act (1920) unilaterally declared all Indians citizens, including the Six Nations Iroquois. After unsuccessful protests to the governor general and other officials at Ottawa, Deskaheh crossed the ocean to ask for the British Crown's support since Iroquois sovereignty had been guaranteed in Article 9 of the Treaty of Ghent (1815). He entered Great Britain in late May 1921 on a Six Nations passport. However, the authorities in London stated that they regarded it as a domestic Canadian problem and refused to help. Disappointed, Deskaheh returned to Grand River. Now he found the Canadians cultivating a small fifth column (disaffected Indians) by means of payments and promises, with the intention that they would at some point ask for Canadian "protection."

After Canada's passage of the Compulsory Enfranchisement Act and the Soldier Settlement Act in 1922, the Iroquois chiefs feared for their sovereignty and their lands. Charles Steward of the Indian Department told them that Canada was willing to go to arbitration over the council's unwillingness to accept the new legislation. The chiefs accepted, but then the deputy superintendent, Duncan Campbell Scott, told them that rather than go to arbitration, the matter would be taken up by a Royal Commission composed of the judges of the Ontario Supreme Court. This the chiefs rejected. At the very end of 1922, Iroquois chiefs at Caughnawaga demanded home rule "similar to Ireland" in a letter to the Ministry of Indian Affairs.

In 1923, eight troops of the Royal Canadian Mounted Police (RCMP) set out from Brantford, Ontario, for Ohsweken, to establish a post to "maintain law and order" at Grand River. Sympathizers alerted Deskaheh of the coming raid, and he escaped across the border to Rochester, New York. A number of houses, including Deskaheh's, were raided and searched, supposedly for illegal beverages. The RCMP built barracks for themselves as an occupying force.

By an order of September 17, 1923, the Canadian government purported to abolish the traditional Iroquois Council. George P. Decker, a white lawyer in Rochester, was the Council's attorney. Financed by funds donated by Iroquois and their supporters, Decker and Deskaheh, the latter still traveling on his Iroquois passport, went to Geneva in September 1923, intending to plead the Iroquois case before the League of Nations. This was around the time when President Woodrow Wilson had spoken in favor of the sovereignty of small nations. Deskaheh spent the winter and spring preparing his case. By June, he was working with a Swiss attorney on a statement of the Six Nations's case in French. He also used the time to reach out to the public and to the diplomatic corps. By the end of the year, based on an ancient condolence wampum he had found in the Museum of the American Indian in New York City, Deskaheh had secured the cooperation of the Netherlands to bring the matter before the League of Nations. Albania also cooperated. Ultimately, however, no foreign government recognized the Iroquois claim.

The chiefs also rejected the attempts of Colonel Andrew Thompson, the new Indian commissioner, in 1924 to conduct an independent investigation and hold hearings. The chiefs complained that Thompson was only willing to listen to people who for one reason or other were disaffected with the traditional chiefs.

In October 1924, while Deskaheh was away, the Canadians again raided the reserve and held elections for a new "democratic" government band council installed under Canadian federal law. This vote was supposedly held in the name of "enfranchising" the people. Mainly on the advice of Deskaheh, the traditionals, who were greatly in the majority, refused to participate. Only 400 of 4,500 people at Grand River accepted this "enfranchisement," the great majority not wanting to be subject to the laws and taxation of the Canadian government. Nevertheless, the traditional chiefs were forced out of their council house at Ohsweken and the council house was encircled by a guard of 20 police. Longhouse officials were asked to show the records and sacred wampum of the Six Nations, upon which the Canadians confiscated the wampum and refused to return it.

Meanwhile, things were not going well in Geneva. The secretariat refused to let Deskaheh petition before a plenary session of the League of Nations, nor would they let him or George Decker into the gallery as observers. In desperation, the two men called their own public meeting at the Salle Centrale in Geneva, where Deskaheh presented their case, as well as the whole story of Canadian actions against the Iroquois over the previous few years. The public response was overwhelming. At the end of his presentation, Deskaheh was given a long standing ovation. But there was no official response, and he left for home in late 1924, dejected, disillusioned, and with his health shattered.

Until 1924, U.S. officials had let Canadian-born Indians enter the United States freely without being legally considered aliens, but in 1924 there arose a legal bind because, according to the 1924 Immigration Act, no alien ineligible for citizenship was to be admitted as an immigrant. The 1924 Indian Citizenship Act extended citizenship only to noncitizen Indians "born within the United States." Official interpretation of the two acts taken together was that Indians born in Canada could not be admitted as immigrants. This absurd situation would not remedied until the 1927 Diabo decision reaffirmed Article 3 of the Jay Treaty (1794), which states that Indians on both sides of the border may pass freely (see IRON-WORKERS, AMERICAN INDIAN). Deskaheh could not go back to Grand River, however, and remained in New York. His brother Alex made many attempts to cross the border to be with him as much as possible, sometimes succeeding, sometimes not.

On the night of March 10, 1925, Deskaheh gave his last speech, a radio broadcast from Rochester. Suffering from pleurisy and pneumonia, he was brought next morning to the Rochester Homeopathic Hospital. Six weeks later, still not recovered, he asked to be brought back to Tuscarora chief CLINTON RICKARD's house on the Tuscarora reservation in New York State. At Deskaheh's request, Rickard got two medicine men from Six Nations to come down. They stayed with him in his room for a week, and when they came out, Deskaheh came with them. After that, another medicine man made three trips down. After six weeks at Rickard's, Deskaheh was in good spirits and recovering, but one day while eating he was handed a letter. It said that the medicine men would henceforth not be allowed to cross the border. Without finishing the meal, he went to bed and never got up again.

Deskaheh's wife, children, and brother Alex tried to get to Tuscarora to be with him at his death, but at Niagara Falls they were denied permission to cross the border. Levi General died on June 27, 1925, of pulmonary hemorrhage. His last words were "fight for the line"—meaning the U.S.-Canada border. Clinton Rickard heard those words and followed the directive for the rest of his life. At last, Deskaheh was able to come home: His body was laid to rest in the burial ground by the Cayuga Longhouse.

See also SOVEREIGNTY, INDIGENOUS AND TRIBAL.

Further Reading

Smith, Donald B. "Deskaheh." In *Dictionary of Canadian Biography*, edited by Ramsey Cook, and Real Belanger, 15, 278–280. Toronto: University of Toronto Press, 1998.
Wanamaker, Tom. "Indian Law Scholars Comment on Proposed Passport Regulations." *Indian Country Today*, 30 November 2005, B2.

General Federation of Women's Clubs, Indian Welfare Committee

The General Federation of Women's Clubs (GFWC), the world's oldest nonpartisan, nondenominational women's volunteer service organization, was founded in New York City in 1890 by delegates from 61 women's clubs around the United States. In 1917, Stella Atwood of Riverside, California, became chair of the Indian Welfare Committee of the Southern California District of the GFWC. By 1921, she had convinced the federation to establish a national committee on Indian welfare. GERTRUDE BONNIN, who had left the SOCIETY OF AMERICAN INDIANS in 1920 after major leadership changes, played a large role in the establishment of this committee. At the GFWC's annual meeting in Salt Lake City, Bonnin, who had long sought their support in the fight for Indian citizenship, was called to the platform. With tears in her eyes, she cried, "It has begun. Nothing now can stop it. We shall have help." Stella Atwood was elected chair.

The committee's main goal was economic improvement, including "keeping for the Indians the land which they still possess . . . [,] getting for them the land of which they have been illegally dispossessed, and . . . fostering the Indian arts and crafts." The members labored for Indian enfranchisement; for improvement in education, health care facilities, and hospitals; for home demonstration agents to teach mainstream homemaking skills to Indian women; for resource conservation; for preservation of tribal culture; and for help in marketing Native products. In addition, the legislative committees in the various states were to track Indian-related legislation and mobilize members on important legislative issues. The GFWC's importance for Indian legislation would emerge in the fight against the BURSUM BILL, a federal law that affected the land rights of the New Mexico Pueblo. The committee also had a particular interest in health issues among reservation Indians, including trachoma, tuberculosis, and malnutrition, all very serious problems during the 1920s (see HEALTH, AMERICAN INDIAN).

By 1922, state Indian welfare committees had been established in all the western "Indian country" states but one, as well as in Maine and Pennsylvania. In May 1922, Atwood obtained a copy of the Bursum bill and discussed it with JOHN COLLIER. That same month, the GFWC hired Collier as a consultant to investigate the Pueblo crisis over the Bursum bill. Two articles by Atwood (on the GFWC's Indian reform program and on Pueblo art) as well as Collier's "The Red Atlantis," appeared in the October 1922 issue of the *Survey*, a magazine edited by Collier's friend Paul Kellogg.

At the GFWC's 1922 convention at Chautauqua, New York, Bonnin appealed to the clubwomen to help in the fight against peyote and the peyote cult (see NATIVE AMERICAN CHURCH). She secured their support for an investigation by the INDIAN RIGHTS ASSOCIATION and the American Indian

Defense Association on the situation of Indians in Oklahoma. The report was published by the Indian Rights Association in 1924 under the title *Oklahoma's Poor Rich Indians*. Meanwhile, Atwood advocated in 1923 for PIMA WATER RIGHTS, because their supply of water was being appropriated by settlers.

Although Atwood, who was basically a charity woman rather than a specialist on Indian affairs, advanced no new ideas, her support in the Pueblo crisis was crucial. She also tried to mobilize the women's clubs against the DANCE ORDERS of 1923, federal regulations that affected the cultural rights of the New Mexico Pueblo. At the 1924 GFWC convention, however, members of the Indian Rights Association split the federation by bringing with them representatives of the General Council of Progressive Christian Indians, who alleged that "pagan" traditional chiefs were violating their right to RELIGIOUS FREEDOM. As a result, the federation took no action on the dance order, and Collier's contract was terminated a few months later.

After WORLD WAR II, many clubs and state federations began providing scholarships to Indian students and assisting Indians who had relocated off the reservation. In 1948, women's clubs gave generously to help alleviate problems among the Navajo, who were affected by a series of harsh winters that had led to food shortages.

In 1950, ELIZABETH BENDER CLOUD, a member of the National Congress of American Indians (NCAI) and chair of Indian welfare in the Oregon Federation of Women's Clubs, was elected chair of what was now called the Indian Affairs Division. In this position, which she would hold for the next eight years, Cloud was able to quietly marshal the support of American clubwomen for the policies of the NCAI. She continued to raise the legislative awareness of the state women's clubs and to encourage them to provide scholarships for deserving Indian college students.

The GFWC's Indian Welfare Committee became inactive around 1970.

Further Reading

Jacobs, Margaret D. *Engendered Encounters: Feminism and Pueblo Cultures, 1879–1934*. Lincoln: University of Nebraska Press, 1999.

George, Charles (1932–1952) *Cherokee Medal of Honor winner*

Born to Mr. and Mrs. Jacob George in Cherokee, North Carolina, on August 23, 1932, Charles George was raised in the Birdtown community of the Qualla Boundary on the Cherokee Reservation. He attended Cherokee schools before enlisting in the U.S. Army. George became a member of the 45th Infantry Division, the same division as WORLD WAR II Medal of Honor winners VAN T. BARFOOT, ERNEST CHILDERS, and JACK MONTGOMERY.

George was sent to Korea after the outbreak of the Korean War in 1950. On the night of November 30, 1952, PFC George was assigned to a raiding party near Songnae-dong, Korea,

Private First Class Charles George, a Cherokee and Medal of Honor winner during the Korean War, participating in a training exercise in Japan. *(AP/Wideworld)*

to engage the enemy and capture a prisoner for interrogation. Fighting its way to enemy lines, the unit suffered severe casualties. When they were ultimately ordered to withdraw, George and two others stayed behind to cover the others. As the three began to pull back themselves, a grenade was thrown into their midst. Private George threw himself on the grenade. He saved the lives of his comrades, but was himself mortally wounded. He was awarded the Medal of Honor posthumously on March 18, 1954. In 2007, the Veterans Affairs Medical Center in Ashville, North Carolina, was renamed the Charles George Department of Veterans Affairs Medical Center in his honor.

George, Dan (Geswanouth Slahoot) (1899–1981) *Coastal Salish actor*

Chief Dan George, as he was popularly known, was a Coastal Salish actor best known for his portrayal of a Northern Cheyenne elder in the film *Little Big Man*. He was born Geswanouth Slahoot on July 24, 1899, near Vancouver, British Columbia. His father, George Tslaholt, was chief of the Tell-lall-watt band of the Burrard Tribe of the Coastal Salish Indians.

George grew up on the Burrard Reserve. His last name was changed to George when he entered a boarding school at the age of five. After leaving school, he found work as a longshoreman in Vancouver, joining the union in 1920, the

Coastal Salish actor Chief Dan George (in costume) as he appeared in the 1971 film *Little Big Man. (AP/Wideworld)*

year after he was married. His work on the docks was often interrupted by the labor unrest of the period and then by the Great Depression, but George found occasional work as a lumberjack. He built his own home out of scraps of lumber and hunted and picked berries to provide food for his family when work was scarce. Like his father and grandfather, he was a champion canoe builder. An accident while loading a ship in 1947 forced him to retire from the docks permanently, and he turned to construction work, driving a school bus, and working as a musician. George was appointed chief of the Tell-lall-watt band by his father in 1951, but he gave up that position in 1963 in favor of his younger brother, John.

George began his acting career in 1964 when his son, who had a role in the Canadian Broadcast Corporation series *Caribou Country*, suggested that the 63-year-old novice be cast in the part of the elderly Indian, Ol' Antoine. In 1967, George appeared in the original production of the play *The Ecstasy of Rita Joe*, in which his acting was highly praised. George then revived the role of Ol' Antoine in the Walt Disney film *Smith*, starring Glenn Ford. In 1970, George was chosen to play Old Lodge Skins, after Laurence Olivier turned down the role, in the film *Little Big Man*. The movie, which starred Dustin Hoffman, was a departure for Hollywood films about Indians and won George the New York Film Critics Award for best supporting actor as well as an Academy Award nomination in 1971.

While George did not become involved in the militant political movements of the day and indeed frowned upon such

tactics, he was an advocate for Native rights and the environment. He also was particular about the roles he played, insisting on the accurate portrayal of Native peoples, and he sought to improve the image of Indian people in the media. In 1971, the Canadian Council of Christians and Jews awarded him their Human Relations Award. Dan George made numerous film and television appearances, including a film version of the *Ecstasy of Rita Joe*; *Harry and Tonto*; *Cold Journey*; and *The Outlaw Josey Wales*, in which he starred opposite Clint Eastwood. He also authored two books of prose poetry, *My Heart Soars* (1974) and *My Spirit Soars* (1982). George died on September 23, 1981, in Vancouver.

Further Reading

Mortimer, Hilda, with Chief Dan George. *You Call Me Chief: Impressions of the Life of Chief Dan George.* Toronto: Doubleday Canada; Garden City, N.Y.: Doubleday, 1981.
Newhouse, David, Cora Jane Voyageur, and Daniel J. K. Beavon, eds. *Hidden in Plain Sight: Contributions of Aboriginal Peoples to Canadian Identity and Culture,* Vol. 1. Toronto: University of Toronto Press, 2005.

Gerard, Forrest J. (1925–2013) *Blackfeet assistant secretary of the Interior for Indian affairs*

Forrest J. Gerard was born on January 15, 1925, in Browning. Montana, to Fred Gerard, a mixed French-Blackfeet rancher, and Rose (Douglas) Gerard, a Blackfeet woman. During WORLD WAR II, Gerard became a decorated pilot in the U.S. Army Air Corps, flying 35 combat missions. He graduated from Montana State University in 1949 and then attended the National Tuberculosis Association Training Institute. Gerard began his long public health career by serving as executive secretary of the Wyoming Tuberculosis and Health Association and later as a staff member of the Montana Tuberculosis Association. In September 1957, he joined the Public Health Service in Washington, D.C., serving for six years as a tribal relations officer; he succeeded PERU FARVER. Gerard eventually became chief of the tribal relations division for four years.

In 1965, Gerard was awarded a fellowship that allowed him to study the operations of Congress for one year. The next year, he was appointed legislative liaison officer for the BUREAU OF INDIAN AFFAIRS (BIA), then headed by ROBERT LAFOLLETTE BENNETT. In 1967, Gerard moved back to the Department of Health, Education, and Welfare to become director of its Office of Indian Affairs. On July 12, 1977, he was appointed by President Jimmy Carter to become the first assistant secretary for Indian affairs, a new position that had superseded the position of commissioner of Indian affairs. Gerard replaced BENJAMIN REIFEL, who had been commissioner for only one year. Under Gerard, the two Indian commissioners, Martin Seneca, Jr. (Seneca) and WILLIAM EDWARD HALLETT (Chippewa), had little to do, and the office was abolished near the end of Gerard's term.

Gerard led the BIA through its most productive period. Under his administration, the total spending for federal

Indian programs peaked at $4.46 billion per year. In 1979, he helped to distribute $143.3 million in economic development grants to INDIAN RESERVATIONS.

During Gerard's tenure, a number of important bills were passed, such as the American Indian Religious Freedom Act, and settlements reached, such as the Maine Indian Claims Settlement Agreement of 1980. Most important was the expansion of government services and programs, through either the BIA or other government programs like Head Start, which directly benefited Indian people. The percentage of Indian families living below the poverty level on reservations declined to 24 percent, the lowest since these statistics were maintained. Budget cuts under his successor, KENNETH L. SMITH, would undo much of Gerard's work.

After leaving office, Gerard started his own consulting firm, Gerard, Bayler and Associates, and served as the head of Arrow, Inc., a nonprofit Indian educational organization founded by Flathead D'ARCY McNICKLE, WILL ROGERS, JR., and Robert LaFollette Bennett. He died December 28, 2013, in Albuquerque, New Mexico.

Further Reading

Reynolds, Jerry. "Forrest Gerard Speaks about Early Lobbying in Washington." *Indian Country Today*, 6 December 2006, A4.

Irahant, Mark. *The Last Great Battle of the Indian Wars: Henry M. Jackson, Forrest J. Gerard and the Campaign for Self-Determination of America's Indian Tribes*. Fort Hall, Idaho: The Cedars Group, 2010.

Trimble, Charles. "Unsung Heroes—Forrest Gerard: A Humble Icon of Achievement." *Indian Country Today*, 12 November 2004, A5.

Giago, Tim (Nanwica Keiji) (1934–) *Oglala Lakota Sioux journalist, publisher, columnist*

An Oglala Lakota Sioux born on July 12, 1934, on the Pine Ridge Reservation in South Dakota, Tim Giago was sent as a boy to the Holy Rosary Indian Mission School, and later to a Jesuit high school. He left the reservation to join the U.S. Navy, serving in the Korean War before returning to the United States and attending San Jose Junior College and the University of Nevada, Reno.

Giago began his JOURNALISM career in 1979 as an Indian affairs columnist for the *Rapid City Journal*. In 1981, he borrowed $4,000 from a childhood friend and established the *Lakota Times*, a weekly newspaper that eventually grew into the largest Indian newspaper in the United States. In 1992, the *Lakota Times* was purchased by the Gannett newspaper syndicate, and the paper was renamed *Indian Country Today*, changing its format to serve a national audience.

Giago attended Harvard University as a Nieman Fellow from 1990 to 1991, the first Native American to be accepted into that program. One of the most prominent Indian journalists, he was the first president of the Native American Journalists Association (NAJA) when it was formed in 1984. His weekly political column, "Notes from Indian Country," is syndicated by Knight Ridder Tribune News. In 1998, Giago sold *Indian Country Today*, and in 2000 he started the weekly *Lakota Journal*. In addition to his journalism work, Giago has written several books, including *The Aboriginal Sin: Reflections on the Holy Rosary Indian Mission School* (1978), *Notes from Indian Country* (1982), *The American Indian and the Media* (1991), and *Children Left Behind: Dark Legacy of Indian Mission Boarding Schools* (2006). He has won the H. L. Mencken Award and the University of Missouri Distinguished Journalism Award.

Gilmore, Melvin Randolph (1868–1940) *ethnobotanist, Indian rights advocate*

Born on a farm in Valley, Nebraska, in 1868, Melvin Randolph Gilmore became interested in ethnology and graduated from Cotner College in Bethany, Nebraska, in 1904. He then taught botany at Cotner and ran the college museum before studying under Charles E. Bessey at the University of Nebraska, receiving his M.A. in 1909 and his Ph.D. in 1914.

Between 1905 and 1910, Gilmore lived among the Omaha on their reservation in Missouri, where his interest in ethnobotany was awakened. After that, he worked among the Lakota Sioux on the Pine Ridge Reservation in South Dakota. In 1913, with a grant from the state of Nebraska, he traveled among the Pawnee, Teton Lakota, Ponca, Santee Dakota, Omaha, and Winnebago. From 1911 to 1916, Gilmore was director of the Nebraska State Historical Museum, where he became involved in a controversy over a FILM about the events at Wounded Knee in 1890. In October 1913, a film crew under the direction of Buffalo Bill Cody, working with the U.S. Army, engaged the local Oglala Lakota to stage a typical "Wild West" battle. The film purported to be a historical reenactment of the events at Wounded Knee, but evidently few if any of the Indians understood that. Perhaps this was due not only to their ignorance of English, but also to the fact that, since Wounded Knee was not a battle but a massacre of unarmed Indians, it never occurred to them that this was what they were supposed to be "reenacting." Realizing they had been duped, the Indians complained. Gilmore came to their aid by gathering Indian eyewitness accounts of the massacre along with additional evidence, which he used to condemn the film before a 1916 session of the Nebraska State Historical Society and in the Lincoln *Daily Star*.

From 1923 to 1928, Gilmore was a member of the scientific staff of the Museum of the American Indian, Heye Foundation, where he grew American Indian plant varieties from seeds in typical Indian gardens. From 1928 to 1937, he worked at the University of Michigan, Ann Arbor, where in 1931 he set up a major ethnobotanical laboratory.

Gilmore greatly respected Native American herbalists and was so well versed in plant lore that they trusted him with their special knowledge. In turn, he came to believe that people must respect the land and live within its historical biological limits. Rather than change the environment to suit new introduced plants (through intensive irrigation, for example), society should follow the Indian way of developing indigenous plants to coexist with the natural environment. In this, Gilmore anticipated the views of such modern researchers as Gary Nabhan of Native Seeds/SEARCH, Wes Jackson of the Land Institute in Salinas, Kansas, and JANE MT. PLEASANT of Cornell University. Around 1937, Gilmore retired to Lincoln, Nebraska, where he died in 1940 after a long illness (see INDIGENOUS ECONOMICS).

Further Reading

Erickson, David L. Melvin. "Randolph Gilmore, Incipient Cultural Ecologist: A Biographic Analysis." Ph.D. dissertation, University of Nebraska, 1971.

Gilmore, Melvin R. *Uses of Plants by the Indians of the Missouri River Region.* 1919. Reprint, Lincoln: University of Nebraska Press, 1991.

Will, George F. "Melvin Randolph Gilmore." *North Dakota Historical Quarterly* 8, no. 3 (1941): 179–183.

On the fraudulent Wounded Knee film:

Beeker, Thomas, ed. "In the Old Army." *Nebraska History Magazine* 71 (1990): 13–22.

Brownlow, Kevin. *The War, the West, and the Wilderness.* New York: Random House, 1979.

Wooster, Robert. *Nelson A. Miles and the Twilight of the Frontier Army.* Lincoln: University of Nebraska Press, 1996.

Gordon, Philip B. (Ti-bish-ko-gi-jik, "Looking into the Sky") (1886–1948) *Chippewa Roman Catholic priest, reform activist*

A Chippewa born on March 31, 1886, in Gordon, Wisconsin, one of 14 children, Philip B. Gordon was given the name Ti-bish-ko-gi-jik (Looking into the Sky) at birth. He was educated at St. Mary's Mission School on the Bad River Reservation and ordained a priest on December 8, 1913, leading his first mass at Bad River the next year. He then attended the Catholic University in Washington, D.C., and served as a chaplain at the Carlisle Indian School in Pennsylvania.

From 1915 to 1917, as assistant director of Catholic Indian welfare, Gordon was assigned to visit Indian reservations and agencies for the Bureau of Catholic Indian Missions. In 1915, he also became a member of the SOCIETY OF AMERICAN INDIANS, a pan-Indian reform group. Gordon joined CARLOS MONTEZUMA, a hard-line assimilationist, in taking control of the group around 1919, and Gordon effectively ran the organization until its demise a few years later.

In 1916, Gordon served as chaplain to the Haskell Institute in Lawrence, Kansas, where he denounced the sorry conditions at the boarding school, which led to a federal government investigation and reform. Known as "Wisconsin's Fighting Priest" because of his activism, Gordon was reassigned by the church to duties not related to Indians, until in 1918 he was given a parish among the Chippewa (Ojibwa) at the Lac Courte Oreilles Reservation near Hayward, Wisconsin. There he oversaw the building of the St. Francis Solanus mission church, which is constructed out of pipestone. He remained

there until 1925, when he became pastor of the Church of St. Patrick in Centuria, Wisconsin, where he remained for the rest of his life.

In 1923, Secretary of the Interior Hubert Work appointed Gordon to the COMMITTEE OF ONE HUNDRED, which reviewed federal Indian policy, and the next year he campaigned successfully for the Indian Citizenship Act, which made all Indians citizens of the United States (see CITIZENSHIP), completing a lifelong dream. Gordon then retired from political activity to concentrate on his parish duties, although in June 1943 he appeared before Congress as one of the first Indians to give an opening prayer to a session of the House of Representatives. Philip Gordon died on October 1, 1948, in St. Paul, Minnesota; he was buried in Gordon, Wisconsin.

Further Reading

Delfeld, Paula. *The Indian Priest Philip B. Gordon 1885–1948.* Chicago: Franciscan Herald Press, 1977.

Gorman, R. C. (Rudolph Carl Gorman) (1931–2005) *Navajo painter, sculptor*

Navajo artist R. C. Gorman was born Rudolph Carl Gorman on July 26, 1931, near Chinle, Arizona, on the Navajo Reservation. His mother, Adelle Katherine Brown, was a Navajo from Tsaile, Arizona. His father, Carl Nelson Gorman, was himself a distinguished artist and one of the famed Navajo code talkers of WORLD WAR II (see CODE TALKERS). Gorman grew up in a traditional Navajo (Dineh) hogan, herding sheep for his grandmother. At three years of age, he was already drawing. He attended school at Chinle before graduating from Ganado Mission High School in 1950.

Gorman served in the U.S. Navy from 1952 to 1956, attending Guam Territorial College while in the service. After studying at Arizona State College and San Francisco State College, he won a scholarship from the Navajo Tribal Council to study at Mexico City College (now the University of the Americas) in 1958. Following a short stay in Mexico, he returned to San Francisco State College, and by the early 1960s he had begun to establish himself in the Bay Area art scene. In 1964, Gorman and his father held a combined show at the prestigious Philbrook Art Center, and the next year they exhibited together at the Heard Museum's Gallery of Indian Art in Phoenix, Arizona. In 1968, Gorman opened a gallery in Taos, New Mexico, and his work began to appear in publications such as *Western Review* and *Southwestern Art*.

Gorman was one of the first Native artists to expand beyond the Santa Fe Studio school popularized by PABLITA VELARDE and fellow Navajo HARRISON BEGAY, and to experiment with new styles, creating a bridge between traditional art and the avant-garde. His early attempts to change the concept of Indian art, like those of OSCAR HOWE and WALTER RICHARD WEST, SR., met with protests from art critics for not being "Indian enough." He was also the first Indian painter to paint nudes. By the end of the 1960s, Gorman had abandoned his more surreal influences, and by the end of the 20th century, he was best known for his abstract portraits of Indian women, often with subtle washes of color. He worked in many media, including watercolor, oil, pen and ink, and pastel, in addition to doing prints and bronze sculptures.

In 1973, Gorman was the only living Indian artist to be represented in the show "Masterworks of the Museum of the American Indian," held at the Metropolitan Museum of Art in New York City, and he was the first American Indian to be represented in the museum's permanent collection. Two years later, the Museum of the American Indian featured Gorman in the first of its series of solo exhibitions on Indian artists. He was exhibited in museums and galleries worldwide, and his work is held in numerous permanent collections, including the Indianapolis Museum of Art, the Philbrook Museum of Art, and the Museum of New Mexico.

German's work has been published in numerous books, including an illustrated cookbook called *Nudes and Foods* (1989), and in 1992 he released a book about his life and philosophy, *The Radiance of My People*. In 1995, Gorman sculpted a monument to the code talkers in Flagstaff, Arizona. R. C. Gorman died on November 3, 2005. He remains one of Native America's most popular artists.

Further Reading

Greenberg, Henry, and Georgia Greenberg. *Carl Gorman's World*. Albuquerque: University of New Mexico Press, 1984.
Romancito, Rick, and Virginia L. Clark. "R. C. Gorman, 1931–2005: A Taos Original." *Taos News*, 3 November 2005.

Gover, Kevin (1955–) *Pawnee-Comanche lawyer, head of the Bureau of Indian Affairs*

Born in Lawton, Oklahoma, on February 16, 1955, Kevin Gover was the son of a Comanche and Pawnee father and a non-Indian mother, both of whom worked at Fort Sill (where Geronimo was once held captive). When Kevin was a teenager, a member of the Volunteers in Service to America (VISTA, the domestic Peace Corps) helped him enter St. Paul's School, a private institution in Concord, New Hampshire. He later attended Princeton University, receiving his B.A. in public and international affairs from the Woodrow Wilson School of Government in 1978.

After receiving his law degree from the University of New Mexico, Gover served as a law clerk under U.S. District Court judge Juan G. Burciaga. From 1983 to 1986, he worked for the Washington, D.C., law firm of Fried, Frank, Harris, Shriver and Jacobsen. In 1986, along with young Harvard-trained lawyer Suzan Williams, he founded the law firm Gover, Williams, and Jonov in Albuquerque, New Mexico. The firm became influential in Indian natural-resource issues as well as environmental and housing law on INDIAN RESERVATIONS.

Gover's father died in a drunk driving accident in 1981 at the age of 47. Gover himself had an alcohol abuse problem until he finally gave up drinking in September 1992.

Gover is known for representing Indians in environmental disputes, largely in cases dealing with the use of reservations as dump sites or for other controversial purposes. For example, Gover represented the Campo Band of Mission Indians in Southern California in their attempt to open a commercial landfill.

During the 1992 presidential campaign, Gover organized "Native Americans for Clinton and Gore," and four years later he campaigned again for the Democratic ticket. Not long after that, Secretary of the Interior Bruce Babbitt approached him about the assistant secretary's job, heading the BUREAU OF INDIAN AFFAIRS (BIA). In October 1997, Gover was nominated to succeed ADA DEER as assistant secretary for Indian affairs.

Gover continued Deer's policies of strengthening Indian self-government and defending sovereignty from state encroachment (see SOVEREIGNTY, INDIGENOUS AND TRIBAL). He also fought to protect Indian sacred lands from cultural and environmental desecration.

Gover made news when, on September 8, 2000, during a ceremony for the 175th anniversary of the BIA, he apologized for the bureau's past actions toward Indians. In his speech, he said, "This agency set out to destroy all things Indian. . . . The legacy of the misdeeds haunts us. . . . Our hearts break." His apology to American Indians for the bureau's historic misconduct—the first time any BIA head had done such a thing—won widespread praise. Gover specifically expressed sorrow over past agency policies that "forbade the speaking of Indian languages, prohibited the conduct of traditional religious activities, outlawed traditional government and made Indian people ashamed of who they were."

After his term ended in 2000, Gover joined the law firm Steptoe and Johnson, LLP, as a partner and leader of its American Indian practice. Gover was selected to join the faculty of the Arizona State University College of Law in July 2003. On September 11, 2007, he was named director of the Smithsonian's National Museum of the American Indian, replacing Richard West, Jr.

Further Reading

Gourneau, Dwight A. "Kevin Gover Unquestionably Best Choice to Run NMAI." *Indian Country Today*, 26 September 2007, A5.

Grass, Luther Burbank (1926–2002) *Cherokee soil scientist*

The son of Benjamin Grass, a full-blood Cherokee, and Ethel Hart Grass, who was half-Cherokee, Luther Burbank Grass was born in Arkansas City, Kansas, on March 2, 1926. When he was one year old, the family moved back to the homestead at Locust Grove, Oklahoma, where he grew up in an agricultural environment. His father, who died when he was four years old, was an admirer of the famous horticulturalist Luther Burbank. His grandfather was a small farmer of little formal education but of an experimenting frame of mind. One of his discoveries, for example, was that mixing the petals of a flower from a certain tree in a bag of beans would increase the nitrogen-fixing capacity of the beans, producing more vigorous plants.

Grass's interest in science was first awakened in a general science class at Locust Grove High School, and he went on to get B.S. and M.S. degrees in soil science at Oklahoma State University. In 1952, he entered the University of California, Davis, where he did four years of postgraduate research on the genetics of disease resistance in oil crops (flax, safflower, and sunflower).

Grass developed as his field of special expertise the effect of salt on soil, water, and plant growth. In summer 1956, he got a position with the western regional office of the U.S. Department of Agriculture (USDA) Agricultural Research Service (ARS) at Pomona, California. His first assignment was a project to determine the cause of an extreme rise in soil acidity on a stretch of shallow tidal marshlands next to San Francisco Bay, north of Oakland. Among other problems he focused on during his years with the USDA were the difficulties caused by irrigating food crops with salty water from the Colorado River and methods of dissolving iron and manganese from tile drains. His last research project, carried out at the ARS station at Brawley, California, a wing of the USDA salinity laboratory, dealt with the effects of salt buildup and other stress factors on the irrigated cultivation of the rubber-producing guayule plant.

Luther Grass was also prominent in supporting Indian science education. In 1973, the ARS's southwestern regional office established its first advisory committee on equal employment opportunity (EEO) to try to recruit qualified minority agricultural scientists. Grass urged the agency to include its first program for Indians. Other regions of the ARS followed suit with their own EEO programs for Indians, and nationwide conferences were held every few years, some of which were also attended by RICHARD E. FRENCH of the U.S. Forest Service.

Grass served as manager of the ARS's American Indian Program from 1975 until 1984. When the AMERICAN INDIAN SCIENCE AND ENGINEERING SOCIETY was founded in 1977, he coordinated its recruiting program, helping a few Native American graduates find employment in the ARS. In 1983, he received the Francis X. Guardipee Gray Wolf Award for distinguished service to American Indian youth.

Grass retired in 1984 to live in Brawley, California. He died in July 2002. His younger brother, Buster Grass (1928–2003), was a champion Oklahoma western swing fiddler.

Graves, Peter (Sha-ga-na-she, "Englishman")

(1872–1957) *Chippewa political leader, activist*
Born on the Red Lake Reservation in Minnesota on May 20, 1872 (the official date, 1870, is incorrect), Peter Graves was the son of a Scottish follower of Métis revolutionary Louis Riel and a full-blood Chippewa mother from Leech Lake. His name in Ojibwa (the language of the Chippewa), Sha-ga-na-she, means

"Englishman" (literally, "Blown into Sight," the name given to the English troops under General James Wolfe when they suddenly appeared "out of nowhere" on the Plains of Abraham in Quebec in 1763). After the hopes of the Métis that they might gain title to their lands were dashed by the failure of the Riel rebellion in 1885, Graves's father, Joe Omen, like many other Métis, fled Canada to northern Minnesota.

Graves's father returned to Canada after five years, but his mother preferred to stay at Red Lake. When an Episcopal mission was founded there in 1877, she was baptized and given the name Elizabeth Graves after a Boston woman who did Indian charity work. Her son, baptized a Catholic at eight months, now took communion in the Episcopal church. He was given the name Peter Graves when he entered the Episcopal school. After graduating, he spent 10 months at Jubilee College near Peoria, Illinois, in 1884, then transferred to the Lincoln Institute in Philadelphia, where he stayed until 1889. There he learned the trades of carpentry and cigar-making and for a while played professional baseball with the Middle States League in Hazelton, Pennsylvania.

Returning to Minnesota, Graves worked at logging camps on or near the reservation in the 1890s, then became janitor and disciplinarian at the Red Lake boarding school from 1896 to 1898. During the 1890s, he also worked for the Indian police. He went to Washington, D.C., in 1899 as the official interpreter of a delegation from Red Lake.

In 1899, jurisdiction over the Red Lake Reservation was transferred from the White Earth Agency to the Leech Lake Agency, and in 1904 the Red Lake band sold 11 western townships (256,152 acres) to the federal government. This "Diminished Red Lake Reservation," now consisting of 573,238 acres, was allowed to remain independent of the other Chippewa reservations. Starting about this time, Graves served as a representative for the chiefs and the band in official business with the United States and with nongovernment organizations. To the end of his life, he was one of the few leaders of this very conservative band who could speak English fluently as well as Ojibwa. Also about this time, Graves moved to Onigum on the Leech Lake Chippewa Reservation, where for the next 13½ years, he served as assistant clerk, property clerk, and chief of the Indian police. He also fought the liquor traffic, which was a serious source of trouble on the reservation. In 1918, he resigned to work full time to oppose the claims of the Minnesota Chippewa against the Red Lake band.

In northern Minnesota, entrepreneurial mixed-bloods had long detested the Indian Office (later the BUREAU OF INDIAN AFFAIRS) for classifying them as wards and severely curtailing their ability to do business. After the passage of the Nelson Act of 1889, which provided for the division of Minnesota Indian lands into ALLOTMENTS, these experienced speculators (known as "progressives") became notorious for the systematic land frauds they perpetrated against more traditional Indians (see BEAULIEU, GUS H.). At Red Lake, however, the traditional chiefs successfully resisted negotiating a plan to allot tribal lands. Thus, the traditionals at Red Lake, on the principle of "the enemy of my enemy is my friend," saw the paternalistic Indian Office as their protector. Graves and the seven chiefs of the tribal council pursued this policy so effectively that Red Lake was never allotted.

In 1918, a renegade "Chippewa Legislative Committee" supporting Allotment was set up by Benjamin Fairbanks and Clement and Gus Beaulieu, allies of John G. Morrison, Jr., postmaster and leader of the progressive faction at Red Lake. On April 25, 1918, a council of 77 delegates from northern Minnesota reservations met at Ball Club on the White Oak Point Reservation and voted to oust this committee and to replace Morrison with James Coffey, who supported the traditionals. Federal government inspectors who were present recognized this decision as representing the views of "real Indians."

When the General Council of Red Lake was officially organized on April 13, 1918, Graves became its first treasurer. (The first chair was Joseph B. Jourdain.) It consisted of seven hereditary chiefs, each of whom could appoint five councilmen. Because Red Lake's tribal constitution dates from this time, it was never incorporated under the INDIAN REORGANIZATION ACT of 1934.

In summer 1918, Red Lake withdrew from the Grand Council of Minnesota Chippewas, which had been formed in 1913 to represent bands that were subject to the Nelson Act. This move was resented by the progressives. Graves suggested quieting these "clamoring mixed bloods" by giving them their proportionate share of tribal funds.

Under the new government, Red Lake established its own commercial enterprises, a fishery association, and a sawmill. The Red Lake Fisheries Association, originally established in 1917 under state law, came under federal supervision the following year. The tribal sawmill was set up under federal supervision in 1925 and came to be the band's most important source of income. By 1950, it employed 97 men. All profits went to an account managed by the federal government. Meanwhile, Graves became a director of the Red Lakes Fisheries Association in 1929. The operation brought more than $80,000 per year into the reservation. Five percent of the gross profits went to an account with the federal government.

From 1920 until his death, Graves held the office of secretary-treasurer of the Red Lake General Council. From 1936 to 1943, he served as a tribal judge.

Graves's main opponents were the progressives of the Red Lake Tribal Business Association, who disliked the whole system of governing the reservation and considered him a dictator. Their influence remained limited, however, in part because the tribe had developed successful business enterprises and in part because at Red Lake it was the traditionals, not the progressives, who were close to the Indian Bureau. "I was a policeman when I was 21 years of age," Graves stated in a 1950 interview. "I grew up to civilize these Indians here, and I'm always on the side of the government. . . . I was always on the side of the government, and a lot of them doesn't like it."

In a 1952 article, the agency superintendent Frel M. Owl (Eastern Cherokee) wrote of Graves: "His opposition to allotment and alienation of Indian lands is a mania; his opposition to State authority on the reservation is almost of similar proportions; his defense of an Indian's reservation rights is mighty, and his support of the Indian Bureau policies is consistent as long as the policy appears to be of benefit to the Red Lake Indians. [He] is loved by most of the Indians, disliked by others. He has been a powerful leader in the affairs of the Red Lake Band."

The high degree of sovereignty maintained by Red Lake even in the perilous days of TERMINATION is suggested by the fact that when Public Law 280, giving the states jurisdiction over criminal and civil matters on reservations in the states of California, Minnesota, Nebraska, Oregon, and Wisconsin, was passed on August 15, 1953, Red Lake was one of only three reservations exempted.

Peter Graves remained active until the end of his life. He last attended a council meeting on February 24, 1957. He died on March 14, 1957, and was buried in Red Lake Episcopal Cemetery, Red Lake, Minnesota.

See also JOURDAIN, ROGER; SOVEREIGNTY, INDIGENOUS AND TRIBAL.

Further Reading

Brill, Charles. *Red Lake Nation: Portraits of Ojibway Life.* Minneapolis: University of Minnesota Press, 1992.

Taylor, Graham O. *The New Deal and American Indian Tribalism: The Administration of the Indian.* Lincoln: University of Nebraska Press, 2001.

Great Lakes Indian Fish and Wildlife Commission (GLIFWC)

The Great Lakes Indian Fish and Wildlife Commission (GLIFWC) is an organization that coordinates and assists 13 Chippewa (Ojibway) tribal governments in the management of natural resources on off-reservation lands in the states of Michigan, Wisconsin, and Minnesota. Its headquarters are on the Bad River Reservation in Odanah, Wisconsin. The member bands are Mille Lacs and Fond du Lac in Minnesota; Red Cliff, St. Croix, Lac Courte Oreilles, Bad River, Lac du Flambeau, and Sokaogon (Mole Lake) in Wisconsin; and Lac Vieux Desert, Keweenaw Bay, and Bay Mills in Michigan.

Under the treaties of 1836, 1837, 1842, and 1854, by which most of the Great Lakes Chippewa bands ceded lands to the United States, they also reserved the legal right to hunt, fish, and gather on these lands. These federal treaty rights had been dormant for many years, and tribal members faced prosecution by the states for exercising them. However, when tested in 1974 by brothers Frederick and Michael Tribble, members of the Lac Courte Oreilles band of Chippewa, the federal district court, after a number of judgments and appeals, in 1983 reaffirmed the treaty rights in *Lac Court Oreilles Band of Chippewa v. the State of Wisconsin*, or what has come to be known as the Voigt Decision (after Lester B. Voigt, secretary of the Wisconsin Department of Natural Resources and defendant under the original suit). The court affirmed that the rights include the harvest of all types of natural resources sufficient to provide a moderate standard of living.

GLIFWC assists member tribes in the conservation, enhancement, safe harvest, and environmental comanagement of fish, wildlife, and other natural resources, as well as protection of the ecosystem. It also facilitates the development of institutions of tribal self-government to ensure continued sovereignty in the regulation and management of natural resources, infusing all implementation of its mission with traditional Anishinabe (Chippewa) culture and values.

GLIFWC is the descendant of two earlier organizations: the Great Lakes Indian Fisheries Commission and the Voigt Intertribal Task Force (headed by James Schlender). The Fisheries Commission was founded in 1982 by two officials at Red Cliff, tribal attorney Henry Buffalo, Jr., and tribal biologist Tom Busiahn. The Voigt Inter-Tribal Task Force was founded in February 1983 immediately after the Voigt Decision, when Gordon Thayer, tribal chairman of Lac Courte Oreilles, called a meeting of all affected tribes. GLIFWC is the product of their merger in 1984.

On the heels of the Voigt Decision, the new organization was immediately faced with the need to provide biological data, develop ordinances governing harvesting seasons, train enforcement personnel, and seek adjudication by tribal courts—a difficult task, especially since the Voigt Decision stirred up tremendous antagonism from non-Indians in these states, particularly Wisconsin, greatly affecting the atmosphere in which the new organization had to develop.

GLIFWC is a remarkable organization in that it institutionalizes the traditional Native connection between ecology and sovereignty within the framework of U.S. law and uses scientific techniques of resource management in order to implement traditional Anishinabe values, assisting its members to exercise tribal sovereignty over natural resources off the reservations.

See also HUNTING AND FISHING RIGHTS; SOVEREIGNTY, INDIGENOUS AND TRIBAL.

Further Reading

"From Weeds to 'Spirit Food': Wild Rice Restoration; Removing Competing Plants Is Helping the Staple of Tribal Spiritual Life Make a Comeback." *Saint Paul Pioneer Press* (Minnesota), 2 September 2002.

Thompson, Abbey. "King of Fish to Return to Northern Wisconsin Tribal Lakes." *Indian Country Today*, 3 March 2004, D1.

Zorn, James E. "Statement of Policy Analyst James E. Zorn, Great Lakes Indian Fish and Wildlife Commission." In *Hearing before the Committee on Indian Affairs, United States Senate, on Status of Tribal Fish And Wildlife Management Programs across Indian Country, June 3, 2003.* U.S. Senate, Committee on Indian Affairs, 22–25. Washington, D.C.: U.S. Government Printing Office, 2003.

Greene, Graham (1952–   ) *Oneida actor*

Graham Greene is an Oneida actor best known for his portrayal of Kicking Bird in the film *Dances with Wolves*. He was born in Ohsweken on the Six Nations Reserve in Ontario, Canada, on June 22, 1952, to Lillian and John Greene. His father was an ambulance driver and maintenance man. Graham Greene dropped out of school at age 16 and drifted to Rochester, New York, where he worked in a carpet warehouse for a short time. He spent the next six years in Canada as a welder, steelworker, bartender, and sound engineer, before taking his first acting role in a small Toronto theater company in 1974.

In Toronto, Greene acted in numerous stage productions, including *The Crackerwalker* (1980) and *Jessica* (1982), as well as building sets and operating the theater lights. His first film role came in 1982, when he played a friend of BILLY MILLS in the film *Running Brave*. However, the death of his father in 1984 led Greene into a period of, in his words, "fast cars and guns" as he drifted around. By 1989, however, he was again making strides as an actor. Three important events occurred that year: he had a small role in the landmark independent film *Powwow Highway*; he received the Dora Mavor Moore Award of Toronto for best actor for his performance in Tomson Highway's play *Dry Lips Oughta Move to Kapuskasing*, in which Cayuga actor GARY FARMER was a fellow cast member; and he played the role of a Lakota Sioux holy man who befriends Kevin Costner in *Dances with Wolves*. The film, which was released in 1990, featured Native actors speaking Lakota, which Greene had to learn. The film transformed the genre of the Western by focusing on Indian society for its human interest and by portraying Indians as major characters rather than villains or bit players. Greene's portrayal of Kicking Bird as a wise, funny, and ultimately tragic figure did much to help the film win the Academy Award for best picture in 1991. Greene himself was nominated for the Academy Award for best supporting actor that year, only the third Native American to be nominated after DAN GEORGE in 1971 and WILL SAMPSON in 1974.

Greene followed this success by playing Ishi in the film *Last of His Tribe* (1992). In *Thunderheart* (1992), his role as a tribal policeman opposite Val Kilmer's FBI agent also won wide praise. Currently Native America's most recognizable actor, Greene has also appeared in the films *Cooperstown* (1993); *Benefit of the Doubt* (1993); and *Maverick* (1994), with James Garner, Mel Gibson, and Jodie Foster. He also made appearances on the highly regarded television series *Northern Exposure* (1990–95).

In 1995, Greene appeared in the movie *Die Hard with a Vengeance*, and in 1997 he was seen in *The Education of Little Tree* and *Clearcut*. Also in 1997, Greene suffered an attack of depression and had to be hospitalized. He soon recovered and subsequently starred in the film *The Green Mile* (1999), with Tom Hanks. His portrayal of Magie Yellow Lodge, an alcoholic Vietnam veteran, in Northern Cheyenne director Chris Eyre's film *Skins* (2002) once again won him critical acclaim. In recent years, he has appeared frequently on television and in films, including *Transamerica* (2005), *A Lobster Tale* (2006), and *Just Buried* (2007). In 2007, he appeared in the Stratford Theater Festival of Canada's productions of *The Merchant of Venice* and *Of Mice and Men*.

Grinnell, George Bird (1849–1938) *writer,
anthropologist, naturalist*

Born on September 20, 1849, in Brooklyn, New York, George Bird Grinnell played as a child in the woods of the old John James Audubon estate on the Upper West Side of Manhattan, where his father had bought a house in 1859 and where he lived until 1909. In 1870, as a Yale University undergraduate, Grinnell went fossil collecting with the team of Professor Othniel Charles Marsh (the first professor of paleontology in the United States and the second in the world). This was the start of a series of expeditions to the western United States that would eventually total 40. Two years later, he accompanied a group of Pawnee on a buffalo hunt. He entered his father's dry-goods business, as he was expected to do, but in 1873 he sold it and returned to Yale for graduate studies in paleontology at his own expense, completing a Ph.D. dissertation in 1880 on the osteology of the roadrunner.

In 1874, Grinnell was invited to join General George Armstrong Custer in exploring the Black Hills. Custer hoped to find gold, but Grinnell confined his interest to fossils. He turned down Custer's invitation to revisit the area in 1876, the year Custer and his troops were killed by Sioux warriors at Little Bighorn. By then, Grinnell was working at Yale's Peabody Museum as an expert in osteology. In 1876, he was made natural history editor of *Forest and Stream*, becoming editor when he purchased the magazine in 1879. In 1885, he first traveled to northern Montana, where the Grinnell Glacier now bears his name. With his friend Theodore Roosevelt, Grinnell founded the Boone and Crockett Club in 1887, a society for the promotion of big-game hunting, the study of natural history, and game animal preservation. He also started the first Audubon Society in 1886 and helped to found the Bronx Zoo in 1895. As a conservationist, he became influential in encouraging the passage of the Lacey Act of 1900, which outlawed the killing of game for profit and the killing of birds for ornamental plumage.

During 1883–84, Grinnell waged a campaign on behalf of the starving Blackfeet, helping them to obtain rations and remove an obstructive agent. In appreciation, Chief Last Gun White Calf (see WHITE CALF JAMES; WHITE CALF, JOHN) made Grinnell an honorary chief of the Blackfeet and gave him the name Pinut-u-ye-is-tsim-o-kan (Fisher Hat) in 1885. Ten years later, President Grover Cleveland appointed him to negotiate the purchase of what became Glacier National Park in Montana from the Blackfeet. In 1890, he accompanied the expedition of E. H. Harriman to Alaska, later publishing a number of papers on Alaska Natives as part of the records of the expedition. After Theodore Roosevelt became president in 1901, Grinnell wrote the sections on Indian affairs in the president's annual addresses to Congress in 1902 and 1904. He also recommended FRANCIS ELLINGTON LEUPP for the post of Indian commissioner in 1904.

Grinnell made an effort to learn Indian spoken and sign languages. In 1889, he published his first book, *Pawnee Hero Stories and Folk Tales*. He later published a similar collection, *Blackfoot Lodge Tales* (1892), and three notable works of history and ethnology on the Cheyenne: *The Fighting Cheyennes* (1915), *The Cheyenne Indians* (1923), and *By Cheyenne Campfires* (1926.) All these books contain material collected by Grinnell from Indians of his acquaintance.

Grinnell was one of a circle of writer-naturalists, including CHARLES ALEXANDER EASTMAN, HAMLIN GARLAND, and ERNEST THOMPSON SETON, who worked for better understanding of American Indians in the early 20th century. In the foreword to his first book on the Cheyenne, Grinnell remarked, "Since the Indians could not write, the history of their wars has been set down by their enemies, and the story has been told always from the hostile point of view. . . . Evidently there is another side to this history, and this other side is one which should be recorded." (In this, he was a forerunner of WILLIAM CHRISTIE MACLEOD.) Throughout his writings, Grinnell objected strongly to the unsympathetic viewpoint, superficiality, and factual errors of many existing descriptions of Indians. Mari Sandoz, author of *Cheyenne Autumn*, regarded Grinnell's work on the Cheyenne as "the finest body of material on any American tribe." His book *The Indians of To-day* (1900) is a survey of the histories and living conditions of Indian tribes at the beginning of the 20th century. Grinnell also published three volumes of frontier history, the best known being *Two Great Scouts and Their Pawnee Battalion* (1928) an account of the exploits of brothers Luther and Frank North, who led a company of Indian Scouts. He also wrote the Jack Danvers series of Western adventure stories for children.

In failing health in his last years, Grinnell died in New York City at the age of 88 on April 11, 1938. His ethnological collections on the American Indian were bequeathed to the American Museum of Natural History in New York and the Peabody Museum at Yale University, New Haven, Connecticut. Five decades later, in 1988, Grinnell's great-nephew Skuyler M. Meyer, Jr., and Pat Trudell Gordon (Santee Dakota) established in his memory the George Bird Grinnell American Indian Children's Education Foundation.

In 1992, Dr. Lonewolf (Dorothy) Miller, a Blackfeet educator, wrote of Grinnell: "He saved Glacier National Park—if only he could have understood that the Blackfeet's spiritual life was there, as the Sioux are related to the Black Hills, the Navajos to the Four Sacred Mountains. He was a man of his times, but he could appreciate different drums, albeit faintly."

Further Reading

Smith, Sherry L. *Reimagining Indians: Native Americans through Anglo Eyes 1880–1940*. New York: Oxford University Press, 2000.

Guyon, Joe (Joseph Napoleon Guyon, O-Gee-Chidaha, "Brave Man") (1892–1971)
Chippewa football player

Joe Guyon was born Joseph Napoleon Guyon on November 26, 1892, in Mohnomen, on the White Earth Reservation in northern Minnesota. His parents gave him the Ojibwa name O-Gee-Chidaha (Brave Man). In 1904, his older brother, Charles, enrolled at the Haskell Indian school in Lawrence, Kansas, where he became an outstanding football player. Charles later transferred to the Carlisle Indian Institute in Pennsylvania. There Joe joined him in 1912, competing on the football and track teams under coach POP WARNER. When the great JIM THORPE graduated in 1913, Guyon replaced him as halfback, leading the Indians to a 10-1-1 record and scoring two touchdowns to hand mighty Dartmouth College its only defeat. Guyon earned All-America honors in both 1912 and 1913.

In order to get his grades up so that he might enter a major university, Guyon left Carlisle in 1914 to enter the Keewatin Academy in Prairie du Chien, Wisconsin. (The school did not have a football team.) After finishing there, Guyon was offered scholarships by a number of universities and went to visit some of them. En route to North Carolina, he met with his brother, who had meanwhile become an assistant coach to legendary coach John Heisman at Georgia Tech. Joe was persuaded to enroll at Tech, where he became an All-American tackle and halfback on their undefeated team of 1917, which outscored opponents 491-17 on the way to a national title. In a game against Vanderbilt, Guyon rushed for 344 yards on only 12 carries, setting a record that would stand until 1937. Big, fast, and an exceptional blocker, the 5 foot 10 inch, 195-pound runner was considered by Heisman to be among the three or four greatest football players of all time.

Guyon was signed by the Canton Bulldogs professional football team in 1919, joining Thorpe and PETE CALAC in an all-Indian backfield that brought Canton an undefeated season and the championship. In 1920, Guyon—a versatile player who joked that he "did everything except sell programs"—set the record for longest punt, 95 yards, a mark that stood for 50 years.

Guyon moved to the Cleveland Tigers in 1921 before joining the all-Indian OORANG INDIANS when they were formed the next year. Although injuries kept him out of all but three games, he still managed to be among the league leaders in rushing and points scored. Guyon rejoined the faltering Indians at the end of the 1923 season to lead them to their only two wins. When the team folded, he moved to the Rock Island Independents and then to the Kansas City Cowboys. In 1927, his final year, he threw the touchdown pass that gave the New York Giants their bitterly fought victory over the Chicago Bears and their first National Football League (NFL) crown. After his retirement, Guyon, along with Thorpe, was named to the 1920s NFL All-Pro Team.

Guyon was also a successful baseball player. He played four seasons with the Louisville Colonels (1925–28), leading the team to two American Association pennants, though it was a baseball injury in summer 1928 that ended his football career. Later, he coached high school football in Louisville and served as a bank guard. He also become an accomplished golfer. Guyon was inducted into the Pro Football Hall of Fame in 1966 and into the College Football Hall of Fame in 1971. He died on November 27, 1971, in Louisville, Kentucky, of injuries suffered in an auto accident.

Further Reading

Adams, David Wallace. "More Than a Game: The Carlisle Indians Take to the Gridiron, 1893–1917." *Western Historical Quarterly* 32, no. 1 (Spring 2001): 25–53.

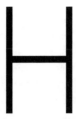

Hagerman, Herbert James (1871–1935) *New Mexico territorial governor, BIA negotiator, chair of Pueblo Lands Board*
Herbert James Hagerman was born in Milwaukee, Wisconsin, on December 15, 1871, the son of James John and Anna Hex (Osborne) Hagerman. His father was in mining and railroads. Herbert Hagerman went to school in Milwaukee and Colorado and obtained a B.Litt. in 1894 and an LL.B.in 1895 from Cornell University. After briefly practicing law in Colorado Springs (1897–98), he served as second secretary in the U.S. embassy in St. Petersburg, Russia (1898–1901).

Returning to the United States, Hagerman took up ranching and fruit growing at Roswell, New Mexico (1901–05), until President Theodore Roosevelt appointed him governor of the Territory of New Mexico. After one year, however, he had to resign because of timber scandals, although he himself was not involved. He resumed ranching and fruit growing until January 3, 1923, when Secretary of the Interior ALBERT BACON FALL appointed him federal commissioner to the Navajo (serving until 1932) and later special commissioner to negotiate with various southwestern tribes (1923–30). In addition, from 1926 to 1932, Hagerman represented the secretary of the interior on the Pueblo Lands Board, which had emerged as the compromise solution, after the defeat of the notorious BURSUM BILL, to adjudicate the rights of the Pueblo and non-Indian settlers on Pueblo lands.

Hagerman's appointment as special commissioner to the Navajo came shortly after oil was discovered on their lands. Federal oil leasing had been a source of massive corruption during the tenure of Secretary Fall, and the fact that Hagerman, his appointee, had responsibility for oil and gas development on Indian land raised suspicions. Hagerman, however, had a reputation for honesty and integrity, and, since he was appointed *after* the oil-leasing Teapot Dome scandal broke, it seems that this is exactly why he was chosen.

Hagerman set up the Navajo Tribal Council, the first tribal council in the United States, specifically to sign oil and gas leases. It could be convened only by him and could not legally function without his presence. At the first meeting, the council members gave him the power to sign leases on behalf of the tribe. Although the arrangement was paternalistic and much to the benefit of the oil companies, Hagerman was an intelligent and broad-minded person who liked and respected Indians and their culture. Not only was he highly regarded by most knowledgeable white Indian supporters, but the tribal council had much popular support among the Navajo (Dineh) themselves. It was their first unified tribal government, for the reservation had previously consisted of six separate jurisdictions, which the Indians had no say in governing. On Hagerman's tribal council, all six reservation districts were represented, and the first tribal chairman was the popular HENRY CHEE DODGE (1923–28).

Hagerman's good reputation notwithstanding, he had been thrown into a den of thieves. In October 1923, he sold rights to a parcel of Navajo land at Rattlesnake Dome to a friend for $1,000; the friend then transferred the rights to Continental Oil (a Rockefeller subsidiary) for $4 million. When called upon to explain, Hagerman pointed out that prior to selling the tract, he had put it up for sale in public auction but had received no bids. It seems likely that some kind of collusion had occurred behind Hagerman's back.

In 1931, Hagerman came under attack from the Democratic-controlled Senate Indian Affairs Committee, chaired by Senator Burton K. Wheeler and advised by JOHN COLLIER, head of the American Indian Defense Association. As Collier later explained in his memoirs, the Pueblo Lands Board had restored some lands to the Pueblos but had in many cases legitimated non-Indian claims. By 1931, Collier considered Hagerman the single key to success or failure in the hearings of the Senate Indian Investigating Committee. Yet even Collier did not accuse him of corruption, but rather of failing to protect the financial interests of the Navajo. Collier, though he had thus far supported Indian commissioner CHARLES JAMES RHOADS, broke with him over Hagerman.

On January 21, 1931, Senator Lynn J. Frazier introduced a rider to an appropriations bill to eliminate Hagerman's salary. OLIVER LA FARGE, adviser to Rhoads and recently appointed director of the Eastern Association on Indian Affairs, had investigated conditions among the Navajo the previous year and strongly defended Hagerman in a letter to the *New York Times*. When the inexperienced La Farge and other members of his association appeared before the committee several days later, Wheeler, with Collier at his side, tore them to pieces.

Hagerman's reputation was defended by New Mexico senators Bronson M. Cutting and Sam G. Bratton. Besides La Farge, Rhoads, and JOSEPH HENRY SCATTERGOOD, many others, including Indian rights advocate HAROLD SELLERS COLTON, writer Mary Austin, Robert Murray Haig of Columbia University, H. Alexander Smith of Princeton University, the INDIAN RIGHTS ASSOCIATION, the New Mexico Association on Indian Affairs (NMAIA), and the New Mexico State Senate, publicly came to Hagerman's defense. Members of NMAIA burned Collier in effigy in the plaza at Santa Fe. Hagerman's salary was restored on February 14. But when Senators Lynn J. Frazier, Burton K. Wheeler, John W. Thomas, and Henry F. Ashurst held hearings at Oraibi (Hopi territory) on May 18, 1931, Frazier, with Collier's help, again attacked Hagerman.

Surviving for the time being, Hagerman continued working on the Hopi-Navajo land dispute issue. He proposed a partition plan, which embodied Colton's suggestion that the Hopi should retain rights to their sacred sites and the gathering of wood in the Navajo area. He continued to serve as Navajo commissioner and chair of the Pueblo Lands Board until 1932.

Harold Colton, though impressed with Hagerman's character, thought him "not tough enough for the job." Hagerman died of a stomach ailment in Santa Fe, New Mexico, on January 28, 1935. Colton went so far as to blame John Collier for having hastened his death.

See also BIG MOUNTAIN; OIL, AMERICAN INDIANS AND.

Further Reading

Chamberlain, Kathleen P. *Under Sacred Ground: A History of Navajo Oil, 1922–1982*. Albuquerque: University of New Mexico Press, 2000.

Keleher, William Aloysius. *The Fabulous Frontier: Twelve New Mexico Items*. New York: Rydal Press, 1945.

Philp, Kenneth R. *John Collier's Crusade for Indian Reform, 1920–1954*, 103–111. Tucson: University of Arizona Press, 1977.

Richardson, Elmo R. *The Politics of Conservation: Crusades and Controversies, 1897–1913*. Berkeley: University of California Press, 1962.

Halfmoon, Frank L. (1929–2010) *Nez Perce–Cayuse biologist*

A Nez Perce–Cayuse, Frank Halfmoon was born on February 13, 1929, in Pendleton, Oregon, one of 13 children of Otis A. Halfmoon and Mary Joshua Halfmoon. He studied music and Russian at Gonzaga University in Spokane, Washington. He served two tours overseas with the U.S. Air Force. He later studied biology at Creighton University in Omaha, Nebraska, where he received a B.S. in 1962. He also won a Bausch and Lomb Science Award.

Halfmoon took a job as branch chief for fisheries in the Portland area office of the BUREAU OF INDIAN AFFAIRS, where his responsibilities involved him in developing recommendations on policies affecting tribal fishing, state programs, and foreign governments. While his own research focused on the Columbia River ecosystem, he also worked on fisheries issues with 57 tribes across the country. In 1991, Halfmoon received the Award of Excellence from the Western Division of the American Fisheries Society. At the time of his retirement in 1991, he was very much in demand as a hatchery manager, but despite offers from the U.S. Fish and Wildlife Service, the American Fisheries Society (as a consultant), and the Colville Indian Reservation, he retired completely, living in Coulee Dam, Washington, on the Colville Reservation. Halfmoon was a champion POWWOW dancer in both traditional and fancy-dance styles. His wife, Anna Ruth Halfmoon (1920–2006), a skilled bead worker, was active in the Nez Perce Longhouse in Nespelem, Washington.

Frank Halfmoon died at his home in Coulee Dam, Washington, on January 31, 2010.

Hallett, William Edward (1942–1992) *Chippewa commissioner of Indian Affairs*

William E. Hallett, a Chippewa (Ojibway) from the Red Lake Reservation in Minnesota was born on May 18, 1942. He received a bachelor's degree in business administration from Bemidji State College in 1965 and then joined the Chicago Police Department as a personnel technician. From 1967 to 1968, he was director of housing and manpower programs for the Red Lake Band of Chippewa Indians, where he set up and directed the Tribal Home Construction Company.

Hallett then became director of industrial development for the NATIONAL CONGRESS OF AMERICAN INDIANS (NCAI). He left NCAI in 1970 to become a consultant to the National Council on Indian Opportunity and the President's National Advisory Council on Minority Business Enterprise. From 1970 to 1975, Hallett also worked for the BUREAU OF INDIAN AFFAIRS (BIA) as a special assistant to the regional administrator for Indian affairs for Region VIII in Denver, Colorado. In 1975, he became assistant regional administrator for Region VIII.

In 1979, Hallett was appointed by President Jimmy Carter as commissioner of the BIA. He was to be the last commissioner of Indian Affairs. Under the Carter administration, his position was already superseded by the new office of assistant secretary for Indian Affairs. The assistant secretary position was created in 1972, and FORREST J. GERARD was appointed to that post. Hallett served under Gerard and then Gerard's successor, Thomas W. Frederick. Under Hallett, total federal spending for Indians peaked at $4.5 billion per year, and Indian poverty levels fell to their lowest point to date. Spending for Indian economic development programs peaked at $143.3 million in 1979. However, after his tenure, budget cuts under Assistant Secretary for Indian Affairs KENNETH L. SMITH seriously increased Indian poverty. He died on February 7, 1992, from injuries suffered in an automobile accident near Bemidji, Minnesota.

Harjo, Chitto (Wilson Jones) (1846–1909?) *Creek leader of the Crazy Snake Rebellion*

Chitto Harjo, also known as Wilson Jones, was born in 1846 in Arbeka on the Deep Fork River, in Indian Territory (now Oklahoma), near the town of Boley. His father was Ahrlock Harjo, a farmer. Chitto Harjo became a farmer as well.

In 1899, Harjo was selected as the spokesman for his community, Hickory Ground, by its chief, Lahtah Micco. The next year, when Micco fell ill in Washington, D.C., Harjo became chief. Harjo and the Hickory Ground Creeks were opposed to the ALLOTMENT process set in motion by the CURTIS ACT of 1898. They rejected the agreement signed by Pleasant Porter, principal chief of the Creek, on May 25, 1901, which mandated the dissolution of the Creek Nation and the division of Creek lands among individuals. Mostly full-bloods, they viewed with mistrust the machinations of educated mixed-bloods such as ALEX POSEY. They sought to reestablish the traditional government and strict enforcement of the Treaty of 1832, which guaranteed Creek lands in Indian Territory. By fall 1900, Harjo had united a large number of Creek, and they established their own Snake Government, complete with a legislature, judiciary, and police department, at Hickory Ground.

The Snakes, as the traditionalists came to be known, also sought to combine forces with dissidents of the four other "Civilized Tribes" such as the Nighthawk Keetoowah Cherokee under REDBIRD SMITH. This brought a military response from the federal government, which feared an insurrection. On January 25, 1901, U.S. soldiers invaded Hickory Ground and captured Harjo and 100 other Snakes without a fight. On February 2, they were tried and found guilty of insurrection, though their sentences were suspended and they were allowed to return to their homes.

Thus began what was known as the Crazy Snake Rebellion. More a movement than an actual armed rebellion, for the next nine years the Snakes resisted implementation of the Curtis Act. The rebellion takes its name from Chitto, meaning "recklessly brave" or "crazy" in Creek, and Harjo, meaning "snake." Harjo and nine other Snakes were rearrested in February 1902, and this time served 10 months in prison. Harjo then tried to plead the Snakes' case to the federal government, meeting with President Theodore Roosevelt in 1905 and making an impassioned, highly publicized speech on November 26, 1906, before a Senate hearing in Tulsa.

The creation of the state of Oklahoma in 1907 ushered in an orgy of looting of Indian lands through legal sleights of hand or even outright violence. Many Snakes who had rejected the Allotment agreement of 1901 found themselves without land, assigned to lands they did not want (see BARNETT, JACKSON), or quickly defrauded of the lands they did get by non-Indian carpetbaggers or "boosters" who descended on the new state. Discontent among the Snakes and mistrust on the part of local non-Indians, who feared a new rebellion, led to the "Smoked Meat Rebellion" in March 1909. The loss of 100 pounds of bacon from a white town led to accusations that the Snakes or freedmen blacks had stolen it, and a posse descended on Hickory Ground, this time killing a dozen men and arresting 42 more. Harjo was blamed, and on March 27 the posse surrounded his cabin. A shoot-out ensued. Two members of the posse were killed, and Harjo was wounded, probably fatally, but somehow escaped. Fred S. Barde reported in the *Kansas City Star* (1915) that Harjo died of a gunshot wound at the home of his friend Daniel Bob (Choctaw) on April 11, 1911, and was buried in the yard. There seems little reason to doubt this, except the correct year is more likely 1909.

The Snake movement continued under the aegis of the Four Mothers Society, led by Eufaula Harjo (no relation to Chitto Harjo), who joined with Redbird Smith and the Keetoowah and supporters of traditional government from the Choctaw and Chickasaw nations.

Further Reading
Harring, Sidney L. "Crazy Snake and the Creek Struggle for Sovereignty: The Native American Legal Culture and American Law." *American Journal of Legal History* 34, no. 4 (1990): 365–380.
Zissu, Erik March. *Blood Matters: Five Civilized Tribes and the Search for Unity in the Twentieth Century.* New York: Routledge, 2001.

Harjo, Joy (1951–) *Creek poet*

An acclaimed poet whose work features social and feminist themes woven into Native American myths and symbols, Joy Harjo was born in Tulsa, Oklahoma, on May 9, 1951. Her father, Allen W. Foster, was Creek, and her mother, Wynema (Baker) Foster, Cherokee; she was enrolled in the Creek Nation. At age 16, she was sent to the Institute of American Indian Arts in Santa Fe, where she began to paint. She then studied at the University of New Mexico, earning her bachelor's degree in 1976 while raising two young children. While in Albuquerque, she sought out her great-aunt, Lois Harjo Ball, who was also a painter. Ball would influence the young artist profoundly, introducing her to the "dream world," which would later play a large role in Harjo's poetry.

In 1975, Harjo published her first collection of poetry, *The Last Song*, a surprisingly mature work that featured her fluid, graceful style and rich thematic approach. Her second collection, *What Moon Drove Me to This*, was published in 1980 and included all of the material in *The Last Song* along with new poems. The release in 1983 of *She Had Some Horses* brought her national attention and firmly established her as one of Native

America's leading poets. Her singular use of metaphors and the lyrical quality of her poetry, often combined with a traditional chanting style, helped her explore the alienation, abuse, heartbreak, and loneliness that often figure in many Native American women's lives.

In 1989, Harjo turned to prose poems, accompanied by photographs of the Southwest by Stephen Strom, in *Secrets from the Center of the World*. This collection highlights a favorite idea: that the vibrancy of the land can be a source of strength for people in their search for freedom and empowerment. Between *She Had Some Horses* and *Secrets*, Harjo wrote a number of dramatic screenplays for television, including *Maiden of Deception Pass* in 1985 and *The Runaway* in 1986.

Her 1990 collection of prose poems, *In Mad Love and War*, touched on a wide range of subjects, from the Ku Klux Klan to Nicaragua, from jazz great Charlie Parker to murdered Indian rights activist ANNA MAE AQUASH, or returning to the dream world of "The Deer Dancer." The collection met with instant critical acclaim, winning the William Carlos Williams and Delmore Schwartz awards for poetry.

In 1991, Harjo became a full professor in the department of English at the University of New Mexico. An accomplished musician, she plays tenor saxophone in the jazz group Poetic Justice. In 1994, she released a collection of poems, *The Woman Who Fell from the Sky*, along with an audiocassette of her work performed to music. In 1996, Poetic Justice released the CD *Letter from the End of the Twentieth Century*, and for the next few years Harjo toured with her band. In 1998, she edited the collection *Reinventing the Enemy's Language: Contemporary Native American Women's Writings of North America*.

Harjo returned to poetry with her acclaimed *Map to the Next World: Poems* in 2000. Released in paperback the next year with additional prose material and renamed *Map to the Next World: Poems and Tales*, the work featured a more mature, wiser voice and some of Harjo's strongest poems ever. She wrote the children's book *The Good Luck Cat* in 2000 with illustrator Paul Lee, and in 2002 a collection of her works, *How We Became Human: New and Selected Poems: 1975–2001*, was published. In 2008, she released a CD of music, *Winding through the Milky Way*, and in 2010, *Red Dreams, A Trail Beyond Tears*.

Harjo's rich, personal style, which frequently incorporates Native imagery and oral traditions, and her ability to capture the texture and life of the land have made her a leading figure in the renaissance of Native American poetry that characterized the last quarter of the 20th century.

Further Reading

Harjo, Joy. "Ordinary Spirit." In *I Tell You Now: Autobiographical Essays by Native American Writers*, edited by Brian Swann and Arnold Krupat, 263–270. Lincoln: University of Nebraska Press, 1987.

Pettit, Rhonda. *Joy Harjo*. Boise, Idaho: Boise State University Press, 1998.

Schröder, Nicole. "'Webs of Motion': Joy Harjo's Poetic Landscapes." In *Spaces and Places in Motion: Spatial Concepts in Contemporary American Literature*, 49–110. Tübingen, Germany: Gunter Narr, 2006.

Wilson, Norma C. "Joy Harjo." *Dictionary of Literary Biography: Native American Writers of the United States*. Vol. 175, edited by Kenneth Roemer. Detroit, Mich.: Gale Research, 1997.

Harjo, Suzan Shown (1945–) *Cheyenne-Creek journalist, legislative activist*

Suzan Shown Harjo was born Suzan Douglas on June 2, 1945, in El Reno, Oklahoma. Her father, Freeland Douglas, a cryptographer for the U.S. Army, was Hudolgee Muskogee (Creek), and her mother, Susie Eades Douglas, was Cheyenne and Pawnee. Suzan Douglas lived in Oklahoma as a young child and then in Hawaii from 1952 to 1954. In 1956, her father was stationed in Naples, and the family lived in Italy until 1960.

Suzan moved to New York in the late 1960s, and with her husband, Frank Ray Harjo, a Wotko Muskogee, she coproduced the first regularly scheduled Indian news and analysis radio show in the country, *Seeing Red*, on WBAI-FM. For the radio show, she covered many of the leading events of the day, including the TRAIL OF BROKEN TREATIES demonstration in 1972, when the headquarters of the BUREAU OF INDIAN AFFAIRS (BIA) was taken over and ransacked. While living in New York, she helped Murial Miguel, Gloria Miguel, and Lisa Mayo create the Spiderwoman Theater, now the longest-running Native women's theater group in the country.

In 1974, Harjo moved to Washington, where she replaced RICHARD VANCE LACOURSE as news director of the American Indian Press Association. She then worked as a legislative liaison for a Washington law firm. In 1977, she joined the administration of President Jimmy Carter as special assistant for Indian legislation and liaison under the assistant secretary for Indian affairs, FORREST J. GERARD. In 1978, Harjo played an important part in the passage of the AMERICAN INDIAN RELIGIOUS FREEDOM ACT, and in 1979 she authored Carter's *President's Report to Congress on American Indian Religious Freedom* (see RELIGIOUS FREEDOM, AMERICAN INDIAN).

After working for the NATIVE AMERICAN RIGHTS FUND, Harjo became executive director of the NATIONAL CONGRESS OF AMERICAN INDIANS (NCAI) in 1984, succeeding JOSEPH BURTON DELACRUZ. During her five-year tenure, she fought President Ronald Reagan's efforts to defund the BIA, eliminate federal Indian health and housing programs, and turn over the responsibility for managing tribal and federal schools to the states. She clashed repeatedly with BIA head Ross O. SWIMMER, who favored the privatization of Indian services, and she sought to expose the rampant corruption in the bureau. She also successfully defended Indian treaty rights from a rising tide of anti-Indian hate groups that formed in response to tribal HUNTING AND FISHING RIGHTS victories in the 1970s. As a board member of the Museum of the American Indian (Heye Foundation) in New York City, Harjo was instrumental in getting the failing institution incorporated within the Smithsonian Institution in Washington, D.C., in

1989 as the National Museum of the American Indian. While serving as a trustee of the new museum from 1990 to 1996, she authored its policies on REPATRIATION (1991), Indian identity (1993), and exhibits (1994).

Harjo left NCAI in 1989 to become head of the Morningstar Foundation, a group she founded in 1984 to commemorate her husband, who had died in 1982, and to advocate for cultural rights. She successfully fought for the passage in 1990 of the Native American Graves Protection Act, which helped tribes regain lost cultural objects.

Harjo helped lead the Native American resistance to the Columbus Quincentenary in 1992. That same year, she filed suit against the National Football League in an attempt to change the name of the Washington, D.C., professional football team, the Redskins. Declaring the name demeaning, Harjo and other national Indian leaders opposed the use of Indians as mascots for any professional or amateur sports team. The suit, *Harjo et al. v. Pro Football Inc.*, sought to have the U.S. Patent and Trademark Office remove trademark protection for the Washington Redskins. In 1999, the Trademark Trial and Appeals Board canceled the registration of the Redskins trademark, handing Harjo another important victory, although the team appealed the verdict. In 2003, a federal judge sided with the Redskins and overturned the Trademark Appeals Board ruling, dismissing the case. Harjo then appealed that decision, and in 2005 a federal appeals court agreed to reinstate the suit. In 2009, the Supreme Court declined to hear the case; however, a new case Blackhorse et al. v. Pro Football is working its way through the courts.

Harjo was a Dartmouth College Montgomery Fellow in 1992 and a Stanford University Visiting Mentor in 1996. She was also the curator of the Peabody Essex Museum's 1996 exhibition, "Gifts of the Spirit: Works by Nineteenth-Century and Contemporary Native American Artists." That year, her lobbying efforts helped to persuade President Bill Clinton to sign Executive Order 13007 on Indian Sacred Sites, which required federal agencies to accommodate access to Indian sacred sites by Indian religious practitioners. The agencies were also instructed to avoid adversely affecting the site's physical integrity and to maintain their confidentiality.

Harjo is the author of "Fighting Name-Calling: Challenging 'Redskins' in Court, The Native American Mascots Controversy" (2001). An accomplished poet, her verses have appeared in numerous collections, and her political commentary has been featured regularly in a column in the newspaper *Indian Country Today*. In 2008, she was named the first Vine Deloria, Jr. Distinguished Indigenous Scholar at the University of Arizona, and in May 2011 she received an honorary doctorate from the Institute of American Indian Arts in Santa Fe, New Mexico. One of the most effective Native activists of her time, Suzan Shown Harjo has conducted hundreds of successful legislative efforts to protect American Indian lands and cultures. On November 24, 2014, Harjo was awarded the Presidential Medal of Freedom, the nation's highest honor, by President Barack Obama.

Further Reading

Harjo, Suzan Shown. "Fighting Name-Calling: Challenging 'Redskins' in Court." In *Team Spirits, the Native American Mascots Controversy*, edited by Richard King and Charles F. Springwood, 189–207. Lincoln: University of Nebraska Press, 2001.

Harris, LaDonna (LaDonna Crawford) (1931–)
Comanche political activist, feminist

LaDonna Harris, née Crawford, was born on February 15, 1931, in Temple, Oklahoma. Her mother, Lily Tabbytite, was Comanche, and her father, Don Crawford, Irish American. An only child, LaDonna was raised by her maternal grandmother because of her parents' early separation. Her grandmother, Wick-kie Tabbytite, was a devout Christian who spoke only Comanche. Young LaDonna Crawford was educated in the customs of her tribe and did not learn English until she started school at the age of six. In 1949, she graduated from high school and married Fred Roy Harris, the son of a sharecropper. She helped him graduate from the University of Oklahoma in 1952, and he received his law degree from that school in 1954. After practicing law in Lawton, Oklahoma, Fred Harris was elected to the Oklahoma State Senate in 1956.

A born organizer, LaDonna Harris established an intertribal organization, Oklahomans for Indian Opportunity (OIO), in 1965. The first intertribal organization in the state, with members from 60 tribes, OIO sought to improve economic conditions for Indians and overcome discrimination. When her husband was elected to the U.S. Senate in 1964, Harris moved to Washington, D.C., where she worked in the civil rights struggles of the time and joined the National Women's Political Caucus. She also became involved with the National Rural Housing Conference, the National Association of Mental Health, and the National Committee Against Discrimination in Housing, and she chaired the National Steering Committee of the Urban Coalition. In 1967, President Lyndon B. Johnson appointed her to chair the National Woman's Advisory Council on the War on Poverty, and the next year she was appointed to the National Council on Indian Opportunity, through which she aided Taos Pueblo in its struggle to regain BLUE LAKE. Located in northern New Mexico, the lake, along with 50,000 acres of Taos land, was seized by the federal government in 1906 in order to create the Carson National Forest.

In 1970, expanding on her efforts in Oklahoma, Harris founded Americans for Indian Opportunity (AIO), an organization devoted to the economic development of INDIAN RESERVATIONS. That same year, she helped the social reformer John W. Gardner, with whom she had worked at the Urban Coalition, create the public advocacy group Common Cause. Harris supported the AMERICAN INDIAN MOVEMENT (AIM) during its takeover of the BUREAU OF INDIAN AFFAIRS (BIA) headquarters in 1972 (see TRAIL OF BROKEN TREATIES) and aided AIM chairman REUBEN SNAKE in his efforts to create a self-sufficient economy for the Winnebago tribe. She played an important role in the fight to restore the tribal status of the

Menominee after their TERMINATION, successfully lobbying President Richard Nixon to sign the Menominee Restoration Act in 1973 (see DEER, ADA ELIZABETH; WASHINAWATOK, JAMES A.). Also in 1973, the *Ladies' Home Journal* selected Harris as one of its seven Women of the Year.

In 1974, Harris helped to form the National Indian Housing Council, an organization that advocated for and provided safe, sanitary, and affordable housing for Native Americans. The next year, President Gerald Ford named Harris to the U.S. Commission on the Observance of National Women's Year. After her husband's failed bid for the U.S. presidency in 1976, the couple moved to New Mexico, where Harris began to concentrate on the work of her organization, Americans for Indian Opportunity.

Concerned about the disadvantageous contracts that Indian tribes had signed with energy companies, Harris had AIO hire three interns from Dartmouth University to review federal surveys of Indian mineral deposits. The results made tribes aware of the magnitude of the potential wealth under their lands. In summer 1975, after an unsuccessful meeting with officials from the Department of Energy, Harris organized a meeting with Navajo (Dineh) chairman PETER MACDONALD and other leaders of energy-rich tribes that led to the creation of the COUNCIL OF ENERGY RESOURCE TRIBES (CERT) in 1976.

Under the administration of President Jimmy Carter, Harris served on the Commission on Mental Health and was the U.S. representative to the United Nations Educational, Scientific and Cultural Organization (UNESCO). In 1980, she became the first Native woman to run for the vice presidency, joining Barry Commoner on the ticket of the Citizen's Party. They managed to garner a total of 232,538 votes, approximately two-tenths of 1 percent of the total cast, finishing a distant fifth to Ronald Reagan.

During the 1980s, Harris's work with CERT and law firms that promoted Indian sovereignty (see SOVEREIGNTY, INDIGENOUS AND TRIBAL) at the expense of environmental regulations raised some controversy. In 1990, she formed the National Tribal Environmental Council to enhance Indian tribes' ability to preserve their environment and promote the wise management of their resources.

By 1990, Harris, a proponent of technology as a means to benefit Indian people, had been considering ways to use the Internet to aid Indians. In 1993, AIO hosted the first Native American Telecommunications Forum, funded by the National Science Foundation. That same year, Harris persuaded Apple Corporation's Libraries of Tomorrow program to donate a computer to AIO for the creation of INDIANnet, a national Internet network.

In recent years, AIO's main work has been its Ambassadors Program, a leadership training program created in 1993. Each year, advisers to the program choose approximately 30 young professional men and women from tribes throughout the United States. Each then serves as an "ambassador" for a year, during which time they go to Washington, D.C., and learn about the political process. They also tour reservations around the country and visit selected tribal groups in Central and South America.

Among the most influential Indian women in the country, Harris serves on the boards of numerous international development organizations, including UNESCO and Save the Children, as well as political organizations such as the National Organization for Women (NOW) and Common Cause. Under President Bill Clinton, Harris served on the board of the Institute of American Indian Arts, the Advisory Council on the National Information Superstructure, and the Secretary of Energy Advisory Board. In 1994, she moved the AIO to the Santa Ana Pueblo in New Mexico, where she continued to work on economic development initiatives. In 2002, LaDonna Harris stepped down as the president of AIO in favor of her daughter, Laura Harris.

Further Reading
Harris, LaDonna. *LaDonna Harris: A Comanche Life*, edited by H. Henrietta Stockel. Lincoln: University of Nebraska Press, 2000.

Harvey, Raymond (1920–1996) *Chickasaw war hero soldier*

Raymond Harvey was born in Ford City, Pennsylvania, on March 1, 1920, to Frank and Frannie (Thomas) Harvey. His father, a non-Indian, was in the construction business, and his mother, a Chickasaw, had been born near the community of Nebo, Oklahoma. After living in Ford City for four years, the family moved to Frannie Harvey's hometown of Sulphur, Oklahoma, where Raymond attended high school.

Harvey enlisted in the U.S. Army on August 16, 1939. Mustered into the 79th Infantry Division, he fought in Europe during WORLD WAR II. Harvey landed on Utah beach in Normandy on June 13, 1944, one week after D-day. With the 79th Division, he fought his way across France and into Germany, participating in some of the heaviest fighting of the war, including the battles of Cherbourg, Fort du Roule, La Haye-du-Puits, Charmes, Hagenau, and the Battle of the Bulge. For his heroic service, he was awarded the Distinguished Service Cross, the military's second-highest award for valor, as well as two Silver Stars and two Purple Hearts. After the war, he was a civilian for only a short time. In 1947, he joined the army reserves and was recalled to active duty in 1948 as a quartermaster.

After the outbreak of the Korean War, Harvey went ashore with the Seventh Division in the daring amphibious assault of Inchon in September 1950. Harvey, now a captain, took command of C Company, First Battalion, 17th Infantry Regiment, in November, just before the Chinese entered the war. He led the company out of North Korea during the subsequent retreat of U.S. and UN forces. When the United States went back on the offensive early the next year, C Company soon gained a reputation for aggressiveness.

On March 9, 1951, Harvey's company was the lead unit in the battalion's attack on Hill 1232 near Taerni-dong, South

Korea. When enemy machine guns pinned the company down, Harvey moved forward alone. He killed the crew of one machine gun with grenades. Advancing to a second position, he killed five of the enemy with his carbine. He had just eliminated a third position when he was shot through the lung. Seriously wounded, Harvey was still able to direct his company, enabling the men to destroy the remaining enemy positions. Only when assured the objective had been taken did Harvey consent to be evacuated. For his heroic actions on Hill 1232, Harvey was presented with the Medal of Honor by President Harry S. Truman at the White House on July 5, 1951.

Harvey was assigned by the U.S. Army to be military technical adviser to Samuel Fuller for his Korean War film *Fixed Bayonets* (1951), a film loosely based on Harvey's own experiences. The two of them struck up a friendship, and Harvey also became technical adviser on Fuller's *Verboten!* (1958). After the war, Harvey remained with the U.S. Army, eventually rising to the rank of lieutenant colonel. Later, he was employed by Northrup Corporation in California and also worked as a self-employed investment banker. He served as the director of Indian affairs for the Arizona Division of Emergency Services until a stroke forced his retirement in 1981.

Not merely the most decorated Native American serviceman, Harvey is one of the most highly decorated soldiers in American history, one of only a handful to win both the Medal of Honor and the Distinguished Service Cross. In addition, he was awarded three Silver Stars (the nation's third-highest award for valor in combat), three Bronze Stars, three Purple Hearts, 10 Campaign stars, two Presidential Unit Citations, the Croix de Guerre with Palm (from the government of France), the Chung Mu Distinguished Service Medal with Gold Star (by the government of South Korea), as well as eight additional medals. Raymond Harvey died on November 18, 1996, in Scottsdale, Arizona. He is buried in Arlington National Cemetery.

Hastings, William Wirt (1866–1938) *Cherokee leader, U.S. congressman*

William Wirt Hastings was born on December 31, 1866, on a farm in Benton County, Arkansas, near the boundary of Indian Territory (now Oklahoma). The son of William Archibald Yell Hastings, a white man, and Louisa J. (Stover) Hastings, daughter of a prominent Cherokee, he grew up in Beatties Prairie, Cherokee Nation, in Indian Territory, where he attended Cherokee common schools. Hastings graduated from the Cherokee Male Seminary in Tahlequah, Indian Territory, in 1884. He taught in Cherokee schools for a year before receiving a law degree from Vanderbilt University in 1889. He also formed a law partnership with the Cherokee leader E. C. Boudinot and served as the attorney general for the Cherokee Nation from 1891 until the tribal government was dissolved in 1907 under the CURTIS ACT. Following this, he served the tribe as its chief counsel.

Hastings won election to the U.S. House of Representatives in 1915, joining CHARLES DAVID CARTER and ROBERT L.

OWEN, as one of the first Indians in Congress. During his tenure in the House, Hastings did little to stop the looting of Indian lands by carpetbaggers drawn to the breakup of Indian Territory. In 1918, he helped to overturn the reforms enacted by Indian Commissioner CATO SELLS, who sought to protect Indian ALLOTMENTS and restrict the role of the professional "guardians" who oversaw the allotments made to Indian children. Hastings was defeated for reelection in 1921. He regained his seat in 1923, serving until his retirement in 1935. William Wirt Hastings died on April 8, 1938, in Muskogee, Oklahoma, and was buried in Tahlequah.

Further Reading

Cravens, Dollye Hefner. "Standard Bearer of the Cherokees: The Life of William Wirt Hastings." M.A. thesis, Oklahoma Agricultural and Mechanical College, 1942.

Hatcher, Eddie (Eddie Clark) (1957–2009) *Lumbee political activist*

A Lumbee who identified as a Tuscarora, Eddie Clark was born in Robeson County, North Carolina, on September 26, 1957. He and his two siblings were largely raised by their mother, Thelma Hatcher Clark, a textile-mill worker who put herself through nursing school and became a registered nurse. Upon the death of his grandfather Ted Hatcher in 1985, Eddie changed his surname from Clark to his mother's maiden name, Hatcher.

Hatcher began to challenge the racism prevailing in Robeson County when, in 1986, he started working with Concerned Citizens for a Better Government, a group formed after the shooting death of an unarmed Lumbee Indian by police. On February 1, 1988, along with fellow Lumbee Timothy Jacobs, he occupied the offices of a local newspaper in the county capital of Lumberton, North Carolina, holding 19 employees hostage for more than 11 hours. Accusing the Robeson County sheriff's office of allowing the county to be turned into a haven for drug smugglers, Hatcher demanded a state investigation into the numerous unsolved murders of black and Indian residents. Though Jacobs and Hatcher were armed, their peaceful demeanor and sincerity brought them national sympathy, and after receiving promises of a state investigation, they surrendered. The incident, in which no one was harmed, provided disclosure of rural southern justice and shed new light on North Carolina's political inequalities.

Robeson County, where fully two-thirds of the population was black or Indian, was run by a white minority. It includes the largest concentration of Indians in the Southeast, the Lumbee, who are descended from a mixture of tribes that included many Tuscarora, Cherokee, and Catawba. In the town of Pembroke, the Lumbee had founded their own university, Pembroke State University (begun as the Croatan Normal School in 1909 and later called Pembroke State College). Despite this, and despite the overwhelming majority of Lumbee in the town, whites had managed to control it since its founding in 1895. At first, they simply prevented the

Lumbee from voting. When that failed in 1917, they persuaded the state legislature to change the town's election laws, giving the governor of the state the power to choose the mayor and other high officials. When direct elections were finally held in Pembroke in 1947, a Lumbee was elected mayor.

The federal government did not recognize the Lumbee as a tribe until 1956, but the legislation denied them any federal services. The Lumbee were also affected by North Carolina's Jim Crow laws, which barred African Americans and Indians from many employment opportunities and imposed racial segregation. In 1958, the Lumbee gained fame when they shut down a Klu Klux Klan (KKK) rally and chased KKK Grand Dragon James W. "Catfish" Cole out of Robeson County. Yet despite the gains the Lumbee made in the 20th century, by 1988 the county was still largely controlled by the white minority. That it was dangerous to challenge this system was made clear that year when Julian Pierce, a popular Lumbee leader, was murdered during his campaign for county judge.

Eddie Hatcher and Timothy Jacobs became the first people to be prosecuted under the federal Anti-Terrorist Act of 1984, which included the crime of "overt acts against the United States" as well as kidnapping. Both were acquitted after a three-week trial, the jury finding that fear for their lives, and their need to expose the corrupt public officials, justified the occupation.

For Hatcher, the victory of the trial was not enough. He launched a very public campaign to have the sheriff removed, using every opportunity he could find to denounce corruption in Robeson County. But his flamboyant style and difficult personality made him few friends and many enemies. As he lost community support, the state took the opportunity to reindict him and Jacobs in late 1989. Fleeing across the country, often staying on INDIAN RESERVATIONS, yet always falling out with his hosts, Hatcher was arrested in California after trying to seek asylum in the consulate of the Soviet Union.

In 1989, Hatcher was tried and convicted in North Carolina on state kidnapping charges stemming from the 1988 occupation and sentenced to 18 years in jail. Once in prison, he was attacked, stabbed, and seriously wounded. Though he alienated family, friends, and supporters, his actions provided the spark to change a system of southern white rule maintained in Robeson County since its founding in 1787.

Seriously ill from AIDS, Hatcher was paroled from prison in North Carolina in May 1995. Although the terms of his parole required him to stay away from Robeson County, he moved back and quickly found himself in trouble. In November 1998, Hatcher was shot in the arm in an incident he described as "a private matter." No charges were filed. In May 1999, he was involved in an altercation with a 12-year-old whom Hatcher had accused of stealing. Hatcher fired a weapon during the dispute and was arrested by the police.

On June 1, 1999, police arrested Hatcher and charged him with the drive-by shooting death of 19-year-old Brian McMillian near Maxton and the wounding of 15-year-old Amelia Travis. In May 2001, he was convicted of first-degree murder and sentenced to life without parole.

By 2008, after a six-year investigation, 22 Robeson County lawmen were arrested and convicted for crimes ranging from kidnapping, assault, drug trafficking, and theft. "Eddie Hatcher was right all those years ago," Robeson County district attorney Johnson Britt told the *Raleigh News and Observer* in June 2008. "He just went about it the wrong way."

Eddie Hatcher died at the Central Prison in Raleigh, North Carolina, on the morning of May 1, 2009. He had stopped taking AIDS medication two years earlier and was very sick.

Hayes, Ira Hamilton (1923–1955) *Pima soldier*

A Pima, Ira Hamilton Hayes was born on the Gila Reservation in Arizona on January 12, 1923. His parents, Joe and Nancy Hayes, were cotton farmers, and Ira grew up in a traditional adobe house in the reservation town of Bapchule. The oldest of four brothers, Hayes enlisted in the U.S. Marines in August 1942, during WORLD WAR II, and shipped out to the South Pacific in March the next year as part of the 3rd Parachute Battalion. Completing a tour of duty that saw him participate in the assault on the island of Bougainville, in the Pacific, he returned to the United States in January 1944.

Assigned to the 28th Marine Division, Hayes returned to active duty in time for the assault on the heavily guarded island fortress of Iwo Jima, site of one of the bloodiest battles in the war. Hayes landed with the first troops on February 20, 1945. After three days of heavy fighting, the marines managed to capture Mount Suribachi, the highest point on the island, and plant an American flag. The next day, Hayes was sent with five other men to plant a larger flag on top of the mountain. The event was captured by photographer Joe Rosenthal and became one of the most famous images of the century. Hayes and the two other surviving marines who planted the flag became instant heroes and were sent on a promotional tour to sell war bonds around the United States.

Hayes, shy by nature, was uncomfortable in the spotlight. He began to drink heavily. After his discharge from the marines in December 1945, he returned to his family farm to pick cotton. His alcoholism landed him in jail numerous times, and the lack of jobs on the reservation forced him to apply for relocation to Chicago under the Indian Relocation Act. He could not escape the pressures of fame, and he soon lost his job in Chicago and found himself once again in jail for alcohol abuse.

After his release, Hayes returned to his reservation. On the night of January 23, 1955, after a bout of heavy drinking, Hayes fell into an irrigation ditch. He was found dead, face down in two inches of water. His death became a symbol of the tragedy that culture shock and alcohol have brought to many Indian lives. A film, *The Outsider*, starring Tony Curtis as Ira Hayes, is based on his life, as is the song *The Ballad of Ira Hayes* written by Peter La Farge and recorded by Johnny Cash.

Further Reading

Hemingway, Albert. *Ira Hayes, Pima Marine*. Lanham, Md.: University Press of America, 1988.

Pima war hero Ira Hayes was one of six marines who raised the U.S. flag on Mount Suribachi on Iwo Jima during World War II. *(AP/Wideworld)*

Marling, Karal Ann, and John Wefenhall. *Iwo Jima: Monuments, Memories, and the American Hero.* Cambridge, Mass.: Harvard University Press, 1991.

Wenz, Karen L. "Ira Hayes: His Story and a Detailed Bibliography." M.A. dissertation, St. Cloud State University, St. Cloud, Minnesota, 1998.

Hayward, Richard Arthur (Skip Hayward)

(1948–   ) *Mashantucket Pequot tribal chair*

Born on November 28, 1948, in Groton, Connecticut, Richard "Skip" Hayward was the grandson of Elizabeth George Plouffe, who along with her half sister, Martha Langevin Ellal, led the Mashantucket Pequot through most of the 20th century. In 1900, fewer than 20 Pequot were living at Mashantucket. Their number declined further, until only 10 remained on their small landholdings, which total about 250 acres. By 1947, Elizabeth Plouffe and Martha Ellal was the only ones left, and in 1973, when Plouffe died, Ellal was the last Pequot on the reservation. But Hayward had promised her that he would not let the land fall into the hands of the state.

In August 1974, Hayward, at that time working as a pipe fitter, called together as many uncles, aunts, and cousins as could be located in nearby towns, to a meeting on the reservation. A year later, there were 55 people of at least 1/16 Pequot blood on the tribal rolls. Hayward had reorganized the tribe. Now began a long fight for federal recognition, and one of the most unlikely stories in American Indian history.

Hayward was elected tribal chair by the Pequot in 1975. The next year, the tribe approved a new constitution. In 1976, the Pequot filed suit against the state of Connecticut for the return of 800 acres. Hayward then sued property owners in Ledyard to recover 989 acres of Pequot land that had been sold by the state of Connecticut in 1856. He led the Mashantucket's attempts to attain economic self-sufficiency by promoting the sale of firewood, maple syrup, garden vegetables, and swine, and by opening a hydroponic greenhouse. On January 15, 1979, the tribe filed a petition for federal recognition. With the help of the NATIVE AMERICAN RIGHTS FUND (NARF), the Pequot prevailed and were granted federal recognition in 1983. In 1988, Hayward became chair of the board of directors of NARF.

In 1985, following the lead of Seminole gaming pioneer JAMES BILLIE, Hayward led the Mashantucket Pequot tribe in opening the first bingo hall in the Northeast, an effort the state government of Connecticut attempted in vain to stop, fighting Hayward until finally losing in the U.S. Court of Appeals. Immediately after passage of the Indian Gaming Regulatory Act in 1988, the Pequot applied to the newly formed gaming commission to open a casino of a kind that could only be found in Nevada or Atlantic City, upgrading from a bingo hall. When Connecticut refused to negotiate with the Indians as prescribed by the law, the Pequot went to court again. In May 1990, a federal court ruled that Connecticut was obligated to negotiate with the tribe, and two months later Connecticut lost on appeal. When the U.S. Supreme Court refused to hear the case, the state was forced to the bargaining table.

In return for a payment of $100 million per year to Connecticut and state supervision of their operations, the Pequot opened what proved to be the single most profitable casino in the country. Within three years of the court ruling, the Foxwoods Casino had become one of Connecticut's largest industries, employing almost 2,000 people and netting more than $1.6 million per day. The $100 million per year that the state received turned out to be a godsend to a local economy that had fallen victim to a deep recession. The Pequot subsequently expanded into various forms of local and national businesses, including a shipbuilding enterprise at the site where the defunct defense contractor Electric Boat was once a mainstay of the Connecticut economy. Hayward himself became one of the most important Indian leaders in the country, contributing heavily to the Democratic Party and meeting regularly with Bill Clinton while he was president.

In 1998, Hayward was defeated by Kenneth Reels in the election for tribal chair and had to settle for the post of vice chairman. He sought the top position in 2002 but was again beaten, this time by Michael Thomas. Despite the recent reversals, Hayward continues as a key figure in Pequot politics and one of the most influential Indian leaders of the new millennium.

See also GAMING ON INDIAN RESERVATIONS.

Further Reading

Eisler, Kim Isaac. *Revenge of the Pequots: How a Small Native American Tribe Created the World's Most Profitable Casino.* New York: Simon & Schuster, 2001.

Fromson, Brett Duval. *Hitting the Jackpot: The Inside Story of the Richest Indian Tribe in History.* New York: Grove Press, 2004.

Hauptman, Laurence M., and James Wherry, eds. *The Pequots in Southern New England: The Fall and Rise of an American Indian Nation.* Norman: University of Oklahoma Press, 1993.

health, American Indian

At the start of the 20th century, the health and nutrition of American Indians in the United States, as well as their population, had reached a historic low point. Before the arrival of Europeans, Indians enjoyed generally good health. But by 1900, the average death rate among Indians was over 30 per 1,000, more than double the average rate of white Americans, and the average life expectancy was only 30 years—less than that of people in England in the 11th century. Infectious diseases, such as pneumonia and trachoma in adults and gastroenteritis in children and infants were particularly prevalent on INDIAN RESERVATIONS. Tuberculosis was the single largest killer of Indians; in 1906, 72 percent of all Indian deaths in the Southwest were attributed to the disease. ALCOHOLISM was a significant health problem, aggravated by desperate poverty brought about by the dismantling of Indian traditional economies and the loss of their land base.

For most of the 19th century, the Indian Office, as the BUREAU OF INDIAN AFFAIRS (BIA) was then known, did not have a medical division. For a short period, from 1873 to 1877, a medical and educational division existed, but for the most part medical services were administered by local Indian agencies and schools, and they in turn were often dependent on army doctors.

Like most other government services that dealt with Indians at the start of the 20th century, the medical service was rife with corruption. Medicines, if they could be found, were generally stale, and surgical equipment was often obsolete or unusable. Dentists were almost nonexistent. Pay for medical professionals in the Indian Service was very low, thus tending to attract only the least capable and least interested, and they were virtually without supervision. In addition, most Indian Service doctors focused their attention on the white government employees. The Dakota physician CHARLES ALEXANDER EASTMAN, upon being appointed to the Pine Ridge Agency in South Dakota in 1890, found that his predecessor, rather than examining and diagnosing Indian patients, had been, as Eastman put it, "practicing his profession through a small hole in the wall between his office and the general assembly room of Indians."

Indian Commissioner WILLIAM ARTHUR JONES attempted to improve the standards of medical professionals as well as fight the endemic corruption. In 1909, he made the education division responsible for Indian health. In 1911, Commissioner FRANCIS ELLINGTON LEUPP established the first sanitoriums for tuberculosis. However, in 1912 a congressional survey of Indian reservations found that Indian Bureau medical services were still substandard and inadequately staffed. The survey found, moreover, that more than 14 percent of the Indians in the country had tuberculosis and an additional 22.7 percent had trachoma, although the rates for the two diseases varied widely from state to state and from tribe to tribe.

The congressional survey of 1912 also found sanitary conditions on the reservations to be very poor, particularly in schools and hospitals. Leupp's successor, ROBERT GROSVENOR VALENTINE, made the first attempt to deal systematically with these serious problems. Valentine persuaded President William Howard Taft to support an ambitious program of preventive medical education, and the Indian Bureau made improvements in sanitary waste disposal, proper food storage, adequate ventilation in schools and other buildings, and other measures. However, Valentine's far-reaching attempts to overhaul the bureau led to a backlash and his dismissal. Under his successor, CATO SELLS, the medical service was allowed to decline once more.

The terrible world influenza epidemic of 1918 struck Indian reservations hard, leaving thousands dead. Along with the faltering health system, the rise in infectious diseases was responsible for a serious decline in Indian populations between 1910 and 1920. In 1921, Congress passed the Snyder Act (Public Law 67-85)—named for its sponsor, Congressman Homer P. Snyder of New York, chair of the House Indian Affairs Committee (who would also sponsor the American Indian Citizenship Act of 1924)—in an attempt to reorganize Indian health care and to provide money for Indian health. The Snyder Act authorized regular appropriations for "the relief of distress and conservation of health" of Indians and set up administrative mechanisms that allowed the Indian Office to pay contractors. In 1924, a separate medical division under Dr. Robert Edward Lee Newberne (1855–1926), was finally created. However, Commissioner CHARLES HENRY BURKE, facing political pressure to save money and reluctant to ask for increased appropriations, allowed the nutrition and health of Indians to slip further. In December 1922, admitting that the Indian Office could not "afford salaries that command the service of enough high-class physicians and trained nurses," he announced that he had secured the help of the Red Cross to survey conditions on reservations. By 1927, funding shortages had become so serious that in some cases they were preventing the purchases of food for Indian schoolchildren. Moreover, the salaries of Indian physicians and nurses were so low that in 1927 alone the turnover rate was 57 percent for physicians and an astounding 127 percent for nurses. Although funds were received for a new tuberculosis sanitarium and three new hospitals, they did little good in the chaotic and corrupt administrative climate of Burke's administration. Under Sells and Burke, Indian death rates soared, reaching 37 per 1,000 among the Sioux and an alarming 55 per 1,000 among the Blackfeet (Siksika).

Burke's policies came under attack from the American Indian Defense Association (see COLLIER, JOHN), and he requested that each superintendent name a committee of local citizens to report on conditions on each reservation. In 1929, at a new but underfunded tuberculosis hospital in Kayenta, New Mexico, Indian rights advocate HAROLD SELLERS COLTON and his wife found only one patient, because the Navajo (Dineh) were afraid to go there, and at both institutions they encountered serious health and sanitation problems. Burke did launch a crash program against trachoma, using a new surgical technique to perform thousands of eye operations in the Southwest, but the disease continued to spread. It infected Indians at a rate of between 18 to 25 percent of the population until the development of sulfanilamide in 1938 by Dr. Fred Loe, who discovered it while practicing on the Rosebud Reservation in South Dakota. Research on sulfanilamide and trachoma was also being conducted by Dr. Phillips Thygeson on the Fort Apache reservation in Arizona.

Under Commissioner CHARLES JAMES RHOADS, some strides were made in the medical division, now under the directorship of reformer Dr. Marshal C. Guthrie, including the hiring of new doctors and nurses. The number of Indians receiving medical assistance grew during Rhoads's tenure. In particular, the emphasis on preventive care achieved some success. However, Rhoads was hampered by Michigan congressman Louis C. Cramton's stranglehold on the Indian Bureau's budget, which left the agency still unable to provide fully for the nutritional needs of Indian schoolchildren. Despite the increase in hospitals and sanitoriums, the rate of tuberculosis infection continued to hover at around 10 percent. In 1931, the medical division was renamed the health division.

The JOHNSON-O'MALLEY ACT of 1934 allowed the bureau—now the BIA—to contract its health service to the states, and in 1936 President Franklin D. Roosevelt allowed Indian health workers to hold the same jobs with state health agencies as well, thereby allowing the BIA to hire more qualified professionals and to expand its reach. Although still much higher than for the general population, by 1938 the death rate among Indians had been lowered by half from what it was at the turn of the century, to 1,490 per 100,000 population. In 1940, the health division was brought under the Community Services Branch.

The years of WORLD WAR II brought heavy budget cuts to the BIA and the loss of much of its staff. At the half-century mark, the health of Indians on reservations continued to be poor. Trachoma cases increased from the previous decade, and the tuberculosis death rate among Indians in the Southwest and on the Great Plains was more than seven times the national rate. In Alaska, the tuberculosis mortality rate was an astounding 688 per 100,000 of the population, or 20 times the national average. Pneumonia death rates were between five and six times the national average, and typhoid on Indian reservations was four times the national rate. One-quarter of the infants on most reservations died before their first month, usually of gastroenteritis. The winter of 1948–49 in the Southwest was particularly hard, leading to starvation on many reservations, particularly among the Navajo.

The poor state of Indian health led Dr. Fred T. Foard, director of the BIA's medical services, to state in 1949 that the "lack of health facilities for Indians is a disgrace to the nation. Our government has spent tens of millions to improve health conditions throughout the world, yet stands indicted for conditions such as existing among the Papago [Tohono O'odham] Indians" where "the average life expectancy of a Papago infant is 17 years, whereas that of a non-Indian infant in the United States is over 60 years."

Indian health programs were woefully underfunded. The 70 Indian hospitals in the continental United States and Alaska were so understaffed that most had to make do with only one doctor, and they operated at only one-quarter of their theoretical manpower. From 1949 to 1955, the department responsible for Indian medical services was known as the Branch of Health and was under the Community Services Division of the BIA.

As a part of the federal TERMINATION policy, the responsibility for providing health care to Indian people was transferred in 1955 to the Department of Health, Education, and Welfare's Public Health Service, allowing Indian care to be merged into the nation's growing health care system. During the 1960s, the Great Society programs of the John F. Kennedy and Lyndon B. Johnson administrations brought increases in funding to public health programs, greatly improving the scope and quality of care (see BENNETT, ROBERT). Beginning in 1959, the Indian Health Service (IHS) began to upgrade Indian homes with running water, sewage, and solid waste disposal systems; by 1990, the IHS had upgraded more than 182,000 Indian houses. Also during the 1950s and 1960s, newly developed antibiotics and vaccines became effective against the infectious diseases that afflicted Indians.

The Indian Self-Determination and Education Assistance Act, passed in 1975, allowed for tribes to operate their own health facilities under contract from the IHS. The next year, the Indian Health Care Improvement Act was passed; among other things, it increased the health service's budgets, provided capital funds for the upgrade of marginal facilities, and mandated that the government raise the standard of health care for Indians to that of the general U.S. population. The law also provided financial and other incentives to increase the number of Indian health professionals.

The changes in the health care system and the conquest of many infectious diseases led to an increased life expectancy among American Indians and contributed to the surge in population in the last half of the century (see DEMOGRAPHICS). Infant mortality began to decline in the 1950s and more so in the 1960s, falling from 97 per 1,000 live births before World War II to 22.2 per 1,000 in 1971, eventually reaching 9.3 per 1,000 in 1996. Yet this was still about 22 percent higher than the U.S. rate for all races, which stood at 7.6 per 1,000. By 2004, the infant mortality rate had fallen to 8.4 per 1,000, still higher than the general population rate of 6.8 per 1,000. Deaths from gastroenteritis declined dramatically, from more than 20 per 100,000 in 1955 to less than 2 per 100,000 in 1991. Tuberculosis mortality dropped even more dramatically, from 200 per 100,000 in 1935 to only 2.7 per 100,000 in 1991. The overall death rate also fell to 1,007 per 100,000 in 1972 and then all the way to 700 per 100,000 in 1998, to 663.4 per 100,000 in 2005. Since 1955, the life expectancy of Indian men has increased more than 17.8 years, to 69.1, and more than 25.6 years among women, to 77.5 years. As of 1998, the life expectancy of American Indians and Alaska Natives, men and women, was 71.1 years. This was still 4.7 years lower than the general population and 5.4 years less than U.S. whites.

A number of outstanding American Indian health workers were active in this period, such as LUCILLE JOHNSON MARSH (Tuscarora), LILLIE ROSA MINOKA-HILL (Mohawk), and ANNIE DODGE WAUNEKA (Navajo).

After World War II, the rising acculturation of Indian people and consequent changes in diet and lifestyle led to an increase in chronic diseases, with heart disease, cancer, and diabetes now becoming the leading causes of death. By 2005, heart disease (141.8 deaths per 100,000) was the leading killer, followed by cancer (123.2 per 100,000), cirrhosis of the liver and other chronic liver diseases (122.6 per 100,000), and diabetes mellitus (41.5 per 100,000). The diabetes mortality rate, however, does not convey the impact of diabetes on Indian populations; since World War II, this disease, once virtually unknown among Indians and Alaska Natives, has become an epidemic. Believed to be caused by dietary changes, in particular by the use of processed foods and sugars and a high fat intake, diabetes has been called "a disease of civilization." It is currently estimated that 11 percent of Indian men and 13 percent of Indian women are diabetic.

Alcoholism is still one of the greatest health problems Indian people face today. In addition to chronic liver diseases, accidents, most of which are alcohol-related, rank third as the leading cause of death for Indian people (54.7 per 100,000). During the period from 1994 to 1996, there were 158 male deaths and 46 female deaths due to HIV infection, and the incidence of infection in 2005 was 2.7 per 100,000, or about the same as the rate among whites. However, the incidence among Indians was increasing at a higher rate than among whites.

As of 2002, more than half of all Indians received their health care from the Indian Health Service, and the service operated 36 hospitals, 63 health centers, and 44 clinics. The health service also contracted to certain tribes the operations

of an additional 12 hospitals, 155 clinics, and 160 Alaska Native village clinics. The IHS employed more than 950 physicians—12 times the number employed in 1950—2,687 nurses, 424 pharmacists, and 319 dentists, totaling more than 15,000 personnel. There had also been a revival in the use of indigenous healing on various reservations, particularly among the Navajo (Dineh), and traditional healing, alongside Western medicine, was becoming more accepted in IHS facilities.

In the 21st century, the IHS did not generally provide health care for urban Indians, having only 13 primary care programs in urban communities, and although the care of reservation Indians had improved dramatically in the 20th century and early 21st century, the quality is still lower than that of the general population. Despite the fact that Indian health care is part of the "trust" aspect of Indian–federal government relations, and health care is generally considered to be a treaty obligation, during the 1980s and 1990s, Indians had to lobby vigorously to prevent the IHS from being dismantled. Its annual budget of $2.8 billion remained largely unchanged from the mid-1990s through 2002, leading to cutbacks in services and diminishing its ability to improve Indian health in the new millennium. The enacted budget for 2008 was $3.35 billion.

Further Reading

Benson, Todd. "Blinded with Science: American Indians, the Office of Indian Affairs, and the Federal Campaign against Trachoma, 1924–1927." *American Indian Culture and Research Journal* 23, no. 3 (1999): 119–142.

Day, Priscilla A., and Hilard N. Weaver. *Health and the American Indian*. Philadelphia: Haworth Press, 1999.

DeJong, David H. *If You Knew the Conditions: A Chronicle of the Indian Medical Service and American Indian Health Care, 1908–1955*. Lanham, Md.: Lexington Books, 2008.

Gray, Sharon A. *Health of Native People of North America: A Bibliography and Guide to Resources*. Lanham, Md.: Scarecrow Press, 1996.

Joe, Jennie R., and Robert S. Young. *Diabetes as a Disease of Civilization: The Impact of Culture Change on Indigenous Peoples*. Berlin, N.Y.: Mouton De Gruyter, 1994.

McConnell, Edwin A., and Teddy Jones. *A Stone for Every Journey: Traveling the Life of Elinor Gregg, R.N.* Santa Fe, N.Mex.: Sunstone Press, 2005.

Nebelkopf, Ethan, and Mary Phillips. *Healing and Mental Health for Native Americans: Speaking in Red*. Lanham, Md.: Rowman Altamira, 2004.

Rhoades, Everett R. *American Indian Health: Innovations in Health Care, Promotion, and Policy*. Baltimore, Md.: Johns Hopkins University Press, 2000.

Rife, James. *Caring & Curing: A History of the Indian Health Service*. Landover, Md.: Public Health Service, Commissioned Officers Foundation, 2009.

Sandefur, Gary D., Ronald R. Rindfuss, and Barney Cohen, eds. *Changing Numbers, Changing Needs: American Indian Demography and Public Health*. Washington, D.C.: National Academy Press, 1996.

Trafzer, Clifford E., and Diane Weiner. *Medicine Ways:*

Disease, Health, and Survival Among Native Americans. Walnut Creek, Calif.: AltaMira Press, 2001.

Vernon, Irene S. *Killing Us Quietly: Native Americans and HIV/AIDS.* Lincoln: University of Nebraska Press, 2001.

Young, T. Kue, ed. *The Health of Native Americans: Toward a Biocultural Epidemiology.* New York: Oxford University Press, 1994.

Heap of Birds, Edgar (Hachivi) (1954–)
Cheyenne-Arapaho artist, teacher

Also known as Hachivi, Edgar Heap of Birds was born on November 22, 1954, in Wichita, Kansas, the son of Charles and Margaret Heap of Birds. Educated at East High School in Wichita, he graduated in 1972 and attended the Haskell Institute in Lawrence, Kansas. In 1974, he transferred to the University of Kansas, where he received his B.F.A. in 1976. Heap of Birds then studied at the Royal College of Art in London for one year, returning to the United States to attend Temple University, where he received his M.F.A. in 1979.

After graduation, Heap of Birds moved to the Arapaho reservation in Oklahoma, where the rugged canyon landscape became an important influence on his paintings. He used his work to explore what it means to be a Native American artist. Although he began as a painter, he largely abandoned "pictures" in favor of incorporating Native American and English words into his work. Labeled a deconstructionist, Heap of Birds focused on how these words could be influential and intimidating.

A popular artist, Heap of Birds's works have been exhibited extensively, often out of doors as installation pieces and most prominently in museums such as the Museum of Modern Art in New York City and the Denver Art Museum. Since 1989, Heap of Birds has been an associate professor of art at the University of Oklahoma in Norman, Oklahoma.

He married Shanna Ketchum, a Navajo (Dineh) critic and art historian, in a traditional Navajo ceremony at Kayenta on the Navajo reservation in Arizona on June 3, 2006.

Further Reading
Murg, Wilhelm. "Painted Words: Interview with Artist Edgar Heap of Birds." *Native American Times* (Tulsa, Oklahoma), 1 January 2002, 2B.

Henderson, James Youngblood (Sákéj) (1944–)
Chickasaw-Cheyenne legal scholar, attorney

James Youngblood Henderson, a Chickasaw-Cheyenne, member of the Bear Clan of the Chickasaw, was born on his family's allotment in Oklahoma on December 20, 1944, the son of James Young Henderson and Edna Corrine Henderson. He received a B.A. from the University of Oklahoma in 1967 and a J.D. from Harvard University in 1974.

At Harvard, Henderson met RUSSEL LAWRENCE BARSH, who was also working on a law degree. After completing law school in 1974, they jointly wrote *The Road: Indian Tribes and Political Liberty.* Published by the University of California Press in 1978, it is an important study of the historical development of Native American sovereignty as an American constitutional doctrine. Elsewhere, Henderson has stated: "Very few American Indians get their cases published in works of legal materials. However, their plight is directly related to the fundamental concept of political liberty and constitutional liberty. That is the course I am following."

Around the same time, Henderson met Marie Battiste, a Micmac (Mi'kmaq) then studying in Harvard's Indian Education Program. Born in Eskasoni, Cape Breton, Nova Scotia, and raised in Maine, she had graduated from the University of Maine before coming to Harvard. A few years later, she and Henderson both moved to California. In 1978, they were both employed at the University of California at Berkeley. She then enrolled at Stanford University, receiving a doctorate in education in 1984. (Since 1999, she has been professor in the Department of Educational Foundations, University of Saskatchewan.)

A short time later, they married and moved to Marie's home village of Eskasoni, where she was hired to run an elementary school teaching in the Mikmaw (Micmac) language, and Henderson became a legal adviser to Alex Denny, grand captain of the Mi'kmaq Grand Council; he was given the Mikmaw name Sákej. Working with the council, Henderson's attention was drawn to the history and present position of indigenous peoples under international law, and he became a member of the United Nations (UN) Working Group on Indigenous Populations (WGIP).

The WGIP met for the first time in Geneva in 1982 to review developments concerning the promotion and protection of human rights and fundamental freedoms of the world's indigenous peoples and to develop new standards for indigenous rights. With the WGIP, Henderson took part in the creation of the Indigenous and Tribal Peoples Convention in 1989; the writing of a special chapter for indigenous peoples programs in Agenda 21, adopted by the UN Conference on the Environment in 1992; the drafting of a declaration by the UN General Assembly of the International Year of the World's Indigenous Peoples in 1993; and the declaration of an International Decade of the World's Indigenous Peoples, 1995–2004, one of the main objects of which was to "educat[e] indigenous and non-indigenous societies concerning the situation, cultures, and languages, rights and aspirations of the indigenous people." He also worked for the inclusion of traditional ecological knowledge of indigenous peoples in the 1992 UN Convention on Biological Diversity, contributing to a special UN study done between 1993 and 1996 on how to protect the heritage and treaties of the indigenous peoples, as well as on land and natural resource issues.

Henderson also participated in the WGIP's most complex project, the creation of a Draft Declaration on Indigenous Rights to serve as an interpretive tool for applying the UN human rights covenants to the indigenous peoples of the world. It took 12 years for the participants to reach a consensus on the text, which sets forth minimum standards of human rights for indigenous peoples in 45 articles. Their work finally culminated in the adoption of the United Nations Declaration on the Rights of Indigenous Peoples on September 13, 2007. His book *Indigenous Diplomacy and the Rights of People Achieving UN Recognition* (2010) documents this struggle.

In addition to *The Road*, Henderson's most important publications include *First Nations' Legal Inheritance* (1991), *Indian Land Claims Policy in the United States* (1992), and *The Mikmaw Concordat* (1997). He was a coeditor of *Continuing Poundmaker and Riel's Quest: Presentations Made at a Conference on Aboriginal Peoples and Justice* (1994). With Marjorie L. Benson and Isobel M. Finlay, he published *Aboriginal Tenure in the Constitution of Canada* (2000), and with Marie Battiste, *Protecting Indigenous Knowledge and Heritage* (2000). At present, Henderson teaches at the University of Saskatchewan, Canada. He won a National Aboriginal Achievement Award in 2006.

See also SOVEREIGNTY, INDIGENOUS AND TRIBAL.

Further Reading
Frideres, James S. Review of *Aboriginal Tenure in the Constitution of Canada*. *Canadian Ethnic Studies Journal* 32, no. 2 (2000): 140.
Henderson, James (Sákej) Youngblood. "Proving a Constitutional Right to the Land for Aboriginal Peoples of Canada." Available online. URL: http://www.deigamuukw.org/research/proof.pdf. Accessed on 15 February 2003.
Valpy, Michael. "Aboriginal Academics Breathing New Life into Canada's Ivory Tower." *Toronto Globe and Mail*, 1 June 2007.

Herrington, John Bennett   *See* POGUE, WILLIAM REID.

Hewitt, John Napoleon Brinton (1859–1937)
Tuscarora ethnologist, linguist
Born in Lewiston, New York, on December 16, 1859, John Napoleon Brinton Hewitt was the eldest of five children. His mother, Harriet Brinton Hewitt, was of French, English, and Tuscarora descent; his father, Dr. David Brainard Hewitt, was a Scottish physician adopted by the Tuscarora. Hewitt was educated in the public schools of Niagara County and in 1865 entered the Wilson Academy in Wilson, New York. He then attended the Lockport Union Academy in Lockport, New York, but poor health forced him to give up his studies and return to the reservation. Between 1876 and 1879, he worked as a farmer and newspaper correspondent and conducted a private night school for young men at Lewiston. Later, he lived at Suspension Bridge, New York, and in Jersey City, New Jersey.

Hewitt had intended to follow in his father's footsteps and study medicine, but in 1880 he was engaged by ethnologist Erminie A. Smith to help record Iroquois materials (1880–84). After her death in 1886, the Bureau of American Ethnology (BAE) in Washington, D.C.—which had been founded only

seven years earlier by Major J. W. Powell—asked Hewitt to continue her work. He did so for the next 51 years.

Hewitt was soon internationally recognized as the leading authority on all aspects of Iroquois lore. He had a deep knowledge of the six Iroquois languages, spoke Mohawk and Onondaga fluently, and made extensive studies of many other indigenous languages, including Ojibway, Creek, Delaware (Lenni Lenape), Maya, Seri, Waicure, and the Polynesian languages. In a paper of 1887, Hewitt was the first to demonstrate conclusively that Cherokee is an Iroquoian language.

While extremely knowledgeable about the history of all the eastern Indians, Hewitt, from the closing years of the 19th century until the end of his life, focused most of his attention on the Iroquoian languages and cultures. Due to his extremely detailed approach, only a small part of his work ever appeared in print. From 1894, Hewitt was in charge of the BAE manuscript collections and became official custodian in 1903. From 1907 to 1910, he contributed more than 100 articles to the *Handbook of the American Indians North of Mexico*. He was a member of the Museum of Natural History in New York and a founder of the American Anthropological Society and the Anthropological Society of Washington, of which he was treasurer from 1912 to 1926 and vice president and president from 1932 to 1934. He also served on the executive committee of the U.S. Board of Geographic Names, representing the Smithsonian Institution. Deeply religious, he was a Unitarian and a Mason.

Although in failing health during the last two years of his life, Hewitt continued working up to the day of his death. He died of a bronchial attack on October 14, 1937, in Washington, D.C.

Further Reading
Moses, L. G., and Raymond Moses, eds. *Indian Lives: Essays on Nineteenth- and Twentieth-Century Native American Leaders*. Albuquerque: University of New Mexico Press, 1985.
Swan, Brian, ed. *Voices from Four Directions: Contemporary Translations of the Native Literatures of North America from Western Folklore*. Lincoln: University of Nebraska Press, 2004.
Tooker, Elizabeth, and Barbara Graymont. "J. N. B. Hewitt." In *Histories of Anthropology Annual*, edited by Regina Darnell and Frederic W. Gleach, 70–98. Lincoln: University of Nebraska Press, 2007.

higher education

At the opening of the 20th century, only a miniscule number of Indians had received a university education. Indian college graduates such as JOHN MILTON OSKISON, HOWARD EDWARDS GANSWORTH, HENRY CLARENCE ROE CLOUD, CARLOS MONTEZUMA, SHERMAN COOLIDGE, LAURA MIRIAM CORNELIUS KELLOGG, and CHARLES EDWIN DAGENETT formed a tiny elite; and even within this elite, views on the importance of higher education differed. Some, like Coolidge and Montezuma (both raised by white foster parents), were total assimilationists (see ASSIMILATION); others, like Arthur C. Parker (who had attended but not graduated from Dickinson Seminary), believed in a brilliant future for Indians if only their leaders would get a higher education; Kellogg urged educated Indians to help rebuild and protect their traditional cultures.

As early as 1911, August Breuninger (Menominee) advocated an Indian university with Indian cultural emphasis. Another advocate was Parker, but in the meantime he saw a "white man's education" as essential to survival and independence. "Not every Indian ought to go to college," he wrote in 1913, "any more than every white . . . but there should be as many Indian college men in proportion to the number of Indians as there are white college graduates in proportion to the number of white Americans." Although arch-assimilationist RICHARD HENRY PRATT helped a small number of highly capable Carlisle Indian School graduates (such as Howard Gansworth) get into universities, he opposed the idea of an Indian university because it went against his goal of completely assimilating Indians into mainstream American culture.

Even the best federal Indian schools had only eight grades. The first, Carlisle Indian School in Pennsylvania, was founded in 1879, and by 1900 there were 26 of these schools. However, they provided vocational training, not college preparation, and only a handful of students went on to college. Some Indians went to state colleges and universities, but their numbers were small, and few of them returned to their communities.

Reverend Walter C. Roe had dreamed of founding an Indian high school to develop Christian Indian leadership. In 1915, his protégé Henry Roe Cloud founded the Roe Indian Institute (later American Indian Institute) a college preparatory high school for Indian boys, in Wichita, Kansas. Cloud's article "Education of the American Indian" in the July–September 1914 issue of *American Indian Magazine* is one of the best discussions from that period.

The Creek Nation had granted land for a postsecondary Baptist institution, Bacone College in Muskogee, Oklahoma, as early as 1880. In the 1920s, its ambitious expansion plan was thwarted by the federal court's refusal to allow an endowment from wealthy Creek JACKSON BARNETT.

In 1928, students of Haskell Institute, in Lawrence, Kansas, wanted to turn the school into a junior college. While this was not done, a junior college program was set up that year, graduating its first class of 28 in June 1929. It was abolished in 1932 because the BUREAU OF INDIAN AFFAIRS (BIA), still influenced by the Pratt philosophy, believed it impeded assimilation. In the 1940s, ARCHIE PHINNEY urged the BIA to set up an "Indian Service College" to provide an intellectual basis for the administration of Indian affairs. It would offer such courses as colonial administration, ethnography, Indian Service administration, race relations, and comparative educational systems, and while intended primarily for American Indians and would also be open to interested non-Indian students from the United States and abroad. The guiding principle would be "ethnic democracy." (Although the college never materialized, Phinney's idea of "ethnic democracy"

was embodied in the NATIONAL CONGRESS OF AMERICAN INDIANS, founded in 1944.)

As late as 1932, there were only 385 American Indian and Alaska Natives in college and only 52 known college graduates. Scholarships for Indians were offered at five institutions of higher learning. In that year, the BIA instituted a program to provide loans for higher education and training (see BRONSON, RUTH MUSKRAT). Under the INDIAN REORGANIZATION ACT (1934), $250,000 was set aside for college loans, a program that continued until 1952. In 1934–35, there were still only 515 American Indian college students, 181 of whom were receiving federal or tribal assistance.

In 1940, the Cherokee Indian Normal School located in Robeson County, North Carolina, began to confer four-year college degrees, and in 1941 the name of the school was changed to Pembroke State College for Indians. The school had been originally founded in 1887 as the Croatan Normal School to train Native, mostly Lumbee, public school teachers. The scope of the college was widened in 1942, when non-teaching baccalaureate degrees were added, and in 1945, when enrollment, previously limited to the Indians of Robeson County, was opened to people from all federally recognized Indian tribes. Up until 1953, Pembroke was the only state-supported four-year college for Indians in the nation. In 1953, the school, succumbing to the desegregation pressures of the time, approved the admission of white students up to 40 percent of the total enrollment. The next year, following the Supreme Court's decision on desegregation, *Brown v. Board of Education of Topeka*, Pembroke became open to all qualified applicants, regardless of background.

After WORLD WAR II, Indian veterans went to college under the GI Bill. The BIA instituted a new higher education scholarship grant program in 1948. Under TERMINATION, Indians could not aim for Indian-controlled education. The goal was simply survival. However, this increased effort to survive paid off: Of all items on the Indian agenda in the second half of the century, education would make the most substantial gains. Eventually, true Indian control and content would be achieved. In the mid-1950s, Indian college enrollment increased, but observers were disturbed to find the dropout rate high and apparently unrelated to academic ability. By 1955, there were about 2,000 American Indians in postsecondary education, but the ratio of degree graduates was small. Only 66 Indian students graduated from four-year institutions in 1961.

In 1955, Ruth Bronson and representatives of support organizations suggested a summer workshop to investigate the problem, and plans were drawn up under the direction of SOL TAX. Students attended these Workshops on American Indian Affairs from 1956 through 1963 (see THOMAS, ROBERT KNOX). The workshops found that most Indian students suffered from confused identity and loss of cultural moorings. In March 1957, the Fund for the Republic formed a commission to appraise the status of Indians; its summary report on education (written by WILLIAM ALOYSIUS BROPHY and Sophie D. Aberle and published in 1961) condemned previous policies and recommended enlisting "the support of the Indian community, its neighbors, and tribal and local government officials."

In 1961, JACK D. FORBES (Lenni Lenape–Powhatan) wrote an article entitled "Proposal to Create an Indian University," stating that it should be "Indian-centered and Indian controlled." (His efforts culminated in the founding of D-Q University at Davis, California, in 1971.) By 1965, postsecondary enrollment had increased to 7,000 nationwide, but the number of graduates from four-year institutions had not: In 1968, there were only 181. Enrollment continued to grow rapidly: By 1970, there were approximately 15,000 Indian college students. Several thousand received degrees in the 1960s, but in their final Fund for the Republic report of 1966, Brophy and Aberle still reported a dropout rate of 60 percent.

In the mid-1960s, the United Scholarship Service was the only national Indian organization involved in Indian higher education. In May 1965, the Economic Opportunity Act made major non-BIA funding available to Indians for the first time. Educational opportunities came especially through the Head Start Program. The dropout rate, however, remained high.

The Higher Education Act (1965) set aside Title III (a federal grant program) funds for Indian colleges. In July 1968, Navajo Community College became the first college founded and controlled by an Indian tribe. In 1969, the report on hearings of the Special Subcommittee on Indian Education (of the Senate Committee on Labor and Public Welfare) suggested improvements in the BIA's granting of scholarships and called for programs in Native American studies, more Indian community colleges, and "special recruiting and orienting programs." It also urged that higher education programs for Indians be included in Title III (Developing Institutions) of the Higher Education Act (1965), which would take some power away from the BIA. Funds from the Vocational Education Act (1963) and Higher Education Act were to be used to support BIA programs.

Thus, at the height of Termination, all advisory studies recommended strengthening community control of Indian education. Public concern increased, and programs were introduced. Of course, the 1960s and 1970s saw increasingly vocal discontent and resistance by Indians themselves.

The National Indian Education Association was founded in 1969. Termination ended in 1970. In fall 1972, Native American studies programs in a number of universities attempted to form a national organization to represent them and to get Title III funding. Seeing a threat, Indian colleges, supported by the National Indian Education Association, moved to found the American Indian Higher Education Consortium (AIHEC), officially established in January 1973 to (1) help Indian-controlled junior colleges get accreditation, possibly becoming an accrediting body itself; (2) help find general funds; (3) help develop curriculum; and (4) coordinate communication and contacts among the colleges.

By the early 1970s, there were more than 10 tribally controlled community colleges and D-Q University, Indian but not under tribal control. (In 2005, D-Q University lost its accreditation and soon closed.) Partly as a result of pressure from AIHEC, the Tribally Controlled Community College

Assistance Act was passed in 1978, authorizing funding for all Indian community colleges either chartered or sanctioned by tribal governments. Colleges sanctioned by a tribal government are not under its control—the only leverage being the threat to withdraw the sanction. As of 1997, AIHEC had 29 member institutions.

Aside from state colleges and universities in states with high Indian populations, several other postsecondary institutions have predominantly Native American student bodies, the most important of which are Sheldon Jackson College (Alaska), Fort Lewis College (Colorado), and NAES College (Chicago, Twin Cities, Fort Peck, Menominee).

Sheldon Jackson College, the oldest school in Alaska, was founded in 1878 as a grade school for Tlingit Indians. Upgraded first to a high school, then to a two-year college, it has been a fully accredited four-year college since 1984. Formerly Presbyterian, it has not been directly affiliated with the church since 1972. Serving Alaska Natives is an explicit element of the school's mission. About 30 percent of its students are Alaska Natives.

Fort Lewis College (FLC) in Colorado was converted from a military post to a boarding school for Indians in 1891. In 1911, Congress deeded the school to the state of Colorado, and it became an agricultural high school open to all students, with the charter proviso that any American Indians who met admission standards would continue to receive free tuition. Since 1933, FLC has offered college courses exclusively. In 1948, it became a junior college, and in 1956 the campus moved from Hesperus to Durango. FLC began to offer four-year liberal arts degree programs in 1962, graduating its first baccalaureate class in 1964. From 1986 to 2000, it was part of the Colorado State University system. In 1997, about 12 percent of the 4,400 students were Native American.

NAES College opened in 1975 as Native American Educational Services, originally affiliated with Antioch College. It descends directly from the summer Workshops on Indian Affairs. SOL TAX and ROBERT K. THOMAS were active on its board of directors. Robert V. Duncan, one of its founders and a participant in the 1960 workshop, stated: "We have modelled NAES on this notion—the functional role of tribal knowledge and learning for the student and the community." Accredited since 1984 to grant a B.A. in community studies, NAES has branch campuses at Ft. Peck, Montana (1978), Northern Cheyenne (1980), Minneapolis-St. Paul, Minnesota (1988), and Menominee, Wisconsin (1989). NAES Chicago lost its accreditation in 2005 and closed in 2007.

See also EDUCATIONAL POLICY, AMERICAN INDIANS AND.

Further Reading

Beck, David R. M. "American Indian Higher Education Before 1974: From Colonization to Self-Determination." *Australian Journal of Indigenous Education* 27, no. 2 (1999): 12–23.

Churchill, Ward, and Norbert S., Hill, Jr. "A Historical Survey of Tendencies in Indian Education: Higher Education." *Indian Historian* 12, no. 1 (Winter 1979): 37–46.

Stein, Wayne J. *The Renaissance of American Indian Higher Education: Capturing the Dream.* Philadelphia: Lawrence Erlbaum Associates, 2003.

Talahonga, Patty. "From the Past, into the Future." *Tribal College Journal of American Indian Education* (August 2009).

Wollock, Jeffrey. "Protagonism Emergent: Indians and Higher Education." *Native Americas* 14, no. 4 (Winter 1997/98): 12–23.

Hightower, Rosella (1920–2008) *Choctaw ballerina*

Rosella Hightower, the only child of Charles Edgar and Eula May Flanning Hightower, was born in Durwood, Oklahoma, on January 20, 1920. She came to ballet comparatively late: It was after seeing the Ballet Russe in Kansas in 1933—when both Leonide Massine and George Balanchine were resident choreographers—that she decided to become a dancer. She studied in New York with Mikhail Fokine before joining the Ballet Russe de Monte Carlo, and by 1946 she was working with Massine, Balanchine, and German (Gerry) Sevastianov.

In 1947, Hightower joined the Grand Ballet de Marquis de Cuevas, at the time the only professional American ballet company based in Europe. She worked there through the 1950s as leading ballerina and artistic consultant. When the company was dissolved following the benefactor's death in 1962, Hightower set out to create a dance school in Cannes, France, based on the multidisciplinary training of the traditional conservatories of Europe and Russia. From its inception, the Centre de Danse Internationale attracted dancers of the first rank, including Rudolph Nureyev, who had recently defected from the Soviet Union. Nureyev became one of a quartet with Hightower, Erik Bruhn, and Sonia Arova, and they performed a series of galas during 1963.

The school rapidly consolidated its position as an institution of international stature, numbering members of most of the major European ballets among its alumni. In 1980, concurrent with her work at the school, Hightower was made director of the Paris Opera ballet for a three-year term, becoming not only the first American Indian but the first American to occupy this position. She was succeeded by Rudolph Nureyev. In 1986, Hightower was awarded the highest class of the French Légion d'honneur for her services to international ballet, and in 1990 the French awarded her the Grand Prix National de Danse.

In 1991, Hightower established the École Supérieure de Danse de Cannes; she served as its artistic director until 2001. During this period, she also directed ballets at the Marseille Opera and at La Scala in Milan. She died at her home in Cannes on November 4, 2008.

Further Reading

Livingston, Lili Cockerille. *American Indian Ballerinas.* Norman: University of Oklahoma Press, 1997.

Hill, Charlie (1951–2013) *Oneida-Cree comedian*

Born on July 6, 1951, in Warren, Michigan, Charlie Hill was the grandson of physician LILLIE ROSA MINOKA-HILL and the brother of educator NORBERT S. HILL, JR. His father, Norbert Hill, Sr., was an Oneida, and his mother, Eileen Johnson Hill, was a Canadian Cree.

Even as a child, Hill wanted to become a comedian. He traveled to New York City to pursue acting as a prerequisite to his goal. In New York, Hill worked in experimental theater at La Mama and met young comedians Jay Leno, Richard Belzer, and Elayne Boozler, who helped him with his career. He then moved to Los Angeles, where he continued to pursue acting as well as comedy, though he turned down many movie roles that he found demeaning or stereotyped. Hill honed his talents at the Comedy Shop, a club in Los Angeles. He was the lead actor in the cult classic Indian movie *Harold of Orange* (1989), written by GERALD ROBERT VIZENOR.

Hill was a staff writer for the *Roseanne* show and other TV shows. In 1998, he founded Club Red, a comedy show featured on National Public Radio stations. *On and Off the Res with Charlie Hill*, a 70-minute video documentary about his life as a comedian, directed by Sandi Osawa (Makah), with music by FLOYD RED CROW WESTERMAN, was released in 2000 to great acclaim. As a comedian, Hill has appeared on both the *Tonight Show* and *The Late Show with David Letterman* and in comedy clubs across the country. Hill called himself an "activist disguised as a comedian" and he lived with his wife, a Navajo, and their four children in the BIG MOUNTAIN region of the Navajo Reservation, where Hill long championed the cause of Navajo facing relocation. Charlie Hill died on December 30, 2013, in Oneida, Wisconsin, of lymphoma.

Further Reading

Koch, John. "Comic Stands Up for Native Americans." *Boston Globe*, 21 November 1990.

Hill, David Russell (1874–1950) *Onondaga leader, musician*

David Russell Hill was born on the Onondaga Reservation in central New York State in 1874 (the year 1878 is sometimes given). After graduating from Hampton Institute in Virginia in 1895, Hill taught at federal Indian schools—two years at the Teller Institute in Colorado, one year at Fort Lewis, also in Colorado, and eight years at Mt. Pleasant, Michigan. While teaching in Indian schools, he also became an accomplished bandmaster, taking his school's orchestras to concerts throughout the Midwest. In 1905, he was appointed by the Department of the Interior to distribute $100,000 to Indians of the Onondaga reservation.

In 1906, Hill was appointed conductor of the Onondaga Indian Concert Band, founded in 1840, the oldest all-Indian band in the United States at the time. The band played to capacity crowds throughout New York, including a two-week engagement at Madison Square Garden in New York City in 1909. In summer 1910, the band did a 12-week tour of France, Germany, and Italy. In 1910, Hill organized the American Indian Concert Band, which over the next two years played under his direction in 38 cities in the United States and 36 cities in Belgium, France, Germany, Austria, and Poland. The band won several gold medals in American tournaments.

After serving in the U.S. Army in WORLD WAR I, Hill was appointed by New York's governor, Alfred E. Smith, to represent the Six Nations Iroquois in New York State on the Everett Commission to confer with congressional committees on Indian affairs. Like progressive ARTHUR C. PARKER, the other Indian member of the commission, Hill supported citizenship for the Iroquois and state jurisdiction over tribal lands, which put him at odds with the Iroquois Grand Council, headed by GEORGE A. THOMAS. Hill criticized commission chair Edward Everett, who had come to sympathize with Grand Council aims, and he later refused to sign the Everett report, which reaffirmed Iroquois claims to 6 million acres of land in New York State (see KELLOGG, LAURA MIRIAM CORNELIUS).

Hill served as vice president of the Iroquois Indian National Convention, which represented the progressive element in furthering educational projects for Indian children. At various times, he served as clerk for the Onondaga council of chiefs or acted as interpreter for Indians in federal and state courts. When Allied Chemical proposed running a pipeline through the Onondaga reservation, Hill promoted the idea, which eventually brought each resident an annuity of $400. He died of a heart attack on October 14, 1950, in a restaurant in Syracuse, New York. (See also WHEELOCK, DENNISON).

Hill, Norbert S., Jr. (Onan-quat-go, Big Medicine)

(1946–) *Oneida-Cree guidance counselor, educator*
Norbert S. Hill, Jr., was born on November 26, 1946, in the Detroit suburb of Warren, Michigan. His father, Norbert S. Hill, Sr., was a son of Oneida physician LILLIE ROSA MINOKA-HILL; his mother, Eileen Johnson Hill, was a Cree from Canada. Hill's father started the North American Indian Club, a support network that played an important role in the urban environment in which Hill grew up. He first experienced reservation life at age 16, when he moved with his family to the Oneida reservation in Wisconsin and attended high school there.

Hill attended the University of Wisconsin at Oshkosh, where he studied sociology and anthropology, receiving his B.A. and an alumni award in 1969. After earning an M.A. in guidance and counseling at the same campus, he was hired as guidance counselor at the high school in Port Washington, Wisconsin, and later was counselor to American Indian students at the Green Bay campus of the University of Wisconsin, near the Oneida reservation. He served as assistant to the dean of students there for five years.

Hill was chair of the Oneida tribal education committee from 1970 to 1974. In 1977, he went to the University of Colorado at Boulder to direct the American Indian Education Opportunity Program there and to begin working toward a Ph.D. From 1983 to 1998, Hill was executive director of the AMERICAN INDIAN SCIENCE AND ENGINEERING SOCIETY (AISES). He founded the society's magazine, *Winds of Change,*

in 1986. He was also chair of the board of the Smithsonian National Museum of the American Indian. Since 2000, he has been executive director of the American Indian Graduate Center in Albuquerque, New Mexico. In 1999, he wrote *Words of Power*, published by Fulcrum Press.

CHARLIE HILL, the well-known comedian, was Norbert Hill's brother. Another brother, Richard Hill, a former Oneida tribal chair, later served as chair of the National Indian Gaming Commission. Roberta Hill, his first cousin, is a well-known poet.

Hogan, Linda (1947–) *Chickasaw poet, novelist, social commentator*

Linda Henderson was born on July 16, 1947, in Denver, Colorado. Her father, Charles Henderson, was a Chickasaw, and her mother, Cleo Bower Henderson, was of German descent. Her father was in the army, so her youth was spent moving from post to post. While in her early 20s, Hogan moved to California, where she became a nurse's aide and began writing poetry. Around this time, she married Pat Hogan, whom she later divorced. She received her master's degree in creative writing from the University of Colorado at Boulder in 1978, and the next year she released her first book of poems, *Calling Myself Home*. In 1981, she released a collection of poems *Daughters, I Love You*—an indictment of nuclear proliferation—and a three-act play, *A Piece of the Moon*. The next year, she became an associate professor of American studies at the University of Minnesota.

Hogan deftly combines her activist leanings with her poetry, championing the natural world and tribal life and traditions. Like the Laguna Pueblo poet LESLIE MARMON SILKO, Hogan's vision of the nuclear threat has transformed her vision of nature, in which the relationship between humans and their environment is complex and precarious. Hogan believes that women, as the givers of new life, should combine spirituality with political commitment, and her work, in the words of Laguna-Sioux poet PAULA GUNN ALLEN, "resolves the conflict that presently divides the non-Indian feminist community."

In 1983, Hogan published her third book of poems, *Eclipse*, and in 1985 her fourth collection, *Seeing through the Sun*, won an American Book Award from the Before Columbus Foundation. In 1984, she began teaching at the University of Colorado at Boulder and joined the board of directors of the Denver Indian Center. Hogan began publishing short stories in 1985 with the release of *The Horse*, following that up with *The Big Woman* in 1987. After publishing *Savings*, a collection of poems, in 1988, Hogan released her first novel, *Mean Spirit*, in 1990. *Mean Spirit*, a mystery story set in Oklahoma, documents the theft of Indian land during the oil boom of the 1920s (see OSAGE REIGN OF TERROR). It was nominated for a Pulitzer Prize in 1991. Hogan subsequently released two volumes of poetry, *Red Clay: Poems and Stories* (1991) and *The Book of Medicines* (1993).

Hogan's second novel, *Solar Storms*, was published in 1994. In 1995, she released two collections of essays, *From Women's*

Experience to Feminist Theology and *Dwellings: A Spiritual History of the Natural World*. In 1998, she published her third novel, *Power;* in 2001, a memoir, *Woman Who Watches over the World;* and in 2010, *Walk Gently Upon the Earth*. A writer of enormous scope, Hogan has made important contributions to the development of contemporary Native American writing through her literary criticism, which, along with her poetry and fiction, have helped to make her one of the most prominent figures in modern Native American literature.

Further Reading

Beadling, Laura L. "The Aesthetics of Translating Cultural Trauma: Traumatized Communities in Twentieth-Century Fiction and Film." Ph.D. dissertation, Purdue University, 2007, 80–131. "Imagining the Conquest Undone: Trauma, Time and Politics in Linda Hogan's *Solar Storms.*"

Hogan, Linda. "First People." In *Intimate Nature: The Bond Between Women and Animals*, edited by Linda Hogan, Deena Metzger, and Brenda Peterson, 6–19. New York: Ballantine Books, 1998.

———. "An Ethical Regard for the Land." In Lee Schweninger. *Listening to the Land: Native American Literary Responses to the Landscape*, 1–15. Athens: University of Georgia Press, 2004.

Jensen, Derrick. *Listening to the Land: Conversations about Nature, Culture, and Eros*, 122–130. White River Junction, Vt.: Chelsea Green Publishing, 2004.

Schweninger, Lee. "'Changed by the Wild': Linda Hogan's Spirit of Renewal." In Lee Schweninger. *Listening to the Land: Native American Literary Responses to the Landscape*, 184–201. Athens: University of Georgia Press, 2004.

Hokeah, Jack   *See* Kiowa Five.

Honganozhe   *See* Ballard, Louis Wayne.

Hoover Commission (1947–1949)

In a fall 1948 editorial, the Association on American Indian Affairs noted that "Indian policy and administration need objective review and reform today." The authors hoped that a long-awaited report by a commission chaired by former president Herbert Hoover would be in "the tradition of the Meriam Report . . . [,] a landmark [that could] help to build a tradition of nonpartisanship in Indian Affairs." However, it proved to be not at all like the Meriam Report. Instead, it was one of the earliest official manifestations of the postwar policy of Termination, which would dominate especially during the presidencies of Harry S. Truman and Dwight D. Eisenhower and would not be officially rescinded until 1971.

The Hoover Commission, officially the Commission on Organization of the Executive Branch of the Government, was established in 1947 with the goal of extensively reorganizing the federal government and cutting federal spending. The commission issued policy recommendations in March 1949; the report of its special task force on Indian affairs was under the chairmanship of George A. Graham, a professor of political science at Princeton University, who had no previous experience in Indian affairs. The guiding philosophy of the report was that assimilation was inevitable and therefore "must be the dominant goal of public policy." Indians comprised less than 3/10 of 1 percent of the population of the United States, and traditional tribal organization no longer existed. The report noted: "The only remaining questions are: What kind of assimilation, and how fast?"

The report described tribal governments as temporary training grounds for the transformation of Indians from federal wards to fully integrated, taxpaying citizens. In the meantime, Indian social programs should be taken over by the states and the role of the Bureau of Indian Affairs (BIA) be diminished. Much stress was laid on the need for relocation to urban areas.

The Indian task force was endorsed by the Hoover Commission as "the keystone" of federal Indian policy. Three members of the commission—Dean Acheson (vice chair), James Forrestal, and James H. Rowe, Jr.—voiced strong dissent, on the grounds that neither the commission nor the task force had the competence or authority to make substantive policy recommendations. However, this dissent was left out of the general report of the Hoover Commission, which was distributed to the public nationwide.

Although self-categorized as "practical" and "moderate," the Hoover Commission report signaled a full-scale reversal of the Indian policy of John Collier, Nathan Margold, and Felix Solomon Cohen, which was based on inherent tribal sovereignty and the binding nature of treaties, and which accepted tribal governments and reservations as potentially permanent parts of the American fabric (see sovereignty, indigenous and tribal).

Just as the report was issued, John Ralph Nichols, who had been a member of the Hoover Commission Indian Task Force, took over as BIA commissioner from William Aloysius Brophy. Nichols served only 11 months and was succeeded by arch-terminationist Dillon Seymour Myer.

Further Reading

Fixico, Donald R. *Termination and Relocation: Federal Indian Policies, 1945–1960*. Albuquerque: University of New Mexico Press, 1986.

Koppes, Clayton R. "From New Deal to Termination: Liberalism and Indian Policy, 1933–1953." *Pacific Historical Review* 46, no. 4 (November 1977): 543–566.

McCoy, Donald R., and Richard T. Ruette. *Quest and Response: Minority Rights and the Truman Administration*. Lawrence: University Press of Kansas, 1973.

Nash, Bradley De Lamater, and Cornelius Lynde. *A Hook in Leviathan: A Critical Interpretation of the Hoover Commission Report*. New York: Macmillan, 1950.

Philp, Kenneth R. *Termination Revisited: American Indians*

on the Trail to Self-Determination, 1933–1953. Lincoln: University of Nebraska Press, 1999.

Horn, Michael Hastings (1942–   ) *Cherokee marine biologist, conservationist, educator*

A Cherokee, Michael Hastings Horn was born in Tahlequah, Oklahoma, on November 14, 1942. His parents, Tom and Mary Garrison Horn, were teachers. A high school biology teacher in Stillwell, Oklahoma, first interested him in becoming a scientist. He went on to earn a B.S. in biology from Northeastern State University in Oklahoma in 1963, an M.S. in zoology from the University of Oklahoma, and a doctorate in biology from Harvard University in 1969. Since 1970, Horn has taught biology at California State University at Fullerton. He has received several teaching awards, among the most important of which have been the Outstanding Professor Award (1980) and the Lynne K. McVeigh Award for Exceptional Service to Students (1990).

Horn's special expertise lies in the relationship between fish and algae in temperate oceans. He is a member of the Society for Conservation Biology, and in both his teaching and his research, he is centrally interested in problems of conservation. He has conducted research in ichthyology at the Woods Hole Oceanographic Institution in Massachusetts; studied natural history at the British Museum in London; and in 1986 traveled to Oban, Scotland, to carry out a program of research at the Dunstaffnage Marine Research Laboratory, on a grant from the National Geographic Society. He serves on the board of governors of the Southern California Academy of Sciences and was book review editor of *Copeia*, the journal of the American Society of Ichthyologists and Herpetologists, from 1985 to 1992. Horn has published numerous papers in scientific journals. His study *The Ecology of Fishes in Upper Newport Bay, California* was published by the California Department of Fish and Game in 1981. With Karen Lynn Martin, he edited *Intertidal Fishes: Life in Two Worlds*, which appeared in 1999; and in 2006 he edited *The Ecology of Marine Fishes: California and Adjacent Waters* published by the University of California.

Houser, Allan (Allan Haozous) (1914–1994) *Apache painter, sculptor*

Allan Houser, a Fort Sill Chiricahua Apache, was born Allan Haozous on June 30, 1914, near Apache, Oklahoma. His father, Sam Haozous (the name Haozous means "the sound of pulling roots" in Apache), was a grandson of the great Apache leader Mangas Coloradas and a nephew of Geronimo. Sam Haozous and his wife, Blossom, lived on an allotment on the former Kiowa, Comanche, and Apache reservation and raised their son in the Chiricahua and Warm Springs Apache traditions. Allan Haozous was later sent to public school in nearby Boone, Oklahoma, before attending the Chilocco Indian School in Oklahoma and the Haskell Indian Institute in Lawrence, Kansas, but he had to cut his studies short to work on the family farm.

In 1934, determined to become an artist, Haozous went to the Santa Fe Indian School, where he studied under the influential DOROTHY DUNN and began to use his pseudonym, Allan Houser. While at Santa Fe, his paintings were exhibited in San Francisco and at the National Exhibition of American Art, held in New York City in 1937, where Houser was the only Indian represented. He left Santa Fe in 1938, his reputation as an artist already established, and the next year his paintings were exhibited at the National Gallery of Art in Washington, D.C.; at the Art Institute of Chicago; and at the World's Fair in New York City. Houser initially worked within the strict confines of the Santa Fe (or Studio) school of painting, but gradually he began to add movement and energy to his compositions—a departure from the flat, immobile style championed by Dunn—drawing instead on painters such as Frederick Remington and Charles Marion Russell for inspiration.

Also in 1938, Houser painted murals in the Department of the Interior building in Washington, D.C., and returned to paint others in 1940 before working with Norwegian muralist Olle Nordmark at the Fort Sill Indian School in Oklahoma. Nordmark taught Houser to work in oil, fresco, egg tempera, and gouache, and the muralist urged him to try sculpture. Houser began carving in wood, though professionally he continued to be a painter, executing murals at a number of Oklahoma and Arizona Indian schools before moving to Los Angeles during WORLD WAR II, where he worked as a pipefitter. At the war's end, he entered the competition to design a memorial sculpture for war veterans for Haskell Institute. Although he had never worked in stone before, Houser carved the masterpiece *Comrade in Mourning* out of a four-ton marble block, using only the few carving tools he had managed to acquire. Completed in 1948, the work set the pattern for Houser's future sculptures—massive pieces with understated, sensitive lines, generally featuring Native American figures in unsentimental, dignified poses.

In 1949, Houser's paintings won the grand prize at the Philbrook Arts Center's Annual Indian Art Competition, which led to a Guggenheim fellowship. The next year, he was commissioned to create four dioramas for the Southern Plains Museum in Anadarko, Oklahoma.

Houser began his teaching career at the Inter-Mountain School in Brigham City, Utah, in 1951. In 1954, he received the Palmes Académiques from the French government, and in 1958 he illustrated *The Cave*, a novel by Elizabeth Coatsworth. In 1961, he left the Inter-Mountain School to become head of the sculpture department at the newly organized Institute of American Indian Art at Santa Fe, where he taught until his retirement in 1975. During this period, Houser created some of his finest sculptures, concentrating on smaller works with rough textures, out of which would rise the smooth forms of Apache women, eagles, or horses. In 1968, he began to work in bronze, and the following year his welded steel sculpture *Buffalo Dancer*, crowned by a headdress made of masonry nails, brought new abstract elements to Houser's now-trademark style.

In 1979, Houser served as artist in residence at Dartmouth

College, and in 1985 his large bronze, *The Offering of the Sacred Pipe*, was dedicated at the U.S. Mission to the United Nations in New York City. His flowing sculptures bridged the gap between traditional Indian art and mainstream art—profoundly influencing a new generation of Indian sculptors—and his works are included in some of the most important collections in the world, including the Metropolitan Museum of Art in New York City, the Dahlem Museum in Berlin, and the British Royal Collection in London. During his later years, Houser continued to expand artistically, experimenting with different stones, including black marble, alabaster, and limestone, and exploring various combinations of realism, surrealism, and abstraction.

The preeminent Native American sculptor of the 20th century, Allan Houser was presented with the National Medal of Art by President George H. W. Bush in 1992. Houser died of cancer on August 22, 1994, in Santa Fe, New Mexico.

Further Reading

Baldit, Catherine. "Twentieth-Century American Indian Artists: An Issue of Identity." *Journal of American Studies of Turkey* 5 (1997): 27–41.
Haozous, Phillip M., executive producer. *Allan Houser Haozous: The Lifetime Work of an American Master*. Video Documentary. Santa Fe, N.Mex.: Phil Lucas Productions, 1998.
Lowe, Truman, ed. *Native American Modernism: The Art of George Morrison and Allan Houser*. Seattle: Smithsonian NMAI and University of Washington Press, 2004.
Perlman, Barbara H. *Allan Houser*. Boston: David R. Godine, 1987.
Rushing, W. Jackson III. *Allan Houser, An American Master (Chiricahua Apache 1914–1994)*. New York: Harry N. Abrams, 2004.

Howe, Oscar (Mazuha Hokshina, "Trader Boy")

(1915–1983) *Yankton Nakota Sioux painter, muralist, educator*
A Yankton Nakota Sioux, Oscar Howe was born on May 13, 1915, in Joe Creek, on the Crow Creek Reservation in South Dakota. His father, George Tikute Howe, and mother, Ella Fearless Bear, gave him the Yanktonai name Mazuha Hokshina (Trader Boy). Young Howe, who was raised speaking the Nakota language, attended the Pierre Indian School, where like many Indian children of the day, he suffered under their strict policy of forced ASSIMILATION. A serious skin condition made him a recluse, and he found comfort in drawing. He eventually transferred to the Santa Fe Indian School, where he began to paint under the influential DOROTHY DUNN.

After graduation from Santa Fe in 1938, Howe returned to Crow Creek and became an art instructor at Pierre. He was commissioned in 1940 to paint murals in the Carnegie Public Library in Mitchell, South Dakota, and in a new civic center in Mobridge, South Dakota. He illustrated two books, *Legends of the Mighty Sioux* (1941) and *The Lost Little Sioux* (1942), and was featured in *Indian Art of the United States*

(1941) by Frederic Douglas and René D'Harnoncourt, before serving in the U.S. Army in WORLD WAR II.

In 1947, Howe's painting *Dakota Duck Hunt* won the prestigious Grand Purchase Prize at the Philbrook Indian Art Annual, leading to his being appointed artist in residence at Dakota Wesleyan University, where he received his B.A. in 1952. The same year, Oscar Jacobson's two-volume *North American Indian Costumes* was published, featuring 50 of Howe's illustrations and bringing him international recognition. After being featured in OLIVER LA FARGE's *Pictorial History of the American Indian* (1956), Howe's reputation as an artist was firmly established, and he went on to illustrate or have his work included in 27 books and more than 100 journals in his lifetime. In 1957, he was appointed to the faculty of the University of South Dakota, and a major exhibition of his art was held in Santa Fe.

The 1954 painting *Victory Dance* had marked a break in Howe's work, which had begun in the "point and line" style of traditional Sioux (Dakota, Lakota, Nakota) art. His art was evolving, and he had begun incorporating abstract geometrical designs in combination with Native American themes. His later work involved a circular composition style, which he termed Tahokmu (spiderweb), or the ultimate combination of line, circle, and triangle. Labeled an "Indian cubist," Howe rejected the notion of European influences, arguing that his art flowed from traditional Native American abstraction.

In 1958, the Philbrook Indian Art Annual rejected his painting *Umine Wacipi* for not being "traditional Indian art," igniting a controversy that would change the way Indian art was perceived and open the door for Native artists to explore less formulaic styles. The art historian Frederick J. Dockstader argues that "no single living Indian artist exerted a greater force to open up Indian easel art and to effect its general acceptance as a free aesthetic than Oscar Howe."

In 1960, South Dakota honored Howe as its artist laureate (one of 28 awards he received during his life), and he was featured on the television show *This Is Your Life*.

A successful as well as an influential artist, he had 47 solo exhibits in cities across the country, and his art is held by numerous public collections, including the Denver Art Museum and the Museum of New Mexico. Plagued by illness in his later years, including Parkinson's disease, which forced him to give up painting, Oscar Howe died on October 7, 1983.

Further Reading

Anthes, B. *Native Moderns: American Indian Painting, 1940–1960*. Durham, N.C.: Duke University Press, 2006.
Milton, John R. *Oscar Howe*. Minneapolis, Minn.: Dillon Press, 1972.

hunting and fishing rights

The right of Indians to hunt and fish on lands they have ceded was a source of conflict throughout the 20th century, as non-Indian development of these lands threatened the natural resources upon which Indian people depended, and as the commercialization of those resources took precedence over Indian prior rights of usage. Moreover, the early 20th-century American policy of ASSIMILATION pressured Indians to abandon hunting and fishing in favor of farming and wage laboring.

During the 18th and 19th centuries, it was understood by all parties to Indian treaties that Indians could maintain certain rights to lands they were ceding, including the important rights of hunting, fishing, and gathering. Many of the 19th-century treaties were very specific about such rights. For example, the 1837 and 1842 treaties between the U.S. government and the Lake Superior Chippewa provided that "The privilege of hunting, fishing, and gathering the wild rice, upon the lands, the rivers, and the lakes included in the territory ceded, is guaranteed to the Indians, during the pleasure of the President of the United States." The Treaty of 1855 with tribes of the Northwest Coast secured for Indians the "right to take fish at all usual and accustomed grounds and stations." Even after 1871, when treaties were no longer made, executive agreements between Indian tribes and the United States still often incorporated the rights of Indians to hunt and fish in their usual and accustomed places.

As fishing and hunting resources began to be depleted by the expanding non-Indian population, states imposed hunting and fishing regulations on Indians, and tribes started to fight these regulations in court. The first challenges arose in the 1930s, when the state of Washington attempted to require Indians who fished off reservation to purchase a license and comply with state fishing laws. Sampson Tulee, a Yakima Indian arrested and convicted for fishing without a license, took the state to court, claiming that his status as an Indian exempted him from state fishing laws. Tulee's appeal went before the U.S. Supreme Court in 1942 as *Tulee v. Washington*, and although the Supreme Court overturned the conviction, the majority opinion held that states did have some rights to regulate Indian fishing if this was done for the purpose of conservation.

In 1940, Thomas L. St. Germaine, a Chippewa lawyer from Lac du Flambeau, argued before the Wisconsin Supreme Court that 19th-century treaties had given the Wisconsin Chippewa the right to hunt and fish unhindered both on and off their reservations. The court, however, ruled that the Chippewa had rights to hunt and fish only on their reservations.

In the late 1950s, Alaska attempted to outlaw the use of salmon fish traps. In this instance, the U.S. Supreme Court, in two separate decisions—*Metlakatla Indian Community v. Egan* (1961) and *Organized Village of Kaka v. Egan* (1962)— again supported the state in its attempt to regulate Indian fishing. In 1962, in *United States v. Dion*, the Court also upheld the federal government's legislative fiat over Indian treaties when it ruled that amendments to the Bald and Golden Eagle Protection Act applied to INDIAN RESERVATIONS.

During the 1950s and 1960s, Indian activists such as DAVID SOHAPPY, BILLY FRANK, JR., JANET MCCLOUD and HANK ADAMS began to mobilize against the increasingly restrictive practices of the states of Washington and Oregon,

which sought to exclude Indians, often through violent harassment, from the valuable fishing stocks in the region. The state of Washington began to sue Indians for violating state fishing regulations, and in 1968 the first of three cases entitled *Puyallup Tribe v. Department of Game* came before the U.S. Supreme Court. The first *Puyallup* case was decided in 1968, with the Court ruling that the state had the right to regulate Indian fishing only for the purposes of conservation and that state regulations could not discriminate against Indians. Because in this instance the state had enacted regulations aimed only at Indians, they were overturned. The case settled little and was returned to the Supreme Court in 1973. In *Puyallup II*, the Court clarified its views toward Indian fishing, ruling that the state's attempts to regulate net fishing, which only Indians used, without attempting to similarly regulate hook-and-line fishing, largely used by non-Indians, was discriminatory. *Puyallup III* was decided in 1977, and the Court extended the state's regulatory powers onto the reservation itself, but only for conservation purposes.

In the meantime, the tribes of the Northwest had won an important victory in 1969 in *United States v. Oregon*, in which the Supreme Court clarified the source of Indian fishing rights. These were not delegated to Indians by the United States, but were inherent, preexisting rights guaranteed by treaties signed by the two parties (see SOVEREIGNTY, INDIGENOUS AND TRIBAL). The Court ordered federal governments, state governments, and Indian governments to cooperatively manage fish resources. In *Kimball v. Callahan* (1974), federal courts ruled that those members of the Klamath tribe who had not agreed to TERMINATION continued to enjoy their treaty rights to hunt and fish on their trust lands (see EMMONS, GLENN LEONIDAS). Also in 1974, attempts by the state of Washington to ban Colville Indians from hunting deer out of season, a right guaranteed by an 1891 agreement between the tribes and the United States, was struck down by the Supreme Court, which argued in *Antoine v. Washington* that an agreement had the same status as a treaty and therefore maintained Indian prior rights to the game.

As the states of Washington and Oregon stepped up their efforts to harass Indian fishermen and drive them out of the fishing industry by the use of discriminatory conservation laws, the stage was set for the landmark decision *United States v. Washington*. Presided over by federal district judge George Boldt in 1974, the case, which has come to be known as the Boldt Decision, finally determined what exactly were the Indians' prior rights to the fish in the Northwest. Boldt ruled that Indian treaties in effect gave Indians the right to one-half of the harvestable off-reservation catch of salmon. He further ruled that the authority to regulate tribal fishing, whether on or off the reservation, was held by the tribes, not the state. The decision raised a storm of protest from the states and the powerful commercial and sport fishing interests that had for so long tried to regulate Indian fishing out of existence. Boldt directed the state of Washington to negotiate a salmon-management plan with the Indian tribes, and when the state refused to do so, Boldt himself took over the state's regulatory authority.

The Supreme Court upheld this view of Indian fishing rights, extending it in 1979 by ruling that the use of modern technology by Indians to catch fish did not impair these rights. That same year, the federal court ruled that the state of Michigan could not regulate Indian hunting and fishing.

Since then, Indians have had to turn back many challenges to the regulation of hunting and fishing on their own reservations. In 1983, the U.S. Supreme Court found, in *New Mexico v. Mescalero Apache Tribe*, that reservation, not state, hunting and fishing regulations apply to non-Indians on Indian reservation. That same year, the court defeated attempts by the state of Wisconsin to regulate Indian hunting and fishing by upholding the bitterly fought case *Lac Court Oreilles Band of Chippewa v. Wisconsin*. Known as the Voigt Decision (after Lester B. Voigt, secretary of the Wisconsin Department of Natural Resources and the defendant in the original suit), the Supreme Court upheld the ruling by the U.S. Court of Appeals for the Seventh Circuit that Wisconsin not only had no rights to regulate fishing on Chippewa reservations, but also that the treaties with the Chippewa guaranteed them the right to use traditional means to hunt and fish off their reservations for subsistence purposes.

Despite the court rulings, Indians continued to suffer harassment while exercising their treaty rights. During the late 1980s and early 1990s, violent protests led by white hate groups, such as Protect Americans' Rights and Resources (PARR) and Stop Treaty Abuse (STA), sought to intimidate Indian spearfishermen in northern Wisconsin, but their efforts failed. Because of the court rulings, Indians are now among the leaders in protecting natural resources such as fish stocks, and organizations such as the Northwest Indian Fisheries Commission and the GREAT LAKES INDIAN FISH AND WILDLIFE COMMISSION have done much to preserve North America's endangered natural bounty. (See also BRESETTE, WALT).

Further Reading

Arey, Bette B. *Chippewa Off-Reservation Treaty Rights: Origins and Issues. Research Bulletin 91-1*. Madison: State of Wisconsin Legislative Reference Bureau, 1991.

Cohen, Fay. *Treaties on Trial: The Continuing Controversy over Northwest Indian Fishing Rights*. Seattle and London: University of Washington Press, 1986.

McDonald, David K. "Native American Fishing/Hunting Rights: An Annotated Bibliography." *Indian History* 11, no. 4 (1978): 57–62.

Montgomery, David R. *King of Fish: The Thousand-Year Run of Salmon*. Boulder, Colo.: Westview Press, 2003.

Nesper, Larry. *The Walleye War: The Struggle for Ojibwe Spearfishing and Treaty Rights*. Lincoln: University of Nebraska Press, 2002.

Ryser, Rudolph. *The Anti-Indian Movement on the Tribal Frontier*. Occasional Paper No. 16. Olympia, Wash.: Center for World Indigenous Studies, 1993.

Wunder, John R., ed. *Recent Legal Issues for American Indians, 1968 to the Present*. New York: Garland Publishing, 1996.

Huron cemetery dispute

The Wyandot, known also by their French name of Huron, were once a powerful confederacy in the Great Lakes region of Canada. Remnants survive today as the Huron Wendat of Wendake, Quebec, Canada; the Wyandot Nation of Kansas; the Wyandot Nation of Anderdon, Michigan; and the Wyandotte Nation of Oklahoma. From the end of the 19th century to the end of the 20th, a parcel of land in downtown Kansas City, Kansas, was the object of a dispute between the Kansas Wyandot and the Oklahoma Wyandotte. Even after the two tribes settled their differences, the issue continued as a dispute over the right of the Oklahoma Wyandotte to open a casino in Kansas City that pitted them against the state of Kansas and the rest of the Indian tribes in the state.

Driven out by the Iroquois in 1649–50, the Wyandot wandered homeless through the territory of Wisconsin, Minnesota, and upper Michigan until they settled in the Ohio Valley in 1701. With the incursion of settlers in Ohio, they ceded these lands in 1842 in return for land west of the Mississippi, including a tract that had belonged to the Delaware (Lenni Lenape) and which today comprises the first through sixth wards of Kansas City, Kansas. By a treaty of February 1, 1855, the Wyandot, who had been well trained in modern agricultural methods by a Methodist Episcopal mission on their former lands in Ohio, opted for ALLOTMENT in severalty (conversion of tribal land to individual ownership), thus legally terminating the tribe and becoming U.S. citizens. However, the same treaty stipulated that a two-acre plot, established as a burial ground in 1843 after a devastating epidemic, would be "permanently reserved and appropriated for that purpose."

In 1867, about 200 of the 700 Kansas Wyandot voluntarily moved to Indian Territory (near present-day Miami, Oklahoma). By this time, the downtown district of Kansas City had grown up around the old cemetery, and it had become a valuable property. In 1899, the lawyer William E. Connelly went to Indian Territory and promised the group there that he would help them regain tribal status if they would authorize him to have the graves moved and sell the cemetery.

Strong protests from the Kansas Wyandot and others spurred the formation of the Wyandot Cemetery Association to protect the burial ground, and the city fathers temporarily relented. At that point, a young Wyandot woman named LYDA B. CONLEY decided to go to law school in order to defend the burial ground. She graduated with honors from the Kansas City School of Law in 1902 and was admitted to the Missouri bar the same year.

In 1905, after three years of agitation by "progressive" citizens, the city approved the removal of the bodies to another cemetery. The following year, sale of the property was authorized by an act of Congress. In response, Lyda Conley and her two sisters entered the cemetery and padlocked the gates. They built a shack, which they named Fort Conley, over their parents' graves and threatened to shoot any trespassers. They were soon arrested and removed, but Lyda immediately filed suit in federal court against the secretary of the interior. The sisters returned and made Fort Conley their legal residence. Armed with shotguns, they remained even through the winters.

In 1918, after Congressman CHARLES CURTIS used his influence to get the congressional sale-authorization law repealed in the Senate, the city agreed to care for the plot in perpetuity. Yet even now the burial ground was not safe. In January 1946, just a few months before Lyda Conley's death, a plan was proposed which would have reduced it by half, and some civic leaders opted for its complete elimination. In 1947, Congressman George Schwabe and Senator Elmer Thomas of Oklahoma introduced bills authorizing the cemetery's sale, with the proceeds to go to the Oklahoma Wyandotte. This was opposed, however, by formal protests from the mayor of Kansas City and the two Kansas senators. In 1949, a bill to make the cemetery a national monument received the support of President Harry S. Truman.

The issue continued to simmer throughout the 1950s, with the Interior Department actually soliciting and receiving bids for the land in 1959. Kansas City sought an injunction. The burial ground was declared a national historic site in August 1972. Nonetheless, in 1994, the Wyandotte tribe of Oklahoma again expressed interest in the land, now for the purpose of gaming (see GAMING ON INDIAN RESERVATIONS). In 1996, the BUREAU OF INDIAN AFFAIRS approved the tribe's application to purchase—with INDIAN CLAIMS COMMISSION moneys—a half acre immediately adjacent to the cemetery, next to the City Hall building and occupied by the former Masonic Temple, and to have it placed in trust status for high-stakes gaming, or what is called a class III casino. This move was opposed not only by the Kansas Wyandot, but also by all the other Indian tribes of Kansas—the Kansas Kickapoo, who had just opened their own gambling operation on their reservation near Topeka; the Sac and Fox (Mesquakie); the Iowa; and the Prairie Band Potawatomi.

The bitter, century-old dispute between the Kansas and Oklahoma branches finally came to an end in 1998, when they reached a legally binding agreement providing for the permanent protection of the cemetery. In June 1999, representatives of the communities of Quebec, Michigan, Kansas, and Oklahoma met at Wendake, Quebec, for a historic three-day ceremony of reconciliation. From then on, the Oklahoma Wyandotte continued to pursue the matter simply as a gaming issue.

In February 2001, a federal appeals court ruled that the Wyandotte's two acres could not be used for a casino because although the tribe owned the property, the Department of the Interior had not had the authority in 1996 to deem it a reservation that could support gambling. According to the appeals court, only the National Indian Gaming Commission could settle such matters. An Interior Department ruling in March 2002 gave the Wyandotte the right to operate a casino in downtown Kansas City, but the state of Kansas and several Kansas tribes sued the department over this ruling. In April 2002, the Wyandotte had 200 slot machines delivered to the building they owned next to the burial ground, but they soon decided the move was premature and had them removed, announcing that they intended to operate a class II casino featuring electronic pull-tab machines in trailers at another location, but that they still aimed to eventually open a high-stakes (class III) casino. Their strategy appeared to be to use the threat of a casino downtown as a bargaining chip to force the Kansas legislature to allow expanded gambling at the Woodlands Race Track or elsewhere in western Wyandotte County. In October 2008, a federal judge ruled that the Wyandotte have the right to open a casino in downtown Kansas City.

Further Reading

Dayton, Kim. "'Trespassers, Beware!': Lyda Burton Conley and the Battle for Huron Place Cemetery." *Yale Journal of Law and Feminism* 8, no. 1 (1996): 1–30.

English, James K. "A Brief Chronological Overview of the Wyandot Nation of Kansas and the Huron Indian Cemetery." Available online. URL: http://www.wyandot.org/cemetery.html. Accessed 15 February 2003.

Shin, Clara. "Lyda Burton Conley: In Defense of Huron Place Cemetery" (Fall 1998). Available online. URL: http://womenslegalhistory.stanford.edu/papers/conley.pdf. Accessed 28 October 2007.

Indian Arts and Crafts Board (IACB)

Established by Congress in 1935 "to promote the economic welfare of the Indian Tribes and the Indian wards of the government through the development of Indian arts and crafts and the expansion of the market for the products of Indians arts and craftsmanship," the Indian Arts and Crafts Board (IACB) helps Native craftspeople organize; offers aid in design, production, and management; and promotes marketing of Native arts.

The IACB was the product of a long evolution, from the foundation of the INDIAN INDUSTRIES LEAGUE in 1893; to WARREN KING MOOREHEAD's 1910 efforts to promote the commercial possibilities of traditional arts and crafts and set up a government Bureau of Indian Arts and Industries; to writer Mary Austin's efforts (starting in 1919) to get federal support for Native American arts, leading to the foundation of the Indian Arts Fund in Santa Fe (1924); to the MERIAM REPORT (1928), which deplored the loss of Indian arts and crafts. The immediate ancestor of the IACB was the Herbert Hoover administration's Frazier-Leavitt bill, which unsuccessfully tried to create an Indian crafts board in 1930. In 1934, Indian Commissioner JOHN COLLIER asked James Young, a member of the American Indian Defense Association, to chair a committee to study Indian arts and crafts from both the economic and cultural points of view.

Prior to the introduction of the Indian Arts and Crafts bill, Collier's daughter-in-law had been involved in promotional work and exhibits of Indian arts and crafts in 1933. She subsequently prepared a detailed plan to employ Indian artists who could not find work. Work-relief arts and crafts projects of this kind became a reality on various reservations with funding from the Works Progress Administration (WPA). For example, Seneca JESSE CORNPLANTER was an instructor in the WPA Seneca Arts and Crafts Project at New York's Tonawanda and Cattaraugus Reservations headed by ARTHUR C. PARKER from 1935 to 1941. Another such project was the Indian Weaving Unit on the Chippewa (Ojibway) reservation at Lac du Flambeau, Wisconsin, from 1939 to 1941.

House and Senate bills to create the Indian Arts and Crafts Board, introduced in early March 1935, gained wide support, with opposition coming mainly from western traders. The bill creating the board became law on August 27, 1935, and the actual board was established in 1936. It consisted of five members appointed by the secretary of the interior, with Collier as chair. Its purpose was to promote Indian arts and crafts and expand their market, undertake market and technical research, coordinate with relevant public and private agencies, assist with projects, provide managerial help, make loan recommendations, uphold standards of quality, and provide guarantees of authenticity and penalties for counterfeit goods.

The IACB did not really get under way, however, until museum director, curator, and lecturer René d'Harnoncourt was appointed general manager in June 15, 1937. Typical of early development projects was Mohegan ethnologist GLADYS TANTAQUIDGEON's 1938 efforts to revive and develop handicrafts in the northern Plains area (Dakotas, Montana, Wyoming).

Genuine Indian articles were to carry the label "U.S. Dept of the Interior, Indian Arts and Crafts Board, Certified Indian Enterprise." The board created a certificate of authenticity for Navajo rugs and licensed traders to use them. Many crafters were trained in Indian Bureau schools. Many of the IACB's activities were aided by a revolving loan fund, and the board sponsored a series of outlets or sources of supply for Indian arts and crafts products.

The 1990 Indian Arts and Crafts Act, sponsored by then representative BEN NIGHTHORSE CAMPBELL and Representative John Kyl of Colorado, attempted to strengthen the trademark-creating powers of the IACB in order to combat the widespread imitation of Indian artwork, particularly Navajo, Zuni, and Hopi jewelry, by foreign manufacturers. It gave the IACB the power to enforce criminal penalties and required it to establish a definition of who can claim to be an Indian artist.

The most controversial feature of the law was the definition of an Indian artist as any individual who is a member of an Indian tribe or certified as an Indian artisan by a federally recognized tribe. Because the sponsors were from the West, they overlooked the issue of nonfederally recognized tribes, which tend to be concentrated in the East. Although the definition was later expanded to include state-recognized tribes, many Indian artists still did not have the technical qualifications or tribal affiliations needed to qualify as officially "Indian" under the act, and many more objected to being required to prove their ancestry, something artists of other ethnic origins are not required to do. At least one Indian artist moved to Europe in protest (see DURHAM, JIMMIE). The Five Civilized Tribes Museum in Muskogee, Oklahoma, estimated that one-third of the master artists whose works are exhibited there had difficulties with certification.

The IACB runs three museums: the Southern Plains Indian Museum in Anadarko, Oklahoma; the Sioux Indian Museum in Rapid City, South Dakota; and the Museum of the Plains Indians in Browning, Montana. It sponsors sales exhibits and publishes a source directory for American Indian arts organizations and activities. The IACB's success in promoting Native arts and crafts has been much debated. While its supporters maintain that it has helped maintain a high standard of art, its critics contend that it is a culturally imperialist organization focused on gearing Indian art to non-Indian consumers.

Further Reading

Jacobs, Margaret D. *Engendered Encounters: Feminism and Pueblo Cultures, 1879–1934,* 149–179. Lincoln: University of Nebraska Press, 1999.

Meyn, Susan Labry. "More Than Curiosities: A Grassroots History of the Indian Arts and Crafts Board and Its Precursors, 1920 to 1942." Ph.D. dissertation, University of Cincinnati, 1997.

Schrader, Robert Fay. *The Indian Arts and Crafts Board: An Aspect of New Deal Indian Policy.* Albuquerque: University of New Mexico Press, 1983.

Indian Bill of Rights   *See* INDIAN CIVIL RIGHTS ACT.

Indian Child Welfare Act (1978)

Under the ASSIMILATION policies of the early years of the 20th century, the federal government encouraged the placement of Indian children in boarding schools, often from the age of five until they reached adulthood. Since the early 1900s, the BUREAU OF INDIAN AFFAIRS (BIA) had also encouraged the adoption by non-Indians of Indian children as a means of assimilating Indian children and stamping out Indian culture. However, there was no mechanism in place to carry out this policy, and adoptions were mostly for orphans and not

very common. In 1958, during the TERMINATION era, the BIA united with the Child Welfare League of America to establish a program to accelerate the adoption of Indian children by non-Indian families. The new policy allowed for the rights of Indian parents to be terminated, often without their consent or understanding. Over the next 10 years, non-Indians adopted more than 1,000 children under this program. On some reservations, as many as 35 percent of the children were placed in foster care.

This BIA program followed on the heels of a wide-scale adoption program to place Indian children with Mormon families. That concept, which originated in 1947 with informal arrangements between beet farmers in Utah and migrant Navajo (Dineh) pickers to allow their children to continue attending schools in Utah, was formalized in 1954 as the Mormon Indian Student Placement program. Baptism of the children into the Mormon faith was a requirement. (Many Mormons believe that American Indians are descendants of the Lamanites, who were, according to a doctrine unique to that church, members of one of the lost tribes of Israel; they also believe that the Indians' dark complexions and aboriginal traditions reflect punishments by God for the evil and greed of their ancestors and, consequently, that Mormons who convert Indians receive special privileges in heaven.)

Starting in the 1970s, the Mormon program came under criticism for pressuring Indian parents to give up their children. In 1977, the federal government commissioned a study under the auspices of the Association of Administrators of the Interstate Compact for the Placement of Children (a professional organization ensuring that children adopted or placed in foster homes across state lines are placed with suitable persons). The study exonerated the placement program and allowed it to continue. Nevertheless, the program went into a gradual decline because of changing social attitudes as well as the improvement of reservation schools; it was finally abandoned in 1996, by which time it had placed some 70,000 Indian children, the great majority of them Navajo, with white families.

Under the BIA program, meanwhile, numerous cases of abuse and serious psychological damage to adopted Indian children were reported. By the early 1970s, Indian rights activists had targeted it as one of many examples of BIA mismanagement. Congress responded to growing Indian demands for control over the adoption process by passing the Indian Child Welfare Act of 1978. The act gave broad powers to tribal governments to determine what is best for the tribe's children. The legislation granted tribal courts the authority to decide the placement of Indian children and forced state and other courts to respect tribal decisions. The principle surrounding the legislation was that in cases where adoption was a necessary alternative, placement with the child's extended family, in accordance with Indian traditions, or among other Indians was to be pursued before adoption by non-Indians could be considered.

The act ended the heavy-handed policies of the BIA and other social agencies, which could no longer remove a child without the permission of the tribal courts. Some social organizations criticized the legislation for putting tribal sovereignty before the best interests of the child and for being overly complicated and onerous. However, the Mormon Church was uniquely exempted from the act, and its long-term adoption program continues.

In a celebrated case, *Mississippi Band of Choctaw Indians v. Hollyfield et al.*, the U.S. Supreme Court decided that tribal jurisdiction extended to any child who is a member of the tribe, regardless of whether he or she lives on the reservation. The case revolved around twin Choctaw children who had been born off the reservation in 1985 to unmarried members of the tribe. The parents signed consent forms allowing Mississippi state social services to place the twins with a non-Indian family, who adopted the children the following year. The Choctaw tribe contested the adoption process, and the case wound its way through courts before being decided three years later. The decision proved difficult for the non-Indian family, who had to give up the children after having cared for them for three years, and it led to new criticism of the act.

The act came under assault by the Clinton administration, which proposed granting more power to the states and argued that state courts should have jurisdiction when the child's parents do not have a significant association with the tribe. In 1996, the NATIONAL CONGRESS OF AMERICAN INDIANS managed to defeat proposed amendments to the act that would have eroded tribal sovereignty.

See also SOVEREIGNTY, INDIGENOUS AND TRIBAL.

Further Reading

Allen, James B. "The Rise and Decline of the LDS Indian Student Placement Program, 1947–1996." In *Mormons, Scripture, and the Ancient World: Studies in Honor of John L. Sorenson*, edited by Davis Bitton, 85–119. Provo, Utah: FARMS, 1998.
Chadwick, Bruce A., Stan L. Albrecht, and Howard M. Bahr. "Evaluation of an Indian Student Placement Program." *Social Casework* 67, no. 9 (1986): 515–524.
Cope, Arianne. *The Coming of Elijah*. St. George, Utah: Bentley Enterprises, 2006.
Jones, B. J. *The Indian Child Welfare Act Handbook: A Legal Guide to the Custody and Adoption of Native American Children*. New York: American Bar Association, 1995.

Indian Civilian Conservation Corps (Indian Emergency Work Program, Indian CCC)

The Emergency Unemployment Act of March 31, 1933, created a new independent agency, the Emergency Conservation Work Program, to help relieve the unemployment caused by the Great Depression and to restore the country's natural resources. In June 1937, the agency was renamed the Civilian Conservation Corps (CCC), by which name this program is now best known. Although only one of the many new agencies created around that time, such as the Works Progress Administration (WPA) and the Public Works Administration (PWA), the CCC was the ideal agency for employing Indians because of its focus on conservation and rural work. BUREAU OF INDIAN AFFAIRS

(BIA) commissioner JOHN COLLIER assisted in the formation of a special Indian branch, known as the Indian Emergency Work Program but usually referred to as the Indian CCC, which focused on land management and conservation on INDIAN RESERVATIONS.

Beginning in late 1933, Indians were placed in charge of each of the 40 Indian CCC camps that had been established on 69 Indian reservations as rapidly as men were found to qualify as camp managers. The Indian CCC, though run on a shoestring budget, was very successful. Not only did it bring badly needed money to the reservations, but its success strengthened Collier's hand, especially by giving a non-BIA federal entity a stake in the outcome of important Indian programs. Providing Indians with the opportunity to develop their own conservation programs allowed Collier to test his ideas about community decision making on soil conservation, forestry, roads, and bridges. Through the biweekly *Indians at Work*, which first appeared in August 1933 and was funded jointly by the CCC and the BIA, Collier publicized the program and its philosophy. Furthermore, the CCC provided vocational education, and through it many Indians were trained as mechanics, carpenters, surveyors, and engineers. In all, some 85,000 Indians took part in the Indian CCC over the nine years of its existence.

The program survived until 1942. By that time, with all focus on the war effort, federal funding could no longer be justified; however, the availability of war-related work continued to provide economic opportunity for Indians.

Further Reading

Bromert, Roger. "The Sioux and the Indian-CCC." *South Dakota History* 8, no. 4 (1978): 340–356.
Gower, Calvin W. "The CCC Indian Division: Aid for Depressed Americans." *Minnesota History* 43 (Spring 1972): 3–13.
Hanneman, Carolyn G. "Baffles, Bridges and Bermuda: Oklahoma Indians and the CCC—Indian Division." *Chronicles of Oklahoma* 77 (Winter 1999): 428–449.
Parman, Donald L. "The Indian and the Civilian Conservation Corps." *Pacific Historical Review* 40, no. 1 (February 1971): 39–56.
Sypolt, Larry N. *Civilian Conservation Corps: A Selectively Annotated Bibliography*. Westport, Conn.: Praeger/Greenwood, 2005.

Indian Civil Rights Act (Indian Bill of Rights) (1968)

Also known as the Indian Bill of Rights, the 1968 Indian Civil Rights Act extended American constitutional protections to INDIAN RESERVATIONS, where they had previously not been in force. The act also amended Public Law 280, passed in 1953 (which allows a number of specifically named states to exercise limited jurisdiction over federally recognized Indian reservations), by providing that states that had not extended criminal jurisdiction to reservations by 1968 could not do so in the future without the consent of the tribes affected (see EMMONS, GLENN LEONIDAS; TERMINATION). The bill was controversial, however, in that it further extended federal laws onto reservations, limiting Indian self-government and diminishing Indian sovereignty (see SOVEREIGNTY, INDIGENOUS AND TRIBAL).

For most of the 20th century, federal courts had ruled that the constitutional protections of the Bill of Rights did not apply to Indian governments. The precedent for this was set in 1896, under *Talton v. Mayes*, when the U.S. Supreme Court ruled that Bob Talton, a white man convicted of murdering a Cherokee on Cherokee reservation land, could not invoke the Fifth Amendment—which accords certain protections to criminal suspects—to overturn his conviction. In 1959, the U.S. Court of Appeals ruled that First Amendment guarantees of freedom of religion did not apply to the Navajo reservation, where the use of peyote had been banned and where three members of the NATIVE AMERICAN CHURCH had been arrested and convicted for conducting ceremonies with the sacred plant.

The ruling clashed with a growing civil rights movement in the country, however, and led to Senate hearings in 1961 on the issue of civil rights on Indian reservations. The hearings proved to be a flash point for disaffected members of Indian reservations, who successfully argued that many Indian governments were tyrannical or despotic. Congress conducted more than six years of hearings before passing the Indian Civil Rights Act in 1968, on the premise of protecting the rights of individual Indians from "arbitrary and unjust actions of tribal governments."

Attempting to strike a balance between the self-government of Indian tribes and the extension of individual protections, Congress did not include in the act four individual rights normally accorded to American citizens—the Establishment Clause of the First Amendment, which prohibits the government from sponsoring churches (although individual religious freedom was guaranteed); the right to an attorney free of charge in case the plaintiff should be indigent; the right to a trial by jury in civil cases presented before tribal courts; and the right to a grand jury in criminal cases. The act did extend all other constitutional rights to reservations, such as the right of protection from unlawful search and seizure, freedom of speech and assembly, and other well-known protections.

The act allowed for a prisoner to use the rights of habeas corpus—that is, to petition a court—to freedom from any arbitrary or unjust imprisonment. But since it carried no penalties to the offending tribal government should it act against an individual, accusations of despotic behavior continued to be made against some tribal governments. The act also opened the door to lawsuits against Indian tribes, on the ground that the tribal governments had waived their sovereign immunity. This led to 10 years of unprecedented litigation against Indian tribes, until the Supreme Court affirmed Indian tribal immunity in the landmark decision *Santa Clara Pueblo v. Martinez* in 1978. Since then, litigation under the act has been limited.

Further Reading

Burnett, Donald L., Jr. "An Historical Analysis of the 1968 'Indian Civil Rights' Act." *Harvard Journal on Legislation* 9 (May 1972): 557–626.

Crawford, James. "The Aborigine in Comparative Law." In *Law and Anthropology: Internationales Jahrbuch für Rechtsanthropologie*, 18–23. Vienna, 1987.

Richland, Justin B., and Sarah Deer. *Introduction to Tribal Legal Studies*, 247–252. Walnut Creek, Calif.: AltaMira Press, 2004.

Shattuck, Petra T., and Jill Norgren. *Partial Justice: Federal Indian Law in Liberal Constitutional System*, 164–189. Providence, R.I.: Berg, 1993.

Indian Claims Commission (ICC)

A quasijudicial agency of Congress, the Indian Claims Commission (ICC) was established in 1946 after a long series of discussions among U.S. administrators. Indian tribes had struggled throughout the 19th century for the right to sue the U.S. government in pursuit of their treaty rights. The Choctaw, the most active in this process, made a breakthrough in 1881, when a special judicial act of Congress allowed them to present a case in the U.S. Court of Claims. This cumbersome method was then used by other tribes through the first half of the 20th century. A few tribes did receive favorable judgments, though they found that even when successful, their claims were reduced by the General Accounting Office, which subtracted "gratuities"—a variety of expenses the government claimed it had incurred for the benefit of the tribe. This procedure was encouraged by legislators and officials who feared the effect on the federal budget of large payments with interest. Between 1929 and 1935, in all but two cases, these offsets for "gratuities" were greater than the award (for example, see WHITE CALF, JAMES).

A new agency dedicated to resolving tribal claims was first proposed in 1910 by Indian commissioner FRANCIS ELLINGTON LEUPP. From the first, it was thought of as a way to extinguish Indian treaty claims, which were seen as an obstacle to ASSIMILATION. The MERIAM REPORT called for such a commission again in 1928. In 1929, attorney Nathan R. Margold was asked to study the subject and draft a bill. His version called for a commission of six that would function for 15 years. Indian commissioner CHARLES JAMES RHOADS encouraged Congress to take some such action in 1930 and 1931, but in vain. His successor, JOHN COLLIER, included in the proposed INDIAN REORGANIZATION ACT a special Indian court that would have jurisdiction over claims and other matters affecting the tribes, but this provision was eliminated from the final version of the bill. A separate attempt to legislate an Indian Claims Commission was defeated in 1937.

After a 20-year debate over whether a new court or a commission should be set up, Congress passed a bill organizing the ICC in 1946. In the 1945 debate, one of the most experienced Washington attorneys practicing Indian law, Ernest I. Wilkinson—outraged by a recent Supreme Court decision against the Shoshone that refused to recognize either aboriginal title or the treaty as an enforceable contract—spoke in favor of the bill. Associate Solicitor General FELIX SOLOMON COHEN reported on the bill's amendments. Undoubtedly, the passage of the ICC bill at this time was greatly aided by the support of congressmen who understood the close relation of the ICC to TERMINATION.

Although Cohen stated in 1945 that the title of any lands purchased from Indians should not be in doubt, even if the compensation had been grossly inadequate, the fact is that a large portion of the United States had been taken through fraudulent treaties or without any legal transfer or compensation at all, including much of the Southwest and California. The government was aware that its title to these lands was not fully secure—hence Native historian JACK D. FORBES's remark that Congress saw the ICC as a way not merely to compensate the tribes but in many cases to transfer the aboriginal title to the United States for the first time.

As constituted in 1946, the ICC had three commissioners, none of them Indian or experienced in Indian law. The first chief commissioner was Edgar E. Witt, a former lieutenant governor of Texas. He was replaced in 1957 by ARTHUR VIVIAN WATKINS of Utah, who had been one of the most prominent supporters of Termination in Congress and who attempted to streamline the commission's procedures.

Although it had been set up as a commission, the ICC in fact functioned as a court, in which government lawyers argued against those employed by the tribes. The Indians' attorneys, who were regarded with suspicion as potential exploiters of their clients, had their fees limited to 10 percent of the amount awarded in a successful claim. The commission heard two main types of cases: claims that land ceded by treaty had been undervalued and that the government owed the tribe further compensation, and claims that tribal funds had been mishandled by the government in its role as legal guardian of Indians. The issue of interest on moneys owed had never been settled by Congress and was not considered; the act establishing the ICC had eliminated a number of categories of gratuities, and by the 1960s they were almost entirely eliminated. Appeals were handled by the federal court of claims. The tribes were given five years to prepare their cases. By 1951, 852 claims had been presented. The ICC, renewed three times, finally expired on September 30, 1978, and the outstanding claims cases were passed to the court of claims.

The Commission's general procedure in disputes over undervalued land was to consult records, along with historians, anthropologists, and land appraisers, to determine the tribal location and the value of the land in dispute at the time of the treaty. If this value differed greatly from the amount paid by the government, the difference was to be awarded to the tribe by Congress.

Never consulted in the design of the ICC, Indians became more and more vocal in their criticisms of it through the 1950s, 1960s, and 1970s. One obvious flaw was that the ICC only envisioned itself as awarding money, whereas most Indians wanted land returned. This led some tribes, notably the Oglala Sioux and the Western Shoshone, to refuse awards from the ICC (see BATTLE MOUNTAIN). Since the ICC would base the amount of the judgment on the value of the land at the time it was taken in the 18th or 19th century—usually less than a dollar an acre—and since it did not award interest on the judgment, the money that eventually went to the tribe did not come close to compensating them for their loss, while still generating hefty fees for their lawyers. Far from bringing an end to Indian claims against the federal government, the experience of dealing with the ICC enhanced the legal expertise of many tribes, leading to increasingly sophisticated forms of litigation.

Further Reading

Barney, Ralph A. "Legal Problems Peculiar to Indian Claims Litigations." *Ethnohistory* 2, no. 4 (Fall 1955): 315–325.

Lurie, Nancy O. "Problems, Opportunities, and Recommendations." *Ethnohistory* 2, no.4 (Fall 1955): 357–375.

Steward, Julian H. "Anthropology and Indian Claims Litigation: Papers Presented at a Symposium Held at Detroit in December, 1954." *Ethnohistory* 2, no. 4 (Autumn, 1955): 292–302.

Philp, Kenneth R. *Termination Revisited: American Indians on the Trail to Self-Determination, 1933–1953*. Lincoln: University of Nebraska Press, 1999.

Rosenthal, Harvey D. *Their Day in Court: A History of the Indian Claims Commission*. New York: Garland, 1990.

Indian Industries League (IIL)

The Indian Industries League (IIL) was a Protestant Indian welfare organization dedicated to promoting and supporting craft and handicraft industries on reservations, particularly among Indian women, with the aim of enabling them to become economically self-sufficient. An offshoot of the Boston-based Women's National Indian Association (WNIA), its original aims were purely assimilationist (see ASSIMILATION). In 1891, the novelist Frances Campbell Sparhawk started a Division of Indian Industries under the WNIA's Department of Libraries, which she headed. Her philosophy was similar to that of educator RICHARD HENRY PRATT, except that she was more interested in the education of girls, on which she placed particular importance because of her belief—widely shared at the time—that women and the "feminine virtues" were the very basis of civilization.

In the federal schools, Indians were being taught the "arts of civilization," with special emphasis on agriculture for boys and housekeeping for girls. But there was a great fear that, once returned to the reservation, they would "go back to the blanket." This was especially true for women, since there was a widespread prejudice that Indian women were treated as "squaw drudges" in traditional Indian society.

In 1893, the IIL became a separate organization under Sparhawk's direction but still affiliated with the WNIA. By January 1895, it had 109 white and 38 Indian members, mainly women. In 1901, bolstered by some success in fund-raising, the IIL struck out on its own.

Because the league's resources were too limited to provide enough capital for training and materials, leaders had to abandon notions of teaching "civilized" arts such as lace-making and look to traditional tribal arts in which Indians were already highly skilled. This was the only practical way to alleviate the Indians' economic distress while at the same time providing funds to the IIL. Since Indian baskets, blankets, and other handicrafts were becoming popular with eastern consumers, league members were able to offer craftswomen much better prices than they could get from western traders, and sometimes the league would even reduce their own profit to nothing. The league helped Josephine Foard, an employee of the Indian Service (as the BUREAU OF INDIAN AFFAIRS was known at the time), to move from the East Coast to Laguna Pueblo, where she taught the local potters new glazing techniques that made their wares more commercially attractive.

The promotion of traditional Native arts could not be justified by mere pragmatism, however, because to some members and supporters it seemed to undercut the organization's mission by encouraging Indian women to backslide into "savagery." Thus, the IIL was forced to develop a position defending Indian arts, if only to show that it would not undermine the goals of "civilizing the Indian." Once set upon this line of thinking, however, it was but a short time before many members were arguing in defense of Indian cultures in general and even criticizing the civilization of modern America (see DU BOIS, CONSTANCE GODDARD). Reverend Walter C. Roe, a vice president of the IIL, who with his wife fostered traditional Indian beadwork at John Seger's Colony at Colony, Oklahoma, was perhaps the leading figure in promoting these ideas. Even Sparhawk, who was far more prejudiced against Native cultures than most of the organization's field matrons, gradually came to terms with this new perspective.

The difference was dramatized by the fact that in her novels, Sparhawk had always portrayed older Indian women as villains intent on dragging young, progressive women back into tribalism and savagery. Yet by 1901, IIL field matrons were helping to reestablish traditional family ties, placing young Indian women as apprentices to elder craftswomen. Intimate contact with Native Americans was giving missionaries respect for Indian cultures.

Field matrons facilitated the development of industries on many reservations—for example, pottery and textiles at Acoma, Laguna, and other pueblos; beadwork among the Cheyenne and Arapaho; rugs and silversmithing among the Navajo; and basketmaking among the Pima and the Kumeyaay (Diegueño) at Mesa Grande. The league served as a collection, marketing, and distribution agency, and it provided small loans to individual artists. Some Native American women were hired as field matrons.

In 1910, the IIL sold off its stock of Indian goods, though it continued to sell Navajo rugs on a small scale up to about 1918. Though not officially dissolved until 1922, it had effectively ceased operation by 1919. Ironically, the league was by then in better financial shape than it had ever been, but most of the leading members were growing old and lacked the energy to continue.

In its two decades of work, the IIL could claim some important accomplishments. First and foremost, it had done a great deal to change public attitudes about Indian cultures and cultural values. With increasing frequency, the argument was made that the survival of traditional Native American cultures was both a benefit to Indians and a great asset to all Americans. Second, the league's work had paved the way for the AMERICAN INDIAN ARTS AND CRAFTS BOARD, created by Congress in 1935.

Further Reading

Holm, Tom. *The Great Confusion in Indian Affairs: Native Americans and Whites in the Progressive Era.* Austin: University of Texas Press, 2005.

Lanmon, Dwight P., et al. *Josephine Foard and the Glazed Pottery of Laguna Pueblo.* Albuquerque: University of New Mexico Press, 2007.

Meyer, Carter Jones, and Diana Royer, eds. *Selling the Indian: Commercializing and Appropriating American Indian Cultures.* Tucson: University of Arizona Press, 2001.

Trump, Eric Krenzen. "The Indian Industries League and Its Support of American Indian Arts, 1893–1922: A Study of Changing Attitudes toward Indian Women and Assimilationist Policy." Ph.D. dissertation, Boston University, 1996.

Indianist music

American Indian music supplied the original impulse for the rise of modernism in American art music in the first quarter of the 20th century and also influenced light and popular music of the time. The Czech composer Antonin Dvorak (1841–1904), while artistic director of the National Conservatory in New York (1892–95), was perhaps the first to express the opinion that a truly American musical art could develop only out of black and American Indian music. A decade later, in a February 1906 speech to black students at the Industrial Institute in Manassas, Virginia, President Theodore Roosevelt, influenced by a recent conversation with visiting French musicologist Julien Tiersot (1857–1936), said much the same thing. At this time, a number of American composers were concerned with the problem of developing a distinctive national idiom in music instead of imitating European models. Ironically, it was the authority of Europeans such as Dvorak and Tiersot that made them look to both African-American and American Indian music as potential sources of a truly American music.

An Omaha Indian, the ethnologist FRANCIS LA FLESCHE (1857–1932), played the central role in transmitting knowledge of Native music to American composers, along with musicologist John Comfort Fillmore (1843–98) and ethnologists Alice C. Fletcher (1838–1923), Frances Densmore (1867–1957), Natalie Curtis (1875–1921), and Harold Amasa Loring (1879–1934). Among the leading composers in this so-called Indianist movement were Carlos Troyer (1837–1920), Frederick Russell Burton (1861–1909), Preston Ware Orem (1862–1938), Harvey Worthington Loomis (1865–1930), Charles Sanford

Skilton (1868–1941), Henry F. B. Gilbert (1868–1928), Robert Elmer Smith (1881–1964), Arthur Nevin (1871–1943), Arthur Farwell (1872–1952), Blair Fairchild (1877–1933), Thurlow Lieurance (1878–1963), Homer Grunn (1880–1944), and Charles Wakefield Cadman (1881–1946). Ironically, Edward MacDowell (1861–1908), whose *Indian Suite*, first performed in Boston in January 1895, is perhaps the best piece of American music based on Indian themes, kept aloof from this school, believing that a national art arises only from the genius of gifted individuals and cannot be prescribed by ethnic theories.

In this period, most American social scientists, influenced by the theories of the English philosopher Herbert Spencer and the American anthropologist Lewis Henry Morgan, believed that all peoples in their historical development go through the same stages, so that at any given time, some cultures are at higher and some at lower (more primitive) stages (see BOAS, FRANZ). This idea also influenced the Indianist composers. While traditional Indian music is unharmonized, and thus "primitive" according to this view, John Comfort Fillmore, seconded by La Flesche, believed that "primitive" music potentially or ideally implies harmonies that would be expressed if the society were at a "more advanced" level of civilization. The composer's task was to discover these "implied" harmonies.

While all the Indianists accepted this procedure, which they called *idealization*, there were two contrasting approaches. Fillmore himself assumed that 19th-century Western harmony was the ideal or most perfect form and interpreted Indian melodies accordingly. Among the composers, Cadman and Lieurance were the best-known exponents of this method. Cadman's 1915 statement is typical: "Only one-fifth of all Indian thematic material is valuable in the hands of the composer—is suitable for harmonic investment. It becomes necessary to choose an Indian song or chant that will stand alone by virtue of its inherent melodic line, and is fairly good in symmetry, otherwise the idealizer is confronted with a formidable problem."

Not surprisingly, the result of this technique sounds nothing like genuine American Indian music, except where certain authentic vocal and rhythmic nuances were brought to it by the Indian singers and musicians who often performed it. It has a faintly exotic quality that was undoubtedly more striking to the early 20th-century mainstream American ear than to today's. Some songs, such as Cadman's "From the Land of the Sky-Blue Water," became extremely popular.

Idealization took a different path, however, in the hands of such composers as Farwell and Loomis (Dvorak's leading pupil in New York). As Loomis stated in his program notes for a concert in New York (April 27, 1905), "Indian music may smell of sweet grass or a revival meeting, according to who harmonizes it." The inevitable conclusion of Fillmore's logic was that music of all nationalities should be harmonized in the same way. Rejecting this, Farwell and others pointed out that composers such as Mussorgsky, Grieg, and Dvorak were developing distinctive national styles of harmonization. Of course, the folk music of these nations already had harmony; Indian music did not. Art music (i.e., "serious" concert music),

according to Western tastes at the time, must have harmony. But rather than dilute the distinctive American Indian melodies with Western chord structure, one should search within these melodies for suggestions of new and unusual harmonizations organically related to them, a process the composers often enhanced by trying to cultivate a somewhat mystical appreciation of a particular Native culture. These composers were not afraid to break the rules of contemporary Western harmonic practice. Their use of exotic harmonies and rhythms, traditional Indian instruments for "color," and sometimes vocal techniques that sounded more Indian led to what was referred to by at least one critic as a "beautiful ugliness."

Composers such as Farwell and Loomis (although their compositions are rarely heard today) thus represent the beginnings of modernism in American music. Though not comparable in genius, they occupy a position in the history of American music not unlike that of Modest Mussorgsky in Russian music or Bela Bartok in Hungarian music. Much of the work of the 37 composers in the catalog of the Wa-Wan Press (named after an Omaha peacemaking ceremony), founded by Farwell explicitly to foster American music, is based on Indian themes or topics. Farwell himself, having learned much from his studies of Indian music, left the confines of the explicitly Indianist genre.

A number of composers, including Cadman, Lieurance, Farwell, and Loomis, traveled around the country, giving what they called "Indian music lectures," bringing with them other musicians, a collection of Native instruments, and presenting through this music their theories of aesthetics and civilization. Such lectures had their greatest vogue from about 1905 until 1930 but in one form or another remained popular throughout the 20th century. When possible, an Indian performer would be featured. Among the most famous were Tsianina Redfeather (see BLACKSTONE, TSIANINA EVANS), who worked for years with Cadman; Princess Watahwaso (see POOLAW, LUCY NICOLA), who performed and even recorded with Lieurance (ca. 1914–18); and IRENE EASTMAN (Taluta), whose promising career was cut short by her untimely death at the age of 24.

In 1911–12 and 1912–13, photographer Charles Curtis toured with what he called a "musicale" or "picture opera." His tour, *A Vanishing Race*, was a montage of lectures, photographs, and motion pictures accompanied by the music of Henry F. B. Gilbert, a composer from Farwell's Wa-Wan movement. Robert Elmer Smith was still doing such lectures with (non-Indian) soprano Louise Merrill Cooper as late as 1950. One of the few composers of the Indianist school who was actually an Indian was Miami-Quapaw violinist FRED CARDIN.

From a present perspective, this music was a distortion, based on romantic stereotypes and exploitation of Indian culture. As Bunny McBride puts it in her biography of MOLLY SPOTTED ELK, "They picked up the bodies (notes) but not the souls of native songs, then adapted them for white audiences by replacing the original souls with white or generic ones." This characterization was more true of the Cadman/Lieurance approach than that of Farwell and Loomis. But even Cadman came to regard his "idealization" as something more than a purely musical problem. In a letter to La Flesche (August 19, 1908), he wrote: "I hope the work will go on until man is forced to see that unity and brotherhood are inevitable. Until that time there is no such thing as civilization . . . I am so glad if I can have a small part in the great awakening . . ." The Indian Music lectures popular in the early 20th century presented Native performers, costumes, and instruments to the early 20th-century American public, portraying Indian culture for mainstream and acculturated Native audiences in what was then seen as a positive light, and Indianist numbers were featured in the repertoire of virtually all Indian concert performers along with European classical music. By the end of the 20th century, though isolated numbers were still occasionally performed, the Indianist repertoire had been largely forgotten.

Further Reading

Chase, Gilbert. "The Native Americans." In *America's Music, from the Pilgrims to the Present*, 385–401. New York: McGraw-Hill, 1955.

Daniels, Valerie. "A Vanishing Race." Available online. URL: http://xroads.virginia.edu/~MA02/daniels/ curtis/musicale.html. Accessed 24 September 2002.

Levine, Victoria Lindsay, ed. *Writing American Indian Music: Historic Transcriptions, Notations, and Arrangements.* Middleton, Wisc.: A–R editions, 2002.

Pisani, Michael V. *Imagining Native America in Music.* New Haven, Conn.: Yale University Press, 2006.

Further Listening

Muller, Dario. *The American Indianists*, 2 vols., Marco Polo 8.223715 and 8.223738 (released 1996).

Indian New Deal

The Indian New Deal is the name commonly given to a series of sweeping reforms in U.S. Indian policy that were conceived in the late 1920s and implemented during the 1930s. During the first quarter of the 20th century, federal policy toward Indians was focused on complete ASSIMILATION of Indians into mainstream American society. The process of destroying the ancient Indian way of life was to be accomplished by the breakup of their vast landholdings under the policy of ALLOTMENT, the extinction of their languages and cultures through harsh education policies, the banning of their traditional religions, and other repressive measures (see EDUCATIONAL POLICY, AMERICAN INDIANS AND; RELIGIOUS FREEDOM, AMERICAN INDIAN).

The suffering of Indians under assimilation was exacerbated by the corruption endemic in the Indian Office, as the BUREAU OF INDIAN AFFAIRS (BIA) was known at the time. Numerous frauds were perpetrated under the guise of bringing civilization to Indians, particularly the theft of their lands and resources. The despoliation of Indian Territory, after its dissolution and incorporation into the new state of Oklahoma in 1907,

led to calls by some Indian rights advocates for the reform of the Indian Office (see BONNIN, GERTRUDE; CURTIS ACT). The corruption at the Indian Office reached new heights with the appointment of ALBERT BACON FALL as secretary of the interior in 1921. His scandalous tenure, combined with the desperate conditions for Indian people at that time, led to the formation of the COMMITTEE OF ONE HUNDRED in 1923 to review federal Indian policy. Their report only fueled the growing clamor for reform, leading to the landmark MERIAM REPORT of 1928.

The Meriam Report advocated a significant shift in Indian policy by calling for an end to allotment and the forcible assimilation of Indians. In 1929, President Herbert Hoover appointed CHARLES JAMES RHOADS as commissioner of Indian Affairs with the specific mission of instituting the recommendations of the Meriam Report. Rhoads's appointment was heralded as a "New Deal for Indians," and thus the term actually precedes by several years the "New Deal" programs enacted by Hoover's successor, President Franklin Delano Roosevelt. But despite vigorous attempts, Rhoads was not able to implement the most important recommendations of the report, an end to allotment and forced assimilation. That would have to wait until the more favorable political climate created by Roosevelt's election in 1932.

The Indian New Deal found its champion in Roosevelt's new commissioner of Indian affairs, JOHN COLLIER, appointed in 1933. Under Collier, federal Indian policy was no longer based on the dissolution of Indian lands and cultures but on their preservation, and the disastrous Allotment policy was finally brought to an end. Bans on Indian religions were lifted, and the forced assimilation policies in education were halted. The centerpiece of the Indian New Deal, the INDIAN REORGANIZATION ACT—which made Indian tribes self-governing—was passed in 1934. Other important initiatives included the creation of the INDIAN ARTS AND CRAFTS BOARD, the INDIAN CIVILIAN CONSERVATION CORPS, and the JOHNSON-O'MALLEY ACT. New legal paradigms developed by FELIX SOLOMON COHEN, associate solicitor for the Interior Department, enhanced the rights of Indians and recognized their SOVEREIGNTY over their own lands, a significant break from previous policy.

Collier and the Indian New Deal lost much of their political support when Roosevelt died in 1945. Yet attempts during the 1950s and 1960s to overturn the gains made under the New Deal, through the federal policy called TERMINATION, largely failed. The policies enacted under the Indian New Deal, for the most part, remain in force today.

Further Reading

Britten, Thomas A. "Hoover and the Indians: The Case for Continuity in Federal Indian Policy, 1900–1933." *Historian* 61, no. 3 (Spring 1999): 518–538.

Indian Reorganization Act (IRA, Wheeler-Howard Act) (1934)

The most important piece of Indian legislation of the 20th century, also known as the Wheeler-Howard Act, the Indian

Reorganization Act (IRA) was the centerpiece of President Franklin D. Roosevelt's INDIAN NEW DEAL. Drafted by BUREAU OF INDIAN AFFAIRS (BIA) commissioner JOHN COLLIER and his staff, principally FELIX SOLOMON COHEN, the act prohibited any further ALLOTMENT of tribal lands; facilitated consolidation of fractionated lands and tribal purchase of necessary lands; established a revolving credit fund for tribes; encouraged tribes to adopt constitutions and form themselves into governments "in the nature of municipal corporations"; allowed tribes to charter corporations for economic enterprises; gave tribes authority over various BIA, state, and local functions; and also gave tribes the right to prior review of annual appropriation requests by the BIA.

Collier's original bill envisioned reform in four areas: tribal self-government, landholding, education, and the establishment of a special court of Indian affairs to preside over Indian cases in place of federal district courts. Congress significantly altered the bill, and the only provision to pass unchanged was the one ending Allotment. Collier's proposed court of Indian affairs was eliminated altogether. After much debate, the bill was enacted on June 18, 1934.

The IRA entitled tribes to adopt their own constitutions and engage in self-government of a limited kind. This legislation went beyond Collier's proposal to give the new tribal governments unrestricted powers to negotiate with federal, state, and local governments and to exercise the same powers as existing tribal governments. These "unrestricted powers" were left unclear at the time, but Nathan R. Margold, the solicitor general of the Department of Interior, later issued an opinion defining them. The legislation also directed the secretary of the interior to revise the BIA's standards for employment so that a greater number of qualified Indians could be hired at the BIA.

Among its economic provisions, the IRA returned certain surplus lands to tribes and set up a credit fund of $10 million to fund tribal projects and provide annual appropriations for the purchase of additional tribal lands. This funding was later scaled back. Collier's educational projects were also scaled back, particularly the funding for grants to Indian students and for the encouragement of Indian culture, but the IRA did offer $250,000 a year in low-interest loans for education "in recognized vocational and trade schools."

All tribes were to be given the chance to vote within the year on whether or not to accept the IRA, and unless a majority of adult tribal members voted against it, the legislation would go into effect. This provision favored the "progressive" members of any tribe, since traditional Indians, who were more likely to vote against the IRA, often boycotted such elections. The IRA was in fact ratified by a minority of tribal members in the case of 17 tribes.

Implementation of the IRA by the BIA began with attempts to clarify some of the act's vague language. Nathan Margold worked with Collier to produce a 32-page opinion entitled "Powers of Indian Tribes," issued on October 25, 1934. In this document, Margold defined the scope of the new tribal governments. He identified these powers as "inherent powers of a limited sovereignty which has never been extinguished" rather than powers granted by Congress. In this way, the opinion recognized some form of original and lasting Indian sovereignty (see SOVEREIGNTY, INDIGENOUS AND TRIBAL). Among the specific tribal powers acknowledged were the right to establish their own forms of government, offices, and procedures; define membership and voting rights; regulate inheritance, fees, taxes, domestic relations, and the use of property; administer justice; and define the duties of federal employees when these were not established by the Department of the Interior. Through this opinion, Collier reestablished many of his original ideas that had been removed from the IRA in congressional discussions. He also established the vital concept of tribal sovereignty as a power not derived from Congress but inherent in tribes.

In the tribal elections of 1934–35, the BIA, through local superintendents and agents of its organization division, promoted the IRA (see FARVER, PERU; LA FARGE, OLIVER; PHINNEY, ARCHIE). It was eventually ratified by 181 tribes and rejected by 77, including such major tribes as the Klamath, the Crow, and the Navajo (Dineh). Those that ratified it were then visited by field agents, sometimes anthropologists from Collier's applied anthropology staff (see ANTHROPOLOGISTS AND AMERICAN INDIANS), who were to act as advisers in the development of tribal constitutions. The constitutions were then supplied by attorneys at the Department of the Interior, based in many cases on a "boiler-plate" tribal constitution already drafted by government employees. Only 96 of the tribes who passed the IRA actually adopted such government-approved constitutions, and only 73 were given corporate business charters, entitling them to participate in the revolving credit fund.

The IRA did not remove outdated laws, guarantee that treaties would be kept, or extend Indians' civil rights. It did, however, give the tribes greater economic and political liberties.

The IRA's historical context is perhaps best seen by examining the complaints of its detractors. As early as 1937, Senator Burton K. Wheeler, one of the bill's original sponsors, called for its repeal. In a report of Wheeler's hearing of June 22, 1944, the act was blamed for perpetuating a system of indefinite land titles that ensured permanent government supervision and control; complete incompatibility of Indian land policies with the American system of LAND TENURE; placing more than 500,000 acres of land under BIA supervision, much of which would go unused; providing for complete regimentation of Indians through the system of loans; and strengthening and perpetuating the reservation system.

These criticisms reflect the very philosophy that the bill had been meant to defeat in the first place. Before 1934, or at least before the MERIAM REPORT of 1928, the Indian Bureau, in theory, had but one mandate—to assimilate the Indian out of existence (see ASSIMILATION) and put itself out of business. Intimately familiar with the damage done by previous policies, Collier instead tried to upgrade and redefine the BIA in positive terms. He put it to work to reverse the loss of tribal lands, encourage the development of tribal cultures, and develop an enlightened administration.

Collier, however, held an attitude, characteristic of American political philosophy, that if a government is democratic in form, it will be a good government. The IRA envisioned tribes adopting constitutions modeled on that of the United States, rather than promoting traditional forms of government. In fact, for many tribes, the democratic form of government established by the IRA constitutions was just another imposition.

As Cherokee anthropologist ROBERT KNOX THOMAS wrote in *Eastern American Indian Communities* in 1974:

> When tribal groups have had the autonomy to be able to use their own institutions or to develop new institutions so they could learn together as communities about their new environment, a civilization, then they have been able to make adjustments to the outside and handle the internal effects brought about by the presence of that outside force.

But this has rarely happened. On most reservations, all previous institutional structures were destroyed by governmental agencies and new institutions were not allowed to develop. Thus, Thomas continued:

> So-called tribal governments are creations of the Federal governments—set up by urban people who do not value harmony in human relationships, as reflected by such secular notions as individual and secret balloting, majority rule and representation by geographical area instead of kin group. Such outside created structures have been simply dropped on the heads of Indians and not only function as the internal arm of the Federal government, but are socially destructive as well to Indians.

In 1989, performance artist JAMES LUNA expressed it this way:

> Originally, authority was determined by ancestry, though one might be able to "understudy" with a leader, a dancer, a hunter, or a healer. When the U.S. Bureau of Indian Affairs came in and set up tribal councils, in an attempt at democracy, this was yet another source of ambivalence for us. The establishment of reservations gave us certain rights and encouraged stability, but the idea of ownership was foreign to Indians and it brought with it a kind of devastation. We knew the points of our world because they were established by landmarks, and we believed the territory within belonged to all of us, both personally and collectively.

For Indians, the greatest benefits of the IRA in the 1930s was not in the text alone but in Margold and Cohen's legal interpretation of the act. After WORLD WAR II, however, the

BIA began a new policy called TERMINATION that aimed to assimilate Indians, terminate the special trust relationships the tribes enjoyed with the government, and sell off reservations. Instead of trying to repeal the Indian Reorganization Act, the act's opponents found ways to use the New Deal machinery to their advantage. In particular, these opponents sought to integrate Indian policy more smoothly into the whole fabric of U.S. law regarding federal lands. Although the IRA system of constitutional governments for tribes was not designed to open Indian lands to corporate exploitation, it was increasingly used for that purpose in the growing postwar economy.

See also JOHNSON-O'MALLEY ACT.

Further Reading

Deloria, Vine, Jr., and Clifford M. Lytle. *The Nations Within: The Past and Future of American Indian Sovereignty.* 1984. Reprint. Austin: University of Texas Press, 1998.

Rusco, Elmer R. *A Fateful Time: The Background and Legislative History of the Indian Reorganization Act.* Reno: University of Nevada Press, 2000.

Taylor, Graham D. *The New Deal and American Indian Tribalism: The Administration of the Indian Reorganization Act, 1934–1945.* Lincoln: University of Nebraska Press, 1980.

Indian reservations

Reservations are lands exclusively set aside for Indian use and generally protected from alienation and taxation; they are currently recognized by the federal, state, and local governments as Indian lands. Reservations were created for Indians as early as the 17th century, in order to protect them from constant settler encroachment. However, the greatest period of reservation creation occurred during the latter half of the 19th and the early 20th centuries.

Reservations vary in the manner of their creation, the type of land ownership that exists within them, and the degree of protection accorded them by the various governments. The very earliest reservations were created by treaties between Indians and various colonial governments and later became state reservations. After the creation of the United States, federal reservations were set aside by treaties between Indian tribes and the federal government. Later reservations were often created by legislation or, more commonly, by executive order. Pueblos and rancherias, Indian lands in the Southwest that were recognized by Spain and Mexico before their incorporation into the United States, have a similar legal status to reservations, although they go back to Spanish or Mexican land grants. Lands owned by the tribes living on a reservation are generally under federal jurisdiction and therefore not subject to state and local taxation or most state civil laws. As a legacy of the ALLOTMENT period, when policy makers sought to break up Indian reservations, many lands on Indian reservations became the property either of individual Indians (rather than the tribe) on a "fee simple" basis, or of non-Indians (see LAND TENURE).

As a consequence of the INDIAN REORGANIZATION ACT (1934), tribal governments exert jurisdiction over Indians and Indian land on Indian reservations; however, their jurisdiction over non-Indians has been successively limited by federal courts and legislation. In the case of Oklahoma, where most reservations were dissolved under the CURTIS ACT (1898), Indians may live in "Indian historical areas." These areas may or may not have tribal land held in trust, like reservations. In the late 1940s and 1950s, known as the TERMINATION era, the federal government attempted once again to break up Indian reservations.

At the start of the 21st century, the United States recognized 280 Indian reservations, and the states recognized several dozen more.

There are also 223 federally recognized Alaska Native villages formed under the previsions of the ALASKA NATIVE LAND CLAIMS SETTLEMENT ACT of 1971.

See also MINING, AMERICAN INDIANS AND; OIL, AMERICAN INDIANS AND; SOVEREIGNTY, INDIGENOUS AND TRIBAL.

Further Reading

Frantz, Klaus. *Indian Reservations in the United States: Territory, Sovereignty, and Socioeconomic Change.* Chicago: University of Chicago Press, 1999.

Kickingbird, Kirke, and Karen Ducheneaux. *One Hundred Million Acres.* New York: Macmillan, 1973.

Sutton, Imre. "Land Tenure, Tribal Sovereignty, and the States." In *Law in the Western United States*, edited by Gordon Morris Bakken, 251–266. Norman: University of Oklahoma Press, 2000.

United States Bureau of the Census, "Chapter 5." In *Geographic Areas Reference Manual.* Washington: U.S. Dept. of Commerce, Economics and Statistics Administration, Bureau of the Census, 1994. Available online. URL: http://www.census.gov/geo/www/GARM /Ch5GARM.pdf. Accessed 29 October 2007.

Indians in Science   *See* SCIENCE, AMERICAN INDIANS AND.

Indian Rights Association (IRA)

The Indian Rights Association (IRA) was a non-Indian advocacy organization that from 1882 until 1994 dedicated itself to protecting the rights of Indian peoples. It exercised a significant influence on government policy toward Indians during the latter part of the 19th century and the first quarter of the 20th century. The IRA was founded on December 15, 1882, in Philadelphia by Herbert Welsh (1851–1941), a wealthy Philadelphian artist, and Henry Spackman Pancoast (1858–1928), a lawyer and author. Welsh was the nephew of William Welsh, a prominent member of the Episcopal Church who helped formulate President Ulysses S. Grant's Peace Policy toward Indians during the 1870s.

The IRA grew out of a tour Welsh and Pancoast made in summer 1882 visiting Episcopalian missionaries among the Sioux in North and South Dakota. This experience embued them with the belief that Indians could be "civilized" through just, wise, and consistent government policies and the extension of missionary efforts. To build public sentiment for government reform, Indian education, the protection of individual Indian's land rights, and, ultimately, CITIZENSHIP for all Indians, they formed the IRA.

The organization's founding coincided with a growing public backlash over federal Indian policy, which if anything was geared to defrauding Indians and aiding the armies of speculators, squatters, and carpetbaggers who clamored for Indian land. In 1879, the Women's National Indian Treaty-Keeping and Protective Association (later shortened to the Women's National Indian Association) was founded in Philadelphia by two non-Indian women, Mary Bonney (1816–1900) and Amelia Stone Quinton (1833–1926), to try to stop the illegal settlement of INDIAN RESERVATIONS and to force the government to uphold Indian treaties. Also in 1879, RICHARD HENRY PRATT opened the first federal boarding school for Indians at Carlisle, Pennsylvania, with the goal of "saving" Indian children by training them, by force if need be, to integrate into mainstream society (see EDUCATIONAL POLICY, AMERICAN INDIANS AND). The reform movement gathered steam with the activist work of Helen Hunt Jackson (1830–85) and the outrage that followed the publication of her bitter indictment of the U.S. government's treatment of Indian peoples, *A Century of Dishonor*, in 1881.

In 1883, Welsh attended the first Lake Mohonk Conference of the Friends of the Indian, held in upstate New York. Organized by Quaker educator Albert K. Smiley (1828–1912), the Lake Mohonk Conference brought the various new reform groups and sympathetic government officials together to try to develop a new Indian policy. These reformers, liberal by the standards of their day, believed that the then-current government policy of warfare and military occupation should be replaced with one that focused on the education and Christianization of Indians. In their view, the only way to protect Indians from the conservatives, who advocated their complete extinction, was to force Indians to adopt Anglo-American ways (see ASSIMILATION).

The reformers sought the breakup of Indian reservations and the end of communal Indian landholdings through the allotment of Indian lands into small individual holdings. This, they thought, would take Indian lands out from under the corrupt management of Congress and the Indian Office (as the BUREAU OF INDIAN AFFAIRS was known at the time) and place it under the general protections accorded to individual property (see LAND TENURE). It would also force Indians to give up their traditional lifestyle and become farmers or laborers.

At a time when the federal government was spending almost nothing on Indian education, the reformers advocated education for all Indians, with the goal of eradicating Indian culture and preparing young Indians for work in mainstream society. At the same time, Indians had virtually no rights under the law and were effectively wards of the government, and so the reformers aimed to end the Indians' dependence on the Indian Office and to help them become full, productive citizens with all the same rights as other Americans. Thus, the reformers proposed concrete solutions to genuine problems but did so from their own cultural perspective, with only the most limited understanding of Indian cultures and with almost no Indian input. Although these policies were seen as the only options to protect Indians from extinction, they would have many negative consequences for Indian peoples and their cultures.

The IRA was intensely practical from the beginning, opening an office in Washington, D.C., in 1884 and hiring Congregational minister and former abolitionist Charles Cornelius Painter (1883–95) as their lobbyist. Their first president was Wayne MacVeagh (1833–1917), a prominent Pennsylvania lawyer and Civil War hero who had been ambassador to Turkey under President Grant and attorney general under President James A. Garfield. Welsh served as corresponding secretary, a position that gave him considerable influence, and Pancoast was their legal counsel. The IRA immediately went to work to try to stop the numerous frauds being perpetrated against Indians by launching investigations and sending its members across the country to expose wrongdoing. The group was aided by the publication in 1884 of Helen Hunt Jackson's *Ramona*, a tragic novel of two Indian lovers persecuted by non-Indians, which became a national best seller and galvanized public sentiment around the growing movement to protect Indian rights.

In late 1885, MacVeagh stepped down as president of the IRA in favor of James E. Rhoads (1828–95), a prominent Quaker and the president of newly created Bryn Mawr College. The organization began publishing a newsletter, *Indian Truth*, and began printing special reports on Indian issues. Within a few years, they were distributing more than 40,000 pamphlets a year, a prodigious output for the time. Their agents made regular field trips to reservations, bringing a critical eye to the Indian Office's activities and reporting instances of incompetence and graft. The IRA became masters at effective use of the press, often embarrassing the office and Congress into action.

IRA agents investigated timber and mineral sales on Indian reservations, a common source of fraud, and fought off numerous attempts by the Indian Office to use funds earmarked for Indians to pay for projects benefiting non-Indians. By publicly exposing the deplorable conditions under which 447 Apache prisoners of war, most of them women and children, were confined in an old fort in St. Augustine, Florida, the IRA managed to secure their transfer to better quarters in Indian Territory (now Oklahoma) in 1894. The following year, they stopped a gang of speculators and politicians known as the Durango Ring from forcibly evicting the Southern Ute from Colorado. Beginning in 1898, the IRA worked to help the Gila River Pima safeguard their water rights, eventually securing the removal of, and a criminal indictment against, the reservation's superintendent (see PIMA-MARICOPA WATER RIGHTS). In two particularly egregious cases in 1906, they managed to prevent Congressman ALBERT BACON FALL from turning the Mescalero Apache Reservation into his own

personal park, and derailed Congressman CHARLES HENRY BURKE's attempts to sell off a million acres of the Rosebud Reservation in South Dakota to some of his friends.

The IRA won a major victory with the passage of the General Allotment Act of 1887, also known as the Dawes Act, and the inauguration of ALLOTMENT, a transformative policy that would remain in force for almost 45 years. By the time Indian commissioner WILLIAM ARTHUR JONES took office (1897) the political power of the IRA was so great that he was grudgingly forced to accommodate the organization's demands for the extension of civil service reforms to the Indian Office, and for the creation of day schools on Indian reservations.

In 1891, the IRA secured the passage of the Act for the Relief of the Mission Indians, which directed the government to set aside lands for the Mission Indians of California, who were facing extinction. The organization attempted to uphold Indian treaties by financing the landmark case *Lone Wolf v. Hitchcock* through the court system, but their loss before the U.S. Supreme Court was a bitter blow to Indian rights (see SOVEREIGNTY, INDIGENOUS AND TRIBAL).

The deaths in 1895 of their energetic Washington lobbyist, Painter, and their president, Rhoads, did not stop the IRA. They found equally capable replacements in newspaperman FRANCIS ELLINGTON LEUPP, who succeeded Painter as Washington agent, and longtime IRA member Philip C. Garrett (1834–1905), a prosperous Quaker who succeeded Rhoads. Leupp left the IRA in 1898 and was replaced as Washington agent by the even more formidable Samuel M. Brosius (1851–1936), a prominent Quaker attorney. Although Welsh became president when Garrett died in 1905, he had by that time become immersed in other causes. He left the running of the organization to Brosius and longtime IRA investigator and author Matthew K. Sniffen (1867–1942), who succeeded Welsh as corresponding secretary.

When their former Washington agent, Leupp, became Indian commissioner in 1905, the IRA was at the height of its power. Both Leupp and his successor, ROBERT GROSVENOR VALENTINE, worked closely with the IRA, even asking the organization to conduct investigations on behalf of the Indian Office. However, the Progressive Era commissioners found it impossible to reform the Indian Office, and the IRA eventually turned on Valentine after he proved ineffective.

Under Brosius and Sniffen, the IRA remained ardently assimilationist, vetoing Omaha attorney THOMAS SLOAN's 1920 bid to become Indian commissioner on the grounds that Sloan was too accommodating to Indian use of peyote (see NATIVE AMERICAN CHURCH). Instead, they supported arch-assimilationist Charles Henry Burke, Sloan's rival, despite the former congressman's previous attempts to defraud Indians. Commissioner Burke's efforts to stamp out Indian religions through his infamous DANCE ORDERS had the wholehearted backing of the IRA.

In 1924, the IRA achieved one of its long-standing goals with the passage of the Indian Citizenship Act, drafted by Brosius, which conferred citizenship on all Indians born in the United States. By the mid-1920s, however, fraud in the government's Indian administration had reached new heights, in part because of wheeling and dealing by Burke and his superior, Interior Secretary Albert Fall, and in part because the Allotment policy championed by the IRA was a fount of corruption. As early as 1903, the IRA was forced to investigate government officials for speculating in Indian lands marked for allotment under the CURTIS ACT. The act, which opened up Indian Territory, led to such massive fraud that the IRA launched an investigation that culminated in the report, *Oklahoma's Poor Rich Indians: An Orgy of Graft and Exploitation of the Five Civilized Tribes, Legalized Robbery.* Written in part by Dakota activist GERTRUDE BONNIN, its release in 1924 led to a large public outcry.

The dismal state of Indian affairs led President Warren Harding to appoint Sniffen to a special panel, the COMMITTEE OF ONE HUNDRED, to examine government Indian policy. In the resulting shakeup, Interior Secretary Ray Lyman Wilbur called for a "new deal for Indians" (see INDIAN NEW DEAL) and named two long-standing members of the IRA to top positions in the Bureau—CHARLES JAMES RHOADS, son of former IRA president James Rhoads, and JOSEPH HENRY SCATTERGOOD. Although this was an important victory for the IRA, their assimilationist policies were by this time falling out of favor. Despite heavy lobbying by the IRA to keep Rhoads on as commissioner, in 1932 incoming President Franklin Delano Roosevelt appointed in his stead JOHN COLLIER, an activist who believed that Indian lands and cultures should be preserved rather than given up. Under Collier, assimilation and allotment, the foundations of the IRA's Indian policy, were overturned. The IRA bitterly fought Collier's efforts to transform the bureau, and as a consequence lost virtually all its political power and influence.

In the 1940s, as its leading members began to die off and as Indian rights groups led by Indians, such as the NATIONAL CONGRESS OF AMERICAN INDIANS, were established, the IRA faded into the background. It continued to advocate for Indian rights and to keep a critical eye on the Bureau of Indian Affairs, largely through the tireless efforts of longtime members and prominent Quakers, Lawrence E. Lindley and Theodore Hetzel. Under their leadership the IRA fought for the return of BLUE LAKE to Taos Pueblo and tried to stop the flooding of Seneca lands by the KINZUA DAM. The group also fought for greater expenditures by Congress for Indian health and education programs. After their deaths, the IRA finally dissolved in 1994. The organization's legacy, however, was immense, and its effect on Indian policy in the early 20th century cannot be overstated. It did much to stop the most egregious abuses against Indians, and many tribes, such as the Mission Indians in California, owe their continued existence to the IRA. However, the Allotment and assimilation policies promulgated by the IRA led to a massive loss of Indian lands and irreplaceable cultural losses, some of which continue to plague Indian people to this day.

See also BURSUM BILL; COLTON, HAROLD SELLERS; DU BOIS, CONSTANCE GODDARD; INDIAN INDUSTRIES LEAGUE; MCKENZIE, FAYETTE AVERY; MOOREHEAD, WARREN KING.

Further Reading
Hagan, William Thomas. *The Indian Rights Association: The Herbert Welsh Years, 1882–1904.* Tucson: University of Arizona Press, 1985.

Indians of All Tribes

Indians of All Tribes, a short-lived militant rights organization, was founded in the wake of the second OCCUPATION OF ALCATRAZ ISLAND. Originally proposed by Belvia Cottier, a Lakota woman involved in the planning of the occupation, the name was meant to reflect the diversity of the group that landed on the island in November 1969. Leadership of the organization, which was formed shortly after the occupation began on November 22, was restricted to the occupiers of the island, mostly young Indian students from California colleges who were followers of Mohawk activist RICHARD OAKES. Unlike the Bay Area Indians, who had for years hoped to gain the island for the community, the members of Indians of All Tribes, true to their college-oriented, 1960s style of protest, were more interested in promoting broader Indian rights and self-determination, seeing the occupation as a larger, symbolic effort.

Indians of All Tribes was incorporated on January 15, 1970. The original board of directors was composed of Stella Leach (Colville-Lakota Sioux) and her son David, Alan Miller (Seminole), Judy Scraper (Shawnee), Ray Spang (Northern Cheyenne), Denis Turner (Luiseño), and Richard Oakes. However, by that time, under a cloud of jealousy and resentment from the other occupiers, Oakes had already left the occupation in the wake of the accidental death of his stepdaughter. The group's leadership then fell to Stella Leach, an abrasive and bitter woman who had advocated the TERMINATION of the Colvilles during the 1950s, and who at 50 was far older than the others; JOHN TRUDELL, who started a radio show; and Shoshone-Bannock activist LaNada Means, a student at Berkeley.

Means's attempts to negotiate the transfer of the island to Indian peoples were subverted by the other leaders, who mistrusted her plans to turn it into a cultural center and preferred to maintain the occupation for as long as possible. As a consequence, negotiations with the federal government achieved nothing, in marked contrast to the takeover of Fort Lawton in Washington State, launched in the wake of Alcatraz, which secured the return of land for the Native community there.

Indians of All Tribes experienced enormous turmoil during the 19-month takeover. The creation of a tough security force under David Leach only added to the problems, leading to the defection of most of its founders and the gradual collapse of the occupation. When the takeover ended on June 11, 1971, its most prominent member, Trudell, joined the AMERICAN INDIAN MOVEMENT (AIM), and Indians of All Tribes ceased to exist as an effective organization. Despite all its problems, Indians of All Tribes marked the beginning of a new era in the RED POWER MOVEMENT, one that added the tactics and rhetoric of the 1960s antiwar protest movement to the demands for sovereignty and justice for Indian people. This explosive mix was ignited shortly thereafter with the TRAIL OF BROKEN TREATIES and the OCCUPATION OF WOUNDED KNEE.

Indians of All Tribes should not be confused with United Indians of All Tribes, a nonprofit foundation based in Seattle, Washington, and founded in 1970.

Indian Welfare Committee   *See* GENERAL FEDERATION OF WOMEN'S CLUBS, INDIAN WELFARE COMMITTEE.

indigenous economics

The term *indigenous economics* refers to the traditional thought and practice of indigenous peoples relating to economic issues, as well as to the branch of social science that studies this aspect of human culture. Most mainstream economic theories are based on a model of "rational economic man" that always seeks economic advantage in market exchanges measured in units of monetary value. While this reflects certain realities of life under industrial capitalism, it often misses important value considerations even in industrial societies. When applied to peasant and indigenous societies, it is seriously inadequate. It is true that indigenous exchanges are also based on value, but these values are often specific to particular cultures and not easily understood by others. In addition, resources in a particular indigenous culture are allocated according to practical, religious, and social values that are unique to that culture and can only be determined by the indigenous people themselves. Economic life is organically connected to all other aspects of life, and many values considered exchangeable and quantifiable by mainstream economics are regarded by indigenous cultures as nonexchangeable and unquantifiable. Those who study indigenous economics must use anthropological methods to try to understand the entire culture.

It has been found that despite the tremendous diversity of indigenous peoples and environments around the world, the traditional economic thought and practice of indigenous peoples share certain basic principles, generally referred to by the scientists who study them as "traditional ecological knowledge." Traditional rural cultures tend to see humans as an integral component of the ecosystem, not above and apart from it; nature itself is viewed as the primary and fundamental producer of wealth; and the labor and technology that modify the products of nature are seen as themselves part of nature and therefore must keep within nature's laws. From this standpoint, the term *economic development* means maintaining the ecosystem at a maximum degree of complexity, harmony, and balance, preserving and enhancing the productive powers of nature while developing and applying technology in such a way as to extend rather than diminish these powers.

Traditional ecological knowledge sees the entire ecosystem as a sphere of common good, a community. Thus, community building is both the method and the goal of indigenous economic development. But community in Native thought has a far wider meaning than in most Western thought: a

community in which not only humans but all other creatures have both rights and responsibilities.

In order to subjugate Indian tribes in the 19th century, federal Indian policy encouraged the destruction of traditional Native economic systems. For example, the mass slaughter of the buffalo was seen as the best means to force Plains Indians onto reservations, where decades of paternalistic Indian Bureau (later BUREAU OF INDIAN AFFAIRS [BIA]) management badly eroded the viability of traditional leadership and the capacity of communities to set their own priorities and act on them. With their traditional economies curtailed, reservation Indians became dependent on government rations. Economic development plans, such as leasing, were primarily designed to make profits for non-Indians with, at best, some side benefits for the tribe. Those development plans were based on culturally alien models imposed by the mainstream society as a means of ASSIMILATION.

At the very start of the 20th century, attempts were begun to find ways of economic development for Indians that would be more in harmony with traditional values, as well as to preserve and adapt arts and techniques that were threatened with extinction (see GARLAND, HAMLIN). One of the earliest areas of indigenous economic development was in traditional arts and crafts, spearheaded by the INDIAN INDUSTRIES LEAGUE. Shortly thereafter came the program of LAURA CORNELIUS KELLOGG and CHESTER POE CORNELIUS among the Keetoowah (traditional Cherokee) in Oklahoma and Arkansas in the 1910s and 1920s. From the 1930s to the 1950s, there was a conscious revival of community development, spurred by JOHN COLLIER's desire to apply new concepts from the social sciences to problems of Indian administration, and by the community work of people such as RUTH MUSKRAT BRONSON, GEORGE P. LAVATTA, D'ARCY MCNICKLE, ANNIE DODGE WAUNEKA, and SOL TAX.

With the failure of TERMINATION in the 1950s and of the BIA-promoted economic development campaigns of the 1960s and early 1970s (essentially top-down industrialization and tourism schemes), and with tribes facing increased pressure from multinational resource-extraction cartels, the last decades of the 20th century saw a revival of traditional Native culture and cultural values. But no culture can survive without an economic base. As the Seneca journalist JOHN MOHAWK wrote in 1978 in *Akwesasne Notes*, "Even spiritual life revolves to a considerable extent around the ways that people see their lives supported."

However, the economic mode of mainstream society is in many ways destructive of traditional culture. Mohawk also notes, "Economic policies such as industrialization were introduced to Native communities with the full weight of the federal government. The major target of those programs was the replacement and destruction of the traditional economies, and to that end, the programs were surprisingly successful. . . ."

Since traditional culture always had an economic base, advocates of indigenous economics sought the roots of a culturally compatible economic system in Native tradition itself. Though conditions have changed greatly, the principles themselves can still be applied. Thus, indigenous economics was proposed as a working model for Native communities. As Paula Hammett (then a staff member at the Tribal Sovereignty Program) and Cayuga leader DANIEL R. BOMBERRY wrote in the opening editorial of the first issue of *Native Self-Sufficiency* (April 1978), "The roots of self-sufficiency are deep within our cultures and traditional economies. With a little nurturing and some cross-fertilization from the contemporary 'back-to-the-land' movement they can once again sprout new economies that can sustain our people in the future."

Tradition is thus the first source. The second, out of which culturally appropriate methods can be adapted, is the economic reform movements that have arisen as Western culture's own response to the excesses of capitalism and industrialism and that tend to be compatible with traditional community economics—reforms such as the cooperative movement, credit associations, appropriate technology, the back-to-the-land movement, traditional foods and agricultural practices, and community building or regeneration.

As Cherokee leader WILMA MANKILLER wrote in *Native Self-Sufficiency* (Spring 1987), economic development means rebuilding a people and a nation, their faith in themselves and their own ability to do things. A business is not in and of itself economic development. Housing, water systems, community centers, and HEALTH, nutrition, and alcohol programs are economic development. In general, strengthening the leadership ability and the creativity of the people themselves is economic development.

"Successful economic development projects," noted Victoria Bomberry and Jacques Seronde in *Native Self-Sufficiency* (Spring 1988), "must be planned, managed, evaluated and owned by the community people themselves, the process must be broadly comprehensive or integrative of all appropriate needs, aspirations, capabilities, and resources. A sustainable economy has to allow the people to flourish, to use their talents, to solve their own problems, to express their spiritual side of life, to ask for appropriate technical help and get it, all on the community's terms."

The community has to start from wherever it is and go step by step, piece by piece, doing what works, Mankiller believes. As she put it, "You don't start by having General Motors come in. GM isn't going to come to Eastern Oklahoma, and I'm not sure we want them to. No one looks at our economic development system, what we had for thousands and thousands of years. These systems that we are adopting today are relatively new. We need to go back and look at our own indigenous forms of economy and begin to rebuild those. What seems impossible is entirely possible. We can rebuild our Nation."

The government's role, in this view, is simply to facilitate this process through partnership, not to do what the community ought to be doing for itself. Government can raise money, organize, and act as facilitators if the community itself commits to building what it needs. Every family should participate, for such community effort transcends factionalism. Everyone does what they can according to their abilities. In this way, they begin to realize they have the power to change their communities.

With the revival of indigenous economics, the concept was extended to techniques of wealth creation that are more remote from tradition but, if managed according to general principles of community economics, can still be compatible with it: elements such as trust funds, credit institutions, tribal philanthropy, marketing and other business techniques, and, in some cultures, gaming. The Blackfeet and others have shown that even factory production, when developed and managed according to traditional principles, can be compatible with traditional values.

Among the organizations supporting indigenous economics projects are the Seventh Generation Fund, First Nations Financial Development Institute, and Native Seeds/SEARCH. Writers and thinkers who have contributed to this movement include John Mohawk, Daniel Bomberry, Victoria Bomberry, Paula Hammett, Jacques Seronde, Wilma Mankiller, Gary Nabhan, Wes Jackson, Jane Mt. Pleasant, Mahina Drees, Rebecca Adamson, Sherry Salway Black, Peggy Berryhill, Tom Barry, JAMES S. WILLIAMSON, and others. Of all tribal leaders, Winnebago REUBEN SNAKE was probably the most supportive of this philosophy of economic development. The greatest contribution of all, however, has come from traditional elders, who continue teaching the basic principles of harmony with all life.

Further Reading

"Indigenous Economics: Toward a Natural World Order." *Akwe:kon Journal* 9, no. 2 (Summer 1992).

Johansen, Bruce E. *The Encyclopedia of Native American Economic History*. Westport, Conn.: Greenwood Press, 1999.

Mohawk, John. "Regaining Control of Our Lives: The Promise of Alternative Technology." *Akwesasne Notes* (Autumn 1978): 4–6.

Underwood, Paula. "Creation and Organization: A Native American Looks at Economics." *Perspectives on Business and Global Change* 10, no. 4 (1996): 24.

Wuttunee, Wanda Ann. *Living Rhythms: Lessons in Aboriginal Economic Resilience and Vision*. Montreal: McGill–Queens University Press, 2004.

Indigenous Environmental Network (IEN)

Based in Bemidji, Minnesota, the Indigenous Environmental Network (IEN) is an alliance of grassroots Native environmental organizations. Its mission is to protect the sacredness of the Earth from contamination and exploitation by strengthening, maintaining, and respecting traditional teachings and natural laws. At a grassroots level, IEN seeks to educate and empower indigenous peoples to address and develop strategies to protect the environment; to reaffirm traditional and natural laws according to indigenous cultural traditions; to recognize, support, and promote environmentally sound lifestyles and economic livelihoods; to influence all politics that affect indigenous peoples on a local, regional, national, and international level; and to protect Native peoples' rights to practice their spiritual beliefs. It tries to include youth and elders in all levels of its activities.

IEN acts as a national clearinghouse of information; maintains a resource and referral network for technical information and fact sheets; provides national, regional, and local advocacy on indigenous grassroots issues; and gives referrals and support for grassroots organizing, training, and strategizing. It also keeps abreast of indigenous grassroots environmental groups and environmental programs of tribal governments.

In the late 1980s, national and multinational corporations began systematically targeting indigenous peoples' lands as sites for toxic dumps and other environmentally hazardous projects. IEN grew out of attempts by Indian communities to fight these projects. In June 1990, Diné CARE (Citizens Against Ruining the Environment), a grassroots Dineh (Navajo) community organization that had recently prevented the building of a toxic waste incinerator and landfill on tribal lands, hosted a gathering on Dineh Nation territory at Dilkon, Arizona. The idea of holding yearly gatherings for Native communities to educate one another about environmental issues was born here. Since then, each of its annual gatherings has been held on or near a threatened site in order to educate the environmental community, Native and non-Native, about the particular problems involved, as well as other problems in different parts of Indian country.

The second annual gathering, "Toxic Threat to Indian Lands," was hosted near Bear Butte, South Dakota, in June 1991, by two Lakota organizations, the Native Resource Coalition (from the Pine Ridge Reservation) and the Good Road Coalition (from the Rosebud Reservation), the latter of which had stopped the siting of a 5,000-acre toxic landfill on their lands. This conference officially established the IEN and adopted an environmental code of ethics that affirmed the commitment of indigenous peoples to the protection of the Earth and emphasized the distinctive indigenous world view based on natural law and reflected in ancestral teachings and knowledge of traditional elders.

The IEN code of ethics further calls for a multicultural coalition of peoples, including religious coalitions, to defend the Earth. It supports indigenous self-determination and in particular urges indigenous peoples to speak for themselves and not let non-Native environmental organizations make decisions for them. IEN supports environmental justice regardless of race, economic position, gender, or national identity; rejects any accommodations or deals with polluters; and considers violations of environmental justice to be against international law, the UN Universal Declaration of Human Rights, and the UN Convention on Genocide.

The third annual gathering, held in 1992 at the village of Celilo Falls, Oregon, was hosted by the Columbia River Defense Project—an organization defending the traditional hunting, fishing, and gathering rights of the Klickitat and Cascade peoples—and the Indigenous Peoples Alliance. At this meeting, the task force was increased to 17 members, reflecting a wider regional representation. A small group, the Native American Energy Coalition, was formed to fight the extraction, processing, and transportation of radioactive materials within indigenous territories.

IEN's fourth conference, the first hosted by a tribal government, was held at Stroud, Oklahoma, in June 1993 and was sponsored by the Sac and Fox Nation and the Oklahoma Environmental Network. The fifth gathering (1994), hosted by the Sokagaon band of Chippewa, the Midwest Treaty Rights Group, Anishnabe Niiji, and other indigenous communities in Wisconsin, was held at Mole Lake, Wisconsin, where Rio Tinto Zinc was threatening to develop a copper mine that would have destroyed the reservation's wild rice resource. Gatherings have continued at different locations each year.

Since passage of the North American Free Trade Agreement (NAFTA) in 1993 and the Uruguay Round of the General Agreement on Tariffs and Trade (GATT 1994), IEN has been particularly concerned about the effects of the globalization of international trade on indigenous peoples, including such issues as diminishing biodiversity and exploitation of indigenous intellectual property, especially with regard to indigenous crop varieties and medicinal plants.

See also ENVIRONMENTAL MOVEMENT, AMERICAN INDIANS AND THE; LADUKE, WINONA.

Further Reading

Cole, Luke W., and Sheila R. Foster. *From the Ground Up: Environmental Racism and the Rise of the Environmental Justice Movement*, 134–140. New York: New York University Press, 2001.

Gedicks, Al. *The New Resource Wars: Native and Environmental Struggles against Multinational Corporations*. Montreal, Canada, and Cheektowaga, N.Y.: Black Rose Books, 1994.

indigenous language use

The number of speakers of Indian languages as a percentage of the total American Indian population has undergone a catastrophic decline since the beginning of the 20th century. By the century's end, many languages had become extinct or were on the verge of extinction. Loss of language diversity is a global trend, and it has been estimated that, at current rates, the 5,500 currently living languages will be reduced in a century or two to just a few hundred. American Indian languages have been especially hard hit.

Of the world's languages that are considered nearly extinct, more than one-quarter are indigenous languages of the United States. The exact numbers are difficult to determine, in part because of differences among scholars as to what constitutes a language and what a dialect, but also because there are great differences in competence and fluency among speakers of a language and because many surveys rely on self-evaluation.

It is believed that at the time of Christopher Columbus's voyage in 1492, North America was among the most linguistically diverse regions in the world, with at least 300 indigenous languages being spoken in what is now the United States alone. By the end of the 20th century, there were approximately 150, and of those, one-third had fewer than 100 fluent speakers and were considered near extinction. More ominous, 28 Native languages had 10 or fewer speakers and were in critical danger of disappearing within the next few years.

The decline in American Indian language use is a direct result of federal policies of ASSIMILATION, begun in the 1880s. Before that time, the decline of North American Indian languages followed the decline of Indian populations; that is, there were fewer Indian language speakers simply because they had died or been killed off. Despite the steep drop in Indian populations since the 15th century, the tribe, unless it was entirely exterminated, usually managed to maintain its language thanks to the strong sense of cultural preservation characteristic of most Indian societies.

Thus, at the beginning of the 20th century, there were relatively few Indians who could not speak their own language and, indeed, a sizable percentage of Indians unable to speak English. In 1910, of the 188,704 Indians over the age of 10, 59,055, or 31 percent, could not speak English. The tribes in the Southwest had the fewest English speakers, among them the Navajo (Dineh), where 88.2 percent of the population did not speak English; the Zuni (81.4 percent); Keresan Pueblo (70.1 percent); Tohono O'odham (Papago) (72.3 percent); and Apache (61.8 percent). English speakers were somewhat more common among northwestern and north central Indians, such as the Crow (51.6 percent), Sioux (Lakota, Nakota, Dakota) (43.4 percent), and especially Chippewa (Ojibwa) (26.5 percent).

Among the Five Civilized Tribes (as the Cherokee, Creek, Choctaw, Seminole, and Chickasaw were known), with their strong educational system, the rates of non-English speakers were comparatively low, with the Chickasaw (6.2 percent) having the smallest number, followed by the Cherokee (12.1 percent), Choctaw (21.4 percent), and Creek (27.8 percent). Eastern groups such as the Iroquois (11.8 percent) also had low rates of Native monolinguals. Among these groups, however, indigenous language retention remained high because many people were bilingual. Rates of non-English speakers on the West Coast were comparatively low, though they varied from tribe to tribe; for example, in Oregon the Salishian (16.9 percent) was much lower than the Shahaptian (32.6 percent).

By 1901, the federal government's assimilation policy was completely geared toward stamping out Indian languages and all other aspects of Indian culture. Since a language once learned is usually not lost, in order to completely rid Indians of their languages, the children had to be denied the opportunity to learn them.

In his landmark book *Reversing Language Shift* (1991), the sociologist Joshua Fishman has noted that languages go through stages of decline that pass through a number of generations. In the first stage, language use is vigorous throughout the community and is used by both young and old. In the second stage, children have stopped learning the language. In the third stage, only adults beyond childbearing age speak the language fluently. In the fourth stage, only a few elders still speak the language, and it is on the verge of disappearing. Therefore, the most important indicator of language health is its use among children, because once the children are no longer learning the language, it is on a slow but inexorable path toward extinction unless extraordinary measures are taken.

In 1901, with the exception of most of the California and East Coast tribes, which had extensive non-Indian contact, and tribes such as the Chippewa and Cherokee, which had large mixed-blood contingents, the vast majority of Indian children could speak their traditional languages. Federal education policy turned to the use of boarding schools to prevent Indian children from using their languages (see PRATT, RICHARD HENRY). The 26 federal boarding schools forbade the use of these languages, even among children speaking to one another, through strict military discipline and corporal punishment. Although sometimes not as harsh, reservation day schools, public schools, and mission schools also strictly forbid Indian language use (see EDUCATIONAL POLICY, AMERICAN INDIANS AND).

Despite this treatment, the ability of Indian children to speak their indigenous languages remained steady through the first quarter of the century, as most of their parents still spoke English only as a second language if they spoke it at all, and consequently spoke to their children in their indigenous tongue. For example, in 1910, 54 percent of U.S. Chippewa children between the ages of five and 15 were capable of speaking Ojibwa, as the language is known. By 1930, the rate of language use among Chippewa children, although declining, was still a healthy 41 percent.

As the generation of Indians that grew up after 1890, many of them under the boarding school system, started having children of their own, they were less inclined to speak the indigenous languages to their children, and thus the rate of language use among these children began to drop significantly. In addition, the process of ALLOTMENT had destroyed the land base of entire reservations and seriously disrupted tribal cultures. Bans on Indian religious ceremonies, especially harsh during the 1920s, also had a negative effect on Indian culture and language use (see RELIGIOUS FREEDOM, AMERICAN INDIAN). Therefore, despite attempts by Indian commissioner JOHN COLLIER during the 1930s to reverse the assimilationist policies of his predecessors, by 1940 Indian language use among children had begun to show a steep decline in many tribes.

In 1940, according to the BUREAU OF INDIAN AFFAIRS and U.S. Census figures, fewer than 20 percent of Chippewa children between the ages of five and 15 were able to speak Ojibwa. The Cherokee fared even worse: Only 4 percent of their children could speak Cherokee. The Choctaw/Chickasaw language fared somewhat better, with 11 percent of the children able to speak it. Among the old Five Civilized Tribes of Oklahoma, Muskogee, the language of the Creek and the Seminole, held up best, with 16 percent of the children capable of speaking it. In the Midwest, the Dakota language (spoken by the Sioux and including, for the purposes of census enumeration, all three dialects—Dakota, Lakota, and Nakota) had a speaking rate of 31 percent for children ages five to 15, far below that of 30 years earlier, when virtually every Sioux child could speak the language. Among the eastern tribes, 16 percent of Mohawk children spoke Mohawk and 13 percent of the Seneca children spoke Seneca, but only 2 percent of Potawatami children spoke Potawatami. In the Southwest, the particularly harsh attempt to stamp out traditional Hopi culture had taken some effect, with Hopi children growing up speaking the language at a 68 percent rate. Other tribes in the region, such as the Zuni (93 percent) and Navajo (90 percent) managed to maintain very high speaking rates among their children.

WORLD WAR II and its aftermath saw the rapid URBAN-IZATION of Indians, encouraged by the federal government under its Relocation policy. Before World War II, only 7 percent of all Indians lived in cities, but by 1960 the number had risen to 30 percent, and by 1970 to 44.5 percent. For many reasons, language use is much harder to maintain in urban areas than on the reservations. The postwar TERMINATION philosophy, while not as harshly assimilationist as that of the early part of the century, actively discouraged Indian cultural activity. Thus, despite the slow phasing out of boarding schools, local reservation schools did not encourage Indian language use and did not offer language programs. More and more Indian children were enrolling in public schools, especially in urban areas, which also was a great disincentive to Native language use.

Racism and stereotyping by non-Indians further discouraged language use among Indians. It was not until the late 1960s, with the emergence of the RED POWER MOVEMENT, that cultural attitudes toward Indians shifted away from assimilation. By then, however, language use among most tribes had undergone further serious declines, a trend that would continue through to the end of the century.

According to the census of 1990, 281,990 Indians spoke their indigenous languages. Because of population growth, this number is actually greater than the total number in 1900, when the entire population of Indians was less than 240,000, but as a percentage it shows a great decline, amounting to only 14 percent of the current Indian population. The raw numbers are also misleading because the language of half the current speakers is Navajo, by far the most widely spoken Indian language, with 142,886 speakers. Along with Navajo, the top 20 Indian languages spoken in 1990 were Dakota (including its three main dialects Lakota, Nakota, and Dakota), with 13,387 speakers; Pima (11,449); Cherokee (9,285); Keres, spoken by most of the Pueblo Indians in New Mexico (8,346); Choctaw/Chickasaw (8,147); Zuni (6,343); Hopi (5,264); Muskogee, the language of the Creek and Seminole (4,706); Ojibwa, the language of the Chippewa (4,518); Crow (4,143); Tewa (3,447); Tiwa (2,338); Shoshone (2,142); Ute (1,814); Cheyenne (1,570); Paiute (1,534); Mohawk (1,504); Towa, spoken at Jemez Pueblo (1,390); and Havasupai (1,324). These 20 Indian languages accounted for 92 percent of all Indian-language speakers. Of the remaining 128 Indian languages for which figures were available, 115 were spoken by fewer than 500 speakers and 88 by fewer than 100 speakers. Languages such as Chumash, Wyandot (Huron), Atsugewi, and Catawba have become extinct in recent years (see RED THUNDER CLOUD), and 28 languages, including

Eyak, Wintu, Kalispel, Mandan, and Cowlitz, had 10 or fewer speakers in 1990, all of them elderly people.

Total numbers are not necessarily an indicator of language health, as a language with a small group of speakers may remain healthy if enough of the children speak it. However, even among the more frequently spoken languages, use by children is dropping, raising concerns that they may be on the road to extinction as well. New cultural factors, such as the universal ownership of television sets, have begun to exert a powerful if subtle assimilative effect on Indian children. Although Navajo (61 percent) and Zuni (86 percent) are still spoken among young people, among the Hopi, only 32 percent of the children now speak the language. Fewer than 4 percent of Chippewa children can speak Ojibwa, and only a little more than 1 percent of Cherokee children can speak Cherokee. Among the Plains tribes, fewer than 6 percent of Sioux children can speak Sioux, and only 4 percent of Cheyenne children speak Cheyenne. Forty-six indigenous languages are not spoken by children at all, including Cayuga, Coeur d'Alene, Maidu, Maricopa, and Miwok.

By the end of the 20th century, recognition that languages were disappearing led tribes to attempt to develop strong language programs in schools. The Akwesasne Freedom School, formed in 1982 by Mohawk chiefs TOM PORTER and Ron LaFrance on the St. Regis Mohawk Reservation in New York State, began with a "Mohawk-first, English-second" approach to language teaching that has proven very successful. Tribes with endangered languages, such as Onondaga, Quinault, Wichita, Cupeño, Ahtena, and Penobscot, began intensive language training among youth that may help to bring these languages back from the brink of extinction.

Among other tribes with strong language programs, helped in some cases by gaming revenue (see GAMING ON INDIAN RESERVATIONS) or federal grants, are the Menominee and the Crow. Since the late 1970s, the Crow have had a bilingual educational system using funding from the federal government under its Title VII program. With more than 50 percent of Crow children fluent in the language, the success of the Crow program is clear. Also in the 1970s, the Menominee launched their bilingual education program, employing the few remaining elders fluent in Menominee to train teachers for schools. Later, with the help of gaming revenue, they hired linguists to help develop curriculum and textbooks. In 1996, the Menominee tribal legislature went so far as to pass an ordinance, the Menominee Language and Culture Code, that makes Menominee the official language of the tribe. It requires that the language be taught in all the schools on the reservation and that it be used in tribal business whenever possible.

After more than a century of official hostility to Indian language use, the federal government passed the Native American Languages Act of 1990, which recognizes the language rights of American Indians, Alaska Natives, and Native Hawaiians. However, the legislation provided no funding or new programs for language revitalization. In addition, the only national survey of language use is that of the U.S. Census Bureau, which is hampered by budget cuts and is unable to provide up-to-date and accurate statistics. Despite this lack of federal interest, preserving indigenous languages had become a high priority among many tribes and Native organizations, though it remains to be seen whether it will be possible to resist the strong process of cultural assimilation that is occurring all around the world.

As of 2000, there were 322,054 speakers of American Indian languages in the United States, according to the Census Bureau. Of these speakers, 173,800 spoke Navajo (Dineh); 17,466 Dakota; 13,681 Apache; 12,009 Cherokee; 9,272 Choctaw/Chickasaw; 9,220 Pima; 6,919 Ojibwa; 6,903 Zuni; 5,120 Hopi; 5,009 Muskogee; 4,149 Crow; 3,736 Tewa; 2,075 Cheyenne; 1,995 Tewa; 1,995 Towa; and 1,792 Ute. However, the methodology of the 2000 Census is controversial, and its tabulation of American Indian demographics is open to question.

See also DEMOGRAPHICS; RADIO, AMERICAN INDIANS AND.

Further Reading

Bradley, David, and Maya Bradley. *Language Endangerment and Language Maintenance*. New York: Routledge, 2002.
Fishman, Joshua A., ed. *Can Threatened Languages Be Saved? Reversing Language Shift, Revisited: A 21st Century Perspective*. Clevedon, U.K., and Buffalo, N.Y.: Multilingual Matters, 2001.
Hinton, Leanne. *The Green Book of Language Revitalization in Practice*. St. Louis, Mo.: Elsevier, 2001.
Krauss, Michael E. *Alaska Native Languages Past, Present and Future*. Fairbanks: Alaska Native Language Center, 1980.
Kroskrity, Paul V., and Margaret C. Field, eds. *Native American Language Ideologies: Belief, Practices, and Struggles in Indian Country*. Tucson: University of Arizona Press, 2009.
U.S. Department of the Census. *Characteristics of American Indians by Tribe and Language: 1990 Census of Population*. Washington, D.C.: U.S. Government Printing Office, 1997.

Indigenous Women's Network   *See* WOMEN OF ALL RED NATIONS.

International Indian Treaty Council (IITC)

Founded in the mid-1970s, the International Indian Treaty Council (IITC) represents the American Indian perspective to the international community and has been instrumental in influencing the United Nations to discuss the rights of indigenous peoples. In 1974, the First International Indian Treaty Conference, sponsored by the AMERICAN INDIAN MOVEMENT (AIM), was held on the Standing Rock Sioux (Lakota) Reservation in South Dakota. One of the largest Indian gatherings of its kind, almost 3,000 Indians—representatives and members of more than 97 tribes—attended. At the conference, the International Indian Treaty Council was formed to lobby the United Nations to recognize the sovereign rights of indigenous peoples. The new organization established a New York City headquarters under its director, JIMMIE DURHAM.

The council passed a major milestone in 1977, when the United Nations recognized it as a nongovernmental organization (NGO) on its Economic and Social Council. That same year, the IITC working with ROBERT COULTER and LEE A. LYONS, sponsored an International Non-Governmental Organizations Conference on the Indigenous Peoples of the Americas in Geneva, Switzerland, which brought indigenous people together from around the world to share their concerns. The conference helped move the United Nations to a more sympathetic posture toward indigenous peoples, despite the opposition of countries with large indigenous populations, such as the United States and Canada.

Growing out of this conference, a UN Working Group on Indigenous Populations was established in 1981, which began working on, among other things, a draft of the UN Declaration on the Rights of Indigenous Peoples (which was not adopted until September 2007). By 1981, however, the IITC had undergone a number of defections, particularly that of the Iroquois Confederacy, and was dominated by former members of AIM, which was itself in the process of disintegrating. After the departure of Durham in 1979, the IITC was led by WILLIAM MEANS. Despite the aid of local New York City organizations such as the American Indian Community House, the council was unable to raise the necessary resources to continue functioning, and it suffered a major blow when it was evicted from its New York offices in 1985. That same year, the IITC aligned itself with the leftist government of Nicaragua in their war against the Miskito Indians, causing a serious loss of American Indian support.

The IITC reformed itself in San Francisco in 1987, and in 1992 Andrea Carmen (Yaqui) became the executive director and Antonio Gonzales (Seri/Chicano) the director of operations. The organization then began to focus on developing a network of activists and Indian organizations. It continues to be an important source of news and information about indigenous peoples' struggles worldwide, although its role in international affairs has been largely superseded by the work of the individual Indian nations themselves. See also WASHINAWATOK, INGRID.

Further Reading

Brysk, Alison. "Turning Weakness into Strength: The Internationalization of Indian Rights." *Latin American Perspectives* 23, no. 2 (Spring 1996): 38–57.

ironworkers, American Indian

In 1850, Canadian business interests decided to span the St. Lawrence River with a rail bridge. They contracted with Mohawk river pilots from the Akwesasne Reservation in upper New York State and the Kahnawake Reserve in Canada, who were well known for their ability to navigate the fierce currents, to help transport materials for the bridge. Developers of the Victoria Bridge, one of the largest and most ambitious projects of its day, had trouble keeping local Quebecois workers, who were afraid to work on the tall supports, and construction began to fall behind schedule. One day, the lead engineer spotted a small group of men on the top of the structure, not holding onto dear life like most the workers but calmly gazing across the river. They were the Mohawk pilots, who were curious about how the bridge was being constructed and had climbed up to get a good view of the whole thing. The engineer offered to hire them on the spot and, since most of them spoke only Mohawk, decided to replace the entire crew with Mohawk workers, also hiring a foreman who was fluent in French and Mohawk. Their reputation assured, Kahnawake and Akwesasne Mohawk workers built bridges for Canadian railways for the next 50 years.

In 1886, more than 50 Mohawk helped build the Sault Ste. Marie Bridge connecting Michigan with Ontario. In 1897, the Dominion Bridge Company built its steel fabrication plant along the Lachine Canal, across the St. Lawrence from Kahnawake, and began using Mohawk crews to construct their steel bridges, employing them as riveters. On August 29, 1907, a bridge being built by the Phoenix Bridge Company over the St. Lawrence collapsed while under construction. Known as the Quebec Bridge Disaster, the collapse killed 96 men, including 33 Mohawk.

Following the Quebec Bridge Disaster, Mohawk ironworkers found employment with the McClintock Marshall Company (later Bethlehem Steel) and U.S. Steel. In 1912, Paul Diabo—the first Mohawk "boomer," or freelance ironworker—traveled to New York City, lured by the rush to build the tallest buildings in the world. In 1915, he was joined by his brother and then by two more Mohawk to work on the Hell Gate Bridge connecting Queens and the Bronx, via Randall's and Wards Islands.

By the early 1920s, there were three "gangs" (a group consisting of one riveter and three assistants) of Mohawk in New York City, and eventually more than 150 Mohawk ironworkers settled with their families in Brooklyn, New York. Although Mohawk were the most numerous, other Iroquois, particularly Seneca and Tuscarora, also flocked to the trade. Mohawk ironworkers worked on the Empire State Building, the George Washington Bridge, the Triboro Bridge, and Rockefeller Center. Mohawk began to travel across the country for jobs, including work on the Golden Gate Bridge in San Francisco. Since many of the ironworkers were from Canada, they faced harassment by border officials from Canada and the United States, and in 1926 the United States attempted to deport Diabo to Canada as an illegal immigrant. With the help of the Grand Council of the Iroquois at Onondaga, Diabo fought his deportation in court, and on July 8, 1926, a federal judge dismissed the case against the ironworker on the grounds that the Jay Treaty of 1794 allowed Indians free passage across the border. In October 1927, the case, appealed by the Department of Immigration, was settled by the U.S. Court of Appeals for the Third Circuit, which found the Mohawk were imperium in imperio, a nation within a nation, and thus have free rights of passage across the border.

Meanwhile, the lucrative pay of ironworking, compared with the limited opportunities on INDIAN RESERVATIONS, and the guarantee of a job thanks to the Mohawk's reputation, began to draw Indians from the entire East Coast to New York City. Mohawk brought their families and began to settle in the neighborhood of North Gowanus, now called Boerum Hill, in Brooklyn. By the 1950s, North Gowanus was home to more than 700 Mohawk.

In 1967, the New York Thruway was completed to connect New York City with upstate New York and Canada, cutting the 12-hour drive to the upstate and Canadian Mohawk reservations in half. The ironworkers would no longer have to relocate their families. In the 1970s, as the great building boom in New York City began to fade and as more modern and safer techniques and machinery replaced the riveting gangs, the Mohawk neighborhood in North Gowanus, Brooklyn, began to disperse.

However, Mohawk and other Iroquois continue to work as ironworkers throughout the East Coast and Canada. During the new building boom in New York City in the late 1990s, more than 250 Mohawk from Kahnawake commuted from their reservation every weekend to work in the city during the week.

Further Reading

Einhorn, Arthur C. "Warriors of the Sky: The Iroquois Iron Workers." *European Review of Native American Studies* 13, no. 1 (1999): 25–34.
Mitchell, Joseph. "The Mohawks in High Steel." In *Apologies to the Iroquois*, by Edmund Wilson, 1–36. New York: Farrar, Strauss and Cudahy, 1960.

Iroquois Confederacy   *See* SHENANDOAH, LEON; SOVEREIGNTY, INDIGENOUS AND TRIBAL; THOMAS, GEORGE A., THOMAS, GEORGE E.

Iroquois Nationals Lacrosse Team

The national LACROSSE team of the Iroquois Confederacy, established to compete against other national teams and promote Iroquois sovereignty, was created in 1983. On an invitation by the Lacrosse Hall of Fame, the Iroquois Nationals came together to compete in an international competition hosted by Johns Hopkins University, ending a century-long ban on Indian players in international competition. (In 1880, the National Lacrosse Association of Canada had ruled that only amateur teams could compete in international competition, which effectively excluded Indian teams, who did not have the luxury of private income.) The confederacy welcomed the opportunity to pit its team against the likes of Syracuse University, at that time national champion; Team Canada, a collection of Canadian all-stars; and Hobart College, Class III national champions. By then, the Iroquois were used to playing only box lacrosse, a version of the game played with fewer men on a smaller field, but a decade earlier they had formed their own league of competing Iroquois teams in field lacrosse, the standard for international competition, and many of their young men had gone on to college to become stars.

Largely on the initiative of former lacrosse All-Americans OREN LYONS, JR., and Sidney Jemison, who became the Nationals coach, along with Rick Hill and Wes Patterson, a Tuscarora lacrosse stick maker, the confederacy put together a team of young Iroquois players—including collegiate All-Americans Greg Tarbell, Travis Solomon, Fred Upson, David Brey, and David White—to compete in the exhibition match. The Nationals' inexperience as a team led to resounding defeats, first against Syracuse, 28-5, and then against Hobart, 21-14, but the Iroquois were determined to improve.

Their next opportunity came during the 1984 Olympics, when the Los Angeles World Lacrosse Championships were held in conjunction with the Jim Thorpe Memorial Games to commemorate the posthumous return of Thorpe's gold medals (see THORPE, JIM). The Nationals beat a California all-star team in the first game, then lost to both Australia and Canada. In the fourth game, they rebounded to beat England, and they gave the United States its toughest competition of the match, losing 21-15. With this, the Nationals, proving themselves capable of playing on an international level, applied to be admitted into the International Lacrosse Federation as a national team. They were denied admittance but, undaunted, they toured England, where a century earlier an Iroquois team had introduced the sport to the country. They scored an important victory for sovereignty when the British honored their Iroquois passports (see GENERAL, LEVI).

In 1987, the Nationals were admitted into the international federation, and in 1990 they competed in the World Championship games in Australia. They also competed in World Cup competitions in Japan in 1994 and in the United States in 1998, where they finished fourth. In 2002, they again finished fourth in the World Championship games in Australia. In addition to being a showcase for Iroquois sovereignty, the Iroquois Nationals have become an important binding force in the Iroquois community. In 2010 they were denied entry to Great Britain on their Iroquois-issued passports and so had to forfeit the competition.

Further Reading

Harris, Othello, Claire Elaine Nolte, and George B. Kirsch. *Encyclopedia of Ethnicity and Sports in the United States*, 240–241. Santa Barbara, Calif.: Greenwood Press, 2000.

Malloy, Daniel. "Iroquois Shedding Light on Roots of Lacrosse." *Boston Globe*, 9 October 2007, F1.

Johnson-O'Malley Act (1934)

Passed on April 16, 1934, the Johnson-O'Malley Act was the centerpiece of Indian commissioner JOHN COLLIER's efforts to reform Indian education. The act authorized the secretary of the Interior to negotiate contracts with states or territories to fund Indian education in public schools, and in some cases to provide funding for medical, agricultural, and social welfare services.

Developed largely by progressive educator WILL CARSON RYAN, JR., who wrote the education section of the MERIAM REPORT (1928) and served as superintendent of Indian education under Commissioner CHARLES JAMES RHOADS, the act was an attempt to move away from BUREAU OF INDIAN AFFAIRS (BIA) boarding schools, which, with their assimilationist policies and often substandard facilities, had become a flashpoint for critics. The act was designed to offset the costs to states of educating Indian students and streamline a cumbersome process of contracting for the education of Indian children, until then carried out for the most part in hundreds of separate school districts. By 1928, there were already more Indian students enrolled in state public schools than in BIA schools. However, the Indian students often received a substandard education, if they received any at all, because the states discriminated against Indian students or would not let them attend classes.

Although conceived by Ryan during the Rhoads administration, the act had to await the favorable political climate created by the administration of Franklin D. Roosevelt, (see INDIAN NEW DEAL; INDIAN REORGANIZATION ACT). The first state to contract for Johnson-O'Malley funds was California in 1934, followed by Washington in 1935, Minnesota in 1937, and Arizona in 1938.

By the end of the 20th century, 26 states, representing approximately 225,000 Indian students, were receiving Johnson-O'Malley funds. Like many other initiatives of the Indian New Deal, the Johnson-O'Malley Act, born of great promise, has had only mixed results. Despite the act's continual structural problems and inadequate funding, Indian tribes have begun to take control of Johnson-O'Malley funds. As the tribes take control, they have been able to use these funds to address their needs as they see them.

In 2007, the Johnson-O'Malley program received $16 million to help the approximately 350,000 Indian students attending state public schools. Attempts by the administration of George W. Bush to eliminate the program were unsuccessful.

See also EDUCATIONAL POLICY, AMERICAN INDIANS AND.

Further Reading

Olson, James Stuart, and Raymond Wilson. *Native Americans in the Twentieth Century*. Champaign: University of Illinois Press, 1986.

Jones, Paul (1895–1971) *Navajo political leader*

Paul Jones was born on the Navajo (Dineh) reservation near Tohatchi, New Mexico, on October 27, 1895. He attended the Christian Reformed Church Missionary School on the reservation and, after becoming proficient in English, served for three years as interpreter for the school's doctor. Jones then left the reservation to enter high school in Englewood, New Jersey. He obtained his college education at Calvin College in Grand Rapids, Michigan.

Jones served in the U.S. Army during WORLD WAR I, seeing action in Europe, where he was seriously injured by mustard gas. After the war, he spent two years on the reservation recovering from his injuries. His health restored, Jones went back to Grand Rapids to attend business college, then moved to Chicago. In 1933, he returned to the Navajo reservation to take a position with the BUREAU OF INDIAN AFFAIRS (BIA), eventually rising to district supervisor at Piñon, Arizona.

Jones was elected Navajo tribal chairman in 1955, defeating

the incumbent, Sam Ahkeah, who had become tribal chairman in 1947 after the death of HENRY CHEE DODGE. Jones expanded Ahkeah's policies of opening the reservation to mineral development. Under Jones's tenure as tribal chair of the Navajo reservation, the tribe received almost $200 million in oil and gas revenues. Jones fought off attempts to split the oil and mineral royalties on a per-capita basis, preferring instead to use the money to invest in economic development, schools, roads, and other Navajo needs. He established a tribal park in Monument Valley, built new waterworks, community centers, and health facilities, and started a tribal work program that guaranteed any Navajo who needed it 10 days of work per month. Jones was criticized for spending the money from oil and gas developments lavishly on himself and other members of the tribal council and for being a tool of long-time tribal attorney Norman M. Little, a former assistant U.S. attorney general who had been counsel to the Navajo since 1947. Little persuaded Jones to try to gain a portion of the valuable mineral deposits in Black Mesa, where thousands of Navajo lived, but which was in part located on the neighboring Hopi Reservation.

Jones lobbied Congress to enact legislation that would allow the two tribes to sue each other, which Congress passed on July 22, 1958. Soon after, Hopi chair Dewey Healing, represented by attorney JOHN BOYDEN, sued Navajo tribal chair Paul Jones. The suit, *Healing v. Jones*, inaugurated the bitterly contested BIG MOUNTAIN dispute and led to the largest forcible relocation of Indians in the 20th century. Little had a direct interest in the suit, as he had carefully reworked his contract with the Navajo to stipulate that he would receive 10 percent of the value of the total Navajo claim. Congress found out about the provision, however, and forced Jones to delete it.

Jones was defeated for reelection as tribal chair by RAYMOND NAKAI in 1963. By the time of his defeat, revenue from oil and gas exploration had grown to $25 million per year. He later served on Richard M. Nixon's President's Committee of Job Opportunities and later on the New Mexico Commission on Indian Affairs. Jones died in November 1971 in Window Rock, Arizona.

Further Reading

Iverson, Peter. *Diné: A History of the Navajos*. Albuquerque: University of New Mexico Press, 2002.

Jones, William (Megasiáwa, "Black Eagle")

(1871–1909) *Fox anthropologist*
William Jones was born on the Sac and Fox Reservation in Indian Territory (now Oklahoma) on March 28, 1871, the son of a Fox (Mesquakie) father, Henry Clay Jones (Bald Eagle), and an English mother, Sarah Penny. His mother died when he was still a baby, and he was given to his grandmother Katiqua, a medicine woman of the Eagle Clan, who raised him in the traditional ways. His Mesquakie name was Megasiáwa (Black Eagle), and he grew up speaking only the Mesquakie language.

When Jones was nine, his grandmother died, and he was

sent to live with his father, who by that time had remarried. That arrangement did not work, so at age 10 he was sent to a Quaker boarding school for Indians in Wabash, Indiana. After three years there, he returned to help his father herd cattle.

Jones worked about five years as a cowboy, but in October 1889, eager for more education, he enrolled at the Hampton Institute in Virginia. In his third year there, he became a Christian and joined the Episcopal Church. Hampton did not offer college preparatory courses, so in fall 1892, Jones entered Phillips Andover Academy in Andover, Massachusetts. A bright and highly motivated student, Jones excelled there, and in fall 1896 was admitted to Harvard University. He intended to study medicine but, failing to obtain a scholarship, opted instead for anthropology, which his advisers had all along encouraged him to study. Receiving his B.A. in 1900, Jones proceeded to Columbia University, where FRANZ BOAS headed the anthropology department. In New York, Jones became a close friend of western artist Edwin Willard Deming.

Jones received his M.A. from Columbia in 1901, was appointed university fellow in anthropology for 1902, and in 1904 became one of the earliest Americans—and the very first American Indian—to earn a Ph.D. in anthropology, with his thesis on *Some Principles of Algonquian Word Formation*. In Algonquian studies, Jones was the immediate predecessor of FRANK GOULDSMITH SPECK, who received his B.A. at Columbia that same year.

While still a student, Jones did fieldwork among the Fox, Sac, Kickapoo, and other tribes. With the great advantages of his ethnic kinship and native fluency in the language, he went far in his study of Fox religion, working with the very traditional community in Tama, Iowa. He described the Fox ceremonies with great precision and subsequently published *Fox Texts* (1907) and other treatises on Algonquian linguistics, religion, and culture. Boas called this work "the first considerable body of Algonquian lore published in accurate and reliable form in the native tongue, with translation rendering faithfully the style and the contents of the original." He went on to state that "In form, and so far as philological accuracy is concerned, these texts are probably among the best North American texts that have ever been published."

As a research assistant of the Carnegie Institution in Washington, D.C., Jones went on to the northern shore of Lake Superior, where he learned the local Ojibwa dialect and recorded many tales and other texts. He then wanted to go to Labrador to study the traditional religion of the Naskapi but was unable to get funding or employment to do so. During this period, Boas tried repeatedly to help Jones secure a position with the Carnegie Institution or the Bureau of American Ethnology, but to no avail. Instead, Jones applied in 1906 to the Field Museum in Chicago, where Dr. G. A. Dorsey gave him three choices, none of which were related to his field of expertise, Algonquian studies—Africa, the South Pacific, or the Philippines. Jones opted for the last.

The United States had annexed the Philippines in 1898 after a short war with Spain. But from 1899 to 1901, the Filipinos fought the Americans in what became known as the

Philippine-American War. In the years following, the United States built up a colonial government that lasted until the Japanese occupation of 1941 to 1945. (The Philippines became an independent republic on June 12, 1946.) Thus, Jones's scientific assignment was closely bound up with the development of the U.S. colonial administration in the Philippines. After a year of preparation in Chicago, Jones left for the West Coast. In August 1906, he embarked on the Japanese steamer *Aki Maru*, docking in Manila on Friday, September 13, 1907.

Jones worked for a year and a half in four neighboring hamlets of the Ilongot, a Negrito-Malay people inhabiting an uncharted area of northern Luzon Island along the Cagayan River, south of the town of Echague in southern Isabela Province. The Ilongot were headhunters, and Jones had to be constantly on his guard. He never showed any sign of fear, even when he learned in August 1908 of a failed plot to kill him. Jones finished his research in spring 1909. It was the height of headhunting season, and there was additional tension due to fear of a cholera epidemic that was raging downstream.

Having completed his research, Jones packed his specimens in crates at Dumabato (now Maddela, in the present Quirino Province) and arranged for the Ilongot to bring them down the Cagayan River on their bamboo rafts to the headwaters at Echague, whence they would be shipped to Manila and from there to the United States. Despite all assurances, the rafts arrived late and there were not enough of them. Jones lost his temper. Unable to control himself, he unwisely grabbed the arm of Tacadan, a respected elder, and threatened to hold him until the promised rafts arrived. This was the evening before his departure.

On March 29, 1909, as Jones was about to board a boat on a sand spit at Pung-gu near the hamlet of Panipagan, he was approached by three Ilongot. They appeared friendly and said they wanted to talk to him about the rafts. Suddenly, one of them, Palidat, hit Jones over his left eye with a *bolos* (a large knife used in headhunting); Magueng speared his left arm, and Gacad speared him in the abdomen. Jones's assistant, Romano, warded off another *bolos* blow aimed by Palidat, and Jones drove off the assassins with several shots from his revolver. In gratitude, Jones gave Romano his wristwatch. He also gave him instructions for the care of his notes and specimens, took medicine, and even bandaged Romano's hand. He then left in a boat with some Ilongot companions, but his wounds proved fatal, and he died later that day in the boat en route to Echague, where he was buried on April 1, 1909.

Jones was killed as a direct consequence of his anthropological work, or rather, of the tensions that grew between him and his Ilongot subjects as a result of that work and the way it was carried out. Jones's personal journals reveal some ambivalent feelings toward the Ilongot, but such subjective reactions are not uncommon among anthropologists, and the fact that he recorded them seems more a mark of his honesty than a significant influence on his scientific work. Certainly his intentions were benevolent; suggestions he made to Governor-General James F. Smith resulted in legislative and administrative changes beneficial to the Ilongot, and Jones used his influence to make peace between the communities of Dumabato and Panipagan.

More to the point were the pressures Jones put on the four communities to provide him with craftworks and artifacts for his museum collection. Most of the Ilongot always treated him with respect, at the beginning even with reverence, and he took advantage of this. He commissioned craftworks and artifacts in exchange for useful goods like beads and cloth but would frequently express dissatisfaction with the quality or quantity of what was brought in, would shame the community by telling them that another hamlet had done better work, and so on. In this way, he did get a better collection, but he also made people angry.

It was the problem of transportation that proved the greatest irritant and led to his death. By spring 1909, Jones had amassed a considerable collection, but he needed many shallow-draft bamboo rafts to transport it. All such rafts in the area had been taken to Echague the previous fall by Jones's friend Captain George B. Bowers, commander of the army post there—which meant that the Ilongot would have to make many new ones. Their first new rafts were washed away by the spring floods; it was not easy to obtain sufficient bamboo to make more, and it would take several weeks to cure it so as to be suitable for construction. As a result, progress in delivering the boats was slow and uncertain, Jones became more and more frustrated, and finally he lost his temper.

The three killers were caught, tried, and sentenced to death, but the Philippine Supreme Court commuted the sentences to 17 years and four months in prison and payment of a fine to Jones's heirs. However, they escaped en route to Manila's Bilibid Prison, and in retaliation, the U.S. military authority ordered the Ilongot houses in the area where Jones was killed to be burnt down. Innocent tribesmen held the murderers responsible, and the U.S. Philippine Constabulary used this conflict to divide and conquer, that is, to strengthen its control over the area. The result was a minor civil war during which Ilongot heads were sometimes delivered to the U.S. authorities by other Ilongot.

Though his life was cut short and he did not live beyond the first decade of the 20th century, Jones was younger than Native anthropologists FRANCIS LA FLESCHE, JOHN NAPOLEON BRINTON HEWITT, or fellow Hampton alumnus JAMES R. MURIE, and all his work was published in the 20th century. Jones's Ojibwa texts did not appear until 1916, 1917, and 1919; his collected writings on the Fox, edited by Margaret Welpley Fisher, were published as *Ethnography of the Fox Indians* in 1939 as Bulletin 125 of the Bureau of American Ethnology. Shortly after his death, two of Jones's fellow-students from Harvard, William Morrow and Raynal Bolling, commissioned a memorial biography from another of his Harvard friends, novelist Henry Milner Rideout; it was published in 1912.

There was much trouble over Jones's will, but his personal effects and papers eventually went to his fiancée, Caroline Andrus, a non-Indian member of the Hampton Indian program staff. In 1948, shortly before her own death, she instructed the curator of the Peabody Museum in Boston to burn hundreds of Jones's letters, which would probably have helped to provide a better understanding of his state of mind during the Ilongot expedition.

A 58-minute video documentary of this extraordinarily complex story by Collis Davis, an American media artist and two-time former Fulbright scholar based in the Philippines, is near completion. Davis's prospectus and a review of his own research is published on the Internet.

See also ANTHROPOLOGISTS AND AMERICAN INDIANS.

Further Reading

Boas, Franz. "William Jones." *American Anthropologist* 11 (1909): 137–139.
Davis, Collis H. "Headhunting William Jones." Available online. URL: http://www.okara.com/portfolio/html /wmjones.html. Accessed 13 August 2009.
Kramer, Paul A. "The Pragmatic Empire: U.S. Anthropology and Colonial Politics in the Occupied Philippines." Ph.D. dissertation, Princeton University, 1998.
Rideout, Henry Milner. *William Jones, Indian, Cowboy, American Scholar and Anthropologist in the Field.* New York: Frederick A. Stokes, 1912.
Rosaldo, Renato I. *Ilongot Headhunting: 1883–1974. A Study in Society and History.* Palo Alto, Calif.: Stanford University Press, 1980.

Jones, William Arthur (1844–1912) *commissioner of Indian affairs*

William A. Jones was born in Pembrokeshire, Wales, on September 27, 1844, to John P. and Phoebe Davies Jones. His family immigrated to the United States in 1851 and settled in Wisconsin. Jones attended Platteville Normal School in Wisconsin and graduated in 1872. Jones eventually became a successful banker and founded a large zinc mining company. His ties to the Wisconsin Republican Party and his support for William McKinley's presidential campaign earned him the post of head of the Indian Bureau (later the BUREAU OF INDIAN AFFAIRS [BIA]). His extraordinary political and administrative skills quickly silenced the many critics of his nomination, who believed he got the job only as a political favor.

When Jones assumed office on May 3, 1897, federal policy toward Indians in the United States was well established. Jones, like most non-Indians of the day, was a firm proponent of the philosophy that Native Americans should cease to exist as separate peoples and assimilate themselves into mainstream American culture (see ASSIMILATION). ALLOTMENT, the breaking up of INDIAN RESERVATIONS into individually owned plots, was the means by which Indians would be transformed from a reservation-based collective economy into, in Jones's words, "farmers, stockraisers, or laborers." Children were enrolled in schools that attempted to "kill the Indian" in order to "save the man," according to RICHARD PRATT's well-known motto for the Carlisle Indian School. The reservation system, "conceived in inequity," was to be abolished so that Indians would eventually become "self-supporting, useful member[s] of society." Although the policy had been in place for 10 years, what Jones sought to bring was a measure of businesslike efficiency to the process and to the problem-plagued Indian Office.

The previous commissioner had been Daniel M. Browning, an Illinois judge whose primary concern while in office was to place as many of his friends and supporters as possible in lucrative positions in the department. Jones managed to replace many politically appointed agents with career civil service employees, winning support from reformers such as the INDIAN RIGHTS ASSOCIATION while deftly assigning the friends of powerful congressmen to minor positions. He personally supervised many of the purchases of goods destined for reservations, goods which in the past had often been substandard if not totally worthless, and also managed to reform somewhat the corrupt system of licensed traders, eventually securing the passage of legislation that promoted free trade on reservations.

Jones originally favored off-reservation boarding schools such as Carlisle in Pennsylvania, with its "outing" program, as the best means for assimilating young Indians (see PRATT, RICHARD HENRY), but toward the end of his tenure he began to see reservation boarding schools as more useful and cost-effective. A Presbyterian, Jones sharply reduced the role of mission schools—which were mostly Catholic—in educating Indian students, while increasing enrollment in government schools by more than a third. In 1901, in a highly publicized directive, he ordered that young male Indians enrolled in government schools must cut their long hair and look more like white men. Believing that ancient Indian traditions were "barbarous," the commissioner also banned Indian participation in Wild West spectacles, such as those produced by Buffalo Bill Cody, and enacted a number of civil ordinances, such as requiring marriage licenses, designed to force Indian customs to conform with prevailing U.S. laws.

Jones attacked the issuance of rations to Indians, often guaranteed by treaty, as an impediment to moving them into the labor force. In 1901, he instructed agents on Indian reservations to begin culling the ration rolls of able-bodied and self-supporting Indians, instantly cutting off thousands and forcing them to find work or starve. Annuity funds, (funds paid to individual Indians out of treaty obligations) were likewise curtailed, as were the funds derived from the leasing of grazing lands or timber sales.

Like most observers of Indian affairs of that time, Jones felt that Allotment was the final solution to the "Indian Problem." It would make Indians self-supporting and would sell off "surplus" lands that were considered "unused," or lease them to (often unscrupulous) white people. Jones threw himself and the department behind Allotment, and under his tenure, tribal land holdings fell from more than 82 million acres in 1897 to only 58 million by 1905.

Unlike some of his predecessors, who sought to protect allotments from alienation—that is, transfer from Indian to non-Indian ownership—Jones approved regulations that allowed for the sale or lease of allotted Indian lands, as well as legislation that allowed an allottee's heirs to sell off their inheritance. Under his watch, serious frauds occurred regarding the transfer of allotted lands. In the end, the net result of Jones's policy was the wholesale loss of Indian lands at fire-sale prices, largely benefiting politically connected locals who took advantage of one of the most massive transfer of lands in American history, while leaving Indians more destitute than ever.

By the end of his tenure, it was Jones's businesslike political skills that drew the most attention; the department had been streamlined, losing a full third of its agencies while increasing productivity and to some extent limiting the pervasive internal corruption and patronage. His political skills were also borne out in the increasing appropriations he exacted from Congress, rising from $7.4 million per year in 1897 to $9.8 million in 1904, with the bulk of the increase going to education. But for Indians, the processes of Allotment and assimilation were disastrous, and the efficiency he brought to these policies only made things worse.

Having served longer than any other previous commissioner, Jones resigned on January 1, 1905. He was replaced by FRANCIS ELLINGTON LEUPP. Upon leaving office, Jones returned to the Mineral Point Zinc Company and his other business interests in Wisconsin. William Arthur Jones died on September 17, 1912, at Mineral Point.

Further Reading
Hoxie, Frederick E. *A Final Promise: The Campaign to Assimilate the Indians, 1880–1920.* Lincoln: University of Nebraska Press, 2001.

Josephy, Alvin M., Jr. (1915–2005) *author, historian*
Born on May 18, 1915, in Woodmere, New York, the elder of two sons of Alvin M. and Sophia Knopf Josephy, Alvin M. Josephy attended Harvard College until the stock market crash of 1929 left him without tuition money. Encouraged by his uncle, the publisher Alfred Knopf, to pursue a career in writing, he worked as a journalist, screenwriter, and short fiction writer. As a correspondent in Mexico for the *New York Herald Tribune*, he interviewed the exiled Russian leader Leon Trotsky. During WORLD WAR II, Josephy served as a war correspondent with the U.S. Marine Corps. He joined *Time* magazine in 1951, working as an associate editor for nine years. He then became editor in chief of the American Heritage Publishing Company, serving as its head until his retirement in 1979. He also served as commissioner of the INDIAN ARTS AND CRAFTS BOARD from 1966 until 1970.

Josephy is best known for his numerous books on the West and on Indian culture and history. In 1961, he edited *The American Heritage Book of Indians*, which featured an introduction by President John F. Kennedy. *The Patriot Chiefs*, also released in 1961, brought Josephy acclaim. A sympathetic portrayal of historic Indian leaders, the book was a direct rebuke to the TERMINATION policies of the day. It became highly popular among Indians, and in 1964 the NATIONAL CONGRESS OF AMERICAN INDIANS awarded Josephy its Eagle Feather Award. Josephy's

1971 book, *Red Power*, helped to give the growing RED POWER MOVEMENT important credibility, and he was present at the takeover of the BUREAU OF INDIAN AFFAIRS in Washington, D.C., during the TRAIL OF BROKEN TREATIES. A prolific author, Josephy also wrote *The American Heritage History of the Great West* (1965) and *Now That the Buffalo's Gone* (1982).

Alvin M. Josephy, Jr., died at his home in Greenwich, Connecticut, on October 16, 2005. His anthology, *Lewis and Clark through Indian Eyes*, with essays by nine contemporary Indian writers, was published posthumously in 2006.

Further Reading
Adams, Jim. "Noted Historian Deepened Meaning of America." *Indian Country Today*, 2 November 2005, C4.
George, Emma. "Indian Battle for Survival Is Not Over Says Historian." *Sho-Ban News* (Fort Hall, Idaho) 6 March 1998, 8.
Peavey, Diane Josephy, and Allison Wolowitz. "The Life of Alvin M. Josephy, Jr., Authoritative Interpreter of History." *Indian Country Today*, 2 November 2005, C4.

Jourdain, Roger (1912–2002) *Chippewa tribal leader, political activist*
Roger Jourdain was born on July 27, 1912, in the village of Little Rock on the Red Lake Chippewa Reservation, northern Minnesota, the son of Joe and Maggie Jourdain. Joe Jourdain had attended school in Fort Totten, North Dakota, and later at Haskell Institute in Lawrence, Kansas. In 1912, he became one of the first at Red Lake to take up farming. He also worked for the Indian Bureau (later the BUREAU OF INDIAN AFFAIRS [BIA]) agency there at various times.

Roger Jourdain began his education at the Red Lake Catholic mission school. He was an altar boy and began learning English from hymns his mother taught him. When he was nine, his parents moved to Cross Lake (now Ponemah), Minnesota, where his father was disciplinarian of the Catholic mission school and his mother was the school matron. Jourdain was a good student and an avid reader. His parents expected him to set an example, but his good grades only caused the other students to pick on him, and when he was 13 his parents transferred him to the boarding school at Tomah, Wisconsin. The next year he rejoined them when they moved back to Red Lake, where his father worked as a carpenter and a mechanic.

In 1927, Jourdain began high school at the Flandreau Indian School in South Dakota. Though he did well, he ran back home with two other boys from Red Lake at the end of the term because one of them had failed his courses. Nonetheless, he finished high school. His father wanted him to go on to Haskell Junior College, but Jourdain preferred to get a job. At his father's suggestion, he worked at a lumber camp, but one winter of that was enough for him. From 1934, he worked on road construction for several years with the INDIAN CIVILIAN CONSERVATION CORPS and learned how to supervise a road construction crew. He was postmaster at Red Lake for a while and served on the local school board for 10 years.

Jourdain's interest in politics began in the late 1930s. He used to go to all the meetings of the chiefs, bringing along his father-in-law, Paul H. Beaulieu, whom he called "a walking encyclopedia on Red Lake's history and politics."

During WORLD WAR II, Jourdain obtained a job with the Bechtel Corporation on a secret project in the Northwest Territories of Canada (the CANOL pipeline), where he braved frequent snowstorms and temperatures often as low as -80°.

After the war, when veterans returned to the Red Lake Reservation, they were frustrated with the lack of economic development. Many blamed the hereditary chiefs, each of whom, under the 1918 constitution, appointed his own council members. The chiefs, under head chief August King's leadership, voluntarily decided to relinquish their control and let the Red Lake people select their own council, with the chiefs remaining as advisers, "to avoid a factional fight," as Jourdain explained in a 1984 interview. But the "Graves council" (see GRAVES, PETER) would not accept the chiefs' plan.

As a council member from 1952 to 1954, Jourdain, working with Senator Leonard R. Dickinson and Representative John McKee, helped create the Minnesota Indian Scholarship Program. Starting in 1955 with $5,000, it had reached $1.6 million by 1990.

When treasurer Peter Graves, who had effectively led the council for nearly 40 years, died in 1957, leadership was assumed by chair Joseph Graves and secretary-treasurer Rose Graves. However, this attempt to continue the family dynasty and old form of council against the wishes of the hereditary chiefs provoked opposition from council members who had either resigned or been ousted. Under Jourdain's leadership, this group organized its own council, which disputed the legality of the Graves council. After an investigation in February 1958, the Department of the Interior ruled that neither council was legally constituted. Because the old constitution contained no provision for the election of council members by secret ballot, the band had to either amend the 1918 constitution or draw up a new one. A seven-member constitutional committee, including Jourdain, was established. The constitution was duly revised and amended, and it was approved by ballot on October 14, 1958.

When the election was held on January 6, 1959, Jourdain, running for the chairmanship against Royce Graves and Louis Stately, an independent candidate, won by a large majority. Ten other members were elected to the new council. Their first priority was to come to a new understanding with the BIA, which soon learned that Jourdain was not a man who could be pushed around.

Jourdain was not only an effective leader on his own reservation; he soon became a prominent figure in national Indian politics. He rallied Red Lake around the Minnesota Democratic Farm-Labor Party (DFL), beginning a long association with Minnesota senator Hubert H. Humphrey. The friendship bore fruit when Humphrey became vice president in 1964 under Lyndon B. Johnson, and Johnson's Great Society programs began to improve the health and welfare of Indian people (see BENNETT, ROBERT LAFOLLETTE).

Jourdain's influence was so great that in 1964 Humphrey stated, "Before we act on Indian legislation, we must first check with Chairman Jourdain."

Jourdain led the growing wave of powerful tribal chairs, such as RAYMOND NAKAI and WENDELL CHINO, who were prominent in national politics and whose growing influence began to force Congress and the Johnson administration to effectively curtail the government's TERMINATION policy, which had been in place since the end of World War II. Jourdain's effectiveness led VINE DELORIA, JR., to state: "We need about 50 Roger clones to turn loose in Indian Affairs." In 1971, Jourdain was a founder of the NATIONAL TRIBAL CHAIRMEN'S ASSOCIATION. In the 1970s, with the participation of the White Earth and Leech Lake Chippewa, he led a successful boycott of businesses in Bemidji, Minnesota, to protest racism against Indians.

In 1979, after treasurer Stephanie Hanson was removed by the Red Lake council for alleged irregularities and improprieties in tribal accounts, the Hansons led a dissident faction on a two-day rampage (May 19–20) that resulted in two fatalities and $2 million of property damage. Dissidents occupied a BIA law-enforcement center and burned the police station. Jourdain's home was burned to the ground, and all his files, including many priceless old tribal records, were destroyed. His car was also burned. Jourdain subsequently moved to Bemidji. Stephanie Hanson's husband, Harry, was later convicted of arson.

Deciding a suit filed in 1981 at Jourdain's insistence, the court held that the FBI's depriving the reservation of police protection was the proximate cause of the looting and burning that had occurred. In a separate judgment rendered on March 22, 1990, the tribe was awarded damages of $689,274.62 for the loss of the police station, Young Adult Conservation Corp (YACC) office and equipment, a Red Lake builder's warehouse, and other incidental losses. It was one of the few cases ever decided against the FBI for negligent law enforcement and believed to be the first case obtained against the United States for failure to supply adequate law enforcement on an INDIAN RESERVATION.

Hanson supporters formed a constitutional committee to press for reforms and a BIA audit of tribal funds, but in the 1982 elections, which were monitored by the BIA without any finding of improprieties, none of their candidates were elected, and all the former council members were returned.

Red Lake is one of only two totally closed reservations in the United States (the other being Mescalero Apache reservation in Arizona). Red Lake was the first tribe to issue its own license plates and has always charged lower fees than those charged for state plates. Red Lake Hospital, dedicated in 1981, was the first hospital built by an Indian tribe. An adjacent state-funded, tribally managed nursing home facility was dedicated June 17, 1989. The tribe took over administration of the hospital from the Indian Health Service in March 1990.

Jourdain joined Wendell Chino, chair of the Mescalero Apache, in opposing the Indian Gaming Regulatory Act (S-555), which President Reagan signed into law on October 17,

1988, as PL 100–497. They considered it a blow to Indian self-determination and tribal self-governance (see GAMING ON INDIAN RESERVATIONS). Jourdain also played an important leadership role in fighting the opponents of Indian treaties, who became extremely vocal in the late 1980s and 1990s. In 1986, after a long fight, Red Lake won clear title to 32,000 acres in northern Minnesota.

Jourdain wanted Congress to abolish all BIA area offices (originating from the decentralization of the bureau that occurred in 1946 at the onset of Termination) and to give funding directly to tribal programs or administration training programs. He foresaw corporate attempts to use Indian land as industrial waste dumps and landfills and fought the proposal of a nuclear repository at Red Lake in the late 1980s (see NUCLEAR INDUSTRY, AMERICAN INDIANS AND THE).

In May 1990, in a challenge backed by the Graves family faction, Jourdain lost the election for tribal chair by 136 votes (with about 2,200 votes cast) to Gerald "Butch" Brun, a reservation logger who had been on the council for 14 years. Jourdain filed a complaint alleging irregularities, but a tribal judge determined the election had been fair.

As chair at Red Lake for more than 31 years, Jourdain brought in more than $100 million in federally funded projects. Other achievements included the first urban Indian health program in the country and the first tribal community health program.

Roger Jourdain died at a hospital in Bemidji on March 21, 2002. Among the most influential tribal chairs of the 20th century, he was described by former U.S. vice-president Walter Mondale from Minnesota as "the elder statesman, a man of the people, the dean of Indian politics."

Further Reading
Wilkinson, Charles F. *Blood Struggle: The Rise of Modern Indian Nations.* New York: W. W. Norton, 2005.

journalism

At the start of the 20th century, Indian Territory, now the state of Oklahoma, was already a hotbed of Indian journalism. The Cherokee alone had more than half a dozen newspapers, most printed in both Cherokee and English. In the early 20th century, the official Cherokee newspaper was the venerated *Cherokee Advocate*, published since 1844 under the successive editorship of William T. Loeser, G. O. Butler, and W. J. Melton. Other Cherokee papers included the *Tahlequah Telephone*, begun in 1887; the *Daily Capital;* the *Tahlequah Courier*, founded in 1893; the *Capital City News;* and the *Tahlequah Arrow*, begun in 1888 and surviving until 1920. The *Daily Indian Chieftain* (1891–1913) although owned by non-Indians, featured a number of prominent Cherokee journalists as editors, including William P. Ross and ROBERT LATHAM OWEN, JR.

The *Indian Citizen*, begun in 1886 by Choctaw politician J. S. Stanley and his son-in law Butler S. Smiser, covered the affairs of the Choctaw and Chickasaw nations. The *Indian Journal* (1876–1972) a Creek newspaper, had a circulation of 5,000 and boasted one of the most gifted Indian journalists, ALEX POSEY, first as editor and later as owner and publisher. Chickasaw FINIS FOX edited the *Ardmore Appeal* during its short existence (1901–03). Other important Indian newspapers in Indian Territory included the *Osage Journal* (1898–ca. 1905). *Fort Gibson Post* (1897–1920) out of Muskogee, and the *Herald* (1895–ca. 1902) out of Miami.

During this time, most non-Indian newspapers in the western United States were virulently anti-Indian, advocating the abolishment of INDIAN RESERVATIONS and the extermination of Indian people. The Native newspapers in Indian Territory were important in countering the non-Indian "boomer" presses, which sensationalized and fictionalized Indian crimes and conditions on Indian lands.

This golden era of Indian journalism was destroyed, along with the governments of the Five Civilized Tribes (as the Cherokee, Choctaw, Creek, Chickasaw, and Seminole were known), by the implementation of the CURTIS ACT in the first decade of the 20th century, which broke up their reservations through the ALLOTMENT process. The *Cherokee Advocate*, which had vigorously fought Allotment and had sought to further the Cherokee language and culture, was ordered closed by the U.S. government, and the newspaper complied on March 4, 1906. The *Indian Citizen* closed the next year. While some papers held on, and new ones such as the *Cheyenne and Arapahoe Carrier Pigeon* were formed, Indian newspapers would never again attain their former level of readership or influence.

The Five Civilized Tribes maintained excellent schools, but outside of Indian Territory Indian journalism was hampered by the lack of educational opportunities available on Indian reservations (see EDUCATIONAL POLICY, AMERICAN INDIANS AND). Whatever education did exist was generally geared toward craft-making or vocational skills. Despite this, Indians managed to publish a few newspapers during the early years of the century, including the *Tomahawk*, founded in 1903 by GUS H. BEAULIEU; the *Winnebago Chieftain*, founded by Roy Stabler in 1907; the *Nez Perce Indian*, begun in 1914; the *Tulalip Bulletin* (1916–19); and the *Quileute Independent*, founded in 1908 by Webster Hudson, and its successor the *Quileute Chieftain* (1910).

During the course of the Progressive Era, the early part of the 20th century before 1918, federal policy toward Indians became somewhat less heavy-handed, and new journals were begun in order to counter the harsh stereotypical view of the vast majority of contemporary non-Indian newspapers and magazines. Organizations such as the SOCIETY OF AMERICAN INDIANS (SAI) published the important *Quarterly Journal*, later renamed the *American Indian Magazine* (1913–20), under the editorship of ARTHUR C. PARKER. The *Journal* largely concurred with the assimilationist policy of the federal government at the time; however, it also sought to portray Indians in a favorable light and protect Indians from the fraud endemic at the BUREAU OF INDIAN AFFAIRS (BIA).

After splitting from the SAI, CARLOS MONTEZUMA published his journal, *Wassaja* (1916–22), to further his assimilationist views. A number of journals highlighting Native

American culture began around this time, including the U.S. Department of Education's *The Eskimo* (1916–47); *Indian Life* (1912–60), by the Inter-tribal Indian Ceremonial Association out of Gallup, New Mexico; and the short-lived *California Indian Herald* (1922–24).

Among the many Indian school magazines, a number were highly admired, such as Bacon College's *Baconian* (1898–ca. 1903), the Sherman Institute's *Sherman Bulletin* (1907–ca. 1963), Haskell College's *The Indian Leader* (founded 1897), and the *Carlisle Arrow and Red Man* (1904–18). Churches put out a number of newspapers for Indians, including the *Iapi Oaye*, published from 1871 to 1939 by the Dakota Mission; the *Indian Advocate*, published from 1889 to 1910 by the Benedictine Fathers of Sacred Heart, Oklahoma; and the *Indian Sentinel*, published (1902–62) by the Bureau of Catholic Missions.

During the 1920s, Cherokee Will Rogers (see ROGERS, WILLIAM PENN ADAIR) rose to fame on the strength of his witty travelogues and newspaper columns championing the "little man." The 1920s brought about the return of the assimilationist policies of the late 19th century and a harsh government repressions of Indian religions. This time, however, journals began to appear that championed Indian rights and promoted Indian culture. Among those journals were the *Alaska Fisherman* (1923–ca. 1932); *American Indian Life* (1925–36), published by the American Indian Defense Association; *Indian Outlook* (1923–ca. 31); the *Indian Teepee* (1920–28), edited by several hands, including JOSEPH STRONGWOLF; the *American Indian* (1926–31), published by Joseph Bruner in Tulsa; and the INDIAN RIGHTS ASSOCIATION's *Indian Truth* (1924–80), all of which began to champion the reform of Indian affairs.

Indian policy relaxed with the advent of the administration of Franklin Delano Roosevelt in 1932, although Indians in journalism and Indian journals remained rare as the number of educated Indians was still very low. From March 1935 to March 1936, Choctaw BEN DWIGHT edited the biweekly *Tushkahomman* out of Stroud, Oklahoma. That same year, *Talking Leaf*, the newsletter of the Los Angeles Indian Center, made its debut. The BIA also began to publish a magazine, *Indians at Work*, beginning in 1934, which promoted the INDIAN NEW DEAL policies of Commissioner JOHN COLLIER. The New Deal led to the creation of tribal governments, some of which began to publish newspapers, for example the *Narraganset Dawn* and Colville's *Independent American*. In 1944, the *Adhoniigii*, a monthly newspaper printed in the Navajo language, made its appearance, and it still appeared irregularly after 1946. *Smoke Signals* was begun in 1947 in California by Marie Potts, a Maidu.

The onset of TERMINATION during the late 1940s, a policy that once again sought to assimilate Indians and dissolve Indian reservations, led to the creation of new periodicals that advocated Indian rights. Among the most prominent were the *NCAI Bulletin* and the magazine the *NCAI Sentinel*, both of which made their debut in 1947 on behalf of the NATIONAL CONGRESS OF AMERICAN INDIANS. The year 1949 saw the first appearance of *Indian Affairs*, the magazine of the ASSOCIATION ON AMERICAN INDIAN AFFAIRS. These journals sought to preserve the gains made during the Indian New Deal and fought against Termination at every turn. A number of important newspapers were born in the 1950s, including the *Navajo Times* in 1959, funded by the Navajo Tribal Council. The *Navajo Times* would eventually become the most important Indian newspaper in the country and the only Indian daily.

It was not until the 1960s that Indian journalism again reached the level of influence that it had achieved at the turn of the century. A growing militancy, especially among Indian youth, coupled with a new generation of college-educated Indians, characterized some of the most important Indian journals published between 1960 and 1980. The NATIONAL INDIAN YOUTH COUNCIL's *Indian Voice*—founded in 1961 and succeeded in 1968 by *ABC: Americans Before Columbus*—led the militant wave. The *Tundra Times*, founded by Inupiat HOWARD ROCK in 1962, advocated for the rights of Alaska Natives. *Wassaja, the Indian Historian* (1964–80), founded by Cahuilla/Cherokee Jeanette Henry and Cahuilla RUPERT COSTO, made its debut in 1964.

The year 1968 saw the debut of *Akwesasne Notes*, the most influential Indian paper of the latter half of the century. *Akwesasne Notes* began as a compilation of news clippings pertaining to the CORNWALL BRIDGE BLOCKADE by militant Mohawk. Under its first editor, Jerry Gamble, a non-Indian better known as Rarihokwats, *Akwesasne Notes* became an important source of information about the activities and demands of the Indian militants of the RED POWER movement. The paper's circulation soared from 900 in 1968 to 7,000 in 1969, to 56,000 in summer 1973 after the siege of WOUNDED KNEE. It became the center of a large publishing operation that included books, calendars, posters, pamphlets, and even a traveling lecture group known as the White Roots of Peace. Although *Akwesasne Notes* won a number of awards, including the Robert F. Kennedy Memorial Foundation Journalism Award Citation in 1972, by 1976 Gamble had been removed as editor following accusations that he had mismanaged the magazine's many extensive operations.

After Gamble left, Seneca journalist JOHN MOHAWK reoriented *Akwesasne Notes*—still the most important source of news on Indian events—to the task, in Mohawk's words, "of confronting the Indian movement with some serious thinking about the unique world view that emerges from ancient Indian community traditions." With associate editor JOSÉ BARREIRO, Mohawk sought to promote constructive means of enhancing the future of Indian communities at a time when the AMERICAN INDIAN MOVEMENT (AIM), with its militant pan-Indianist perspective, was disintegrating as a national force. Another outgrowth of this perspective was *Native Self-Sufficiency*, a seminal journal of Indian economic development, which made its debut in 1978 under editors Paula Hammett and Cayuga DANIEL BOMBERRY. It continued until 1988; *Akwesasne Notes* until 1997.

As Indian journalism began to gather momentum, in 1970 Oglala Lakota Charles Trimble, the editor of the *Indian*

Times out of Denver, Colorado, founded the American Indian Press Association (AIPA), the first such organization. However, Trimble had difficulty securing funding for the association, and it folded in 1976. In 1984, prominent Yakima journalist RICHARD LACOURSE, formerly AIPA's Washington Bureau chief, formed the Native American Press Association, with Oglala Lakota TIM GIAGO as its first president and Navajo journalist Loren Tapahe as vice president. The association eventually changed its name to the Native American Journalists Association (NAJA).

In 1981, the weekly *Lakota Times*, under the editorship of TIM GIAGO, made its debut. It was bought by *USA Today* in 1992, and the name was changed to *Indian Country Today*. In late 1998, it was sold to the Oneida Nation of New York. Under the editorship of Mohawk Tim Johnson, *Indian Country Today* became the leading Native newspaper in the country.

The *Northeast Indian Quarterly*, renamed *Akwe:kon* and later *Native Americas*, was begun in 1984 by José Barreiro at Cornell University as an academic journal but later took on a more general-interest approach. It ceased publication in 2004. *Aboriginal Voices* was begun by Cayuga GARY FARMER to be a leading Indian journal of the arts. *Native Peoples*, a quarterly journal portraying Indian arts and lifeways, has been published in Phoenix, Arizona, since 1987.

In 1995, Osage Elizabeth Gaines Gray and her husband, James Gray, on Osage chief, began publishing the *Oklahoma Indian Times*. In 2001, they turned it into a national newspaper, *Native American Times*, which has become one of the leading American Indian newspapers.

By the mid-1980s, nearly every tribal government was publishing a newspaper for its own community. However, conflicts between newspapers and tribal councils became commonplace as newspapers sought to exercise their rights to free speech and incumbent councils tried to censor them. The most dramatic conflict came in 1986, when Navajo tribal chair PETER MACDONALD accused the *Navajo Times* of favoring his rival, PETERSON ZAH, during an election campaign. The *Times*, then the only daily Indian newspaper (boasting a circulation of 14,000), was summarily shut down by MacDonald. Although *Times* editor Mark Trahant (Shoshone-Bannock) tried to form an alternative, the *Navajo Nation Today*, it could not duplicate the success of the *Times*. Trahant soon left to take the post of managing editor of the *Salt Lake Tribune*, becoming the first Native American journalist to head a major metropolitan newspaper.

In 1994, under the leadership of Chippewa PAUL DEMAIN, editor of the Wisconsin Oneida *News from Indian Country* (1977–), the Native American Journalist Association participated in a historic UNITY conference in Atlanta, which combined the black, Hispanic, and Asian journalist associations. Since that time, the various associations have held more joint conventions. In 2001, the American Society of Newspaper Editors conducted a survey that found 249 Native American journalists working for mainstream newspapers. Hundreds more work for tribal newspapers. By the beginning of the 21st century, the Native American Journalist Association has 600 members, as growing numbers of Indians enter the field.

Further Reading

Danky, James Philip, and Maureen E. Hady. *Native American Periodicals and Newspapers, 1828–1982: Bibliography, Publishing Record, and Holdings.* Santa Barbara, Calif.: Greenwood Press, 1984.

Greco, Stephanie. *Media & Minorities: The Politics of Race in News and Entertainment.* Lanham, Md.: Rowman & Littlefield, 2006.

Murphy, James Emmett. *Let My People Know: American Indian Journalism, 1828–1978.* Norman: University of Oklahoma Press, 1981.

Trahant, Mark N. *Pictures of Our Nobler Selves.* Nashville, Tenn.: Freedom Forum First Amendment Center, 1995.

Weston, Mary Ann. *Native Americans in the News: Images of Indians in the Twentieth Century Press.* Santa Barbara, Calif.: Greenwood Press, 1996.

Jumper, Betty Mae Tiger (1923–2011) *Seminole tribal leader*

Betty Mae Jumper (née Tiger) was born on April 27, 1923, in Indiantown, Florida. Her mother, Ada Tiger, was a full-blood Seminole; her father was white. Miscegenation was strictly forbidden among traditional Seminole, and there was doubt whether the lives of Betty or her younger brother, Howard, would be spared, but they were protected by their Seminole grandfather, who was a Baptist. They were raised in a traditional Seminole environment, with no exposure to mainstream American culture.

When Betty Mae was five, her family moved onto the newly formed Dania (now Hollywood) reservation. The Tigers eventually became devout Christians and joined the Baptist Church. Determined to go to school, something her traditional grandmother vehemently opposed, Betty Mae prevailed upon her mother to let her and her younger brother attend a day school near Indiantown. When that school closed in 1936, she and her brother were sent to an Indian boarding school in Cherokee, North Carolina. Though they found the cool mountain climate difficult to get used to, they were cheered by the friendship of the four other Seminole children at the school. An enthusiastic student, Betty Mae and a cousin became the first Florida Seminole to graduate from high school (1945).

After a year's study of public-health nursing at the Kiowa Indian Hospital in Oklahoma, Betty Mae returned to Florida. There she married Moses Jumper, one of her fellow Seminole students from the Cherokee boarding school, and worked as a public-health nurse on the three Florida reservations (Dania, Big Cypress, and Brighton), as well as caring for the Miccosukee living along the Tamiami Trail.

When the Seminole Tribe was organized in 1957, Jumper was elected to the tribal council. She became vice chair in 1959 and from 1963 to 1967 was also secretary-treasurer. From 1959, she also served on the tribal board of directors. In 1967,

Betty Mae Jumper, longtime leader of the Florida Seminole tribe, stepped down from her position as tribal chair in 1971. *(AP/Wideworld)*

Jumper became the first Seminole woman elected to the tribal chair, serving for four years. She was also active in the National Tribal Chairmen's Association and was a founder of United Southeastern Tribes (now United Southern and Eastern Tribes), an organization begun to help counter the tremendous influence of Western tribes in national Indian affairs. In 1970, Jumper was appointed by President Richard Nixon to his newly formed National Congress on Indian Opportunity, an organization designed to help streamline federal Indian policy.

When she left the tribal chairship in 1971, Jumper continued to serve the tribal council as the director of its communication department (from 1971) and editor in chief of the biweekly *Seminole Tribune*. In 1984, her history of Christianity among the Seminole, *And with the Wagon Came God's Word*, was published by the Seminole Print Shop. During the 1980s and 1990s, she became known throughout Florida as a lecturer on Seminole history and culture as well as many aspects of contemporary Indian affairs, often appearing with a family singing group. She is also widely recognized for her English-language presentation of traditional Seminole stories.

Betty Mae Tiger Jumper died at her home in Hollywood, Florida, on January 14, 2011.

Further Reading
Jumper, Betty Mae Tiger, and Patsy West. *A Seminole*

Legend: The Life of Betty Mae Tiger Jumper. Gainesville: University Press of Florida, 2001.

Junaluska, Arthur Smith (Arthur Freeman Smith)
(1912–1978)   Cherokee playwright, director, actor, choreographer, producer
Arthur Freeman Smith was born at Cherokee, North Carolina, on November 30, 1912, the eldest son of Jacob Lawrence Smith, an electrical engineer, and Olive L. Smith. After receiving elementary education at a government boarding school, he studied at Okmulgee Junior College (Oklahoma) and received a B.Sc. from Maryville College in Tennessee.

Enlisting in the army in Tulsa, Oklahoma, in December 1942, Smith served in the medical branch of the U.S. Army Air Corps (stationed in England) during WORLD WAR II. After the war, he returned to the United States, where he worked for the New York City Department of Health and hoped to enter medical school. Discouraged by long waiting lists, however, he returned to England. There he enrolled in the School of Medicine at King's College, University of London. Subsequently, he worked as a staff research hematologist and serologist at the South London Blood Transfusion Depot.

On July 12, 1948, Smith married Betty Wright, an English nurse he had met during the war, in her native city of Exeter, Devonshire, England. It was around this time that he adopted the name of his great-great-grandfather, Cherokee chief Junaluska. Depressed by the austerity of postwar England, he and Betty left for New York in December 1949.

There Junaluska resumed his work as a medical technician and even developed a modified serological testing procedure later used in commercial blood banks. But he had long had a passionate interest in the stage, and in 1955 he gave up medical work to devote himself to a theatrical career. Even while a student at Maryville College, he had written some plays that were performed on a radio station in nearby Knoxville. Now he began to act in Shakespearean drama with a small theater group, gradually working up to legitimate theater, off-Broadway, Broadway (*The Strong Are Lonely* at the Broadhurst Theatre in 1957), television, and films. He is the only Indian to have played in the Shakespearean Repertory Company.

Junaluska's chief interests, however, remained writing and directing, and in New York in the 1950s he became one of the founders of the contemporary Indian theater movement. In 1956, Junaluska organized the American Indian Drama Company and directed and played a leading role in its first production, *The Arrow Maker*. In 1958, as director of a drama workshop at South Dakota Wesleyan University, he staged *Thunder in the Hills*, a historical drama about Plains tribes, for the ASSOCIATION ON AMERICAN INDIAN AFFAIRS. Among other plays he wrote are: *The Medicine Woman*, *The Spirit of Wallowa*, *The Man in Black* (drama), *Shackled* (documentary), *Hell-Cat of the Plains*, *Spectre in the Forest* (drama), and the dramatic pageant *Grand Council of Indian Circle*. He also organized the American Indian Theatre Foundation.

Junaluska had always been interested in dance. He is said to have taught Indian dance steps to Helen Tamiris, choreographer of the classic Broadway musical *Annie Get Your Gun* (1946). His first venture as a choreographer in his own right came in 1961 with his narrated folk ballet *Dance of the Twelve Moons*, which played in New York City, at Cherokee, North Carolina (1962), and in the Northwest, with an all-Indian troupe, the American Indian Society of Creative Arts. In the early 1960s he was director and coordinator of the Indian Village at Freedomland (an amusement park in the Bronx) in New York City. He also wrote, produced, and directed plays unrelated to Indians.

In March 1970, Junaluska was one of the invited participants in the first Convocation of American Indian Scholars, organized at Princeton University by RUPERT COSTO, Jeannette Henry, BEATRICE MEDICINE, ALFONSO ORTIZ, and others. He played the role of Mr. Blacktree in the 1971 film of Paddy Chayefsky's comedy-drama *The Hospital*.

His wife worked for a nursing agency in New York, for a while attending the composer Igor Stravinsky in his last days (he died in 1971). But she missed her family, and in 1972 they returned to England. Attempts to promote his career there met with little success, through he gave some lectures and recitals.

In 1976, Junaluska issued a double-cassette sound recording, *Great American Indian Speeches*, read by himself and VINE DELORIA, JR.

Arthur Junaluska died in Exeter, England, on July 1, 1978. For the remainder of her life, Betty made efforts to get his work performed in Europe and the United States. She died in 2005.

Further Reading

Heard, Nick. "Arthur Junaluska and Betty Wright." Available online. URL: http://www.heardfamilyhistory.org.uk /Junaluska.htm. Accessed 13 May 2009.

Kabotie, Fred (Nakayoma, "Day after Day"; Tawawiiseoma, "Trailing Sun") (1900–1986)

Hopi painter, craftsperson, teacher

Born in Shungopovi, Arizona, on February 20, 1900, Fred Kabotie had two Hopi names, Nakayoma (Day after Day) and Tawawiiseoma (Trailing Sun). His parents belonged to the traditional faction from Shungopovi that moved to Oraibi to join YOUKIOMA in opposing "progressive" influences under WILSON TEWAQUAPTEWA. After being evicted from Oraibi along with the rest of Youkioma's followers, Kabotie and his family were among those who founded the village of Hotevilla. Kabotie herded sheep far from the village during the day to avoid the "school police," but in 1913 he was finally caught and, because of his stubborn refusal to go to school, was sent to the federal Indian boarding school at Santa Fe, New Mexico. There he showed promise and was encouraged by the superintendent and his wife to develop his artistic talent. After graduating, he turned to art as a source of income.

From 1920 through 1926, Kabotie was engaged to paint Indian dances for the permanent collection of the School of American Research (Santa Fe) and for the Archaeological Society of New Mexico (Albuquerque). He soon became widely known for his watercolors and tempera on paper, though he also worked in pen and ink, oil, and acrylic. Using exquisite care and intense colors in painting the dancers, Kabotie made them appear to float in white space, as his backgrounds lacked all detail, even a horizon line.

In 1928 and 1929, Kabotie was engaged by the Museum of the American Indian (Heye Foundation) to paint scenes of Hopi life and ceremonial dances. In 1937, he became the art instructor at the Hopi reservation high school, where he taught, among others, Charles Loloma (see LOLOMA, CHARLES, AND OTELLIE LOLOMA). In 1940, he reproduced Hopi paintings from the Awatobi ruins for the Peabody Museum (New Haven, Connecticut), and in 1945 he was awarded a Guggenheim fellowship.

In 1949, Kabotie established the Hopi Silvercraft Guild at Second Mesa. In addition to teaching silver design to the guild members, he was also the guild's manager. He later founded the Hopi Cultural Center at Second Mesa, becoming its first president. His works are displayed in numerous collections, including the Museum of Modern Art in New York City, and his paintings have been featured in more than 50 books and magazines. Kabotie's son Michael, born in 1942, is also a prominent artist. Fred Kabotie died in Shungopovi on February 28, 1986.

Further Reading

Anthes Bill. *Native Moderns: American Indian Painting, 1940–1960.* Durham, N.C.: Duke University Press, 2006.

Kabotie, Fred. *Fred Kabotie, Hopi Indian Artist: An Autobiography Told with Bill Belknap.* Flagstaff: Museum of Northern Arizona, 1977.

Katchongva, Dan (Dan Qöchhongva, Dan Kochongva, "White Cloud Above the Horizon")

(1865–1972) *Hopi political leader, silversmith*

Born in Oraibi in 1865 to YOUKIOMA, Dan Katchongva (White Cloud Above the Horizon, with many variant spellings, including Qöchhongva and Kochongva) was a member of the traditional faction of Oraibi Hopi who lost the famous "pushing match" in 1906 to the progressive faction led by WILSON TEWAQUAPTEWA. Katchongva himself was knocked unconscious during the scuffle, and the defeated traditionals were forced to leave Oraibi and establish the town of Hotevilla. The people of Hotevilla continued to resist the harsh assimilationist policies of the day (see ASSIMILATION) and were repeatedly punished for refusing to cut their hair or send their children to school. Shortly after they moved from Oraibi, Katchongva and 100 other men from Hotevilla were marched more than

30 miles to Keams Canyon, where they were shackled together and consigned to hard labor for more than a year.

After Youkioma died in 1929, Poliwuhioma of the Spider Clan ascended to the title of kikmongwi or village chief. Katchongva was already an influential force in the village, however, and by 1936 he had become its de facto leader. Although a member of the relatively minor Sun Clan, Katchongva also belonged to the powerful Two Horn Society, which had the responsibility of installing chiefs. Furthermore, his traditional credentials were impeccable, as he was not only the son of Youkioma but also married to the niece of 19th-century resistance leader Lomahongyoma. In 1943, he installed James Pongyayouma of the Fire Clan as kikmongwi, but 10 years later, when Pongyayouma married a woman from Santo Domingo Pueblo and moved away, Katchongva returned to the position of kikmongwi, which he held until 1971.

In 1936, Katchongva and other Hotevilla leaders rebuffed the attempts of BUREAU OF INDIAN AFFAIRS (BIA) emissary OLIVER LA FARGE to get their support for the new Hopi council, a creation of the policies of BIA commissioner JOHN COLLIER under the INDIAN REORGANIZATION ACT. The idea of a tribal council was foreign to the Hopi, among whom each of the eight major villages, governed by the kikmongwi and other religious leaders, was politically autonomous (see COLTON, HAROLD SELLERS). The town of Hotevilla, along with traditional strongholds Shungopovi, Mishongnovi, Oraibi, and Lower Moencopi, would boycott the council during most of three decades, forcing the tribal council to lose its official recognition in 1940 and disband in 1943. Katchongva also opposed the sheep stock-reduction plans under Collier, which fell heavily on the towns of the Third Mesa. During WORLD WAR II, Katchongva encouraged the Hopi to become conscientious objectors, and many ended up in prison for refusing to serve in the military.

In 1948, following the announcement by Shungopovi religious leader Andrew Hermequaftewa that the exploding of the atomic bomb over Japan was the prophesied "gourd of ashes" that would fall from the sky—a sign that the Hopi must reveal certain knowledge to the people of the world—Katchongva organized a meeting of more than 20 Hopi religious leaders. The group selected his protégé, THOMAS BANYACYA, and three others for the task of interpreting Hopi prophesies to the outside world. In 1950, Katchongva led a delegation of traditional Hopi leaders to visit the United Nations (UN) in an attempt to fulfill their sacred mission to inform the world of their prophecies. Although they were denied an audience with the world body, they used the opportunity for a side-trip to upstate New York, where they met with the Iroquois Confederacy and formed an important alliance that would come to exert a great influence on young Iroquois activists such as WILLIAM RICKARD, MAD BEAR ANDERSON, and TOM PORTER.

Later, Katchongva fought against Salt Lake City lawyer JOHN S. BOYDEN in his work to revive the dormant Hopi Tribal Council, as well as Boyden's attempts to settle land claims, lease lands for energy development, and have the tribal council run the Hopi reservation over the authority of the village kikmongwis (see SEKAQUAPTEWA, EMORY). In 1955, when the BIA instituted a permit system of livestock grazing on the reservation, Katchongva met with BIA commissioner GLENN EMMONS and managed to get the policy revoked. That same year, a special investigative team, formed by Emmons, heard testimony from all the Hopi villages except Oraibi concerning the newly revived tribal council, stock reductions, and other issues. Despite testimony of the majority of Hopi against the recognition of the tribal council, Emmons went ahead and recognized the council as the Hopi's only government, dealing the traditional Hopi leaders a severe setback.

In 1956, Katchongva organized a "Meeting of Religious People" in Hotevilla that helped galvanize support for the growing traditional movement, and between 1959 and 1963 he organized three "Meetings of Indian Brothers" that began to spread the Hopi traditional philosophy of resistance among other Indian tribes across the country. Among those who attended was Tuscarora activist William Rickard, an important champion of Iroquois sovereignty. In 1964, Katchongva, as well as the kikmongwis of Shungopovi, Mishongnovi, Oraibi, and Sipaulovi, filed suit in U.S. District Court in an attempt to prevent mineral leasing of Hopi lands at Black Mesa, charging the United States with "overthrowing their ancient government." However, despite Katchongva's abilities to mobilize support, from both traditional Hopi and outsiders, he was unable to stop the tribal council, which was largely funded and advised by energy interests, from leasing Hopi lands for mining and exploration. (See BIG MOUNTAIN; MINING, AMERICAN INDIANS AND.)

In the late 1960s, Katchongva went so far as to oppose the introduction of electricity, running water, sewage, and other modern conveniences to Hotevilla, leading to a loss of support for the traditional movement in the town and somewhat breaking the solidarity between Katchongva and the kikmongwis of Shungopovi and Mishongnovi. To make matters worse, despite his fierce determination to save the Hopi from modern American influences, Katchongva was unable to stem the growing process of acculturation that was under way in every Hopi town, including Hotevilla, and that was leading to the loss of important ceremonies and a drift away from traditional values. In 1970, Katchongva wrote down the philosophy to which he struggled to hold the Hopi true, entitled *From the Beginning of Life to the Day of Purification*. However, after his death in February 1972, the movement he led began to unravel, as his successors, Tewangyouma and David Monongye, were unable to prevent the growing schisms from taking hold in the town.

Although founded in order to get away from the "progressives" and their Americanized values, Hotevilla, like the other traditional centers Shungopovi and Mishongnovi, became deeply divided.

Further Reading

Katchongva, Dan. *From the Beginning of Life to the Day of Purification: Teaching, History and Prophecies of the Hopi People.* Translated by Danaqyumptewa. Los Angeles: Committee for Traditional Indian Land and Life, 1972.

Treat, James. *Around the Sacred Fire: Native Religious Activism in the Red Power Era.* New York: Palgrave Macmillan, 2003.

Keeler, William Wayne (1908–1987) *Cherokee political leader, oil industry executive*

William Wayne Keeler was born on April 5, 1908, in Dalhart, Texas. Both his parents were part Cherokee; Keeler himself was one-sixteenth Cherokee by blood. His grandfathers were white men who had immigrated to Indian Territory (later Oklahoma); both of them married women who were one-eighth Cherokee.

Keeler's paternal grandfather, George Keeler, was in the forefront of the Cherokee oil boom. When oil was discovered in the area, he leased more than 200,000 acres from the Cherokee Nation, then persuaded the U.S. secretary of the Interior to approve drilling on the land. George Keeler and his partner, Michael Cudahy, made the first big strike in the area in 1897.

William Keeler's maternal grandfather, Nelson Carr, settled in Indian Territory in the late 1860s, opening the first trading post in his area. Though he married his Cherokee wife in 1867, Carr remarried her according to the laws of the Cherokee Nation in order to be able to obtain land as a Cherokee citizen. He then proceeded to buy all the Indian land he could, eventually owning 5,000 acres. Once oil was discovered, he began leasing it to oilmen (see OIL, AMERICAN INDIANS AND).

When William Keeler was still a small child, the family moved to Bartlesville, Oklahoma. There he attended elementary and high school. In 1924, still a high-school student, Keeler took a part-time job with the engineering department of Phillips Petroleum. Graduating in 1926 as class valedictorian and entering the University of Kansas the same year, he earned a degree in chemical engineering. In 1929, he began working full time at the Phillips refinery in Kansas City.

During the 1930s, Keeler rose from chemist to engineer to supervisor of various Phillips refineries. During WORLD WAR II, he was named director of refining for the U.S. Petroleum Administration, which controlled the nation's wartime oil production, and also served as chairman of the Military Petroleum Advisory Board. Keeler worked his way up the corporate ladder at Phillips until he became vice president of the refining division in 1947. In 1951, he was elected to the board of directors, becoming executive vice president in 1956. In 1960, Keeler headed the first U.S. Petroleum Industry Exchange Delegation to tour and study the oil industry of the Soviet Union. He became chairman of the board and chief operating officer at Phillips in 1968, a position he would hold until his retirement in 1973.

While pursuing his top-level corporate career, Keeler also became an important figure in Cherokee and national Indian politics. Since election of Cherokee officials had ended with the abolition of the Cherokee government in 1908 (see CURTIS ACT), the principal chief was appointed directly by the president. In 1949, President Harry S. Truman named Keeler

to this position. Concerned that Congress would terminate the Cherokee (see TERMINATION), Keeler set up a Cherokee Foundation to provide welfare and other services to the tribe.

In 1961, Secretary of the Interior Stuart Udall appointed Keeler to serve on a presidential task force to reorganize the BUREAU OF INDIAN AFFAIRS (BIA). This task force ended up strongly condemning the Termination policy currently in place. The next year, Keeler served on a task force that investigated the conditions of Alaska Natives and their land claims (oil having recently been discovered in Alaska—see ALASKA NATIVE CLAIMS SETTLEMENT ACT). In 1964, Keeler served as chairman of the U.S. delegation to the Inter-American Indian Conference in Quito, Ecuador. He also served on various advisory committees under President Lyndon Johnson and Richard Nixon.

When the Cherokee government was reconstituted in 1971, Keeler won election as principal chief. With his protégé ROSS SWIMMER, tribal attorney and president of Tahlequah's First National Bank, Keeler formed a trust company called the Jelanuno Cultural and Economic Development Authority, which soon came under criticism for not having the Cherokee Nation as its beneficiary and appearing to swindle tribal assets. In 1972, for only one dollar, Jelanuno became the trustee for all property and proceeds of the Cherokee Nation Historical Society; in 1973, for 10 dollars, the society secured title to the Cherokee Nation land on which the nation's restaurant, craft shops, and motel were situated, after which the Cherokee Nation was obliged to lease the land back from Jelanuno at more than $11,000 a month.

Keeler's connections with President Nixon allowed him to place his friend Marvin Franklin as head of the BIA in 1972. (See THOMPSON, MORRIS). In 1973, Keeler was found guilty of making illegal contributions to Richard Nixon's campaign. That same year, the Securities and Exchange Commission found that Keeler and two associates had siphoned almost $3 million from Phillips Petroleum, funneled it to Swiss banks, and used most of it for political contributions. Keeler along with Phillips later pled guilty to the charge of concealing the funds from the U.S. Internal Revenue Service.

In 1975, Keeler lost his position as principal chief of the Cherokee Nation to Ross Swimmer. Keeler died in Bartlesville on August 24, 1987.

Further Reading

Lowe, Marjorie J. "Let's Make It Happen: W. W. Keeler and Cherokee Renewal." *Chronicles of Oklahoma* 74, no. 2 (Summer 1996): 116–129.

Keetoowah Society *See* SMITH, REDBIRD.

Kellogg, Laura Miriam Cornelius (Minnie Cornelius, Wynnogene) (1880–1947) *Oneida social and political thinker, writer, claims advocate*

Laura Miriam "Minnie" Cornelius (Oneida name Wynnogene)

was born into a prosperous farming family on the Oneida reservation near Green Bay, Wisconsin, in 1880, the daughter of Adam Poe and Celicia Bread Cornelius. After graduation from Grafton Hall in Fond du Lac, Wisconsin, she had planned to go straight on to college, but for health reasons a mild climate was recommended, and she enrolled as a teacher at the Sherman Indian School at Riverside, California, where she taught for two years (1903–05). On May 12, 1903, some 80 miles southeast of Riverside, the Indian Bureau (now BUREAU OF INDIAN AFFAIRS [BIA]) evicted a community of Cupeño Indians from their traditional home on the Warner Springs Ranch. Cornelius was present and is reported to have played a role in persuading the Indians not to resist relocation to the Pala Reservation 40 miles away.

Already at this time, Cornelius intended to help the tribes understand their rights. In an article in the *Los Angeles Times*, December 28, 1904, she stated her hope to become the first American Indian woman to study law. Unknown to her, that honor had already been achieved by LYDA CONLEY, admitted to the Missouri bar in 1902. Cornelius enrolled at Barnard College in New York City in 1906, still intending to study law, but in fact she never obtained a law degree.

Cornelius also attended Stanford University, the New York School of Philanthropy (forerunner of Columbia's School of Social Work), Cornell University, and the University of Wisconsin. In 1910, when Buffalo Bill Cody asked her, "What tribe do you belong to?," she replied, "I don't belong to any tribe. . . . We were called the Six Nations because we long ago had left the tribal state of society when the Europeans found us."

In 1911, Cornelius became one of the six founding Indian members of the SOCIETY OF AMERICAN INDIANS (SAI) and a member of its first executive committee. At the society's first convention in 1911, she showed her genius for adapting contemporary Western ideas to traditional Native values in a paper entitled "Industrial Organization for the Indian," which proposed turning INDIAN RESERVATIONS into self-governing "industrial villages" that would interact with the market economy, along the lines of English social reformer Robert Owen's Rochdale cooperative. The type of industry would be geared to local needs, skills, and the stage of development of the particular community. Indians could thus adopt beneficial elements of mainstream society while avoiding such evils as the factory system, urban congestion, and class conflict between labor and capital. "We believe the greatest economy in the world is to be just to all men," she wrote.

On April 24, 1912, at Stevens Point, Wisconsin, she married Orin J. Kellogg, a wealthy white attorney from Seymour, Wisconsin. After the wedding, they spent several months traveling on the Pacific coast.

At the education session of the second SAI conference in October 1912, Laura Cornelius Kellogg, now president of the educational division, declared the concept of the acculturated "new Indian" "a fake": "I am not the new Indian, I am the old Indian adjusted to new conditions." The ideas she presented at these Indian conferences were far from the assimilationist

emphasis of most other participants and drew little response there. As she continued to develop her vision over the next several years, she drew both support and criticism. The critical reaction of GUS BEAULIEU in his assimilationist Indian newspaper *The Tomahawk* (White Earth, Minnesota), November 7, 1918, is typical:

> . . . we consider professional and industrial pursuits or occupation, for any race of people, [superior] to the pursuit of superficial or medieval craft or art; we believe that the citizen who can properly cultivate an acre of ground and make it yield grain and garden truck or the citizen who can fill an artisan's position of far more consequence and value to the country than the product of "segregated limits." [N]o man, whatever his race, creed, or previous condition, can ever know the value of a dollar until surrounding circumstances prompt him to labor for every cent which compose that dollar.

In 1913, Thomas Sloan, an Indian attorney and SAI member then serving as special representative of the joint congressional commission to investigate Indian affairs chaired by Arkansas senator Joseph T. Robinson, delegated the Kelloggs as advance investigators. Oklahoma was a nest of corruption in Indian affairs, and on October 11, 1913, after several weeks investigating oil leases at Pawhuska, the agency of the Osage tribe (see OSAGE REIGN OF TERROR), the Kelloggs were arrested by the local marshal on orders of the federal district court in Pueblo, Colorado, on charges of obtaining money under false pretenses and impersonating federal officials. They asserted to the *Daily Oklahoman*, October 12, 1913, that this was no more than a frame-up instigated by the Indian Bureau, "another move in the game now being played in Osage County between the department of the Interior, various big factors in the oil world, and the advance guard of the Robinson investigating committee." They did not resist or seek bail in Oklahoma but accompanied federal agents to Colorado, where they were released on bail. At the U.S. District Court at Denver, Colorado, on January 31, 1914, Judge R. E. Lewis ordered the jury to acquit the Kelloggs.

By this time, they had moved to Washington, D.C., to devote themselves to lobbying for better Indian legislation. There, later in 1914, they met REDBIRD SMITH, leader of a traditionalist Cherokee faction in Oklahoma known as the Nighthawk Keetoowah. Laura and her brother CHESTER POE CORNELIUS were invited to come down to work with Smith and his community and implement some of her economic development ideas. The people there gave her the Cherokee name "Egahtahyen" ("dawn"). But she maintained her residence in Washington and continued to be involved in legislative matters. In particular, she strongly advocated a bill introduced by Senator Harry Lane that would abolish the Indian Bureau and replace it with a commission, under direct control of Congress, to consist of three men selected from among five nominees chosen by a council of Indians. A report in the Portland *Oregonian* for February 14, 1916, characterizes this Indian council as "a protected autonomous [Indian] government."

The most extensive presentation of her vision, which she called the Lolomai Plan (later spelled Lolomi—the word means "good, beautiful, wise" in the Hopi language) is given in her 1920 book *Our Democracy and the American Indian;* (A work "lovingly dedicated" to the memory of Chief Redbird Smith "who preserved his people from demoralization, and was the first to accept the Lolomi.") Its foreshadowing of JOHN COLLIER's later INDIAN REORGANIZATION ACT (1934) is unmistakable, but in its time it stood alone. Although some artists, writers, and scientists such as ERNEST THOMPSON SETON and FRANK G. SPECK had similar views, none had framed them into a comprehensive program of action.

The Dawes Act of 1887 (see ALLOTMENT) destroyed the Wisconsin Oneida's tribal land base, and the New York Oneida had lost almost all their land in the 18th and 19th centuries. Kellogg began to study the Oneida land claims in New York State. In 1920, two events raised hopes. The United States Court of Appeals for the Second Circuit, in *U.S. v. Boylan*, denied New York courts jurisdiction to dispose of Indian property or remove Indians without the consent of the federal government; and in August, the Everett Commission of the New York State Assembly concluded that the Six Nations Iroquois were entitled to 6 million acres in New York, due to illegal dispossession after the 1784 Treaty of Fort Stanwix. (See also THOMAS, GEORGE E.).

Kellogg and her husband determined to pursue an Iroquois claim to 18 million acres in New York and Pennsylvania. Setting up headquarters at Onondaga, the traditional capital of the Six Nations, they traveled out to every Iroquois community in New York, Quebec, Ontario, Wisconsin, and Oklahoma to gather support and funds. A superb orator in both Oneida and English, Kellogg had an unusual ability to communicate equally well with both Indians and non-Indians. She collected large sums for the project, and her followers became known as the Kellogg Party. In 1925, as a test case, they instituted a class action in the court for the Northern District of New York (*James Deere v. St. Lawrence River Power*), on behalf of the Iroquois confederacy, to eject a subsidiary of Alcoa Aluminum and other occupants from a small parcel of land. The case foundered on technicalities, and in October 1927 the court claimed lack of jurisdiction and dismissed it. Assemblyman Edward A. Everett, the Indians' chief counsel, died a short time later, and subsequent appeals got nowhere. As Kellogg's great plan lost momentum, support dwindled. Because much of the money collected was never used for its intended purpose, she was accused of fraud. In 1927, she, her husband, and her brother were actually indicted in Canada, though they were later acquitted. But after having convinced many Iroquois that the claims case could not lose, she had nothing to show for it. Non-Indian welfare organizations attacked her for misleading thousands of Iroquois, and she had alienated important traditional figures such as CLINTON RICKARD because she had never gone through traditional Iroquois protocol. The constant string of defeats in the courts did not help.

Turning to Congress, Kellogg managed to get a hearing before the Senate Subcommittee on Indian Affairs on March 1, 1929. There she outlined the Oneida claims before the Senate and secured a congressional investigation into New York Indian affairs, John Collier, then head of the American Indian Defense Association, helped organize these hearings. Kellogg's testimony, however, alienated most of the senators as well as E. B. Merritt, assistant commissioner of Indian Affairs, who accused her of fraud and tried to launch a federal investigation.

The last blow to Kellogg's project was the INDIAN NEW DEAL itself. She had always decried the Bureau of Indian Affairs, arguing that her project was the only way for her followers to get money. In fact, she had taken money from them. Now the government was providing money and programs that addressed the Iroquois' immediate needs.

Under other circumstances, a person like Kellogg might have made great contributions to the Indian New Deal, Ernest Thompson Seton's Woodcraft movement, and Clinton Rickard's Indian Defense League of America, but her determination to stay an increasingly unpopular course estranged her from all of them. By the 1940s, Kellogg was, according to historian Lawrence Hauptman, "a broken woman, who had outlived her time in history and dissipated both her fame and the money that had come with it." She died, almost forgotten, in New York City in 1947.

Nevertheless, in historical perspective, Kellogg emerges as an important figure. Her Lolomi Plan showed a viable way for the survival and development of Indian cultures in the modern world. She also wrote many valuable articles and several books. Her leadership reactivated the dormant claims issue and kept it alive under great adversity for as long as possible; it drew together the scattered Oneida bands and developed contacts with the state and federal governments on their behalf.

Years later, her legal reasoning was also vindicated. The Oneida went back to federal court in 1970 to sue for the rights to 270,000 acres around Verona and Vernon, New York. Though *Oneida Indian Nation v. County of Oneida* (1974) was dismissed for lack of jurisdiction, the U.S. Supreme Court ruled that it was indeed a federal question whether the Indian Trade and Intercourse Act had been violated. A further decision, *Oneida Nation v. County of Oneida* (1977), held that according to the Intercourse Act, the landowners could not have acquired good title from the state and were therefore trespassers on Oneida land. Adjudication of damages began in 1981. This, too, went to the Supreme Court. In March 1984, the judgment was upheld, and in 1986 the Oneida won the right to sue for damages in the U.S. Supreme Court. Negotiations continued, but nothing significant happened until December 1998, when the Oneida and the U.S. Department of Justice named 20,000 local landowners as defendants, intending to pressure New York State to work out a settlement. In *Sherill v. Oneida Nation* (2005), the Supreme Court stated concern about the "disruptive" nature of the Oneida claims. Based on this, Judge Lawrence Kahn of the District Court for the Northern District of New York on

May 21, 2007, dismissed the Oneidas' possessory claims to the land (which would give them right of eviction), but upheld their right to trespass damages. The U.S. Court of Appeals for the Second Circuit heard the appeals of both plaintiffs and defendants on June 3, 2008, and dismissed the case in a split decision in 2010. In 2011, the Supreme Court refused to hear the Oneida's appeal, but they continue to press their claims through other legal avenues.

Further Reading
Hauptman, Laurence M. "Designing Woman: Minnie Kellogg, Iroquois Leader." In *Indian Lives: Essays on Nineteenth and Twentieth-Century Native American Leaders*, edited by George Moses and Raymond Wilson, 159–188. Albuquerque: University of New Mexico Press, 1985.
Holm, Tom. *The Great Confusion in Indian Affairs: Native Americans & Whites in the Progressive Era*. Austin: University of Texas Press, 2005.
McLester, Thelma Cornelius. "Oneida Women Leaders." In *The Oneida Experience: Two Perspectives*, edited by Jack Campisi and Laurence M. Hauptman, 109–111. Syracuse, N.Y.: Syracuse University Press, 1988.
Stovey, Patricia. "Opportunities at Home: Laura Cornelius Kellogg and Village Industrialization." In *The Oneida Indians in the Age of Allotment, 1860–1920*, edited by Lawrence M. Hauptman and L. Gordon McLester, 143–175. Norman: University of Oklahoma Press, 2006.

Kenny, Maurice Francis (1929–) *Mohawk-Seneca poet, playwright*
Maurice Kenny was born on August 16, 1929, in Watertown, New York, to a Mohawk father and a Seneca mother. After earning his B.A. in English literature from Butler University in 1956, Kenny moved to New York City, where he came under the influence of poet Louise Bogan and other well-known writers of the 1950s.

In 1958, Kenny's first collection of poetry, *Dead Letters Sent, and Other Poems*, made him the first Native American poet to be published in the period after WORLD WAR II. The next year, he released *With Love to Lesbia*. For the next 15 years, he worked as the personal secretary for author Willard Motley and as a journalist for the *Chicago Sun*.

In 1976, Kenny published *I Am the Sun*, a collection that found a wide audience. He also established Strawberry Press to provide an outlet for a new generation of Indian writers. During this time, he served as coeditor of the poetry magazine *Contact II*. After releasing *Only as Far as Brooklyn* (1979) and *Kneading the Blood* (1981), Kenny published his most important work, a combination of poetry and drama, *Blackrobe: Isaac Jogues, b. March 11, 1607*, in 1982. *Blackrobe* was nominated for the Pulitzer Prize and received the National Public Radio Award in 1984. Kenny's collection *Is Summer This Bear* (1985) best characterizes his use of Native American imagery to, in the words of critic James Ruppert, "express the tension between Native perceptions and the contemporary American world, a

world that Native people cannot ignore." Kenny's tireless championship of young Indian poets, as well as his emphasis on the idea of poetry as an oral art compatible with Native American traditions, made him an important catalyst in the renaissance of Native American poetry in the last quarter of the 20th century.

Further Reading
Grant, E. "He Walks in Two Worlds: An Interview with Maurice Kenny." *Studies in American Indian Literature* 7 (1995): 17.
Kenny, Maurice. *Blackrobe: Isaac Jogues, b. 11, 1607*. Saranac Lake, N.Y.: North Country Community College Press, 1982.
———. *Carving Hawk: New & Selected Poems, 1953–2000*. Buffalo, N.Y.: White Pine Press, 2002.
———. *Is Summer This Bear*. Saranac Lake, N.Y.: Chauncy Press, 1985.
Nowak, Mark. "Historian of Home: A Talk with Maurice Kenny." *River City* 17, no. 1 (Winter 1997): 20–22.
Roemer, K. M. *Native American Writers of the United States*. Detroit, Mich.: Gale Research, 1997.
Swann, Brian, and Arnold Krupat. *I Tell You Now: Autobiographical Essays by Native American Writers*. Lincoln: University of Nebraska Press, 2005.

Kickingbird, K. Kirke (1944–) *Kiowa attorney, educator*
A Kiowa, K. Kirke Kickingbird was born in Wichita, Kansas, in 1944, the son of Carl and Sue (Katherine Suzanne) Kickingbird. His mother, whose maiden name was Burnette, came from a distinguished, traditional citizen Potawatomi family. His great-great-grandfather Chief Kickingbird took part in negotiations of the Little Arkansas and Medicine Lodge treaties.

After receiving his B.A. (1966) and law degree (1969) from the University of Oklahoma, Kickingbird worked for the BUREAU OF INDIAN AFFAIRS (BIA) Office of Congressional Relations from 1969 to 1971. In 1971, he cofounded with VINE DELORIA, JR., the Institute for the Development of Indian Law, originally under the name Indian Legal Information Development Service, in Washington, D.C., serving as its executive director from 1971 to 1975 and from 1978 onward.

In 1971, the institute began publishing a periodical, the *Legislative Review*. A second periodical, the *Education Journal of the Institute for the Development of Indian Law* first appeared on August 28, 1972. In 1975, they were merged to become the *American Indian Journal (AIJ)*, which continued until 1983, was suspended 1983–85, then resumed through autumn 1987. Kickingbird was editor-in-chief from 1975 to 1981. An extremely interesting, well-researched, and well-written publication, the *AIJ* ranked as one of the best American Indian periodicals, and it played an important role in the development of a new consciousness. By working to formulate the legal arguments for Native sovereignty (see SOVEREIGNTY, INDIGENOUS AND TRIBAL), the magazine helped to expand the struggle for Indian rights beyond the activist movements of the day and toward a broader recognition of the role of treaty rights, economic development, environmental protection, and education in helping to sustain Indian cultures (see BRESETTE, WALT; BARREIRO, JOSÉ).

In addition, Kickingbird did fund-raising and public relations, litigation, research, writing, and editing for the institute, which has issued, in addition to the *AIJ*, a large number of pamphlets, booklets, and audiovisual materials on various aspects of Indian law and public affairs.

In the mid-1970s, Kickingbird, along with Vine Deloria, Jr., was one of the formative intellectual influences in the planning of the AMERICAN INDIAN POLICY REVIEW COMMISSION, and was on its staff. He also worked for the Legal Service Corporation. In 1988, he was appointed director of the Native American Legal Resource Center as well as assistant professor at the School of Law of Oklahoma City University. He was chairman of the Oklahoma Indian Affairs Commission and in 1995 was named by Oklahoma governor Frank Keating as special counsel on Indian affairs. From 1996 until 2000, he served on the board of governors of the American Bar Association.

Kickingbird has also been interested in problems of indigenous peoples in other countries. He has provided technical assistance to more than 150 indigenous government, not only in the United States but also in Siberia, Namibia, Australia, New Zealand, and Japan, through his consulting firm, Kickingbird Associates.

Kirke Kickingbird is currently an attorney with the law firm Hobbs, Straus, Dean, and Walker. His books include *One Hundred Million Acres* (1973, with Karen Ducheneaux), *Economic Perspectives of American Indian History* (1979), and *Indians and the United States Constitution: A Forgotten Legacy* (1987, with Lynn S. Kickingbird). He also contributed to Vine Deloria, Jr.'s *Behind the Trail of Broken Treaties* (1974).

Kidwell, Clara Sue (1941–) *Choctaw-Chippewa educator, historian of science*

Clara Sue Kidwell was born on July 8, 1941, at Tahlequah, Oklahoma, the daughter of Hardin Milton Kidwell (Choctaw) and Martha Evelyn St. Clair (Chippewa), both graduates of the Haskell Institute in Lawrence, Kansas. Both of her parents worked, so Kidwell was raised by her Choctaw grandmother in Muskogee, Oklahoma.

As a junior high and high school student, Kidwell began to develop an interest in science, which she pursued as an undergraduate and graduate student at the University of Oklahoma at Norman, ultimately focusing on the history of science as her area of research. At the University of Oklahoma, Kidwell received her B.A. in 1962, M.A. in 1966, and Ph.D. in 1970. She later taught the history of science and Western civilization at the Kansas Art Institute (1966–68), and American and Indian history at Haskell Indian Junior College (1970–72). From 1974 to 1993, she was associate professor of Native American studies at the University of California at Berkeley, where she taught Native American philosophy and medicine,

also serving as associate dean of the graduate division. She held a Rockefeller Humanities Fellowship in 1977–78 and a University of California Regents humanities fellowship in 1978. In 1993, she became assistant director for cultural resources at the Smithsonian National Museum of the American Indian in Washington, D.C. She was a professor of history and directed the Native American Studies Programs at the Universities of Oklahoma and North Carolina.

Kidwell is a member of the Native American Science and Engineering Society, the History of Science Society, and the American Society for Ethnohistory. She currently directs Bacone College's Indian Studies division. In addition to numerous articles on various subjects, she has published several books, including *The Choctaws: A Critical Bibliography* (1980, with Charles Roberts); *Choctaws and Missionaries in Mississippi, 1818–1918* (1995); and *A Native American Theology* (2001, with Homer Noley and George E. Tinker).

Kinzua Dam

The building of a dam near the Allegany Seneca Reservation in upstate New York was proposed as early as 1908 and studied throughout the 1920s. Attempts during the 1930s to build a dam were blocked by Secretary of the Interior Harold Ickes and the JOHN COLLIER–controlled BUREAU OF INDIAN AFFAIRS. In 1941, however, legislation was passed in Congress that authorized a dam on the Allegheny River as part of a flood-control program for the Ohio River Basin. WORLD WAR II intervened, postponing the project until 1956.

The dam was to be constructed in Pennsylvania at a narrows called the Kinzua, on the Allegheny River only 12 miles downstream from the Allegany Seneca Reservation. The resulting lake would flood more than 9,000 acres of the reservation, leaving only 2,300 acres habitable. The graves of Cornplanter and other Seneca leaders, as well as ancient ceremonial sites, would be flooded as well, and 130 Seneca families would lose their lands and be forced to move. Moreover, the flooding of the Seneca Reservation would violate the Treaty of Canandaigua, signed in 1794 between the Iroquois Confederacy and the newly established United States.

Led by their president, Cornelius Seneca, and his successors George Heron and Basil Williams, the tribe had two prominent engineers, Arthur E. Morgan, former chair of the Tennessee Valley Authority (TVA), and Barton Jones, construction engineer for the TVA, conduct a study, which found the proposed Kinzua Dam was needlessly expensive and other, cheaper and better, flood-control options were available that would not flood the reservation.

Despite the report, the project proceeded—largely, as many believed, because flood control was never the sole object of the dam. Pittsburgh manufacturers wanted the project as a way to mitigate pollution from Pennsylvania coal mines that was fouling their boilers.

The Army Corps of Engineers hired an independent engineering firm to examine Morgan's alternative, but the firm, founded by three ex-corps generals, refused to criticize the

Kinzua site. The Seneca fought the Army Corps of Engineers in court, arguing that congressional legislation was required to condemn Indian land. However, they lost on appeal when the court ruled that by merely appropriating the money for the dam's construction, Congress had already authorized the land cession.

Although the case caused a national outcry and won support from, among others, social critic Edmund Wilson in his *Apologies to the Iroquois*, and from Brooks Atkinson, the distinguished *New York Times* theater critic, the power of the Army Corps of Engineers and their supporters in Congress was too great, and the dam was completed in 1965. After it was built, Congress belatedly awarded the Seneca $15 million in compensation. While this money was useful to the tribe, nothing could replace the lost land. To this day, many Seneca remain bitter over Kinzua Dam. But the battle had galvanized Indians across the country, and it helped fuel the militancy of the RED POWER MOVEMENT then under way.

Further Reading

Bilharz, Joy Ann. *The Allegany Senecas and Kinzua Dam: Forced Relocation through Two Generations*. Lincoln: University of Nebraska Press, 1998.

Hauptman, Lawrence M. "General John S. Bragdon, the Office of Public Works Planning, and the Decision to Build Pennsylvania's Kinzua Dam." *Pennsylvania History* 53, no. 3 (1986): 181–200.

Kiowa Five

The term "Kiowa Five" refers to a group of Kiowa artists who founded the Kiowa School of painting, which exerted a strong influence on 20th-century Indian art. These artists, all from distinguished traditional Kiowa families, were Spencer Asah, born around 1907, the son of Jim Asah, a leader of the Kiowa Buffalo Medicine Cult; James Auchiah, born on November 17, 1906, the son of Mark Auchiah and grandson of famous Kiowa chief Satanta; Stephen Mopope, born on August 27, 1898, the grandson of noted Kiowa warrior Appiatan, who raised him; Jack Hokeah, born on December 4, 1901, the grandson of warrior White Horse; and Monroe Tsatoke, born on September 29, 1904, the son of Tsa To Kee, a scout for General George Armstrong Custer.

As children, the young boys, along with a sixth child, Louise Smoky (born on April 8, 1907, the daughter of Enoch Smoky), were already influenced by the developing Indian art world in Anadarko, Oklahoma. Ledger drawings had become an established local art form by the late 19th century, with the return of Plains Indian prisoners from Fort Marion in Florida, where they had been given paper and colored pencils by educator RICHARD HENRY PRATT. The vivid pictographic compositions, often drawn in ledger books furnished by military personnel, were rooted in the traditional culture of the Plains Indians. The children received encouragement from their families, many of whom still lived in the traditional manner. Hokeah was orphaned while a young boy and reared by his

grandmother, while Mopope learned to paint on skins in the Kiowa way from his great-uncles Silverhorn, a noted Anadarko artist, and Hakok. The children attended St. Patrick's Indian School, where they were further encouraged in their artwork by Father Isadore Richlin and Sister Olivia Taylor, teachers at the boarding school.

In 1916, Susie Peters, a matron at the Anadarko, Oklahoma, Indian agency, began teaching art classes to the six children at St. Patrick's, even organizing a fine arts club to help give them lessons and encouragement. (Peters would eventually help other young Indians become artists, including WOODY CRUMBO.) Impressed by their talent, Peters took some of the children's paintings to Taos, New Mexico, in 1918, where she sold them to a dealer. In 1926, Oscar Jacobson, director of the art department at the University of Oklahoma, invited four of the boys—Asah, Mopope, Hokeah, and Tsatoke—to Norman, Oklahoma, to develop their skills. Smoky joined them the next year, though she faced resentment from the other four, as in Kiowa culture it was not customary for women to paint or draw in a representational style. Smoky (she would later sign her works Lois Smokey) soon dropped out and was replaced by Auchiah, and the Kiowa Five were established.

In 1927, the group held a show at the American Federation of Arts Convention in Denver, and the next year they were featured in an international exposition in Prague, Czechoslovakia, that later traveled throughout Europe. It was the first international showing of American Indian art. In 1930, at the Exposition of Indian Intertribal Arts in New York City, the group's work reached a wide audience, including DOROTHY DUNN, who helped establish the Studio (or Santa Fe) school of Indian art a few years later.

The style of the Kiowa Five was based on the pictographic Plains drawings of the 19th century. It is characterized by a two-dimensional aspect, usually without perspective or background, thus giving its figures the appearance of floating in space.

Like Dunn's Studio school, the Kiowa Five helped reverse the trend toward the ASSIMILATION of Indian culture by returning to traditional techniques and subjects in their art and by helping to popularize Indian paintings as a distinct and valuable art form. Jack Hokeah later traveled to the Southwest to study under Dunn, bringing the Studio style back with him to Oklahoma.

The individual success of the five artists fluctuated throughout their lives. Monroe Tsatoke became ill with tuberculosis and joined the NATIVE AMERICAN CHURCH. His paintings of peyote road men, as spiritual leaders in the church are called, are among the best known of the style. He also became a well-known traditional singer. Tsatoke died of tuberculosis on February 3, 1937, at the age of 33.

In 1930, Jack Hokeah went to Santa Fe to attend a fiesta and met renowned potter MARIA MARTINEZ of San Ildefonso Pueblo. He stayed at San Ildefonso Pueblo for the next 10 years, living with the Martinez family. He also became known as an exceptional dancer, which led to his withdrawal from painting and the art world in his later years. He died on December 14, 1969. Stephen Mopope also became well known as a traditional dancer, though he also continued to paint for the rest of his life. Between 1936 and 1937, he painted 16 murals on the upper walls of the Anadarko Post Office. Assisted by Spencer Asah and James Auchiah, the murals portray various aspects of Kiowa Indian life. Mopope died on February 3, 1974. Spencer Asah became a farmer and died in 1954 in Norman, Oklahoma. James Auchiah became a teacher and a museum curator. He died on December 28, 1974.

Lois Smoky's art career was brief; after leaving the University of Oklahoma, she married and devoted herself to her family. She died on February 1, 1981.

Further Reading

Berlo, Janet Catherine, and Ruth B. Phillips. *Native North American Art*. Oxford: Oxford University Press, 1998.
Jacobson, Oscar Brousse. *Kiowa Indian Art: Watercolor Paintings in Color by the Indians of Oklahoma*. Nice, France: C. Szwedzicki, 1929.

LaCourse, Richard Vance (1938–2001) *Yakama journalist*

A Yakima (later Yakama), Richard LaCourse was born on September 23, 1938, in Toppenish, Washington. He attended San Luis Rey College from 1957 to 1961, studying later at Portland State University and, from 1964 to 1968, at the University of Washington. He then joined the *Seattle Post-Intelligencer* as a news copy editor and correspondent, becoming managing editor of the *Confederated Umatilla Journal* in 1971, and later, managing editor of the *Yakima Nation Review*, one of the most respected tribal Indian newspapers in the country.

LaCourse was an early member of the American Indian Press Association (AIPA), an organization created to help promote Indian JOURNALISM, and he helped to found the Native American Press Association (now known as the Native American Journalist Association), writing the group's charter, code of ethics, and business plan. From 1972 through 1974, he was AIPA's news director and reported from Washington, D.C.

In 1977, LaCourse founded and managed the *Manatabla Messenger* for the Colorado River Tribes in Arizona. He began his own company, LaCourse Communications, in 1983. It provided design, research, and marketing help to tribal newspapers. Considered the dean of Indian journalists in his time, LaCourse worked to raised the standards of Indian journalism, particularly among tribal and organizational newspapers and newsletters.

Richard LaCourse died on March 9, 2001, in Seattle, Washington, while undergoing heart surgery.

Further Reading

Harjo, Suzan Shown. "Richard V. LaCourse (1938–2001)
 Indian Journalist." *Indian Country Today*, 21 March
 2001.

lacrosse

Lacrosse, one of today's fastest-growing sports, with approximately half a million players worldwide, is an indigenous Native American game. At the time of the first European contact, lacrosse was played by tribes in the Southeast, the western Great Lakes, and in the St. Lawrence valley area. Each region had a different variant of the game. In general, lacrosse had a profound religious and mystical basis in tribal culture and ceremony.

By the late 19th century, the game was in decline among Indian nations, despite its central cultural role. As traditional cultures eroded, betting and violence began to increase to unmanageable levels. Around 1900, for example, the Oklahoma Choctaw began to attach lead weights to their sticks to use them as skull crackers, leading to the banning of the game in that area. Government officials and missionaries began to see lacrosse as a catalyst for antisocial behavior and as yet another aspect of Native American life that needed to be stamped out.

Non-Indians, on the other hand, had been playing lacrosse for some time, after Canadians in Montreal picked it up from the Mohawk. For non-Indians, lacrosse was something that needed to be "civilized" by a set of rules and regulations. William Beers, a Montreal dentist, formulated the laws of present-day lacrosse with this aim in mind, observing, "Only a savage people could, would or should play the old game; only such constitutions, such wind and endurance, could stand its violence." Duly gentrified, the sport was declared the national game of Canada on the same day that the Dominion came into being: July 1, 1867. In its new "refined" version, lacrosse quickly became popular and spread throughout the Commonwealth and Europe.

Non-Indian enthusiasm for lacrosse went hand in hand with a consistent hostility to Indian participation in the game.

As early as 1866, one of Beers's rules stated that no Indian must play for a white club, "unless previously agreed on." That agreement was never intended to be reached, although for many years white teams made extensive use of Indian "ringers"; the colonists were bent on establishing the lacrosse team as a gentleman's club. But Indians, not having the luxury of a private income, needed to be paid for travel to matches. When the National Lacrosse Association of Canada ruled in 1880 that only amateurs could play, Indian teams were effectively maneuvered out of international competition for more than a century.

Despite this, Indians continued to play competitive lacrosse. At the turn of the century, POP WARNER was an advocate of the game and its ability to develop players in other sports. While he coached sports at the Carlisle Indian School, Warner fielded some powerful lacrosse teams. Among the best were the 1909–12 teams that featured JIM THORPE and Onondaga brothers Isaac and Jesse Lyons. Around this time, EDWARD CORNPLANTER captained the lacrosse team for Newtown, a traditional stronghold on the Cattaraugus Seneca Reservation in New York. In 1932, lacrosse was featured in the Olympic games, and Indians had one of their brief chances to compete internationally when they fielded an Indian all-star team.

In the contemporary game, there are two distinct worlds of lacrosse. The first is that played, mostly on reservations, by Indians. Although the Great Lakes game is virtually extinct, in the Southeast lacrosse is still a vital part of tribal culture and religious ceremony, as it is in the Northeast for the Iroquois. The second world exists in one of two forms: either box lacrosse (in Canada), or field lacrosse (in the United States), the latter played by the international "lacrosse community" and dominated by Euro-Americans, with minimal Indian participation. It is this community that controls the rules and regulations, manufactures and sells the equipment, and financially supports the institutions where field lacrosse is played. For the most part, its members are only minimally aware of or indifferent to the history of this major contribution of the American Indian to world sport. Since the 1980s, however, with the formation of the IROQUOIS NATIONALS LACROSSE TEAM, Indians have returned to international competition.

In 1993, Onondaga goalie OREN LYONS, JR., was be inducted into the Lacrosse Hall of Fame, joining Cherokee Leon Miller as the only other Indian so honored.

Further Reading

Fisher, Donald M. *Lacrosse: A History of the Game*. Baltimore, Md.: Johns Hopkins University Press, 2002.

LaDuke, Vincent   *See* SUN BEAR.

LaDuke, Winona (1959–) *Chippewa (Anishinabe) activist, author, vice-presidential candidate*

Winona LaDuke was born on August 18, 1959, in Los Angeles,

Winona LaDuke and her son, Aajuawak Kapashesit, on the White Earth Reservation, Minnesota, in 1992. *(Ronnie Farley)*

California, the daughter of Mississippi Band Chippewa author Vincent LaDuke (see SUN BEAR) and artist Betty Bernstein LaDuke. Her parents separated when Winona was five years old, and LaDuke was raised by her mother in Ashland, Oregon. At 17, she enrolled in Harvard University, completing a B.A. in Native economic development in 1982. She also managed the men's hockey team. In 1983, she won a fellowship to the Massachusetts Institute of Technology (MIT) and later earned a master's degree in rural development at Antioch College in Ohio.

LaDuke was a member of the INTERNATIONAL INDIAN TREATY COUNCIL delegation that spoke on indigenous issues before the United Nations (UN) in Geneva in 1977. She was commissioned by the Treaty Council to write a report on the activities of multinational corporations on INDIAN RESERVATIONS. Also in 1977, she spent a summer in Nevada campaigning against mining on Indian lands in the Southwest (see MINING, AMERICAN INDIANS AND).

In 1982, LaDuke moved back to her father's reservation, White Earth in Minnesota, and became the principal of the reservation high school. She quickly became involved with a lawsuit to recover Chippewa lands taken fraudulently through the ALLOTMENT process (see BEAULIEU, GUS H.); however, the case was dismissed four years later.

An extremely effective organizer, LaDuke became involved

in many of the Native struggles of the 1980s, including the Hopi-Navajo land dispute at Big Mountain, as well as opposition to the effects of the nuclear industry on Indian lands (see nuclear industry, American Indians and the). She was among the first U.S. Indian activists to speak out against the James Bay II hydroelectric project in Quebec—a megadevelopment program that would have devastated huge tracts of Cree lands–and she played an important part in the project's demise in 1993. (In 2002, however, Quebec began negotiating with the Cree to restart the project, although as of 2015 its future remains uncertain.)

In 1989, LaDuke was honored for her activism with the first Reebok Human Rights Award, presented to outstanding activists under 30 years of age. With the award money, she initiated the White Earth Land Recovery Project in an attempt to regain the lands lost to her home reservation. Since then, the project has repurchased about 1,200 acres. The Recovery Project has also created programs aimed at reviving Chippewa culture and language. In addition, the project supports sustainable economic development activities, such as an organic raspberry farm and a maple sugar operations, and ecological restoration, such as the restocking of sturgeon and modification of dams.

LaDuke has also written prolifically in Indian publications such as *Akwesasne Notes*, *Daybreak*, and *Native Americas* magazine, as well as general publications such as *Cultural Survival*. In 1997, she published a novel, *The Last Woman Standing*; in 1999, *All Our Relations*, a survey of Native resistance to corporate domination, cultural loss, and environmental degradation; in 2007, *Recovering the Sacred*, about traditional beliefs; and in 2011, *The Militarization of Indian Country*. A former member of Women of All Red Nations (WARN), LaDuke was a founder and cochair, with Ingrid Washinawatok, of the Women's Indigenous Network. Her emphasis on the environment led her to found the Indigenous Environmental Network and to join the board of directors of the environmental group Greenpeace. In 1993, to raise awareness to the issue of radioactive contamination in the community of Point Hope, Alaska (see Rock, Howard), LaDuke organized the first Honor the Earth tour with the folk-rock group the Indigo Girls. Subsequent Honor the Earth tours and a compact disk, *Honor 1*, to raise funds for the Indigenous Environmental Network, the Seventh Generation Fund, and a host of other Native grassroots groups.

In 1994, LaDuke was named by *Time* magazine as one of America's 50 most promising leaders under 40 years of age. Two years later, she was one of six vice presidential candidates, each representing a region of the United States, who ran with Ralph Nader on the Green Party ticket. In 2000, she again joined the Green Party ticket with Nader, this time as his sole running mate, and they received almost 3 percent of the ballots cast. In September 2007, LaDuke was inducted into the National Women's Hall of Fame.

Uncompromising in her political outlook, Winona LaDuke has become one of the most effective and prominent Indian leaders in the struggle to maintain Native traditions and preserve Indian lands. In her diverse and far-reaching work, she has managed to bridge the gap between the powerful environmental movement and the Indian rights movement, which were often at odds. Although inspired by the activism of the American Indian Movement (AIM), she represents the less confrontational style of the next generation of Indian activists who have focused on networking and coalition building rather than militancy to achieve their goals.

See also environmental movement, American Indians and the.

Further Reading

LaDuke, Winona. *All Our Relations: Native Struggles for Land and Life*. Cambridge, Mass.: South End Press, 1999.
Ritter, Peter. "The Party Crasher." *City Pages* (Minneapolis/ St., Paul), 11 October 2000.
Silverstone, Michael. *Winona LaDuke: Restoring Land and Culture in Native America*. New York: Feminist Press, 2001.

La Farge, Oliver (1901–1963) *anthropologist, novelist, Indian rights activist*

Oliver La Farge was born in New York City on December 19, 1901, the son of Christopher Grant and Florence Bayard Lockwood La Farge. He graduated from the Groton School, Massachusetts, in 1920, earned his B.A. from Harvard University in 1924, his M.A. in 1929, and received an honorary M.A. from Brown University in 1932. From 1926 to 1928, La Farge was an assistant in ethnology in the Department of Middle American Research at Tulane University in New Orleans. He made several archaeological and ethnological expeditions to Mexico, Guatemala, and Arizona between 1926 and 1932.

In February 1930, La Farge became a member of the board of directors of the Eastern Association on Indian Affairs (New York City) and served as director from 1930 to 1932. In the latter year, the name was changed to National Association on Indian Affairs. From shortly after its founding in 1922 to fight the Bursum bill, as a close ally of the New Mexico Association on Indian Affairs, this organization was often at odds with the American Indian Defense Association (AIDA), due largely to friction with AIDA director John Collier.

From 1929 through 1933, La Farge was special adviser to Bureau of Indian Affairs (BIA) commissioner Charles James Rhoads. After Collier became commissioner in April 1933 and the Indian Reorganization Act (IRA) became law in 1934, La Farge was more or less satisfied with the legislation and reconciled with Collier. In connection with the IRA, people were needed to go out across Indian country and persuade tribes to accept a constitution and hold a vote on it. In 1936, Collier hired La Farge to draft a tribal constitution for the Hopi and lobby for its adoption. This was just one of a number of assignments La Farge carried out for Collier between 1936 and 1937, but it was a particularly difficult one and had fateful consequences.

La Farge had first visited the Four Corners region of the Southwest in 1921 on a Harvard archaeological field trip. On his return in 1924, he found himself so interested in Navajo (Dineh) culture that he decided to make it his special study. (The considerable knowledge he acquired became the basis for his successful novel *Laughing Boy*, published in 1929.) He had investigated the Hopi and Navajo in 1930 for Commissioner Rhoads.

Certainly Collier, knowing the Hopi situation would be a challenge, appreciated La Farge's energy and organizational talents. A trained anthropologist, keen student of character, and clever negotiator, La Farge was able to get the job done, but he himself knew that the project was badly flawed. In an unpublished narrative of the project, he wrote:

> The Hopis are going to organize, first because John Collier and a number of other people decided to put through a new law. . . . These Indians didn't think this up. We did . . . I said all the right things—"this is your decision, it is up to you"—but my manner was paternal and authoritarian. . . . We bring to these Indians a question which . . . includes a world-view and a grasp of that utterly alien, mind-wracking concept, Anglo-Saxon rule by majority vote, with everything that follows in the train of that.

The central flaw of the new Hopi constitution was its attempt to create one federally chartered tribal council to govern 11 separate villages. As HAROLD SELLERS COLTON of the INDIAN RIGHTS ASSOCIATION understood, the Hopi villages were every bit as distinct from one another as the Rio Grande pueblos were, the main difference being that the Hopi had rejected Christianity and therefore did not have Spanish land grants. Most Hopi showed their opposition by not voting, so the results were hardly representative (see KATCHONGVA, DAN; TEWAQUAPTEWA, WILSON). The elected tribal council consisted of those who had supported the act. A tribal council that was imposed on top of the traditional governments was felt by most Hopi to be an unwarranted intrusion. Thus, the council soon ceased functioning—until artificially revived years later by attorney JOHN STERLING BOYDEN.

In 1937, La Farge's National Association on Indian Affairs merged with Collier's American Indian Defense Association to form the American Association on American Indian Affairs (AAAIA), of which La Farge was president from 1937 to 1942. During WORLD WAR II, La Farge served with the Army Air Corps. In 1946, the AAAIA shortened their name to the ASSOCIATION ON AMERICAN INDIAN AFFAIRS (AAIA).

Apart from his novels and stories, La Farge's work with AAIA was probably his most lasting achievement, and it is doubtful how much he really did after World War II. The anthropologist Alexander Lesser, AAIA director from 1947 to 1955, undoubtedly did a tremendous amount of the hard work. It was Lesser who brought in FELIX SOLOMON COHEN as counsel and anthropologist Clyde Kluckhohn as a board member. La Farge showed an amazing lack of appreciation of Cohen, so it was Lesser who had to keep defending him and reminding La Farge how crucial he was in the fight against TERMINATION and BIA commissioner DILLON SEYMOUR MYER.

La Farge worked on Taos Pueblo's BLUE LAKE land claim case from the early 1950s until the end of his life. It seems, however, that his secretary, Corinne Locker, was the real moving force in the fight for trust status. Whatever the case, by 1963, the year of his death, La Farge had become more "radical" than Collier on Taos, for Collier counseled the Indians to be satisfied with mandatory-use permits and not go for trust-status legislation.

D'ARCY MCNICKLE, who became La Farge's somewhat reluctant biographer, provides an incisive evaluation of the man. Writing to a friend while at work on the book in February 1969, he stated:

> I find that I am beginning to admire the guy a great deal, which was not the case when I began to dig into his background. I still don't like his attitude toward the Indians, in spite of what he accomplished on their behalf and the undoubted sacrifices which his Indian work required of him. He seems never to have acquired humility, which is always a great lack in a human being. But he was fearless, faithful, and a hell of a hard worker. One can settle for that.

La Farge was indeed a difficult, imperious, and paradoxical personality. Over a lifetime of Indian work, he had proved himself an administrator and fighter of exceptional talent, yet he continued to have a paternalistic attitude and to believe in the ultimate disappearance and assimilation of Native American cultures.

La Farge's other biographer, Robert A. Hecht, argues that witnessing the effects of Termination (which he had at first supported), along with the growing effectiveness of Indian resistance spearheaded by the NATIONAL CONGRESS OF AMERICAN INDIANS (NCAI), altered La Farge's attitude in the last decade of his life. In particular, he was genuinely surprised to realize that Indians did not consider ASSIMILATION inevitable, and that they preferred to adapt and contribute to American culture rather than assimilate. As allies in the fight against Termination, the relationship of the AAIA to the NCAI gradually changed from paternalism to partnership, and by 1954, La Farge supported the addition of Indians to the board of the AAIA.

Oliver La Farge died on August 2, 1963, in New York City. His son, Peter La Farge, became an important folk singer, writing, among other songs, "The Ballad of Ira Hayes" (See HAYES, IRA).

Further Reading

Hecht, Robert A. *Oliver La Farge and the American Indian: A Biography*. Metuchen, N.J.: Scarecrow Press, 1991.
Parker, Dorothy R. *Singing an Indian Song: A Biography of D'Arcy McNickle*. Lincoln: University of Nebraska Press, 1992.

Trump, Erik. "The Laying Aside of a Shield: Ethnographic Power Struggles in Oliver La Farge's Indian Fiction." *American Indian Quarterly* 22, no. 3 (1998): 326–342.

La Flesche, Francis (Zhogaxe, "Woodworker")

(1857–1932) *Omaha ethnologist*

Born on December 25, 1857, on the Omaha reservation in Nebraska, Francis La Flesche was the youngest of five children of Joseph La Flesche (Iron Eye) and Elizabeth Esau (Tainne) La Flesche. His Omaha name was Zhogaxe (Woodworker). Physician SUSAN LA FLESCHE was his half sister.

La Flesche's father, Iron Eye (Estamaza or Inshtamaza), was the son of a French fur trader, also named Francis La Flesche, and an Omaha woman, Waoo-winchtcha. Iron Eye had grown up in two worlds, working and traveling with his father in St. Louis and elsewhere. Though he spoke French and became a Christian, he chose to live as a traditional Omaha and had several wives. In 1853, Omaha chief Big Elk named Iron Eye his successor, and he became the tribe's last chief, serving until 1864. He was one of the Indian leaders who negotiated an 1854 treaty by which a number of tribes relinquished their traditional territories in exchange for reservations.

Though Iron Eye preferred traditional ways, he knew mainstream American culture would soon become dominant, and he understood it well enough to make sure that his children were adequately prepared. His son Zhogaxe—Francis La Flesche—learned English at the Presbyterian mission school in Bellevue, Nebraska, yet still participated in traditional culture, including dances, ceremonies, and the annual buffalo hunts. Years later, Francis would write about his experiences in *The Middle Five: Indian Boys at School* (1900).

In 1879, when Ponca chief Standing Bear traveled to Washington and other eastern cities to protest against forced Indian removals such as the one his people had undergone in 1877, La Flesche and his half sister Susette (not to be confused with Susan) accompanied the chief as interpreters. (The Ponca and the Omaha speak the same language.) In 1881, a congressional committee held hearings to investigate the Ponca removal, and La Flesche was again brought in to act as interpreter. He did so well that the chairman, Senator S. J. Kirkwood, who was appointed secretary of the interior a short time later, gave La Flesche a job as a copyist in the Office of Indian Affairs (later the BUREAU OF INDIAN AFFAIRS [BIA]), where he would remain for the next 30 years. Several years after taking this job, he entered the National University School of Law in Washington, D.C. (now George Washington University Law School), receiving a law degree in 1893.

On their eastern tour in 1879, La Flesche and Susette had met Alice C. Fletcher (1838–1923), an ethnologist associated with Harvard University's Peabody Museum. She told them that she was eager to do fieldwork among Indian tribes, and two years later she toured Omaha communities in Nebraska. Out of these experiences came a desire to help the Omaha. Afraid that their lands might be taken, Fletcher drafted a bill that would allot the tribal lands to individual Indian homesteaders. Passed by Congress in 1882, the Omaha Allotment Act was the model for the Dawes Act of 1887 (see ALLOTMENT).

In 1883, President Chester A. Arthur appointed Fletcher to supervise the Allotment process on the Omaha reservation. Francis La Flesche went with her. While there, she suffered an attack of inflammatory rheumatism, and La Flesche took care of her during her illness. This established the foundations of a relationship that grew so close that Fletcher wanted to adopt La Flesche as her son. Although he declined, mainly because he did not want to give up the La Flesche family name, she eventually established a life trust for him.

As a Christian, Iron Eye had opposed the Omaha cult of the Sacred Pole, but as an ethnologist La Flesche had long taken a special interest in it. In September 1888, a disturbing incident occurred. Alice Fletcher wanted to transfer the pole to the Peabody Museum, and a meeting was arranged on the reservation, attended by her; La Flesche; his father, Iron Eye; and Yellow Smoke, custodian of the pole. Traditions of the pole were recited, and a solemn transfer ceremony was held. Immediately afterward, Iron Eye fell ill, and two weeks later he died in the same room.

On Fletcher's visit to the Omaha reservation in 1897, she was forced to admit that Allotment had failed. Far from smoothing the path to ASSIMILATION, it had caused great suffering and hardship and had led to the retrenchment of the traditionalists and the rise of the peyote religion (see NATIVE AMERICAN CHURCH; SLOAN, THOMAS L.). La Flesche himself became a member of the Native American Church.

In 1910, La Flesche was transferred from the Office of Indian Affairs to the Bureau of American Ethnology. He remained there until his retirement on December 26, 1929.

La Flesche's career as an ethnologist can be separated into two somewhat overlapping parts. The first consists of his 40-year collaboration with Fletcher, in which he assisted her in her work among the Omaha. La Flesche deserves most of the credit for gathering the materials, for the almost unlimited access to informants Fletcher enjoyed, and for her authoritative interpretations made possible by La Flesche's intimate knowledge of Omaha language and traditional culture.

The second part of La Flesche's legacy consists of his own studies of the rituals of the Osage, a culture closely related to his own. Amounting to some 1,600 pages, they appear in volumes 36, 29, 43, and 45 of the Annual Reports of the Bureau of American Ethnology. They combine the clarity and care of a superlative scholar with the penetration and closeness of a cultural insider. La Flesche's interest in Osage ritual was sparked by his meeting with Saucy Calf, a member of an Osage delegation to Washington, in 1900. They found they had many intellectual interests in common, and when Saucy Calf asked La Flesche if there was an Omaha corn song, La Flesche sang it for him. Saucy Calf not only invited him to visit the Osage reservation to learn more about Osage rituals, but adopted La Flesche as his ceremonial son and visited him again in Washington. Saucy Calf made an enormous contribution to the recording of Osage rituals before he was murdered and his house was burned down in February 1912. (The perpetrator was rumored to be a jealous girlfriend, but many Osage saw a deeper cause in the fact that Saucy Calf had given his songs away.) Saucy Calf's death was a great personal blow to La Flesche, but he was able to continue his work with other Osage informants. His study of the Osage comprises what may well be, in the words of Hartley Burr Alexander, professor of philosophy at the University of Nebraska, "the most complete single record of the ceremonies of any North American Indian people."

La Flesche also helped a number of ethnomusicologists and composers gain cultural access to the Omaha—which is why so many of the tribal melodies used by American composers are of Omaha origin (see INDIANIST MUSIC). La Flesche himself wrote an opera on Indian themes, *Da-o-ma* (1912), but it was never performed. He died at the home of his brother Carey, near Macy, Nebraska, on September 5, 1932.

Further Reading

Bailey, Garrick. *The Osage and the Invisible World: From the Works of Francis La Flesche.* Norman: University of Oklahoma Press, 1999.

Green, Norma Kidd. *Iron Eye's Family: The Children of Joseph La Flesche.* Lincoln, Neb.: Johnson Publishing Company, 1969.

Mark, Joan. "Francis La Flesche: The American Indian as Anthropologist." *Isis* 73 (1982): 497–510.

Walcott, Ronald. "Francis La Flesche: American Indian Scholar." *Folklife Center News* 4, no. 1 (January 1981): 10–11.

La Flesche, Susan (1865–1915) *Omaha physician*

The youngest daughter of Joseph La Flesche (Iron Eye) and Mary Gale (Hinnuaganun, or One Woman), Susan La Flesche was born on the Omaha reservation in Nebraska on June 17, 1865. Her older half brother was ethnologist FRANCIS LA FLESCHE. After learning English in reservation schools, Susan was sent, like her sisters Susette and Marguerite, to the Elizabeth Institute for Young Ladies in Elizabeth, New Jersey. From there, she went on to the Hampton Institute in Virginia, where she was salutatorian of her graduating class. On a scholarship provided by the Women's National Indian Association, she entered the Women's Medical College of Pennsylvania in Philadelphia. When she received her M.D. in 1889, not only was she first in a class of 36 women, but she had become the first American Indian woman in history to receive a medical degree. She served her internship at Women's Hospital (1889–90). Both CARLOS MONTEZUMA; (Yavapai), at Chicago Medical College, and CHARLES ALEXANDER EASTMAN (Wahpeton-Mdewakanton Sioux), at Boston College, received their M.D. degrees about the same time, Montezuma in 1889 and Eastman in 1890.

Susan La Flesche was appointed resident physician at the school on the Omaha reservation and was later a federally appointed physician for the Omaha tribe, riding around the reservation for five years seeing patients. She married Henry Picotte, a farmer of French and Sioux ancestry, in 1894. They lived among the Omaha briefly, then moved to Bancroft, Nebraska, where La Flesche set up a private practice treating both Indian and non-Indian patients.

After her husband's death in 1905, La Flesche moved to the new town of Walthill on the Omaha reservation, where she built a home across the street from her sister Marguerite. A crusader for public health, Susan La Flesche was one of the organizers of the county medical society, became chair of the board of health, and lobbied the state legislature on public health legislation. She also lobbied for temperance, and her testimony before a congressional committee in 1906 helped secure a congressional ban on the sale of liquor on the Omaha and Winnebago reservations.

La Flesche never shied away from controversy. In 1909, she accused fellow Omaha and Hampton alumnus THOMAS L. SLOAN of having "defrauded, coerced and exploited the Omaha Indians for a number of years." In 1910, when the 25-year trust period preventing the sale of Omaha allotments had run its course, and the federal government attempted to extend it for another 10 years, La Flesche protested vociferously on behalf of those who wanted to profit by selling their land.

Though her career was devoted to maintaining and restoring health, her own was not good. As she grew older, she lost her hearing and suffered from a painful disease of the facial bones. In 1913, with the help of the Presbyterian Board of Home Missions, La Flesche founded a hospital in Walthill. She died in that same hospital on September 18, 1915. After her death it was renamed in her honor.

Further Reading

Tong, Benson. *Susan La Flesche Picotte, M.D.: Omaha Indian Leader and Reformer.* Norman: University of Oklahoma Press, 1999.

Lame Deer, John Fire (1903–1976) *Lakota Sioux spiritual leader*

A Lakota Sioux, John Fire Lame Deer was born on March 17, 1903, to Sally Red Blanket and Silas Fire in a log cabin between the Rosebud and Pine Ridge reservations. His father, also known as Silas Let-Them-Have-Enough, was a Hunkpapa Lakota, and his mother was a Minneconjou Lakota. John Fire was one of 10 children and raised in large part by his maternal grandparents, Good Fox and Plenty White Buffalo. After six years at a local Indian Bureau school, he attended boarding school for two years before running away.

When John Fire was 16, he undertook a vision quest in which his great-grandfather, Miniconjou Lakota chief Lame Deer (Tahca Ushte), appeared before him and instructed him to become a medicine man and teacher. Fire took on the name Lame Deer and eventually became an important religious teacher. For most of his youth, however, he led a wandering life. He was variously a rodeo clown, a tribal policeman, and a bootlegger. In 1930, he was convicted of car theft and jailed for nine months in Chillicothe, Ohio. During WORLD WAR II he was drafted and served in the U.S. Army.

Lame Deer's son, Archie Fire (1935–2001), also became a medicine man, though he was dogged by controversy. Fire was the spiritual leader of the AMERICAN INDIAN MOVEMENT (AIM) camp at Box Canyon, California, where a white man was brutally murdered in 1974 (see BOX CANYON MURDER). Archie Fire was later accused of teaching sacred Lakota ways to non-Indians, including the publication of a book of Sioux tarot cards. In 1978, a diabetic man died after four days without food while on a vision quest Fire conducted in California.

John Fire Lame Deer told his life story to Richard Erdoes, who in 1972 published *Lame Deer, Seeker of Visions*, and Archie Fire did the same in 1992, in a book entitled *Gift of Power*. John Fire Lame Deer appeared in the 1976 feature film *Return of a Man Called Horse*, directed by Irvin Kershner. John Fire Lame Deer died on December 15, 1976.

See also NEW AGE MOVEMENT.

land tenure

Every society recognizes certain moral and legal conditions under which land may be held, but the customs and laws of land tenure, as well as the philosophies and spiritual beliefs on which they are based, can vary widely from one culture to another. In the United States, land tenure assumptions of the European colonists were very different from those of traditional Native cultures. European colonists generally assumed that their rights to the lands of the Western Hemisphere took precedence over those of its original inhabitants.

The starting point for all Euro-American land tenure systems in the Western Hemisphere and the belief that European settlers had rights to these lands begin with Pope Alexander VI in the document *Inter Caetera* (1493), in which the pope presumed the authority to apportion all parts of the world that remained to be discovered and "gave" them to Spain and Portugal. France, however, rejecting the power of the pope over temporal matters, made claims of its own to Western lands based on the notion of "discovery"—that is, whoever gets there first, owns it. With the religious Reformation of the 16th century, Protestant colonizers such as Britain and Holland, while denying papal authority, made similar claims for themselves.

As a general rule, European powers did not recognize one another's "right of discovery," but only saw "effective occupation" as true ownership—which, of course, required either the agreement of the indigenous inhabitants or their conquest. The cruelty of the early Spanish conquistadores toward Indians led *Inter Caetera*, based on legal notions developed during the Crusades, to be crucially revised by the papal encyclical *Sublimis Deus* (1537), which defended the rights of indigenous peoples to their lands. Colonial powers, whether Catholic or Protestant, gradually adopted into their laws the doctrine that forcible acquisition of territory from peaceful indigenous peoples was not valid. Even so, attempts to conquer Indians and seize their lands did not stop, but the Indians in what is now the United States managed to resist through a combination of remoteness, military prowess, alliances, and diplomatic skills, exploiting the competition between the various European powers.

In the 17th and 18th centuries, European governments were increasingly forced to respect the reality of indigenous land systems ("aboriginal title"). They began to purchase the lands they needed, and most of the lands they owned were lands they had bought, albeit in many cases the Indians were swindled. These negotiated land purchases often took the form of treaties between Britain, and later the United States, and Indian nations. When the United States grew more powerful in relation to Indian tribes, the treaties became mere formalities, as the Indians were under enormous pressure to sell or face extermination.

In 1823, in the case *Johnson v. M'Intosh*, Chief Justice John Marshall enunciated the previously unheard of doctrine that "discovery equals conquest"—in other words, that the bare claim of ultimate dominion inherited by the United States from European colonial powers would from now on be considered effective occupation. In that same year, the Monroe Doctrine—a unilateral executive statement that the United States would no longer recognize any new claims of European powers to territory anywhere in the Western Hemisphere—was announced. These new policies posed an ominous threat to aboriginal title. In effect, the United States was saying that aboriginal title was nothing but the legal capacity of a particular indigenous people to transfer land to the United States.

Nevertheless, up to 1868, the United States at least negotiated and made treaties with Indian tribes under the same constitutional provision as with foreign powers in order to ensure the legal validity of the transactions. This acknowledged the sovereignty of Indian tribes or nations, since a sovereign can make treaties only with other sovereigns (see SOVEREIGNTY, INDIGENOUS AND TRIBAL). However, many of these treaties were fraudulent or were signed by Indians under duress, for they faced certain war if they did not sell. In return for giving up most of their aboriginal lands, tribes singly or in combinations were allowed to retain some land, protected by the federal government, as a "reservation." In cases where a tribe gave up all aboriginal title, it would be granted a reservation elsewhere on land already owned by the federal government (see INDIAN RESERVATIONS).

Near the end of the 19th century, due to ever-increasing pressure from speculators and settlers, Indian land rights began to deteriorate. In 1871, Congress passed a law prohibiting any further treaties with Indian tribes. From then on, new reservations could be created only by executive order or act of Congress. In 1887, Congress passed the Dawes Act, which began the breakup of Indian lands, despite their protection by treaty, through the process of ALLOTMENT. The aim of this and further legislation such as the CURTIS ACT was to destroy all vestige of traditional Indian land tenure through the absolute power of the sovereign, by way of what is called the plenary power of Congress. In 1889, the Supreme Court determined, in *Chae Chan Ping v. United States*, that Congress had the power to unilaterally override treaties, even with foreign nations. Thus, Allotment took precedence over all previously agreed-to land settlements. In terms of legal theory, the breaking of treaties (contracts between sovereigns) in this way was not unlike the Renaissance doctrine of the divine right of kings; that is, that the ultimate foundation of law is the whim of the sovereign—even if the sovereign happens to be democratic in form.

The ideology behind Allotment found its classic statement in chapter 5 of John Locke's *Second Treatise on Government*, itself based on Puritan interpretations of the Bible that colonists used as early as the 17th century to justify the taking of Indian lands. According to Locke, God gave the earth to all humanity in common, but each person acquires a claim to individual property by transforming a piece of the earth through personal labor, or as much of it as can be used without its spoiling. Through this transformation of nature, people create wealth. The flip side, as Locke himself maintained, was that "Land that is left wholly to Nature . . . is called . . . waste; and we shall find the benefit of it amount to little more than nothing." According to this philosophy, Indians no longer had a right to their land because they were "wasting" it by not industriously converting it into farms and cities as Europeans were. These ideas found themselves transformed into the legal principles of colonialism through jurists such as Emerich de Vattel, who wrote in his *Law of Nations* in 1733 that no nation "may appropriate to themselves more land than they have occasion for, or more than they are able to cultivate or settle."

As Senator Henry Dawes complained about the Cherokee in 1893, under Native forms of land tenure, "There is no enterprise to make your home any better than that of your neighbors. There is no selfishness, which is at the bottom of civilization. Till this people will consent to give up their lands, and divide them among their citizens so that each can own the land he cultivates, they will not make much more progress." With this argument, the most liberal thinkers of the 1870s and 1880s transformed raw competition for land into a "humanitarian" act, seeing it as their moral duty to "relieve" the tribes of as much of their remaining land as possible, in order for them to "progress."

From the traditional Indian perspective, on the other hand, the constant land hunger of non-Indians only proved that they did not know how to use the land they already had. Indians saw it as unfair that those who properly cared for land should constantly have to give up more to a people who did not. The economic basis of Anglo-American society was the idea of continual growth, of transformation and conquest of a "frontier" or "wilderness," rather than living within the limits of the land. By the first decade of the 20th century, ethnologists such as MELVIN RANDOLPH GILMORE, FRANK GOULDSMITH SPECK, Mary Watkins, and CONSTANCE GODDARD DuBOIS, and Native thinkers such as CHARLES ALEXANDER EASTMAN and LUTHER STANDING BEAR were already beginning to interpret this fundamental Native idea to the American public, but it did not really begin to get through to any serious extent until about 1970, when some of the adverse ecological consequences of the Anglo-American system began to become unavoidably evident to the general public (see ENVIRONMENTAL MOVEMENT, AMERICAN INDIANS AND).

Before 1871, most Indian land rights were based on federal treaties. But in the Allotment period, these Indian treaties were regarded as essentially bills of sale, on which the government still owes the seller certain services—education and material aid—until such time as the Indian has been assimilated into the larger community (see ASSIMILATION). At that point, the "bill" would be considered "paid in full." The reservation, in other words, was a temporary or transitional arrangement. Allotment was designed to break up tribes and create individuals, and the words *allotment*, *education*, and *assimilation* were spoken in the same breath. Yet even on its own terms, Allotment was self-defeating. It led to fractionated heirship, which damaged and wrecked the ability of individuals to use the land; and to large-scale fraud, which deprived Indians of the real or imagined benefits they were supposed to get from their land. By the time of the MERIAM REPORT (1928), this was universally admitted; but neither the report nor the administration of Indian commissioner CHARLES JAMES RHOADS under President Herbert Hoover achieved a solution.

Unlike any previous commissioner, JOHN COLLIER, Franklin Roosevelt's commissioner of Indian affairs, aimed to save and restore tribal lands. In fact, he saw the principles of Indian community life as a model for community life in America and the modern world. He therefore tried to establish somehow, in U.S. law, the Indian understanding of the relationship with the federal government. With the INDIAN REORGANIZATION ACT of 1934, Collier put an end to the disastrous policy of Allotment. FELIX SOLOMON COHEN, associate solicitor of the Interior Department, took the lead in working out the administrative details of the new system.

Collier called this new approach "reestablishing the contractual relationship." It sought to end the unilateral relationship that had existed between the tribes and the federal government under Allotment. Cohen strove to reestablish the ethical foundations of Indian land tenure by reconstructing the moral logic of its legal sources. Nevertheless, the perfect solution eluded them. They were operating under one major constraint: the Department of the Interior. Whatever beneficial changes in the administration and adjudication of Indian affairs they might bring about, inevitably it had to be conceived within Interior's mission of administering all federal lands. So Indian land rights would have to be upheld through the integration of tribal holdings into a unified federal land system.

Despite this, Cohen and Collier argued that Indians maintained certain rights to their lands, one of which was that they could determine for themselves the manner in which these lands would be held, whether in communal ownership or as private property. Moreover, the United States had a government-to-government relationship with the tribes and must therefore negotiate with them for any land cessions. The new Collier land policy was criticized by conservatives for reasons similar to those put forth during the Allotment era: that he was trying to secure "socialism" on the reservation, and that by perpetuating tribal land tenure he was interfering with the "Americanization" of the Indian. These criticisms were revived after WORLD WAR II with the onset of TERMINATION.

Although Termination led to the dispossession of a few tribes, notably the Menominee and the Klamath, it did the greatest damage to Indian land rights through the INDIAN CLAIMS COMMISSION. Among and even beyond the well-meaning humanitarians who sought to compensate tribes for wrongs done to them, there were those who realized that federal title to many Indian lands rested on tenuous legal doctrines or outright fraud. The commission quieted these claims with monetary compensation to tribes, of which lawyers received a hefty share. By accepting this compensation—pitifully low, given the actual value of the lands—tribes often abandoned strong, but far less convenient, legal positions. In some cases, when Indian communities realized this, they refused to accept the claims awards (see BATTLE MOUNTAIN).

Currently, U.S. law recognizes six different sources by which Indian tribes may hold title to their land. The first is by aboriginal possession—that is, having lived on the land "since time immemorial," although in practice this title is rarely upheld in its own right. The second is by treaty, which may either recognize aboriginal possession or may involve a transfer or outright grant of lands to tribes. Other sources are acts of Congress, executive orders, purchases by tribes, or the action of a colony, state, or foreign power. These lands are held in many different ways, ranging from common tribal ownership to fee-simple allotments, to shareholding in business corporation (see ALASKA NATIVE CLAIMS SETTLEMENT ACT). There are tribes that continue to hold certain important use rights (hunting, fishing, gathering and trapping) on off-reservation land (see GREAT LAKES INDIAN FISH AND WILDLIFE COMMISSION; HUNTING AND FISHING RIGHTS).

Under the premise of eminent domain, the United States argues that ultimately it owns all lands within its boundaries, Indian lands included, and if need be, may dispossess them yet again. The country still maintains that all Indian land was obtained "by conquest," despite the historical and legal inaccuracy of this view. The only thing really obtained by conquest—of colonial powers—was the right to negotiate with Indian tribes in what is now the United States. Unable to find a legal remedy in U.S. courts, which created the legal doctrines that dispossessed Indians of their lands, Indian activists and the Iroquois Confederacy began to seek out international forums such as the United Nations to uphold the validity of indigenous land rights. (See also BARSH, RUSSEL LAWRENCE; GENERAL, ALEXANDER; GENERAL, LEVI; HENDERSON, JAMES YOUNGBLOOD; INTERNATIONAL INDIAN TREATY COUNCIL.)

Further Reading

Banner, Stuart. *How the Indians Lost Their Land: Law and Power on the Frontier.* Cambridge, Mass.: Harvard University Press, 2005.

Holly, Marilyn. "The Persons of Nature versus the Power Pyramid: Locke, Land and American Indians." *International Studies in Philosophy* 26, no. 1 (1994): 13–31.

Squadrito, Kathy. "Locke and the Dispossession of the American Indian." In *Philosophers on Race: Critical Essay,* edited by Julie R. Ward and Tommy L. Lott, 101–124. Oxford: Blackwell, 2002.

Sutton, Imre, ed., with Theodore S. Jojola, et al. *Irredeemable America: The Indians' Estate and Land Claims.* Albuquerque: University of New Mexico, 1985.

Sutton, Imre. "The Continuing Saga of Indian Land Claims: Not All Aboriginal Territory Is Truly Irredeemable." *American Indian Culture and Research Journal* 24, no. 1 (2000): 129–162.

University of Oklahoma Law Center. Native American Constitution and Law Digitization Project. *American Indian Territoriality, an Online Research Guide.* Available online. URL: http://thorpe.ou.edu/treatises/AIT%20 hdr%20pdfs/index.htm. Accessed 3 May 2009.

Larkin, Moscelyne (1925–2012) *Shawnee-Peoria ballerina*

Edna Moscelyne Larkin was born in Miami, Oklahoma, on January 14, 1925. Her father, Reuben "Babe" Larkin, a stenographer, was Shawnee-Peoria, and her mother, Eva Matlagova, was a Russian dancer. At the age of 15, Larkin joined the Ballet Russe, rising to soloist and first ballerina. She then joined Alexandra Danilova in the Ballet Russe de Monte Carlo and toured the world with Danilova's Great Moments of Ballet. In 1956, Larkin and her husband, Roman Jasinski of the Ballet Russe, founded the Tulsa Ballet. The next year, Larkin founded the Oklahoma Indian Ballerina Festival. When Oklahoma celebrated its 60th year of statehood in 1967, she danced in an original ballet, *The Four Moons*, written by Quapaw-Cherokee composer LOUIS WAYNE BALLARD. With her husband, Larkin was honored with the prestigious Dance Magazine Award in 1988. When he died in 1991, Moscelyne Larkin retired from directing the Tulsa Ballet.

Moscelyne Larkin died on April 25, 2012, of pneumonia at her home in Tulsa.

Further Reading

Larkin, Moscelyne. *Private Musings.* Tulsa, Okla.: s.n., 2003.

LaVatta, George P. (1894–1993) *Shoshone-Bannock Bureau of Indian Affairs official*

A Shoshone-Bannock, George P. LaVatta was born on the Fort Hall Reservation in Idaho, son of Ed and Nettie LaVatta, on July 24, 1894. After graduating in 1913 from Carlisle Indian School in Pennsylvania, he returned to the reservation, where he was struck by the sense of hopelessness that was so pervasive there. Inspired by the gospel of Carlisle head RICHARD HENRY PRATT and Indian Service agent CHARLES EDWIN DAGENETT, he regarded work and organization as the salvation of any people and wanted to inspire the people of his own reservation with this ideal.

LaVatta's first job was as a clerk in a store. With much

persistence, he finally got himself hired by the Union Pacific Railroad in 1914. After several promotions, he reached a position in which he was responsible for organizing employee safety, welfare, and goodwill programs. At night he took organization and personnel courses. In 1926, he received the company's meritorious service button.

While still with Union Pacific, LaVatta voluntarily organized work programs on the Fort Hall Reservation and helped young people find employment. In 1929, he joined the Indian Service (later the BUREAU OF INDIAN AFFAIRS [BIA]) as assistant guidance and placement officer, obtaining employment for Fort Hall Indians and organizing work projects, 4-H Club, and Stock Association work. He was subsequently promoted to field agent, then to the superintendency of the 10-reservation Toholah district in Washington State, for which he organized many constructive programs in education and vocational training. He took pride in the fact that by the mid-1930s, the Shoshone-Bannock had almost eliminated the ration system.

In the later 1930s, LaVatta was an organizational field agent in connection with the INDIAN REORGANIZATION ACT. He received the Indian Achievement Award of the Indian Council Fire in 1938. He played a prominent role in the fifth Inter-Tribal Conference of Council Representatives, Carson Jurisdiction, held at Stewart, Nevada, in 1940. LaVatta was also one of the original organizers of the NATIONAL CONGRESS OF AMERICAN INDIANS in 1944. By 1960, LaVatta was BIA area administration officer out of Portland, Oregon. He was greatly interested in the preservation of Indian arts and crafts, legends, and folklore, and wrote many magazine articles on these subjects.

LaVatta was married to Viola F. Welch of Cambridge, Kansas. Their son, George LaVatta, Jr., the youngest lawyer in Oregon and the first Indian to pass the Oregon bar, died tragically at the age of 23. George LaVatta died in January 1993 in Beaverton, Oregon, a suburb of Portland. His grand-nephew Mark Trahant was the editor of the *Navajo Times* and, since 2003, editorial page editor with the *Seattle Post-Intelligencer*.

Further Reading
Trimble, Charles. "Remembrance of a Little Big Man." *Indian Country Today*, 24 August 2007.

Leupp, Francis Ellington (1849–1918) *commissioner of Indian affairs*

Francis Ellington Leupp was born on January 2, 1849, in New York City. He became interested in Indian cultures when, as a teenager, he made several visits to INDIAN RESERVATIONS in the state. After graduating from Williams College in Massachusetts and Columbia Law School in New York, Leupp joined William Cullen Bryant's *New York Evening Post* in 1870 and became editor and part owner of the *Syracuse Herald* in 1878. In 1885, he moved to Washington, D.C., and in 1889 he became the Washington correspondent for the *Post*, a position he held for the next 15 years.

Leupp was a strong advocate of the Progressive Era governmental reforms, serving as the editor of *Good Government*, the official organ of the National Civil Service/Reform League. He participated in a number of the Lake Mohonk Conferences. These forums for Indian reform organizations called for a merit-based civil service to replace the entrenched patronage system at the Office of Indian Affairs (later the BUREAU OF INDIAN AFFAIRS [BIA]), which Leupp blamed for the office's notorious corruption and inefficiency.

In 1895, Leupp's friend Charles C. Painter, Washington agent of the INDIAN RIGHTS ASSOCIATION (IRA), suddenly died, and Leupp was asked to fill the position pro tempore. Leupp's political connections as well as his interest in Indian affairs made him a good choice, and his blunt and energetic personality were well suited to protecting Indian rights in the face of land- and mineral-hungry speculators. Leupp defended the Southern Ute of Durango, Colorado, against removal to Utah. He also successfully represented two Cheyenne River Sioux (Miniconjou Band of Lakota) unjustly accused of murder and investigated timber sales for the Lac Courte Oreilles Chippewa at La Pointe, Wisconsin.

In 1896, Leupp was appointed to the Board of Indian Commissioners, a largely symbolic regulatory agency for Indian affairs, where he continued to lobby for civil service reforms. This brought him into conflict with RICHARD HENRY PRATT, the popular founder of the Carlisle Indian School, who in fall 1896 had dismissed two civil service appointees and had publicly criticized the merit system. Leupp also opposed Pratt's educational philosophy of forced ASSIMILATION, believing that day schools that would lessen the cultural shock that distant boarding schools instilled in both the returning Indian children and their parents.

Leupp's disapproval of President William McKinley's appointment of WILLIAM ARTHUR JONES as commissioner of Indian affairs, and his clash with newly appointed Secretary of the Interior Cornelius S. Bliss, led to his resignation from both the Board of Indian Commissioners and the IRA by 1898. He returned to his work at the *Post*, where he had been under criticism for spending too much time on Indian affairs, but on January 1, 1905, at the request of his friend Theodore Roosevelt, then the U.S. president, Leupp replaced Jones as commissioner.

Despite his initial criticism of Jones, Leupp largely maintained his policies. In keeping with the philosophy of "bringing civilization to the Indian," Leupp continued Jones's shift away from off-reservation boarding schools such as Carlisle—despite their strong congressional support—by sending children to on-reservation boarding schools or day schools, and he supported the more liberal policies of ESTELLE REEL, the superintendent of Indian schools and a critic of Pratt. Leupp stepped into the bitter conflict between Roman Catholics and Protestants over the lucrative federal funding of mission schools and the control of teaching positions within the Indian Office, which were generally given to missionaries. Leupp enacted a set of regulations for teachers that, by forbidding the wearing of religious garb and symbols, were a thinly disguised attempt to restrict the participation of Catholic priests and nuns in Indian education. The regulations caused a storm of protest and had to be rescinded by Roosevelt.

Like Reel, Leupp did not hold to the simplistic view of ultra-assimilationists, such as Jones and Pratt, that ending all distinctions between non-Indians and Indians—while harshly suppressing any signs of Indian culture—would solve the "Indian problem" quickly and absolutely. For Leupp, assimilation had to come gradually and benevolently, and for him many aspects of Indian culture were worth preserving, even if only as tokens. He therefore loosened the ban on the wearing of Indian clothing and the participation of Indians in Wild West shows, and he expanded the nascent arts and crafts industries begun by Jones, all of which to a small extent fore-shadowed the policies of JOHN COLLIER during the INDIAN NEW DEAL of Franklin D. Roosevelt's administration.

However, Leupp intervened forcibly in a bitter factional dispute on the Hopi reservation, where traditional Hopi had refused to send their children to school. When Leupp failed to persuade the "hostiles" that they must end their resistance to education, he sent troops to punish the resistors and imprisoned 17 of their leaders. (See YOUKIOMA.)

More important, Leupp continued Jones's policy of breaking up Indian reservations, going so far as to favor the Burke Act of 1906, which removed the few protections Indian tribes had from the ALLOTMENT process. Under Leupp's management, Indian land holdings continued to decline at the rate of almost 3 million acres per year, much of that lost through fraud.

Leupp replaced the Indian Office's inept and corrupt system of managing Indian forests with the new scientific forestry ideas of Gifford Pinchot of the National Forest Service, but the program backfired when Pinchot persuaded Roosevelt to transfer to the Forest Service more than 15 million acres of Indian timber on executive order reservations. When Leupp endorsed the sale of 1 million acres of the Rosebud Reservation to politically connected friends of congressman and future Indian commissioner CHARLES HENRY BURKE, he lost the support of the IRA, who felt the deal should at least have been bid out competitively. And when IRA leader S. M. Brosius, believing that the Crow reservation was being illegally controlled by a ring of cattle ranchers, was evicted by Indian Office agents from the reservation, Leupp found himself increasingly under attack. His reputation suffered more in the By-a-li-le affair, in which Navajo leader By-a-li-le, who led a band of Navajo accused of refusing to send their children to school, stealing livestock, and other criminal deeds, was tracked down by soldiers and surrendered peacefully. Leupp sentenced By-a-li-le and his followers to prison without a trial, doing little to dispel critics' charges that he ruled the office arbitrarily and with an "iron hand."

Having made few friends and many enemies during his tenure, Leupp resigned in favor of his protégé ROBERT GROSVENOR VALENTINE in 1909, when it became clear that newly elected President William Howard Taft would not support him. Although he brought some improvements to the lives of Indians, largely in the area of health care, liquor control,

and education, Leupp's temper and autocratic manner eventually turned his commissionership into a string of political and personal battles. After leaving office, he kept up his interest in Indian affairs, writing the *The Indian and His Problem* (1910) and *In Red Man's Land* (1914). Francis Ellington Leupp died on November 19, 1918, in Washington, D.C.

See also EDUCATIONAL POLICY, AMERICAN INDIANS AND.

Further Reading
Hoxie, Frederick E. *A Final Promise: The Campaign to Assimilate the Indians, 1880–1920.* Lincoln: University of Nebraska Press, 2001.
Kvasnicka, Robert M., and Herman J. Viola. *The Commissioners of Indian Affairs, 1824–1977.* Lincoln: University of Nebraska Press, 1979.

Lewis, Robert E. (1914–1996) *Zuni-Cherokee politician*

Born on August 24, 1914, in Zuni Pueblo, Robert Edward Lewis was the son of William Lewis (Lawetetsagte), a Zuni, and Margaret A. Lewis, a Cherokee. He attended the Phoenix Indian School in Phoenix, Arizona. After serving in WORLD WAR II, Lewis returned to participate in Zuni politics. In 1965, he was elected governor of the Zuni tribe, a position he held until 1974. He regained the governorship for one term in 1979, losing his position in 1982 but regaining it again in 1989.

Under Lewis's tenure, the Zuni successfully pursued their land claims against the United States and were able to secure the return of nearby Salt Lake in 1978. In 1984, a sacred area known as Kolhu/wala:wa, where Zuni spirits are believed to reside after their deaths, was transferred back to the Zuni reservation, and four years later the Zuni received a $25 million settlement from the INDIAN CLAIMS COMMISSION for lands lost during the 19th century, as well as an additional $25 million from Congress to establish sustainable development programs and restore degraded lands. Also under Lewis, the Zuni adopted a constitution and established a number of tribally and individually owned businesses. In addition, in 1980 the Zuni established their pueblo as a state public school district, allowing them to control their own education and successfully maintain the Zuni language and traditions while still receiving moneys from the state of New Mexico.

Robert E. Lewis died on January 8, 1996, in Zuni Pueblo.

Further Reading
Aarons, Leroy F. "The Zuni Story: A Beginning for Self-Reliance on the Reservation." *Washington Post,* 1 April 1973.

Loloma, Charles (1921–1991) and Otellie Loloma (1921–1993) *Hopi artists*

Charles Loloma, a potter, painter, and illustrator best known for his jewelry making, was born on January 7, 1921, in the Hopi village of Hotevilla at Third Mesa. His father was Rex Loloma (Sand and Tobacco Clan), and his mother was Rachel

(Badger Clan). Charles's grandfather, Loloma, was the leader of the "progressive" faction that forced the traditionals out of Oraibi in 1906 (see TEWAQUAPTEWA, WILSON).

Loloma began to paint at age seven, when his aunt gave him a box of colors. He attended Hopi High School in Oraibi, where he studied art with distinguished Hopi artist FRED KABOTIE. He then transferred to the Phoenix Indian School in Phoenix, Arizona, where he studied under LLOYD KIVA NEW. In 1939, Loloma worked with Kabotie and René d'Harnoncourt, of the Museum of Modern Art in New York City, painting murals for the Federal Building at the 1939 Golden Gate Exposition in San Francisco. Loloma also attended summer school at Fort Sill, Oklahoma, where he studied with muralist Olle Nordmark. He illustrated Edward Kennard's *Hipihoya* before graduating from Phoenix Indian School in 1940, and he illustrated the same author's *Little Hopi* in 1948. In 1942, he married Otellie Pasivaya. During WORLD WAR II, Loloma served as an engineer in the Aleutian Islands.

Both Charles and Otellie Loloma attended the School for American Craftsmen at Alfred University, in Alfred, New York, where Charles, influenced by his wife, a potter, worked on pottery making, an unusual art for a Hopi man. In the early 1950s, he began making jewelry, specializing in silver, and using traditional Hopi designs. He soon began to experiment widely, using gold, precious stones, ivory, coral, lapis lazuli, and other materials, piecing his work together in interlocking puzzlelike designs that became extremely popular. Often hiding his stones on the inside of a bracelet, he worked to give his pieces "hidden beauty," or to express the "inner beauty" of his art. His innovative designs and use of nontraditional materials were controversial, and he was criticized by many art dealers for "not being Indian enough." Loloma's work was rejected by the Gallup Intertribal Art Show three times.

Otellie Pasivaya Loloma, a Hopi born on December 30, 1921, in the town of Shipaulovi on Third Mesa, became one of the country's finest and most influential potters. Her father, El Capitan Pasivaya, was a trader, and her mother, Suzan Mesabenka, was a midwife. Although a gifted artist from childhood, she worked little in pottery until she left her post as a substitute teacher at local Indian schools to study ceramics at the School for American Craftsmen in Alfred, New York. There she met Charles. Upon her return to the Hopi reservation, she taught her students to work in clay. Otellie later attended the College of Santa Fe and Northern Arizona University, where she worked in printmaking and painting. In addition to pottery, she became well known for her clay sculptures, sometimes dressed in leather or cloth and often using traditional Hopi young women as a subject.

In 1954, Charles and Otellie moved from Hotevilla to Scottsdale, Arizona, where they opened a ceramic studio. After setting up shop in Scottsdale, the Lolomas became internationally recognized for their art, known as Lolomaware, and were among the first Native American artists to combine originality with a strong business acumen. After the couple divorced in 1965, each became known as an influential art instructor. In 1986, Charles Loloma was severely injured in an auto accident and had to give up working. He died on June 9, 1991. Otellie Loloma died on January 30, 1993, in Santa Fe, New Mexico, after a long hospitalization.

Further Reading
Pardue, Diane F. *Contemporary Southwestern Jewelry*. Layton, Utah: Gibbs Smith, 2007.

Longest Walk (1978)

This 1978 march on Washington, D.C., commemorated the 1972 TRAIL OF BROKEN TREATIES and protested a number of anti-Indian bills in Congress at the time. Organized by AMERICAN INDIAN MOVEMENT (AIM) leader DENNIS BANKS, the walk began in San Francisco in February 1978, with Washington, D.C., as its destination. Along the way, walkers offered teach-ins and other assorted events. On July 14, 1978, they arrived at a Greenbelt Park in Maryland, near Washington, D.C., where they would camp out for the next week. Unlike the Trail of Broken Treaties protest, in which government opposition and lack of support led to a riot, for the Longest Walk the federal government provided the campground, food, and free buses to activities in Washington. The marchers had come to lobby Congress in an effort to stop 11 bills, mostly sponsored by representatives from Washington State, which attempted to overturn recent court decisions favoring Indian HUNTING AND FISHING RIGHTS and that sought to restrict Indian SOVEREIGNTY.

On July 15, more than 800 Indians, along with 2,000 non-Indian supporters, gathered near the Washington Monument in Washington. The group included almost all of the prominent RED POWER MOVEMENT activists, as well as celebrities such as Marlon Brando and Muhammad Ali. The highlight of the gathering was a moving speech by Creek spiritual leader PHILIP DEERE. The next few days featured more speeches and workshops, and the gathering lasted until July 27, when Greenbelt Park was reopened to the public. The peaceful, spiritual nature of the protest was in marked contrast to the violent upheavals of the past decade, and the march was effective in stopping the anti-Indian legislation. Yet the Longest Walk proved to be the last gasp of the Red Power movement, whose tactics were becoming increasingly less effective and whose leadership was under constant harassment by the FBI. It would be the last major national demonstration by Indians in the 20th century. In 2008, Dennis Banks organized the Longest Walk 2, to commemorate the 30th anniversary of the Longest Walk.

Long Lance, Sylvester (Sylvester Clark Long)

(1890–1932) *Lumbee journalist, author, movie actor*

Sylvester Clark Long was born on December 1, 1890, in Winston (now Winston-Salem), North Carolina. His father was Joseph S. Long, a school janitor, and his mother was Sally Carson Long. His ancestry is widely misunderstood, due in part to the misleading system of racial classification that existed at the time; due also to the origin of the Croatan people themselves (now known as Lumbee), the remnants of various Carolina tribes, with admixtures of white and black blood, who then had only limited recognition as Indians; due finally to his misrepresentation of himself, especially in later life. Research by author Donald B. Smith indicates that Long's father was of mixed Cherokee and white ancestry and that his mother was three-quarters white and one-quarter Croatan (Lumbee). There is some evidence to suggest that his father may also have had Catawba ancestry.

At age 12, Long joined a Wild West show, where he learned the Cherokee language from some of the performers. He later applied to Carlisle Indian School in Pennsylvania as a Cherokee, graduating in 1912. Having changed his name to Long Lance, he spent a year at Dickinson College, also in Carlisle, before winning a scholarship to St. John's Military Academy in Wisconsin. In 1915, rather than enter West Point, where he was a candidate, Long Lance, like many Indians at the time, joined the Canadian army and shipped out overseas with the Canadian Expeditionary Force to fight in WORLD WAR I. Rising to the rank of staff sergeant, Long Lance was wounded twice before being sent to Calgary, Alberta, where he was discharged.

Long Lance then became a successful reporter for the *Calgary Daily Herald*. There he became friendly with the Indian tribes of the northern plains. Long Lance wrote many articles defending Indian rights and advocated for the preservation of Native cultures. He was adopted by the Blackfoot of the Blood Reserve, who gave him the name Buffalo Child and made him an honorary chief in 1922. Long Lance then left the *Herald* to do freelance work. He coached football for the Calgary Canucks and became a press representative for the Canadian Pacific Railway. Long Lance also began writing for major magazines, such as *Maclean's* and *Cosmopolitan*. His reputation as a writer and reporter of Indian life grew, as did his identification as a Blackfoot chief. When his publishers, the Cosmopolitan Book Company, changed a fictional work he had submitted to *Long Lance: The Autobiography of a Blackfoot Indian Chief*, he went along without complaint. The book, published in 1928, was both a popular and scholarly success, and Long Lance became a celebrity, boasting such famous friends as actor Douglas Fairbanks, boxer Jack Dempsey, and actor-director Charlie Chaplin.

In 1930, Long Lance starred in a film, *The Silent Enemy*, which was a dramatic success. This film also featured Penobscot actress MOLLY SPOTTED ELK and Sioux Chief CHAUNCEY YELLOW ROBE. Directed by Henry P. Carver and written and produced by W. Douglas Burden, this docudrama tried to realistically portray the traditional life of the Ojibwa of Canada. Yellow Robe was antipathetic to Long Lance's advocacy for Indian rights, having been an ardent supporter of the destruction of traditional Indian cultures through the federal policy of ASSIMILATION. During the shooting of the film, Yellow Robe became suspicious of Long Lance's claims to be a full-blood Blackfoot and alerted Paramount Studios, which launched an investigation. Paramount had planned for Long Lance to star in a film about an Indian flying ace during World War I. He quickly learned how to fly, and before shooting the film, vacationed in high style in Europe. After his return to the United States, discovering that he was about to be exposed as a "non-Indian," he committed suicide on March 20, 1932, at the Anoakia ranch in Arcadia, California.

While Long Lance misrepresented himself, first as a Cherokee and then as a Blackfoot, by today's standards he was certainly an Indian. The Lumbee, although one of the largest Indian tribes in the country, were not granted federal recognition until 1994. Long Lance, a gifted writer who possessed an engaging personality, felt that he had to transform himself into the Indian stereotype of the day in order to be successful and did so to such a remarkable degree that ultimately he could not escape the image he had created.

Further Reading

Cook, Nancy. "The Only Real Indians Are Western Ones: Authenticity, Regionalism, and Chief Buffalo Child Long Lance, or Sylvester Long." In *True West: Authenticity and the American West*, edited by William R. Handley, 140–156. Lincoln: University of Nebraska Press, 2007.

Garroutte, Eva Marie. *Real Indians: Identity and the Survival of Native America*. Berkeley: University of California Press, 2003.

Ling, Amy. "Creating Oneself: The Eaton Sisters." In *Reading the Literatures of Asian America*, edited by Shirley Geoklin Lim and Amy Ling, 305–318. Philadelphia: Temple University Press, 1992.

Smith, Donald B. *Chief Buffalo Child Long Lance: The Glorious Impostor*. Calgary, Alberta, Canada: Red Deer Press, 1999.

Looking Horse, Arvol (1954–) *Miniconjou Lakota holy man*

Born one of eight children to Stanley and Celia (Shoots the Bear) Looking Horse, Arvol Looking Horse, a Lakota Sioux, grew up in poverty in the Moreau River Valley on the Cheyenne River Sioux Reservation in South Dakota. Raised by his paternal grandparents, Thomas and Lucy Looking Horse, to become a traditional Lakota spiritual leader, Looking Horse was 12 when he became keeper of the sacred Ptehinchala Huhu Chanupa, or Buffalo Calf Pipe, of the Sioux (Dakota, Lakota, Nakota) people.

The pipe is believed to have been handed down to the Sioux by the legendary White Buffalo Calf Woman, and for most of the 20th century it was kept by the family of renowned Sioux spiritual leader Elk Head. When Elk Head, also known as Red Hair and Old Man Elk Head, died in 1916, the pipe was passed to his daughter, Martha Bad Warrior. She in turn passed it on to her son, Ehli Bad Warrior, upon her death in 1936. When Ehli Bad Warrior died in 1959, the Buffalo Calf Pipe bundle went to his sister, Lucy Looking Horse, Arvol Looking Horse's grandmother. Just before Lucy Looking Horse died in 1966, she chose not to give the pipe to her son, Stanley, but gave it instead to her grandson. Elk Head was reputed to have been the eighth keeper of the Buffalo Calf

Pipe, making Arvol Looking Horse the 12th keeper, although some accounts have him as the 19th keeper. Looking Horse is a direct descendant of the first pipe keeper, Buffalo Standing Upright.

Looking Horse became a rodeo rider, but his career ended in 1983 when a horse fell on him, crushing three of his vertebrae and leaving him temporarily paralyzed. After he healed, he dedicated himself to fulfilling his responsibility as a Sioux spiritual leader. Concerned largely with his duties as a medicine man, Looking Horse began to play a more active role outside of the Cheyenne River Sioux community from 1986 on. That year he helped to initiate the Big Foot Memorial Ride, which retraced the route taken in 1890 by Miniconjou chief Bigfoot and his band before the massacre at Wounded Knee, South Dakota. In 1992, he led prayers at the United Nations, where Indian leaders such as OREN LYONS, JR., and THOMAS BANYACYA opened the United Nations Year of Indigenous People. Two years later, Looking Horse led the prayers at a historic meeting between President Bill Clinton and more than 300 Indian leaders, the largest gathering of tribal leaders ever held in the White House.

Looking Horse's activities on the international stage, in particular his association with the NEW AGE MOVEMENT, have led to criticism from his own community. His decision to allow non-Indians to participate in Sioux ceremonies has drawn fire from other traditional Sioux spiritual leaders as well as from respected Sioux scholars, such as BEATRICE MEDICINE.

Further Reading

Gonzalez, Mario, and Elizabeth Cook-Lynn. *The Politics of Hallowed Ground: Wounded Knee and the Struggle for Indian Sovereignty.* Lincoln: University of Nebraska Press, 1998.

Lookout, Fred (Wy-hah-shah-shin-kah, "Little Eagle That Gets What He Wants") (1861–1949) *Osage chief*

Born on November 17, 1861, near Independence, Kansas, to Wahkasetompahpe (The Eagle That Dreams), an important Osage chief, and Metsahehum, who died when he was very young, Fred Lookout was given the name Wy-hah-shah-shin-kah (Little Eagle That Gets What He Wants), which was eventually translated into Fred Lookout. After the Osage were forced to relocate to Indian Territory (now Oklahoma) in 1871, Lookout attended the Osage Boarding School in Pawhuska before being sent to Carlisle Indian School in Pennsylvania in 1879. After attending White's Quaker Institute in Salem, Iowa, he returned to the Osage reservation shortly before his father's death in 1884. Lookout married Julia Pryor (Mo-se-che-he), an Osage member of the Bear Clan, and the couple settled on a small farm near Pawhuska.

Lookout was elected to the Osage Tribal Council in 1896 and became assistant principal chief in 1908. A protégé of James "Big Jim" Bigheart, leader of the full-blood, anti-ALLOTMENT faction of the Osage tribe, Lookout was with Bigheart in Washington when the old chief suffered a fatal stroke in 1906. That year, along with full-blood chief Ne-Kah-wah-she-tun-kah and adopted mixed-blood Sioux John Palmer, Lookout helped the Osage tribe hold on to their subsurface mineral rights after their reservation was allotted. After his term as assistant chief expired in 1910, he declined to run for another term and stepped down.

Lookout became head chief of the tribe in 1914, after the previous council, led by BACON RIND, had been removed by the Interior Department for fraudulently approving oil leases on the oil-rich reservation. Appointed by Secretary of the Interior W. C. Fisher along with a new council to replace the old regime, Lookout rejected attempts by the oil companies to extend a disadvantageous blanket lease. He ensured that oil leases were auctioned off to the highest bidder, enacted regulations to cut down on pollution and spills, and hired inspectors and lawyers to assure they were not being bilked by the oil companies. Lookout lost his bid for reelection in late 1914 but regained the chieftainship in 1916. During WORLD WAR I, the Osage gave the federal government 5,000 acres of oil land for an oil reserve, and the tribe and individuals purchased $2.5 million worth of Liberty Bonds. Lookout was replaced as chief in 1918 and then served on the council from 1920 until 1922. He was elected principal chief again in 1924.

In 1925, Congress passed the Osage Guardianship Act, which regulated the appointment of guardians—a fount of corruption in Oklahoma—and afforded the tribe's lands a degree of trust protection. Despite some high-profile cases (see OSAGE REIGN OF TERROR), the Osage managed to survive the plague of con men, thieves, and murderers that descended on oil-rich reservations, and by 1925 they had become the wealthiest tribe in the country, with the average Osage family receiving more than $50,000 a year from oil royalties, an enormous sum in those days. However, the distribution of oil royalties on a per-capita basis led to a spending spree labeled the "Great Frenzy," and the tribe eventually squandered its money.

Lookout led the Osage through the Great Depression, when the collapse of oil prices ended the period of fabulous wealth, and into WORLD WAR II, in which the Osage fought with great distinction. A cattle rancher and a devout member of the NATIVE AMERICAN CHURCH, Lookout was widely admired for his integrity and his political skills. Head chief from 1916 to 1918, and again from 1924 until his death on August 28, 1949, in Pawhuska, Lookout was able to skillfully bridge the two political factions, full-bloods and mixed-bloods, that divided the reservation.

See also OIL, AMERICAN INDIANS AND.

Further Reading

Wallis, Michael. *Oil Man: The Story of Frank Phillips and the Birth of Phillips Petroleum.* New York: St. Martin's Press, 1995.

Wilson, Terry P. "Chief Fred Lookout and the Politics of Osage Oil, 1906–1949." In *Indian Leadership*, edited by Walter L. Williams, 46–53. Manhattan, Kans.: Sunflower University Press, 1984.

Luna, James (1950–) *Luiseño-Diegueño painter, performance artist*

James Luna was born in 1950, one of six children of a Mexican father and a Luiseño (Payomkowishum) mother of the Sobenish Clan. He was raised in Fountain Valley, California, an agricultural community in Orange County, in a house next door to his mother's parents, who had made a living there since the 1940s as agricultural workers and house movers. Though the children were raised Catholic, their mother regularly took them back to the reservation at La Jolla for traditional feasts and ceremonies. Luna identified with his Indian grandparents. He stayed at their house periodically, and it was from them that he absorbed traditional teachings.

Luna's Mexican father, who had been criticized by his own family for marrying an Indian, was more assimilation-minded, and the family was not outwardly different from many others in the neighborhood. James was president of his high school's junior class and cofounded a student organization of Chicanos, Samoans, and Indians known as the Brown Culture Society. He composed an epic poem about 1950s culture icons Hank Williams, Dave Brubeck, Jack Kerouac, and Elvis Presley and was targeted as a likely minority scholarship candidate by a recruiter from the University of California at Los Angeles (UCLA). However, Luna preferred the less prestigious UC-Irvine, and there he began studying art. But after a short time he dropped out to work as a union organizer for Cesar Chavez's United Farm Workers. In 1975, Luna moved to the La Jolla reservation in Pauma Valley, California. Thanks to the influence of his grandparents, as he later stated, "When I moved to the reservation . . . it was as if I had been there all my life."

The following year, Luna resumed his studies at UC-Irvine, where he was greatly influenced by artist-in-residence Basjan Addur, a Dutch conceptualist of East Indian origin. Luna's work in performance art grew out of sensory improvisation exercises taught by Addur: "Addur taught me to lower my guard and drop pretenses. I had to look within myself and be willing to show myself to other people."

Through he received a bachelor of fine arts degree from Irvine, the prevailing taste for formalism in modern art and its isolation from social reality drew Luna away from painting. Enrolling in San Diego State University, he received a degree in counseling. Since 1983 he has been an academic counselor at Palomar College in San Marcos near his home.

Toward the end of the 1980s, contemporary art criticism began to catch up with Luna's conviction that an artist should consciously interact with his environment. In 1988, when he, David Avalos, Deborah Small, and historian William E. Weeks presented *California Mission Daze*, they received national attention. The show was an artistic protest against the Catholic Church's beatification of Father Junípero Serra, a Franciscan who established the California mission system in the 18th century. To the Mission Indian community, Serra was guilty of many calculated cruelties that ill suited beatific status or the designation of "Blessed." The mixed-media event, held in San Diego, was timed to coincide with the beatification ceremonies at the Vatican on September 25, 1988, and the collaboration of a Chicano, white male, white female, and Indian was intended to show that the concerns were not limited to just one group.

Since then, Luna has continued to develop as a performance artist. His work is characterized by the use of ritualized self-disclosure, performances and installations that explore the perceptual reality of life in two worlds (if not more), the simultaneous coexistence and creative interaction of rootedness and uprootedness, an artistic theme that has broad social resonance in this country of immigrants.

Luna participated in the 2005 Venice Bienniale art exhibition, with *Emendatio*, a piece with three installations and a performance, devoted to the life of Pablo Tac (1822–41), a gifted Luiseño scholar who died in Rome, Italy, at the age of 19.

In a 1989 interview, Luna said, "I am not timid about the idea that art is teaching—a 'showing,' a demonstration, in which talk is minimal. But I'm just a circuit that channels energy. I pass it on for people to make their own decisions. I have no 'knowledge' to pass on. I just act and learn by doing."

Further Reading

Blocker, Jane. "Failures of Self-Seeing: James Luna Remembers Dino." *Performing Arts Journal* 23, no. 1 (January 2001): 18–22.
Garoian, Charles R. "Performing a Pedagogy of Endurance." *Teacher Education Quarterly* 29, no. 4 (2002): 161–173.
Haas, Lisbeth, et al. *James Luna: Emendatio*. Washington, D.C.: Smithsonian National Museum of the American Indian, 2006.
Smith, Donald. "James Luna: Correcting the Erroneous in a One-Man Show." *Inside Smithsonian Research, Quarterly Newsletter on Science, History and the Arts* 9 (2005): 16–18.

Lyons, Lee A. (Jonohndawde) (1931–1985) *Seneca activist, Iroquois political representative*

Lee Lyons was born in 1931 on the Onondaga Reservation in upstate New York. His father, Oren Lyons, Sr., was an Onondaga of the Eel Clan, and his mother, Winifred (Gordon) Lyons, was Seneca and a member of the Wolf Clan. His brother, OREN LYONS, JR., became an influential Onondaga chief. Lee Lyons was given the Seneca name Jonohndawde and, following the Iroquois matrilineal tradition, he became a member of the Seneca Wolf Clan. He grew up and went to school on the Onondaga Reservation. In 1951, he joined the U.S. Army, serving with the 82nd Airborne Division. A highly decorated Korean War and Vietnam War veteran, Lyons won the Distinguished Service Cross, the Silver Star, and two Bronze Stars with oak-leaf clusters.

Discharged from the army in the late 1960s with the rank of sergeant first class, Lyons worked for the Iroquois Confederacy as an adviser and researcher on issues of REPATRIATION, treaty rights, and education, helping to make the confederacy a model for other Indian nations in their struggle for sovereignty (see SOVEREIGNTY, INDIGENOUS AND TRIBAL).

He was a member of the Iroquois delegation that went to WOUNDED KNEE in 1973 and helped to organize the beleaguered encampment.

Lyons became one of the main architects in developing Iroquois international policy, which sought to use the United Nations (UN) as a forum for addressing Indian issues. He helped to found the INTERNATIONAL INDIAN TREATY COUNCIL and organized the landmark International Non-Governmental Organizations Conference on the Indigenous Peoples of the Americas held at the United Nations in Geneva in 1977. He also served as a strategist and negotiator for the Iroquois in their battles with New York State during the 1970s and early 1980s and was a negotiator at GANIENKEH and the siege of AKWESASNE.

By the mid-1980s, Lyons's organizational skills had helped to make the confederacy the most autonomous and influential Indian government in the country. One of the few traditional governments recognized by the United States (see INDIAN REORGANIZATION ACT), the confederacy repudiated federal and state jurisdiction over their lands and even issued their own passports for travel around the world.

On December 9, 1985, Lee Lyons died of complications from heart surgery. At the time, he was working on his master's degree at the University of Buffalo and planning the Iroquois strategy for bringing land claims against the state of New York in the hopes of regaining lands stolen in the 1800s. His death was a severe blow to the aspirations of the Iroquois in their quest for sovereignty and international recognition. Since then, the federal and state governments have slowly chipped away at the many gains he helped to achieve.

See also SHENENDOAH, LEON.

Lyons, Oren, Jr. (Jo Ag Quis Ho) (1930–)
Onondaga politician, activist, artist, educator

Born Jo Ag Quis Ho (Bright Sun Makes a Path in the Snow) on March 5, 1930, Oren Lyons, Jr., is a member of the Wolf Clan of the Seneca and a chief of the Onondaga. His father, Oren Lyons, Sr., an Onondaga, left the family when Lyons was only 10. His mother, Winifred Gordon Lyons, was Seneca and a member of the Wolf Clan. Lyons, the oldest of eight children, took up hunting to help feed the family, then dropped out of school in the eighth grade to work. In 1950, he joined the U.S. Army, becoming a member of the elite 82nd Airborne Division. He returned to the Onondaga Reservation near Syracuse, New York, at the age of 23, painting boxers' portraits for local bars to support his family.

Lyons came from a family of LACROSSE players: His grandfather Isaac Lyons and granduncle Jesse Lyons both played with JIM THORPE on the Carlisle Indian School's powerful

Oren Lyons speaks at the American Indian Movement's International Treaty Conference in Mobridge, South Dakota, on June 12, 1974. *(AP/Wideworld)*

lacrosse team, and his father was a champion goalie. Lyons was recruited to play for Syracuse University by coach Roy Simmons, who helped him enter the School of Fine Arts. He become a All-American goalie in 1957 and 1958. In 1957, along with All-Americans Roy Simmons, Jr., and future football star Jim Brown, Lyons led Syracuse to an undefeated season and the national title. He was inducted into the Lacrosse Hall of Fame in 1993, joining Leon Miller as the only other Indian so honored. Lyons's son Rex would also become an All-American lacrosse star at Syracuse.

After receiving his B.A. from Syracuse in 1959, Lyon moved to New York City, where he worked as an artist for Norcross Greeting Cards, eventually rising to the position of head planning director for seasonal lines for the company. In 1967, Onondaga Turtle Clan mother Betty Jacobs summoned Lyons back to the reservation to sit on the Onondaga Council of Chiefs as the representative of the Turtle Clan. Although a Wolf Clan Seneca under the matrilineal system of the Iroquois, Lyons was "borrowed" into the Onondaga Nation, as is the right of a clan mother to do. Lyons is therefore a member of the Onondaga and a chief of the Turtle Clan.

By this time, the Iroquois Confederacy was undergoing a period of renewed militancy, sparked in part by the unsuccessful movement to prevent the Allegany Seneca Reservation from being flooded by the KINZUA DAM and in part by a traditional revival movement led by militant Iroquois such as WILLIAM RICKARD. The strength of the confederacy increased when the Onondaga successfully blocked attempts by New York State to expand Interstate 81 onto the reservation in 1968. The ascension in early 1969 of Eel Clan chief and longtime activist LEON SHENENDOAH to the position of Tadadaho, the highest-ranking chief of the Iroquois Confederacy, marked a turning point for the Iroquois in which they began to regain the sovereignty they had been forced to yield to New York State in preceding decades. (See SOVEREIGNTY, INDIGENOUS AND TRIBAL.)

With THOMAS BANYACYA and MAD BEAR ANDERSON, Lyons helped to organize the North American Indian Unity Caravan, which traveled across the country in 1969, visiting Indian reservations and advocating a return to Indian traditions. Lyons was present when the TRAIL OF BROKEN TREATIES arrived in Washington in 1972, and after the BUREAU OF INDIAN AFFAIRS (BIA) headquarters was occupied, he helped negotiate a peaceful conclusion to the demonstration.

In 1972, Lyons recruited activist lawyer William Kunstler to defend a group of Onondaga IRONWORKERS accused of assaulting police in Philadelphia. The Onondaga had been watching the making of a movie from the balcony of their hotel rooms when a disturbance from an unruly party broke out nearby, and the police were called. Assuming that this was the fault of the Onondaga, the police climbed the balcony and viciously beat the ironworkers. Leroy Shenendoah, a decorated Vietnam veteran, was shot and killed, but the police charged the Onondaga with assaulting them. What the prosecution did not know was that the film crew had shot the entire event. Kunstler could not participate in the trial, which was held in 1973, but the defense

stunned the court when it presented the film, which showed Shenendoah, before he was shot, being punched and kicked by the police while lying unconscious on the floor of the balcony. Charges against the Onondaga were dismissed.

In 1973, Lyons, his brother LEE LYONS, and Onondaga chief William Lazore led an Iroquois delegation to WOUNDED KNEE, giving the AMERICAN INDIAN MOVEMENT (AIM) occupiers an important boost. The delegation helped organize the beleaguered camp, which had fallen into disarray, with petty squabbles among the leadership. After the occupation ended, Oren Lyons recruited Kunstler to defend AIM leaders in the Wounded Knee trials. In 1984, Lyons persuaded the Council of Chiefs at Onondaga to grant AIM leader DENNIS BANKS asylum from government prosecution on the reservation. He also helped lead the successful Iroquois negotiations with Lieutenant Governor Mario Cuomo and New York State over the Mohawk occupation of GANIENKEH and the siege of AKWESASNE.

Lyons was the driving force behind Iroquois efforts to gain international recognition for their sovereign status, and his international presence has influenced indigenous movements worldwide. Along with Lee Lyons, and Seneca journalist JOHN MOHAWK, Oren Lyons organized the Iroquois delegation to the United Nations in Geneva in 1977. He played an important role in the founding of the INTERNATIONAL INDIAN TREATY COUNCIL and the United Nations Working Group on Indigenous Populations, and led indigenous efforts to secure passage of the Draft Declaration on Indigenous Rights at the United Nations. (This was finally adopted on September 13, 2007, as the United Nations Declaration on the Rights of Indigenous Peoples.) His influence and stature helped persuade the UN General Assembly to declare 1993 the International Year of the World's Indigenous Peoples. In New York City on December 11, 1992, Lyons led the distinguished group of worldwide indigenous leaders who addressed the UN General Assembly for the year's inauguration.

Through his speeches and lectures, Lyons, a superb orator, has exerted an important influence on Indian thought. In particular, he has sought to educate the world about the Iroquois concept of "natural law." Like Western concepts of natural law, such as is found in the American Declaration of Independence, the laws of nature are "self-evident," and humans are "endowed by their creator with certain inalienable rights." However, according to Lyons, humans are also given "responsibilities," a part of the "original instructions" the Creator once gave all peoples. In addition, Lyons extends the idea of the laws of nature, with its inherent rights and responsibilities, beyond the narrow bounds of human society, to all living things. Among other responsibilities, humans are required to protect the "life-giving forces of the planet," lest humanity should perish. Under Lyons's concept of the laws of nature, for example, the pollution of water is illegal and is an offense ultimately punished by disease, mutation, and starvation. For Lyons, "the seed is the law," and all things begin with the creative power of life; he admonishes people to "not be the generation that allows the seed to fail."

Lyons's traditional views made him a leading critic of the NEW AGE MOVEMENT that began to appear during the 1970s and 1980s, and in 1989 he debated Chippewa SUN BEAR in New York City over the question of non-Indians participating in Indian ceremonies. Working with Leon Shenandoah, Irv Powless, Jr., and other prominent Onondaga chiefs, Lyons played an important role in the formation of Iroquois policy during the last quarter of the 20th century, but his attempts to rein in Iroquois "businessmen" who began to challenge the authority of the confederacy during the late 1980s and 1990s made him a lightning rod for Iroquois discontent. Although he is not himself an organizer, the number of prominent Indian organizations Lyons has helped bring to life is remarkable. They include the Traditional Circle of Indians and Youth, the Indian Law Resource Center, the Native American Council of New York City, (see RICHMOND, ROSEMARY; WASHINAWATOK, INGRID) and the IROQUOIS NATIONAL LACROSSE TEAM, to name a few.

With John Mohawk, Lyons cofounded *Daybreak* magazine and edited the book *Exiled in the Land of the Free* (1992). An associate professor at the State University of New York at Buffalo,

Lyons chaired the American Indian Studies Department and is now Professor Emeritus of American Studies. In 1993, he delivered the commencement address and was awarded an honorary doctor of laws degree from Syracuse University. He is highly regarded as a painter as well, his art having been published in *Daybreak, Akwesasne Notes,* and *Native Peoples* magazines.

An Indian leader of international standing, Lyons worked with such notable figures as Nobel laureate Archbishop Desmond Tutu, Soviet Union president Mikhail Gorbachev, Harry Belafonte, Marlon Brando, and John Lennon. Few people have been as prominent as Lyons in the 20th-century struggle on behalf of traditional Indian cultures.

Further Reading

Smith, Huston. "Redeeming The Future. The Traditional Instructions of Spiritual Law: A Conversation with Chief Oren Lyons." In *A Seat at the Table: Smith in Conversation with Native Americans on Religious Freedom,* edited by Huston Smith, 162–182. Berkeley: University of California Press, 2006.

MacDonald, Peter (Haskohazohi
Betani) (1928–   ) *Navajo chair, founder of the Council of Energy Resource Tribes*

Born Haskohazohi Betani (his mother and father's respective clan names) in May 1928 at Teec Nos Pos on the Navajo Reservation, Peter MacDonald was the son of Daghalani (Many Whiskers Sons) Begay and his wife Glen-Habah (Many Warriors over the Hill). Because he was born while his family was moving their herds of sheep toward summer pastures, Haskohazohi's birth date was not registered until December 16 of that year. He grew up in the seminomadic traditional Navajo (Dineh) way of life. When he was two, his father died after being crushed by a horse, and when he was four his younger sister died following a serious burn from the campfire, an accident that profoundly affected him.

In school, the teachers gave Haskohazohi a number of names, including Peter Tent and Peter Donald, until the other schoolchildren finally named him MacDonald from the children's song "Old MacDonald Had a Farm." At age 15, MacDonald joined the Marine Corps, becoming one of the Navajo Code Talkers (see CODE TALKERS) just before the end of WORLD WAR II. After the war, he attended Bacone Junior College, where he converted to Christianity. Completing a degree in electrical engineering from the University of Oklahoma in 1957, MacDonald went on to become a successful engineer at Hughes Aircraft in Southern California. In 1963, he returned to the Navajo Reservation to work for new tribal chair RAYMOND NAKAI. In 1965, Nakai appointed MacDonald to head the Office of Navajo Economic Opportunity. After control of the program was wrested from the BUREAU OF INDIAN AFFAIRS (BIA), the office was soon netting $12 million a year in federal grants, catapulting MacDonald into the tribal chair's office in 1970.

A harsh critic of the BIA and its close ties to powerful mining and oil industries, MacDonald renegotiated many of the unfavorable leases for coal and oil that had been granted on Navajo land and fought to uphold Navajo rights to water from the Colorado River. Demonstrating his independence from the BIA, in 1975 during the great energy crisis, he founded, with the help of LA DONNA HARRIS, the COUNCIL OF ENERGY RESOURCE TRIBES (CERT), a consortium that aimed to turn energy-resource-producing tribes into an "Indian OPEC." MacDonald was elected CERT's first chair. A firm proponent of Indian sovereignty, he also began to tax the big multinational energy corporations that operated on the reservation, an action they vigorously opposed until the Ninth Circuit Court of Appeals upheld the taxing policy in 1982.

MacDonald was an advocate of bringing private investment to the reservation, and in 1987 he organized a successful Navajo Economic Summit that attracted business and political leaders from across the country. MacDonald developed a number of Navajo-owned businesses, including the Navajo Nation Shopping Centers Enterprise and the Navajo Engineering and Construction Authority. His vision for a self-sufficient Navajo reservation, however, was undercut by the collapse of energy prices in the 1980s. By the end of his tenure, unemployment on the reservation stood at more than 40 percent.

In 1972, during the TRAIL OF BROKEN TREATIES, MacDonald broke with the NATIONAL TRIBAL CHAIRMEN'S ASSOCIATION, which had condemned the AMERICAN INDIAN MOVEMENT'S (AIM) takeover of the BIA headquarters in Washington, D.C. MacDonald called AIM's actions a justified response to the incompetence and fraud at the bureau. He refused to order BIA police to attack AIM in 1971 when, led by Navajo Larry Anderson, they seized the Fairchild Instrument plant on the reservation, in protest against the exploitation of its workers. Although a peaceful settlement was reached, the action backfired for AIM—the company closed the plant, taking its 1,200 badly needed jobs elsewhere. Despite his sympathy to the movement, MacDonald disapproved of AIM's tactics, believing them to be unfocused, while AIM found

Navajo leader Peter MacDonald *(left)* shook hands with Hopi tribal chair Abbott Sekaquaptewa after a meeting in 1974. *(AP/Wideworld)*

MacDonald too pro-business and accused him of furthering "the destruction of Mother Earth" by creating CERT.

A Republican, MacDonald worked for the reelection of Richard Nixon in 1972 but incurred the wrath of Arizona's powerful Republican senator, Barry Goldwater, over the Big Mountain dispute between the Navajo and the Hopi, when MacDonald helped kill a relocation bill introduced that year by Arizona congressman Sam Steiger. After this, he switched to the Democratic Party, beginning a voter registration drive among the Navajo that enabled a Democrat to win the Arizona governor's office in 1974. After MacDonald brought the AFL-CIO to the reservation to help organize Navajo workers at the Bechtel-run Salt River generating station, Goldwater became an implacable foe. Because MacDonald's lavish lifestyle lent credibility to charges that he was abusing the power of his office and aggrandizing himself at the expense of his people, Goldwater in 1976 instigated a criminal investigation of MacDonald for falsifying travel vouchers, but MacDonald was acquitted with the help of famed attorney F. Lee Bailey.

After three terms in office, MacDonald lost a close election for the chairmanship to PETERSON ZAH in 1982, though he returned to defeat Zah four years later. MacDonald alienated the rest of the tribal council when he shut down the tribal newspaper *Navajo Times Today*, ostensibly for financial irregularities, when it had thrown its support behind Zah. Claiming that MacDonald had accepted kickbacks from contractors and corporations, in 1988 the council suspended him. He refused to step down, creating a yearlong crisis in which both factions fought for control.

In 1989, in the aftermath of a large corruption scandal at the BIA that surfaced during the tenure of Commissioner Ross O. SWIMMER, congressional hearings investigating misconduct at the bureau focused instead on MacDonald's misdeeds in office. MacDonald's close friend and fund-raiser, Bud Brown, along with MacDonald's son, Peter, Jr., had brokered the sale of the Big Boquillas Ranch to the Navajo tribe. From the sellers, the intermediaries had received a kickback of almost $7 million, only a tiny bit of which went to Peter, Jr, while Peter, Sr., in financial straits at the time, had been loaned money by the principals involved in the transactions. In 1990, both MacDonalds were convicted of corruption in both federal and Navajo tribal courts and given long prison sentences. MacDonald chose to serve his term in the tribal prison. In January 2001, President Bill Clinton commuted MacDonald's sentence, and he was freed after serving seven years.

Despite his controversial tenure, MacDonald was at the forefront of a movement by tribal chairmen to free themselves from the domination of the BIA, an institution in which the corruption was far greater and more systematic than anything the tribes could accomplish on their own. His pragmatic actions on behalf of Indian self-rule were arguably more significant than the actions of his contemporaries in AIM. Although one of the most powerful Indian leaders of his time, MacDonald's maverick political style won him few friends and numerous powerful enemies, who brought his downfall in the end.

Further Reading

MacDonald, Peter. *The Last Warrior: Peter MacDonald and the Navajo Nation.* New York: Crown, 1993.
Wilkins, David Eugene. *The Navajo Political Experience.* New York: Rowman & Littlefield, 2003.

Macleod, William Christie (1892–1951) *scholar*

A neglected but very original scholar interested in American Indian and indigenous issues, William Macleod, Jr., was born in Philadelphia on January 22, 1892. He was the son of William Christie Macleod and Sarah J. Macleod, both born in Ireland. He received a B.A. from Swarthmore College in 1914 and earned a Ph.D. at the University of Pennsylvania in 1924 under anthropologist FRANK GOULDSMITH SPECK, with a thesis entitled *The Origin of the State Reconsidered in the Light of the Data of Aboriginal North America.* He was assistant professor of finance at the Wharton School of Business of the University of Pennsylvania from 1924 to 1935.

In 1928, Macleod published *The American Indian Frontier*, stating: "This volume represents the first attempt at an analysis of American frontier history made particularly from the viewpoint of the Indian side of the frontier development." In the tradition of historian Frederick Jackson Turner—a tradition that dominated American writing of frontier history throughout most of the 20th century—American Indians were portrayed as obstacles in the way of progress. They were denizens of the wilderness who simply had to go, because (in the familiar phrase) that was "how the West was won." They were opponents (or allies) in the wars of the dominant Euro-American society or conquered peoples to be "removed." But although a start was made by GEORGE BIRD GRINNELL, they were never viewed as protagonists of their own histories with their own points of view, until Macleod's *American Indian Frontier*. The book was dedicated to Edward Sherwood Mead, a professor of finance at Wharton and the father of the anthropologist Margaret Mead.

Unfortunately, Macleod was too far ahead of his time. As Kerwin L. Klein notes in his 1997 book *Frontiers of Historical Imagination*, Macleod's *American Indian Frontier* was largely ignored by historians. It was only in the last part of the 20th century that the book began to be recognized as one of the forerunners of ethnohistory (history viewed from the perspective of ethnic minorities, especially indigenous peoples).

In 1936, Macleod published the first paper wholly devoted to, as he called it, "Conservation among Primitive Hunting Peoples" (see ENVIRONMENTAL MOVEMENT, AMERICAN INDIANS AND THE). He also published numerous other papers on indigenous topics. William Christie Macleod died on September 8, 1951.

Further Reading

Klein, Kerwin Lee. *Frontiers of Historical Imagination: Narrating the European Conquest of Native America, 1890–1990.* Berkeley: University of California Press, 1997.

Mankiller, Wilma Pearl (1945–2010) *Cherokee principal chief*

Wilma Pearl Mankiller was born on November 18, 1945, at Hastings Indian Hospital in Tahlequah, Oklahoma. Her father, Charley Mankiller, was a full-blooded Cherokee, and her mother, Clara Irene (Sitton) Mankiller, was a non-Indian of Dutch-Irish descent. The sixth of 11 children, Wilma Mankiller grew up in poverty in Mankiller Flats, a 160-acre tract allotted to her grandfather, John Mankiller, after the dissolution of the Cherokee lands in 1907 (see CURTIS ACT). She attended the local Rocky Mountain School, located in the rural community of Rocky Mountain in Adair Country, Oklahoma.

Needing to find steady work, Charley Mankiller moved the family to San Francisco in 1956 under the controversial Relocation program of the day (see URBANIZATION, AMERICAN INDIANS AND), and Wilma Mankiller grew up in various towns around the Bay Area. She was unhappy with the change and took to running away, eventually living with her maternal grandmother for a year on her ranch in Riverbank, California. Mankiller graduated from high school in 1963 and then married a well-to-do Ecuadorian college student Hugo Olaya de Bardi. After the birth of her second daughter in 1966, she attended Skyline Junior College and then San Francisco State University.

Along with her sisters, Linda and Vanessa, and her brothers, Richard and James, Wilma Mankiller participated in the 1969 OCCUPATION OF ALCATRAZ ISLAND. Richard Mankiller served on the Alcatraz Council and later participated in the siege of WOUNDED KNEE (1973). The Alcatraz occupation was a turning point in Mankiller's life, and she began to work with Bay Area Indian activist groups. She helped AMERICAN INDIAN MOVEMENT (AIM) leader BILL WAHPEHPAH with various Indian youth and adult educational projects, eventually cofounding the American Indian Community School in Oakland with him. She also became the director of Oakland's Native American Youth Center.

From 1972 through 1977, Mankiller helped Raymond Lego and the PIT RIVER Indians in their bitter land-claims fight with the powerful California utility, Pacific Gas and Electric. In 1974, she divorced Hugo Olaya, and following a dispute with him over the custody of their daughter, Gina, she returned to Oklahoma in 1977 with both her children. There she worked in community development for the Cherokee Nation. In 1979, Mankiller completed her B.S. in social work and began graduate work at the University of Arkansas at Fayetteville. That same year, she was severely injured in a car accident and shortly afterward contracted myasthenia gravis, a neuromuscular disorder. After a long recuperation, she returned to her job with the Cherokee Nation, and in 1981 she founded the Cherokee Nation Community Development Department and became its director. She helped to obtain large development grants for the Cherokee, including the building of a 26-mile waterline for the rural Cherokee community of Bell.

The success of her grassroots community-renewal efforts led Mankiller to gain recognition as a pioneer in the field of, or the modern application of, the traditional economic thought of indigenous peoples. A central aspect of INDIGENOUS ECONOMICS is its focus on community building while at the same time preserving if not enhancing the natural ecosystem. Mankiller based her community development efforts on the Cherokee concept of *gadugi*—that is, their tradition of working collectively. Rather than a top-down system of authority, in which community development "experts" would decide what was best, the goal, explained Mankiller, "was to bring members of the community together so they could solve their common problems." The community was expected "not only to develop long-range plans, but also to implement their community renewal, with our staff members acting only as facilitators and funding brokers." Placing the responsibility for the success or failure of the project on the community itself gave them the determination and self-confidence necessary to carry out the tasks.

Mankiller's vision of economic development required the use of local labor rather than outside contractors, allowing the moneys raised for community projects to circulate within the community. The use of alternative technologies was also important, and Mankiller oversaw the construction of new, energy-efficient homes on the reservation. Her effectiveness at community development and garnering federal grants brought her to the attention of Cherokee chief Ross SWIMMER. He asked her to run as his deputy in his bid for reelection, and after a hard-fought election, on August 14,

1983, Mankiller was sworn in as the first woman deputy chief of the Cherokee Nation.

Mankiller's two-year stint as deputy chief was difficult, not least because, despite being running mates, Swimmer, a conservative Republican, and Mankiller, a liberal Democrat, did not share the same perspective. In addition, the deputy chief serves as president of the tribal council, but most of the 15-member tribal council had supported Mankiller's opponents in the election, and they regarded her, a political newcomer, with hostility. In spite of the political climate, Mankiller was effective in helping to administer the tribe's vast operations, which included more than 40 tribally run programs. In 1984, at Red Clay, Tennessee, she helped to facilitate the first joint council meeting in 146 years between the Eastern Band of Cherokee, located in North Carolina, and the Cherokee Nation of Oklahoma. In 1988 and 1989, the two bands commemorated together the 150th anniversary of the Trail of Tears, the removal of the Cherokee to Oklahoma.

In September 1985, Swimmer was asked to join the Reagan administration as head of the Bureau of Indian Affairs (BIA). Mankiller replaced him as principal chief on December 5, 1985, becoming the first woman principal chief of the Cherokee. Her first priority was the economy of the tribe and rural development, and over the next two years tribal revenue rose by $6 million, in part through the growing profitability of Cherokee Industries, a tribally owned electronic firm. In 1986, Mankiller married Charlie Soap, a full-blooded Cherokee community organizer. The next year, she was elected to a four-year term, and in 1991, despite undergoing a kidney transplant the previous year, she was again reelected, this time with 83 percent of the vote.

Under Mankiller's tenure, the Cherokee Nation's budget doubled to $75 million per year, with more than 1,200 employees spread over an area of 7,000 square miles. She signed an important self-determination agreement with the BIA in which the tribe took over the management of BIA programs among Cherokee people. She also expanded the Cherokee rolls, and along with the natural increase in population, tribal membership tripled while she was in office. However, Mankiller extended the practice, begun by Swimmer, of disenfranchising the descendants of Cherokee Freedmen (Cherokee slaves who were freed after the Civil War and made citizens of the Cherokee Nation under the Cherokee Constitution of 1866) by requiring all enrolled members to have a "Certificate of Degree of Indian Blood" card.

Mankiller's popularity helped to unify the fractious tribe, and when she declined to run again in 1995, it led to a serious destabilization of the Cherokee government under her successor, Joe Byrd. She went on to serve on the board of numerous influential groups, including the Ford Foundation and the Ms. Foundation, and in 1996 she became a visiting professor of Native American studies at Dartmouth College. Her lifelong struggle with poor health did not abate, and that same year she was treated for cancer. The chemotherapy caused her transplanted kidney to fail, and in 1998 she underwent another transplant operation.

Despite her ill health, Mankiller reentered Cherokee politics in 1999 to campaign for Chad Smith, the great-grandson of traditional leader REDBIRD SMITH, and helped him defeat Joe Byrd and end his tumultuous four-year term as principal chief. One of the best-known and most respected Native leaders of her day, Wilma Mankiller was the recipient of numerous awards, including the Presidential Medal of Freedom, given to her by President Bill Clinton in 1998. She continued to battle with cancer, and in 2007 she underwent a second operation for breast cancer. In March 2010, Mankiller was diagnosed with advanced metastatic pancreatic cancer and was given only a few months to live. Rather than go through another debilitating round of chemotherapy, she decided to spend her remaining time with her family and friends. Wilma Mankiller died on April 6, 2010, at her home in Adair County, Oklahoma.

Further Reading
Mankiller, Wilma, and Michael Wallis. *Mankiller: A Chief and Her People.* New York: St. Martin's Press, 1993.

Marsh, Lucille Johnson (1896–1965) *Tuscarora pediatrician*

Estella Lucille Johnson was born on March 10, 1896, in Dundee, Michigan, the elder of two children of Dr. Philip T. Johnson, a Tuscarora chief, and Minnie Johnson, who was half-Tuscarora. Her father, who graduated as president of his class at the Cleveland College of Homeopathic Medicine, was one of the first American Indian physicians. The family moved to Erie, Pennsylvania, near the Tuscarora reservation in western New York State, and Dr. Johnson maintained a highly respected practice in that city.

Lucille Johnson attended high school in San Antonio, Texas, graduating in 1914. Encouraged by her father to enter the medical profession, she enrolled in the University of Texas later that year. In 1917, she transferred to Ohio State University for her senior year, receiving her B.A. in 1918. She entered the College of Medicine at Ohio State that year, earning an M.D. in 1923. Johnson went on to study children's diseases at the Sanitarium for Sick Children at Lincoln Park in Chicago and decided on a career in pediatrics. She married Hubert R. Marsh, and they had a daughter, Phyllis.

Lucille Marsh began her career in private practice, but by 1936 she was director of the Infant Welfare Clinic in Miami, Florida. In 1938, she was put in charge of the infirmary at the Florida State College for Women in Tallahassee (now Florida State University), one of the largest women's colleges in the United States at the time. By 1944, Marsh had become the director of Maternal and Child Care for the Florida State Board of Health. Moving on to the U.S. Department of Health, Education, and Welfare, she advanced rapidly over the next decade, becoming medical director of the Atlanta office of the Children's Bureau and then chief of the Bureau's Program Services Branch in Washington, D.C. In the mid-1950s, she transferred to the Indian Health Service, where she served as chief of the Maternal and Child Health. Her paper

"Health Services for Indian Mothers and Children" was published in the journal *Children* in 1957. Returning to the U.S. Department of Health in 1962, she was appointed regional medical director of the Children's Bureau, Regional Office V in Chicago. For a time, after the death of ROSA MINOKA HILL in 1952, Marsh was the only American Indian woman physician in the United States.

Marsh was active in the Medical Women's National Association (later American Medical Women's Association), of which she was Florida state director from at least 1936. She was later a fellow of the American Public Health Association and held a diploma from the American Board of Preventive Medicine. She was also head of the Miami branch of the Zonta Club, an organization that promotes the professional advancement of women, and a director of the Jacksonville, Florida Historical Society.

After a long and distinguished career in public health, Lucille Johnson Marsh died in Washington, D.C., on September 21, 1965. She was buried in Arlington National Cemetery.

Martin, Phillip (1926–2010) *Mississippi Band of Choctaw leader*

A Choctaw, Phillip Martin was born on March 13, 1926, in Philadelphia, Mississippi, the third son of Willie and Mary Martin, full-blood Choctaw. He attended the Cherokee Boarding School in North Carolina, graduating in 1945. He then joined the U.S. Air Force, serving for 10 years. Upon his discharge in 1955, Martin attended Meridian Community College in Mississippi for two years. In 1957, he was elected to the Choctaw tribal council, and in 1959 he won his first term as tribal chief.

The Mississippi Band of Choctaw are descended from the 5,000 Choctaw who were not removed to Oklahoma during the infamous Trail of Tears, lasting from 1831 to 1834. They continued to hold on to their lands under a section of the 1830 Treaty of Dancing Rabbit Creek, which provided for the allotment of lands to individual Choctaw. Mississippi refused to recognize the claims of these Indians or grant them their allotments, and they were eventually dispossessed. The Mississippi Band of Choctaw was forced to live as squatters on whatever lands they could find, enduring a life of poverty and hardship. An attempt by Mississippi to remove the Choctaw to Oklahoma at the turn of the century led to a federal investigation of the plight of these landless Indians. The federal government then granted them status as a band, a form of federal recognition, and established an agency for them in Philadelphia, Mississippi. During the 1920s and 1930s, the BUREAU OF INDIAN AFFAIRS (BIA) established schools and an Indian hospital. The tribal government was set up in 1945, when its members ratified a constitution and created bylaws.

Martin served as chief until 1965 and then became head of the Choctaw Community Action Agency. In 1971, he regained his position as principal chief for four years, only to lose it again in 1975. He once again became tribal chair in 1979 and continued to serve in his position for the remainder of the 20th

century. When Martin first assumed his position as tribal chief in 1959, most Mississippi Choctaw were poor sharecroppers. He helped set up a number of economic development initiatives, including the establishment of an industrial park, a tribally owned construction company, tribal utilities such as a transit authority, and tribal water and power.

Martin was also the president of the successful Chata Development Company, a private Choctaw stock company, created in 1969 under the authority of the tribal government in order to fund development projects. He successfully formed partnerships with large corporations—for example, Choctaw companies built automotive wiring harnesses for General Motors as well as small motors for United Technologies. Martin even began the Choctaw Greetings Enterprises, which hand-finishes greeting cards for the American Greeting Corporation.

On July 1, 1994, the Mississippi Band of Choctaw Indians launched its first gaming operation, the Silver Star Hotel and Casino, which quickly became the largest and most profitable Choctaw tribal enterprise to date. In 2002, the tribe built its second casino, the Golden Moon Hotel and Casino, along with a world-class golf course and resort. The resort and casinos currently employ approximately 8,000 people, making the Choctaw the fifth largest employer in the entire state of Mississippi. In his more than 40-year tenure as leader of the Mississippi Choctaw, Phillip Martin transformed the poor former sharecroppers into one of the most economically successful and politically powerful tribes in the United States. In July 2007, Martin lost his bid for reelection by only 211 votes to challenger Beasley Denson. He died on February 4, 2010, after suffering a stroke.

See also GAMING ON INDIAN RESERVATIONS.

Further Reading
Ferrara, Peter J. *The Choctaw Resolution: Lessons for Federal Indian Policy.* Washington, D.C.: Americans for Tax Reform Foundation, 1998.
Williams, Rudi. "Former Sergeant Leads Destitute Tribe to Economic Prosperity, Self-Respect." *American Forces Press Service,* 20 November 2002.

Martinez, Maria Montoya (Maria Antonia Montoya, Poveka, "Pond Lily") (ca. 1887–1980) *San Ildefonso Pueblo potter*

Born Maria Antonia Montoya in San Ildefonso Pueblo, New Mexico, the second daughter of Tomas and Reyecita Peña Montoya. Her Tewa name was Poveka, or Pond Lily. The date of her birth is unknown, but her baptism is recorded as having taken place in 1887. Maria herself chose April 5 as the date to celebrate her birthday.

Maria began making her first pottery as a child under the influence of her aunt, Nicolasa Peña Montoya. Her aunt did not use a potter's wheel, but as was the tradition in that area, painstakingly arranged hand-coiled ribbons of clay in a circular fashion to build up the pot shapes. Maria Montoya went to the local pueblo school before being selected to attend

St. Catherine's Indian School in Santa Fe. After graduating, she briefly considered becoming a teacher.

While at St. Catherine's, Maria met Julian Martinez, a laborer from San Ildefonso, and in 1904 they were married. The son of a saddle maker, Julian Martinez was born about 1883. While young, he had taken up painting with watercolors and tempera on paper. The couple spent their honeymoon at the 1904 World's Fair in St. Louis, Missouri, where they demonstrated Pueblo pottery-making techniques and Pueblo dancing. They would be invited to every subsequent World's Fair until the outbreak of WORLD WAR II.

When anthropologist Edgar Hewett began excavating ancient Pueblo sites on the Pajarito Plateau in 1907, Julian worked on the excavation as a laborer. Hewett asked Julian and Maria to try to re-create the ancient pottery. Experimenting with different clays, firings, and polishing, the Martinezes successfully duplicated this thin, hard, and more lustrous pottery.

In 1911, Julian was hired as a janitor for the Museum of New Mexico in Santa Fe, which gave the couple the opportunity to demonstrate their craft and sell their pottery. The two collaborated closely, with Maria producing, shaping, and polishing the vessels and Julian decorating and helping to fire them. Constantly experimenting, Maria began developing larger and larger vessels in elegantly proportioned and perfectly balanced shapes, although like her aunt, she did not use a potter's wheel. She meticulously burnished her pots to eliminate any traces of tool marks. Julian adapted traditional designs, such as the feathers found on prehistoric Mimbres pottery or the figure of Avanyu, a mythical water snake, painting them onto the clay.

In 1919, the Martinezes developed a style of black pottery vessel, upon which Julian painted black designs; it was then finished to a satiny luster. The blackware was fired with dried horse manure, and the carbon from the heavy black smoke colored the clay throughout. John D. Rockefeller purchased the first nine pieces of black-on-black pottery, and it became their signature design as well as one of the most coveted styles of Indian art.

Maria's first award came at the Santa Fe Indian Market in 1922 for pottery she had created with other family members. In 1933, she and Julian displayed their works to popular acclaim at the Century of Progress Exhibit in Chicago. Demand for their pottery grew to such an extent that they began to teach others in San Ildefonso. During Maria Martinez's youth, the lack of opportunities had led most young people to leave the pueblo, and by 1900 the population had fallen to below 100. Maria felt her skills should be used to help her pueblo. As she told Richard Spivey in his biography of her, *Maria* (1979), "I said to my God, the Great Spirit, my Mother Earth gave me this luck. So I'm not going to keep it. I take care of our people."

The efforts of the Martinezes transformed the poor, agriculturally based pueblo into one of the largest arts and crafts centers in the United States, and Julian was eventually elected governor of San Ildefonso Pueblo. He died, after years of alcoholism, on March 6, 1943. Maria then began to collaborate with her daughter-in-law, Santana Martinez. In 1954, she was awarded the Palmes Académiques by the French government. In 1956, when she began to collaborate with her son Tony, better known by his Pueblo name Popovi Da (1923–1971), her work achieved its highest level. Their pottery was exhibited in the Smithsonian Institution in 1979.

In her lifetime, Maria Montoya Martinez brought about the revival of Native pottery making while at the same time transforming it into a high art. She died on July 20, 1980, at the age of 94. Her legacy continues with her grandson Tony Da and great-granddaughter Barbara Gonzales, both now world-renowned potters.

See also INDIAN INDUSTRIES LEAGUE.

Further Reading

Jacobs, Margaret D. *Engendered Encounters: Feminism and Pueblo Cultures 1879–1934*. Lincoln: University of Nebraska Press, 1999.
Marriott, Alice. *Maria: The Potter of San Ildefonso*. Norman: University of Oklahoma Press, 1948.
Spivey, Richard L. *Maria*. Flagstaff, Ariz.: Northland Press, 1979.
———. *The Legacy of Maria Poveka Martinez*. Flagstaff, Ariz.: Museum of New Mexico Press, 2003.

Mathews, John Joseph (1894–1979) *Osage rancher, writer*

John Joseph Mathews was born in Pawhuska, Indian Territory, on November 16, 1894, the son of William Shirley and Eugenia Girard Mathews, a prosperous couple who ran a trading post. His great-grandfather, William Shirley Williams, was a fur trader and missionary who had translated the Bible into Osage and married A-Ci'n-Ga, a Buffalo Clan woman of the Big Hill band. Osage clans being patrilineal, the Mathews family, whose Osage connection was through a female line, did not participate in traditional life. They did, however, respect it and were respected in turn by the full-blood members. Though only one-eighth Osage by blood, Mathews spoke Osage, spent much time with traditionals, and learned tribal history and lore from them. Outwardly, however, he lived the life of a non-Indian. Like all Osage, Mathews received an equal share of the tribe's oil royalties (see OSAGE REIGN OF TERROR), which allowed him to be financially independent.

A geology student at the University of Oklahoma when the United States entered WORLD WAR I, Mathews enlisted as an officer in the aviation section of the U.S. Signal Corps, trained as a pilot, and served in France, reaching the rank of second lieutenant. (See AVIATION, AMERICAN INDIANS IN.) After the war, he returned to the university, receiving a B.A. in 1920. He went on to Oxford University, where he studied natural sciences, earning a second B.A. in 1923. After studying international relations at the University of Geneva in summer 1923, he toured Europe and Africa, visiting archaeological sites. Against the exotic backdrop of North Africa, Mathews was suddenly moved to go back home and investigate the traditions of his own people.

From 1926, Mathews sold real estate in southern California, but in 1928 he returned home, putting all his efforts into "Osage culture rescue." He built a house a few miles outside Pawhuska, where he studied and wrote. When retired Indian agent Major Laban J. Miles, who became the Osage agent in 1878 and lived until 1931, gave Mathews his journals, Joseph Brant, editor of the University of Oklahoma Press, encouraged Mathews to write a book based on them. Published in 1932 as *Wah'kon-tah: The Osage and the White Man's Road*, it won high critical acclaim and was a Book of the Month Club selection, the first published by a university press and the first written by an Indian.

In 1934, Mathews published his only novel, *Sundown*, drawn in part from his own life experiences. It was one of the first, and is still considered one of the best, portrayals of an Indian "between two worlds." His other nonfiction books also deal with Osage themes: *Talking to the Moon* (1945); *Life and Death of an Oilman: The Career of E. W. Marland* (1951); and *The Osages: Children of the Middle Waters* (1961), a comprehensive history from an Osage perspective, based on extensive oral accounts and carefully evaluated documentary sources. The product of more than three decades of work, *The Osages* won the Award of Merit of the American Association for State and Local History (1962).

A Democrat, Mathews was a member of the Osage tribal council during the time when JOHN COLLIER was commissioner of Indian Affairs (1934–42). In 1938, with no encouragement or support from the tribal council, he opened an Osage museum in Pawhuska, subsequently devoting much of his time to its development. In the 1950s, other Osage finally began to appreciate the museum and give it their support.

Mathews died in Pawhuska on June 11, 1979. At the time of his death, he was at work on *Boy, Horse and Dog*, the first book of what he planned as a three-volume autobiography.

Further Reading

Blackburn, Bob L. "Oklahoma Historians Hall of Fame—John Joseph Mathews." *The Chronicles of Oklahoma* 74, no. 3 (Fall 1996): 332–334.

Parker, Robert Dale. *The Invention of Native American Literature*. Ithaca, N.Y.: Cornell University Press, 2003.

Warrior, Robert Allen. *Tribal Secrets, Recovering American Indian Intellectual Traditions*. Minneapolis: University of Minnesota Press, 1995.

Maytubby, Floyd Ernest (1893–1963) *Chickasaw leader*

Born in Caddo, Indian Territory (now Oklahoma), to Samuel and Lula (Maben) Maytubby on November 27, 1893, Floyd Ernest Maytubby attended the Harley Institute in Tishomingo, Oklahoma. After graduation, he became a banker. Maytubby married Frances Elizabeth Leecraft in Oklahoma City on June 30, 1917. He served in World War I as a field artillery officer. In 1939, President Franklin Delano Roosevelt appointed Maytubby governor of the Chickasaw Nation, a position he held for 24 years. Maytubby succeeded Douglas H. Johnston, who had been appointed in 1906 and served for 33 years. While governor, Maytubby promoted legislation that gave the Department of the Interior the authority to negotiate with the Chickasaw and Choctaw for the sale of their coal deposits. He also worked for the passage of legislation that would lead to the formation of the INDIAN CLAIMS COMMISSION. Upon his retirement from Chickasaw politics, Maytubby entered the insurance business. He died on February 24, 1963.

Further Reading

Green, Richard. "Tribal Historian: Historic 1959 Tribal Meeting of Ada's Aldridge Hotel." *Chickasaw Times* 42, no. 9 (September 2007): 34–35.

McCloud, Janet (Janet Renecker, Yet Si Blue)

(1934–2003) *Tulalip-Nisqually fishing-rights activist*

Janet Renecker, a Tulalip-Nisqually, was born on the newly created Tulalip reservation in Washington on March 30, 1934. A descendant of the great Suquamish leader Chief Seattle, she received the name Yet Si Blue, or "Woman Who Talks," from her grandmother. Both her parents were alcoholics, and Janet, the oldest of three children, grew up in foster homes. After a brief marriage and divorce, she married Don McCloud, a Puyallup-Nisqually truck driver, and the couple lived in Seattle. After their third child was born, the family moved to Frank's Landing, on the Nisqually River, where Don's former father-in-law, Billy Frank, Sr., owned some land.

The Franks were staunch traditionalists who lived off the land and by fishing, and their way of life captivated Janet McCloud, who had been raised in urban areas. She abandoned Catholicism for the traditional religion of the Nisqually. Don McCloud held a number of jobs, and the family finally saved enough money to buy a home a few miles away in Yelm, Washington, where Janet gave birth to the rest of her eight children. The family turned to fishing to help supplement their income, and their use of nets, as well as their refusal to purchase permits, soon drew the scrutiny of the Washington State Fish and Game Commission, which claimed they were violating the state's fish and game laws.

Although the right to fish in their "usual and accustomed" places was guaranteed by 19th-century treaties, Indians who attempted to do so were often arrested by Washington State game wardens. In 1937, gillnetting, a traditional form of fishing, was outlawed by the state, leading to many arrests. In the mid-1950s, Puyallup activist Robert Satiacum began net fishing on the Puyallup River. His arrest in 1954 led to a decision by the Washington Supreme Court that prohibited state regulation of Indian fishing, unless for conservation. Yet the state continued to harass Indian fishermen.

In January 1961, Washington State police arrested a number of Indians, including McCloud's in-laws. McCloud and other Indian women began to fish in place of the men. On January 7, 1962, the state game wardens launched their largest sting to date, using reconnaissance planes and walkie-talkies and deploying almost 100 men along the Nisqually River. Five Indians were arrested for illegal fishing. Along with Nisqually activists Al Bridges, Billy Frank, Sr., BILLY FRANK, JR., and Columbia River activist DAVID SOHAPPY, the McClouds became two of the leaders of the fishing rights movement. In 1964, with HANK ADAMS, Janet McCloud organized the Survival of American Indians Association to uphold Indian fishing rights. The group began organizing "fish-ins" with celebrities such as Dick Gregory and Marlon Brando.

In a two-year period, groups of Indians were arrested 16 times for illegal net fishing on the Nisqually, leading to the "Battle of Frank's Landing" on October 13, 1965. At Frank's Landing, dozens of state agents surrounded 50 Indians, mostly women and children who were participating in a fish-in. When nets began to lower into the river, state game department boats rushed in and violently broke up the protest, viciously beating the protesters. Six Indians, including Janet McCloud, were taken into custody and charged with resisting arrest and illegal fishing. After several delays, her case finally went to trial in 1969, when she was found not guilty of all charges. The protests continued until the Boldt Decision of 1974, which established that Indian treaties set aside half the harvestable catch in the rivers of Washington State for Indians.

Following her trial, McCloud helped to put together *Our Brother's Keeper*, a scathing report on the dismal social conditions of INDIAN RESERVATIONS, for the NATIVE AMERICAN RIGHTS FUND. She also helped to organize the Brotherhood of American Indian Prisoners in 1971. She joined the AMERICAN INDIAN MOVEMENT (AIM), although she was dissatisfied with the lack of women among its leadership and founded WOMEN OF ALL RED NATIONS (WARN) in 1978 in an attempt to redress the imbalance. Despite this, she defended AIM and in particular its confrontational tactics, arguing: "Few acknowledge that real change began to take place only after the tremendous sacrifices of the young warriors of the American Indian Movement. . . . We need our warriors, and where are they? In prisons, in hiding, pursued relentlessly by the FBI." In 1978, McCloud also helped AIM leader DENNIS BANKS to organize the LONGEST WALK, a national demonstration intended to duplicate the TRAIL OF BROKEN TREATIES protest of 1972.

Deeply influenced by the traditional teachings of Hopi THOMAS BANYACYA, McCloud became a founding member of the Traditional Circle of Elders and Youth. She traveled extensively to promote the rights of indigenous peoples, making numerous trips to Africa and Europe. Her land in Yelm has been transformed into a community center, the Sapa Dawn Center, where women from all over the world come to discuss indigenous, environmental, and family issues. A tireless activist, she also helped to found the Northwest Indian Women's Circle. Janet McCloud died on November 25, 2003, at her home in Yelm.

See also HUNTING AND FISHING RIGHTS.

Further Reading

Kamb, Lewis. "Janet McCloud, 1934–2003: Indian Activist Put Family First." *Seattle Post Intelligencer*, 27 November 2003.
Katz, Jane, ed. *Messengers of the Wind: Native American Women Tell Their Life Stories*. New York: Ballantine Books, 1995.

McGinnis, Duane   *See* NIATUM, DUANE.

McKenzie, Fayette Avery (1872–1957) *sociologist*
Born in Montrose, Pennsylvania, on July 31, 1872, the son of Edwin and Gertrude Avery McKenzie, Fayette Avery McKenzie received his B.S. from Lehigh University in 1895, an LL.D. from Lehigh in 1916, and a Ph.D. from the University of Pennsylvania in 1906. He began his career in 1897 as an instructor of modern languages at Juniata College in Huntingdon, Pennsylvania. In 1903–04, he taught at the federal Indian school on the Wind River (Eastern Shoshone) Reservation in Wyoming. Appointed professor of economics and sociology at Ohio State in 1905, McKenzie published his doctoral thesis, *The American Indian in Relation to the White Population of the United States*, three years later, and in 1910 he coauthored the Indian Census Report for the U.S. Bureau of the Census, the most comprehensive census of American Indians ever issued.

McKenzie was a typical reformer of the Progressive Age. He was an avowed assimilationist (see ASSIMILATION) and proponent of ALLOTMENT. He viewed tradition and custom as "the social tyranny of the tribe." In McKenzie's view, tribalism and citizenship were incompatible. By removing all traces of traditional culture, the Indian should "vanish" and become a citizen.

Among social scientists, it was typically anthropologists who studied Indians, but in the early part of the century hardly any anthropologists were interested in assimilation and culture change (see ANTHROPOLOGISTS AND AMERICAN INDIANS). McKenzie, probably the only sociologist of his time who worked with Indians, was very interested in culture change, but not in anthropology or Indian culture. As part of his assimilationist outlook, McKenzie conceived of an organization of Indian professionals and began working to bring it about, beginning with correspondence in 1908 or 1909. In 1911, he invited LAURA MIRIAM CORNELIUS KELLOGG, CHARLES ALEXANDER EASTMAN, CARLOS MONTEZUMA, CHARLES EDWIN DAGENETT, THOMAS L. SLOAN, and Henry Standing Bear to a meeting that launched the SOCIETY OF AMERICAN INDIANS (SAI). The first annual conference was held in Columbus, Ohio, in October 1911. McKenzie attended it, as well as the next three, keeping a generally low profile but exercising an important mediating influence among the widely contrasting Indian and non-Indian participants.

McKenzie left Ohio State for Fisk University (Nashville, Tennessee) in 1915. Although from then on he no longer participated in the SAI, he served in 1923 as chair of the resolutions subcommittee of the COMMITTEE OF ONE HUNDRED, and in 1926 and 1927 he was a member of the research committee for the MERIAM REPORT. He was also a member of the INDIAN RIGHTS ASSOCIATION. In 1927, McKenzie rejoined the faculty of Juniata College, where he taught until his retirement in 1941.

Fayette Avery McKenzie died in Huntingdon, Pennsylvania, on September 1, 1957. His papers were donated to the Tennessee State Library and Archives in 1960.

McLendon, Mary Stone (Ataloa, "Little Song")
(1895–1967) *Chickasaw artist, educator, singer*

A Chickasaw, Mary Stone McLendon was born in Duncan, Oklahoma, to Wiliam F. Stone, a white man, and Josephine (Smith) Stone, one-quarter Chickasaw. Raised by her Chickasaw grandmother, she was educated at public and private schools, then went on to the Oklahoma College for Women, the University of Redlands in California (B.A.), and Columbia University Teachers College (M.A.). At the age of 17, she married Ralph McLendon, who joined the army and died a year later; she never remarried. Later, she received an honorary scholarship to the International Institute at Columbia. While studying in New York, McLendon—who became better known by the name her grandmother gave her, Ataloa ("Little Song" in Chickasaw)—spoke out on Indian issues and made efforts to present Native American culture to the wider public. A recital at International House on January 16, 1927, included such "idealized" INDIANIST MUSIC numbers as "By the Weeping Waters," "Invocation to the Sun God," "Indian Spring Song," and the canoe song from Charles Wakefield Cadman's *Shanewis*. In March 1927, she presented a recital with fellow student and good friend, TE ATA, another Chickasaw from Oklahoma.

Ataloa had gone to Columbia intending to return to Oklahoma to teach. From 1927 to 1935, she taught English and philosophy at Bacone College in Muskogee, then the only accredited college for Indians in the United States (see HIGHER EDUCATION), and coached dramatics, elocution, and other extracurricular activities. She traveled extensively on fund-raising missions for the college at a time when a planned expansion had been handicapped by the government's withholding of a large donation by Creek millionaire JACKSON BARNETT, who had been judged incompetent to manage his oil wealth.

In the capacity of field secretary, Ataloa collected items for a planned Indian museum on the Bacone campus. It became a reality with the opening of the Art Lodge on December 2, 1932. The building was designed by Ataloa herself, and the interior furnishings were crafted and developed from her designs by Indians. A fireplace in the lodge was built out of stones sent in from nearly every place and tribal territory important to Indian history. After her death, it was renamed the Ataloa Art Lodge, and later it became the Ataloa Lodge Museum. It now houses more than 20,000 pieces of traditional and contemporary American Indian Art.

Ataloa served on the Oklahoma State Welfare Committee in 1934 and 1935 at the appointment of the governor. During WORLD WAR II, she worked for the Relocation Authority (see MYER, DILLON S.) and the United War Chest. In the 1950s, she moved to Los Angeles, where she served in California schools as a consultant and lecturer on intercultural education and played a major part in the development of the Los Angeles Indian Center and the Commission on Indian Work of the Southern California Council of Churches. She was a member of the Intercultural Club of Pasadena and the National Congress of American Indians.

Mary Stone McLendon died in Los Angeles in 1967.

McNickle, D'Arcy
(1904–1977) *Cree-Flathead social scientist, national community organizer, historian, novelist*

D'Arcy McNickle was born January 18, 1904, on the Confederated Tribes Reservation in Montana. His parents were William James McNickle, son of Scotch-Irish immigrants, and Philomene Parenteau, a Métis-Cree. William McNickle had been employed as a maintenance engineer at the Catholic mission school at St. Ignatius, on the reservation. Philomene was a student at the school. They married in 1899. Though of Cree descent through his mother, McNickle was an enrolled Flathead through legal adoption into that tribe in 1905. He first attended the Indian mission boarding school at St. Ignatius, but after his parents' divorce in 1913, the agency superintendent and mission authorities placed him and his two sisters in the federal boarding school at Chemawa, Oregon, to get them away from their mother, whom they considered a bad influence. Ironically, although his parents had wanted to raise him as a non-Indian, he passed his entire childhood as an Indian and also spent time with his Métis (Cree-French) grandparents. His mother, who had remarried, finally took custody of him in 1916. In 1918, his mother and stepfather took McNickle to Langley, Washington, where he enrolled in a high school and was for the first time in an environment with very few Indians. He studied violin, developing what would be a lifelong love of classical music, and did well in school. A few years later, the family moved to Missoula, Montana, where he finished high school in 1921.

McNickle enrolled in Montana State University, studying history and literature (1921–25), but did not graduate. Harold G. Merriam, chair of the English Department, nurtured his writing talent and recommended him to Oxford University. In fall 1925, he studied privately at Oxford but was discouraged when he learned it would take two years just to earn a bachelor's degree. After several months in Paris, he returned to the United States, spending most of the next six years in New York. In 1929, he enrolled at Columbia University, where he took history courses through 1931. Seven months in Philadelphia as an automobile salesman made him realize how alienated he was from the values of salesmanship and moneymaking. He then returned to New York City to work in publishing. The stock market crash of 1929 convinced him he was right about the falsity of modern American society.

In the late 1920s, McNickle began working on his first, strongly autobiographical novel, *The Hungry Generations*, which eventually became *The Surrounded*, published in 1936. While working on the novel, McNickle developed an interest in anthropology. In 1934, he became enthusiastic about the work of anthropological linguist William Gates of Johns Hopkins University, initiating a correspondence with him that provided further inspiration. About the same time, he applied for a job with the BUREAU OF INDIAN AFFAIRS (BIA). Meanwhile, in September 1935, McNickle was hired by the Works Progress Administration's Federal Writers Project, and he moved to Washington, D.C. His BIA application was approved in February 1936, and he became administrative assistant in the Indian organization division, often working with the tribal relations division as well.

One month before McNickle was hired, the BIA set up its Applied Anthropology Unit (AAU). Although the AAU proved a failure and was closed at the end of 1937, McNickle continued to believe that field agents working on tribal reorganization should be instructed in the culture of the particular tribe by knowledgeable anthropologists (see ANTHROPOLOGISTS AND AMERICAN INDIANS). In 1939, he became one of the nucleus of a group, mainly BIA employees, who began to discuss the possibility of a national pan-Indian lobbying organization. The eventually became the NATIONAL CONGRESS OF AMERICAN INDIANS (NCAI), founded in 1944.

For several months in 1945–46, due to the illness of Commissioner WILLIAM ALOYSIUS BROPHY, McNickle was in effect acting commissioner of Indian affairs. He was particularly active on Alaskan issues. In 1949, he published *They Came Here First*, the first history of Indian–non-Indian relations from a Native American point of view written by a Native American. In 1950, at the urging of RUTH MUSKRAT BRONSON and ELIZABETH BENDER CLOUD, McNickle formed a new organization, American Indian Development, Inc. (AID), to secure foundation funds for community development projects.

With the administrations of Harry S. Truman and Dwight D. Eisenhower came a major shift in Indian policy (see TERMINATION). McNickle had been acting chief of tribal relations in 1949–50. He became chief of tribal relations in 1950 and was in line for assistant commissioner, but he did not like the direction federal Indian policy was taking. He stayed on for another two years as a moderating influence, but his position became increasingly difficult, and in March 1952 he left government service in the belief that he might be able to accomplish much more on the outside through AID.

McNickle decided to use health education as the basis of an overall community development project somewhere on the Navajo (Dineh) reservation. There was an especially great need for this among the eastern Navajo, most of whom were not even living within the reservation boundaries and had been much neglected. This eventually became the Crownpoint Project, centering on the Crownpoint Hospital. To be nearer to the project, McNickle moved to Boulder, Colorado. With McNickle working closely with the new Navajo Tribal Health Committee and its chair, ANNIE DODGE WAUNEKA, the project got under way in 1953. It would continue through 1960.

While McNickle was in Colorado, leadership workshops for Indian college students, initially organized by SOL TAX in 1956, were held at the University of Colorado in Boulder. Preoccupied with Crownpoint, McNickle was not much involved at the start (though he was visiting lecturer from 1956 to 1959), but from 1959 to 1961, he mediated the funding through AID, and from 1960 he directed the entire program (see THOMAS, ROBERT KNOX).

McNickle chaired the steering committee of the AMERICAN INDIAN CHICAGO CONFERENCE, organized by Tax with NCAI, and held in June 1961 at the University of Chicago. He scheduled the 1961 workshop so that its first week coincided with the conference and students could attend as observers. Because the first stirrings of the RED POWER MOVEMENT pushed the conference beyond what he had foreseen, and because he felt that Tax had not sufficiently appreciated his work, McNickle was disappointed. It proved to be a historically important event, however, propelling the momentum set up by supporters of JOHN COLLIER and continued by NCAI to a new level with the establishment of the NATIONAL INDIAN YOUTH COUNCIL by radical college students later that year.

Since he did not have a college degree, McNickle had never sought an academic position. As a proven administrator, however, and (through his work with AID and the Crownpoint Project) an effective "action anthropologist," he was offered and accepted the chairmanship and an associate professorship in the new Department of Anthropology at the University of Saskatchewan in 1965. That same year, he received an honorary degree from the University of Colorado.

In 1967, McNickle returned to the summer workshop, where he found that the growing Red Power movement created a stormy atmosphere. In 1965, the Indiana University Press, on the recommendation of ALVIN M. JOSEPHY, JR., had asked him to write a biography of OLIVER LA FARGE, but the Saskatchewan appointment had left him no time to finish it. He took unpaid leave from the university in 1968–69, and the book was published as *Indian Man* in 1971. McNickle returned to Saskatchewan in fall 1969 but retired in 1971 and went back to Albuquerque, after two years of high political tension in Indian affairs in both the United States and Canada. He published *Native American Tribalism* in 1973.

D'Arcy McNickle died in Albuquerque on October 18, 1977, of a massive heart attack. He had been about to travel to Chicago to accept a nomination as distinguished research fellow of the Newberry Library, which would have provided a stipend, free accommodation in Chicago, and freedom to work on his own projects. His novel, *Wind from an Enemy Sky*, was published shortly after his death. McNickle's papers are at the Newberry Library.

Further Reading

Cowger, Thomas W. *The National Congress of American Indians: The Founding Years*. Lincoln: University of Nebraska Press, 2001.

Parker, Dorothy. *Singing an Indian Song: A Biography of D'Arcy McNickle*. Lincoln: University of Nebraska Press, 1992.

Purdy, John, ed. *The Legacy of D'Arcy McNickle: Writer, Historian, Activist*. Norman: University of Oklahoma Press, 1996.

Ruppert, James. *D'Arcy McNickle*. Boise, Idaho: Boise State University Press, 1988.

Wilkinson, Charles F. *Blood Struggle: The Rise of Modern Indian Nations*. New York: W. W. Norton, 2005.

Means, Russell (Wanbli Ohitika, "Brave Eagle")

(1939–2012) *Oglala Lakota–Yankton Dakota Sioux activist, prominent member of the American Indian Movement, actor*
Born in Porcupine, South Dakota, on November 10, 1939, on the Pine Ridge Reservation, Russell Means was given the name

Wanbli Ohitika (Brave Eagle). His father, Walter "Hank" Means, was part Oglala Lakota Sioux and part Irish, and his mother, Theodora Louise Feather, was Yankton Dakota Sioux. His family moved to Oakland, California, shortly after his birth, where Hank Means worked in the shipyards during WORLD WAR II. When the war ended, they returned to South Dakota. Means attended an all-white school in Huron, near the Yankton Sioux reservation, where his exposure to racism made a deep impression on him. The family returned to the San Francisco Bay Area in 1947, and Means attended public schools in San Leandro, California.

In 1959, Means drifted to Los Angeles, where he worked for an oil company and then in a paint factory. In 1964, he accompanied his father and a small group of Sioux during the first attempt to occupy Alcatraz Island on behalf of the Bay Area Indian community (see ALCATRAZ ISLAND, OCCUPATION OF). Afterward, Means returned to South Dakota and worked for the Rosebud Reservation's tribal council before moving to Cleveland, Ohio, in 1968, where he became the head of the Cleveland Indian Center.

While attending a business meeting in Minneapolis in 1969, Means met DENNIS BANKS and CLYDE BELLECOURT—who had recently founded the AMERICAN INDIAN MOVEMENT (AIM) to monitor police brutality against Indians in that city—and returned to Cleveland to start AIM's second chapter. He then launched a $9 million suit against the Cleveland Indians baseball team, claiming that their mascot, Chief Wahoo, was demeaning to Indian people. Though the suit failed to get any support, his next moved displayed the genius for dramatic media events for which he would soon become famous. On Thanksgiving Day 1970, Means and a small group of cohorts seized the *Mayflower II* berthed in Plymouth, Massachusetts, and renamed the holiday the "National Day of Mourning."

In June 1971, Means led an occupation of Mount Rushmore, and in September that year, he barged into BUREAU OF INDIAN AFFAIRS (BIA) headquarters in Washington, D.C., and attempted to make a citizen's arrest of prominent BIA functionary JOHN CROW as well as WILMA VICTOR, former headmistress of the notorious Intermountain Boarding School, whom Means accused of being a "dictatorial sadist."

Along with Dennis Banks, Means led a massive three-day demonstration in Gordon, Nebraska, in March 1972, demanding that the killers of RAYMOND YELLOW THUNDER be brought to justice, an ultimately successful protest that made AIM a household word among Indians. Means joined Indian leaders from across the country in helping to organize the TRAIL OF BROKEN TREATIES, a national protest march on Washington, D.C., in November 1972 that culminated in the occupation of BIA headquarters for more than a week. The image of Means guarding the BIA entrance with a club and a large photograph of President Richard Nixon as a shield became one of the symbols of the takeover, and the demonstration catapulted AIM into the forefront of the Indian political world.

In January 1973, Wesley Bad Heart Bull was stabbed to death in Buffalo Gap, South Dakota. When his assailant, a

Russell Means *(left)* and Dennis Banks listened to testimony during their trial in Minnesota in 1974 on conspiracy charges stemming from the occupation of Wounded Knee the previous year. *(AP/Wideworld)*

white man, was charged with only second-degree manslaughter, Means and Banks organized a protest in front of the county courthouse in Custer that turned into a fiery riot when police attempted to break up the peaceful gathering.

After the riot, Means and Banks led 200 Indians to occupy the small hamlet of WOUNDED KNEE. As early as 1971, Means had been toying with the notion of "liberating" an Indian reservation, and he had considered Wounded Knee—the site of a massacre of more than 150 Sioux by the U.S. Army in 1890 and located in one of the poorest reservations in the country—as the place with the most symbolic value. He knew he could count on the support of the traditional Oglala of Pine Ridge, who, under the leadership of PEDRO BISSONETTE, were attempting to overthrow the increasingly repressive and corrupt administration of tribal chair RICHARD WILSON.

Expecting, indeed encouraging, a violent reaction from the U.S. government, Means issued a statement at the beginning of the occupation. "I hope by my death," he said, "and the deaths of all these Indian men and women, there will be an investigation into corruption on the reservations, and there is no better place to start than Pine Ridge." Yet his charismatic personality and blunt outspokenness during the 71-day standoff helped draw tremendous support for the activists and prevented bloodshed.

When the siege ended, the U.S. government began a campaign to harass and ultimately destroy AIM. In the two years after Wounded Knee, Means was arrested 12 times and had to undergo seven different trials, though he was convicted of only one crime—rioting at the Custer courthouse. Means was also shot four times, including once by a policeman, and stabbed while in prison. Yet he refused to stop his activism. In February 1974, he lost a highly charged election for the tribal presidency of Pine Ridge against Wilson, who publicly despised Means and all that he stood for. In April 1981, he occupied a portion of the Black Hills in South Dakota, where he established Camp Yellow Thunder.

Meanwhile, AIM, riddled with government informers and provocateurs, was beginning to disintegrate. Means broke with most other AIM members in 1985, when he backed the Miskito Indians in their war against the Sandinista government of Nicaragua. In 1987, Means sought the nomination of the Libertarian Party for president, and although he attracted considerable support, he lost to Congressman Ron Paul. He left what remained of the AIM in 1988, feeling that he had accomplished what he set out to do.

In 1992, Means won widespread acclaim for his portrayal of Chingachgook in the film *The Last of the Mohicans*, and he has since had important roles in Oliver Stone's *Natural-Born Killers* and in Disney's animated film *Pocahontas*. His autobiography, *Where White Men Fear to Tread*, written with Marvin J. Wolf, was released in 1997.

The actions of Russell Means and AIM drew a great deal of attention to the plight of Native people and helped bring a resurgence of self-confidence among Indians, new pride in their heritage, and respect for their cultures. With a flair for publicity and a gift for making inflammatory statements, Russell Means served more as a dynamic catalyst for change than as a true Indian leader. A master at manipulating the U.S. media, with natural charisma, flamboyance, and photogenic features, he helped to redefine the image of a "militant Indian" and made himself virtually synonymous with Indian activism during the 1970s.

Means continued to be active in politics. He unsuccessfully ran for governor of New Mexico in 2001. Into the 21st century, he also still managed to generate publicity. In 2007, he and a small group of Lakota activists declared the Lakota to be a sovereign nation and broke off all relations with the United States, at least temporarily. In 2000, he appeared in the British film *Billy and The Magic Railroad* and in 2007 in the film *Pathfinder*.

In mid-2011, Russell Means was diagnosed with esophageal cancer; it was reported in remission by September 2011, but he died at his ranch in Porcupine, South Dakota, on October 22, 2012.

Further Reading

Means, Russell, with Marvin J. Wolf. *Where White Men Fear to Tread: The Autobiography of Russell Means*. New York: St. Martin's Press, 1995.
Wilkinson, Charles F. *Blood Struggle: The Rise of Modern Indian Nations*. New York: W. W. Norton, 2005.

Means, Ted   See MEANS, WILLIAM.

Means, William (Bill Means) (1946–   ) *Oglala Lakota–Yankton Dakota Sioux activist, member of the American Indian Movement*

The younger brother of RUSSELL MEANS, Bill Means, with his twin brother Ted, was born on August 9, 1946, in Huron, South Dakota, near the Yankton Sioux reservation. His father, Walter "Hank" Means, was part Oglala Lakota Sioux and part Irish, and his mother, Theodora Louise Feather Means, was a Yankton Dakota Sioux. Shortly after the twins' birth, Hank Means, who had worked in the San Francisco shipyards during WORLD WAR II, decided to return to the shipbuilding trade and moved the family to California. The Means twins grew up first in San Francisco and then in Oakland but spent their summers on the Yankton Sioux and Pine Ridge reservations.

Both Bill and Ted Means attended Black Hills State College in South Dakota. Bill Means then joined the U.S. Army, becoming a paratrooper with the elite 101st Airborne Division and serving in Vietnam.

Like their brother Russell, Bill and Ted Means joined the AMERICAN INDIAN MOVEMENT (AIM) and participated in most of the major events of the movement, including the siege of WOUNDED KNEE in 1973, and both suffered persecution after Wounded Knee. Ted Means was charged with inciting a riot in Sioux Falls during the trial of Sarah Bad Heart Bull, the mother of slain Indian Wesley Bad Heart Bull, who was herself charged with inciting the riot in Custer that had directly led to the Wounded Knee siege. In 1981, Bill Means led the occupation of Camp Yellow Thunder, which attempted to secure for the Sioux an 800-acre tract of Forest Service land in the Black Hills on which to hold religious ceremonies. The Forest Service, which had slated the land for timber cutting and grazing, refused the requests of Mathew King and other Sioux spiritual leaders for use of the tract, even though the Forest Service provided camps for mainstream religions.

Both Ted and Bill Means served as directors of the INTERNATIONAL INDIAN TREATY COUNCIL, a successor to AIM. Bill Means later became the principal of the Heart of the Earth School in Minneapolis, Minnesota, known for its traditional Native curriculum. In 1992, as director of the Treaty Council, Bill Means spoke before the United Nations at the inaugural ceremony of the "Year of Indigenous People."

Bill Means served as executive director of American Indian Opportunities Industrialization Center, the Minneapolis affiliate of a national network (Opportunities Industrialization Centers of America) founded in 1979, which places people in full-time employment. He remains on the board of directors of the Treaty Council and serves on the board of the World Archaeological Congress. Ted Means died of a stroke on November 29, 2011, in Rapid City, South Dakota.

Medicine, Beatrice (1924–2005) *Lakota scholar, anthropologist*

Beatrice Medicine was born on August 1, 1924, in Wakpala, South Dakota, on the Standing Rock Reservation. Her parents, Martin Medicine, Jr., and Anna Grace (Gabe) Medicine, brought her up in the traditions of the Sihasapa Teton Lakota Sioux. After attending public elementary and high schools in

Wakpala, she enrolled in South Dakota A&M (now South Dakota State University), earning a B.S. in 1945.

After graduation, she became an instructor at the Haskell Indian Institute in Lawrence, Kansas. Later, she taught at other Indian schools, including the one at Flandreau, South Dakota. While teaching at Santo Domingo Pueblo, she pursued studies in anthropology at the University of New Mexico. She subsequently studied at the University of Washington and at Michigan State, where she earned an M.A. in 1954. Medicine went on to teach anthropology at a number of universities, including the University of South Dakota, San Francisco State University, the University of Washington, Michigan State, Stanford, Dartmouth, and in Canada at the University of British Columbia and the Mount Royal College in Calgary. In 1983, while teaching at the University of Wisconsin, Madison, she completed a Ph.D.

A prolific scholar, Medicine wrote more than 60 articles, largely on the role of women in Indian societies, but also on such diverse subjects such as alcoholism, homosexuality, education, and Native art. In 1978, she authored *Native American Women: A Perspective*, and in 1983, she edited, with Patricia Albers, *The Hidden Half: Studies of Plains Indian Women*. Medicine's work is known for its attempts to combat the reductive, patronizing views of American Indians perpetuated by many anthropologists in the early and middle years of the 20th century. Not content with studying the past, she focused as well on contemporary Indian issues, such as ASSIMILATION, bilingual education, and the adaptive strategies employed by Indians in the attempt to preserve their languages and cultures. She is also known for promoting the perspective that Native people should speak for themselves rather than having experts speak for them and that they are equipped to solve their own problems if allowed to do so.

Medicine was active in the communities in which she lived, helping to found American Indian centers in Seattle, Vancouver, and Calgary. In 1974, she served as an expert witness for the defense in the federal case brought against members of the AMERICAN INDIAN MOVEMENT for their OCCUPATION OF WOUNDED KNEE in 1973. In her home town of Wakpala, she helped found a new public school and served on the local school board as well as on the Wakpala District Elder's Organization.

In 1991, Medicine was appointed to chair the Women's Branch of the Royal Commission on Aboriginal Peoples for the Canadian government, a task force whose recommendations, published in 1996, would lead to important reforms in Canadian Indian policy. That same year, she received the Franz Boas Award for Exemplary Service to Anthropology from the American Anthropological Association (AAA). Medicine has received numerous other awards, including the Bronislaw Malinowski Award for Lifetime Achievement from the Society for Applied Anthropology, the Honoring Our Allies Award from the National Gay and Lesbian Task Force, and the Outstanding Woman of Color Award from the National Institute of Women of Color. In 1998, Medicine received an honorary doctorate in the humanities from the University of Michigan for her contributions to anthropology. In 2001, she published *Learning to Be an Anthropologist and Remaining "Native,"* a collection of her previously published works. In 2005, she received the Spindler Award for Education in Anthropology from the AAA.

Beatrice Medicine died on December 19, 2005, during emergency surgery at MedCenter One Hospital in Bismarck, North Dakota. At the time of her death, she was professor emeritus of anthropology at California State University at Northridge. Her book *Drinking and Sobriety among the Lakota Sioux* appeared posthumously in 2006.

Meriam Report (*The Problem of Indian Administration*) (1928)

Issued in 1928, this massive and authoritative study of the administration of Indian affairs was one of the most influential documents of the 20th century concerning federal Indian policy. More than 800 pages in length, its official title is *The Problem of Indian Administration*, but it is more often referred to by the name of its chief investigator, social scientist Lewis Meriam. An outgrowth of the clamor for reform that followed in the wake of the 1923 report of the COMMITTEE OF ONE HUNDRED, the Meriam Report was undertaken at the request of the secretary of the interior, prepared by a research panel of the Brookings Institute, and funded by philanthropist John D. Rockefeller, Jr. Rockefeller had previously funded the INDIAN RIGHTS ASSOCIATION, but he was persuaded to support a more scientific approach after social work and future Indian commissioner JOHN COLLIER convinced him that the association's missionary concerns (see DANCE ORDERS) were counterproductive to the solution of the most important problems of Indian administration.

For seven months, Meriam and a team of social scientists traveled around the country observing conditions on INDIAN RESERVATIONS. They found that the ALLOTMENT policy had caused great hardship and that large numbers of Indians were living in poverty, poor health, and malnutrition. The report criticized the Allotment policy and recommended that it be terminated but made no concrete proposals. It recommended increased congressional funding for Indian health and education and encouraged the development of Native American arts. The main philosophical emphasis was that the task of the Office of Indian Affairs (later the BUREAU OF INDIAN AFFAIRS) should be primarily educational. The section on education in the Meriam Report was written by WILL CARSON RYAN, JR., who would later be appointed head of the Indian Office's educational work by incoming secretary of the interior Ray Lyman Wilbur and Commissioner of Indian Affairs CHARLES JAMES RHOADS (see EDUCATIONAL POLICY, AMERICAN INDIANS AND).

The Meriam Report shifted the balance in Indian affairs and supplied the impetus for a powerful reform movement, the so-called INDIAN NEW DEAL initiated under the administration of Herbert J. Hoover's Indian commissioner, Charles Rhoads, and assistant commissioner, JOSEPH HENRY SCATTERGOOD. Under Hoover, the Indian Office was given the explicit mission of instituting the policy recommendations of this groundbreaking report. This the commissioners set out to do in all good conscience, but they met with only limited success because of intransigence within the Indian Office and because the House of Representatives was reluctant to provide money for Indian programs.

The Meriam Report also foreshadowed Collier's INDIAN REORGANIZATION ACT of 1934 and served as the starting point for discussions when Collier first took office in 1933 as commissioner of Indian affairs. They ultimately diverged in a number of important ways, however. Although the Meriam Report broke new ground on the question of ASSIMILATION, the basic goal of federal policy since the beginning of the 20th century—recommending for the first time that Indians who wanted to go on being Indians should not be prevented from doing so—it was still oriented toward assimilation. Collier, on the other hand, actually advocated strengthening of Indian societies and culture. The supporters of the Meriam Report tended to concentrate on family life, education, and community without concerning themselves with the effect that resource-extracting economies had on Indian life in all these areas. This "live and let live" approach was not enough for Collier. A definite effort had to be made to correct the continuing abuse of Indian land and resources or restore a measure of power to the tribes. As Collier later wrote in his 1954 memoir, *From Every Zenith*, the Meriam Report "cast decisive illumination upon Indian education, Indian health work, Indian income and living standards, and the deficiencies of [the] Indian Service, [but left] somewhat vague the core subjects of Indian land tenure and Indian tribal or corporate organization."

Historians VINE DELORIA, JR., and Clifford Lytle list six points on which Collier advanced on the Meriam Report: the continued existence, regeneration, and usefulness of Indian societies is important; tribes should have status, responsibility, and power; land is fundamental; Indians should have all freedoms, including cultural and religious liberty; tribes should have the freedom to organize, extend credit, and provide civic and business technical assistance; and tribes should be governed by responsible democracy. In sum, Collier wanted government to help Indians "recapture their own genius."

Meriam went to such lengths to avoid the appearance of bias that, remarkably, there was only one Indian on the commission—HENRY CLARENCE ROE CLOUD—and a few minor Indian consultants. Also, in contrast to the Committee of One Hundred, there were no anthropologists.

A companion study, *The Office of Indian Affairs*, by Laurence F. Schmeckebier (1927), is a comprehensive history of the Bureau of Indian Affairs but contains no policy recommendations.

See also MOOREHEAD, WARREN KING.

Further Reading
Deloria, Vine, Jr., and Clifford Lytle. *The Nations Within: The Past and Future of American Indian Sovereignty.* New York: Pantheon Books, 1998.
Deloria, Vine, Jr., and Daniel Wildcat. *Power and Place: Indian Education in America.* Golden, Colo.: Fulcrum Resources, 2001.
Reyhner, Jon Allan, and Jeanne M. Oyawin Eder. *American Indian Education: A History.* Norman: University of Oklahoma Press, 2004.
Szasz, Margaret Connell. *Education and the American Indian: The Road to Self-Determination Since 1928.* 3rd ed. Albuquerque: University of New Mexico Press, 1999.

Meyers, John Tortes (Chief Meyers) (1880–1971)
Cahuilla baseball player

John Tortes Meyers was born on July 29, 1880, in Riverside, California. His father, John Mayer (not Meyers), was a German-American Civil War veteran from Terre Haute, Indiana, who owned a saloon in downtown Riverside. His mother, Felicite Tortes Mayer, was an accomplished Cahuilla (Iviatim) basket maker from Spring Rancheria (now on the Santa Rosa Reservation). After John Mayer died in 1887, Felicite was forced to find work in a hotel to support her three children. Young John Tortes Mayer attended the Sixth Street Grade School in Riverside, where a teacher misspelled his name as Meyer, and it eventually became Meyers. He attended Riverside High School and played on the baseball team, but he never graduated, as the family moved to the Santa Rosa Reservation.

At the age of 18, Meyers began playing semi-pro ball for the Santa Rosa Reservation team and then the Riverside town team. He bounced around California, working, among other things, at a raisin factory while playing semi-pro ball in Fresno. From 1902 through 1904, he played in San Diego. After a short stint in El Paso, Texas, he signed on in 1905 to the Phelps-Dodge Copper Company ball club based in Clifton, Arizona. There he was spotted by Dartmouth University football star Ralph Glaze, who convinced him to play for Dartmouth. Meyers entered Dartmouth in September 1905 with a fake high school diploma provided by Glaze. When the deception come to light, Meyers was permitted to stay but barred from participating in sports. After only a year, he had to leave to care for his mother, who had become ill. She recovered, but it was too late to return to Dartmouth, so Meyers played for minor league clubs in Harrisburg, Pennsylvania; Butte, Montana; and St. Paul, Minnesota.

It was not until he was 28 that "Chief" Meyers (as he would be known throughout his career) broke into the Major Leagues, joining the New York Giants in 1908. Playing sporadically in 1909, he became a regular in 1910, batting .285 and establishing himself as the best hitter on the Giants team and one of the best-hitting catchers in baseball. In 1911, Meyers batted .332, leading the Giants and finishing a close third in league standings, behind Doc Wilson (.333) of Boston and Honus Wagner (.334) of Pittsburgh. In 1912, he finished second in the league with a career-high .358 average. On June 10, 1912, Meyers became the first Major League catcher to hit a home run, triple, double, and single in one game (known as "hitting for the cycle").

Between 1910 and 1915, Meyers caught in practically every game that the Giants played, earning the title "Ironman." An excellent defensive player, he was best known as the catcher that Hall of Fame pitcher Christy Mathewson relied on. In 1911, he was catching when Mathewson out-dueled CHARLES ALBERT BENDER of the Philadelphia Athletics to take the first game of the World Series. In that series Meyers threw out 12 base runners, setting the Major League record for most assists in a six-game World Series—a mark that still stands. From 1911 through 1913, Meyers led the Giants to three straight National League pennants, but they lost in the World Series each time. In 1913, Meyers had the distinction of rooming with the great Olympian JIM THORPE, then a rookie outfielder for the Giants. Meyers tried to assuage Thorpe's grief at being stripped of the gold medals he won in the Olympics of 1912, an action as Meyers recalled that "broke Jim's heart," and from which "he never recovered."

Meyers was featured in numerous advertisements and promotions and was famous enough even for the vaudeville circuit, participating in sketches with Christy Mathewson and actress May Tully. In 1915, age and the wear and tear of being a catcher caught up with him, and that season he batted only .232. The next year, he was traded to the Brooklyn Dodgers, and with them participated in his fourth World Series. Meyers finished his Major League career with the Boston Nationals in 1917. After that, he played on Minor League teams in Buffalo, New York, and New Haven, Connecticut.

In November, 1918, after the United States entered WORD WAR I, Meyers joined the marines. Discharged in March 1919 without having seen action, he ended his Major League career that year with a .291 lifetime batting average.

Meyers found work as a construction foreman for the San Diego Consolidated Gas and Electric Company, but he lost his life savings in the stock market crash of 1929, and in 1931, as the Great Depression deepened, he found himself without a job. Returning to the Riverside area in 1933, Meyers became police chief for the Mission Indian Agency. Still enjoying a following, he barnstormed with other notable baseball old timers around the country and played a small role in the film *Laughing Boy* (1934), a story based on a novel by OLIVER LA FARGE. Meyers then worked for the BUREAU OF INDIAN AFFAIRS, eventually rising to the rank of supervisor.

Known as Jack to his friends, among whom were baseball greats Babe Ruth and Honus Wagner as well as celebrities such as entertainers Lillian Russell, W. C. Fields, and WILLIAM PENN ADAIR ROGERS, the warm and affable Meyers was the most popular catcher of his era. With his love of fine art and classical philosophy, quick wit, and dignified demeanor, Meyers did much to shatter the stereotype prevalent at the time that Indians were "dumb" or "savages." John Meyers died on July 2, 1971, in San Bernardino, California.

Further Reading

Koerper, Henry G. "The Catcher Was a Cahuilla: A Remembrance of John Tortes Meyers (1880–1971)." *Journal of California and Great Basin Anthropology* 24, no. 1 (2004): 21–40.
Simon, Thomas P. *Deadball Stars of the National League:*

The Society for American Baseball Research. Dulles, Va.: Potomac Books, 2004.

Mills, Billy (William Mervin Mills, Makata Taka Hela, "Loves His Country") (1938–) *Oglala Lakota Sioux Olympic gold medalist, record-holding long-distance runner*

William Mervin Mills was born on the Pine Ridge Indian Reservation in South Dakota on June 30, 1938, one of eight children. His mother, who was one-quarter Sioux, died when Billy was only seven. His father, a boxer who was three-quarters Sioux, passed away when Billy was 12. He was raised by his sister and then sent to Indian boarding schools. A "mixed-blood," Mills felt rejected by both the Indian and non-Indian communities and turned to running to find his own identity. While in high school at the Haskell Indian Institute in Lawrence, Kansas, Mills soon became the finest long-distance runner in the state, winning the two-mile cross-country championship three times and the mile twice. He then led the University of Kansas track team to two national titles, setting a conference record in the 10,000 meters. A three-time collegiate All-American in long-distance running, for two of those years he was the only American to hold the distinction (at that time foreign students were eligible to become All-Americans).

Mills joined the U.S. Marine Corps after graduation, and as a marine he continued to compete in interservice meets. In 1964, he made the U.S. Olympic team and went to Tokyo to run in the 10,000 meters. Mills was a virtual unknown in a 36-member field that was among the strongest in Olympic history. No American had ever won the race in Olympic competition, and LOUIS TEWANIMA's silver medal in 1912 marked the only time an American had finished among the top three. With favorites such as the 1960 Olympic champion Pyotr Bolotnikov of the Soviet Union, 5,000-meter champion Murray Halberg of New Zealand, Mohamed Gamoudi of Tunisia, gold medalist in 1968, and reigning world-record holder Ron Clarke of Australia, not a single reporter bothered to interview Mills before the event.

Clarke set a world-record pace for much of the race, and by the halfway mark he had managed to shake off everyone except Gamoudi, Mills, future gold medalist Mamo Wolde of Ethiopia, and local favorite Kokichi Tsuburaya. As the race wore on, Tsuburaya and Wolde began to falter, and Clarke needed only to break away from Mills and Gamoudi, neither of whom had ever run the race in under 29 minutes. In an electrifying finish, Clarke and Mills were abreast in the final lap, with Gamoudi right behind, when Clarke shoved Mills in order to get around a straggler, almost knocking Mills to the ground and seemingly out of contention. Gamoudi took the opportunity in the confusion to grab Clarke and push his way to a 10-yard lead. Clarke raced to close the gap, finally passing Gamoudi at the homestretch, but Gamoudi, sensing a victory, pulled up and passed Clarke again. Unnoticed by either of them, Mills had recovered and, in a furious sprint, passed them both just 50 yards before the finish line, breaking

Billy Mills *(right)* edges Gerry Lindgren, setting the world record for the six-mile run at the 1965 national Amateur Athletic Union (AAU) track-and-field meet in San Diego, California. *(AP/Wideworld)*

the tape in an Olympic record time of 28:24.4 and scoring one of the greatest upsets in the history of the Olympic Games.

Proving that his Olympic win was not a fluke, the next year Mills bettered Clarke's world record in the six-mile run by six seconds at the Amateur Athletic Union meet in San Diego, California. That year, Mills received his greatest reward, a ring made of Black Hills gold given to him by his Oglala elders, along with the name Makata Taka Hela, Loves His Country.

Mills finished his career in the U.S. Marine Corps as an officer assigned to the Department of the Interior. As a civilian, he became a successful life insurance salesman. Since his triumphs, Mills has devoted much of his time to Indian causes and working to raise young Indians' self-esteem, establishing a running program for reservation Indian youth. A tireless fund-raiser, Mills has raised millions for charity, helping to send medical supplies and food to strife-torn regions around the world. His life story was made into the movie *Running Brave* in 1983, and in 1994 he published his autobiography, *Wokini, A Lakota Journey to Happiness and Self-Understanding.*

Billy Mills was inducted into the U.S. Olympic Hall of Fame in 1984 and is a member of the U.S. Track and Field Hall of Fame, the National Distance Running Hall of Fame, the Kansas Hall of Fame, the San Diego Hall of Fame, and the National High School Hall of Fame. He and his wife, Patricia, live in Sacramento, California, where he owns and operates the Billy Mills Speakers Bureau. In 2005, he expanded on themes developed in his autobiography, in a novel, *Lessons of a Lakota: A Young Man's Journey to Happiness and Self-Understanding*, a story about Lakota traditions and how they can help young people succeed in life.

mining, American Indians and

Before the 1891 Indian Leasing Act, valuable mineral resources found on American Indian lands were simply sold outright by the government, generally without the tribe's consent and without compensation. Lands that contained gold and other precious metals, such as those found during the late 19th century on the Great Sioux Reservation, the Crow Reservation, or the Fort Belknap Reservation, were detached from the reservations and sold to speculators. Likewise, newer INDIAN RESERVATIONS, such as those of the Tohono O'odham (Papago) in Arizona or the Ute in Colorado, were structured so as to exclude valuable copper or silver deposits. Only the Five Civilized Tribes (Cherokee, Choctaw, Chickasaw, Creek, and Seminole) managed to maintain some control over mining on their lands under laws they adopted in 1869. The Choctaw, for example, had by 1891 contracted with 39 companies to produce more than 1.5 million tons of coal per year.

The 1891 act allowed for leasing of Indian lands for mineral and oil production without requiring the wholesale cession of lands, thus providing a brake of sorts on the hordes of illegal miners trespassing on many Indian reservations. The law also authorized the leasing of Indian ALLOTMENTS, a practice that would become a fount of corruption once oil was discovered in Indian Territory (see CURTIS ACT; OIL, AMERICAN INDIANS AND).

Beginning with Commissioner WILLIAM ARTHUR JONES, who ended the distribution of per-capita Indian annuities, and throughout the first three-quarters of the 20th century, the general federal policy had been to use the proceeds from mineral development, if there were any, to pay for government services, generally leaving the leasing tribe with little or no economic benefits.

Under Indian Commissioner ROBERT GROSVENOR VALENTINE, the Indian Omnibus Act of 1910 was passed, which for the first time geared the Office of Indian Affairs (later the BUREAU OF INDIAN AFFAIRS [BIA]) toward resource development by creating a technical staff to scientifically oversee the exploitation of Indian lands. Under other Progressive Era legislation, the federal government in 1912 extended to Indian reservations its policy of reserving for itself the mineral rights to public lands, regardless of surface use. Indian tribes thereafter maintained their valuable subsurface rights even on allotted or homesteaded lands, a policy known as *split estates*. In 1916, the government further provided that Indians could retain mineral rights to certain ceded Indian lands that were still in the public domain. By 1919, however, Congress, dominated more and more by Western interests, opened executive-order reservations to precious-metal and coal mining and returned to the policy of selling rather than leasing resources. Attempts by Westerners such as ALBERT BACON FALL during the early 1920s to liberalize leasing even further, in particular oil leasing, led instead to a backlash, resulting in stronger protections and higher royalties for Indians.

In 1938, at the urging of Indian Commissioner JOHN COLLIER, the Omnibus Tribal Leasing Act was passed. It restricted leases to 10 years, with approval from the secretary of the interior and disallowing state taxation of Indian mineral resources. Although the act required competitive bidding and stipulated that successful bidders post performance bonds, the long leases still proved disadvantageous to Indians, as the prices, set during the Great Depression, were out of proportion to the demand generated by WORLD WAR II and the expanded postwar economy. As mineral prices rose during the 1940s and 1950s, many tribes found themselves saddled with unfavorable contracts.

Moreover, during the TERMINATION era of the 1950s and 1960s the cozy relations between mining companies and the Interior Department returned. The arrangement was aided by cold war imperatives, which foresaw the creation of National Sacrifice Areas—mineral-rich lands located almost exclusively in regions of the Southwest and Great Plains with large Indian landholdings, which for security reasons would be developed without regard to environmental or social consequences. As mining companies moved to exploit the vast Indian energy reserves, Indians not only found themselves without government protection but realized that their legal and political representatives were beset with conflicts of interest that would deprive them of the full value of their resources (see BOYDEN, JOHN STERLING).

The movement of vast energy consortiums onto Indian lands led to growing activism by traditional Indian leaders and members of militant groups, such as the AMERICAN INDIAN MOVEMENT (AIM), who opposed the large mining operations on environmental and cultural grounds. The renewed activism provoked bitter struggles during the 1970s and 1980s, including Sokaogon Chippewa attempts to block Exxon and Kennecott from mining zinc and copper near their reservation in Wisconsin, and traditional Hopi attempts to stop the stripmining of Black Mesa by Peabody Coal. The same factors figured prominently in the BIG MOUNTAIN dispute between the Navajo (Dineh) and Hopi tribes.

During the 1970s, tribal councils began to assert more control over mining and its impact on Indian reservations. In 1973, the Northern Cheyenne successfully sought to terminate coal leases recently approved by the Department of the Interior that would have paid the Cheyenne only 17.5 cents per ton, a minuscule fraction of the market value for the coal, which at the time was $26 per ton. Three years later, the tribe redesignated its air-quality standards as Class I, the same as a national park or wilderness area, forcing the nearby coal-mining and electrical power plants to install pollution-control devices.

Using the Indian Self-Determination and Education Assistance Act of 1975, Midwestern tribes began forming joint companies with energy corporations. In the same year, the Jicarilla Apache began to impose a severance tax on oil companies operating on their lands, including industry giants Amoco and Marathon. The Navajo, in the meantime, began adding a business-activity tax to energy companies such as Kerr-McGee, which were mining coal on their lands. The energy companies bitterly fought the new tribal taxes in court, but in 1985 the U.S. Supreme Court handed the Apache a victory in *Merrion v. Jicarilla Apache Tribe*, and in 1985 the Court upheld the Navajo's right to tax in *Kerr-McGee v. Navajo Tribe*. The tribes also fought off attempts by the states to help themselves to Indian resources, and in 1985 the courts, in *Montana v. Blackfeet Tribes*, rejected Montana's claim to levy a tax on tribal income derived from reservation oil and natural gas royalties.

With the help of a vigorous lobbying effort by the COUNCIL OF ENERGY RESOURCE TRIBES (CERT), which had ambitious plans to create an "Indian OPEC," in 1982 Congress passed the Indian Mineral Development Act and the Federal Oil and Gas

Management Act, which allowed for the renegotiation of royalty contracts and the establishment of joint ventures between mining companies and tribes, created a technical training program for tribes, and established a revolving fund to improve reservation infrastructure. However, CERT itself was accused of serious conflicts of interest, and the exemption from certain environmental laws granted to tribes under the 1982 acts only served to further alienate the organization from traditional leaders (see McDONALD, PETER).

The 1982 acts were the highwater mark in Indian efforts to gain control of their mineral resources. The subsequent collapse of energy prices, along with the 1980s budget cuts led by Indian commissioners KENNETH L. SMITH and ROSS O. SWIMMER, brought deep financial hardships to those tribes that had become dependent on mining income and erased any gains they may have made during the preceding decade.

Under the Clinton administration, the AMERICAN INDIAN RELIGIOUS FREEDOM ACT of 1978 was strengthened to allow the secretary of the interior to deny mining permits on federal lands in order to protect Native religious, cultural, or historic sites. The Interior Department was also given the authority to prevent mining for environmental reasons as well, and the legislation made mining companies, including parent firms and affiliates, liable in case of a mining disaster. Under these new regulations, Secretary of the Interior Bruce Babbitt stopped the planned Imperial Project gold mine in Imperial County, California, which had been opposed by the local Quechan Indians. Babbit also closed the White Vulcan pumice mine on the San Francisco Peaks, which are sacred to many Arizona tribes. However, these regulations were quickly overturned by Babbitt's successor under President George W. Bush, Gale Norton, and many rejected mine projects, such as the Imperial Project, were revived.

Mining has left great environmental damage on many Indian lands and serious health problems for their peoples. For example, the largest Superfund (federally designated hazardous waste) site in the United States is on the land of the Quapaw in Oklahoma, 72 million tons of toxic mining waste. See BIG MOUNTAIN; BRESETTE, WALT; BUTLER, NILAK; LaDUKE, WINONA; nuclear industry, AMERICAN INDIANS AND; oil, AMERICAN INDIANS AND.

Further Reading

Colomeda, Lorelei Anne Lambert. *Keepers of the Central Fire: Issues in Ecology for Indigenous Peoples.* Sudbury, Mass.: Jones and Bartlett Publishers, 1999.

Fixico, Donald. *The Invasion of Indian Country in the Twentieth Century: American Capitalism and Tribal Natural Resources.* Niwot: University Press of Colorado, 1998.

Gedicks, Al. *The New Resource Wars: Native and Environmental Struggles against Multinational Corporations.* Boston: South End Press, 1993.

Grinde, Donald A., and Bruce Johansen. *Ecocide of Native America: Environmental Destruction of Indian Lands and Peoples.* Santa Fe, N.Mex.: Clear Light, 1995.

Jorgensen, Joseph G., ed. *Native Americans and Energy Department.* Cambridge, Mass.: Anthropology Resource Center, 1978.

———. *Native Americans and Energy Development II.* Cambridge, Mass.: Anthropology Resource Center, 1984.

———. "Energy Developments in the Arid West: Consequences for Native Americans." In *Paradoxes of Western Energy Development: How Can We Maintain the Land and the People If We Develop?* edited by Cyrus M. Mckell, 297–322. Boulder, Colo.: Westview Press for the American Association for the Advancement of Science, 1984.

Leubben, Thomas E. "Mining Agreements with Indian Tribes." *American Indian Journal* 2, no. 5 (1976): 2–8.

Minoka-Hill, Lillie Rosa (Rosa Minoka) (1875–1952)
Mohawk physician

The second American Indian woman ever to become a physician, Rosa Minoka was born August 30, 1875, on the St. Regis (Akwesasne) Reservation in northern New York State, the daughter of a Mohawk woman who died a short time after she was born. She was adopted by a Quaker physician from Philadelphia, Joshua Allen, who wanted to give her a good education. After graduating with a diploma from the Grahame Institute in Philadelphia in 1895, Rosa attended the Woman's Medical College of Philadelphia, where she received an M.D. in 1899. She did her internship at Women's Hospital, Philadelphia, in 1900. Omaha physician SUSAN LA FLESCHE had done her medical training at the same two institutions a decade earlier.

Minoka set up a private practice in Philadelphia in 1900. In 1905, she married Charles Abram Hill, a Wisconsin Oneida, and moved with him to Oneida, Wisconsin. Though she gave up formal practice at that time, she continued to provide medical care to neighbors and relatives while raising her six children. When her husband died in 1916, she went back to full-time medical practice, setting up a clinic in her home. After 1917, she was the only doctor at Oneida. Her patients, who were nearly all poor, usually paid her in kind (with goods rather than money).

In 1934, Minoka-Hill took the Wisconsin medical license examination, upon which she received some federal support for her medical work. After suffering a heart attack in 1946, she retired from active practice but continued her home clinic, treating both Oneida and non-Oneida patients. She was also active in public health, educating people about nutrition, sanitation, and general preventive medicine.

Minoka-Hill won local and national recognition for her work in the community and was adopted by the Oneida tribe. She received the Indian Council Fire Award in 1947 and was the first woman ever to be made an honorary life member of the Wisconsin State Medical Society (1949).

Rosa Minoka-Hill died on March 18, 1952, in Oneida, Wisconsin. After her death, grateful patients erected a monument to her memory outside Oneida. The comedian CHARLIE HILL and the educator NORBERT S. HILL, JR., are her grandsons.

Further Reading

Hill, Roberta Jean. "Dr. Lillie Rosa Minoka–Hill: Mohawk Woman Physician." Ph.D. dissertation, University of Minnesota, 1998.

Ogilvie, Marilyn Bailey, and Joy Dorothy Harvey. *The Biographical Dictionary of Women in Science: Pioneering Lives from Ancient Times to the mid-20th Century.* New York: Taylor & Francis, 2000.

Mofsie, Louis (Cloud Standing Straight in the Sky, Green Rainbow) (1936–   ) *Hopi-Winnebago educator, performer, founder of several important New York City Indian institutions*

A Hopi-Winnebago born on May 3, 1936, in Brooklyn, New York, Louis Mofsie was the son of Morris Mofsie, a Hopi from Arizona, and Alvina Lowry Mofsie, a Winnebago from Nebraska. His Hopi name is Cloud Standing Straight in the Sky, and his Winnebago name is Green Rainbow. He attended the State University of New York at Buffalo, receiving a B.S. in 1958. He then enrolled at the Pratt Institute before earning his master's degree at Hofstra University. Mofsie attended the landmark AMERICAN INDIAN CHICAGO CONFERENCE in 1961 on behalf of the growing New York City urban Indian community. That same year, he founded the Thunderbird American Indian Dancers, a performing troupe that raised money for scholarships for Indian students. The oldest continuously functioning organization of its kind, the Thunderbird Dancers have been highly influential in Indian dance, and their alumni include the renowned choreographer HANAY GEIOGAMAH.

Mofsie's mother, Alvina Mofsie, was a prominent member of the United Association of the American Indian, one of the first urban pan-Indian organizations in the United States. Begun in New York City in 1934 by Jules Haywood (One Arrow), a Cherokee, the organization grew to include affiliated councils, or longhouses as they were known, on Long Island and in northern New Jersey. During the 1950s, the organization became known as the United Association for the Advancement of the American Indian. Along with Poosepatuck Howard Treadwell, Sr., Shinnecock Henry Best, Nipmuc Zara Ciscoebrough, and Mohawks Earl and John Two Bears, the association sponsored events such as an annual American Indian Day celebration in Inwood Park, Manhattan. Based on Pacific Street in Brooklyn, the organization became a prominent voice for urban Indian concerns, and its events were attended by politicians such as New York City mayor Robert Wagner. The organization raised money for various Indian causes, including helping Iroquois who had to relocate after the building of the St. Lawrence Seaway. The organization gradually died away in the 1960s.

In 1969, Louis Mofsie helped to found the American Indian Community House (AICH), one of the largest and most successful Indian urban centers in the United States. A service organization that provides job training and substance-abuse programs for Indians, the AICH is nationally known for its support of Indian artists, musicians, as well as its commitment to Indian rights.

Mofsie, a retired instructor of art in New York City public schools, has illustrated books for authors such as DEE BROWN, as well as illustrating Mary Elting's *The Hopi Way* (1970).

See also URBANIZATION, AMERICAN INDIANS AND; RICHMOND, ROSEMARY.

Further Reading

Adams, Jim. "Thunderbird Dance Troupe: Keeping Native Hearts Beating in Downtown Manhattan." *Indian Country Today*, 25 February 2004.

Mohawk, John C. (Sotsitsowah) (1945–2006) *Seneca journalist, author, philosopher*

John Mohawk, whose Seneca name is Sotsitsowah, was born on August 30, 1945, in Buffalo, New York, and raised on a farm near the traditional stronghold of Newtown on the Cattaraugus Seneca Reservation. His parents, Ernest and Elsie Mohawk, were important members of the Newtown Longhouse, one of the original longhouses of the Code of Handsome Lake (also known as the *gaiwiio*—the teaching of the Seneca prophet Handsome Lake [1735–1815]). Mohawk, a member of the Turtle Clan, grew up steeped in the ancient Iroquois religion.

Mohawk received a B.A. from Hartwick College in Oneonta, New York, in 1968. In 1971, he edited the book *The Red Buffalo*, part of a series published by the American Studies Program of the State University of New York (SUNY) at Buffalo, where he had begun to work on his Ph.D. In 1974, he was the keynote speaker at the First International Indian Treaty Conference, held on the Standing Rock Sioux Reservation in South Dakota and attended by representatives and members of more than 97 tribes. Sponsored in part by the AMERICAN INDIAN MOVEMENT (AIM), this conference gave rise to the INTERNATIONAL INDIAN TREATY COUNCIL. By this time, Mohawk was beginning to be known as one of the most articulate exponents of the Iroquois concept of sovereignty (see SOVEREIGNTY, INDIGENOUS AND TRIBAL) and a leading critic of Western thought from an Indian perspective. He was not a member of AIM and indeed would criticize the movement for its lack of coherent political understanding; yet his speech, "The Sovereignty Which Is Sought Can Be Real," deeply influenced AIM leaders such as JOHN TRUDELL. In that speech, Mohawk argued that real power, even political power, ultimately comes from the earth's ability to create life, a power that can be understood and harnessed in traditional Indian ways. His conclusion, that in order for Indians to be sovereign "we have to have our self-sufficiency and our spirituality," would help begin to lead the movement away from its 1960s-based radicalism toward a more traditional, community-based activism.

In 1976, Mohawk gave up his graduate studies when he was invited by the Mohawk chief's council at the Akwesasne

Reservation (St. Regis) to take over the editorship of the troubled national Indian magazine, *Akwesasne Notes* (see JOURNALISM). Under Mohawk, *Akwesasne Notes*, though still the most important source of news on Indian events, dedicated itself to the task, in his words, "of confronting the Indian movement with some serious thinking about the unique world view that emerges from ancient Indian community traditions." With associate editor JOSÉ BARREIRO, Mohawk sought to promote constructive means of enhancing the future of Indian communities at a time when AIM and its pan-Indianist perspective was disintegrating as a national force. In a series of articles in *Akwesasne Notes*—"The Future Is the Family" (1977), "Regaining Control of Our Lives: The Promise of Appropriate Technology" (1978), and "Technology Is the Enemy" (1979)—Mohawk outlined both his critique of Western economies and his understanding of Native economic thought, or INDIGENOUS ECONOMICS, a perspective that would influence such writers and activists as Cayuga DANIEL BOMBERRY and his wife Victoria Bomberry, Cherokee community organizers WILMA MANKILLER and Rebecca Adamson, and would give rise to organizations that put these economic theories into practice, notably the Seventh Generation Fund and the First Nations Financial Development Institute.

In "Native People and the Right to Survive" (*Akwesasne Notes*, 1979), Mohawk criticized Western thought for viewing "living things and the things that support life (water, etc.) as objects to be transformed and consumed." He contrasted that with Native spiritualism, which "carries with it an understanding that all forms of life are sacred and require a great deal of human support, and that in the absence of that support, all life will suffer, including human life." For Mohawk, an economic system that destroyed natural resources without replenishing them was ultimately self-defeating. The alternative was to work with nature to maximize its wealth for the benefit of humanity.

Under Mohawk and Barreiro, *Akwesasne Notes* also became a means to funnel aid and assistance to Indians throughout the hemisphere, and they set up an emergency response network to help bring political pressure to aid Indians in such politically repressed countries as Guatemala and Nicaragua. An important political advisor for the Iroquois Confederacy, Mohawk served as a negotiator for the Mohawk Council of Chiefs during the two-year SIEGE OF AKWESASNE, which began in 1979.

Mohawk worked with the Grand Council of Chiefs of the Iroquois Confederacy to produce *A Basic Call to Consciousness*, a message presented by an Iroquois delegation to the United Nations in Geneva, Switzerland, in 1977. An important and unique summary of the Iroquois world view, *A Basic Call to Consciousness* was published as a book in 1978. In November 1980, Mohawk addressed the Fourth Russell Tribunal, held in Geneva, which documented the struggles of indigenous people from across the world.

Mohawk stepped down as editor of *Akwesasne Notes* in 1983 to take a teaching position at SUNY-Buffalo and to complete work on his Ph.D. Along with Onondaga chief OREN

LYONS, JR., Barreiro, and Tuscarora artist and writer Rick Hill, Mohawk established *Daybreak Magazine* in 1987. An eclectic collection of articles centered around the protection of the environment and indigenous cultures, *Daybreak* was published by Mohawk from Buffalo with the help of his wife, Yvonne.

In *Exiled in the Land of the Free* (coedited with Oren Lyons, 1992), Mohawk wrote that the history of contact between Indians and Europeans had been "powerfully influenced by the ideas and attitudes the West has constructed to explain who the Indian was/is in relation to the Europeans." Consequently, "This history informs us more about European attitudes and ideas than it does about the reality of the Indian." Dismissing the notion of a "one-way street" where Europeans migrated to the Americas and then "forged the foundations of the modern world" with "no influence or contributions from non-Western cultures," Mohawk argued, to the contrary, that Indians exerted an important influence on the creation and evolution of American democracy.

Mohawk was a popular keynote speaker at Indian conferences and events, and his influence among Indians was due in large part to his numerous lectures and speeches. A traditional singer active in his community's cultural and religious life, Mohawk was one of a small group of Indian thinkers fully versed in both Western and traditional Indian thought and able to translate the essentials of the latter to a non-Indian audience without distortion. Far from the anger and bitterness that characterized the Indian thinkers of the early years of the RED POWER MOVEMENT, he offered a positive vision for the world, based in part on the Iroquois concept of the "clear mind." For Mohawk, Western and Indian worlds did not necessarily have to clash but, rather, should learn from each other. According to Mohawk, if people would only reject the intolerance that is at the heart of most modern Western ideologies and "trust themselves to do their own thinking," they could instead "take all of the experience, information, and knowledge of the whole of the family of mankind and start plotting a better future."

Mohawk was not a primitivist, and as he wrote in "Looking for Columbus" (*Native Nations*, February 1991), new technologies offered the hope of communicating with virtually all the people of the world, no matter how isolated, giving us "a wonderful opportunity to amalgamate and pull things together and to make the world our library." Mohawk's critique of Western thought received its fullest exposition in his book *Utopian Legacies: A History of Conquest and Oppression in the Western World*, published in 1999.

John C. Mohawk died on December 10, 2006, in Buffalo, New York.

Further Reading

Jackson, Bruce. "Saying 'Oh!': John Mohawk, 1944–2006." *Artvoice* 5, no. 51 (21 December 2006). Available online. URL: http://artvoice.com/issues/v5n51/saying_oh. Accessed 3 October 2009.

Lyons, Oren, and Mohawk, John, eds. *Exiled in the Land of the Free*. Santa Fe, N.Mex.: Clear Light Press, 1991.

Mohawk, John. *A Basic Call to Consciousness.* Rooseveltown, N.Y.: Akwesasne Notes, 1978.

———. "The Indian Way Is a Thinking Tradition." In *Indian Roots of American Democracy,* edited by José Barreiro. Ithaca, N.Y.: Northeast Indian Quarterly, 1992.

———. *Utopian Legacies: A History of Conquest and Oppression in the Western World.* Santa Fé, N.Mex.: Clear Light Press, 1999.

Momaday, N. Scott (Navarre Scott Momaday, Tsoai-talee, "Rock Tree Boy") (1934–) *Kiowa author, poet, philosopher, Pulitzer Prize winner*

Navarre Scott Momaday was born on February 27, 1934, in Lawton, Oklahoma. His father, Alfred Momaday, was Kiowa, and his mother, Mayme Natchee Scott Momaday, was part Cherokee. While still a baby, Momaday was given the name Tsoai-talee (Rock Tree Boy) by a Kiowa elder after Devil's Tower (Rock Tree, or *Tsoai* in Kiowa), the prominent Wyoming landmark that lay on the Kiowa's ancestral migration route. Momaday's parents would take him to Devil's Tower as a child so that he could make contact with his ancient traditions, and that experience would be among the most important of his formative influences.

Both of Momaday's parents were teachers, and in 1936 they moved to the Navajo reservation, where the stark redrock landscape would make a lasting impression on the child. In 1946, Alfred Momaday became the principal and art teacher, and Mayme became the grammar teacher for the Jemez Pueblo Day School in New Mexico. Young Momaday later wrote that he could not imagine a more beautiful or exotic place than Jemez Pueblo, surrounded by steep canyons and volcanic outcroppings and vibrant with tradition and ceremonial dance. He attended high school in Santa Fe and then the Augusta Military Academy in Virginia. Returning to the Southwest, Momaday graduated with a B.A. in political science from the University of New Mexico. He then taught school at the Jicarilla Apache Reservation for one year, adding another important experience to his unique background.

Momaday studied under the poet Yvor Winters at Stanford University, receiving his first award, the Academy of American Poets prize, for his poem "The Bear" in 1962. He earned his doctorate in English in 1963 and began to teach at the University of California at Santa Barbara. In 1965, his dissertation on a reclusive New England naturalist, *The Complete Poems of Goddard Tuckerman,* was published, and the following year he studied at Harvard University under a Guggenheim Fellowship.

Momaday returned to Santa Barbara in 1967, publishing a selection of Kiowa folktales, *The Journey of Tai-me,* before releasing his first novel, *House Made of Dawn,* in 1968. The novel, a cryptic story of a young, estranged Jemez Pueblo man who must suffer the consequences, both legal and spiritual, when he kills another Pueblo man whom he had mistaken for a magical being, won instant acclaim and the Pulitzer Prize in 1969. Momaday incorporated Native storytelling techniques and mythical characters; used a circular, nonlinear narrative and multiple storytelling voices for the novel; and focused on the question of Indian identity and its meaning in the modern world. All of this would profoundly influence other Native writers, such as LOUISE ERDRICH and LINDA HOGAN.

In 1969, Momaday released *The Way to Rainy Mountain,* which featured pen-and-ink illustrations by his father. A combination of oral history, poetry, and autobiography, it relates the story of the Kiowa people from ancient times, beginning near Yellowstone, Montana, and journeying over 200 years until reaching Rainy Mountain, Oklahoma, finally ending with the extermination of the buffalo—the focus of Kiowa spirituality—by white hunters in modern times. *The Way to Rainy Mountain,* Momaday's most popular book, examined a second great theme that runs throughout his works, the human relationship to the natural world, especially the relationship to animals, articulating his philosophy on the environment.

In 1969, Momaday was initiated into the Gourd Dance Society, the ancient fraternal organization of the Kiowa.

Momaday moved to the University of California, Berkeley, in 1969, where he worked as a professor in the English department until 1973, then moved to the University of Arizona. He continued his philosophical explorations with the 1970 essay "A Man Made of Words," examining the place of language in the sphere of existence, and in 1973 he collaborated with photographer David Muench to produce *Colorado: Summer, Fall, Winter, Spring.* The next year, he released his first chapbook of poetry, *Angle of Geese,* and in 1976 he released his second, *The Gourd Dancer.* His essay "A First American Views the Land," written for the bicentennial issue of *National Geographic* in 1976, expanded on his views in *The Way to Rainy Mountain,* arguing that Native Americans, at home with nature, care for the environment as an inherent part of their culture. (See ENVIRONMENTAL MOVEMENT, AMERICAN INDIANS AND THE.) Also in 1976, Momaday published *The Names: A Memoir,* which personalized his history of Kiowa people in an extended prose narrative of his personal genealogy.

It was not until 1989 that Momaday wrote his second true novel, *The Ancient Child,* which expanded on the themes present in *House Made of Dawn.* In 1997, *Conversations with N. Scott Momaday* was published. The author also released a collection of essays and stories, *The Man Made of Words,* that same year.

An accomplished painter as well as writer, Momaday has illustrated a number of his own books, including *In the Presence of the Sun* (1993), a collection of poems and short stories, and *Circle of Wonder: A Native American Christmas Story* (1993). In 1999, he released *In the Bear's House,* a mixed-media collage of paintings, dialogue, poems, and prose on the subject of the bear, an animal of spiritual significance to American Indians. In 2007, he was awarded the National Medal of the Arts by President George W. Bush. He currently heads the Rainy Mountain Foundation, a nonprofit organization that works to preserve Native cultures. Momaday's deeply philosophical and autobiographical writings have become the focus of intense study and numerous books, and his works continue to influence a new generation of Native American writers, poets, and activists.

Further Reading

Cutter, Martha J. *Lost and Found in Translation: Contemporary Ethnic American Writing and the Politics of Language Diversity.* Chapel Hill: University of North Carolina Press, 2005.

Isernhagen, Hartwig. *Momaday, Vizenor, Armstrong: Conversations with Native American Writers.* Norman: University of Oklahoma Press, 1999.

Maitino John R., ed. *Teaching American Ethnic Literatures: Nineteen Essays.* Albuquerque: University of New Mexico Press, 1996.

Nelson, Robert M. *Place and Vision: The Function of Landscape in Native American Fiction.* New York: Peter Lang, 1995.

Roemer Kenneth M., ed. *Approaches to Teaching Momaday's The Way to Rainy Mountain.* New York: MLA, 1988.

Scarberry-Garcia, Susan. *Landmarks of Healing: A Study of* House Made of Dawn. Albuquerque: University of New Mexico Press, 1990.

Schubnell, Matthias. *N. Scott Momaday: The Cultural and Literary Background.* Norman: University of Oklahoma Press, 1986.

Singh Amritjit, ed. *Memory and Cultural Politics: New Approaches to American Ethnic Literatures.* Boston: Northeastern University Press, 1996.

Velie, Alan R. *Four American Indian Literary Masters: N. Scott Momaday, James Welch, Leslie Marmon Silko, and Gerald Vizenor.* Norman: University of Oklahoma Press, 1982.

Vizenor, Gerald, ed. *Narrative Chance: Postmodern Discourse on Native American Indian Literatures.* Albuquerque: University of New Mexico Press, 1989.

Montezuma, Carlos (Wassaja) (ca. 1867–1923)
Yavapai physician, author, political activist

A Yavapai born in the Superstition Mountains in central Arizona in either 1866 or 1867, Carlos Montezuma was given the name Wassaja by his father, Cocuyevah, and his mother, Thilgeyah. In 1871, Wassaja was captured by some Pima (Akimel O'odham), and while searching for him, his mother was killed by an Indian scout. Wassaja briefly lived with the Pima along the Gila River before being taken to Adamsville, Arizona, where he was sold to a photographer and part-time prospector named Carlo Gentile for $30. Gentile renamed the boy Carlos Montezuma and took him east, moving first to Chicago and finally settling in New York City. Montezuma attended public schools in Chicago and New York. Gentile eventually committed suicide after a fire destroyed his business, and young Montezuma was cared for by a family named Baldwin until Baptist missionary George W. Ingalls placed him with William H. Steadman, a minister in Urbana, Illinois.

Montezuma was a brilliant child, and after only two years of private tutoring by Steadman, he enrolled in a college preparatory program for the University of Illinois. Majoring in chemistry, he graduated with a bachelor of science degree in 1884 at 18, after which he worked part time in a pharmacy to help support his studies at the Chicago Medical College.

Upon earning an M.D. from Chicago in 1889, Montezuma opened a private practice, but he left it to accept an appointment as a physician and surgeon at the Fort Stevenson Indian school in North Dakota. He embarked on his new duties with great zeal but became disillusioned by the desperate conditions of his Indian patients and the incompetence of the government's supervision of the reservation. The next year, he was transferred to the Western Shoshone Agency in Nevada, and three years later he moved to the Colville Agency in Washington State. Tired of working out west, he transferred in 1894 to the Carlisle Indian School in Pennsylvania, where he met GERTRUDE BONNIN and RICHARD HENRY PRATT. Montezuma became a close friend of Pratt as well as a staunch advocate of his ultra-assimilationist creed (see ASSIMILATION).

In 1896, Montezuma returned to Chicago, opening a successful private practice with a specialty in intestinal diseases and eventually being appointed professor of the College of Physicians and Surgeons there. Becoming active in Indian affairs, he called for the immediate abolition of the Office of Indian Affairs (later the BUREAU OF INDIAN AFFAIRS), the dissolution of the reservation system, and CITIZENSHIP for all Indians.

In 1901, he reached out to his friend at Carlisle, Gertrude Bonnin, and they became engaged for a short time before she broke it off. Despite some bitterness on his part, they would maintain their friendship. Although their differing views on assimilation would never be reconciled, as she favored the preservation of Native culture whereas Montezuma sought to extinguish it, Bonnin did inspire Montezuma to seek out his Yavapai roots. That same year, he went to Arizona and tracked down some of his distant relatives. In 1903, Montezuma helped to create the Fort McDowell Yavapai Reservation.

In 1911, Montezuma joined with other leading Indians of the day to form the SOCIETY OF AMERICAN INDIANS, the first pan-Indian organization in the United States. However, his radical prescription for the failures of the Indian Office led to disagreements with other members, who favored a more gradual process of assimilation and the reform of the Indian Office rather than its immediate abolishment. By 1915, his hard line had alienated him from moderates such as Bonnin and CHARLES ALEXANDER EASTMAN, and by 1919 they had left the group and allowed control to pass to Montezuma and PHILIP B. GORDON. Weakened, the society would last only a few more years.

In 1914, Montezuma published *Let My People Go*, the best-known of his three books. In April 1916, he also founded the Indian magazine *Wassaja*, which in Yavapai means "to signal," to promulgate his assimilationist views. Montezuma was popular in Congress and among policy makers, who were anxious to solve the "Indian problem" once and for all. Both Theodore Roosevelt and Woodrow Wilson considered him for the position of commissioner of Indian affairs, but he was too idealistic to want to direct an agency he sought to abolish.

Montezuma was married twice, both times to white women. Near the end of his life, he moderated his hard-line stance and eventually became a strong advocate for Yavapai rights. He deserves a great deal of credit for protecting the reservation from non-Indian encroachment and the usurpation of its water. In 1922, suffering from diabetes and seriously ill from tuberculosis, Montezuma returned to Fort McDowell to live out his remaining months. He died there on January 31, 1923.

Further Reading

Iverson, Peter. *Carlos Montezuma and the Changing World of American Indians*. Albuquerque: University of New Mexico Press, 1982.
Speroff, Leon. *Carlos Montezuma, M.D.: A Yavapai American Hero—The Life and Times of an American Indian, 1866–1923*. Portland, Oreg.: Arnica Publishing, 2003.

Montgomery, Jack Cleveland (1917–2002) *Cherokee*
Medal of Honor winner

A Cherokee, Jack Cleveland Montgomery was born in Long, Oklahoma, on July 23, 1917. He attended the Chilocco Indian School and Bacone College in Muskogee before earning his B.A. in physical education from the University of Redlands, California.

A member of the Oklahoma National Guard, Sergeant Montgomery was activated during WORLD WAR II and assigned to the U.S. Army's 45th Infantry Division, the same division to which Medal of Honor winners ERNEST CHILDERS and VAN T. BARFOOT belonged. Montgomery saw his first action in Sicily as a platoon sergeant and received a battlefield commission as a second lieutenant shortly before participating in the invasion of Salerno in southern Italy in September, 1943. After the landings he was promoted to first lieutenant. In January 22, 1944, he participated in the daring Allied assault of Anzio, near Rome.

During the Battle of Anzio, one of the deadliest of the war, the Allies sustained more than 72,000 casualties, nearly five times the number suffered at Normandy in the D-day invasion. Unlike D-day, the landing near Anzio was quickly blunted by German reinforcements, and the Allies ended up stuck near the beach and subjected to an intense pounding by the Germans. In late February, the Germans counterattacked, attempting to drive the Allies into the sea. During the desperate fighting that ensued, Montgomery's platoon advanced about two miles inland, to the small town of Padiglione.

Two hours before daybreak, on February 22, 1944, the platoon encountered German troops armed with heavy machine guns occupying strong defensive positions. Montgomery singlehandedly attacked a German machine-gun emplacement, killing eight soldiers and capturing four more. He then advanced on a house that was full of German soldiers, capturing seven, killing three more, and silencing two machine-gun nests guarding the house. Next, he attacked the house by himself, capturing an additional 21 German soldiers. That night, the Germans counterattacked, and Montgomery was struck by shrapnel from a mortar shell and seriously wounded. He received the Medal of Honor on January 15, 1945, from President Franklin D. Roosevelt at the White House.

One of the most decorated soldiers in World War II, Montgomery also won the Silver Star, Bronze Star, and the Purple Heart with Oakleaf Clusters. He returned to active duty during the Korean War. Later, he worked for the Veterans Administration. Jack Montgomery died in Muskogee, Oklahoma, on June 11, 2002. The Veterans Health Administration medical center in Muskogee, Oklahoma is named in his honor.

Further Reading

Martin, Douglas. "Jack Montgomery, 84, and Gino Merli, 78, Two Medal of Honor Winners, Are Dead." *New York Times*, 17 June 2002.

Moore, Russell (Big Chief Moore) (1912–1983) *Akimel O'odham (Pima) jazz trombonist, vocalist*

An Akimel O'odham (Pima), Russell Moore was born at Komatke on the Gila River Reservation near Sacaton, Arizona on August 13, 1912. His parents, J. Newton and Elizabeth Moore, were both from Gila River. Russell Moore's father died when Russell was only 11. At 12, he moved to Blue Island, Illinois, where his uncle, William T. Moore, taught him trumpet, piano, euphonium, trombone, drums, sousaphone, and French horn. He was especially drawn toward the trombone after hearing Pawnee-Otoe JOSEPH SHUNATONA playing with Lillian Scott's orchestra.

After doing some work on the railroads, Moore attended high school at the Sherman Institute in California. At graduation, he determined to go into music, especially jazz. Beginning his career with Tony Corral's Band in Tucson, he moved to southern California, playing first with local bands at the Hollywood Casino and Million Dollar Theatre, then with the band at Sebastian's Cotton Club in Hollywood. In 1935, he was in one of Lionel Hampton's first bands, and he did a brief stint with Eddie Barefield's Big Band in summer 1936. After gigging in California, Moore toured the West Coast with Noble Sissle's orchestra in 1938. The following year, he did a long tour with Eli Rice. When it ended abruptly in Monroe, Louisiana, Moore went on to New Orleans. In 1939–40, he worked there with Dixieland great Oscar "Papa" Celestine and got to play with many of the older generation of jazzmen. It was a revelation. In his own words, he "played from sundown to sunrise, and listened to jazz" as he "had never heard it played before."

After brief stints with Harlan Leonard and Ernie Fields, Moore rejoined Noble Sissle (1939–41). Then Louis Armstrong heard about him and sent for him to play in his band at the Club Zanzibar in New York. Moore toured coast to coast with Armstrong's Big Band from 1944 to summer 1947 as first trombonist, with featured solo spots. When the band broke up, he stayed in New York, working occasionally with Sidney Bechet (1947–49, 1951).

Russell "Big Chief" Moore, right, performs with jazz great Charlie Parker on the opening day of the International Jazz Festival in Paris on May 8, 1949. *(AP/Wideworld)*

Moore was honored with an invitation to play, along with jazz greats from several countries of the world, at the Paris Jazz Festival in May 1949. After that, he led his own band for a while, working occasionally with such greats as Eddie Condon, Buck Clayton, Red Allen, Hot Lips Page, Wild Bill Davison, and Tony Parenti. In late 1952, he was with Pee Wee Russell and Ruby Braff, and he toured Europe with Mezz Mezzrow beginning in February 1953. In Paris, Moore organized a band of French musicians and toured with them through North Africa, Italy, Switzerland and Belgium, afterward doing night-club engagements in Paris. He recorded there as well as in the United States. In 1954, he played with Jimmy McPartland, and in the late 1950s he worked with Lester Lanin's Society Orchestra, playing "for all social events of the wealthy families in and about New York."

Moore was honored by the Pima Tribal Council in 1957. In 1959, he went to South Dakota and Arizona on a good-will trip for the NATIONAL CONGRESS OF AMERICAN INDIANS (NCAI). For part of the 1960s, he did guest dates in Canada. His reputation as a jazzman was further enhanced when Louis Armstrong chose him to play with his All Stars (January 1964–spring 1965). After a spell in the hospital in late 1965, Moore resumed leading his own bands, recording occasionally into the 1970s. Despite ill health, he kept working in 1981 and 1982, which included a tour of Europe with Keith Smith.

Russell Moore died at Nyack, New York, on December 15, 1983. He was married to Ida Powlas, an Oneida, of Oneida, Wisconsin.

Moore's discography remains to be compiled, but among his solo albums are *His Way*, with Sidney Bechet, recorded at the Storyville Club, Boston, in 1951 but not released until 1977; *Russell "Big Chief" Moore* (1953–74); and *Russell "Big Chief" Moore's Pow Wow Jazz Band* (1973), featuring his celebrated trombone solo on "Wabash Blues," "Big Chief Stomp," and "Chant for Wounded Knee." The Russell Moore Music Fest is held annually on the Gila River Indian Reservation at Sacaton, Arizona.

Moorehead, Warren King (1866–1939) *archaeologist, explorer, Indian rights advocate*

Warren King Moorehead was born in Siena, Italy, on March 10, 1866, the son of William Galoughly and Helen (King) Moorehead. He received an M.A. from Denison University and honorary degrees from Dartmouth and Oglethorpe.

Though an archaeologist by profession, Moorehead was also intensely interested in contemporary Indian problems. In 1890, he published a novel *Wanneta, the Sioux*, which led to a commission by a national magazine to write about the Ghost Dance, a religious revival movement underway at that time among the Plains Indians. In the days leading up to the Wounded Knee massacre (December 1890), he was one of the few non-Indians who, on several occasions, talked directly with the Indians camped there. He found them absolutely peaceful.

In 1901, Phillips Academy, in Andover, New Hampshire, named Moorehead curator of their newly established department of archaeology. In 1907, he was made director of the department, a position which he held until his retirement in 1938.

Moorehead strongly supported traditional Native American culture. At a time when ASSIMILATION was the national policy, he opposed forced ALLOTMENT and supported Native dances and ceremonies. He also defended the religious use of peyote where it was prevalent. A strong supporter of traditional arts and crafts, Moorehead was a member of the executive committee of the INDIAN INDUSTRIES LEAGUE (IIL) from 1907 to 1915. In that capacity, he advocated a national marketing strategy in which a federal Bureau of Indian Arts and Industries, with himself at the head, would form partnerships with department stores in major eastern cities. A direct marketing effort, which he launched in 1907, though well conceived, was undercut by the financial panic of that year.

In 1908, Moorehead began to lobby for a position on the Board of Indian Commissioners. Supported by the IIL, he was appointed by President Theodore Roosevelt in 1909; he remained on the board until its dissolution in 1933. As a commissioner, Moorehead investigated conditions at the White Earth Chippewa Reservation in 1909 (see BEAULIEU, GUS H.; BEAULIEU, THEODORE H.) and was instrumental in removing several non-Indians who had fraudulently gained control of large parcels of Indian land. Information supplied by Moorehead resulted in their prosecution by the Justice Department.

Moorehead was particularly interested in developing a crafts industry among the Navajo (Dineh). Unable to get financial support from the IIL, he corresponded with Indian Commissioner ROBERT GROSVENOR VALENTINE in 1910, and prepared a report for him on the feasibility of developing Native American arts and crafts through a Bureau of Arts and Industries. This bureau would encourage older people skilled in beadworking and the making of baskets, blankets, and moccasins, to work "in their own way, with absolutely no supervision upon our part." (The idea of complete creative control by Native artists had been advocated by Candace Wheeler, a leading figure in the Arts and Crafts movement, as early as 1901.)

Over the next 25 years, Moorehead wrote reports on reservation conditions in many parts of the country, most of which were not published. He was an early supporter of the SOCIETY OF AMERICAN INDIANS (1911) and a member of the INDIAN RIGHTS ASSOCIATION.

In addition to his many papers on Indian archaeology, Moorehead published pamphlets and articles on contemporary Indian affairs, such as *The Lesson of White Earth*, his address at the 30th Annual Lake Mohonk Conference of the Friends of the Indians, (1912); *Our National Problem: The Sad Condition of the Oklahoma Indians* (1913), a report on the Five Civilized Tribes (Cherokee, Chickasaw, Choctaw, Creek, and Seminole); "Indians in War Service" (1919); and "Congress and the Indian" (1929), the latter two in the *Phillips Academy Bulletin*. His major work was *The American Indian in the United States, Period 1850–1914*, published in 1914.

In 1928, Moorehead prepared an analysis of the 870-page MERIAM REPORT, available from him only as a 22-page mimeographed typescript. Although he agreed with most of the report's conclusions, he noted a number of important issues that had been omitted, and he regretted that more recognition had not been given to the efforts of those who had worked so hard over the past several decades to improve conditions.

Warren King Moorehead died in Andover, New Hampshire, on January 5, 1939.

Further Reading

Byers, Douglas S. "Warren King Moorehead." *American Anthropologist* 41 (1939): 286–294.
Conn, Steven. *History's Shadow: Native Americans and Historical Consciousness in the Nineteenth Century.* Chicago: University of Chicago Press, 2004.
Weatherford, John W. "Warren King Moorehead and His Papers," *Ohio Historical Quarterly* 65 (1956): 179–190.

Mopope, Stephen   *See* KIOWA FIVE.

Morgan, Jacob Casimera (1879–1950) *Navajo missionary, educator, tribal leader*

Jacob Casimera Morgan was born in Nahódeshgizh, on the Navajo (Dineh) reservation near Crownpoint, New Mexico. His father was a member of the Meadow clan and young Jacob belonged to the Salt clan. He entered the Fort Defiance school when he was five. After one year there Morgan was transferred to a school at Grand Junction, Colorado, where he learned to speak English and play the cornet. There he became a Christian. In 1898, at age 19, Morgan went to Hampton Institute in Virginia to learn carpentry. He graduated in 1900 but returned a short time later to take a business course. After two years, due to health problems, he left without finishing.

In this era, the goal of all Indian schools, federal and private, was ASSIMILATION (see PRATT, RICHARD HENRY). Morgan's commitment to assimilation was not nuanced, however—it was wholehearted. In this respect he may be compared with CARLOS MONTEZUMA, except that whereas the latter, until near the end of his life, was largely divorced from the local affairs of his Yavapai people, Morgan was always deeply involved in Navajo affairs.

In 1904, Morgan was hired by the Office of Indian Affairs (later the BUREAU OF INDIAN AFFAIRS [BIA]) as a clerk and interpreter, and for a while, he ran a trading post. From at least 1910, when he began working with Reverend L. P. Brink, on a Navajo translation of the Bible, he was a member of the Christian Reformed Church. From 1914, he taught shop classes at the Crownpoint school, and under his direction the school band became a local attraction.

In 1923, Morgan won a seat on the newly formed Navajo Tribal Council (see HAGERMAN HERBERT JAMES), where he quickly established himself as a foe of the traditional HENRY CHEE DODGE. Morgan left government service in 1925 to work with Reverend Brink at a new mission in Farmington, New Mexico, where he taught children and wrote for church publications.

As a conservative Protestant, Morgan, like the missionaries and converts who had supported the DANCE ORDERS of the 1920s, never ceased to attack Navajo medicine men and traditional ceremonies. Thus, he was horrified by JOHN COLLIER's support of traditionalism. When Collier became Indian commissioner in 1934, Morgan and others formed the AMERICAN INDIAN FEDERATION to oppose what they considered his anti-Christian and pro-Communist policies. Morgan also condemned Collier's highly unpopular livestock-reduction program, claiming that it was illegal. In this way, he gathered support, successfully blocking Navajo ratification of the INDIAN REORGANIZATION ACT.

In 1937, Morgan was bitterly disappointed not to have been named to succeed the recently deceased Brink as missionary of the Christian Reformed Church at Shiprock and Farmington. Morgan started his own mission at Shiprock, New Mexico.

When Collier ordered new council elections in September 1938, Morgan easily won the chairmanship. Though he still condemned the BIA in his inaugural speech, he soon began to cooperate with the government and for the first time began to get a perspective on the full range of Navajo problems and what the federal government was trying to do. He enjoyed being in the leadership position, worked hard, and was scrupulously honest. A milestone of Morgan's chairmanship was the beginning of tribal business development. Aside from the Navajo Tribal Fair of 1938, the first tribal enterprise to be approved—though it was not opened until July 22, 1940—was a sawmill to process timber from the Fort Defiance Plateau on the Navajo Reservation. It created 100 jobs and was an object of tribal pride. The council also built a small flour mill on the reservation at Round Rock, which began operating in the winter of 1939–40, and a cannery operation at Many Farms, also on the reservation.

Morgan was absolutely opposed to the peyote religion, which had appeared on the Navajo Reservation shortly after the 1933 and 1934 stock reductions, and he campaigned to outlaw it. On this issue, he had the support of the traditionalists as well (see NATIVE AMERICAN CHURCH). The council passed a ban, and Collier supported it as a right of self-government, but as an attack on religious freedom he would not allow E. Reesman Fryer, the reservation superintendent, to help them enforce it.

By 1940, Morgan had come to accept most of the INDIAN NEW DEAL policies, even the livestock reductions. After the United States entered WORLD WAR II in December 1941, he gave his full support to the war effort. However, his cooperation with the government had cost Morgan the support of a large number of disaffected Navajo, and when he announced his bid for reelection in 1942, he was not even nominated.

After leaving the tribal council chairmanship, Morgan went back to his mission at Shiprock. His son Buddy died in a Japanese prison camp in 1943. In September the following year, Morgan was ordained as a minister. He continued his missionary work, including translation and Bible instruction. Jacob Morgan died on May 10, 1950.

Further Reading

Bailey, Garrick, and Roberta Glenn Bailey. *A History of the Navajos: The Reservation Years.* Santa Fe, N.Mex.: SAR Press (School of American Research), 1986.

Iverson, Peter. *Diné: A History of the Navajos.* Albuquerque: University of New Mexico Press, 2002.

———. *"For Our Navajo People": Letters, Speeches, and Petitions, 1900–1960,* edited by Peter Iverson and Monty Roessel. Albuquerque: University of New Mexico Press, 2002.

Mountain Wolf Woman (Xehaciwinga, "To Make a Home on the Mountain as a Wolf Does") (1884–1960) *Winnebago (Ho-Chunk) autobiographer, spiritual seeker*

Mountain Wolf Woman, a Winnebago (Ho-Chunk), was born in April 1884 in East Fork River, Wisconsin, to Charles Blowsnake, a member of the Thunder Clan, and Lucy Goodvillage. The youngest of four sisters and three brothers, she was named Haksigaxunuminka, or Little Fifth Daughter. When still a baby, she contracted an illness and was cured by a Ho-Chunk

healer, Wolf Woman. The healer renamed the young child, Xehaciwinga, or To Make a Home on the Mountain as a Wolf Does—translated as Mountain Wolf Woman. Shortly thereafter, the family moved to Black River Falls, Wisconsin, where they engaged in a traditional lifestyle of hunting and fishing.

At age nine, Mountain Wolf Woman began attending school in nearby Tomah. Although she liked school, the family's nomadic life forced them to take her out after only two years. When she was a teenager, she attended school again for a short time at the Lutheran Mission School in Wittenberg, Wisconsin. However, an arranged marriage forced her to drop out of school, a turn of events she bitterly resented. Eventually, after her second child, she left her husband and married again, this time happily. With her second husband, Mountain Wolf Woman was introduced to the NATIVE AMERICAN CHURCH and the peyote religion, which had a profound effect on her beliefs, though she continued to practice Christianity, as well as the traditional Ho-Chunk religion, for the remainder of her life.

Mountain Wolf Woman had 11 children, three of whom died young. Although brought up in a traditional Indian lifestyle, she adapted well to modern Western society. She was one of the first Winnebago women to own a car and once took a bus to visit her daughter in Oregon. In her autobiography, she noted the differences between the two societies, and even in her later years, she still held a deep attachment to the traditional Indian values of her youth.

The autobiographies of Mountain Wolf Woman's two brothers, Jasper Blowsnake and Sam Blowsnake, were taken down and translated by anthropologist Paul Radin. Jasper Blowsnake's short account was published in 1913. Sam Blowsnake, like Mountain Wolf Woman, was an adherent of the Native American Church, and his account of his life, *The Autobiography of a Winnebago Indian* (1920), was both an important scholarly work and a popular success. In 1945, Mountain Wolf Woman met Nancy Lurie, an anthropologist studying Ho-Chunk culture, although it would be 13 years before she told Lurie her life story.

Mountain Wolf Woman, Sister of Crashing Thunder: The Autobiography of a Winnebago Woman was published in 1961 to wide acclaim. Mountain Wolf Woman was by then dead, having passed away on November 9, 1960. She was buried in a Christian cemetery, after receiving Christian, peyote, and traditional Winnebago funeral rites. Nancy Lurie went on to become a prominent activist anthropologist, helping SOL TAX organize the influential AMERICAN INDIAN CHICAGO CONFERENCE (1961) and working with the Menominee to help them win reinstatement as a tribe after their TERMINATION in 1963.

Mount Graham

Located next to the San Carlos Apache Reservation in the Coronado National Forest, Mount Graham, home to a number of rare plant and animal species including a unique variety of red squirrel, is believed by the Apache to be the home of their guardians, the Gan, or Mountain Spirit Dancers. The mountain, known in Apache as Dzil Nchaa Si An, was originally part of the San Carlos Apache Reservation but was taken by the U.S. government under an executive order in 1873.

In 1988, the federal government began construction of a large observatory on Mount Graham consisting of three telescopes. The third and largest, a $60 million binocular telescope, became the main focus of a dispute between the Apache and the U.S. government. Built by an unlikely consortium including the University of Arizona, the Max Planck Institute in Germany, and the Vatican in Rome, the project's proponents, skirting the AMERICAN INDIAN RELIGIOUS FREEDOM ACT, were able to persuade the Forest Department to allow the observatory to be located in an ecologically sensitive part of the National Forest and to have Congress exempt the project from both the Endangered Species Act and the National Environmental Policy Act. The Catholic Church, which is financing one of the telescopes and had dubbed their observatory the Columbus Project, is planning to use it in the hope of sighting life in other parts of the universe.

Apache opposition was led by elder Ola Cassadore Davis and the Apache Survival Coalition, although for the first five years there was little they could do to stop construction of the first two telescopes. In 1993, the observatory consortium attempted to move the construction site of the third telescope a quarter mile from its original location in order to get a better view, and the Forest Department cleared hundreds of trees from the area. The coalition and 18 environmental groups sued the Forest Service for illegally clearing the site, and federal courts stopped the project on the grounds that the new site was outside the area exempted from federal environmental laws.

In an attempt to circumvent the court's rulings, Representative Jim Kolbe of Arizona added an amendment to the House Interior Appropriations Bill of 1994 authorizing the project and extending the exemptions from federal environmental laws. The chair of the House Appropriations Committee, Ralph Regula, then quietly inserted the rider in the Interior Department's appropriation bill. The rider drew protests from environmental groups across the country and was vetoed by President Clinton on February 19, 1995. In 1998, Clinton vetoed a congressional appropriation of $10 million, a large portion of which was slated for the Mount Graham project. The protests against the telescope made it increasingly difficult for the University of Arizona to find partners and the additional funding needed to complete the project. More than 40 lawsuits filed by environmentalists as well as the San Carlos Apache tribe also slowed the project but could not halt it. The observatory was completed in 2005 and began operation in 2006. The coalition continues to oppose any further extensions of the project.

Further Reading

Norrell, Brenda. "Apache Reject Money and Bring Honor to Mount Graham." *Indian Country Today*, 26 May 2004.
———. "Mount Graham Sacred Run." *Indian Country Today*, 18 August 2004.
Rotstein, Arthur A. "Long-Embattled Mount Graham Telescope Dedicated." *USA Today*, 15 October 2004.

Mt. Pleasant, Jane (1950–) *Tuscarora agronomist, soil scientist*

Jane Mt. Pleasant was born in Syracuse, New York, on July 26, 1950. Her father, Carl Vincent Mt. Pleasant, a Tuscarora from the reservation near Buffalo, was a factory foreman; her mother, Ruth Dennison Mt. Pleasant, of European ancestry, was a nurse. In the 1960s, Jane enrolled in American University in Washington, D.C., as a political science major, but she dropped out after one term and moved to New York City. There she drove a taxi for eight years and fought corruption as a union shop steward.

While still driving cabs, Mt. Pleasant started taking various night courses at City College, including an introduction to geology. One day, looking through a list of occupations with her future husband, she became intrigued by the idea of studying soil science. She enrolled in the interdisciplinary American Indian Program at Cornell University, where she studied soil science along with a mix of courses related to American Indians. Although her only previous connection with indigenous agriculture was that her father loved to eat corn soup, she had a first-hand initiation into agricultural work at school. Mt. Pleasant was fascinated by the subject, going on to get a doctorate at North Carolina State University with research on farming methods in the Amazon Basin of Peru. In 1987, she and her husband moved back to Cornell, where she joined the faculty.

Mt. Pleasant's research specialty is soil and cropping-systems management, with an emphasis on sustainability based on the principles derived from indigenous agriculture. In her research on indigenous agriculture, she has worked closely with the few Iroquois farmers who still follow the ancient system and grow the old varieties, and she is making sure these are supported and are not lost. Corn and the "Three Sisters" cropping system (corn, beans, and squash), used by the Iroquois and many other Indian cultures of eastern North America, have been a particular focus of her research. She is especially interested in the old Iroquois white flour corn.

Mt. Pleasant's work has proved to be of great practical potential. Agricultural science went overboard for high-input monocropping in the 1950s and 1960s, but some of the drawbacks are now starting to become apparent. Such monocropping is expensive in terms of chemical and energy input, and it is predicted that the world phosphate supply will be exhausted in 50 years. Certainly yield is very high, but it comes at great cost to the soil and the water. Plowing without cover crops causes erosion: the soil's organic content is depleted, and heavy application of chemicals poisons the water table. Further, hybrid, genetically identical monocrops are highly vulnerable to epidemics. In 1970, southern corn leaf blight killed 15 percent of the U.S. crop. These systems do not appear to be sustainable, and new ones have to be found.

The indigenous agricultural systems have exactly the opposite characteristics. They are labor intensive, energy efficient, genetically variable, and based on polycropping (mixed plantings, like the Three Sisters). Thus these ancient, sustainable systems are becoming the key to the future of agriculture.

Particularly interested in the use of cover crops in corn-based systems, Mt. Pleasant conducts experimental research based on polyculture. She has proved that polyculture prevents erosion, adds nutrients and organic matter to the soil, controls weeds, and maintains relatively high yield. The results have been made available to the state's farmers through the New York State Agricultural Extension Service and have already given them a better way to grow cover crops.

Since 1994, Mt. Pleasant has been director of the American Indian Program and associate professor of soil, crop, and atmospheric sciences at Cornell University. In 1997, she was awarded the Ely S. Parker Award by the AMERICAN INDIAN SCIENCE AND ENGINEERING SOCIETY for her contributions to Native American peoples. In 2005, *Smithsonian Magazine* named her one of "35 People Who Made a Difference in the World."

See also INDIGENOUS ECONOMICS.

Further Reading

Eames-Sheavly, Marcia. *The Three Sisters, Exploring an Iroquois Garden*. Ithaca, N.Y.: Cornell Cooperative Extension, 1993.

Mt. Pleasant, Jane. "The Three Sisters. Care for the Land and the People." In *Science and Native American Communities: Legacies of Pain, Visions of Promise*, edited by Keith James, 126–136. Lincoln: University of Nebraska Press, 2001.

———. "Traditional Iroquois Methods Work for Today's Farmers." *Science Daily*, 16 February 2004.

Muldrow, Hal (Henry Lowndes Muldrow, Jr.)

(1905–1983) *Choctaw U.S. Army officer, war hero*

A Choctaw, Henry Lowndes Muldrow, Jr., was born on May 31, 1905, in Tishomingo, Oklahoma. One of five children, four sons and a daughter, his father, Henry Lowndes Muldrow, was a white insurance agent, and his mother, Mary Daisy Fisher, came from a prominent Choctaw family. He served in the Reserve Officer's Training Corps (ROTC) while attending the University of Oklahoma and received a B.S. in Business in 1928. Upon graduation he was commissioned in the army as a second lieutenant in field artillery. Muldrow later left the army to become an athletic coach, and in 1932 he opened an insurance agency. He married Claramae Bell, a Chickasaw.

At the outbreak of WORLD WAR II, Muldrow was reactivated as an artillery battalion commander in the 45th—or "Thunderbird"—Division. Over 20 percent of the Thunderbird Division was of Indian heritage, and it was among the most decorated divisions in the war, producing three Indian Medal of Honor winners—VAN T. BARFOOT, ERNEST CHILDERS, and JACK CLEVELAND MONTGOMERY.

In 1943, Muldrow's artillery battalion landed with the 45th Division on the strategic beach at Salerno in Sicily. The Germans, however, had laid a trap and surprised the landing party with a powerful force of tanks and infantry. They were on the verge of driving the American forces into the sea when Muldrow, ordering his artillery to stand their ground, fired point-blank into the tanks, stopping their advance. Regrouping the scattered infantry, he then directed a fierce counterattack, driving the German units back and securing the beachhead. Muldrow then braved enemy fire to set up a forward observation post and relay data back to his battalion, which could then fire accurately on enemy positions.

Muldrow participated in the landing at Anzio Beach, the battle for Rome, and the march through France and the battle of the Ardennes. He won both the Silver Star and the Bronze Star with Oak Leaf Clusters, and by the end of the war he had been promoted to colonel.

Muldrow served with the American forces occupying Japan before being promoted to brigadier general in command of the 45th Division Artillery during the Korean War. During that conflict, he won three additional Bronze Stars and received a special citation from the president of South Korea. After the war, he was given the command of the entire 45th, and he held that post longer than any previous commander. Muldrow retired from the army in 1960 with the rank of major general, sharing with CLARENCE LEONARD TINKER the honor of being the highest ranking Indian in the U.S. Army in the 20th century. Hal Muldrow died in Norman, Oklahoma, in October 1983. The Oklahoma National Guard helicopter training base in Lexington, Oklahoma, is named after him.

His younger brother, Alvin Montgomery Muldrow, also served with distinction in World War II, rising to the rank of lieutenant colonel by the end of the war.

Murie, James R. (1862–1921) *Pawnee ethnographer*

James R. Murie was the son of Anna Murie, a Pawnee full-blood of the Skiri band, and James Murie, a Scotsman who had commanded Pawnee scouts under Major Frank North. He was born in Grand Island, Nebraska, then still Pawnee territory. After his father abandoned his wife and infant son to go to California, the family took refuge with Anna's brother. Although his uncle had adopted non-Indian customs, Murie recalled at least one childhood buffalo hunt. He also attended day school at the Indian agency at Genoa. He continued his schooling at different agency schools after the family was relocated to the new Pawnee reservation in Indian Territory (Oklahoma) in 1874, where he also served as interpreter for the agent.

In October 1879, Murie was admitted to Hampton Institute in Virginia, where he worked at the school's printing office and was a successful student. Graduating in 1883, he returned home and worked first as a bookkeeper and clerk in a store, then as a teacher of English. The next year, he took a group of older students with him to Haskell Institute in Lawrence, Kansas, where he spent two years as assistant disciplinarian and drillmaster. In 1886, hoping to study for the ministry, he again traveled east but, promised a teaching appointment, returned to the reservation. When the appointment fell through, he tried farming but eventually became an employee of the agency, assisting in the ALLOTMENT program of 1893. He later worked as a bank cashier and interpreter in the town of Pawnee.

In 1887, Murie married Mary Esau, with whom he had eight children, four of whom died young.

Around 1895, Murie met anthropologist Alice Fletcher (see FRANCIS LA FLESCHE), who had come to the region to study Pawnee ceremonies and who remembered him from Hampton. He worked with her from 1898 to 1902, introducing her to informants, transcribing and translating traditional songs and texts, and in general acting as an ethnographic assistant. In 1902, he started to collaborate with George A. Dorsey, curator of anthropology at the Field Museum of Natural History in Chicago, initially serving as Dorsey's assistant on field trips to study the myths and rituals of the Pawnee. From 1902 to 1909, he acted as a field researcher, occasionally moving to Chicago with his family to work at the museum. In 1903 and 1905, Murie also carried out a valuable research project in North Dakota among the Arikara, staying at Fort Berthold with Strikes the Enemy, who adopted him and initiated him as a priest. Of the many notes, recordings, and transcriptions on the subject of Pawnee and Arikara religion and language that Murie supplied to Dorsey, some appeared in Dorsey's articles and in a posthumous monograph on Skiri society by Dorsey and Murie, but much remains unpublished.

In 1910, Murie, now working on his own, became a part-time field researcher for the Bureau of American Ethnography. He supplied material on three ceremonies of the South Bank Pawnee, among them one that may have been the last performance of the Bear Dance of the Pitahawirata band. In 1912–14, he worked on a paper on Pawnee societies under the editorship of Clark Wissler, curator of anthropology at the American Museum of Natural History. In 1919, he divorced his wife Mary and married Josephine Walking Sun, the daughter of Old Lady Washington, who kept one of the Pawnee Morning Star bundles. Murie died soon after completing his major ethnographic project, *Ceremonies of the Pawnee*, which was to be published by the Bureau of American Ethnology but did not actually appear in print until 1981.

James Murie is remembered as a man of great charm who preserved a valuable body of Pawnee traditional lore that would otherwise have been lost. Although he was active among the progressive faction of the tribe and was an Episcopalian and a Freemason, later in life he performed a number of the ceremonies he had been taught, trying to carry on the traditions he recorded.

Further Reading

Boughter, Judith A. *The Pawnee Nation: An Annotated Research Bibliography*. Lanham, Md.: Scarecrow Press, 2004.

Weltfish, Gene. *The Lost Universe: Pawnee Life and Culture*. 1965. Reprint, Lincoln: University of Nebraska Press, 1977.

Myer, Dillon Seymour (1891–1982) *commissioner of Indian affairs*

The son of strict Methodist parents, Dillon Seymour Myer was born in Hebron, Ohio, on September 4, 1891, and grew up on a farm. He attended Ohio State University, majoring in agronomy, and graduated in 1914. Myer then worked for the Department of Agriculture in its extension programs at Ohio State and Purdue University, a position that secured him a draft deferment during WORLD WAR I. In 1925, he enrolled in Columbia Teachers College, where he received a master's degree in education. He taught agronomy at Kentucky Agricultural College before returning to the Department of Agriculture in 1933.

Myer moved to Washington, D.C., in 1934, becoming assistant chief of the Soil Conservation Service before WORLD WAR II. In June 1942, he replaced Milton S. Eisenhower as director of the infamous War Relocation Authority (WRA), after Eisenhower resigned when the injustice of his task began to wear on his conscience. Myer's zeal and the authoritarian manner in which he relocated and incarcerated 120,000 Japanese Americans during the war did much to exacerbate their suffering, and the relocation centers were dubbed "America's concentration camps." Although with time the United States would acknowledge its mistake and compensate the surviving Japanese-American victims for violating their constitutional rights, Myer was awarded the Medal of Merit by President Harry S. Truman immediately after the war for his efficient handling of "the most distasteful of all war jobs." He then served as head of the Federal Housing Administration until 1947, when he became coordinator of the Institute of Inter-American Affairs.

With nothing more than the most limited and prejudiced understanding of Indians, Myer was installed by Truman on May 8, 1950, to replace Indian Commissioner JOHN RALPH NICHOLS and provide the BUREAU OF INDIAN AFFAIRS (BIA) with the leadership stability it had been lacking since the departure of JOHN COLLIER five years earlier. Following the lead of a restive Congress that was now coming under the sway of McCarthyism and was intent on repealing the "leftist" policies of President Franklin D. Roosevelt, Myer began to revive the discredited agenda of ASSIMILATION that had been in place before the INDIAN NEW DEAL (see INDIAN REORGANIZATION ACT). Myer had no love for Collier, who had publicly condemned Myer's heavy-handed attempts to subvert Japanese-American culture inside the WRA camps and who now called Myer's new "Programming for Indian Independence" a "hoax" that simply disguised "as *a new policy* those social genocides of the earlier generations of dishonor toward Indians."

Myer's "Programming for Indian Independence" actually meant that the BIA should simply "get out of business as quickly as possible," and he promised to bring "a new broom" to the bureau. In an action that did not bode well for Native Americans, Myer replaced the widely known and trusted assistant commissioner, William Zimmerman, with Erwin J. Utz, formerly chief of the WRA Operations Division, and sacked BIA chief counsel Theodore H. Haas, who had collaborated with FELIX SOLOMON COHEN on the landmark *Handbook of Federal Indian Law*, replacing him with former

WRA solicitor Edwin E. Ferguson. Surrounding himself with other colleagues from the WRA, including anthropologist John H. Provinse, public relations officer Morrill M. Tozier, and "relocation expert" and lobbyist H. Rex Lee, Myer made a clean sweep of the upper echelon of the Collier administration, driving from the BIA a whole group of skilled reformers who had transformed it over the preceding two decades.

In August 1950, Myer aligned himself with freshman congresswoman Reva Beck Bosone from Utah in sponsoring the Bosone Resolution (H.J. 490), which aimed to initiate a "procedure for the final termination of Federal supervision and control of the American Indian." Although the bill was killed by opposition from the tribes and their allies, Myer made it clear the bureau would go ahead and embark on the TERMINA- TION policy anyway, and after the passage of the Navajo-Hopi Reorganization Act in 1951, which provided $88 million for education, health, and agricultural projects on the reservations, he ended all development projects for Indians.

Beginning in 1952, Myer offered to withdraw the "trusteeship responsibility" of the bureau from any tribe. When no tribe took up the offer, Myer supported House Resolution 698 (introduced on July 1, 1952), which allowed the BIA to identify those tribes "qualified for withdrawal" and to submit, without the tribes' approval, a proposal for their Termination. The resolution also empowered the BIA to draw up a list of services provided to Indians that could be discontinued or transferred to the states. Myer then began the process of transferring Indian children from Indian schools to state public schools systems, and under Public Law 291, passed on April 3, 1952, he began the process of transferring Indian Service hospitals to state control. Myer also supported attempts by states to gain criminal and civil jurisdiction over INDIAN RESERVATIONS, which prior to his tenure were subject exclusively to federal law, and in 1950 Congress granted New York State courts criminal jurisdiction over the Indian reservations within its boundaries (see SOVEREIGNTY, INDIGENOUS AND TRIBAL).

Myer opened up vast Indian tracts to mining and other leasing operations—in 1952 alone, he leased more than 600,000 acres for oil and gas exploration on reservations in the Midwest and Southwest. He encouraged tribal governments and Indian individuals to seek loans from private banks and other lending institutions, going so far as to allow them to put up trust land as collateral. However, this attempt to allow Indian lands to be put up for sale was killed by the tribes' vigorous opposition. Myer also inaugurated "Operation Relocation," which drew on WRA techniques to encourage Indians to migrate off their reservations and into American cities, a program which later swelled under his successor, GLENN LEONIDAS EMMONS. (See URBANIZATION, AMERICAN INDIANS AND.)

Myer threw his support behind his friend and mentor, Nevada senator Pat McCarran, by attempting to transfer the Carson Agency's superintendent, E. Reesman Fryer, who was helping the Paiute try to regain their lands surrounding PYRAMID LAKE, and, when that failed, by forcing Fryer to resign. Myer even went so far as to try to remove the Paiute's tenacious lawyer, James A. Curry, from the case by withholding

money due the tribe. Creatively rewriting an obsolete 1872 statute, the commissioner also attempted to handpick attorneys for other Indian tribes that were "fomenting trouble," including the Blackfeet, who had hired Felix Cohen to represent them. The tactics caused an uproar, leading 44 prominent Indian leaders to meet with Secretary of the Interior Oscar Chapman in January 1952 to demand Myer's removal.

Having aligned himself with the formidable anti-Indian bloc in Congress—led by Oklahoma's Toby Morris, chair of the Indian Affairs Subcommittee in the House; Utah senator ARTHUR VIVIAN WATKINS; and New Mexico senator Clinton P. Anderson, chair of the Senate Indian Affairs Committee—Myer easily rebuffed Chapman's attempts to get him fired. Truman himself had little love for Indians and saw the commissioner's job as "dirty work" that a man like Myer was good at. In a seemingly contradictory move, the president rewarded Myer by doubling the bureau's budget.

Myer responded to the growing chorus of condemnation from Indians by having Senator McCarren introduce in Congress S. 2543, "A Bill to Authorize the Indian Bureau to Make Arrests without Warrant for Violation of Indian Bureau Regulations, etc." which drew fire from, among others, the American Civil Liberties Union, the National Association for the Advancement of Colored People, and the American Bar Association for its broad use of police powers. The prickly Myer also sought to smear his worst critics, in particular Felix Cohen, on whom he tried to set the FBI. But the tactic backfired when it became clear to the press that Cohen's integrity was unimpeachable.

In the end, Myer's attempt to singlehandedly dismantle the protections Indian people had painstakingly fought for over the past 30 years led to a wide mobilization of Native Americans under RUTH MUSKRAT BRONSON and the NATIONAL CONGRESS OF AMERICAN INDIANS, who were augmented by the efforts of non-Indian supporters led by OLIVER LA FARGE and the ASSOCIATION ON AMERICAN INDIAN AFFAIRS. Together they succeeded in having incoming president Dwight Eisenhower remove Myer in March 1953. His Termination policy, however—now firmly in place—would continue to unfold under his successor, Glenn L. Emmons.

Myer subsequently became the executive director of the Group Health Association and worked briefly for the United Nations and the Organization of American States before retiring in 1964 and settling near Washington, D.C. In his later life, he unsuccessfully fought any legislation that would have offered apology or compensation to the Japanese-American victims of the WRA. He died of a heart attack on October 21, 1982, in Washington, D.C.

Further Reading
Philp, Kenneth R. "Dillon S. Myer and the Advent of Termination: 1950–1953." *Western Historical Quarterly* 19, no. 1 (1988): 37–59.

Nakai, Raymond (1918–2005) *Navajo politician*
Raymond Nakai was born on October 12, 1918, in Lukachukai, Arizona, on the Navajo Reservation, one of eight children of John and Bilthnedesbah Nakai. He attended reservation schools in Fort Wingate and Shiprock before joining the U.S. Navy. During WORLD WAR II, Nakai served aboard the light carrier the USS *Ommaney Bay* and participated in the Battle of Samar in October 1944, in which Cherokee commander ERNEST EDWIN EVANS and his ship the *Johnston* were lost. Three months later, on January 2, 1945, the *Ommaney Bay* was struck by a Japanese kamikaze and sunk, and Nakai was among the survivors pulled from the water. Nakai was then transfered to the destroyer USS *Dale*. After the war, he returned to the reservation to become a disc jockey in Flagstaff, Arizona. His popularity as a radio announcer among the Navajo (Dineh) led him to try his hand at politics, and in 1963, after two previous unsuccessful tries, he won a bid to serve as chair of the Navajo Tribal Council, in an upset election in which he ousted the heavily favored two-term incumbent, PAUL JONES.

By 1963, the Navajo population had grown to more than 92,000, split between the growing, affluent sector of Navajo associated with the tribal council, which had been set up in 1923 for the express purpose of facilitating oil and mineral development (see BURKE, CHARLES HENRY; HAGERMAN, HERBERT JAMES), and the great majority of Navajo, who still lived a traditional lifestyle on a per capita income of less than $100 per year. Nakai shook up the tribal government, ousting longtime tribal attorney Norman M. Little, a former assistant U.S. attorney general, who had been counsel to the Navajo since 1947 and whom Nakai accused of actually running the tribal council.

Nakai was by then prominent in the Democratic Party and a personal friend of President John F. Kennedy, who called him one of the finest political speakers he had ever met. Taking full advantage of the Democratic presidency and the Great Society programs under Kennedy's successor, Lyndon B.

Johnson—programs that funneled millions of dollars to the impoverished tribe—Nakai virtually revolutionized the Navajo nation during his eight years in office. He built the first reservation post office and instituted the Navajo's first social security program. Nakai developed reservation housing using the government Housing and Urban Development (HUD) program. He wrested control of Navajo livestock management from the ossified hands of the BUREAU OF INDIAN AFFAIRS (BIA). He replaced boarding schools, many of them notorious for their mismanagement under the BIA, with Navajo day schools. He encouraged a return to traditional crafts such as weaving and silversmithing through the formation of the Navajo Arts and Crafts Board.

Under Nakai, the Navajo established the first Indian banks and shopping centers, as well as the first tribal college in the United States (1968), the Navajo Community College at Many Farms, Arizona (see HIGHER EDUCATION). The following year saw the founding of one of the first tribal libraries, the Navajo Library at Window Rock. Nakai legalized the NATIVE AMERICAN CHURCH, which had been severely repressed on the reservation, and established a Navajo Bill of Rights. In 1969, he had the name of the Navajo tribe officially changed to the Navajo Nation. His attempt to draft a new constitution, however, met defeat through fear that his extensive power would become dictatorial.

Nakai brought back to the reservation talented and educated Navajo who had left for lack of work, using them to help manage the tribe. He brought in PETER MACDONALD to run the new Office of Navajo Economic Opportunity and Peter Allen to revamp the tribe's legal system. With all these achievements, however, it was in economic development that Nakai brought about the most important changes. He established a giant irrigation system to help Navajo farmers and built roads to get their products to market. He promoted tourism on the reservation, building motels and parks, and encouraged many traditional people, whose lifestyle depended on herding sheep, off their lands. In 1966, Nakai was reelected to a second term, narrowly defeating longtime candidate Samuel W. Billison, who accused him of voting irregularities. However, he was defeated for a third term by his protégé MacDonald in 1971. Unable to unseat MacDonald in either the 1974 or the 1978 election, Nakai retired from politics after a dismal showing in 1982. Possibly the most influential tribal chairman of the 20th century, his tenure brought far-reaching changes to the Navajo people.

Raymond Nakai died on August 14, 2005, and was buried in Lukachukai Community Cemetery. His son, R. CARLOS NAKAI, is a popular composer and musician.

Further Reading
Shaffer, Mark. "Raymond Nakai, 86, Influential Navajo Tribal Leader." *Arizona Republic*, 16 August 2005.

Nakai, R. Carlos (Raymond Carlos Nakai)
(1946–) *Navajo-Ute composer, flutist, recording artist*
Raymond Carlos Nakai was born in Flagstaff, Arizona, on April 16, 1946. His father was longtime Navajo tribal chairman RAYMOND NAKAI, and his mother, Ella Crawford Nakai, was Navajo and Ute. Nakai learned to play trumpet as a child and later played in the Flagstaff High School band. He served in the U.S. Navy from 1966 to 1971 and then attended Northern Arizona University (NAU), receiving a B.S. in 1979. He later attended the University of Arizona from 1987 to 1992, earning a master's degree in American Indian studies.

In 1973, while studying trumpet and cornet at NAU, Nakai began to play the Native American wooden flute, adapting the traditional flute melodies of the Plains and Woodland Indians to his own unique style. He produced his first recordings in 1980, making his own cassette tapes and selling them himself in the Southwest. In 1982, he was signed by Canyon Records and released his debut album, *Changes*, the next year. *Changes* was an album of solo flute recordings that included traditional Zuni, Blood, and Lakota melodies along with Nakai's own impressionistic compositions. In 1985, Nakai released *Cycles*, and the next year he issued *Journeys*, this time featuring only his own compositions with the addition of a synthesizer reproducing the sounds of nature, the wind, and the ocean.

In 1987, Nakai's album *Earth Spirit* brought him critical acclaim, and in 1989 *Canyon Trilogy* became the first Native American folk album to be certified a gold record. In 1988, Nakai began to collaborate with guitarist-harpist William Eaton, releasing *Carry the Gift* (1988) and *Winter Dreams* (1990), a collection of Christmas songs. Nakai's collaboration with Eaton and the Black Lodge Singers, *Ancestral Voices*, was a finalist in the Best Traditional Folk Music category in the 1994 Grammy awards.

Beginning in 1989, Nakai began to work with classical pianist Peter Kater. They released *Natives* in 1989, *Migrations* in 1992, *Honorable Sky* in 1994, and *Song for Humanity* in 1998. *Migrations* won the National Association of Independent Record Distributors Indie Award for Best New Age Album.

Raymond Nakai prepared to give his inaugural address as Navajo tribal chair in 1963. Seated behind him was the former chair, Paul Jones. *(AP/Wideworld)*

corporations to settle on the reservation, including military contractors General Dynamics and Fairchild Semiconductor.

Nakai continued the tribal council's heavy emphasis on mineral leasing, working to maximize production of Navajo uranium, coal, gas, oil, and timber, which made the Navajo government self-sufficient. He liberally signed leases for energy development on the reservation but was unable to change entrenched federal policy that allowed energy companies to pay Indian tribes far less than market value for the resources.

In 1969, Nakai agreed to have the world's largest coal-fired electric generating plants built on reservation land near Page, Arizona. The plants, which supplied power to cities as far away as Los Angeles, were supplied with coal from Navajo strip mines on Black Mesa by water slurry. The plants soon became the single largest source of air pollution in the world, and the water slurry began to deplete the aquifer on which both the Navajo and Hopi depended for farming. The strip mines badly scarred the delicate desert and forced the relocation of thousands of self-sufficient Navajo sheepherders. Moreover, few Navajo used the electricity created, and the capital-intensive projects brought few jobs to the rapidly growing Navajo population.

While his social programs did much to incorporate the Navajo into mainstream American life, Nakai's development policies ultimately did little to help the average Navajo, most of whom still lived in poverty by the end of his term, and drove

Island of Bows (1994), recorded in Kyoto's Hounji Temple, brought Nakai together with the Wind Travelin' Band and two traditional Japanese musicians, Shonosuke Ohkura and Oki Kano. In 1995, *Feather, Stone & Light*, a musical trialogue with longtime collaborators William Eaton and Will Clipman, was noted as a Billboard Critic's Choice and debuted on Billboard's Top New Age Albums chart, remaining there for 13 weeks. In fall 1996, Nakai started a band called the R. Carlos Nakai Quartet to produce a jazz album, *Kokopelli's Café*.

Nakai is generally considered to be a New Age composer (see NEW AGE MOVEMENT), but as with many modern artists, he has largely avoided the controversy connected with that movement because his work does not purport to be anything other than original creations based in part on traditional art forms. His music is known for its use of modern instruments, such as the electronic synthesizer, to add subtle effects and create various moods reflecting his attachment to nature and natural landscapes. Nakai recorded two albums, *Sundance Season* and *Desert Dance*, for the Celestial Harmonies label, a prominent New Age recording company. He also formed a jazz ensemble, Jackalope, which has released two albums, *Jackalope* and *Weavings*.

Nakai's composition "Cycles" was set to dance by the Martha Graham Company in October 1988, and he has composed numerous soundtracks, primarily for documentaries. A popular performer and one of America's best-known Indian musical artists, he regularly tours North America, Europe, and Japan. In 1993, Nakai was the soloist with the Phoenix Symphony for the world premier of a concerto for the cedar flute composed by James DeMars. DeMars and Nakai's album *Spirit Horses* had been chosen by *Pulse* magazine as one of the top albums of 1991.

Nakai has done a significant amount of research on Native American flute music and lectures on the subject. In 1997, he published a book called *The Art of Native American Flute*. He continues to be a prolific composer. With jazz multi-instrumentalist Amo Chip Dabney, he released *Edge of the Century* in 2001, and in 2002, this time backed by a symphony orchestra, he released *Fourth World*. Nakai works with musicians from around the globe including Tibetan flutist Newang Khechog, Hawaiian slack guitarist Keola Beamer, and Israeli cellist Udi Bar-David. He has received more than seven Grammy Award nominations including *Ancestral Voices* (1994 Best Traditional Folk Album), *Inner Voices* and *Inside Monument Valley* (both for 2000 Best New Age Album), *In a Distant Place* (2001 Best New Age Album), *Fourth World* (2002 Best New Age Album), *Sanctuary* (2003 Best Native American Album), and *People of Peace* (2004 Best New Age Album). Through such achievements, Nakai has been responsible for popularizing the use of traditional Native American music as a mainstream art form and has brought the wooden flute, traditionally used for courting and healing, new international renown.

Further Listening
Nakai, R. Carlos. *Canyon Trilogy*. Canyon Records, 1989.
———. *Changes*. Canyon Records, 1983.
———. *Earth Spirit*. Canyon Records, 1987.

Further Reading
Murg, Wilhelm. "Interview with R. Carlos Nakai." *Indian Country Today*, 11 February 2004.

Nampeyo ("Snake That Does Not Bite"; Tsu-mana, "Snake Girl") (ca. 1860–1942) *Hopi-Tewa potter*

Nampeyo was born in the Tewa village of Hano on the First Mesa in Arizona; her year of birth is not known but is believed to be 1859 or 1860. Her mother was Kotsakao, a Tewa, and her father was Kotsvema, a Hopi from neighboring Walpi. Nampeyo (Snake That Does Not Bite) was her Tewa name, but she also carried a corresponding Hopi name, Tsu-mana (Snake Girl). Her brother, Captain Tom, became a prominent traditional leader of their village.

As a girl, Nampeyo learned traditional Hopi pottery-making from her grandmother at Walpi, showing exceptional skill at a young age. With the opening nearby of Keam's Canyon Trading Post in 1875, she found a market for her pottery and began to experiment with new styles. In 1881, after a failed first marriage, Nampeyo married Walpi native Lesou, and the two settled below the mesa in nearby Polacca.

By 1890, Nampeyo had emerged as the foremost potter on First Mesa and had begun to grow beyond the Walpi style, producing a few vessels with the characteristic yellow color and painted designs from the ancient village of Sikyatki. In 1895, the anthropologist Jesse W. Fewkes began excavating the Sikyatki ruins, uncovering great quantities of the exquisitely painted polychrome pottery shards. Nampeyo visited the dig, at which her husband Lesou labored, and copied designs of these prehistoric wares to use as inspiration for her own designs. She also traveled throughout the countryside seeking the clays needed to capture the fine detail of the ancient pottery. Unlike the then-current Hopi style, which used two kinds of clay, Nampeyo used four different types of clay in her work, including the white *hisat chuoka* (ancient clay), which had been used by the Sikyatki potters. Fewkes later claimed credit for inspiring Nampeyo by "allowing" her to copy the ancient designs produced by his dig, a claim now largely refuted.

Demand for her work led Nampeyo to teach others at Hano her new style and techniques, leading to the "Sikyatki Revival" and a renaissance in Hopi ceramics. In 1898, George Dorsey, curator of anthropology at Chicago's Field Museum, arranged for Nampeyo and Lesou to exhibit their craft in the Chicago Coliseum. Nampeyo returned to Chicago in 1910, appearing at the Chicago Land Show. She now had an international reputation, and her pottery was highly sought after by collectors. With visitors regularly coming to her house to view her at work and make purchases, she began to commission family members to paint the pottery in order to keep up with the demand.

Around 1920, Nampeyo's eyesight began to fail, and she spent the next 20 years virtually blind. She continued to mold the pottery, but Lesou, who had mastered her style, did the painting. Upon his death in 1932, her daughters, Fannie, Annie, and Nellie, took over the painting process. Nampeyo's last years were spent under her children's care, although she continued to shape vessels until almost the day of her death on July 20, 1942. Her descendants, accomplished potters themselves, have continued her tradition. Nampeyo's skill and success paved the way for Indians to be recognized as individual artists and helped turn pottery-making into one of the most vibrant and successful of Indian artistic art forms.

Further Reading

Blair, Mary Ellen. *The Legacy of a Master Potter: Nampeyo and Her Descendants.* Tucson, Ariz.: Treasure Chest Books, 1999.

Graves, Laura. *Thomas Varker Keam, Indian Trader.* Norman: University of Oklahoma Press, 1998.

Kramer, Barbara. *Nampeyo and Her Pottery.* Albuquerque: University of New Mexico Press, 1996.

Nash, Philleo (1909–1987) *commissioner of the Bureau of Indian Affairs*

Philleo Nash was born in Wisconsin Rapids, Wisconsin, on October 25, 1909. His family was in the cranberry business, and his grandfather, T. E. Nash, was the founder of the Nekoosa-Edwards Paper company. Nash graduated from the University of Wisconsin in 1932, earning a B.A. in anthropology, before moving to Chicago and earning a Ph.D. in anthropology from the University of Chicago in 1937. He lived for a year on an Indian reservation in Oregon, completing his dissertation on the Klamath Ghost Dance of 1870, which he contended was a response to the tribe's contact with non-Indians.

Nash lectured in anthropology at the University of Toronto before moving to Washington, D.C., at the outbreak of WORLD WAR II. There he became special assistant to Elmer Davis in the Office of War Information, where he used his anthropological skills to write pamphlets such as "Enemy Japan" and "The Command of Negro Troops." Nash stayed on in government service after the war, serving as special assistant in the White House for the Department of the Interior from 1946 to 1952. He was an administrative assistant to President Harry S. Truman from 1952 to 1953, working on reports concerning civil rights.

In January 1952, Nash became the first member of the Truman staff to be accused by Senator Joseph McCarthy of Wisconsin of being a communist, a charge Nash denounced as a "contemptible lie." The attack prompted Truman to defend his adviser and call McCarthy a "pathological character assassin."

After the election of Dwight D. Eisenhower to the presidency, Nash returned to Wisconsin and his family's cranberry business, the Biron Cranberry Company. He also entered state politics, becoming state chair of the Democratic Party in 1955 and serving as lieutenant governor from 1958 to 1960. By this time, Nash had become active on Indian issues as a member of the board of directors of the ASSOCIATION ON AMERICAN INDIAN AFFAIRS and as vice chairman of the Menominee Indian Tribal Trust.

The election of President John F. Kennedy in 1960 meant the departure of GLENN LEONIDAS EMMONS as commissioner of the BUREAU OF INDIAN AFFAIRS (BIA), but Interior Secretary Stewart Udall allowed the position to go unfilled for seven months. Cherokee JOHN ORIEN CROW filled it temporarily while the new administration sought to develop an Indian policy. Udall created a task force on Indian affairs composed of Cherokee leader WILLIAM WAYNE KEELER; William Zimmerman, former assistant commissioner under JOHN COLLIER; James E. Officer, an anthropologist; and Nash. The task force recommended that the administration move away from the policy of TERMINATION promoted by Presidents Truman and Eisenhower, and instead support economic development efforts on INDIAN RESERVATIONS.

By this time, the AMERICAN INDIAN CHICAGO CONFERENCE had made it clear that as far as Indians were concerned, the Termination policy had to go, and the task force report was warmly received by Indians. Nash, when he was finally nominated for commissioner on July 31, 1961, was considered an excellent choice. Nonetheless, he endured a bruising confirmation hearing in Congress, where Termination had strong support, and powerful senators such as Clinton P. Anderson (D-N.Mex.), chairman of the Interior Committee, and Henry Jackson (D-Wash.), who was seeking to terminate the Colville, did not welcome him at all.

Nash attempted to implement the task force suggestions, beginning with the ambitious economic development programs. Between 1961 and 1965, he helped to establish 51 industrial plants on Indian reservations, more than eight times the existing number, and he persuaded the Area Redevelopment Administration (later the Economic Development Administration) to make development loans to Indian communities. He also pushed for the Public Housing Administration to provide housing on Indian reservations, and 80 tribes took advantage of the new opportunity.

In education, Nash was able to increase school enrollment figures for Indian children from 85 percent under Emmons to more than 90 percent by 1965. He also established summer schools for Indian children in an effort to keep them from falling behind non-Indians. Under Nash, the Institute of American Indian Art opened its doors in 1962; it would go on to lead a revolution in Indian art. In 1965, Haskell Institute became Haskell Junior College. College enrollment jumped from 600 in 1961 to 2,900 in 1962, and college grants began their increase from $296,000 in 1962 to $1,998,800 in 1967. Between 1961 and 1966, the number of Indian college graduates doubled.

Nash convinced President Lyndon B. Johnson to make Indian communities one of the first battlegrounds in Johnson's ambitious "War on Poverty" programs, and he steered the Head Start, Jobs Corps, and other programs to Indian reservations. Nash's achievements, however, were overshadowed by his continuing battles with Congress, largely over his vocal opposition to Termination and his attempts to end it. He gradually lost Udall's support, and the secretary began to look for someone less likely to antagonize Congress. When Nash was dismissed on March 15, 1966, replaced by ROBERT

LaFollette Bennett, Indian leaders felt they had lost a true friend in the administration. Fortunately, as it turned out, Bennett continued Nash's policies.

After leaving the BIA, Nash opened a consulting business in Washington and headed a program at American University for students with special education needs. He returned to Wisconsin in 1977 to once again manage the family cranberry business. Philleo Nash died of cancer on October 12, 1987, at a hospice in Marshfield, Wisconsin.

Further Reading

Allen, Ray A. "Whither Indian Education? A Conversation with Philleo Nash." *The School Review* 79, no. 1 (1970): 99–108.

Clarkin, Thomas. *Federal Indian Policy in the Kennedy and Johnson Administrations, 1961–1969.* Albuquerque: University of New Mexico Press, 2001.

Officer, James. "Philleo Nash (1909–1987)." *American Anthropologist* 90, no. 4 (1988): 952–956.

National Congress of American Indians (NCAI)

The largest national Indian organization in the United States, the National Congress of American Indians (NCAI) was founded in 1944 to preserve the gains made under the Indian New Deal (see Indian Reorganization Act). Its origins go back to a walkout of Indian delegates at a conference hosted by the University of Toronto and Yale in 1939. (See Phinney, Archie.) The NCAI was organized by New Dealers D'Arcy McNickle, Ruth Muskrat Bronson, Robert LaFollette Bennett, Ben Dwight, Archie Phinney, George P. LaVatta, and Judge N. B. Johnson, who hoped that it would provide political backing to the administration of Indian Commissioner John Collier, which was under increasing attacks from conservative members of Congress.

With the departure of Collier from the Bureau of Indian Affairs (BIA) in 1945, the government's federal policy once again turned back to the assimilation policies of the earlier 20th century. This time, however, the policy was called Termination, and its goal was the dissolution of the tribes' trust status with the U.S. government and complete assimilation of all Indians into mainstream society. The NCAI was forced to become increasingly active in order to preserve any Indian rights at all. In 1946, the NCAI helped secure the creation of the controversial Indian Claims Commission. During the early 1950s, it fought against the policies of Indian Commissioner Dillon Seymour Myer, eventually securing his removal in 1952. The next year, the organization managed to overturn the BIA prohibition against the use of liquor by Indians, believing the law to be discriminatory.

Cheyenne activist Helen White Peterson became the executive director of the organization in 1953, succeeding Bronson, and with NCAI president Joseph Richard Garry, she tried to mitigate the Termination policies of the new commissioner of Indian Affairs, Glenn Leonidas Emmons, with no small degree of success. NCAI was a major force in putting together the historic American Indian Chicago Conference of 1961, but the organization was unprepared for the militancy espoused by Indian students led by Ponca Clyde Warrior and the Iroquois-style sovereignty demands articulated by Tuscarora William Rickard. The Chicago Conference led to changes in the NCAI, as a result of which the old guard was effectively weakened and young activists such as Robert Phillip Burnette and Vine Deloria, Jr., came to the fore. NCAI, however, soon lost its leadership position to the Red Power groups that emerged in the late 1960s and early 1970s, which quickly seized the initiative in rolling back Termination.

Under BIA commissioners Robert LaFollette Bennett and Louis Rook Bruce, Jr., NCAI was successful in establishing programs for the growing population of urban Indians, including increased government benefits for relocatees (see Urbanization, American Indians and). In 1971, a number of tribal chairs, unhappy with what they felt was NCAI's excessive attention to urban issues, formed the National Tribal Chairman's Association (NTCA). Deloria's attempts to forge a coalition of militants, NCAI, and old-guard groups such as the NTCA foundered after the Trail of Broken Treaties occupation of BIA headquarters in 1972.

NCAI continued to do what it did best, lobbying Congress for concrete gains for Indian people, such as the Indian Self-Determination and Education Act of 1975. The organization, however, was caught badly off guard by the Reagan administration's attempts to drastically weaken tribal governments, this time through massive budget cuts. NCAI regained strength under the leadership of Quinault Joseph Burton DeLaCruz and Cheyenne-Creek Suzan Shown Harjo, who managed to fight off some of the most dangerous legislation. After Harjo was ousted in the late 1980s, NCAI fell into a period of decline and has not regained its former standing. In the 1990s, tribes that turned to gaming on Indian reservations, such as the Mashantucket Pequot, became more and more influential in their own right, preferring to use their own lobbyists rather than rely on a national organization.

Further Reading

Cowger, Thomas W. *The National Congress of Americans Indians: The Founding Years.* Lincoln: University of Nebraska Press, 2001.

Fahey, John. *Saving the Reservation: Joe Garry and the Battle to Be Indian.* Seattle: University of Washington Press, 2001.

National Indian Youth Council (NIYC)

Organized in Gallup, New Mexico, on August 13, 1961, in response to the American Indian Chicago Conference, the National Indian Youth Council (NIYC) was the first pan-Indian organization to arise from the Red Power movement. Founded by Ponca Clyde Warrior, Paiute Mel Thom, Navajo Herbert Charles Blatchford, Mohawk Shirley Hill Witt, Tuscarora Karen Rickard (the sister of William Rickard), and other Indian youth, the organization had a decidedly militant cast. In addition to providing a more confrontational opposition to the TERMINATION policy then under way, NIYC believed in strengthening Indian heritage and sovereignty (see SOVEREIGNTY, INDIGENOUS AND TRIBAL).

The organization drew support from the Southwestern Regional Youth Conference, which had organized large gatherings of Indian youth during the late 1950s in New Mexico and Arizona, and of which Blatchford was the president. With Thom as Chair and principal organizer, NIYC began to use its new militant tactics effectively when its leaders recruited Assiniboine–Dakota Sioux activist HANK ADAMS to help organize "fish-ins" in the Northwest. These demonstrations were instrumental in helping to restore Indian HUNTING AND FISHING RIGHTS. More than simply activists, the founders of NIYC had a scholarly bent, and the council's newsletters, *America Before Columbus* and *The Aborigine*, played an important role in developing a distinct Indian philosophy of political struggle that would come to fruition in the 1970s and 1980s.

NIYC continued organizing among Indian youth, and by 1970 had a membership of more than 2,000, mostly between the ages of 17 and 25. In 1967, the group received a grant from the Carnegie Foundation to study the problems of schools and address the issue of ASSIMILATION. The group also sought to close some of the more notorious boarding schools, filing suit to close the Intermountain Indian School in 1971. NIYC began to lose its militancy in the early 1970s, when its founders dropped out to concentrate on other issues, and its vanguard role was superseded by the AMERICAN INDIAN MOVEMENT (AIM).

Headquartered in Albuquerque, New Mexico, NIYC began to work on environmental issues during the 1970s and 1980s, bringing lawsuits in an attempt to stop uranium and coal strip mining on INDIAN RESERVATIONS. In 1983, the group founded an Indian Voter Project. By the late 1980s, the NIYC had become a service organization, conducting numerous leadership training programs among youth, but by the late 1990s it had become relatively inactive, though it remains in existence today. The records of the NIYC are now held by the Center for Southwest Research at the University of New Mexico.

Further Reading

Cobb, Daniel M. *Native Activism in Cold War America: The Struggle for Sovereignty*. Lawrence: University Press of Kansas, 2008.

Shreve, Bradley Glenn. "Up against Giants: The National Indian Youth Council, the Navajo Nation, and Coal Gasification, 1974–77." *American Indian Culture and Research Journal* 30, no. 2 (2006): 17–34.

Shrere, Bradley Glenn, and Shirley Hill Witt. *Red Power Rising: The National Indian Youth Council and the Origins of Native Activism*. Norman: University of Oklahoma Press, 2011.

National Tribal Chairman's Association (NTCA)

Founded in February 1971, the National Tribal Chairman's Association (NTCA) is a national organization of Indian leaders originally formed as a conservative counterweight to the growing RED POWER MOVEMENT of the 1960s and 1970s. Its first president was William Youpee (Sioux-Assiniboine), chair of the Fort Peck Reservation. The founders of NTCA had grown disenchanted with the NATIONAL CONGRESS OF AMERICAN INDIANS (NCAI), the leading national Indian organization of the day, which they felt was becoming too concerned with urban Indian issues (see URBANIZATION, AMERICAN INDIANS AND). The tribal chairmen believed that the increase in federal programs for urban Indians spurred by NCAI and implemented by Indian Commissioners ROBERT LAFOLLETTE BENNETT and LOUIS ROOK BRUCE, JR., was siphoning off badly needed funds from INDIAN RESERVATIONS.

NTCA condemned the takeover of the BUREAU OF INDIAN AFFAIRS (BIA) headquarters in Washington, D.C., after the TRAIL OF BROKEN TREATIES march in November 1972. Its public denouncement of the militants in a widely covered press conference shortly after the takeover brought NTCA a serious loss of credibility among Indian people, particularly after PETER MACDONALD, chair of the Navajo (Dineh) tribe, broke with the association and supported the goals, if not the tactics, of the demonstrators. NTCA was further put on the defensive by the AMERICAN INDIAN MOVEMENT (AIM), which attacked many of the tribal chairmen as corrupt despots and puppets of the U.S. government.

NTCA also badly miscalculated when, in 1980, it supported the administration of President Ronald Reagan and the ambitious plans of his Indian commissioner, KENNETH L. SMITH. By the time NTCA grasped the effects of Smith's dramatic budget cuts, the political initiative had been seized once again by NCAI, under the leadership of JOSEPH DELACRUZ (Quinault) and SUZAN SHOWN HARJO (Cheyenne-Creek). During the 1990s, as many of the political activists of the Red Power era assumed positions of leadership on Indian reservations, the political conservatism that had characterized tribal chairmen of the 1960s and 1970s began to erode, leaving NTCA without a common political agenda. Therefore NTCA, although potentially a powerful force in Indian politics, largely failed to live up to its promise. It gradually lost the support of the tribes and is now defunct.

See also CHINO, WENDELL; JOURDAIN, ROGER.

Native American Church

Conceived in Oklahoma on October 10, 1918, by Frank Little Eagle (Ponca), Mack Haag (Cheyenne), George Pipestem (Otoe), and Louis McDonald (Ponca), with the aid of anthropologist James Mooney, the Native American Church was founded in an attempt to protect the growing peyote religion from the intense efforts of the U.S. government to suppress it.

Although the sacred use of peyote was traditionally confined to the ancient Mexican Indian cultures, by the late 19th century, Indians north of Mexico had begun to incorporate it as part of a new religious movement that blended Christian and traditional Indian beliefs. In the last decade of the 19th century, the religion was formalized under two men: Quanah

Parker (Comanche), who advocated the Half-Moon, or Tipi, Way; and Nishkuntu, or John Wilson (Caddo-Lenni Lenape), who introduced the Big Moon, or Cross Fire, Way. The religion, however, was not exclusive, and the rituals varied from tribe to tribe. Because its religious leaders, or "road men," proselytized among different tribes, and early peyotists advocated the replacement of traditional Indian religions with peyotism and also encouraged the destruction of sacred objects such as medicine bundles, peyotism often found itself opposed by followers of traditional Indian religions.

By 1888, the Indian agency overseeing the Kiowa, Comanche, and Wichita in Indian Territory (now Oklahoma), where peyotism was well established, had outlawed its sale or possession, threatening to cut off the annuities or rations of any offenders. Two years later, the Office of Indian Affairs prohibited use of peyote on all federal reservations, though Indian agents had no legal authority to punish peyotists. In 1897, Indian Commissioner WILLIAM ARTHUR JONES began to selectively harass peyote users under bills designed to prevent the intoxication of Indians. On a number of occasions, peyote users managed to successfully fight the cases against them. In 1916, South Dakota representative Harry L. Gandy and Kansas senator W. W. Thompson introduced bills to make it a federal crime to use peyote, but the measures were defeated. Nevertheless both the states and Indian agents continued to arrest, harass, and otherwise attempt to disrupt the religion, and numerous peyotists were arrested and imprisoned.

In this climate, the Native American Church was founded to "foster and promote the religious belief of the several tribes of Indians in the State of Oklahoma, in the Christian religion with the practice of the Peyote Sacrament." Although not the first incorporated peyote religion church—the Otoe First Born Church of Christ holds that distinction, having been incorporated in 1914—the Native American Church was the first to seek adherents from more than one tribe. Other churches soon followed, including the Peyote Church of Christ, incorporated by Winnebago in Nebraska in 1921, the first outside of Oklahoma. Peyotism flourished in the first part of the century, so that by the late 1920s, the religion had spread to the Omaha, Menominee, Chippewa, Crow, Wind River Shoshone, Blackfeet, and even to Indians in Canada.

The peyote religion stressed sobriety and "right living," and on those reservations where it became established, it proved to be an important force in countering the serious effects of ALCOHOLISM. As a consequence, its use was advocated by many leaders, such as Omaha attorney THOMAS L. SLOAN. However, Christian groups, government officials, and some prominent Indians, including CHARLES ALEXANDER EASTMAN and GERTRUDE BONNIN, agitated for its ban.

Peyotism met stiff resistance among the Navajo (Dineh) and the Pueblos, led by writer and arts patron Mabel Dodge Luhan, who had married Taos Pueblo leader Antonio Luhan. When Taos elected peyotist Geronimo Gomez as governor in 1934, Dodge prevailed upon Commissioner JOHN COLLIER to remove him from office. Collier then worked out an agreement allowing peyotists to hold meetings in the pueblo on the condition they refrain from proselytizing. Three years later, Dodge persuaded New Mexico senator Dennis Chavez to introduce legislation banning peyote use, but the measure failed.

Dodge's campaign achieved success when the Navajo tribal council, led by chairman JACOB CASIMERA MORGAN, passed a law forbidding the practice in 1940. In 1958, Navajo tribal police raided a peyote ceremony, leading to the convictions of three Navajo in tribal court. The case, *Native American Church v. Navajo Tribal Council*, was appealed to federal courts, where the U.S. Court of Appeals found that First-Amendment protections of religious freedom were not applicable on INDIAN RESERVATIONS. The Navajo anti-peyote ordinance was not repealed until 1968, when the INDIAN CIVIL RIGHTS ACT extended constitutional protection to reservations.

In 1944, the Native American Church amended its charter, becoming the Native American Church of the United States. In 1955, in order to include Canadian peyotists, it changed its name to the Native American Church of North America. Persecution of its adherents continued, however. In 1962, three Navajo—Jack Woody, Leon B. Anderson, and Dan Dee Nez—were arrested and convicted in California for violating that state's anti-peyote laws. Although their conviction was upheld in the state's court of appeals, the California Supreme Court, under *People v. Woody*, overturned their convictions in August 1964 on the grounds that the state had violated their First Amendment rights. Under the Drug Abuse Control Act of 1965, however, peyote was classified as a controlled substance, and Indians continued to be arrested and harassed.

The passage in 1978 of the AMERICAN INDIAN RELIGIOUS FREEDOM ACT did little to uphold peyotists' rights to conduct their rituals without government interference. In 1986, federal courts ruled that prison inmates' right to the use of peyote was superseded by prison security needs. Nor did the act stop states from exacting civil penalties for peyote use. In a landmark case, *Employment Division, Department of Human Resources of Oregon v. Smith* (1990), the U.S. Supreme Court allowed Oregon to terminate the employment of two Indians for participating in a peyote ceremony, a violation of state employment guidelines. In 1994, after several conflicts with states who continued to aggressively enforce their anti-peyote laws, Congress amended the American Indian Religious Freedom Act so that "the use, possession, or transportation of peyote by an Indian for bona fide traditional ceremonial purposes in connection with the practice of a traditional Indian religion is lawful, and shall not be prohibited by the United States or any State."

The Native American Church of North America continues to grow, with chapters in 23 states, Canada, and Mexico. Along with its cohort the Native American Church of Navajoland (incorporated in 1973) and the Native American Church of Oklahoma (separated from the national organization in 1950), it is estimated that as many as 200,000 Indians belong to one of the three churches.

See also RELIGIOUS FREEDOM, AMERICAN INDIAN.

Further Reading

Slotkin, James. *The Peyote Religion: A Study in Indian-White Relations.* Glencoe, Ill.: Free Press, 1956.

Smith, Huston, and Reuben Snake, eds. *One Nation under God: The Triumph of the Native American Church.* Santa Fe, N.Mex.: Clear Light Press, 1996.

White, Phillip M. *Peyotism and the Native American Church: An Annotated Bibliography.* Santa Barbara, Calif.: Greenwood Press, 2000.

Native American Rights Fund (NARF)

In 1970, the Ford Foundation commissioned California Indian Legal Services to develop a program that would recognize the distinct legal challenges faced by Indian tribes and provide legal services to tribes and individuals, ostensibly bypassing the non-Indian attorneys who were viewed as having their own agenda. Begun by David Getches, then a professor at the University of Colorado School of Law, and David Risling, Jr. (Hupa), the Native American Rights Fund (NARF) formally separated from the California group in 1971 and incorporated in Colorado, making Denver its headquarters. It quickly grew from a three-attorney pilot project to a major law firm with 18 attorneys. Joined by JOHN ECHOHAWK (Pawnee), Robert Pelcyger, Bruce Green, Joe Brecher, and Charles Wilkenson, NARF quickly became active in protecting the HUNTING AND FISHING RIGHTS of Indian tribes.

From 1971 to 1973, NARF attorneys worked to restore the Menominee to federal tribal status after they had been terminated (see TERMINATION). In 1973, NARF aided the Bay Mills Chippewa in securing fishing rights to the Great Lakes under *United States v. Michigan.* NARF also helped Winnebago leader REUBEN SNAKE prevent the Army Corps of Engineers from condemning Winnebago land for a proposed flood-control project on the Missouri River.

In 1971, Thomas Tureen, an attorney at a federally funded legal services group in Maine, joined NARF. Tureen had come to the conclusion that the Non-Intercourse Act of 1790 made state treaties with Indians, unless ratified by Congress, illegal. Since a large portion of the land in the Northeast had been acquired from Indians through treaties made by the states, this opened the door to major land claims in the Northeast. NARF filed suit behalf of the Penobscot and Passamaquoddy tribes, seeking to recover land from Maine (see STEVENS, JOHN W.).

With the help of a grant from the Carnegie Corporation, NARF founded the National Indian Law Library in 1972, to house materials devoted exclusively to Indian law.

NARF attorneys won important decisions on the rights of tribal courts to handle adoption cases (*Fisher v. Montana,* 1976), and for the rights of Indians to their burial grounds and remains (*Charrier v. Bell,* 1982). They helped a number of non-federally recognized tribes win recognition, including the Mashantucket Pequot.

In 1984, NARF attorney Arlinda Locklear (Lumbee), became the second Indian woman, after Wyandot LYDA B. CONLEY, to argue a case before the U.S. Supreme Court,

successfully challenging South Dakota's attempt to extend its criminal jurisdiction over Indians on land opened up to non-Indians but still within the original boundaries of the Cheyenne River Reservation. The following year, Locklear won another stunning victory before the Supreme Court. Arguing on behalf of the Oneida, the Court found that New York State could be sued for damages regarding lands taken unlawfully (see KELLOGG, LAURA MIRIAM CORNELIUS).

Despite achieving significant legal victories for Indian tribes, notably helping the Penobscot and the Passamaquoddy win an $81 million land claims settlement against the state of Maine in 1980 and the Pequot gain federal recognition in 1983, NARF's growing power also sparked controversies. Regularly litigating against the U.S. government on behalf of Indian tribes, yet at the same time receiving a substantial portion of its funds from the very same American government, the group was accused by some of working under a conflict of interest. NARF's growing political role also led to controversy, especially with activists who found the organization too moderate and with traditional leaders who felt it represented tribal government interests even when they conflicted with traditional culture. NARF's handling of the Native American Graves Protection and Repatriation Act (NAGPRA), for example, drew the ire of traditional leaders such as Onondaga OREN LYONS, JR., for compromising Indian rights in favor of powerful political organizations such as the Smithsonian Institution.

During the 1990s, however, a period when Indian sovereignty rights were under incessant attack from the courts and Congress, NARF emerged as one of the strongest and most able defenders of Indian sovereignty (see SOVEREIGNTY, INDIGENOUS AND TRIBAL). Among the most powerful and well-funded Indian organizations in the United States, NARF represents a new form of Indian organization that combines great legal expertise with strong political connections able to lobby for Indian rights.

Further Reading

Johnson, Jean. "Native American Rights Fund Celebrates 35 Years: Modern-Day Warrior Society Establishes Strong Legal Foundation for Indian Law." *Indian Country Today,* 31 August 2005.

New, Lloyd Kiva (Lloyd Henry New) (1916–2002)
Cherokee artist, craftsperson

Lloyd Henry New was born on February 18, 1916, in Fairland, Oklahoma, to a Cherokee mother and a father of Scots-Irish descent. After hopping a freight train to Chicago to attend the World's Fair while in his teens, New discovered the Art Institute of Chicago and became determined to enroll some day. He attended Oklahoma State University (1933–34), the Art Institute of Chicago (1934–35), the University of New Mexico (1937), and the University of Chicago, where he received his B.A.E. in 1938. During WORLD WAR II, New served in the Navy.

After studying at the Museum of Indian Arts and Culture's Laboratory of Anthropology in Santa Fe, New Mexico,

New taught at the Phoenix Indian School for two years. In 1945, changing his name to Kiva, he established the Lloyd Kiva Studio in Scottsdale, Arizona, where he instructed prospective art teachers on behalf of the BUREAU OF INDIAN AFFAIRS (BIA). While at the Phoenix Indian School he realized that, although Indians could be master artists and craftsmen, they had few outlets for their work. He developed the theory that Indian arts and crafts could be incorporated into Western culture by using Indian motifs on fashion items such as handbags. With his first wife, Betty, he began crafting leather goods from his studio, and soon his handbags were featured in top fashion magazines such as *Harper's Bazaar*. He pushed his theory of bringing Indian art into the mainstream fashion world by having wool, featuring Native patterns and woven by Indians in Oklahoma, cut into jackets and coats.

In 1947, New became the director of the Arizona State Fair's Indian exhibits. He transformed the staid exhibits by placing Indian rugs, baskets and other articles in a living room decked out with contemporary furniture from a local furniture store and by dressing mannequins in stylish Adrian suits while sporting Indian jewelry. In 1959, he became codirector of the influential Southwest Indian Arts Project at the University of Arizona, which was sponsored by the Rockefeller Foundation.

New established the Institute of American Indian Arts (IAIA) in 1962 with longtime BIA educator George A. Boyce. The addition of ALLAN HOUSER and FRITZ SCHOLDER, turned it into an important center for modern Indian art. They expanded the student body to include Indians from across the country, not simply the Southwest, and gave instruction in art forms other than painting. The IAIA helped to pave the way for new artistic styles to supplant the "Studio" school fostered by DOROTHY DUNN which had dominated Indian painting until then. The school originally began as a two-year program offering high school diplomas, but is now a four-year college. New served as president of AIA from 1967 until 1978, and after retiring remained president emeritus.

In 1968, under the name Lloyd H. New, he published *Institute of American Indian Arts: Cultural Difference as the Basis for Creative Education*, which outlined some of his groundbreaking ideas for teaching Indian art students. New also served as an adviser on the creation of the National Museum of the American in Washington, D.C. In 2000, he was awarded an honorary doctorate by the Art Institute of Chicago. His poetry has been set to music by Cherokee/Quapaw composer LOUIS WAYNE BALLARD.

Known for his unique crafts and fashion accessories, such as his "Kiva bags," Lloyd Kiva New was one of the 20th century's most successful marketers of Indian arts. He died on February 8, 2002, in Santa Fe, New Mexico.

Further Reading
Avey, Gary. "Lloyd Kiva New." *Native Peoples Magazine.* Available online. URL: http://www.nativepeoples.com/article/artieles/l30/1/Lloyd-Kiva-New. Accessed 5 December 2009.

Metcalfe, Jessica R. *Beyond Buckskin: About Native American Fashion*. Available online. URL: http://beyondbuckskin.blogspot.com. Accessed 20 February 2010.

New Age movement
In the last quarter of the 20th century, American Indians increasingly felt the impact of the New Age movement, a vaguely defined trend characterized by a turn toward spiritual sources and practices unconventional by Western standards. New Age thought superficially resembles ancient traditions, but its basic tendencies are Western, and its structures and procedures parallel general economic and social trends of the contemporary world.

New Age, in its most recent phase, began in the mid-1970s as more conservative trends began to overshadow the revolutionary atmosphere of the 1960s counterculture. Despite the eclectic, fluid, and often inarticulate nature of New Age thought, what its myriad forms have in common is an intense subjectivity. New Agers do not believe in any real or ultimate truth. As theological critic Elliot Miller puts it, "Anything can be true for the individual, but nothing can be true for everyone." On a cosmic level, New Agers embrace holism, monism, pantheism, cosmic evolution, and the desire to unlock hidden potentials in the mind. They emphasize experience over doctrine, a value often expressed in such terms as *self-actualization, human potentiality, the higher self, inner harmony, gnosis, enlightenment, human divinity, self-improvement,* and *therapy* (the human potential movement, with its mecca at the Esalen Institute in Big Sur, California). Many believe in reincarnation. They seek unity of religions in a "wild eclecticism" that is drawn from a smorgasbord of spiritual traditions but remains in essence antitraditional.

The underlying philosophy of New Age combines three fundamentally Western traits, the first of which is optimism, an attitude that blends easily with humanistic utopianism but also reflects liberal Christian postmillennialism, which foresees a second coming of Christ after a period of social improvement. The second trait is evolutionism, the idea of improvement through a natural and inevitable process of change. The last is Theosophy, a doctrine that the earth is entering a new age of enlightenment brought on by a cosmic spiritual evolution, of which the evolution of natural forms is only an outer manifestation.

The term *new age* was first popularized by the New Jerusalem Church (Swedenborgian) and appears in titles of numerous publications of the late 19th century. Features of what would become the New Age movement—altered states of consciousness, communication with other realms (in Theosophy, with what are called "ascended masters"), alternative medicine, divinity of man—were already typical of the "New Thought" movement that developed in Boston in the late 19th century out of transcendentalism, Swedenborgianism, Christian Science, and other forms of liberal Christianity, with Darwinian evolutionism adding a scientific veneer. But it was Madame Helena Petrovna Blavatsky's *Isis Unveiled* (1877) and

The Secret Doctrine (1888), the "bibles" of her Theosophical movement, that supplied the exotic, pseudoesoteric elements that would later come to distinguish today's New Age.

Images of American Indians as highly spiritual, morally superior beings, possessing supernatural powers and the secrets of health, were part of popular culture in 19th-century America and a stock in trade of the snake-oil salesman. In New Age's earlier phase, in which spiritualism (the supposed communication with spirits of the dead, and other such phenomena of suggestion) played a prominent role, the American Indian often figured as a spirit guide appearing to the medium who was supposedly receiving messages from the souls of the departed, or as the messenger himself. As early as 1891, medium Kate R. Stiles published *Sitting Bull's Message from the Spirit Life* in Boston.

After WORLD WAR I, ARTHUR C. PARKER was prominent in developing fraternal organizations that incorporated Masonic rituals with Indian trimmings. The American Indian Association (see TIPI ORDER OF AMERICA) welcomed whites (blacks were excluded), aiming to foster a new type of identity among urban Indians while furthering Indian-white contacts. As the esoteric element undoubtedly appealed to some whites, such fraternal societies helped to integrate the Indian image into New Age thought. Meanwhile, in the 1920s, Katherine Tingley's School of Antiquity at Point Loma, California (run by the Universal Brotherhood and Theosophical Society, an American group that seceded from the original Theosophical Society in 1899), became a center for fanciful (as well as genuine) research on pre-Columbian civilizations.

Around 1929, a "spirit" known as White Eagle, identified as an Indian chief and member of the White Brotherhood of the Great White Lodge (a nonexistent "spiritual center" that plays a central role in Theosophical doctrine), began delivering messages through spiritual medium Grace Cooke at Burstow in Surrey, England. (White Eagle Lodge, with headquarters in Liss, Hampshire, England, today claims more than 100 branches worldwide.) Her *Sun-Men of the Americas* (1975) represents their version of American Indian spirituality. Because the "spirit guides" are believed to be, in Theosophical parlance, "highly evolved entities," the pronouncements attributed to them are considered authoritative. Thus, New Age devotees will always give them precedence over genuine traditional American Indian world views. Yet they have nothing whatever to do with Indian culture, being a conglomeration of various spiritual traditions with an underpinning of Blavatskian Theosophy.

After WORLD WAR II, several new trends came together to give the New Age movement its late 20th-century form. The definitive union between humanistic psychology and Eastern mysticism occurred in 1962 when psychologist Abraham Maslow and Michael Murphy (owner of a bohemian colony at Big Sur in northern California and a student of Eastern religions) founded the Esalen Institute. Another early supporter was Aldous Huxley, author of *The Doors of Perception* (1956). Huxley, whose interest in Eastern esotericism, hallucinogenic plants, and alternative perception went back to 1930s London, was then teaching at the University of California at Santa Barbara. Out of these influences, the Human Potential movement arose in California and spread rapidly.

Interest in American Indian spirituality emerged in the early 1960s, mainly under the rubric of *shamanism*. CARLOS CASTAÑEDA, then an undergraduate at the University of California, Los Angeles, interviewed his first California Indian informants in 1960. Although Castañeda was not yet New Age at that time, his series of books featuring the Yaqui Shaman Don Juan served as a major catalyst for the neo-shamanism of the 1990s. Writer Evelyn Eaton (1902–82), a Theosophist, first encountered Paiute and Arapaho medicine people in 1962 in Owens Valley, California. She studied with medicine men Raymond Stone (Paiute) and Red Eagle (Apache), and was a close friend of New Age writer HYEMEYOHSTS STORM. The publication of Andrija Puharich's *The Sacred Mushroom* in 1959 and Frank Waters's *Book of the Hopi* in 1963, as well as the republication in 1962 of John Neihardt's *Black Elk Speaks*, also attracted the human potential movement to shamanism, identified with the traditional religious practices of indigenous peoples.

In the 1960s, large numbers of young people, frustrated with the conformity of the postwar period and opposed to the war in Vietnam and racism at home, became alienated from mainstream American culture. This loss of faith in traditional institutions—from mainstream religions to rationalism, secular humanism, science, and progress—brought a new interest in esotericism and exotic spiritual traditions. This was the seedbed of the modern New Age. "In 1966," wrote VINE DELORIA, JR., in *Custer Died for Your Sins* (1969), "strange beings began to appear on Indian land, proclaiming their kinship to redskins in no uncertain terms." Around that time, hippies began frequenting the gatherings of Indians and non-Indians held by Hopi traditional leaders DAN KATCHONGVA and "Grandfather David" Monyonge. (His hippie followers cost David Monyonge the chance to become kikmongwe of Hotevilla Pueblo.) These hippies included Oh-Shinnah Fastwolf, a white woman who later became well known in the New Age "Indian" movement.

Within the New Age Indian leadership can be found some with genuine Indian backgrounds, such as SUN BEAR (Chippewa); WALLACE BLACK ELK (Lakota Sioux); and Archie Fire (Lakota Sioux), son of JOHN FIRE LAME DEER. However, the vast majority can only make unsupported claims of ancestry or some kind of "spiritual" connection. New Age publications that exploit Indian traditions include Lynn Andrews's *Medicine Woman*, the works of Jamake Highwater, Brooke Medicine Eagle, Dhyani Ywahoo (who mixes Cherokee and Tibetan traditions), and many others.

In the 1980s, human potential became a goal of those who could afford it. Alienated from accustomed social roles, such people took refuge in a commercialized spirituality, pursuing personal rather than community-oriented ideals and seeking easy access to shamanic power from increasingly exotic sources. Career advancement and a comfortable lifestyle could now be achieved with the help of psychotechnologies such as hypnosis and biofeedback; by meditation and exercise; and by purchasing the books, lectures, seminars, videotapes, audiotapes, kits, and paraphernalia, all suited to a rationalized, commercial mass-market consumer society.

New Age belief thus became a commodified "spirituality," a market of products to be collected piecemeal. A 1994 advertisement in *Shaman's Drum* magazine epitomized these trends. Readers were invited to

> take the shamanic voyage of discovery . . . trade in Indian villages . . . participate in all-night ayahuasca ceremonies guided by real Amazonian shamans. . . . Travel through worlds in which spirit animals are your teachers and flying saucers are your classrooms all while living in comfort on our beautiful mahogany river boat with two shamans, ten Amazonian crew members, a fleet of motorized canoes, open bar, laundry service, and all-natural gourmet meals.

In 1980, the Traditional Circle of Indian Elders and Youth issued a resolution condemning the commercialization of traditional ceremonies, and in 1984 the AMERICAN INDIAN MOVEMENT (AIM) drew up its own resolution in support of the Traditional Circle. The NATIONAL CONGRESS OF AMERICAN INDIANS (NCAI) condemned non-Indians for the New Age distortion of Indian traditions. This has not stopped the New Age movement from continuing to expropriate or misrepresent Indian ceremonies and religions. New Agers do not see indigenous traditions as the cultural property of a particular tribe; rather, they view spiritual traditions as being in the public domain, and thus believe they have some kind of equal-access "right" to sacred knowledge. The poet Gary Snyder's statement that "Spirituality is not something that can be 'owned' like a car or a house . . . [but] belongs to all humanity equally" reflects the Western, nontraditional origin of New Age thinking. By this logic, the traditional Indians are unfairly keeping their spirituality from other people.

The confrontation between Indians and New Agers has reached the point of physical interference. In 1994, in one of many such demonstrations, Indian protesters accused New Age enthusiasts of desecrating Bear Butte, a sacred site now in a South Dakota state park, and excluding traditional Indians.

Further Reading

Aldred, Lisa. "Plastic Shamans and Astroturf Sun Dances: New Age Commercialization of Native American Spirituality." *American Indian Quarterly* 24, no 3 (2000): 329–352.

Bell, Diane. "Some Readings on Cultural Appropriations, Native America, and the New Age." Bibliography. Available online. URL: www.hanksville.org/sand/intellect/NAbibBell.html. Accessed on 15 March 2007.

Jenkins, Philip. *Dream Catchers: How Mainstream America Discovered Native Spirituality*. New York: Oxford University Press, 2004.

Shaw, Christopher. "A Theft of Spirit?" *New Age Journal* (July/August 1995): 84–92.

Smith, Andrea. "For All Those Who Were Indians in a Former Life." In *Ecofeminism and the Sacred*, edited by Carol Adams, 168–171. New York: Continuum, 1993.

Niatum, Duane (Duane McGinniss) (1938–   )
S'Klallam (Jamestown Band) poet, editor

A member of the S'Klallam Jamestown Band of the Klallam, Duane McGinniss was born in Seattle, Washington, on February 13, 1938. His parents divorced when he was five, and he was raised by his maternal grandfather, Francis Patsy, who taught him hunting, fishing, and Klallam traditions. McGinniss spent a good part of his youth in and out of reform school before joining the U.S. Navy at the age of 17. He returned from the service to enroll at the University of Washington, where he studied under poets Theodore Roethke and Elizabeth Bishop and produced his first work, an experimental verse drama, in 1968. After receiving his B.A. in 1970, he attended Johns Hopkins University in Baltimore, Maryland, where he received his M.A. in 1972.

In 1970, still using the name McGinniss, Duane published *After the Death of an Elder Klallam*, a book of poems eulogizing his grandfather. The next year, he changed his name to Niatum, his maternal great-grandfather's Indian name. In 1973, he issued two chapbooks of poetry, *A Cycle for the Woman in the Field* and *Taos Pueblo and Other Poems*. That year, Niatum was named editor of Harper and Row's Native American Authors Series, for which he put together an anthology of young Indian writers, *Carriers of the Dream Wheel*, in 1975. Illustrated by WENDY ROSE (Hopi-Miwok), the anthology immediately became an important text in the field of American Indian literature. In 1988, Niatum published an expanded version, *Harper's Twentieth Century Native American Poetry*.

Niatum continued to write poetry, releasing *Digging Out the Roots* (1977), *To Bridge the Dream* (1978), and *Pieces* (1981). His poem collection *Songs for the Harvester of Dreams* won the 1982 Before Columbus Foundation's American Book Award. A prolific poet whose works largely explore the meaning of Native American identity in the United States, Niatum also published *Drawings of the Song Animals* (1991). In 2000, he released another book of poetry, *The Crooked Beak of Love*. He published a chapbook, *Journeys That Criss-Cross Darkness and Light*, in 2004.

Further Reading

Niatum, Duane. "The Transformational Tracks of a Marginalized Life." *Paradoxa* 7, no. 3 (1998): 75–85.

Nichols, John Ralph (1898–1968) *commissioner of Indian affairs*

Born on September 18, 1898, in New York City, John Ralph Nichols earned a B.S. in agriculture in 1922 from Oregon State Agricultural College. In 1925, he received a master's in education from Stanford University, and in 1930 he earned his Ph.D.

He was appointed president of Idaho State College in 1934 and later served as dean of the southern branch of the University of Idaho. In 1943, Nichols earned another master's in international administration from Columbia University before serving in WORLD WAR II in the U.S. Navy, where he attained the rank of commander. He remained in Japan after the war as an adviser on education to General Douglas McArthur.

From 1947 to 1949, Nichols was president of the New Mexico College of Agriculture and Mechanical Arts (now New Mexico State University) at Las Cruces. At that time he also served on the HOOVER COMMISSION, which advocated the ASSIMILATION of Indians, a break from the policies of the INDIAN NEW DEAL (see INDIAN REORGANIZATION ACT). The mood in Congress had shifted away from the culturally based policies of Indian New Deal architect JOHN COLLIER and toward a new vehicle of assimilation known as TERMINATION. Nichols himself favored assimilation. Unlike the terminationists, however, he felt that it should come benevolently and not be forced upon the Indians. Nominated in 1949 by President Harry S. Truman to serve as Indian commissioner, Nichols attempted to grasp the complexities of an assimilationist policy that would effectively integrate Indians into the mainstream. After some study, he concluded that a comprehensive assimilation policy, involving many branches of government, including the building of adequate schools and provision of basic services still unavailable to Indians, would cost more than $150 million, a sum Congress was not prepared to pay.

Less than a year into his administration, Nichols was appointed special assistant to the secretary of the interior to study the transfer of jurisdiction of Pacific trust territories from the navy to the Interior Department. It was therefore Nichols's successor, DILLON SEYMOUR MYER, who implemented the Termination policy. After leaving the Interior Department, Nichols worked in private industry. He died in New York City on May 5, 1968.

Further Reading

Koppes, Clayton R. "From New Deal to Termination: Liberalism and Indian Policy, 1933–1953." *Pacific Historical Review* 46, no. 4 (1977): 543–566.

Officer, James E. "The Bureau of Indian Affairs Since 1945: An Assessment." *Annals of the American Academy of Political and Social Science* 436, no. 1 (1978): 61–72.

Nighthawk Keetoowah   *See* SMITH, REDBIRD.

Nordwall, Adam   *See* FORTUNATE EAGLE, ADAM.

Northrup, Jim   (1943–   ) *Chippewa humorist, author, radio commentator, video producer*

A Chippewa born April 28, 1943, on the Fond du Lac Reservation, Jim Northrup joined the U.S. Marine Corps in 1961, serving in Vietnam and rising to the rank of sergeant before his discharge in 1966. Northrup's syndicated column "Fond du Lac Follies" appeared in three northern Indian newspapers, including *News from Indian Country* (see DEMAIN, PAUL). A satirical look at local Indian affairs from a folksy reservation point of view, the "Follies," in the best tradition of Will Rogers (see ROGERS, WILLIAM PENN ADAIR), liberally skewered the antics of political leaders, large and small, in a disarmingly friendly way. After a 25-year run, the column ended in August 2014.

Northrup has broadcast over public radio, and his snippets of local reservation life have been turned into a number of locally produced videos, including *Warriors* (1988), *Diaries* (1991), *Zero Street* (1993), and *With Reservations* (1994). He has also published two books of poetry, *Frags and Fragments* (1990), about his experiences in Vietnam, and *Days of Obsidian, and Days of Grace* (1994). Other books are *Touchwood* (1987), *Three More* (1992), *Walking the Rez Road* (1993), *The Rez Road Follies: Canoes, Casinos, Computers, and Birch Bark Baskets* (1999), and *Dirty Copper* (2014). His play *Shinob Jep*, an Ojibwa parody of the television game show *Jeopardy*, preceded by an interview, was broadcast on KFAI radio (Minneapolis/St. Paul, Minnesota) on October 25, 2009.

Further Reading

Thompson, Abbey. "Catching Up with Writer Jim Northrup." *Indian Country Today*, 2 October 2003.

nuclear industry, American Indians and the

There is a close historical association between the nuclear industry and American Indians. First, more than half of all the uranium in the United States lies beneath or immediately adjacent to INDIAN RESERVATIONS. Second, the remoteness of many Indian reservations has made them attractive sites for the many toxic stages in the processing and disposal of nuclear products. The effects of the nuclear industry on Indians have been almost uniformly negative, and the few jobs created, usually the lowest-paying and most dangerous, do not begin to compensate for the permanent damage done to many Indian communities by the nuclear industry.

Mining of uranium on Indian lands began in 1920, when the Carriso Uranium Company and the Radium Ores Company staked claims for mines on the Navajo (Dineh) Reservation. Mining of uranium in the United States remained at a low level until WORLD WAR II, but during and after the war the race to arm America with atomic weapons led to an escalation of mining on reservations, with little regard for safety and health concerns. Indian miners dug the uranium ore by hand in the small mines called "dog holes," breathing radon gas and contaminated dust. Many of the miners eventually suffered painful, drawn-out deaths from their exposure to radiation.

Lax environmental and safety regulations led to numerous accidents, such as one in June 1962, when 200 tons of radioactive waste washed into the Cheyenne River near the Pine Ridge Reservation in South Dakota. The largest such accident, and possibly the worst nuclear accident in

In this 1953 photo, Navajo uranium miners at the Kerr McGee mine at Cove on the Navajo (Dineh) Reservation pull ore out of the mine—unaware that this would lead to serious health problems for many of them from exposure to radioactivity. *(AP/Wideworld)*

U.S. history, occurred in July 1979, when a United Nuclear Corporation dam holding 100 million gallons of radioactive water and 1,100 tons of radioactive waste burst, spilling into the Rio Puerco on the Navajo Reservation. The spill killed more than 1,000 sheep, horses, and other livestock that drank from the river and forced the evacuation of 1,700 Navajo.

By the end of the mining boom, in the early 1980s, there were more than 1,200 abandoned uranium mines on the Navajo Reservation alone. These mines would be left uncovered with exposed piles of highly radioactive tailings nearby, some containing as much as 2 million tons of radioactive waste. When the Jackpile Mine in New Mexico, once the largest open-pit uranium mine in the world, was abruptly abandoned by the Anaconda Mining Company in 1981, it left contaminated the Laguna Pueblo's water sources, as well as the tribal council building, the community center, and other buildings. Anaconda had also used low-grade uranium ore to "improve" the road system leading to the mine and village, forcing the Laguna Pueblo people to launch a reclamation project.

In addition, the milling process, the step in which usable uranium is extracted from uranium ore, was carried out in places such as the Susquehanna Mills Processing Plant, located next to the Wind River Reservation of the Shoshone and Arapaho in Wyoming. Susquehanna, when closed, left more than 900,000 tons of radioactive tailings on that reservation alone.

The enrichment process and the use of fission to create plutonium posed special hazards. The Hanford Nuclear Reservation, built during World War II next to the Yakama Reservation in Washington State, and its sister processing plant, Sequoyah Mills near Cherokee lands in Oklahoma, produced plutonium with such a total disregard for environmental controls that they have become two of the most toxic sites on Earth. Also during World War II, military police evicted Shoshone ranchers and herders from lands in southern Nevada in order to secure a test site for the new weapons. The former Shoshone lands were subjected to more than 700 nuclear tests, above and below ground, a greater number than any other region on the planet.

By the early 1970s, an antinuclear movement had arisen, largely spawned by a new environmental consciousness and by the threat to public safety that commercial reactors posed. Indians themselves began to mobilize against the threat to their lands. Hopi traditional leader David Monongye spoke out against mining when uranium was discovered near Hopi lands in 1979, arguing: "We who believe in the sacred instructions of the Great Spirit must resist and protest, for the sake of all life, both present and future." Also in 1979, in Nevada, the Western Shoshone mobilized against a proposed MX missile silo that would have been sited on their lands. The Shoshone also began hosting demonstrations against the Nevada Test Site, on lands that they still claim under the 1863 Treaty of Ruby Valley (see BATTLE MOUNTAIN).

Attempts to expand the Hanford Nuclear Reservation in 1980 found Yakama councilman Russell Jim and Columbia River traditional leader Wilbur Slockish among Hanford's most bitter critics. At the same time, in Oklahoma, Cherokee activist Jesse Deer-in-Water launched Native Americans for a Clean Environment (NACE) to fight the Sequoyah Mills weapons plant. In these two cases, Native people became effective organizers for campaigns that publicized the weapons plants' notoriously bad safety and environmental records and helped lead to their closing.

A major confrontation now revolved around what to do with the high-level radioactive wastes. The Mdewakanton Dakota Sioux of Prairie Island, Minnesota, led an unsuccessful campaign against the attempt of Northern State Power to build a storage depot adjacent to their reservation. Numerous attempts had been made to place the nuclear waste products from both commercial reactors and arms manufacture on Indian lands, and the Nuclear Waste Policy Act was initiated in 1982. In 1987, the United States selected seven potential sites for a permanent high-level waste dump, four of which were on Indian reservations. While searching for a suitable permanent site, the United States negotiated with 26 Indian reservations for a temporary federal depository. Grassroots Indian activism spread to all 26 Indian reservations that were being considered for temporary sites, leading 23 reservations to withdraw themselves from consideration and forcing Congress to defund the proposal to create a temporary depository. The Mescalero Apache's efforts to become a "private" depository outside of federal and state control met with fierce local opposition (see CHINO, WENDELL).

Since there is currently no solution for dealing with the deadly end products of the uranium cycle, it is likely that Indians and the nuclear industry will continue to do battle well into the 21st century.

See also MINING, AMERICAN INDIANS AND.

Further Reading

Anon. "Minnesota Indian Tribe Calls on President Obama to Find Solution to Nuclear Waste Issue." *PRNewswire* (October 15, 2009). Available online. URL: http://www.prnewswire.com/news-releases. Accessed 31 October 2011.

Churchill, Ward, and Winona LaDuke. "Native North America: The Political Economy of Radioactive Colonialism." In *The State of Native America: Genocide, Colonization, and Resistance*, edited by M. Annette James, 241–266. Boston: South End Press, 1992.

Eichstaedt, Peter. *If You Poison Us: Uranium and Native Americans.* Santa Fe, N.Mex.: Red Crane Books, 1994.

Kuletz, Valerie. *The Tainted Desert: Environmental Ruin in the American West.* New York: Routledge, 1998.

Smithson, Shelley. "Radioactive Revival in New Mexico." *Nation* 288, no. 25 (June 29, 2009): 16–20.

Oakes, Richard (1942–1972) *Mohawk political activist*
Born on May 22, 1942, at Akwesasne (St. Regis Reservation) in northern New York, Richard Oakes left school at age 16 to become a construction worker. After traveling throughout New England, he attended Adirondack Community College and Syracuse University in New York. Moving to San Francisco, California, he found work in high-steel construction and as a truck driver before becoming a bartender at Warren's Bar, a popular hangout for Indians, in the Mission District of San Francisco. There Oakes and other young Indians formed a club modeled after the popular motorcycle clubs of the day; they called it Indians and Half Breeds of San Francisco.

By 1968, many universities across the country were experiencing unrest and violence, generally focused around protests against the Vietnam War. On November 6, 1968, students went on strike at San Francisco State College (SFSC), demanding, among other things, the creation of a department for ethnic studies. Although not a student, Oakes sympathized with the goals of the striking students, known as the Third World Liberation Front, and joined their efforts. As a result of the five-month strike, the college agreed to create a number of new departments, including a Native American Studies Department (now called the American Indian Studies Department).

With the help of a sympathetic anthropology professor, Luis S. Kemnitzer, Oakes organized the Native American Studies Department, recruiting Indian scholars Jeanette Henry (Eastern Cherokee) and RUPERT COSTO (Cahuilla) to serve as advisers. Oakes also brought in his friends and acquaintances, including Al Miller (Seminole), Gerald Sam (Round Valley), Joe Bill (Inuit), Deanna Francis (Maliseet), Mickey Gemmill (Pit River), Robert Kaniatobe (Choctaw), Ronald Lickers (Seneca), and Joyce Rice (Winnebago), and together they became the core student body of the new department. During this time, Oakes married a Kashia Pomo woman, Annie Marufano, and adopted her five children.

In fall 1969, shortly after the new Native American Studies Department began holding its first classes, Oakes discovered that the White Roots of Peace, an Iroquois lecture group led by Mohawk chief TOM PORTER, was coming to the area. At Oakes's behest, Professor Kemnitzer arranged the group's appearance at SFSC; Mill College; the University of California, Santa Cruz; and the University of California, Berkeley. The White Roots of Peace's impact on American Indian students at these schools was, in the words of Kemnitzer, "electrifying," inspiring Oakes to organize Indians outside of the college. His leadership ability was by this time well known among the local Bay Area Indian leaders, who were planning an OCCUPATION OF ALCATRAZ ISLAND. The former prison had closed in 1963 and had been declared surplus property by the U.S. government. In late October 1969, ADAM FORTUNATE EAGLE (Chippewa) asked Oakes to recruit Indian students and lead the occupation attempt.

On November 9, 1969, Oakes and 75 Native students and activists gathered on the San Francisco docks, ready to occupy the island, but none of the boats Oakes and Fortunate Eagle had arranged for showed up. The press did show up, however, so Oakes kept the media entertained while Fortunate Eagle searched for transportation to the island. Oakes read a proclamation in which the activists offered to buy Alcatraz from the federal government for $24 in beads and cloth, the same amount the Dutch paid the Delaware (Lenni Lenape) Indians for Manhattan Island in 1626. Likening the barrenness of the island to conditions on most INDIAN RESERVATIONS, he wryly noted that their offer to purchase Alcatraz, at approximately $1.24 per acre, was substantially greater than the federal government's offer of 47 cents per acre to settle land claims with the California tribes. Eventually Fortunate Eagle managed to persuade the owner of the *Monte Cristo*, a three-masted sailing ship, to circle Alcatraz with the activists. Oakes then jumped overboard and tried to swim to shore, followed by some of the students. Although they misjudged the tide and had to be pulled from the frigid waters, the group was undeterred, and they landed on shore later that night.

Oakes and 13 other Indians left the island the next day, but when negotiations over its future failed to materialize, he led another attempt on November 20, this time determined to stay. For Oakes, the Alcatraz occupation was a symbolic act, geared not so much to recover the island for Indians to use, as older leaders such as Fortunate Eagle had hoped, but as a way to send a message to the American people. In his view, "Alcatraz is not an island, it's an idea. It's the idea that you can control your own destiny, and self-determine your future."

Handsome and articulate, Oakes became a celebrity during the first few months of the occupation. His defiant words "We Hold the Rock!" became the motto of the occupation, but his celebrity status quickly became a source of friction between him and the other occupiers. In addition, a struggle for leadership emerged in INDIANS OF ALL TRIBES, the organization he had helped create to oversee the takeover.

In January 1970, Oakes's stepdaughter Yvonne died of a head injury after falling down a stairwell on the island, and he left the occupation. Oakes then joined the PIT RIVER Indians' efforts to regain land near Mt. Shasta, California, helping them organize demonstrations, drumming up support in San Francisco, and on June 12, 1970, even making a citizen's arrest of the president of Pacific Gas and Electric, one of the companies operating on the contested lands. In fall 1970, Oakes was relaxing in Warren's Bar when he got into a fight with another customer and was badly beaten. He remained in the hospital in a coma for several days until a visit by Tuscarora activist MAD BEAR ANDERSON. Anderson brought with him a traditional healer who helped Oakes regain consciousness.

Though now partially paralyzed, Oakes remained involved in Indian issues and antiwar organizing. On September 20, 1972, in Mendocino County, he became embroiled in a confrontation between some Indian youths and officials at a YMCA camp over the Indian children's unauthorized riding of the camp's horses. Oakes was there simply to pick up a friend, but when the argument grew heated, a security guard for the camp shot the unarmed Oakes dead. His killer, a non-Indian named Michael Morgan, claimed that Oakes had ambushed him. Initially Morgan was charged with murder, but the charge was changed to involuntary manslaughter. Although there was no evidence of a struggle, Morgan's attorneys argued self-defense before a jury of non-Native citizens. In the end Morgan was acquitted. Oakes's death stunned members of the RED POWER movement, which at the time had become factionalized and uncertain of its direction, and an attempt to commemorate his death led directly to the TRAIL OF BROKEN TREATIES later that year.

Though his life was short, Oakes had a profound impact on the struggle for Indian rights, and his actions inspired such groups as the AMERICAN INDIAN MOVEMENT (AIM) to try to duplicate his success. On November 20, 1999, the 30th anniversary of the takeover of Alcatraz, San Francisco State University (formerly San Francisco State College) established the Richard Oakes Multicultural Center in his honor.

Further Reading
Johnson, Troy R. *The Occupation of Alcatraz Island: Indian Self-Determination and the Rise of Indian Activism.* Champaign: University of Illinois Press, 1996.

oil, American Indians and
Unbeknownst to the 19th-century policy makers who established it as a home for relocated tribes, the lands of Indian Territory (now Oklahoma) held one of the greatest concentrations of oil and gas in the Western Hemisphere. Before the mass production of automobiles, oil was in little demand, and during the late 19th century drilling proceeded slowly. The first petroleum enterprise organized in Indian Territory was the Chickasaw Oil Company, founded by Robert M. Darden in 1872. His contract with the Choctaw and Chickasaw allowed him to drill for oil in return for a royalty to the two tribes equivalent to half the total oil production. The company failed to produce oil, however. Other unsuccessful ventures included the National Oil Company, founded by H. W. Faucett of New York City in 1883 to drill on Choctaw land, and an attempt by Michael Cudahy, owner of a large packing company, who came up dry on Creek land near Muskogee.

The first commercially successful oil well in Indian Territory was opened by Edward Byrd in November 1889 on Cherokee lands north of Spencer Creek. Byrd held a blanket lease on 94,000 Cherokee acres, signed by Chief Bushyhead, but the validity of the lease was contested by the Department of the Interior. With the venture held up by red tape, Byrd abandoned the field. In 1891, seeking to protect Indian interests, Congress passed an Indian oil-leasing act that placed a 10-year limit on all leases and set other minimum regulations.

George Keeler, as owner of a trading post, had become adept at circumventing the Office of Indian Affairs (later the BUREAU OF INDIAN AFFAIRS [BIA]). He persuaded Cudahy to try his luck again on the same Cherokee lands near Bartlesville that Keeler had leased. In March 1897, the first well came in, bringing 150 barrels a day from a depth of 1,400 feet. In 1896, the newly formed Phoenix Oil Company began to drill test wells on the Osage reservation, and high-quality oil was found on Creek lands as well. News of these strikes and the potential bonanza they represented was kept quiet while attempts were made to lease larger reservation tracts at low prices.

In May 1905, the Standard Oil Company prevailed upon the Theodore Roosevelt administration and Secretary of the Interior Ethan Allen Hitchock to renew the Osage blanket lease, which most oilmen knew to be severely undervalued. Later that year, the discovery of the Glenn Pool near Tulsa blew the lid off the secret, spurring a massive oil rush. Harry Sinclair, founder of Sinclair Oil, was drawn to the rush. He soon became adept at using the guardianship process to bilk Cherokee minors and other "incompetents" out of their oil-rich allotments (see ALLOTMENT). Brothers Frank and

L. E. Phillips organized Phillips Petroleum in 1917 to capitalize on their vast holdings on Osage lands. E. W. Marland successfully drilled for oil on the Ponca lands he leased.

The discovery of oil led to a vast looting spree, as Indian allotments were snapped up by speculators and con men. The disastrous "competency commissions" under Indian Commissioner CATO SELLS fed into the frenzy of theft and violence, as thousands of oil-rich Indians were removed from federal trust protections and allowed to sell their valuable allotments for a pittance. An entire industry of "guardians" grew up in Oklahoma, dedicated to managing individual Indian assets while actually milking them (see CURTIS ACT). Some criminals even married into Indian families and murdered them for their allotments. An epidemic of kidnapping, forgery, and murder plagued Indian Territory throughout the first three decades of this century (see OSAGE REIGN OF TERROR). Although a few Indians, such as Creek JACKSON BARNETT, became fabulously wealthy, even they were dogged by gold diggers and grifters.

Only the Osage, under leaders Big Jim Bigheart and FRED LOOKOUT, managed to preserve tribal control over their oil wealth and somewhat minimize the thievery. As a consequence, the Osage became staggeringly wealthy, and with more than 3,000 oil wells on their lands, by 1917 the average Osage was earning between $5,000 and $10,000 per year from oil royalties, a hefty sum in those days.

The 1920s was the period of the "great frenzy" among the Osage and those individual Indians who had managed to maintain their oil-producing allotments. By 1925, the Osage were averaging a per-capita payment of $50,000 per year, and most were spending their money as fast as they could. The decade was also the heyday of "Big Oil," and the administration of President Warren G. Harding, who took office in 1921, was filled with representatives of the oil companies, leading one Mexican newspaper to wryly note that ALBERT BACON FALL's appointment as secretary of the interior "smells of petroleum."

Secretary Fall tried to capitalize on newly discovered oilfields in the Southwest, but the Navajo proved intransigent. Fall then turned to Congress for help, securing passage in 1922 of a bill that not only permitted oil and gas leasing on Navajo lands but authorized Fall himself to negotiate the leases. In 1923, he placed HERBERT JAMES HAGERMAN in charge of leasing the Navajo Reservation to oil interests and forming a Navajo tribal council to approve the leases. The move led to controversy when the leases were found to be grossly undervalued.

Fall also issued a controversial administrative order that allowed executive-order reservations to be drilled under the General Leasing Act. This caused another storm of controversy, and the order had to be rescinded by his successor, Hubert Work. (See CURTIS, CHARLES.) However, Congress overrode Work's attempts to create a manageable policy that would award all leasing revenue to the tribes. Instead it passed the Indian Oil Leasing Act of 1924, which amended the 1891 act, eliminating the 10-year limit on leasing and allowing

states to impose a tax on Indian oil revenues. Attempts to further liberalize leasing on Indian lands and to allow states to receive 37.5 percent of Indian oil revenues ran into a fierce storm of protest, led in part by JOHN COLLIER. After Fall's involvement in the infamous Teapot Dome scandal became public, attempts to reform the leasing policy led to the Indian Oil Leasing Act of 1927, which awarded to Indians nearly all revenues gained from oil leasing. The Great Depression and the collapse of oil prices ended the oil boom on INDIAN RESERVATIONS.

Through congressional legislation in 1938, Collier, now Indian commissioner, managed to remedy a number of the disadvantages of the 1924 and 1927 Indian oil-lease acts, opening up the process to competitive bidding and ending state taxation of Indian oil royalties. However, during WORLD WAR II, Collier liberally leased Indian oil lands to the War Department in the vain hope of currying favor with the government, which was rapidly turning against his ambitious reform policies.

During the postwar TERMINATION era, Congress loosened the restrictions on the leasing and alienation of Indian allotments. This led to the removal of more than 2.6 million acres of allotted land, most with considerable energy reserves from trust protection, largely in Oklahoma and the northern Great Plains. Attempts made during this time to terminate the Osage and other energy-rich tribes were mostly fought off. The period is also notable for reviving the BIA's cozy partnership with oil companies, characterized by lax supervision and numerous conflicts of interests (see BOYDEN, JOHN STERLING).

The discovery of oil in Alaska during the 1960s required the resolution of the state's questionable title to most of its land. The result was the controversial ALASKA NATIVE LAND CLAIMS SETTLEMENT ACT of 1971. With the rise in energy prices during the 1970s, long-term leases, many signed in the 1950s, began to seem anachronistic. Indians attempted to gain control of their energy resources through organization such as the COUNCIL OF ENERGY RESOURCE TRIBES (CERT).

The huge increases in oil prices after the Arab oil boycott of 1973 and the political militancy of the Organization of the Petroleum Exporting Countries (OPEC) in the early 1970s brought renewed efforts to fleece Indian oil holdings. In 1980, the Jicarilla Apache assumed complete ownership and control of their oil production when it was discovered that one of the oil companies operating on their lands had underpaid them by $600,000. This was but a small amount compared to the sums claimed to have been stolen from the Wind River Reservation (Eastern Shoshone and Northern Arapaho)—about $3 billion between 1960 and 1980. The government turned a blind eye to the allegations until 1987, when the *Arizona Republic* charged that oil companies with concessions on Indian reservations had systematically swindled Indian tribes of almost $6 billion in oil revenues between the years 1981 and 1986 (see SWIMMER, ROSS O.). Although the findings created a national outcry, Congress managed to derail any investigation into the matter, preferring instead to focus on the business dealings of Navajo tribal chair PETER MACDONALD. The collapse of oil prices during the late 1980s and through the 1990s led the oil-rich tribes into an economic recession from which they have yet to recover.

See also MINING, AMERICAN INDIANS AND.

Further Reading
Chamberlain, Kathleen. *Under Sacred Ground: A History of Navajo Oil, 1922–1982*. Albuquerque: University of New Mexico Press, 2000.
Colby, Gerard. *Thy Will Be Done: Nelson Rockefeller and Evangelism in the Age of Oil*. New York: HarperCollins, 1995.
Glasscock, Carl B. *Then Came Oil: The Story of the Last Frontier*. Indianapolis and New York: Bobbs-Merrill, 1938.
Leubben, Thomas E. *American Indian Natural Resources: Oil and Gas*. Washington, D.C.: Institute for the Development of Indian Law, 1980.
Wilson, Terry P. *The Underground Reservation: Osage Oil*. Lincoln: University of Nebraska Press, 1985.

Old Coyote, Barney (1923–2012) *Crow educator, Bureau of Indian Affairs administrator*

Barney Old Coyote was born in St. Xavier on the Crow reservation in Montana on April 10, 1923, to Barney Old Coyote, Sr., and Mae Takes the Gun Childs. He attended Big Horn County public schools. In 1938, Old Coyote went with Crow medicine man William Big Day to ask Wind River Shoshone medicine man JOHN TREHERO to bring the Sun Dance back to the Crow Reservation. At 18 years of age, Old Coyote enlisted in the Army Air Corps on the day after the bombing of Pearl Harbor. His zeal for combat drew the attention of Secretary of the Interior Harold Ickes, who used Old Coyote to help publicize Indian contributions to the war effort (see WORLD WAR II, AMERICAN INDIANS AND). Trained as a pilot during the war, Old Coyote completed 72 combat missions, receiving 17 combat awards, including the Air Medal with Oak Leaf Clusters. After his discharge in 1946, he entered the Haskell Institute in Lawrence, Kansas, before transferring to Morningside College in Sioux City, Iowa, where he received a B.S.

Old Coyote then began his long service in the BUREAU OF INDIAN AFFAIRS (BIA), working as an engineer, a realty officer, and, eventually, a superintendent. From 1964 to 1969, he served as special assistant to the secretary of the Interior, coordinating a Jobs Corps training program. In 1968, he received a Distinguished Service Award from the department. In 1969, he was promoted to assistant area director of the BIA office in Sacramento, California, in time to witness the OCCUPATION OF ALCATRAZ ISLAND. Sympathetic to the aims of the occupiers, he attempted to help them win the island for the Bay Area Indian community. However, the protesters, mostly college students interested in symbolic, rather than concrete results, did not trust anyone connected with the government and rebuffed his offers to help.

After retiring from the BIA in 1970, Old Coyote became the founder and first president of the short-lived American Indian National Bank, chartered in 1973. Initially a success, enabling Indian tribes to receive capital support largely unavailable from regular banks, the American Indian National Bank was unable to attract sufficient investment to make it financially viable and was dissolved in the late 1980s. In 1970, Old Coyote became professor and director of the American Indian Studies program at Montana State University in Bozeman.

In 2003, Old Coyote and his brother Henry published *The Way of the Warrior: Stories of the Crow People*, edited by his granddaughter, Phenocia Baverle. Barney Old Coyote died at Crow Agency, Montana, on August 5, 2012.

Further Reading
"Barney Old Coyote and the American Indian National Bank." *Banker's* 157 (Autumn 1974): 17–18.
McCleary, Carrie Moran. "Crow Landscapes Not Forgotten: Project Preserves Traditional Names." *Indian Country Today*, 3 January 2001.
Old Coyote, Barney, and Willard Fraser. "Reminiscences of Barney Old Coyote, Crow Tribe of Montana." (Microfiche reproduction.) *American Indian Oral History Research Project* II, no. 102. Sanford, N.C.: Microfilming Corp. of America, 1979.

Old Person, Earl (1929–) *Blackfeet tribal leader*

Born in Browning, Montana, on April 13, 1929, to Juniper and Molly (Bear Medicine) Old Person, Earl Old Person attended the local Starr School on the Blackfeet Reservation and graduated from Browning High School. As a child, Old Person performed traditional Blackfeet songs and dances at statewide events. He was elected to the Blackfeet Tribal Business Council in 1954. In 1964, he became its chair and continued to hold that position, with the exception of only two years, until 2008.

Under Old Person's tenure as tribal chair, the Blackfeet constructed an industrial park, housing developments, tourist facilities, and a community center. He also brought small-scale manufacturing plants to the reservation, bringing the Blackfeet renown not only for their pencils, pens, and markers (Blackfeet Writing Instruments, Inc.), but also for their cooperative management. The Blackfeet-owned Pikuni Industries shapes metal into farm items such as corrals, gates, calving pens, and branding irons and recently expanded into making modular homes. Old Person also brought the Headstart program to the reservation and established the Blackfeet Community College. He has created numerous housing, alcohol prevention, and other social-service programs.

Old Person was elected president of the NATIONAL CONGRESS OF AMERICAN INDIANS (NCAI) in 1969, serving for two years. In 1990, he was elected vice president. Old Person's successful leadership of the Blackfeet for over five decades has made him one of the most respected and admired tribal chairmen in the United States. In 1978, the family of former chief JOHN TWO GUNS WHITE CALF bestowed on Old Person the chieftainship of the Blackfeet, an important traditional position of leadership that is held for life. In 1998, the American Civil Liberties Union of Montana gave him its most prestigious award, the Jeanette Rankin Civil Liberties Award, and in 2007, he was inducted into the Montana Hall of Fame.

Further Reading

Anon. "Longtime Blackfeet Chair Earl Old Person Ousted in Elections." *News from Indian Country*, 9 July 2008.
Selden, Ron. "Blackfeet Pencil Factory Competes in Volatile Industry." *Indian Country Today*, 29 March 2000.

Oorang Indians

An all-Indian football team that was one of the National Football League's (NFL) earliest franchises, the Oorang Indians were organized in 1922 by Sac and Fox athlete JIM THORPE and Walter Lingo, owner of the Oorang Airedale Kennels, in Larue, Ohio. The Oorang Indians were to a large extent created as a publicity stunt to promote a special strain of large airedale terrier dog known as the Oorang Airedale. Thorpe, by then 34, was to be the coach. He built the team around many of his teammates from his college days a decade earlier (see WARNER, POP), as the closing of the Carlisle Indian School in 1918 had shut off the flow of great Indian players to professional sports.

With a starting lineup that featured such former stars as Chippewa JOE GUYON at quarterback and Mission Indian PETE CALAC at halfback, the team was largely past its prime. Others on the team included Mission Indian Reggie Attache as the other halfback, Cherokee Stillwell Sanook at right end, Chippewa Xavier Downwind at right tackle, Santee Sioux Ted Lone Wolf at right guard, 37-year-old Chippewa Ted St. Germaine at center, Pomo Elmer Busch at left guard, Nick Lassa from the Flathead Indian Reservation at left end, Chippewa Baptiste Thunder at tackle, and Iroquois Asa Walker, Mohawk Joe Little Twig, and 49-year-old Seneca Bemus Pierce as backups.

Despite the ages of their players, the Indians managed to win four games in their first season, mostly on the running of Guyon and Calac and the return of Thorpe to the playing field. In 1923, with the retirement of almost all of the linemen and lacking Guyon for most of the season, the Indians fell to a dismal 2-10 record, and the team subsequently disbanded. Despite its gimmickry, the Oorang Indians were the most popular of the early NFL franchises, played more games than any other NFL team in their two seasons, and did much to boost attendance to the nascent sport of professional football.

Further Reading

Springwood, Charles Fruehling. "Playing Football, Playing Indian: A History of the Native Americans Who Were the NFL's Oorang Indians." In *Native Athletes in Sport and Society: A Reader*, edited by Richard C. King, 123–144. Lincoln: University of Nebraska Press, 2005.
Whitman, Robert L. *Jim Thorpe and the Oorang Indians: The N.F.L.'s Most Colorful Franchise*. Mount Gilead, Ohio: Marion County Historical Society, 1984.

Ortiz, Alfonso (1939–1997) *Tewa anthropologist, author*

A Tewa born on April 30, 1939, in San Juan Pueblo to Sam and Lupe (Naranjo) Ortiz, Alfonso Ortiz came from an ancient line of traditional religious leaders on his father's side. He excelled as a high school student in nearby Española, New Mexico, received a B.A. from the University of New Mexico in 1961, and studied at Arizona State before receiving a master's degree in anthropology from the University of Chicago. In 1964, he earned the Roy D. Albert Prize for best M.A. thesis. He received a Ph.D. there in 1967. Ortiz taught at Princeton University for seven years before becoming a professor at the University of New Mexico in 1974.

In 1969, scientific knowledge of the culture of the Tewa was vague, if not completely incorrect. Previous anthropologists who had studied the Tewa, such as John P. Harrington and Elsie Clews Parsons, found that the Indians delighted in leading anthropologists, in the words of Parsons, "down the garden path with fabricated wisdom." Ortiz, as a member of the San Juan Pueblo, found it easy to penetrate the secrets that the Tewa had formerly withheld from anthropologists and other investigators, using extensive fieldwork to supplement the knowledge handed down to him by his family. His landmark 1969 work, *The Tewa World: Space, Time, Being, and Becoming in a Pueblo Society*, revealed the beautiful intricacy of the Tewa cosmology and its relationship to the sacred landmarks that surrounded their homelands. The work was hailed by anthropologists as a unique insight into another culture, but Ortiz was criticized by some of the tribal elders in the pueblo for betraying religious secrets (see ANTHROPOLOGISTS AND AMERICAN INDIANS).

Ortiz published *New Perspectives on the Pueblos* in 1972 and edited two volumes of the Smithsonian Institution's *Handbook of North American Indians* (1978–2004). His collaboration with Richard Erdoes on the book *American Indian Myths and Legends* (1984) was widely praised and furthered his reputation as Native America's most distinguished anthropologist. He won many awards, research grants, and scholarships, including a postdoctoral fellowship from the John Simon Guggenheim Memorial Foundation and a MacArthur Foundation "genius grant."

Ortiz was keen to use his academic training to try to help Indian people solve their problems. As vice president and then president of the ASSOCIATION ON AMERICAN INDIAN AFFAIRS, he helped to lead the fight to return BLUE LAKE to the Taos Pueblo and to pass the Native American Child Welfare Act. Ortiz was active as an advisory board member of the NATIVE AMERICAN RIGHTS FUND (NARF) and a fellow of both the American Anthropological Association and the Royal Anthropological Institute (U.K.). He was also a board member of Cultural Survival, an indigenous-rights advocacy group founded by anthropologists at Harvard University, as well as a board member of Harvard Peabody Museum and the National Museum of the American Indian. He worked to encourage Indian youth to pursue careers in academia and served as an adviser for the award-winning film documentary *Surviving Columbus: The Story of a Pueblo People* (1993).

Alfonso Ortiz died on January 27, 1997, in Santa Fe, of a long-standing heart ailment. In 1999, the University of New Mexico established the Alfonso Ortiz Center for Intercultural Studies in his honor.

Further Reading

Biolsi, Thomas. *A Companion to the Anthropology of American Indians.* Boston: Blackwell Publishing, 2004.

Erdoes, Richard, and Alfonso Ortiz, eds. *American Indian Myths and Legends.* New York: Pantheon Books, 1984.

Ortiz, Alfonso. *The Tewa World: Space, Time, Being, and Becoming in a Pueblo Society.* Chicago: University of Chicago Press, 1969.

Ortiz, Simon J. (Simon Joseph Ortiz) (1941–)

Acoma Pueblo poet, short story writer

Simon Joseph Ortiz was born on May 27, 1941, in McCartys (Deetzeyaamah), near Albuquerque, New Mexico. His father, Joe L. Ortiz, and his mother, Mamie Toribio Ortiz, both spoke Keres, the language of Acoma, at home. His father, a railroad worker and a woodcarver, was a religious leader of the Eagle or Dyaamih Clan. At age seven, Ortiz attended the Bureau of Indian Affairs (BIA) day school in McCartys before being sent to St. Catherine's Indian School in Santa Fe. From there, he went on to Grants High School in Grants, New Mexico. After graduating, he worked in the local uranium mining industry as a rock crusher.

In 1962, Ortiz attended Fort Lewis College, majoring in chemistry, before enlisting in the U.S. Army. After entering the University of New Mexico in 1966, he received a fellowship to the University of Iowa, where he earned an M.F.A. in 1969. To support himself, Ortiz worked as a teacher of writing at San Diego State University, Navajo Community College, and at the Institute of American Arts in Santa Fe. He first attracted attention in 1969 when some of his poems were published in a special Indian issue of *South Dakota Review*. In 1971, he released *Naked in the Wind*, a chapbook, and he was subsequently featured in several anthologies before *Going for the Rain*, his first full-length collection of poetry, was released in 1976.

In *Going for the Rain*, Ortiz uses oral histories, narratives, and memories of his youth to create a journey that follows the cycles of the *shiwana*, or Cloud People, upon whom the Acoma depend for rain and subsistence. Making use of the humorous and versatile coyote, an important hero among many Native American peoples, the poems become a search for a new means of survival, for the culture and the community as much as for the individual Indian.

In 1977, Ortiz released his second volume of poetry, *A Good Journey*, in which there emerged a major and recurring theme, the poet's voice as a channel through which the earth can speak and discuss its often-estranged relationship with humanity. In 1978, Ortiz published a collection of stories, *Howbah Indians;* a children's book, *The People Shall Continue;* and a collection of essays, *Song, Poetry, Language: Expression and Perception.*

Ortiz's *Fight Back: For the Sake of the People, for the Sake of the Land* (1980), a collection of poems and prose, documents the struggle of Mexicans, blacks, and Indians against corporate exploitation and the destruction of the environment. In 1981, Thunder's Mouth Press released Ortiz's *From Sand Creek: Rising in This Heart Which Is America*, a series of poems in which he reflects on his yearlong stay at Fort Lyons Veterans Hospital in Colorado, located near the site of the 1864 Sand Creek massacre of Cheyenne and Arapaho by a Colorado militia unit. Other collections of Ortiz's poetry included *Woven Stone*, released in 1991, and *After and Before the Lightning* in 1994. In 1999, he released a collection of short stories, *Men on the Moon*, and, in 2002, a collection of essays and poems. *Out There Somewhere.*

In 1988, Ortiz was appointed tribal interpreter for the Acoma Pueblo, and, in 1989, he became first lieutenant governor. Although not as familiar to the general public as other modern Indian poets, among American Indians themselves Ortiz is possibly the best known. A leading voice in the struggle to preserve traditional Indian values and cultures, he has, however, managed to do without the militancy and self-righteousness characteristic of many of his contemporaries. His ability to extend an Indian perspective to the problems of modern-day America through the gentle rhythms and reassuring optimism of his work has influenced poets as diverse as Abenaki Joseph Bruchac and Laguna Pueblo–Sioux Paula Gunn Allen.

Further Reading

Smith, Patricia Clark. "Simon Ortiz: Writing Home." In *The Cambridge Companion to Native American Literature*, edited by Joy Porter and Kenneth M. Roemer, 221–232. New York: Cambridge University Press, 2005.

Wiget, Andrew. *Simon Ortiz.* Western Writers Series. Boise, Idaho: Boise State University Press, 1986.

Osage Reign of Terror (1912–1923)

An oil strike in Osage County, Oklahoma, in 1906 made the 2,000 members of the Osage tribe listed on the tribal roll on July 1, 1907, the richest group of people on Earth in their day (see OIL, AMERICAN INDIANS AND). It also inaugurated a period that has been called the Osage Reign of Terror. The Bureau of Investigation (BOI), the forerunner of the FBI, estimated that hundreds of Osage Indians were killed for their mineral headrights during the first two decades of the 20th century, though other estimates range from a dozen to 60. Also killed were several white investigators and witnesses who attempted to report evidence of the crimes. The last of these murders, of Osage Agency investigator and ex-judge William W. Vaughn, finally aroused the interest of the BOI. On the night of June 29, 1923,

Vaughn was thrown from a train between Oklahoma City and Pawhuska as he returned from a deathbed interview with George Bigheart, son of James Bigheart, the last Osage hereditary chief. Vaughn's body was so badly damaged that a coroner's jury could not determine the cause of death.

In 1870, the Osage sold their land in Kansas to the U.S. government for the then-generous sum of $1.25 an acre. The tribe purchased land for a new reservation from the Cherokee in Oklahoma. Because they owned their land outright, the Osage were exempt from the Dawes Act of 1887. They agreed to accept ALLOTMENT in 1906, but under terms that divided the land of the reservation equally among members of the tribe rather than selling off any "surplus" to whites. Because oil had been discovered on their land in 1897, the Osage Allotment Act of 1906 also reserved mineral rights to be held in common by tribal members. As the reservation stood on one of the largest oil fields in the United States, this meant that each allotment, or "headright," would be worth millions of dollars. Indians who were minors or who could not prove themselves mentally competent were assigned white guardians to manage their assets.

During the boom years, beginning in 1912, as oil companies competed for the right to drill on Osage land, many white guardians of Indians arranged the murders of their wards, often by means of poisoned alcohol or faked suicides, in order to cover up their embezzlement or to inherit a headright from an Indian wife or other relative. The deaths tended to be officially ascribed to bad bootleg whiskey. Twenty-four local businessmen and attorneys were arraigned by the Department of the Interior in 1924 for stealing from their Osage wards, but they all settled out of court.

A two-year BOI investigation under the auspices of the young J. Edgar Hoover eventually resulted in the 1926 trial and conviction of the three most flamboyant murderers: cowboy-turned-rancher William K. Hale; his nephew, Ernest Burkhart; and their accomplice, John Ramsay. (Hale was not finally convicted until January 1929.) They were sentenced to life in prison for the murders of three Indians and two whites: the shootings of Burkhart's Osage sister-in-law, Anna Brown, and her cousin, Henry Roan Horse, on whom Hale had taken out a $25,000 life insurance policy; and the murder of Bill Smith, his wife, Burkhart's other sister-in-law Rita Smith, and their white housekeeper by blowing up their house.

None of the other white "guardians" who profited by the suspicious deaths of their Osage "wards" were ever investigated.

Further Reading

Broad, William. "The Osage Oil Cover-up." *Science* 208, no. 4,439 (1980): 32–35.
Fixico, Donald Lee. *The Invasion of Indian Country in the Twentieth Century: American Capitalism and Tribal Natural Resources.* Boulder: University Press of Colorado, 1998.
Hogan, Laurence J. *The Osage Indian Murders: The True Story of a 21-Murder Plot to Inherit the Headrights of Wealthy Osage Tribe Members.* Frederick, Md.: Amlex, 1998.
Hogan, Linda. *Mean Spirit* (novel). New York: Atheneum, 1990.
McAuliffe, Dennis. *Bloodland: A Family Story of Oil, Greed and Murder on the Osage Reservation.* Tulsa: Oklahoma Council Oak Distribution, 1999. (Previously published under the title *The Deaths of Sibyl Bolton: An American History.* New York: Times Books/Random House, 1994.)

Oskison, John Milton (1874–1947) *Cherokee writer*

John Milton Oskison was born on September 21, 1874, at Pryor Creek, Vinita, Indian Territory (now Oklahoma). His father, John Oskison, was an English immigrant, and his mother, Rachel Connor Crittenden Oskison, was one-quarter Cherokee. After a somewhat irregular schooling, Oskison entered the new Willie Halsell College at Vinita, where he met WILLIAM PENN ADAIR ROGERS, who became a lifelong friend. Oskison graduated with the first class in 1894. Later that year, he went to Stanford University, receiving a B.A. in 1898. He did a year of graduate work in English literature at Harvard University (1898–99) and in 1898 won a contest for college graduates sponsored by the *Century Magazine* with his short story "Only the Master Shall Praise."

Home from Harvard, Oskison began writing for local and Indian papers. To pursue a career in JOURNALISM, he decided to move to New York City, where from 1903 to 1906 he was an editor and editorial writer with the *New York Evening Post.* He won the Black Cat Prize for his short story "The Greater Appeal" in 1904. From 1907 through 1912, Oskison was first associate editor, then financial editor, of *Collier's Weekly.* Later he was a syndicated columnist on economic and financial topics. An advocate of equal opportunity for Indians in the professions, Oskison was an early member of the SOCIETY OF AMERICAN INDIANS and participated in its first conference (1911).

Although well over 40 when the United States entered WORLD WAR I, Oskison joined the U.S. Army, where he was made a lieutenant and given command of a machine-gun company. He went overseas with the American Expeditionary Forces, and he worked in and wrote about the relief effort in France. He was discharged on September 23, 1919.

Oskison objected to the depredations and encroachments of settlers on Indian land that followed the passage of the CURTIS ACT of 1898 and forced ALLOTMENT on the Cherokee. He believed, however, that "racial preservation" could only be achieved through adaptation to and competition with whites. Like the majority of educated Indians at the time, he completely accepted the dominant ideology of ASSIMILATION and equated tribalism with "dependence."

While Oskison wrote numerous essays on Indian affairs for various magazines and newspapers and was best known in his own day as a journalist, he is today chiefly remembered for his fictional portraits of life during those last years of the Cherokee Nation. Aside from numerous stories that have never been collected together, Oskison wrote "The Passing of the Old Indian" (1914) and published three novels—*Wild Harvest: A Novel of Transition Days* (1925), *Black Jack Davy* (1926), and *Brothers Three* (1935)—as well as two biographies—*A Texas Titan: The Story of Sam Houston* (1929) and *Tecumseh and His Times: The Story of a Great Indian* (1938).

Raised in the frontier environment himself, having experienced the pain and prejudice of growing up on the Indian side, Oskison nevertheless gave Indians only bit parts in his three novels and in many of his stories, and he portrayed Indian life only as a part of the whole frontier situation. However, some of his short stories have more Indian content. His popular story "The Problem of Old Harjo" (1907) was set in Indian Territory and humorously reflected the culture clash between the Christian white settlers and a polygamous full-blood Creek. While most critics find Oskison's three novels weak, some of his stories have been favorably compared with those of famed writer Bret Harte.

At the time of his death in Tulsa, Oklahoma, on February 27, 1947, he was working on his autobiography.

Further Reading

Etulain, Richard W., and N. Jill Howard. *Bibliographic Guide to the Study of Western American Literature*. Albuquerque: University of New Mexico Press, 1995.

Ronnow, Gretchen. "John Milton Oskison, Cherokee Journalist: Singer of the Semiotics of Power." *Native Press Research Journal* 4 (Spring 1987): 1–14.

Ottipoby, James Collins (1900–1960) *Comanche educator, army chaplain, missionary*

James Collins Ottipoby was the son of Otipoby (later known as Bob Otipoby) and his wife Pedday, old-time Comanche of the Penateka Band led by Quanah Parker. After the Penateka camp was captured in 1876 and forcibly relocated to Fort Sill, Indian Territory (later Oklahoma), they settled near Lawton, along East Cache Creek north of the military reservation. Born in Elsin on October 26, 1900, James Ottipoby began life as a traditional plains Comanche. When he and his brother Hugh reached the age to be enrolled at the Fort Sill Indian Boarding School, their parents were reluctant to let them go, and the boys hid until they were found and taken off to school by the agency's Indian police. James continued at the school until he was about 14, when he was adopted by foster parents Mr. and Mrs. Peter Van Donselaar, who brought him to the Dutch community of Sioux Center, Iowa. He attended public school there and later in Pella, Iowa, where he studied at Central College in 1921 and 1922 and played on the college basketball team. He then moved with his foster parents to Holland, Michigan.

Ottipoby entered Hope College in Holland in 1922, where he excelled in football, basketball, and baseball. He received his B.A. in 1925, the first Comanche ever to earn a college degree. He subsequently studied for the ministry at Western Theological Seminary in Pittsburgh, graduating in 1927. For the next few years he was a supervisor and coach at HENRY CLARENCE ROE CLOUD's American Indian Institute in Wichita and at the Indian school in Rapid City, South Dakota.

Ottipoby began missionary work in 1934, with pastorates in Lawton, Anadarko, and Fletcher, Oklahoma. He studied sociology and physical education at a YMCA college and the Methodist School for Pastors in Chicago and was for some years a pastor and missionary of the Methodist Church. Ordained at the Marble Collegiate Church, New York City, on November 15, 1938, he was the second Indian to be ordained in the Reformed Church in America. The first was Robert Paul Chaat, another Comanche, who had been ordained at Marble Collegiate on November 20, 1934. Ottipoby subsequently served as a missionary to the Winnebago reservation in Nebraska and the Mescalero Apache reservation in New Mexico.

In 1943, during WORLD WAR II, Ottipoby enlisted in the armed forces, becoming the first American Indian chaplain in the U.S. Army. During three years of service with an infantry division, he saw duty in the Philippines campaign and the occupation of Japan, eventually attaining the rank of major. Discharged in 1946, he was sent by the Presbyterian Board of National Missions to Laguna Pueblo, New Mexico, where his pastorate consisted of three churches. He was pastor of the Casa Blanca Church in Laguna until 1957. From then until his death, he was pastor of the Bethany Presbyterian Church in Albuquerque, serving a mixed Anglo and Spanish community. Ottipoby died there of a massive heart attack on October 6, 1960.

Further Reading

Koopman, LeRoy. *Taking the Jesus Road: The Ministry of the Reformed Church in America among Native Americans*. Grand Rapids, Mich.: Eerdmans, 2005.

Owen, Robert Latham, Jr. (1856–1947) *Cherokee leader, U.S. senator*

Born in Lynchburg, Virginia, on February 2, 1856, Robert Latham Owen, Jr., was the son of Robert Latham Owen, president of the Virginia & Tennessee Railroad, and Narcissa Chisholm Owen, who was part Cherokee. Owen attended private schools in Virginia and the Merillat Institute in Baltimore before graduating as valedictorian from Washington and Lee University in 1877. After earning his law degree there as well, Owen moved to Indian Territory (later Oklahoma), where he became principal of the Cherokee Orphan Asylum at Grand Saune. He began practicing law in 1880 and that same year won a case against the federal government (known as the Leased District Case) that secured almost $3 million in compensation for the Choctaw and Chickasaw. He would later win two similar land-claims settlements, realizing more than $824,000 for the Western Cherokee and $5 million for the Eastern Cherokee.

From 1881 to 1884, Owen was secretary of the board of education of the Cherokee Nation. After briefly becoming editor of *The Indian Chieftain*, a daily newspaper published in Vinita, Owen served from 1885 to 1889 as U.S. Indian agent overseeing Indian Territory. As Indian agent, Owen opposed the ALLOTMENT of the land of the Five Civilized Tribes (Creek, Choctaw, Chickasaw, Seminole, Cherokee), arguing that their communal landholding policy was better suited to their needs and would best protect them from the army of "boomers" then trying to take their lands. In 1887, while still in public service, Owen also managed to establish for himself a ranch in Craney Valley that would eventually encompass more than 10,000 acres.

Owen sought to modernize Indian Territory, helping to establish its first bar association and bring the territory under the regulations of the National Banking Act. After leaving the Indian Service, Owen organized the First National Bank of Muscogee in 1890; and served as its president until 1900. As he became more prominent in the local Democratic Party— he served on the territory's Democratic National Committee from 1892 to 1896—Owen began to favor the Allotment policy, eventually supporting the CURTIS ACT of 1898.

By then, Owen had also begun to see the opportunities that the dissolution of the Five Civilized Tribes might bring. In 1895, he went before the Dawes Commission to enroll the Mississippi Choctaw into the Choctaw Nation in Indian Territory so they might be able to share in any Choctaw assets distributed upon the breakup of the tribe. When it was discovered that Owen had arranged a contingency fee entitling him to 50 percent of the proceeds that the impoverished Mississippi Indians might receive, the Dawes Commission dismissed the claim.

Although Owen attended the convention of 1905 in which the Creek, Cherokee, and Choctaw sought to create the separate state of "Sequoyah" in a desperate attempt to evade the Curtis Act, Owen's politics by then strongly reflected the views of the white "boosters" who were clamoring for an end to the Indian governments. By publicly calling for an end to restrictions placed on the sales of Indian allotments, Owen brought on the ire of full-bloods such as Moty Tiger, head chief of the Creek, who upon Owen's nomination as senator prophetically noted that "posterity will only remember him for his avarice and his treachery."

By then, Owen had formed the Indian Land and Trust Company, designed to fleece Indian minors under the corrupt guardianship process. He had also moved to protect his large ranch from being broken up under the Curtis Act by arranging for desperate Cherokee to be allotted his land, which he then leased back from them at a pittance.

Owen was elected to the U.S. Senate in 1907 as one of the first two senators of the new state of Oklahoma. In the Senate he was placed on the important Indian Affairs Committee. As the breakup of the Five Civilized Tribes began to descend into a frenzy of looting and violence, Owen, along with the rest of the Oklahoma congressional delegation, fought federal attempts to regulate the disposition of Indian property. In 1908, when the federal government brought suit to invalidate 25,517 conveyances of Indian land comprising 3,842,553 acres, Owen and Chickasaw congressman CHARLES DAVID CARTER led the attempt to limit the right of the federal government to bring suit in cases of possible fraud against Indians. That same year, Owen helped pass the Removal of Restrictions Act, making thousands of Indian allotments available for sale in Oklahoma and leading to a massive loss of Indian land.

In 1909, Owen used his influence to try to derail the federal prosecution of a group of influential Oklahoma citizens, including Governor Charles Haskell, who had been accused of illegally acquiring valuable "town lots." The case was effectively stalled until the statute of limitations expired.

Owen did secure from the secretary of the interior an accounting of the Five Civilized Tribes' moneys managed by the Indian Service in the 10 years subsequent to the passage of the Curtis Act, confirming the Indians' worst fears that the majority of their funds had been squandered or used to benefit the non-Indians in the state. In 1913, he also moved to squelch the attempts of thousands of white "claimants" to reopen the tribal rolls in order to share in the disbursement of tribal assets.

However, Owen led the attempt to overturn the reforms enacted by Indian Commissioner CATO SELLS in 1914. By 1918, working in concert with the other members of his delegation— including Cherokee WILLIAM WIRT HASTINGS, who became a member of Congress in 1915, and Charles D. Carter—Owen had succeeded in eliminating the use of federal probate attorneys to monitor guardians, allowing the process to degenerate to its previously corrupt state.

In other political matters, Owen was known for his support of President Woodrow Wilson's attempts to include the United States in the League of Nations, as well as his promotion of a national health service, womens suffrage, and stronger child labor laws. In 1913, as chair of the Senate Committee on Banking and Currency, he sponsored the Federal Reserve Act, known at the time as the Glass-Owen Bill, arguably the most important banking legislation of the 20th century. In 1919, he wrote a short book, *The Federal Reserve Act*, in which he praised the value of a central bank. However, Owen would soon regret creating the Federal Reserve. Under Republican president Warren Harding and his successors, who advocated a laissez-faire approach to the economy, Owen felt the Fed had become a tool of the big banks, and he blamed the Fed's monetary policies for leading to the Great Depression. He retired from the Senate in 1924. His successor, W. B. Pine, a wealthy oilman elected with the support of the Ku Klux Klan, continued to protect Oklahoma's corrupt Indian policy through the remainder of the 1920s. Owen remained in Washington, D.C., working as a lawyer and a lobbyist. He supported Republican Herbert Hoover for president in 1928 but returned to the Democratic fold after Franklin D. Roosevelt's election. Robert Latham Owen died in Washington, D.C., on July 19, 1947, of complications following prostate surgery.

Further Reading

Brown, Kenny Lee. "Robert Latham Owen, Jr.: His Careers as Indian attorney and Progressive Senator." Ph.D. dissertation, Oklahoma State University, 1985. Available online. URL: http://proquest.umi.com/pqdlink?did=744025031&Fmt=7&clientId=79356&RQT=309&VName=PQD. Accessed 12 May 2012.

Owen, Narcissa. "Excerpts from the Memoirs of Narcissa Owen." In *Native American Women's Writing: An Anthology c. 1800–1924*, edited by Karen L. Kilcup, 90–109. Hoboken, N.J.: Wiley, 2000.

P

Parker, Arthur C. (Arthur Caswell Parker, Gawaso Wanneh) (1881–1955) *Seneca anthropologist, author, pan-Indian reformer*

Born April 5, 1881, on the Cattaraugus Reservation in New York, Arthur Caswell Parker was the son of Frederick Ely Parker (Seneca), an accountant for the New York Central Railroad, and Geneva H. Griswold, a woman of Scottish and English ancestry who had been a teacher on the Seneca reservations at Cattaraugus and Allegany. Brigadier General Ely S. Parker was his granduncle. The general's brother, Nicholson H. Parker, a graduate of the State Normal School at Albany, was Arthur's grandfather. A farmer, U.S. interpreter, and clerk of the Seneca Nation, Nicholson Parker greatly influenced Arthur's early interest in natural science, Iroquois history, and traditions.

Parker began his schooling on the reservation. After his father was transferred to White Plains, New York, in 1892, he attended White Plains High School, graduating in 1897. His minister having recommended the ministry as a career, Parker entered Dickinson Seminary at Williamsport, Pennsylvania, in 1899 but decided against it in 1902 and ended his studies. Though he never formally earned a degree, Parker eventually received an honorary M.S. from the University of Rochester in 1922 and honorary doctorates from Union College (Schenectady, New York) in 1940 and Keuka College (Keuka Park, New York) in 1945 in recognition of his contributions to anthropology and museology.

After briefly working for the *New York Sun*, Parker was drawn back to his early interest in anthropology and archaeology. In New York City, he was a frequent visitor at the home of Indian rights advocate Harriet Maxwell Converse, whom he had known since school and whose salon attracted ethnologists such as Mark R. Harrington, FRANK GOULDSMITH SPECK, and Alanson B. Skinner. Harrington and Skinner became Parker's lifelong friends.

Though he had the opportunity to work with anthropologist FRANZ BOAS at Columbia University, Parker preferred to study informally with Frederick W. Putnam, professor of anthropology at Harvard University and at that time temporary curator at the American Museum of Natural History. Parker's choice may have had something to do with Boas's hostility to ethnographer Lewis Henry Morgan's theory of social evolution: Parker venerated Morgan, whose main source on the Iroquois had been his granduncle Ely S. Parker, and whose theories helped him make sense of his own sort of Indian identity, allowing him to rationalize his deep interest in Iroquois traditions while still considering them relics of a bygone age and no longer viable in the modern world. With the emergence of anthropology as an academic field in the 20th century, Parker's neo-Morganic slant on American Indian culture change and the study of culture change in general—that is, the idea that social change must inevitably follow the path of Western culture—was falling out of favor.

In 1903, Putnam sent Parker to assist Mark Harrington on his first archaeological field trip to Long Island. Over the next few years, Parker directed excavations at Iroquois sites for Harvard's Peabody Museum. He began collecting Seneca oral texts during his excavations at Cattaraugus. In 1904, he was appointed ethnologist at the New York State Library in Albany, and in 1906 he became New York State archaeologist.

Parker was one of the founders of the SOCIETY OF AMERICAN INDIANS (SAI) in 1911. He edited and wrote voluminously for its journal during the organization's first several years. Here he was able to outline a sense of Indian identity very different from that of the academic anthropologists—one that centered on acculturation and change. Especially interested in improving education, codifying federal Indian law (see CARTER, CHARLES DAVID), and furthering the land claims process, Parker assumed that a significant Indian identity would survive the process of ASSIMILATION and contribute to the American melting pot. However, as the intellectual leader of the SAI, his writings show the extreme ambiguity on this subject that would become typical of that organization. Contemporaries such as Charles Alexander Eastman and Luther Standing Bear were far more articulate in defining areas where traditional Native American culture could significantly influence the larger society, while at the same time defending the validity and viability of traditional culture.

Parker seems more an apologist for the dominant society, with which he very much identified. Although a pan-Indianist and a proud authority on the Iroquois past, he was no less proud of his Anglo-Saxon and Scottish ancestry, favoring Indian amalgamation with northern European stocks. Consistent with this view, he was an ethnic chauvinist, and in the 1920s he opposed immigration from southern and eastern Europe and disparaged Indians who had any admixture of African ancestry. Like many other prominent Indians, Parker was a Freemason; during the 1920s, he seems to have been an important link between that society and the Tipi Order of America.

During the crises caused by World War I and the usurpation of the traditional Longhouse government in Canada (see General, Alexander; General, Levi), Parker opposed the traditional sovereignty of the Six Nations and supported the imposition of American and Canadian citizenship. Files discovered after his death revealed that he had spied for the U.S. government during World War I, monitoring draft registration on the Iroquois reservations at a time when the traditionals opposed U.S. jurisdiction to impose registration (see Schanandoah, Chapman).

Undoubtedly there were deep personal reasons for Parker's outlook. He was a descendant of illustrious Iroquois ancestors (including Handsome Lake, Cornplanter, and Red Jacket), but only through the male line. Since his paternal grandmother and mother were white, Christian women, he could never hold a significant position in the traditional matrilineal Iroquois system. Although adopted into the Bear Clan under the name Gawaso Wanneh (Big Snow-snake) and, in his mid-20s, into the Little Water Society, Parker's status as a Seneca was always problematic.

In May 1923, Parker chaired the Committee of One Hundred, set up by Secretary of the Interior Hubert Work. Later he was involved, though not in a major way, in the founding of the National Congress of American Indians and attended its opening convention in Denver in 1944.

From 1906 to 1925, Parker was archaeologist of the New York State Museum, where he wrote many Iroquois studies of high quality. From 1925 to 1946, he directed the Rochester Municipal Museum (later the Rochester Museum of Arts and Sciences). Edward Cornplanter and Jesse Cornplanter of Cattaraugus were his main informants, and he kept the whole Cornplanter family employed in collecting and making objects for his museums.

As director of the Seneca Arts Project (1935–41), sponsored by the Rochester Municipal Museum and funded by the Works Progress Administration, Parker supervised more than 100 Iroquois artists at Tonawanda and Cattaraugus reservations in the production of approximately 5,000 works of art, either traditional or (if representational) with a traditional theme. (See Bruce, Louis Rook, Jr.; India New Deal.) Jesse Cornplanter was also employed on this project, which Parker hoped would in some measure compensate for the tragic loss of the Lewis Henry Morgan collection of Iroquois artifacts in a fire at the State Capitol in 1911. Ironically, much of Parker's Seneca collection was itself destroyed in a fire on the Tonawanda Reservation in 1941.

Parker retired in 1946 to his home in Naples, New York. Author of 14 books, including children's literature, and almost 300 articles, he continued to write and be involved in Indian affairs up to his death of a heart attack on New Year's Day 1955.

In 1998 the Society for American Archaeology established the Arthur C. Parker Scholarship, which provides funds to Native Americans for training in archaeology.

See also anthropologists and American Indians; higher education.

Further Reading

Hertzberg, Hazel W. *The Search for an American Indian Identity: Modern Pan-Indian Movements.* Syracuse, N.Y.: Syracuse University Press, 1971.

Porter, Joy. *To Be Indian: The Life of Seneca-Iroquois Arthur Caswell Parker, 1881–1955.* Norman: Oklahoma University Press, 2002.

Thomas W. Stephen. "Arthur Caswell Parker: 1881–1955. Anthropologist, Historian and Museum Pioneer." *Rochester History* 17, no. 3 (July 1955): 1–20.

Parker, Gabe Edward (1878–1953) *Choctaw educator, financial officer, Indian agency superintendent*

Gabe Edward Parker born in Fort Towson, Indian Territory (now Oklahoma), on September 29, 1878, the son of John Clay and Eliza E. Willis Parker. As an infant, he moved with his family to a ranch near Nelson, Indian Territory. After graduating from Spencer Academy at Nelson in 1894, he was able, with the financial support of the Choctaw Nation, to go on to Henry Kendall College, then at Muskogee, Indian Territory, earning a B.A. in 1899.

Parker intended to study law, but his mother's death forced him to accept a position in 1899 as assistant teacher at the Spencer Academy, where he was promoted to principal teacher after three months. When the academy was destroyed by fire in 1900, Parker was appointed principal of the Choctaw Nation's Armstrong Male Academy near Durant, Oklahoma, becoming superintendent in 1904. He remained there through 1913. When Indian Territory officially became the state of Oklahoma in 1907, Parker was chair of a committee in the Oklahoma Constitutional Convention and was one of the designers of the state seal. A Democrat, he was named registrar of the U.S. Treasury in 1913, but was replaced in 1915 by Cherokee Houston Teehee after being made superintendent of the Five Civilized Tribes (Cherokee, Creek, Seminole, Choctaw, and Chickasaw) at Muskogee, the largest Indian agency in the United States, with jurisdiction over approximately 100,000 Indians. Parker held this position through 1920, when, with the inauguration of Republican president Warren G. Harding, he was replaced as superintendent of the Five Civilized Tribes by Choctaw Victor M. Locke. During his tenure, Parker handed over $200 million in tribal funds, including royalties for gas, oil, coal, and asphalt and other payments, to members of tribes. During WORLD WAR I, he invested more than $11 million of Indian money in Liberty Bonds for the war effort.

A member of the SOCIETY OF AMERICAN INDIANS, Parker was the society's vice president for education in 1918. In the 1920s, Parker worked for the Pacific Mutual Life Insurance Company in Tulsa. He returned to government service in the mid-1930s as superintendent of the Winnebago Indian agency in Nebraska, retiring in 1950.

After his retirement, Parker went back to Oklahoma. He died in Oklahoma City on May 8, 1953, suffering a heart attack after learning that his son, GABE EDWARD PARKER, JR., had died earlier that same day in England.

Parker, Gabe Edward, Jr. (1904–1953) *Choctaw army officer, insurance executive*

Gabe E. Parker, Jr., was born in Armstrong, Indian Territory (now Oklahoma), on April 19, 1904, the son of GABE EDWARD PARKER. He attended the Armstrong Academy, where his father was on the faculty, as well as public schools in Washington, D.C., and Muskogee, Oklahoma. Parker entered the U.S. Military Academy at West Point in July 1921. He was manager of the cadet football teams of 1924, 1925, and 1926, receiving the coveted army letter, and was also a soloist in the 1926 West Point choir.

Upon graduation, in June 1926, Parker was assigned to the regular army, 12th Field Artillery, Second Division, at Fort Sam Houston in San Antonio, Texas. Later he served as reserve officer of the 160th Field Artillery, Oklahoma National Guard. Following his military service, Parker worked for the Pacific Mutual Life Insurance Company in Tulsa, as his father had done. Later he served as procurement officer for the state of Oklahoma. He was subsequently appointed civilian manager of Burtonwood Air Force Base near Liverpool, England.

Parker died suddenly of a heart attack in England on May 8, 1953. His father, on hearing the news, suffered a heart attack himself and died later the same day.

Paytiamo, James (Flaming Arrow, Ah-shrah-ne, "Wheat Sprout") (ca. 1891–1965) *Acoma singer, author*

James Paytiamo was born on August 2 (or September 1), in either 1891 or 1892, at Acoma Pueblo, New Mexico, the eldest child of Luciano and Maria Paytiamo. His legal name was Santiago Paytiamo, and his Keres-language baby-name was Ah-shrah-ne (Wheat Sprout). The family was well to do and possessed many sheep and cattle.

After a traditional Pueblo boyhood, Paytiamo was educated at the Haskell Institute in Lawrence, Kansas. He then returned to New Mexico. Around 1917, when he was working as a shepherd at Acomito in Socorro County, he was briefly married and fathered a son.

By all accounts, Paytiamo was an outstanding singer in the traditional style. Influenced by many compliments from tourists, he decided to take singing lessons and was taught the obligatory INDIANIST MUSIC repertoire, including such songs as Charles Wakefield Cadman's "From the Land of the Sky Blue Waters." (Indianist music, popular in the early part of the 20th century, was a style of composition based on Indian melodies and rhythms but adapted to Western style harmonies and musical forms.) Paytiamo married his teacher, Larue I. Simmons (née Payne), in Kansas City, Missouri, in November 1926. It was she who anglicized his name to James. Paytiamo wrote and illustrated a book called *Flaming Arrow's People* (1932), in which he told about his childhood—the stories he had heard and the ceremonies he had seen and sometimes taken part in. *Flaming Arrow's People*, the only book published by a Pueblo Indian in the first half of the 20th century, was widely reviewed and very favorably received.

Paytiamo is also known for his association with ERNEST THOMPSON SETON, writer and advocate of American Indian culture. Seton settled in the place later known as Seton Village, about eight miles southeast of Santa Fe, in February 1930. It is known that as of April of that year, the Paytiamos were farming in or near Glorieta, very close to there. In October they sold a meteorite in their possession (known as the Santa Fe meteorite) to the National Museum in Washington.

In summer 1932, Seton and his wife Julia founded the Seton College of Indian Wisdom (later the Seton Institute of Indian Lore) as a summer training institute for leaders in the Woodcraft Indians and other youth organizations. It is not know exactly when or how Paytiamo and Seton met, but it must have been around this time, since LaRue Paytiamo published an article on "Foods of the Pueblo" in the January 1933 issue of the *Totem Board*, a magazine issued at Seton Village.

According to a story later published in *The Daily Oklahoman* (June 25, 1936), when the Paytiamos called on the Setons at their home one evening, Paytiamo was asked to sing. After he obliged with a few Indianist numbers, Julia handed him a drum and asked for some traditional chanting. As he began, not only his voice but his entire personality changed. Soon afterward, he took the course on Indian dancing at Seton Institute. Paytiamo and his wife subsequently entered show business with this act and did very well. As Julia commented, "That's what people want, the real thing."

Attitudes to Indian culture were changing. For several decades, only the extremely diluted repertoire of the Indianists was deemed palatable for a "civilized" audience. As recently as 1923, the Indian Office, as the BUREAU OF INDIAN AFFAIRS (BIA) was known at the time, supported by Indian and white welfare organizations, had conducted an anti-dance campaign, which both Seton and his friend, anthropologist F. W. Hodge, opposed (see DANCE ORDERS). The policy was officially rescinded by JOHN COLLIER in 1933 after he became head of the BIA.

Paytiamo became well known in the East, where he toured with his own Pueblo company, sponsored by the Swarthmore Chautauqua lecture circuit. A biographical notice states: "He presents, in authentic portrayal, those songs and dances of his tribe that are not prohibited from use by religious decree." He joined Seton's Woodcraft League of America, attracted by its interest in Indian lore and its program based on Indian ritual. He taught courses in the College of Indian Wisdom.

In 1936, the Paytiamos traveled in South America, where, according to the *Sarasota Herald* of January 21, 1937, they "made a comparative study between the customs and dress of the South and North American Indians," including music and dance. They returned to the United States in May 1936.

For three summers, Paytiamo was featured in the "Indian Hill Ceremonials" at the Wisconsin Dells. There, in 1946, Charles Hoffman, a folklorist specializing in American Indian music, and Leland Coon, Professor of Music at the University of Wisconsin, recorded him singing Acoma, Shoshone, Hopi, and Navajo (Dineh) songs. Hoffman, in an article in *The Journal of American Folklore* published in the summer of 1947, identified Paytiamo as "a silversmith from the Acoma pueblo" and described his vocal delivery as somewhat westernized compared to most of the other Indian singers who also recorded. "The raucous vocal quality was lacking and the intervals seemed more properly placed and more in keeping with westernized scales."

Nothing is known about the last part of Paytiamo's life, except that he died in 1965. His wife, Larue Paytiamo, who was about 13 years his senior, passed away in April 1973 at the age of 95 in Cottonwood, Arizona.

Peltier, Leonard (1944–) *Chippewa-Sioux activist*

A member of the AMERICAN INDIAN MOVEMENT (AIM) who was imprisoned on charges that he participated in the murder of two Federal Bureau of Investigation (FBI) agents in 1975, Leonard Peltier became a cause célèbre and his case turned a spotlight on the FBI's deadly campaign to discredit AIM. Born on September 12, 1944, in Grand Forks, North Dakota, Leonard Peltier was the son of Leo Peltier, a Turtle Mountain Chippewa (Ojibway). His mother, Alvina Robideau, was Sioux. Peltier's parents separated when he was four, and he and his younger sister, Betty Ann, were raised by their paternal grandparents, Alex and Mary Peltier, on the Turtle Mountain Reservation. The two children had a traditional upbringing until Alex Peltier's death in 1952, when they were sent to a boarding school in Wahpeton, North Dakota. At age 14, Leonard moved to the northwest coast, where his mother and her brothers had settled. By 1965, he was part owner of a body shop in Seattle that became known as a place local members of the Indian community could stay and find work.

Peltier was introduced to the surging Indian activism of the day when he participated in the successful takeover of Fort Lawton, just outside Seattle, in 1970. There he met RICHARD OAKES and Indian activist MAD BEAR ANDERSON. Hearing about the exploits of the newly formed AIM, Peltier traveled to their office in Denver, where Vernon Bellecourt, brother of AIM founder CLYDE BELLECOURT, invited him to join the group. Peltier participated in AIM's abortive attempt to help the Chippewa at Leech Lake, then traveled with DENNIS BANKS on fund-raising trips to the Southwest and Los Angeles. In early November 1972, Peltier joined the TRAIL OF BROKEN TREATIES; he was put in charge of security when the protest reached Washington, D.C.

On November 22, shortly after the demonstration in Washington, Peltier and two Indian friends were involved in a minor fracas with two off-duty policemen in a restaurant in Milwaukee; Peltier was arrested and charged with attempted murder. After serving five months in prison when the Milwaukee AIM chapter could not raise bail, Peltier left the state rather than be prosecuted on what he insisted were trumped-up charges.

By this time, the FBI had turned its infamous counterintelligence program, known by its acronym, COINTELPRO, against AIM. Established during the 1960s in an attempt to discredit the Civil Rights movement, COINTELPRO included among its tactics the attempted sexual blackmail of Martin Luther King, Jr., and the violent suppression of the Black Panthers. The dubious legality of many aspects of the program would lead Idaho senator Frank Church, chair of the Senate Select Committee on Intelligence, to investigate the FBI in 1975. The Church investigation subsequently concluded that the COINTELPRO program was nothing less than "a sophisticated vigilante operation."

While Peltier was in jail in Milwaukee, AIM occupied the village of WOUNDED KNEE on the Pine Ridge Reservation in South Dakota. After his release, Peltier shuttled back and forth between the West Coast and South Dakota before joining Dennis Banks's camp on Calvin Jumping Bull's ranch, Pine Ridge Reservation, in late 1974.

In early June 1975, Peltier attended the AIM convention in Farmington, New Mexico, where he was once again placed in charge of security. The discovery that member Douglass Durham had been an FBI informer during the Wounded Knee trials made AIM members suspect the group was riddled with provocateurs and informers, leading to an atmosphere of tension and paranoia. Given the task of confronting ANNA MAE AQUASH over rumors that she was working for the FBI, Peltier asked her to leave the convention. On June 8, just as the convention was starting, AIM leader RUSSELL MEANS was shot in the back and severely wounded by a BUREAU OF INDIAN AFFAIRS (BIA) police officer on the Standing Rock Reservation. After this, AIM chairman JOHN TRUDELL decreed that its members should begin to shoot back, even if the assailants were police officers.

The Pine Ridge AIM contingent—consisting of Peltier; Banks and his wife, Kamook Nichols; Mike Anderson, Wilford "Wish" Draper, Norman Brown, and Lena Funston, all Navajo; two Sioux children from Rapid City, Jean Bordeaux and Jimmy Zimmerman; and Peltier's cousin Bob Robideau—returned from New Mexico to South Dakota, where they joined up in the camp with Joe Killsright Stuntz, a 21-year-old

Coeur d'Alene; Darrelle Dean "Dino" Butler, a Tututni from Oregon; and Butler's Inupiat Eskimo wife, NILAK BUTLER. In the meantime, tensions on Pine Ridge had begun to reach a boiling point. Following the Wounded Knee occupation, the reservation had become locked in a virtual civil war, pitting Pine Ridge tribal chair Dick Wilson and his armed gang of GOONS (Guardians of the Oglala Nation), backed by a large contingent of BIA police and FBI agents, against the AIM militants, who had strong support from the reservation's impoverished and disenfranchised traditionals. Dennis Banks was leading the resistance to Wilson, who in June 1975 was secretly preparing to turn over a large tract of the reservation to the federal government. The escalating violence had led to the deaths of more than 60 Oglala, including Wounded Knee leader Pedro Bissonette, who was shot by BIA police.

On the morning of June 26, 1975, while seeking a petty criminal, two FBI agents, Ronald Williams and Jack R. Coler, pursued a red pickup truck onto the Jumping Bull property, a known stronghold of AIM and its traditional supporters. An exchange of fire between the driver of the pickup and the agents drew both the Oglala who lived at the Jumping Bull ranch and the AIM members camped nearby. Approximately two dozen armed Indians, including Peltier, Bob Robideau, and Dino Butler, joined the shoot-out, holding FBI and police reinforcements at bay and wounding the two FBI agents. The unknown driver of the pickup, who was apparently ferrying dynamite, is believed to have then killed the wounded agents and driven off. An FBI and police assault mounted on the AIM camp later that day ended in the death of Killsright Stuntz, but the Oglala and the rest of the AIM encampment managed to escape.

Calling the killings "a cold-blooded ambush," the FBI mounted a massive manhunt to try to catch the perpetrators. As with the BOX CANYON MURDER, the deaths of the agents were pinned only on Indians clearly identified with AIM—Peltier, Robideau, and Butler. The resulting bad publicity damaged AIM's reputation and ended congressional support for the Church investigation into FBI misconduct. On September 5, 1975, Butler was arrested at LEONARD CROW DOG's camp on the Rosebud Reservation, and a short time later Robideau was caught in Wichita, Kansas. Peltier, in the meantime, had fled to Canada.

The trial of Robideau and Butler began in Cedar Rapids, Iowa, on June 7, 1976, under Judge Edward McManus, who was known for his quick trials and for the earlier convictions of AIM members Leonard Crow Dog, Carter Camp, and Stan Holder. With a strong legal team headed by William Kunstler and John Lowe, the defense managed to persuade McManus that the AIM members had acted in self-defense, and that the FBI COINTELPRO program was an attempt to "neutralize" AIM leaders by any means possible. Judge McManus even allowed Kunstler to take the unprecedented step of forcing Clarency Kelly, the director of the FBI, to testify about COINTELPRO. The trial disclosed a history of FBI provocations, "dirty tricks," use of provocateurs, "excessive force," tampering with witnesses, perjury by special agents, and the

manufacturing of evidence, all to destroy AIM. To the consternation of the FBI, Butler and Robideau were acquitted on all counts in the slayings of the agents.

Leonard Peltier would not be so fortunate. Captured in Canada on February 7, 1976, he was not extradited back to the United States until December 16, and then on the basis of a false affidavit from Myrtle Poor Bear, a mentally unstable young woman whose testimony was later also used by the FBI to convict AIM leader Richard "Dick" Marshall of murder. Judge Paul Benson, unlike McManus, would not allow Peltier's defense team to use the self-defense argument, nor to introduce the verdict or testimony from the trial of Butler and Robideau as evidence. Without Kunstler and Lowe, who were unavailable to the defense, the perjury, witness tampering, and manufacturing of evidence that had previously backfired on the FBI and the prosecution in the Butler-Robideau trial, now won Peltier's conviction on two counts of murder in the first degree.

Convicted on April 18, 1977, Peltier was sentenced to two life terms in prison. In 1979, he received an additional seven years when he was apprehended after escaping from prison for five days. He was sent to prison, first at Marion, Illinois; then at Lompoc, California; and finally at Leavenworth, Kansas. During his imprisonment, Peltier survived two assassination attempts and a severe beating that permanently damaged one of his eyes. Despite a lawsuit filed under the Freedom of Information Act, which forced the FBI to release thousands of pages of secret documents concerning the Peltier case, and an evidentiary hearing before an appeals court that subsequently determined the FBI had largely manufactured the case against Peltier and might be protecting the identity of the real killer, the courts have steadfastly refused to grant him a new trial.

Peltier's case has attracted international attention and widespread support, including at one time that of more than 50 U.S. congressman who sought to have his case reopened. People from Mother Teresa and the Dalai Lama to Willie Nelson and Robert Redford have voiced their support for Peltier. The FBI, however, remains opposed to any effort that could lead to freedom for Peltier or further disclosures about the COINTELPRO program and continues to withhold, on the grounds of national security, more than 6,000 pages of vital documents concerning the case.

Peltier was once again denied parole on June 12, 2000; the parole examiner refusing to consider pleas from Amnesty International and more than 10,000 letters of protest. In January 2001, President Bill Clinton left office without granting Peltier a pardon.

In 2003, after journalist PAUL DEMAIN wrote in *News from Indian Country* that Anna Mae Aquash was murdered to cover up Peltier's guilt, Peltier filed a libel lawsuit and DeMain was forced to issue a statement disclaiming Peltier's involvement in the Aquash murder and acknowledging that Peltier had not received a fair trial. In the trial of Aquash's killers, in 2004, Darlene "Kamook" Nichols, the former wife of Dennis Banks, testified that she heard Peltier brag that he shot the agents. It was later revealed that she had been paid $42,000 by the FBI for her testimony. She subsequently married Robert Ecoffey, the BIA police officer in charge of the Aquash investigation. In 2006, the FBI won a court ruling that prevented the release of documents sought by Peltier's defense team, again citing "national security." Peltier was again denied parole in 2009 and will not have another parole hearing until 2024.

Further Reading

Hendricks, Steve. *The Unquiet Grave: The FBI and the Struggle for the Soul of Indian Country.* New York: Thunder's Mouth Press, 2006.

Matthiessen, Peter. *In the Spirit of Crazy Horse.* New York: Viking, 1991.

Pepper, Jim (James Pepper) (1941–1992) *Kaw-Creek jazz musician*

Born James Gilbert Pepper in Salem, Oregon, on June 18, 1941, to Gilbert Pepper, a Kaw, and Floy Pepper, a Creek, both employees of the BUREAU OF INDIAN AFFAIRS (BIA), Jim Pepper grew up in Oregon, though in summers his parents sent him to his relatives in Oklahoma so he could learn his tribes' traditions. His parents later left the BIA and settled in Portland, where Jim would listen to Sonny Rollins, Gene Ammons, and John Coltrane on the radio. He taught himself to play the tenor saxophone on borrowed instruments.

In 1964, Pepper moved to New York City, where his distinctive sax playing, known for its crying tone, soon established his reputation. He joined guitarist Larry Coryell, drummer Bob Moses, and bassist Columbus Baker to form one of the first jazz-rock fusion groups, the Free Spirits, which made a record for ABC/Paramount in 1966 called *Out of Sight and Sound.* Encouraged by saxophonist Ornette Coleman, Pepper frequently worked with trumpeter Don Cherry (himself part Choctaw), saxophonist Dewey Redman, and drummer Paul Motian. He released his classic album, *Pepper's Powwow,* on Atlantic Records in 1971, featuring his signature song, "Witchi-Tai-To," based on a peyote chant his Kaw grandfather used to sing. It became a hit in the United States and Europe.

In 1971, Pepper performed with Coryell, and for the next two decades he played in San Francisco, Portland, and Vienna. He also began working with Indian children in Alaska and Oregon, helping them to build their self-esteem through music. Popular in Europe, Pepper released his *Coming and Going* album there in 1983, featuring Cherry, English guitarist John Scofield, and Brazilian percussionist Nana Vasconcelos. He also collaborated in Europe with visionary pianist Mal Waldron, releasing several records on the Enja and Tutu jazz labels. In 1989, Pepper returned to the United States, where he performed with bassist Charlie Hayden's Liberation Music Orchestra.

Jim Pepper died on February 10, 1992, of lymphoma at his home in Portland, Oregon. His album *The Path* was released posthumously in 1993. Pepper's life is featured in a documentary made by Makah filmmaker Sandra Johnson Osawa, *Pepper's Pow Wow,* released in 1996. In 2007, at a ceremony honoring his musical legacy, Pepper's saxophone was enshrined in the National Museum of the American Indian in Washington, D.C.

Further Reading

Olding, Jim. "Jim Pepper's Legacy in Recorded Music, A Treasure Chest: Discography of Jim Pepper's Music." *In Motion Magazine.* Available online. URL: http://www.inmotionmagazine.com/pepper.html. Accessed 5 December 2009.

Siegel, Bill. "Jim Pepper: The Man Who Never Sleeps." *In Motion Magazine.* Available online. URL: http://www.inmotionmagazine.com/siegel.html. Accessed 5 December 2009.

———. "Jazz and the Politics of Identity: The Musical Legacy of Jim Pepper." *In Motion Magazine.* Available online. URL: http://www.inmotionmagazine.com/ac04/bsiegel_id.html. Accessed 5 December 2009.

Perry, Ted (1937–) *screenwriter, educator*

Ted Perry was born in New Orleans, Louisiana, on June 4, 1937. He received a B.A. from Baylor University in Texas and an M.A. and Ph.D. in speech and dramatic arts from the University of Iowa. Perry began teaching at the University of Texas at Austin in 1971. Later he chaired the film department at New York University and for a while directed the film department at the Museum of Modern Art. Since 1978, he has taught at Middlebury College in Vermont. While he has done some work for the theater, he writes mainly for film and video.

Perry is the real author of what has been widely believed to be a speech or letter by the 19th-century Chief Seattle, one of the most eloquent statements in the English language on the importance of the natural environment. Constantly quoted, it is often referred to as the gospel of the environmental movement.

In 1854, Sealth (Seattle), a 68-year-old Suquamish chief and baptized Roman Catholic, delivered an oration in the Lushootseed language at a place that now lies within the city that bears his name. It was simultaneously translated into Chinook Jargon, a trade language with a limited vocabulary, and then rendered from Chinook into English. The only known record of the speech was made by Seattle physician Henry Smith in the form of notes that are now lost. The chief died in 1866. Years later, Smith composed or reconstructed the speech in a somewhat flowery Victorian style from his notes and published it in the *Seattle Star* of October 29, 1887, under the title "The Indian's Night Promises to Be Dark."

The origins of what is now known as Chief Seattle's speech go back to a rally at the University of Texas on the first Earth Day (1970), where the classicist William Arrowsmith read his own reedited version of Smith's reconstruction of Seattle's address. Arrowsmith's version was substantially the same as Smith's but altered in syntax and wording to more closely resemble the speech of Indians of the region in the time of Chief Seattle. Perry, Arrowsmith's friend, was then working on a film project on environmental pollution for the Southern Baptist Radio and

Television Commission. When he heard the speech, said Perry in an unpublished interview with Jeffrey Wollock (March 6, 1997), "I realize now that it already had overtones of the Bible and Milton, which must have been put in by Smith, but with Arrowsmith reading it in that context, I found it so beautiful and eloquent and so much what Earth Day was about, that I asked him if I could use it for the film project."

Chief Seattle's speech was a response to the government's offer (or demand) to buy his people's land. Seattle's main concern was the fate of his people and their relations with whites; he refers to land and nature only incidentally. At one point, comparing attitudes to the departed among whites and Indians, Seattle says, in the Arrowsmith version, "Our dead never forget this beautiful Earth. It is their mother. They always love and remember her rivers, her great mountains, her valleys." Further on, he says, "Every part of this Earth is sacred to my people. Every hillside, every valley, every clearing and wood, is holy in the memory and experience of my people. The ground beneath your feet responds more lovingly to our steps than yours, because it is the ashes of our grandfathers. Our bare feet know the kindred touch. The Earth is rich with the lives of our kin." With the exception of the reference to "bare feet," these are sentiments that, taken literally, might have been found in a patriotic speech of any nationality. They do, however, reflect a spiritual as well as physical connection with the land that (as Perry says) was greatly enhanced by the Earth Day context in which he first heard it.

In his script for the film *Home* (1971), Perry imaginatively transformed the speech into a letter from Chief Seattle to President Franklin Pierce. No such letter existed in reality. Inspired by Arrowsmith's reading, Perry embroidered and expanded on the ecological overtones with sentiments that the chief no doubt believed but did not actually express. Then John Stevens, the producer, changed Perry's version somewhat. He shortened it and inserted references to God as well as the line "I am a savage and do not understand." Nothing in the film credits indicated that the chief's "letter" had been written by Perry; they merely stated that the script had been "researched" by Perry. On top of that, 18,000 copies of the fictitious letter, attributed to Seattle, were sent out for promotional purposes without Stevens's knowledge or permission. The film was eventually shown on ABC network television.

The film version of the "letter" next appeared in the November 11, 1972, issue of *Environmental Action* magazine. After that, it was reprinted in other environmental magazines as a letter or speech of Chief Seattle. Its publication in *Passages*, the magazine of Northwest Airlines, under the title "The Decidedly Unforked Message of Chief Seattle," disseminated it not only across the country but around the world. In that publication, it was identified as an "adaptation of [Seattle's] remarks based on an English translation by William Arrowsmith." Perry's name did not appear.

Thus, this speech, which has since become world famous as that of Chief Seattle, is in reality by Ted Perry (as altered by John Stevens), inspired by William Arrowsmith's adaptation of Henry Smith's re-creation of a speech by Chief Seattle.

Perry eventually published his original, longer text in the *Middlebury Magazine* under his own name in the early 1990s.

In 1984, a German historian named Rudolf Kaiser traced the environmental version to Perry. Contacted by Kaiser, Perry stated, "I wrote a speech which was fiction," adding that he was horrified when he realized the speech had been attributed to Chief Seattle rather than to Ted Perry.

When organizers of Earth Day 1992 asked religious leaders around the world to read the famous "letter from Indian Chief Seattle to President Franklin Pierce," Kaiser and other historians protested. Yet the organizers, after checking with some American Indians, decided to send it out anyway, noting that the sentiments were "attributed" to Chief Seattle. Ironically, Indians in general were not bothered. In the March 1997 interview, Perry recalled a visit to an Indian school where he observed a lower-grade class reading his "letter." In the discussion that followed, the teacher asked the class, "Did Chief Seattle really say this?" The children all said no. Then she asked, "Does it matter?" and they all said no.

The Perry speech is not a hoax. It was written as part of a legitimate work of fiction, the author of which, unfortunately, was not credited. No clearly deceptive intent appears in what followed, only a chain of misunderstandings and face-savings. The attribution of the fictional speech and its great popularity arose from a genuine cultural need and can best be explained as a kind of folk phenomenon with a momentum of its own. Although the attribution to Seattle is historically incorrect, the philosophy and mode of expression is clearly Indian. That it could have been written by a non-Indian is a tribute to the influence of American Indian thought as well as the author's poetic imagination. That Perry's work quickly became a classic demonstrates how vital to world consciousness the Native environmental message had become by the early 1970s.

See also ENVIRONMENTAL MOVEMENT, AMERICAN INDIANS AND THE.

Further Reading

Gifford, Eli, and Michael R. Cook, eds. *How Can One Sell the Air? Chief Seattle's Vision.* Summertown, Tenn.: Book Publishing Company, 2005.

Kaiser, Rudolf. "Chief Seattle's Speech(es): American Origins and European Reception." In *Recovering the Word: Essays on Native American Literature*, edited by Brian Swann and Arnold Krupat, 497–536. Berkeley: University of California Press, 1987.

Scull, John. "Chief Seattle, er, Professor Perry Speaks: Inventing Indigenous Solutions to the Environmental Problem." In *Gatherings: Seeking Ecopsychology*. Available online. URL: http://www.ecopsychology.org/ journal/gatherings2/scull.htm. Accessed 7 December 2009.

Peterson, Helen White (1915–2000) *Cheyenne activist*

A Cheyenne/Lakota Sioux born on the Pine Ridge Reservation in South Dakota on August 3, 1915, Helen Louise White was enrolled in the Oglala Lakota Sioux tribe. She was raised by her

Cheyenne grandmother, Lucille Mae White, a niece of Chief Black Kettle, in Chadron, Nebraska. Helen was given the Cheyenne name, Wachi or "Trustworthy." She graduated cum laude from Chadron State Teachers College in Nebraska and later attended the University of Colorado and the University of Denver Law School.

In 1941, Peterson became director of Rocky Mountain Council on Inter-American Indian Affairs, located at the University of Denver, and worked with politician Nelson Rockefeller, founder of the council, who had a deep interest in Indian lands and, in particular, Indian oil. In 1940, Rockefeller had been named director of the newly created Office of Inter-American Affairs (OIAA), which helped to shape U.S. policy toward Latin America during WORLD WAR II. Peterson worked with Rockefeller to have the OIAA take over the funding and mission of the National Indian Institute (NII), an organization created in the wake of the historic First Inter-American Indian Congress. The conference, held in 1940 in Pátzquaro, Mexico, under the leadership of Mexico's president and champion of Indian rights, Lázaro Cárdenas, and organized by JOHN COLLIER and Mexican anthropologist Manuel Gamio, was dedicated to the protection of Indian cultures and their lands. An important treaty, the Inter-American Convention on Indian Life, formulated at the conference, mandated among other things the creation in the United States of the NII to promote the development of education, health, and agricultural projects and to revitalize Indian arts and crafts throughout the Western Hemisphere. However, Collier failed in his attempts to get it funded by Congress. Under Rockefeller and Peterson, the OIAA then took the initiative and focused on counteracting Nazi Germany's attempts to win Indian support in South America. When the war ended, the OIAA was defunded. On behalf of the Rocky Mountain Council, Peterson attended the Second Inter-American Indian Conference in Cuzco, Peru, in 1949, advising the U.S. delegation and presenting a resolution on Indian education that was adopted by the body.

By 1949, the second conference, convened by Peruvian dictator and former head of the military police General Manuel Odría, was intended to promote a policy of rapid assimilation of Indians, reflecting the onset of the TERMINATION policy in the United States. Peterson did not object when the head of the American delegation, Assistant Secretary of the Interior William E. Warne, argued at the conference that Indians must modernize because "the Indian way, valid though it may have been for the times in which it flourished unchallenged, will not suffice." Underscoring the main point of ASSIMILATION, Warne stated that Indians should "share with us the riches yielded by the good American earth." Although Congress provided funds for the National Indian Institute in 1950, funding was discontinued in 1951.

Peterson also founded the Colorado Field Service Program in the Denver area that sponsored cultural programs, helped minority and disenfranchised groups to register to vote, and worked with them to pass progressive legislation, such as fair housing laws.

Peterson allied herself with the anti-Terminationists when she was appointed executive director of the NATIONAL CONGRESS OF AMERICAN INDIANS (NCAI) in 1953. Her skills as an organizer helped transform the organization, which by then was nearly bankrupt, into a major lobbying force in Washington, D.C. Along with RUTH MUSKRAT BRONSON and JOSEPH GARRY, Peterson successfully limited the ambitious plans of Indian commissioner GLENN LEONIDAS EMMONS to overturn the gains of the INDIAN NEW DEAL (see INDIAN REORGANIZATION ACT) and eliminate Indian reservations. Eminently practical in navigating the political currents of the day, Peterson made sure that NCAI, unlike many other reform groups of that era, would not come under suspicion of Communist influences: she kept the House Un-American Activities Committee (HUAC) and the State Department informed of any potentially subversive groups or individuals who contacted the group with offers of aid. In 1956, with Flathead scholar D'ARCY MCNICKLE, Peterson helped to organize an influential summer workshop program in Colorado, the Workshop on Indian Affairs, for Indian college students (see THOMAS, ROBERT KNOX).

Peterson also helped to organize the AMERICAN INDIAN CHICAGO CONFERENCE of 1961, one of the most influential Indian gatherings of the 20th century. Before and during the conference, she clashed with Tuscarora activist WILLIAM RICKARD, who was organizing a coalition of Eastern tribes and who sought to bring a more traditional perspective to the meeting. Through the agitation of students such as Ponca CLYDE WARRIOR and Paiute MEL THOM, this conference unleashed a new, more militant approach to Indian politics and gave birth to the RED POWER MOVEMENT.

Peterson resigned from her powerful position in the NCAI shortly after the conference, yielding to the militant wave led by VINE DELORIA, JR. She returned to Denver to become director of the city's Commission on Community Relations. In 1970, Peterson became the first woman to be appointed assistant commissioner for Indian affairs, serving under LOUIS ROOK BRUCE, JR. She retired from the BUREAU OF INDIAN AFFAIRS in 1985.

Peterson served on the boards of numerous organizations, including the National Committee on Indian Work of the Episcopal Church, the National Lutheran Board, the National Council of Churches Commission on Race and Religion, and the Girl Scouts. She received a number of awards including honorary doctorate degrees from the University of Colorado in 1973 and from Chadron State College in 1994. She was inducted into the Colorado Women's Hall of Fame in 1986. Helen White Peterson died on July 10th, 2000, after a long battle with Parkinson's disease.

Further Reading

Varnell, Jeanne. *Women of Consequence: The Colorado Women's Hall of Fame*. Boulder, Colo.: Johnson Books, 1999.

Peyote   *See* NATIVE AMERICAN CHURCH; RELIGIOUS FREEDOM, AMERICAN INDIAN.

Phinney, Archie (Kaplatsilpilp) (1903–1949)
Nez Perce leader, anthropologist, scholar, cofounder of the National Congress of the American Indians

Archie Phinney (Kaplatsilpilp) was born September 4, 1903, at Culdesac, Idaho, on the Nez Perce reservation. Raised in a traditional home, he was fully immersed in the tribe's cultural life, spoke Nez Perce fluently, and heard many legends and tales from his mother, Wayi'latpu. He attended the reservation school at Lapwai and at age 14 won the gold medal in the Idaho state public spelling tournament, competing with students from public schools throughout the state. After graduating from high school, unable to afford tuition at the state university, Phinney secured a special arrangement whereby he could matriculate at the University of Kansas while living at the Haskell Institute, a federal Indian secondary school in Lawrence, Kansas. (This would later become a standard procedure.) He majored in sociology and was lettered in three years of varsity sports. He received a B.A. in 1926, becoming the first Indian ever to graduate from the University of Kansas.

Phinney then went to Washington, D.C., to work for the BUREAU OF INDIAN AFFAIRS (BIA) while taking evening graduate courses in ethnology and philosophy at George Washington University. From 1928 to 1932, he worked part time for New York University's extension division doing community social work while continuing graduate studies in ethnology under FRANZ BOAS at Columbia University. He did research in historical processes in race and cultural contacts, with special emphasis on Indian reservation life. Boas even had him record samples of the Nez Perce language at the Victor recording laboratory in Camden, New Jersey.

In 1934, Phinney, with the help of his mother, then 60, published *Nez Perce Texts*. His introduction to this work is in itself an important document. He also wrote several semi-technical papers and articles, including some for the BIA newsletter, *Indians at Work*. While living in New York, Phinney spent many seasons as counselor and head counselor of various boys' camps in New York State, was assistant scout director of the Washington Boy Scout Camp, and organized and led boys' clubs in New York City.

In 1932, Phinney received a fellowship under a cooperative arrangement between Columbia and the Leningrad Academy of Sciences to study "the primitive races of the Union of Soviet Socialist Republics." Between 1932 and 1937, he did 18 months of field research on Siberian tribes, consulted with Soviet scientists and officials, and lectured in different institutions of the academy, including the Institute of Anthropology and Ethnography, the Institute of Language and Thought, and the Institute of History and Philosophy. In 1937, he received a degree equivalent to the Ph.D. He remained an associate of the academy for the rest of his life.

Phinney rejoined the BIA in October 1937, working in the organization division. As agent for the Great Lakes Area, he worked with, among others, Chippewa MARK L. BURNS. He married Ellen French at Minneapolis on December 5, 1939; they had one daughter, Mary Ellen. In 1941, Phinney was transferred to the Southwest Field Training Program. In 1942,

he investigated the problem of the rejection of the INDIAN REORGANIZATION ACT (IRA) by the New York Indians. In 1943, as assistant supervisor of Indian education for in-service training, he directed a training program for Latin Americans in Indian education, agriculture, and soil conservation on southwestern and Plains reservations.

In January 1944, Phinney was appointed superintendent of the Fort Totten Reservation, North Dakota, and in November was promoted to superintendent of the Northern Idaho agency, his home reservation of Nez Perce. There he tried to help organize a government under the IRA and worked to help the tribe preserve their traditions, setting up a museum and a library.

In 1939, Phinney was one of several Indian delegates appointed by Indian Commissioner JOHN COLLIER to attend a conference on North American Indians in Toronto, hosted jointly by the University of Toronto and Yale University. A walkout and separate meeting of the Indian delegates on the last day (including D'ARCY MCNICKLE, ARTHUR C. PARKER, LOUIS ROOK BRUCE, JR., David Owl, and RUTH MUSKRAT BRONSON) produced the germ of the idea for what would later become the NATIONAL CONGRESS OF AMERICAN INDIANS (NCAI). The group discussed the possibility of a national pan-Indian organization that could lobby for legislation in Congress. Phinney, by this time superintendent to the Nez Perce, was one of the most active founders of the NCAI and was elected councilman at the organization's constitutional convention in 1944. He received the Indian Council Fire's Achievement Award in 1948. His untimely death at St. Joseph's Hospital on October 29, 1949, was the result of a hemorrhage caused by an ulcer, among other complications.

Phinney summed up his life in these words: "While the Indian people are drifting toward the complete loss of racial and cultural identity, and blindly clutching vapid fetishes of traditional Indian glories, my biggest achievement, I think, has been to preserve an Indian personality and integrity, having both meaning and élan in modern life. To have Indian blood in one's veins is of little moment when one does not know and feel the traditional Indian life, its language, ideology, folklore, etc." Phinney Hall, the anthropology building at the University of Idaho, is named in his memory.

Further Reading

Crum, Steven. "Archie Phinney and His 'New Indian Case.'" *La América Indígena* 2, no. 1 (2003): 28–42.
Willard, William, and J. Diane Pearson. *Remembering Archie Phinney, a Nez Perce Scholar.* Salinas, Calif.: Coyote Press, 2004. (Originally published as volume 37, no. 2, of the *Journal of Northwest Anthropology*.)

Pick-Sloan plan (Pick-Sloan Missouri Basin Program)

In 1944, the U.S. Army Corps of Engineers began implementing a plan for flood control and reshaping of the Missouri River Basin, developed in conjunction with the Bureau of

Reclamation under the Flood Control Act of 1944. The architect of the plan, Colonel (later General) Lewis A. Pick, was best known at that time as the designer of the Ledo Road in Burma during WORLD WAR II; he was not trained as a hydrological engineer. Pick's ambitious plan for the Missouri basin led to his appointment as chief of the Corps of Engineers in 1949, and he would retire as a three-star general in 1953.

Pick's flood-control project was combined with a rival plan submitted by the Reclamation Bureau, completed by William Glenn Sloan, assistant director of the bureau's office in Billings, Montana. The resulting package was criticized by engineers, politicians, and affected residents as having retained all the worst features of both proposals. The plan, officially known as the Pick-Sloan Missouri Basin Program, provided for the construction of 107 dams, additional levees, the dredging of a new navigational channel, and hydroelectric and irrigation programs. Efforts to create a Missouri Valley Authority that might function like the Tennessee Valley Authority were defeated by opponents fearful of creating a new bureaucracy. Although the projects were to have a great impact on a number of Indian tribes, they had no opportunity to comment on the proposals. BUREAU OF INDIAN AFFAIRS (BIA) officials, disrupted by the wartime conditions and isolated in temporary offices in Chicago, knew that the plan required the flooding of Indian lands, but they failed to object while Pick-Sloan was being debated by Congress in 1944 and did not report to the affected tribes until 1947.

At first many Indians welcomed the idea of the Pick-Sloan plan, believing that it would bring benefits to their reservations. They soon discovered that this was not so. The Army Corps of Engineers, exercising its power to take property by eminent domain, proceeded to evict Indians from the Fort Berthold, Standing Rock, Cheyenne River, Lower Brulé, Crow Creek, and Yankton reservations in the Dakotas and to flood their best agricultural lands. On more than one occasion, the corps began construction before even entering into negotiations with the tribes on whose lands they were operating. The Indians lost the best lands on their reservations in return for inadequate monetary assessments of the value of their property. Promises of future profits in the form of irrigation, flood control, and the development of navigation and tourism in the area never materialized. Besides losing their homes and the plant and wildlife resources of the bottomlands, many communities were forced to relocate their burial grounds. The Sioux (Dakota, Lakota, Nakota) also lost water rights, despite the legal precedents of the WINTERS DOCTRINE, which should have guaranteed them. The Oahe Dam flooded more Indian land than any previous public works project, and the three Pick-Sloan dams at Oahe, Fort Randall, and Big Bend covered more than 202,000 acres of Sioux reservation bottomlands in all. Most damaging of all may have been the GARRISON DAM in western North Dakota, which required relocation of 80 percent of the population of the Three Affiliated Tribes (Mandan, Arikara, Hidatsa) of the Forth Berthold Reservation and which flooded 94 percent of their agricultural lands.

Conceived and begun in the wartime atmosphere of total military mobilization, designed and executed by a branch of the U.S. Army, the Pick-Sloan plan was truly a war against Indians and against the natural environment.

See also DAMS ON AMERICAN INDIAN LANDS; TERMINATION.

Further Reading
Lawson, Michael. *Dammed Indians: The Pick-Sloan Plan and the Missouri River Sioux, 1944–1980.* Norman: University of Oklahoma Press, 1982.
Wilkinson, Charles F. *Blood Struggle: The Rise of Modern Indian Nations.* New York: W. W. Norton, 2005.

Pima-Maricopa water rights
The question of the water rights of the Salt River Pima-Maricopa Indians attracted wide attention throughout the 20th century. The Gila River Pima, or Akimel O'odham, for centuries an agricultural people in what is now the state of Arizona, depend primarily upon the waters of the Gila River for their subsistence. When the Spaniards first came to the area at the end of the 17th century, the Pima were settled farmers. A large proportion of their food came from their own fields, supplemented with wild plants and animals. Around the beginning of the 19th century, they were joined by a small number of Maricopa, who share their way of life as well as their problems.

After Indian-settler contact in the mid-19th century, the U.S. government created an agency for the Pima-Maricopa but did nothing to help them safeguard their water, and it was encroached upon by settlers. By 1871, diversion of water from the Gila caused the Pima to run out of water at planting time. Alarmed, several villages moved to the Salt River later that year, founding the Salt River community of Pima and Maricopa. But by 1878, 50,000 acres of the 70,000-acre reservation were worthless because of the shortage of water. Even native wild plants were being affected, and the Pima were already destitute. In the 1880s, greater rainfall somewhat alleviated the situation, and the Pima Agency helped by providing better agricultural tools, technical instruction, a small agency demonstration farm, and, in 1883, a dam and a canal. Nevertheless, the problem remained serious.

In 1898, the INDIAN RIGHTS ASSOCIATION began to help the Pima-Maricopa ensure a water supply as guaranteed by treaty. By 1911, the Pima on the San Carlos Reservation were also starving and in a pitiful condition. There, too, settlers had diverted so much water from the Gila River that the Pima could no longer irrigate their crops. The government had put in an irrigation system fed by wells, but it was useless because the water was salty. Indian Commissioner ROBERT GROSVENOR VALENTINE asked Matthew Sniffen of the Indian Rights Association to help Indian Inspector Edward B. Linnen investigate. They found serious problems with the administration of reservation superintendent J. B. Alexander and his staff; Alexander was suspended and removed. In 1914, the Indian Rights Association urged construction of a dam in the Box Canyon of the Gila River to provide water for the Pima.

In 1919, just before Commissioner CATO SELLS's retirement, the Indian Rights Association charged that Pima agent Frank A. Thackery, a part owner of the Shannon Ranch, was knowingly diverting Pima water from the Gila River onto his own property. Sells transferred him to the Crow Reservation in Montana but did not fire him. By 1923, the situation was attracting the attention of other Indian welfare organizations. An article by Stella Atwood of the Indian welfare committee of the GENERAL FEDERATION OF WOMEN'S CLUBS, "The SOS of the Pimas: They Must Have Water for Their Crops to Avoid Starvation and Beggary," appeared in *Sunset Magazine* in April 1923.

The construction of the San Carlos Dam, later renamed the Coolidge Dam, was partly meant to fulfill the government's treaty obligation for water. The Coolidge Dam was formally dedicated in February 1930 and ready to operate by July. In March 1931, President Herbert Hoover granted the Pima relief from a lien of $1,388,000 for Gila River bridge and irrigation costs that had been assigned to the Pima as "reimbursable charges" (see RHOADS, CHARLES JAMES). In March 1936, it was announced that the Salt River community would get additional water.

Meanwhile, Phoenix, Arizona, was growing into a major city just 15 miles southwest of the Salt River Reservation, and together with other nearby urban communities and agricultural lands, it exerted a tremendous demand for water.

Tribal rights to water were set forth in the WINTERS DOCTRINE, which had resulted from a Supreme Court decision of 1907. The Salt River Pima-Maricopa Indian Water Rights Settlement Act of 1988 provided for settlement of the community's claims, with participation of Maricopa County municipalities; the Roosevelt Water Conservation District; the state of Arizona; and the Salt River Project, an agency that delivers water for power generation, irrigation, municipal, and other uses to 1.6 million people in the cities of Phoenix, Mesa, Chandler, Tempe, Gilbert, Scottsdale, Tolleson, and Avondale as well as to agricultural and recreational areas. Today, some of the Salt River Pima-Maricopa community's water comes from the Roosevelt Dam and Reservoir (completed in 1911), managed by the Salt River Project.

Around 1990, the cities of Phoenix and Tucson, along with the Salt River Project, negotiated with six INDIAN RESERVATIONS, including the Salt River community, over their substantial rights to the Gila River. As a result, the Salt River Pima-Maricopa community now leases water to the cities of Phoenix and Scottsdale. The Salt River community completed its own $10 million delivery system for Salt River Project water in the late 1990s.

The Salt River Pima-Maricopa also leased its entire water allocation from another management system, the Central Arizona Project, to cities in the Phoenix area, with delivery begun in 2000. A water rights settlement provided the Pima-Maricopa community with an additional yearly allotment of 38,000 acre-feet from the Salt and Verde Rivers.

Further Reading

Dejong, David H. "'Abandoned Little by Little': The 1914 Pima Adjudication Survey, Water Deprivation, and Farming on the Pima Reservation." *Agricultural History* 81, no. 1 (2007): 36–69.

———. "The Sword of Democles? The Gila River Indian Community Water Settlement Act of 2004 in Historical Perspective." *Wicazo Sa Review* 22, no. 2 (2007): 57–92.

Dobyns, Henry F. *The Pima-Maricopa*. New York: Chelsea House, 1989.

Myers, John L. *The Salt River Pima-Maricopa Indians: Legends, Reflections, History, Future*. Phoenix, Ariz.: Life's Reflections, 1988.

Pit River

During the latter half of the 20th century, a bitter land-claims battle raged in northern California between the Achumawi and Atsuge (also known as the Pit River Indians) and a number of large utility and logging companies.

In the mid-19th century, the Pit River Indians were forcibly removed from their homelands in and around the northwest corner of California and forced to live under wretched conditions, suffering a 90 percent drop in population between 1850 and 1900. Not until 1944 were they compensated for their losses. The settlement, which applied to all surviving California Indian tribes, effectively provided only $5 million, or $150 per remaining Indian, to compensate for the acquisition of the entire state. So small was the award that many California Indians sued in the court of claims and were awarded an additional $29 million.

However, many of the Pit River Indians refused to accept the claims award and demanded the creation of a 3.4-million-acre reserve. In 1963, they hired San Francisco attorney Louis Phelps to represent their claims, but Phelps betrayed them and reached an agreement with Ramsey Clark, assistant U.S. attorney general for land claims, for a monetary settlement and the merger of their claim with other California Indians, a settlement a majority of the Pit River Indians opposed but could not prevent.

The Pit River Indians, led by community leaders Willard Rhoads and Raymond Lego, replaced Phelps with celebrated attorney Melvin Belli, but the BUREAU OF INDIAN AFFAIRS had him removed from the case on the grounds that they had not approved him as counsel for the Pit River Indians. Belli appealed the removal all the way to the Supreme Court, but he lost in 1969. Meanwhile, Rhoads and Lego began to block timber harvesting of the Mount Shasta region, arguing that it was destroying the Pit River's forests, and won a compromise from the U.S. Forest Service.

In 1970, in the wake of the OCCUPATION OF ALCATRAZ ISLAND, Lego, Rhoads, and a party of 100 Achumawi and Wintun attempted to occupy a small portion of the Lassen National Forest, but they were met by a large force of armed police and federal marshals and instead occupied another piece of contested land owned by Pacific Gas & Electric (PG&E) at the Big Bend of the Pit River. The next day, a large force of police raided the camp and arrested Lego, Rhoads, and 35 other occupiers. The following day brought a replay of the occupation and subsequent arrests, this time joined by Alcatraz leader RICHARD OAKES (Mohawk).

In October 1970, 150 Pit River Indians occupying another parcel of PG&E property near Burney, California, were set upon by 400 police wielding clubs. Attempts to prosecute the leaders on the grounds of criminal trespass or assaulting the police largely failed, and the occupations continued without police interference. In 1971, Lego led an occupation of a Kimberly-Clark logging holding near Montgomery Creek, California.

The federal Department of Labor offered to transfer an abandoned jobs corps site, earlier occupied by a group of Wintun, to settle the lands claim. The Pit River Tribal Council accepted the offer over the objections of Rhoads, Lego, and their followers, and the site was turned over on May 26, 1973. Unbowed, Lego continued his militant tactics, holding out at Montgomery Creek and then occupying a 900-acre PG&E site near Big Bend shortly before his death on June 13, 1980.

Further Information

Callister, Lee, and Wendy Carrel. *Forty-Seven Cents* (film). 25 min. University of California Extension Media Center, 1973.

The Dispossessed (film). 33 min. University of California, 1970.

Protect Medicine Lake! Available online. URL: http://protectmedicinelake.org. Accessed 25 April 2015.

Further Reading

Chavers, Dean. "What Does Federal Money Really Buy?" *Indian Country Today*, 24 August 1994.

Garner, Van Hastings. *The Broken Ring: The Destruction of the California Indians.* Tucson, Ariz.: Westernlore Press, 1982.

Jaimes, Annette, M. "The Pit River Indian Land Claim Dispute in Northern California." *Journal of Ethnic Studies* 14, no. 4 (1987): 68–85.

Lego, Raymond, Charles Buckskin, and Willard Rhodes. "A Plea for Land: Pit River Indian Spokesmen Address the Public." Interviewed by Hoyt Elkins, February 6, 1974. *Oral History Program, Northeastern California Project.* Chico, Calif.: Association for Northern California Records and Research and California State University, Chico, 1974.

Olsen, Nancy, and Tom Izu. "Legends, Landscapes, and Wisdom: An Interview with Darryl Babe Wilson." *Indian Times* 16, no. 3 (2007): 1–3.

Pogue, William Reid (1930–2014) *Choctaw pilot, astronaut*

William Pogue, the first American Indian in space, was born to Alex W. and Margaret Pogue on January 23, 1930, in Okemah, Oklahoma. His mother was part Cherokee and his father part Choctaw. Encouraged to become a scientist by his high-school physics teacher, Pogue received a B.S. from Oklahoma Baptist University in 1951 and immediately enlisted in the U.S. Air Force. He received his commission in 1952 and served until 1975, piloting fighter bombers during the Korean War with the Fifth Air Force (1952–54) and flying with the air force's Thunderbirds exhibition team from 1955 to 1957. After graduating from the Empire Test Pilot's School in Great Britain in 1962 under a U.S. Air Force–Royal Air Force exchange program, he served as a test pilot for the British Ministry of Aviation from 1962 to 1965.

In 1966, then an instructor at the U.S. Air Force Research Pilot School, Pogue became one of 19 astronauts selected by NASA for the Apollo space program. He served on the support crew for the *Apollo 7*, *11*, and *14* missions. He piloted *Skylab 4*, the last of the three manned visits to the Skylab orbital workshop and up to that time the longest manned flight in the history of the space program. It was launched on November 16, 1973, and returned to Earth on February 8, 1974, a mission of 84½ days. For the flight he carried with him a flag representing the 67 Indian tribes of Oklahoma. He retired from the U.S. Air Force on September 1, 1975.

From 1976 to 1980, Pogue continued with NASA as a civilian astronaut. He was installed in the Oklahoma Aviation and Space Hall of Fame in 1980. Pogue published *Astronaut Primer* in 1985 and *How Do You Go to the Bathroom in Space? Answers to Real Questions Kids Have about Living in Space* in 1991. Later he moved to northwest Arkansas, where he worked as a consultant on space exploration to energy and aeronautics firms, and then to Florida. William Pogue died in Cocoa Beach, Florida, on March 3, 2014.

Chickasaw John Bennett Herrington (1958–), who subsequently followed Pogue into space, was the first tribally enrolled Indian astronaut. He carried the flag of the Chickasaw Nation on a mission to the International Space Station from November 23 to December 4, 2002, and made three spacewalks in his five days at the station.

Poolaw, Horace (Kaw-au-in-on-tay) (1906–1984) *Kiowa photographer*

The first American Indian to win recognition as a professional photographer, Horace Poolaw was born on March 13, 1906, at the Kiowa Indian Agency in Anadarko, Oklahoma. His father, George Poolaw, was a traditional healer and former Indian scout who married two sisters, the daughters of a Mexican captive. Horace Poolaw was given the Kiowa name Kaw-au-in-on-tay and grew up in the traditions of his people, as his mother spoke only Kiowa. Poolaw's family danced in the last Ghost Dance held by the Kiowa before its ban in 1923 (see DANCE ORDERS; RELIGIOUS FREEDOM, AMERICAN INDIAN).

Apprenticed at age 17 to landscape photographer George Long and later to Long's successor, John Coyle, Poolaw began taking pictures of Kiowa daily life during the 1920s. In 1929, when the American Indian Exposition, an annual celebration of Indian culture in Anadarko, first opened, he was its official photographer. He served in WORLD WAR II in the U.S. Army Air Corps, teaching aerial photography. After the war, he returned to his family in Anadarko, where he raised cattle. There he documented the transition of Kiowa culture into the postwar American scene. In 1978, failing eyesight from diabetes finally forced him to put down his camera.

Horace Poolaw died in January 1984 in Anadarko. After his death, his daughter, Linda Poolaw, arranged to have his photographs printed, cataloged, and exhibited. The exhibit *War Bonnets, Tin Lizzies and Patent Leather Pumps: Kiowa Culture in Transition 1925–1955*, traveled around the country in the early 1990s and was the subject of a major documentary video. His work has also been featured in other exhibits, including *Spirit Capture: Native Americans and the Photographic Image* shown at the National Museum of the American Indian in New York in 2002. His grandson Tom Poolaw (Kiowa–Lenni Lenape) is a recognized painter.

Further Reading

Smith, Laura E. "Obscuring the Distinctions, Revealing the Divergent Visions: Modernity and Indians in the Early Works of Kiowa Photographer Horace Poolaw, 1925–1945." Ph.D. dissertation. Indiana University. Bloomington, 2008.

Poolaw, Lucy Nicola (Princess Watahwaso, Watawaso, "Bright Star") (1882–1969) *Pen obscot mezzo-soprano*

Known professionally as Princess Watahwaso (Bright Star), Lucy Nicola (sometimes spelled Nicolar) was born on June 22, 1882, at Indian Island, Maine. She was the daughter of Joseph Nicolar, governor of the Penobscot, representative to the Maine state legislature, and author of *Life and Traditions of the Red Man*, and Elizabeth (Josephs) Nicolar. Her father died when she was eight.

The first female resident of the island to attend school in nearby Old Town, Maine, Nicola left when she was 15 to work as a stenographer and typist for the naturalist Montague Chamberlain, secretary of the Lawrence Scientific School and clerk of the summer school at Harvard University. He was particularly interested in helping her because one of her ancestors had fought with, spared the life of, and adopted one of his ancestors. Living with the Chamberlains brought her great educational advantages.

Endowed with a beautiful natural mezzo-soprano voice, Nicola went on to study singing in Chicago. "No one 'discovered' me; I just knew I could sing," she said in a 1966 interview. Nicola enrolled in Radcliffe College in fall 1901 but did not stay very long. She later studied piano at the Sherwood Music School in Chicago.

Over the course of her career, Nicola used three spellings of her Penobscot name. Up to around 1914, it was Wah-ta-waso. From then until about 1926, the period when she was concertizing and recording, it was Watahwaso. After that, it was Watawaso.

About 1913, Nicola joined the Redpath Lyceum Chautauqua circuit, a popular form of educational entertainment, performing in cities and towns from Jacksonville, Florida, to Chicago. Working for Redpath, she met composer Thurlow Lieurance, who was their musical director during 1914. Lieurance was one of the leading composers of INDIANIST MUSIC, a style that adapted traditional American Indian melodies to Western scales and musical forms. After three years of Chautauqua touring, Lucy went to study voice again in New York.

Impressing everyone with her exquisite voice, Nicola was signed by Harold D. Smith of the Victor recording company. In her first three recordings of Indian songs, recorded in October and November 1917, she is accompanied at the piano by Lieurance, many of the songs being his own arrangements, and by the flutist Hubert Small. These were released in May 1918. Nicola also recorded for Victor in 1920, 1921, 1922, 1924, and 1930, but only the last of these sets was ever released.

Victor also arranged concert tours for her in the United States and Mexico, and she gave a number of concerts in Havana, Cuba. Nicola made her New York debut at Aeolian Hall on April 19, 1920, accompanied by Francis Moore at the piano. She received glowing reviews, but though she continued to give classical recitals into the 1930s, she did not meet with the level of success she deserved, no doubt because she was typecast as an Indian "princess."

Working in an Indian troupe for the Keith Vaudeville Circuit in the 1920s with Penobscot dancer MOLLY SPOTTED ELK, also from Indian Island, Nicola met Bruce Poolaw, a Kiowa and former rodeo champion from Oklahoma some 20 years her junior. Nicola and Poolaw then spent a lot of their time on Indian Island. In the early 1930s, Nicola built a bungalow on the shore of the island facing Old Town. She began directing the annual three-day all-Indian pageants there in 1933, with Poolaw playing a very active role in the proceedings. She returned to the island for good in 1935. Poolaw and Nicola married in 1937 and started a trading post to sell the local sweetgrass baskets and other crafts.

On the island, Lucy Poolaw became active in charitable, religious, and political affairs, founding the Indian Island Women's Club and helping to integrate the Indian schools into the public school system, for until then all Indian schools in Maine had been Catholic. In 1937, she was instrumental in beginning Baptist services on the long-Catholic Island, and after a Baptist church opened in 1942 she served as its organist for years. From 1932, she advocated a bridge to the island; one was finally built in 1950. Poolaw lobbied to obtain federal voting rights for Maine Indians, which did not come until 1954. She also was active in the effort to get a specific commission of Indian Affairs established in Maine; this became a reality in 1965.

After her death in March 1969, Bruce Poolaw went back to Oklahoma, where he died in 1987.

Further Reading

McBride, Bunny. "Lucy Nicolar: The Artful Activism of a Penobscot Performer." In *Sifters: Native American Women's Lives*, edited by Theda Perdue, 141–159. Oxford: Oxford University Press, 2001.

Spottswood, Richard K. *Ethnic Music on Records*. Vol. 5. Urbana: University of Illinois Press, 1990.

Pop Chalee ("Flower Blue," Merina Luján) (1906–1993) *Taos Pueblo artist, singer, textile designer*

Pop Chalee was born Merina Luján on March 20, 1906, in Castle Gate, Utah, the daughter of Merea (Myrtle) Margherete Luenberger, a Mormon of primarily Swiss descent, and Joseph Cruz Luján, a Taos Pueblo ranch hand, coal miner, and Spanish-American war veteran who had made the charge up San Juan Hill with Teddy Roosevelt. Her parents separated when Merina was very young, and the girl went to live with her father briefly in Taos. In 1911, she began to attend the Santa Fe Indian School, graduating in 1920. She was then sent with her three sisters to Salt Lake City to live with their mother. At age 16, she rebelled against her mother and married Otis Hopkins, a Mormon metal and wood craftsman.

In 1928, with her husband, Merina visited Taos to find that her father had become one of the founders of the All-Pueblo Council, formed to protect Pueblo lands, and her uncle Tony Luján [Luhan] had married wealthy society matron and champion of Indian rights Mabel Dodge (see BURSUM BILL).

In 1935, she moved back to New Mexico and enrolled again in the Santa Fe Indian School, this time to study art under influential teacher DOROTHY DUNN alongside Dunn's distinguished pupils in the "Studio," HARRISON BEGAY, OSCAR HOWE, and PABLITA VELARDE. Graduating in 1937, Merina began using her Tiwa-language name, Pop Chalee, or "Flower Blue," and established a small studio with fellow graduates ALLAN HOUSER and Gerald Nailor. She soon became part of a growing Santa Fe art scene that included Georgia O'Keeffe, Fremont Ellis, Olive Rush, and Alfred Morang, and in 1939, she was one of seven artists chosen to represent New Mexico at the New York World's Fair.

In 1941, Pop Chalee had a one-woman show at the Museum of Fine Arts in New Mexico. By then she had branched out into designing textiles, working with Al Momaday (father of Kiowa author N. SCOTT MOMADAY), José Ray Toledo, Bob Chavez, and BEATIEN YAZZ. During WORLD WAR II, her husband, Otis, by then an accomplished metalsmith, was recruited to work on the atomic bomb, and she moved with him to Los Alamos for two years.

After the war, Pop Chalee's fame grew, and she appeared in a number of promotions, including publicity events for movies such as *Annie Get Your Gun* (1950) and tourism publicity for the Santa Fe Railroad. In 1947, she divorced Hopkins and married Ed Natay, a Navajo medicine man and teacher. She encouraged him to sing and record his music. Natay was the first artist recorded on Canyon Records, a label begun in 1951 by Phoenix studio owner Ray Boley to showcase traditional Indian music.

Though her early paintings follow the Studio style encouraged by Dunn, Pop Chalee soon developed distinctive paintings of deer, horses, and other animals in deep, unusual colors such as blue and featuring humanlike eyes and expressions. In later years, she drew criticism for working in the "Bambi style." If anything, it was the other way around: Walt Disney himself tried to recruit Indian painters from Dunn's workshops, and he purchased one of Pop Chalee's forest scenes in 1937, a year before *Bambi* was begun and four years before it was released. The artist was well known for her murals and painted murals for the Albuquerque, Roswell, and Santa Fe airports; the Santa Fe Railroad (now in the Wheelwright Museum collection); the New Mexico State Capitol Building; the Grand Hotel in Mackinac Island, Michigan; and many others.

Pop Chalee continued to paint in her later years, though she preferred to lapse into obscurity. A vibrant artist who successfully marketed herself to become one of the best-known Indians of her day, Pop Chalee died on December 11, 1993, in Santa Fe, New Mexico.

Further Reading

Cesa, Margaret. *The World of Flower Blue: Pop Chalee, an Artistic Biography*. Santa Fe, N.Mex.: Red Crane Books, 1997.

Porter, Tom (Sakokwenionkwas, The One Who Wins) (1944–) *Mohawk chief*

Tom Porter was born Sakokwenionkwas (The One Who Wins) in 1944 on the St. Regis (Akwesasne) Mohawk Reservation, a member of the Bear Clan. Porter was raised by his grandmother, Hattie Chubb, who spoke only Mohawk. His uncle was Mohawk chief and ironworker Francis Johnson, alternately known as Frank Thomas or Standing Arrow, who led a failed occupation of contested land in the Mohawk Valley in upstate New York in 1954. Standing Arrow also led the Mohawk protests over their displacement by the St. Lawrence Seaway project in the late 1950s. As a young man, Porter was influenced by the cultural revitalizing efforts of teacher and historian RAY FADDEN. In 1966, at the urging of Hopi religious leader DAN KATCHONGVA, he helped found the White Roots of Peace, a traveling group of speakers and elders who sought to bring the traditional Iroquois perspective to Indian people around the country. An eloquent speaker even by the high standards of the Iroquois, Porter was one of the group's main organizers as well as one of its lecturers from 1966 until 1970.

While the idea of a traveling lecture group had been anticipated a few years before by Mohawk Chief Ernest Benedict in his attempts to form the North American Indian Traveling College, a rail car that would travel across Canada teaching Native traditions, and by the Unity Caravans conceived by Tuscarora activist WILLIAM RICKARD, the White Roots of Peace was to have the most success. Aided by a non-Indian employee of the Canadian Department of Indian Affairs, Jerry Gambill (also known as Rarihokwats), a group of young Mohawks including Porter, Mike Mitchell, Ron La France, and Francis Boots traveled to Indian reservations, urban Indian centers, schools and colleges across the United States, Canada, and even into Central and South America. Mixing talks about Indian rights and values with traditional dancing and singing, the group attempted to foster pride among young Indians about their heritage. Along with its national newspaper, *Akwesasne Notes*, founded in 1968 following the CORNWALL BRIDGE BLOCKADE, the White Roots of Peace deeply influenced the RED POWER MOVEMENT of the 1960s and 1970s. The group's visit to San Francisco in 1969 created a lasting impression on Mohawk activist RICHARD OAKES and helped galvanize the Indian community there prior to the takeover of Alcatraz Island.

In 1970, Porter and Chief Benedict led an occupation of Stanley Island in the St. Lawrence River. The peaceful occupation forced the Canadian government to recognize Mohawk claims to the land. As chief of the Bear Clan, Porter defended the Akwesasne Reservation from attempts by New York State to extend its criminal jurisdiction over the reservation in 1979. The resulting standoff led to a two-year confrontation with New York State police (see AKWESASNE, SIEGE OF). The leadership of Porter and other Mohawk chiefs, such as JAKE SWAMP, eventually led the state to withdraw its forces and recognize the authority of the traditional Longhouse government, a major victory for the traditional movement (see SHENAN-DOAH, LEON).

The victory, however, had a destabilizing effect as the Longhouse government struggled to maintain its authority over the fractious reservation itself. The Mohawk chiefs' council was unable to prevent the nearby territory of GANIENKEH from dissolving into bitter infighting. Furthermore, the council was unable to stop the lucrative smuggling operations that began to spring up on the reservation. Despite this, Porter continued his work of revitalizing Mohawk culture. In 1981, he and Mohawk Wolf Clan chief Ron La France founded the Akwesasne Freedom School, one of the most successful indigenous language schools in the country (see INDIGENOUS LANGUAGE USE). The next year, his book *Our Ways* was published by the North American Indian Traveling College, and in 1986 *Cycle of Ceremonies* appeared.

Porter led the traditional faction of Mohawk who opposed the spread of gaming on the reservation, a dispute that eventually erupted into a full-scale civil war in 1990 (see GAMING ON INDIAN RESERVATIONS). The bitter fighting led to numerous demonstrations, the burning down of a gaming hall, and a shootout in which two Mohawk died. Sick of the infighting, Porter in 1993 led some traditional members of the tribe back to their ancestral homeland, the Mohawk Valley, purchasing a property they called Kanatsiohareke (Clean Pot), where they could maintain a traditional life.

Porter's third book, *Trading Eyes: Alternative Visions of Native Americans*, was published in 1989. His fourth, *Clanology*, appeared in 1992. In 1998, Porter launched the Iroquois Immersion Program at Kanatsiohareke, likening it to a Carlisle Indian boarding school in reverse (see ASSIMILATION). A much-sought-after lecturer, Tom Porter continues to successfully advocate the Iroquois perspective and encourage young Indians to return to tradition. In 2008, he published a new book entitled, *And Grandma Said*, about Iroquois teachings.

Further Reading

Hauptman, Lawrence M. *Seven Generations of Iroquois Leadership: The Six Nations since 1800.* Syracuse, N.Y.: Syracuse University Press, 2008.

Posey, Alex (Alexander Lawrence Posey) (1873–1908) *Creek humorist, poet, newspaper publisher, politician*
Alexander Lawrence Posey was born on August 3, 1873, near Eufaula, Indian Territory (now Macintosh County, Oklahoma), the son of Lewis Henderson Posey, a mixed Scottish-Creek farmer, and Nancy Phillips, a full-blooded Creek from the prominent and politically powerful Wind Clan. Posey grew up on the family farm near Tuskegee, where his father, fluent in Muskogee, and his mother, a devout Baptist who did not speak English, brought him up speaking only Muskogee until he was in his early teens.

After private tutoring and a period at the Creek National School in Eufaula, Posey spoke English well enough to enroll in Indian University (later Bacone College) in Muskogee at the age of 16. By then, he had already developed his writing talents working for the Eufaula *Indian Journal*, and at Indian University he began setting type for the school newspaper, *The BIU Instructor.* He contributed a number of poems to the *Instructor*, including "The Comet's Tail," "Death of a Sea God," and his satiric "Death of the Window Plant," which established his literary reputation. Posey's unmatched oratorical powers, especially his commencement speech on June 21, 1893, on the subject of Cherokee leader Sequoyah, attracted widespread attention and brought him celebrity among his people. It was also at Indian University that he developed the first of his popular characters, "Chinnubbie Harjo," through which he expressed his gift for political satire.

After leaving Indian University in 1894, Posey was elected to the House of Warriors (the lower house of the Creek legislature) on September 3, 1895. His support of ALLOTMENT in the politically tense climate surrounding the passing of the CURTIS ACT and the establishment of the Dawes Commission was not enough to tarnish his popularity with the Creek leadership. Posey believed that it would do little good to oppose the Dawes Commission, which the majority favored, and thought a negotiated settlement inevitable. He soon left the legislature to take a post at the Creek Orphan Asylum, where he returned to his writing.

In 1899, Posey took over the supervision of the Creek National High School at Eufaula. His poems "My Hermitage" and "The Blue Jay" achieved national recognition at this time. By then, however, Posey was becoming more interested in prose writing and had already abandoned poetry. He was also becoming interested in local politics. In 1902, he bought the *Journal* and turned it into a regional newspaper. In October 1902, Posey brought out another of his satirical characters, "Fus Fixico." In his Fus Fixico letters, he reached the height of his literary powers. The 81 printed letters are among the finest examples of American political satire, humorously skewering both regional and national political leaders and trends.

Although a "progressive" newspaperman, Posey sympathized with the "nostalgic" aims of the leaders of the Crazy Snake Rebellion, referring to CHITTO HARJO as "the last true Creek." However, he also considered their goals—the reestablishment of the traditional government and the strict enforcement of the treaty of 1832, which guaranteed Creek lands in

Indians territory—hopelessly outdated, and he lamented that their followers were "too numerous for councilors and too few for war."

In 1904, recognizing that "the old days are gone" and that "the new Indian must meet the new condition, not as an Indian, but as an American citizen," Posey decided to shift careers and work for the Dawes Commission as an interpreter and enrollment officer. This two-year experience brought him into direct personal contact with the Snakes and other conservatives and made him more appreciative of their stubborn refusal to give up the traditional way of life. Nevertheless, Posey himself was bent on capitalizing on the opportunities presented by the end of the Creek nation and the birth of the new state of Oklahoma.

After helping to draft the Creek Constitution at Muskogee in 1905, Posey withdrew from politics to speculate in real estate, joining the International Land Company, which focused on Creek lands. Although his involvement with the company was short-lived, his association with Land Company president C. M. Bradley—known as the "King of Grafters" and later indicted for forgery and conspiracy involving freedmen's allotments—damaged Posey's reputation. Brushing aside any criticism that he was selling out his own people, he went to work as an agent for the Palo Alto Land Company, which purchased allotments from full-blooded Oklahoma Indians. Anticipating the end of restrictions on purchasing allotments, he also became involved in oil exploration, founding his own company, Posey-Thornton Oil and Gas.

In 1908, Posey returned to the *Indian Journal*, which he had sold five years before, and while continuing his various business pursuits, he seemed ready once again to make use of his great literary skills. However, on May 27, 1908, while attempting to cross the flood-swollen North Canadian River in a rowboat, Posey and one of his boatmen lost control of their small craft and drowned.

Further Reading

Kosmider, Alexia. "Hedged in, Shut up and Hidden from the World: Unveiling the Native and Landscape in Alex Posey's Poetry." *Poetry and Poetics* 21, no. 1 (1996): 3–19.

Littlefield, Daniel F. *Alex Posey: Creek Poet, Journalist, and Humorist.* Lincoln: University of Nebraska Press, 1992.

Posey, Alexander Lawrence. *The Fus Fixico Letters: A Creek Humorist in Early Oklahoma*, edited by Daniel F. Littlefield, Jr., and Carol A. Petty Hunter. Norman, Okla.: Red River Books, 2002.

Powers, Mabel (Yehsennohwehs) (1872–1966) *author, storyteller, historian*

Mabel Powers was born on July 23, 1872, at Hamburg, New York, the daughter of Richard F. and Lydia Post Powers. Upon graduating from Buffalo Normal College, she decided on a career in public speaking. After attending the Shoemaker School of Elocution and Oratory, Philadelphia, she lectured and gave dramatic readings throughout Pennsylvania and New York and also wrote for magazines and newspapers.

While reading Longfellow's *Hiawatha* at an Iroquois council meeting at Rochester, New York, Powers made such an impression that the Seneca adopted her, giving her the name Yehsennohwehs ("storyteller"). Such adoptions of non-Indians were far more common then than today and for the most part had no deep significance. At the time, Powers thought of it mainly as good publicity. However, she soon became deeply interested in the history, customs, religion, ritual, and stories of the Iroquois.

During the winters, traditional storytelling time, Powers, with the help of an interpreter, heard many tales from the elders and became skilled at retelling them and educating the general public on Iroquois culture and history. She also published some stories. She became an advocate of traditional Iroquois sovereignty and emphasized that all information in her lectures and writings was given to her directly by her Indian friends. A sensitive interpreter of Iroquois traditions, she emphasized that "their religious and esthetic life was so intimately related to their industrial and social order that the result was a completely integrated culture" (*The Portage Trail*, 1924).

For many years, Powers's lectures were a popular part of the program at the Chautauqua Institution in upstate New York. She first spoke in 1917 and, from the early 1920s, lived in a bungalow on Chautauqua Lake. She loved the outdoors and believed in its benefits. She was a "guide" of the Wahmeda "tribe" of Woodcrafters (members of the Woodcraft League, founded by ERNEST THOMPSON SETON), offering hospitality at her place to Woodcrafters and others, particularly girls who could not afford all expenses at Chautauqua. Organized by "tribes," such as the Wahmeda (named after a lake near Chautauqua), the Woodcrafters were the precursors to outdoor organizations such as the Boy Scouts.

A direct outgrowth of Powers's association with the Iroquois was her work in the international peace movement after WORLD WAR I, and she represented the Seneca at the World Peace Congress of the International League for Peace and Freedom in 1924. She was a member of the Six Nations Association, the Women's National League for Justice to the American Indian, and the National Council for Prevention of War.

Aside from articles on Indians for *Outlook* (1916–21) and other magazines through the 1920s and 1930s, Powers published *Stories the Iroquois Tell Their Children* (1917), *Around an Iroquois Story Fire* (1923), *The Portage Trail* (1924), and *The Indian as Peacemaker* (1932). She also wrote "The Original American Blueprint for Peace" for *Common Ground* (originally published in Spanish in Mexico). Mabel Powers died on August 24, 1966, in Jamestown, New York.

powwows

Powwows are festivals of Native American music and dance that have become emblematic of the Indian cultural renaissance of the last 30 years. Although rooted in ancient forms, the powwow is a modern pan-Indian cultural manifestation that is continually adapting to reflect forces at work in contemporary Native life. The word *powwow* comes from the Algonquian *pauwau*, meaning "he dreams," referring to a traditional healer or a traditional healing ceremony. Early non-Indian settlers had little understanding of Indian rituals, and in 1646 the Massachusetts General Court decreed "that no Indian shall at any time *pawwaw*, or perform outward worship to their false gods, or to the devil." The word *powwow* was often used to describe any Native council or ceremony, but by the 20th century, it specifically came to refer to a secular social gathering featuring singing and dancing by men, women, and children.

The modern powwow has its roots in the Omaha Grass Dance, a fusion of a late-summer harvest celebration with a Hethu'shka warrior society dance, in which the Omaha warriors wore only a breechcloth with a long bunch of grass attached at the waist. The men would dance free-style to the beat of the drum, moving like a blade of grass in the wind. The Grass Dance was a social dance, and although vastly different in style, was similar in concept to the social gatherings of eastern tribes, where the community could get together, socialize, dance, and sing. The Omaha celebration, begun in 1804 in Nebraska, is currently the longest continually running powwow in the country.

By the 1860s, the Grass Dance was common throughout the Plains. In 1867, one of the first Sioux powwows, the Sisseton-Wahpeton Oyate Powwow, was begun on the Lake Traverse Reservation in South Dakota. The Grass Dance spread among the Indians living in Indian Territory (now Oklahoma) through the Omaha's close relatives, the Ponca, who also had a Hethu'shka warrior society. In 1872, the Quapaw Tribal Powwow was begun in Quapaw, Indian Territory, and in 1877 the Ponca Fair and Powwow was inaugurated in Ponca City. Early powwows varied greatly in style and in the types of dances. The Ponca Fair, generally considered the first modern powwow, was made up mostly of Hethu'shka warrior dances, such as the Grass Dance. Powwows soon began to spread throughout Indian Territory; in 1884 the Choctaw held their first powwow in Tushka Homma, and the Osage held their first gathering the next year in Pawhuska. Buffalo Bill's Wild West shows, begun in 1883, and "Indian Congresses," usually held in conjunction with major fairs or expositions, featured Indian dancers among the performers. These shows and exhibitions, which usually included performers from many different tribes, helped to spread the Grass Dance style across the country. They also influenced Indian powwows by adding an element of showmanship and promotion. The "grand entry" of the modern powwow is believed to be derived from the opening parades through town typical of the early Wild West shows and circuses.

In the late 19th century, the federal policy of ASSIMILATION led to the banning of Indian religious and cultural events on reservations. By 1891, an attempt by the Flathead to hold a Fourth of July celebration powwow in Arlee, Montana, was broken up by police from the Indian Bureau (later the BUREAU OF INDIAN AFFAIRS [BIA]). The bans were relaxed somewhat after 1905 by Indian Commissioner FRANCIS ELLINGTON LEUPP, and powwows began to start up once more. In 1916, a number of Indian tribes in southwestern Oklahoma began a powwow in Anadarko that eventually became the Anadarko Indian Fair, and in 1920 an intertribal powwow was established at Dietrich Lake. In 1919, the first annual Crow Fair was held in Crow Agency, Montana, and over time it became one of the largest powwows in the country.

Powwows were largely spared from the DANCE ORDERS of the early 1920s, which were targeted at religious ceremonies, and they continued to expand and diversify. During this time, railroad companies began to promote Indian culture as a way to attract tourists to remote locations and helped to organize and publicize Indian fairs and powwows throughout the West and Southwest.

New dances began to make their appearances as well, including the Fancy Dance, now a staple of every powwow. It was created by three Ponca dancers—Gus McDonald, Dennis Rough Face, and Henry Snake—who began competing with each other to develop a livelier, more creative form of expression than the Grass Dance upon which it is based. In 1926, at the Haskell Institute in Lawrence, Kansas, the first world championship Fancy Dance contest was held; it was won by McDonald. The Fancy Dance also inaugurated a new era of competition in powwows, where dancers and singers traveled to compete for prize money.

As powwows spread to the North and Southwest, tribes from different regions began to incorporate versions of their traditional dances into them. The Jingle Dance, a woman's dance that came from the Chippewa and became popular throughout the country during the 1920s and 1930s, featured a dress sewn with metal "jingles" made of the lids of tin cans. The Gourd Dance was adapted from the ceremonies of the Cheyenne, Kiowa, and Comanche.

As the assimilation policy came to an end after the election of President Franklin Delano Roosevelt in 1932 and the appointment of JOHN COLLIER as Indian commissioner, powwows began to spread further and grow in size. Backed by 15 tribes, the Anadarko Indian Fair became the American Indian Exposition in 1935, one of the largest gatherings of Indians in the country. By the time of WORLD WAR II, most reservations had a local powwow. Powwows became a focal point for celebrating the safe return of the many Indian soldiers who served the war effort, and since then, powwows often include a special place for Indian veterans in the grand entry.

After the war, most powwows began to develop from local social gatherings into more competitive contest powwows, featuring prize money for dancers and singers. The contest powwows quickly led to the establishment of a "powwow circuit," with Indian performers traveling from powwow to powwow in search of prize money. Powwows also began to grow in size, some becoming huge intertribal festivals, such as Crow Fair, attracting tens of thousands of Indians from across the country. Hundreds of Indian families began to live by following the circuit, competing in the events and selling crafts to Indian and non-Indian spectators. This in turn led to the standardization of powwows, and although they varied somewhat from region to region, by the 1960s most followed the general outline of the style originated by the Ponca in Oklahoma. Powwows had become a truly pan-Indian form of cultural expression, and the Oklahoma style of powwow spread to the East Coast, in some cases supplanting the traditional "socials" of eastern tribes.

Although there are still many differences, generally the modern powwow is held in a circular dance area, the larger ones surrounded by seats or grandstands. Usually there is a master of ceremonies; a head judge and other judges; and two lead dancers, one male and one female. One or more host drum groups provide the music and singing that is essential to the powwow. Male dancers compete for prizes in dances such as the Grass Dance, Fancy Dance, and Men's Traditional Dance, and women compete separately in the Jingle Dance, Shawl Dance, and Women's Traditional Dance. Drum groups also compete for prizes. Dances such as the Round Dance and the Two-Step are noncompetitive dances that everyone is usually welcome to join. Sometimes special dances, such as the Hoop Dance, originally from the Hopi tribe, are performed to entertain the spectators who surround the dance circle. There is usually an area for vendors to sell food, artworks, and crafts, and an area where people can camp.

By the 1970s, as the American Indian population became increasingly urbanized (see URBANIZATION, AMERICAN INDIANS AND), large powwows began to be organized in cities. Today some of the largest powwows are held in urban areas, such as the Red Earth powwow in Oklahoma City and the Gathering of Nations in Albuquerque, New Mexico. Large or small, virtually every Indian community, and every city with an Indian population, now has a powwow. In many ways, the powwow reflects the resilience and adaptability of Indian cultures during the 20th century, and from its local roots in Nebraska, it has spread nationwide to become one of the most powerful modern symbols of Indian pride and identity.

Further Reading

Browner, Tara. *Heartbeat of the People: Music and Dance of the Northern Pow-Wow.* Urbana: University of Illinois Press, 2002.
Knopff, Bradley D. "Reservation Preservation: Powwow Dance, Radio, and the Inherent Dilemma of the Preservation Process." Ph.D. dissertation. Lund University, Sweden, 2001.

Pratt, Richard Henry (1840–1924) *educator, founder of Carlisle Indian School*

Richard Henry Pratt was born in Rushford, New York, on December 6, 1840, the son of Richard S. and Mary Herrick Pratt, and was raised in Logansport, Indiana, where he learned tinsmithing. During the Civil War, Pratt served in the Indiana Volunteers, rising to captain. Reenlisting in 1867, he commanded a troop in the Tenth Cavalry, a black regiment in Indian Territory. In 1875, he led Indian scouts in the capture of 72 militant Cheyenne, Kiowa, Arapaho, and Comanche, some of whom he later took to Fort Marion in St. Augustine, Florida, as prisoners of war.

Over the next three years, Pratt set up an educational program for the captured Indians, bringing in local teachers to provide basic academic skills, and local craftspeople to teach them trades such as carpentry, tailoring, baking, and masonry. They were also encouraged to draw. When these Indians were ordered released in 1878, Pratt placed some with white families and others with the Episcopal church. He brought 17 to the Hampton Institute in Virginia, a school for blacks, mainly former slaves, directed by General S. C. Armstrong. In 1879, after Pratt had taught the Indians for a year, the War Department authorized him to open a school on an abandoned military post at Carlisle, Pennsylvania—the first federal boarding school for Indians. Eleven of the former prisoners went with him.

By 1900, Carlisle had 1,024 pupils. Its football team, led by coach POP WARNER, already showed signs of future greatness and increased Carlisle's prestige among both Indians and non-Indians: ". . . if the Indians could kick themselves into civilization through football," wrote Pratt to Yavapai physician-writer CARLOS MONTEZUMA in November 1896, "let them do it." Pratt succeeded in building up an esprit de corps at Carlisle.

By 1901, Carlisle had become the flagship of a system of 26 federal Indian boarding schools. However, the federal boarding school was not the only type of Indian school: It had less-expensive rivals in reservation boarding schools, reservation day schools, and the regular public schools. Carlisle was by now in a position to siphon off the "best and the brightest" from the reservation schools, so those schools' response to its recruitment drives was grudging. Some critics objected that the boarding schools were elitist and expensive; others, that Pratt's policies were cruel and destructive of a great cultural resource.

One of the most unusual features of Carlisle, which Pratt regarded as the key to the whole, was the "outing system"—whereby students were placed with white families. Based on the principle of apprenticeship, which had been Pratt's own main education, its aims were to encourage Indian-white contact, further the students' education, force them to speak English, enable them to earn a little money, and instill what Pratt called the "courage of civilization"—not to fear whites, to be able to compete, and to do without the support of the tribe. Pratt claimed to have conceived the idea from observing the experience of immigrants from abroad. Both students and families were carefully selected; Pratt often scouted the families himself, usually Quaker farming families in Pennsylvania. The "outing" was presented to the students as a challenge to their persistence and their ability to make the most of opportunities. Basic placement was for the summer, after which the student could either return to Carlisle or stay on until November, when he or she would be enrolled in the local school. Pratt expected the student to be treated like a son or daughter of the family, not a servant.

The outing system was admired even by Pratt's greatest critics, such as FRANCIS ELLINGTON LEUPP. It was adopted at the Haskell Institute in 1889, and in 1894 the secretary of the Interior directed agents and school superintendents to use the system. But it was difficult to administer and not successful in the West—largely, it would seem, because Western whites did not relate well to Indians. When Leupp became Indian commissioner, he tried unsuccessfully to develop it at reservation schools. It was successful only in the specialized form developed by Leupp's appointee CHARLES EDWIN DAGENETT, who would find labor-intensive projects such as railroad or dam construction, and bargain with the employers to hire Indians.

Pratt was a radical assimilationist. He saw no value in tribalism or Native culture. To him, these were simply negative conditions, and to "relieve" Indians of these "burdens" was the best thing one could do for them. And he felt that it should be done fast. Impressed with what he saw of the progress of former black slaves living among whites, Pratt did not accept the idea of leading the Indian through "stages of civilization." His philosophy was dramatically simple: apply a type of "shock treatment." He advocated education in citizenship and the arts of mainstream American culture for all Indians, in order that they might be placed in the midst of white society as soon as possible; and he wanted all Indians to be given allotments rapidly and at the same time, thus breaking up tribal society and the tribes themselves. "The individual is the unit," he wrote in an 1894 letter, "not the tribe or the race."

Pratt's criticisms of the Dawes General Allotment Act (1887) were all to do with its being far too slow and not providing enough education or the right kind of education. (For example, he disagreed with the emphasis on farming.) Property holding was an education in itself, and if Indians lost their land, well and good—it would teach them a lesson about civilization. Indian property holding should therefore not be restricted in any way. For these reasons, by the late 1880s, Pratt had disassociated himself from supporters of ALLOTMENT—the humanitarian and religious groups, their missions and contract schools, and even the army itself. He also attacked Hampton Institute and its director, General Armstrong. All, in his view, were holding the Indian back from the goal—ASSIMILATION.

Moreover, Pratt opposed the move to adopt civil service principles in the Indian Bureau (later the BUREAU OF INDIAN AFFAIRS [BIA])—supported by the INDIAN RIGHTS ASSOCIATION (IRA)—because he did not believe that merely improving the administration of affairs would solve the "Indian problem." More particularly, it interfered with Pratt's running of Carlisle.

Pratt's program was controversial from the start, and his imperious temperament made him many enemies as well as friends. As early as 1894, Herbert Welsh, director of the IRA confided to Leupp that Pratt "has long overdrawn the deposit of favor which charity should set to his account." His opposition to civil service reform also annoyed Theodore Roosevelt, a member of the Civil Service Commission, but by 1898, Pratt still had sufficient power to secure the dismissal of Superintendent of Indian Education William N. Hailman, a civil service man.

When Theodore Roosevelt was elected president in 1901, Pratt became vulnerable (see REEL, ESTELLE). He withstood calls for his resignation from the army in 1903, but in 1904 he was dismissed for insubordination when, at a conference of Baptist ministers in New York City, he called for the abolition of the Indian Bureau. He left Carlisle that year.

Pratt might seem to belong to the 19th century, not the 20th: His thought was formed in the atmosphere of post–Civil War egalitarianism and a reaction to President Ulysses S. Grant's Peace Policy, which emphasized confining Indians to reservations. By 1900, Carlisle had already been operating more than two decades. Pratt was retired from active duty and directorship of Carlisle by 1904 and the school itself was closed in 1918. Nevertheless, Pratt occupies an important place in any history of American Indians in the 20th century. Not only did he continue to actively promote his radical assimilationist philosophy right up to his death in 1924, but his ideas continued to guide attitudes and policies long after that. Most members of the SOCIETY OF AMERICAN INDIANS, representing the Indian elite of the first quarter of the century, were strongly under Pratt's influence, and despite his differences with the Christian welfare organizations, they were much affected by him as well. Author-activist Elaine Goodale Eastman was still preaching his gospel and using it to criticize JOHN COLLIER when the latter was Indian commissioner (see her *Pratt, the Red Man's Moses*, 1935). Graduates of Carlisle and other federal Indian boarding schools continued in important positions well into the 20th century for example, Charles Dagenett and GEORGE P. LAVATTA both high-ranking officials in the Bureau of Indian Affairs.

Even the sink-or-swim spirit of TERMINATION in the 1950s and 1960s was basically a postwar version of the Pratt philosophy. It was argued that only by terminating the existence of the tribes would Indians and non-Indians achieve harmonious relations and Indians learn to stand on their own feet; but in both cases, this independence was to be achieved at the expense of Indian cultural identity.

Pratt died in San Francisco on March 15, 1924, and was buried in Arlington National Cemetery. A subscription drive to erect a monument over his grave drew contributions from more than 600 former Carlisle students and other Indians.

Further Reading

Eastman, Elaine Goodale. *Pratt, the Red Man's Moses*. Norman: University of Oklahoma Press, 1935.

Pratt, Col. Richard H. *Battlefield and Classroom: Four Decades with the American Indian, 1867–1904*. 1964. Reprint, Norman: University of Oklahoma Press, 2003.

Reyhner, Jon. "Reconsidering Indian Schools." *History of Education Quarterly* 45, no. 4 (2005): 636–642.

Presidential Commission on Indian Reservation Economies (1983–1984)

This nine-member panel, set up by President Ronald Reagan in 1983, epitomized the approach of the "Reagan revolution" to Indian economic development. Previously, the energy crisis of 1973 had once again thrown INDIAN RESERVATIONS into sharp relief as an important source of strategic resources for a worried corporate America (see MINING AMERICAN INDIANS AND; OIL, AMERICAN INDIANS AND). That year, beer manufacturer Joseph Coors founded the Heritage Foundation, one of the first of a network of closely linked conservative think tanks with a common vision of deregulation and laissez-faire economics. Part of its stated agenda, as later published in *Mandate for Leadership* (1980) was to open energy development on public lands to private enterprise, without interference from government agencies such as the Environmental Protection Agency (EPA), the Department of Energy (DOE), or the Department of the Interior (DOI), and to bring Indian resources into the larger economy through Indian "economic self-sufficiency." Main contributors to Heritage included Chase Manhattan Bank, Gulf Oil, Sun Oil, Mobil Oil, Mellon Bank, Fluor Corporation, Reader's Digest, and many other Fortune 500 companies.

Coors also founded the Mountain States Legal Foundation in 1977 to promote the interests of large energy corporations. Its stated mission was "to fight in the courts those bureaucrats and no-growth advocates who create a challenge to individual liberty and economic freedom." Among the principal contributors were Occidental Petroleum, Gulf, Amoco, Conoco, and AMAX.

When Ronald Reagan was elected president in 1980, he appointed more than a dozen Heritage Foundation stalwarts to his transition team. Many later found positions in his administration. Shortly after the election, Heritage issued the 1,000-page *Mandate for Leadership: Policy Management in a Conservative Administration*. No private organization not officially connected with a new president had ever before presented such a detailed and comprehensive plan for government policy. It was, in effect, the blueprint of the Reagan administration. In a foreword to the second edition (1984), Ed Feulner, Heritage's director, noted that nearly two-thirds of the more than 2,000 specific recommendations in the original *Mandate for Leadership* either had been or were in process of being translated into government policy.

On January 14, 1983, by Executive Order 12,401, Reagan set up the Presidential Commission on Indian Reservation Economies "to identify obstacles to Indian reservation economic development and to promote the development of a healthy private sector on Indian reservations." It consisted of nine commissioners, six Indian and three non-Indian. Reagan's Indian policy speech of January 24, 1983, prepared by Indian Commissioner KENNETH L. SMITH, "set the parameters within which the recommendations would be made." In reality, the commission had a fairly good idea what its recommendations would be before starting its investigation—specific applications of the *Mandate* philosophy to Indian policy.

The commission was made up, in the words of Cayuga-Salish activist DANIEL BOMBERRY, "primarily of individuals with a lot more Republican than Indian blood" (see INDIGENOUS ECONOMICS.) The non-Indians were Bob Robertson (cochair), Manuel H. Johnson, and B. Z. (Bud) Kastler. The Indians were ROSS SWIMMER (Cherokee, cochair), Daniel Alex (Athabascan), Ted Bryant (Cherokee-Choctaw), David J.

Matheson (Coeur d'Alene), Neal A. McCaleb (Chickasaw), and Walter B. McCay (Cherokee).

Bob Robertson was a vice president of Armand Hammer's Occidental Petroleum, which had major interests in oil shale. (Eighty percent of America's oil shale reserves lie under public lands.) Robertson had been executive administrator for Paul Laxalt when the latter was governor of Nevada, and in 1969 he headed the National Council on Indian Opportunity, which was run through the office of Laxalt's close friend Spiro Agnew, Richard Nixon's vice president. Robertson was later special assistant to interior secretaries Rogers C. B. Morton, Stan Hathaway, and Thomas Kleppe.

Manuel Johnson was at that time serving on the U.S. cabinet as assistant secretary of the treasury for economic policy. A professor of economics at George Mason University and active member of the Heritage Foundation, he was brought in to give the commission intellectual credibility. Nevertheless, the report would later be criticized for its weak methodology.

Bud Kastler was a Mormon attorney from Utah and chair of the board of Mountain Fuel Supply, Utah's largest gas supplier. A company in which the Mormon church had heavy investments and numerous interlocking directors, Mountain Fuels had many leases on Ute lands. Kastler, a key member of Coors's Mountain States Legal Foundation, was also a founder of the Western Regional Council (WRC), a consortium of utilities and the mining and drilling companies that supplied them—the largest corporations in the West, including regional vice presidents of the biggest multinational energy corporations. After the EPA, backed by clean-air regulations, refused in 1976 to grant a permit for the Kaiparowits power plant in southern Utah, Kastler, former Utah governor Calvin Rampton, and executives from Kennecott copper (a heavy air polluter and major player in Utah) founded the WRC to oppose environmental interests blocking Western energy projects and to seek special easing of regulations for their desired projects. Denver banker Bruce Rockwell soon brought in Colorado interests, greatly increasing WRC's influence with WESTPO, the Western Governors Policy Office, through Colorado governor Richard Lamm. Over the next few years, while cultivating a sophisticated, "reasonable" image, WRC continued to attack coal-leasing and air-quality regulations and to push for huge strip mines, coal slurries, and power plants throughout the Southwest, some of them on or near Indian reservations. At the same time, a number of tribal governments were organizing an institutional base compatible with this new policy push (see COUNCIL OF ENERGY RESOURCE TRIBES; MACDONALD, PETER).

Cochair Ross O. SWIMMER was principal chief of the Cherokee Nation of Oklahoma and vice chair of Council of Energy Resource Tribes (CERT) and later head of the BUREAU OF INDIAN AFFAIRS (BIA) in Reagan's second term.

Daniel Alex (Athabascan) was a major Indian entrepreneur, head of both Eklutna Utilities and ERCO, a construction company. Involved with the planning of the controversial ALASKA NATIVE LAND CLAIMS SETTLEMENT ACT from its inception, Alex was president of the Alaska Native

Land Managers Association and a former president of the Eklutna Native Corporation.

Ted Bryant (Cherokee-Choctaw) worked for the Denver office of Deloitte, Haskins and Sells, an accounting firm, as director of Native American programs. He was a specialist in management-capacity building, president of the American Indian National Republican Federation, and a member of the Economic Development Committee of the NATIONAL CONGRESS OF AMERICAN INDIANS (NCAI).

David J. Matheson was chair of the Coeur d'Alene tribe, a member of CERT, and former director of planning and natural resources for the tribe. He had previously served on the City of Coeur d'Alene's Panhandle Area Council, the planning body for the economy of northern Idaho. Matheson was the only member of the commission who would eventually turn against the consensus.

Neal A. McCaleb (Chickasaw) was an engineer and the head of an architectural and engineering firm, McCaleb and Associates, in Edmond, Oklahoma. He served eight years in the Oklahoma State Legislature, four of them as Republican floor leader in the House of Representatives. President Nixon appointed him to National Council on Indian Opportunity in 1971. He was later Oklahoma secretary of transportation and head of the BIA under President George W. Bush from July 2001 to December 2002.

Walter B. McCay (Cherokee) was the head of Agricultural Products, Ltd., of Paradise Valley, Arizona. In addition to major interests in a large farming operation and a luxury vehicle-leasing firm, McCay had many international business interests. He was an advance man for Ronald Reagan, covering his domestic and foreign trips, and had done the same for Reagan when he was governor of California (1976–79).

The commission issued its report on November 30, 1984, after over a year of activity including 16 hearings, in which most of those interviewed were either with tribal government or with corporate business. The report identified 2,320 major obstacles "that adversely affected competitive returns to land, labor and capital" on Indian reservations. While many of these obstacles, such as a shortage of skilled labor on reservations, "incompetent BIA asset management and technical assistance," and inadequate federal funding were incontrovertible, others, such as tribal sovereign immunity to lawsuits, "legal protection of Indian natural resources," "federal environmental protection," "excessive federal regulation," and "cultural dissonance" were seen as attacking rights garnered after decades of struggle. Among the goals of the report were "to promote business development on reservations by Indian and non-Indian entrepreneurs; and the importance of extending to tribal governments the regulatory and financial incentives available to other governments." The report did not encourage tribally owned enterprises. The report listed 37 recommendations, some of them far reaching and controversial, including the dissolution of the BIA and its replacement with an "Indian Trust Services Administration," private ownership of lands and resources still held in common by Indian tribes, and the waiver of tribal sovereign immunity in certain cases.

The report was followed up by bills introduced in 1987, among them the Indian Economic Development Act (H.R. 1759 and S. 788), calling for "Indian enterprise zones," including foreign trade zones within Indian enterprise zones. (The father of the "enterprise zone," a designated area in which labor and environmental laws would not apply, was the Heritage Foundation's Stuart Butler.) Other associated legislation included the Indian Development Finance Corporation Act (S. 721), which set up a loan corporation with startup capital from the U.S. Treasury, and the Indian Gaming Regulatory Act (H.R. 1079 and S. 555; see GAMING ON INDIAN RESERVATIONS).

The Commission was a product of the very forces that had stymied the AMERICAN INDIAN POLICY REVIEW COMMISSION (AIPRC) a few years earlier. Whereas the AIPRC was originally intended to work from the grass roots up, the new version was a top-down effort. Whereas the former was congressional and intended to take a comprehensive look at all aspects of Indian life, even to reexamine all treaties and the very foundations of federal Indian law, the latter was executive, regulatory (or rather, deregulatory), and narrowly focused on the promotion of corporate-style economic development.

The Commission was the latest of the 20th-century series of Republican policy-making efforts against "big government," against the BIA and in favor of individual enterprise. Ironically, the fact that the BIA was not a responsible trustee of tribal resources had previously been to the advantage of the energy companies. With the establishment of the Department of Energy in 1977, however, the energy industry no longer needed the BIA. The Commission thus reflected an important structural change. Until that time, big business forces had always aimed at eventually eliminating tribes. However, the failure of TERMINATION and the rapid rise of a corps of young, educated Indians who believed in tribalism in one form or another, meant that the tribes were here to stay. Working with organizations such as CERT, the big energy companies hoped they could perhaps co-opt the tribes rather than eliminate them. The tribes could be treated as the Heritage Foundation recommended treating Third World countries: as pools of cheap labor and resources. In this sense, the Reagan administration had an interest in fostering government-to-government relations with tribes.

The Commission's proposals were not well received by most Indian leaders, and organizations such as the NCAI managed to mitigate its most far-reaching efforts.

Further Reading

Cook, Samuel R. "Ronald Reagan's Indian Policy in Retrospect. Economic Crisis and Political Irony." *Policy Studies Journal* 24, no. 1 (1996): 11–26.

Stockes, Brian. "Commission Report May Haunt BIA Nominee." *Indian Country Today*, 9 May 2001.

United States Presidential Commission on Reservation Economies. *Report and Recommendations to the President of the United States*. Washington, D.C.: Government Printing Office, November 1984.

Problem of Indian Administration, The   See
Meriam Report.

psychology, American Indians in

During the early part of the 20th century, the field of psychology in the United States showed little interest in the relationship between culture and the workings of the human mind, preferring to leave this study to anthropology. Research generally focused on innate, generic characteristics of the mind, seeking universal principals driving human behavior that crossed cultural boundaries, and tended to ignore the question of culturally specific factors. The dominance of this approach in part reflected the "melting pot" ideology during this period of high immigration and assimilation. While many psychologists continue to hold this perspective, by the early 1970s, driven in part by the growing number of psychologists from different ethnic minorities, a new subdiscipline, known as cultural (or cross-cultural) and ethnic psychology, began to appear. This investigates, and accommodates in practice, differences that cultural and ethnic lifeways can make to human psychology.

American Indian psychologists have played a role in developing this line of inquiry, in part because of the need to address specific social issues, such as the loss of self-esteem, high suicide rates, alcoholism, and other social ills that plague Indian people and that may be ameliorated by psychological counseling (see ALCOHOLISM, AMERICAN INDIANS AND; HEALTH, AMERICAN INDIAN). Many of these psychologists also believe that particular kinds of psychological traumas are connected with the lingering effects of colonization and forced ASSIMILATION of Indians into Western culture. In addition, the breakup of Indian lands and their ALLOTMENT left most Indian people impoverished, making life on Indian reservations more difficult than in other communities. Chippewa professor of psychiatry at the University of Colorado, Spero Manson, argued in an interview published in *Winds of Change* in 2000, that Indian psychological problems were unique in that "The environment in which most Indian people live is more stressful than any other environment in the United States. Death is a regular companion. There are vehicle accidents and many other accidents. The health care structures are spread thin. The safety net during times of crisis is inadequate. There's a growing awareness that grief and trauma can be transmitted through the generations."

In addition, the fact that American Indian attitudes toward Western psychological counseling have been generally ignored by non-Indian psychologists may limit the effectiveness of standard treatments. Many Indians believe that conventional psychological counseling shapes behavior in ways that conflict with Indian cultures. The Indian Health Service (IHS) has had a mental health program since 1955, but it is generally considered grossly underfunded and inadequate, and many American Indian psychologists have been active in trying to get Congress to remedy the situation.

One of the pioneers in the field of ethnic psychology was Joseph E. Trimble (Lakota), professor of psychology at Western Washington University. Trimble, who received a Ph.D. in social psychology from the University of Oklahoma in 1969, is the coeditor of the *Handbook of Racial & Ethnic Minority Psychology* (2004), an important work on the subject. A leader in promoting psychological research among indigenous peoples, Trimble has proposed developing what he calls a more "inclusive psychology." Giving more attention to what he calls "diversity issues" will further advance the whole field of psychology he says, because "by exploring psychological processes across diverse populations and contexts, we can gain deeper insights into how these processes operate."

This research has spawned new approaches to the counseling of mental distress among Indians. Clinical psychologist Eduardo Duran (Apache/Tewa) uses what he calls a "culture-specific" approach to provide therapy for prevalent problems on INDIAN RESERVATIONS, such as substance abuse, intergenerational trauma, and internalized oppression. The IHS has in recent years allowed the use of traditional Native healers to treat psychological and other disorders. More recently, psychologists such as Tawa Witko (Lakota) have expanded the research on indigenous peoples to include urban Indian populations in the United States.

It is believed that the first American Indian to enter the field of psychology was Carolyn L. Attneave (Cherokee-Delaware), who received her doctorate in clinical psychology from Stanford University in 1952, following a stint as an officer in the U.S. Coast Guard during WORLD WAR II. Attneave worked for state mental health services in Oklahoma and Massachusetts before becoming a professor of psychiatry at the University of Washington, as well as director of the University's American Indian Studies program. In 1970, she founded the *Network of Indian Psychologists*, a newsletter providing information about psychological services available to Native communities; she also helped found the Boston Indian Center the same year. A tireless worker, Attneave conducted studies for the Indian Health Service (IHS), including an annotated and computerized bibliography of American Indian and Alaska Native mental health research sponsored by the National Institutes of Mental Health. She died in 1992.

Marigold Linton (Cahuilla-Cupeño) earned a Ph.D. in experimental psychology from the University of California at Los Angeles in 1964. In 1970, she helped found the National Indian Education Association, an advocacy organization aimed at ensuring that American Indian, Alaska Native, and Native Hawaiians have a voice in their education. In 1974, Linton joined the psychology faculty of the University of Utah—the first woman to be hired by that university as a full professor. She later taught at Arizona State University and the University of Kansas.

The first American Indian man to earn a Ph.D. in psychology was Arthur L. McDonald (Oglala Lakota), at the University of South Dakota in 1966. McDonald later served as head of the department (1968–71). He helped found Dull Knife Memorial College on the Northern Cheyenne reservation and became its president. In 1996, the American

Psychological Association (APA) honored McDonald with a Lifetime Achievement Award.

Diane Willis (Kiowa) was another early worker in the field. She received her doctorate in experimental psychology from the University of Oklahoma in 1970. Willis has worked with tribes across the country, teaching about infant mental health. She is now professor emeritus of the Health Sciences Center at the University of Oklahoma.

Another prominent Indian psychologist is Marlene Echo-Hawk (Otoe-Missouria), who obtained her doctorate in clinical psychology from Oklahoma State University in 1976. She joined the IHS Mental Health Program in 1986, serving as staff psychologist in the Chinle Comprehensive Health Facility in Chinle, Arizona, on the Navajo Reservation. In 1989, EchoHawk became Mental Health Branch Chief in the IHS Aberdeen Area Office in Aberdeen, South Dakota, where she oversaw 17 tribal mental health programs in 14 states. In 1993, she was recruited as deputy chief of the IHS Alcoholism and Substance Abuse Program. From 1999 to 2009, she worked at IHS Headquarters in Rockville, Maryland, in the Behavioral Health Program. EchoHawk retired from the IHS in 2009.

Carolyn G. Barcus (Blackfeet) is another pioneer in the field. She received her doctorate in counseling psychology from Utah State University at Logan in 1975. In 1986, to address the shortage of Native American mental health professionals and school psychologists, Barcus launched the American Indian Support Project (AISP) at Utah State. She is now clinical assistant professor of psychology there.

The year 1987 saw the founding of the Society of Indian Psychologists of the Americas (SIPA), the combined outgrowth of Carolyn Attneave's network subscriber list and an American Indian interest group that Joseph Trimble had formed in 1971 with the support and cooperation of the Society for the Psychological Study of Social Issues (SPSSI), Division 9 of the APA. Under the leadership of Carolyn Barcus, AISP and SIPA sponsored the first annual convention of American Indian Psychologists and Graduate Students that same year. Also in 1987, Spero Manson founded the National Center for American Indian and Alaska Native Mental Health Research at the University of Colorado in Denver, which since then has published a professionally refereed scientific journal, *American Indian and Alaska Native Mental Health Research: The Journal of the National Center.*

Despite the many attempts to encourage Indians to become mental health professionals, an APA survey in 1989 found that, of the organization's more than 68,000 members, only 91 were of Indian descent. In 1992, after years of lobbying Congress, Arthur L. McDonald secured authorization for Indians In Psychology (INPSYCH), a scholarship program, although it received no funding until 1994. Sponsored by the Indian Health Service under Section 217, Title II of Public Law 102-573, INPSYCH is available at select colleges with a high concentration of Indian students.

In 2002, John Spaulding, then an Indian Health Services psychologist, and others, organized a new section under the APA's Division 18 (Psychologists in Public Service) to advocate for more funding and programs in American Indian and Alaska Native communities. Known as Psychologists in Indian Country, the section now has more than 50 members. The number of Indians in psychology is still nowhere near adequate to the needs of the communities, but it is growing, albeit slowly. In the mid-1960s, there were perhaps 10 or so Indians and Natives with doctoral degrees in psychology; some 45 years later, that number had increased to about 350. In 2004, the APA found that 212 of its members were of Indian descent, more than double the number 15 years earlier.

Further Reading

Duran, Edwardo. *Healing the Soul Wound: Counseling with American Indians and Other Native Peoples (Multicultural Foundations of Psychology and Counseling)*. New York: Teachers College Press, 2006.

Duran, Eduardo, and Bonnie Duran. *Native American Postcolonial Psychology*. Albany: State University of New York Press, 1995.

Grandbois, Donna. "Stigma of Mental Illness among American Indian and Alaska Native Nations: Historical and Contemporary Perspectives." *Issues in Mental Health Nursing* 26, no. 10 (2005): 1,001–1,024.

La Fromboise, Teresa D. "American Indian Mental Health Policy." *American Psychologist* 43, no. 5 (May 1988): 388–397.

La Fromboise, Teresa D., and Joseph E. Trimble. "Carolyn Lewis Attneave (1920–1992)." *American Psychologist* 51, no. 5 (May 1996): 549.

Trimble, Joseph E., and Mary Clearing-Sky. "An Historical Profile of American Indians and Alaska Natives in Psychology." *Cultural Diversity and Ethnic Minority Psychology* 15, no. 4 (October 2009): 338–351.

Pyramid Lake

Pyramid Lake in Western Nevada was the source of a century-long dispute between the Pyramid Lake (Winnemucca Band) Paiute and local non-Indian squatters as well as non-Indian farmers and corporations that had appropriated the lake's water. In 1859, a special Indian agent assigned to Nevada recommended that the land surrounding Pyramid Lake and the delta of the Truckee River, which feeds it—300,000 acres in all—be set aside for the Winnemucca Band of Paiute. The next year, reservation notices were posted. In 1865, the land was surveyed, and the reservation was proclaimed by executive order of president Ulysses S. Grant in 1874. Even before the proclamation, however, whites had begun to squat on the choicest parts of the land, and they would routinely harass and even kill Paiute in order to secure more land.

For the next 50 years, the squatters held on to their lands illegally, and in general the Paiute were powerless to remove them. In addition, as part of the Newlands Project, mandated by the Land Reclamation Act of 1902, the Derby Dam was built on the Truckee River (1903–05), the forerunner of a series of large-scale engineering programs across the United States.

The architect of the project, Francis Griffith Newlands, progressive congressman and senator from Nevada at the turn of the century, believed large-scale irrigation would create vast new farmlands in the arid West. Though the best geologists of his day warned that there was not enough water to go around, Newlands and his allies succeeded in drafting legislation that would lead to a series of environmentally questionable water projects. The Derby Dam was especially harmful to the Paiute, whose livelihood centered around the fish, wildlife, and vegetation on the banks of the Truckee River and Pyramid and Winnemucca Lakes.

The Derby Dam was designed to divert half the flow of the Truckee along a canal leading to the town of Fallon, where free land was being offered to potential homesteaders. As a result of the construction of the dam, Lake Winnemucca vanished completely, and Pyramid Lake, with its population of cutthroat trout and very rare cui-ui fish on which the Paiute depended, suffered striking environmental degradation. In spite of the legal precedent recognizing Indians' prior water rights set by the WINTERS DOCTRINE in 1907, the Indian Office (later the BUREAU OF INDIAN AFFAIRS [BIA]) did not defend the tribe.

In the meantime, the squatters on Paiute land had pressured Congress in 1924 to allow them to purchase the lands they held, but only a few took advantage their victory, and of those who did, all but two families defaulted on their payments. In 1932, BIA commissioner JOHN COLLIER appointed Alida C. Bowers, a former colleague from the American Indian Defense Association, to head up the Carson Agency in Nevada—the first female Indian superintendent. Bowers was appalled at the free use the squatters were making of the Paiute's reservation and promptly moved to have them evicted. The squatters appealed to Nevada senator Patrick A. McCarran, who proposed a bill that would have given the squatters the lands on which they had settled. Although defeated, McCarran managed to have Bowers transferred out of Nevada.

Collier continued Bowers's efforts to get the squatters evicted, and in 1943 the U.S. Circuit Court of Appeals ruled that the land, totaling 2,000 acres, belonged to the Paiute and upheld the eviction orders; however, the squatters then cut off water to the repossessed lands through irrigation ditches. In 1949, E. Reeseman Fryer became superintendent of the Carson Agency and moved to regain title to the irrigation ditches. McCarren then appealed to his friend and new BIA commissioner DILLON SEYMOUR MYER, who attempted to transfer Fryer. RUTH MUSKRAT BRONSON, then head of the NATIONAL CONGRESS OF AMERICAN INDIANS, met with Myer, who denied that McCarran had provoked the transfer, and prevailed on Secretary of the Interior Harold Ickes to countermand Myer's order. Myer still forced Fryer to resign and then attempted to remove the Paiute's able attorney, James E. Curry, forbidding the Paiute from renewing the lawyer's contract when it ran out in February 1951.

Led by Avery Winnemucca, chair of the tribal council, the Paiute managed to force Myer to release funds to pay Curry. However, the victory was short-lived, as Myer and McCarren—with help from their allies, Utah senator ARTHUR VIVIAN WATKINS and New Mexico senator Clinton P. Anderson, chair of the Indian Affairs Subcommittee—embarked on a series of hearings in early 1952 that effectively smeared Curry's reputation and destroyed his legal practice. By then the Derby Dam and the irrigation network had dropped the level of Pyramid Lake more than 50 feet, endangering the survival of the cui-ui, a unique and primitive species of fish surviving from the primeval Lake Lahontan that had covered most of Nevada and Utah in prehistoric times.

It was only with the environmental movement of the 1960s that a climate of opinion favorable to preserving the lake was manifested, and the cui-ui was among the first group of species to be protected by the Endangered Species Act of 1966. This led to the establishment of a BIA-financed hatchery and to court rulings that gave maintenance of the water level of Pyramid Lake priority over other water users. Negotiations led to a settlement, approved by the Senate in 1990, that reapportioned water rights between California and Nevada and gave priority to the reestablishment of the habitats of the cui-ui and cutthroat trout. This settlement requires the Paiute to be consulted in all future decisions regarding water use, and it appears to give them decisive control over the future of land-use planning in the region.

Further Reading

Knack, Martha C., and Omer Call Stewart. *As Long as the River Shall Run: An Ethnohistory of Pyramid Lake Indian Reservation*. Reno: University of Nevada Press, 1999.

Liebling, A. J. *A Reporter at Large: Dateline: Pyramid Lake, Nevada*. Reno: University of Nevada Press, 1999.

Qöyawayma, Alfred H. (1938–) *Hopi engineer, potter*
Alfred Harold Cooyama (Qöyawayma) was born on February 26, 1938, in Los Angeles, California. His mother, Mamie Picklesimer Cooyama, was a BUREAU OF INDIAN AFFAIRS (BIA) employee at Chinle, Arizona, about 40 miles northeast of the Hopi reservation in Arizona. His father, Alfred Cooyama, was a painter, and his aunt, Polingaysi Qöyawayma (Elizabeth Q. White)—author of the autobiography *No Turning Back: A Hopi Indian Woman's Struggle to Live in Two Worlds* (1964) and subject of a 1983 biography by Jo Linder— was a celebrated potter and educator. In the earlier part of his career, at least up to the late 1970s, he was known as Alfred Qöyawayma Colton. (Qöyawayma means Grey Fox Walking at Dawn.) He is more familiarly known as "Al Q."

Qöyawayma's career as a scientist began with an interest in chemistry in the sixth grade, which he pursued with the help of his mother's college-level chemistry books. He received a B.S. in mechanical engineering from California State Polytechnic University in 1961 and an M.S. in engineering from the University of Southern California in 1966.

Working as a project engineer for Litton Systems in Woodland Hills, California, Qöyawayma developed and patented inertial guidance systems and star trackers. In 1977, he became one of the founders of the AMERICAN INDIAN SCIENCE AND ENGINEERING SOCIETY (AISES) and its first chair. The University of Colorado at Boulder awarded him an honorary doctorate of Humane Letters in May 1986 in recognition of this contribution to Indian scientific education. He oversaw environmental, meteorological, and air-quality research programs as manager of the Environmental Services Department of the Salt River Project (Phoenix), America's first (1903) multi-purpose reclamation project. The Salt River Project is now the nation's third largest public power utility and one of Arizona's largest water suppliers. (See PIMA-MARICOPA WATER RIGHTS.)

In 1966, Qöyawayma began to learn traditional Hopi pottery making from his aunt Polingaysi. In 1976, he achieved his first great success at the Scottsdale (Arizona) National Indian Art Show. His pottery became extremely popular in the 1980s, and he was able to pursue the art full time after his retirement in 1990. He became nationally recognized for his exquisitely fashioned "flying saucer" pottery, made with traditional wooden tools and without a potter's wheel. As an expert on ancient Hopi ceramics, he is affiliated with the Smithsonian Institution. He published a booklet, *Al Qöyawayma, Hopi Potter*, in 1984. He received an honorary doctorate in 1986 from the University of Colorado at Boulder, in recognition of his work to increase opportunities for Native people. In 1991, Qöyawayma was awarded a Fulbright scholarship to help the Maori of New Zealand rebuild their traditional art of pottery-making. In 2002. Chickasaw astronaut John Herrington (see POGUE, WILLIAM REID) took one of Qöyawayma's ceramic pots into space aboard the space shuttle. The pot is now in the collection of the National Museum of the American Indian in Washington, D.C.

Further Reading

Hucko, Bruce. "Al Qöyawayma, Engineer and Potter Extraordinaire." *Native Peoples Magazine*, no. 16,157 (November–December 2002): 22–24.

Quintasket, Christine (Mourning Dove)

(1888–1936) *Okanagan-Colville writer, activist*
According to her own account, Christine Quintasket was born in April 1888 near Bonner's Ferry, Idaho, while her family was crossing the Kootenai River in a canoe. Her father, Joseph Quintasket, was a Nicola (an Athabaskan-speaking tribe living among the Okanagan) from British Columbia, and her mother, Lucy Stukin, was a Colville from Washington State. Joseph Quintasket adopted a white orphan boy who helped the

family learn English, teaching the children to read from the penny-dreadful novels (also known as dime novels) of the day.

Quintasket attended various Indian schools before spending three years at the Sacred Heart School in Ward, Washington. In 1902, following the death of her mother, she returned home to care for her siblings for two years before she could attend Fort Shaw Indian School in Great Falls, Montana. While at Fort Shaw, Quintasket met her first husband, Hector McLeod, a Flathead Indian. They married in 1909 but divorced several years letter.

In 1908, after witnessing the roundup of the last remaining wild buffalo in the United States, Quintasket was inspired to write her first novel. Working as a housekeeper, she saved up enough money to buy herself a typewriter. In 1912, she moved to Portland, Oregon, where she adopted the pen name Morning Dove (Humishuma in Okanagan—she would change the spelling to Mourning Dove in 1921) after the legendary wife of the Salmon Chief who welcomed her husband when he returned up the Columbia River from his migration. The next year, she settled in Calgary, British Columbia, attending business school in the hope of improving her writing skills.

In 1914, Quintasket finished the first draft of her novel *Co-Ge-We-A, The Half-Blood: A Depiction of the Great Montana Cattle Range*. A romance told from the perspective of a mixed-blood woman and drawing on the oral history and culture of the Coastal Salish Indians, this groundbreaking work was not published until 1927, in a version unfortunately marred by the heavy editing and elaborate notes of her well-meaning mentor, Lucullus V. McWhorter, founder of the *American Archaeologist*.

Quintasket had married Wenatchee migrant farm worker Fred Galler in 1919 and since then had been living on the Colville reservation. She worked in the fields with her husband through the day and wrote into the night. In 1933, as Mourning Dove, she published a collection of Colville tales called *Coyote Stories*, edited and illustrated by Heister Dean Guie and with a foreword by Teton Lakota Sioux author Luther Standing Bear.

Quintasket turned to activism in the late 1920s, founding the Colville Indian Association in 1930 to seek the return of lands and moneys due the tribe and speaking publicly on issues such as fishing rights. In 1935, she became the first woman elected to the Colville Tribal Council. She continued working on her autobiography and other writings. Her health had never been good, however, and the strain of her hard and active life eventually took its toll. Christine Quintasket died on August 8, 1936. Her manuscript autobiography, long lost, was discovered among the effects of Heister Guie in 1981 and, under the title *Mourning Dove—A Salishan Autobiography*, was finally published in 1990. Another collection of unpublished stories, *Mourning Dove's Stories*, was published in 1991.

Further Reading

Six, Beverly G. "Mourning Dove (Hum-Ishu-Ma): Christine Quintasket (1882?–1936)." In *American Women Writers, 1900–1945: A Bio-Bibliographical Critical Sourcebook*, edited by Laurie Champion and Emmanuel Sampath Nelson, 252–257. Santa Barbara, Calif.: Greenwood Press, 2000.

R

radio, American Indians and

It is not clear who was the first American Indian to speak on the radio. It may have been Dakota Brulé Chief CHAUNCEY YELLOW ROBE, who in 1920 was invited by the State School of Mines in Rapid City, South Dakota, to broadcast some anecdotes from his youth over their new station, WCAT. Growing more and more animated as he went on, Yellow Robe suddenly let out a loud war whoop, which blew out the transmitter tube and ended the broadcast.

The honor was also claimed by Blackfeet actor and celebrity JOHN WHITE CALF. When broadcast programming was in its infancy and Two Guns White Calf, as he was known, was on one of his eastern "goodwill" tours, he was invited to speak on the air. Without hesitating, he stepped up to the microphone and delivered an oration in the Piegan language. Afterward, a journalist asked him what he had said. Through an interpreter, he replied: "Two Guns, he say, yes, this best telephone white man has made, because you get 'em all on the line same time. Two Guns, in his talk, he just finish also mention this to his listeners." When he heard this, the station director realized he had missed an opportunity in not having the speech interpreted on the air. He had merely thought of getting the station some publicity by broadcasting a few words of "Indian" over the air. It had never occurred to him that the chief would actually say something interesting! (Most likely this was in spring 1921, when White Calf was in the East with a contingent of Blackfeet to promote the film *Bob Hampton of Placer*.)

Indians were making use of the new medium virtually from the start of regularly scheduled broadcasting in 1921. Over station WJZ, of Newark, New Jersey, for example, Oskenonton, "Indian Baritone," gave a one-hour evening recital on December 13, 1921; JOSEPH STRONG WOLF broadcast a speech (previously delivered on several stations around the country in September and October) on the evening of October 5, 1922; and a Flathead drum, Chief Michele Crawler, Sam Vincent, and

Sam Nose, in town for the Madison Square Garden Rodeo, performed on November 13, 1923. In Washington, D.C., Osage Nacoomee was heard in her first radio recital in early 1924 over WRC. Deskaheh (LEVI GENERAL) gave a famous speech on Iroquois sovereignty on March 10, 1925, in a broadcast from Rochester, New York.

Among the earliest regularly broadcast Native American radio personalities was JOSEPH SHUNATONA, a Pawnee-Otoe singer, musician, and actor, who played himself as well as his own comic character "Skookum" on the *Cowboy Tom Roundup* successively over WINS, WOR, and WMCA between 1932 and 1935. In the 1930s, concerned to correct biased history books, Nashaweena (a Naragansett whose English name was Sadie E. Barry), secretary of the American Indian Federation of the Northeast, hosted a weekly program of American Indian legends on a Rhode Island station. The program was piped in to school classrooms throughout the state. During the same decade, Seneca JESSE CORNPLANTER was well known as a radio personality in northern New York. Will Rogers (see ROGERS, WILLIAM PENN ADAIR), who began his broadcasting career in 1922, hosted America's first coast-to-coast national radio broadcast in 1926.

A pioneer of Indian radio was Sac and Fox DON WHISTLER, who in 1941 established the *Indian for Indians* radio hour, sponsored by the University of Oklahoma and broadcast weekly through the 1940s over WNAD. Aside from a few non-Indians actively interested in Indian affairs, almost all guests on the program were Indians. A special feature devoted time to Indian news. It was estimated that the program reached approximately 75,000 Indian listeners in Oklahoma, and it was piped into some Indian schools and sanitoriums. In the late 1950s and early 1960s, the *Indian Hour*, hosted by Cochiti Pueblo artist Joe H. Herrera, was a regular program on KTRC, Albuquerque, New Mexico.

By the 1940s, there was already some Navajo-language

radio programming. In 1940 the Navajo established their own radio station, KTGM, broadcasting from Window Rock, Arizona. The station had 40 repeater transmitters that allowed it to be heard across the vast reservation. Traditional Navajo singer Ed Natay and future Navajo chairman RAYMOND NAKAI would became local celebrities through their radio programs. ANNIE DODGE WAUNEKA began her Navajo-language broadcasts over KGAK, in Gallup, New Mexico, in 1960.

From 1967 to 1974, Suzan and Frank Harjo coproduced "Seeing Red," an outstanding bi-weekly American Indian news and public affairs program over listener-sponsored WBAI-FM in New York City (see HARJO, SUZAN SHOWN). It was not until the early 1970s, however, that other Indians were able to begin creating their own community radio stations, beginning with the Alaska Public Radio Network (APRN), with one Native and one non-Native station. Another early Indian station was KTDB 89.7, of Pine Hill, New Mexico, broadcasting much Navajo-language programming. In the same period, Native programming produced by volunteers began to appear on non-Indian public and listener-sponsored stations—weekly programs about their communities, Native music, and interviews. One of the first and most important was Peggy Berryhill's (Muskogee) *Living on Indian Time* (1973–78) over KPFA, in Berkeley, California. Berryhill played an important part in the development of Indian radio as an independent producer, consultant, and trainer of Indians in all aspects of radio production and operation.

Between 1971 and 1985, 13 noncommercial Indian radio stations went on the air in the United States, ranging in power from 100 to 100,000 watts. In 1986, APRN started National Native News, the first nationally syndicated Indian news program. The decade from 1986 to 1996 saw 10 new stations, for a total of 25. (In comparison, Canada has more than 400 stations with some Native language programming.) The first national Indian call-in show, *Native America Calling*, based at KUNM, Albuquerque, New Mexico, began in spring 1995 as the flagship effort of American Indian Radio on Satellite (AIROS), in Lincoln, Nebraska.

The Native American Public Broadcasting Consortium (NAPBC), which funds productions for the Public Broadcasting Service (PBS), started in 1978; in 1984 it began a radio training staff and management program, but NAPBC has emphasized production since 1986. Its Telecommunications Project is a partnership with the American Indian Higher Education Consortium (AIHEC).

Beginning in 1983, APRN's Alaska Native Fellowship Program offered on-the-job training for Native radio staff. It created the Indigenous Broadcasting Center (1991) to recruit Native people for careers in broadcasting, aid their advancement in the field, and strengthen stations.

Beginning in 1991, the ICA (Indigenous Communications Association, Hoopa, California) represented the interests of tribal radio stations, working with APRN and NAPBC to address Native stations' common concerns. Since the Corporation for Public Broadcasting (CPB) provided most of the funding for Indian stations, ICA lobbied them to support the CPB Minority and Rural Initiative, which includes the Native community stations.

At the end of the 20th century, the biggest problems were still lack of training in management, programming, and engineering, as well as lack of money. With federal budget reductions in the late 1990s, money became tighter than ever.

Radio is a technology appropriate to Indian culture, more so than television. Like Indian culture itself, radio is aural: It depends on telling a story well. According to Berryhill, television is intrusive, its images are assimilated passively, and there is little substance to what you hear. Radio, paradoxically, is *more* visual because the listener draws the pictures, and deeper because there is no imposed image to distract attention. It is also a lot less expensive (a community station can be run on $100,000 a year) and thus less mass-oriented.

Radio has proved to be far superior to newspapers in getting news out quickly and promoting community dialogue. Its personal and culturally appropriate programming responds to local needs, providing information on health, weather, and agricultural sales and conditions. A successful station must have audience support, and building an audience takes time. Community outreach is essential, because there must be a give and take as to programming. People like music, but too much music misses the point of public radio, which is to feature indigenous thinking, voices, values, and norms. Above all, elders can be on the air, Indian philosophy can be presented, and the cultural image can be strengthened.

One of the most important contributions of radio to Native culture is in the area of indigenous languages, many of which are endangered. All Native stations make an effort to broadcast indigenous-language programming, and although empirical data is lacking, it appears that the Native stations help stabilize the languages by keeping them in use among speakers, stimulating pride and interest, and providing instructional programming for nonspeakers. KILI, on the Pine Ridge Reservation, for example, has a four-hour program in Lakota every morning; they have also done a language course in conjunction with Oglala Lakota College. All their disc jockeys are bilingual and use both Lakota and English on the air. KWSO, in Warm Springs, Oregon, has a 10-week course in Sahaptin, with coordinated lessons printed in the tribal newspaper. KTDB has mostly Navajo (Dineh) programming and even broadcasts NPR's syndicated program "Morning Edition" in Navajo.

See also INDIGENOUS LANGUAGE USE.

Further Reading

Daley, Patrick J., and Beverly A. James. *Cultural Politics and the Mass Media: Alaska Native Voices.* Urbana: University of Illinois Press, 2004.

Keith, Michael C. *Signals in the Air: Native Broadcasting in America.* Santa Barbara, Calif.: Praeger Publishers, 1995.

Knopff, Bradley D. "Reservation Preservation: Powwow Dance, Radio, and the Inherent Dilemma of the Preservation Process." Ph.D. dissertation. Lund University, Sweden, 2001.

Trahant, Mark N. *Pictures of Our Nobles Selves: A History of*

Native American Contributions to News Media, 20–23. Nashville, Tenn.: The Freedom Forum First Amendment Center, 1995.

Further Listening
North American Indian Radio/TV Online! Available online. URL: http://www.yvwiiusdinvnohii.net/indianradio .html. Accessed 8 May 2005.

Redbone

Redbone was an Indian rock band formed in Los Angeles in 1968 by Yaqui-Shoshone brothers Lolly Vasquez (guitar and vocals) and Pat Vasquez (bass and vocals). Lolly, whose real name was Candido Albelando Vasquez, was born on October 2, 1939, and Patrick Morales Vasquez was born on March 17, 1946, both in Coalinga, California. Their parents were of Mexican Indian descent. The Vasquez brothers grew up in Fresno, about 65 miles northeast of Coalinga. They began their musical careers around 1960 in the touring band of pop idol Jimmy Clanton. Leaving the Clanton band in 1961, they moved to Los Angeles, where their new manager Bumps Blackwell encouraged them to change their name to avoid discrimination. They decided on "Vegas," the name of one of their uncles, and for the next few years they performed and recorded variously as the Vegas Brothers, the Avantis (Regency Records), and the Deuce Coupes (Del-Fi). In fall 1962, they met Bob Bogle, lead guitarist of the Ventures, an instrumental rock band whose classic "Walk Don't Run," was an international hit in 1960 and who became a huge influence in the development of rock music. Bogle had just started his own label, Unity Records, and Pat wanted to record a song he had written, "That Smile." Bogle helped the brothers with the arrangements, and "That Smile," with B-side "The Best Girl in the World," was released on Unity.

In 1964, the brothers joined Leon Russell and Delaney Bramlett in the Shindogs, the house band of "Shindig," a very popular music television show on the ABC network. In 1966, as a duo, the Vegas brothers released the garage rock album, *Pat and Lolly Vegas at the Haunted House.* The next year they appeared in the movie, *It's a Bikini World.* During this time they wrote a number of songs, including "Look at Me" for Dobie Gray in 1963, and "Niki Hoeky," with lyrics by Jim Ford, a top 30 hit for P. J. Proby in 1967. The Vegas brothers appeared frequently in the clubs on Sunset Strip, sharing the bill with legendary bands such as the Doors, Buffalo Springfield, and the Byrds. They were a strong influence on the East L.A. bands Thee Midniters, Cannibal and the Headhunters, and the Premiers.

In the late 1960s, the brothers started The Crazy Cajun Cakewalk Band with drummer Ed Greene. Encouraged by Jimi Hendrix, himself part Cherokee, the Vegas brothers decided to form an Indian-style band in 1968. They added a Mexican American, Tony Bellamy (born Anthony Avila) and Peter "Last Walking Bear" DePoe, a Siletz-Cheyenne from the Neah Bay Reservation in Washington State. DePoe, a ceremonial drummer turned session musician, was playing in Bobby Womack's band at the time.

The name of the band was taken from *rehbon*, Cajun slang for "half-breed," and their early work resembled the bayou rock of Creedence Clearwater Revival. Signed by Epic, they released *Redbone* in 1969, followed by *Potlatch* (1970), *Message from a Drum* (1972), *Wovoka*, and *Beaded Dreams through Turquoise Eyes*, both released in 1974. All of their albums made the charts, and they had three top 40 hits: "Maggie" in 1970, "The Witch Queen of New Orleans" in 1971, and "Come and Get Your Love," which reached the top 5 in 1974.

Many of their songs, such as "Alcatraz" and "Without Reservation" were political, reflecting the RED POWER atmosphere of the day, and in the beginning they performed in buckskins, moccasins, and headdresses. Songs such as "Chant: 13th Hour," which segues from tribal chanting to their funk rock style, anticipates ROBBIE ROBERTSON's similar experiments 20 years later. Lolly Vegas had a distinctive, jazz-influenced guitar style, and he was among the first guitarists to use the Leslie rotating speaker as part of his amplification. DePoe's heavy style of drumming, known as the "King Kong Beat" influenced many later drummers.

In 1973, after recording *Wovoka*, DePoe left the band and was replaced by Butch Rillera, Tony Bellamy's cousin. In 1978, the group switched to RCA, but their album, *Cycles*, was not a success, and they split up. They regrouped in the 1990s, but in 1995 Lolly Vegas had to drop out due to declining health. Tony Bellamy left a short time later, and of the original Redbone, only Pat Vegas is still in the band. In 1994, Rhino Records released *Redbone Live*, the recording of a 1977 concert in Corpus Christie, Texas, and in 2003, Sony released *The Essential Redbone*, a compilation of their greatest hits. Lolly Vegas died of lung cancer on March 10, 2010, in Reseda, California.

Further Reading
Guerrero, Mark. "Redbone: Cajun Funk with a Touch of Latin Soul." Available online. URL: http://www .markguerrero.net/23.php. Accessed 21 March 2010.

Red Bow, Buddy (Warfield Richard Red Bow)
(1949–1993) *Lakota Sioux guitarist, singer*
A Lakota Sioux born on June 27, 1949, on the Pine Ridge Reservation in South Dakota, Buddy Red Bow was abandoned by his mother as an infant at the jail at Pine Ridge. He was adopted by Stephen and Maisie Red Bow, the daughter of one of the jail keepers. His full given name was Warfield Richard Red Bow, but his grandmother preferred to call him Buddy because he was so friendly as a child. Growing up along the banks of the Cheyenne River, Red Bow began performing early in his teens. He was brought up in the traditional religion of the Lakota Sioux and participated in the sun dances led by spiritual leader FRANK FOOLS CROW. In 1966 he married Cheryl Lynne Oyler, with whom he had five children, two of whom died shortly after birth.

His first album, *Buffalo*, was recorded in 1976 but was

never released. He then signed to Etherean Records releasing *BRB*, *Journey into the Spirit World*, and *Black Hills Dreamer* during the 1980s. *Black Hills Dreamer* featured two of his best known songs, "Run, Indian, Run" and "Indian Love Song."

Red Bow was unusual as a popular artist in that many of his songs were sung in the Lakota language. His blend of country music and traditional Indian rhythms proved very popular on INDIAN RESERVATIONS across the country.

Red Bow had a few small film parts, including *Thunderheart* (1992), and the character, Buddy Red Bow (played by A. Martinez), in the classic film, *Pow Wow Highway* (1989), is based on him. Like the character in the movie, Buddy Red Bow struggled with drugs and alcohol most of his life, ultimately leading to his untimely death on March 28, 1993. He was inducted into the Native American Music Awards Hall of Fame in 1998.

Further Reading

"No Royalties Netted from Artist's Legacy." *Indian Country Today*, 27 October 1997.

Stillman, Pamela. "Buddy Red Bow, Lakota Country Western Singer, a Legend in His Time." *Indian Country Today*, 29 June 1994.

Red Cloud, Mitchell (1924–1950) *Ho-Chunk Medal of Honor winner*

A full-blooded Ho-Chunk (Winnebago), Mitchell Red Cloud was born on July 2, 1924, in Hatfield, Wisconsin, the eldest of three sons born to Mitchell Red Cloud, Sr., and Lillian Winneshiek. He grew up in the nearby town of Friendship. At age 17, he joined the U.S. Marine Corps. After the United States entered WORLD WAR II, Red Cloud served with the elite 2nd Marine Raider Battalion for two years in the South Pacific. Known as Carlson's Raiders, after their colorful commander, Lt. Col. Evans Carlson, the battalion was known for their catchword, "Gung-Ho!," a term coined by Carlson (based on a Chinese expression meaning "work together") that has since become a synonym for extreme dedication to a goal. The Raiders, created in the mold of the British Commandos, were an all-volunteer unit trained to infiltrate enemy-held territory; they were the first "special forces" created by the U.S. military in World War II. Mitchell, a machine gunner in "F" Company, participated in the raid on Guadalcanal on November 4, 1942. Known as "The Long Patrol," for the next 30 days the battalion fought in almost impassable jungles and swamps, killing more than 500 Japanese soldiers with the loss of only 19 Marines. The Raiders exploits were made into the movie *Gung-Ho!* (1943).

Red Cloud, suffering from malaria, had lost 75 pounds during the ordeal and was shipped to a hospital in San Diego in January 1943 to recover. While he was in the hospital, the Raiders were disbanded. Red Cloud was transferred to the 29th Marines, 6th Marine Division, a new unit formed to invade Japan. He participated in the invasions of Guam in July 1944, and Okinawa in March 1945. In northern Okinawa, Red Cloud fought in the battles to clear the Motobu Peninsula

of Japanese defenders and then joined the assault on Naha, the capital of Okinawa. On May 17, 1945, during the ferocious Battle for Sugar Loaf Hill, Red Cloud was shot in the shoulder and had to be evacuated to Guam.

Red Cloud was discharged on November 9, 1945, but reenlisted in 1948, this time joining the U.S. Army. When North Korea invaded South Korea in June 1950, Corporal Red Cloud was among the first U.S. troops rushed into the conflict. The U.S. and South Korean forces having been driven back to the very tip of South Korea, Red Cloud fought with the 24th Infantry Division in the desperate attempt to defend the Pusan Perimeter. After the successful counterattack by General Douglas MacArthur at Inchon, the 24th was assigned to protect the Eighth Army's left flank in an ill-fated drive to reach the Yalu River on the Chinese border.

On November 3, Chinese troops attacked the 24th Infantry Division, with Red Cloud's unit—the 2nd Battalion, 19th Regiment—bearing the brunt of the first attacks. After two days of furious fighting, the 2nd Battalion captured a hill north of the Chongchon River, near the town of Chongyon.

In the early morning hours of November 5, most of the troops were resting. Red Cloud, although only a corporal, was among the most experienced men in his unit, and the captain of Company E had placed him outside the company perimeter to try to spot any potential trouble. Shortly after 6 A.M., Red Cloud detected a line of Chinese troops coming up the hill, and, yelling out "Here they come," opened fire with his Browning automatic rifle, killing and wounding dozens of the enemy. His quick action allowed the company to regroup and protect itself, but Red Cloud was hit by a burst of machine-gun fire and collapsed over his gun.

For 15 minutes, the company fought for its survival. Just as it seemed that the troops might be overrun, the soldiers heard Red Cloud's machine gun come back to life. Red Cloud had regained consciousness and despite his wounds, had crawled out of his foxhole. With one arm wrapped around a small tree for support, he now stood firing at the Chinese attackers, and for five minutes, he held back the Chinese troops until he was finally surrounded and killed. That was just enough time for his company to withdraw to safety. When General Omar Bradley presented the Medal of Honor to Mitchell's mother on April 3, 1951, he recalled Mitchell as one of the "great Indian warriors who have died bravely in battle."

At the request of the Red Cloud family, in 1955 his remains were returned from the UN Cemetery in North Korea to Wisconsin for reburial. In 1957, the headquarters of the 2nd Infantry Division stationed in South Korea was named Camp Red Cloud in his honor and, in 1999, the U.S. Navy named a new transport ship, the USS *Red Cloud*, after him.

Further Reading

"A Tale of Two Warriors." *Indian Country Today*, 9 November 1998.

Dan Marsh's Marine Raider Page. "Red Cloud." Available online. URL: http://www.usmcraiders.com/Redcloud1 .htm. Accessed 18 December 2009.

Redfeather, Tsianina   *See* BLACKSTONE, TSIANINA
EVANS.

Red Power movement

The Red Power movement was characterized by a militant
activism and a nationalistic approach that influenced and
eventually dominated the American Indian political landscape from approximately 1961 to 1979. The movement had
its roots in summer workshops for Indian college students led
by Cherokee anthropologist ROBERT KNOX THOMAS during
the late 1950s. Following WORLD WAR II, the federal policy of
TERMINATION had been threatening to break up INDIAN RES-
ERVATIONS and sought to assimilate Native people (see ASSIM-
ILATION). The workshops helped to foster a pride in Indian
identity lacking in most Indian college students of the day and
introduced them to Thomas's concept of "internal colonization," as he described the situation of Native American reservations at the time.

Thomas helped bring young activists such as Ponca CLYDE
WARRIOR, Paiute MEL THOM, Navajo (Dineh) HERBERT
BLATCHFORD, and Cherokee-Catawba GERALD WILKINSON to
the historic 1961 AMERICAN INDIAN CHICAGO CONFERENCE,
where they introduced a militant stance that had only rarely
been seen in Indian politics in the 20th century. In Chicago,
they met Tuscarora activist WILLIAM RICKARD, who added the
hard-line Iroquois concept of sovereignty to the mix (see SOV-
EREIGNTY, INDIGENOUS AND TRIBAL). Together they clashed
with the organizers of the conference, such as social scientist
D'ARCY MCNICKLE and Cheyenne activist HELEN WHITE
PETERSON, whom they saw as too passive and slow-moving.
Later in 1961, Warrior, Thom, Blatchford, and Wilkinson, along
with Rickard's sister, Karen Rickard, founded the NATIONAL
INDIAN YOUTH COUNCIL (NIYC) in Gallup, New Mexico,
determined to see their more militant perspective put into
action. Beginning in 1964, NIYC began organizing fish-ins
on the Northwest Coast under the leadership of Assiniboine-
Dakota Sioux HANK ADAMS, and Tulalip-Nisqually JANET
MCCLOUD. The fish-ins sought to publicize the violations of
Indian treaty rights by state authorities, who regularly arrested
or harassed Indian fishermen (see HUNTING AND FISHING
RIGHTS). The demonstrations led to a violent backlash from
local fishermen and state wildlife officials, who used force to
break them up. Adams and McCloud in turn brought in celebrities to show support for the protesters, which helped to bring
the news media to cover the events and in many cases expose
the brutality of the police and non-Indian vigilantes.

The release of Cree singer BUFFY SAINTE-MARIE's first
album, *It's My Way*, in 1964 marked a cultural watershed, featuring the first modern Indian protest songs such as "Now That
the Buffalo's Gone" and the antiwar song "Universal Soldier."
As the Red Power movement grew, she became even more biting in her criticism of American policy toward Indian people. Also in 1964, William Rickard and flamboyant Tuscarora
activist MAD BEAR ANDERSON began the North American
Indian Unity Caravans, which crisscrossed the country in an
attempt to revitalize Indian traditions and traditional thought.
In 1966, Mohawk TOM PORTER formed the White Roots of
Peace, a traveling speaking and cultural group that also sought
to revive Indian traditions. Rickard and Porter were themselves influenced by the work of Hopi leaders such as DAN
KATCHONGVA, who had been organizing "Meetings of Indian
Brothers" on the Hopi Reservation since the 1950s.

The Iroquois had a long tradition of militant activism, and
during the 1950s, their attempts to block public works projects
on their lands such as the KINZUA DAM had made activists such
as Anderson and Rickard's father, CLINTON RICKARD, well
known to Indian people. In 1968, militant Mohawk organized
the CORNWALL BRIDGE BLOCKADE to protest their denial of
free passage across the Canada-U.S. border, guaranteed by
treaty rights. The protests led to the creation of *Akwesasne
Notes*, a national newspaper published by the Mohawk that
extensively covered the Red Power movement (see JOURNAL-
ISM). Also in 1968, Sioux-Creek Lehman L. Brightman organized United Native Americans in San Francisco as a militant
organization dedicated to spreading Red Power across the
country. Although it never achieved a wide following outside
of the San Francisco Bay Area, its newsletter, *Warpath*, helped
to articulate the growing demands of the movement.

By the late 1960s, Hank Adams's "Red Muslims," as his
supporters became known, had distanced themselves from
the mainstream efforts of groups such as the ASSOCIATION ON
AMERICAN INDIAN AFFAIRS and the NATIONAL CONGRESS OF
AMERICAN INDIANS (NCAI), and preferred forming working
relationships with the increasingly militant Civil Rights and
antiwar movements of the day.

Although local Bay Area Indians planned the OCCUPATION
OF ALCATRAZ ISLAND, its leadership was subsequently assumed
by activists under Mohawk RICHARD OAKES and later Santee
Dakota Sioux JOHN TRUDELL. The Alcatraz occupation was
seen by Oakes and Trudell as a symbolic act, designed to draw
attention to past and present injustices against Indians and far
removed from the practical goals of the previous generation
of activists. The occupation, begun on November 20, 1969,
galvanized Indians across the country, leading to attempted
takeovers in northern California, Washington State, and New
York City. As Indian communities began rising up across the
country, they were met with increasing violence from law enforcement officials. One of the most dramatic takeovers was in
Gresham, Wisconsin, where on January 1, 1975, a group called
the Menominee Warrior Society occupied an unused abbey
belonging to the Alexian Brothers Novitiate in the hope of
converting it into a health center; a violent confrontation with
local and federal police ensued.

In 1970, two films with strong antiwar messages, *Little Big
Man*, starring Chief DAN GEORGE, and *Soldier Blue*, presented
Indians and their struggle for their lands in the 19th century
in a sympathetic light. The publication the next year of DEE
BROWN's book *Bury My Heart at Wounded Knee*, a moving
account of those same 19th-century wars from the Indian
point of view, lent a historical context as well as credibility
to the demands of the Red Power movement. The growing

American Indian Movement (AIM) guards maintained a vigil during the occupation of Wounded Knee in 1973. *(AP/Wideworld)*

movement against the war in Vietnam and the Civil Rights movement, which were both becoming increasingly confrontational, influenced the tactics of the Red Power movement. On the other hand, the late 1960s counterculture lifestyle drew much from American Indians, and Indian-inspired clothes, jewelry, and hairstyles became fashionable. The tribally oriented hippie movement saw Indians as a role model, and many hippies provided support for the diverse components of the Red Power movement.

In the meantime, the AMERICAN INDIAN MOVEMENT (AIM) had been formed in Minneapolis in 1968 by CLYDE BELLECOURT and DENNIS BANKS (both Chippewa) to help combat police brutality by following the lead of the Black Panther's street patrols. Under AIM, the Red Power era reached its zenith. AIM's demonstrations, including a dramatic seizure of the replica of the pilgrim ship *Mayflower* on Thanksgiving Day 1970 by RUSSELL MEANS (Oglala Lakota–Yankton Dakota Sioux) brought the group national attention. Successful rallies for justice in the case of RAYMOND YELLOW THUNDER, an Oglala Lakota Sioux beaten and killed by whites in Gordon, Nebraska, led to increased respect from Indian people. Although AIM was only one of the many organizers of the TRAIL OF BROKEN TREATIES in 1972, in part a commemoration of the death of Richard Oakes, it led the subsequent takeover and ransacking of the headquarters of the BUREAU

OF INDIAN AFFAIRS (BIA) in Washington, D.C., following the march. In 1973, AIM's 71-day occupation of WOUNDED KNEE, a small hamlet on the Pine Ridge Reservation in South Dakota, dominated the national media's coverage of Indians. Taking the Alcatraz occupation a step further, AIM chose Wounded Knee, the site of the massacre of more than 150 Lakota men, women, and children by the Seventh Cavalry in 1890, because of its deep symbolism. Through the occupation, AIM's two charismatic leaders, Dennis Banks and Russell Means, became internationally known.

AIM's flamboyant actions led to a resurgence of pride among Indian youth, who flocked to the organization. It also sparked a renewed interest in Indian tradition and culture, which had been suppressed on many reservations due to the assimilationist policies of the federal government. Early on, AIM leaders sought out religious figures such as PHILLIP DEERE (Creek) and LEONARD CROW DOG (Brulé Lakota Sioux) to provide them with a spiritual direction. Urban Indians, many of them alienated from their tribes, found in AIM the way to get back in touch with their cultures, and young urban Indians would form the core part of AIM's constituency.

After the Wounded Knee occupation, the FBI marked the movement for harassment, culminating in a violent shootout on the Pine Ridge Reservation in South Dakota in 1975 (see PELTIER, LEONARD) and the death of Micmac activist

ANNA MAE AQUASH. The murder of a non-Indian in Northern California in 1974, in which two AIM members were implicated, led to further erosion in AIM support (see BOX CANYON MURDER). With its leaders in jail or in hiding, the movement went into decline. Although AIM would participate in further demonstrations, such as the formation of Yellow Thunder Camp (see MEANS, WILLIAM) in 1981, or the Hopi-Navajo dispute over BIG MOUNTAIN, most of its leaders had left the group by the mid-1980s.

The last successful demonstration of the Red Power era was the LONGEST WALK in 1979, by which time the militant stance was rapidly losing its effectiveness. In summer 1980, the leadership of AIM convened in South Dakota for the Black Hills Alliance Gathering, an attempt to form a coalition with Midwest farmers and ranchers to work on common needs, and a far cry from the militant rhetoric of the preceding decade. New Indian leaders, such as Cheyenne-Creek SUZAN SHOWN HARJO, who revitalized the NCAI, and Chippewa WINONA LADUKE, who sought to network with the powerful ENVIRONMENTAL MOVEMENT, were using less confrontational tactics to gain important political results for Indians. New groups, such as the INTERNATIONAL INDIAN TREATY COUNCIL, sought to organize indigenous people around the world by working with international bodies such as the United Nations.

The militancy of the Red Power era led to dramatic changes in federal Indian policy. It forced the federal government to address Indian issues, which had long been a low priority, and ended Termination. Under Indian commissioners ROBERT LAFOLLETTE BENNETT, LOUIS ROOK BRUCE, JR., MORRIS THOMPSON, and FORREST GERARD, significant gains were made in the areas of hunting and fishing rights, sovereignty, Indian HEALTH, and education (see EDUCATIONAL POLICY, AMERICAN INDIANS AND), and a new era of self-determination dawned for the tribes. The Red Power movement resulted in a renewed sense of Indian identity and ushered in a cultural and social revival among American Indians that continues unabated.

Further Reading

Deloria, Vine, Jr. *Behind the Trail of Broken Treaties: An Indian Declaration of Independence.* New York: Delacorte Press, 1974.

Josephy, Alvin M. *Red Power: The American Indians' Fight for Freedom.* New York: American Heritage Press, 1971.

Nagel, Joane. *American Indian Ethnic Renewal: Red Power and the Resurgence of Identity and Culture.* New York: Oxford University Press, 1996.

Smith, Paul Chaat, and Robert Allen Warrior. *Like a Hurricane: The American Indian Movement from Alcatraz to Wounded Knee.* New York: New Press, 1996.

Steiner, Stan. *The New Indians.* New York: Harper & Row 1968.

Red Star, Kevin (1943–   ) *Crow painter, gallery owner*

Born on October 9, 1943, in Crow Agency on the Crow Reservation in Montana to Wallace Red Star, Sr., and Amy (Bright Wings) Red Star, an accomplished traditional craftswoman, Kevin Red Star grew up on the rugged plains. He worked as a rodeo contestant and a janitor and did other odd jobs before enrolling in the Institute of American Indian Arts in Santa Fe in 1962. Red Star left the Institute in 1965 to attend the San Francisco Art Institute on a one-year scholarship. He then attended Montana State University for a year and Eastern Montana College from 1971 until 1972.

Known for his portraits, Red Star often gets his inspiration from old photographs and old tape recordings of ancient Crow stories. His best-known works are contemporary mixed-media collages, often using paper, pencil, ink, crayons, and oil paint, to create a vivid image of traditional Crow life and culture. A self-described romanticist, he often tries to capture in his paintings the 19th-century Crow way of life before it began to change. In 2009, his life was featured in the documentary, *From the Spirit: Kevin Red Star.*

Further Reading

Carstens, Rosemary. "Decoding Tradition." *Southwest Art.* Available online. URL: http://www.southwestart.com /article/1692. Accessed 30 October 2009.

Red Thunder Cloud (Tez, Cromwell Ashbie Hawkins West, Carlos Ashibie Hawk Westez)

(1919–1996) *linguist, folklorist, herbalist, lecturer*

The man known as Red Thunder Cloud, or "Tez" to his many friends, was one of the most enigmatic figures in 20th-century American Indian history. He was the last speaker of Catawba, a Siouan language from South Carolina, and claimed to be a Catawba on his mother's side. Though he gained the respect and, for a time, the friendship of the Catawba, they never accepted him as one of their own. Four years after his death, anthropologist Ives Goddard conclusively proved that Red Thunder Cloud was not an Indian at all.

Red Thunder Cloud was born Cromwell Ashbie Hawkins West in Newport, Rhode Island, on May 30, 1919, the son of Cromwell Payne West, proprietor of a drugstore, and Roberta M. Hawkins West. Cromwell West was a black man born in Pennsylvania in 1891 who moved to Newport with his parents before 1894. Roberta West came from a distinguished black family. She was born in Baltimore in 1891, the daughter of William Ashbie Hawkins, one of the city's first black lawyers and a well-known civic leader, and Ada M. McMechen of Wheeling, West Virginia, whose younger brother, George William Frederick McMechen, was Ashbie Hawkins's law partner. From 1929 through 1933, it seems that Roberta West lived with her children in North Carolina not far from the Catawba reservation at nearby Rock Hill, South Carolina.

As a junior at Southampton High School in Long Island, New York, West introduced himself to anthropologist FRANK GOULDSMITH SPECK in a 1938 letter. He said he was a Catawba raised among the Narragansett of Rhode Island and that he had been living with the Shinnecock in Southampton since the previous year. He did not provide information about his family background or claim to know any Catawba, but he signed the letter "Chief Red Thunder Cloud." In 1941, he began working with Speck, who took down texts from the last speakers of many eastern tribes. Speck, a gifted linguist, learned Catawba, and Red Thunder Cloud assisted him in his work with Catawba informants. With Speck's training and encouragement, Red Thunder Cloud began doing ethnological work himself.

When anthropologist Frank Siebert, Jr., shortly after a field trip among the Catawba, met Red Thunder Cloud in New York City in 1941, he elicited from him a few dozen Catawba words and numbers, but felt he knew more, "between 100 and 250 words . . . numeral count up to ten, and occasional short expressions."

In 1942, Red Thunder Cloud was commissioned by the Heye Foundation, Museum of the American Indian, to collect surviving material culture items of Montauk and other Long Island Indians. He published several articles on the subject, defending their Indian status. "The Long Island Indians have not become extinct, as writers would have us believe," he declared in 1943, "but are very much alive and significant." For many years, while he was recording Long Island aboriginal culture, especially Montauk and Shinnecock, he lived on the South Fork of Long Island.

With a letter of introduction from Speck, Red Thunder Cloud visited the Catawba for about two weeks in February 1944. Chief Samuel Blue, introducing Red Thunder Cloud at a gathering at the reservation church on February 6, 1944, said (in Catawba) "This man, Red Thunder Cloud, has come to our nation speaking Catawba. This man is of the people who were lost far away. I am sure that this man is Catawba." Then he danced while the chief sang and beat the drum.

It was around this time that Red Thunder Cloud put forth a genealogy. He said he was born in Virginia, the son of Carlos Panchito Westez (originally Sanchez), of Tegucigalpa, Honduras, and Roberta Hawk Westez; that his mother was three-quarters Catawba and one-quarter Congaree, a closely related southeastern Siouan tribe; and that his mother's ancestors left the Catawba reservation at Rock Hill, South Carolina, around 1820 to escape a smallpox epidemic, and settled in Virginia. According to linguist G. Hubert Matthews, Sam Blue found the story plausible. Matthews also says that Red Thunder Cloud told him specifically that he had learned Catawba from Strong Eagle, his maternal grandfather, a lawyer who graduated from Yale Law School and died in 1941. (As noted above, his maternal grandfather was indeed a lawyer and did die in 1941, though he had a law degree from Howard Law School, not Yale. He was not an Indian, however, and did not speak Catawba.)

For about six months, probably in 1945, Red Thunder Cloud studied Catawba intensively with two of the last speakers, Sam Blue and Sally Gordon, according to Chief Gilbert Blue, Sam's grandson. At one time, there was controversy over how well Red Thunder Cloud spoke Catawba. Speck defended Red Thunder Cloud's command of the language. In 1964 and 1965, Red Thunder Cloud met G. Hubert Matthews, a linguist at the Massachusetts Institute of Technology (MIT), and they published a number of Catawba texts together in 1967 in the *International Journal of American Linguistics*. As Matthews stated in an interview, "He could really speak the language—in connected sentences, not just words. He spoke quite fluently. Of course there were some things he just didn't know—but he was straightforward about it, and very consistent."

During the TERMINATION period in the 1950s, Chief Blue and many others advocated Termination for the Catawba. Red Thunder Cloud opposed this, raising the anger of tribal members and leading to a 40-year estrangement. The tribe did not terminate, however.

Red Thunder Cloud later lived in Northfield, Massachusetts. He developed a line of herbal teas, which he harvested and prepared himself and which were sold at POWWOWS and fairs, and at the American Indian Archaeological Institute in Washington, Connecticut. He collected portfolios of old photographs of East Coast Indians, and often appeared in schools as a dancer and interpreter of Indian lore.

One by one, the last speakers of Catawba passed away until by the 1960s there was no one left on the reservation who could speak the language. But even after the tribe inaugurated a language research project in the late 1980s, it was a long while before they contacted Red Thunder Cloud. Eventually he was invited to come to Rock Hill and tell some of his stories in Catawba at the 1995 "Yap Ye Iswa" festival. There he was finally interviewed by linguists working for the tribe. According to his friend Trudy Richmond (Mohawk), director of the American Indian Archaeological Institute, "He was very, very excited that they invited him down—and very nervous. But when he came back he said they'd been very nice to him. He said that when he told the stories in Catawba, some of the older people were crying."

Only a short time later, on January 8, 1996, Red Thunder Cloud died of a stroke in Northfield, Massachusetts.

Further Reading

Goddard, Ives. "The Identity of Red Thundercloud." *SSILA* (Society for the Study of Indigenous Languages of the Americas) *Newsletter* (April 2000).

Perlmutt, David. "Booster of Catawba Language Not Indian?" *Charlotte Observer*, 4 May 2000.

Red Wing   *See* ST. CYR, LILLIAN.

Redwing, Roderic (Red Wing, Rodd Redwing)

(1904–1971) *Chickasaw actor, performer, stunt adviser*
A full-blooded Chickasaw, born in New York on August 24, 1904, Rodd Redwing was the son of circus performers who moved to London shortly after he was born. Redwing attended school in London, acquiring a slight British accent. When the family moved back to New York City, he enrolled in Haaren High School and later graduated from New York University. He acted on Broadway for a time before heading to Hollywood around 1930. Sometimes called "the handsomest Indian in

often Rodd Redwing. He appeared with Mohawk actor JAY SILVERHEELS in the classic film *Key Largo* (1948). Although he acted in many films (and later television), he was not satisfied with the instability of the field, and when the quick draw became a stock feature of Westerns around 1940, Redwing saw an opportunity. As he explained in a 1964 *Newark Evening News* interview, "I created a business within a business—gun coach." He won out over the competition because "They didn't know camera speeds and shortcuts. . . . Sometimes you get a call to teach an actor how to shoot a gun in two hours. That takes shortcuts." He was a technical adviser on countless films and taught many actors to shoot. He was particularly proud of a scene in *Shane*. "I put a wire on Elisha Cook's back. And when Jack Palance shot him with a .45 colt, we pulled Elisha down. We wanted to show the effect of the bullet hitting him." Redwing coached Alan Ladd, Glenn Ford, Henry Fonda, and many other actors.

He also put on exhibits of virtuoso shooting, such as at the National Walk-and-Draw Championship in Las Vegas in 1963. Many of his shows were put on to raise money for charity, particularly Indian causes. Redwing's most famous stunt, documented on film, was to throw a knife and then draw his gun with the same hand. While the knife was still in the air he would fire the gun at a target and the knife would then stick in the bullet hole.

In a career spanning almost 40 years, Redwing appeared in more than 48 films. He also made more than 30 television guest appearances on shows such as *The Cisco Kid, The Life and Legend of Wyatt Earp, Bonanza*, and *Gunsmoke*. On May 30, 1971, on a flight from London en route from Spain, where he had been working in the Robert Dorfmann Western *The Red Sun*, 30 minutes before landing at Los Angeles International Airport Redwing suffered a heart attack and was pronounced dead shortly thereafter.

Reel, Estelle (Estelle Reel Meyer) (1862–1959) *federal superintendent of Indian schools*

Born in Pittsfield, Illinois, in 1862, the daughter of A. L. Reel, a doctor, and Jane R. Scanland Reel, Estelle Reel was educated in Boston and Chicago. Around 1889, she moved to Cheyenne, Wyoming, where her brother was mayor and where she taught in the public schools for six years. A loyal Republican in the first state to give women the vote (1869), she ran for state superintendent of schools in 1895 and became the first woman in the United States ever elected to a state office. She was also registrar of the land board and secretary of charities and reforms, including the prisons and insane asylums.

Reel supported William McKinley in his presidential campaign, and in 1898 he appointed her superintendent of Indian education, the highest federal position filled by a woman up to that time, replacing William N. Hailman (whose dismissal had been arranged by RICHARD HENRY PRATT). Her first assignment was to tour the 250 federal Indian schools, meet their 2,000 teachers, and develop a curriculum for the system's 20,000 pupils.

Chickasaw actor and stuntman Rodd Redwing displaying his shooting style. *(AP/Wideworld)*

films," he was in nearly all of director Cecil B. DeMille's later productions and acquired the reputation of being the fastest draw in the country. He mostly played Indian characters in Westerns.

Redwing's first known film credit is in 1936 in *The White Hunter*, and he was known variously as Red Wing or more

When Theodore Roosevelt became president in 1901, he retained WILLIAM A. JONES as Indian commissioner. Richard Henry Pratt was then the dominant figure in Indian education. Owing to Roosevelt's distaste for Pratt, however, Jones shifted his policies in a way that gave Reel a freer hand to develop her ideas. Her freedom increased under Commissioners FRANCIS ELLINGTON LEUPP, appointed by Roosevelt in 1905, and ROBERT GROSVENOR VALENTINE, appointed in 1909, who continued Leupp's policies. Whereas previous administrations had supported rapid ASSIMILATION, federal authorities now saw it as a long, gradual process in which some elements of Native American culture could be retained. A radical break with home and elders, as in Pratt's system of boarding schools and assimilation in a single generation, was not favored under Roosevelt. Support of home life was seen as a way to influence parents through children. Special attention was paid to the education of Indian girls, under the principle "if you civilize the wife, you civilize the home."

In a 1901 report (which incidentally signaled the beginning of the decline of Pratt's influence), Jones emphasized that Indian education would have an even more practical emphasis than it had previously: "The ground work of all instruction in Indian schools is the systematic inculcation of the principles of work." Industrial training was even to be inserted into all academic subjects—with an emphasis on agriculture and household arts. In addition, Indian pupils were to be indoctrinated with the moral values of work, property, individualism.

While Reel and Leupp believed that a white man's education was simply not suitable for most Indian children, the shift also reflected a general trend in the educational theory of the time. Even as Wyoming's superintendent of education, Reel had been an early proponent of the manual training and home economics movements. In a speech to the Cheyenne high school graduating class in the 1890s, she stated that "application and hard work are forms of genius."

At the same time, "race pride" was to be encouraged. Leupp and Reel encouraged pupils to use tribal legends or aspects of their traditional culture as subjects for English composition, to sing songs in their Native languages, and so on. Above all, she recognized the economic and cultural value of Native arts and crafts.

As early as 1897, Reel's predecessor, Hailman, had suggested that teachers try to take a more positive view of their pupils' cultural heritage, that it was not necessarily lower simply because it was different. This new philosophy was fully embodied in the course of study written by Reel and issued in 1901. Her emphasis on Indian crafts education shows the influence of the INDIAN INDUSTRIES LEAGUE: "The importance of preserving the Indian designs and shapes cannot be overestimated. The object must be to weave the history and traditions of the tribe in all distinctively Indian work, thus making it historical, typical, and of value. The Chinese do not attempt to imitate the works of other nations, nor should the Indians." She joined the league's executive committee in December 1902.

Despite such statements, Reel's thought about Indians was still paternalistic and superficial. Nor did she alter the basic character of the boarding schools. Under Leupp, however, emphasis shifted to the reservation day school for the great majority of Indian children, and plans were discussed to close some of the boarding schools and retain the rest for HIGHER EDUCATION. There was also the beginning of a move to entrust Indian education to the public schools of local school districts, subsidized by the Indian Office.

It must not be forgotten that the fundamental principle of Pratt's policy of deliberate suppression of Indian culture was his conviction that Indians had exactly the same capacities as whites. It was only culture that held the Indian back. The new emphasis on racial difference has to be seen in this light. Moreover, racial inferiority was not regarded as something inevitable, because the red race was considered capable of great progress, and not exactly in the path of whites, either. The race was considered "lower" in the sense of being at an earlier stage of its own cultural evolution, not in its ultimate capacities. But Leupp and Reel seemed to believe this applied to physical evolution as well, and the result was an overemphasis on racial difference (see BOAS, FRANZ).

On a visit to the Yakima Reservation near Toppenish, Washington, Reel met Cort F. Meyer, who ranched sheep on reservation land. She retired from public office in 1910 and married him in Hot Springs, Arkansas. They ranched and farmed together in Toppenish for many years. In her 80s, Reel lost her sight and had to be helped around by her husband. After his death on April 25, 1947, she was effectively incapacitated. She died at the Summitview Nursing Home in Yakima, Washington, on August 2, 1959.

Further Reading

Lomawaima, K. Tsianina. "Estelle Reel, Superintendent of Indian Schools, 1898–1910: Politics, Curriculum, and Land." *Journal of American Indian Education* 35, no. 3 (Spring 1996): 5–32.

Reese, John N., Jr. (1923–1945) *Cherokee Medal of Honor winner*

John N. Reese, Jr., a Cherokee from Muskogee, Oklahoma, was born on June 13, 1923. He was a private in the 37th Army Division during the assault on Manila in the Philippines. On February 9, 1945, Reese's company was pinned down by 300 Japanese soldiers defending the railroad station in the southern part of Paco. Street fighting in Manila, the Philippine capital, was some of the most ferocious of the war, and rather than being shot at, Reese and fellow private Cleto Rodriguez decided to take matters into their own hands.

Making their way through the rubble of the shattered rail yard, they took up positions in a ruined building, allowing them to fire on the Japanese. After killing 35, they attacked a group of the enemy attempting to man a pillbox, killing 40 more soldiers. Finally they attacked the train station itself, killing seven more men and destroying two heavy machine guns. Nearly out of ammunition, they covered each other's retreat until, just yards from safety, Reese was shot and killed. Between the two of them, they had killed 82 enemy soldiers. Reese was posthumously awarded the Medal of Honor on October 19, 1945.

Reifel, Benjamin (1906–1990) *Brulé Lakota Sioux federal official, member of Congress*

Born on September 19, 1906, on the Rosebud Reservation in South Dakota, Benjamin Reifel was the son of William Reifel, a German-American farmer, and Lily Lucy Burning Breast, a Brulé Lakota. His education was informal, and he attended both a Rosebud Reservation boarding school and a county school. He graduated from the eighth grade at age 16. After working on his parents' farm for three years, Reifel entered the School of Agriculture in Brookings, South Dakota. He managed to become clerk at the local trading post and save money to go to South Dakota State College. Reifel graduated in 1932 with a degree in biochemistry and a commission as a second lieutenant in the U.S. Army reserves. A year later, he joined the BUREAU OF INDIAN AFFAIRS (BIA), advising Indian farmers on the Pine Ridge Reservation, and in 1935 he was sent by Commissioner JOHN COLLIER to reservations across the Plains to help implement the INDIAN NEW DEAL (see INDIAN REORGANIZATION ACT).

Reifel was called up for active duty during WORLD WAR II, serving with the military police and reaching the rank of lieutenant colonel. After the war, Reifel was appointed superintendent of the Fort Berthold Reservation, helping the Bureau of Reclamation force an agreement on the Three Affiliated Tribes (Arikara, Hidatsa, and Mandan) for the building of the GARRISON DAM.

In 1949, Reifel received a scholarship to Harvard University's Littauer School of Public Administration, receiving a master's degree in 1950 and a Ph.D. in 1952. He then returned to Fort Berthold before becoming superintendent of Pine Ridge in 1954 and area director in 1955. In 1960, Reifel ran successfully for Congress, where he served until 1971. A conservative Republican, Reifel was mostly involved in local issues during his tenure in Congress, serving on the House Agriculture Committee and pushing for aid to farmers and irrigation projects. After his retirement, he remained active in Indian issues, serving briefly as commissioner for Indian affairs under President Gerald Ford, replacing MORRIS THOMPSON. In 1988, Reifel got some notoriety when the National Taxpayers Union reported that he was the first member of the House to receive more than $1 million in retirement benefits. Benjamin Reifel died on January 2, 1990, in Sioux Falls, South Dakota. His papers are housed at South Dakota State University.

Further Reading
Beckman, Aldo. "South Dakota Congressman Knows Indian Needs." *Chicago Tribune*, 13 July 1969.

religious freedom, American Indian

Notwithstanding constitutional protections for religious freedom, the period of the late 19th and early 20th century was largely characterized by intense government persecution of Native American religions. Throughout this time, U.S. federal policy included the christianization of Indians as one of its primary goals. The ALLOTMENT program, begun in 1880 as a plan to break up Indian reservations, was led in large part by Christian reformers who believed that big reservations encouraged the maintenance of the traditional Indian way of life and hindered the ASSIMILATION of Indians into mainstream American society. (See INDIAN RIGHTS ASSOCIATION.) For much of the 19th century, the education of Indians was overseen by Christian churches, and virtually all of the educated Indians of the early 20th century were Christians, who in turn often agitated on behalf of the non-Indian reform groups to abolish Indian religions.

In 1883, the Court of Indian Offenses was established specifically to eradicate, in the words of then Secretary of the Interior H. M. Teller, "heathenish dances; such as the sun dance" and replace them with Christian practices. By 1890, the use of peyote, a plant used in some religious ceremonies, was banned on Indian reservations. Indian Commissioner WILLIAM ARTHUR JONES, a Presbyterian, considered Indian traditions "barbarous" and, during his tenure at the turn of the century, enacted a number of ordinances designed to prevent ceremonial dances and the wearing of ceremonial garb. Under Progressive Era commissioners FRANCIS ELLINGTON LEUPP, ROBERT GROSVENOR VALENTINE, and CATO SELLS, the persecution of Indian religions and religious leaders abated only slightly; the commissioners believed that the heavy-handed tactics under Jones were counterproductive and cruel, preferring instead a more gradual "phasing out" of Indian beliefs. However, increasing efforts to stamp out the growing peyote religion during this time led to the incorporation of the NATIVE AMERICAN CHURCH in 1918, organized like Christian churches in the hope that it would come under the protection of the First Amendment.

In the 1920s, a time of growing Protestant fundamentalist influence in the United States, Commissioner CHARLES HENRY BURKE represented a return to the policies of Jones and the 19th century. Between 1921 and 1926, he issued a number of DANCE ORDERS, which sought to curtail Indian ceremonial dances, and he personally led raids on Indian ceremonies in the Southwest in an attempt to break them up. Burke also fostered a closer cooperation with Christian denominations and government schools, allowing them to provide teachers for religious instruction. Even by 1921, Christians churches still operated 30 day schools and 51 boarding schools for Indian students. (See EDUCATIONAL POLICY, AMERICAN INDIANS AND.)

It was not until the appointment of JOHN COLLIER as Indian commissioner that overt persecution ended. The INDIAN REORGANIZATION ACT of 1934, which allowed tribes a measure of self-government, also allowed them to practice their religions as they saw fit. The period under Collier led to a rebirth of Indian religions, many of which had for a long time been performed surreptitiously. For example, the Sun Dance began to be performed regularly among the Sioux, and it was reestablished on the Crow reservation in 1941 after an absence of more than 65 years (see TREHERO, JOHN). Collier was less interested in extending protection to adherents of the Native American Church, however. Sympathetic to the traditional Pueblo religion, he had peyotists removed from their offices in Taos Pueblo.

The TERMINATION era, which followed Collier's tenure, was a throwback to the assimilation policies of the 19th and early 20th centuries. Supporters of Termination sought to reduce any sense of tribal identity and were thus inherently opposed to any cultural or religious force that might bind Indians together. With conversion of Indians an explicit goal of Mormon theology, the involvement of powerful Mormon leaders did not escape the notice of Termination's critics, among them O. Hatfield Chilson, an official under Dwight D. Eisenhower, who believed that Utah senator ARTHUR VIVIAN WATKINS's strong advocacy of Termination was in part religiously motivated, in that he believed "he was paying off a debt which the Mormons owed the Indians." Other powerful Mormons influential in the Termination era were Reva Beck Bosone, a Utah congresswoman who coined the term *termination;* Ernest Wilkinson, who helped draft the act that created the INDIAN CLAIMS COMMISSION; and attorney JOHN STERLING BOYDEN.

Indian Commissioner DILLON SEYMOUR MYER, the architect of Termination, was himself a strict Methodist and Commissioner GLENN LEONIDAS EMMONS, who carried out the policy, was an Episcopalian. In 1954, the Mormon Church, in an effort to convert Indian children, established a wide-scale adoption program that coincided with attempts to accelerate Indian adoptions (see INDIAN CHILD WELFARE ACT).

Termination and Relocation (see URBANIZATION, AMERICAN INDIANS AND) policies also struck at the heart of many Indian religions: the sacred association of traditional religious beliefs with the land on which the tribes lived. In the Southwest, where the Terminationists had tangible goals, policies were enacted to overcome traditional Indian religious objections to the sale or mining of sacred sites, such as Black Mesa on the Hopi and Navajo (Dineh) reservation (see BIG MOUNTAIN). Communities that had found ways to use traditional religious and cultural means to successfully manage their natural resources, such as the Menominee and the Klamath, were dissolved and their members scattered. The unpopular Termination policy was overturned in 1970 by President Richard M. Nixon, who in this respect seemed to live up to the continuing tradition of concern shown by other prominent Quakers such as Indian Commissioner CHARLES JAMES RHOADS.

The end of Termination spurred a revival of Indian religious practices, aided this time by books such as *Black Elk Speaks,* by BLACK ELK (reprinted in 1962) and CARLOS CASTAÑEDA's books on Yaqui medicine man Don Juan, which brought Indian religious beliefs wider acceptance among non-Indians. The RED POWER MOVEMENT was greatly influenced by prominent spiritual leaders such as Creek PHILLIP DEERE and Brulé Lakota Sioux LEONARD CROW DOG, and the activists themselves, many of them nontraditional urban Indians, began to return to traditional beliefs.

The protection of Indian sacred sites, however, remained a thorny issue for Indians. Many of the 20th century's most bitterly contested issues, such as BLUE LAKE, PYRAMID LAKE, and Big Mountain, involved expropriation of Indian sacred sites by the United States or private interests. Many sacred areas, such as Devils Tower in Wyoming, Bear Butte in South Dakota, and MOUNT GRAHAM in Arizona, are not on designated Indian lands and have been developed or otherwise desecrated. It was not until 1970, when President Richard Nixon returned Blue Lake to the Taos Pueblo, that the federal government recognized that Indian sacred sites should be accorded any protection at all.

Since then, the Supreme Court has largely blocked executive and legislative protections for Indian religions. In *Lyng v. Northwest Indian Cemetery Protective Association* (1988), known as the "Go Road Decision," the Supreme Court's majority held that Indian sacred sites have no constitutional protections, even if they are central to Indian religious beliefs, and may be destroyed, desecrated, or put to any use, subject only to the provision that the desecrating party was not acting specifically to destroy the religion. It is believed that more than 90 percent of Indian sacred sites, including burial grounds and petroglyphs, have been looted, developed, or desecrated in some way. Despite the passage of the AMERICAN INDIAN RELIGIOUS FREEDOM ACT (AIRFA) in 1978, more than 44 sacred sites are currently under threat from some form of development, including mining on Havasupai sacred land; tourists and logging development near Medicine Wheel, Wyoming; and potential oil drilling near Badger Two Medicine in Montana.

The Supreme Court also ruled against members of the Native American Church in *Employment Division, Department of Human Resources of Oregon v. Smith* (1990). In this and the *Lyng* case, the Court ruled that the AIRFA was simply a "policy statement" of the government and did not in fact extend constitutional protections to Native American religions. In the *Smith* case, the Court further ruled that states and localities no longer had to show a "compelling governmental interest" to justify a law that limited or infringed on religious exercise. In both cases, the Court vacated the judgments of lower courts, which had held that First Amendment guarantees of freedom of religion applied to Indian religious practices. The decisions of the majority of the Court were condemned by the minority justices, Harry A. Blackmun, William Brennan, and Thurgood Marshall, as well as by virtually all mainstream religious groups, who saw the rulings as a threat to religious freedom in general.

Subsequent attempts by Congress and the executive branch to restore protections to Native religions met with mixed success. President George H. W. Bush signed the Native American Graves Protection and Repatriation Act (1990); although it provided some protections to sacred sites on public lands, the act did not apply to state lands or private property (see REPATRIATION). On November 16, 1993, President Bill Clinton signed the Religious Freedom Restoration Act (RFRA), which would have overturned *Smith* and restored the "compelling interest" standard that limits the government's ability to infringe on religious freedom. However, in 1997 the Supreme Court in *City of Boerne v. P. F. Flores* struck down the RFRA as an unconstitutional exercise of congressional powers.

In 1994, the AIRFA was amended to strengthen the protection of sacred sites and peyotists, and in 1996 President Clinton signed Executive Order 13007 which provided further protections and access to sacred sites on federal lands. However, in general Native American religions are accorded protection under the law only when their practices conform to the accepted Western notions of religion. Therefore, there are many exceptions to the right to use sacred plants such as peyote in ceremonies. For example, inmates in prisons where all other forms of worship are allowed may be denied the right to hold peyote ceremonies for prison security (based on the 1986 case *Indian Inmates of Nebraska Penitentiary v. Grammer*). Moreover, Indian religious rights can be subsumed under state laws, such as game and fishing laws, if the state can demonstrate a compelling interest in enforcing those laws.

Further Reading

Hirschfelder, Arlene B., and Paulette F. Molin. *The Encyclopedia of Native American Religions.* New York: Facts On File, 1992.
Michaelsen, Robert S. "The Significance of the American Indian Religious Freedom Act of 1978." *Journal of the American Academy of Religion* 52, no. 1 (1984): 93–115.
Vecsey, Christopher, ed. *Handbook of American Indian Religious Freedom.* New York: Crossroad, 1991.
Wunder, John R., ed. *Native American Cultural and Religious Freedoms.* New York: Garland, 1996.

Relocation   *See* URBANIZATION, AMERICAN INDIANS AND.

repatriation

The repatriation movement has sought the return of Indian religious objects and human remains from museums and other cultural centers. As part of the 19th-century policy of ASSIMILATION, Indians were encouraged to give up their religions and as a consequence their sacred objects. Many such objects were destroyed under Christian persecution, but they were also sought after by private collectors and by new institutions created for the scientific study of these and other objects—the modern museums. Museum researchers also dug up Indian graves as an important source of artifacts and information regarding Indian tribes, modern and ancient.

The most avid private collector of Indian artifacts at the start of the 20th century was George Heye, a wealthy New York entrepreneur who had few scruples as to where or how he obtained his materials. In 1916, he opened the Museum of the American Indian, Heye Foundation, containing the largest collection of Indian objects in the world. Government institutions, such as the U.S. Army, also sponsored collectors of Indian artifacts as well as human remains, and their collections became incorporated into the Smithsonian Museum

of Natural History. Other major collections were established by the American Museum of Natural History in New York, the Peabody Museum in Boston, and the Field Museum in Chicago.

As Indian artifacts grew in value in the early 20th century, laws were passed that protected them from looting. In 1906, the Act for the Preservation of American Antiquities made it a criminal offense to "appropriate, excavate, injure or destroy historic or prehistoric ruins or monuments or objects of antiquity located on lands owned or controlled by the U.S. Government." The legislation, however, effectively transferred ownership of these artifacts from the tribes to the federal government, which still allowed their excavation under permit by a "suitable university, museum or other scientific or educational institution."

Tribal ownership of ceremonial or historical objects was not an accepted legal concept at the time, and thus property that belonged to the entire tribe could be sold off by unscrupulous individual members. In 1891, Onondaga chief Thomas Webster sold four of the most important Iroquois wampum belts, including the Hiawatha Belt, which represented the founding of the Iroquois Confederacy and was possibly more than 500 years old; and the George Washington Covenant Belt, representing a treaty of friendship with the United States. Because of his transgression, Webster was removed as chief in 1897; however, Iroquois attempts to regain the belts, which had passed into the possession of the mayor of Albany, were fruitless. A suit to reassert ownership of the belts was dismissed in 1907 on the grounds that the Iroquois Confederacy had ceased to exist as a legal entity and therefore had no communal property.

The Iroquois had appointed the New York State Board of Regents to act on their behalf to recover the belts and gave them an additional 26 belts for safekeeping. However, in 1909 the Board of Regents persuaded the New York State legislature to pass a law making the state the owner of all Iroquois wampum belts, and over the protests of the Iroquois, all of the belts were transferred to the state museum in Albany. In addition, in 1896, 11 Iroquois wampum belts were taken from the Six Nations Reserve in Canada and, despite the fact that they were known to be stolen, were purchased by George Heye and added to his collection.

Art dealers such as Grace Nicholson and F. M. Noe routinely pilfered graves for human remains and funerary objects, most of which would eventually wind up in museums. During the 1920s and 1930s, more than 70 Zuni "War Gods," wooden carvings of the twin figures of Masewi and Oyoyewi, were stolen from their shrines around Zuni lands. Carved by members of the Deer and Bear Clans, the War Gods were believed to protect the Zuni people and to provide stability and harmony to the world.

The return of sacred objects to Indians was extremely rare. In 1938, George Heye returned a medicine bundle in his collection to the Hidatsa in North Dakota, who were suffering from a severe drought. After the bundle was returned, it rained on the reservation. During and after the 1930s, development on and near Indian reservations through large construction projects, roads, and dams accelerated the transfer of artifacts to museums (see DAMS ON AMERICAN INDIAN LANDS). In 1960, the U.S. Reservoir Salvage Act authorized archaeologists to recover objects, often funerary items and human remains, from construction sites. Furthermore, the ever-increasing demand for Indian antiquities and the lack of protection over these sites had led to the plundering of an estimated 90 percent of them by 1979, leading to the passage of the Archaeological Resources Protection Act that year. Many of these objects had found their way to museums, and an inventory conducted in 1986 found that at least 27,312 human remains and 543,081 burial objects were held in museum collections around the country.

As part of the RED POWER MOVEMENT, a cultural resurgence occurred during the 1960s and 1970s. Along with a growing demand for self-determination in every aspect of their lives, Native communities began agitating for the return of their objects and for the reburial of their ancestors' remains. The Indian repatriation movement coincided with an international repatriation movement, led by the attempts of Jewish communities to secure the return of cultural artifacts stolen under Nazi occupation and by the growing assertiveness of countries such as Greece, which demanded the return of the Elgin Marbles held by the British Museum. Museums, however, vigorously resisted any legislative attempt to redress these demands.

During the 1970s, the financial troubles of the Museum of American Indian, Heye Foundation—discovered to have been selling off portions of its collection to pay operating expenses—undercut arguments from museum advocates that Native objects were safer and better cared for in museums. Furthermore, federal courts increasingly began to recognize the validity of tribal communal property, which put into question the conveyance of title to many of the objects in museums that had been purchased from individual Indians not authorized by the tribe to sell them. In 1976, Lakota Sioux activist Maria Pearson successfully lobbied Iowa to pass the Iowa Reburial Law, which protected Indian grave sites and required the reburial of any American Indian remains uncovered during construction projects, the first such law in the country. Two years later, the AMERICAN INDIAN RELIGIOUS FREEDOM ACT recognized the right of Indians to their cultural patrimony, although it provided no legal remedy for its return.

During the late 1970s and early 1980s, the Zuni began an active campaign to regain their War Gods and were eventually successful in achieving the return of more than 65 of them. After intense lobbying, the Heye Foundation in 1988 returned the 11 stolen wampum belts to the Six Nations Reserve, and the next year the New York State Museum in Albany returned the Hiawatha Belt and other wampum belts to the Iroquois.

In an attempt to suppress the growing repatriation movement, museums in the United States supported federal legislation in 1986 that would have allowed them to keep any objects, regardless of how they were obtained, as long as these objects had been in the possession of the museum for more than three years. The legislation was defeated by a coalition of American Indian and Jewish groups and by opposition from countries

such as Greece and Egypt. Under pressure from Native activists, in particular SUZAN SHOWN HARJO (Cheyenne-Creek) and Richard "Rick" Hill (Tuscarora), the creation of the National Museum of the American Indian (NMAI) out of the Heye and Smithsonian collections in 1989 incorporated many of the demands of the repatriation movement.

On November 16, 1990, President George H. W. Bush signed into law the Native American Graves Protection and Repatriation Act (NAGPRA). This landmark legislation required museums or any other institution receiving federal funding to inventory their human remains and funerary items, notify tribes of their holdings, and return the remains and funerary objects to their original owners. It also provided that any new remains and grave goods found on federal or tribal lands be turned over to their respective tribes for reburial. NAGPRA makes the sale of illegally obtained grave materials a federal crime. The law permits tribes to request the return of objects that are indispensable to the tribe and form part of its cultural patrimony, even if they may have been legally acquired by museums or other institutions. The tribe, on the other hand, must show proof of the need of these objects for their religious life.

Since the legislation, some skeletal remains and cultural objects have been returned to their respective tribes, but the process has been delayed by the slow pace of inventorying the remains and objects. The Smithsonian Institution's Museum of Natural History, which holds the largest collection of Indian remains in the United States, completed its inventory in 1998. Since the act was signed, the Smithsonian has repatriated to tribes only around 6,000 human remains from their collection of approximately 19,000 skeletons and 900 funerary objects. A report by the General Accounting Office (GAO), released in June 2011, criticized the Smithsonian and NMAI for the slow pace of their repatriation efforts. Other museums have also been slowly repatriating remains and object to their respective tribes. Unfortunately, many cultural objects are no longer usable for ceremonies. For most of the 19th and 20th centuries, it was common practice for museums and collectors to preserve artifacts and ward off insects and rodents by applying a variety of toxic pesticides, including mercury, arsenic, and DDT. As a result, when remains or objects are repatriated, they must be kept in special cases or handled with gloves so as not to poison their custodians.

Although by and large the act has been deemed a qualified success by the majority of both the anthropological and Native American communities, NAGPRA became the source of a bitter controversy upon the discovery of an ancient skeleton in 1996. Uncovered on the banks of the Columbia River within the ancestral territory of the Umatilla Indian Nation and under the jurisdiction of the U.S. Army Corps of Engineers, the human skeleton, dubbed Kennewick Man, was found to be more than 9,000 years old. The Nez Perce, Umatilla, Yakama, and Colville tribes moved to have the skeleton reburied under the provisions of NAGPRA, sparking a storm of protest from the archaeological community, which wished to study it further. The dispute went to the courts, and in February 2004 the

U.S. Court of Appeals, Ninth Circuit, ruled that the tribes had failed to establish a cultural link with the skeleton. The tribes dropped their lawsuit, and scientists undertook studies of Kennewick Man in July 2005. The remains, still owned by the Army Corps of Engineers, are housed in the Burke Museum at the University of Washington in Seattle.

See also RELIGIOUS FREEDOM, AMERICAN INDIAN.

Further Reading

Fine-Dare, Kathleen S. *Grave Injustice: The American Indian Repatriation Movement and NAGPRA*. Lincoln: University of Nebraska Press, 2002.
Hill, Richard. "Mining the Dead." *Daybreak* (Summer 1988): 10–14.
———. "Reclaiming Cultural Artifacts." *Museum News* (May/June 1987): 43–46.
Talbot, Steve. "Desecration and American Indian Religious Freedom." *Journal of Ethnic Studies* 12, no. 4 (1985): 1–18.

Revard, Carter Curtis (Nompehwahthe) (1931–)
Osage poet, scholar

Carter Curtis Revard was born on March 25, 1931, in Pawhuska, Oklahoma, to Thelma Camp and McGuire Revard. He is one-fourth Osage on his father's side, and his stepfather, Addison Jump, Sr., was also Osage. Revard and his six brothers and sisters all graduated from the one-room Buck Creek School. Going on to Bartlesville College High, he won a radio quiz scholarship to the University of Tulsa, from which he graduated in 1952. In that year, he was given his Osage name, Nompehwahthe, by his grandmother, Josephine Jump. Revard won a Rhodes Scholarship and earned a second B.A. and an M.A. at Oxford University; he received his Ph.D. in English from Yale University in 1959. In 1956, he married Stella Purce (d. 2014), a fellow doctoral student at Yale; they had four children.

Revard first taught at Amherst College in Massachusetts and later at Washington University in St. Louis, Missouri (1961–97), where he is now emeritus professor of English language and literature. His areas of scholarly expertise include linguistics, Middle English literature, the study of medieval manuscripts and their social context, and American Indian literature.

Carter Revard is active in American Indian affairs in the St. Louis area. During 1973 and 1974, he was one of the founders of what was to become the American Indian Center of Mid-America, serving on the board of directors (1980–81 and 1986–97) and as president (1990–95). The center offers social services, and has been involved in lobbying and mediation on Indian remains and reburial (see REPATRIATION) and on wild-rice harvesting issues. Revard also has worked with the Washington University Center for American Indian Studies, directing its first Plains Indian Powwow in 1991. He became a member of the St. Louis Gourd Dancers in 1978 and regularly participates in POWWOWS.

Carter Revard's stories and poems, many of them autobiographical or focused on Indian experience, have appeared in numerous journals and anthologies. He has published several collections of poems: *My Right Hand Don't Leave Me No More* (1970), *Ponca War Dancers* (1980), *Cowboys and Indians Christmas Shopping* (1992), and *An Eagle Nation* (1993). In addition, he has published a book of essays, *Family Matters, Tribal Affairs* (1998). His book *Winning the Dust Bowl*—a memoir told in poems, prose, and photographs—appeared in 2001 and was a finalist in the nonfiction category for the Oklahoma Book Award in 2002. He also contributed to *Speak to Me Words: Essays on Contemporary American Indian Poetry*, published by University of Arizona Press in 2003. In 2005, he released *How the Songs Came Down*, a compilation of new and older poems. That same year, he received the Lifetime Achievement Award from the Native Writers' Circle of the Americas.

Further Reading

Arnold, Ellen L. *The Salt Companion to Carter Revard*. London: Salt Publishing, 2007.

Reynolds, Allie (Albert Pierce Reynolds, Superchief) (1917–1994) *Creek baseball player*

Allie Reynolds was a member of the powerful New York Yankees baseball team that won six world championships. He was one of the most successful pitchers in World Series history. A Creek Indian, he was born Albert Pierce Reynolds in Bethany, Oklahoma, on February 10, 1917, to David C. Reynolds, who was three-eighths Creek, and Mary Reynolds. His father was a strict Nazarene minister and did not allow Allie to play baseball on Sundays, so he never played for an organized team until he was a junior in college. He went to Oklahoma A&M (now Oklahoma State University) on a track scholarship and became the first player from that school to sign with a major league club, the Cleveland Indians, in 1942.

In 1947, Reynolds was traded to the New York Yankees and dubbed "Superchief" by the New York press, in an allusion to the powerful and fast Santa Fe express train, the Super Chief. He won 19 games in his first season with the Yankees and won the second game of the 1947 World Series in which the Yankees swept the Brooklyn Dodgers in four games. Working as both a starter and reliever, he was a major force on the great Yankee teams of 1949–53 that won an unmatched five World Series in a row. Reynolds's record of World Series success as a starter and reliever may never be equaled. Pitching in 15 games, he won seven, saved four more, and lost only two, all the while posting a 2.79 earned-run average (ERA).

In 1951, Reynolds became the first American League pitcher to pitch two no-hitters in a single season. His second no-hitter came against the heavy-hitting Boston Red Sox, and to end the game and enter the record books, he had to face Ted Williams, the greatest batsman of his time. In a famous play, Williams hit a pop foul ball that Yankee Hall of Fame catcher Yogi Berra dropped, forcing Reynolds to pitch again to the dangerous batter. Williams pop-fouled the next ball, and this time Yogi caught it, preserving Reynolds's no-hitter and the Yankee win.

Allie Reynolds is pictured on February 16, 1947. *(AP/Wideworld)*

In 1952, Reynolds posted a 20-8 record and led the league with a 2.06 ERA, 160 strikeouts, and six shutouts. That year, in the deciding seventh game of the World Series, he beat the Brooklyn Dodgers, which then boasted hitters like Jackie Robinson, Roy Campanella, Duke Snider, and Carl Furillo, considered one of the greatest baseball teams of all time.

At the peak of his ability, Reynolds's career was cut short by a back injury suffered in a crash of the team bus, and he had to retire at the end of the 1954 season. Overall, he won 182 games and posted 49 saves while losing only 107 games; his winning percentage of .630 is 27th on the all-time list. In addition to his World Series triumphs, he was an American League All-Star in 1949, 1950, and from 1952 to 1954.

After his retirement, Reynolds returned to Oklahoma and went into the oil business. He worked for numerous Native American causes and became president of the National Hall of Fame for Famous American Indians. On April 24, 1982, in a ceremony attended by Reynolds and Yankee legend Mickey Mantle, Oklahoma State dedicated its new baseball stadium, the Allie P. Reynolds stadium, and on August 26, 1989, a host of Yankee greats were present when the Yankees dedicated a plaque in his honor in Yankee Stadium's monument park. Allie Reynolds died on December 26, 1994, in his hometown of Oklahoma City.

Further Reading

Burke, Bob, and Royse Parr. *Allie Reynolds: Super Chief.* Oklahoma City: Oklahoma Heritage Association, 2002.

Rhoads, Charles James (1872–1954) *banker, philanthropist, commissioner of Indian affairs*

Born in Germantown, Philadelphia, Pennsylvania, October 4, 1872, Charles Rhoads was the son of James E. Rhoads, the first president of Bryn Mawr College, and Margaret Wilson Ely Rhoads. After graduating from the William Penn Charter School in Philadelphia in 1889, Rhoads went to Haverford College in Pennsylvania. Receiving a B.A. in 1893, he was hired by the Girard Trust Company, Philadelphia, where he worked his way up to vice president. He married Lillie Frishmuth in 1912. In 1914, Rhoads was appointed the first governor of the Federal Reserve Bank of Philadelphia. In 1920, he was appointed director of the Central National Bank of Philadelphia, and from 1921 to 1929 he was a partner at Brown Brothers.

Rhoads's father had served for the last nine years of his life (1885–94) as the second president of the INDIAN RIGHTS ASSOCIATION. Rhoads himself joined the association in 1899, serving as its treasurer for 28 years (1900–27) and as its president from 1927 through April 1929.

In April 1929, President Herbert Hoover named Rhoads commissioner of Indian affairs, with JOSEPH HENRY SCATTERGOOD as assistant commissioner. Promptly confirmed by the Senate, they served from July 1929 into the beginning of the Franklin Delano Roosevelt administration. In these appointments, Hoover, himself a Quaker and committed to implementing the recommendations of the MERIAM REPORT of 1928, made what seemed to be the perfect choice: two devout Philadelphia Quakers who were longtime colleagues and friends, able administrators with broad experience in Indian affairs, and highly knowledgeable and respected in the financial world. Hoover intended a thorough reorganization of the Indian Office (later the BUREAU OF INDIAN AFFAIRS [BIA]) "so that it can and will function along modern lines solely for the benefit of the Indian" (*Indian Truth*, May 1929). To some extent this was accomplished, but the big problem, as with most of Hoover's plans, was that America suffered the worst financial depression in its history shortly after he took office.

On their appointment in spring 1929, Rhoads and Scattergood first looked to the protection of Indian property. In December 1929, the commissioner sent letters to the chairman of the Senate Indian Affairs Committee, Burton K. Wheeler, outlining the need for legislation on claims of tribes against the government, Indian ALLOTMENT, liens on Indian lands, and indivisible tribal estates. They wanted to establish a court of Indian claims in which claims awards would be paid into tribal trust funds, thereby relieving the BIA of the responsibility of safeguarding and managing these funds, a task at which the bureau had shown itself notoriously inept. Neither Rhoads nor even his successor, JOHN COLLIER, succeeded in passing such legislation; it would not become a reality until 1946 (see INDIAN CLAIMS COMMISSION).

Although Allotment was not ended until 1934 under Collier, Rhoads and Scattergood at least tried to end its abuses. They suggested reform legislation that would allow fractionated and dissipated allotments to revert to the tribes. (In theory, these tribal lands were to be reallotted when circumstances warranted.) To increase tribes' independence from the BIA, they suggested tribes be incorporated for the handling of property, each with an Indian board of directors and a three-member non-Indian advisory board, members of which would be appointed, respectively, by the president, the federal district judge, and the tribal stockholders. This legislation also failed to pass.

Another crying financial issue was that of federal claims against the tribes. Previously, it had been standard practice for the government to bill tribes for "reimbursable charges" of capital improvements, mainly bridges and irrigation projects, on Indian lands. If a tribe succeeded in getting a claims award, these reimbursable charges would be deducted, vastly diminishing the amount due the tribe (for example, see WHITE CALF, JAMES). Most of these charges, which by 1930 totaled $40,549,686, were completely unjust, as the beneficiaries of the projects were usually white settlers rather than Indians. In addition, liens on allotted lands totaled more than $25,000,000, with the government holding mortgages on property probably greater than the value of the property. In 1930, the House Committee on Indian Affairs reported favorably on a bill to investigate the whole issue, with the intent of wiping out all spurious or illegal "debts." Again, such a bill was not passed until the Collier administration.

In addition to property issues, Rhoads and Scattergood were concerned with "human relations." In 1930, they commissioned physician and anthropologist ERL A. BATES (also a Quaker) to formulate an extensive national education plan for Indians. Believing Indians should be able to compete with whites, Rhoads and Scattergood sought increased appropriations for postsecondary education loans and vocational education. For the latter, they emphasized skilled mechanical work over high-speed factory work. The BIA's district superintendents would be expected to help find jobs for young Indians who did not return to reservations after leaving school (although the effectiveness of this program must have been marred by the depression). This was basically a continuation and expansion of the program developed by CHARLES EDWIN DAGENETT, who had retired in 1927.

Michigan congressman Louis Cramton, chair of the Interior Subcommittee, House Appropriations Committee, 1921 to 1931, was another great obstacle to Rhoads and Scattergood's intended reforms. He, former commissioner CHARLES HENRY BURKE, and Burke's assistant commissioner, Edgar B. Meritt, had "understood one another and worked together" (Nation, 2 April 1930), and though both administrators were now gone, the congressman was still committed to the old guard. Cramton controlled the purse strings of the Indian administration and, it was alleged, even interfered with personnel matters in the BIA. Rhoads and Scattergood could not stop Cramton from reviving and putting more money into the already debt-ridden irrigation and reclamation projects of the BIA instead of moving them to the Bureau of Reclamation.

Although reorganization was a top concern, no personnel changes were made until March 1931, when, after more than a year's study, the commissioners unveiled a complete reorganization of the BIA. It helped that Cramton had lost his party's nomination in 1930. The reorganization called for two new assistants to the commissioner, one for human relations and the other for property. The first assistant would head field divisions on health, education, and agricultural extension and industry. The second would head a field division on land, irrigation, and forestry. Qualifications and salaries were raised to attract more technically trained people. With his social-service viewpoint, Rhoads wanted to put outstanding social workers in charge of personnel and coordination of existing activities. The four field positions, which had formerly been given almost exclusively to political appointees, were filled now by men and women with special training in social welfare. This group included one of the most distinguished American Indians of the time, HENRY CLARENCE ROE CLOUD, who was named field representative on Indian education in September 1931.

One of Rhoads's most important appointments was WILL CARSON RYAN, JR., as director of education. Ryan had been the education specialist on the Meriam Commission (1926–28) and was the author of the section on education in the MERIAM REPORT. (See EDUCATIONAL POLICY, AMERICAN INDIANS AND.)

Rhoads and Scattergood followed the Meriam Report's recommendation to hire qualified Indians. Among the most important was the appointment of RUTH MUSKRAT BRONSON as guidance and placement specialist in 1930. In 1932, she took over the loan program for postsecondary education that had been authorized by Congress in 1930.

When Rhoads and Scattergood first took office, all the Indian support organizations rallied around them, including John Collier's American Indian Defense Association (AIDA). But Collier and the AIDA campaigned against Cramton and were disappointed at what they considered Rhoads and Scattergood's easy submission to his demands. As Collier stated in his memoir, From Every Zenith, the problem with Rhoads and Scattergood was that the Indian Office bureaucracy resisted, Congress refused to budge, and the commissioners fell to defending the bureaucrats. Collier himself, working closely with the Democrat-controlled Senate Indian Affairs Committee, later became one of Rhoads's harshest critics, although much of his criticism was politically motivated and of doubtful substance (see HAGERMAN, HERBERT JAMES).

After Franklin D. Roosevelt became president, their supporters (especially the Indian Rights Association) lobbied unsuccessfully to keep Rhoads and Scattergood on. They served until April 21, 1933, when they were replaced by Collier.

Rhoads returned to Philadelphia and the banking business. In 1948, he served as a member of the HOOVER COMMISSION, which sought to formulate a new federal Indian policy. Charles James Rhoads died on January 2, 1954.

Further Reading
Britten, Thomas A. "Hoover and the Indians: The Case for Continuity in Federal Indian Policy, 1900–1933." Historian 61, no. 3 (1999): 518–538.
Philp, Kenneth R. John Collier's Crusade for Indian Reform,

1920–1954, 92–112. Tucson: University of Arizona Press, 1977.

Rusco, Elmer R. *A Fateful Time: The Background and Legislative History of the Indian Reorganization Act.* Reno: University of Nevada Press, 2000.

Richmond, Rosemary (Rosemary Martin)

(1937–   ) *Mohawk urban Indian leader*

Rosemary Richmond was born Rosemary Martin in White Plains, New York, on December 19, 1937, to David K. Martin and Mary Elizabeth (Cook) Martin, both Mohawk from the Akwesasne (St. Regis) Reservation in upstate New York. David Martin was a high-steel ironworker in New York City (see IRONWORKERS, AMERICAN INDIAN). Rosemary Martin was raised in Greenwich, Connecticut, and attended Greenwich public schools. After graduation she worked on an assembly line. In 1957, she joined Fawcett Publications, a national book and magazine publisher headquartered in New York City. Beginning as a clerk in the subscriptions department, she headed the department by 1973.

Along with LOUIS MOFSIE, Rosemary Martin was one of the founders of the Thunderbird American Indian Dancers, a New York City dance troupe, in 1961. She married David Richmond (Mohawk) on February 1, 1969. Later that year they worked with Mifaunwy Hines (Pawnee-Otoe), the daughter of JOSEPH BAYHYLLE SHUNATONA; Chy Pells (Wampanoag); Mary Helen Deer (Kiowa Creek); Iola Hill Boyle (Mohawk); Olive Ward (Onondaga); Charmain Lyons (Onondaga); OREN LYONS, JR. (Onondaga); Louis Bayhye, Jr. (Navajo); Louis Mofsie (Hopi-Winnebago); and Robert W. Venables, an anthropologist and historian, to form the American Indian Community House (AICH), an urban Indian center in New York City. David Richmond, one of the original board members, was also among the 20 Indian activists from 14 different tribes who attempted to seize Ellis Island in March 1970, in an effort to duplicate the seizure of Alcatraz by the Indians of San Francisco a few months earlier (see ALCATRAZ, OCCUPATION OF). Ellis Island, located near the Statue of Liberty in New York's harbor, was at the time abandoned and vacant. The attempt failed when the boat the activists had procured developed engine trouble.

In 1973, David and Rosemary Richmond moved from Greenwich to Cold Spring, New York, where they ran a trading post. Two years later, they decided to move to New York City. Rosemary Richmond began working for the Title IV program of the U.S. Department of Education, which provides federal funding for disadvantaged students. As part of this work, she conducted a survey to determine the number of American Indian students in the New York City school system. In 1975, Mifaunwy Hines stepped down as executive director of AICH, having held the post since 1969, and her place was taken by Michael Bush (Mohawk), who had worked with Richmond in the Title IV program. Richmond joined AICH as executive secretary.

Under Bush and Richmond, AICH moved away from being an all-volunteer organization and became a large, professionally staffed entity with numerous departments. It added job placement and training programs; Indian health services; alcohol and substance abuse programs; and food, housing, legal and other services for the New York City Indian community. Aided by a New York State grant, the community house opened an art gallery, which became, under directors Peter Jemison (Seneca) and his successors Lloyd Oxendine (Lumbee) and Joanna Bigfeather (Cherokee), an important showcase for contemporary American Indian art. AICH also opened a theater and hosted a number of theater groups, including Spiderwoman Theater, the oldest continually running Indian woman's theater collective in the United States.

AICH was also active in furthering the rights of indigenous peoples worldwide, providing the funding and support for the INTERNATIONAL INDIAN TREATY COUNCIL while it was located in New York City, and providing important logistical support for Indian struggles such as the REPATRIATION of sacred Indian artifacts from museums, the BIG MOUNTAIN dispute in Arizona and New Mexico, and the cases of LEONARD PELTIER and DAVID SOHAPPY. With their skilled information officer, Rudy Martin (Tewa-Navajo-Apache), AICH became one of the leading publicists for Indian issues and Indian events; their newsletter had a circulation of more than 15,000.

In 1987, Bush left AICH to enter law school, and Richmond became executive director of the organization. Under her leadership, the center continued to expand, and she became the de facto leader of the New York City Indian community, one of the largest and most powerful in the country. AICH was one of the few Indian centers that welcomed Indians from other countries, including Central and South America, and prided itself on helping anyone who professed Indian identity, regardless of whether they were recognized by their governments as Indian or not.

Under Richmond, AICH became one of the most important artistic centers in the United States, hosting virtually every major Indian artist, poet, author, musician, or actor in its theater or gallery. Richmond was also as staunch defender of traditional Indian governments and culture. She threw her support behind the traditional, anti-gambling faction in the dispute over GAMING ON INDIAN RESERVATIONS in upstate New York. AICH hosted a debate in 1989 between Chippewa NEW AGE MOVEMENT leader SUN BEAR and Onondaga Chief Oren Lyons, Jr., over the sale of Indian traditions to non-Indians. She actively aided the efforts of Tonya Gonnella Frichner (Onondaga), president of the American Indian Law Alliance, and INGRID WASHINAWATOK (Menominee) to force the United Nations to address the rights of Indigenous peoples, ultimately leading to the U.N. issuing the Declaration on the Rights of Indigenous Peoples in 2008.

In 1991, after riots in Crown Heights, Brooklyn, New York—a heavily Hasidic area—Richmond worked with New York City mayor David Dinkins to host a Thanksgiving dinner at City Hall featuring Native American foods, where leaders of New York's varied religious and ethnic communities sat and ate together in an effort to ease racial tensions. That same year she founded the Native American Council of New York

City in order to coordinate policy among the many Indian organizations in the city. Richmond brought the full support of the Native American Council to a coalition of New York groups, organized at the behest of Chippewa activist WINONA LADUKE, that forced New York State to drop its support of James Bay II, a hydroelectric megaproject slated to flood Cree and Inuit lands in northern Quebec, Canada. (The project was suspended in 1992.) Also in 1992, in return for acquiescing to the celebrations of the quincentenary of Columbus's first voyage, Richmond secured an apology from King Juan Carlos of Spain for the misdeeds of the Spanish conquistadores.

In 1999, Richmond led attempts to secure the release of Ingrid Washinawatok, kidnapped by guerrillas in Colombia, South America, and, after Washinawatok's murder at their hands, helped to create the Flying Eagle Woman Fund in her memory. Richmond has served on numerous boards, including the American Indian Health Care Association, the New York City Workforce Investment Board, and the Democratic National Committee's American Indian Advisory Council. In 2009, she retired from her position as executive director of AICH and went back to live in Connecticut. Her son Lance Richmond and nephew Kevin Tarrant are noted singers with the traditional drum group, the Silver Cloud Singers (see also ART, VISUAL; DEMOGRAPHICS; URBANIZATION, AMERICAN INDIANS AND).

Rickard, Clinton (1882–1971) *Tuscarora chief, activist*

Clinton Rickard was born on the Tuscarora reservation near Buffalo, New York, on May 19, 1882, the third son of George and Lucy Rickard. George Rickard became a Tuscarora chief in 1885, but in 1886, he joined Buffalo Bill's Wild West Show, leaving the family for years. Lucy Rickard was of the Beaver Clan, and clan membership is matrilineal among the Tuscarora, so Clinton Rickard became a member of that clan.

Rickard attended school on and off until he was 16, receiving no more than a third-grade education. Enlisting in the U.S. Army in 1901, he fought in the Philippines during the Spanish-American War. Returning to the United States, he worked at a quarry, where his boss invited him to become a Freemason; he belonged to that fraternal society for the rest of his life.

During the 1920s, Rickard gave up his quarry job to become a full-time farmer and a chief in the Tuscarora council.

(From left to right) Clinton Rickard, Dave Hill, and Angus Horn led 1,500 Indians through Buffalo, New York, and across the Peace Bridge into Canada in 1946, reasserting the rights of Indians to freely cross the border between the nations. *(AP/Wideworld)*

He opposed measures to confer CITIZENSHIP on all Indians, considering this a violation of Iroquois sovereignty (see SOVEREIGNTY, INDIGENOUS AND TRIBAL), and fought unsuccessfully against the Indian Citizenship Act of 1924. That same year, Congress passed the Immigration Act and ended the free passage Indians had enjoyed between Canada and the United States by effectively excluding Canadian Indians from entering the United States. Rickard worked with Canadian Iroquois leader ALEXANDER GENERAL (Deskaheh) to keep the border open, arguing that the Jay Treaty of 1794 between the United States and Great Britain guaranteed unrestricted passage of Indians and their goods across the Canadian border. In 1926, Rickard and others founded the Six Nations Defense League, which was soon renamed the Indian Defense League of America (IDLA). In 1928, the IDLA secured a victory with the passage of H.R. 11351, which upheld the right of Indians to cross the border freely.

Rickard then successfully worked on the Canadian Cayugas' claim to a share of the annuity granted to the Cayuga living in New York State, managing to obtain a settlement of $100,000 from Governor Franklin D. Roosevelt in 1929. The following year, Rickard became a well-known figure when he managed to persuade the U.S. attorney's office to defend two Seneca women accused of murder. In 1931, he was arrested and jailed in Canada for raising money contrary to the Canadian Indian Act, losing his life's savings in the process. During the Great Depression, despite the considerable hardship suffered by his family, Rickard continued his political activism.

After WORLD WAR II, Rickard fought hard against the TERMINATION policies of Harry S. Truman and Dwight D. Eisenhower. Although he managed to help prevent the federal government from terminating the Tuscarora, he could not stop the closing of the federal Indian office in New York State in 1949 and the transfer of criminal jurisdiction over Iroquois reservations from the federal government to the state in 1948.

In 1957, Rickard joined MAD BEAR ANDERSON in the fight against the New York State Power Authority's attempt to flood one-fifth of the Tuscarora reservation for a reservoir. He later joined with other Iroquois in campaigning against the KINZUA DAM. Rickard's son, WILLIAM RICKARD, introduced the hard-line Iroquois view of sovereignty to the AMERICAN INDIAN CHICAGO CONFERENCE in 1961. Later William and his father, who was a Christian, had a falling out over William's decision to join the traditional Iroquois Longhouse Religion. William's early death in 1964 deeply affected Clinton, whose health deteriorated afterward. Clinton Rickard's other son, Norton, was well known for his fostering of traditional farming practices, including cultivation of a number of age-old varieties of Iroquois corn and potatoes.

Among the best-known Indian leaders of his day, Clinton Rickard died after a series of long illnesses on June 14, 1971.

Further Reading

Rickard, Clinton. *Fighting Tuscarora: The Autobiography of Chief Clinton Rickard.* Syracuse, N.Y.: Syracuse University Press, 1973.

Rickard, William (1917–1964) *Tuscarora activist*

William C. Rickard was born in 1917 on the Tuscarora reservation in upstate New York, the son of Tuscarora leader CLINTON RICKARD and Elizabeth Patterson Rickard, a Tuscarora member of the Bear Clan. As a child, Rickard was severely beaten by other Tuscarora children whose families opposed Clinton Rickard's political activities. Found late at night by his father lying nearly dead in a ditch, William suffered injuries that led first to pneumonia and then to emphysema, and ill health would plague him throughout his life. As a consequence, he was in and out of school throughout his youth.

As a young man, William Rickard fought against New York State's imposition of criminal jurisdiction over INDIAN RESERVATIONS in 1948 and civil jurisdiction in 1950. He became president of the Niagara Chapter of the Indian Defense League in 1954, an organization founded by his father. Along with his father and MAD BEAR ANDERSON, Rickard fought the New York State Power Authority's attempt to seize Tuscarora land for a reservoir. He led the demonstration of April 16, 1958, that battled police and workers attempting to survey the reservation, and he was arrested along with Anderson and John Hewitt, son of JOHN NAPOLEON BRINTON HEWITT.

In 1956, Rickard attended one of the "Meetings of Religious People," organized by Hopi religious leader DAN KATCHONGVA on the Hopi Reservation. There he met and became good friends with Hopi activist THOMAS BANYACYA. His stay at Hopi was a defining moment and led him to seek out his traditional roots. Although baptized and a Freemason like his father, William Rickard became a member of the traditional Longhouse Religion, which he learned from the Tonawanda Seneca. The conversion hurt his father deeply, although they continued to work together to protect both their land base and Indian self-determination.

In 1961, Rickard became the president of the League of North American Indians, a pan-Indian organization founded in 1935 by Mohawk Lawrence Twoaxe on the Caughnawaga Reserve in Quebec, Canada. For the previous 20 years, the league, largely run from Parsons, Kansas, by Tom Pee-Saw, a man of dubious Cherokee ancestry, had fought for the rights of traditional reservation Indians. Although the league had little mainstream credibility due to its hard stance in opposing both the BIA and tribal council governments formed under the INDIAN REORGANIZATION ACT (IRA), many traditional leaders lent it support. After Rickard's death, the presidency of the league passed to his friend and protégé, Alfred Gagne. With Gagne's death in 1970, the league ceased to exist.

Also in 1961, before the historic AMERICAN INDIAN CHICAGO CONFERENCE, Rickard helped to organize Eastern Indians, first in a conference at Pembroke College, Robeson County, North Carolina, hosted by Lumbee judge Lacy Maynor. Maynor was the judge who presided over the trial of James "Catfish" Cole, grand wizard of the South Carolina Ku Klux Klan, a group the Lumbee had recently chased out of Robeson County.

The second meeting was organized by Rickard and Seneca leader George Heron at Haverford College, featuring his father

Clinton as well as Hopi-Winnebago educator Louis Mofsie, Mimi Hines (the daughter of Pawnee-Otoe performer Joseph Shunatona), and Cherokee Clarence Wood, all leaders of the large New York City Indian Community; Mary Red Wing Congdon and Tall Oak, future leaders of the Red Power movement among the Narragansett; Gladys Widdiss of the Gay Head Wampanoag; and Earl Mills of the Mashpee. In the lead-up to the Chicago conference, Rickard clashed with Cheyenne Helen White Peterson of the National Congress of American Indians (NCAI), leader of the "old guard" of NCAI members who had dominated Indian politics during the 1950s and who opposed the inclusion of eastern tribes. At Chicago, Rickard brought the Iroquois concept of sovereignty, in which Indian reservations have the status of autonomous states, to national Indian attention, leading to a breakthrough in Indian politics. The agitation by Rickard in Chicago, as well as by Ponca Clyde Warrior, Paiute Mel Thom, and a new group of militant Indian college students, would lead to a reshaping of Indian political thought, and William Rickard's sister Karen Rickard was among the founders of the National Indian Youth Council, formed shortly after the conference.

After Chicago, Rickard worked with Chief W. R. Richardson of the Haliwa in their struggle for recognition. Shortly before his death, Rickard and George Heron organized the North American Indian Unity Caravans, in which groups of traditional Indians toured the United States over the next seven years. The caravans were influential in helping to reawaken pride among young Indians in their ancient traditions. Led by Seneca chief Beeman Logan, Mad Bear Anderson, and Thomas Banyacya, the first caravan left the Tonawanda Seneca reservation on September 2, 1964, with five carloads of Indians. Following the Canadian-U.S. border, they joined up with a Canadian Indian contingent and traveled all the way to the West Coast before returning back through the Southwest, having visited more than two dozen Native communities along the way. Bringing their blend of hard-line sovereignty centered around traditional religious perspectives, the unity caravans would have a profound and lasting effect on the Red Power movement. Sadly, Rickard was too ill to participate.

After struggling all his life with emphysema, Rickard died on September 18, 1964, of an acute pulmonary edema. His early death was a severe blow to his father, Clinton, who never fully recovered, and cut short one of the most influential Indian lives of the mid-20th century.

Rider, Iva Josephine (Princess Atalie Unkalunt, "Sunshine Rider") (1895–1954) *Cherokee soprano, author, illustrator*

Iva Josephine Rider, sometimes called Sunshine Rider and known professionally as Princess Atalie Unkalunt, was born on the Cherokee estate at Stillwell, Oklahoma, on June 12, 1895. Her father, Thomas Lafayette Rider (Dom-Ges-Ke Un Ka Lunt), was an Oklahoma state senator and descendant of Cherokee chiefs; her mother, Josephine Pace Rider, was

white. Educated at the Thomas School for Girls, San Antonio, Texas; Central High School, Muskogee, Oklahoma; and the Emerson School of Oratory (Boston), Rider went on to study logic, ethics, and psychology at Boston University and voice at the New England Conservatory with Charles W. White, Clarence B. Shirley, and Millie Ryan. After the U.S. entry into World War I in 1917, she worked overseas for the YMCA as a secretary and entertainer for 18 months.

A friend of prominent Indians such as Charles Curtis and Chauncey Yellow Robe, Rider founded, in 1922, the Society of First Sons and Daughters of America, a genealogical organization of which she was the first and only president. She was an ardent promoter of Indian culture, and in 1923 she publicly opposed the dance orders and other attempts to stamp out Indian religions being implemented by the Indian Office (as the Bureau of Indian Affairs [BIA] was then known) under Commissioner Charles Henry Burke. By this time perhaps the foremost Native American soprano (see also Blackstone, Tsianina Redfeather, Eastman, Irene; Poolaw, Lucy Nicola), she was a soloist with the Boston Symphony Orchestra and sang the lead in an opera, *Nitana*, written especially for her by Umberto Vesci and Augustus Post. In 1928, Rider was forced to file for bankruptcy, but the next year she led a group of Indians who performed for the inauguration of President Herbert Hoover in Washington, D.C.

For eight years during the 1930s, Rider led a private theater, group, the Indian Council Lodge, in New York, where she worked with, among others, Chief Yowlachie. She gave recitals and lectures and wrote and illustrated *The Earth Speaks* (1940, a collection of Indian legends); another book *Talking Leaves* (1950) is mentioned by some sources, but was not published. She also wrote the foreword to a collection of poems by Alice Hirsh, *From Pipes Long Cold* (1954). Rider participated in local powwows and dances of the New York City Indian community. She was affiliated with Christ Church in New York City. In the early 1950s she moved to Washington, D.C., where she died on November 6, 1954.

Ridley, Jack R. (1933–1988) *Shoshone crop physiologist, specialist in tribal economic development*

Jack Richard Ridley, a member of the Te-Moak Band of Western Shoshone, was born in Elko, Nevada, on April 16, 1933. He attended the Stewart Indian Boarding School at Stewart, Nevada, on the southern edge of Carson City. Immediately after graduation in 1951, he enlisted in the U.S. Air Force, serving in the Far East as a security radio operator. Returning to civilian life in 1955, Ridley enrolled in the University of Nevada at Reno, earning a B.S. in agricultural education in 1961 and a M.S. in agronomy in 1963. He went on to the University of California at Davis, where he became one of the first American Indians to earn a doctoral degree in science. (See science, American Indians and.) His dissertation was in experimental agronomy: "Effect of Temperature on Flowering Intensity of the Ladino Clover Stolon." In 1966, Ridley received appointments as professor of agronomy at U.C.

Davis and as assistant crop physiologist in the Department of Plant Science, University of Idaho at Moscow, Idaho, where he soon was promoted to assistant professor of plant physiology. He also held the position of research agronomist in the Crops Research Division, Agricultural Research Service, U.S. Department of Agriculture.

Ridley was keenly interested in the problems of American Indians, and his article, "A Plan for National Unity of Native Americans," published in the *Journal of American Indian Education* in 1970, was widely read. He saw the fact that Indians were divided into hundreds of separate communities, having little contact with one another, as a fundamental problem. He proposed the creation of four national organizations: a national reservation organization, a national urban organization, a national college student organization, and a national educational and historical organization, which would all be subdivided among seven geographical regions.

Ridley attended the historic First Convocation of American Indian Scholars, held in Princeton, New Jersey, in 1970, which featured virtually every Native American in academia at the time. At the University of Idaho, Ridley served as president of the Northwestern Native American Graduate Program, the first Indian-planned, organized, and executed graduate program in the United States. (See HIGHER EDUCATION.) In the early 1970s, he worked on development plans for the Coeur d'Alene and Nez Perce Tribes and gave a course on reservation economic development. In 1972, the Center for Native American Development was founded at the University of Idaho under his direction. Records from the center, which remained active through 1978, are housed in Special Collections at the library of the University of Idaho.

In November 1978, responding to recommendations of an Interior Department task force in April of that year that reported a "general management crisis" at the BUREAU OF INDIAN AFFAIRS (BIA), Commissioner of Indian Affairs FORREST J. GERARD appointed Ridley to direct the BIA's Office of Tribal Resources Development, a position that had been vacant. As one of five directors in the bureau's central office, Ridley was the top staff official responsible for assisting tribes with economic development and employment programs. In this position he supervised Indian business enterprise development, credit and finance, job placement and training, and road construction programs. He also oversaw the operation of the Indian Technical Assistance Center in Lakewood, Colorado, which administered the Indian Action Program—a project offering vocational training in many skilled trades to unemployed Indians between 18 and 35. Ridley continued to direct the Office of Tribal Resources Development after President Ronald Reagan took office in 1981. Subsequently he served as special assistant to the deputy assistant secretary of the Interior on Indian Affairs in the area of economic development for Indian tribal governments; and later as a special liaison officer for Indian and tribal affairs between the Bureau of Land Management and the Bureau of Indian Affairs.

Jack Ridley died at his home in Burke, Virginia, on February 28, 1988, of liver and kidney disease.

Further Reading

Ridley, J. R. "A Plan for National Unity of Native Americans." *Journal of American Indian Education* 10, no. 1 (1970): 16–19. ERIC #: EJ028742.

Robertson, Robbie (Jamie Robert Kelgerman)

(1943–) *Mohawk musician*

A prominent musician best known as the lead guitarist in the legendary rock group The Band, Robbie Robertson was born Jamie Robert Kelgerman on July 5, 1943, in Toronto, Canada. His father was Jewish and his mother was Mohawk. He took his stepfather's surname after his mother remarried. As a youth Robertson often spent his summers visiting his mother's relatives on the Six Nations Reserve in Ontario.

In 1960, Robertson joined singer Ronnie Hawkins's backup band, the Hawks, working with Levon Helm, Rick Danko, Richard Manuel, and Garth Hudson. In 1965, Bob Dylan asked Robertson and Helm to perform with him in concert, and eventually Robertson contributed his guitar playing to Dylan's masterpiece album, *Blonde on Blonde*. In 1968, the Hawks renamed themselves The Band, releasing their classic album, *Music from Big Pink*. Their second album, *The Band*, featured a number of songs written by Robertson, including "The Night They Drove Old Dixie Down" and "Up on Cripple Creek."

After The Band broke up in 1976, Robertson went on to a successful solo career, recording *Robbie Robertson* in 1987 and *Storyville* in 1991. In 1994, he worked with an all-star band of Native American musicians, dubbed the Red Road Ensemble, on the soundtrack to the television documentary series *The Native Americans*. In 1998, he released *Contact from the Underworld of Redboy*, an album featuring a number of songs with Native American themes. Robertson has collaborated with filmmaker Martin Scorsese, the director of *The Last Waltz*, a film about The Band, on a number of his films, including writing the score for his classic movie *Raging Bull*. He continues to record and perform, and he was inducted into Canada's Walk of Fame in 2003. He has received numerous honors and in 2007 received the Lifetime Achievement Award at the National Aboriginal Achievement Awards in Canada.

Further Reading

Wilonsky, Robert. "Divide and Conquer: Robbie Robertson Throws History into the Bonfire." *The Dallas Observer*, 7 May 1998. Available online. URL: http://dallasobserver. com/1998-05-07/music/divide-and-conquer. Accessed 4 January 2010.

Robertson, Wesley Leroy (Ishtiopi, Ish-Ti-Opi, "The Ultimate") (1901–1970) *Choctaw singer*

Wesley Leroy Robertson was born in Caddo, Indian Territory (now Oklahoma), on November 6, 1901 (not 1905 as sometimes claimed), of an Indian mother (Vivian Locke) and an English father; his grandfather was a full-blooded Choctaw.

After graduating from high school in Caddo and attending the University of California for one year (1920–21), Robertson transferred to the University of Oklahoma, where he received a B.A. in 1924. He spent four years in New York City studying voice and doing some work on Broadway. He then made two trips to Europe, where he studied and made appearances in several countries. By this time had already begun using his professional name, Ish-Ti-Opi.

In the early 1930s, Robertson coached and studied with noted voice teacher Andres de Segurola in California, supporting himself by working at a millinery shop in Hollywood where he made hats for film actresses. He performed in 1932 at the Hollywood Bowl in Los Angeles with the Hollywood Bowl Symphony Orchestra at the formal opening of the Olympic Games and was heard during the 1930s on several national and international radio broadcasts. From the mid-1930s, he spent most of his time in southern California, where he did film work. The famous "victory yell of the savage bull-ape" in the Johnny Weissmuller *Tarzan* films of the 1930s is actually the dubbed-in voice of Ish-Ti-Opi.

While in England in 1934, Robertson was presented to the royal family by Lady Nancy Astor. He also met future king Edward VIII (later the duke of Windsor). By 1937, he had sung at 343 concerts in the Los Angeles area and made several tours of the Southwest. On June 11, 1939, at the invitation of President Franklin D. and Eleanor Roosevelt, he performed at their estate in Hyde Park, New York, before the king and queen of England, in a program that also included Chickasaw actress TE ATA. Mrs Roosevelt commented in her newspaper column "My Day," on June 13, 1939, that, "Ish-ti-Opi is quite a remarkable actor as well as a singer."

In May 1942, Robertson appeared before the Senate Appropriations Committee and launched an attack on the INDIAN ARTS AND CRAFTS BOARD, charging, among other things, that the board did little to help Indian artists and that its director, René d'Harnoncourt, was not qualified. Robertson was present along with other distinguished Indians, such as D'ARCY MCNICKLE, when on August, 13, 1946, President Harry S. Truman signed the act creating the INDIAN CLAIMS COMMISSION. In 1949, Robertson opened a millinery shop in New York where he sold high-fashion hats that he designed and made himself, many featuring large and colorful feathers. During the 1950s, he was a publicity agent for Universal Studios and traveled across the country to promote Westerns such as *Taza, Son of Cochise* (1954). He died in March 1970 in New York City.

Rock, Howard (1911–1976) *Inupiat publisher, painter, activist*

Born in the Inupiat village of Point Hope, Alaska, on August 10, 1911, Howard Rock was the son of Sam Weyahok Rock and Emma Keshorna Rock. He attended St. Thomas Mission School and the Office of Indian Affairs boarding school near Nome, Alaska, the White Mountain Industrial School. In 1935, he decided to move to Seattle, working on a ship to pay for

his passage. He worked in both Washington and Oregon as a craftsman, taking art classes at the University of Washington. In Oregon he apprenticed with Max Siemes, an established artist from Belgium, in exchange for working on his farm. During WORLD WAR II, Rock became a radio operator for the U.S. Army Air Corps, spending three years in North Africa. After the war, he returned to the Northwest Coast to continue his career as an artist. In 1960 he returned to Point Hope and settled there as an oil painter.

At this time, the United States had plans to use atomic weapons to blast out a harbor near the Inupiat village. The village had organized against this ill-conceived plan with a movement called Inupiat Paitot, or the People's Heritage. Rock was drafted to create a newsletter that would publicize the movement's concerns. In October 1962, with the backing of a friend, he established the *Tundra Times* in Fairbanks. After successfully stopping the Point Hope nuclear tests, the paper became an important advocate for Alaska Natives, fighting for HUNTING AND FISHING RIGHTS and opposing the Rampart Dam, which threatened to flood large areas of Athabaskan lands. The paper also played a prominent role in mobilizing Alaska Natives to protect their land claims. In 1965 in Anchorage, Rock helped to organize the first meeting of Alaska Federated Natives (AFN), an organization that helped to secure the passage of the ALASKA NATIVE LAND CLAIMS SETTLEMENT ACT. He was awarded an honorary doctorate from the University of Alaska and voted "Alaskan Man of the Year" in 1974 and "49er of the Year" in 1975. The *Tundra Times* was nominated for a Pulitzer Prize in 1975. Rock remained a tireless advocate for his people and the editor of the *Tundra Times* until his death in April 1976.

Further Reading

Daley, Patrick J., and Beverley A. James. "Voices of Subsistence in the Technocratic Wilderness: Alaskan Natives and the *Tundra Times*." In *Cultural Politics and the Mass Media: Alaska Native Voices*, edited by Patrick J. Daley and Beverly A. James, 82–138. Urbana: University of Illinois Press, 2004.

Fogarino, Shirley E. "The Tundra Times: Alaska Native Advocate, 1962–1976." M.A. thesis, University of Maryland, 1981.

Hecht, Kathryn A., and Robert M. Fox. "Leadership Programs and Alaska Native Perspectives: A Study to Promote University Awareness." University of Alaska, 1977. Identifier number ED 145992.

Morgan, Lael. *Art and Eskimo Power: The Life and Times of Alaskan Howard Rock*. Fairbanks: University of Alaska Press, 2008.

Rogers, William Penn Adair (Will Rogers) (1879–1935) *Cherokee humorist, political commentator*

Will Rogers was born on November 4, 1879, in Oologah, Indian Territory (later Oklahoma). His father, rancher Clement Vann Rogers, and his mother, Mary America (Schrimsher) Rogers, were both part Cherokee. During the Civil War, Clement Rogers had fought in the Cherokee Mounted Rifle Regiment, the last Confederate Army unit to surrender; he named his eighth and youngest child William Penn Adair Rogers after his commanding officer. After the war, the elder Rogers became one of the most prosperous Cherokee in Indian Territory, his ranch exceeding 60,000 acres. He was prominent in the affairs of the Cherokee Nation, serving on the delegation that met with the Dawes Commission in 1898 (see CURTIS ACT).

Enrolled in the Cherokee nation shortly after his birth, young Will was educated in the one-room schoolhouse in nearby Drumgoole. Rogers would later joke that unlike his classmates, who were mostly full-blooded Indians, "I had just enough white in me to make my honesty questionable." Although not a full-blood, Rogers spoke Cherokee. After one year at Drumgoole, he joined his sister May at the Harrell Institute in Muskogee, Indian Territory, a Methodist boarding school for girls that he was allowed to attend because the school's headmaster had a son with whom he could room.

His mother's death in 1890 was a deep blow. The Cherokee historian EMMET STARR, a friend of the Rogers family, ascribed Will Rogers's talent as a humorist to his mother, who at church gatherings would keep the other ladies in a constant uproar of laughter. In 1891, Rogers attended the Presbyterian Mission School in Tahlequah, Indian Territory, for one year. The next year, he was sent to Willie Halsell College in Vinita, near his hometown, where he met the Cherokee author JOHN MILTON OSKISON. Rogers made the school's honor roll in 1892 and 1893.

In 1893, Rogers attended the World's Columbian Exhibition in Chicago, also known as the Chicago World's Fair, to see Buffalo Bill's Wild West Show. Although already an accomplished roper from working on his father's ranch, at the Wild West Show he encountered famed Mexican cowboy Vincente Oropeza, who performed a dazzling array of rope tricks and inspired Rogers to learn to do the same. Rogers returned to Halsell with only roping on his mind. He developed a whole new repertoire of tricks and would eventually become the world's foremost trick roper.

In 1895, Rogers transferred to Scarritt College in Missouri, but he was not used to being in a non-Indian environment and his nonstop roping caused him to be dubbed "the Wild Indian" by other students. In a last attempt to keep him in school, his father sent him to the Kemper Military Academy in Missouri, where he spent "one year in the fourth grade and one year in the guardhouse." Not inclined to scholastic pursuits, Rogers worked on his father's ranch and on cattle drives across the West before setting off in 1901 on a trip around the world. He drove cattle in Argentina and eventually found himself breaking horses on a ranch in South Africa. There he joined Texas Jack's Wild West Show as a trick rider, but it was his unmatched roping skills that soon earned him his own slot in the show as "The Cherokee Kid."

Rogers returned from his three-year adventure, which included a stint in Australia and New Zealand as part of the Wirth Brothers Circus, broke and "ruined for life, as far as actual work was concerned." In 1904, he joined a Wild West group performing at the St. Louis World's Fair and, when they went to New York City, managed to get himself booked at Keith's Union Square Theater.

In 1908, Rogers married his longtime sweetheart Betty Blake. Three years later WILLIAM VANN ROGERS, was born. In 1912, Will Rogers opened in his first Broadway show, *The Wall Street Girl*, scoring a critical success. In 1915, he appeared in *Hands Up*, where he was spotted by Gene Buck, who booked acts for producer Florenz Ziegfeld. Buck signed Rogers to perform nightly at the *Midnight Frolic*, the most fashionable variety revue in New York City. Rogers enjoyed skewering the high and mighty who came to the show. He was happy to let the blue-blooded patrons know that *his* "ancestors didn't come over on the *Mayflower*—they met the boat." For the country's political leaders, including President Woodrow Wilson, who flocked to his show, Rogers would wryly boast that "America has the best politicians money can buy."

Before long, Rogers became not only the star of the Ziegfeld Follies but an important voice in American politics. He published two collections of his political quips, *The Cowboy Philosopher on the Peace Conference* and *The Cowboy Philosopher on Prohibition*.

Rogers left the Follies in 1919 to pursue a movie career in California. After making 12 films in two years for Goldwyn Studios, Rogers decided to produce his own pictures, a venture that nearly bankrupted him and forced his return to the Follies in 1922. That same year, he began writing a syndicated weekly column and made his first radio broadcast. In 1924, he published *Illiterate Digest* and the next year *Letters from a Self-Made Diplomat to His President*, a collection of humorously perceptive articles written while touring Europe.

Behind Rogers's folksy manner and Oklahoma drawl was a keen mind with a penetrating grasp of contemporary events and mores. Using his powerful position in radio and the press to make himself a voice for the common man, Rogers further extended his popularity and influence. He made his first talking motion picture, *They Had to See Paris*, in 1929. As the country began to spiral into the Great Depression, Rogers became the country's leading box office star, making hits such as *A Connecticut Yankee* (1931) and *State Fair* (1933) for Fox Studios.

Rogers was extremely generous, raising hundreds of thousands of dollars, either from his own pocket or by organizing benefits, for charities and for victims of disasters around the globe. He was also very proud of his Indian heritage, pointing out long before it was fashionable that "you can learn a lot from Indians." Before there was an established notion of environmentalism, for example, he noted—beginning as he often did with the disclaimer, "I hope my Cherokee blood is not making me prejudiced"—that "we are just now learning that we can rob from nature the same way as we can rob from an individual. The pioneer thought that it was nature he was living off, but it was really future generations that he was living off." This was in the early 1930s.

To those who were considering further defrauding Indian people, he issued the stern warning that "if you monkey around, I'm Cherokee too, and a few of us will get together and run you all out of the country, that's all, and take it back over again."

Through his many films, regular Sunday radio broadcasts, a weekly syndicated column, and a daily squib that was carried by most newspapers, Rogers was arguably the most recognizable and most admired figure in America. When his plane crashed near Point Barrow, Alaska, on August 15, 1935, killing him and aviation pioneer Wiley Post, the nation was stunned and united in grief.

Further Reading

Boyd, Danny M. "Enthusiasts work to Boost Interest in Will Rogers." *Journal Record* (Oklahoma City), 27 December 2001.

Petete, Timothy, and Craig S. Womack. "Will Rogers's Indian Humor." *Studies in American Indian Literatures* 19, no. 2 (2007): 83–103.

Rogers, Will. *The Autobiography of Will Rogers*. New York: Lancer Books, 1949.

———. *The Papers of Will Rogers, Wild West and Vaudeville. Volume I, November 1879–April 1904*, edited by Arthur Frank Wertheim and Barbara Bair. Norman: University of Oklahoma Press, 2006.

Rogers, William Vann (Will Rogers, Jr.) (1911–1993)

Cherokee publisher, journalist, member of Congress

Born on October 20, 1911, in New York City, William Vann Rogers was the son of the famed Cherokee humorist and was usually known as Will Rogers, Jr. He moved to Beverly Hills, California, in 1919, when his father began making films in Hollywood and attended school there. He received a B.A. from Stanford University in 1935. After graduation, Rogers worked for the newspaper *Beverly Hills Citizen* for 12 years, rising to the position of publisher. During this time, he successfully ran for Congress, representing California's 16th District from 1942 to 1944. He left his post in Congress to serve in WORLD WAR II, winning a Bronze Star with the U.S. Army. During the war, Rogers was active in the campaign led by Jewish activist Peter Bergson to alert Congress and the American people about the Holocaust, then under way in Germany and German-occupied territories.

Rogers performed in several motion pictures, including playing his famous father (see ROGERS, WILLIAM PENN ADAIR) in *The Will Rogers Story* in 1951. Active in Indian affairs, he was an early supporter of the NATIONAL CONGRESS OF AMERICAN INDIANS (NCAI) and founded ARROW in 1949 with ROBERT LAFOLLETTE BENNETT. ARROW (American Restitution for Righting of Old Wrongs), directed by D'ARCY MCNICKLE, was originally created to help the NCAI solicit funds for the Indians of the Southwest, who were suffering terribly in the winter of 1948–49. ARROW helped to provide scholarships to Indian students and sponsored training workshops for Indians in the legal field, eventually organizing the National American Indian Court Judges Association in 1970.

When Bennett became commissioner of Indian affairs,

Will Rogers is seen in the studios of the NBC Radio Network in New York City, date unknown. *(AP/Wideworld)*

Rogers served as his special assistant from 1967 to 1969. During the 1960s, Rogers also worked with the Alaskan Federation of Natives in their struggle for HUNTING AND FISHING RIGHTS and for title to their lands. Rogers worked with ARROW on educational projects for Indian students up to the end of his life. In his later years, Rogers moved to Tubac, Arizona. In 1991, he suffered a series of strokes, and the next year, a hip implant operation left him in great pain. To end his suffering, he drove into the Arizona desert near Tubac on July 9, 1993, where he committed suicide.

Further Reading

Philp, Kenneth R. *Termination Revisited: American Indians on the Trail to Self-Determination, 1933–1953*. Lincoln: University of Nebraska Press, 2002.

Romero, Juan de Jesus (Deer Bird) (1874–1978)

Taos Pueblo leader, activist

Born in 1874 in Taos, New Mexico, Juan de Jesus Romero was given the Taos name Deer Bird. Trained to become a spiritual leader, Romero inherited the position of cacique, or headman, of the Taos Pueblo upon the death of his grandfather. Only the cacique, responsible for the spiritual life of Taos, fully knows the rituals and traditions of the Pueblo.

According to their spiritual history, the Taos people emerged at the beginning of time from their sacred BLUE LAKE. Blue Lake was seized from the Pueblo by the United

States in 1906 to make the Carson National Forest, a move the Pueblo at first accepted in the hope that the lake would be protected from development. In 1916, when the supervisor of the forest began to allow non-Indians to use the sacred lake and opened the surrounding area to ranching and logging, Romero began to take action for the lake's return. Along with the town governor and councilman Seferino Martinez and secretary Paul Bernal, Romero waged a half-century effort to regain the sacred lake.

As the spiritual leader of Taos, Romero also fought Indian Commissioner CHARLES HENRY BURKE's attempts to stop Taos ceremonies during the 1920s (see DANCE ORDERS). Over the years, he enlisted the aid of powerful political allies, including JOHN COLLIER, OLIVER LA FARGE, Robert F. Kennedy, Ted Kennedy, and Senator Fred Harris, the husband of LaDONNA HARRIS, and in 1970 Romero met with President Richard Nixon to personally plead the case for the Pueblo. Shortly thereafter, Nixon gave his support to the restoration effort, and the lake was returned to the Taos Pueblo in 1971. Romero died in Taos at the age of 103 on July 30, 1978. He was succeeded as cacique by Juan Concha.

Further Reading

"Taos Tribe Leader, in West, at Age 103; Juan de Jesús Romero, a Spiritual Head of New Mexico Indians Responsible for Spiritual Life." *New York Times*, 31 July 1978.

Rose, Wendy (Bronwen Elizabeth Edwards)

(1948–   ) *Hopi-Miwok poet, artist, anthropologist*
Wendy Rose was born Bronwen Elizabeth Edwards in Oakland, California, on May 7, 1948. She had a difficult, lonely childhood. As a teenager in the late 1960s, she dropped out of high school and joined the counterculture of the Bay Area. Under the name Wendy Rose, she published her first book of poetry, *Hopi Roadrunner Dancing*, in 1973, and her second, *Long Division: A Tribal History*, in 1976. That same year, she earned a B.A. at the University of California, Berkeley.

A prolific writer, Rose published *Academic Squaw: Report to the World from the Ivory Tower* in 1977 and *Wendy Rose* in 1978. Also in 1978, she received an M.A. in anthropology from Berkeley and published a history, *Aboriginal Tattooing in California*. The next year, she released a collection of poems, *Builder Kachina: A Home-Going Cycle*. In 1980, *Lost Copper*, another book of poetry, was nominated for the Pulitzer Prize. Other collections include *What Happened When the Hopi Hit New York* (1981), *The Halfbreed Chronicles* (1985), *Going to War with My Relations* (1993), and *Itch Like Crazy* (2002). Rose has also contributed to a number of anthologies, sometimes under the pseudonym Chiron Khanshendel. In 1994, a major retrospective of her work, *Bone Dance: New and Selected Poems 1965–1993*, was released by the University of Arizona Press.

From 1979 to 1983, Rose taught at Berkeley in both the ethnic studies and Native American studies departments. In 1983, she taught at Fresno State University for a year. Since 1984, she has been the coordinator of the American Indian Studies Program at Fresno City College. Known for a biting political style that, in the words of N. SCOTT MOMADAY, "supersedes political hostility and transforms it into literature," Rose has also received critical acclaim for her work as an illustrator of books and journals.

Further Reading

Saucerman, James R. "Wendy Rose: Searching through Shards, Creating Life." *Wicazo-sa Review* 5 (Fall 1989): 26–29.

Wiget, Andrew. "Blue Stones, Bones and Troubled Silver: The Poetic Craft of Wendy Rose." *Studies in American Indian Literatures* 2, no. 5 (Summer 1993): 29–33.

Ross, Mary Golda (1908–2008) *Cherokee aerospace engineer*

Born in Oklahoma on August 1, 1908, Mary Golda Ross was a great-great-granddaughter of Cherokee principal chief John Ross (d. 1866). In high school, she enjoyed mathematics, chemistry, and physics and was the only girl in her mathematics class. She graduated at age 16.

After graduating from Northeastern State Teachers College (later Northeastern State University), Tahlequah, Oklahoma, in 1928, Ross taught mathematics and science in a public school. In 1936, she moved to Washington, D.C., to work in the BUREAU OF INDIAN AFFAIRS (BIA) as a statistical clerk, after which she went to Santa Fe, New Mexico, where she worked as a girls' adviser in a school for Pueblo and Navajo children.

Ross went on to study mathematics at Colorado State Teachers College (now the University of Colorado at Greeley), where she received an M.A. in 1938. In 1942, she was hired by Lockheed Aviation as a consulting mathematician to work on differential equations of motion for fighter and transport planes. Advanced studies in aeronautical and mechanical engineering at the University of California, Los Angeles, sponsored by Lockheed, led to a professional engineering license. Ross went on to become the first woman engineer to work at Lockheed, and in 1954 she was one of the first 40 employees chosen for their new Missile System Division, where she conducted research on ballistic missile and other defense systems, including submarine-launched vehicles.

In 1958, Ross studied satellite orbits and worked on the Agena series of rockets that later launched the Apollo moon program. She was one of the chief designers of the Polaris reentry vehicle, helped develop engineering systems for manned space flights, and she was recognized as a specialist in the effect of underwater explosions. Shortly before her retirement in 1973, she conducted research toward the planning of space probes to study Venus and Mars. Following her retirement, Ross became active as a speaker on engineering to high school and college audiences, especially young women and Native American students.

Ross joined the Los Angeles chapter of the Society of Women Engineers in 1952, later being named a fellow and life member. In 1961, she received the Woman of Distinction award from the *San Francisco Examiner*. She was also honored by the AMERICAN INDIAN SCIENCE AND ENGINEERING SOCIETY and the COUNCIL OF ENERGY RESOURCE TRIBES. She was inducted into the Silicon Valley Engineering Hall of Fame in 1992, won the Trailblazer Award for Honored Alumni from the University of Northern Colorado at Greeley in 1993, and was honored in 1994 as the Distinguished Alumnus at Northeastern State University. Mary Ross died on April 29, 2008, in Los Altos, California.

Ryan, Will Carson, Jr. (1885–1968) *federal director of Indian education*

Will Carson Ryan, Jr., was born on March 4, 1885, in New York City, the son of Will C. and Sarah Hobby Ryan. After receiving a B.A. summa cum laude from Harvard in 1907, he did graduate work at Columbia University (1907–11) and received his Ph.D. from George Washington University in 1918. He taught French and German for a year in a high school in Nutley, New Jersey (1908–09) and German at the University of Wisconsin (1911–12).

After working as a vocational education specialist with the U.S. Bureau of Education from 1912 to 1920, Ryan spent a year as educational editor of the *New York Evening Post*. He was, successively, secretary and president of the National Vocational Guidance Association and a member of the National Education Association's editorial council. During the 1920s, he became known for his research on local educational systems and private and mission schools in the United States, and for his work with educational surveys in Saskatchewan, Puerto Rico, and the Virgin Islands. From 1921 through 1930, Ryan was professor of education and head of the department at Swarthmore College. He was also the delegate from the Progressive Education Association to the World Conference on Education held in 1927 at Locarno, Switzerland.

Ryan was the education specialist on the Meriam Commission (1926–28), set up by Secretary of the Interior Hubert Work to investigate conditions on American Indian reservation and recommend reforms. While conducting research, Ryan visited many Indian Service schools as well as public and mission schools for Indian children. In his section of the MERIAM REPORT, Ryan recommended that education for all age levels, closely tied to the community through day schools,

should be the primary function of the Indian Service (later the BUREAU OF INDIAN AFFAIRS). According to Ryan, the boarding schools should be reformed, with more Indian culture included in the curriculum.

In 1929 and 1930, Ryan served on President Herbert Hoover's committee on child welfare and advisory committee on education. In 1931, he was appointed director of education in the Indian Service under Commissioner CHARLES RHOADS, after passing highest in an open competition examination for the post held by the U.S. Civil Service Commission. Already an educator of international reputation, Ryan appointed an unusually capable staff to direct vocational education, vocational guidance and placement, practical work in home economics, and elementary education.

By the end of 1932, Ryan had changed the entire emphasis of Indian education. He had put into operation an effective program based on local community schools, intended to supersede the obsolete boarding school system. At least 8,000 more Indian children were in school than in 1929, with 2,000 fewer in boarding schools. The number of Indian children in public schools had been greatly increased, saving federal money. Thanks to Ryan's effective plan for cooperation between the Indian Office and state school boards, there were 10,000 more Indian children in public schools than in 1930. Meanwhile, the boarding schools had been greatly improved, especially in quality and quantity of food; educational programs were substituted for forced labor; the standards for the teaching staff were raised; and more attention was given to Native American cultures, particularly as represented in the arts and crafts.

Indian education as developed by Ryan well illustrates how the INDIAN NEW DEAL under Rhoads and JOSEPH HENRY SCATTERGOOD was already on the path it was to take under JOHN COLLIER. Ryan's policy of shifting Indian education from federal boarding schools to state and local public schools was the prototype for the JOHNSON-O'MALLEY ACT, passed in 1934 under Collier. Will Carson Ryan, Jr., died in Alexandria, Virginia, on May 28, 1968.

Further Reading
Szasz, Margaret Connell. *Education and the American Indian: The Road to Self-Determination Since 1928.* 3rd. ed. Albuquerque: University of New Mexico Press, 1999.

S

Sainte-Marie, Buffy (Beverly Sainte-Marie)

(1941–　) *Cree composer, singer, performer, activist*

Beverly "Buffy" Sainte-Marie was born on February 20, 1941, on the Cree Piapot Reserve in Craven, Saskatchewan. Orphaned at only five months of age, she was adopted by Albert C. Sainte-Marie and Winnifred Kendrick Sainte-Marie, who was part Micmac, and raised in Massachusetts by her adoptive parents, who nicknamed her Buffy. By age four, she had taught herself to play the piano and had begun writing poetry. She started to play guitar and compose when her father gave her a guitar for her 16th birthday, teaching herself to play the instrument in a unique style that would become one of her trademarks. Sainte-Marie's musicianship was a reflection of her curiosity about sound. She strung and tuned her guitar in 32 different ways and played a mouth bow, a Native instrument that relies on harmonics and a keen ear.

In 1959, Sainte-Marie enrolled in the University of Massachusetts, graduating with honors in 1963 with a B.A. in philosophy. During her college years, she played in local clubs and coffeehouses, and after graduating she moved to Greenwich Village in New York City, where she became part of the growing folk music scene. Her debut at the Gaslight Café on August 17, 1963, prompted *New York Times* music critic Robert Sheldon to label Sainte-Marie "one of the promising new talents on the folk scene." However, a serious bout with bronchial pneumonia left her almost without a voice. Later, professional voice lessons and vocal exercises helped preserve her singing ability, but during the time of her illness she became addicted to codeine, an experience recounted in her song "Cod'ine."

After attracting a following at such legendary Village clubs as the Bitter End and Folk City, Sainte-Marie was spotted by Maynard Solomon, founder of folk music label Vanguard Records, at a Town Hall performance. Solomon signed her, and her first album, *It's My Way!*, was released in 1964.

The album showed her concern for Indian issues and included her song "Now That the Buffalo Is Gone," regarded as the first modern Indian protest song. *It's My Way!* also featured the antiwar song "Universal Soldier," which was covered by Scottish singer Donovan and became one of the anthems of the Vietnam War protest movements; and "Cod'ine," one of the few 1960s songs to address the dangers of drugs; it was covered by California rock bands Quicksilver Messenger Service and the Charlatans. Accompanied only by her guitar, Sainte-Marie incorporated a singing style that used traditional Indian sounds while mixing in a rich vibrato. With her versatile alto voice, she could come across as sultry, angry, happy, humorous, and much more, but her outspoken lyrics and support for antiwar and Indian issues led to her being blacklisted by the administration of President Lyndon B. Johnson, which pressured radio stations to stop playing her songs.

Sainte-Marie's next album, *Many a Mile* (1965), included her ballad "Until It's Time for You to Go," covered by numerous pop singers, including Elvis Presley. That same year, Sainte-Marie played at Carnegie Hall. Using talented backup musicians Bruce Langhorne, Eric Weissberg, Felix Pappalardi, and Patrick Sky (a Cree who had introduced Sainte-Marie to the mouth bow), her next album, *Little Wheel Spin and Spin* (1966), was notable for the song "My Country 'Tis of Thy People You're Dying," a biting indictment of the United States' mistreatment of Indian people. In 1968, the album *I'm Gonna Be a Country Girl Again* found her moving from folk to a Nashville country sound.

Not content to stand still, Sainte-Marie continued to evolve with her album *Illuminations* (1969), a mystical psychedelic-folk tour de force that was far ahead of its time. In 1970, her mouth bow was featured on the soundtrack of the cult movie *Performance*, starring Mick Jagger. While working on *Performance* she collaborated with Ry Cooder and Crazy Horse (Neil Young's backup band), who would accompany

Buffy Sainte-Marie listens as John Trudell defends the American Indian Movement's (AIM) takeover of the Fairchild Instrument Corporation's electronic plant on the Navajo Reservation in 1975. *(AP/Wideworld)*

Sainte-Marie on her next album, *She Used to Wanna Be a Ballerina* (1971). The bluesy-rock record was coproduced and arranged by her future husband, legendary musician-producer Jack Nitzsche.

During the late 1960s, Sainte-Marie lived on and off in Hawaii, where she married surfing instructor Dewain Kamaikalani Bugbee. In 1972, she and Bugbee divorced; she also scored her only top 40 hit, "Mister Can't You See," from her album *Moonshot*. She left Vanguard and moved to MCA in 1974, releasing *Buffy*, a mainstream rock record. The next year, she married actor Sheldon Peters Wolfchild, with whom she had one son, Dakota Starblanket (Cody). After the release of *Sweet America* in 1976, Sainte-Marie withdrew from the music world to concentrate on acting.

During the 1960s, Sainte-Marie had appeared on several television shows. For one episode of *The Virginian*, she had insisted that all the Indian roles be played by Indians, a stipulation that she enforced in all her subsequent television appearances. In the late 1970s, she became a regular on the children's show *Sesame Street*, on which her son Cody also appeared, teaching children racial tolerance. In 1995, she appeared in the Turner miniseries *The Broken Chain*.

In 1982, she married Jack Nitzsche and returned to composing. The next year, she and Nitzsche won the Academy Award for cowriting the number-one hit, "Up Where We Belong," sung by Joe Cocker and Jennifer Warnes in the film *An Officer and a Gentleman*. Sainte-Marie then wrote the scores for two films, the cult classic *Harold of Orange* (1986), written by Chippewa author GERALD VIZENOR and starring Oneida-Cree comedian CHARLIE HILL, and *Where the Spirit Lives* (1989).

In 1992, after a lapse of 16 years, Sainte-Marie returned to the recording studio to make the critically acclaimed album *Coincidences and Likely Stories*. A hard-hitting condemnation of mindless polluters, dirty politics, and corporate greed, it featured programmed drums and keyboards created at her home recording studio in Hawaii. Her next album, *Up Where We Belong* (1996), was a collection of rerecordings of fan favorites. In 2009, Sainte-Marie released another politically charged album, *Running for the Drum*, featuring the rock songs "No No Keshagesh" and "Cho Cho Fire."

Always active in Indian issues, Sainte-Marie helped organize a benefit concert for the occupiers of ALCATRAZ ISLAND in 1970 and participated in issues such as BIG MOUNTAIN and the case of LEONARD PELTIER. Her song "Starwalker," released in 1976, became one of the anthems of the AMERICAN INDIAN MOVEMENT (AIM). She has also been active in Indian education, organizing benefits for many "freedom schools" (see EDUCATIONAL POLICY, AMERICAN INDIANS AND) and creating the Nihewan Foundation, which offers scholarships to Indian students in law school. She also founded the Native North American Women's Association, which sponsors theater and arts as well as education projects. A tireless worker, she wrote articles for the influential newspaper *Akwesasne Notes* during the 1980s; edited *The Native Voice*, a magazine from Vancouver, British Columbia; and wrote a children's book in 1986 entitled *Nokomis and the Magic Hat*. In 1993, Sainte-Marie worked with the United Nations to proclaim the International Year of Indigenous Peoples. She collaborated with Lakehead University in Canada to produce the *Aboriginal Innovations in Arts, Sciences, and Technology Handbook*, published in 2002.

In the 1990s, Sainte-Marie began to experiment with visual art—by then she had earned a Ph.D. in fine arts from the University of Massachusetts—using a computer to manipulate 19th-century photographs of Indians. In 1996, her art was featured in a one-woman exhibit at the Institute of American Indian Arts Museum in Santa Fe. She remains best known, however, for her musical compositions and her uncompromising defense of Indian peoples and cultures. In 1995, the Canadian music industry inducted this uniquely gifted composer and artist into their Juno Hall of Fame.

Sainte-Marie was featured in 1997 in the Canadian TV special *Buffy Sainte-Marie: Up Where We Belong*, which won a Gemini Award. In 1999, she received a star on Canada's Walk of Fame in Toronto. She was awarded an honorary doctorate of letters from Lakehead University in 2000 and was inducted into the Canadian Country Music Hall of Fame in 2009.

Further Listening
Sainte-Marie, Buffy. *Illuminations*. Vanguard Records, 1969.
———. *It's My Way!* Vanguard Records, 1964.
———. *Little Wheel Spin and Spin*. Vanguard Records, 1966.
———. *Many a Mile*. Vanguard Records, 1965.
———. *She Used to Wanna Be a Ballerina*. Vanguard Records, 1971.
Stonechild, Blair. *Buffy Sainte-Marie: It's My Way*. Markham, Ontario: Fitzhenny and Whiteside, 2011.

Sampson, Will (Kvs-Kvna, "Left-Handed") (1933–1987) *Creek actor, painter*
Born on September 27, 1933, to Mabel Lewis Hill and William "Wiley" Sampson, Will Sampson was raised on the Creek Nation Reservation in Okmulgee, Oklahoma. Given the Muscogee name Kvs-Kvna (Left-Handed), he sold his first painting when he was only three. "Sonny" Sampson, as he was known by his friends and family in Okmulgee, attended the Haskell Institute in Lawrence, Kansas, and later the Los Angeles Art Center School. After briefly serving in the U.S. Navy, he worked variously as a construction worker, rodeo cowboy, lumberjack, and oil-field worker. Above all, however, he was a passionate painter, and by 1968 he had become well enough known to be listed in *American Indian Painters: A Biographical Dictionary*.

In 1974, while Sampson was directing an art exhibition in Yakima, Washington, a rodeo friend told him that producer Michael Douglas was looking for a "big Indian" to play next to Jack Nicholson in his film version of the Ken Kesey novel *One Flew Over the Cuckoo's Nest*. Sampson, at six feet seven, fit the bill. His portrayal of Chief Bromden, the alienated Indian who pretends to be mute to escape from the inhuman treatment of an insane asylum, won him critical acclaim and a nomination for an Academy Award.

His career as an actor assured, Sampson proceeded to play in a number of films, including *The Outlaw Josie Wales* (1976), *The White Buffalo* (1977), *Orca* (1977), and *Fish Hawk* (1979), in which he played the lead role. He had many roles in television, including playing Chief Harlon Two Leaf in the series *Vega$*. Sampson's paintings, mostly Western scenes and landscapes, also became well known and were exhibited at the Smithsonian Institution and the Library of Congress.

In his last years, Sampson suffered from scleroderma—a degenerative fungal infection characterized by swelling of the skin and internal organs. He died of kidney failure on June 23, 1987, in Houston, Texas, less than two months after undergoing a heart and lung transplant.

See FILM, AMERICAN INDIANS AND.

Further Reading
Greb, Jacqueline K. "Will the Real Indians Please Stand Up?" In *Back in the Saddle: Essays on Western Film and Television Actors*, edited by Gary A. Yoggy, 129–144. New York: McFarland & Company, 1998.
Reese, Joel. "Flashback: Look-Alike Son Takes on Dad's Role." *Daily Herald* (Arlington Heights, Ill.), sec. Suburban Living, May 2000.
Taillon, Joan. "Documentary Ensures Actor Is Remembered." *Wind Speaker* 22, no. 6 (2004): 30–31.

Sanderville, Richard (Chief Bull) (1867–1951) *Blackfeet interpreter, sign talker*
Richard Sanderville was born in April 1867, near the mouth of the Marias River in what is now the state of Montana. His father, Isidore Sandoval, was the official interpreter at the Badger Creek Agency in Montana; his grandfather Isidore Leroy Sandoval had also been an interpreter. His mother was Margaret Red Bird Tail. As a child, Sanderville was strongly influenced by his mother's brother Red Paint, who instructed him in the history and traditions of the Blackfeet tribe. Sanderville first attended an off-reservation Catholic mission school in St. Ignatius, Montana, and later a government school on his own reservation. One of the first Blackfeet Indians to attend Carlisle Indian School, he participated in the outing program between 1890 and 1892 (see PRATT, RICHARD HENRY).

Beginning in 1895, Sanderville was employed at the Blackfeet agency as an interpreter, carpenter, and assistant farmer, helping the agent to encourage agriculture. He was one of the organizers of the Piegan Farming and Livestock Association. He was also an elected member of the tribal council, representing on occasion, after the tribal reorganization in 1934 (see

INDIAN REORGANIZATION ACT), the southern community of Heart Butte.

Sanderville became famous as an expert in Indian sign language after he met General Hugh L. Scott, who visited the Badger Creek Agency during the 1920s. Sanderville helped Scott bring together sign talkers from 14 tribes for the Indian Sign Language Council meeting of 1930 at Browning, Montana. After Scott's death, the Smithsonian invited Sanderville to Washington in 1934 to finish Scott's *Dictionary of the Indian Sign Language*. The dictionary, which took the form of a silent film recording sign language gestures, is probably the film by Scott that is now in the National Archives. Another, shorter film in the same location shows Sanderville himself using hand gestures to tell a love story, describe methods of buffalo hunting on foot and horseback, and formally transfer a painted tipi. In the same year, when President Franklin D. Roosevelt visited Glacier National Park, it was Sanderville who performed the ceremony inducting him into the Blackfeet tribe.

The Museum of the Plains Indian, originally requested by the National Park Service for Glacier National Park, was moved to the town of Browning, on the Blackfeet Reservation, thanks to Sanderville's influence. Although he himself was first a Catholic and later a Methodist, he respected indigenous religious traditions and was one of the leaders who succeeded in getting government permission to revive the Blackfeet Sun Dance in 1906. He also organized groups of performers, one of which he led at the National Folk Festival in Constitution Hall in Washington, D.C., and another that was performed for tourists staying at the large hotel at Glacier during the early 1940s.

Sanderville belonged to the mixed-blood faction that followed Three Suns in his rivalry for the Blackfeet chieftainship with JAMES WHITE CALF. After some of the full-blood performers persuaded the hotel management not to rehire Sanderville because he was a mixed-blood, he went on to teach Indian crafts at the summer school of the Culver Military Academy in Culver, Indiana. He died in the Indian Hospital on the Blackfeet Reservation on February 25, 1951. The author JAMES WELCH is his grandnephew.

Further Reading
Johnson, Bryan R. *The Blackfeet: An Annotated Bibliography.* New York: Garland Publishing, 1988.

Scattergood, Joseph Henry (1877–1953) *assistant commissioner of Indian affairs*

Joseph Henry Scattergood was born on January 26, 1877, in Philadelphia, the son of Thomas and Sarah Garrett Scattergood. On his father's side, he was descended from an old English Quaker family that came to America in 1676. His father was the president of a company that manufactured tanners' and textile dyes and extracts, and throughout his career, the younger Scattergood would maintain ties with the dyestuffs industry. After attending private schools in Philadelphia, he majored in mathematics at Haverford College, Pennsylvania, graduating with a B.A. in 1896. He then spent a year at Harvard University (1896–97), where he achieved fame as a cricketer.

During and after WORLD WAR I, Scattergood worked in France, Germany, Poland, and Russia with the reconstruction unit of the American Friends Service Committee (AFSC) and the American Red Cross. Particularly interested in postwar reconstruction in Europe, he spoke to hundreds of chambers of commerce, Rotary Clubs, and other civic organizations across the country to popularize the Dawes Plan (an attempt to collect war reparations from Germany).

Scattergood was long interested in sociological and educational issues and also involved in the financial or executive functions of a number of philanthropic and educational organizations. He served as treasurer of both Haverford College and Bryn Mawr College, the Pennsylvania Working Home for Blind Men, and the Christiansburg Industrial Institute. For a time he was vice principal at the Hampton Institute in Virginia and was a trustee and chairman of the board of that institution.

Like his cousin, museum director and Indian rights advocate HAROLD SELLERS COLTON, Scattergood was an active member of the INDIAN RIGHTS ASSOCIATION. In 1929, he was appointed by President Herbert Hoover, a fellow Quaker, to serve as assistant commissioner of Indian Affairs alongside his friend and colleague CHARLES JAMES RHOADS. The two were chosen on the heels of the MERIAM REPORT, a scathing indictment of federal Indian policy issued in 1928, and tried to implement some of the report's proposals. They sought to overhaul the Indian Office, as the BUREAU OF INDIAN AFFAIRS was known at the time, an effort dubbed the INDIAN NEW DEAL.

In order to improve the dismal state of Indian schools, they appointed WILL CARSON RYAN, an educator with impeccable credentials, as director of education. They tried to end the policy of ALLOTMENT, which had severely diminished the Indian land base, and to move away from the strict ASSIMILATION programs that sought to stamp out Indian culture. They lobbied Congress to end the practice of billing tribes for irrigation and other projects that were often created for the benefit of non-Indians.

By and large their ambitious plans were unsuccessful, in part because of opposition from the chairman of the Interior Subcommittee of the House Appropriations Committee, Michigan congressman Louis Cramton, a diehard assimilationist. It would be up to the incoming administration, led by JOHN COLLIER, to implement the reforms begun by Rhoads and Scattergood.

After leaving office in April 1933, Scattergood worked in insurance and banking. Joseph Henry Scattergood died in Philadelphia on June 15, 1953.

Further Reading
Philp, Kenneth R. *John Collier's Crusade for Indian Reform, 1920–1954*, 92–112. Tucson: University of Arizona Press, 1977.

Schanandoah, Chapman (1870–1953) *Oneida naval engineer, inventor, political leader*

Born on May 16, 1870, at Oneida, New York, Chapman Schanandoah was a direct descendant of Skenandoa (ca. 1706–1816), a famous Oneida chief who sent wagonloads of grain to George Washington's starving troops at Valley Forge. His father was Abram Schanandoah (also spelled Sconondoa) and his mother, Mary Honyoust, also from a distinguished Oneida family, was a member of the Wolf Clan. His brother, Albert Schanandoah (1867–1934) would become an Oneida chief. Chapman Schanandoah entered the Hampton Institute in Virginia in 1888, but left after a year. He reentered Hampton in 1892 and graduated in 1894.

Schanandoah enlisted in the U.S. Navy in 1897 and served in the Spanish-American War. The first American Indian mechanic in the U.S. Navy, Schanandoah saw action on the gunboat USS *Petrel*. In the Philippines, he was one of seven volunteers who poled a small boat across Manila Bay in a daring mission to destroy the remnants of the Spanish fleet damaged in the epic Battle of Manila Bay, fought the day before on May 1, 1898. By laying explosives on the burning hulks, the seven men systematically destroyed the warships *Don Juan de Austria, Isla de Cuba, Isla de Luzon, Marquis del Duero,* and *Velasco.* They captured the transport *Manila,* later converted into an American gunboat. When several Spanish torpedo boats captured at Santiago de Cuba in 1898 were brought to the Brooklyn Navy Yard, Schanandoah captained one of them.

After the war Schanandoah served on the battleship USS *New York*. In 1899, on a trip with the *New York* to the Caribbean, he was accused of public drunkenness while on shore leave in St. Thomas in the Virgin Islands and was sentenced to 15 days in a military brig. Schanandoah's military career was saved only by the intervention of political cartoonist Joseph (Uda) Keppler, Jr., a longtime Indian activist who was an honorary chief of the Seneca.

In 1900, Schanandoah joined the cruiser USS *Atlanta* and in 1901 was promoted to chief machinist's mate. In 1903, he became the machinist on the newly recommissioned cruiser USS *Raleigh*. He also served on board the gunboat USS *Marietta*. In 1907 and 1908, with the navy's "Great White Fleet," Schanandoah, it is believed, became the first Indian to circumnavigate the globe. He was discharged from the U.S. Navy in 1912. After leaving the service, Schanandoah worked at the Frankford Naval Arsenal in Philadelphia. The explosion of the battleship USS *Maine* in Havana harbor in 1898 had dramatized the danger of carrying tons of powder on a warship, and he set out to invent a safer explosive. The result was "Shenandite," an explosive so safe it could be shipped through the mail. It was made of two components, each harmless and nonflammable in itself. When these were combined, however, the result was twice as powerful as dynamite. He also held patents on a megaphone and a compressor.

When the United States entered WORLD WAR I in 1917, Schanandoah worked to clarify the legal status of Indians, most of whom were not citizens, under the selective service draft and labor enrollment. He pointed out that the Onondaga, as a sovereign nation, had already declared war on Germany, the first Indian nation to do so, and that most Onondaga men were either doing war work or were volunteers in the Canadian or U.S. armed services, many at the front. "We are doing our bit as we see it . . . but we must protect our status as Indians," he said. Through his efforts, a settlement was reached whereby 130 Onondaga Indians volunteered to register and submit to enrollment but reserved the right to claim exemption as Indians.

By 1919, Schanandoah was a chief of the Oneida and represented them in meetings with New York State officials. He also worked as a machinist for General Electric in Schenectady, New York. He was married to Bertha Crouse, an Onondaga, and they lived on the Onondaga Reservation. He was active in 4-H Club work at Onondaga; was a leader in the Iroquois Temperance League; and belonged to the Six Nations Association, serving as its president in 1935–36. He died at Syracuse, New York, on February 22, 1953, survived by four sons, a daughter, and nine grandchildren.

Scholder, Fritz (1937–2005) *Luiseño painter, sculptor*

Fritz Scholder was born on October 6, 1937, in Breckenridge, Minnesota, to Fritz William Scholder IV and Ella Mae Haney. Scholder's maternal grandmother was Luiseño, a Shoshonean tribe of California, although Scholder, predominantly of German, English, and French extraction, was raised as a white and described himself as a "non-Indian Indian." His father worked for the BUREAU OF INDIAN AFFAIRS (BIA) as an Indian school administrator. Scholder began to draw as a child growing up in Wahpeton, North Dakota, and in Shawano and Ashland, Wisconsin. In 1950, the family moved to Pierre, South Dakota, where he studied art in high school under Yankton Nakota painter OSCAR HOWE, who encouraged him to make art his career. Scholder attended Wisconsin State University before graduating from Sacramento State College in 1960. In 1964, he received a master of fine arts degree from the University of Arizona. After graduation he taught advanced painting and art history at the newly opened Institute of American Indian Arts in Santa Fe, New Mexico.

Scholder experimented with different themes, beginning with his "New Mexico" series in 1964, followed by the "Butterfly" series in 1966. For Scholder, color was the primary element, with a strong image and subject matter following in importance, and for this reason he is often referred to as a "colorist." In 1967, he began his "Indian" series of portraits, combining surrealism with the pop art popular at the time. The new works broke out of the traditional Santa Fe or Studio style popularized by PABLITA VELARDE (Santa Clara Pueblo) and HARRISON BEGAY (Navajo) and championed by DOROTHY DUNN at the old Santa Fe Indian School. They are really not about Indians, but more of an ironic commentary on the whole genre of "Indian" painting. Scholder continued to paint the "Indian" series until 1980, although he also began working in bronze and mixed media during this time. He left the Indian themes for works on vampires (1972) and dreams (1981), though he returned to Indian subjects in 1994 with his "Red" series.

Among the most distinguished contemporary American painters, Scholder profoundly influenced a new generation of Indian artists, and his "Indian" series effectively inaugurated the era of modern Indian painting. His lithographs made him, along with R. C. GORMAN, one of the best-known Indian artists in the country, with works held in important collections such as the Museum of Modern Art in New York City and the National Museum of American Art, Smithsonian Institution in Washington, D.C. Scholder was the subject of a PBS documentary *Painting the Paradox* (1997). He had a retrospective at the Tucson Museum of Art in 1981, another at the Phoenix Art Museum in 1997, and a major exhibition of paintings and sculpture at the Tweed Museum of Art, University of Minnesota, Duluth, in 2001.

For many years, Fritz Scholder lived primarily in Scottsdale, Arizona. He died in Phoenix on February 10, 2005, from complications of diabetes.

Further Reading

Baldit, Catherine. "Twentieth-Century American Indian Artists: An Issue of Identity." *Journal of American Studies of Turkey* 5 (1997): 27–41.
"Fritz Scholder Tumbles to Realm of Kitsch." *Arizona Republic*, sec. E5, 20 March 1994.
Levin, Eli. *Santa Fe Bohemia: The Art Colony, 1964–1980.* Santa Fe, N.Mex.: Sunstone Press, 2006.
Scholder, Fritz. *Indian Kitsch: The Use and Misuse of Indian Images.* Phoenix, Ariz.: Northland Press, 1979.
Traugott, Joseph. "Native American Artists and the Postmodern Cultural Divide." *Art Journal* 51, no. 3 (1992): 36–43.

science, American Indians and

Not only did the rise of science have a great impact on American Indian life in the 20th century, but Indians also came to affect science, both as working scientists and as critics of the scientific establishment. Many modern scientists now recognize that traditional indigenous cultures have much wisdom, experience, and environmental expertise to contribute to contemporary research. Perhaps if any one trend can be identified in the relationship between Indians and scientists in the course of the 20th century, it is a movement from the idea of the Indian as a primitive and passive object of scientific scrutiny to the Indian as an active participant in reshaping the world of science.

Both Indian and non-Indian scientists have been inspired by Indian attitudes to nature and have explored traditional Indian medicine and other technologies such as horticulture, architecture, and boatbuilding. Indian approaches to science have influenced such fields as solar energy, ethnobiology, ethnobotany (and the related effort to preserve seeds of indigenous varieties), fish and wildlife conservation, and the restoration of degraded environments. Notable scientific studies have been initiated in these fields by organizations such as the GREAT LAKES INDIAN FISH AND WILDLIFE COMMISSION, Native Seeds/SEARCH, and the Society for Ecological Restoration. Traditional Indian forms of architecture and engineering and traditional housing are attracting the attention of physicists as well as architects, particularly those interested in environmental architecture, appropriate technology, and alternative energy sources.

Recent developments in biomedical research, medicine, and public health continue to hold promise for improving the conditions of life for indigenous communities. In other cases, modern science caused the problem in the first place. Of particular concern to Indians are the genetic effects of exposure to radiation, related to the aftereffects of atomic testing on Western Shoshone lands; of uranium mining on Pueblo and Navajo reservations; and of nuclear power plants on the Yakama Reservation (see NUCLEAR INDUSTRY, AMERICAN INDIANS AND THE). Scientists have begun to investigate the medical effects of the abandonment of traditional foodways, with special reference to nutrition and the possible prevention of diseases, such as adult-onset diabetes, now prevalent in Indian populations (see HEALTH, AMERICAN INDIAN). Medical researchers are taking a tremendous interest in exploring the potential of traditional pharmaceuticals. Other scientific fields much indebted to Indians include plant genetics, studies of genetic diversity and biodiversity, resource management, traditional wildlife management, traditional forestry, ecological restoration, animal husbandry (especially the care of sheep, bison, and reindeer), zoology, ecology, and indigenous agriculture.

The Indian critique of "value-free science" has focused in particular on the desecration and looting of ancient Indian sacred sites in the name of archaeology, and on the problematic record of anthropology as a tool for understanding Indians. Indians campaigned successfully for the reburial of Indian remains that had been gathered by museums and universities as exhibits or objects of analysis, leading to the 1990 Native American Graves Protection and Repatriation Act, a law that was opposed by the Smithsonian (see REPATRIATION). Indians have also voiced strong objections to the Human Genome Project, with its accompanying efforts of corporations to patent and obtain commercial profits from genetic material taken from indigenous peoples.

In 1977, the AMERICAN INDIAN SCIENCE AND ENGINEERING SOCIETY (AISES) was founded by a group of Indian engineers, scientists, and educators. Its goal is to support American Indians in science and to encourage Indian students to pursue careers in science and technology.

In 1993, the Packer Foundation instituted the Tribal College Science Program to encourage American Indian students in their science education. One goal of this training was to prepare them to oversee the environmental resources of their reservations. In 1994, the tribal colleges received 11 grants of approximately $50,000 each to support science programs, renewable for up to three years.

Indians can be found in every area of science, but in many cases they seem to be drawn to fields that relate to traditional

Indian attitudes and concerns. At the start of the century, notable American Indian scientists included Oneida naval engineer CHAPMAN SCHANANDOAH and Yavapai physician CARLOS MONTEZUMA. More recent American Indians who have made contributions to science include Hopi-Laguna geneticist and biomedical specialist FRANK C. DUKEPOO, Penobscot-Passamaquoddy geographer and geophysicist CAROL METCALF GARDIPE, Cherokee agronomist LUTHER BURBANK GRASS, Chippewa entomologist and specialist in biological insect control J. E. Henry, Cherokee marine biologist MICHAEL HASTINGS HORN, Saginaw-Chippewa forestry biologist David L. Jackson, Crow geologist Anita Louise Moore-Nall, Tuscarora agronomist JANE MT. PLEASANT, Tuscarora-Seneca professor of biology Clifton Poodry, Shoshone agronomist JACK R. RIDLEY, Cherokee aerospace engineer MARY GOLDA ROSS, Navajo microbiologist O. TACHEENI SCOTT, Santa Clara Pueblo (Tewa) biologist and geneticist AGNES NARANJO STROUD-LEE, and Turtle Mountain Chippewa energy engineer JAMES WILLIAMSON.

See also ANTHROPOLOGISTS AND AMERICAN INDIANS; CAJETE, GREGORY; DELORIA, VINE, JR.

Further Reading

Broadhead, Lee-Anne, and Sean Howard. "Deepening the Debate over 'Sustainable Science': Indigenous Perspectives as a Guide on the Journey." *Sustainable Development* (2009). Available online. URL: http://www3.interscience.wiley.com/journal/122453237/abstract. Accessed 24 February 2010.

Cajete, Gregory, and Leroy Little Bear. *Native Science: Natural Laws of Interdependence*. Santa Fe, N.Mex.: Clear Light, 1999.

Hirsch, Helmut V. B., and Helen Ghiradella. "From Canyon de Chelly to the Science Longhouse at Albany: Educators Look at Contemporary Science Teaching." *Winds of Change* 8, no. 2 (1994): 38–42.

Kidwell, Clara Sue. "Native American and Contemporary Scientific Systems." In *Columbus, Confrontation, Christianity: The European-American Encounter Revisited*, edited by Timothy J. O'Keefe. Tulsa, Okla.: Forbes Mill Press, 1994.

Peat, F. David. *Blackfoot Physics: A Journey into the Native American Worldview*. Grand Rapids, Mich.: Phanes, 2002.

Pruette, Dave, and Ernest Stromberg. Review of Keith James, ed. *Science and Native Communities: Legacies of Pain, Visions of Promise*. Lincoln: University of Nebraska Press, 2001. *Great Plains Research* 13, no. 2 (2003): 342–344.

Simonelli, Richard. "Toward a Sustainable Science." *Winds of Change* 8, no. 2 (1994): 36–37.

Smith, Linda Tuhiwai. *Decolonizing Methodologies: Research and Indigenous Peoples*. London: Zed Books, 1999.

Snively, Gloria, and John Corsiglia. "Discovering Indigenous Science: Implications for Science Education." *Science Education* 85 (2001): 6–34.

Winds of Change: A Magazine for American Indians in Science and Technology (1986).

Scott, Orville Tacheeni (1944–) *Navajo (Dineh) microbiologist*

Navajo (Dineh) Orville Scott was born in Tuba City, Arizona, on May 1, 1944, to Doc and Leora Scott. His father was a medicine man. Scott received his B.A. in 1966 from Westmont College, Santa Barbara, California, struggling against isolation, poor grades, and problems with alcohol, but encouraged by his parents' support. He taught high school biology and physical education in Tuba City (1967–70) and biology at Navajo Community College (1972), before going on to graduate school at the University of Oregon, where he received an M.S. in 1974. Continuing his graduate work at Oregon, he held a Ford Foundation scholarship and a Navajo Tribal Doctoral Fellowship from 1976 to 1979, and from 1980 to 1982 he did postdoctoral research at the University of New Mexico. With the completion of his dissertation in 1981, Scott became the first American Indian to receive a doctorate in microbiology.

While still a graduate student, Scott collaborated with folklorist Barre Toelken on a paper "Poetic Retranslation and the Pretty Languages of Yellowman," published in the book *Traditional Literatures of the American Indians* (1981), edited by Karl Kroeber. A collection of Navajo stories told by a Navajo elder Yellowman, Scott helped Toelken grasp some of the complexities of the Navajo language and thus the deeper meanings associated with the stories. The paper has since been widely cited. The work with Toelken led Scott to become more aware of his own culture, and he began using his clan name Tacheeni. Scott taught biology at Fort Lewis College in Durango, Colorado (1983–84), and at Northern Arizona University in Flagstaff (1984–88), where he was also program director of the Minority Biomedical Research Support Program (1985–87). Since 1989, he has taught biology at California State University, Northridge.

Scott's research focuses on parasitic and photosynthetic bacteria. He sees his research work, however, not in the fragmentary way typically encouraged by Western science but within the universal metaphysical-cosmological perspective of his Navajo (Dineh) culture. He accepts the Gaia hypothesis of British scientist James Lovelock, who first put forth the hypothesis in 1973 to explain why the atmospheres of Mars and Venus consist almost entirely of carbon dioxide (CO_2), while that of Earth contains only a small amount of CO_2 and consists mainly of oxygen. On Earth, the original carbon dioxide was drawn out of the atmosphere and replaced by oxygen through the action of plants and has been incorporated in plants, animals, and the Earth's crust. In light of the transformation of the atmosphere by the combined work of living things, Scott suggests that the Earth may be a single living organism. The universality of chemical processes flowing through all things does not mean that life is reduced to nonlife, but rather that all things are in some sense alive. When asked whether he understands this literally or metaphorically, Scott replied, "I have the option of looking metaphorically or literally because of my dual viewpoint stemming from both cultures."

Further Information

Scott's seminar, *Mother Earth/Father Sun: Cultural Intuition and Codified Knowledge* (1998), is available on audiotape from the Institute for Science and Interdisciplinary Studies. Prescott House D-1, 893 West Street, Amherst, Massachusetts 01002-5001.

Segundo, Thomas (1920–1971) *Tohono O'odham political leader*

Born on April 13, 1920, on the Papago (Tohono O'odham) reservation in southern Arizona, Thomas Segundo soon moved off the reservation with his family, and he was educated in non-Indian schools as well as the Presbyterian Indian Training School in Tucson, Arizona. After high school, Segundo moved to California, settling in San Francisco and working in the shipyards, where he eventually rose to the position of supervisor. During World War II, he served with the Army Corps of Engineers. He was considering pursuing a career in engineering when, in 1946, returning on vacation to his homeland, he was struck by the desperate poverty of his reservation and decided to dedicate his life to improving the conditions of his people. He began with small-scale efforts to improve the ranching industry and educate Tohono O'odham youth. Borrowing a truck, he would purchase hay off the reservation at low prices and sell it cheaply to the Indian ranchers, bypassing the expensive reservation traders. He also organized a football team to cut down on the high teenage delinquency on the reservation. The football team eventually became a state powerhouse.

In 1947, the Tohono O'odham (then still known as the Papago) elected Segundo their tribal chair, the youngest in the country at the time. His first act was to go to Washington, D.C., to try to get the approximately 500 Tohono O'odham World War II veterans their share of federal benefits under the G.I. Bill of 1944. Segundo quickly reorganized the Papago government, which had been dormant for many years. He also managed to significantly increase tribal revenues through taxing non-Indian traders who worked on the reservation. Although they fought him bitterly, even attempting to have the tribal council abolished, Segundo eventually prevailed. Hiring outside attorneys, he reorganized the Papago legal system, codifying a new set of laws. He enacted conservation measures to protect tribal rangeland and inaugurated an irrigation program to help increase agricultural productivity. He also worked to provide training for Tohono O'odham to leave the reservation and find work in nearby towns.

Segundo received the 1952 Indian Achievement Award of the Indian Council Fire in Chicago and that year was a delegate from Arizona to the Democratic National Convention, also held in Chicago. In 1953, he resigned his tribal leadership to study law at the University of Chicago. Segundo quickly became an important leader in the Chicago Indian community. He helped found the first urban Indian center in Chicago, the All Tribes American Indian Center (see WILLIAMS, SCOTT T.), and was its first executive director.

In 1954, Segundo appeared with anthropologist SOL TAX and Cree-Flathead historian D'ARCY McNICKLE on an NBC radio show entitled *The American Indian Now*. That same year he resigned as executive director of the Chicago Indian center to concentrate on his law studies, although he returned to the directorship in 1957. During this time he joined the NATIONAL CONGRESS OF AMERICAN INDIANS and became their Chicago regional representative. Segundo attended the historic AMERICAN INDIAN CHICAGO CONFERENCE of 1961 that would give birth to the RED POWER MOVEMENT.

He returned to his reservation in 1967 and was again elected tribal chairman. A tireless advocate for his tribe, Segundo succeeded in securing more than $23 million in construction projects for the reservation. His dream, which he called "The Plan," was to achieve full economic autonomy for the tribe, based on agricultural production, quality education, and effective public health services. However, after six terms as tribal chair, the plan was tragically cut short when Segundo was killed in an airplane accident on May 6, 1971. Segundo was considered by his contemporaries to be among the most brilliant Indian leaders of his generation; his death dealt a deep blow to the aspirations of the Tohono O'odham. Thomas Segundo Hall, the auditorium for Tohono O'odham Community College, is named after him.

See INDIGENOUS ECONOMICS.

Sekaquaptewa, Abbott (1929–1992) *Hopi leader*

Hopi leader Abbott Sekaquaptewa was born on December 4, 1929, outside the Hopi village of Hotevilla. His father, EMORY SEKAQUAPTEWA, was tribal chair. Abbott was attending the Phoenix Indian school when he was stricken with arthritis and forced to remain bedridden for more than three years. While convalescing, Sekaquaptewa studied radar and electronics from books brought to him by his older brother Wayne. Though he could attend school only on a sporadic basis, he eventually earned a high school equivalency diploma and established a business, Hopitronics, repairing radios and electrical appliances.

Along with his father, Sekaquaptewa became involved with the Hopi Tribal Council, which, after years of nonfunctioning, had been revived and organized in the mid-1950s by Salt Lake City lawyer JOHN STERLING BOYDEN. In 1953, Sekaquaptewa became chairman of the Hopi Negotiating Committee, formed to resolve land disputes with the neighboring Navajo tribe. In 1956, he was appointed secretary to the Hopi Tribal Council. In 1958, he became the clerk of the Hopi Tribal Court and was, from 1961 until 1964, the chairman of the court. Sekaquaptewa then became executive director for the Hopi tribe, a position appointed by the tribal council, after which he served three terms on the council. In 1973, he unseated Clarence Hamilton to become chair, an office he held until 1981, when he lost to IVAN SIDNEY in a close race.

Sekaquaptewa led the tribe through some of its most tumultuous years. He was the main force behind the fight, known as the BIG MOUNTAIN dispute, to evict Navajo (Dineh) from Hopi lands. As a child, Sekaquaptewa had chafed as he saw Navajo gradually encroaching on his father's grazing lands; anthropologist Richard Clemmer described him as "a man who burns with a commitment to Hopi ethnicity and a passion for unremitting vengeance against the Navajo." Tense and tenacious, Sekaquaptewa organized a fierce lobbying campaign that climaxed in 1974 with the Navajo-Hopi Relocation Act, which ordered the partition of nearly 2 million acres of disputed land and forced the relocation of thousands of Navajo. It was a huge victory for the Hopi tribe, more than doubling their land base; yet traditional Hopi largely opposed Sekaquaptewa's efforts, as they also opposed his forceful advocacy of mineral development on the Hopi reservation. This was because both of these efforts were connected with his attempts to usurp the authority of the kikmongwis, or village chiefs. Sekaquaptewa had no patience with kikmongwis, since they refused to recognize the legitimacy of the tribal council. For him, traditionalists such as DAN KATCHONGVA and THOMAS BANYACYA were anachronisms. Sekaquaptewa preached that "the way to survive is to adapt to life as it is today and to learn its ways so you can cope with it. There is no way in the world we can escape from modern society, even if we build a stone wall around the reservation."

Sekaquaptewa worked closely with Hopi attorney Boyden, and after the attorney's death in 1980, with Boyden's partner, John Kennedy, to expand mining on the Black Mesa section of the Hopi Reservation. Sekaquaptewa defended the work of Boyden and Kennedy before a special tribal council hearing in 1984, when it was revealed the attorneys had also been representing the very firms, such as Peabody Coal, that they were negotiating with on behalf of the Hopi. Like Boyden and Kennedy, Sekaquaptewa was a Mormon, a tie that was not unnoticed by Sekaquaptewa's detractors.

After his defeat by Ivan Sidney in 1981, Sekaquaptewa served as executive secretary to the Hopi Tribal Council and as director of the Hopi Office of Economic Opportunity. Failing to unseat Sidney in 1985, Sekaquaptewa retired from active politics, though he continued to try to see the Navajo relocation completed. In addition to managing his family ranch, he worked with a number of public service agencies. He served on the board of directors of Arizona's community colleges and was chairman emeritus of the Heard Museum National Advisory Council. He was also a board member of Futures for Children, which assists Indian young people in North and South America. Fiercely devoted to what he perceived as Hopi interests, Abbott Sekaquaptewa was admired by his supporters and reviled by his enemies. He was killed in an automobile accident near Keams Canyon, Arizona, on August 7, 1992.

Further Reading

Benedek, Emily. *The Wind Won't Know Me: A History of the Navajo-Hopi Land Dispute*. Norman: University of Oklahoma Press, 1999.

Sekaquaptewa, Emory (1895–1969) *Hopi family patriarch, Hopi Tribal Council chair*

Emory Sekaquaptewa was born on July 15, 1895, in the village of Oraibi on the Hopi reservation in northern Arizona. His father, a follower of traditional Hopi leader YOUKIOMA, separated from his wife when Emory was young, and the child was raised in Oraibi by his maternal grandfather, Wickvaya, a heroic Hopi figure and traditionalist. When Emory was only five, he was kidnapped by the "school police" and sent to Keams Canyon, where he was placed in school. He remained there up to the age of 13, then transferred to the Sherman Institute in Riverside, California. Not until he was 16 was he allowed to return home to the reservation. By then, his mother had remarried for the third time. No longer feeling comfortable in Oraibi, young Sekaquaptewa went to live with his cousin and her husband in Bacabi, then for a while attended the Indian school in Phoenix. Next he worked in the Indian school at Hotevilla, where in 1919 he met and married Helen Talashongnewa.

She had been born in Oraibi on January 1, 1898. As a girl, she, with her family, also belonged to the "hostile" faction of Hopi who were forced to move to the new village of Hotevilla that had been founded by Youkioma. She was one of the Hotevilla children rounded up in 1906, shortly after the move, and sent to the boarding school at Keams Canyon. In 1910, she was allowed to visit her family briefly in Hotevilla before returning to Keams Canyon for another three years. She then attended the Phoenix Indian School. By the time she returned to Hotevilla in 1918, after 13 years away from home, she was largely alienated from her family and from Hopi traditional life—so much so that, though she and Emory were married in a traditional ceremony in Hotevilla, their consciences troubled them, and they were subsequently remarried in a Christian ceremony a few days later by a Mennonite clergyman.

After their marriage, the young couple went to Idaho to work in the Indian school on the Nez Perce Reservation. They saved up enough money for Emory, upon their return to Hotevilla, to buy a wagon and four horses and begin a career as a freighter of goods to and from the reservation. Persuading several Hopi not to sell their cattle to the local white trader, who paid very little, Sekaquaptewa helped them drive their cattle to Winslow, Arizona, and board a train to Los Angeles, where they sold the cattle for four times what the trader would have paid them.

Sekaquaptewa's nontraditional bent and his attempts to improve what he saw as the desperate poverty of the village led to clashes with other Hopi, who were suspicious of change. After they began to can peaches, use diapers, and operate a gas-powered washing machine, the couple were accused of becoming *bahannas*, or white people. Chafing under the religious strictures of the village and its unyielding clan system, the family moved in 1935 to their clan lands about 12 miles away. There they began ranching and, through hard work, became one of the largest cattle families on the Hopi reservation. Sekaquaptewa's ranching operation brought him into conflict with the Navajo, whose increasing population had led them to slowly encroach on Hopi lands.

In 1951, led by their son Wayne, the Sekaquaptewas became Mormon converts. That same year, the Hopi Tribal Council, defunct since the 1930s, was reactivated by Salt Lake City attorney JOHN BOYDEN. In 1953, Emory became a tribal judge and soon tribal chair, leading the Hopi on a course that included an aggressive land-claims action against the Navajo, large-scale mineral leasing, and the modernization of the Hopi villages, most of which had no running water or electricity.

After Sekaquaptewa's death in May 1969, his four sons continued to dominate Hopi tribal politics. Wayne Sekaquaptewa (1923–79), after serving during WORLD WAR II as a radar technician in India and China, returned to Oraibi to open a jewelry business. Wayne became president of the Oraibi branch of the Mormon church and eventually rose to the position of bishop. He drew fire from Oraibi traditional leader Mina Lansa, daughter of WILSON TEWAQUAPTEWA, when he attempted to build a Mormon church in Oraibi. He was the majority partner of a construction company that worked for the tribe and also founded a newspaper, *Qua Toqti*, in 1973 to promote his anti-traditional views.

Eugene Sekaquaptewa (1925–93) also served in World War II, participating in the invasion of Iwo Jima. After attending Arizona State University and the Sherman Institute, he returned to work for the Hopi Tribal Council in the office of economic opportunity.

Emory Sekaquaptewa, Jr. (1928–2007), attended the Phoenix Indian School before being accepted at the U.S. Military Academy at West Point, although he was discharged for health reasons. He then attended Brigham Young University in Provo, Utah, returning to teach at Oraibi High School. After attending law school at the University of Arizona, he, like Wayne, went into the business of manufacturing jewelry. He followed his brother ABBOTT SEKAQUAPTEWA in becoming executive secretary of the Hopi tribal council and later became chief judge of the Hopi Tribes Appellate Court. Emory Sekaquaptewa, Jr., is also well known for his extensive writings on Hopi life and traditions. He served on the faculty of the University of Arizona and was cultural editor of the *Hopi Dictionary* (University of Arizona Press, 1998), a massive compendium of 30,000 entries, all with sentences that put Hopi words and phrases into cultural context.

Helen Sekaquaptewa remained a devout Mormon for all of her life, becoming president of the church's relief society on the reservation. In 1969, she wrote her autobiography, *Me and Mine*, published by the University of Arizona Press. She died on March 24, 1991, on the Hopi Reservation.

Sekaquaptewa, Helen   *See* SEKAQUAPTEWA, EMORY.

Sells, Cato (1859–1948) *commissioner of Indian affairs*
Born on October 6, 1859, in Vinton, Iowa, Cato Sells attended Cornell College, a nearby Methodist institution, before apprenticing with a local attorney. Admitted to the bar in 1884, he was elected county attorney in 1891 as a Democrat, remaining in that office until appointed U.S. district attorney by President Grover Cleveland in 1894. In 1899, he returned to private

practice, and in 1907, seeing greater opportunities in Texas, he decided to move there.

In Cleburne, Texas, Sells founded the Texas State Bank and Trust Company and continued his active role in Democratic politics. Sells served during the 1912 general campaign as Woodrow Wilson's fund-raiser, and it was largely thanks to him that Texas went over to Wilson in the Democratic Convention that year. Following Wilson's election to the presidency, Sells, though lacking any previous experience in Indian administration, was rewarded on June 2, 1913, with the position of commissioner of Indian affairs.

By that time the Office of Indian Affairs (later the BUREAU OF INDIAN AFFAIRS), in the aftermath of the controversial tenure of ROBERT GROSVENOR VALENTINE, had been without a commissioner for almost nine months and was badly demoralized. Sells moved quickly to place the Indian Office back on its course of assimilating Indians (see ASSIMILATION) and breaking up tribal lands and governments. The new commissioner accelerated the issuance of "fee patents," taking advantage of the Burke Act of 1906, which authorized him to remove "competent" Indians from the trusteeship restrictions that had been placed on Indians living on allotted lands (see ALLOTMENT). At the behest of Secretary of the Interior Franklin K. Lane, Sells revived Valentine's failed policy of establishing competency commissions to force patents on Indians who had not applied for them, and in 1917 he went so far as to declare all Indians of less than one-half blood competent and even authorized the sale of lands owned by incompetent elderly Indians. Between 1917 and 1921, Sells issued more than 20,000 fee patents, double the number issued in the previous 10 years, leading to widespread losses of Indian allotments.

Despite his policy of withdrawing protections from allotted lands, leaving their owners vulnerable to schemers, sharpers, and bootleggers, Sells found the wholesale looting that characterized the Allotment process in Oklahoma during this time so scandalous that he was moved to try to correct some of the worst abuse (see CURTIS ACT). Much of this was connected with the probate system, which appointed guardians to manage the property of incompetent Indians and minors, largely for their own personal gain (see BARNETT, JACKSON). In 1914, Sells reached an agreement with state judicial officials to safeguard the rights of Indian wards, and the next year he removed 2,500 corrupt court-appointed guardians. He also increased funding for probate attorneys to represent the interests of Indian wards, managing to secure an accounting for 7,500 Indians. By 1919, however, Oklahoma had succeeded in overturning all of his initiatives, and the widespread fraud continued.

Sells did extend protections for thousands of Indians whose 25-year probationary period on their allotments was due to expire, and he secured land for many landless Indians, including the creation in 1916 of the 2-million-acre Papago (now Tohono O'odham) reservation in Arizona—though not without important concessions to mining and livestock interests. To provide income, Sells increasingly turned to the leasing of Indian lands—despite its being a fount of corruption and inherently contradictory to the goal of making Indians self-supporting. By the end of his administration, more than 4.5 million acres of Indian lands were being leased to non-Indians, including 400,000 acres of valuable irrigated land. Sells was able to mitigate only slightly the inequitable system by which the Bureau of Reclamation used tribal moneys to build irrigation projects that mainly benefited non-Indians, a system that caused further leasing of Indian lands to pay for the projects and to protect Indian rights to scarce western water (see WINTERS DOCTRINE).

A prohibitionist, Sells cracked down hard on bootleggers on Indian reservations, using a clause in an 1855 Chippewa treaty to shut down more than 100 saloons bordering Minnesota reservations and securing stronger anti-trafficking laws and increased appropriations for enforcement. When the United States entered WORLD WAR I in 1917, he threw the weight of the Indian Bureau behind the mobilization. Seeing the war as both a heroic cause and a means for furthering Indian assimilation, Sells encouraged Indians to enlist and used Bureau employees to help with the draft. While higher wartime prices benefited the economies of some reservations, such as that of the wool-producing Navajo (Dineh), Sells's expanded leasing of Indian lands to increase agricultural and livestock production led to the "Great Plow Up" that wrecked some reservations, finishing off the Pine Ridge Reservation's successful ranching operations, for example.

Sells was no more enthusiastic about boarding schools than his Progressive Era predecessors—indeed, the most famous, the Carlisle Indian School, was closed under his watch (see PRATT, RICHARD HENRY)—and he limited attendance at federal schools to children whose parents could not afford to send them to a public school or who lived too far away from one. Though he entered office a firm believer in assimilation and the breakup of tribes, calling for the liquidation of all tribal assets, including funds and lands, Sells had come to understand by the end of his tenure that many tribes were not ready for the transition. As a consequence, he fought against the universal granting of CITIZENSHIP to Indians and for continuation of Bureau control over Indian life. Marked by the attempt to bring efficiency and legality to policies that would only later be recognized as failed and misguided, Sells's tenure was full of ambitious initiatives, most of which only further impoverished Indian people in the end. He resigned from office on March 29, 1921, following the election of Warren G. Harding, and was replaced by CHARLES H. BURKE. Sells returned to private life. He died at Fort Worth, Texas, on December 30, 1948.

Further Reading

Britten, Thomas A. "Hoover and the Indians: The Case for Continuity in Federal Indian Policy, 1900–1933." *The Historian* 61, no. 3 (1999): 519–538.

Whisenhunt, William Benton. "Straining at a Gnat and Swallowing a Camel: Progressive Indian Policy under Cato Sells, 1913–1921." M.A. thesis, University of Nebraska at Omaha, 1992.

Seton, Ernest Thompson (Ernest Evan Thompson) (1860–1946) *author, conservationist, Indian rights activist, educator, founder of Boy Scouts of America and the Woodcraft League*

Born on August 14, 1860, in South Shields, Durham, England, Ernest Evan Thompson was the son of Joseph Logan and Alice Snowden Thompson. Years later, in a break with his abusive father, he changed his name to Ernest Thompson Seton. As a boy, he emigrated with his family to Ontario, Canada, living first in Lindsay and then in Toronto. Seton's father opposed his desire to become a naturalist but allowed him to study art. After winning the gold medal at the Ontario School of Art in 1879, Seton proceeded to the Royal Academy in London, returning to Canada in October 1881. He subsequently became successful as an author, artist, and naturalist.

Seton first met Indians in 1882 near Carberry, Manitoba, and he encountered Cree, Ojibwa, and Sioux (Dakota, Lakota, Nakota) on hunting and naturalist trips to Manitoba in 1884 and 1886. One Cree hunter named Chaska, who taught Seton and his brother much woodcraft, made a particularly strong impression; Seton later named both Lake Chaska and a character in his book *The Preacher of Cedar Mountain* (1917) after his Cree friend. Mohawk poet Pauline Johnson, whom Seton met in Toronto in 1893, called him "medicine brother," and her presentation of Indian lore became the model for his own lectures. Johnson instilled in Seton a lifelong admiration for Shawnee leader Tecumseh, whom he came to regard as the most Christlike character in American history.

Seton was outraged at injustices he witnessed at the Crow Reservation in 1897. White Swan, an old Crow scout from the doomed Custer campaign, awakened his interest in Indian sign language.

He was a founding member of the Sequoya League (1901), promoted by journalist and Indian activist Charles F. Lummis and endorsed by President Theodore Roosevelt with the aim to "make Indians better by treating them better."

Seton's friendship with CHARLES ALEXANDER EASTMAN went back to a joint trip to the Pine Ridge Reservation in the summer of 1901. After Seton founded the Woodcraft League (1902), an international recreation/education movement for young people, and played the leading role in starting the Boy Scouts of America (1910), Eastman wrote several articles for *Boy's Life*, the scouting magazine, and a book *Indian Scout Talks* (1914) for the Boy Scouts and their sister organization, the Camp Fire Girls of America. Eastman also spoke to scout troops and served as camp director and national councilman.

During the 1910s, after discovering a record of Indian signs compiled by Lewis F. Hadley, a missionary at Anadarko, Oklahoma, Seton studied sign language, sending a preliminary study (1914) and later a dictionary (1916) based on the Hadley prints, to anthropologist Frederick Webb Hodge at the Smithsonian Institution. On Omaha ethnologist FRANCIS LA FLESCHE's advice, Seton turned to the one-handed Cheyenne code, hiring an Oklahoma Cheyenne named Cleaver Warden to help him. Seton continued interviewing sign talkers in Oklahoma, giving the Smithsonian approximately 800 drawings upon the project's completion in 1918. His *Sign Talk* (1918) remains an important work in the field.

Seton's ideas were very advanced for their day: As Indian cultures did not violate any basic natural laws, they had the right to exist. Each tribe should be allowed to incorporate and hold its land as a tribe. Tribes had the right to their own forms of government, religions, and customs; Indian-controlled schools, museums, and local industry would allow them to preserve their cultures. Following his first visit to the Hopi pueblos in 1914, Seton opposed attempts to allot or break up Indian lands and advocated the return of all land unfairly taken. He favored returning land to the Plains tribes and restocking it with buffalo (a project set in motion back in 1907 by his old friend the zoologist William Temple Hornaday, when he sent a few animals from the Bronx Zoo to Oklahoma). Seton was one of the most important early links between the natural conservation movement and Indians (see ENVIRONMENTAL MOVEMENT, AMERICAN INDIANS AND THE).

Two decades later, the shock of the Great Depression would make it possible to move toward these goals under the new Indian commissioner, JOHN COLLIER. Seton had known Collier since 1910, when they both worked with Luther and Charlotte Gulick, founders of the Camp Fire Girls. During the 1920s, Collier had been extremely interested in Seton and the Woodcraft League. He long remembered a talk Seton gave in 1924 in which the latter "dwelt with insistence and at length upon our U.S. Indians and their hopes, as representative of the Indians of the Western Hemisphere. His was the first voice to speak of the ill effects, from the Rio Grande to Chile, of our victimization of the U.S. Indians."

Among Seton's closest friends were Western regionalists of the Santa Fe art colony, such as Mary Austin, HAMLIN GARLAND, and Charles Lummis, who condemned American materialism and had a strong interest in Indian traditions, encouraged Native American artists, and were politically active, especially with Collier's American Indian Defense Association. They opposed the 1923 DANCE ORDERS. Seton believed that an alliance with the regionalists would make the woodcraft movement more effective in the justice campaign for Indians. In 1927, he decided to investigate establishing national headquarters in the Southwest. After visiting Plains reservations, where he found that Indians under 40 were forbidden to perform dances, he studied music and dance among all the Rio Grande pueblos, where he spoke to the chiefs and other leaders. In August, he attended the Intertribal Indian Ceremony at Gallup.

For several summers, still looking for a site for his headquarters, Seton strengthened his ties with the local Pueblo Indians. Finally, in February 1930, he bought a 2,500-acre parcel seven miles southeast of downtown Santa Fe. His home, known as Seton Castle, built by Pueblo Indians beginning in 1935, eventually had 30 rooms and a village around it called Seton Village. Here Seton's "College of Indian Wisdom" opened in summer 1932. Fully accredited courses were taught by a faculty of 42, and Native American artists taught pottery. Later a camp was added where children were taught aspects of Indian culture

(see PAYTIAMO, JAMES). In 1938, the Setons toured the country with the Pueblo artist PABLITA VELARDE.

Seton continued to tour the country, giving lectures on Indian culture and religious beliefs. "Our civilization is a failure," he used to say in his lecture "The Message of the Redman." "It makes a millionaire and a million paupers wherever pushed to a conclusion. White culture values the amount of property a man has, Indian, how much service you have rendered to your people."

The College of Indian Wisdom became a sounding board for the coming Indian administration. After John Collier became Indian commissioner, he sent BUREAU OF INDIAN AFFAIRS (BIA) employees to take courses there to help in the revival of Native American arts. Collier and his coworkers praised Seton highly, and the commissioner visited the college and spoke there whenever he could.

In his preface to *Rhythm of the Redman* (1930) by Julia Moss Buttree—later his second wife—Seton emphasized that Indian art is symbolic and thus has a deeper intellectual content; she emphasized the importance of dance. The BIA adopted this as a text for Indians. With Julia, whom he married in 1935, Seton wrote *The Gospel of the Redman* (1936), in which he compares the Bible with Indian religious philosophy. Representing the distilled essence of Seton's philosophy, the book was successful with the public and admired by Eastman, Collier, and Hodge, but Seton's friend Stanley Vestal (pen name of Walter S. Campbell) criticized it for exaggerating Indian virtues.

Seton continued giving the "Message" lecture throughout the 1930s. WORLD WAR II brought the College of Indian Wisdom to a sudden end, and it never reopened. Seton died at Seton Village on October 23, 1946.

Julia Seton died on April 28, 1975. That same year, Seton Village was designated a National Historic Landmark. By 2003, the property had dwindled to a core 86 acres of the original 2,500, and the house and lands were in poor condition. In that year, Seton Village was purchased by the Academy for the Love of Learning, which immediately began restoring it. At about noon on November 15, 2005, with the restoration nearly complete, a fire of unknown origin destroyed the big house in less than two hours. Fortunately the contents—books, drawings, manuscripts, and furniture—had been removed to safety years earlier.

Further Reading

Anderson, H. Allen. *The Chief: Ernest Thompson Seton and the Changing West*. College Station: Texas A & M University Press, 1986.

Jehlicka, Petr. "Indians of Bohemia: The Spell of Woodcraft on Czech Society, 1912–2006." In *Sport—Ethnie— Nation: Zur Geschichte und Soziologie des Sports in Nationalitatenkonflikten und bei Minoritäten*, edited by Diethelm Blecking and Marek Waic, 112–130. Baltmannsweiler, Germany: Schneider Verlag, 2008.

Keller, Betty. *Black Wolf: The Life of Ernest Thompson Seton*. Vancouver, B.C., Canada: Douglas and McIntyre, 1984.

Morris, Brian. *Ernest Thompson Seton, Founder of the Woodcraft Movement 1860–1946: Apostle of Indian Wisdom and Pioneer Ecologist.* Lampeter, UK: Edwin Mellen Press, 2007.

Shenandoah, Leon (1915–1996) *principal chief of the Iroquois Confederacy*

Born on the Onondaga Reservation on May 18, 1915, Leon Shenandoah was the second youngest of five brothers and sisters. His parents, Edward and Jessie (Cook) Schenandoah (as their name was spelled at the time), were both full-blood Onondaga. When Shenandoah was a small child, a pot of hot water was accidentally spilled on him, scalding his entire body and nearly killing him. He was taken to a medicine man to be healed, and during the ceremony it was predicted that Shenandoah would hold a special position among his people. He was subsequently sent to a Quaker school but dropped out after the eighth grade when he recognized that it conflicted with the Longhouse, or traditional religion of the Iroquois. Shenandoah worked on his family's farm, then became an ironworker (see IRONWORKERS, AMERICAN INDIAN).

Shenandoah became active in the leadership of the Iroquois Confederacy during the 1950s, when he became a chief of the Onondaga Eel Clan. He helped to organize a number of demonstrations in New York City and in Washington, D.C., to protest New York State's usurpation of sovereignty (see SOVEREIGNTY, INDIGENOUS AND TRIBAL) over Iroquois Confederacy lands and to attempt to prevent the flooding of the Allegany Seneca Reservation by the KINZUA DAM.

In 1968, Shenandoah led the Onondaga demonstrations that successfully defeated an attempt by New York State to expand Interstate Highway 81 onto their lands. The Onondaga blocked the construction crews and seized their heavy equipment. Governor Nelson Rockefeller's tough stance against the demonstration might have ended in violence except that state police called to remove the Onondaga were reassigned to Attica Prison at the last minute to quell a prison riot. In the meantime, the principal chief, Tadadaho GEORGE A. THOMAS, who had been in ill health, died near the end of 1968. On December 7, 1968, Leon Shenandoah became the fourth Tadadaho of the 20th century and the 23rd since the founding of the confederacy.

By then the militancy of the Tuscarora, Seneca, and Onondaga had spread to the Mohawk, who had successfully defended their border-crossing rights during the CORNWALL BRIDGE BLOCKADE in 1968. The revitalizing work of teacher and Mohawk cultural leader RAY FADDEN was bearing fruit, and a new generation of young traditional chiefs, such as TOM PORTER and JAKE SWAMP, began to assert control over the Akwesasne Reservation in opposition to the state-led three-man council. In addition, in 1968 the Mohawk established *Akwesasne Notes*, which would become the most influential Indian magazine in the country and spread the Iroquois view of Indian sovereignty to Indians across the nation (see BARREIRO, JOSÉ; MOHAWK, JOHN C.). On the Tonawanda Seneca reservation, young traditional chiefs such as Bernie

In 1969, Leon Shenandoah became Tadadaho, or principal chief, of the Iroquois Confederacy. He is pictured here holding the traditional headdress of the Tadadaho. *(AP/Wideworld)*

Parker joined established leaders such as Corbett Sundown and replaced the last remnants of Christians who had formed part of the chief's council there. In Tuscarora, where the reservation had been completely christianized by the turn of the 20th century, young activists such as WILLIAM RICKARD and MAD BEAR ANDERSON were leading the reservation back to the Longhouse.

Shenandoah led a new wave of younger, more politically active chiefs in Onondaga, such as Irv Powless, Jr. (whose father, Irv Powless, Sr., was an important chief in his own right), William Lazore, Paul Waterman, Louis Farmer, Ambrose Gibson, and OREN LYONS, JR. A new generation of clan mothers, such as Alice Papineau (Shenandoah's sister), Betty Jacobs, and Audrey Shenandoah, were taking places as leaders as well.

Shenandoah broke with his predecessor, George A. Thomas, who favored a nonpolitical stance and was focused more on the religious aspects of the position of Tadadaho. By contrast, Shenandoah set out to combine the spirituality of the Iroquois with the political demands of the day. His first act after becoming principal chief was to demand, on both religious and political grounds, the return of Iroquois wampum belts taken by New York State at the turn of the century. In 1969, he also convened an important gathering, the "Unity Meeting," held on the Tonawanda Seneca reservation in New York and attended by Indian activists from across North America, where traditional Indian ceremonies were held alongside the political planning for a movement that would unify traditional Indians.

The Iroquois exerted an important influence on the growing RED POWER MOVEMENT, first through the increasingly wide distribution of *Akwesasne Notes* and second through Iroquois activists such as Rickard, Anderson, and RICHARD OAKES. Rickard, Anderson, Lyons, and other Iroquois formed the North American Indian Unity Caravans, and Tom Porter founded the White Roots of Peace, both of which traveled throughout the country in the late 1960s in an effort to promote a return to Indian traditions. When the AMERICAN INDIAN MOVEMENT (AIM) appealed to the confederacy for aid in its occupation of WOUNDED KNEE, Shenandoah issued a statement of support and sent a delegation to the encampment, giving the beleaguered AIM leaders an important boost. Shenandoah agreed to have the confederacy provide asylum for AIM leader DENNIS BANKS in 1984. The confederacy itself, however, had little use for the AIM militants, whose urban 1960s style of radicalism had little in common with the century-long Iroquois struggle for autonomy. Shenandoah rejected AIM aid during the Mohawk confrontations with New York State over GANIENKEH in 1975 and the SIEGE OF AKWESASNE in 1979. During the mid-1970s, the council at Onondaga began to forcibly evict non-Indians and mixed-blood Iroquois (those not affiliated with a clan) from the reservation, leading to sharp divisions in the confederacy.

Seeking to continue its work in the 20th century for international recognition, the confederacy threw its support behind the INTERNATIONAL INDIAN TREATY COUNCIL when it was formed in 1974, but later withdrew when the council became dominated by members of AIM. Shenandoah led the large Iroquois delegation to the United Nations in Geneva in 1977, as part of a gathering organized by the Treaty Council. Under the leadership of Lyons and Tonya Gonnella Frichner, an Onondaga and founder of the American Indian Law Alliance, the confederacy maintained an active presence in the international arena and played a role in the creation of the United Nations Draft Declaration on the Rights of Indigenous Peoples and the establishment of 1993 as the United Nations Year of the World's Indigenous People. Shenandoah led the Iroquois delegation at the inauguration of the Year of the World's Indigenous People in New York City.

Under Shenandoah's leadership, the confederacy became a national stabilizing force as AIM began to disintegrate during the mid-1970s. Through the writings and speeches of Oren Lyons, Tom Porter, Jake Swamp, and John Mohawk, the Iroquois world view became accessible and understood by Indians and non-Indians alike. Mohawk, DANIEL BOMBERRY, and the collective of Iroquois and non-Iroquois thinkers that gathered around *Akwesasne Notes* between 1976 and 1983 began to articulate traditional Indian thought in Western terms, giving rise to new fields such as INDIGENOUS ECONOMICS. What is more, after facing down New York State during the two-year siege of Akwesasne, the confederacy had by 1980 achieved a level of government recognition, and from the state and federal government, relative autonomy not seen since before the

19th century. Asserting its traditional sovereignty, the confederacy could issue its own international passports and have them honored by countries in Europe and Asia. It formed the IROQUOIS NATIONALS LACROSSE TEAM to play in international competition, defeating England in the 1998 World Cup. It also regained the wampum belts taken by New York State in the 1980s (see REPATRIATION).

Unfortunately, Shenandoah and the Iroquois Confederacy could not withstand the national and international market forces that were sweeping over INDIAN RESERVATIONS in the late 1980s and 1990s. The hard-won sovereignty that the Iroquois had helped Indian reservations achieve was used to establish gaming enterprises and other businesses (see GAMING ON INDIAN RESERVATIONS). Under the Code of Handsome Lake, gaming was specifically prohibited to the traditional Iroquois, but individuals, formulating a new interpretation of Iroquois sovereignty that placed the individual over the community, began to reject Shenandoah's leadership and to organize gaming and business enterprises without the confederacy's oversight or, indeed, any government oversight at all. Many of the activists and even some of the chiefs who had led the Iroquois throughout the long struggle for sovereignty became "businessmen" who sought out the lucrative niches that operating on nontaxable Indian reservations could provide. In Akwesasne, gaming operators established private armies to protect their business from competitors and government interference. In the early 1990s, under the ultranationalist Canadian Mohawk Louis Hall, the private security forces morphed into a well-armed "Warrior Society" that began to create its own government and challenge the authority of Shenandoah and the confederacy chiefs.

The clash between the Warrior Society and traditional chiefs led to a virtual civil war in Akwesasne in 1991, leaving two Mohawk dead, and to violent flare-ups on the Onondaga, Tonowanda, and Tuscarora reservations. Ray Halbritter, who had founded a small-scale gaming operation in 1986, spun the Oneida away from the confederacy. Despite Shenandoah's attempts to remove him as leader of the New York Oneida, Halbritter created his own government, which was then recognized by New York State and the BUREAU OF INDIAN AFFAIRS. New York, seeking to regain the power over the confederacy it had only achieved in 1950, began to exploit the divisions among the Iroquois.

Despite assaults on the Iroquois government, under Shenandoah's tenure, the confederacy made a lasting impression on Indian life and Indian thought. Widely renowned as an Indian leader, Leon Shenandoah died on July 22, 1996, at Onondaga. He was succeeded as Tadadaho by Sidney Hill.

Further Reading

Hauptman, Laurence M. *The Iroquois Struggle for Survival: World War II to Red Power.* Syracuse, N.Y.: Syracuse University Press, 1986.

Shenandoah, Leon, and Steve Wall. *To Become a Human Being: The Message of Tadadaho Chief Leon Shenandoah.* Newburyport, Mass.: Hampton Roads, 2001.

Shotridge, Louis (Situwaka) (1886–1937) *Chilkat Tlingit ethnologist*

Louis Shotridge (Situwaka or Stoowokháa, "Ashite One") was born on April 15, 1886 in the village of Klukwan in southwestern Alaska. As a boy, he went to a Presbyterian school near the village. The name Shotridge was an English form of the Chilkat name Tlothitckh (Hard to Kill), a powerful chief of the Chilkat group of Tlingit in southern Alaska. Tlothitckh's nephew was Louis's father George Shotridge, master of the Whale House and head chief of the Raven phratry. (A phratry is a subdivision of the tribe, consisting of two or more distinct clans.) On Tlothitckh's death in 1883, George Shotridge became *yitsati*, or chief ruler, of the Chilkat. When he died in 1917, Shotridge broke custom by leaving his belongings to his eldest son, Louis, rather than to a nephew. Louis's mother, Kudeit Saakw, belonged to the Eagle phratry, the Kaguantan clan and the Finned House. According to Chilkat descendancy laws, this meant that Louis was an Eagle of the Kaguantan clan.

When ethnologist Louis B. Gordon made research trips to Alaska in 1905 and 1907, he met Louis Shotridge and was greatly impressed by his intelligence and learning. After Gordon became director of the University of Pennsylvania's Museum of Archaeology and Anthropology. He hired Shotridge as his assistant in 1912. Shotridge brought his wife Florena with him to Philadelphia. He was promoted to assistant curator in 1915. In 1914, he met FRANZ BOAS of New York and worked with him on Tlingit language and music.

Shotridge's work for the museum became highly controversial among his own people. He was greatly troubled to find that Tlingit ceremonial life had been rapidly eroding and that ceremonial objects were already being sold into private collections. As a member of a family of high social rank, he had access to other such families and was able to buy from them rare old ceremonial objects and regalia that were not even known to collectors. He saw museum preservation as the only alternative to the complete loss of the objects and the traditional knowledge surrounding them. Nevertheless, his activities were bitterly resented by many Indians, who argued that the objects were communal property and ought to stay in the village (see REPATRIATION).

In 1915, Shotridge began a four-year expedition among the Tlingit, Haida, and Tsimshian in Alaska to collect objects as well as the myths and traditions connected with them, traveling mainly by water in his motorboat, the *Penn*. He began another two-year expedition in 1922. While employed by the museum, he spent most of the time in Alaska, with trips to Philadelphia mainly of short duration. In addition, he helped several anthropologists, including Franz Boas, Edward Sapir, and Theresa Durlach, with their Tlingit research.

In 1932, during the Great Depression, the University of Pennsylvania Museum experienced financial difficulties, and most of the staff was fired, including Shotridge, who was then in Alaska. This plunged him into difficulty. Unlike most acculturated Indians, he would not can fish or log, and in his hometown he was ostracized and even threatened with death.

Ironically, he never received much recognition from mainstream society for his important scientific work.

In the early 1930s, Shotridge organized a branch of the Alaska Native Brotherhood in Sitka and served as grand president of the whole organization. (See ALASKA NATIVE LAND CLAIMS SETTLEMENT ACT.) He worked with native groups throughout the Alaska panhandle, recording the Tlingit culture. He earned a living by fishing, doing odd jobs, and the occasional sale of an artifact. In 1935, he took a government job as a stream guard; his task, an unpopular one, was to prevent fishing in restricted areas.

A few years later, Shotridge began to build a small house in a remote spot some 16 miles from Sitka. While working, he suffered a fall in which he broke his neck. His body was not found until a few weeks later. The date of his death was recorded as August 6, 1937. Although the death appeared to be an accident, the local natives believed that he was killed by people from Klukwan who, in the word of Alaska historian Robert De Armon "were very clever at making it look like an accident."

The resentment that surrounded Louis Shotridge in Klukwan descended to his children. When representatives of non-Alaskan interests arrived at Klukwan on May 12, 1976, to buy up the remaining ceremonial treasures of the tribal houses, some of the villagers attempted to block the road with logs. Injunctions were sought, and both buyers and protesters were represented by attorneys, but many objects had already been sold over the previous month at very high prices. It was considered a great loss to the entire state of Alaska. It was said that the people who were now selling these objects were the very ones who had scorned and ostracized Shotridge and his family.

Shotridge's life was dramatized by Anne W. Hanley of Fairbanks in her drama *Shotridge*, which played from April 14 to 30, 1995, at the Second Stage Theatre, University of Alaska Anchorage, under the direction of Michael Hood.

In 2010, the T'akdeintaan clan of Tlingit of Southeastern Alaska sued Penn's Museum of Archaeology and Anthropology for the return of a group of ceremonial objects that Shotridge had acquired on his 1924 expedition.

Further Reading

Enge, Marilee. "Collecting the Past." *Anchorage Daily News*, 6 April 1993.
Kaplan, Susan A., and Kristin J. Barsness. *Raven's Journey: The World of Alaska's Native People*. Philadelphia: University Museum, University of Pennsylvania, 1986.
Milburn, Maureen Elizabeth. "The Politics of Possession: Louis Shotridge and the Tlingit Collections of the University of Pennsylvania Museum." Ph.D. dissertation, University of British Columbia, 1997.

Shunatona, Joseph Bayhylle (Joe Shunatona)

(1901–1969) *Pawnee-Otoe baritone, bandleader, dancer, actor*
A Pawnee-Otoe, Joseph Bayhylle Shunatona was born on January 12, 1901, at Pawnee, Oklahoma. His father, Richard Shunatona, was descended from traditional Otoe chiefs, and

his mother, Jennie Bayhylle, was Pawnee. He and his brother Baptiste, three years his junior, attended the Chilocco Indian School, and Joseph went on to study singing at the Wichita Conservatory of Music. Baptiste went to the Mercersburg Academy on a scholarship, became the first full-blooded Indian to receive a law degree from the University of Oklahoma, and much later served as Oklahoma state commissioner of Indian affairs.

For a while, Joseph Shunatona was the clerk for Pawnee finances at his agency in Oklahoma. After beginning his theatrical career in 1920, he organized, with some Pawnee cousins, the "Four American Indians," a male vocal quartet, and toured the Chautauqua circuit. In 1925, on a trip to the Miller Brothers' 101 Ranch in Oklahoma (a famous "Wild West show" company), he met Penobscot dancer MOLLY SPOTTED ELK. From 1925 to 1927, he played in the Chicago area as a trombonist with Lillian Scott and her Indian orchestra, touring on Martin Beck's RKO Orpheum circuit as a singer, dancer, and instrumentalist around 1926.

In 1928, at the request of Republican organizers of the Hoover-Curtis inaugural ball, Shunatona formed the United States Indian Band to play in honor of Vice President CHARLES CURTIS, a Kaw. After the ball (January 1929), the band toured the country for two years on the Paramount-Publix theater circuit, playing major vaudeville and movie houses. Publix built an entire revue unit around them, with Shunatona as both bandleader and master of ceremonies. While in New York for a few weeks in 1929, they made a one-reel film short for Paramount, *The Moon Bride's Wedding*, directed by Monte Brice.

In 1931, the U.S. State Department organized an American exhibit for the French Colonial Exhibition in Paris, and the band was signed to play. The act, which featured the dancing of Molly Spotted Elk, sometimes joined by Joe Shunatona, was a great success with the French public but a financial failure. While the band found some outside work in Paris, they were poorly paid and in need of money. They secured bookings in London, Berlin, and Rome, but their passports were valid only for France, and then they learned that recent English and German laws limited bookings of foreign talent. As the State Department refused to pay even their basic expenses, and the Indian office (as the BUREAU OF INDIAN AFFAIRS was then known) had always refused to have anything to do with them, they reluctantly left for home on June 9, 1931. The band broke up in January 1932.

On returning to the United States, Shunatona, with his wife, Gwen (Gwendolyn Johnson Shunatona, a Wyandotte), and their two children, settled in New York City. From 1932 to 1935, he played himself (Shunatona) as well as "Skookum," a comic character of his own creation, on the *Cowboy Tom Roundup*, a children's radio program developed by cowboy singer Tex Ritter, with Tom Martin in the title role, which aired on WINS in New York and other East Coast Stations. He also played non-Indian dramatic parts on *Mr. District Attorney* for CBS. In early 1935, he was assistant director for a New York performance of Peter Joseph Engels's three-act Indian opera *Minnehaha*, but it ran for only a few performances.

In 1935, Shunatona returned to Pawnee, where he organized a small Indian band. In 1936, he moved to Tulsa, still playing with the band up to about 1938. He then began producing Indian pageants for conventions and big events, and for many years he was a mainstay of civic and Indian musical entertainments or tribal shows. He also assisted the Tulsa Indian communities in their POWWOWS and other local entertainments.

In the late 1930s and 1940s, Shunatona taught children singing, acting, and comedy, featuring them on a weekly children's radio program he started around 1938 and that continued into the 1940s. During WORLD WAR II, he and the children made appearances to sell war bonds. In the 1950s, Shunatona continued as a children's vocal teacher, and in the 1950s and 1960s he also conducted a large women's choir made up of the best women singers from churches all over Tulsa. He produced a civic pageant in North Dakota in 1963 and another the following year in LaGrande, Oregon.

In 1967, Shunatona moved to Wichita, Kansas, where he directed a federally funded educational program for children up to high-school age. His daughter, Mifaunwy Shunatona Hines, was Miss Oklahoma in 1941 and became the first American Indian to compete in the Miss America Pageant. She reached the semifinals and was chosen "Miss Congeniality." Hines was a participant in the 1961 AMERICAN INDIAN CHICAGO CONFERENCE and founded New York City's American Indian Community House in 1969 (see RICHMOND, ROSEMARY). Joe Shunatona died in Wichita in August 1969.

Further Reading
Troutman, John William. "Indian Blues: American Indians and the Politics of Music, 1890–1935." Ph.D. dissertation, University of Texas at Austin, 2004. Available online. URL: http://hdl.handle.net/2152/1429. Accessed 17 October 2007.

Sidney, Ivan (1947–) *Hopi tribal chair*
Ivan Sidney was born on August 19, 1947, and raised in the Hopi village of Polacca on the Hopi reservation. He attended the Phoenix Indian School, where he met and befriended future Navajo (Dineh) leader PETERSON ZAH. Sidney then joined the Arizona state police force and became a highway patrolman. He eventually returned to the Hopi tribe and became their chief of police. Sidney turned the Hopi police force into a highly organized, professional organization. In 1982, he succeeded ABBOTT SEKAQUAPTEWA as chair of the Hopi Tribal Council.

One of the few Indian leaders who was a member of the Republican Party, Sidney was friendly with Ronald Reagan and was selected as a delegate to the Republican National Convention in 1988. Despite his support, the Hopi reservation suffered under the Reagan administration's budget cuts, administered by assistant secretaries of the interior KENNETH L. SMITH and ROSS O. SWIMMER.

Sidney was elected partly on the strength of his vow to settle the Hopi's bitter BIG MOUNTAIN dispute with the

Navajo by coming to an agreement with his friend Zah, who was by then the Navajo tribal chair. This did not happen, however, and Sidney took a hard line with the remaining Navajo families in the joint-use area, threatening their eviction if they did not accept relocation housing.

Like his predecessors, Sidney was a strong proponent of economic development, negotiating numerous joint ventures with outside companies, including an electronics assembly plant and a hat factory. When he took the side of off-reservation construction companies working on Second Mesa, he came into conflict with Hopi religious leaders, who claimed that the construction was disturbing sacred rattlesnake breeding grounds. Sidney also continued his predecessors' controversial mining policies, which were draining the Hopi's underground aquifers and were largely opposed by religious leaders. In 1988, Sidney was dogged by accusations that he knew Polacca schoolteacher John Boone was molesting Hopi children as early as 1981 but did nothing about it. Not arrested until 1987, Boone was convicted and given a term of life in prison for molesting 94 Hopi boys during an 11-year period.

After serving two terms as tribal chair, Sidney was defeated in 1989 by Vernon Masayesva, the protégé of traditional Hopi spokesman THOMAS BANYACYA. He remained active in the Hopi tribe, serving as the administrator of schools for First Mesa, as well as in the Arizona Republican Party. In 2005, he again became tribal chair when he defeated incumbent Wayne Taylor in a closely contested election. After less than 10 months in office, Sidney was removed by the tribal council for "violating the tribe's constitution and neglecting his duties."

Further Reading

Cole, Cyndy. "Hopis Sack Sidney." *Arizona Daily Sun*, 18 October 2006.

Silko, Leslie Marmon (1948–)   *Laguna Pueblo novelist, poet*

Born in Albuquerque, New Mexico, on March 5, 1948, Leslie Marmon Silko is the daughter of Lee H. Marmon (Laguna and Mexican) and Virginia Marmon, a woman of mixed Indian ancestry from Montana. As a child, Leslie was deeply influenced by her paternal great-grandmother and grandmother, as well as by her grandaunt, all of whom immersed the young woman in Laguna (Keres) lore.

Leslie Marmon attended a Catholic high school in Albuquerque before enrolling in the University of New Mexico in 1965. The next year, at age 18, she married Richard C. Chapman and gave birth to her first son. In 1969, she graduated with honors and published her first story, "The Man to Send Rain Clouds," which brought her a grant from the National Endowment for the Humanities. That same year, she divorced Chapman, and two years later, she married John Silko (a marriage that would also eventually end in divorce). She briefly attended the law school of the University of New Mexico before deciding to devote herself to writing. In 1973, she received a National Endowment for the Arts fellowship. Leslie

Silko taught for two years at Navajo Community College, and in 1974 she published a collection of poems, *Laguna Woman*. The collection won wide acclaim for the narrative poems that drew from the Laguna traditions she had learned as a child.

When her husband was offered a position with the Alaska Legal Services, Silko moved with him to Ketchikan, Alaska, where she completed her first novel, *Ceremony*, which appeared in 1977. Not since N. SCOTT MOMADAY's *House Made of Dawn* had a novel by a Native American been so enthusiastically received. Like Momaday's novel, the story centers around a mixed-blood WORLD WAR II veteran estranged from his Pueblo traditions, but for Silko the emphasis is on the regeneration of tradition through the use of ceremonies, rather than the ambiguity of Native American existence in the modern world. *Ceremony* weaves myths, legends, and stories, often in the form of verse, into the narrative, giving the work a rich, ritualistic texture.

Silko's next work, *Storyteller*, published in 1981, featured poems, short stories, family stories, and photographs. It was widely praised for its success in weaving the oral tradition of storytelling into a literary form. That year, she won a Mac-Arthur Foundation fellowship, which allowed her to devote time to her second novel, *Almanac of the Dead*, a monumental work covering more than 400 years of history, completed in 1991. Silko foresaw a time when Native Americans, following centuries of brutalization, would reclaim their ancestral lands after the contemporary non-Indian world had succumbed to corruption, environmental degradation, and moral decay. Graphic and disturbing, the work extends the theme Silko explored in *Ceremony*—the age-old battle between good and evil—though in *Almanac of the Dead* the battle, instead of being fought inside the mind of a Pueblo veteran, is in the world and for the very future of civilization.

In 1986, Silko's correspondence with poet James Wright, who had died of cancer in 1980, was published as *Delicacy and Strength of Lace*. In 1993, she released a collection of her work, *Yellow Woman*, following it up with a collection of essays on contemporary Native American life entitled *Yellow Woman and a Beauty of the Spirit*, released in 1996. That same year, she also released two collections of poems and short stories, *Rain* and *Love Poem and Slim Canyon*. Her next novel, *Gardens in the Dunes*, was published in 1999. Many regard it as her finest work. *Publishers Weekly* proclaimed that her "integration of glorious details into her many vivid settings and intense characters is a triumph of the storyteller's art." Silko's work is noted for its emphasis on storytelling and the role it can have in healing people and cultures. Often enigmatic as well as profound, she is among the foremost writers to emerge from the Native American literary renaissance of the late 20th century.

Further Reading

Arnold, Ellen L. *Conversations with Leslie Marmon Silko.* Jackson: University Press of Mississippi, 2000.

Romero, Channette. "Envisioning a 'Network of Tribal Coalitions': Leslie Marmon Silko's *Almanac of the Dead.*" *American Indian Quarterly* 26, no. 4 (2002): 623–640.

Silko, Leslie Marmon. *Ceremony*. New York: Viking Press, 1977.

———. *Storyteller*. New York: Seaver Books, 1981.

Slovic, Scott. "Leslie Marmon Silko, *Ceremony* (1977)." In *Literature and the Environment*, edited by George Hart and Scott Slovic, 111–128. Santa Barbara, Calif.: Greenwood Press, 2004.

Teale, Tamara M. "The Silko Road from Chicago or Why Native Americans Cannot be Marxists." *MELUS* 23, no. 4 (1988): 156–166.

Silverheels, Jay Smith (Harold Jay Smith)

(1912–1980) *Mohawk athlete, actor*

Born Harold Jay Smith on May 26, 1912, in Brantford, on the Six Nations Reserve in Ontario, Canada, Jay Silverheels, a Mohawk, was the son of Captain Alexander George Smith, Jr., the most decorated Canadian Indian soldier of WORLD WAR I and a Mohawk chief. There is some confusion as to his actual date of birth. Although his tombstone gives the date as May 26, 1919, his death certificate has it as May 26, 1912. His grandfather, Cayuga chief Alexander George Smith, gave Harold the nickname "Silverheels," because of his high-kicking style when he ran. Several of his brothers were steelworkers in New York City.

Before embarking on an acting career, Smith was a star LACROSSE player as well as a recognized athlete in hockey, football, and track, with honors in boxing and wrestling. He first came to the United States in 1938 while touring with Canada's national lacrosse team. A short time later, he was "discovered" by comedian Joe E. Brown, who got him started in Hollywood.

Smith moved to Hollywood, where he adopted the stage name Jay Silverheels (he made this his legal name only in 1971). His first film is believed to have been a small role in *Sea Hawk*, made by Warner Brothers in 1940 and starring Errol Flynn, although Silverheels is uncredited. His first role credited, as Harry Smith, was in a 12-chapter serial movie made by Republic Pictures called *Daredevils of the West* (1943). He played minor parts in Westerns for seven years before landing his first important role, as an Aztec warrior opposite Tyrone Power in *The Captains from Castile* (1947). Silverheels and Chickasaw actor RODD REDWING played the parts of two Seminole brothers in the classic film *Key Largo* (1948), which starred Humphrey Bogart, Edward G. Robinson, Lauren Bacall, and Lionel Barrymore. In 1949, he became the first American Indian to star in a television series, in the role that made him famous: as Tonto in the popular *The Lone Ranger* program. (The first film Tonto was Cherokee actor VICTOR DANIELS in a 1938 serial; on the origins of the character Tonto, see WILLIAMS, SCOTT T.) The popular television program, with Clayton Moore as the Lone Ranger, ran through 1957—221 episodes in all. Silverheels also appeared with Moore in three feature films: *The Lone Ranger* (1956), *The Lone Ranger and the Lost City of Gold* (1958), and *Justice of the West* (1961). Among his other important films were *Broken Arrow* (1950), in which he played Geronimo; *Indian Paint* (1965); and *Santee* (1973).

Silverheels was in perfect accord with the chivalrous

Mohawk actor Jay Smith Silverheels *(left)*, who played the character Tonto, posed beside the Lone Ranger, Clayton Moore, in 1959. *(AP/Wideworld)*

spirit of the Lone Ranger's creator, Fran Striker. Throughout his career, conscious of the example he was setting for children, Silverheels chose roles that portrayed Indians in a favorable light, avoided violence between Indians and whites, and showed good triumphing over evil.

Silverheels guest-starred on numerous television shows, such as *Daniel Boone* and *Rawhide*, in the 1960s and early 1970s. His last on-screen appearance was in the TV show *Dusty's Trail* in 1974. He did a great deal to further the progress of Indians in film and television. He founded an actors' workshop and helped other Indians get started in Hollywood. On July 21, 1979, a star bearing his name was placed in the Walk of Fame on Hollywood Boulevard, the first time an American Indian actor received this honor. Silverheels died on March 5, 1980, of complications following pneumonia, at the Motion Picture and Television Country House, Woodland Hills, California. He was posthumously inducted into the Hall of Honor of First Americans in the Arts, Beverly Hills, California, on February 21, 1998.

Further Information

Jay Silverheels: The Man beside the Mask. Bio-documentary written and directed by Maureen Marovitch and David Finch. Montreal, Quebec, Canada: Picture This Productions, 2000.

Silverheels, Jay. *"The Fire Plume" and Other Legends of the American Indians.* Phonograph record TC 1451; audio-cassette CDL 51451. Caedmon, 1977.

Further Reading

Klein, Jeff Z. "A Sidekick's Little-Known Leading Role." *New York Times*, late ed. 1 September 2013, Sports, 13.

Petten, Cheryl. "TV Star Paves Way for Indian Actors." *Wind Speaker* 22, no. 8 (2004): 30.

Sloan, Thomas L. (1863–1940) *Omaha attorney*

Born on May 14, 1863, in St. Louis, Missouri, eldest son of John W. and Elizabeth Rogers Sloan, Thomas Louis Sloan lived with his grandmother Margaret Sloan from 1881 until her death in 1898. She was the daughter of a French Canadian, Michael Barada (Michel de Baradat), and Taeglaha Haciendo, a full-blood Omaha woman. In 1857, Margaret settled with her husband, Thomas Sloan, and their children, John (Thomas L. Sloan's father) and Artemisia, on the Nemaha Half-Breed Reservation, a tract created for mixed-race descendants of Indian tribes and French trappers near the present town of Falls City, Nebraska. The Nemaha Reservation was allotted and then disbanded in 1861, and Margaret moved with Thomas L. Sloan to the Omaha Reservation in 1881 to ensure they would be awarded lands when the reservation was allotted, a process that began in 1882 (see ALLOTMENT). Although some records state that Thomas L. Sloan was 1/16 Omaha, he was actually 1/8.

As a teenager, Sloan worked as a herder for white cattlemen who leased grazing lands on the reservation. In fall 1880, the 17-year-old Sloan came upon some members of the Omaha Indian Council discussing how little they had received for the past season's grazing. Sloan knew the exact number of steers on the land, since he and another herder had just counted them. Realizing that there was a big discrepancy between the number he had reported to the agent and the money the latter had paid the owners—one-sixth or less of what they were due—Sloan immediately complained to the Indian affairs commissioner and the interior secretary. Attempts were made to silence him. He was heckled, abused, and even sentenced on trumped-up charges to 30 days in the agency blockhouse. There he found himself in company with another objector, Hiram Chase, son and grandson of Omaha chiefs.

After his release, now realizing the importance of education, Sloan, who had attended only the agency school, requested a scholarship to Hampton Institute in Virginia. It was quickly approved, as the reservation officials were glad to be rid of him, and he was admitted to the junior class. In his final year, as spokesman for the Indian students, he was involved in a controversy with Reverend Dr. Thomas Spencer Childs, who had written a negative report on conditions at the school. Sloan graduated as class valedictorian in 1889.

Returning to the reservation, Sloan found that Hiram Chase had graduated from the Cincinnati Law School and was now in practice. Chase lent Sloan his law books, and the latter was soon arguing cases before the justice of the peace. Two years later, Sloan began law practice as Chase's partner at Pender, Nebraska. He was the first Hampton Indian student to become a lawyer.

When Captain William H. Beck (later appointed brigadier general by Theodore Roosevelt) was sent to the Omaha-Winnebago Reservation to remove trespassers, Sloan worked with him for four years, preparing orders for the Indian police to remove trespassers, seeing to legal details of injunction suits filed against the agent and habeas corpus procedures to release men arraigned by the police. That job done, Sloan was offered a transfer to another division of government service but declined, preferring to resume his law practice, which was almost entirely with local Indians. He argued many successful cases before the Nebraska Supreme Court, the most notable being *Sloan v. United States of America*, the first and leading Indian Allotment case to be decided in federal court.

Throughout his career, Sloan was a controversial figure on two counts. First, there were suspicions that, as a lawyer, he was not averse to exploiting less-educated Indians. In 1909, in letters to the director of the Hampton Institute and to the secretary of the interior, fellow Omaha and Hampton graduate Dr. SUSAN LA FLESCHE accused Sloan of having "defrauded, coerced and exploited the Omaha Indians for a number of years." She alleged that, in anticipation of the expiration of the trust period, Sloan had formed a syndicate to buy up Omaha allotments and had secured the dismissal of an inspector who got wind of the scheme. She further provided particulars of 10 cases in which Sloan had allegedly cheated Indians.

The second cause of controversy was Sloan's support of the peyote religion, of which a christianized version had already been organized on the Omaha Reservation by 1906. Opposed at first, Sloan had even drafted a bill to outlaw peyote in Nebraska, but he changed his mind when he realized it attracted the younger, better educated, more acculturated Omaha, and it combated alcoholism. By 1909, more than half the tribal members belonged, and in 1915 the church was reorganized as the Omaha Indian Peyote Society (see NATIVE AMERICAN CHURCH). Both Sloan and Chase were members.

Despite controversy, Sloan's prominence was such that he was one of the six Indians invited by anthropologist FAYETTE AVERY MCKENZIE to form the SOCIETY OF AMERICAN INDIANS (SAI) in 1911. In 1914, he was sent to Washington as a delegate of the Omaha tribe to secure legislation to allow a claim against the United States in federal claims court. While there, he also went before both the House and the Senate Indian committees on various matters and decided to stay in Washington, giving up his practice to spend his days testifying before congressional committees and the Indian Bureau on behalf of various tribes. He published an article on tribal claims in the *American Indian Magazine* (April–June 1916).

In February–March 1918, Sloan spoke on behalf of peyotism at hearings held on a bill by Representative Carl Hayden (Ariz.) to suppress liquor and peyote. The bill, supported by Sioux GERTRUDE BONNIN and CHARLES ALEXANDER

EASTMAN, was opposed by Sloan and Omaha ethnologist FRANCIS LA FLESCHE.

Most of the white missionaries and reformers who supported the SAI, including the INDIAN RIGHTS ASSOCIATION, regarded Sloan with suspicion, and his defense of peyotists in court incurred their further hostility. Despite this, in October 1919 he was unanimously elected president of the SAI. His ally, Father PHILIP GORDON, nominated THEODORE BEAULIEU as vice president. Anti-peyote campaigner Gertrude Bonnin, who detested Sloan, resigned. While Sloan continued as president of SAI a few more years, the organization lacked direction. At the 1923 convention in Chicago, Sloan spoke before the Chicago Bar Association, trying to interest them in Indian affairs.

In 1921, Sloan was a candidate for commissioner of Indian affairs in the new Warren G. Harding administration; he was strongly opposed by the INDIAN RIGHTS ASSOCIATION. CHARLES HENRY BURKE got the position.

Sloan stated his basic legal philosophy in statements at the SAI's founding conference in 1911. According to Sloan, Indian sovereignty was a fiction that had never been taken seriously by the government, the Indian could never rely on the government for anything, and Indian property rights should be determined by the courts, not by the regulations of a paternalistic Indian Bureau. He was not in favor of breaking up INDIAN RESERVATIONS, but he wanted their administration decentralized. In 1916, he supported legislation that would abolish the Indian Bureau but allow tribes to choose their own agents and superintendents. At congressional hearings in February 1934, he praised JOHN COLLIER's INDIAN REORGANIZATION ACT for its general commitment to tribal self-determination, but criticized it for not going far enough, leaving too much to the discretion of the secretary of the interior.

After he was succeeded by Father Philip Gordon as president of the moribund SAI, Sloan moved to Southern California. In the late 1930s, he joined with the opponents of Collier, becoming attorney for the AMERICAN INDIAN FEDERATION. He died in Los Angeles on September 10, 1940.

Further Reading

Iverson, Peter. *Carlos Montezuma and the Changing World of American Indians*. Albuquerque: University of New Mexico Press, 1982.

Hertzberg, Hazel W. *The Search for an American Indian Identity: Modern Pan-Indian Movements*. Syracuse, N.Y.: Syracuse University Press, 1971.

Tate, Michael. *The Upstream People: An Annotated Research Bibliography of the Omaha Tribe*. Metuchen, N.J., Scarecrow Press, 1991.

Smith, Jaune Quick-to-See (1940–) *French Cree, Salish, and Shoshone artist*
Jaune Smith was born on January 15, 1940, at St. Ignatius on the Flathead Indian Reservation in Montana. She is an enrolled member of the Confederated Salish and Kootenai Tribes of the Flathead Indian Nation. Her father, Alfred Smith, was a horse trader and amateur artist. When she was young, Smith helped her father breed horses and sometimes traveled with him on his frequent and extended trading trips across the Midwest. On other occasions, he would have to leave her behind in foster homes.

After high school, Smith attended Olympia Junior College in Washington State. When she was in her 20s, her grandmother named her Quick-to-See. Over the course of 18 years, while raising a family of three, she worked and attended school, finally earning a B.A. in 1976 in art education from Framingham State College, Massachusetts. In 1980, she earned a master's of fine arts degree in painting from the University of New Mexico.

Smith's work achieved an early following in New York City, where she exhibited at the American Indian Community House Gallery. Her art appeared in the *SOHO Weekly News* and *Artspace* in late 1979 and in *Art in America* in March 1980. Over the next three years, her reputation spread, and she was featured in such publications as *Southwest Art*, *New York* magazine, and *People* magazine.

Smith works in a number of media, such as prints, pen-and-ink, and mixed media, though she is primarily known for her paintings. While her work is abstract in style, her themes are generally based in traditional Native American images, such as animals, rock art, and western landscapes, and her colors tend to reflect the natural hues of the Earth. She frequently explores the relationships between land and people and often returns to images of her childhood, in particular the horses among which she was raised. In the 1990s, her work became more political, with mixed media pieces that criticized polluters, Indian mascots, and the quincentenary celebrations of Christopher Columbus's first voyage. Smith's work has been featured in more than 100 shows, and her paintings are included in notable permanent collections such as the Denver Art Museum, the Heard Museum, and the Corcoran Art Gallery in Washington, D.C.

Smith also works to promote Native American artists and has founded two artists' cooperatives, one on the Flathead Reservation and one in Albuquerque. She has also provided scholarships on her reservation. With feminist painter Harmony Hammond, Smith curated "Women of Sweetgrass, Cedar and Sage" (1985), the first exhibition devoted entirely to the contemporary art of Native American women. In 1987, the American Academy of Arts and Letters awarded her its Purchase Award, and in 1989 Washington University in St. Louis made her an honorary professor. Her painting *Rainbow* was chosen for a series of posters to celebrate President Bill Clinton's reelection in 1992. In 2005, she was a recipient of the New Mexico Governor's Award for Excellence in the Arts and the Allan Houser Memorial Award, named after the distinguished Apache painter and sculptor (see HOUSER, ALLAN). Smith remains to be at the forefront of Native American contemporary art while keeping true to her traditional vision, and she is continually attempting to perfect her technique of finding commonality within differing cultures.

Further Reading

Smith, Jaune Quick-to-See, and Julie Sasse. *Jaune Quick-to-See Smith: Postmodern Messenger.* Tucson, Ariz.: Tucson Museum of Art, 2004.

Smith, Kenneth L. (1936–) *Wasco assistant secretary of the interior for Indian affairs*

A Wasco, Kenneth L. Smith was born on March 29, 1935, in The Dalles on the Warm Springs Reservation in Oregon, where he lived most of his life. He graduated from the University of Oregon in 1959 and then began to work for the Confederated Tribes (Wasco and Paiute) of the Warm Springs Reservation as an accountant. He joined the tribal council in 1965. In 1969, he succeeded Vernon Jackson as the reservation's chief executive officer. He was a board member of the Oregon State Board of Education from 1973 to 1979. In 1975, Smith joined the board of directors of the Oregon Historical Society. He also became president of the Intertribal Timber Council and served as chair of the steering committee of the National Indian Timber Symposium. In 1976, he served on the AMERICAN INDIAN POLICY REVIEW COMMISSION Task Force on Reservation and Resource Development and Protection, along with Navajo (Dineh) PETER MACDONALD and Choctaw PHILLIP MARTIN.

Smith served as Warm Springs's chief executive officer until he was appointed to head the BUREAU OF INDIAN AFFAIRS (BIA) by President Ronald Reagan in spring 1981. When Secretary of the Interior James G. Watt stated on January 18, 1983, that INDIAN RESERVATIONS had become worse examples of failed socialism than the Soviet Union, the NATIONAL TRIBAL CHAIRMAN'S ASSOCIATION called for Watt's resignation and the NATIONAL CONGRESS OF AMERICAN INDIANS (NCAI) expressed strong disapproval. Smith, however, argued that while the manner of Watt's statements may have been offensive, the general principle was true, and he criticized the critics of Watt's diatribe for then coming to the administration "in here the next day with their hands out" (February 17, 1983).

Along with Watt, Smith developed the Reagan administration's policy toward Indians, which called for less "special treatment from Washington" and aimed to "promote more self-government of the reservations and less day-to-day supervision of tribal activities by the Bureau." The new direction was unveiled in a policy statement released in January 1983. It received a mixed reaction from Indian leaders. Smith tried to assuage tribal leaders' fears that the new policies were simply a disguised version of TERMINATION, arguing that "President Reagan's approach has a much greater chance of success than the proven failures of the past. We know paternalism and Indian tribal dependency won't work. We know that from the experience of 200 years."

Although the BIA's budget was not significantly diminished under Smith, the Reagan administration's deep cuts in federal agencies that administered social programs, such as the Departments of Labor, Health and Human Services, and Education, hit Indians particularly hard. Total federal spending on Indians dropped from $3.5 billion in 1981 to $2.5 billion in 1984, and Indian unemployment jumped more than 10 percent during this period.

Smith was particularly interested in the development of the private sector on Indian reservations, and the centerpiece of his policy was a partnership between tribes and corporations aimed at bringing financial independence to reservations (see PRESIDENTIAL COMMISSION ON INDIAN RESERVATION ECONOMIES). The policy met with little success, however. Smith's actions did reinvigorate Indian activism, in particular the NCAI, which, under JOSEPH DELACRUZ and SUZAN SHOWN HARJO, fought against his policies and those of his successor, ROSS SWIMMER.

In 1984, after stepping down from the BIA, Smith returned to the Warm Springs Reservation and formed the company Ken Smith and Associates, a consulting firm for economic development projects. In 1989 he regained his position as chief executive officer of the Confederated Tribes of Warm Springs. As CEO, he was instrumental in the construction of a museum, early childhood education center, and health and wellness center. His economic development efforts helped to bring the Warm Springs Composite Products Company and a casino to the reservation (see GAMING, ON INDIAN RESERVATIONS). In 1995, he was replaced as CEO by Edward Henderson. Smith currently serves as a director of numerous business enterprises.

Further Reading

Cook, Samuel R. "Ronald Reagan's Indian Policy in Retrospect: Economic Crisis and Political Irony." *Policy Studies Journal* 24, no. 1 (1996): 11–26.

Kotlowski, Dean J. "From Backlash to Bingo: Ronald Reagan and Federal Indian Policy." *Pacific Historical Review* 77, no. 4 (2008): 617–653.

Smith, Redbird (1850–1918) *Cherokee leader*

Traditionalist leader of the Cherokee full-bloods in Oklahoma, Redbird Smith was born on July 19, 1850, the son of Pig Smith, a conservative Cherokee leader, and a part-Cherokee woman of the Wolf Clan. His birth occurred while the family was moving from Arkansas to the Cherokee Nation (located in what is now northeastern Oklahoma) and just after they had crossed the border into the Cherokee Nation. The family settled in the Illinois District, where traditional Muscogee (Creek) also lived, along with very conservative remnants of the Natchez, who retained the religious practices of the old southeastern Indians before contact with non-Indians. During the Civil War, Smith's family, along with other conservative Cherokee who opposed the Cherokee Nation's alliance with the Confederate States, fled to Kansas, where they endured severe hardships. When they returned home after the war, they ended up in refugee camps within a devastated landscape. These conditions drew the traditional people from all three tribal traditions closer together.

By the end of the Civil War, Pig Smith had emerged as a major leader of the full-blood Cherokee, in particular its most conservative, non-Christian faction. Among the Cherokee, the terms *full-blood* and *mixed-blood* are not racial; they refer to particular cultural, economic, and political attitudes. The full-bloods were subsistence farmers, strongly opposed to ASSIMILATION and, by a great majority, to slavery. They refused to learn English but were often literate in Cherokee and read the *Cherokee Advocate*. Pig Smith was an important member of the Keetoowah Society, a secret society resurrected just before the Civil War to oppose slavery and the power of wealthy Cherokee "mixed-blood" planters and to restore traditional Cherokee values. Seeking to bring up his son in the most traditional way possible, Pig Smith sent young Redbird to Notchee Town, near Sulphur Springs in the southern Illinois District, to be educated by a Natchez religious leader, Creek Sam. There on Greenleaf Mountain the few remaining Natchez had their sacred fire, and the surrounding area was a stronghold of religiously conservative Cherokee. Redbird married Lucie Fields, who came from a family of mixed Cherokee-Natchez ancestry in what is now Braggs, Oklahoma.

After his father's death in 1871, Smith gradually rose in the leadership of the Illinois District Keetoowah. After the Civil War, two factions developed within the Keetoowah Society, one of which was more political and the other more spiritual. Some of the more spiritual Keetoowah never even joined the original society, seeing it as primarily political. This division was similar to that between the old Cherokee system of White Chief (peace) and Red Chief (war). In 1889, the "White" faction met at Long Valley in the Going Snake District of the Cherokee Nation and drew up an amendment to the constitution stating that the society would be religious as well as political. Now Redbird Smith became more active, developing his own spiritual beliefs along the "White Path." Elected to the Cherokee Council in 1890, he led a religious revival among the most conservative of the Keetoowah, who became known as the Nighthawk Keetoowah, bringing back the Cherokee Stomp Dance in 1896 and rekindling the Cherokee Sacred Fire in 1902.

Around this time, the Four Mothers Society was founded by Natchez people, with some Cherokee and Creek members (see HARJO, CHITTO). Like the Keetoowah Society, the Four Mother was based on the ancient religion of the southeastern Indians and was opposed to assimilation and ALLOTMENT. For a time Smith was active in both organizations.

Smith's "White Path" was the path of nonviolence and good deeds, and he counseled his followers always to avoid the use of witchcraft. He believed that whites had descended on the Cherokee as a punishment for their wrongdoing, but if they could be held off long enough for all Cherokee to return to the White Path, they would survive as a people.

After the CURTIS ACT of 1898 extended the Allotment process to the Five Civilized Tribes (Cherokee, Chickasaw, Choctaw, Creek, and Seminole), the Cherokee became the last of the five to sign an Allotment agreement, in 1901. In the Cherokee Council, Smith had opposed the agreement, refusing to vote on it and then, when it was approved, refusing to sign it, since the full-bloods regarded Allotment as a violation of Cherokee rights under the treaty of 1832. When the

Dawes Commission began enrolling all Cherokee in order to assign them allotments, some Keetoowah complied, but under Smith's leadership, 5,000 refused, withdrawing from all participation in any further tribal business or voting. They also left the Keetoowah Society (which incorporated separately in 1905) and founded the Nighthawk Keetoowah. In 1902, the commission had Smith and other Nighthawk leaders arrested, but the movement continued. The Nighthawk Keetoowah, with the "irreconcilables" of the Creek, Choctaw, and Chickasaw, had belonged to the Four Mothers Society, which continued as a clandestine organization for many years thereafter (and still exists today), calling for the creation of a territory within Oklahoma where full-bloods could hold their lands in common. Later in 1902, Smith broke with them—not over goals, however, but over procedures. He also wanted the Keetoowah to be more Cherokee and less Natchez in their traditions. A ceremonial fire was established in 1902 on Blackgum Mountain, near Smith's home.

In 1910, Smith went to Mexico with a document which some of his followers believed gave them valid title to land in Mexico, but he could not establish the claim and soon returned. With the outbreak of the Mexican Revolution shortly thereafter, the document, which had been left in the hands of a Mexican lawyer, was lost. That same year, seeing that resistance to the federal government was becoming futile, Smith accepted his allotment.

In 1914, Smith went to Washington, D.C., in a last effort to present the full-blood position to the U.S. government. Indian Commissioner CATO SELLS wrote a sympathetic letter to the president but did not give his support. In Washington, Smith met Oneidas LAURA CORNELIUS KELLOGG and her brother CHESTER POE CORNELIUS, who would have a great influence on him and the Nighthawk Keetoowah movement. Persuading Smith that the Keetoowah were the "lost fire" of the Iroquois, Cornelius brought ashes from an Iroquois fire to the Blackgum Mountain fire of the Keetoowah, and in some important observances replaced the old Natchez beliefs and practices with Iroquois ones.

In addition, under the guidance of the two Oneidas, Smith implemented one of the earliest plans for "culturally appropriate" community economic development, emphasizing the need for good land and education; this was based on Kellogg's "Lolomi Plan." The Nighthawk Keetoowah already raised their own food and paid cash for their supplies. In 1917, they bought 200 head of Black Angus cattle, the first of a number of community investments. After Redbird Smith died on November 8, 1918, his son Sam continued the project with Cornelius, intending for the Keetoowah to practice modern farming and become known for the excellence of their poultry, stock, and produce, and even to develop a Keetoowah brand for their products. However, the project failed when several community investments turned sour, and since the group had never incorporated, many individuals were saddled with heavy losses.

The Nighthawks have maintained their resistance to assimilation into the 21st century.

Further Reading

Hendrix, Janey. *Redbird Smith and the Nighthawk Keetoowahs.* Welling, Okla.: Cross-Cultural Education Center, 1983.

Minges, Patrick Neal. "The Keetoowah Society and the Avocation of Religious Nationalism in the Cherokee Nation, 1855–1867." Ph.D. dissertation, Union Theological Seminary, New York, 1994.

Myers, Donna J. *The Nighthawk Keetoowah Society: Symbols of Identity.* Norman: University of Oklahoma Press, 1996.

Starr, Emmet. *Starr's History of the Cherokee Indians.* Fayetteville, Ariz.: Indian Heritage Association, 1967.

Smoky, Lois (Lois Smokey)   See KIOWA FIVE.

Snake, Reuben (Kikawa Unga, "To Rise Up")

(1937–1993) *Winnebago political, religious leader*
Born on January 12, 1937, in Winnebago, Nebraska, to Reuben Harold and Virginia Greyhair Snake, Reuben Snake was baptized three months later in the peyote tradition of the NATIVE AMERICAN CHURCH and given the name Kikawa Unga (To Rise Up). His parents divorced when he was four, and Snake was shuttled between his father and his mother, both of whom moved from place to place in the Midwest in search of work. He attended a local mission school in the Winnebago reservation before being sent to Haskell Institute in Lawrence, Kansas, at age 13. In 1954, he joined the U.S. Army and became a Green Beret. After his discharge in 1958, Snake attended Northwestern Junior College in Iowa before moving to Omaha in 1960 with his new bride Winnebago Kathy McKee. There he founded the Omaha Indian Center. After attending the University of Nebraska, he returned to the Winnebago Reservation in 1967.

In 1969, Snake led a successful Winnebago boycott of Walhill, Nebraska, a racist border town, and turned toward political activism. In 1970, in another successful fight against the Army Corps of Engineers, which wanted to annex Winnebago lands on the Missouri River, Snake established a "Winnebago Navy" to patrol their side of the river. He attended the first national organizational meeting of the AMERICAN INDIAN MOVEMENT (AIM), held in St. Paul, Minnesota, in 1970, and was elected vice chairman of the organization. Snake then returned to the Winnebago Reservation to take control of the tribe's education programs, then being managed by the state of Nebraska in order to receive the lucrative federal funds supplied by the JOHNSON-O'MALLEY ACT (see EDUCATIONAL POLICY, AMERICAN INDIANS AND). Snake used this experience to help train Indian tribes to use their federal money wisely.

After RUSSELL MEANS resigned as AIM chairman in 1972, Snake was appointed to the post. That same year, he was named cochair, along with ROBERT BURNETTE, of the TRAIL OF BROKEN TREATIES, although he was unable to participate because his father-in-law had suffered a debilitating stroke. In the meantime, Snake had become more committed to the Native American Church, of which he was ordained a roadman (spiritual leader) in 1974.

Snake stepped down from AIM to run for the chairmanship of the Winnebago tribe, winning election in 1977. Aided by LADONNA HARRIS, he centralized the different federal programs that provided tribal income, embarking on his goal of economic self-sufficiency for the tribe. Snake's many initiatives for economic development, cultural renewal, and education made the Winnebago a model for other reservations, and he became widely known for his advocacy of sustainable economic development (see INDIGENOUS ECONOMICS).

Snake was elected president of the NATIONAL CONGRESS OF AMERICAN INDIANS (NCAI) in 1985, working with SUZAN SHOWN HARJO. In 1986, however, he suffered the first of two heart attacks and had to give up his post the following year. After his recovery, he became one of the foremost advocates of Indian RELIGIOUS FREEDOM, leading the fight to protect the use of peyote as a sacrament in the Native American Church.

Later, Snake worked for the Institute of American Indian Arts in Santa Fe, New Mexico. But his health worsened, and he returned to the Winnebago Reservation, where he died of heart failure on June 28, 1993.

Further Reading

Reynolds, Jerry. "Reuben Snake Papers Carry His Spirit to National Museum." *Indian Country Today*, 29 December 2006.

Snake, Reuben. *Reuben Snake, Your Humble Serpent.* Santa Fe, N.Mex.: Clear Light Publishers, 1996.

Society of American Indians (SAI)

Founded in Columbus, Ohio, in 1911, the Society of American Indians (SAI) was the first national pan-Indian rights organization in the United States. Since the turn of the 20th century, a small group of English-speaking, highly educated Indians had attempted to assert control over the movement to reform federal Indian policy, a movement that had been dominated by non-Indian groups such as the INDIAN RIGHTS ASSOCIATION (IRA) and the Lake Mohonk Conference of the Friends of the Indian.

Conceived by sociologist FAYETTE AVERY MCKENZIE and some of the most illustrious Indians of the day, including CHARLES ALEXANDER EASTMAN (Santee Dakota Sioux), SHERMAN COOLIDGE (Arapaho), CHARLES EDWIN DAGENETT (Peoria), LAURA CORNELIUS KELLOGG (Oneida), THOMAS L. SLOAN (Omaha), HENRY ROE CLOUD (Winnebago), and GERTRUDE BONNIN (Yankton Nakota Sioux), the SAI was largely progressive in bent—that is, nontraditional—and favored ALLOTMENT, Indian access to greater educational opportunities, and the ASSIMILATION of Indians into mainstream American culture. The group opened a Washington office and established *American Indian Magazine* under the editorship of ARTHUR C. PARKER (Seneca). The SAI then lobbied to open the U.S. court of claims to Indian tribes and threw its weight behind a bill introduced by Oklahoma congressman and SAI member CHARLES D. CARTER (Chickasaw) that would have codified Indian law.

Despite its formidable membership, the SAI achieved little in its short tenure. By and large, the society's views differed only slightly from the prevailing federal policy toward Indians. Hamstrung by a lack of finances and public support, the SAI failed to secure President Woodrow Wilson's backing for its reform agenda, despite a meeting between him and the society's leaders in 1914. Factions arose in the society, beginning with Yavapai CARLOS MONTEZUMA's call in 1915 for the immediate abolition of the Office of Indian Affairs (as the BUREAU OF INDIAN AFFAIRS [BIA] was then known) and Indian assimilation, a course deemed too radical by the rest. Eastman and Bonnin's position in favor of outlawing the use of peyote also created a serious split (see NATIVE AMERICAN CHURCH). The 1919 campaign to make Indians citizens, which deeply divided the members, led to the demise of the group. Although Sloan, Montezuma, and PHILIP B. GORDON (Chippewa) continued on, the SAI declined rapidly, ceasing to function by 1926.

Further Reading

Clark, David Anthony Tyeeme. "Representing Indians: Indigenous Fugitives and the Society of American Indians in the Making of Common Culture." Ph.D. dissertation, University of Kansas, 2003.

Hertzberg, Hazel W. *The Search for an American Indian Identity: Modern Pan-Indian Movements.* Syracuse, N.Y.: Syracuse University Press, 1971.

Holm, Tom. *The Great Confusion in Indian Affairs: Native Americans and Whites in the Progressive Era.* Austin: University of Texas Press, 2005.

Hoxie, Frederick E. *Talking Back to Civilization: Indian Voices from the Progressive Era.* New York: Palgrave Macmillan, 2001.

Larner, John W., Jr. *The Papers of the Society of American Indians* (microfilm). Wilmington, Del.: Scholarly Resources, 1987.

Maddox, Lucy. *Citizen Indians: Native American Intellectuals, Race, and Reform.* Ithaca, N.Y.: Cornell University Press, 2005.

Sockalexis, Andrew (1891–1919) *Penobscot distance runner, Olympic athlete*

Andrew Sockalexis, a Penobscot, was born on January 11, 1895, in Old Town, Maine. His first cousin was Louis Sockalexis, the late 19th-century baseball player after whom the Cleveland Indians are named. Andrew Sockalexis began his running career at age 10, training during the winter on the frozen Penobscot River. He is best known for placing second in the Boston Marathons of 1912 and 1913 after heartbreakingly close and dramatic races. He also competed on the 1912 Olympic team that featured Jim Thorpe (see THORPE, JAMES FRANCIS), LOUIS TEWANIMA, and Native Hawaiian swimmer Duke Kahanamoku. A marathon runner, he finished fourth in the event. In 1916, he beat the great marathoner Clarence DeMar in a 15-mile race, but by then Sockalexis was already suffering from the effects of tuberculosis. He died of the disease on August 16, 1919, at age 27. He was inducted into the Maine Sports Hall of Fame in 1984.

Further Reading

Fleitz, David L. *Louis Sockalexis: The First Cleveland Indian.* Jefferson, N.C.: McFarland, 2002.

Rice, Ed. *Andrew Sockalexis.* Charleston, S.C.: Book Song Publishing, 2008.

Sohappy, David (1925–1991) *Wanapum fishing rights activist, traditional leader*

Born on April 25, 1925, on the Yakima Reservation in Washington State, David Sohappy was raised in a traditional Wanapum family that practiced the Dreamer Religion of his great-granduncle Smohalla. His grandparents had little use for non-Indian culture and, once he had learned to read and write, took David out of school after the fourth grade to keep him from "having his mind changed" to the government's "way of thinking." His father, Jim Sohappy, fished in the age-old style, living on the banks of the Columbia River in a longhouse and using nets made by hand. During WORLD WAR II, while David Sohappy served in the U.S. Army, the family was evicted from their traditional fishing camps near Priest Rapids to make way for the Hanford Nuclear Reservation (see NUCLEAR INDUSTRY, AMERICAN INDIANS AND THE).

Upon his return from the war, Sohappy worked in a sawmill until he was laid off in the early 1960s. He returned to fishing to sustain his family of nine children. In 1957, the new Bonneville Dam had flooded Celilo Falls, the greatest Native fishing grounds on the continent, driving most Indians out of the fishing industry and forcing the Sohappy family to settle on a small parcel of federal land at Cooks Landing. Although the federal government had promised to replace Indian fishing villages destroyed by the building of dams on the Columbia, they never did, and Sohappy's existence on the river was tenuous.

Washington State fish and game officials, who regulated the fishing on the river, raided the camp often, confiscating more than 230 nets, beating family members, and finally arresting Sohappy in 1968 for fishing out of season. Sohappy argued that the Walla Walla Treaty of 1855 guaranteed his rights to fish undisturbed (see HUNTING AND FISHING RIGHTS). In 1969, the case he brought, *Sohappy v. Smith,* won an important ruling that prohibited the states of Oregon and Washington from interfering with Indian fishing except for purposes of conservation.

With the ruling affirmed by the Boldt Decision of 1974, which established that Indian treaties set aside half the harvestable catch in the Columbia River for Indians, Sohappy's struggles should have ended. However, Washington State police continued to raid Sohappy's house and harass him and his family, though they never took him to court. Finally, in 1981 state and federal undercover agents set up a salmon scam buying operation directed specifically at Sohappy. In 1983, quietly amending a federal law to make the interstate sale of fish a crime, they arrested Sohappy and his son, David, Jr.,

Wanapum fishing rights activist and traditional leader David Sohappy and his wife, Myra, after David Sohappy's release from prison in 1988 for attempting to exercise his right to fish. *(Ronnie Farley)*

for selling fish out of season. The fact that the sting operation had begun eight months before the law was changed to make Sohappy's actions a criminal offense marks the action as simply a vendetta by fish and game officials.

Unable to pay for an experienced lawyer, Sohappy was convicted in 1987 of selling fish taken in violation of state law (though he was acquitted of the charge of selling the fish in violation of state law and was found to be in compliance with tribal fishing regulations). Sentenced to five years in prison, he suffered two debilitating strokes while behind bars, and his case attracted international attention for its injustice. Intervention by Senator Daniel K. Inouye (Hawaii), then chair of the Senate Subcommittee on Indian Affairs, Senator Brock Adams of Washington State, and attorney Thomas Keefe, Jr., finally secured his release in May 1988.

Still not finished, the government attempted to evict Sohappy from his house on Cooks Landing, though he took them to court and beat them one last time. He died of a stroke on May 6, 1991, in Hood River, Oregon. His wife, Myra, died on March 28, 2005.

Further Reading

Hart, John. "Salmon and Social Ethics: Relational

Consciousness in the Web of Life. *Journal of Society of Christian Ethics* 22 (2002): 67–93.

Hunn, Eugene S. "What Ever Happened to the First Peoples of the Columbia?" In *Great River of the West: Essays on the Columbia River*, edited by William L. Lang and Robert C. Carriker, 18–35. Seattle: University of Washington Press, 1999.

Ulrich, Roberta. *Empty Nets: Indians, Dams, and the Columbia River*. 2nd edition. Corvallis: Oregon State University Press, 2007.

sovereignty, indigenous and tribal

Sovereignty, in terms of a political body, includes the power to select a form of government, administer justice, determine membership, tax, control domestic relations, hold relations with other sovereign nations, wage war, extradite, and enter into treaties. Most Indian tribes have exercised most if not all these powers at some time, and Indian tribal sovereignty is legally recognized by the United States.

The Supreme Court in *Cherokee Nation v. Georgia* (1831) defined Indian tribes as sovereign—but domestic and dependent—nations. However, a weaker state does not necessarily surrender its independence by putting itself under the protection of a stronger one. Until 1831, Congress had legislated on Indians according to international law and with the consent of tribes. After *Cherokee Nation v. Georgia*, Congress continued to make treaties with Indian tribes on a government-to-government basis, but by the end of the 19th century, Congress had begun to put the emphasis on the "domestic" and "dependent" aspects of the Supreme Court definition. Regarding individual Indians as its own wards rather than citizens of sovereign entities, Congress began to exercise "plenary," or absolute, powers over the tribes without their consent—not according to treaty, but for its own unilateral expediency.

The Supreme Court decision in *Ex parte Crow Dog*, 109 U.S. 557 (1883), which recognized tribal jurisdiction over Indian lands, led Congress to pass the Major Crimes Act in 1885, extending federal criminal jurisdiction over major crimes on INDIAN RESERVATIONS. Despite this, the Supreme Court continued to uphold Indian sovereignty, ruling in *Talton v. Mayes*, 163 U.S. 376 (1894) that Indian courts were not bound by the provisions of the U.S. Constitution. The court finally reversed itself in *Lone Wolf v. Hitchcock*, 187 U.S. 553 (1903), ruling that Lone Wolf, a Kiowa, could not obstruct the implementation of ALLOTMENT on Kiowa land, regardless of Kiowa consent. The case firmly established Congress's power to unilaterally break treaties and exercise complete control over Indian peoples.

The ideology emphasizing that Indians were wards of the federal government reigned for the first 30 years of the 20th century. This period coincided with the federal policy of Allotment and a repressive attempt to break up Indian tribes. Under congressional plenary power, Indian sovereignty was treated virtually as a legal fiction, and Indian governments were ignored. Indian reservations were run by agents chosen by the Indian commissioner. These agents exercised dictatorial powers as they sought to undermine Indian traditions, religions, and forms of governance. If, on some reservations, Indians happened to have their own governments, the sovereign powers that they exercised were, according to Congress's interpretation of sovereignty, entirely delegated by Congress, and therefore could be altered and even dissolved by act of Congress. The unilateral dismantling of the governments of the Five Civilized Tribes (Cherokee, Choctaw, Chickasaw, Creek, and Seminole) under the CURTIS ACT (1898) and their subsequent despoliation represent the most extreme example of this trend.

The INDIAN REORGANIZATION ACT (IRA) of 1934 marked a change in federal policy, establishing tribal governments that had powers over their respective territories. Radical critics have charged that the IRA was simply a more sophisticated form of colonial administration. It certainly was that, but to ignore the tremendous reprieve from cultural and territorial disintegration that it granted is to miss one of the defining moments of American Indian history in the 20th century.

The new tribal governments often did come at the expense of traditional systems of governance, and attempts to implement the IRA were themselves sometimes heavy-handed, such as in the notorious case of the Hopi (see LA FARGE, OLIVER). For Indian Commissioner JOHN COLLIER, who promoted and implemented the legislation, the kind and degree of sovereignty these new governments would enjoy was never fully resolved. Although at one time Collier argued that the IRA was merely recognizing the inherent sovereignty of Indian tribes, he would also refer to the IRA as similar to state and federal delegations of power to municipalities—in effect, creations of the federal government. As attorneys RUSSEL BARSH and JAMES YOUNGBLOOD HENDERSON put it, "He was unable to propose a consistent theory of power."

There are two sources of sovereignty: inherent (residual) and delegated. The first has existed "from time immemorial" and cannot be destroyed so long as the tribe exists. Attorney FELIX COHEN, in his *Handbook of Indian Law*, called inherent powers "the most basic principle of all Indian law." Congress turned to Nathan Margold, solicitor of the Interior Department, to interpret the basis of tribal powers under the IRA. Margold came to the conclusion that "those powers which are lawfully vested in an Indian tribe are not, in general, delegated powers granted by express acts of Congress, but rather inherent powers of a limited sovereignty which have never been extinguished." The decision of the Interior Department's solicitor—that Indian sovereignty was inherent rather than delegated by the federal government—achieved a greater influence in the theory of tribal sovereignty than the IRA itself did.

Cohen, in drafting the influential *Handbook of Indian Law*, followed Margold closely, emphasizing the tribes' inherent sovereign powers, although he still recognized that federal plenary power could in theory always overrule tribal sovereignty. Despite the limits to sovereignty under the IRA and the interpretations of Margold and Cohen, the new concept of sovereignty was anathema to state governments, which had hoped for a transfer of federal powers over reservations to the states, and to assimilationists, who wished to see an end to Indian reservations. Once Collier stepped down as commissioner in 1945, the tide turned in favor of those who sought wide use of Congress's plenary powers. The subsequent TERMINATION era was just that—an attempt to terminate Indian tribes as political entities and thus terminate their sovereignty. Although Termination did not accomplish its ultimate goal of destroying Indian tribes, it did place limits on Indian sovereignty and gave many states broad powers over tribes. The heaviest blow to Indian sovereignty during this era was Public Law 280 (1953), which granted states criminal jurisdiction over Indian reservations.

During the 1960s, as the Termination era waned, the doctrine put forward by Cohen and Margold regained force and began to be refined by Indian legal thinkers such as HANK ADAMS (Assiniboine-Dakota Sioux) and VINE DELORIA, JR. (Yankton Nakota Sioux). For Deloria, the relationship between Indians and the United States was one of government to government. Congressional legislation should thus give way to direct negotiation and treaties with the federal government on a tribal or regional basis. Deloria went so far as to suggest that Indian governments are akin to "international protectorate[s]." For the TRAIL OF BROKEN TREATIES protest in 1972, Adams helped draft the "Twenty Points," which advocated a return to the "treaty relationship" and demanded the repeal of the 1871 legislation that forbade making treaties with Indian tribes.

Although treaty making was not revived, the concept of a government-to-government relationship became the official policy of the federal government after President Richard Nixon called for the repeal of Termination in 1970. The HUNTING AND FISHING RIGHTS struggles of the 1960s and 1970s gave rise to court decisions reaffirming Indian sovereignty rights as inherent rather than delegated. However, these rights continue to be limited by the same federal courts, in particular in areas of civil and criminal jurisdiction. During the 1980s, legislation affecting Indian economic development, in particular the gaming industry (see GAMING ON INDIAN RESERVATIONS), as well as attempts by states to tax Indian commerce, also limited the powers of Indian governments.

Another concept of sovereignty that has gained force since the 1970s is based directly on Indian traditions. Although sovereignty may seem to be a Western concept, legal expert Charles Wilkinson has found expressions of sovereignty in traditional thought, such as the Sahaptin concept put forward by Delbert Frank, Warm Springs tribal councilman: "At the time of creation the Creator placed us in this land and He gave us the voice of this land and that is our law."

Like traditional Western concepts of sovereignty, traditional Indian sovereignty is traced to a spiritual source. The difference of emphasis in the two spiritualities is that Native American traditions place more emphasis on the spiritual nature of the Earth itself. In addition, whereas the more humanistic Western concept of sovereignty focuses on rights, the Indian concept is more ecological and focuses on responsibilities. For this reason, it is to secure their ability to continue carrying out their responsibilities to their lands, that Indian nations must have sovereignty and jurisdiction over them. As Seneca author JOHN MOHAWK put it in a speech to the AMERICAN INDIAN MOVEMENT (AIM) in 1974, to be sovereign, "we must have self-sufficiency and our spirituality."

During the first three decades of the 20th century, when sovereignty was at its lowest ebb, it was still kept alive in theory and in actual practice by a few traditional governments, such as the Iroquois Confederacy (see THOMAS, GEORGE E.), the traditionalists of the Five Civilized Tribes (for example, the Nighthawk Keetoowah; see SMITH, REDBIRD), the Red Lake Chippewa, the Florida Seminole, and the Pueblo (including the Hopi). Important expressions of traditional Indian sovereignty can be found throughout the early part of the 20th century—for example, the Iroquois struggle against draft registration in WORLD WAR I, LEVI GENERAL's attempts at the League of Nations to gain international recognition for the Iroquois, and the Pueblo fight against missionaries and against the notorious BURSUM BILL.

Before WORLD WAR II, both the Iroquois and the Florida Seminole challenged the U.S. Selective Service Act of 1940. They took the position that selective service did not apply to them because, like the 1924 Citizenship Act, which they also did not recognize, it had been passed unilaterally and without their knowledge or consent.

Traditional sovereignty, coming from other and higher sources, may sometimes find itself at odds with the delegated sovereignty of tribal governments. As Diné CARE, a grassroots indigenous environmental organization, stated in its newsletter, "politicians and bureaucrats have the wrong idea about sovereignty. . . . True sovereignty can only come from within. . . . [Tribal governments] make convenient use of political sovereignty by shirking their responsibility to take care of the land as U.S. environmental laws say they should."

Yet this is far from saying that individuals may "take the law into their own hands." In the climate of "me first" fostered by the Ronald Reagan administration during the 1980s, the traditional Iroquois theory of sovereignty was distorted in just this way. Groups such as the Warrior Society used this new interpretation of "personal sovereignty" to justify their rejection of any attempts to tax them, even by their own Iroquois communities, invoking sovereignty to profit at the expense of the community as a whole. (See SHENANDOAH, LEON.) The real origin of this theory of "personal sovereignty" or "sovereign citizen" was the extreme right-wing Posse Comitatus movement; it was first articulated by Christian Identity minister William Potter Gale in the 1970s. As John Mohawk put it, "While individuals can assert group rights, individuals are not the group." Sovereignty is the community's will. Without this, "there can be no Mohawk sovereignty. There can only be competing groups of individuals who are ultimately hostile to the will of the whole and, inadvertently, to the sovereignty of the whole."

Given inherent sovereignty based on traditional cultural and religious values, the definition of Indian sovereignty cannot be purely constitutional. As Potawatomi attorney ROBERT COULTER writes, "The question whether as a legal matter Indian nations have retained sovereign rights has been regarded by some as a question entirely governed by United States law. The more contemporary view is that Indian rights are properly questions of international law."

In recent years, indeed, indigenous peoples not only in the United States but all over the world, following the lead of the Iroquois of the 1920s, have vastly developed their presence in the international law community. International instruments such as the United Nations Charter and the 1960 Declaration on the Granting of Independence to Colonial Countries and Peoples say a nation cannot preempt exercise of sovereignty of another nation.

No nation can unilaterally extinguish another's sovereignty, and Indians have not willingly relinquished theirs. At the creation of the United Nations Working Group on Indigenous Populations in 1981 (see DEERE, PHILLIP), the United States and Canada insisted on the use of the term *populations*, not *peoples*, so that any work done in the United Nations would be considered as relating to "domestic minorities." The Draft Declaration on the Rights of Indigenous Peoples, approved by indigenous delegates in 1993 and adopted by the

Working Group and its parent group, the Subcommission on Prevention of Discrimination and Protection of Minorities, ran afoul of nation-state reviewers from the Commission on Human Rights, which balked at features the U.S. representative said conflicted with conventional American legal doctrine. The attempt by the United States to make the Declaration on the Rights of Indigenous Peoples a projection of its own internal policy precipitated a mass walkout of Native delegates, who stopped the process. Nonetheless, the United Nations Declaration on the Rights of Indigenous Peoples was finally adopted on September 13, 2007.

Further Reading

Anaya, S. James. *Indigenous Peoples in International Law.* New York: Oxford University Press, 1996.

Barsh, Russel Lawrence, and James Youngblood Henderson. *The Road: Indian Tribes and Political Liberty.* Berkeley and Los Angeles: University of California Press, 1980.

Deloria, Vine, Jr., and Clifford M. Lytle. *The Nations Within: The Past and Future of American Indian Sovereignty.* Austin: University of Texas Press, 1984.

d'Errico, Peter. "Native Americans in America: A Theoretical and Historical Overview." In *American Nations: Encounters in Indian Country, 1850 to the Present,* edited by Frederick E. Hoxie, Peter C. Mancall, and James H. Merrell, 481–499. New York: Routledge, 2001.

Ivison, Duncan, Paul Patton, and Will Sanders, eds. *Political Theory and the Rights of Indigenous Peoples.* Cambridge: Cambridge University Press, 2000.

Taiaiake, Alfred. "Sovereignty." In *A Companion to American Indian History,* edited by Philip Joseph Deloria and Neal Salisbury, 460–474. Malden, Mass.: Blackwell Publishing, 2004.

Wilkins, David E. *American Indian Sovereignty and the United States Supreme Court: The Masking of Justice.* Austin: University of Texas Press, 1997.

Wunder, John R. *Native American Sovereignty.* New York: Routledge, 1999.

Speck, Frank Gouldsmith (1881–1950) *naturalist, anthropologist, linguist*

Frank Gouldsmith Speck was born in Brooklyn, New York, on November 8, 1881. Between the ages of eight and 15, he spent the summers in the Mohegan-Pequot community of Mohegan Hill near New London, Connecticut, with Fidelia Fielding, an old friend of his family. Fielding, one of the last speakers of her tribal language and one of the last repositories of traditional Mohegan lore, taught him to see the natural world through different eyes and gave him a critical perspective on mainstream American society. She also taught him the Mohegan-Pequot language.

Speck went on to study at Columbia University. In his third year, he took a linguistics course under J. Dyneley Prince, a specialist in American Indian languages. Astounding Prince with his firsthand knowledge of two nearly extinct Algonquian languages (Mohegan-Pequot and Delaware-Mohican), Speck soon cowrote three papers with him and published a fourth in *American Anthropologist* under his sole authorship. Though he was still an undergraduate, the pattern of his life's work was set: learning to speak Indian languages and rescuing them and the cultures they embodied from oblivion by collecting texts and other ethnographic information. He would go on to study and record not only many other Eastern Algonquian languages, but also four other language families: Yuchian, Muskogean, Iroquoian, and Eastern Siouan (such as Catawba).

While still in college, Speck met Seneca anthropologist ARTHUR C. PARKER at the home of Indian rights advocate Harriet Maxwell Converse. Their views on the relation of Indians to the larger American society were quite different. Parker, though passionately interested in indigenous traditions, saw them as history; they had lost their validity for the present, and modern Indians must strive toward ASSIMILATION, achieving racial pride by successfully competing in the non-Indian world. Speck, on the other hand, found traditional Native American religion and lifeways far more worthwhile and meaningful than most of what mainstream American culture had to offer. They were precious resources in the fund of human knowledge, and traditional ways of life should be kept alive to the extent possible. "Anybody who advocates total tribal disintegration," he stated in a paper read at a meeting of the SOCIETY OF AMERICAN INDIANS in 1914, "is manifestly advocating race murder..." (the term *genocide* had not yet been coined). "Might as well some powerful foreign nation establish propagandist centers in the United States, trying to convert us to some foreign ideas that we should dissolve our national feelings for the sake of assimilating its higher life."

Speck received his B.A. in 1904, and on Prince's recommendation was accepted into the graduate program at Columbia under noted anthropologist FRANZ BOAS. Upon receiving his M.A. in 1905, he did further fieldwork in Oklahoma among the Yuchi, Creek, Chickasaw, and Osage, under Boas's supervision. Offered a research fellowship at the University of Pennsylvania in 1907, Speck earned his Ph.D. there in 1908 with a thesis on Yuchi ethnography (see BROWN, SAMUEL WILLIAM, JR.) and later that year was appointed instructor in anthropology and assistant at the university museum. He left the museum in 1911, when he became assistant professor. He became full professor in 1925. To all intents and purposes the founder of the anthropology department at the University of Pennsylvania, Speck was department chair nearly the whole time from 1911 to his death.

An informal, unassuming man, always sociable with students and popular with Indians, Speck hoped to develop an Indian intelligentsia that could help Native American people better appreciate the value of their own cultures at a time when nearly all Indian education was aimed at assimilation. To this end, he tried to inspire promising Native American students to study anthropology, he helped them to get funding and to navigate the university bureaucracy. Among these were GLADYS TANTAQUIDGEON (Mohegan) and MOLLY SPOTTED ELK (Penobscot). He also taught RED THUNDER CLOUD (Cromwell West) and WILLIAM CHRISTIE MACLEOD.

While Speck's interests were encyclopedic, he came to focus on the Eastern Woodland Algonquians. He visited every Eastern Algonquian community at least once and often many times, from Labrador in the north to North Carolina in the south, no matter how acculturated the community. He gathered virtually every type of information, from myth and folklore texts to lifeways and land tenure to physical objects. Among his fundamental contributions was his study of Algonquian hunting territories.

From his work among the more southerly Algonquians, Speck realized that they were strongly tied to the southeastern cultures, and this revived his interest in the whole Southeast cultural area, including the Gulf of Mexico, to which he had already been introduced in Oklahoma. For this he had to turn to three other linguistic families: Eastern Siouan (including Catawba), Yuchian, and Iroquoian (including Cherokee). His work on the Cherokee led him back to the study of Iroquois ceremonialism that he had begun at the Sour Springs Cayuga Long House about 1924 under the guidance of Cayuga-Oneida leader ALEXANDER GENERAL.

Speck was always centrally interested in American Indian religions, and he received full cooperation from traditionalists because of his highly respectful attitude. In fact, religion was really the key to everything he did. His extraordinary linguistic ability brought great strength to these studies. What Speck had to say to the general society about Indians went against every stereotype prevalent at the time. He understood traditional cultures as high cultures, treasuries of wisdom that compared favorably with the classical cultures of the Old World, but with the immeasurable benefit that they were still living cultures.

Speck was too absorbed in his chosen work to be a political activist, but although he always looked for the intellectual and spiritual content of everything he studied, he was also well aware of the political implications of his traditionalist perspective. For example, Speck was one of the few white men to understand that in most of the Algonquian cultures, the LAND TENURE system was usually based on clearly delineated, hereditary family hunting territories. He explained how this form of ownership required hunters to think and act in an ecologically sound manner (see ENVIRONMENTAL MOVEMENT, AMERICAN INDIANS AND THE). Finally, he saw that colonial authorities had frequently made territorial transfer agreements with Native American individuals who had absolutely no right to dispose of the lands they purported to transfer.

For the last several years of his life, Speck suffered from a serious heart condition. In late January 1950, he and his wife, Florence, went to the Seneca midwinter ceremonies at the Coldspring Long House near Red House, New York. There he became ill and had to be brought back to Philadelphia, where he died on February 6, 1950, at the University Hospital.

Further Reading

Blankenship, Roy, ed. *The Life and Times of Frank G. Speck.* Philadelphia: Department of Anthropology, University of Pennsylvania, 1991.

McNab, David T. "The Perfect Disguise: Frank Speck's Pilgrimage to Ktaqamkuk—the Place of Fog—in 1914." *American Review of Canadian Studies*: 85–104.

Obermeyer, Brice. "Salvaging the Delaware Big House Ceremony: The History and Legacy of Frank Speck's Collaboration with the Oklahoma Delaware." In *Histories of Anthropology Annual*, Vol. 3, edited by Regna Darnell and Frederic W. Gleach, 184–198. Lincoln: University of Nebraska Press, 2007.

Pulla, Siomonn. "'Would You Believe That, Dr. Speck?': Frank Speck and *The Redman's Appeal for Justice.*" *Ethnohistory* 55, no. 2 (2008): 183–201.

Spopee ("Turtle") (1850–1915)   *Blackfeet prisoner*

Spopee, a Blackfeet, was born in 1850 on Blackfeet lands in what is now the state of Montana. The Blackfoot or Niitsitapi (officially called Blackfeet by the U.S. government) are a confederacy of four tribes in Montana and Alberta, Canada—the Piegan (Canadian spelling: Peigan) or Pikunis, North Piegan, Kainai (Blood), and Siksika (Blackfoot)—all of whom speak the same language. According to James W. Schultz, in his book *My Life as an Indian* (1907), a highly reliable source, Spopee was actually a Blood (Kainai). In the time of Spopee's youth, there were few, if any, non-Indian settlers in the region, and he grew up in the traditional lifestyle of the Blackfeet.

On January 23, 1870, U.S. cavalrymen attacked a peaceful group of Blackfeet camped on the Marias River in the vicinity of what is now Shelby, Montana (the exact location is unknown). Most of the men were away, so the majority of those attacked were women and children. In the slaughter that followed, approximately 200 Blackfeet, mostly women and children, were killed. Spopee himself was shot and wounded. According to Ella Clark, a Blackfeet who later provided the best-known though not the most reliable account of Spopee's life, his mother was killed during a massacre, presumably this one. This unprovoked attack, known as the Marias Massacre (or Baker Massacre after the commanding office, Major Eugene F. Baker), left a traumatic mark on the Blackfeet people, though it went largely unnoticed in the U.S. press.

Spopee eventually married a Blackfeet woman, Different Cuts (also known as Strange Cut or Cuts Different). In 1877, they had a daughter, Mary.

In September 1879, a white miner named Charles Walmsley was found murdered on Cut Bank Creek, near the encampment where Spopee lived. According to Schultz, suspicion fell upon Spopee and another Blackfeet, Good Rider, who had been observed together purchasing hundreds of dollars worth of goods at nearby Fort Benton in the days after the murder. Schultz was living in the Blackfeet camp at the time and in his book documents the arrest of Spopee and Good Rider by Fort Benton sheriff John J. Healy, who then transported the two suspects to Helena, Montana Territory, for trial.

During the trial, held in 1880, Good Rider claimed that Spopee had shot Walmsley in the back while the latter was cooking supper. Spopee did not deny killing Walmsley. In his statement during the trial, a portion of which was printed in the *Anaconda Standard* of July 14, 1914, he said, "I did kill the white man, for I thought he would kill me; he told me he would do so." Spopee claimed he only acted in self-defense after they had stopped to ask for some food and that Walmsley attacked them with an ax. Spopee was convicted, sentenced to life imprisonment, and transferred to a jail in Detroit.

Knowing no English and believing he would soon be tortured and put to death, Spopee prepared himself and decorated his prison garb with buttons and other items that would befit a brave warrior. This, along with his stoic silence and his few attempts to communicate with guards in sign language, which the guards could not understand, were interpreted as evidence that Spopee was losing his mind. After two years in Detroit (1879 to 1881) he was transferred to the Federal Hospital for the Insane (St. Elizabeth's Hospital) in Washington, D.C.

Spopee did not understand why he was being moved, and he maintained complete silence. To the Blackfeet, Spopee's fate remained a mystery; most assumed he had died in Detroit. As he later explained, having no one to converse with for decades, he gradually forgot much of his own language. Years went by and the silent Indian in the hospital became a curiosity pointed out to visitors. He was comforted by his religion, and at night, despite the din of the asylum, as he later stated in an interview, "I knew the Great Spirit was in me and I could go to sleep."

One Blackfeet, Robert J. Hamilton, a graduate of Carlisle Indian School in Pennsylvania and an interpreter for the tribe, began about 1904 to inquire after Spopee at every federal penitentiary in the country. Unfortunately, Spopee had never been held in a federal prison.

It was not until 1913, when a delegation of sightseeing Indians visited the hospital and a guard led them to Spopee, that he was rediscovered. According to one version of the story, the Indians were Sioux; in another, they were Blackfeet and included Ella J. Clark and her husband, Malcolm W. Clark, both Carlisle graduates in their 40s, who were visiting Washington after having escorted a contingent of new Blackfeet students to the Indian school in Carlisle, Pennsylvania. Possibly the group included both Blackfeet and Sioux. In any case, they could not converse with Spopee—if Sioux, because they did not know the Piegan language; if Blackfeet, because Spopee had forgotten his own language. In both versions, the visitors established that the prisoner was Blackfeet by singing tribal songs. Clark says, more specifically, that she sang him Blackfeet lullabies and spoke to him as a mother speaks to a child, awakening in him the first recollections of his native tongue.

Hamilton was notified of the discovery, as was CATO SELLS, the commissioner of the Indian Office (as the BUREAU OF INDIAN AFFAIRS was known at the time). Sells took a great personal interest in the case and carried out an investigation. Visited frequently by Hamilton, Spopee gradually regained the ability to speak. After a few months, Sells applied to the Justice Department for an unconditional pardon on Spopee's behalf.

Spopee was unwavering in his claim that he had killed Walmsley only in self-defense. Furthermore, Sells determined that the body had actually been found on the Canadian side of the border and thus that the Montana court that sentenced Spopee had been without jurisdiction. The Justice Department's decision was favorable, President Woodrow Wilson signed a pardon on July 7, 1914, and it was delivered to Sells two days later.

The presidential pardon was widely publicized and made Spopee a celebrity. He was released on July 13, given an automobile ride around Potomac Park, taken to dinner at the Capitol Hotel, feted by Indian rights advocates, and brought to meet commissioner Sells, with Hamilton as interpreter and journalists present.

Spopee's ordeal was further publicized by Ella Clark, whose version of the story first appeared as "The Story of Spo Pee" in the *New York World* in early July 1914, just prior to his release. Her account is highly stylized and melodramatic, and many statements are clearly incorrect. According to Clark, immediately after a massacre of the Blackfeet, in which Spopee's mother is killed, Spopee vows vengeance and kills the next white man he sees. (In reality, the two events occurred a decade apart.) Convicted of murder, he is spared a hanging because of a certain justness to his action.

After his release, Spopee was escorted back to Montana where he was reunited with his daughter, now Mrs. Takes Gun of Browning, Montana. The Blackfeet received him with much rejoicing. On July 18, the tribal council legally adopted him as a member of the tribe, and he was granted an allotment of 320 acres. Sadly, the years spent in confinement had made it impossible for Spopee to readjust to life on the reservation. He had dreamed of once again living in a tipi, making bows and arrows, and hunting buffalo, but this old way of life was gone. At the same time, he preferred wearing modern clothing and wearing his hair in the American style. He became depressed and did not mingle with his people. Although he had appeared in good health at the time of his liberation, Spopee died less than one year later in Browning, Montana, on May 29, 1915, of a combination of heart, gallbladder, liver, and kidney diseases.

Further Reading

Anon. "Greatly Interested in Spo Pee's Case. Montana Indian Who Has Just Been Pardoned Is Interviewed by Writers." *Anaconda Standard* (Anaconda, Montana), 14 July 1914, p. 7.

Gibson, Stan. "An Uncelebrated Anniversary." Available online. URL: http://www.dickshovel.com/parts.html. Accessed 10 March 2010.

Gibson, Stan, and Jack Hayne. "Witnesses to Carnage: The 1870 Marias Massacre in Montana." Available online. URL: http://www.dickshovel.com/parts2.html. Accessed 10 March 2010.

Schultz, J. W. *My Life as an Indian: The Story of a Red Woman and a White Man in the Lodges of the Blackfeet.* London: John Murray, 1907.

Wessel, Thomas R. "Political Assimilation on the Blackfoot Reservation, 1887–1934." In *Plains Indian Studies: A Collection of Essays in Honor of John C. Ewers and*

Waldo R. Wedel, edited by Douglas H. Ubelaker and Herman J. Viola, 59–72. *Smithsonian Contributions to Anthropology* 30. Washington, D.C.: Smithsonian Institution Press, 1982.

sports, American Indians and

The early part of the 20th century was a golden era for Native American athletes, who dominated many sports, especially football. The game had become popular among colleges at the end of the 19th century, and between 1893 and 1914, the Carlisle Indian School assembled some of the most powerful teams ever to play in college competition. Under their legendary coach, POP WARNER, the team would showcase a string of all-Americans, including GUSTAVUS WELCH (Gus Welch, Chippewa), WILLIAM DIETZ (Lone Star Dietz, Oglala Lakota Sioux), PETE CALAC (Pedro Calac, Luiseño), and JOE GUYON (Chippewa). Carlisle also fielded a formidable track team, which featured one of America's finest long-distance runners, LOUIS TEWANIMA (Hopi).

Indians also dominated long-distance running, a field in which the United States had long lagged behind the rest of the world. Tom Longboat (Canadian Onondaga), ANDREW SOCKALEXIS (Penobscot), and ELLISON BROWN (Tarzan Brown, Narragansett) all won fame in the Boston Marathon, the premier long-distance race in America. Indians also ran in popular "bunion" marathon races, such as the 480-mile race from Milwaukee in 1927, which was won by Karok runner Mad Bull. That same year, Chief Tall Feather (Levi Parker Webster), a 43-year-old Oneida from Green Bay, Wisconsin, another Carlisle graduate, broke the record for the Milwaukee-to-Chicago nonstop marathon, 94 miles in 19 hours and 47 minutes. Twenty years before, Tall Feather had set the record for the mile run with a time of four minutes, 13 seconds. In 1928, Cherokee Andrew Hartley Payne was the winner of the Great Cross-Country Marathon Race from Los Angeles to New York City. Payne finished the 3,442-mile race in 573 hours and four minutes.

A number of Indians were prominent in major league baseball in the early part of the 20th century, including ZACK WHEAT (Cherokee), CHARLES ALBERT BENDER (Chief Bender, Chippewa), and JOHN TORTES MEYERS (Chief Meyers, Cahuilla).

In professional football, Carlisle stars such as Guyon and Calac helped the Canton Bulldogs become the winningest team in the pre–National Football League (NFL) era. After the NFL was born, one of the first franchises was an all-star Indian team known as the OORANG INDIANS.

The greatest sports figure of the first quarter of the 20th century was the legendary JIM THORPE (Sac and Fox). A football and track star for Carlisle, he was also an Olympic gold medal winner and one of the founders of the NFL. His feats on the athletic field were so remarkable that he was dubbed "the world's greatest athlete," an honor that went unchallenged while he lived.

The 1918 closing of the Carlisle Indian School, the premier forum for Indian amateur competition, largely shut off the flow of great Indian athletes into professional sports. During the 1920s and 1930s, the Haskell Institute in Oklahoma boasted a number of great athletes, including all-American running backs John Levi (Arapaho) and Louis "Rabbit" Weller (Caddo) and runner WILSON D. CHARLES (Buster Charles, Oneida). In the 1940s, Jack "Indian Jack" Jacobs (Creek) was a standout quarterback, defensive back, tailback, and halfback at the University of Oklahoma. Drafted in the second round by the Cleveland (now St. Louis) Rams in 1942, Jacobs had a long career in the NFL, playing for the Washington Redskins and Green Bay Packers. In the 1950s, he moved to the Canadian league, where as a quarterback he led the Winnipeg Blue Bombers to the Grey Cup five times. Jesse "Cab" Renick (Choctaw) was an all-American basketball player at Oklahoma A&M (now Oklahoma State University) in 1939 and 1940. In 1948, Renick won a gold medal as team captain of the undefeated U.S. Olympic basketball team.

Creek athlete ALLIE REYNOLDS ("Superchief") was a major force behind the most successful baseball team of all time, the 1949–53 New York Yankees, who won an unmatched five World Series in a row. In 1957, Onondaga OREN LYONS, JR., was an all-American goalie for the undefeated Syracuse University LACROSSE team, one of the greatest lacrosse teams on record. In the 1964 Olympic games, Oglala Lakota Sioux BILLY MILLS won the 10,000-meter run, scoring one of the most dramatic victories in Olympic history. At the Tokyo games, Northern Cheyenne BEN NIGHTHORSE CAMPBELL competed in judo. Other athletes of note include Gene Locklear, a Lumbee who played professional baseball during the 1970s; Alex "Sonny" Sixkiller, Cherokee quarterback for the University of Washington and later an NFL player; Ron Curl, a Wintu professional golfer; and Micmac PATTI DILLON, the premier American woman long-distance runner in the early 1980s.

In hockey, Chippewa HENRY BOUCHA won an Olympic silver medal in 1972 and became an all-star player for the Minnesota North Stars. Cherokee stuntwoman and racecar driver Kitty O'Neill, dubbed "The Fastest Woman on Earth," set the record for the quarter mile in 1977, 3.22 seconds at a speed of 412 MPH, one of many records she would set. Al Waquie (Jemez Pueblo) won three consecutive Pike's Peak Marathons (1979–81) and five consecutive Fleet Empire State Building Run-Ups (1983–87). During the 1980s, the IROQUOIS NATIONAL LACROSSE TEAM was formed to allow Indians to compete internationally in the sport of lacrosse.

Further Reading

Adams, David Wallace. "More Than a Game: The Carlisle Indians Take to the Gridiron, 1893–1917." *Western Historical Quarterly* 32, no. 1 (2001): 25–53.

Bloom, John. *To Show What an Indian Can Do: Sports at Native American Boarding Schools.* Minneapolis: University of Minnesota Press, 2000.

Deloria, Philip J. *Indians in Unexpected Places.* Lawrence: University of Kansas Press, 2004.

Harris, Othello, Claire Elaine Nolte, and George B. Kirsch.

Encyclopedia of Ethnicity and Sports in the United States. Santa Barbara, Calif.: Greenwood Press, 2000.

King, C. Richard. *Native Athletes in Sports and Society: A Reader.* Lincoln: University of Nebraska Press, 2005.

Oxendine, Joseph B. *American Indian Sports Heritage.* Champaign, Ill.: Human Kinetics Books, 1988.

Powers-Beck, Jeffrey P. "'Chief': The American Indian Integration of Baseball, 1897–1945." *American Indian Quarterly* 25, no. 4 (2001): 508–538.

Spotted Elk, Molly (Mary Alice Malledellis Nelson, Molly Nelson) (1903–1977) *Penobscot dancer, actress*

Mary Alice Malledellis Nelson was born on Indian Island, Maine, on November 17, 1903. She was the eldest of eight children of Philomene Saulis Nelson (Penobscot-Maliseet) and Horace Nelson (Penobscot-Passamaquoddy), and later Penobscot representative to the Maine state legislature (1921–22) and tribal governor (1939–40). Horace Nelson's father, Peter "Dindy" Nelson, was also a tribal governor, elected in 1905.

As a child, Molly Nelson played bit parts in several Indian films made in the area. She went to public school in Old Town, Maine, and graduated Old Town Junior High in 1917. After working as a governess in Swampscott, Massachusetts, for a year, she toured with a vaudeville company, returning to Indian Island in September 1920. Immediately entering high school, she left after two terms to join the Boston-based road show of Milton Goodhue. She returned to high school at the end of summer 1922 but dropped out in fall 1923.

In September 1924, invited by her friend FRANK SPECK, Nelson took some courses at the University of Pennsylvania, where she became friends with Mohegan GLADYS TANTAQUIDGEON. She stayed only one semester, spending the rest of 1925 with her sister in the Miller Brothers 101 Ranch Wild West Show, and returned east that December (see EAGLE SHIRT, WILLIAM). In winter 1926, now calling herself Molly Spotted Elk, she moved to New York City, where she worked as an artist's model and danced in the 16-member Foster Girls precision troupe at the Hippodrome. In May, she was sent to the Aztec Theater in San Antonio, Texas, for eight months, returning to New York in January 1927, only to hit the road with fellow Penobscot LUCY NICOLA POOLAW (Princess Watahwaso), touring on the Keith-Albee-Orpheum circuit in Ohio, Michigan, and New York State for two months. Back in New York in May 1927, she appeared with various revues, did some modeling, and briefly worked with composer Charles Wakefield Cadman (see INDIANIST MUSIC) in late 1927.

Spotted Elk also performed in speakeasies, notably those of Texas Guinan. Mary Louise "Texas" Guinan was a former chorus girl and silent film actress who had opened a speakeasy the 300 Club at 151 West 54th Street in New York City at the onset of Prohibition. The club became a hangout for movie stars and the wealthy elite of New York. At Guinan's club in 1928, Spotted Elk met Douglas Burden, who was so impressed with her that he offered her the role of the female lead in his film *The Silent Enemy*, also featuring CHAUNCEY YELLOW ROBE and SYLVESTER LONG LANCE. On this very long location job (1928–29), she became close to Yellow Robe and developed a long-lasting infatuation with Burden.

Back in New York in spring 1929, Spotted Elk returned to work with Texas Guinan. On September 17, 1929, she opened on Broadway in *Fiesta*. She was a hit, but the show ran only five weeks. When the stock market crashed a week later, Spotted Elk was already booked in the Guinan Girl dance troupe for *Broadway Nights*, which enjoyed 130 performances followed by a successful road tour. She was nearly signed for director Cecil B. DeMille's *The Squaw Man* but was replaced at the last minute by Lupe Velez. In early 1930, she made promotional appearances for *Silent Enemy* and devoted the year to writing and the study of voice.

In spring 1931, Spotted Elk was the featured dancer with the band of JOSEPH SHUNATONA in Paris, and when the band found itself stranded, she managed to find work in Paris and was fairly successful. She became involved with French journalist Jean Archambaud and soon found herself pregnant. Spotted Elk traveled to Los Angeles in May 1934 to be with her sister, only to discover that her sister had moved to New York. Penniless and nearly alone, Spotted Elk gave birth to a daughter at the end of May. After a few weeks her sister joined her, but things were difficult, and in November she went to Maine. She spent 1935 and 1937 shuttling back and forth between Maine and New York and most of 1936 with her sister in California, where she landed minor roles in several well-known Hollywood films.

Meanwhile, Archambaud was becoming mired in the dangerous politics of prewar France. Suspected of knowing too much, he became involved with a female spy and was carefully watched. In 1936, he quit his political activities. Through their four-year separation, Spotted Elk and Archambaud kept up a correspondence. In 1937, she nearly despaired of their relationship, but a letter from his parents convinced her of his love, and after many difficulties, she and her daughter arrived in France about the beginning of July 1938. The couple married in September 1939, a few weeks after the start of WORLD WAR II.

As Hitler's armies advanced through Europe, Spotted Elk and Archambaud made plans to escape. They had intended to sail for the United States from Bordeaux, but Jean was denied a visa, and Molly refused to leave him. They went to stay with Jean's parents in Royan. After the partition of France, fearing for her daughter's safety, Molly left with the girl on June 30, 1940, and, after a long and difficult foot journey across the Pyrénées, reached Spain. They sailed for New York City in July. Archambaud, ill and unable to leave France, died in October 1941. Spotted Elk received the news in December.

Molly Spotted Elk never fully recovered from this tragedy. After a disappointing love affair, she suffered a nervous breakdown in 1948 and was hospitalized for a year. She returned to New York but could not find a job and never performed again. Eventually she returned to Indian Island, where she died on February 27, 1977, after a fall.

Further Reading

McBride, Bunny. *Molly Spotted Elk: A Penobscot in Paris.* Norman: University of Oklahoma Press, 1995.

Standing Bear, Luther (Ota Kte, "Kills Plenty")

(1868–1939) *Teton Sioux chief, author, lecturer, educator, actor*
Luther Standing Bear was born Kills Plenty (Ota Kte) in Fort Robinson, Nebraska, at the Spotted Tail Agency, Rosebud Reservation, in December 1868. His mother was named Pretty Face; his father, Standing Bear, who took part in the defeat of George Armstrong Custer at Little Big Horn, was leader of the Wears Salt band of the Brulé, one of the seven branches of the Teton Lakota Sioux nation. Kills Plenty was raised in the traditional way, participating in one buffalo hunt and a war party against the Ponca that was called back before reaching its destination. However, the agency had been established in the year of his birth, and his whole youth was a time of deepening white impact and interference with traditional life and the authority of traditional chiefs.

Without even understanding what a school was, Kills Plenty volunteered to become a member of the first class to enter Carlisle Indian School in Pennsylvania (1879), regarding it, in the traditional Lakota sense, as an act of bravery in which he would probably die. He was given the name Luther Standing Bear after he picked the name Luther from a list of names on a blackboard. He then spent six years there, learning the tinsmith's trade. His sister, Victoria, and two brothers, Henry and Willard, also attended Carlisle. Leaving in 1885, he worked for a while at a Wanamaker's store in Philadelphia, then returned to Rosebud, where he taught school. Later he moved to Pine Ridge, where the rest of his family was already living.

Standing Bear was with Buffalo Bill's Wild West Show as an official interpreter and manager of the Indian contingent on its 11-month tour in 1902, which took him to New York and England. He rejoined them for the 1903 season but left the company after being seriously injured in a railway accident in Illinois in which several other Indians were killed. In 1905, after his father's death, Standing Bear was selected to replace him as chief. Not long afterward, he moved to Sioux City, Iowa, and then lived in Walthill, Nebraska, between 1907 and 1911 where he worked as a store clerk. He nonetheless remained involved in reservation affairs, participating in a protest against the government's move to open more lands at Pine Ridge to non-Indian settlers. As a result of friction with superintendent John Brennan, who had failed to secure enrollment and an allotment for his wife, Mary Splicer, Standing Bear decided to leave the area.

After a brief stint with the Miller Brothers 101 Ranch in Oklahoma, a famous Wild West show, Standing Bear was invited by film producer Thomas Ince in 1912 to join his studio in California (see also EAGLE SHIRT, WILLIAM). In subsequent years, he not only acted in silent films (including a several that starred William S. Hart), but also spoke on the lecture circuit, acted in a play in New York (*The Race of Man)*, worked with

Chief Luther Standing Bear is seen in this file photograph from First National Pictures movie studio, date unknown. *(AP/First National Pictures)*

the Boy Scouts and the Girl Scouts, and owned a business in Venice, California.

Among his films were *White Oak* (1921), *Santa Fe Trail* (1930), *The Conquering Horde* (1931), *Texas Pioneers* (1932), *Laughing Boy* (1934), and *Murder in the Private Car, Circle of Death, Cyclone of the Saddle, Fighting Pioneers,* and *The Miracle Rider* (all 1935). He was the founder of the Indian Actors' Association (affiliated since 1936 with the Screen Actors Guild).

Still more important was Standing Bear's contribution as a writer. The publication of his books *My People, the Sioux* (1928), *My Indian Boyhood* (1931), *Land of the Spotted Eagle* (1933), and *Twenty True Stories* (1934) coincided with the reform of Indian administration under Indian Commissioner CHARLES RHOADS and the INDIAN NEW DEAL (see also INDIAN REORGANIZATION ACT) under JOHN COLLIER, a time when the American public was open to a defense of traditional Native American life that was more than mere nostalgia. Standing Bear also advocated far-ranging reforms on the reservation that would give Indians control over their own lives and restore their own languages, histories, and cultures while training them in the skills of modern life. Finally, he advocated educational reforms to teach non-Indian schoolchildren about the history, society, culture, and arts of American Indians.

Unlike his Carlisle classmate CHAUNCEY YELLOW ROBE, Standing Bear was one of the relatively few prominent Sioux of the time who remained traditional; he was also one of the few Hollywood "chiefs" who really was a chief. He found a way to function in non-Indian society and to work for his people while remaining true to his cultural values. He sought the spotlight mainly because he saw it as the best position available to him to educate the American public about his people in an accurate way. His books had the same purpose. He defended the permanent value of Lakota culture, criticized white culture, spoke out against ASSIMILATION, and detailed a clear and influential vision of the Sioux relationship to the Earth (see ENVIRONMENTAL MOVEMENT, AMERICAN INDIANS AND THE).

Standing Bear died in Huntington Park, California, on February 20, 1939, while engaged in production of the film *Union Pacific*. He was survived by a son.

Further Reading

Maddox, Lucy. *Citizen Indians: Native American Intellectuals, Race, and Reform.* Ithaca, N.Y.: Cornell University Press, 2005.

Rosenthal, Nicholas G. "Representing Indians: Native American Actors on Hollywood's Frontier." *Western Historical Quarterly* 36, no. 3 (2005): 329–352.

Starr, Emmet (1870–1930) *Cherokee physician, historian*

Emmet Starr was born on December 12, 1870, in the Going Snake district of the Cherokee Nation, Indian Territory, the son of Judge Walter Adair and Ruth (Thornton) Starr. His parents were both mixed-blood Cherokee. Educated in the Cherokee schools, Starr completed his studies at the Cherokee National Male Seminary in 1888 and received his M.D. at Barnes Medical College in St. Louis in 1891. He practiced medicine for five years, but as soon as he started, he also began to collect material for a history of the Cherokee Nation. At the time, he was serving on the Cherokee National Council and as a delegate to the Sequoyah Convention, which met at Muskogee, Oklahoma, in 1905 to draft a constitution for the proposed state of Sequoyah, to be formed out of the old Indian Territory. Starr was an active participant in this campaign for a separate Indian state, and its failure was a great blow to him, as was the loss of the Cherokee national government in 1907. (See CURTIS ACT.)

Starr's most important book on the Cherokee is *History of the Cherokee Indians and Their Legends and Folklore* (1921). He also wrote three shorter works: *Early History of the Cherokees* (1917), *Cherokees West* (1910), and *Encyclopedia of Oklahoma* (1912). Starr's access to traditional Cherokee informants and materials is remarkable, especially his contacts with the Nighthawk Keetoowah (see SMITH, REDBIRD). His work is exceptional for its time in its outspoken criticism of the Baptist missionaries' influence on his fellow Cherokee. He was regarded by Cherokee historians as the highest authority on tribal history and genealogy.

After helping to support and educate his younger brothers and sisters, Starr eventually moved back to St. Louis where he opened a bookstore. He died there on January 30, 1930, and was buried in Clarence, Oklahoma.

Further Reading

Blackburn, Bob L. "Oklahoma Historians Hall of Fame, Emmet Starr." *Chronicles of Oklahoma* 75, no. 2 (1997): 220.

Meredith, Howard L. "Emmet Starr's Manuscript Essay on the Texas Cherokees." *Indian Historian* 10, no. 1 (1977): 14–16.

Smith, Micah Pearce. "The Latter Days of Dr. Emmet Starr." *Chronicles of Oklahoma* 8, no. 3 (September 1930): 339–342.

Starr, Emmet. *History of the Cherokee Indians and Their Legends and Folklore.* 1921. Reprint, Baltimore, Md.: Genealogical Publishing Co., 2003.

———. *Old Cherokee Families. Notes of Dr. Emmet Starr*, edited by Jack D. Baker and David Keith Hampton. Oklahoma City: Baker Publishing Company, 1988.

Strickland, Rennard, and Jack Gregory. "Emmet Starr, Heroic Historian." In *American Indian Intellectuals*, edited by Margot Liberty, 120–131. St. Paul, Minn.: West Publishing Company, 1976.

St. Cyr, Lillian (Rupa-Hu-Sha-Win, "Red Wing") (1884–1974) *Winnebago actress*

Lillian St. Cyr was born Margaret Lilly St. Cyr on the Winnebago reservation in Nebraska on February 13, 1884. In the course of her life her name was also spelled Lily and she was alternatively known as Lilian or Lillian, with Lillian the most common version. According to her own account, her father was a Winnebago chief named Wank-Shik-Sto-He-Gah (He Who Gathers His People) and her mother Nah-Guh-Pingah (Pretty Hair Woman). Census records indicate that her father, whose English name was Mitchel St. Cyr, was half-Winnebago and half-Métis, and that her mother, whose maiden name was Julia DeCora, was Winnebago. Both parents were descended from prominent Winnebago chiefs, spoke Winnebago, and raised their children in the Winnebago language and culture. Lilly St. Cyr, the youngest of seven children, was given the Winnebago name Rupa-Hu-Sha-Win; the name has also been given as Ah Hoo Souch Wing Gah.

Her mother died only a year after her birth in June 1885, and her father died in 1889 when she was only five. She apparently lived for a time with her older brother, David, a graduate of the Hampton Normal and Agricultural Institute in Virginia and the first Indian to serve as an election official in Nebraska. Their sister Julia also attended Hampton, where she mentored their cousin, aspiring Winnebago artist ANGEL DECORA. After graduating from Hampton in 1885, Julia joined the Indian Office (as the BUREAU OF INDIAN AFFAIRS was known at the time) as a teacher at Indian boarding schools. She passed the bar in Nebraska in 1906, thus becoming, after LYDA B. CONLEY, the second American Indian woman lawyer in the United States.

As a girl, St. Cyr became the protégé of Anna Bache Long, the wife of Kansas congressman Chester Long, learning high society manners in their house. She was put through private school in Philadelphia by Episcopal missionaries and later attended the Carlisle Indian School in Pennsylvania. At Carlisle, where she was registered as Lilian M. Saint Cyr, she became friends with Chippewa baseball star, CHARLES A. BENDER. Graduating in 1902, she returned to Kansas to live with the Long family. When Chester Long was elected to the Senate in 1903, she moved with them to Washington, D.C.

On April 9, 1906, in Washington, D.C., St. Cyr married actor JAMES YOUNG DEER (Delaware). As an actress, St. Cyr took the screen name Princess Red Wing (later dropping the "Princess"). She debuted in the film *The White Squaw* in 1908. Her next film, *The Falling Arrow* (1909), was produced by Lubin, an independent company in Philadelphia noted for using real Indians (usually from vaudeville) to portray Indian characters at a time when most companies used white actors. Other early films were *For Her Sale, or Two Sailors and a Girl* (Vitagraph, 1909) and *An Apache Father's Revenge* (year and production company unknown). With her husband, she played in one of D. W. Griffith's early films, a story with all Indian characters entitled *The Mended Lute* (Biograph, 1909), and starred in *Red Wing's Gratitude* (Vitagraph, 1909), directed by Young Deer.

From 1909 to 1911, Red Wing and Young Deer played in a series of pictures for Bison Films, founded in 1907 by Adam Kessel, Charles Bauman, and Fred Balshofer as an offshoot of their New York Motion Picture Company. Balshofer knew the couple from Lubin. In his book *One Reel a Week*, he says he first used them in supporting roles in *The True Heart of an Indian* (starring Charles Inslee and Evelyn Graham), shot for Bison at Ft. Lee, New Jersey, in 1909. Red Wing helped design the sets.

Later that year, Bison became one of the first film companies to relocate to Southern California. Red Wing's Bison films, which won high critical praise, were *The Flight of Red Wing*, *For the Honor of Red Wing*, *Red Wing's Loyalty*, *Red Wing's Constancy*, all released in 1910; and *Little Dove's Romance* (1911), in which Young Deer also starred. At a screening of this film for the American Society of Cinematographers in 1965, Balshofer, then 86, praised Red Wing's talent and described some of the difficulties of getting the company and its equipment to the location site at Big Bear Lake, California.

Also in 1910, Red Wing played a major part in another Griffith film, the Biograph production of *Ramona*, with Mary Pickford in the title role. Subtitled "A Story of the White Man's Injustice to the Indian," this was the first of four screen versions (1910, 1916, 1928, 1936) of an extremely popular novel by Helen Hunt Jackson (1884) and may have been the first film for which the producers bought motion picture rights from the publisher. Red Wing would also play in the second *Ramona*, directed by Donald Crisp.

Red Wing appeared in a series of films for the French film company Pathé, whose western division was now under her husband's management and direction. She starred in *The Girl from Arizona* (1910), the first Pathé film made in America. Young Deer directed her second Pathé film, *White Fawn's Devotion: A Play Acted by a Tribe of Red Indians in America*, released in mid-1910. They costarred in *Back to the Prairie* (1911), and Young Deer directed *The Unwilling Bride* (1912). The next four—*The Frame-Up*, *The Penalty Paid*, *A Redskin's Appeal*, and *The Pioneer's Recompense*, all filmed in July and August 1912—were written and directed by Young Deer as a vehicle for Red Wing and leading man George Gebhart (as "Young Buffalo").

That same year, she played in *Red Wing and the Paleface* for Kalem, followed by *An Indian's Honor* (1913) for Kay-Bee (a later incarnation of Bison), codirected by Frank Montgomery and Jack Conway; the Tom Mix film *In the Days of the Thundering Herd* (1914, Selig); and what would prove her most famous role, as Nat-U-Rich opposite Dustin Farnum in *The Squaw Man* (1914, Lasky), directed by Cecil B. DeMille and Oscar Apfel and said to be the first feature-length film ever made in Hollywood as well as the first film with screen credits. Red Wing had not been DeMille's first choice to play Nat-U-Rich. He had originally asked her great rival, Josephine Akley, a non-Indian who went by the name of Princess Mona Darkfeather, but Akley was too busy.

Like most actors of the day, Red Wing often performed her own stunts. During the filming of *The Squaw Man* she was accidentally shot in the arm, but the wound was not serious. Though widely acclaimed for her portrayal of Nat-U-Rich, this would be her last major role. Her husband had been implicated in a scandal, and they were both dropped by Pathé. Young Deer managed to find work in Europe, but Red Wing, who remained in California, had trouble getting film parts. In the six years from 1908 through 1914, Red Wing had made almost 50 films, including 20 in 1910 alone. The year after *The Squaw Man*, she made only one, *Fighting Bob* for Rolfe Photoplays. In 1916, her only film role was in Donald Crisp's *Ramona*, made by Clune Films. After Young Deer's return from Europe she appeared with him in the film *Under Handicap*, made by the Yorke Film Corporation in 1917. Although Young Deer had by then been absolved of any wrongdoing, their careers were effectively over.

One of Red Wing's last screen roles was in *White Oak* (1921, Artcraft), starring William S. Hart. After retiring from films in the early 1920s, she returned to New York, where, resuming the name Lillian St. Cyr, she designed and made Indian costumes of very high quality for the F.A.O. Schwarz toy store and the Eaves Theatrical Costume Company. Eventually, however, the buyers who knew her died off, and it became harder for her to find work. She continued making costumes and regalia for a wide variety of clients, including her own tribe.

James Young Deer died in New York on April 6, 1946. St. Cyr, who lived and worked in an apartment on West End Avenue in Manhattan, was active in Indian affairs in New York and Washington. She died at St. Vincent's Hospital in New York on March 12, 1974, at age 90. A pioneer in the film industry, St. Cyr was one of Hollywood's first film stars. Along with her husband, she tried to present in their films a sympathetic portrayal of Indian culture and life, in marked contrast to the then current picture of Indians in most other mainstream media as senseless savages. Indians would never again play such a major role in the development of the Hollywood film industry.

See FILM, AMERICAN INDIANS AND.

Further Reading

Aleiss, Angela. *Making the White Man's Indian: Native Americans and Hollywood Movies*. Santa Barbara, Calif.: Praeger Publishers, 2005.

Stevens, John W. (1933–) *Passamaquoddy tribal leader*

A Passamaquoddy, John Stevens was born on August 11, 1933, in Washington County, Maine. His father, George Stevens, Sr., was an important tribal leader. John attended the local schools before joining the U.S. Marines in 1951. Serving in Korea, he won a number of military decorations, including the Presidential Unit Citation and the United Nations Medal. After his return in 1954, he became active in Passamaquoddy politics and was elected chief in 1955, a position he held for the next 43 years. He also worked for the local paper mill.

By 1955, the tribe had fallen on hard times. Since 1820, when Maine gained statehood, the Passamaquoddy had been under the guardianship of the state, which in 1929 had assigned the Forestry Department to oversee them, and then in 1932 the Health and Welfare Department. In 1936, the state issued free hunting and fishing licenses to the Passamaquoddy, but during WORLD WAR II, the U.S. government annexed a part of Indian Township for a German prisoner of war camp and after the war sold the land to non-Indians. Maine was the last state to allow Indians to vote, ratifying the 1924 United States Citizenship Act only in 1953 after years of intensive lobbying by the Penobscot. (See POOLAW, LUCY NICOLA.)

By this time, Indian Township (also known as Motahkok-mikuk) was mired in severe poverty, and with the economy based largely on hunting and farming, young Passamaquoddy began to abandon the area to such an extent that by 1960 the population had declined to around 200. Stevens began the process of trying to reclaim Indian Township land, organizing a demonstration in 1964 to protest the state's appropriation of 6,000 acres. Stevens's great-aunt, Louise Sockabesin, provided him with documents she had been keeping for the tribe, including letters from George Washington to the Passamaquoddy written during the Revolutionary War and an original copy of a treaty between the nascent state of Maine and the Passamaquoddy signed in 1794. Stevens found numerous disparities between the lands guaranteed by the treaty and lands actually held by the Passamaquoddy. He recruited a non-Indian law student, Thomas N. Tureen, to research the Passamaquoddy land claims. In 1972, the two worked with the NATIVE AMERICAN RIGHTS FUND to file suit for the tribe against the United States, arguing that Maine had violated the 1790 Non-Intercourse Act when it seized Passamaquoddy and Penobscot lands. After arguments by Tureen, the federal district court ruled in the tribes' favor, holding that they had

a valid claim to more than two-thirds of the state. Maine then chose to settle, and in 1980 President Jimmy Carter signed the Maine Indian Claims Settlement Act. Each tribe received $13.5 million in funds and $26.5 million to purchase 150,000 acres as trust land. Both tribes also received federal recognition, leading to a new relationship with the state. However, under the settlement, the Indian governments are municipalities of the state and do not have the sovereign rights of reservations as in other states.

Since then the Passamaquoddy have acquired more than 134,000 acres of land as well as a number of investments, including the Dragon Cement Plant, which they sold at a profit, and Northeastern Blueberry Farms. The tribe also opened a gaming hall, thanks to which it became comparatively well off, funding its own health and education programs and establishing a museum and cultural and language revival programs.

In 1998, Stevens stepped down as governor of Indian Township, but he continues to be active on the tribal council.

Further Reading

Brodeur, Paul. *The Land Claims of the Mashpee, Passamaquoddy, and Penobscot Indians of New England*. Boston: Northeastern University Press, 1985.

Stigler, William Grady (1891–1952) *Choctaw lawyer, political leader, U.S. congressman*

William Grady "Bill" Stigler was born in Newman, Indian Territory, on July 7, 1891, the son of Joseph Simeon and Mary Jane (Folsom) Stigler. Joseph Stigler was the town's first postmaster and a former deputy marshal who had served under infamous "Hanging Judge" Isaac Parker. The name of the town, Newman, was changed in 1893 to Stigler in honor of Joseph. Mary Jane Stigler was part Choctaw, and William Stigler, one-quarter Choctaw, became an enrolled member of the tribe.

Stigler attended Northeastern State College in Oklahoma, where he received a teaching certificate in 1912. He studied law at the University of Oklahoma in 1915 but did not receive a degree. Stigler also worked for the Oklahoma Department of the Interior. In 1917, he attended officers' training school and became a second lieutenant in the 357th Infantry of the 90th Division. During WORLD WAR I, he fought in France in the Battle of Saint-Mihiel and participated in the Meuse-Argonne offensive. After the war, Stigler attended the University of Grenoble in France. He returned to Oklahoma in 1919 and was admitted to the bar in 1920.

Stigler was active in local politics, becoming city attorney to the town of Stigler. In 1924, he was elected Democratic senator to the Oklahoma state legislature and became president pro tem. of the senate in 1931. He served as lieutenant colonel in the 45th Division of the Oklahoma National Guard from 1925 until 1938. On March 28, 1944, Stigler was elected to represent Oklahoma's Second District in the U.S. House of Representatives, filling a seat left vacant after the resignation of Jack Nichols, who had become vice president of Trans World Airlines. Stigler was sworn in on April 12, 1944.

As congressman, Stigler played an important role in the shaping of federal Indian policy. He was a supporter of TER-MINATION, a series of new initiatives that sought to dismantle the gains of the INDIAN NEW DEAL, end federal obligations to Indians, and ultimately dissolve Indian reservations. He sought unsuccessfully to terminate the Osage, along with their valuable mineral rights (see OIL, AMERICAN INDIANS AND). One of his first acts in Congress was to introduce a bill for the federal government to purchase Choctaw and Chickasaw coal and asphalt lands (see DURANT, WILLIAM ALEXANDER). In 1945, Stigler introduced the controversial INDIAN CLAIMS COMMISSION bills H.R. 1198 and 1341 in the House, which were designed to end Indian claims to disputed lands. He did advocate proper oversight of the Interior Department's disbursements to Indians and adequate compensation for the use of natural resources extracted from tribal lands. He also introduced an unsuccessful bill to authorize federal recognition of the United Keetoowah Band of Cherokee (see SMITH, REDBIRD).

In addition to holding a seat on the House Indian Affairs Committee, Stigler also served on the Roads, World War Veterans Legislation, Public Works, and Appropriations committees. He was reelected to the House three consecutive times and served until his death. Stigler died in his hometown on August 21, 1952, after several months of ill health and was buried in Stigler Cemetery. His papers are housed at the William G. Stigler Collection, Carl Albert Center Congressional Archives at the University of Oklahoma.

Further Reading

Philp, Kenneth R. *Termination Revisited: American Indians on the Trail to Self-Determination, 1933–1953*. Lincoln: University of Nebraska Press, 2002.

St. James, Red Fox (Francis Fox James, Chief Red Fox Skiuhushu) (ca. 1889–ca. 1949) *activist, minister*

The life story of Red Fox St. James is shrouded in mystery. His name underwent many changes throughout his career, and his real birth name is not known, but independent sources agree that he was born about 1889. In a letter of July 24, 1913, he told Indian Affairs commissioner CATO SELLS that his father was James Thomas St. James, of Welsh descent and one-sixteenth American Indian blood, and that his mother was a Northern Blackfeet who was apparently half-white and who left the reservation when she married. He described himself as "one-quarter degree Indian blood and more white," who "never had any connection with the Reservation" and was "raised the same as any child born of white people." However, there is no evidence to support any of this. He also claimed to have attended the Carlisle Indian School, but there is no record of it, and the claim is contradicted in an article about him in the *Fort Worth Star-Telegram* from April 24, 1914, where he is said to have attended a college in Spokane, Washington. He is also said to have joined the Catholic Church in 1909 and acquired the name Francis, only to develop a strong anti-Catholic bias and revert to Protestantism after a few years.

In a letter to ex-governor James H. Hawley of Idaho, sent from Nevada, Missouri, excerpts of which were printed in the *Idaho Statesman* on November 30, 1912, he represented himself as Francis Fox James, a cowboy from the town of Blackfoot, Idaho, member of the American National Livestock Association, and "a booster for the commercial industry of our great little rich state . . ." He had taken it upon himself to ride on horseback from Blackfoot to Washington, D.C., to greet newly elected president Woodrow Wilson on behalf of the people of Idaho. The article notes: "In an interview published in a Topeka newspaper, Mr. James [favors] open range and gra[z]ing lands in the west, protection for the Indians, and woman suffrage. . . . Mr. James is a pen and ink artist and also a poet."

St. James did have an informal connection with the Crow reservation in Montana. By 1914, the Crow in the Big Horn country of southern Montana were already developing a prosperous livestock industry, and he rode the range there. Thus, on his second horseback trip to Washington, D.C., he was accompanied by two Indians from the Crow reservation and carried a message to President Wilson from Plenty Coups, the Crow chief. Setting out on March 30, 1914, now as "Red Fox James," he and his companions rode to Washington, D.C., to advocate for a bill to establish an American Indian Day. This cause had been adopted by the SOCIETY OF AMERICAN INDIANS (SAI), of which Red Fox had become a member, and although the publicity trip was his own idea, the SAI backed it and reported on it in their journal. Red Fox and his friends also advocated for two other causes on their journey—the completion of the Lincoln Highway, the first transcontinental highway in the United States, the proposed route of which they followed for much of their ride; and the expansion of Young Men's Christian Association (YMCA) services in Indian country, with the Crow reservation to be the center for all reservations in the vicinity.

The trip, which took more than 10 months, attracted a great deal of national publicity. Red Fox finally arrived in Washington, D.C., on December 18, 1914, and presented the White House with the endorsements of 24 state governors for a bill to recognize American Indian Day. In 1915, the SAI, at their annual meeting in Lawrence, Kansas, issued a statement by founder SHERMAN COOLIDGE supporting the holiday, and the fourth Friday in September was suggested as the date. In 1916, New York became the first state to officially adopt it. Other states followed, but it never became a national holiday because the consensus in Congress was against giving up another workday for a federal holiday.

After bringing his message to the president, Red Fox stayed in the East and was present on January 18, 1915, when the first all-Indian Boy Scout troop was formed at the Carlisle Indian School. Later that year, in New York City, where he visited the YMCA headquarters, he is believed to have formed the TIPI ORDER OF AMERICA as a secret, fraternal youth group to study Indian culture.

Red Fox spent the next few years traveling the country giving speeches while unsuccessfully pushing for federal recognition of American Indian Day. On Independence Day,

1917, he addressed more than 35,000 people at City College Stadium in New York, urging the acceptance of American Indian fighters into the armed services and, in particular, the creation of Indian units to patrol the borderlands with Mexico to counter the perceived threat of a possible alliance between Germany and Mexico.

In 1918, Red Fox was ordained a minister in the Disciples of Christ and, with his so-called cousin Black Hawk (George Rothman), worked at a mission of that denomination on the Yakima (now Yakama) reservation at White Swan, Washington (which still exists as the Yakama Christian Mission Log Church). However, at the same time (as shown in surviving correspondence from 1918 and 1919 with Paul Sperry, minister of the Swedenborgian New Church at Washington, D.C.), Red Fox was falling under the sway of the Swedenborgians, a liberal Christian denomination. Only two years later, Red Fox and Black Hawk would be forced to leave the mission, according to the *Messenger News*, "because the American Christian Missionary Society did not like their New Church doctrines."

In a letter of December 11, 1918, Red Fox invited Sperry to attend a meeting of the Indian Grand Council of the Tipi Order of America. By 1919, he had established chapters of the Tipi Order in various cities in Washington State and transformed it into an adult fraternal organization. The order was closely akin to Freemasonry, and evidence that Red Fox was himself a Freemason is seen in a letter to Governor Davis of Idaho advocating American Indian Day. Published in the *Idaho Statesman* on January 26, 1919, the letter concludes, "Sincerely, I am, A.F. & A.M. Chief Red Fox Skiuhushu . . ." (A.F. & A.M. means Ancient Free and Accepted Mason.) The nature of the various organizations Red Fox founded cannot be fully understood without taking into account their Masonic roots. Under the Tipi Order, he had now become Red Fox "Skiuhushu" and its "Most High Chief." The addition of Skiuhushu to his name he explained as meaning "Red Fox in the Indian tongue." In 1920, as "Head Chief of the Federated Tribes of Indians," he worked for the presidential campaign of Warren G. Harding.

Red Fox edited the Tipi Order's magazine, originally named *American Indian Tipi*, from 1920 through 1923, was succeeded as editor by JOSEPH STRONGWOLF, then resumed editorship from 1925 to 1927. The magazine often followed Red Fox's mystical interests, with articles on religion bearing the hallmarks of Freemasonry, Rosicrucianism, and other esoteric philosophies, as well as often sharing his bias against immigrants, Catholics, and African Americans. He also continued to travel around the country, lecturing on American Indian subjects, often in full "Indian" regalia. He was a strong advocate for CITIZENSHIP and the right of Indians to vote. In 1922, Red Fox founded the American Indian Association (AIA) as an advocacy group modeled upon the SAI, which was by then in decline.

In 1925, Red Fox was ordained a deacon in the newly formed Anglican Universal Church, a mystical Christian sect founded by George Winslow Plummer, who also founded the Societas Rosicruciana in America. By then he was using the name Reverend Red Fox St. James. Red Fox was apparently insecure about his Indian heritage, or lack of it. Nor did he have a typically Indian appearance. As a consequence, he developed a number of theories to bolster his Indianness, including the concept that the Welsh were in America before Columbus and were therefore Indians. He also accumulated titles, such as head chief, and names such as Red Fox. However, by 1926, many Indians, including the well-known Yankton Nakota Sioux advocate GERTRUDE BONNIN, had begun to suspect that Red Fox was an imposter. In 1927, when the officers of the Tipi Order decided that no national office could be held by a non-Indian, Red Fox resigned.

By this time, Red Fox had already founded a social club in New York City with another celebrity of dubious Indian heritage, Princess MARY CHINQUILLA, under the auspices of the AIA. One of the first urban Indian centers, it had recreational facilities and a place where visiting Indians could gather. The club had another purpose, however, and that was to explore the mystical and occult aspects of Indian and Christian religions. According to an article in the *New York Times* on February 6, 1927, "Dr. Skiuhushu is supervisor and chaplain of the clubhouse and holds both a Christian and an Indian religious service in the club's reading room every Sunday morning." Along with Joseph Strongwolf, another member of the AIA, Red Fox became a superior of the Order of White Friars (OWF), a pseudo-Catholic group that blended Indian and Christian rites and also operated under the auspices of the AIA.

Red Fox continued to advocate for a national American Indian Day and was a fixture in New York City's American Indian Day celebrations. In 1928, he wrote a long letter to the *New York Times* on American Indian Day, signing it Francis Red Fox St. James (Skiuhushu). However, he appears from this point on to have turned his attention away from advocacy and more to the esoteric and mystical religious aspects of his organization.

An article in the *New York Times* on September 28, 1936, regarding the proposal for an American Indian Day, contains the first mention of a new organization, the Indian Association of America (IAA). Two months later, Red Fox wrote another letter to the *New York Times* about American Indian Day, this time as the Reverend Barnabas Skiuhushu, president of the Indian Association of America. He also began using the name Barnabas St. James. Two years later, his name morphed into Barnabas S'hiuhushu, often preceded by "Dr.," although he held no doctoral degree.

In 1938, the IAA also began issuing a magazine, *The Indian Speaking Leaf*, which published articles on history and symbolism. A number of St. James's articles on these topics appeared during the 1940s in the *Rosicrucian Digest*, published by the Ancient and Mystical Order Rosae Crucis (AMORC). The *Indian Speaking Leaf* continued publication into 1949. It may be that Red Fox died about this time or could no longer run the magazine. The date of his death is not known.

Despite his dubious identity, the fact is that Red Fox St. James was one of the best-known advocates on behalf of American Indian rights in the period from 1914 through 1927.

His mystic and occult interests, although seemingly out of place today, were common and widespread at the time and, in many respects, continue to this very day, albeit in different forms (see NEW AGE MOVEMENT). He argued forcefully for many of the goals of Indians of that day such as the granting of citizenship and the abolishment of the Office of Indian Affairs, as the BUREAU OF INDIAN AFFAIRS was known at the time. His role in organizing urban Indians and his establishment of one of the nation's first urban Indian centers is of real historical importance, although his effort to promote an American Indian Day is better known.

Further Reading

Hertzberg, Hazel W. *The Search for an American Indian Identity: Modern Pan-Indian Movements.* Syracuse, N.Y.: Syracuse University Press, 1971.

Storm, Hyemeyohsts (Charles Storm) (1935–)
New Age writer

Hyemeyohsts Storm was born on May 23, 1935, in Lame Deer, Montana, on the Northern Cheyenne Reservation, the son of Arthur Charles and Pearl Eastman Storm. His father, a carpenter, came originally from northern Germany, and his mother was of Northern Cheyenne, Sioux, and Irish descent. Known as Chuck Storm, he grew up on the Northern Cheyenne and adjoining Crow Reservations, later spending short periods at Eastern Montana College in Billings and Oakland City College in California. He tried to enlist in the military during the Vietnam War but was rejected for poor eyesight. After college, he remained in northern California.

In 1972, Storm published *Seven Arrows*, a long novel with a complex structure. It was his ironic achievement to have written one of the most popular works of Native American literature, but one that has been strongly condemned by many Indians, especially by the Northern Cheyenne themselves. This is because, while it is interesting as a work of literature, the book falsely pretends to portray traditional Cheyenne religion and spirituality. Storm's initial defense, that he is an enrolled member of the Northern Cheyenne Tribe, is beside the point.

Seven Arrows was one of the most widely acclaimed novels of 1972. Critic William F. Smith, Jr., wrote: "*Seven Arrows* is doubly a masterpiece as a historical novel, both in the obvious sense of its content and also in the subtle way it combines various forms to produce a virtual microcosm of Indian literary history." However, it provoked harsh criticism from those who knew anything about Cheyenne religion and art. According to anthropologist William H. Sturtevant, while the book contains "a few traditional elements of Cheyenne and other Plains Indian culture," it consists chiefly of "pompous and rather patronizing instructions in the pseudo-religious mysteries which are said to be exemplified in a long boring story." Sturtevant describes its illustrations in the form of Plains shields as "odd kaleidoscopic, psychedelic designs and colors in a saccharine and very self-consciously pseudo-Indian style."

According to anthropologist John H. Moore, "The philosophical framework . . . is primarily Buddhist, with a large component of yoga, some primitive Christianity, and a dash of Manicheism. . . . Several books would be required to correct the compounded inaccuracies of Storm's version of Cheyenne tradition." Historian RUPERT COSTO also condemned it.

VINE DELORIA, JR., however, defended Storm in a *New York Times* review: "*Seven Arrows* is a religious statement, not a statement about religion." This somewhat fine distinction misses the critical objection. As a historical novel about the Cheyenne, the book pretends to be a portrait of the Cheyenne spiritual tradition, but it is not.

After his second novel, *Song of Heyoehkah* (1979), was panned even by his admirers, Storm defied his critics in *Lightningbolt* (1994), his spiritual autobiography. Here, Storm described his teacher, the wise woman Estcheemah, as a "Zero Chief" of the "Flower Soldiers." He defends the teachings of the Flower Soldiers as the true, most ancient, and universal ones, whereas the traditionalists are "fanatics," full of "racial bigotry," and have no future. The autobiographical motivations for this self-serving doctrine are clear enough. Later, Storm and his wife, Swan, led a "plastic Indian" cult in California; and there are numerous allegations of child abuse against them in connection with this cult's activities.

Whatever the ethnic status of the author, and whatever the literary merits of his books, they are typical pseudo-traditional products of the New Age movement. Storm never again achieved the success of his first book, but *Seven Arrows* has become something of a classic, still in print decades after its first appearance.

Further Reading

Moore, John H. "*Seven Arrows* by Hyemeyohsts Storm." *American Anthropologist* 75, no. 4 (1973): 1,040–1,042.
Peyer, Bernd. *Hyemeyohsts Storm's* Seven Arrows: *Fiction and Anthropology in the Native American Novel.* Wiesbaden, Germany: Franz Steiner Verlag, 1979.

Strickland, Rennard (1940–) *Osage-Cherokee historian, law professor*

An Osage-Cherokee, Rennard Strickland was born on September 26, 1940, in St. Louis, Missouri, the son of R. J. Strickland, a businessman, and Adell G. Strickland, director of programs for senior citizens. He received his B.A. from Northeastern State College (now University) in Tahlequah, Oklahoma, in 1962; his doctorate in law (J.D.) from the University of Virginia in 1965 (S.J.D., 1970); and his M.A. from the University of Arkansas in 1966. He began his teaching career as assistant professor and coordinator of basic speech at the University of Arkansas in 1965. He subsequently became professor of law at the University of Tulsa (1972–75) and associate professor at the University of Washington, Seattle (1975–76). From 1976 to 1985, he was John W. Shleppey Research Professor of Law and History at the University of Tulsa, and from 1985 to 1988, he was dean of the School of Law at Southern Illinois University.

From 1988 to 1990, he was professor of law at the University of Wisconsin, Madison.

Strickland is known chiefly for his research into the history, art, and literature of the Cherokee and other Indian nations, as well as studies of traditional Native American legal systems and the history and current practice of federal Indian law. He is considered a pioneer in introducing American Indian law into university curricula. Strickland is the only person to have received both the Society of American Law Teachers Award and the American Bar Association's Spirit of Excellence Award. He directed the Indian Heritage Association from 1966 to 1984.

Among his writings are *Sam Houston with the Cherokees, 1829–1833* (1967), *Cherokee Spirit Tales* (with Jack Gregory, 1969), *Creek-Seminole Spirit Tales* (1971), *Choctaw Spirit Tales* (1973), *American Indian Spirit Tales* (1973), *The Cherokee People* (with Earl B. Pierce, 1973), *Fire and the Spirit: Cherokee Law from Clan to Court* (1975), *Magic Images: Contemporary Native American Art* (1982), *Savages, Sinners, and Redskinned Redeemers: Images of the Native American* (1991), *Indian Dilemma: Rhetoric and Reality of Cherokee Removal* (1991), and *Shared Visions: Native American Painters and Sculptors in the Twentieth Century* (with Margaret Archuleta, 1991). He was editor in chief of *The Handbook of Federal Indian Law* (1982).

Strickland served on the board of governors of the Society of American Law Teachers from 1997 to 1999 and on the board of trustees of the Law School Admission Council (the nonprofit corporation that administers the LSAT law school admission test) from 1995 to 2002. From 1997 to 2002, he was dean of the law school at the University of Oregon. He is currently distinguished professor emeritus at Oregon.

Further Reading

Cronley, Connie. "Rennard Strickland: Doctor, Lawyer, Art Collector and Storyteller." *Sooner Magazine* 30, no. 1 (2009): 25.

Schwartz, Berl. "Professor Sees 'Dances' as First Step," United Press International, 31 March 1991.

Shannon, Tad. "Uncommon Law: Rennard Strickland's Eclectic Interests and Easygoing Demeanor Have Boosted Morale Since He Became Dean of the University of Oregon School of Law." *Register-Guard* (Eugene, Oregon), 22 February 1998.

Strongheart, Nipo Tach Tachnum Chtutumnah
(Neehah, George Mitchell, Jr.) (1891–1966)
Yakama actor, technical adviser, collector, researcher

Nipo Strongheart, whose English name was George Mitchell, Jr., was born on May 15, 1891, in White Swan, Washington, on the Yakima (now Yakama) Reservation, the son of George and Leonora Williams Mitchell. His paternal grandfather, Robert Mitchell, was a Hudson Bay Company agent in Canada; his mother, a Yakama, was the daughter of Chief Owhi, a signer of the Treaty of 1855. After he lost his mother, he was adopted by a Yakama woman, Kate Williams, and given the name Neehahpouw (Nipo) Tachnum Chtutumnah. Neehahpouw was said to mean "messenger of light," but it is not clear where he got the name Strongheart. He was educated at the Fort Simcoe Indian Industrial School on the Yakima Reservation but otherwise had little formal education.

Strongheart spent almost his entire life in show business. In 1902, age 11, he was billed as the "kid rider" or "kid bandit" when he went with his father on a European tour with Buffalo Bill's Wild West Show. Afterward, he toured North and South America and other countries with Major Gordon William Lillie's Pawnee Bill Shows.

When the Lubin Company of Philadelphia went to the Carlisle Indian School in Pennsylvania (see PRATT, RICHARD HENRY) in 1905 to film *The White Chief*, young Strongheart was asked to be technical adviser and interpreter for the many student extras who barely spoke English. Soon he repeated the task when the Vitagraph Company of Brooklyn filmed at Carlisle.

Enlisting as a scout with the U.S. cavalry in 1909 at Lawton, Oklahoma, Strongheart policed the Mexican border with the U.S. Border Patrol, established by President Theodore Roosevelt. After leaving the service, he worked in a stage production of *The Heart of Wetona* for director David Belasco (1915).

The United States entered WORLD WAR I on April 6, 1917. Like many reservation Indians, Strongheart was not a citizen, but in May he offered to reenlist for overseas service, and in June he registered for the draft in New York City. Rejected because of an old leg injury from his cavalry days, Strongheart voluntarily visited more than 200 military installations to entertain the troops with Indian stories. Later, he toured the East, recruiting men and selling Liberty Bonds and war savings stamps for the war effort. It was reported that 233 men enlisted after he gave a speech in front of the New York Public Library.

When the war was over, Strongheart moved to Hollywood but continued to lecture on the Lyceum and other Chautauqua circuits. From 1921 to 1923, he toured the western Canadian provinces for the Dominion Chautauquas. In his lectures, he advocated support for American Indian CITIZENSHIP, which was finally granted by Congress on June 2, 1924.

In 1925, Strongheart assisted in writing the scenario of Cecil DeMille's *Braveheart*, a story of his own Yakama people starring Rod La Rocque, with Strongheart playing a medicine man. He continued his lecture tours with the Redpath Lyceum Circuit in the late 1920s and with the Dixie Lyceum Bureau of Dallas, Texas, in 1928 and 1929.

The addition of sound to movies around 1930 presented new opportunities. Strongheart became a technical adviser to the major studios, trying to prevent false portrayals of Indians that "[offend] our intelligence and sense of pride." He not only helped find Indian extras, he also went to reservations to sign them up and supervised them while they lived at the studio (as before). Now, however, he also had to research dialogue in Indian languages and coach actors in these languages. When it was too difficult for the actor, Strongheart overdubbed the lines himself. He also translated or found others who could translate dialogue into Indian languages. Often he did historical research for scripts—for example, finding the sign language used by a now-extinct tribe. Often he would take a small part in the film as well.

Strongheart was proudest of his work on MGM's *Across the Wide Missouri* (1950), starring Clark Gable and Ricardo Montalban, and directed by William Wellman. Responsible for authenticating the portrayal of three tribes—Nez Perce, Shoshone, and Blackfoot—he had to get much dialogue translated into these languages and coach the actors in them just for auditions. He kept a detailed log of all coaching. For seven weeks, all day every day, actors came to him; he made house calls in the evenings. The leading lady, María Elena Marquéz, who was Mexican but played a Blackfoot woman, required her own Spanish interpreter to explain the meaning of the Indian lines. Strongheart also authenticated the wardrobe and props, makeup, hair, and music. He spent a full day with the director going over the timing of the Indian dialogues: Lines that were too long were revised or mixed with sign language. Everything had to be ready before going on location in Durango, Colorado. There, 100 Sioux extras had to be transformed into Blackfoot. During pre-scene rehearsals, Strongheart carefully watched for errors in speech, sign talk, or character. During shooting, he was on permanent standby from dawn to dusk.

When engaged by Twentieth Century Fox for *Pony Soldier* (1952), directed by Joseph Newman, Strongheart wrote a lengthy critique, and the script was rewritten at the last minute. He also suggested the insertion of a new character, which, as Strongheart wrote, "is seldom if ever seen in a Movie where Indians are concerned. An old, old Lady whose wisdom would be respected in a Tribal Council." The change was approved by Darryl F. Zanuck, head of Twentieth Century Fox.

Throughout his career, Strongheart was an inveterate collector, saving newspaper clippings, articles, flyers, pamphlets, and books relating not only to his career but virtually anything to do with Indians. Eventually, it consisted of about 100 trunks of costumes, arts and crafts, and 12,000 books, as well as documents and other printed materials, occupying three floors of a building in Los Angeles.

Strongheart's first wife was Inez Wiley Strongheart, daughter of Chief Wiley of the Colusa Indians of California. They divorced in 1926. His second wife was Marion Campbell Winton, a singer and president of the Women's National League for Justice to the American Indian. They divorced in 1933.

Strongheart founded the Inter-American Research Institute and the American Indian Arts Academy. He died on December 30, 1966, in the Motion Picture Country Hospital, Canoga Park, California. As a medicine priest of the Dreamer Society, he received a traditional Longhouse burial at Satus Point Cemetery on January 7, 1967. His entire collection was bequeathed to the Yakama Nation, with $15,000 to establish a Yakama Nation Memorial Library and Museum. In 1970, these materials were transported to the reservation, and in 1980 the Yakama Cultural Center, including the museum and library, was opened at Toppenish, Washington.

Further Reading

Rosenthal, Nicholas G. "Representing Indians: Native American Actors on Hollywood's Frontier." *Western Historical Quarterly* 36, no. 3 (2005): 329–352.

Strongwolf, Joseph (Guy-you-ma-wanda) (ca. 1890– unknown) *Ojibwa (Chippewa) lecturer, teacher, priest*

Joseph Strongwolf was born around 1890, but details about his birthplace, parentage, and early life are unknown. He claimed to be Ojibwa (Chippewa), although according to a 1924 report in the *Christian Science Monitor*, he was "brought up on the Menominee Reservation, in Wisconsin." If that is the case, then Strongwolf may have attended a mission run by a lapsed Catholic priest named Joseph-René Vilatte at the Church of the Precious Blood in Brussels, Wisconsin, about 45 miles southeast of the Menominee Reservation. Vilatte later became a bishop in the scarcely known Christian denomination into which Strongwolf was ordained a priest in 1926. But this Menominee story may also simply reflect Strongwolf's later involvement in the church rather than the truth. He also claimed that he graduated from Leland Stanford University in California.

In 1914, shortly after WORLD WAR I had begun in Europe, Strongwolf was hired as cattle foreman aboard the SS *Raeburn*, transporting horses for the British cavalry. The *Raeburn*, under Captain William Jardine, was a Lamport and Holt freighter out of Liverpool, England, which, while docked in New Orleans, Louisiana, shortly after the outbreak of the war, was chartered by the French government. It subsequently ran six transports of mules and horses from Newport News, Virginia, to Bordeaux, France. Thus, Newport News is probably where Strongwolf shipped out. On his second voyage out, Strongwolf decided to join the British army. He enlisted in December 1914, eventually seeing action in France.

In 1922, the TIPI ORDER OF AMERICA organized a cross-country tour to advocate CITIZENSHIP, religious rights, and greater tolerance for American Indians. Strongwolf was their spokesman. While the tour generally stopped at venues such as local fraternal organizations, a brand-new medium, RADIO, was just then coming into general use. Appreciating its power to reach a larger audience, Strongwolf spoke on the radio whenever possible, and whatever the truth about his identity, he is considered one of the first Indians to do so. Exactly when and where he made his first broadcast is not certain, but he spoke on several stations, including KDKA in Pittsburgh, Pennsylvania, in August 1922; WJZ, Newark, New Jersey, on October 5, 1922; and WOR, Newark, on January 5, 1923. He always made a great impression.

Strongwolf ended his WJZ speech with these words:

> Let the Great Spirit look down upon you all and bless each and every one of you, and may He give you the eyes of the eagle that you may see clearly and keenly all the unjust things that have been done in the past and are being done today to a race of men who had such a great love for their native land that 17,500 of them went across the water to fight for someone else's liberty when they did not have liberty themselves.

In the 1920s, Strongwolf lived in or near Philadelphia and frequently took part in commemorative events in Pennsylvania. When Indians became eligible to vote in 1924, he cast his vote in Narberth, a Philadelphia suburb. In October 1926, at the Armenian Cathedral in New York, Strongwolf, described as "the newly elected Superior in the Order of White Friars," was ordained a priest in the American Catholic Church by Archbishop Gregory Lines. This denomination had been founded in Illinois in 1915 by F. E. J. Lloyd, who received his consecration from Bishop Vilatte, who had consecrated Lines in 1923.

The Order of White Friars was not the traditional Catholic Carmelites but a small group conducting religious services described as a "beautiful blending of the Ancient Indian ceremonial with the Christian Eucharist Service" at the headquarters and under the auspices of the American Indian Association (AIA) in New York City. In 1927, the head chief of the AIA was Strongwolf and the superior of the Order of White Friars was AIA founder RED FOX ST. JAMES.

Strongwolf was also something of a poet. His "Indian Prayer" was published on the fourth page of the September 1954 issue of *Good Housekeeping*, and one of his texts is used for the second movement of composer Jacob Avshalomov's *Praises from the Corners of the Earth* (1965) for chorus and orchestra. Like his colleague Red Fox St. James, Strongwolf taught Indian lore and crafts at summer camps. After World War I, he ran Camp Strongwolf for boys at Sumneytown, Pennsylvania. In 1931, he taught at the YMCA Camp Billings in Thetford, Vermont. There is a 1931 photograph of Strongwolf with a group mostly composed of Chinese students at International House, Philadelphia, a group affiliated with the YMCA.

An enigmatic item in the *New York Times* on June 11, 1934, reported that New Jersey state police at Newark were seeking relatives of Chief Strongwolf, who had been overcome by heat in Glens Falls, New York, and appeared to be suffering from amnesia. He recovered, and was still giving speeches as late as 1957, if not later.

See also URBANIZATION, AMERICAN INDIANS AND.

Further Information

Hertzberg, Hazel. *The Search for an American Indian Identity: Modern Pan-Indian Movements.* Syracuse, N.Y.: Syracuse University Press, 1971.

"How an Indian Feels about Radio." *Literary Digest* 76 (24 February 1923): 29.

"Indian Chief." *Pennsylvania Heritage Magazine* (Summer 1996): 4, 5.

Letter from "Chief Strong Wolf, American Indian Association, Newark, N.J." to conservationist John M. Phillips, October 6, 1922. Record Group 161, Pennsylvania State Archives.

"Portrait." *Radio Broadcast* 2 (December 1922): 131.

Stroud-Lee, Agnes Naranjo (1922–)

Santa Clara Pueblo (Tewa) biologist
Born on July 23, 1922, the eldest of seven children, Agnes

Stroud-Lee had strong childhood interests in science, which in college led to involvement in a professor's research project testing the effects of chemicals on plant growth. Dr. Stroud-Lee attended Albuquerque High School and then obtained a B.S. in biology from the University of New Mexico in 1945. She went on to receive a doctorate in biological sciences from the University of Chicago in 1966 and for many years worked in the biology division of the Argonne National Laboratory operated by the university. Subsequently, she served as research scientist at Los Alamos National Laboratory in New Mexico until her retirement in 1979. Her work on ionizing radiation and cytogenetics is important for the understanding of chromosome abnormalities and for the prevention of cancer and birth defects. Dr. Stroud-Lee has written that she believes Indian scientific aptitude draws on ancient Indian cultural traditions. She was active as a pilot and artist but in later years became troubled by failing eyesight. She lives in Belen, New Mexico.

Further Reading

Verheyden-Hilliard, Mary Ellen. *Scientist from the Santa Clara Pueblo, Agnes Naranjo Stroud-Lee.* Bethesda, Md.: The Equity Institute, 1985.

Sun Bear (Vincent LaDuke, Gheezis Mokwa)

(1929–1992) *Chippewa activist, author, New Age proponent*
Sun Bear was born Vincent LaDuke on August 31, 1929, on the White Earth Reservation in northern Minnesota. His father, Louis LaDuke, was Chippewa, and his mother, Judith, was of German and Norwegian descent. Young Vincent was given the name Gheezis Mokwa (Sun Bear) by his uncle, a prominent Chippewa medicine man. LaDuke was raised on his father's allotment, and after high school he displayed the beginnings of his political activism by refusing to serve in the Korean War and going absent without leave. Living on the run, Sun Bear moved to Los Angeles, where he worked as a bit player in Hollywood films and televisions shows until he was finally caught. He served six months in Lompoc Prison in 1956.

Sun Bear returned to Los Angeles, where he continued to find steady work as a bit player, appearing in such notable films as *Spartacus* and in the TV westerns *Maverick* and *The Rifleman*. In 1959, his wife Betty gave birth to their daughter, WINONA LADUKE, who would later become a prominent Indian rights activist. Sun Bear also became involved in the local Los Angeles Indian community, publishing a newsletter in 1961 called *Many Smokes*, which would be transformed into a national publication covering Indian events and issues. Between 1965 and 1972, Sun Bear lived part time in Reno, Nevada, where he began to formulate his synthesis of Indian thought and apocalyptic environmentalism, a perspective that would be published in another newsletter *The Native Nevadan*. In 1969, Sun Bear visited the occupiers of ALCATRAZ ISLAND, and in 1973 he covered the occupation of WOUNDED KNEE for *Many Smokes*.

In the late 1960s, Sun Bear taught in the Tecumseh Indian Studies Program at an experimental college at the

University of California at Davis, the immediate forerunner of D-Q University (see Forbes, Jack D.). There his students, interested in alternative lifestyles, encouraged him to begin a group he called the Bear Tribe Medicine Society. In 1971, the "tribe," through the help of concerts organized by New Riders of the Purple Sage and other bands, swelled to more than 200 people, almost exclusively non-Indians, living in 17 different camps. Led by his visions of a coming "cleansing" of the Earth, Sun Bear felt the need, as he put it, to "teach people from all walks of life, to communicate to them the fact that technology's excesses were rapidly bringing on disaster." By 1972, however, the Bear Tribe was racked by drugs and dissension, and he was forced to dissolve it and start all over.

In 1976, Sun Bear established a religious retreat he called Vision Mountain near Mount Shasta, California, with a few of his group members, where he began to hold seminars on self-reliance and spirituality. By 1980, he started his Medicine Wheel Gatherings, which featured programs such as the vision quest and sweat lodge ceremonies, though few Indians attended. A prolific author, Sun Bear wrote numerous books about his beliefs, including *The Path of Power*, an autobiography, and *The Medicine Wheel: Earth Astrology*, about his prophesies of the coming cleansing. *Many Smokes* became *Wildfire*, a magazine largely devoted to his teachings. He also began to apprentice people in the "paths of power" that he followed, and many students went on to form their own groups.

Sun Bear's activities drew great criticism from traditional Indian leaders who felt his actions were that of a "plastic medicine man" catering to the materialism of a Western society that saw Indian spirituality as simply another commodity. His recruitment of Lakota Sioux medicine man Wallace Black Elk to his gatherings only increased the consternation of traditional spiritual leaders, who were concerned that the ceremonies designed to hold nations together were becoming merely entertainment. Despite the traditional trappings, Sun Bear's teachings were more akin to the self-help therapy that is the core of the New Age movement than to Native American thought.

In a debate with Iroquois spokesman Oren Lyons, Jr., at the American Indian Community House in New York City in 1989, Sun Bear argued that Indian traditions should be open to all people as a means to better the world. His followers also maintained that they had the "right" to follow Indian traditions, in much the same way their rights to the free exercise of religion are embodied in the U.S. Constitution. Lyons countered that the supposed "right" that Sun Bear and his followers claimed to possess was simply another reflection of the Western, not Indian, thinking that permeates New Age religions. For Lyons, these ceremonies were given by the Creator to the particular Indian communities to serve important functions, such as maintaining the delicate social and ecological balance of the community, and are responsibilities to be carried out properly, rather than rights to be enjoyed.

Condemned by the Grand Council of the Iroquois Confederacy, as well as Indian activists Russell Means and Janet McCloud, for selling traditions that were the common property of Indian people, Sun Bear was forced to respond that

most of his teachings were not truly of traditional origin but came largely from his visions.

Despite his controversial status among Indians, Sun Bear was revered by his followers. He died of intestinal cancer on June 19, 1992, in Spokane, Washington.

Further Reading
Jenkins, Philip. *Dream Catchers: How Mainstream America Discovered Native Spirituality*. New York: Oxford University Press, 2004.
Sun Bear. *The Path of Power: As Told to Wabun and to Barry Weinstock*. Spokane, Wash.: Bear Tribe Publications, 1983.

Swamp, Jake (Tekaronianeken) (1941–2010)
Mohawk chief, Iroquois spokesperson

Born on October 18, 1941, on the Akwesasne Reservation in northern New York State, Jake Swamp was given the name Tekaronianeken. Although raised a Catholic, Swamp was influenced as a youth by the traditional views of Ray Fadden. One of the many Mohawk "high-steel" workers, Swamp worked as a welder in New York City and on projects along the St. Lawrence Seaway (see ironworkers). He was at the Cornwall Bridge Blockade in 1968, where Mohawk protested over their rights to free passage from the United States into Canada. In the early 1970s, Swamp was appointed a "Pine Tree Chief," or subchief of the Wolf Clan of the Mohawk Nation. He participated in the Trail of Broken Treaties in 1972 and was a member of the Iroquois delegation that lent support to the American Indian Movement (AIM) in their encampment at Wounded Knee in 1973. Swamp was present at the Longest Walk, a national march that arrived in Washington, D.C., in July 1978. He also spoke at the Fourth Russell Tribunal, an international forum held in the Netherlands in November 1980, that examined the rights of Indians in North America. Along with Mohawk chiefs Tom Porter and Loran Thompson, Swamp was a prominent leader of the traditionalists' encampment during a two-year standoff between New York State and the reservation in the late 1970s (see Akwesasne, siege of).

With Mohawk chief Ron LaFrance, Swamp helped to create an effective means of passing on Mohawk tradition and culture, the Akwesasne Freedom School (see educational policy, American Indians and; indigenous language use). He also directed CKON, a "pirate" Mohawk radio station. In 1982, Swamp founded the Tree of Peace Society, an organization dedicated to spreading Iroquois teachings of peace throughout the world. It was under a white pine tree that the Mohawk, Cayuga, Oneida, Seneca, and Onondaga ended their historic enmity by burying their weapons and founding the Iroquois Confederacy, giving rise to the expression "bury the hatchet." Trees of Peace have been planted by Swamp in Philadelphia near Independence Hall, in New York City in Central Park's Strawberry Fields, and many other places.

Swamp was one of many traditional leaders opposed to bringing the gaming industry (see gaming on Indian reservations) onto the Akwesasne (St. Regis Reservation), a dispute that turned into a virtual civil war in 1990, leading to the deaths of two Mohawk. An important Iroquois religious leader, Swamp traveled extensively as a spokesman for Indian rights and the environment, speaking before the United Nations and other important international forums. He appeared on the television documentaries *Ancient Prophecies* (1994), *Finite Oceans* (1994), and *Five Hundred Nations* (1995). He also authored the children's book *Giving Thanks, a Native American Good Morning Message* in 1997.

Jake Swamp died on October 15, 2010, in Akwesasne, from a heart attack.

Swimmer, Ross O. (1943–) *principal chief of the Cherokee Nation of Oklahoma, special trustee for American Indians*

Ross Owen Swimmer was born on October 26, 1943, in Oklahoma City, Oklahoma. His part-Cherokee father, Robert O. Swimmer, and his mother, Virginia Pounder Swimmer, were both lawyers. Ross Swimmer attended public schools in Yukon, Oklahoma, and Oklahoma City. He enrolled at the University of Oklahoma in 1961, earning a degree in political science before entering the university's law school in 1965. After admission to the bar, Swimmer worked in private practice, joining the firm of Hansen, Peterson, and Thomkins in Oklahoma City. He left the firm in 1972 to become general counsel of the Cherokee Nation.

Swimmer was president of the First National Bank of Tahlequah before succeeding WILLIAM WAYNE KEELER as principal chief of the Cherokee in 1975. He won reelection to two more terms, in 1979 and in 1983, with running mate WILMA MANKILLER, though both elections were bitterly contested and brought charges of electoral fraud. During his tenure, Swimmer passed the new Cherokee constitution drafted under Keeler, and it was ratified by the Cherokee people in June 1976. An advocate of Indian self-determination, he quadrupled the annual budget of the Cherokee tribe, reducing its dependence on the federal government. He also won for the Cherokee the right to royalties from minerals taken from the Arkansas River.

A staunch Republican, Swimmer was sought after by the administration of Ronald Reagan for his pro-business orientation, and he was appointed cochair of the PRESIDENTIAL COMMISSION ON INDIAN RESERVATION ECONOMIES in 1983. After the departure of KENNETH L. SMITH, Reagan named Swimmer assistant secretary of the interior for Indian affairs. He took office on December 6, 1985. Federal budget cuts under the Reagan administration had led to an increase in poverty among Indians, and attempts by Swimmer to restructure the BUREAU OF INDIAN AFFAIRS (BIA) and grant the $3 billion federal budget directly to the tribes were blocked because of fears that this was simply a disguise for more cuts. The fact that Swimmer himself favored the privatization of services to Indians made him deeply unpopular with tribal leaders. In October 1984, Reagan vetoed the reauthorization of the Indian Health Care Act, a move widely criticized by Indians.

In 1987, a series of articles in the *Arizona Republic* entitled "Fraud in Indian Country" documented a veritable morass of fraud and waste at the BIA. Among the paper's charges was that energy and oil companies enjoying concessions on INDIAN RESERVATIONS had systematically swindled Indian tribes of almost $6 billion in royalty moneys during the preceding five years. Investigations into these charges were derailed by the Senate Select Committee on Indian Affairs, chaired by Arizona senator Dennis DeConcini, who in 1989 chose instead to investigate the questionable business dealings of Navajo leader PETER MACDONALD.

Swimmer's denial of BIA wrongdoing provoked criticism from SUZAN SHOWN HARJO, head of the NATIONAL CONGRESS OF AMERICAN INDIANS, who accused Reagan of fostering the "worst administration for Indians since the days of outright warfare and extermination." While his stated goal of improving the BIA's leaky accounting system was well received, Swimmer's attempt to place more than $1.7 billion of Indian assets in the financially troubled Mellon Bank brought a storm of condemnation. Swimmer was also deeply embarrassed by the president's remarks in the Soviet Union on May 31, 1988, where, in response to a question about the situation of American Indians, Reagan told students at Moscow State University that many Indians were wealthy from oil and suggested that "maybe we made a mistake" and "should not have humored them" in trying to maintain their "primitive lifestyles."

By the time Swimmer left office in 1989, the policies of the Reagan administration had resulted in the increase of Indian unemployment on reservations to almost 50 percent, from 39 percent in 1979. Swimmer reentered private law practice, then became the head of Cherokee Industries, the tribe's electronics company, at the behest of Chief Mankiller. From 1995 to 2000, he served as president of the Cherokee Group L.L.C., a consulting and lobbying firm for Indian tribes.

In 2001, under President George W. Bush, Swimmer returned to the Department of the Interior as director of the Office of Indian Trust Transition. In January 2003, he was named to the post of special trustee for American Indians, created in 1994 under the Interior Department as part of the settlement of the lawsuit *Cobell v. Salazar*, which accused the Interior Department of mismanaging Indian trust assets. The special trustee oversees the trust funds held by the United States on behalf of Indian tribes and individual Indians. (The resolution of *Cobell v. Salazar* was the largest class action settlement in American history.)

Further Reading

Lee, Jodi Rave. "They Resurrected Ross Swimmer." *Lincoln Journal Star*, 30 September 2002, p. 8.

"Swimmer Legacy Still Haunts BIA." *Indianz.com*, 12 February 2002. Available online. URL: http://64.38.12.138/News /show.asp?D=polo2/02/22002-1. Accessed 31 March, 2010.

Tallchief, Maria (Elizabeth Maria Tall Chief)

(1925–2013) *Osage dancer, ballet director*

Maria Tallchief was born Elizabeth Maria Tall Chief on January 24, 1925, in Fairfax, Oklahoma, to Osage chief Alexander Tall Chief and a Scots-Irish mother, Ruth Porter. Tallchief was discovered to have perfect pitch and trained for the piano from a very young age, beginning private dance lessons shortly after. She and her younger sister, MARJORIE TALLCHIEF, became accustomed to public performance while still children, and when the family moved to Los Angeles, Tallchief began to train with the grande dame of Russian ballet, Bronislava Nijinska, who recognized her exceptional talent.

At the age of 17 at a time when America was not considered capable of producing ballerinas of the highest standard and imported Russians were all the rage, Tallchief was accepted by Serge Denham's Ballet Russe de Monte Carlo, then based in New York because WORLD WAR II was raging in Europe. She danced her first major role as an understudy for an established Russian dancer, which in itself caused a minor furor. The *New York Times* dance critic subsequently described her as "the discovery of the season." She made an unprecedented rise through the ranks of the Ballet Russe (while at the same time learning from its Russian members how to play a tough game of poker).

In 1944, George Balanchine joined the company as resident choreographer. The innate musicality of his style made an immediate impression on Tallchief; he responded to her musical background. Balanchine began to create ballets for her, and the two had already developed a close professional partnership by the time they married in 1946. That same year, Tallchief joined the Paris Opera as the first American guest ballerina in more than a century.

Tallchief joined Balanchine's new company, the New York City Ballet, as prima ballerina. The leading role she created for *The Firebird* in 1949 made it the company's first major popular success, and she won acclaim as the epitome of the Balanchine ballerina. Between 1947 and 1957, Tallchief created leading roles in 22 ballets choreographed for her by Balanchine. His style exhibited a special attack, speed, and heightened silhouette that reflected the vitality and rhythms of American life. Tallchief was noted for the bravura of her performance, the qualities of force and speed in her technique, and the intensity of her temperament. Balanchine's choreography and her performance fused into a style that became regarded as quintessentially American.

Although Tallchief and Balanchine separated in 1952, their professional relationship remained as close as ever. Balanchine created his ballet *The Nutcracker* in 1954, with Tallchief immortalizing the role of the Sugar Plum Fairy. The ballet was a phenomenal success and became a classic. *Newsweek* dedicated its 1954 cover story to ballet and called Tallchief "the finest American-born ballerina the twentieth century has produced." The New York City Ballet was now a major force in world ballet.

Tallchief retired from performance in 1965, and in that year she received the Capezio Award, the highest honor in the American dance world. The citation paid tribute to the way her exceptional talents had raised American dance to a new standard of excellence and established it as an international force. After moving to Chicago in 1974, she started working with dancers at the Chicago Lyric Opera and was instrumental in founding the Chicago City Ballet. She continued to teach and coach until 1993.

In 1992, just before her final retirement, Maria was inducted into the Oklahoma Hall of Fame and, with her sister Marjorie, attended the unveiling of Gary Larsen's mural *Flight of the Spirit* to honor the state's Native American ballerinas. In 1997, she received the Presidential Medal of Honor. It was a fitting recognition of her landmark contribution to American ballet. In 2006, she was honored by New York's

Ballet dancer Maria Tallchief of the New York City Ballet. 1951 file photograph. *(AP/Wideworld)*

Metropolitan Museum of Art with "A Tribute to Ballet Great Maria Tallchief." Her extraordinary partnership with Balanchine was a perfect synthesis of talents, enabling both to take American ballet in an entirely new direction that was to transform the art. Her daughter, Elise Paschen, by her second husband, Henry Paschen, is a well-known poet. Maria Tallchief died in Chicago on April 11, 2013.

Further Reading
Livingston, Lili Cockerille. *American Indian Ballarinas.*
    Norman: University of Oklahoma Press, 1997.

Tallchief, Marjorie (Marjorie Tall Chief) (1927–)
Osage dancer, ballet teacher
Born on October 19, 1927, in Denver, Colorado, the daughter of Alexander and Ruth Porter Tall Chief, Marjorie Tallchief shared her early childhood training in dance with her sister, MARIA TALLCHIEF. When the family moved to California, Tallchief began to make a name for herself in films but turned down a long-term movie contract in order to study as a ballerina.

In 1944, Marjorie joined Lucia Chase and Richard Pleasant's Ballet Theatre in Montreal, Canada, as a soloist, and she became leading soloist with the Ballet Russe de Monte Carlo two years later. In Monte Carlo, she met and married George

Skibine, with whom she developed a critically acclaimed dancing partnership. Together, they joined the Marquis de Cuevas's Grand Ballet, and the company's Paris opening was a critical triumph for Tallchief.

Marjorie confirmed her place as one of Europe's major dance stars when, in 1956, she joined other ballet luminaries—including Alicia Markova, Margot Fonteyn, Anton Dolin, and John Gilpin—in London at the Stoll Theatre for a gala performance honoring Anna Pavlova. Later that same year, she became the first American ballerina invited to join the Paris Opera with the title of première danseuse étoile.

In 1964, Tallchief and her husband were invited to take the helm of a new American company being formed by arts patron Rebekah Harkness. In October that year, the new company gave a gala performance at the White House, and the following year the Harkness Ballet made a triumphant debut at Cannes. In 1966, Tallchief resigned from the company and moved to Dallas with her husband, ostensibly to retire. However, her work there as a teacher and performer became the catalyst for the formation of the Dallas Civic Ballet, later to become fully professional as the Dallas Ballet. She continued to teach until her final retirement in 1993. Tallchief's son, Alex Skibine, became active in Indian affairs.

Further Reading
Livingston, Lili Cockerville. *American Indian Ballerinas.*
    Norman: University of Oklahoma Press, 1997.

Taluta *See* EASTMAN, IRENE.

Tantaquidgeon, Gladys (1899–2005)
Mohegan herbalist, anthropologist
A descendant of famous sachem Uncas (ca. 1606–ca. 1682) and Mohegan minister Samson Occum (1723–92), Gladys Tantaquidgeon was born in New London, Connecticut, on June 15, 1899, one of seven children of John and Harriet Fielding Tantaquidgeon. When she was five, Gladys was selected by her great aunt Fidelia Fielding (1827–1908) and two other elders, Emma Baker and Merch Ann Nonesuch, for training in herbal medicine and other traditional knowledge. All three women had themselves been trained by Martha Uncas (1761–1859), a very important link in the chain of Mohegan traditional knowledge. Fielding was the last of the Mohegans to live in a traditional log house and one of the last who could speak Mohegan-Pequot. Although she did not teach Gladys to speak the language, claiming she did not want the girl to suffer discrimination, Fielding did teach it to the young FRANK SPECK, later chair of anthropology at the University of Pennsylvania.

Gladys Tantaquidgeon had been close to Speck since childhood. Although she never went to high school, she later studied with him at the university between 1919 and 1927, exploring other Algonquian cultures—the Montagnais-Naskapi (Innu) of Quebec; the Wampanoag of Gay Head and Mashpee, Massachusetts; the Nanticoke of Delaware; and

Mohegan elder Gladys Tantaquidgeon standing next to a portrait of her brother, Harold Tantaquidgeon, in 1992. *(AP/Wideworld)*

with one of the original thirteen colonies, did not have a direct government-to-government relationship with the United States. Not until 1984 did the tribe submit a petition for federal recognition. In 1989, this was denied, ostensibly because the tribe had not maintained a cohesive community and political influence between the 1940s and the 1970s. Tantaquidgeon was able to supply additional documentation, and the decision was reversed. In March 1994, the Mohegan received federal recognition.

Gladys Tantaquidgeon died on November 1, 2005, at her home in Uncasville, Connecticut. She was 106 years old.

Further Reading

Kehoe, Alice. "A Mohegan Anthropologist at Work." *Anthropology of Work Review* 22, no. 2 (2001): 29–31.

Tantaquidgeon, Harold (1904–1989) *Mohegan chief, museum director, educator, military hero*

Harold Tantaquidgeon was born on June 18, 1904, in Montville, Connecticut, the son of John and Harriet Fielding Tantaquidgeon and a direct descendant of famous chief Uncas and minister Samson Occun. In 1931, Harold and his sister, GLADYS TANTAQUIDGEON, helped their father start the Tantaquidgeon Indian Museum at Uncasville, Connecticut.

A veteran of WORLD WAR II and the Korean War, Tantaquidgeon served in the U.S. Army Air Corps and the U.S. Air Force as a tail gunner on a B-25 bomber and a turret gunner on a P-61 Black Widow night fighter. In some of the fiercest fighting in the Pacific theater, he was shot down in the jungles of New Guinea but kept himself alive through the use of survival skills learned from Mohegan elders. He was a recipient of the Purple Heart and the Air Medal.

As the Tantaquidgeon Indian Museum curator, Tantaquidgeon lectured to visiting groups on the ethnology, lore, and history of the Indians of southern New England. He was active with the Boy Scouts and 4-H clubs, teaching New England Native American stone and woodworking techniques as well as survival skills.

Harold Tantaquidgeon was active in Mohegan affairs, including the restoration of the Mohegan Church. He served as Mohegan chief from 1952 to 1970. He died at his home in Uncasville on April 4, 1989. A novelized biography *Mohegan Chief: The Story of Harold Tantaquidgeon* (1965) was written by Virginia Frances Voight. A second edition, published by the Mohegan Tribe in 2004 in honor of the centennial of Tantaquidgeon's birth, includes an afterword covering the last 24 years of his life.

the Lenni Lenape of Ontario and Oklahoma (originally from southern New York and New Jersey).

In 1931, Tantaquidgeon, her father, John, and brother HAROLD TANTAQUIDGEON opened a museum, said to be the first in the United States to be founded and run by Indians. In 1935, she did community work on the Yankton Sioux reservation in South Dakota, and in 1938 she was hired by the INDIAN ARTS AND CRAFTS BOARD to work on the revival and development of handicrafts in the Northern Plains area. She returned to Connecticut in 1947, at first doing social work at a women's prison but soon returning to the Indian museum to work with her brother. She published numerous papers on Mohegan and Delaware crafts, medicine practices, and folk beliefs, and in 1972 she published a book on Native medicine entitled *Folk Medicine of the Delaware and Related Algonkian Indians.*

The Women's Studies Program at the University of Connecticut established the Gladys Tantaquidgeon Award in 1986. In 1994, Yale University awarded her an honorary doctorate for research on indigenous medicine.

While Tantaquidgeon's contribution to the Mohegan was already immense, she was not yet finished. The Mohegan tribe, like many other eastern groups that had treaty relationships

Tapahonso, Luci (1953–) *Navajo poet, educator*

Luci Tapahonso was born on November 8, 1953, in Shiprock, New Mexico, to Eugene Tapahonso and Lucille Deschenne. The sixth of 11 children, fluent in the Navajo language, she grew up on the Navajo (Dineh) reservation. Tapahonso attended the Navajo Methodist Mission in Farmington, New Mexico, before graduating from Shiprock High School in 1971. She then studied at the University of New Mexico, where Laguna Pueblo novelist LESLIE MARMON SILKO encouraged her to change her major from journalism to English. She received her B.A. from New Mexico in 1981 and her M.A. in 1983.

In 1981, Tapahonso published her first book of poetry, *One More Shiprock Night*, in which she established what would become a recurrent theme in her poetry: the sense of home, the land, the family, and the curative effect on the soul of returning to one's home. The following year, she released *Seasonal Woman*, which featured drawings by Navajo artist R. C. GORMAN. In 1983, she published her master's thesis, *A Sense of Myself*, which featured poetry and also a short play written with dialogue in both English and Navajo, which was performed and taped for television. *A Breeze Swept Through*, published in 1987, was a collection of poetry that presented vignettes about life among Indian communities in areas such as Gallup and Albuquerque, as well as on the Navajo reservation. Tapahonso's fourth book, *Sáanii Dahataal, The Women Are Singing*, published in 1993, received widespread acclaim for its expressive use of the English language.

A professor of English first at the University of Kansas, then at the University of New Mexico, Tapahonso has published numerous anthologies. She produced a children's book, *Navajo ABC: A Dine Alphabet Book*, in 1995. Two years later, she released a collection of poems and stories, *Blue Horses Rush In*. In 2006, Tapahonso received the Lifetime Achievement Award from the Native Writers Circle of the Americas.

Further Reading
Fast, Robin Riley. "The Hand Is Full of Stories: Navajo Histories and the Work of Luci Tapahonso." *Women Studies* 36, no. 3 (2007): 185–211.

Tax, Sol (1907–1995) *anthropologist, Indian rights activist*
Sol Tax was born in Chicago on October 30, 1907, the son of Morris Paul and Kate Hanowitz Tax, and grew up in Milwaukee. He received a Ph.D. in 1931 from the University of Wisconsin for fieldwork among the Apache, and a Ph.D. in 1935 from the University of Chicago for his work among the Fox (Mesquakie) in 1932–34.

As an ethnologist for the Carnegie Institution, in Washington, D.C. (1934–46), Tax carried out fieldwork in Guatemala and Chiapas, Mexico. He was a research associate at the University of Chicago from 1940 to 1944, an associate professor from 1944 to 1948, and a professor from 1948. During the 1940s, he studied Mayan civilization and trained many of Mexico's early anthropologists. Tax directed the Fox Indian Project in Tama, Iowa, from 1948 to 1962. This was a community-based project using anthropology to analyze the problems of the Fox and to develop culturally appropriate solutions. It was the beginning of what Tax called "action anthropology," or applied anthropology. He directed the Man-Nature project in Chiapas from 1956 to 1959, and in 1958 and 1959 he was president of the American Anthropological Association.

Tax studied cultures around the world, but his main specialization was the social anthropology of North and Central American Indians. His action anthropology method attempted to reconcile the work of the anthropologist with that of an administrator working to solve problems that had been identified by the people being studied. "By definition, action anthropology is an activity in which an anthropologist has two coordinate goals, to neither one of which he will delegate an inferior position," Tax said in a 1950 paper delivered to the American Anthropological Association. "He wants to help a group of people to solve a problem and he wants to learn something in the process."

A consummate organizer and facilitator, Tax was able to bring diverse gatherings of people together to discuss important issues. In 1956, RUTH MUSKRAT BRONSON and representatives of support organizations enlisted his help in setting up a six-week summer workshop to investigate the problem of a high dropout rate among Native American college students. These Workshops on American Indian Affairs were successful and continued through 1967 (see THOMAS, ROBERT K.).

Tax's greatest organizing achievement came in 1961, when he, along with anthropologists Robert Rietz, Nancy Lurie, and Albert Wahrhaftig, as well as D'ARCY McNICKLE of the NATIONAL CONGRESS OF AMERICAN INDIANS (NCAI), coordinated the AMERICAN INDIAN CHICAGO CONFERENCE. The philosophy of the organizers was already stated in an article Tax had published in *The American Indian* (Winter 1958/59), the magazine of the ASSOCIATION ON AMERICAN INDIAN AFFAIRS, in which he characterized TERMINATION as "the sink-or-swim policy . . . that has never worked and never can." He added: "It is not for any white man, or Congress, or the Indian Bureau to demand that Indians either remain Indians or stop being Indians. . . . What folly it has been to demand that Indians cooperate in plans for making them into something they do not want to be."

The biggest error in the management of Indian affairs, Tax pointed out, remained the fact that non-Indians, not Indians themselves, had decided what the goals should be and the methods by which they would be reached. Decisions important to the community thus continued to be made by outsiders, a state of affairs that went against the very meaning of community and meant that leaders competed for outside sources of power instead of resolving issues and carrying out responsibilities within the community.

Thus, the 1961 conference was itself conceived as a project in action anthropology. Anthropologist Wilcomb Washburn denied the scientific validity of the anthropological observations of action anthropology because Tax and Lurie had interfered by participating in the project themselves and thus altered the relation of Indian to Indian and Indian to white. The fact is, however, that the anthropologist cannot gather data *without* interacting with the community, whether he or she likes it or not. The point of Tax's action anthropology is that as long as interaction is inevitable, why should it not be an interaction that helps the community and elicits information that will benefit the community?

When NAES College, an outgrowth of the summer Workshops on Indian Affairs, was opened in 1975 as Native American Educational Services, affiliated with Antioch College, Tax and another longtime colleague, Cherokee anthropologist Robert K. Thomas, were active members of its board of directors.

Tax served as director of the Smithsonian Institution's Center for the Study of Man, an interdisciplinary research and educational institution in the human sciences, from 1968 to 1976. He served on President Lyndon B. Johnson's Special Task Force on American Indian Affairs (1966). He served as a consultant for the U.S. Office of Education, the U.S. Bureau of Indian Affairs, the National Institutes of Mental Health, and the Smithsonian Institution.

Sol Tax died on January 4, 1995, in Chicago.

See also ANTHROPOLOGISTS AND AMERICAN INDIANS.

Further Reading

Chapman, Michael, Terry Straus, and Ron Bowan. "Anthropology, Ethics, and the American Indian Chicago Conference." *American Ethnologist* 13, no. 4 (1986): 802–804.

Cowger, Thomas W. *The National Congress of American Indians: The Founding Years.* Lincoln: University of Nebraska Press, 2001.

Lurie, Nancy Oestreich. "Sol Tax and Tribal Sovereignty." *Human Organization* 58, no. 1 (Spring 1999): 108–117.

Stapp, Darby C. "A Tribute to Sol Tax." *Society for Applied Anthropology Newsletter* 11, no. 1 (February 2000): 4–5.

Te Ata (Mary Thompson Fisher) (1895–1995)
Chickasaw dramatic storyteller

Mary Thompson was born in a log cabin near the old Chickasaw capital of Tishomingo, Oklahoma, on December 3, 1895. Her Chickasaw name, Te Ata, means "bearer of the morning." Her father, Thomas Benjamin Thompson, also known as Chief Luksi, was treasurer of the last council of the Chickasaw Nation. Her mother, Lucy Alberta (Freund) Thompson, was white, but with a small amount of Osage blood. Te Ata studied at Chickasaw Day School, Chickasaw Boarding School (Bloomfield Academy, a tribal school near Red River), and Tishomingo High School. She received a B.A. from Oklahoma College for Women in 1919 and studied ethnology at Columbia University.

Te Ata first became interested in dramatics as a student at the Oklahoma College for Women, Chickasha (now University of Science and Arts of Oklahoma) when Frances Dinsmore Davis, a young instructor who had joined the drama faculty in 1914, started a "little theater" there as part of the nationwide Little Theater movement. From their first performance, *The Piper* (1916), they staged about four plays a season, with all-female casts. Te Ata helped with various aspects of production but did no acting until Davis asked her to perform in several Indian plays. She later attended the theater school at the Carnegie Institute of Technology in Pittsburgh. After that, she settled in New York.

In New York and elsewhere, Te Ata landed a few minor roles in plays, *The Trojan Women* being one of the few that had a successful run, but she finally abandoned the theater because, as the *New Yorker* later wrote (June 10, 1939), "her natural Indian reserve made her feel uncomfortable in the presence of hardboiled agents and casting directors, who took her, variously, for a Japanese, an Italian, and a Russian." Though based in New York, she went back home every year to visit her family, help with the little theater at Chickasha, and learn more legends and stories from elders. From about 1929, now known as "Princess" Te Ata, she developed a one-woman show, dramatizing Indian legends, including songs, which she rendered to the accompaniment of tom-toms.

On September 28, 1933, Te Ata married Dr. Clyde Fisher, director of New York's Hayden Planetarium. As a performer, she appeared throughout the country at colleges, schools, town halls, and women's clubs. Some of her performances were given in private homes, and in this way she met then-governor of New York Franklin D. Roosevelt and his wife, Eleanor, who subsequently invited her to the executive mansion in Albany and later, during British prime minister Ramsay MacDonald's American visit, to the White House. Roosevelt was so impressed that he named Lake Te Ata near Bear Mountain, New York, after her. Also at the invitation of the Roosevelts, Te Ata and Choctaw baritone Ish-Ti-Opi (see ROBERTSON, WESLEY LEROY) performed for King George VI and Queen Elizabeth on June 11, 1939, at their home in Hyde Park, New York.

Interpreting the folklore, songs, and dances of various American Indian tribes, Te Ata appeared throughout the United States, as well as in Denmark, Sweden, England, and Scotland. She visited most INDIAN RESERVATIONS in the United States and Canada, examined remains of the Inca empire in Peru and the Aztec and other ancient civilizations in Mexico, and was with the 1944 American Museum of Natural History expedition to the active volcano Paricutín in Mexico.

Te Ata was inducted into the Oklahoma Hall of Fame in 1957 and the Alumni Hall of Fame at Oklahoma College for Women (now University of Science and Arts of Oklahoma) in 1972. She received special recognition for lifelong contributions to the arts by the Oklahoma State Arts Council in 1976, and was named the first "Oklahoma Treasure" by Governor Henry Bellmon in September 1987. Te Ata was a member of the Society of Women Geographers and of the NATIONAL CONGRESS OF AMERICAN INDIANS. She was also the author of *Eagle Feather, the Story of a Navajo Boy*, and she wrote articles and book reviews for *Natural History* magazine.

When asked about the designation "Princess," Te Ata told the *New Yorker* in 1939, "Every Indian entertainer is called a princess." To Indians, she explained, she was known simply as Te Ata, "which is her full name and should properly be used in both formal and informal conversation." In fact, Te Ata was one of the first Native American woman performers to drop the "Princess" before her name.

Te Ata died in Oklahoma City on October 26, 1995, one month short of her 100th birthday. The 30-minute film *God's Drum* (1995, Shawnee-Brittan) is about her.

Further Reading

Green, Richard. *Te Ata: Chickasaw Storyteller, American Treasure*. Norman: University of Oklahoma Press, 2002.
Oliva, Judy Lee. "Te Ata—A Chickasaw Indian Performer: From Broadway to Back Home." *Theatre History Studies* 15 (1995): 3–26.

Teehee, Houston Benge (1874–1953) *Cherokee attorney*

Houston Benge Teehee was born in Sequoiah County, Cherokee Nation, on October 31, 1874, the son of Stephen and Rhoda Benge Teehee. His father, whose Cherokee name was Di-hi-hi (Killer), fought on the Union side during the Civil War. The American soldiers, having difficulty pronouncing his name, shortened it to Tehee. Later an enrollment clerk added the extra *e* to the first syllable.

Teehee lived on his father's farm until age 18. As a boy, he spoke no English, only Cherokee, but he enrolled at the federal school, and through hard work he learned English. In an interview in 1919, he stated that "learning the English language was the most difficult thing I had to do. . . . The only way I could continue the study of my country's language after leaving the school-room in the evening was by reading." At 18, Teehee went to the Cherokee National Male Seminary at Tahlequah for two years (1893–94), clerking in a store in Tahlequah in his spare time and saving his meager salary, which he then used to attend Fort Worth University in Texas (1895–96). Afterward he returned to the store, making a few dollars a week. While still working there (1904–05), he served as alderman for the village of Tahlequah. In 1906, he began to study law, while at the same time working as a cashier in a local bank. In 1908, he left the bank to begin his legal practice.

When Tahlequah became a city in 1908, Teehee served as its first mayor (1908–10). In that year, he extricated himself from the hands of a government-appointed guardian by getting himself declared competent by the secretary of the interior (see ALLOTMENT). He was elected to the Oklahoma legislature in 1911 but resigned to fill an unexpired term as county attorney. He was reelected to the legislature in 1912.

In 1914 and 1915, Teehee was appointed U.S. probate attorney for the Oklahoma Cherokee under the Interior Department, resigning only to succeed Choctaw GABE PARKER as register of the U.S. Treasury. He was sworn in on March 24, 1915, and served until 1919. During the 1920s, he was president and treasurer of the Continental Asphalt and Petroleum Company of Oklahoma City. From January 1, 1926, to June 1, 1927, he was assistant attorney general of Oklahoma, and from June 1, 1927, through December 31, 1931, he was a member of the Supreme Court Commission of Oklahoma for the First Supreme Court Judicial District. In 1932, he resumed his law practice at Tahlequah.

A Democrat, Presbyterian, and Mason, Teehee died in November 1953.

Further Reading

Starr, Emmet. *History of the Cherokee Indians and Their Legends and Folk Lore.* 1921. Reprint, Baltimore, Md.: Genealogical Publishing Co., 2003.

Tehanetorens   *See* FADDEN, RAY.

Termination

Inaugurated after World War II, the U.S. federal policy of Termination sought to end federal trusteeship over Indian tribes, abolish the BUREAU OF INDIAN AFFAIRS (BIA), and dissolve INDIAN RESERVATIONS and governments. The policy was actually a return to the philosophy of assimilation that reigned during the first quarter of the century, and an attempt to undo the reforms of the INDIAN NEW DEAL enacted by Commissioner of Indian Affairs JOHN COLLIER. Like the earlier policies, Termination aimed to solve the "Indian problem" once and for all by ensuring that under American law there would be no Indians. All distinctions between Indians and other Americans would be ended, and any "special treatment" that Indians were receiving would cease.

The Termination policy had its antecedents before the war, when Congress began to grow uneasy over the far-reaching effects of the Collier reforms. By 1937, only three years after he had cosponsored the INDIAN REORGANIZATION ACT (IRA), Montana senator Burton K. Wheeler was advocating its repeal. The IRA, combined with new legal paradigms introduced by attorney FELIX COHEN, was threatening to give Indians a degree of sovereignty (see SOVEREIGNTY, INDIGENOUS AND TRIBAL) not anticipated by the conservatives in Congress, who in a 1940 report issued by the Senate Committee on Indian Affairs opposed the IRA's "attempts to set up states or nations within a nation, which is contrary to the intents and purposes of the American republic."

Although Indians contributed heroically to the war effort, World War II itself severely weakened the Collier BIA, unable to compete with other government departments for war dollars, and finished off the special relief measures Collier had been using to help Indians. The overwhelming Indian participation in the war also led to calls to "free" Indians from their "enslavement" by the bureau and to the assumption that if Indians were capable of taking on the Axis, surely they were able to adjust to American life. By the end of the war, articles by Oswald Garrison Willard in the *Christian Century* and O. K. Armstrong in the *Readers Digest* began using the Indians' war experiences to make the case for a return to the policies of assimilation, including the abolition of the BIA.

In 1946, Congressman Francis Case, a Republican from South Dakota, introduced four separate bills to "emancipate" Indians from BIA control, and Oregon Republican senators Wayne Morse and Guy Gordon submitted a bill that would provide for the "liquidation of tribally held property" among the Klamath. Although defeated, the bills were a portent of the new mood in Congress, which, though couched in terms of aiding and freeing the Indian, was actually a return to the land-grab atmosphere of pre-Collier days. The next year, the Senate directed acting commissioner William Zimmerman (Commissioner WILLIAM ALOYSIUS BROPHY was ill) to compile a list of tribes ready for Termination, and in 1949 the HOOVER COMMISSION, using the language of the early part of the century, recommended integration as the "best solution to the Indian problem."

Termination began in earnest with the ascension of DILLON SEYMOUR MYER to the commissioner's office in 1950. An avowed assimilationist who had directed the notorious internment camps for Japanese Americans during the war, Myer sacked most of the remaining high-ranking Collier appointees, who had thus far successfully helped stall Termination, and immediately aligned himself with Republican conservatives calling for the BIA's abolition. Myer inaugurated "Operation Relocation," which would transfer thousands of Indians from their homes on reservations into America's urban areas (see URBANIZATION, AMERICAN INDIANS AND). He supported House Resolution 698 (introduced on July 1, 1952), which allowed the BIA to submit, without the tribes' approval, proposals for their termination. He worked to have states extend their jurisdiction over Indian reservations and services, and in 1950 Congress granted New York State courts jurisdiction over the Indian reservations within its boundaries. He also supported Public Law 291, passed on April 3, 1952, which allowed for the transfer of Indian Health Service hospitals to state control.

Myer aroused a storm of criticism from Indian rights advocates (see ASSOCIATION ON AMERICAN INDIAN AFFAIRS) and the newly formed NATIONAL CONGRESS OF AMERICAN INDIANS (NCAI), and in 1953 he resigned. But this did not halt the Termination process. The election of Dwight Eisenhower in 1952 added a Republican president to the Republican majorities in Congress, and conservative Republicans now controlled both Indian affairs committees: E. Y. Berry of South Dakota in the House and ARTHUR VIVIAN WATKINS of Utah in the Senate. Eisenhower selected GLENN LEONIDAS EMMONS, a proponent of Termination, as his Indian affairs commissioner.

Emmons moved quickly with Congress to begin dismantling Indian protections gained in the preceding decades. In 1953, Congress passed Public Law 280, which granted states criminal jurisdiction over Indian reservations, dealing a serious blow to Indian sovereignty. In 1954, following the lead of House Resolution 108, passed in 1953, which advocated phasing out the BIA and liquidating Indian reservations, Emmons, Watkins, and Berry proposed 13 separate Termination bills, six of which passed. By 1962, 14 bills had been passed terminating 109 tribes and bands. Many of these were smaller or more assimilated—the total number of Indians terminated by 1960 was some 13,000, compared to 533,000 tribal members still enrolled—but the number included some large tribes with valuable resources, such as the Klamath and Menominee. To these, Termination was a disaster.

In 1959, the Klamath were terminated. More than 78 percent of their reservation was sold outright, with rich timberlands going largely to the U.S. government and the Crown Zellerbach Corporation. The 1,660 Klamath each received $44,000; most members either squandered the money or were beset by carpetbaggers, and the majority eventually became destitute. The 473 Klamath who had refused to go along with the Termination plans and not accepted the per capita payments organized a nonprofit trusteeship, retaining 143,000 acres of timber and ranchland. The Termination of the Klamath, however, ended up costing the federal government far more money than the reservation had cost. The administrative expenses for Klamath Termination were $3.4 million, not including purchasing the timber, which ended up costing $69 million. Since the reservation had previously received almost no money from the BIA other than $200,000 per year for roads and conservation, Termination was by no means the bargain promised. As for Klamath, by the end of the 20th century they had still not fully recovered from the effects of Termination.

Meanwhile, BIA hospitals and clinics had been transferred to the Public Health Service in 1955, restrictions on the leasing, selling, and mortgaging of Indian lands were loosened, and in 1958 the BIA established a policy of accelerated adoptions of Indian children into non-Indian homes. However, the Termination policy, harshly criticized by Indians as well as by church groups and other advocates, began to lose steam in the second half of the decade. In 1958, Secretary of the Interior Fred Seaton began to move away from some of the most extreme aspects of Termination, and in 1961, with the election of President John F. Kennedy and the appointment of PHILLEO NASH as commissioner, it lost the support of the executive branch. Termination was still a powerful force in Congress, though, and remained official government policy until President Richard Nixon called for its repeal in June 1970, effectively ending the era (see BRUCE, LOUIS ROOK, JR.). In 1973, the Menominee won a major victory when they were restored to trust status (see WASHINAWATOK, JAMES A.), and in 1978 Congress restored the status of the Modoc, Wyandotte, and Peoria. In 1986, Congress provided a partial restoration for the Klamath, doing the same for the Alabama-Coushatta of Texas the following year. House Resolution 108 was not actually repealed until 1988.

In the end, only a small portion of Indian land was terminated, and almost all of the tribes that were liquidated were smaller rancherias in California (under the California Rancheria Act of 1958) and small bands in Oregon. Although Termination weakened many Indian rights as well as to some extent the BIA, its sponsors never achieved their ambitious goals. Indeed, to a large extent their effort to destroy Indian reservations was the catalyst for the rise of a powerful Indian-based political movement, led by groups such as the NCAI and the NATIONAL INDIAN YOUTH COUNCIL—a movement that would culminate in the militancy of the RED POWER MOVEMENT of the 1960s and 1970s. Thus, the end of Termination also effectively marked the end of the long era in which large non-Indian support groups dominated the formulation of Indian policy.

Further Reading

Cowger, Thomas W. *The National Congress of American Indians: The Founding Years*. Lincoln: University of Nebraska Press, 2001.

Drinnon, Richard. *Keeper of the Concentration Camps: Dillon S. Myer and American Racism*. Berkeley: University of California Press, 1989.

Fixico, Donald L. *Termination and Relocation: Federal Indian Policy, 1945–1960*. Albuquerque: University of New Mexico Press, 1986.

Hasse, Larry J. "Termination and Assimilation: Federal Indian Policy, 1943 to 1961." Ph.D. dissertation, Washington State University, 1974.

Hauptman, Laurence M. *The Iroquois Struggle for Survival: World War II to Red Power*. Syracuse, N.Y.: Syracuse University Press, 1986.

Peroff, Nicholas C. *Menominee Drums: Tribal Termination and Restoration, 1954–1974*. Norman: University of Oklahoma Press, 1982.

Philp, Kenneth R. *Termination Revisited: American Indians on the Trail to Self-determination, 1933–1953*. Lincoln: University of Nebraska Press, 1999.

Wilkinson, Charles F. *Blood Struggle: The Rise of Modern Indian Nations*. New York: W. W. Norton & Company, 2005.

Louis Tewanima, in New York City to help raise funds for U.S. athletes competing in the 1956 Olympics, visited Times Square with model Frances White. *(AP/Wideworld)*

Tewanima, Louis (c. 1882–1969) *Hopi athlete*

Louis Tewanima was born into the Sand Clan in Shongopovi, on the Second Mesa of the Hopi Reservation. His date of birth is not known. The year 1888, commonly given, rests on doubtful authority. His obituary in the *Arizona Champion-Daily Sun* gave the date as January 1, 1878. However, BIA census documents from the early 1930s suggest he was born around 1882. Tewanima's parents, like many traditional Hopi, kept him out of school. But he was curious about world beyond the reservation: As a child, he ran to Winslow, Arizona, 60 miles away, just to get a glimpse of the steam trains that passed through the town.

He was among the resisters who, when rounded up by the army in 1906, were given the choice of going to prison or going to boarding school. Louis chose school. He attended Carlisle Indian School in Pennsylvania between 1907 and 1912, and along with JIM THORPE and GUSTAVUS WELCH, formed one of college history's most formidable track teams (see WARNER, POP). Tewanima once missed the train for a competition but ran 18 miles to the event in time to enter and win a two-mile race. In 1909, the team was booked to meet powerful Lafayette College in Easton, Pennsylvania, and in an encounter that would become legendary, they surprised the local welcoming committee—who expected at least a dozen or more competitors—when only the three Indians got off the train. The trio proceeded to beat Lafayette 71-41, with Thorpe winning six

events and Tewanima and Welch two apiece. They then finished the season by defeating ruling college powers Harvard, Georgetown, Johns Hopkins, and Syracuse Universities. Later that year, Tewanima competed in Madison Square Garden in New York City, where he set the indoor world record for the 10-mile run.

Tewanima was a member of the 1908 U.S. Olympic team and placed ninth in the marathon. He then joined Thorpe, ANDREW SOCKALEXIS, and Native Hawaiian swimmer Duke Kahanamoku in the memorable 1912 Olympics. Tewanima won the silver medal in the 10,000 meters, a feat that would not be equaled by an American until BILLY MILLS won the gold in 1964. Later in 1912, Tewanima easily defeated American cross-country champion Fred Bellars in a five-mile match race at Motordome Stadium in Valisburg, New Jersey. Tewanima came in first in the famous "Bunion Derby" from New York to California in 1925, but he was disqualified for "running too fast" and completing the race before the sponsor could set up the finish line and recruit a paying audience.

In the film *Jim Thorpe—All-American* (1951), actor Al Mejia played the role of Tewanima. In 1954, Tewanima was named to the Helms Foundation All-Time U.S. Track and Field Team. In 1957, he was inducted into the Arizona Sports Hall of Fame. After his running career ended, he returned to Shongopovi, becoming a farmer and traditional religious leader. He died on January 18, 1969, of injuries sustained in a fall from one of the steep mesa cliffs while returning home late at night from a Hopi ceremony.

See also SPORTS, AMERICAN INDIANS AND.

Further Reading
Oxendine, Joseph B. *American Indian Sports Heritage.* Lincoln: University of Nebraska Press, 1995.

Tewaquaptewa, Wilson (Tawakwaptiwa, "Sun in the Sky") (1873–1960) *Hopi political leader*

Wilson Tewaquaptewa was born in 1873 in Oraibi, then the largest and most influential of the Hopi villages. His father was Cheauka of the Bear Clan, among the most important Hopi clans. In 1904, Tewaquaptewa was named a village chief, or kikmongwi, succeeding his uncle, Lololma, a "progressive," or "friendly," who had died the previous year. Like Lololma, Tewaquaptewa, while a firm believer in maintaining Hopi culture, favored a compromise with the ASSIMILATION policies of the U.S. government against the hard line of the "traditionals," or "hostiles," led by YOUKIOMA, who would have absolutely nothing to do with American ways. The heavy-handed tactics of U.S. government officials, who repeatedly imprisoned the traditional leaders for refusing to allow Oraibi's children to attend school, polarized the Hopi factions.

When Youkioma began to conduct important Hopi ceremonies in his own kiva and then invited members of the neighboring town of Shongopovi to swell the traditional ranks, it gave Tewaquaptewa the excuse he needed to expel the traditionals. Bolstered by reinforcements from Moencopi and given tacit support by reservation superintendent Theodore Lemmon, on September 7, 1906, Tewaquaptewa's supporters marched into a home where the traditionals had gathered and demanded the expulsion of the Shongopovi supporters. When the demands were refused, Tewaquaptewa ordered Youkioma and his men seized and expelled. As the threat of violence escalated, Youkioma challenged the progressives to a pushing match, on the condition that the losers would have to leave Oraibi. The progressives won.

The traditionals moved out and founded a new village, Hotevilla, nearby. Commissioner of Indian Affairs FRANCIS ELLINGTON LEUPP then "rewarded" Tewaquaptewa for his triumph by forcing him to attend the Sherman Institute in Riverside, California, with the hope that the experience would make him a better leader. In fact, it embittered the Hopi leader for the rest of his life. With Tewaquaptewa gone, Oraibi fell into dissension. After a failed attempt by the old traditional leader Lomahongyoma to assume Tewaquaptewa's place as kikmongwi, Lomahongyoma established another village, Bacavi, in 1909, under the leadership of Kawonuptewa of the Sand Clan.

Tewaquaptewa returned from Riverside that summer, now antagonistic to the progressive policies he had endorsed before his removal. This created further divisions at Oraibi. After he ordered all Christian converts to leave the town, many of his former supporters moved to a new village, Kykotsmovi (New Oraibi), or to Moencopi.

The conversion of his brother Charles Fredericks to Christianity and his attempt to become the leader of Oraibi further alienated Tewaquaptewa from his own people and eventually led him to a reconciliation with his former rivals in Hotevilla. However, Hopi ceremonial life continued to disintegrate in Oraibi, culminating on August 27, 1922, with the public burning of the Bow Clan altar and the ceremonial objects of the One Horn and Two Horn Societies—objects so ancient and sacred only a few Hopi had ever see them—by Bow Clan chief Tuwaletstiwa, who had converted to Christianity.

Tewaquaptewa opposed the formation of the Hopi Tribal Council under the INDIAN REORGANIZATION ACT of 1934 (see LA FARGE, OLIVER), and along with traditional strongholds Hotevilla, Shongopovi, and Mishognovi, he boycotted the council. His power declined throughout the years, however, as his people defected from his authority or moved to New Oraibi, where modern conveniences were available. By 1940, the population of Oraibi, once greater than 1,000, had dwindled to only 100.

In his later life, Tewaquaptewa became known for his carvings of Kachina dolls, which he sold to collectors. He withdrew from political activity, believing that he was destined to be the last kikmongwi of Oraibi, and that the ancient community, the oldest continuously inhabited village in North America would soon wither away.

Tewaquaptewa's death in Oraibi on April 30, 1960, without a chosen successor, led to further schisms in the village. His daughter Mina Lansa ascended to the position of kikmongwi over her brothers Myron Polequaptewa, who was a supporter of the Hopi Tribal Council, and Stanley Bahimptewa, who did not reside in the town. A fierce advocate of Hopi ways, Lansa closed the village to outsiders and added Oraibi and Lower Moencopi, which she led after the loss of its kikmongwi, to the traditional resistance movement led by DAN KATCHONGVA, who opposed the Hopi Tribal Council and its longtime lawyer, JOHN BOYDEN. With THOMAS BANYACYA, she lent her support to the Navajo in the BIG MOUNTAIN dispute. Sadly, after Lansa's death on January 8, 1978, Wilson Tewaquaptewa's house was looted of many of its valuable and sacred Hopi ceremonial objects.

See also SEKAQUAPTEWA, EMORY.

Further Reading
Dockstader, Frederick J. *The Kachina and the White Man: A Study of the Influences of White Culture on the Hopi Kachina Cult.* Bloomfield Hills, Mich.: Cranbrook Institute of Science, 1954.
Gilbert, Matthew Sakiestewa. *Education Beyond the Mesas: Hopi Students at Sherman Institute, 1902–1929.* Lincoln: University of Nebraska Press, 2010.
Whiteley, Peter. *Bacavi: Journey to Reed Springs.* Flagstaff, Ariz.: Northland Publishing, 1988.

Thom, Mel (1938–1984) *Paiute cofounder of the National Indian Youth Council*

A Paiute, Melvin Daris Thom was born on July 28, 1938, and

raised on the Walker River Reservation in Nevada. Growing up in the desert that makes up much of the reservation, he eventually became a cowpuncher and construction worker. After graduating from Lyon County High School in Yerington, Nevada, Thom studied civil engineering at Brigham Young University. While there, he became president of the Southwestern Youth Conferences. In 1961, he attended the historic AMERICAN INDIAN CHICAGO CONFERENCE, where he met NATIONAL INDIAN YOUTH COUNCIL (NIYC) cofounders HERBERT BLATCHFORD, SHIRLEY HILL WITT, and CLYDE WARRIOR.

Thom was the organizational leader behind the NIYC, formulating its principles and becoming the group's chair. Rather than an organization, Thom proposed that the NIYC be a movement, foreshadowing the rise of the AMERICAN INDIAN MOVEMENT (AIM) 10 years later. According to Thom, "Organizations rearrange history. Movements make history." The group was to be a return to traditional means of political activity. As he put it, "Long ago the Indians knew they had to use direct action. You might say that was the traditional way Indians got things done. . . . The younger Indians got together in the Youth Council because they didn't feel the older leadership was aggressive enough. And we felt that Indian affairs were so bad that it was time to raise some hell." Thom's embrace of confrontational tactics and his organizational abilities earned him the nickname "Mao Tse Thom."

Thom led the NIYC in its first and most successful area of direct action, fish-ins in Washington State, where the council aided Bruce Wilkie and other Makah in their efforts to organize the tribes in the Northwest to fight together for their fishing rights (see HUNTING AND FISHING RIGHTS). The project, begun in February 1964, was dubbed the Washington Project, and Thom tapped Assiniboine-Dakota Sioux HANK ADAMS to coordinate it.

While Thom continued to work with the NIYC, he stepped down from active participation in order to pursue his career in engineering, eventually becoming an assistant resident engineer for the Federal Aviation Agency (later Administration). Thom later returned to the Walker River Reservation to become director of the Office of Economic Opportunity for the Paiute, and in 1967 he was elected tribal chair. He died in Schurz, Nevada, on December 17, 1984

Further Reading

Mencarelli, James, and Steve Severin. *Protest 3: Red, Black, Brown Experiences in America*. Grand Rapids, Mich.: Eerdmans, 1975.

Shreve, Bradley Glenn, and Shirley Hill Witt. *Red Power Rising: The National Indian Youth Council and the Origins of Native Activism*. Norman: University of Oklahoma Press, 2011.

Thomas, George A. (1911–1968) *principal chief of the Iroquois Confederacy*

Born on July 21 or 23, 1911, on the Onondaga Reservation,

George Alanson Thomas, a chief of the Eel Clan, was the third Tadadaho, or principal chief, of the Iroquois Confederacy in the 20th century, succeeding his father, GEORGE E. THOMAS, in 1957. The elder Thomas had served as Tadadaho from 1917, after the death of Frank Logan, until his own death in 1957.

By the time the younger Thomas became Tadadaho, the confederacy was being assailed on many fronts. After numerous attempts throughout the earlier part of the 20th century, New York State succeeded in 1950 in establishing jurisdiction over Iroquois lands. Massive development projects that coincided with the TERMINATION policy of the late 1940s and 1950s were threatening many Iroquois reservations. Beginning in 1957, Thomas fought the state of New York over an attempt to impose a sales tax on the reservation and demanded the return of the Iroquois wampum belts held by New York State (see REPATRIATION). He also fought off attempts by the BUREAU OF INDIAN AFFAIRS (BIA) to overturn the confederacy by replacing it with an elective system of government. However, the Iroquois continued to suffer defeats. The greatest of these was the flooding of the best part of the Allegany Reservation by the KINZUA DAM in 1963.

Thomas was known more as a spiritual than a political leader, his time as Tadadaho coinciding with a revival of the traditional Longhouse religion under the liberalizing currents of the 1960s (see RELIGIOUS FREEDOM, AMERICAN INDIAN). Young Iroquois activists such as WILLIAM RICKARD and MAD BEAR ANDERSON began to abandon Christianity, which had made deep inroads into the confederacy during the 19th and early 20th centuries, for the Longhouse. Rickard's work in preparation for the historic AMERICAN INDIAN CHICAGO CONFERENCE in 1961 and his organizing of the North American Indian Unity Caravans also began to spread the traditional Iroquois philosophy to other Indian communities, with the Iroquois concept of sovereignty striking a particularly strong chord (see SOVEREIGNTY, INDIGENOUS AND TRIBAL). Thomas, however, would not live to see the fruits of the revival of Iroquois traditions, and it would be up to his successor, LEON SHENANDOAH, to bring the confederacy to its height of power and prestige. Hospitalized in Syracuse in July 1968, George A. Thomas died on October 22, 1968.

Further Reading

Fenton, William N. "The Funeral of Tadadaho: Onondaga of Today." *Indian Historian* 3, no. 2 (1970): 43–47, 66.

Hauptman, Laurence M. *The Iroquois Struggle for Survival: World War II to Red Power*. Syracuse, N.Y.: Syracuse University Press, 1986.

Thomas, George E. (1886–1957) *principal chief of the Iroquois Confederacy*

From 1917 to 1957, George E. Thomas, as the Iroquois Confederacy's Tadadaho, or principal chief, led the Grand Council of Chiefs through a number of bitter battles between the confederacy and the state of New York as the two vied for control over the Iroquois reservations. According to census records, George E. Thomas was born on July 8, 1886, on the Onondaga Reservation in upstate New York, the son of John Thomas and Charlotte Mt. Pleasant Thomas. It appears that he later lived with his grandfather, a gardener named Louis Thomas, in Lafayette, New York, about seven miles southeast of the reservation, and he went to school near there.

As Thomas was growing up, the Iroquois Confederacy, or Six Nations, was being hard-pressed by the forces of christianization and by New York State, which had long wanted to extinguish the power of the traditional chiefs of the Onondaga, Seneca, Mohawk, Cayuga, Oneida, and Tuscarora Nations. By 1900, the Iroquois Confederacy chiefs maintained power only on the Onondaga and Tonawanda Seneca Reservations. While the Cayuga and Oneida were represented by traditional chiefs, they had no reservations and lived either on scattered plots of land or at Onondaga, and although the Tuscarora maintained the ancient system of chiefs as well, they had abandoned the Longhouse religion and were almost exclusively Baptist. The Seneca of Cattaraugus and Allegany had split off in the 19th century and organized a separate, republican form of government. At about the same time, a large segment of Oneida had left the confederacy and moved to Wisconsin. The Akwesasne (St. Regis) Mohawk still retained the ancient system of chiefs, but the reservation was actually run by a three-man council set up by the state. Among the Mohawk, all except a handful had become Roman Catholic, but because of their close association with the French and the less onerous nature of Catholic proselytizing, the Mohawk were the most fluent in their language and retained a great amount of their traditional culture. In Canada, a sizable Iroquois community had been well established since the Revolutionary War and over time created their own system of chiefs.

Thomas lived on the Onondaga Reservation near Syracuse, the "firekeeper," or center, of the confederacy where the grand council of the chiefs of the Six Nations meets. It is also home to the Tadadaho, who at the turn of the century was Frank Logan (1857–1917). The Onondaga remained the most traditional and least christianized of the Iroquois, with more than three-quarters of its members still practicing the Longhouse religion and the government still run under the ancient system of chiefs selected by clan mothers. Although a certain degree of coexistence had been maintained between the Christian and traditional Iroquois, the attempt by New York State, backed by Christian elements, to reorganize the Onondaga government in 1882 led to a serious political schism. An Onondaga chief had to be a member of the Longhouse religion, and any who converted were quickly deposed.

On the Tonawanda Seneca Reservation, the traditionals managed to maintain tenuous control of the council, although the reservation itself was split evenly between Christians and traditionals. On the Allegany Seneca Reservation, although it was not a part of the Iroquois Confederacy, one-third of the members were still traditionals, and at the Cattaraugus Seneca Reservation, the community in Newtown was a traditional stronghold. The Oneida who lived off the Onondaga Reservation were all Christian. Thomas was among the Iroquois who remained traditional and fought off attempts to be christianized.

In 1897, the Iroquois suffered a significant loss when their valuable wampum belts, which are ceremonial objects as well as historical records and important symbols of the confederacy government, were appropriated by New York State (see REPATRIATION). On three occasions between 1902 and 1914, the federal government attempted to extend the ALLOTMENT policy to the Iroquois, but the enabling legislation foundered over competing claims to the land. In particular, the Ogden Land Company, which in the 19th century had acquired vast Iroquois tracts, claimed a large portion of Seneca land. The manner in which the Ogden Company and New York State had dispossessed the Iroquois in the previous century, first by violating the Indian Non-Intercourse Act of 1790, which forbade the purchase of Indian lands by any entity other than the federal government, and second through the use of fraudulent treaties (that is, treaties approved by the state without the formal consent of the Indian tribe), would become a serious point of legal and political contention between New York and the Iroquois throughout the 20th century.

The Iroquois Confederacy not only rejected attempts by New York to impose jurisdiction, they vigorously attempted to maintain their sovereign status as an independent nation within the United States, a political position unique among American Indian communities at the time (see SOVEREIGNTY, INDIGENOUS AND TRIBAL). Honoring their historic alliance with the British, the Iroquois Confederacy declared war on Germany well before the American entry into WORLD WAR I, and hundreds of American Iroquois served in the war.

Thomas attended the Carlisle Indian Industrial School in Pennsylvania, where he played football with his friend, the great Sac and Fox athlete JIM THORPE. He graduated in 1910 and married his wife Margaret the same year. Following the death of Frank Logan in 1917, Thomas ascended to the position of Tadadaho, which he would hold until his death in 1957. His appointment was not universally welcomed. Many of the hard-line Iroquois traditionals felt he would not be strong enough to fend off the demands by New York State and Christian advocates to remove the traditional form of government and replace it with one controlled by the state.

Thomas's first challenge as leader came after a federal court ruled that Iroquois land fell under federal trust status, overturning New York State's position that all lands within the state's boundaries belonged to the state and that the state had jurisdiction over these lands (see LAND TENURE). The ruling led to the creation of the New York State Indian Commission, led by Edward A. Everett, a member of the state assembly, and included other high-ranking state officials, and Seneca anthropologist ARTHUR C. PARKER and Onondaga DAVID RUSSELL HILL as the Indian members. Parker, who had agitated for the complete christianization of the Iroquois, was one of the confederacy's most vocal critics, and Hill was not sympathetic to the aims of the confederacy chiefs.

The commission investigated the relationship between the Indians and the state, and the Iroquois chiefs, although suspicious that the intention was simply to establish state jurisdiction and induce the Indians to accept citizenship, agreed to meet with the commission on their respective reservations. Led by Thomas, Onondaga chief Jesse Lyons, and Oneida chief Marshal John, and aided by experts such as attorney John Snyder and physician ERL BATES, the Iroquois convinced Everett that not only did New York not have jurisdiction over or title to Iroquois lands, but that the Iroquois had a valid claim to more than 6 million acres of state land that had been taken from them in the previous century.

The Everett Report, released in 1922, created a sensation and heightened tensions between the Iroquois and the state of New York. Everett himself was ousted from his seat in the assembly by angry New York voters. Subsequent attempts by the Iroquois to pursue the land claims led to serious splits in the Grand Council. While Thomas backed Oneida activist LAURA CORNELIUS KELLOGG's attempts to pursue the claim in court, Jesse Lyons and other chiefs withheld their support. Thomas's backing of Kellogg led to a serious destabilization of the confederacy. A rival Onondaga chief, Joshua Jones, tried to have Thomas removed as Tadadaho and claim the title for himself. The two would vie for control of the confederacy for the next 15 years.

The Iroquois rejected the 1924 Indian Citizenship Act (see CITIZENSHIP), and Thomas sent a delegation under Lyons to Washington, D.C., to reaffirm their sovereignty. In an effort to overcome the Indian Citizenship Act, Tuscarora chief CLINTON RICKARD and Canadian Iroquois chief ALEXANDER GENERAL became active in seeking international recognition of their sovereignty. During the 1920s, the confederacy won a few victories when American courts recognized the rights of Iroquois members to cross the border between the United States and Canada freely, as well as allowing Canadian Iroquois IRONWORKERS to work in the United States without a visa.

Under Thomas, Iroquois joined with the Six Nations Association, formed in 1925 by Reverend William B. Newell of the American Indian Defense Association, and W. David Owl, leader of the Cattaraugus Seneca, to fight successfully against the attempt by the city of Syracuse to construct dams on the Onondaga Reservation for flood control. In 1930, Thomas and Lyons led the Confederacy delegation to Washington, D.C., that defeated the Snell bill, an attempt by New York State to gain criminal and civil jurisdiction over the reservations.

During the Great Depression, the Iroquois, still largely a farming economy, benefited from the increased employment offered by public works projects, and Thomas backed the National Youth Administration (NYA) programs under the supervision of LOUIS ROOK BRUCE, JR. Bruce initiated 26 separate work programs that employed hundreds of Iroquois youth, including a camp counselor program that was helpful in rekindling tribal and cultural identity—beginning the important work of RAY FADDEN among the Mohawk—as well as building a youth center in Onondaga where traditional leaders could instruct Onondaga children in their heritage.

Unlike the Hopi (see LA FARGE, OLIVER), the Iroquois Confederacy managed to avoid the INDIAN REORGANIZATION ACT of 1934. Although Thomas did not support BUREAU OF INDIAN AFFAIRS commissioner JOHN COLLIER's policies, his rival for Tadadaho, Joshua Jones, was an even fiercer opponent of Collier's plans for the INDIAN NEW DEAL. Jones joined the AMERICAN INDIAN FEDERATION (AIF) where he worked with Seneca activist and agitator for Indian Christianization Alice Lee Jemison to attack Collier's efforts to promote the reorganization act. In the mid-1930s, when the AIF was found to have ties with pro-Nazi organizations, Jones and Jemison were effectively discredited, and Jones dropped his attempts to overthrow Thomas.

Fighting any infringement of their sovereignty, the Iroquois opposed efforts by the United States to draft their men into the service before WORLD WAR II. Following the attack on Pearl Harbor, the Iroquois renewed their declaration of war against the Germans and declared war against the other Axis powers. After the war, New York State managed to capitalize on the growing TERMINATION sentiment in the U.S. Congress and in 1948 finally gained criminal jurisdiction over the Iroquois. Although the Grand Council continued to oppose the legislation, they forged a cooperative agreement with the state to manage crime control. In 1948, with the help of Rickard and the Indian Defense League, the Iroquois began making trips to the United Nations, seeking to overturn the infringements on their sovereignty. In 1949, they attended the cornerstone-laying for the UN headquarters in Manhattan. In 1950, when the state gained civil jurisdiction over the Iroquois, the confederacy protested to the United Nations. That same year a delegation of Hopi led by DAN KATCHONGVA met with Thomas and the Grand Council after their unsuccessful attempt to meet with the United Nations. This sowed the seeds of an important renewal in Indian political thought as the two staunchly traditional peoples sought to work together to oppose infringements on their sovereignty. In 1952, the confederacy petitioned to become members of the United Nations. As the Termination era reached its height and development projects such as the KINZUA DAM threatened the integrity of Iroquois reservations, there arose a militant wave of new activists such as WILLIAM RICKARD and MAD BEAR ANDERSON.

George Thomas died in Syracuse, New York, on July 4, 1957, after a three-month illness. He was succeeded as Tadadaho by his son, GEORGE A. THOMAS.

Further Reading

Hauptman, Laurence M. *Seven Generations of Iroquois Leadership: The Six Nations since 1800.* Syracuse, N.Y.: Syracuse University Press, 2008.

Thomas, Robert Knox (1925–1991)
Cherokee anthropologist, educator, philosopher

A Cherokee born in Mount Sterling, Kentucky, on November 26, 1925, while his mother was on a visit, Robert Knox Thomas was raised in Oklahoma. His parents, Florence and Robert Lee Thomas, were both Cherokee, and he was brought up in a traditional manner. He was taught Cherokee healing traditions by his grandmother and aunt, who were herbalists and midwives. As a young man, Thomas was influenced by George Smith, a Cherokee ceremonial leader and friend of the family. After graduating from high school, he enlisted in the U.S. Marines and saw service in World War II. He fought in the battle of Guadalcanal in the Pacific and then spent time in New Zealand, where he got to know some Maori people.

Thomas was discharged in 1944 and became a horse wrangler in the Midwest and Canada, where he befriended some Chippewa and Métis. He moved to Tucson, Arizona, where he married a Tohono O'odam woman. He received his B.A. (1950) and M.A. (1954) from the University of Arizona and in 1953 was admitted to the Ph.D. program at the University of Chicago, working with anthropologist Sam Stanley. (He never completed his dissertation.) Thomas became an active member of the Chicago Indian Center, the most important urban Indian center at the time (see SEGUNDO, THOMAS).

Thomas was one of a group of anthropologists and sociologists from the University of Chicago, including SOL TAX, Rosalie and Murray Wax, Robert J. Havighurst, Frederick O. Gearing, and Robert Rietz, who worked to change the direction of Indian affairs during the TERMINATION period in the late 1950s and early 1960s. In 1956, Thomas and Stanley compiled data for an important map, showing the location and distribution of the Indian population in the United States, published by the university's anthropology department. From 1957 through 1958, Thomas conducted fieldwork among the Cherokee in the Great Smoky Mountains of North Carolina. He became a leading figure in the summer Workshops on American Indian Affairs as director of the second session in Boulder, Colorado, in 1957, assistant director in 1961, and regular lecturer thereafter. With this group, he helped organize the famous 1961 AMERICAN INDIAN CHICAGO CONFERENCE, and he had a close relationship with Ponca activist CLYDE WARRIOR (an active participant in both the 1961 and 1962 Workshops) and with the NATIONAL INDIAN YOUTH COUNCIL in the 1960s.

The workshop staff found that most Indian students suffered from confused identity and loss of cultural moorings, knowing little of their history and culture and internalizing media stereotypes. In the workshops, they strove to give students a clearer sense of Indian identity by explaining both Native and mainstream American cultures objectively. The response was very positive. Ironically, it was this mainly non-Indian staff who were able to reawaken a sense of self-confidence in Indian identity and understanding of Native values and history in the largely acculturated students. Thomas, however, actually played the central role. Cree-Flathead social scientist D'ARCY MCNICKLE, who observed the evolution of the workshops from 1960 through 1963, described Thomas as having "most influenced the shaping of the workshop as a center for discovery and understanding. The teaching faculty looked to him for intellectual challenge, while the students responded by improving academic performances. . . . [He was] equally capable of reaching students and encouraging them to stretch their intellectual grasp." Thomas's students would come to form the nucleus of the new RED POWER MOVEMENT.

By 1961, Thomas was professor of anthropology at Montieth College, Wayne State University, Detroit, where he coined the term *internal colonization* to describe the situation of American Indians and other indigenous peoples in the modern world. His writings, especially the article "Colonialism: Classic and Internal" (*New University Thought*, 1966/67 issue), played a seminal though underappreciated role in the development of the militant pro-sovereignty movement of the 1970s.

Thomas helped establish a traditional activist organization in Oklahoma, the Five County Northeastern Oklahoma Cherokee Organization, later known as the Original Cherokee Community Organization. The group began to assert Cherokee HUNTING AND FISHING RIGHTS and tackle other long-standing grievances.

In 1967, Thomas attended a unity conference at the Tonawanda Seneca Reservation in upstate New York. The conferences, conceived by Tuscarora activist WILLIAM RICKARD, sought to bring a traditional religious slant to activist organizing. Impressed by this combination of spirituality and grassroots organizing, Thomas organized a similar gathering in Oklahoma the next year. He began working in Canada, joining with Wilf Pelletier, an Ottawa from Ontario, and Ian MacKenzie, an Anglican priest, in an attempt to establish an ecumenical movement that would embrace all religions, including traditional Indian religions, in an effort to recognize Indian rights.

As a field anthropologist, Thomas worked with the Sac and Fox of Oklahoma, the Sioux of South Dakota, and the Cherokee of North Carolina and Oklahoma. In the 1960s, he was codirector of the Carnegie Corporation Cross-Cultural Exchange Project, studying literacy and education process among Indians, especially the Oklahoma Cherokee. He also edited the monthly *Indian Voices*, published by the University of Chicago. Thomas was a Newberry fellow in the 1960s, and from 1975 he was an active member of the board of directors of NAES (Native American Education Services) College, essentially an outgrowth of the workshops; its academic degree program for Indian students has been accredited since 1984. From 1981 until his death, Thomas was director of the American Indian Studies Program at the University of Arizona at Tucson.

In 1991, suffering from tumors in his lungs and brain, Thomas, confined to a wheelchair, took sick leave and returned to Oklahoma, where he stayed about a month. He was returning to Arizona in August 1991 when he passed away on the road while traveling through the Texas panhandle. According to another passenger, Thomas was looking out the window and the sun was setting; just before he died, he turned and said, "Beautiful."

Robert K. Thomas was in a unique position to aid in cultural communication. As a traditional Cherokee fluent in the Cherokee language, yet well educated in the Western sense and fully conversant in the theories and techniques of anthropology, he was a highly knowledgeable and sophisticated thinker and a gifted teacher. His efforts to combine traditional Indian thought with grassroots social organizing influenced a host of young Native activists and had a major impact on the political movements of the 1960s and 1970s, which in the end transformed the lives of Indian peoples throughout the country.

Further Reading

Cobb, Daniel M. "Devils in Disguise: The Carnegie Project, the Cherokee Nation, and the 1960s." *American Indian Quarterly* 31, no. 3 (2007): 465–490.

Pavlik, Steve, ed. *A Good Cherokee, a Good Anthropologist: Papers in Honor of Robert K. Thomas.* Los Angeles, Calif.: American Indian Studies Center at UCLA, 1998.

Tax, Sol, and Robert K. Thomas. "Education 'for' American Indians: Threat or Promise?" *Florida FL Reporter* (Spring/Summer 1969): 15–19, 154.

Thomas, Robert K. "Eastern American Indian Communities." In *Indian Education Confronts the Seventies*, vol. 1, edited by Vine Deloria, Jr., 149–194. Oglala, S.Dak.: American Indian Resource Associates; Traile, Ariz.: Navajo Community College, 1974.

———. "Pan-Indianism." In *The American Indian Today*, edited by Stuart Levine and Nancy Lurie, 77–85. Detroit: Everett, 1965.

———. "Powerless Politics." *New University Thought* 1, no. 4 (Winter 1966–1967): 37–44.

Treat, James. *Around the Sacred Fire: Native Religious Activism in the Red Power Era.* New York: Palgrave Macmillan, 2003.

Thompson, Morris (1939–2000) *Athabaskan engineer, commissioner of Indian affairs*

Born in Tanana, Alaska, on September 11, 1939, to an Athabaskan mother, Morris Thompson attended Bureau of Indian Affairs (BIA) schools in Alaska, graduating from the bureau's Mount Edgecumbe Boarding School. He studied engineering at the University of Alaska, then worked for the National Aeronautics and Space Administration (NASA) in Fairbanks as an electronics technical assistant. He also worked for the Alaska state government, serving as deputy director of the Alaska Rural Development Agency.

Thompson joined the federal government in 1969, working on Indian affairs as an assistant to Richard Nixon's interior secretary Walter J. Hinckel. Joining reform-minded Indian commissioner Louis Rook Bruce, Jr., he played an important role in drafting Nixon's progressive Indian policy. Thompson helped formulate Nixon's self-determination message in 1970 ending the era of Termination and restoring Blue Lake to the Taos Pueblo. He also helped the Nixon administration negotiate the controversial Alaska Native Land Claims Settlement Act of 1971. In addition to being involved in the negotiations to return Blue Lake, Thompson helped to regain Mount Adams for the Yakama. He then served as the Alaska area director for the BIA from 1971 until December 3, 1973, when Nixon appointed him to head the BIA.

Thompson, at 34, was the youngest person ever to become commissioner of Indian affairs. The office had been vacant since December 1972, when Bruce was fired after the sacking of

BIA headquarters by militant Indian leaders during the Trail of Broken Treaties. In the interim, the bureau had been headed by Marvin Franklin, former chair of the Iowa Tribal Council and an executive of Phillips Petroleum. Franklin, a friend of Phillips's chairman and Nixon supporter, William Wayne Keeler, worked closely with Secretary of the Interior Rogers C. B. Morton, who created the position of assistant secretary of the interior for Indian affairs for Franklin. Franklin attempted a vast reorganization of the bureau but was forced to step down after South Dakota senator James Abourezk, chair of the Senate Indian Affairs Committee, accused him of holding the office of commissioner illegally in an attempt to bypass Senate confirmation hearings.

Thompson became Indian commissioner at a low point in the BIA's history, when morale was poor and the bureau itself deeply divided. Franklin's reorganization, which included heavy budget cuts as well as an Indian hiring-preference program, had polarized relationships between the non-Indian and Indian staffers, as both competed fiercely for dwindling jobs. BIA employees were further divided between those who supported militants such as the American Indian Movement (AIM) and those who opposed them. Franklin had stood by helplessly when AIM members occupied Wounded Knee, South Dakota, and the BIA found itself not only under heavy criticism for its inability to deal with Indian problems, but also shunted aside by the Justice Department and other hard-line government institutions.

Thompson attempted to strengthen the BIA's credibility with Indian people by appointing Indians to five of its six top area directorships, but a yearlong delay in finding and placing these directors only added to the bureau's ineffectiveness. He also sought to prevent future incidents like Wounded Knee by strengthening the management skills of Indian tribal chairs, and he continued Franklin's policy of reporting directly to Morton instead of to the assistant secretary for land management, raising the bureau's prestige. Thompson was unable to deal with the historical problems that underlay many Indian issues, however, and the relocation of Navajo from Big Mountain began under his tenure.

Despite the political obstacles, Thompson continued the Nixon administration's strong support for Indian self-determination, helping to pass the Indian Self-Determination and Education Act of 1975. The act allowed Indian tribes to manage many federal Indian programs themselves, under contract from the bureau, and was an important legislative victory for Indians (see educational policy, American Indians and; health, American Indian).

Thompson resigned on November 3, 1976, to work for Alaska's growing oil industry, which he helped to foster through his settlement of the Alaskan land claims. A champion of Indian governments, he had played an important role in formulating Indian policy during the historic Nixon administration.

Thompson, who had been vice president of his Native corporation, Doyan, since 1981, became president in 1985. He retired in 2000. On January 31, 2000, Thompson, his wife, Thelma, and their daughter, Sheryl, were returning from a vacation in Mexico on Alaska Airlines flight 261 when their plane crashed into the Pacific Ocean off the California coast. All on board perished.

In 2008, the Morris Thompson Cultural and Visitors Center was dedicated in downtown Fairbanks.

Further Reading

Kane, Roger. "In Memory of Morris Thompson." *Alaska Business Monthly* 16, no. 9 (2000): 17.

Thornton, Joe Tindle (1916–) *Cherokee archery champion*

Joe Tindle Thornton, a Cherokee, was born in Stilwell, Oklahoma, on August 2, 1916. As a youth he attended the Seneca Indian School in Wyandotte, Oklahoma, and Chilocco Indian School. At Chilocco, Thornton made crude homemade bows and arrows for hunting. Graduating in 1934, he joined the army and spent three years at Fort Sill as a field radio operator. After leaving the service, he moved to Stilwell, Oklahoma, and then to Tahlequah, but rejoined the military after the outbreak of WORLD WAR II and served in the Signal Corps. He received a Presidential Unit Citation Award for his service.

When the war ended, Thornton returned to Tahlequah and opened a radio and TV repair business. He began entering archery competitions in the mid-1950s, winning the Oklahoma state tournament in 1960. In 1961, he set three world records on the way to winning the sport of archery's world championship in Oslo, Norway. The next year, he won the British International Trials Championship. In 1963, he finished second in the World Championships, and in 1965 he again missed being champion, this time losing by a slender margin to Matti Haikonen of Finland. Thornton was a member of the 1967 and 1971 U.S. archery teams that won the World Championship. In 1970, at the age of 54, he won the U.S. archery championship.

Thornton operated a television business in Tahlequah, Oklahoma. Now retired, he gardens and makes Indian jewelry. His wife, Helen, is also a champion archer. Thornton was inducted into the American Indian Athletic Hall of Fame in 1978 and in 2004 into the Oklahoma State Archery Association Hall of Fame, along with his wife.

Further Reading

"Thornton, Cherokee from Tulsa, Breaks World Archery Mark in Norway." *New York Times*, 13 August 1961.

Thorpe, Grace (No Teno Quah, "Wind Woman") (1921–2008) *Sac and Fox-Potawatomi antinuclear and Indian rights activist*

Grace Francis Thorpe was born in Yale, Oklahoma, on December 10, 1921, the youngest of three daughters of JIM THORPE and his first wife, Iva Miller, whose mother was one-half Eastern Cherokee. Given the Sac and Fox name No Teno Quah (Wind Woman), Grace Thorpe grew up with her mother. During WORLD WAR II, she joined the Woman's Army Air Corps and

Sports star Jim Thorpe holds his daughter Grace Thorpe, who would later become a noted Indian rights activist. *(AP/Wideworld)*

was stationed in New Guinea, and after the war, she served as a member of General Douglas MacArthur's staff in occupied Japan, returning to the United States in 1950 and settling in Pearl River, New York. While in the military, Grace Thorpe married Fred Seeley. The couple had one daughter and one son before divorcing.

Thorpe became active in the Indian land-recovery movement in the mid-1960s, helping to acquire property in California for what would become D-Q University (see HIGHER EDUCATION). After working briefly for the NATIONAL CONGRESS OF AMERICAN INDIANS (NCAI), she joined the OCCUPATION OF ALCATRAZ ISLAND in 1970, also participating in the successful takeover of Fort Lawton in Washington State that same year. Around that time, she was arrested during the occupation of Pacific Gas and Electric Company lands claimed by the PIT RIVER Indians.

Thorpe subsequently served as a legislative assistant to the U.S. Senate Subcommittee on Indian Affairs before being appointed to the AMERICAN INDIAN POLICY REVIEW COMMISSION. She returned to Oklahoma in 1980 and served as a tribal court judge and health commissioner of the Sac and Fox tribe. Also in 1980, Thorpe received a bachelor's degree in history from the University of Tennessee at Knoxville.

Along with her sister Charlotte, Thorpe was instrumental in 1983 in securing the return of the Olympic medals that had been unfairly taken from her father in 1913. She became active in the antinuclear movement in 1992 when the Sac and Fox tribe applied for a grant to study the feasibility of housing a monitored retrievable storage (MRS) facility for nuclear waste. The grant was part of a large Department of Energy plan to site high-level nuclear wastes on Indian lands. Thorpe managed to rally her people against the proposal, and the grant was returned. She then went on to work nationally to get other tribes and the NCAI to back out of the program, serving as president of the National Environmental Coalition of Native Americans (see NUCLEAR INDUSTRY, AMERICAN INDIANS AND THE).

Grace Thorpe's daughter Dagmar Thorpe is an influential member of the Native American philanthropic community and the author of *People of the Seventh Fire*, a collection of interviews with Native American leaders published in 1996.

Grace Thorpe died on April 8, 2008, in Claremore, Oklahoma.

Further Reading

Rogers, Keith. "Thorpe Battles Nuclear Waste." *Las Vegas Review Journal*, 8 April 1996.

Thorpe, Grace. "Radioactive Racism? Native Americans and the Nuclear Waste Legacy." *Indian Country Today*, 16 March 1995.

Thorpe, Jim (James Francis Thorpe, Wa-tho-huck, "Bright Path") (ca. 1888–1953) *Sac and Fox-Potawatomi athlete, Olympian, sports legend*

Jim Thorpe's date of birth is not clear, and no birth certificate has yet come to light. According to his own account, he was born on May 28, 1888, near Prague, Oklahoma (at that time known as Indian Territory). Later documents, including his international travel documents for 1912 and his gravestone, reflect this date. His baptismal record, on the other hand, gives the date as May 22, 1887. Other early documents, such as the June 1900 BUREAU OF INDIAN AFFAIRS (BIA) census and his Haskell school records, also indicate that he was born in 1887. The BIA census of 1900 lists his tribal membership as Citizen Band Potawatomi. His father, Hiram Thorpe, was half-Irish and half–Sac and Fox, and his mother, Charlotte Vieux Thorpe, was part Potawatomi. At his birth, Jim Thorpe was enrolled in the Sac and Fox tribe and given the name Wa-tho-huck, or Bright Path. Along with three brothers and two sisters, he grew up on his father's farm, becoming an expert hunter and horseman while still young. At age six, he was sent to the Sac and Fox Indian Agency School near Tecumseh, Oklahoma, though he eventually ran away. A defining moment in his life came at age eight, when his twin brother and constant companion, Charles, died of pneumonia.

Thorpe attended the Haskell Indian Institute in Lawrence, Kansas, and after his mother's death in 1900, a public school near his home. In 1904, he enrolled in the Carlisle

Jim Thorpe is pictured during his time playing with the Carlisle Indian Industrial School's football team. *(AP/Wideworld)*

Indian Industrial School in Pennsylvania. Over the next three years, he was sent to live and work with neighboring white families under the school's "outing system" (see PRATT, RICHARD HENRY). He caught the attention of Carlisle coach POP WARNER in 1907 when, walking back from class, he casually cleared a 5'9" high-jump bar that had been left standing on the athletic grounds, besting the school record. By the 1908 track season, Thorpe was virtually a one-man team, regularly winning four or more events each meet to help Carlisle defeat the ruling college powers (see TEWANIMA, LOUIS). He also played football that year, winning third-string All-America honors and earning varsity letters in 11 different sports.

Never fond of the outing system, Thorpe left Carlisle to play minor league baseball in North Carolina until the league abruptly folded. He returned to Carlisle in 1911 and led the football team to within one point of having an undefeated year, attracting national attention when he kicked four field goals and scored a touchdown to upset Harvard, the defending national champions, and leading Harvard coach Percy Haughton to say that he had finally seen "the theoretical superplayer in flesh and blood."

In 1912, Thorpe, along with Hopi Louis Tewanima and Penobscot ANDREW SOCKALEXIS, joined the U.S. Olympic team, traveling to Stockholm to compete in the pentathlon and decathlon. There, Thorpe put on such a display of athletic prowess that the 1912 games became known as "the Olympics of Jim Thorpe." He won four of the five pentathlon events outright, tripling the score of the runner-up. In the decathlon, considered the ultimate Olympic test, he scored a record 8,412.955 points. To put this achievement in perspective, Thorpe's 1912 decathlon performance would still have been good enough 36 years later to earn him the silver medal in the 1948 Olympics.

Thorpe returned from Sweden an international hero and was honored with a ticker-tape parade in New York City. He solidified his title as the "world's greatest athlete" by winning the Amateur Athletic Union's All-Around Championship in track and field with a record score. In the fall, Thorpe returned to the Carlisle football team and again led it to within one game of an undefeated season. He opened the season by recovering a fumbled snap and running it 110 yards for a touchdown against Dickinson, and followed that by intercepting four passes against Rose Bowl–bound Washington and Jefferson. He then scored four touchdowns against Springfield and three each in games against Syracuse, Pitt, and Brown. He returned an interception 110 yards for a touchdown against Lehigh and played brilliantly when Carlisle upset Army, then considered the finest team in the country, 27 to 6 at West Point. Thorpe finished the season with 198 points, a collegiate record that would stand until 1988. He was awarded All-American honors for the second year in a row.

Thorpe's luster was dimmed in 1913 when the American Athletic Union (AAU), having learned of his short stint with semiprofessional baseball in North Carolina, stripped him of his Olympic gold medals. Unlike many college athletes, who played professional sports under assumed names, Thorpe had never made his baseball playing a secret and had not expected that it would affect his amateur status in track and field. The decision created a furor that bitterly divided the sports world, many of whom felt the AAU was making Thorpe a scapegoat. In stripping Thorpe of his medals, the AAU had violated its own guidelines, which allowed only 60 days to challenge a competition. Thorpe did not know the statute of limitations had expired, and, following the advice of Pop Warner, he returned his medals. While he publicly accepted the decision, the loss of the medals was a severe personal blow.

That summer, Thorpe began to play baseball with the New York Giants, though his six-year record in the major leagues would be modest. In football, however, Thorpe had no equal, and while still playing baseball, he joined the Canton Bulldogs in 1915 for the princely sum of $250 a game. He was football's biggest attraction, drawing thousands of fans to the sport. In 1916, joined by Carlisle teammates Gus Welch (GUSTAVUS WELCH) and PETE CALAC, Thorpe led the Bulldogs to an undefeated season and the world championship, the first of a string of championships. The next year, however, he suffered one of his many personal tragedies when his young son died of pneumonia.

Football's growing popularity led team owners in 1920 to organize the American Professional Football Association, soon renamed the National Football League (NFL), with Thorpe as its first president. Thorpe organized his own NFL team, the OORANG INDIANS, in 1922, and played for a number of teams before retiring in 1929 at age 41.

After his athletic career ended, Thorpe fell on hard times, working as a laborer and Hollywood bit player during the Great Depression. Always a warm and generous man, he became involved in numerous causes, not the least of which was Indian rights, and spent much of his last years traveling the lecture circuit and hosting charity events. Thorpe's fame never faded. In 1950, he was voted by the nation's sportswriters the greatest athlete and greatest football player of the first half of the century. In 1951, the Warner Brothers film, *Jim Thorpe—All-American*, starring Burt Lancaster, was a popular success.

Thorpe was married three times and had seven children, including Jack Thorpe, who became president of the Sac and Fox tribe, and GRACE THORPE, who became a leading Indian rights activist. Jim Thorpe died of a heart attack on March 28, 1953, at his home in Lomita, California.

In 1955, the NFL created its Most Valuable Player award, naming it the Jim Thorpe Trophy, and in 1963 he was enshrined in football's Hall of Fame in Canton, Ohio. On January 13, 1983, the International Olympic Committee returned Thorpe's gold medals to his family and restored his achievements to the record books. A soft-spoken man who was as widely admired for his sportsmanship and integrity as he was for his athletic skills, Jim Thorpe was the world's first international sports celebrity.

Further Reading

Mallon, Bill, and Ture Widlund. *The 1912 Olympic Games—Results for All Competitors in All Events*. New York: McFarland & Company, 2002.

Newcombe, Jack. *The Best of the Athletic Boys: The White Man's Impact on Jim Thorpe*. New York: Doubleday, 1975.

Rubinfeld, M. "The Mythical Jim Thorpe: Representing the Twentieth Century American Indian." *International Journal of the History of Sport* 23, no. 2 (2006): 167–189.

Schoor, Gene, with Henry Gilford. *The Jim Thorpe Story: America's Greatest Athlete.* New York: Messner, 1951.

Wheeler, Robert W. *Jim Thorpe: World's Greatest Athlete.* Norman: University of Oklahoma Press, 1979.

Whitman, Robert L. *Jim Thorpe and the Oorang Indians: The N.F.L.'s Most Colorful Franchise.* Mount Gilead, Ohio: Marion County Historical Society, 1984.

Tiger, William Buffalo (1920–2015) *Miccosukee activist, political leader*

The son of Tiger Tiger, William Buffalo Tiger was born on March 6, 1920, in Dade County, Florida. Named Heenehatch, he was raised in a traditional family, learning English while working as a house painter in Miami. His people, the Miccosukee (also spelled Mikasuki), are a distinct tribe that broke away from the Creek Confederacy in the early 18th century. Although traditional foes of the Florida Muskogee, they

joined the Seminole Nation for survival from the time of the First Seminole War, which began in 1818, and established a reputation as the fiercest warriors. The traditional language of the Miccosukee is Hitchiti, while that of the other Seminole is Muskogee (Creek); the two languages are not related. Yet because most of the Seminole who remained in the impenetrable Everglade swamps after removal to Oklahoma were Miccosukee, and owing to extensive intermarriage, many non-Miccosukee Seminole today also speak Hitchiti.

The present Miccosukee tribe broke away from the Cow Creek Seminole in the mid-1930s, when the latter adopted a constitution under the INDIAN REORGANIZATION ACT, swore loyalty to the United States, and were granted legal rights to territory. This territory included the Miccosukee homelands in Big Cypress Swamp, which became part of a new Everglades National Park. The Miccosukee, who refused to join the Seminole Tribe but were not recognized as a separate tribe, were evicted.

(From left to right) William Buffalo Tiger, Howard Osceola, Sam Willie, and Henry Nelson Panther in 1958 in front of the British Embassy in Washington, D.C., where they sought British aid for their land disputes with the state of Florida. *(AP/Wideworld)*

In 1950, when the Seminole Tribe filed a claim with the INDIAN CLAIMS COMMISSION, the Miccosukee repudiated it, noting that they were still legally at war with the United States and that "it is not their desire or intention, now or in the future, to accept any money from the United States government." Tiger was the official interpreter for the group (which also included Cory Osceola, JOSIE BILLY, and his brother Ingraham Billy, chief medicine man) who spoke for the Miccosukee.

The following year, the tribe protested to President Dwight D. Eisenhower, in what has come to be called "the Buckskin Declaration," against "the deliberate confusion of our Mikasuki Tribe of Seminole Indians . . . with the Muskogee Tribe of Seminole Indians in order to avoid recognition of our tribal government, independence, rights, and customs." After investigation by Indian Commissioner GLENN L. EMMONS, it was determined that the Miccosukee should not have been evicted when their territory was turned over to the federal government. After a December 1954 meeting with the Everglades Miccosukee General Council, a group which did not include Cory Osceola or his followers, the federal government for the first time acknowledged the distinct existence of the Miccosukee. Nevertheless, this was ignored by the Indian Claims Commission, and the National Park Service refused to grant them HUNTING AND FISHING RIGHTS in the park.

Tiger became head of the General Council in 1957. In 1958, working with MAD BEAR ANDERSON, the Miccosukee, backed by treaties with Great Britain and Spain, the 1823 Treaty of Moultrie Creek, and the 1842 Macomb-Worth Agreement, threatened to sue the United States in The Hague World Court. In 1959, Tiger, Howard Osceola (a first cousin on his mother's side), Homer Osceola, and other Miccosukee, accompanied by Anderson, went to Cuba, where Fidel Castro had just won his revolution, and signed a treaty of peace and friendship. Embarrassed by the publicity, the state of Florida finally recognized the Miccosukee, although just three years earlier they had rejected them and their request for 143,500 acres in the Forty-Mile Bend region north of the Tamiami Trail. Now the federal government was clearly interested in recognition. Tiger was the leader of the group pursuing these negotiations.

Devastation by Hurricane Donna in September 1960 drove many Miccosukee to support Tiger. The government established a school and a clinic for them at that time. The Miccosukee Tribe was granted official federal recognition on February 11, 1962, at the same time making peace with the United States. However, the land award was minuscule—a strip five miles long by 500 feet deep along the south edge of the trail at Forty-Mile Bend, with little security—and it was held on a 50-year lease from the National Park Service. By the time the agreement was signed, Tiger had lost the support of the traditional followers of Ingraham Billy and even most of the General Council, including Howard Osceola. Only 300 Miccosukee registered as tribal members. Aside from those who had previously gone over to the Seminole Tribe, many others remained "traditional Miccosukee," to this day unrecognized by the federal government. Most of these lived around Big Cypress Bend, near the western end of the highway.

In January 1983, the state of Florida granted the Miccosukee Tribe a lease on 189,000 acres along with $975,000 in economic development funds. The agreement to lease what were legally their own lands was regarded with contempt by the Osceola family group and other traditionals.

William Buffalo Tiger served as Miccosukee chair for 23 years. He was succeeded in 1985 by Sonny Billie, a construction contractor and traditional medicine man. During Tiger's term, the ecology of the Everglades continued to deteriorate, due to commercial overdevelopment and ill-advised large-scale federal engineering projects. The Miccosukee were still excluded from nearly all their traditional hunting grounds and most, attracted by mainstream American life, distanced themselves from their traditions. By the 1990s, scarcely anyone lived in a *chickee* (traditional Seminole house). Tiger himself had been married twice, both times to white women. None of his five children spoke the Hitchiti language. He lived near Miami, drove a Cadillac, and ran an airboat business.

In 1996, Tiger mused: "I remember when I was a boy that there were so many fish that you could just rock the canoe, and the fish would just pour into the canoe. . . . The water has gone bad now. . . . There are chemical fertilizers washing down from the north where the sugar farmers are. There is even mercury in the water. This will all be like a desert some day. It isn't long until the Breathmaker returns. He's going to destroy the earth." Buffalo Tiger died on January 6, 2015.

Further Reading
Dustin, Daniel L., and Robert M. Wolff. "Buffalo Tiger's Dilemma—Miccosukee Indian Tribe." *Parks and Recreation* 33, no. 9 (1998): 6–8.

Kersey, Harry A. "The Havana Connection: Buffalo Tiger, Fidel Castro, and the Origin of Miccosukee Tribal Sovereignty, 1959–1962." *American Indian Quarterly* 25, no. 4 (2001): 491–507.

Lourie, Peter. *Everglades: Buffalo Tiger and Its River of Grass.* Honesdale, Pa.: Boyd Mills Press, 1998.

Tiger, Buffalo, and Harry A. Kersey, Jr. *Buffalo Tiger: A Life in the Everglades.* Lincoln: University of Nebraska Press, 2002.

Tinker, Clarence Leonard (1887–1942)
Osage war hero

An Osage, Clarence Leonard Tinker was born south of Elgin, Kansas, on November 21, 1887, to George Edward and Sarah Ann (Nan) Tinker. He attended the Elgin, Kansas, public school and the Osage Indian Boarding School for Boys in Pawhuska, Indian Territory (later Oklahoma). In 1900, he enrolled in the Haskell Institute in Kansas. Tinker was offered an appointment to the U.S. Military Academy at West Point, but in 1906, undecided over a military career, he chose instead to attend the Wentworth Military Academy in Lexington, Missouri, where he would not incur an obligation to the service. Tinker graduated in May 1908 and accepted a commission in the Philippine Constabulary as a third lieutenant. In

1912, he joined the U.S. Army as a second lieutenant and was stationed in Hawaii. He took up flying as a captain in 1919 and was transferred to the new Army Air Service the next year, with the rank of major.

In 1926, while in London serving as air attaché to the American embassy to Great Britain, Tinker received the Soldier's Medal for rescuing a navy commander from a burning plane, an act in which Tinker himself was seriously injured. He was appointed brigadier general in 1940, and on December 19, 1941, shortly after the Japanese attack on Pearl Harbor, he became major general.

One of the few generals in the army who was also a pilot, Tinker was placed in command of the remnants of the air forces in Hawaii, which had previously been commanded by an infantry officer. He reorganized the remaining forces into a highly disciplined fighting unit, now known as the Seventh Air Force, in time for the Battle of Midway in June 1942. After the successful defense of Midway Island, Tinker personally led a bomber squadron on a daring but ill-fated attack on Wake Island on June 7. His B-24 Liberator failed to return, and he was awarded the Distinguished Service Medal posthumously on November 10, 1942. His son, Major Clarence Leonard (Bud) Tinker, Jr., also a war pilot, lost his life when his plane was shot down over the Mediterranean during the Battle of Pantelleria in May 1943.

General Tinker, along with HAL MULDROW, was the highest-ranking Indian in the U.S. Army in the 20th century. Tinker Air Force Base in Oklahoma is named for him.

Further Reading

Crowder, James L. *Osage General: Maj. Gen. Clarence L. Tinker*. Oklahoma City: Office of History, Oklahoma City Air Logistics Center, 1987.

Tipi Order of America (Tepee Order of America)

The Tipi (or Tepee) Order of America, which flourished in the early 20th century, was a large and important fraternal, pan-Indian organization that also encouraged white membership. It spawned a number of branches and offshoots, including the American Indian Association, a New York–based organization that became well known, and the American Indian Order, a Rosicrucian research organization devoted to the study of American Indian symbolism.

Evidence discovered by historian Hazel W. Hertzberg suggests that the Tipi Order of America was founded in 1915 in New York City as a group for American-born Protestant young people to study American Indian culture. The difficulty in determining with accuracy the details of the order's founding is directly related to the enigmatic background of its founder, RED FOX ST. JAMES, who claimed to be Blackfoot but whose real origins are unknown. According to Hertzberg, the purpose of the youth organization was to study "the early history of the natives of America, its languages, customs, and to put into practice the activities of Indian outdoor life." There is little doubt that it had similarities to the newly formed Boy

Scouts of America (see SETON, ERNEST THOMPSON). Red Fox had attracted their support during a cross-country ride and participated in the ceremonies at the Carlisle Indian School on January 18, 1915, that inaugurated the first all-Indian Boy Scout troop. The Tipi Order of America differed from the Boy Scouts in that it was to be directed by Indians and only assisted by whites, although ironically, the main director would always be Red Fox, whose Indian identity was highly dubious. It differed from the Boy Scouts also in that it was a secret fraternal organization, complete with its own ceremonies, with officers holding titles such as "head chief" or "medicine man." When the Tipi Order was founded, CHARLES EASTMAN apparently held the title of "head chief," which was probably no more than an honorary role. Red Fox was active in the Young Men's Christian Association (YMCA), advocating greater outreach to INDIAN RESERVATIONS, and Eastman had strong ties to both the YMCA and the Boy Scouts, largely through his friend, educator Luther Gulick, who was also YMCA national secretary.

In 1918, Red Fox St. James worked at the Yakima Reservation mission in White Swan, Washington, where he continued to expand the Tipi Order. Lucullus Virgil McWhorter, in his 1920 pamphlet *The Discards*, refers to the "Tepee Association" as

> . . . a body of its own, entirely distinct and separate from the [White Swan] Mission. . . . The Tepee will work in unison with the Mission and kindred organizations for the uplift of the Indian and for a more liberal recognition of his rights. Not only must the coming Indian be prepared by education for a higher plane in life, but the public must also be enlightened to his needs and to the fact that the Indian can never be a man until delivered from the unreasonable trammelings of the Indian Bureau.

Like the Boy Scouts, the Tipi Order promoted outdoor life and sports. But whereas the Scouts had been the formative influence on the Tipi Order as a youth organization, now the Improved Order of Red Men (IORM) became the main influence. The IORM, a fraternal society established in Baltimore, Maryland, in 1834, claims direct descent from the Sons of Liberty (a secret organization of American patriots that originated in the thirteen colonies before the American Revolution) through an earlier organization, the Society of Red Men, founded in 1813. Dedicated to conserving the history, customs, and virtues of American Indians, IORM, ironically, barred Indians from its membership. IORM featured an elaborate system of degrees, such as sachem and keeper of wampum, and used a special calendar.

The Tipi Order also sought to preserve Indian rituals and legends. It also admitted whites, initiating high-ranking individuals such as state senators and city councilmen. Like the IORM, the Tipi Order ritual and initiation were closely related to Freemasonry—a trend influenced by ARTHUR C. PARKER and Red Fox St. James, both Masons. In 1919, St. James was setting up chapters of the Tipi Order in Washington State cities, including Bellingham and Olympia. By 1920, according to

McWhorter, "The Tipi Order of America opened a new Council in Tacoma. . . . It started with 30 charter members, many of them identified with the [Improved Order of Red Men]."

The new Tipi Order sought to imitate the work of the SOCIETY OF AMERICAN INDIANS (SAI), the first and most illustrious of the early pan-Indian organizations. The SAI, however, was an advocacy organization, not a fraternal one, dedicated to advancing the rights and welfare of Indian people. Composed primarily, though not exclusively, of Indians, it did not confer titles or engage in ceremonies and initiation rites, and it was in fact a progressive organization with little interest in preserving traditional Native culture. In many ways, the two groups saw themselves as direct competitors, and their relationship was strained.

In organization, the Tipi Order bore a greater resemblance to the short-lived Brotherhood of North American Indians, another pan-Indian organization formed in 1911. Founded by Richard C. Adams, a member of the Delaware Tribe in Oklahoma, the brotherhood was, like the SAI, an Indian-only advocacy organization, but it also tried to promote a feeling of friendship, brotherhood, and good citizenship among the Indian tribes and to perpetuate ancient traditions. At its national convention, the Indian members would elect 20 national chiefs and council officers with titles such as great sachem, chief historian, and great chaplain. In most cases, the political objectives of the Brotherhood of North American Indians were similar to the SAI—making the federal government fulfill its treaty obligations by allowing tribes to press claims in the U.S. Court of Claims, having Indian children attend public schools, and allowing Indians the right to vote and to have full CITIZENSHIP—although the brotherhood wanted special Indian delegates in Congress, with one delegate representing every 60,000 Indians. Virtually alone among the mainstream groups of the day, the brotherhood advocated the preservation of the reservation system, earning the ire of the Indian Bureau (later the BUREAU OF INDIAN AFFAIRS [BIA]), the SAI, and other Indian support groups such as the INDIAN RIGHTS ASSOCIATION, and leading to its collapse after only two years.

The Tipi Order of America under Red Fox St. James managed to incorporate the most useful aspects of these organizations while advocating popular political goals, such as full citizenship for Indians and the abolishment of the Indian Bureau. By 1920, the SAI was disintegrating, and the new Tipi Order quickly stepped in to replace it as the most influential pan-Indian organization, much to the disgust of Arthur C. Parker, who, in a letter to Peoria Indian agent CHARLES DAGENETT on October 13, 1921, referred to St. James and his men as "Bolshevists," as if to liken their methods to those of the Bolsheviks who had recently taken over in Russia.

The order now began to recruit former SAI members, such as Arapaho SHERMAN COOLIDGE and James J. Irving, a Sioux judge who had been SAI's vice president. They also began to become more public in their advocacy, issuing in 1920 a 12-page manifesto penned by "Strong Wolf, Chief of the Ojibwa" (see STRONGWOLF, JOSEPH) entitled "A Little General Information for the Benefit of Those Who May Be Interested in Present-Day Conditions of the North American Indian." Also that year they began publishing a magazine, *American Indian Teepee*, which underwent a series of name changes through 1928. St. James, Strongwolf, and Francis Valle Boyce rotated as editor, and the paper was published in various places during its existence. William Madison, a Chippewa who was the SAI's secretary, was an associate editor.

Despite this higher political profile, the Tipi Order was still interested in combining esoteric and mystical aspects of Native and non-Native religions, following the lead of St. James. To better attract former SAI members who might be less inclined to join a secret fraternal organization, St. James, Sherman Coolidge, and Joseph Strongwolf in 1922 founded the American Indian Association (AIA), with Coolidge as head chief. The new association presented itself as SAI's continuation, since that organization was falling apart (see GORDON, PHILIP). It had a similar platform, advocating citizenship, recognition of Indian rights, and an Indian claims court. However, whereas many in the SAI opposed peyote, traditional dances, and all non-Christian religious practices, the AIA (no doubt encouraged by the widespread negative reaction to Indian Commissioner CHARLES HENRY BURKE's notorious DANCE ORDERS) was for religious liberty for all Indians and very positive about Native culture. Also, the AIA dropped one of the main demands of the SAI, as well as of the Tipi Order in the past—abolishing the Indian Bureau—and where the SAI was for ALLOTMENT and almost complete ASSIMILATION, the AIA advocated "giving the Indians a voice in reservation affairs," land for landless Indians, increased holdings for those with insufficient land, and a system of welfare for elderly, dependent Indians. It had little lobbying capability but good public outreach. It also sponsored the observance of American Indian Day every September. A ladies' auxiliary, headed by Princess MARY CHINQUILLA, was known as the Daughters of Sacajaweah.

The politics of the AIA were right-wing and Republican—anti-immigrant, antiblack, and opposed to all leftist radicalism. The Indian, as "the original American," was understood to symbolize these values, with northern Europeans as the only immigrants who could measure up to the "true American." This explains a number of peculiarities of the organization: their strict exclusion of persons of African ancestry; passionate advocacy of "Americanism" for Indians, embodied in their campaign for universal Indian citizenship and voting rights; welcoming of whites interested in Indian lore and symbolism; and the assumption of "Indian" identity by whites—notably the leader, Red Fox St. James (whose connection with the Blackfoot existed mainly in his imagination—McWhirter soon became convinced that he was not what he claimed to be). Nevertheless, in the climate of the 1920s, when conditions for Indians were mostly very bad and they were themselves the objects of racism and disrespect, the AIA was an important voice in Indian affairs.

In 1926, Red Fox and Princess Chinquilla, under the auspices of the AIA, rented a house at 72 Grove Street, just south of Sheridan Square in the Greenwich Village section of Manhattan, as a social club for Indians resident in New York and a port of call for transient and newly arrived Indians. This became one of the first urban Indian centers (see URBANIZATION, AMERICAN INDIANS AND). Other branches of the Tipi Order sprang up in cities across the United States, including Philadelphia, Pennsylvania; Minneapolis, Minnesota; Detroit, Michigan; Cincinnati, Ohio; Denver, Colorado; and Long Beach, California. There was considerable variety in each of these local orders, with some emphasizing the fraternal and secret aspects of the Tipi Order and others following the lead of the AIA and focusing on advocacy. William C. Hartmann in his *Who's Who in Occultism* described the esoteric component of the AIA, known as the American Indian Order, as "an international masonic organization, which receives both men and women," the object of which was "to preserve Indian Occult Rituals and Freemasonry."

In 1927, the officers of the AIA decreed that non-Indians could not hold office in the organization, and St. James subsequently resigned from the AIA and the Tipi Order, which by now were effectively the same organization. Without its tireless champion, the Tipi Order and the AIA soon fell into obscurity, although the American Indian Order would still exist for many more years. The clubhouse in New York City also continued for some time. When the AIA moved to new quarters on East 62nd Street in January 1931, the executive director was Francis Running Bear (Francis Valle Boyce), the last editor of the association's magazine. Red Fox created a new offshoot, the Indian Association of America, around 1936, and a new magazine, *Smoke Signals*, was published from 1949 to 1961, under the editorship of Frank E. Becker in Staten Island, New York.

The AIA, like most Indian organizations of the day, protested the heavy-handed tenure of DILLON MYER as commissioner of Indian affairs in the late 1940s, and it continued to play a role in local Indian activities for a while, but its national role was long over. The influence of the Tipi Order in developing urban Indian groups and places where Indians could gather, however, was felt throughout the remainder of the century, as urban pan-Indianism began to become a major force in Indian politics.

See MOFSIE, LOUIS.

Further Reading

Hertzberg, Hazel W. *The Search for an American Indian Identity: Modern Pan-Indian Movements*. Syracuse, N.Y.: Syracuse University Press, 1972.

traditional movement, Hopi   See BANYACYA, THOMAS; KATCHONGVA, DAN; YOUKIOMA.

Trail of Broken Treaties (1972)

The Trail of Broken Treaties was a national protest, begun as a caravan from various points on the West Coast to meet in Washington, D.C., in November 1972, which ended with the occupation and ransacking of the headquarters of the BUREAU OF INDIAN AFFAIRS (BIA).

At a meeting on the Rosebud Reservation during the summer of 1972, Brulé Lakota activist ROBERT BURNETTE suggested a march culminating in a peaceful demonstration in Washington, D.C., just before the presidential elections. The death of Mohawk activist RICHARD OAKES in September 1972 galvanized the various Indian protest groups, which by that time had become factionalized, and gave impetus to the effort, known as the Trail of Broken Treaties and the Pan-American Quest for Justice. Burnette and Winnebago leader REUBEN SNAKE were appointed cochairs of the march. In late October, Assiniboine-Dakota Sioux HANK ADAMS, who drafted the "Twenty-Points," a set of Indian demands for the demonstration, led one caravan of cars from Seattle. Chippewa DENNIS BANKS and Tuscarora WALLACE MAD BEAR ANDERSON led a second one from San Francisco. The 20-points set of Indian demands largely centered around the repeal of TERMINATION era laws that had diminished Indian sovereignty and the return to a relationship between Indians and the federal government that was based on treaties (see SOVEREIGNTY, INDIGENOUS AND TRIBAL).

As the groups began to wend their way across the country, Assistant Secretary of the Interior Harrison Loesch decided to take a strong stand against them, ordering the BIA to refuse the caravans any assistance. Loesch was growing concerned about the militancy of the RED POWER MOVEMENT as well as the reforms being initiated by Indian Commissioner LOUIS ROOK BRUCE, JR., whom Loesch felt was too sympathetic to the militants. He had therefore transferred his assistant, JOHN O. CROW, back to the BIA in order to keep an eye on Bruce. Loesch, who ran the Bureau of Land Management, which at that time oversaw the BIA, was himself a target of the activists for his liberal leasing policies on Indian lands. In 1971, in approving oil and gas leases on 89,535 acres of Apache land, Loesch had ruled that the environmental impact statements required by the National Environmental Policy Act did not apply, a determination he had also made on the lands of the Tesuque Pueblo and the Northern Cheyenne.

When the Trail of Broken Treaties caravan arrived in St. Paul, Minnesota, on October 23, AMERICAN INDIAN MOVEMENT (AIM) members led by Chippewa CLYDE BELLECOURTE and his brother Vernon occupied and ransacked the BIA building, a portent of things to come. In the meantime, Burnette, the Washington, D.C., point man for the demonstration, was hamstrung by the lack of support from the BIA, although Burnette's team suffered from poor planning as well.

When the caravans arrived in Washington on November 3, the only place to stay was a rundown, rat-infested church basement. The protesters then stormed the BIA building and occupied it for five days, during which they ransacked it thoroughly. Loesch and Bruce fought bitterly over how to handle the situation: Loesch wanted to take the building by force; Bruce wanted to negotiate. In the end, Bruce had his way, and the BIA gave the protesters $66,000 to leave town peacefully.

Marchers on the Trail of Broken Treaties stood in the front of the Bureau of Indian Affairs (BIA) headquarters in 1972, after they had occupied it for lack of a place to stay. *(AP/Wideworld)*

The activists used part of the money to rent a truck, which they proceeded to fill with thousands of BIA documents. These documents would later confirm Indian suspicions of BIA corruption and mismanagement.

After the occupation, President Richard Nixon fired both Loesch and Bruce. He also ordered the FBI to try and recover the stolen documents, which led to the deployment of the infamous COINTELPRO counterinsurgency program against Indians.

The Trail of Broken Treaties gave a tremendous boost to AIM, which, thanks to their flamboyant leaders RUSSELL MEANS and Dennis Banks, garnered most of the publicity from the takeover, in the end setting the stage for a greater confrontation at WOUNDED KNEE the following year.

Further Reading

Burnette, Robert, with John Koster. *The Road to Wounded Knee.* New York: Bantam Books, 1974.

Deloria, Vine, Jr. *Behind the Trail of Broken Treaties: An Indian Declaration of Independence.* New York: Delacorte Press, 1974.

Grossman, Mark. *The ABC-CLIO Companion to the Native American Rights Movement.* Santa Barbara, Calif.: ABC-CLIO, 1996.

Nagel, Joane. *American Indian Ethnic Renewal: Red Power and the Resurgence of Identity and Culture.* New York: Oxford University Press, 1996.

Olson, James S., ed. *Encyclopedia of American Indian Civil Rights.* Westport, Conn.: Greenwood Publishing Group, 1997.

Trail of Broken Treaties: BIA, I'm Not Your Indian Anymore. Mohawk Nation, Rooseveltown, N.Y.: Akwesasne Notes, 1973.

Wilkinson, Charles F. *Blood Struggle: The Rise of Modern Indian Nations.* New York: W. W. Norton & Company, 2005.

Trehero, John (John Truhujo, Rainbow, Two Belly)
(1887–1985) *Wind River Shoshone medicine man*
John Pablo Trehero was born on August 14 (or October 7), 1887, at Fort Washakie, Wyoming, on the Wind River Reservation. (Both 1871 and 1883 are sometimes given as the year of his birth, but they are incorrect.) His father, Joe Truhujo, was part Mexican, and his mother, Mary Morton, was the granddaughter of Shoshone chief Yellow Hand, who had introduced the Sun Dance to the Shoshone people in 1800. His name also has various spellings, and he is sometimes known as Rainbow or by his Crow name, Two Belly (or Middle of the Belly).

When Trehero was six years old, his father died, and the boy was sent to a boarding school in White Rock, Utah. Later he returned to Fort Washakie, where he enrolled in a mission school. In the reservation census of June 30, 1906, he is listed for the first time as married to Eva Trehero; he is 19, she is 16.

Although Trehero was baptized in the Episcopal Church at age 15, he was more interested in his people's traditional beliefs. He began participating in the Sun Dance in 1906. After curing Aimee Yellowtail, the sister of ROBERT YELLOWTAIL, of a serious illness, Trehero stayed at the Crow Reservation (about 250 miles north of Fort Washakie) with relatives from his father's previous marriage. Upon his return to the Shoshone in 1920, his mother gave him the sacred medicine bundles that had been passed down in her family. She died in 1922. Trehero became the preeminent Shoshone Sun Dance chief.

In 1938, a Sun Dance at Fort Washakie that Trehero conducted was attended by Crow medicine man William Big Day. Big Day asked Trehero to bring the Sun Dance back to the Crow Reservation, where it had not been held since 1875. In 1941, Trehero conducted his first Sun Dance on the Crow Reservation. He continued to lead the ceremonies until his retirement in 1969, when he handed the reins to Thomas Yellowtail, brother of Robert Yellowtail. Trehero died on the Wind River Reservation in Wyoming in January 1985.

Further Reading
Brown, Joseph Epes. *The Spiritual Legacy of the American Indian*. New York: Crossroads Publishing Company, 1984.
Hultkrantz, Eke. *Shamanic Healing and Ritual Drama: Health and Medicine in Native North American Religious Traditions*. New York: Crossroads Publishing Company, 1992.
Voget, Fred. "A Shoshone Innovator." *American Anthropologist* 52, no. 1 (1950): 53–63.
Yellowtail, Thomas. *Native Spirit: The Sun Dance Way*. Bloomington, Ind.: World Wisdom, 2007.

Trudell, John (1946–) *Santee Dakota Sioux activist, poet*
John Trudell was born on February 15, 1946, in Omaha, Nebraska. His father, Thurman Clifford Trudell, was Dakota; his mother, who was of Mexican descent, died when he was six. Trudell spent his youth shuttling between Omaha, where his father worked as a truck driver, and his grandparents' house on the Santee Sioux Reservation. Graduating from high school in 1963, Trudell joined the U.S. Navy, where he served off the coast of Vietnam on a ship doing search-and-rescue missions for downed pilots. After his discharge in 1967, he moved to Southern California, drifting between school and jobs. In 1969, with his wife Felicia "Lou" Ordoñez and two young daughters, he took part in the OCCUPATION OF ALCATRAZ ISLAND.

At Alcatraz, Trudell found his calling, launching the radio program *Radio Free Alcatraz* and becoming the spokesman for the occupying organization, INDIANS OF ALL TRIBES.

Seeing the takeover as a powerful symbol of Indian resistance, Trudell stayed on the island until the ignominious end. His wife gave birth to their third child, Wovoka, during the occupation. After Alcatraz, Trudell joined the AMERICAN INDIAN MOVEMENT (AIM), participating in the TRAIL OF BROKEN TREATIES in 1972.

Shortly after the siege of WOUNDED KNEE in 1973, Trudell was elected cochair of AIM, along with Carter Camp. By 1975, he was national chair. Although overshadowed by the flamboyant DENNIS BANKS and RUSSELL MEANS, Trudell was arguably AIM's most effective organizer. An incendiary speaker, he broadened AIM's support among Indians and non-Indians while providing the organization with a coherent political perspective. For Trudell, governments and the corporations that supported them had only the "illusion of power." The real power came from the natural forces of the Earth. In an electrifying speech at the Black Hills Survival Gathering in 1980, Trudell synthesized his understanding of the Indian struggle, and indeed the struggle of all oppressed peoples: "There is no such thing as military power; there is only military terrorism. There is no such thing as economic power; there is only economic exploitation." Rather than succumb to illusions of power, "only by understanding our connection to the Earth can we ever create a fair system that is going to be good to the people. We must go beyond the arrogance of human rights; we must go beyond the ignorance of civil rights; and we must step into the reality of natural rights because all of the natural world has a right to existence and we are only a small part of it."

A hard-line advocate of armed self-defense, Trudell himself eschewed violence, though he was arrested in Nevada for discharging a weapon while aiding the Duck Valley Reservation in a long-running water rights dispute.

In February 1975, Trudell helped Navajo AIM member Larry Anderson take over Fairchild Corporation's electronics plant in Shiprock, New Mexico, which had been laying off Indian union organizers, but the action backfired when Fairchild shut down the plant and moved its operations offshore. (See MACDONALD, PETER.) By this time, Trudell had split up with his wife Lou and had married Shoshone-Paiute activist Tina Manning.

Trudell coordinated AIM support for the trials of activists LEONARD PELTIER, Dino Butler, and Bob Robideau, also serving as a witness for the defense. At Peltier's trial in Fargo, North Dakota, Trudell was sentenced to 60 days in prison for contempt of court after objecting to the petty demands of a federal marshal that he leave the courtroom area while the trial was in recess.

On the night of February 11, 1979, hours after Trudell burned an American flag on the steps of the FBI headquarters in Washington, D.C., during a vigil for Peltier, a suspicious fire on the Duck Valley Reservation in Nevada took the lives of his pregnant second wife, Tina, her mother, and their three children. This tragedy was a defining moment in Trudell's life. He stepped down as chair of AIM and turned to writing poetry; his first book of poetry, *Living in Reality*, was published in 1981. He also started a musical poetry group with Warm Springs traditional singer Quiltman Sahmee, and they released their first cassette tape, *Tribal Voice*, in 1983.

In 1985, Trudell joined forces with Kiowa guitarist JESSE ED DAVIS to form Grafitti Man, a rock and roll group. In 1986, they released their first tape, *AKA: Grafitti Man*, on their own label, the Peace Company, to critical acclaim. Trudell continued working with Tribal Voice, releasing *But This Isn't El Salvador* on the Peace Company label in 1987. That same year, Trudell and Davis released *Heart Jump Bouquet*.

The following year, Davis was found dead, apparently of a drug overdose. Though his death came as another deep blow, Trudell managed to continue his work with Grafitti Man, collaborating with guitarist Mark Shark on *Fables and Other Realities* in 1991. With the help of longtime friend Jackson Browne, Trudell released a compilation of Grafitti Man's work on the Rykodisc label in 1992. Also entitled *AKA: Grafitti Man*, this album was a critical success, receiving four stars from *Rolling Stone* magazine, which called it "a moving, shapeshifting, rock and roll treatise on the state of the world."

In June 1992, Trudell was the keynote speaker at the New Music Seminar in New York City, and in the same year he, Quiltman, and Shark collaborated on the Peace Company tape *A Child's Voice*, which featured the voices of Trudell's young daughters Sage, Song, and Star.

By this time, through speaking engagements and through a series of articles in *Native Nations* magazine, Trudell had articulated a philosophy of the historical confrontation between the Indian and non-Indian world, introducing his concept of the "Predator"—or, as he later called it, the "Spirit Eater." The Predator is the means by which civilization corrupts and manipulates people into serving what has become an industrial machine, in the process separating people from their true source of strength and well-being, the Earth.

For Trudell, the war between the industrialized world and tribal peoples, though it has its material aspects, is in reality a spiritual war, and the Predator is in essence a form of spiritual cancer, a "diseased mind-set" that is spreading across the world from its roots in Europe. The Predator attacks individuals by destroying their self-esteem, and the attack can take many forms, including advertising. According to Trudell, "Every commercial that goes on television is telling us that we are worth *less*. We would be worth *more* by consuming the product put in front of us." This "constant barrage" eventually breeds insecurities and paranoias in the individual, a negative spiritual energy that the Predator then feeds upon to make our industrial system run and destroy the natural world.

In 1994, Trudell issued his second album on Rykodisc, *Johnny Damas and Me*, which sold more than 100,000 copies. This was followed in 1999 by *Blue Indians* and in 2001 by *Bone Days*, both on independent labels. In 2001 he released *Madness and the Moremes*, a double album. He published *Stickman*, a compilation of his poetry and writings in 1994.

An actor as well as a poet, Trudell has appeared in a number of films, including *Pow Wow Highway* and *Smoke Signals*, but he is best known for his portrayal of a militant activist alongside Val Kilmer and GRAHAM GREENE in the movie *Thunderheart*. Trudell testified for the prosecution in the 2004 trial of Arlo Looking Cloud, a Lakota member of AIM who was subsequently convicted of the murder of ANNA MAE AQUASH. His testimony also figured in the extradition of AIM member John Graham, who was convicted of Aquash's murder in 2010. One of the best-known American Indian artists and performers of his time, Trudell has influenced poets as diverse as JOY HARJO and SHERMAN ALEXIE, and his political vision continues to inspire new generations of Indians. In 2005, a documentary about him entitled *Trudell* was released.

Further Information

Malkin, John. *Sounds of Freedom*. Berkeley, Calif.: Parallax Press, 2005.

Trudell, John. *Stickman*. New York: Inanout Press, 1994.

Trudell John. *A.K.A. Grafitti Man*. Rykodisc Records, 1992.

———. *Blue Indians*. Dangerous Discs, 1999.

———. *Bone Days*. ASITIS Productions, 2001.

Tsatoke, Monroe   *See* KIOWA FIVE.

Tsianina   *See* BLACKSTONE, TSIANINA EVAN.

United Association of the American Indian, United Association for the Advancement of the American Indian   *See* MOFSIE, LOUIS.

Unkalunt, Princess Atalie   *See* RIDER, IVA JOSEPHINE.

urbanization, American Indians and

In 1900, there were only about 1,000 American Indians living in urban areas in the United States, representing less than half of 1 percent of the entire Indian population at the time. The country was still largely rural. Sixty percent of the American population, Indian and non-Indian, lived in small towns or on farms, and only 40 percent lived in cities. While the 20th century saw the rapid urbanization of the United States as a whole, the shift was especially dramatic with regard to American Indian populations.

By 1910, the total urban Indian population had grown to 11,925, or 4.5 percent of the total Indian population, and by 1920, urban Indians numbered 15,219 (6.2 percent of the total Indian population). Educational programs such as boarding schools began to bear fruit, and educated Indians began to migrate to cities for economic opportunities that were usually nonexistent on INDIAN RESERVATIONS (see ASSIMILATION; EDUCATIONAL POLICY, AMERICAN INDIANS AND; PRATT, RICHARD HENRY). Wild West shows, and their successor in the film industry, the Western, drew hundreds of Indian performers to New York and Los Angeles (see FILM, AMERICAN INDIANS AND).

Many Indians living in urban areas, taking advantage of the political opportunities afforded by large cities, became active in the important Indian issues of the day. In 1911, in Columbus, Ohio, a group of educated, urban Indians founded the SOCIETY OF AMERICAN INDIANS as an advocacy group for Indian rights. The growing urban Indian population also led to the creation of Indian organizations to maintain cultural traditions and social ties. Most of these early organizations were fraternal societies such as the TIPI ORDER OF AMERICA, founded by RED FOX ST. JAMES in New York City in 1915. Dedicated to instructing youth in some aspects of Indian culture, the Tipi Order also admitted whites interested in Indian culture although it was largely run and organized by Indians.

The Tipi Order spread to several cities and inspired the creation of other similar organizations in the 1920s, such as the Wigwam Club in Los Angeles. Like the Tipi Order, the Wigwam Club provided youth with educational and social activities, sponsored talks by prominent Indian leaders, and held monthly dances. Another early urban Indian organization was the American Indian Association. Begun by Arapaho SHERMAN COOLIDGE, Ojibwa JOSEPH STRONGWOLF, and Red Fox St. James as a Christian fraternal order that sought to study Indian history, languages, and customs and to plan outdoor activities, it was headquartered in New York and had clubhouses in many eastern and midwestern cities. In 1926, with the help of MARY CHINQUILLA, the association opened a clubhouse in New York City, possibly the first urban Indian center. The growing Indian population in Minneapolis led to the creation in 1930 of the Twin Cities Chippewa Council, with F. W. Peake as vice president. In Los Angeles, the War Paint Club was founded by Indian movie actors in an attempt to protect Indian employment in movies and discourage the use of non-Indians to portray Indians. (See STANDING BEAR, LUTHER.)

During the 1920s, the number of Indians living in urban areas continued to grow rapidly, reaching 32,816 (9.9 percent of the total Indian population) in 1930. Shortly thereafter, however, the loss of job opportunities during the Great Depression forced thousands of Indians to return to their reservations, where government work programs, such as the INDIAN CIVILIAN CONSERVATION CORPS, were available. By

1940, the number of urban Indians had declined to approximately 24,000, or 7.2 percent of the population. This trend was quickly reversed by the entry of the United States into WORLD WAR II. Soaring demand for workers in the arms industry led thousands of Indians to migrate to cities, and many of them stayed on after the war. By 1950, the number of urban Indians had more than doubled from the previous decade, to 56,000, or 13.4 percent of the population.

Despite the steady growth of urban Indian populations, the major impetus to the urbanization of Indians came through the BUREAU OF INDIAN AFFAIRS (BIA) relocation programs of the 1950s and 1960s, which were a deliberate attempt to draw Indians off of reservations and into cities. Relocation began as a pilot program after the disastrous winter of 1947–48, which struck the Navajo (Dineh) reservation particularly hard. The winter exposed the deep poverty in which the Navajo were living and the lack of arable land to sustain themselves by farming and ranching. To encourage Navajo to leave the reservation for urban areas, the BIA set up employment offices in Los Angeles, Denver, and Salt Lake City and attempted to find employers willing to hire them. As jobs turned up in these cities, BIA agents on the reservation would find interested people to relocate and take the jobs.

In 1949, the BIA received more funding for job placement, adding offices in Aberdeen, South Dakota; Billings, Montana; and Portland, Oregon. With high hopes for the program, Indian Commissioner DILLON SEYMOUR MYER made it a cornerstone of his TERMINATION policy, aimed at the ultimate dissolution of Indian reservations. The relocation budget grew to $500,000 in 1952, and in that year the program provided jobs for some 400 Indians in cities. It continued to expand under Myer's successor, GLENN LEONIDAS EMMONS, and by 1956 more than 12,000 Indians had been relocated, and Congress was providing the program with over $3.5 million per year. Also in 1956, Congress passed Public Law 84-959, the Indian Adult Vocational Training Act, which allowed industries to be reimbursed for training Indians in vocational jobs.

In terms of numbers, the program was a great success. By 1960, the number of urban Indians had increased almost threefold, to 146,000, or 27.9 percent of the total Indian population. However, critics argued that the relocation program amounted to little more than a one-way bus ticket to an urban area. Much of the money earmarked by Congress had gone for glossy brochures and sophisticated advertising promising Indians high-paying, often white-collar jobs, large new homes, and a good education. On arrival in a city, relocatees would be met by a BIA agent, who would purchase some essentials for them and provide them with one month's rent. After that, the Indians were on their own. With few skills and no money, most were able to find only the most menial work, if any at all, and many ended up returning home or succumbing to crime and poverty (see CRIME AND CRIMINALITY).

Despite a phasing out of Termination during the 1960s, the relocation program continued to grow. Between 1960 and 1969, more than $161 million was spent on the program, over six times the sum spent in the previous decade. Under Lyndon B. Johnson's "Great Society" program, Relocation expanded its benefits, covering moving expenses and living expenses until the Indians had found work, in addition to greater counseling and job training. In 1967, the government also offered financing for Indians to purchase their homes. Between 1960 and 1970, the urban population of Indians more than doubled, increasing from 146,000 to 340,000. By 1970, 44.5 percent of all Indians were living in urban areas.

The federal policies of Relocation and Termination led to a politicization of Indians, especially in urban areas. Disaffected urban Indian youth formed the backbone of the RED POWER MOVEMENT of the 1960s and 1970s, spawning groups such as the AMERICAN INDIAN MOVEMENT (AIM). Another outgrowth of the expansion of urban Indian populations was the creation of urban Indian centers, which tried to provide services such as job training, health care, and housing to Indians relocating to cities.

Urban centers also became places for Indians to socialize and maintain their traditions. Among the earliest urban Indian centers was the Lowansa Tipi, founded in 1935 by Oklahoma Kickapoo Mira Frye Bartlette as a meeting place for the large Los Angeles urban Indian community, many of whom worked in Hollywood. An initial grant from the Religious Society of Friends allowed the Lowansa Tipi to begin providing a broad range of services. After World War II, the organization, renamed the Los Angeles Urban Indian Center, grew with the corresponding influx of population, many of them war workers who decided to remain in the city, and it became a part of the relocation program. By 1971, the dispersion of the large Indian population throughout greater Los Angeles, along with the increasing demand for services, forced the center to break up into smaller, separate centers.

The American Indian Center of Chicago was founded in September 1953 by THOMAS SEGUNDO, then a law student; Babe Begay (Navajo); Eli Powless (Oneida); and others with the help of the American Friends Service Committee (AFSC). The center moved into its current spacious headquarters in 1966. It was the most influential Indian urban center during the 1960s and 1970s, sponsoring POWWOWS, traditional schools, Indian art galleries, and other cultural programs now common in urban areas. The AFSC also helped to establish the Intertribal Friendship House in Oakland, California, in 1955. The Seattle Indian Center was organized in 1972 by the American Indian Woman's Service League, which had been in existence there since 1960. In 1969, the Minneapolis Indian Health Board was founded to serve the health needs of the local Indian community and eventually led to the formation of the Minneapolis American Indian Center in 1975.

New York City, which had one of the most established urban Indian populations, was the home of a number of urban Indian organizations, including the United Association of the American Indian, founded in 1934, and its successor, the United Association for the Advancement of the American Indian. They in turn led to the creation of the Indian League of the Americas, headed at one point by Cherokee playwright ARTHUR SMITH JUNALUSKA, which sponsored monthly meetings as well as social gatherings. In 1968, the American Indian Women's League was founded in New York City by Mifaunwy Hines, Pawnee-Otoe daughter of JOSEPH SHUNATONA and a member of the Indian League of the Americas. Hines, who had an exhibit in the 1964 World's Fair, had been running the American Indian Information Center from her home in Queens along with Chy Pells (Wampanoag), Mary Helen Deer (Kiowa-Creek), and Iola Hill Boyle (Mohawk). In 1969, they founded the American Indian Community House (AICH) with Olive Ward (Onondaga), Charmaine Lyons (Onondaga), OREN LYONS, JR. (Onondaga), Louis Bayhye, Jr., and LOUIS MOFSIE (Hopi-Winnebago). Under the leadership of Hines, Michael Bush (Mohawk), and later ROSEMARY RICHMOND (Mohawk), AICH became one of the largest and most important Indian centers in the country. Providing a great variety of services, including job training, adult education, health services, and a legal aid service, it also housed an important art gallery and a number of nationally known theater and music companies.

Although the federal Relocation program was phased out in the early 1970s, the growth in the number of urban Indians continued unabated. The rapid growth of the total Indian population, aided by advancements in Indian health care, also contributed to the increase in the number of urban Indians (see DEMOGRAPHICS; HEALTH, AMERICAN INDIAN). In 1980, more than 690,000 Indians, or 49 percent of all Indians, were urban, and by 1990 that number had reached 1,101,000, or 56.2 percent of the total Indian population. Urban Indian communities have been affected by many of the same problems as most reservation communities, poverty, lack of health care, and ALCOHOLISM, but (generally speaking) to a lesser degree. Only 20 percent of the urban Indians lived below the poverty line in 1990, compared to 50 percent of those living on reservations. On the other hand, cultural loss, including language loss, has been far greater in urban communities than on reservations (see INDIGENOUS LANGUAGE USE). By 2000, 1,560,000 Native Americans, or 63 percent of the total American Indian and Alaska Native population, were living in urban areas. The cities with the largest urban Indian and Alaska Native populations in 2000 were: New York (41,289), Los Angeles (29,412), Phoenix (26,696), Anchorage (18,941), Tulsa (18,551), Oklahoma City (17,743), Albuquerque (17,444), Tucson (11,038), Chicago (10,290), and San Antonio (9,584).

Further Reading

Danziger, Edmund Jefferson. *Survival and Regeneration: Detroit's American Indian Community.* Detroit, Mich.: Wayne State University Press, 1991.

Fixico, Donald L. *The Urban Indian Experience in America.* Albuquerque: University of New Mexico Press, 2000.

Hertzberg, Hazel W. *The Search for an American Indian Identity: Modern Pan-Indian Movements.* Syracuse, N.Y.: Syracuse University Press, 1971.

LaGrand, James B. *Indian Metropolis: Native Americans in Chicago, 1945–75.* Champaign: University of Illinois Press, 2002.

Lobo, Susan, and Kurt Peters, eds. *American Indians and the Urban Experience.* Walnut Creek, Calif.: Altimira Press, 2001.

Philp, Kenneth R. "Stride toward Freedom: The Relocation of Indians to Cities, 1952–1960." *Western Historical Quarterly* 16, no. 2 (1985): 175–190.

Thornton, Russell, Gary D. Sandefur, and Harold G. Grasmick. *The Urbanization of American Indians: A Critical Bibliography.* Bloomington: Indiana University Press, 1982.

Waddell, Jack O., and O. Michael Watson, eds. *The American Indian in Urban Society.* Boston: Little, Brown, 1971.

Valentine, Robert Grosvenor (1872–1916)
commissioner of Indian affairs

Robert Grosvenor Valentine was born in West Newton, Massachusetts, on November 29, 1872. He attended Harvard University and then taught English literature at the Massachusetts Institute of Technology (MIT) before working for the Union Pacific Railroad and National City Bank in New York. In 1901, Valentine returned to MIT, but he spent his summers in New York City working with the settlement house movement in Greenwich Village and aiding the mayoral campaign of reform candidate Seth Low.

Moving to Washington, D.C., in 1904, Valentine met FRANCIS ELLINGTON LEUPP at a civil service reform meeting. Leupp hired Valentine to work for him at the *New York Evening Post*. When Leupp was appointed commissioner of Indian affairs in 1905, Valentine became his personal secretary. Under Leupp, Valentine advanced rapidly, becoming the superintendent of Indian schools and, in 1908, assistant commissioner. After four years of nonstop political battles, the combative Leupp resigned in favor of his protégé, and Valentine assumed the commissionership of Indian affairs on June 19, 1909.

Valentine was a proponent of the ASSIMILATION policies of the day. Though he continued to advocate the Progressive Era reforms favored by Leupp, his businesslike manner and support for scientific management was more reminiscent of Leupp's predecessor, WILLIAM ARTHUR JONES. Valentine strove to increase the professionalism of the Indian Bureau (later the BUREAU OF INDIAN AFFAIRS), and he did much to encourage Indians to work for the department; under his tenure, they eventually came to comprise 30 percent of the workforce.

Valentine saw assimilation as the only alternative to extinction for Indian people. He was not, however, an ultra-assimilationist: Like Leupp, he disagreed with those who wanted to "turn Indians into whites" and argued that his goal was to make them "better Indians" (see EDUCATIONAL POLICY, AMERICAN INDIANS AND). Valentine expanded Leupp's arts and crafts policy (see MOOREHEAD, WARREN KING) as well as the industrial education program (see DAGENETT, CHARLES EDWARD). He also supported the Indian Omnibus Act of 1910, which created a technical staff within the Indian Bureau to oversee the exploitation of Indian resources. The bureau was soon filled with foresters, irrigation engineers, geologists, and other specialists dedicated to maximizing Indian assets.

Along with most Indian observers of the day, Valentine advocated ALLOTMENT—the breaking up of INDIAN RESERVATIONS, owned in common by the Indian tribes, into individual parcels of land that would either be farmed or ranched by Indians or sold off to non-Indians—as the best means for assimilating Indians and the best possible use for vast tracts of land "that were going to waste." He established competency committees to review the issue of granting allotments to Indians declared "competent"—and therefore free to sell their property—but that did little to stop the fraud and abuse brought about by the relaxation of protections for Indian allotments under the Burke Act of 1906. In 1912, the policy exploded in his face when Warren K. Moorehead of the Indian Board of Commissioners, aided by the INDIAN RIGHTS ASSOCIATION (IRA), charged Valentine with doing nothing to stop the wholesale "perjury, fraud, and forced signings" used to transfer allotted land from the White Earth Reservation in Minnesota to lumber companies and non-Indian settlers (see BEAULIEU, GUS H.).

Valentine's business acumen was not backed up by political skills. He proved unable to secure appropriations from Congress to realize his goal of hiring more capable personnel. His attempts to manage Indian forests through contracts with the Forest Service, then headed by Gifford Pinchot, led to a revolt in the Indian Bureau. Valentine did manage to have 2 million acres of forestland restored to Indians after they had been seized by President Theodore Roosevelt and added to the national forest system (see BLUE LAKE). However, he came under fire from the IRA for failing to secure water rights for the Pima in Arizona, where the Gila River had been diverted to non-Indian settlers (see PIMA WATER RIGHTS).

Valentine's ambitious attempts to streamline the Indian Bureau ran aground when he clashed with his superior, Secretary of the Interior Richard A. Ballinger. Valentine's attempt to audit the claims of Indian traders, which his experience had shown to be often fraudulent, swamped his undermanned central office, and his attempts to stop the sale of alcohol to Indians by invoking police jurisdiction over non-Indian lands, including the city of Minneapolis, caused an uproar in Congress. Valentine further alienated church groups when in 1912 he forbade teachers in Indian schools from wearing religious garb or displaying religious insignia.

Under assault from all sides, Valentine was charged by Congress with being an inefficient and wasteful administrator, as well as having committed petty acts of abuse against his office. Although the charges were largely trumped up, they sapped the commissioner's strength and eventually broke his health. He resigned as commissioner on September 10, 1912, to work in private industry. He had entered the commissioner's office with high hopes of reforming the wasteful and corrupt Indian Bureau, but in the end it was the bureau that destroyed him. He never recovered from his arduous tenure in the Indian Office, dying of a heart attack on November 14, 1916, in New York City, at age 44.

Further Reading

Hoxie, Frederick E. *A Final Promise: The Campaign to Assimilate the Indians, 1880–1920*. Lincoln: University of Nebraska Press, 2001.

Putney, Diane T. "Robert Grosvenor Valentine." In *The Commissioners of Indian Affairs, 1825–1977*, edited by Robert M. Kvasnicka and Herman T. Viola, 233–242. Lincoln: University of Nebraska Press, 1979.

Vegas, Pat and Lolly   See REDBONE.

Velarde, Pablita (Tse Tsan, "Golden Dawn")

(1918–2006) *Santa Clara Pueblo painter, muralist*
Pablita Velarde was born on September 19, 1918, in Santa Clara Pueblo, New Mexico, to Herman and Marianita Velarde. Her grandmother gave her the Tewa name Tse Tsan (Golden Dawn). When she was only three years old, her mother died of tuberculosis, and Pablita herself was stricken by an illness that caused temporary blindness. In 1924, her sight regained, she was sent along with her two older sisters to St. Catherine's Indian School in Santa Fe. Summer visits with her traditional grandmother Qualupita, who was a medicine woman, and the ancient stories of the Pueblo that she heard from her father would remain lasting influences.

At age 14, Velarde was sent to the Santa Fe Indian School. There, she studied painting under the influential DOROTHY DUNN, who encouraged her to draw on her tribal culture for inspiration. Velarde was also inspired by San Ildefonso Pueblo painter Tonita Peña, who visited the Indian school. In 1933, although only 15, she was selected to work with artist Olive Rush on murals for the Chicago "Century of Progress" World's Fair. The following year, she continued the collaboration with Rush, working on Works Progress Administration (WPA) art projects.

In 1936, Velarde graduated from the Santa Fe Indian School and began to teach at the Santa Clara Day School. In 1938, she traveled across the United States for four months with naturalist ERNEST THOMPSON SETON and his wife, returning to Santa Clara to build a studio and collaborate again with Rush on the Maisel Trading Post mural. In 1939, the Park Service of New Mexico commissioned her to paint murals for the Bandelier National Monument visitor's center, depicting the ancestral life of the Pueblo people in Frijoles Canyon.

Velarde was known for her attention to detail and knowledge of Pueblo ways, and her themes generally revolved around the historical, mythical, and ceremonial lives of her pueblo. She worked primarily in casein and tempera, beginning first in the two-dimensional style and pastel coloring of the Santa Fe (or Studio) school promoted by Dunn. In 1956, Velarde began shifting to a subtle three-dimensionality enhanced by "earth color" shadings from paints made from local rocks, mixed with water and glue for a plastic effect, and then applied to masonite.

After the U.S. entry into WORLD WAR II, Velarde lost her position at the Park Service, and she moved to Albuquerque. Working as a telephone operator to support herself, she met and married Herbert Hardin in 1942. They had two children but divorced in 1959.

In 1948, Velarde won first prize at the prestigious Philbrook Art Center's Annual Indian Art Show, and in 1954 she received the Ordre des Palmes Académiques award from the French government. The next year, she was featured in the magazine *National Geographic*. In 1960, she collaborated with her father to illustrate the highly acclaimed *Old Father, the Storyteller*, a book of Tewa legends. She exhibited across the country, and her work is held in numerous public collections, including the Museum of New Mexico and the Museum of the American Indian.

Up to her death, Velarde was generally regarded as the leading Indian woman painter of the Southwest, her style evoking, according to Dorothy Dunn, "the poise and gentle strength of a Pueblo woman." Her works were also a means to record and preserve traditions and practices that have been slowly disappearing. In 1984, she was featured in the short film *Pablita Velarde: An Artist and Her People*, sponsored by the National Park Service. In 1993, the Wheelwright Museum in Santa Fe did a retrospective exhibition of her work, which was also reproduced as a book, *Woman's Work: The Art of Pablita Velarde*. Her own book, *Pablita Velarde: Painting Her People*, featuring 28 of her paintings, was published in 2001. Her daughter, Helen Hardin, has become a prominent painter in her own right.

Pablita Velarde died in Albuquerque on January 10, 2006.

Further Reading

Santiago, Soledad. "Pablita Velarde, 1918–2006: Painter 'Blazed a Trail' for Indian, Female Artists." *New Mexican* (Santa Fe), 13 January 2006.

Victor, Wilma L. (1919–1987) *Choctaw educator, Bureau of Indian Affairs administrator*

A Choctaw born in Idabel, Oklahoma, on November 5, 1919, Wilma Victor attended Haskell Institute in Lawrence, Kansas, and then the University of Kansas. She received her B.S. from the University of Wisconsin and earned a master's degree in school administration from the University of Oklahoma in 1952. She eventually earned her Ph.D. from Utah State University. While completing her master's degree, she had also begun to work for the BUREAU OF INDIAN AFFAIRS (BIA) on the Navajo Reservation. With the outbreak of WORLD WAR II, she joined the Women's Army Corps (WACs). At the war's end, Victor returned to the BIA, becoming deputy director of the Phoenix office.

In 1950, Wilma Victor was appointed superintendent of the Intermountain Indian School, which opened that year in Brigham City, Utah. A pet project of powerful Utah senator ARTHUR WATKINS, one of the chief proponents of TERMINATION, the boarding school was a throwback to the days of RICHARD HENRY PRATT and his enforcement of ASSIMILATION. A converted military hospital, the school was more than 700 miles from the Navajo (Dineh) Reservation, where the majority of its students came from, and specialized in providing a vocational education. Intermountain, which at its peak housed more than 2,100 students, became notorious for its brutality, its assimilationist bent, and for the proselytizing by the local Mormon population, from among whom much of its staff was derived.

Victor left the school to become principal of the Institute of American Indian Arts in Santa Fe. She returned to her position at Intermountain in 1964. In the early 1960s, the school became the focus of a campaign by the NATIONAL INDIAN YOUTH COUNCIL to close it down. In 1972, the Navajo tribe passed a resolution that blocked their children from being sent to Intermountain, and in February 1975, the school's students rioted, leading to a steep drop in enrollment. The school was closed in 1984.

Victor left Intermountain in 1970 to return to the BIA, where she became acting director of Indian education. She was a member of the "old guard" in the BIA, those who opposed the reforms of Commissioner LOUIS ROOK BRUCE, JR., appointed by President Richard Nixon in 1969. She sided with deputy commissioner JOHN O. CROW, another longtime BIA functionary, in his power struggle with Bruce. Her assimilationist policies led activist RUSSELL MEANS to call her a "vicious sadist" and to attempt to "arrest" her in September 1971 for mismanagement of Indian schools. That same year, Crow managed to ease out Bruce's patron, Secretary of the Interior Walter Hickel. With the help of Crow, Victor then became special assistant for Indian affairs to the new secretary of the interior,

Rogers B. Morton. Together, they began to block Bruce's attempt to placate the growing militancy of the RED POWER MOVEMENT. After the BIA mishandled the TRAIL OF BROKEN TREATIES demonstration in Washington, D.C., in 1972, and Crow and Bruce were both fired, Victor left the bureau and returned to Oklahoma. Wilma Victor died on November 15, 1987, in Idabel. In the early 1980s, she was interviewed by the Women in the Federal Government Oral History Project, and her tape and transcript are located in the Schlesinger Library at the Radcliffe Institute at Harvard University.

Further Reading

Collier, Peter. "Wounded Knee: The New Indian War." *Ramparts* 11, no. 1 (1973): 25–29, 56–59.

Vizenor, Gerald Robert (1934–) *Chippewa novelist, poet, satirist*

One of the leading Native American writers of the 20th century, Gerald Vizenor was born on October 22, 1934, in Minneapolis, Minnesota. Vizenor is a descendant of journalist THEODORE H. BEAULIEU. His father, Clement William Vizenor, was a Chippewa housepainter from the White Earth Reservation; his mother, LaVern Peterson, of French-Canadian descent, was from Minneapolis; she was only 17 when she married Clement. Gerald's childhood was a hard and lonely one. When he was only two, his father was murdered by an unknown assailant. His mother would leave him for long stretches of time with his paternal grandmother on the White Earth Reservation. She remarried, but when Gerald was eight years old, his mother left both her second husband and her son.

After his stepfather died in a work accident, Vizenor, only 15, was left to fend for himself. He ended up joining the National Guard, and from 1952 to 1955, he served with the U.S. Army in Japan. While there, Vizenor became fascinated by Japanese literature, especially the simple verse and meditative style of the Japanese poetry known as haiku. The traditional forms of Japanese literature made him further appreciate his own tribal culture and led him to writing. Vizenor would eventually produce several volumes of haiku, including *Two Wings of the Butterfly* (1962); *Raising the Moon Vines* and *Seventeen Chirps*, both published in 1964; *Slight Abrasions* (1966); *Empty Swings* (1967); and *Matsushima*, released in 1984.

Following his service in the army, Vizenor attended New York University for a year, then transferred to the University of Minnesota, where he received his B.A. in 1960. He continued with graduate studies at Minnesota and briefly attended Harvard University. During this time, he was also employed as a social worker in St. Paul, Minnesota. In 1960, he became a corrections agent in the Minnesota State Reformatory at St. Cloud. Vizenor's first book of poems, *Born in the Wind*, was privately printed in 1960. The next year, *The Old Park Sleepers*, another collection of poetry, appeared. A focus on the destructive impact of the dominant society on Indian culture, in particular the disintegration of Indian life in urban areas, emerged in his early poems.

In 1968, Vizenor became a staff writer for the Minneapolis *Tribune*, where he remained for two years. He then shifted his focus from poetry to commentaries on Chippewa life. In 1968, he edited *Escorts to White Earth, 1868–1968: 100 Year Reservation*, and he released a collection of essays, *Thomas James White Hawk*. Two collections of traditional Chippewa poems and stories he had compiled and reinterpreted during the 1960s were published in 1970 as *Anishinabe Adisokan: Tales of the People* and *Anishinabe Nagomon: Songs of the People*.

In 1978, Vizenor published his first novel, *Darkness in Saint Louis Bearheart*, a darkly humorous account of a minor BUREAU OF INDIAN AFFAIRS (BIA) functionary and his violent futuristic vision of America. In *Darkness*, Vizenor employed to the fullest extent yet his concept of the "trickster," a mythic Indian archetype, both savior and scoundrel, clown and philosopher, that has been handed down in stories for centuries. Although the trickster motif has been used by other Native American authors, notably N. SCOTT MOMADAY in *House Made of Dawn*, Vizenor would not only feature the trickster as a character in much of his fiction but also extend the trickster vision to the very language he uses. He liberally coined new terms and phrases to create a surreal world full of odd people facing some of the most bizarre situations imaginable. In *Bearheart*, Vizenor employed two trickster characters, each representing an aspect of the Chippewa trickster Naanabozho. Proude Cedarfair, the hero of the novel, represents the heroic side of the trickster, while the character Bigfoot represents the trickster as a clown and a villain. The novel includes Indian characters who are lustful, violent, greedy, and cowardly, as well as a heavy dose of sick humor and shocking violence. Vizenor's extensive use of wordplay and complex imagery, as well as his departure from traditional realism and narrative structures, has earned him the label of "postmodern" novelist. Paradoxically, his novels are also considered among the most traditional in Indian writing. This juxtaposition effectively captures the upside-down trickster world of the old stories. (Vizenor himself has commented on the relationship of postmodernism with contemporary Indian works in his book *Narrative Chance: Postmodern Discourse on Native American Indian Literatures*, released in 1989.)

Also in 1978, Vizenor published *Wordarrows: Indians and Whites in the New Fur Trade*, a collection of stories that satirically explores the conflict between tribal Indian people and the dominant society, seen largely through the desolate urban landscape in which Indians unsuccessfully struggle to live. In 1981, Vizenor published another collection of stories *EarthDiver: Tribal Narrative on Mixed Descent*, and in 1984 he edited *The People Named the Chippewa: Narrative Histories*.

In 1987, after a teaching engagement in China, Vizenor wrote *Griever: An American Monkey King in China*, in which the main character, Griever de Hocus, is a trickster who finds himself teaching English at the Zhou Enlai University in Tianjin. He defies the oppressive Chinese political atmosphere by attempting to save everything, from political prisoners to chickens, from the executioner's block. The critically acclaimed *Griever* won the American Book Award for 1988. Vizenor's next book, *The Trickster of Liberty* (1988), a series of character sketches, features Vizenor at his language-bending best, this time returning the trickster motif to the White Earth Reservation.

As an essayist and social commentator, Vizenor is best known for challenging conventional notions of contemporary Native American life. Vizenor, although not an assimilationist, has challenged those who view mixed-blood Indians as somehow inferior and "impure." During the 1970s, he poked fun at the AMERICAN INDIAN MOVEMENT (AIM) and their leaders—almost all assimilated urban mixed-bloods—over their stereotypical posturing as "traditionals" and their cliché-ridden pan-Indian ranting, which to Vizenor bore little resemblance to the views of reservation Indians.

Vizenor wrote the script for the classic cult film *Harold of Orange*, a mocking view of the philanthropic community released in 1984 and featuring Seneca comedian CHARLIE HILL, with a musical score by BUFFY SAINTE-MARIE. Vizenor's third novel, *The Heirs of Columbus* (1991), employs the trickster imagery to deconstruct the Christopher Columbus mythology in time for the quincentennial of the sailor's famous voyage in 1992. His fourth novel, *Dead Voices: Natural Agonies in the New World*, explores the war between Western words, or the "dead voices," and the tribal and natural world. In 1995, Vizenor served as coeditor on *Native-American Literature: A Brief Introduction and Anthology*, which included some of his own drama. His novel *Hotline Healers: An Almost Browne Novel* was published in 1997, and *Fugitive Poses: Native American Indian Scenes of Absence and Presence* in 1998. In 2000 *Chancers: A Novel* was released, and in 2006, he published two collections of poetry, *Bear Island* and *Almost Ashore*.

Vizenor is now a professor emeritus of Native American literature in the ethnic studies department at the University of California at Berkeley, and his prolific and wide-ranging works defy any conventional description. Although they remain largely unknown to the wider American public, they have exerted a lasting influence on a new generation of Indian writers.

Further Reading

Blaeser, Kimberley. *Gerald Vizenor: Writing in the Oral Tradition*. Norman: University of Oklahoma Press, 1996.

Lee, A. Robert. *Loosening the Seams: Interpretations of Gerald Vizenor*. Bowling Green, Ohio: Bowling Green State University Press, 2000.

Purdy, John, and Blake Hausman. "The Future of Print Narratives and Comic Holotropes: A Conversation with Gerald Vizenor." *American Indian Quarterly* 29, no. 1 (2005): 242–258.

Velie, Alan R. *Four American Indian Literary Masters: N. Scott Momaday, James Welch, Leslie Mormon Silko, and Gerald Vizenor*. Norman: University of Oklahoma Press, 1982.

Wahpepah, Bill (1937–1987) *Kickapoo-Sac and Fox leader of the American Indian Movement and International Indian Treaty Council*

Of Kickapoo and Sac and Fox ancestry, Bill Wahpepah was born on December 23, 1937, near Shawnee, Oklahoma. As a child he was sent to the Pawnee Indian School in Pawnee, Oklahoma, then attended Shawnee High School, where he was expelled and sent to reform school. He graduated in 1958 and moved to Oakland, California. In Oakland, he was a drifter who suffered from bouts of alcoholism and drug addiction.

The OCCUPATION OF ALCATRAZ ISLAND in 1969 inspired Wahpepah to become an organizer, and he joined a mainstream Bay Area group called Native American Concerned Parents. Wahpepah soon became an influential member of the Bay Area Indian community, founding the American Indian Adult Education Program, a child development center in Oakland, and an AMERICAN INDIAN MOVEMENT (AIM) "freedom school." His hard work and dedication to the community inspired many others, including WILMA MANKILLER and the Pulitzer Prize–winning author Alice Walker.

As the more flamboyant members of AIM began to drop out in the late 1970s, Wahpepah worked quietly to spread the AIM vision to indigenous movements across the world. His good-natured personality made him the unofficial ambassador of the group's successor, the INTERNATIONAL INDIAN TREATY COUNCIL, and he played a key role in its early success of spreading the American concept of Indian sovereignty (see SOVEREIGNTY, INDIGENOUS AND TRIBAL) to worldwide indigenous rights movements.

Bill Wahpepah died on January 2, 1987, of complications from bleeding ulcers. While in the hospital in Alameda, California, for treatment of the ulcers, Wahpepah suffered a heart attack; he had to wait more than three hours before being treated, and the delay resulted in his death. He was only 49 years old. Wahpepah's untimely death sparked outrage from Native leaders across the country, who felt the poor treatment was due to his being an Indian and lacking health insurance.

Further Reading

Walker, Alice. "My Big Brother Bill." In *Living by the Word*, 41–50. Philadelphia: Harvest Books, 1989.

Warner, Pop (Glenn Scobey Warner) (1871–1954) *college football coach*

One of the most successful football coaches in college history, Glenn Scobey Warner was born on April 5, 1871, near Springfield, Illinois. He attended Cornell University, where he played football and received the nickname "Pop" because he was older than most of his teammates. Pop Warner graduated from Cornell with a law degree in 1894. He briefly coached at the University of Georgia and at Cornell before being hired by educator RICHARD HENRY PRATT in 1899 to coach at Carlisle Indian School in Pennsylvania. Carlisle had started to play football only in 1893, led by Seneca All-American Bemus Pierce and White Earth Chippewa Ed Rogers, but within a few years the football team had begun to show promise on the gridiron, bringing the school much-needed recognition and revenue.

Warner brought to Carlisle one of the most innovative minds in the history of football. He had been looking for a team that could put into place many of his new ideas, and shortly after he arrived at Carlisle he exclaimed to his wife, "This is a new kind of team. They're light, but they're fast and tricky." Warner found that unlike the "stand-patism" typical of non-Indian teams, "the most remarkable thing about the Indians was their receptiveness to new ideas." He found the Indian youths to be, in his words, "born lovers of the game. They have speed and skill in use of hands and feet. They also

450

have highly developed powers of observation, handed down through generations."

With the "speed and daring" offered by his Indian athletes, Warner invented the single-wing and double-wing formation, the spiral pass and spiral kick, the three-point stance, the "body block," new conditioning techniques, and specialized equipment such as helmets and mud cleats. Because "the Carlisle bunch dearly loved to spring surprises," he created a repertoire of trick plays that befuddled opponents. Led by All-Americans Martin Wheelock (Oneida), Frank Hudson (Laguna Pueblo), and Jimmie Johnson (Stockbridge Munsee), in Warner's first five years the team won a respectable 32 games to 18 losses and three ties. The highlight of this period was when the team pulled the "hidden ball trick" to stun mighty Harvard University.

In 1904, Warner returned to coach his alma mater, Cornell, for three years before Pratt lured him back with a hefty raise. Pratt felt that sportsmanship was an important aspect of the assimilationist philosophy he espoused. By showing non-Indians that Indian youths could play sports and not fight back despite the taunts and insults hurled at them by opposing teams, Pratt felt he was dispelling the notion that Indians could not "rise above savagery."

In 1907, the Carlisle team shot to national prominence when they won 10 games and lost only one, handing the University of Pennsylvania (Penn) its only defeat, crushing perennial powers Harvard, Penn State, Syracuse University, and University of Minnesota, and topping the season off by beating Amos Alonso Stagg's undefeated "Chicago Eleven" in the final game. Featuring ALBERT EXENDINE (Delaware) at end, Frank Mt. Pleasant (Tuscarora) at quarterback, Albert Payne (Umatilla) at halfback, and Peter Hauser (Cheyenne) at fullback, the team was so powerful that a young Sac and Fox athlete named JIM THORPE would spend most of the season on the bench. In 1908, with Thorpe the regular halfback, the team had a record of 10-2-1. Thorpe's absence from Carlisle during the next two years left the team with ordinary seasons, but his return in 1911 brought them back to the top.

With a strong supporting cast of Gus Welch (GUSTAVUS WELCH) (Chippewa) at quarterback, Stansil "Possum" Powell (Cherokee) at fullback, Alexander Arcasa (Colville) and Joel Wheelock (Oneida) as halfbacks, and Sam Burd (Blackfeet), Ike Lyons (Onondaga), Emer Busch (Pomo), and WILLIAM DIETZ (Oglala Lakota Sioux) anchoring the line, Thorpe opened the season with an 85-yard run for a touchdown to beat nearby Dickinson College. Carlisle then proceeded to crush its next six opponents, including mighty Penn and University of Pittsburgh (Pitt)—where Thorpe amazingly fielded his own 50-yard punt and ran it an extra 20 yards for a touchdown—by the combined score of 228-10. Thorpe kicked four field goals and scored a touchdown to shock the defending national champions Harvard, 18-15, but the Indians then lost to Syracuse by one point, 12-11. They rebounded to beat Johns Hopkins University and Brown University and ended the year winning 11 games and losing only one while scoring 298 points and conceding only 49.

As good as the 1911 Carlisle team was, the 1912 team was even better, with PETE CALAC (Luiseño) and JOE GUYON (Chippewa) joining All-Americans Welch, Powell, Arcasa, Busch, and the inimitable Thorpe. The team destroyed its first six opponents by the combined score of 227-0 and tied Rose Bowl–bound Washington and Jefferson College 0-0 before manhandling Pitt 45-8. After routing Georgetown University, the Indians played in the first-ever international football game, defeating the University of Toronto 49-1. Carlisle then beat Lehigh 34-14, before causing a national sensation by trouncing Army at West Point 27-6. They were then upset by Penn but came back to defeat Springfield and shut out a powerful Brown team. Consistently playing more games and facing tougher competition than any other school—always on the road, as they had no home stadium—tiny Carlisle had produced one of the finest football teams in college football history.

Warner also coached 11 other sports, including Carlisle's powerful LACROSSE team, as well as guiding the track and field team, which featured Thorpe, Welch, Guyon, and LOUIS TEWANIMA (Hopi), and the baseball team, which boasted alumni such as CHARLES ALBERT BENDER (Chippewa).

In 1913, the football team had another outstanding season, as Guyon replaced Thorpe at halfback and the team went 10-1. In 1914, however, Carlisle became the focus of a Senate investigation, led in part by some of its students, including quarterback Welch, that accused the school of, among other things, overemphasis on athletics and providing undue favoritism to the school's athletes. The 1914 team won only four games, the worst record in almost 15 years, and Warner left to become head coach at Pitt. The 1915 team fared even worse, going 3-6-2, and in 1916 the squad fell to a dismal one win, three losses, and one tie. During its final season, in 1917, winless Carlisle failed to score in the last seven games, and by the next year the school itself would be closed. Despite its inglorious end, in 25 years of playing football Carlisle had compiled a 167-88-13 record, for an astonishing .647 winning percentage.

Pop Warner went on to even greater fame at Pitt and Stanford University and ended his coaching career at Temple University. When he retired in 1939, he was the most successful coach in college history, with a combined record of 313-106-32. Yet his fondest memories would always be of his years at Carlisle. Though he started with "all of the prejudices of the average white," he found that after "14 years of intimate association, I came to hold a deep admiration for the Indian."

The Carlisle students' "fierce determination to show the palefaces what they could do when the odds were even" was, for Warner, the key to their success:

On the athletic field, where the struggle was man to man, they felt that the Indian had his first even break, and the record proves they took full advantage of it. For fifteen years little Carlisle took the measure of almost every big university, with student bodies of four and five thousand to draw from; and to this day

Jim Thorpe, Bemus Pierce, Frank Hudson, Jimmie Johnson, Mt. Pleasant, Exendine, Lone Star, and Pete Hauser still rank among the all-time stars of football.

Inducted into both the College Football Hall of Fame and the National Football Hall of Fame, Pop Warner died on September 7, 1954, in Palo Alto, California.

See also SPORTS, AMERICAN INDIANS AND.

Further Reading

Jenkins, Sally. *The Real All Americans: The Team That Changed a Game, a People, a Nation.* New York: Doubleday, 2007.

Warner, Glenn S. *Pop Warner, Football's Greatest Teacher: The Epic Autobiography of Major College Football's Winningest Coach, Glenn S. (Pop) Warner.* New York: McBride, 1942.

Warrior, Clyde (1939–1968) *Ponca activist, cofounder of the National Indian Youth Council*

One of the earliest leaders of the RED POWER MOVEMENT, Clyde Warrior advocated confrontational tactics and direct action that would influence the course of Indian politics throughout the 1960s. Born on August 31, 1939, near Ponca City, Oklahoma, to Gloria Collins, he was raised by his traditional Ponca grandparents, Bill and Metha Collins. As a youth, Warrior became a champion fancy dancer and traditional singer. He attended Cameron Junior College in Lawton, Oklahoma. In 1960, he became involved with the Southwest Regional Indian Youth Council, where he met Navajo (Dineh) HERBERT BLATCHFORD. In 1961, Warrior also attended the influential Summer Workshop on American Indian Affairs in Boulder, Colorado, where he came under the influence of Cherokee anthropologist ROBERT K. THOMAS.

In 1961, Warrior and Blatchford attended the AMERICAN INDIAN CHICAGO CONFERENCE, where they met fellow students MEL THOM, SHIRLEY HILL WITT, and WILLIAM RICKARD, all of whom shared the same activist bent. Out of this historic gathering grew the NATIONAL INDIAN YOUTH COUNCIL (NIYC), founded in Gallup, New Mexico, later that year. Warrior attended the Gallup meeting and was elected an officer of the NIYC. The group began to advocate a more militant approach to defending Indian rights. Among their first projects was to assert Indian HUNTING AND FISHING RIGHTS by fishing and hunting in places where these activities had been permitted under Indian treaties that were no longer being honored. Along with Thom, Warrior played an important role in organizing these so-called fish-ins in the Northwest coast, where he worked with Assiniboine-Dakota Sioux activist HANK ADAMS.

In addition to being an activist, Warrior, like the other founders of the NIYC, was also a scholar. He worked with Robert Thomas on the University of Chicago study of the Cherokee known as the Carnegie Project, then became a researcher for the University of Kansas. With Thomas, Warrior was editor of *Indian Voices*, published by the University of Chicago. He attended the University of Oklahoma and then Northeast State University in Tahlequah, Oklahoma, graduating in 1966.

Warrior also served on the Indian Advisory Board to Upward Bound and acted as an adviser to the NATIONAL CONGRESS OF AMERICAN INDIANS. With Hank Adams, he helped to organize Indians around the Poor People's Campaign, a project envisioned by Martin Luther King, Jr. Warrior's perspective on political activism was articulated in an article he wrote for *Americans Before Columbus*, the NIYC newsletter, in December 1964. In the article, entitled "Which One Are You? Five Types of Young Indians," Warrior attempted to formulate his concept of the ideal young Indian. He rejected sellouts, whom he labeled the "fink of finks"; the "hood," who drops out of school and succumbs to alcohol and crime; the "joker," who defines himself by the demeaning "cues society gives him" and acts like a clown; the "ultra-pseudo-Indian" who is proud to be Indian but does not know how to be one and as a consequence must turn to non-Indian sources in order to "act Indian"; and the "angry nationalist," who, though closer to being a true Indian than the others, views Indian life "with bitter, abstract and ideological thinking." Warrior argued that what was needed instead among Indian youth was an activism "based upon true Indian philosophy geared to modern times." Calling for a "Greater Indian America" that rejected the "horror of American conformity" and found a renewed sense of pride from being Indian, he asked Indian youth, "How about it? Let's raise some hell!"

Unlike many Indian activists, Warrior worked well with traditional elders and urged Indian youth to follow the guidance of traditional Indian leadership. In 1966, he aided Finis Smith, a traditional Cherokee chief, founder of the Five County Cherokee Movement and grandson of REDBIRD SMITH, who sought to reestablish a traditional Cherokee government in the hills of Oklahoma. In the late 1960s, Warrior dropped out of NIYC because he felt it was losing its activist leanings, only to be elected president by its membership in 1967. By then, however, alcoholism had saddled him with serious health problems. Clyde Warrior died of liver failure in Enid, Oklahoma, in July 1968.

Further Reading

Billings, Thomas A. "Eulogy for Clyde Warrior." July 9, 1968. "Indians" folder, box 481. Records of the Indian Division Relating to Public Relations, 1965–1970, Records of the Office of Operations, Records of the Office of Economic Opportunity, Record Group 381, National Archives and Records Administration II, College Park, Maryland.

Cobb, Daniel M. "Devils in Disguise: The Carnegie Project, the Cherokee Nation, and the 1960s." *American Indian Quarterly* 31, no. 3 (2007): 465–490.

Smith, Paul Chaat, and Robert Allen Warrior. *Like a Hurricane: The Indian Movement from Alcatraz to Wounded Knee.* New York: New Press, 1996.

Warrior, Clyde. "We Are Not Free." In *Red Power*, edited by Alvin Josephy. New York: McGraw-Hill, 1971.

———. "Which One Are You? Five Types of Young Indians." *ABC: Americans Before Columbus* 4 (December 1964).

Washinawatok, Ingrid (Ingrid Washinawatok El-Issa, O'Peqtaw-Metamoh, "Flying Eagle Woman")

(1957–1999) *Menominee activist*

Ingrid Washinawatok was born on July 31, 1957, at the Indian Hospital in Keshena, Wisconsin, the daughter of JAMES A. WASHINAWATOK and Gwendolyn Dodge Washinawatok. She was given the Menominee name O'Peqtaw-Metamoh (Flying Eagle Woman). At the time of Ingrid's birth, the family lived in Chicago, but Gwendolyn Washinawatok wanted her two daughters to be born on the Menominee reservation. Ingrid attended Darwin Public School, St. Sylvester, a Catholic elementary school, and Alvernia, another Catholic girls school, all in Chicago. She then attended JFK Preparatory High School, a boarding school in St. Nazianz, Wisconsin, graduating in 1975.

After her father helped form Determination of Rights and Unity for Menominee Shareholders (DRUMS) in 1970 to overturn the TERMINATION of the Menominee tribe, the family traveled from Chicago to Keshena every weekend for the next year to protest the selling of lakefront property to non-Indians at Legend Lake. In 1972, Ingrid marched with her mother and father and other DRUMS members from Keshena to Madison, Wisconsin, to bring recognition to the Menominee restoration movement. The family moved to Madison in 1975, and Ingrid worked with the rest of her family at the American Indian Child Placement and Development Inc. The next year she moved to Minneapolis, Minnesota, and began working with the local American Indian community there. In Minneapolis she met AMERICAN INDIAN MOVEMENT (AIM) activists WILLIAM MEANS and CLYDE BELLECOURT, who were in the process of forming the INTERNATIONAL INDIAN TREATY COUNCIL (IITC).

In 1980, Washinawatok was asked by the IITC to go to Cuba to study Spanish at the University of Havana and become an interpreter. There she met her future husband, Palestinian activist Ali El-Issa. She left Havana in 1981 and moved to New York City to work at the IITC office. In summer 1982, she traveled to Lebanon to meet up with El-Issa, and they were married in the fall in Damascus, Syria. Washinawatok returned to New York to become the coordinator of the New York Treaty Council office, and she was joined by El-Issa in December 1983.

In 1985, Washinawatok started to work for MADRE, a human rights organization for which she helped to deliver food and supplies to war-torn Nicaragua. During her many international travels with the Treaty Council and MADRE, she met and befriended a number of Latin American Indian leaders, including exiled Guatemalan Maya Indian and future Nobel laureate Rigoberta Menchu. She served as escort when Menchu returned to Guatemala in 1988.

Washinawatok worked for the American Indian Community House in New York City before moving back to Wisconsin to work in the special education program in the Menominee school system. She returned to New York City in 1992 and worked for the Solidarity Foundation before joining the Fund of the Four Directions, the private philanthropic foundation of Anne Roberts Rockefeller, daughter of former New York governor Nelson Rockefeller. Washinawatok transformed the

Ingrid Washinawatok listens to the opening words of the Indigenous Delegation at the Quincentenary of Columbus's first voyage to the Americas, in New York City, October 1992. *(Estate of Ingrid Washinawatok)*

fund so that it would benefit Native people, in particular to aid in the revitalization of North American Indian cultures. Under Washinawatok's direction, Four Directions began to devote its grants solely to Native nations and indigenous-controlled, community-based, local, regional, and national organizations, working on important issues such as language restoration (see INDIGENOUS LANGUAGE USE). She was a founder and the cochair of the Indigenous Women's Network and was also the chair of Native Americans in Philanthropy.

A leader of New York's large urban Indian community, Washinawatok was a member of the Native American Council of New York City and sat on the board of directors of the American Indian Community House with ROSEMARY RICHMOND. Active in efforts by Indian nations to achieve international recognition, she was a member of the Indigenous Initiative for Peace convened by Rigoberta Menchu. Washinawatok also organized and participated in the first, second, and third State of the World Forums. In 1994, she became the chair of the United Nations–sponsored Committee of the International Decade of the World's Indigenous Peoples, and she was also a delegate for the Commission on Human Rights and the Working Group on Indigenous Populations.

As part of her philanthropic and international work, Washinawatok traveled extensively. On February 25, 1999, while working with the U'wa Indians in northeast Colombia, Washinawatok, Native Hawaiian activist Lahe'ena'e Gay (director of the Hawaii-based Pacific Cultural Conservancy International), and environmentalist Terence Freitas were kidnapped by the Revolutionary Armed Forces of Colombia (FARC). FARC, a Marxist guerrilla army founded in 1964, notorious for assassinations, kidnappings, bombings, and other brutalities, marched Washinawatok and her companions across the border to Venezuela, where they were killed on March 4, 1999.

Ingrid Washinawatok was among the most beloved and respected activists of her generation, and her death stunned the international Indian community and cut short the life of one of Native America's most promising leaders. Her numerous friends and associates established a foundation, the Ingrid Washinawatok El-Issa Flying Eagle Woman Fund for Peace, Justice, and Sovereignty, which continues her work.

Further Reading
Native Americas 16, no. 2 (Summer 1999): special issue.

Washinawatok, James A. (Jim White, Enaehmakiw, "Thunderer") (1924–1997)
Menominee supreme court justice, tribal activist
Justice of the supreme court of the Menominee nation and a leader in the fight to reinstate the tribe after it was terminated in 1961, James A. Washinawatok was born on March 4, 1924, in Neopit, Wisconsin, on the Menominee reservation. His parents, Peter and Elizabeth (Warrington) Washinawatok, gave him the Menominee name Enaehmakiw (Thunderer). Peter Washinawatok was raised in part by an aunt named White, and he had been given the surname White while he was in school, although he remained Washinawatok on the tribal rolls.

James White Washinawatok attended Shawano High School and then Flandreau Boarding School in South Dakota, where he was known as Jim White. In 1942, Jim Washinawatok enlisted in the U.S. Navy, and as a gunner's mate he participated in the D-day invasion of Normandy in 1944. Honorably discharged in 1948, he enrolled in Michigan State University, where he graduated in 1956 with a B.S. in police administration and political science. He then moved to Chicago, where he worked first as an insurance adjuster and then for the state government until 1970, when he helped to create Determination of Rights and Unity for Menominee Shareholders (DRUMS).

At the beginning of the 20th century, the Menominee reservation consisted of approximately 233,000 acres in northern Wisconsin, more than 90 percent of it prime timber. In 1908, aided by the Forest Service, which under Gifford Pinchot was experimenting with scientific management of forests, the tribe initiated a sustained-yield harvesting program. (See VALENTINE, ROBERT GROSVENOR.) The BUREAU OF INDIAN AFFAIRS (BIA) also constructed a sawmill that became the major source of employment for the tribe. Under BIA control, the forest declined during the 1920s, and the Menominee filed suit in 1934 in the U.S. Court of Claims, charging the BIA with mismanagement. In 1951, the Court of Claims ruled in the tribe's favor, awarding them $7.65 million.

The Menominee were by then one of the most self-sufficient tribes in the country. In addition to their sustainable logging operation, they had accumulated $10 million on deposit with the U.S. Treasury. Like the Klamath, their rich forests made them a prime target for TERMINATION, which was then becoming government policy under Indian commissioners DILLON S. MYER and GLENN L. EMMONS. Utah senator ARTHUR WATKINS, the main congressional proponent of Termination, refused to allow the release of the Court of Claims money unless the Menominee agreed to be terminated. Watkins and other congressmen managed to sway many in the tribe by sponsoring legislation that would have distributed the claim on a per-capita basis, and they dangled the possibility of a $1,500 lump-sum payment to each tribal member. In the end, the Menominee General Council, under pressure to formulate a Termination plan before one was forced upon them, agreed to accept Termination.

The Menominee Termination Act was signed by President Dwight D. Eisenhower on June 17, 1954, although it was not fully implemented until May 1, 1961. As part of the Termination agreement, the Menominee reservation became a new county within the state. The tribe also transferred as much of their assets as they could to a new corporation, Menominee Enterprises.

Whereas before Termination the Menominee had been relatively self-sufficient, the transfer of assets to the corporation—although effectively protecting the land—and the loss of federal services under the Termination agreement, led to the impoverishment of the Menominee people, many of whom were forced to go on welfare. Moreover, debts incurred in preparation for Termination, and the inability to make the sawmill operation competitive in the open market, forced the corporation to begin selling off some of its most valuable land. This led to a split among the Menominee and a movement for reinstatement as a tribe.

DRUMS was established in the Menominee urban communities of Chicago and Milwaukee in summer 1970 with help from action anthropologist Nancy Lurie (see TAX, SOL) and a legal service called Wisconsin Judicare. James Washinawatok, one of the founders and president of the Chicago chapter, led demonstrations at Legend Lake, where they successfully prevented the corporation from selling valuable lakefront property. DRUMS challenged the leadership of Menominee Enterprises, which was unpopular on the reservation for its mismanagement of tribal resources and for the reservation's high unemployment and poverty rates, quickly winning the support of the vast majority of Menominee.

Elected president of DRUMS, Washinawatok moved back to Wisconsin. Along with Menominee activist ADA DEER, he recruited support from prominent Indians such as VINE DELORIA, JR., LaDONNA HARRIS, and BUFFY SAINTE-MARIE, as well as senators such as Edward Kennedy. Washinawatok testified on behalf of the Menominee before the Senate. At that time, the administration of Richard Nixon was open to ending the policy of Termination (see BRUCE, LOUIS ROOK, JR.). After a vigorous lobbying effort, Nixon signed the Menominee Restoration Act on December 22, 1973, reinstating the tribe and reestablishing nearly the entire reservation.

Washinawatok then worked at a variety of occupations in Chicago before traveling first to Denver and then to Fort Washakie, Wyoming, where he worked on the Wind River reservation. Returning to the Menominee reservation in 1982, he joined the Trust and Management Department. He was elected to the Menominee Tribal Legislature in 1986, appointed to the Menominee Tribal Court in 1988, and named to the Menominee Supreme Court in 1995.

James Washinawatok died on July 8, 1997, after a long bout with lymphomic cancer. His daughter, INGRID WASHINAWATOK, was herself a prominent rights activist, helping to found such important groups as the Indigenous Women's Network and Native Americans in Philanthropy.

Further Reading
Beck, David R. *The Struggle for Self-Determination: History of the Menominee Indians since 1854.* Lincoln: University of Nebraska Press, 2005.

Watahwaso, Princess   *See* POOLAW, LUCY NICOLA.

Watkins, Arthur Vivian (1886–1973) *U.S. senator*
Arthur Vivian Watkins was born in Midway, Utah, on December 18, 1886, the son of Arthur and Emily Gerber Watkins and grandchild of early Utah pioneers. He studied at Brigham Young University and New York University, earned an LL.B. at Columbia University in 1912, and received an honorary LL.D. from the University of Utah in 1959. Admitted to the bar in 1912, Watkins began his law practice in Vernal, Utah. During the following decades, he engaged in newspaper and agricultural work, was assistant county attorney of Salt Lake County in 1914, served as district judge for the Fourth Judicial District of Utah from 1928 to 1933, and made an unsuccessful run for Congress in 1936. A Republican, he was elected to the U.S. Senate in 1946 and served two terms, from 1947 to 1959.

The most important development in Indian affairs in the aftermath of WORLD WAR II was the move to end the legal existence of tribes and reservations known as TERMINATION. By the early 1950s, a number of related policies were already in place, such as the PICK-SLOAN PLAN (beginning in 1944) and the INDIAN CLAIMS COMMISSION ACT (1946), but it was the 1953 House Concurrent Resolution 108, expressing Congress's sense that federal responsibility for Indians should be terminated with all possible speed, that officially introduced Termination. In the Senate, the principal sponsor of Termination was Arthur V. Watkins. Hearings on Termination began in 1954, when a bill to terminate Indians in Utah—which had been drafted at Watkins's request—was brought to the floor for consideration.

The Indian Claims Commission Act was seen as another piece of the Termination package. Watkins was one of a number of high-ranking Mormons involved in the claims process. Others included Ernest Wilkinson, who as attorney for the Ute assisted in the writing of the Claims Act, and JOHN S. BOYDEN, Wilkinson's partner who, as a very busy Indian claims attorney, was a major beneficiary of the act, since lawyers received from 7 to 10 percent of all claims awarded. The firm of Wilkinson, Cragun and Barker represented a number of Indian tribes in these claims proceedings (see BATTLE MOUNTAIN).

Indian claims and Termination were so closely linked in the minds of their originators that in 1954 Senator Watkins took the unusual step of going out to the Menominee reservation to persuade the Indians that they could not receive the claims judgment they had already won unless they agreed to their own Termination. This was not true, but the result was that, at a meeting representing about 8 percent of the tribe, a vote was taken to accept Termination. Two months after the hearings had ended, on June 17, 1954, the Menominee tribe was terminated (see WASHINAWATOK, JAMES A.).

As Termination wore on, its damaging effects and its rejection by the great majority of Indians became obvious. In a 1957 letter, Indian rights activist OLIVER LA FARGE called it "a program of horrifying inhumanity."

Watkins's desire to terminate the tribes was undoubtedly inspired by his interest in Western water rights. As manager of commercial orchards and a turkey farm (from 1919 to 1932) and counsel to the Provo River Water Users Association from 1935, Watkins understood that the WINTERS DOCTRINE gave Indian tribes a major claim to Western water. Control of water in the arid West would depend on evading these claims. After entering the Senate, Watkins became Utah's chief spokesperson on water issues, cosponsoring the Colorado River Water Storage project and numerous other reclamation projects.

Watkins is best remembered for his 1955 censure of Senator Joseph McCarthy, who gained great power for a time by falsely accusing many members of the government and the U.S. Army of being communists and traitors. Watkins, who was not afraid of McCarthy, was able to put an end to the power of that troublesome senator by leading a censure resolution in the Senate. His role in Indian affairs, on the other hand, is much less known, though of great historical importance—and the two issues are connected. In the mid-1950s, the states of Utah, Arizona, and New Mexico supported the proposal for a Colorado River Storage Project (CRSP) and were against the proposed Navajo Indian Irrigation Project (NIIP) on the San Juan River, a tributary of the upper Colorado River. This was because the Navajo tribe, according to the Winters Doctrine, would have "prior and superior" rights to Colorado River water. At first, President Dwight D. Eisenhower did not support the CRSP, but Watkins agreed to step in as the much-needed hatchet man against Senator McCarthy only on the condition that the president would support the CRSP, which was passed in 1956. From that time on, the Bureau of

Reclamation did much to diminish and delay the NIIP. The Termination policy made this easier.

Watkins can best be understood as promoting the same philosophy of full Indian ASSIMILATION as had educator RICHARD HENRY PRATT in the early part of the century and the AMERICAN INDIAN FEDERATION in the 1930s, and as his contemporaries Indian commissioners DILLON S. MYER and GLENN L. EMMONS were then doing. All of them believed the solution to "the Indian problem" lay in eliminating special status for Indians, including all reservations, and ultimately the BUREAU OF INDIAN AFFAIRS itself. Not by coincidence, Watkins was the driving force behind the creation in 1949 of the Intermountain Indian School in Brigham City, Utah, based on the boarding school concepts developed by Pratt. (See VICTOR, WILMA L.)

Watkins believed that the Citizenship Act of 1924 (see CITIZENSHIP) had rendered all Indian treaty rights null and void, an interpretation diametrically opposed to that established by Indian Commissioner JOHN COLLIER and Department of Interior lawyer FELIX COHEN in the 1930s. As D'ARCY MCNICKLE explained in *Native American Tribalism*, 1973,

> It was [Watkins's] view that Indians could not hope to have an identity separate from the mainstream of American life, and that those who encouraged such hopes by helping Indians to develop their communities were doing a mischief. He regarded the Indian programs of the Roosevelt administration as misdirected social experiments that perpetuated the illusion of a future for Indians as Indians. He looked to Congress as the agency to deliver the Indians out of bondage and free their property from government surveillance. As [Watkins] summarized the situation, "Unfortunately, the major and continuing congressional movement toward full freedom was delayed for a time by the IRA [INDIAN REORGANIZATION ACT] of 1934 . . . Amid the deep social concern of the depression years, Congress deviated from its accustomed policy under the concept of promoting the general Indian welfare. In the post-depression years Congress—realizing this change of policy—sought to return to the historic principles of much earlier decades."

Though Watkins lost his Senate seat in 1958, he was not yet through with Indian affairs. In 1959, President Eisenhower appointed him an associate member of the Indian Claims Commission, and he became chairman in 1960. He retired as chief commissioner in 1967.

Upon his retirement, Watkins moved to Salt Lake City and then to Orem, Utah. He died in Orem on September 1, 1973.

Further Reading

Metcalf, R. Warren. *Termination's Legacy: The Discarded Indians of Utah*. Lincoln: University of Nebraska Press, 2002.
Watkins, Arthur V. "Termination of Federal Supervision: The Removal of Restrictions over Indian Property and Person." *Annals of the American Academy of Political and Social Science* 311, no. 5 (1957): 47–55.

Wauneka, Annie Dodge (1910–1997) *Navajo public health activist, tribal council member*

Annie Dodge was born on April 10, 1910, on the Navajo (Dineh) Reservation near Old Sawmill, Arizona, the daughter of Navajo leader HENRY CHEE DODGE and K'eehabah, his third wife. THOMAS H. DODGE, Navajo Tribal Council chair from 1933 to 1936, was her half brother. Annie Dodge was enrolled at the reservation school in 1918, the same year that a terrible influenza epidemic ravaged the country. There were many deaths throughout the population, including numerous American Indians (for example, IRENE EASTMAN, the family of JESSE CORNPLANTER, and ANGEL DECORA). Many pupils at her school died as well, but Annie suffered only a mild case, and after recovering, the eight-year-old girl helped nurse her suffering classmates. This was the beginning of her lifelong interest in public health.

Later, Dodge attended the Albuquerque Indian School in New Mexico. During her time there, her father became chair of the first Navajo Tribal Council (1923). Traveling with him throughout the reservation, where nearly everyone still lived without plumbing or electricity in the traditional one-room round wooden hogans, she became aware of many public health problems.

At the Albuquerque school, Dodge met George Wauneka, another Navajo student. They graduated after completing the 11th grade and married in October 1929. After living two years at Sonsela Butte, they settled at her father's ranch at Tanner Springs, where they managed large herds of horses, sheep, and cattle and raised a family of eight children.

Annie Dodge Wauneka had grown up bilingual in Navajo and English and fully conversant with the traditional life of the tribe. With her ability to bridge linguistic and cultural barriers, she became an effective community worker. During the 1930s, she participated in outreach activities connected with the controversial Navajo livestock grazing regulations, which required careful interpretation and translation between English and Navajo languages and their value systems. But it was in the field of public health that she made her greatest contribution.

In 1951, Wauneka was elected to represent the Klagetoh District on the 74-member Navajo Tribal Council, becoming the first woman ever to serve on it. She was soon chosen as chair of the council's health committee. At that time, the Navajo were still suffering many serious public health problems, including high incidences of trachoma, tuberculosis, and infant mortality, and Wauneka traveled throughout the enormous reservation to speak on health issues, acted as a personal liaison between people and medical staffers, persuaded patients in clinics not to run home with contagious diseases, worked with health professionals to make public education films for the Navajo, and explained Western medicine to Navajo medicine men. Much of this work was part of

Annie Dodge Wauneka speaks with Surgeon General Leroy E. Burney (far left), on September 26, 1956, in Washington, D.C., while Cheyenne River Sioux Tribal Chairman Frank Ducheneaux looks on. *(AP/Wideworld)*

the Crownpoint Project (1953–60) sponsored by a new agency that had been set up by Cree-Flathead social scientist D'Arcy McNickle, American Indian Development, Inc. (AID).

The biggest problem was tuberculosis. After her election, Wauneka spent three months studying the disease with the U.S. Public Health Service. Then she worked out how to convey this knowledge to the Navajo people in their own language. The first problem was to explain why the traditional medicine men were unable to cure the disease, without being disrespectful to them or the great majority of Navajo who put their trust in them. She explained that tuberculosis was a very powerful disease that affected people around the world. Therefore, the medicine men would need help from other medical systems that had experience with the disease. She also had to address the difficult task of translating modern medical and health concepts into the Navajo language. For instance, she translated germs as "bugs that eat the body."

Wauneka believed that prevention was no less important than treatment. Through her efforts in communication,

the people were persuaded to get diagnostic chest X-rays and other medical help from the new hospitals and clinics that the Indian Health Service was building on the reservation, and many lives were saved. Through her efforts, eye, ear, and dental programs were also set up. In the midst of all this—and also while raising a family—Wauneka earned a B.S. degree in public health at the University of Arizona. She later received several honorary degrees, including a doctor of humanities from the University of Albuquerque in 1972 and a doctor of law from her alma mater, the University of Arizona, in 1996.

For her second term on the tribal council, Wauneka ran against her own husband, George Wauneka, and defeated him. In all, she served four two-year terms.

Beginning in 1960, Wauneka had her own Navajo-language health education program every Sunday on radio station KGAK in Gallup, New Mexico. Since large numbers of Navajo could not read or even speak English, while nearly everyone had a RADIO, this was the most effective vehicle for public health education. Wauneka discussed all kinds of medical topics—nutrition, water purification, pregnancy, care of infants and children, childhood immunizations, home cleaning and ventilation, public sanitation, and many more.

Having played a major part in helping to eliminate tuberculosis from the reservation, Wauneka was named to the board of the National Tuberculosis Association (now American Lung Association). She then turned to other health problems. Through her efforts, fatalities from dysentery among the children were also greatly reduced.

Wauneka's work received much national attention. In 1959, she spoke on one of the most popular television news programs, Walter Cronkite's *Twentieth Century*. She was awarded the Presidential Medal of Freedom by President John F. Kennedy in 1963, the first Indian to be so honored. She also held an honorary lifetime membership in the Society for Public Health. Beginning in the 1970s, she worked to fight drug abuse and ALCOHOLISM, which she called "the number one killer on the reservation today."

Annie Dodge Wauneka died on November 10, 1997. She was posthumously inducted into the National Women's Hall of Fame at Seneca Falls, New York, on October 7, 2000.

See also HEALTH, AMERICAN INDIAN.

Further Reading

Niethammer, Carolyn J. *I'll Go and Do More: Annie Dodge Wauneka, Navajo Leader and Activist.* Lincoln: University of Nebraska Press, 2001.

Witt, Shirley Hill. "An Interview with Dr. Annie Dodge Wauneka." *Frontiers: A Journal of Women Studies* 6, no. 3 (1981): 64–67.

Welch, Gustavus (Gus Welch) (1892–1970)
Chippewa football player, coach

Born in Spooner, Wisconsin, Gustavus "Gus" Welch played on the great Carlisle Indian School football teams at the beginning of the 20th century and went on to become an acclaimed football coach. His actual date of birth, although usually given as December 23, 1892, is recorded on his death certificate as December 23, 1890. Welch grew up in the northern Wisconsin woodlands. His father was of Irish descent and a logger, and his mother was a full-blood Chippewa. Welch was orphaned when he was young. His father was killed in a logging accident, and his mother and five of his siblings died of tuberculosis. Welch was quarterback for Carlisle from 1911 to 1914, when the team fielded legendary players JIM THORPE, JOE GUYON, and PETE CALAC. Under Welch, Carlisle won 33 games, lost only three, and tied two more (see WARNER, POP). A versatile athlete, Welch was also a sprinter on the powerful Carlisle track teams that featured Thorpe, Guyon, and LOUIS TEWANIMA. In 1912, illness forced him to withdraw from tryouts for the same 1912 U.S. Olympic team that sent Thorpe, Tewanima, and ANDREW SOCKALEXIS to Stockholm. In 1913, he became a second team All-American in football, finally breaking free of Thorpe's long shadow.

In 1913, Welch led the call by students for an investigation

Chippewa football star Gus Welch became head football coach for the Haskell Institute in 1933. *(AP/Wideworld)*

into the Carlisle academic programs, charging that Indian students had been physically and verbally abused at the school, moneys for student activities were being misappropriated, and teaching standards were lax. The subsequent investigation led to the school's closing four years later.

During 1914, Welch attended Dickinson College, where he also starred in football. The following year, he joined Thorpe on the Canton Bulldogs, a professional football team. In 1916, Welch and Thorpe led a Canton defense so tenacious that it was not only undefeated but not even scored upon the entire year, winning the national title. With the addition of Pete Calac, the Bulldogs repeated as world champions the following year. Welch retired from the Bulldogs after the 1917 season. That same year, he graduated from Dickinson Law School.

When the United States entered WORLD WAR I in April 1917, Welch joined the U.S. Army, doing his military training at the Fort Niagara camp, where he reached the rank of second lieutenant. Later he was transferred to the cavalry at Camp Meade. In June 1918, he was promoted to captain, the first Indian in the cavalry to reach this rank. In 1923, Welch married Julia Carter, the daughter of Chickasaw congressman CHARLES DAVID CARTER.

From 1919 to 1923, Welch was the football coach at Washington State College, the same school where WILLIAM LONE

STAR DIETZ had coached a few years previously. He coached and was director of athletics at Randolph-Macon College from 1930 through 1934, and he coached lacrosse and football at the University of Virginia in 1935 and 1936. In 1937, Welch became athletic director and football coach at American University in Washington, D.C., but he resigned late the following year due to a shortage of players. In 1938, Welch become director of athletics and head football coach at the Haskell Institute in Lawrence, Kansas, before moving on to the Georgetown Prep School and then Georgetown University. He ran a boys camp in Bedford County, Virginia, bought a farm and retired there.

Gus Welch died on Janauary 29, 1970. He was posthumously inducted into the College Football Hall of Fame in 1975. His papers were donated to the McFarlin Library at the University of Tulsa.

Welch, James P., Jr. (1940–2003) *Blackfeet-Gros Ventre (Atsina) novelist, poet*

James P. Welch, Jr., was born on November 18, 1940, in Browning, Montana. His father, James P. Welch, Sr., was a Blackfeet rancher, and his mother, Rosella O'Bryan Welch, was Gros Ventre and worked for the BUREAU OF INDIAN AFFAIRS. After graduating from high school in Minneapolis in 1958, James Welch attended the University of Minnesota and Northern Montana State University before receiving his B.A. from the University of Montana. In 1971, he published a collection of poems *Riding the Earthboy 40*, which featured his signature style of surrealistic imagery wrapped around themes of grief, despair, anger, and hope. In 1974, expanding from his poetry, he published his first novel, *Winter in the Blood*, a bleak, gripping meditation on Indian identity and its estrangement from the modern world. The novel met with critical acclaim, and Welch followed his success with an equally vivid and unsparing depiction of Indian reservation life, *The Death of Jim Lonely*, in 1979.

In 1986, Welch published a historical novel, *Fools Crow*. Based in part on the life of Welch's great-grandmother, the book details the escape of a small band of Blackfeet Indians from the Marias River Massacre of 1870 and the disintegration of their once-pristine existence. That same year, he coedited a nonfiction work, *The Real West Marginal Way*, a biography of his former professor at the University of Montana, poet Richard F. Hugo. In 1990, Welch released his fourth novel, *The Indian Lawyer*, a tale of intrigue in the prisons and court systems of Helena, Montana, where Indians and non-Indians coexist in sharply differing worlds.

In 1994, Welch wrote a nonfiction account of the Battle of Little Bighorn, called *Killing Custer*. His novel *The Heartsong of Charging Elk* (2001) is an anthropological study of Western culture through the eyes of a Sioux Indian left behind on a Wild West tour of Europe organized by Buffalo Bill. Welch's works, which feature an unsentimental, bitterly humorous look at the clash between Native and non-Native cultures, made him one of Native America's most critically acclaimed novelists. James P. Welch, Jr., died on August 4, 2003, in Missoula, Montana, after a long battle with lung cancer.

Further Reading
Lupton, Mary Jane. "Interview with James Welch (1940–2003): November 17, 2001." *American Indian Quarterly* 29, no. 1 (2005): 198–211.
Welch, James. *Fools Crow*. New York: Viking, 1986.
———. *Winter in the Blood*. New York: Harper & Row, 1974.

West, Walter Richard, Sr. (Dick West, Wapah Nahyah, "Lightfoot Runner") (1912–1996)
Cheyenne painter, teacher

A Cheyenne, Walter Richard West was born Wapah Nahyah (Lightfoot Runner) on September 8, 1912, near Darlington, Oklahoma. His father, Lightfoot West, was a marathon runner, and his mother was Rena Flying Coyote. Young West attended the Concho Indian School in El Reno, Oklahoma, and the Haskell Institute in Lawrence, Kansas, graduating in 1935. He went to Bacone College in Muskogee, Oklahoma, and from there transferred to the University of Oklahoma, where he received his B.A. in 1941. West became an art instructor at the Phoenix Art School, but his career was interrupted by WORLD WAR II. After serving four years in the U.S. Navy, he returned to the Phoenix Art School for one year before becoming chairman of the art department at Bacone in 1947, a position he would hold until 1970. His first illustrated book, *The Thankful People*, was published in 1950.

Though he began painting in a traditional "Indian school" style, West also worked in many contemporary styles, such as abstract; and in many media, including wood and metal. West felt that "the Indian artist must be allowed to absorb influences outside of his own art forms and develop them in his own manner." His work was featured in the Denver Art Museum, and his paintings and sculptures exhibited internationally. His return to Haskell in 1970 as director of the art department allowed him to pursue his philosophy of preserving Indian culture through art and artistic expression. In 1987, he illustrated *The Wolves of Heaven*, one of more than 33 books in which his art has appeared. Popular magazines such as *National Geographic* (1955), *Life* (1959), and the *Saturday Review* (1963) also published his work.

Dick West died of cancer on May 3, 1996, at his home in Tijeras, New Mexico. His son, W. Richard West, is a noted attorney and was the director of the National Museum of the American Indian in Washington, D.C.

Further Reading
Anthes, Bill. *Native Moderns: American Indian Painting, 1940–1960*. Durham, N.C.: Duke University Press, 2006.

Westerman, Floyd Red Crow (Kanghi Duta) (1936–2007) *Dakota Sioux singer, songwriter, actor*

Known for his politically charged folk songs and in his later years a successful actor, Floyd Westerman was born on August 17, 1936, on the Sisseton-Wahpeton Reservation in northeastern South Dakota. He was given the name Kanghi

Floyd Westerman accepts the Silver Bear Award on behalf of the actor and director Kevin Costner for their work on the movie *Dances With Wolves* at the Berlin Film Festival in February 26, 1991. *(AP/Wideworld)*

Duta (Red Crow). Orphaned at age 10, he was sent to the Wahpeton Boarding School, where he met Chippewa DENNIS BANKS. He later attended high school on the Flandreau Sioux Reservation in South Dakota, graduating in 1955. Westerman then served in the marines for two years. He attended Northern State College (later University) in South Dakota, receiving a degree in secondary education.

Westerman began his musical career in Denver, Colorado, and signed a record contract in New York City in 1969. His first album, *Custer Died for Your Sins*, appeared in 1970, shortly after the release of VINE DELORIA, JR.'s book of the same name (1969). The album included stinging songs such as "Missionaries," "BIA," "Here Come the Anthros," and "They Didn't Listen," about the destruction of the environment, with Westerman's resonant bass-baritone featured in simple country-folk style arrangements.

Westerman's second album, *This Land Is Your Mother* (1982) continued where *Custer Died for Your Sins* left off. The album contained some of Westerman's best-known songs, including "Wounded Knee" and "How Long Have You Been Blind." While never a household name, Westerman became a favorite with other musicians, performing in concerts with

Jackson Browne, Bonnie Raitt, Willie Nelson, Joni Mitchell, and Kris Kristofferson and opening for pop superstar Sting on his worldwide tour in support of the Amazon rain forest. A strong supporter of the AMERICAN INDIAN MOVEMENT (AIM) and its successor, the INTERNATIONAL INDIAN TREATY COUNCIL, Westerman organized hundreds of benefits around Indian issues worldwide. His many trips to the United Nations in Geneva have helped bring the AIM perspective to national governments and indigenous leaders alike.

In 1989, Westerman appeared in the film *Renegade*, and the same year he provided the voice of a Cheyenne prophet in the landmark film *Pow Wow Highway*. His role as Ten Bears in the film *Dances with Wolves* (1990) won him critical acclaim and international recognition. Westerman continued his busy acting schedule, playing alongside Chuck Norris in the television show *Walker, Texas Ranger* and appearing in films such as the *The Doors* (1991), *Clearcut* (1991), *Lakota Woman* (1994), *Grey Owl* (1999), and *The Tillamook Treasure* (2006). He also appeared in several television series, including *The X Files* (1995–99).

Floyd Red Crow Westerman died of leukemia on December 13, 2007. In January 2008, the TV miniseries *Comanche Moon* was aired, with Westerman in his last appearance on film.

Further Reading

"An Appreciation of Floyd Westerman." *Indian Country Today*, 27 April 2005.

Figueroa, Ana. "A Hollywood Studio with a Heart?" *Newsweek* 128 (September 2000): 60.

Wheat, Zack (Zachariah Davis Wheat) (1888–1972)
Cherokee baseball player

Zachariah "Zack" Davis Wheat was born on May 23, 1888, near Hamilton, Missouri, the eldest of three sons of Basil Curtis Wheat, Sr., a farmer and descendant of Moses Wheat, a Puritan from England who founded Concord, Massachusetts, in 1653. Zack Wheat's mother, Julia Dee (Scott) was a full-blood Cherokee. When Zack was 16, Basil Wheat died, and the family moved to Kansas City. In order to support them, Wheat began playing semipro baseball, at first with the Kansas City Union Club. In 1906, he joined the Enterprise, Kansas, semipro team, where he earned $60 per month, a decent wage for those days. The next year, Wheat played in Wichita, and in 1908 he jumped to the Shreveport Pirates of the Texas League. In 1909, he played for the Mobile Sea Gulls of the Southern Association. While Wheat was playing for Mobile, a scout for the Brooklyn Superbas (later the Dodgers) of the National League saw him, and on August 29, 1909, the team purchased Wheat's contract for $1,200, a handsome sum at the time.

Wheat made his major league debut as a left fielder with the Superbas on September 11, 1909, playing in 26 games that year and batting .304. A Brooklyn paper wrote of Wheat that, "He is an Indian . . . and a quiet and refined gentleman." Known for his grace as an outfielder, *Baseball Magazine* once called him "the finest mechanical craftsman of them all." Wheat also developed into one of the most dreaded hitters in the National League. In a period known as the "Deadball era," when bunting and hitting for singles was the norm, Wheat changed the way the game was played. As he explained, rather than bunting and trying to beat the ball out, "I adopted an altogether different style of hitting. I stood flatfooted at the plate and slugged." Wheat, although he threw the ball right-handed, batted left-handed, which, in baseball, gives a batter numerous advantages.

In 1910, Wheat's first full season, he led Brooklyn with a .284 average, garnering 172 hits, 36 doubles, and 15 triples. Over the next six years, he was consistently among the league leaders in batting average, home runs, triples, doubles, and runs batted in. In 1912, he married Daisy Kerr Foreman, who became his agent and successfully encouraged him to hold out for more money, so that by 1926 he was making $16,000 per year. Wheat's younger brother, Mack Wheat (1893–1979), joined Brooklyn as an outfielder and catcher in 1915, and the two brothers played together until 1920, when Mack was traded to Philadelphia.

In 1916, Zack Wheat batted .312, leading the league in total bases and slugging average and helping Brooklyn win the pennant. In the World Series, they were defeated by a powerful Boston Red Sox team that featured a pitching rotation that included Ernie Shore, Dutch Leonard, Carl Mays, and Babe Ruth. The next year, Wheat led the league in batting with a .335 average, but his style of hitting was still ahead of its time. In 1919, baseball adopted a new, livelier ball that complemented sluggers like Wheat. Wheat batted .328 in 1920, leading Brooklyn to the pennant, but they lost again in the World Series, this time to the Cleveland Indians. He hit .320 in 1921 and .335 in 1922. In 1923, he batted .375, finishing second to the great Rogers Hornsby, but he was out with injury much of the year. The next year, Wheat led the league in hits with 149. He also batted .375 for the second consecutive year but again finished second to Hornsby, who set the modern major league record for highest batting average, .424, a mark that still stands. In 1925, at the ripe age of 37, Wheat hit .359, finishing third.

Wheat played baseball at a time when Indians such as CHARLES ALBERT BENDER, JOHN TORTES MEYERS, and JIM THORPE were among its biggest stars. Considered the finest and most graceful outfielder in the league during his prime, Wheat was thought to owe his prowess as a hitter and fielder to his Indian heritage. *Baseball Magazine* wrote in 1917 that, "The lithe muscles, the panther-like motions of the Indian are his by divine right."

In 1926, Wheat, then 38 years old, batted .290, and Brooklyn released him. He then signed with the Philadelphia Athletics, where in 1927, his last year in the majors, he hit .324 in part-time duties. He played one more year of minor league ball before retiring. Wheat finished with a career batting average of .317. His 2,884 hits and his 4,100 total bases were among the top 10 totals at the time he finished playing. After his career in baseball was over, Wheat retired to his farm in Polo, Missouri. When the Great Depression came, he was forced to sell it. He moved to Kansas City, where he opened a bowling alley. Later he became a police officer. While chasing a suspect in 1936, his police car crashed and he suffered nearly fatal injuries. After spending five months in the hospital, he resigned from the force and moved to Sunrise Beach, Missouri, where he opened a hunting and fishing resort.

Wheat was unanimously inducted into the Baseball Hall of Fame in 1959, only the second Indian, after Albert Bender, to be so honored. Zack Wheat died of a heart attack on March 11, 1972, at a hospital in Sedalia, Missouri.

In 1981, Lawrence Ritter and Donald Honig included him in their book *The 100 Greatest Baseball Players of All Time*. In 2006, the stretch of Route 13 that runs through Caldwell County, Missouri, was named the Zack Wheat Memorial Highway. As of 2015, Wheat remained the Dodgers' all-time franchise leader in games played, plate appearances, at bats, hits, singles, doubles, triples, total bases, and runs created. He was second in runs scored and extra-base hits and third in runs batted in.

Further Reading

Enders, Eric. "Zack Wheat." In *Deadball Stars of the National League*, edited by Tom Simon, 287–290. Dulles, Va.: Brassey's, 2004.

Wheelock, Dennison (1871–1927) *Oneida musician, attorney*

Dennison Wheelock, the son of James and Sophie Charles Wheelock, was born on June 14, 1871, at the Wheelock homestead on the Oneida reservation nine miles west of De Pere, Wisconsin. He attended the Methodist Episcopal mission school until the age of 12, and in 1883 he went with his brothers James and Charles to the Carlisle Indian School in Pennsylvania, where he distinguished himself as a cornet soloist in the band and one of the school's most talented musicians. While still a student, he also served the government as the school's financial clerk, traveling the country in that capacity.

After graduating from Carlisle in 1890, Wheelock stayed on at the school, organizing and directing the Carlisle Indian Band, a 70-piece ensemble representing 48 tribes. For several years, this was his full-time job. The band had a long engagement at the Chicago World's Fair in 1893, played at the Pan-American Exposition in Buffalo in 1901, and subsequently toured all the major cities of the United States.

For a few years at the end of the 19th century, Wheelock ran his father's farm. In 1904, he presented his farewell concert at Willow Grove Park, Philadelphia, where he was given a gold medal and a loving cup. He declined an offer to take the leadership of the U.S. Marine Corps Band.

After ending his connection with Carlisle in 1907, Wheelock began studying law in Baltimore in the offices of John R. Miller. After passing the bar, he set up practice in De Pere. In 1911, he was admitted to practice before the Wisconsin Supreme Court and in 1919 before the U.S. Supreme Court. He later moved his practice to Green Bay, but he continued living in De Pere. Wheelock served as attorney for many tribes, appearing before the Indian Office, the Supreme Court, and the Court of Claims, pursuing claims worth millions and recovering great sums for his clients. In December 1923, Wheelock served on the COMMITTEE OF ONE HUNDRED.

For the last four years of his life, Wheelock was attorney for many tribes with claims against the federal government and the state of New York. Not long before his death, he acted as attorney in the claim of a tribe of Indians from which Peter Minuit purchased Manhattan Island for $24, demanding a more just compensation from New York State.

Dennison Wheelock died suddenly in Washington, D.C., on March 10, 1927, and was buried in Woodlawn Cemetery, Green Bay, Wisconsin. Besides two children and his wife, he was survived by his brother, James Riley Wheelock, head of the Wheelock Indian Band, which played at the Philadelphia sesquicentennial.

Further Reading

Hauptman, Laurence M. "From Carlisle to Carnegie Hall: The Musical Career of Dennison Wheelock." In *The Oneida Indians in the Age of Allotment, 1860–1920*, edited by Laurence M. Hauptman and L. Gordon McLester, 112–138. Norman: University of Oklahoma Press, 2006.
Troutman, John William. "'Indian Blues': American Indians and the Politics of Music, 1890–1935." Ph.D. dissertation, University of Texas at Austin, 2004.

Whistler, Don (Kishkekosh, "Cloven Hoof") (1894–1951) *Sac and Fox tribal chief, radio broadcaster, ethnologist*

Don Whistler was born on December 9, 1894, at the Sac and Fox Agency, Indian Territory (now Oklahoma), in the first house ever built there. He was the son of Leo and Maude Marie Mayes Whistler and the great-grandson of Captain John Whistler, builder of Fort Dearborn. His Indian name Kishkekosh (Cloven Hoof) was that of a famous warrior, and among his ancestors were both Black Hawk and Keokuk.

Whistler's father was treasurer of the Sac and Fox Nation in the 1880s. He prepared tribal rolls for the federal government entirely from memory, supplying names of parents and grandparents in every case. Don Whistler attended a Quaker mission school. After his parents were divorced in the early 1900s, his mother moved to Norman, Oklahoma, so the children could get a better education. Whistler attended the School of Engineering at the University of Oklahoma, but he interrupted his studies to serve in WORLD WAR I. During the war, his mother opened a boarding house, which later became the Teepee Restaurant. She also built and ran the famous old "Campus Corner" at Boyd and Asp Streets, a university landmark, until she had to sell the business in the late 1930s.

After the war, Whistler returned to the university, where he took up journalism. He spent most of his time, however, researching the history of the Sac and Fox and collecting Indian artifacts, many of them purchased in Arizona and Mexico in the 1920s and 1930s. Wishing to become an anthropologist, inspired no doubt by the example of Fox ethnologist WILLIAM JONES, Whistler applied to the University of Pennsylvania. Rather than accepting a stipend, he took a job in the American Indian division of the university museum, beginning in late October 1924. He prepared exhibits, gave educational tours to children, and lectured outside. Although he was not matriculated at the university, he probably attended some lectures. He and Mary Alice York (Kitinsi), a Choctaw student, performed stories of Indian life, legends, songs, and dances.

After less than a year at the museum, Whistler took a leave of absence to go home and build some houses for his mother. Shortly after arriving home, he and Kitinsi were married. His stay in Norman was prolonged by his mother's business difficulties in the Great Depression, which kept him from ever returning to the university.

In his spare time, Whistler studied writing and worked as a freelance writer. About 1942, he started a RADIO program, *Indians for Indians*, broadcast over KNOR and later WNAD in Norman; it ran through the early 1970s. Transcriptions from this program comprised probably the largest collection of Indian music in Oklahoma, but according to Whistler's son William, most of the material was later lost through the gradual deterioration of the magnetic wire on which it was recorded. Fortunately, some of the old shows had been pressed onto 78-rpm discs, and the later ones were recorded on reel-to-reel tape. A collection of over 100 hours of Native American music is preserved in the Western History Collections of the University of Oklahoma; 121 discs (programs from August 1943 to October 1950) are in the Archive of Folk Culture, American Folklife Center, Washington, D.C.

Whistler was elected principal chief of the Sac and Fox in August 1939 and reelected annually many times thereafter, serving until his death on June 21, 1951. His brother Rex Whistler (1903–71) was principal chief from 1957 to 1963.

Whistler's collection of artifacts was destroyed or badly damaged by a fire at his mother's house in Norman in 1976. Almost everything salvageable was donated to the Stovall Museum (now the Oklahoma Museum of Anthropology) in Norman. His son, William Judson Whistler of Vinita, who was a judge in the 12th judicial district of Oklahoma (Mayes, Craig, and Rogers Counties) for 18 years, kept a few rugs, pots, and baskets.

Further Reading
Murg, William. "Preserving Oklahoma's Ancestral Voices." *Indian Country Today*, 23 July 2003.

White Calf, James (Running Wolf, Last Gun White Calf) (ca. 1863–1969) *Piegan Blackfeet chief*

The son of Last Gun White Calf (Onistaipokah), chief of the Skunk Band of Piegan Blackfeet and later head chief of the Piegan, and Black Snake Woman, his second wife, James White Calf was said to have been born at a camp on the Milk (Teton) River in what is now Montana on May 10, 1857. However, his death certificate lists his date of birth as July 2, 1863, and the Blackfeet tribal rolls list his birth year as 1865. The tribal rolls also list James White Calf as the eldest of four children, a brother, Jimmy White Calf, and two sisters, Diving Around Behind and Hides Behind Blanket. In addition, he appears to have had two half brothers, Wolf Tail and Two Guns, and a half sister, Blanche Stealing Inside, from his father's first wife, Caught One Another, as well as other siblings from his father's other wives, False Piegan, Two Catcher or Double, and Holds Them Together. The exact number and relationship between his siblings are not clear, as White Calf's father is believed to have had as many as six wives and 19 children. White Calf attended Fort Shaw Indian School for a brief period as an adult, but he never learned enough English to function without an interpreter. His baptism, along with seven of his brothers and sisters, by the Jesuit missionary C. Imoda near Two Medicine River is recorded as December 31, 1875. He took Running Wolf, his uncle's name, as his Indian name.

As a young man, White Calf participated in 14 war parties, beginning around the age of 14, including one in 1877 that captured Hunkpapa Lakota Sioux holy man Sitting Bull and another led by the most famous of all Blackfoot horse raiders, White Quiver. Another of his raids, in spring 1889, may have been the last recorded Plains Indian war party to take a scalp. In 1899, he married Kit Fox Woman in a Christian ceremony, and by 1900 he had built a house near Starr School in

Montana. Their first child, a daughter, died in 1901. They had a son, James White Calf, Jr., in 1915.

After his father died in Washington, D.C., in 1903, James White Calf became the Piegan chief. Although he was not the eldest son, his father had named him, in a document of October 19, 1897, as most suitable to succeed him. Despite this, he was involved in a rivalry with Three Suns over the chieftainship.

White Calf served as captain of the Indian police on the Blackfeet reservation, an office appropriate to his tribal position as head of the warrior society of the Crazy Dogs, which traditionally performed police functions. Conflicts between northern and southern divisions of the reservation and between full-bloods and mixed-bloods also preoccupied him; he was especially concerned to protect the rights of the full-bloods. He participated in the Sign Language Council in Browning, Montana, in 1930, organized by Blackfeet interpreter RICHARD SANDERVILLE, and his footprints are preserved in cement at the Museum of the Plains Indians in Browning along with those of the other participants.

The INDIAN REORGANIZATION ACT of 1934 took away White Calf's authority as chief, replacing him with a tribal council controlled largely by the progressives and mixed-bloods, but he still attended council meetings and retained his ceremonial and personal authority. He came into conflict with the council over its leasing of Indian lands to non-Indian ranchers; White Calf wanted more land to be made available to Indian cattlemen. He also became an unflagging critic of corruption on the part of certain council members. His outspokenness at one point may have provoked an opponent to shoot at his house.

In 1935, White Calf traveled to Washington, D.C., to demand full payment of Blackfeet claims against the government. He met with Indian Commissioner JOHN COLLIER and succeeded in obtaining a check representing the claim in question, diminished from $6 million to $600,000 by deductions for "gratuities," assorted government fees, and expenditures.

As hereditary chief, White Calf continued to engage in frequent correspondence and discussions with local and national politicians and officials and was active in the selection of tribal representatives to attend meetings. He was still regularly attending and speaking at Tribal Council meetings in 1962, when he was somewhere around 100 years old. He adopted the linguist and writer Richard Lancaster as his son while the latter was a graduate student at the University of Texas; Lancaster wrote at length of his visits and conversations with White Calf in *Piegan* (1966). James White Calf died in August 1969.

Further Reading
Lancaster, Richard. *Piegan: A Look from within at the Life, Times and Legacy of an American Indian Tribe.* Garden City N.Y.: Doubleday, 1966.

White Calf, John (Two Guns White Calf)
(1872–1934) *Blackfeet orator, statesman*
Born in 1872 in Canada, John White Calf was the son of Many

Chief and Red Otter Woman, both Northern Blackfoot. (In the United States, the Blackfoot are officially known as the Blackfeet.) Two Catcher, the third wife of Last Gun White Calf (Onistaipokah), chief of the Skunk Band and later head chief of the Piegan Blackfeet, adopted him as a baby when her own baby died, naming him Two Guns. His adoptive brother was JAMES WHITE CALF.

A superb orator, highly respected in his own community, Two Guns White Calf enjoyed much wider publicity during the 1910s and 1920s. This was due to two factors: his striking features and his association with railroad entrepreneur James Jerome Hill and his son Louis Warren Hill, who became president of the Great Northern Railroad in 1907 and whom Two Guns first met about 1913 at the newly opened Glacier Park Lodge in Montana. Including Blackfeet hunting grounds, Glacier National Park was created by act of Congress in 1910, largely at the urging of the Great Northern. Louis Hill was interested in attracting tourists and vacationers to the park, a business in which he held a near-monopoly in both transportation and facilities. Hill hired Two Guns to promote the park, thus helping to make it known throughout America.

Around 1913, Hill brought Two Guns east on a publicity tour. According to James White Calf, Hill told Two Guns to say that the face on the newly issued Indian-head nickel was his. This was taken as fact by many, especially in and around Browning, Montana, who bought and sold photographs of him.

However, in a letter dated 1931, James Earle Fraser, the designer of the coin, stated, "I have never seen Two Guns Whitecalf (*sic*), nor used him in any way, although he has a magnificent head. I can easily understand how he was mistaken in thinking that he posed for me. A great many artists have modeled and drawn from him, and it was only natural for him to believe that one of them was the designer of the nickel. I think he is undoubtedly honestly of the opinion that his portrait is on the nickel."

According to a granddaughter of Two Guns's wife, interviewed in the 1960s, Two Guns was aware that the Indian on the nickel was a composite of several heads, but he believed that one of the photographs used by Fraser, ostensibly that of Two Moons (a Cheyenne chief who died on April 28, 1917) had been mislabeled and that it was actually a photograph of himself. While there is no proof of this, the image on the nickel does not look like Two Moons at all, but does resemble both Iron Tail and Two Guns. There is also a resemblance to another claimant, JOHN BIG TREE.

In 1913, Geoffrey O'Hara, music instructor with the Office of Indian Affairs, came to the Blackfeet reservation and made some sound recordings of Two Guns and several other tribesmen singing traditional Blackfeet songs, some of which were commercially released on the Victor label. Two Guns is also thought by some to be the first American Indian to speak on RADIO, as well as the first Indian to fly in an airplane. On a tour east in June 1914, Two Guns was camped with his Blackfeet contingent on the roof of the 25-story McAlpine Hotel in New York. The Thomas hydroplane company wanted some publicity for a new flying boat. Having won a contest

John White Calf, 1921. *(Library of Congress)*

with Chief Lazy Boy of the Indian police, Two Guns was invited to go up for a spin. The entire group of Blackfeet went with him to Dobbs Ferry, New York, and watched as the plane rose into the sky and flew around. In its descent, however, an air pocket caused interference, and the plane dropped the last 150 feet rapidly and fell into the Hudson River with a great splash. The pilot, Ralph M. Brown, was visibly shaken, but Two Guns, though soaked, was serene, unaware that this was not the normal way to come down.

He made another trip to Boston and New York in April–May 1921, to promote the film *Bob Hampton of Placer*, in which he played Chief Sitting Bull (see FILM, AMERICAN INDIANS AND).

For many years, Two Guns spent his summers greeting tourists at the entrance to the hotel in Glacier Park, and nearly every winter for the last 20 years of his life he toured with an entourage of Blackfeet performers. In 1927, he toured the East Coast with "Indian Princess Dawn Mist"—actually a Blackfeet woman named Irene Goss Mendenhall—appearing with her at an exposition in Baltimore sponsored by the Great Northern. Billed as "The Indian on the Nickel," Two Guns was given a tour of the U.S. Mint, received by President Calvin Coolidge, and given a large replica of the Indian Head nickel, which he wore as a pendant for the rest of his life. Because of his touring, he was the most famous Indian of his time, and because of his perceived "ideal Indian" looks, the most widely drawn, painted, and photographed.

Two Guns was more than just a symbol, however. He was an important Blackfeet leader. He was involved in the negotiations that resulted in the transfer to the government of the land that was to become Glacier National Park. To the day of his death, the government had not paid a balance of $1.5 million due the Blackfeet, and Two Guns spoke out about this at every opportunity. An accomplished orator, he usually spoke in the Blackfeet (Piegan) language and used an interpreter, as he knew little English. He was an exceptionally skilled practitioner of Indian sign language. General Hugh L. Scott, who had a reputation as the best non-Indian sign talker, stated that Two Guns was the most rapid signer he had encountered.

Two Guns White Calf died at the Blackfeet Hospital on March 11, 1934, of influenza following a long bout with pneumonia. He was buried in a Methodist burial ground on the southwest edge of Browning, Montana. The exact location of the grave is lost to history, as all trace had disappeared by the mid-1960s.

Further Reading

Hungry-Wolf, Adolf. *The Blackfoot Papers—Volume Four: Pikunni Biographies.* Browning, Mont.: Good Medicine Foundation, 2008.
Van Ryzin, Robert R. *Twisted Tails: Sifted Fact, Fantasy, and Fiction from U.S. Coin History.* Iola, Wis.: Krause Publications, 1995.

White Earth Reservation *See* BEAULIEU, GUS H.; LADUKE, WINONA; MOOREHEAD, WARREN KING.

Wilkinson, Gerald (1939–1989) *Cherokee-Catawba activist*

Gerald Wilkinson was born on February 9, 1939, in Statesville, North Carolina, to Virginia and Harold Curtis Wilkinson. He grew up in Greer, North Carolina, then returned to Statesville to attend the local high school. Playing football on the high school team, he injured his eye, eventually losing it. He attended Duke University on a scholarship and graduated in 1961 with a B.A. in history. He then attended Columbia University Law School and the University of Limoges in France.

In 1968, Wilkinson became the youth coordinator for Oklahomans for Indian Opportunity, an organization founded by LADONNA HARRIS. The next year he succeeded HERBERT BLATCHFORD as executive director of the NATIONAL INDIAN YOUTH COUNCIL (NIYC). Under Wilkinson's direction, the NIYC undertook a number of important causes, including attempting to prevent the Army Corps of Engineers from placing dams on the Arkansas River and aiding Indian voter registration in the Southwest. Wilkinson's work on voter registration influenced and inspired Hispanic political leader Willie

Velasquez, who formed the Southwest Voter Registration and Education Project in 1974. Wilkinson helped to stabilize the NIYC's funding and contributed regularly to its publication *Americans Before Columbus.* A writer on international Indian issues, Wilkinson was part of a special delegation invited in 1985 by then-president of Colombia Belisario Betancourt as an observer at negotiations between the Miskito Indians and the Nicaraguan government held in Bogotá. He also served as adviser on Indian issues to Massachusetts governor Michael Dukakis in his unsuccessful bid for the presidency in 1988. Wilkinson died of a heart attack in Washington, D.C., on April 27, 1989.

Further Reading

Philp, Kenneth R. *Indian Self-Rule.* Salt Lake City, Utah: Howe Brothers, 1986.
Wilkinson, Gerald. "Colonialism through the Media." *Indian Historian* 7, no. 3 (1974): 29.

Williams, Robert A. (1955–) *Lumbee legal scholar, historian*

Robert A. Williams was born on March 11, 1955, in Baltimore, Maryland, to Robert Anthony Williams, Sr., and Sallie Williams. He received his B.A. in 1977 from Loyola College, Baltimore, and his J.D. in 1980 from Harvard Law School, after which he taught at Boston College and the Camden, New Jersey, campus of Rutgers University.

In 1980, Williams was appointed assistant professor of law at the University of Wisconsin, Madison. Presently he is the E. Thomas Sullivan Professor of Law and American Indian Studies in the College of Law, University of Arizona. In 2002, he was a visiting professor at Harvard Law School. His important book, *The American Indian in Western Legal Thought: The Discourses of Conquest,* published in 1990, traces the derivation of fundamental concepts of federal Indian law from the English and wider European legal traditions. It received the Gustavus Meyers Human Rights Center Award as one of the outstanding books published in 1990 on the subject of prejudice in the United States. Another book, *Linking Arms Together: American Indian Treaty Visions of Law and Peace, 1600–1800,* was published in 1997.

Williams is coauthor, with Charles Wilkinson and David Getches, of *Federal Indian Law: Cases and Materials.* In addition, he has published more than 30 articles, book reviews, and other works on American Indian rights and indigenous peoples' rights under international law. In 2005, he published *Like a Loaded Weapon: The Rehnquist Court, Indian Rights and the Legal History of Racism in America.*

As an attorney, Williams represents Indian tribes and other indigenous peoples in various parts of the world, including the O'odham Nation of Mexico, the Native Hawaiian Advisory Council, and the Sawridge Band of Cree in Alberta, Canada. He also serves as chief justice in the court of appeals of the Pascua Yaqui Indian Tribe and judge pro tempore for the Tohono O'odham (Papago) Indian Nation.

Williams, Scott T. (Chief Thunder Cloud, Scott Thundercloud) (1898–1967) *Ottawa entertainer, community organizer*

An Ottawa (Odawa), Scott Williams was born in Cedar, Michigan, on December 20, 1898, near what is now the reservation of the Grand Traverse Band of Ottawa and Chippewa Indians. His father was an Ottawa of mixed blood, his mother a full-blood Ottawa. Williams grew up in Lansing, Michigan, but spent most of his later life in Chicago. In April 1917, when the United States entered WORLD WAR I and noncitizen Indians were still exempt from the draft, Williams enlisted in the U.S. Army. He later claimed to have been the first Indian to enlist. On January 14, 1920, he appears in the federal census as a patient in the Army General Hospital at Carlisle, Pennsylvania, holding the rank of mechanic. By 1930, married and the father of a four-month-old daughter, he was working as a house painter in Chicago.

Williams claimed to have first conceived the character of Tonto, "faithful Indian companion" of the Lone Ranger, the hero of a famous radio program. According to the announcement that introduced every episode, the Lone Ranger was a mysterious masked man who rode the plains on his fiery horse Silver and "led the fight for law and order in the early West." As first revealed to the listening audience in a 1938 episode on his origins, the Lone Ranger was "in reality" a former Texas Ranger named John Reid, but in the stories his identity is known only to Tonto and faithfully kept secret. The series premiered on January 30, 1933, as a local broadcast three times a week over WXYZ, Detroit, Michigan. Picked up the following year by the Mutual Broadcasting System, it would be nationally syndicated for the next 22 years. Through radio, television, films, and comic books, the Lone Ranger would become one of the most popular fictional characters in America. In the classic television show, which ran from 1949 until 1957, Mohawk actor JAY SILVERHEELS earned lasting fame for his portrayal of Tonto.

According to Williams's obituary, published in the *Chicago Tribune*, February 1, 1967, "his widow Anna said her husband conceived the role . . . and played [it] from 1936 to 1939." But Williams never played Tonto on the radio. That he had a part in the creation of the character, however, is possible. Evidence suggests that he may well have known the program's director, Jim Jewell, and it was Jewell who persuaded scriptwriter Fran Striker to add an Indian sidekick for the Lone Ranger and who introduced the term *Kemosabe*.

For the first 10 Lone Ranger radio episodes, there was no Tonto. But in a letter of February 15, 1933, Jewell suggested to scriptwriter Fran Striker that the Lone Ranger needed a sidekick to help develop dialogue and that the sidekick could be an Indian. Tonto duly appeared for the first time in the broadcast of February 25. Radio historian Jim Harmon states that "the part of Tonto was played from first to last by John Todd," a non-Indian. Fred Foy, the show's announcer, confirms that Todd, an aging Shakespearian actor, was the first Tonto, although at one point, "The role was briefly portrayed by [an] Indian actor . . . but Todd returned . . . when the

college-educated Native American refused to speak Tonto's broken English dialect." Foy identifies this Native American actor as Louis Morango (Pima/Chippewa)—not Williams.

Tonto always addressed the Lone Ranger as Kemo Sabay (as it was spelled in the early scripts—later, Kemosabe). Evidently intended to represent some American Indian language, its meaning was never explained, a fact that has given rise to numerous jokes; but clearly it was intended as a term of respect, and in the earliest episodes both characters addressed each other as Kemo Sabay. Tonto continued to address the Lone Ranger as Kemosabe through all the films, books, comic books, and the television series.

It was Jim Jewell who suggested the term to scriptwriter Fran Striker. As Jewell explained to radio historian David Rothel, his father-in-law Charles Yeager, athletic director at the Detroit University School (now University Liggett School), ran a summer camp and "school of woodcraft" (see SETON, ERNEST THOMPSON) called Kamp Kee-Mo Sah-Bee at Mullet Lake, Michigan, just south of Mackinac, from 1911 through 1940 or 1941. Jewell understood the name to mean "trusty scout."

It is not known for sure where Yeager got this name. Over the years, a number of linguists specializing in American Indian languages tried to figure out what language—if any—Kemo Sabay comes from, which would at the same time reveal its meaning and Tonto's tribe. The answer was discovered independently by linguists Robert Malouf and Richard Rhodes, who suggested that it came from Ojibwe or a closely related language. The word *giimoozaabi* means "he looks in secret" in the Odawa (Ottawa) dialect of Ojibwe—by extension, "spy or scout." Tonto had been identified as a Potawatomi in the early radio series, books, and comics, though this detail later fell away. Potawatomi and Odawa are very closely related dialects, and according to Potawatomi specialist Laura Buszard-Welcher the Potawatomi word for *giimoozaabi* is virtually the same; Rhodes says that in the Potawatomi orthography it is spelled *gimozabe*.

Jewell told Rothel that a number of Indians were employed at Kamp Kee-Mo Sah-Bee. One of these was a "Chief Thundercloud" from Cross Village, about 30 miles west of Mullett Lake, who was brought in to tell "tall stories" to the children: "For example, he would come over and tell them how he'd dug the straits of Mackinaw with nothing but a wooden spoon." According to Jewell, Thundercloud's friends called him *tonto* (Spanish for "foolish" or "wild") when he drank too much; Jewell liked the sound of the word and chose it as the name of his new character. Yet all other sources credit the name to Striker, who is said to have found it on a map of Arizona; and surely it is no coincidence that famous Western writer Zane Grey owned a cabin (now a museum) near the Tonto National Forest and that among his celebrated novels are *Under the Tonto Rim*, *Gun Trouble in Tonto Basin*, and *Stranger from the Tonto*, with Tonto Canyon and Tonto Creek also mentioned in his writings. It seems no less odd that Indians in northern Michigan would use a Spanish epithet or that Jewell would choose a name he himself associated with drunkenness, however much he liked the sound, for the Ranger's sober, ever-resourceful companion. In short, the story seems far-fetched, gratuitously designed to disparage the Indian storyteller and to bring Jewell more credit for the origin of Tonto. All this would make sense if Chief Thundercloud from Cross Village and Williams—whose professional name was indeed Chief Thunder Cloud—were the same person, since Jewell must have known that Williams claimed the credit. Thus, in a backhanded way, Jewell's odd story seems to corroborate Williams's claim to have first conceived the Lone Ranger's Indian companion.

Cross Village is situated on tribal lands (federally recognized in 1994) of the Little Traverse Bands of Odawa Indians. Williams's birthplace was only 100 miles away, and though he resided mainly in Chicago, it is entirely plausible that Williams would spend summers in his home territory. As for Chief Thundercloud from Cross Village being Potawatomi rather than Ottawa, the two groups are closely related and intermarried, and Jewell could easily have been mistaken.

Little is definitely known about Williams's performing career. According to his obituary, he played in vaudeville, rodeos, and Indian productions. During the early 1960s, he used to headline the "Indian show" at the Deer Haven amusement park at Fox Lake, Illinois, about 50 miles northwest of Chicago. That he was an expert teller of "tall tales" can be seen in a humorous interview with him in the *Chicago Tribune*, July 19, 1962, which consists almost entirely of such tales.

Although Williams's obituary claims that he played in many Hollywood Westerns, this is highly doubtful. No evidence has come to light that Williams spent any time in Hollywood, and it is known that at least two of his children were born in Chicago during the period when he was supposedly making films—daughters Violet (1930) and Charlotte (1940)—and that he met his second wife there in the 1930s. Williams is often confused with film actor VICTOR DANIELS, an almost exact contemporary who also used the stage name "Chief Thundercloud" and actually did play Tonto—not on the radio, however, but in a 1938 film serial. Thus many, perhaps all, of the film credits attributed to Williams actually belong to Daniels.

Williams was active in the American Indian community in Chicago, where he was known as Scott or Scottie Thundercloud. In 1946, along with other Chicago Indians, including Willard LaMere (Winnebago) and Benjamin Bearskin (Winnebago/Sioux), Williams founded the North American Indian Council (later the North American Indian Mission) to help host POWWOWS, dances, and other events for the Native community. The new group offered traditional Indians an alternative to the dominant Indian organization in Chicago, the Indian Council Fire (begun in 1923 as the Grand Council Fire of American Indians), which was a proponent of ASSIMILATION. Williams's organizing would eventually result in the creation of Chicago's All Tribes American Indian Center in 1953 (see SEGUNDO, THOMAS).

Williams was married twice. His first wife was named Violet; his second, the former Anna Lapthorne, had been his archery student in Chicago in the 1930s. In her obituary, which appeared in the Chicago *Sun-Times* of April 13, 2003, it stated that "she joined him in many live productions presenting Native American culture, and until his death in 1967 helped make Indian regalia."

Scott T. Williams died January 31, 1967, at Veteran's Research Hospital, Chicago.

Further Reading

Anderson, Loraine. "Woman Retraces Father's Steps to Indian Marker Trees." *Traverse City* (Mich.) *Record-Eagle*, 22 May 2013.

Arndt, Grant. "'Contrary to Our Way of Thinking': The Struggle for an American Indian Center in Chicago, 1946–1953." *American Indian Culture and Research Journal* 22, no. 4 (1998): 117–134.

Harmon, Jim. *Radio Mystery and Adventure and Its Appearances in Film, Television and other Media*. Jefferson, N.C.: McFarland, 2003.

"In the Old Lone Ranger Series, What Did 'Kemosabe' Mean?" Available online. URL: http://www.straightdope.com/columns/read/971/in-the-old-lone-ranger-series-what-did-kemosabe-mean. Accessed April 18, 2010.

Rothel, David. *Who Was That Masked Man? The Story of the Lone Ranger*. Cranbury, N.J.: A.S. Barnes, 1976.

"Thunder Cloud Dies; Radio's First 'Tonto.'" *Chicago Tribune*, 1 February 1967, B7.

Williamson, James S. (Jim Williamson) (1949–   )
Turtle Mountain Chippewa mathematician, physicist, solar energy specialist

A Chippewa, James (Jim) Williamson was born in 1949 on the Turtle Mountain Reservation in North Dakota. The Soviet *Sputnik* satellite launch in 1957 aroused his curiosity about science while he was still in elementary school. Encouraged by his teachers, he studied science and mathematics in high school and at college in Montana. After graduating, Williamson worked for the Atomic Energy Commission on the design of safety systems for nuclear power plants and designed solar energy central receiver test facilities in Albuquerque, New Mexico, and Barstow, California. He also worked on air-conditioning systems that use sunlight to produce electricity and nuclear and solar power systems for space travel to Jupiter, Mars, and Saturn.

In 1978, President Jimmy Carter appointed Williamson to the Domestic Policy Review Panel for Solar Energy Research. During the 1980s, Williamson was particularly interested in working with developing nations on alternatives to fossil fuels, and he directed solar energy research projects involving the United States and Saudi Arabia. He was active in organizing the second SOLERAS Workshop on solar energy applications held at Denver, Colorado, in 1981 and was editor of the workshop proceedings.

After serving as director for science and education at the U.S. Department of Energy's National Renewable Energy

Laboratory at Golden, Colorado, in the 1990s, Williamson went on to found the Heritage Institute, a nonprofit organization in Castle Rock, Colorado, providing technical and financial assistance to American Indian tribes to pursue sustainable, environmentally sound economic development. The institute's InCompass Energy Program helps tribes take an active part in utility operations on their reservations and pursue renewable energy projects and energy efficiency. The program also helps tribal communities improve science and technology-related curricula and the physical infrastructure of their schools. Since 2000, the institute has published a newsletter, *InCompass Energy News*. Williamson is also the founder and CEO of New West Technologies, an energy consulting firm. He emphasizes that all these projects grow out of the Indian heritage of living in harmony with nature.

See also INDIGENOUS ECONOMICS.

Willie Boy (ca. 1882–1909) *Chemehuevi cowboy, outlaw*

Willie Boy was born around 1882 near the Twentynine Palms oasis in the Mojave Desert in California. His mother, Mary Snyder, was Chemehuevi, and his father is believed to have been Paiute. As a child living in the desert of the Kingston Mountains near Nevada, Willie Boy developed into an extraordinary long-distance runner. He attended local Indian schools and later worked as a ranch hand and laborer. Subsequently, he moved to Victorville, California, with his sister Georgia and her family. By 1900, he had married and adopted two children, orphans from another tribe. In 1906, he was arrested in Victorville for "disturbing the peace" and was jailed for 90 days in San Bernardino.

In early 1909, Willie Boy ran off with his 16-year-old cousin Carlotta Mike, daughter of Chemehuevi spiritual leader William Mike, also known as Mike Boniface, who lived in nearby Banning. William Mike objected to Willie Boy's involvement with his daughter, and when she returned, he forbade her to continue seeing the young man. On September 26, 1909, Willie Boy went to William Mike's camp to ask for Carlotta's hand in marriage. An argument ensued, and he shot and killed the old man. Willie Boy and Carlotta fled to the desert, and the next day a posse that included Yaqui tracker John Hyde and Chemehuevi tracker Segundo Chino set out after them. In the Morongo Mountains, Willie Boy left Carlotta near some boulders called the Pipes and went to seek supplies. While he was gone, she was shot and killed by Hyde, who mistook her at long range for Willie Boy. Hyde blamed the deed on the fugitive.

Now believed to be a double murderer who had brutally abducted and then killed a young woman, Willie Boy became the vilified object of a nationally reported manhunt. On October 7, the posse caught up with him, but Willie Boy, hiding behind tall rocks, managed to pin them down, wounding one of the lawmen and killing three horses. As the posse pulled back under cover of darkness, they heard a single shot. When the posse returned a week later, they found that Willie Boy had killed himself.

The tragic story of Willie Boy and Carlotta soon began to be told and retold, becoming more fanciful at each telling. As early as 1911, the Selig Western Company filmed a fictionalized version written and directed by Hobart Bosworth, who also played the part of Willie Boy. In this version, an Indian, after being educated at an Eastern boarding school, is shunned by his tribe. Turning to drink for solace, he commits a murder and is hunted down. The film led to protests by Indians who objected to its antiprogressive slant as well as to the fact that all of the Indian parts were played by non-Indians.

In 1960, Harry Lawton wrote another fictionalized account of the story, *Willie Boy: A Desert Manhunt*, which was made into the film *Tell Them Willie Boy Is Here*, released in 1969 and starring Robert Redford and Katherine Ross, with Robert Blake as Willie Boy.

Further Reading

Sandos, James A., and Larry E. Burgess. *The Hunt for Willie Boy: Indian-Hating and Popular Culture*. Norman: University of Oklahoma Press, 1996.

Wilson, Richard (Dick Wilson) (1934–1990)
Oglala Lakota tribal chairman

Richard "Dick" Wilson was born April 29, 1934, on the Pine Ridge Reservation in South Dakota, the son of a mixed-blood Oglala family. Wilson went to school on the reservation and became a plumber. He also raised cattle and eventually opened a trucking company. Like his father, he acquired a reputation as a bootlegger; the sale of alcohol was illegal on the reservation. He became the head of the tribe's housing authority and at one time was accused of misusing $6,000 in federal funds, although no charges were filed.

The Pine Ridge Reservation had been divided along full-blood and mixed-blood political lines since the creation of the tribal government in 1934 under the INDIAN REORGANIZATION ACT, which replaced the authority of the traditional chiefs, who were usually full-bloods. In 1972, Wilson ran for tribal council presidency and defeated Gerald One Feather, a traditional full-blood. Within days of his inauguration on April 10, 1972, Wilson was stirring up controversy. At Pine Ridge, one of the poorest communities in the United States, with a per capita median income at the time of only $800 per year, the tribal government was one of the few sources of well-paying jobs. Wilson began handing out the patronage jobs almost exclusively to the mixed-blood faction, upsetting the balance that had existed before. Stating that "there is nothing in tribal law against nepotism," Wilson hired his wife, brother, son, a cousin, and a nephew to tribal government positions. He also began to marginalize the rest of the tribal council, refusing to call the council together for meetings and transacting business through the council's executive committee, which he controlled. His attempts to introduce the sale of liquor on the reservation created a backlash, even among his supporters. Wilson clashed with the BUREAU OF INDIAN AFFAIRS (BIA) superintendent for the reservation, Al Trimble, an Oglala and a career BIA bureaucrat who had some sympathy for the traditional perspective. Wilson pressed the BIA to remove Trimble, and they did, transferring him to Albuquerque.

A staunch opponent of the AMERICAN INDIAN MOVEMENT (AIM), which was galvanizing traditional Indians across the country, Wilson fired those, including tribal council vice president Dave Long, who sympathized with the movement. Wilson banned AIM from the reservation and threatened AIM leader and Pine Ridge native RUSSELL MEANS, stating, "If Russell Means ever sets foot on this reservation, I, Dick Wilson, will personally cut his braids off." In November 1972, when Means and AIM leader DENNIS BANKS proposed holding a victory celebration on the reservation after the TRAIL OF BROKEN TREATIES demonstration in Washington, D.C., Wilson used the perceived threat of violence by AIM members to have the tribal council pass a resolution giving him almost dictatorial powers. Using funds meant for highway safety, Wilson created a paramilitary group, the Guardians of the Oglala Nation, known as the "Goons," to keep AIM members off the reservation.

In the meantime, the full-blood camp, led by PEDRO BISSONETTE had started an organization, the Oglala Sioux Civil Rights Organization (OSCRO), to combat the historic low rents paid by non-Indians who farmed on reservation lands. In early 1973, when Wilson refused to allow OSCRO to raise this issue with the BIA, OSCRO tried to have Wilson removed as tribal chairman. OSCRO's efforts, along with Wilson's highhandedness and accusations that he had misused tribal funds, led the tribal council to vote to impeach him. Wilson's acquittal in a controversial trial on February 23, 1973, only served to fan the flames of discontent on the reservation.

To make matters worse, the murder of Wesley Bad Heart Bull by a non-Indian in Buffalo Gap, South Dakota, a border town near the reservation, in January 1973 had raised tensions between Indians and non-Indians around Pine Ridge. AIM members from across the country flocked to Custer, South Dakota, for a demonstration that sought justice for the Bad Heart Bull family. The demonstration, held on February 6, 1973, led to a violent confrontation with police that resulted in the Custer courthouse being burned to the ground (see CUSTER RIOT).

Wilson, concerned that his acquittal might lead to violence, had already called in the Federal Bureau of Investigation (FBI) and federal marshals during his impeachment trial and had fortified the tribal council building with sandbags and machine guns, many of them manned by his Goons. OSCRO and their allies marched on the tribal council building the day after Wilson's acquittal, only to be met by the large armed force. They decided to seek AIM's help in ousting Wilson, since many AIM members were still in the area following the Custer demonstration. AIM's attempts to negotiate with Wilson failed when Goon chief Glen Three Star and other Wilson supporters assaulted Russell Means and a legal aide in Pine Ridge village. The next day, on February 27, 1973, AIM, OSCRO, and other Oglala traditionals decided to occupy the village of Wounded Knee as a symbolic protest against the Wilson administration, leading to a violent, 71-day siege (see WOUNDED KNEE, OCCUPATION OF).

During the siege, Wilson and his armed Goons were augmented by hundreds of extra FBI agents and federal marshals who sought to arrest the AIM occupiers. The undisciplined Goons wreaked havoc by refusing to cooperate with federal law enforcement officials, shooting into the AIM camp and sparking firefights with the occupiers, and frustrating attempts by the federal officers to negotiate a settlement.

The end of the Wounded Knee occupation only worsened the tensions between the two factions. In October, Bissonette was gunned down by a tribal police officer, provoking a broad outcry on the reservation. Russell Means then ran against Wilson in a highly charged campaign but failed to unseat him as tribal chairman. Wilson's reelection in February 1974 led to a virtual civil war that left dozens of Indians on Pine Ridge dead. The violence continued unabated through the summer of 1975, when a shootout killed an AIM member and two FBI agents (see PELTIER, LEONARD). In February 1976, the body of AIM activist ANNA MAE AQUASH was found on the reservation. The killings sparked a massive occupation by federal law enforcement officers who, along with the tribal police and Goons, turned the reservation into a brutal police state.

In 1976, Al Trimble resigned from the BIA to run against Wilson on a reform ticket that sought to relieve the tensions on the reservation. Despite a fierce campaign that included violent attacks by Wilson supporters on Trimble and his family, Wilson was decisively defeated. Upon taking office, Trimble disbanded the Goons, placed the tribal police under firm tribal control, and set up a review commission to examine cases of police brutality. He ended the dictatorial nature of Wilson's regime by decentralizing the government and giving the reservation districts more autonomy. Trimble also closed the liquor store that Wilson had opened.

Wilson went back to work as a plumber. Although he mounted a few campaigns for tribal chairmanship, he would never again hold political office. Dick Wilson died of complications from an enlarged heart and kidney failure on January 31, 1990, in Rapid City, South Dakota.

Further Reading
Paulson, T. Emogene, and Lloyd R. Moses. *Who's Who among the Sioux*. Vermilion: University of South Dakota Press, 1988.

Winters Doctrine (1907)

Formulated by the U.S. Supreme Court in 1907, this doctrine safeguards the water rights of Indians, chiefly for the purpose of irrigation. It was first drawn up in response to the case *Winters v. United States*. Henry Winters, a Montana farmer, had been interfering with the flow of the Milk River and was sued by the Fort Belknap tribe downstream. The Court held that all federal reserves in the West, including parks, national forests, wilderness, and INDIAN RESERVATIONS, are entitled to sufficient water to meet the purposes intended by Congress when they were originally set aside. Since that purpose, in the case of most Indian reservations, was to provide the indigenous peoples with land for eventual agricultural uses, Indians held these rights by virtue of the treaty in which they ceded their lands, and this superior right to water use could not be infringed upon by subsequent state laws. A series of later cases affirmed these rights, notably *Conrad Investment Company v. United States* (1908) and *Arizona v. California* (1963), which ruled that a reservation is entitled to an amount of water sufficient to irrigate all acreage that can be practically farmed.

Nevertheless, especially during the 1920s, many irrigation projects that were authorized for Indian lands under the Winters Doctrine were chiefly for the benefit of whites. This was mainly because the Indians generally had no way of getting the water to their own lands. This problem was investigated in a 1928 report by Porter J. Preston and Charles A. Engle included in *Survey of Conditions of the Indians of the United States* (printed in *Hearings before a Subcommittee on Indian Affairs of the U.S. Senate*, 71st Congress, 2d session [1930], part 6, pp. 2,210–2,661).

In spite of the clear legal precedents, encroachments on Indian water rights were a serious problem throughout the 20th century, as in the case of the Flatheads and the Walker River Paiutes in the 1920s (see BURKE, CHARLES HENRY), the PICK-SLOAN PLAN, the PYRAMID LAKE controversy, Navajo water rights (see WATKINS, ARTHUR VIVIAN), PIMA-MARICOPA WATER RIGHTS, and instances of DAMS ON INDIAN LANDS.

Toward the end of the 20th century, a strong trend developed for Indian tribes to demand compensation for water being illegally used by others and for these claims—often very large—to be settled in court. These resulted in leases that were quite lucrative for the tribes and provided legal security for non-Indian users.

Further Reading

Shurts, John. *Indian Reserved Water Rights: The Winters Doctrine in Its Social and Legal Context, 1880s–1930s*. Norman: University of Oklahoma Press, 2000.

Witt, Shirley Hill (1934–) *Mohawk anthropologist, author, activist*

Shirley Hill Witt was born on April 17, 1934, in Whittier, California, the daughter of Melvin Ward and Cordelia Bertiome Hill. She is a member of the Wolf clan, Akwesasne Mohawk Nation, the Iroquois Long House, and an activist for civil rights, Indian affairs, and women's and family issues.

Witt played an important part in the early RED POWER MOVEMENT. A student attendee at the AMERICAN INDIAN CHICAGO CONFERENCE in 1961, she was one of the founders of the NATIONAL INDIAN YOUTH COUNCIL at Gallup, New Mexico, later that year and served as its first vice president from 1961 to 1964.

Witt attended the University of Michigan receiving a B.A. in 1965, and an M.A. in 1966. She earned a Ph.D. in biological

anthropology from the University of New Mexico in 1969. She was visiting assistant professor of anthropology at the University of North Carolina, Chapel Hill, from 1970 through 1972, and associate professor at Colorado College, Colorado Springs, from 1972 through 1974. In 1976, she coauthored a famous memorandum with William F. Muldrow of the U.S. Civil Rights Commission, "Events Surrounding Recent Murders on the Pine Ridge Reservation in South Dakota" (see PELTIER, LEONARD). Hill was director of the Rocky Mountain Regional Office of the Civil Rights Commission from 1975 until 1983, when she left to accept the position of cabinet secretary for natural resources under New Mexico governor Tony Anaya. In 1977, she was an official observer at the International NGO conference on Discrimination against Indigenous Populations in the Americas in Geneva, Switzerland. In 1985, Witt became a foreign service officer for the U.S. Information Agency, serving in South America and Africa.

A fellow of the American Anthropological Association, she has done research among American Indians and Chicanos, and in the Appalachians, in Costa Rica, and in Canada. She served as a consultant to the Civil Rights Office of the U.S. Department of Health, Education, and Welfare on the American Indian Task Force of the Civil Rights Commission.

Witt wrote scripts for *Silent Heritage: The American Indian*, an 11-part series produced by the University of Michigan Television Center for National Educational Television in 1966–67. In 1967, she published *The Saginaw Band of Chippewa Indians* (US GPO, 1967). With Sam Steiner, she edited *The Way: An Anthology of American Indian Life and Literature* (1972); and that same year issued *The Tuscaroras* (1972). With Gilberto Chavez Ballejos, she published the novel *El Indio Jesus* (in English in 2001). In 2011, with Bradley Glenn Shreve, she published *Red Power Rising: The National Indian Youth Council and the origins of Native Activism*. She also contributes to newspapers under the name Katherine Thundercloud.

Women of All Red Nations (WARN)

Women of All Red Nations (WARN) was a militant rights organization formed in 1978 in Rapid City, South Dakota, as a counterpart to the AMERICAN INDIAN MOVEMENT (AIM). WARN was founded by Pat Ballenger (Chippewa), Madonna Thunder Hawk (Oglala Lakota Sioux), Lorraine Canoe (Mohawk), Lorelie Means (Lakota Sioux), and other members of AIM just as AIM itself was disintegrating and its militant tactics were losing their effectiveness. WARN had its best success in South Dakota, where its Lakota Sioux members confronted issues of involuntary sterilization of Native American women, an issue that surfaced in the mid-1970s when South Dakota senator James Abourezk's hearing on AMERICAN INDIAN HEALTH uncovered massive evidence as part of a BUREAU OF INDIAN AFFAIRS birth control program.

WARN never achieved its full potential, though it did highlight some of the women activists who formed the backbone of the RED POWER MOVEMENT. The organization was superseded by the Indigenous Women's Network (IWN), founded during the late 1980s by Ingrid Washinawatok (Menominee) and Winona LaDuke (Chippewa). Including among its founders prominent veterans of WARN as well as longtime activists Janet McCloud (Tulalip) and Nilak Butler (Inuit), IWN is known for its nonconfrontational style.

Further Reading

Ralstin-Lewis, D. Marie. "The Continuing Struggle against Genocide: Indigenous Women's Reproductive Rights." *Wicazo Sa Review* 20, no. 1 (2005): 71–95.

Ramirez, Renya K. "Race, Tribal Nation, and Gender: A Native Feminist Approach to Belonging." *Meridians: Feminism, Race, Transnationalism* 7, no. 2 (2007): 22–40.

World War I, American Indians and

The war that began in August 1914 and ended with the general armistice of November 11, 1918, was a turning point in world history. Although the United States did not officially enter until April 6, 1917, the war affected the United States and its Indian population from the start. In proportion to their numbers, Indians were heavily involved in the war and the war effort. The United States entered the conflict at a time when the public image of Indians was relatively positive (see Eastman, Charles Alexander; Young Deer), and the impressive war record of American Indians was not ignored by the public. Although the war advanced the assimilation process and proved decisive in the campaign for Indian citizenship, at the same time it promoted both pan-Indianism and the pride of individual tribes.

Even before the U.S. entry, Indians contributed to the Allied war effort in Europe. For example, the Crow were shipping horses to Britain and France, the Lakota at Pine Ridge were selling cattle, and southwestern tribes were exporting cotton. And long before U.S. entry into the war, Indians in the northern borderlands of the United States, especially the Iroquois and Ojibwa, joined their cousins on the Canadian side who were enlisting in large numbers in the Canadian and British armed forces. Among the best known were Enos or Ernest Kick, an Oneida who joined the Thirty-fifth Battalion Indian Company (Middlesex Indians), and Lumbee-Croatan Sylvester Long Lance. Some from Oklahoma enlisted as well: Frank Knight, a Cherokee from Vinita, an officer in an English regiment that served in Flanders, was decorated for bravery. Simon Ralph Walkingstick, a Cherokee from Talequah, grandson of Chief Walkingstick, enlisted while a junior at Dartmouth College and served as a captain in the British army in Mesopotamia. Several Indians served in the aeronautical division of the U.S. Army Signal Corps, forerunner of the Army Air Corps (see Aviation, American Indians in). Leo Maguire (Osage) served as a captain in the French army.

When the United States declared war on Germany on April 6, 1917, the initial Indian response was strong, though some tribes objected to the draft. In most cases, this was due to lack of knowledge among the Indians. In only one instance was a show of force used: At the Goshute Reservation on the Nevada-Utah border, a troop of soldiers arrested four troublemakers for encouraging draft resistance. In Washington and northern Oregon, the Nisqually, Puyallup, Kayapulla, and several others appealed to treaties of 1854–55, by which they agreed to lay down their arms and never "make war against any other tribe except in self-defense." When the government explained that this was a war of self-defense, they agreed to fight. A speech urging draft resistance among the Creek led to reports of a violent antidraft uprising in Oklahoma; the speaker, Ellen Perryman, was arrested as a possible German agent but was later released.

The Iroquois, however, were a special case. Traditional Iroquois did not recognize U.S. jurisdiction under the Selective Service Act, though many enlisted voluntarily. In 1918, after a group of Onondaga traveling with a circus in Germany were mistaken for spies, assaulted, and arrested, the Onondaga and Oneida Nations of the Iroquois Confederacy, manifesting their sovereignty, declared war on Germany and encouraged their young men to enlist in the U.S. armed forces as allies.

In general, however, the Indian response was overwhelming. The total U.S. Indian population at the time was 335,998, of whom only about half were citizens, and only 30 percent could read and write English. Yet 12,000–12,500 Indians served during the war, about 25 percent of the adult male Indian population, the great majority of them volunteers. According to Gabe E. Parker (Choctaw), superintendent of the Five Civilized Tribes (Cherokee, Chickasaw, Choctaw, Creek, and Seminole), of the approximately 100,500 Indians under his charge, more than 1,000 had enlisted in the army or navy, practically every able-bodied man. Those who remained behind turned out bumper crops in farmwork.

For the most part, Indians served alongside whites. Although a movement for segregated units had support from both whites and Indians, for the most part such units were avoided and the assimilationists prevailed. One of the most vocal opponents of segregated Indian units was Arthur C. Parker of the Society of American Indians. In his view, such companies maintained the Indian in an inferior social role and reinforced racial stereotypes. He was supported by Indian Commissioner Cato Sells, General Richard Henry Pratt, and the Indian Rights Association.

Nevertheless, simply by virtue of geography, sizable numbers of Indians clustered in certain units. One such company was "Pershing's Indian Scouts," with Apache and Sioux from Fort Apache, Arizona, who had served with Pershing in Mexico and followed him to France. Some 600–1,000 Indians, many of them from the Five Civilized Tribes, joined the 36th Division, in which Company E of the 142nd Infantry was made up largely of Choctaw volunteers. During their training, Indian and white soldiers from this unit were tested on their ability to reach an objective while blindfolded, and the results confirmed their officers' belief in the Indians' inherent sense of direction. Another unit of Oklahoma Indians, the 358th Infantry, 90th Division, was reported to have suffered 80 percent losses in France.

Other companies with large numbers of Indians included

the Second and Third Battalions of the 42nd Division. In the 34th (Sandstorm) Division from Camp Cody, New Mexico, were soldiers from 12 tribes. Indians also served in the 30th and 88th Divisions. Thirty to 35 Indians of the 165th Infantry, New York's old 69th, were reported to be using "old frontier tactics" against the Germans. Perhaps 1,000 Indians joined the navy. Among these Indian sailors were Wesley Youngbird (Eastern Cherokee) on the battleship *Wyoming* and William Leon Wolfe, a Cree gunner, on the *Utah.*

Largely Indian units were among the first to see action. Menominee John Peters of the 1st Engineers was the first Indian killed in the war. Pershing's Apache scouts were recognized for their service at the Battle of the Marne. Company D, 128th Infantry, of the 32nd Division, with 19 Wisconsin Winnebago (now Ho-Chunk), took part in all of the 32nd's battles and remained with the occupation forces in Germany.

Like the later, more famous Navajo code talkers of WORLD WAR II, Choctaw served as CODE TALKERS. Those from the 142nd Infantry spoke Choctaw on field telephones when their unit was pinned down at Saint-Étienne, baffling German eavesdroppers. In the final months of the war, Sioux, (Dakota, Lakota, Nakota), Cheyenne, Osage, and Comanche soldiers also served in this way.

Among Indian soldiers decorated for valor were Private Pontiac Williams, an Ottawa wounded at Chateau-Thierry, who won the Distinguished Service Cross; as did Ernest Spencer, a Yakama of the Sixth Machine-Gunners Battalion; Sergeant Joseph La Jennesse, a Chippewa; and Jesse A. James, Company L, 4th Infantry, from Eagletown, Oklahoma; Lieutenant Josiah A. Powless, a Wisconsin Oneida physician with the 308th Infantry, was awarded a posthumous Distinguished Service Cross after he was killed while treating a wounded comrade.

Thomas Charges Alone (Thomas E. Rogers, Arikara) of Company A, 18th Infantry, was recognized for singlehandedly capturing German sentinels at night during the Battle of Soissons and bringing them back to the Allied lines. Manuel Cordoba, an Indian from Carson City, brought down two German planes in France.

Private Akoohna, Chiricahua Apache, in the 60th Infantry, set out with his sergeant and seven privates one night to destroy a German operations screen consisting of pine boughs stretched over wires just in front of the enemy trenches. As they approached, the sergeant and several of the privates were killed. Akoohna took command but was later captured. Guarded by a single German, he whipped a Colt out from under his shirt, shot the German in the head, and returned to his own lines.

In another famous exploit during the Battle of Soissons, Joe Young Hawk, a Sioux from Elbowwoods, North Dakota, was captured by five Germans, who took his gun from him. Young Hawk, suddenly surprising his captors, lunged for one and broke his neck. He killed two more with his bare hands by cracking their spines over his knee. He then marched the other two back to the American lines, having been shot through the leg on the way. Later he was seriously wounded, and he died of his wounds in June 1923.

Charles Blackbird, an Omaha, won the Croix de Guerre with palm for bravery at Chateau-Thierry. Private Joseph Oklahombi, a Choctaw from southeast Oklahoma of Company D of the 141st Infantry, 36th Division, was awarded the Croix de Guerre for singlehandedly capturing 50 machine guns, holding them for four days under artillery and gas barrage, and bringing in 171 German prisoners. Sergeant James M. Gordon, a Chippewa from Wisconsin detailed to serve as a motorcycle driver, received the same decoration for his rescue of a wounded French officer under fire.

Military service raised the status of Indian soldiers within their tribes and broadened their contacts with the outside world. A number of those who returned became tribal leaders and spokesmen in the years following the war. Choctaw principal chief Victor M. Locke, Seneca JESSE CORNPLANTER, Osage JOHN J. MATHEWS, Santee Dakota John Mackey, Sr., Cheyenne River Sioux George Jewett, Brulé Lakota Sioux Steve Spotted Tail, and Eastern Cherokee aviator Fred Blythe Bauer were all veterans of World War I.

Indians also made significant contributions to the war effort on the home front, working in agriculture and industry. The Indian workforce was active in war-related industries such as shipyards and aircraft factories. The Carlisle Indian School sent a contingent of students to work in the Ford factory in Detroit under an Indian foreman.

Indian women also took part in the war effort, replacing men at the front in agricultural work and increasing their production of traditional Indian crafts for sale. They knitted and sewed Red Cross garments and planted "victory gardens." A number served in France as nurses; army medical corps nurse Lula Owl was the only Eastern Cherokee officer in the war. Tsianina Redfeather sang for the troops in France (see BLACKSTONE, TSIANINA EVAN).

Indian financial support for the war was significant. Native pride was stirred by the fact that when Creek millionaire JACKSON BARNETT demonstrated his patriotism by buying $650,000 of the first issue of Liberty Bonds in 1917, they were transferred to him by Choctaw superintendent Gabe Parker, and every bond note bore the signature of Cherokee HOUSTON TEEHEE, registrar of the U.S. Treasury. Individual Indians of the Five Civilized Tribes subscribed $1,741,550 to the Liberty Loan program. According to Parker, "There is little doubt that citizen Indians of the Five Tribes, whose transactions do not pass through the government office, invested enough more to raise the total amount . . . to two millions."

Altogether, it was estimated that Indians subscribed more than $13 million to the three Liberty Loans, investing between $30 and $40 per capita. The 2,180 Osage, the richest Indians at the time because of their oil-lease revenues, subscribed $226,000 to the third bond drive. At Camp Travis, one Indian noncommissioned officer in the 358th Infantry regiment, Otis Russell, put his oil revenues of $500–$1,000 a month into Liberty Bonds. In addition, in May 1918, Secretary of State Franklin K. Lane obtained congressional permission to invest tribal funds held by the Interior Department in Liberty Bonds.

Indians not only bought bonds, they also sold them.

Among the Indian celebrities who encouraged the purchase of Liberty Bonds were Cherokee Chief White Elk and his wife Princess Ah-tra-ah-saun (Klamath), Charles Alexander Eastman (Santee Dakota Sioux), and NIPO STRONGHEART (Yakama). William Shelton (Wha-cah-dub), a Snohomish full-blood, became a leader in war bond sales.

It was believed that national service during the war years would hasten the assimilation process, and indeed it exposed Indians to mainstream American society in new ways. At the same time, the war revitalized neglected aspects of Indian culture. Traditional dances and ceremonies were revived to encourage Indian soldiers and honor veterans. The Standing Rock Sioux warrior societies sent inductees off with traditional chants. In November 1918, the Sioux held a victory dance for the first time since the Battle of Little Bighorn. The Apache, Arapaho, Pawnee, and Cheyenne all held dances welcoming their veterans home and recognizing them as warriors.

The Indian rights movement of the time, still strongly assimilationist in character, emphasized the many patriotic services performed by Indians abroad and on the home front to press for full citizenship for Indians. The SOCIETY OF AMERICAN INDIANS and the National Indian Association both argued that Indians now deserved legal emancipation. The INDIAN CITIZENSHIP ACT of 1924 was a response to Indian wartime service.

World War I brought drastic changes in reservation economies. The prospects of war profits influenced Indian policy, as Commissioner Sells sought to greatly expand Indian agriculture, but demand was so heavy that tribes often sold even their breeding stock, making short-term money but depleting their long-term capital. An initial agricultural boom led many tribes to sell their herds and lease land at nominal rates. Following the war, declining prices left these Indians without resources. Educated Indians searching for employment were aided by the general economic boom in manufacturing, as in the automotive field (see DAGENETT, CHARLES EDWIN), but after the war such jobs became harder to find. Joseph Oklahombi (Choctaw), perhaps the most decorated of all Indian veterans of World War I, was destitute in the years following the war.

Further Reading

Britten, Thomas A. *American Indians in World War I: At Home and at War*. Albuquerque: University of New Mexico Press, 1997.

Tate, Michael L. "From Scout to Doughboy: The National Debate over Integrating American Indians into the Military, 1891–1918." *Western Historical Quarterly* 17, no. 4 (1986): 417–437.

Zissu, Erik M. "Conscription, Sovereignty, and Land: American Indian Resistance during World War I." *Pacific Historical Review* 64, no. 4 (1995): 537–566.

World War II, American Indians and

A transformative event in the history of American Indians, World War II affected the lives of virtually every Indian in the United States. More than 155,000, or nearly one-quarter of the total Indian population, were directly involved in the industrial, agricultural, or military aspects of the war effort, and by the war's end almost 29,000 Indians, a larger proportion than any other segment of the American population, were enlisted in the armed forces. The war effort did more to further the ASSIMILATION of Indians into the American mainstream than any previous governmental policy, and it ultimately led to the dismantling of the decade-long reform known as the INDIAN NEW DEAL (see INDIAN REORGANIZATION ACT).

The bombing of Pearl Harbor on December 7, 1941, shocked Indians across the country as it did the rest of America. At least one Indian, Henry Nolatubby, an Oklahoma Choctaw, was killed in the attack. Indian nations across the country, including the Osage, those of Jemez Pueblo, and the Iroquois Confederacy, quickly passed their own declarations of war against the Axis, many of them before the United States did. Sixty-five Seminole registered for the draft, even though their tribe was still technically at war with the United States. Many traditional Hopi, however, became conscientious objectors, refusing to join the military on religious grounds.

The Iroquois, who had previously fought attempts to draft their men, on the grounds that they were a sovereign nation and therefore not subject to conscription by the United States, stated in their own declaration of war against Germany, Japan, and Italy that "It is the unanimous sentiment among the Indian people that the atrocities of the Axis nations are violently repulsive to all sense of righteousness of our people."

Individual Indians flocked to the recruiting stations, leading army officials to state that if everyone enlisted in the armed services at the same rate as Indians, there would be no need for the draft. Indeed, the BUREAU OF INDIAN AFFAIRS (BIA) reported that in many cases Indians were bringing their rifles to the agencies, wanting to sign up and "proceed immediately into the scene of the fighting." Less than six months after Pearl Harbor, there were 7,500 Indians in the armed forces, 40 percent of them volunteers. Indian support for the war came as a surprise to the Axis powers. In a radio broadcast, the Germans, persuaded by their own propaganda (see AMERICAN INDIAN FEDERATION), had confidently predicted "an Indian uprising against the United States" if Indians should be "asked to fight against the Axis." Indeed, Indian participation in the war helped to validate the justness of it as a war against tyranny, and the general consensus among Indians, as expressed by a young Columbia River soldier, was that as badly as they had been treated by the United States, "under Nazism we [would] have no rights at all [and would] be used as slaves."

American Indians were welcomed into the service, due in part to the prevailing stereotype of Indians as fearless warriors and stealthy scouts. Many urban Indians suffered acute embarrassment when called on to show troops how to shoot a bow and arrow or track a person through the woods. Although Indian Commissioner JOHN COLLIER had fought for segregated Indian units as a hedge against assimilation, the armed services preferred to place Indians in integrated units.

Navajo code talkers, Corporal Henry Bahe, Jr., (left) and Pvt. First Class George H. Kirk, operate a portable radio close to the front lines in the island of Bougainville in Papua New Guinea in December 1943. *(AP/Wideworld)*

If anything, the armed forces believed, as did Secretary of the Interior Harold Ickes, that the American Indian had "inherited talents" that made them "uniquely valuable" in the war, for the Indian had "an enthusiasm for fighting" and the "rigors of combat hold no terrors for him." As a consequence of this myth, Indians were often given particularly hazardous assignments as commandos, demolition experts, advance scouts, and paratroopers.

The largest concentration of Indians enlisted in the U.S. Army's famed Thunderbird Division—the 45th Oklahoma Division, over 20 percent of whose members were Indians. The Thunderbirds arguably saw more combat than any other division in the war, landing in North Africa, fighting their way through Sicily, Italy, Southern France, and on into Germany. Along the way 163 Indians of the Thunderbird Division earned Purple Hearts, 10 won the Silver Star, and three received the Medal of Honor. (See BARFOOT, VAN T.; CHILDERS, ERNEST; MONTGOMERY, JACK CLEVELAND.) During the war, HAL R. MULDROW, who eventually reached the rank of major general in command of the 45th Division, was an artillery officer whose decisive action at the beachhead in Salerno saved the invasion from a Nazi trap. Spearheading the American attack through Europe, Indians of the 45th made history: LeRoy Hamlin, a Ute, was the first American soldier to make contact with the

Russians across the Elbe; another Ute, Harvey Narchees, was the first American soldier to reach the center of Berlin.

Indians from the Southwest gravitated toward the U.S. Marines and saw ferocious combat in the Pacific. More than 30 Navajo, as well as four Mescalero Apache, including Homer Yahnozha, a descendant of Geronimo, were trapped in Corregidor in the Philippines and forced to endure the infamous death march and captivity under the Japanese. The Navajo CODE TALKERS, one of many Indian groups formed to maintain secure communications among U.S. units, gained fame in the Pacific Theater for their ability to confound Japanese code breakers. The most famous Indian marine was the Pima IRA HAYES, one of the celebrated group who planted the American flag on Mount Suribachi during the assault on Iwo Jima.

Individual Indians distinguished themselves in combat, sometimes with incredible feats of bravery. On February 9, 1945, U.S. Army private JOHN N. REESE, JR., a Cherokee, together with a fellow private, killed 82 Japanese soldiers in an engagement in downtown Manila. Reese lost his life while attempting to reload; he was awarded a Medal of Honor posthumously. Private Joe Longknife, an Assiniboine from Missouri, won the Silver Star for killing 10 Japanese soldiers with 16 shots from his rifle. Kenneth Scissons, a Sioux from Rapid City, joined a British-trained commando unit and became its leading eliminator of Germans, on one patrol killing 10 Nazis in four minutes. RAYMOND HARVEY, who would later win a Medal of Honor in the Korean War, earned two Silver Stars and the Distinguished Service Cross fighting in Europe. During the Normandy invasion, 13 Indian paratroopers were dropped with demolitions to clear the beaches for Allied landings. Aleut and Eskimos, who joined the Alaska National Guard, defeated Japanese forces attempting to take the Aleutian Islands in the only battles of World War II fought in North America.

Indians were also drawn to aviation (see AVIATION, AMERICAN INDIANS IN), and 34 Indians earned the Distinguished Flying Cross. General CLARENCE TINKER rebuilt Hawaii's destroyed air force after the bombing of Pearl Harbor and led the air defense in the Battle of Midway. Brothers LEAFORD BEARSKIN and LEYLAND S. BEARSKIN became famed bomber pilots during the war, and Admiral JOSEPH CLARK commanded a fast carrier task force that participated in virtually every major air engagement in the Pacific, from the liberation of the Marianas to the end of the war. In addition, more than 2,000 Indians served in the U.S. Navy, including ERNEST EVANS, who won the Medal of Honor for his gallant defense of an embattled carrier group during the Battle of Leyte Gulf. Approximately 500 Indians were killed during World War II, with another 600 wounded. Indians garnered 71 Air Medals, 51 Silver Stars, 47 Bronze Stars, and 5 Congressional Medals of Honor.

The Indian contribution on the home front was just as great. More than 46,000 Indians left their reservations to work in wartime industries, a movement Collier called "the greatest exodus of Indians" in the history of the United States. Despite the critical shortage of manpower on reservations during the war, agricultural production actually doubled, due almost exclusively to the efforts of Indian women. In 1942, Indians planted 5,100 "victory gardens," and by the war's end, fully half of all Indian families in the country had one.

The tribes also threw their support to the war effort by purchasing war bonds. The Yuchi and Creek Indians bought $400,000 worth, the Shoshone $500,000. The Quapaw donated $1 million to the war effort and were only reluctantly persuaded to take the bonds. Between April 1 and June 1, 1942, tribes and individual Indians purchased more than $3.7 million in war bonds, and by April 1943, the total had risen to $12.6 million. By the war's end, Indians around the country had purchased $50 million in war bonds, a staggering sum considering the small numbers and impoverished financial condition of most Indian people.

Indian women also participated in the war effort. More than 12,000 Indian women left their reservations to serve in the war industries, and another 800 joined the Women's Army Auxiliary Corps (WACs). On INDIAN RESERVATIONS, Apache women began to labor in the fields for the first time in their history, and Menominee women took over their famed lumber mills to replace the men going to war.

As thousands of Indians left their reservations, most of them for the first time, they found themselves adapting to mainstream American society, a process many tribes had previously resisted. Many Indians who worked in the war industries did not return to their reservations after the war's end, and many soldiers used the GI Bill and other incentives to remain away from their homes. Never before had Indians undergone a process of assimilation so vast and thorough, and even Collier was forced to admit that "in some areas, this assimilation has gone forward so rapidly that the net result has been a destruction of Indian culture."

Ironically, despite the support of Indian people for the war, the war years devastated the BIA and eventually derailed the ambitious plans for reform hatched by Commissioner Collier under the INDIAN NEW DEAL. In 1942, budget appropriations for the bureau dropped from $33 million to $28 million, where they remained throughout the rest of the war, and the BIA lost some of its most talented personnel to war-related agencies. Many of the Depression-era programs that Collier had used to supplement the meager BIA budget, such as the Works Projects Administration (WPA) and the INDIAN CIVILIAN CONSERVATION CORPS, were shut down. The heaviest blow came in 1942, when demand for space in Washington for more essential agencies forced the BIA to move its offices to Chicago. Lack of funds and manpower resulted in the closing of Indian schools, hospitals, community centers, and Indian agencies across the country.

Collier attempted to secure more funding or equipment for Indians by either handing over Indian facilities for wartime use, developing reservation natural resources, or securing funding for Indian agricultural production. These efforts to integrate the BIA into the war effort were, however, largely unsuccessful, and in the end the federal government simply appropriated Indian assets for war use. Oil and coal, as well as

timber resources, were sold to the Department of Defense, and the mining of uranium was authorized on the Navajo reservation. Collier's efforts to place the War Relocation Authority's (WRA) Japanese-American internment camps in the Gila River and Colorado River Indian Reservations proved a disastrous mistake, made worse by his feud with WRA head and future Indian commissioner DILLON S. MYER.

Worse, the Department of Defense and other agencies simply appropriated Indian lands as they saw fit. In many cases, they never gave them back, even after the war ended. Columbia River Indians were forced off their lands in Washington to make way for the Hanford Nuclear Reservation, and the Shoshone in Nevada were evicted to make way for testing grounds for the atomic bomb. The army purchased more than 400,000 acres of the Pine Ridge Reservation at a pittance for use as a gunnery range, forcing 128 families to move out at short notice. A total of 876,000 acres of Indian land was appropriated for Defense Department use during the war.

The war also strengthened the hands of those opposed to Collier's efforts to maintain Indian tribes and culture, and near the end of the war they began to agitate for the abolition of the BIA and the "emancipation" of Indians from government control. The assimilationists argued that since the Indians had performed so well in fighting the Axis, they did not need federal guardianship to manage their affairs. Sadly, the valiant war efforts of Indians led directly to the era of TERMINATION, a postwar policy that sought to end the federal-Indian trust relationship and to dissolve Indian tribes and their assets.

Further Reading
Bernstein, Allison R. *American Indians and World War II: Toward a New Era in Indian Affairs.* Norman: University of Oklahoma Press, 1991.

Franco, Jere Bishop. *Crossing the Pond: The Native American Effort in World War II.* Denton: University of North Texas Press, 1999.

Townsend, Kenneth William. *World War II and the American Indian.* Albuquerque: University of New Mexico Press, 2000.

Wounded Knee, occupation of (1973)

In 1973, a violent standoff took place in the village of Wounded Knee, South Dakota, between militant members of the AMERICAN INDIAN MOVEMENT (AIM) and officers of the Federal Bureau of Investigation (FBI). The 71-day confrontation was the result of factional tensions on the Pine Ridge Oglala Lakota Sioux Reservation.

On February 21, 1973, the Pine Ridge tribal council met to consider the impeachment of tribal president RICHARD WILSON. When the council failed to reach a decision, activists such as PEDRO BISSONETTE and traditional chiefs led by FRANK FOOLS CROW asked AIM to come to the reservation to aid their cause. AIM had recently been successful in bringing charges against the murderers of RAYMOND YELLOW THUNDER (killed in February 1972) and had led the protest for

Richard Wilson, far right, president of the Oglala Sioux tribal council, directs his supporters in setting up a roadblock in Wounded Knee, South Dakota, on March 27, 1973. *(AP/Wideworld)*

justice in the January 1973 murder of Wesley Bad Heart Bull. A meeting on February 26 between AIM leaders and Wilson ended badly when supporters of the tribal president assaulted AIM leader RUSSELL MEANS near Pine Ridge Village on the reservation. The next morning, AIM and the traditional Oglala chiefs decided that the only way to air their grievances would be through a symbolic confrontation. As the site of their demonstration, they chose the village of Wounded Knee, site of the massacre of more than 150 Sioux by the Seventh Cavalry in 1890. Led by Russell Means, DENNIS BANKS, and Bissonette, more than 200 Indians seized the small, isolated hamlet on February 28, taking 11 hostages and barricading themselves into the church and trading post.

Ever since the TRAIL OF BROKEN TREATIES the year before, when Indian leaders had occupied and ransacked the BUREAU OF INDIAN AFFAIRS (BIA) headquarters in Washington, D.C., the BIA and other U.S. agencies had been taking a hard line against continuing Indian protests. The government quickly

concentrated more than 250 FBI agents, U.S. marshals, and BIA policemen around the village, many of them in armored personnel carriers and carrying heavy weapons. Moreover, Wilson hired and deputized a number of his supporters and local white ranchers, creating a small vigilante force that he vowed would march into Wounded Knee and kick the AIM members off the reservation. Surrounded and supplied with only hunting rifles and small arms, the AIM members and their supporters, many of them recent veterans of the Vietnam War, dug fortifications around the church and the trading post and prepared for a police assault. Most of the hostages were sympathetic to the militants and joined them in fortifying their positions, and hundreds of Indians from the reservation converged on the siege, fearing a massacre.

The police, for their part, were finding it difficult to coordinate the myriad federal and local police involved in the conflict. Rivalry between the Department of Justice and Department of the Interior, each of which claimed jurisdiction over the area, virtually paralyzed the law enforcement effort. Armed vigilantes, impatient with the government inaction, repeatedly opened fire on the besieged Indians, provoking numerous firefights.

The first heavy exchange of gunfire broke out 10 days into the siege, and a young Oglala man was wounded. A cease-fire negotiated on March 10 quickly collapsed when six government agents and two ranchers were caught trying to enter the village, and an exchange of gunfire resulted in the wounding of an FBI agent. Both sides settled in for a long fight.

News of the occupation, and the large paramilitary force assembled to end it, stunned the American public. Sympathy for the Indians began to rise when it became clear that they were hopelessly outnumbered and outgunned, and that they had posed little threat to anyone. Actor Marlon Brando refused to accept his Academy Award for *The Godfather* in protest over the government's actions. Indians nationwide, and groups such as the National Council of Churches, began to organize on behalf of the defenders.

Attempts at negotiations failed throughout the first two months of the siege. The demands of the militants, a review of treaty violations by the United States, were beyond the power of the Interior Department officials who led the negotiations. The Justice Department demanded that the Indians lay down their arms before signing any agreements, but the militants refused. On March 26, a marshal was shot and seriously wounded, possibly by vigilantes, and on April 17, a firefight broke out that killed Frank Clearwater, a Cherokee member of AIM. On April 26, another heavy exchange of gunfire killed a young Oglala man, Buddy Lamont.

As the siege dragged on, the news media tired of the event, and the occupation slipped from the headlines. Both sides had had enough, and finally, on May 4, law officers promised that representatives of the White House would meet with the chiefs of the Lakota concerning the treaty violations. On May 9, tired and hungry, the defenders agreed to lay down their arms and submit to arrest. The siege had lasted 71 days and cost the government more than $7 million, the most expensive single police action mounted up to that time.

The occupation only worsened the tense conditions on the Pine Ridge Reservation. The government reneged on its promise of a treaty review. When Russell Means lost a highly charged election for tribal president against Wilson in February 1974, a virtual civil war broke out among the Oglala, leaving dozens of Indians dead.

The Justice Department was intent on prosecuting those involved in the occupation, especially Banks and Means. Boosted by the flamboyant defense team of William Kunstler, Mark Lane, and Kenneth Tilsen, the trial, beginning in February 1974 and lasting more than eight months, generated almost as much publicity as the occupation itself. The acquittals of both Banks and Means were a vindication for AIM and a serious blow to the Justice Department, which was accused by the trial judge of "misconduct" in its zeal to secure a conviction.

As for AIM, Wounded Knee catapulted the organization to national renown and put its charismatic leaders Russell Means and Dennis Banks into the limelight. The occupation and trials focused national attention on the problems that existed on INDIAN RESERVATIONS and brought about a resurgence of pride among Indians across the country. It also set in motion a counterreaction by the Justice Department and the BIA that would discredit and ultimately destroy AIM.

Further Reading

Burnette, Robert, and John Koster. *The Road to Wounded Knee.* New York: Bantam Books, 1974.
Lyman, Stanley David. *Wounded Knee 1973: A Personal Account.* Lincoln: University of Nebraska Press, 1991.
Smith, Paul Chaat, and Robert Warrior. *Like a Hurricane: The Indian Movement from Alcatraz to Wounded Knee.* New York: New Press, 1996.
Voices from Wounded Knee, 1973, in the Words of the Participants. Rooseveltown, N.Y.: Akwesasne Notes, 1974.
Warrior, Robert. "Past and Present at Wounded Knee." In *Defining Moments in Journalism,* edited by Nancy J. Woodhull. New Brunswick, N.J.: Transaction Publishers, 1998.

Wray, Link Frederick (Lincoln Wray, Jr.)

(1929–2005) *Shawnee guitarist*

A Shawnee, Frederick Lincoln Wray, Jr., was born on May 2, 1929, in Dunn, North Carolina, to Lillie M. Norris and Frederick "Fred" Lincoln Wray. The family later moved to Norfolk, Virginia, where Fred Wray got work in the navy shipyards. Link Wray began his musical career in 1947 playing Western swing in the Ranch Gang Band with brothers Doug and Vernon. He was drafted into the army in 1951, serving first in Germany and then in Korea. During the Korean War, he contracted tuberculosis, which resulted in the removal of a lung in 1955.

With Doug and Vernon Wray, Shorty Horton and Dixie Neale, Link Wray made his first recordings in 1956 as Lucky Wray and the Palomino Ranch Hands for Starday Records. They became the house band on the daily live TV show *Milt Grant's House Party* in Washington, D.C. Backing up cowboy stars such as Lash LaRue and Wild Bill Elliot, Wray would continually burn out his Sears and Roebuck guitar amps because he set the volume too high. Looking for a dirtier sound than that made by the guitars available in the 1950s, Wray played an off-brand Danelectro with long horns and mandolin pick-ups. In 1958, he signed with Cadence, where his debut "Rumble," off *Link Wray and His Ray Men*, made the top 20.

A slow, menacing instrumental, "Rumble" is believed to be the first record to feature a distorted guitar sound, later to become a hallmark of rock and roll and heavy metal. The piece originated as an onstage improvisation on Milt Grant's show for the hit group the Diamonds. When recording the tune in the studio later, Wray was dissatisfied with the sound until he punctured the speakers with a pencil. Later he intensified the effect by loosening tubes inside his amplifier.

When Cadence boss Archie Bleyer insisted that he play

country music, Wray switched to the Epic label. On Epic, his single "Raw-Hide" made the top 25 in 1959. In the 1960s, Wray wrote many songs and recorded many singles on the Swan label, including "Jack the Ripper," a minor hit in 1962. He also worked extensively as a session man and was a major influence on Duane Eddy and later Pete Townshend, Jeff Beck, Dave Davies, and Neil Young. Although Wray never again achieved the sales of his first two singles, he remained a cult figure, with a prolific output of records and CDs. In 1973, he joined Jerry Garcia, David Bromberg, and Commander Cody and the Lost Planet Airmen to release *Be What You Want To*, followed by *The Link Wray Rumble* in 1974.

Wray moved to Denmark in the early 1980s. He continued to issue records, though mostly in Europe, where he maintained a wide following. His album *Live in 85* was released on Ace Records (UK) from Scandinavian concerts. After producing *Indian Child* in June 1993, Wray was "rediscovered" by filmmaker Quentin Tarantino, who featured his music on the soundtrack of *Pulp Fiction*. In 1996, "Rumble" was heard on the soundtrack of the movie *Independence Day*. The following year, Wray released *Shadowman* (Ace Records) and, at the ripe age of 67, successfully toured the United States. In 2000, he released the album *Barbed Wire* (Ace).

Link Wray died at his home in Copenhagen on November 5, 2005. He was posthumously inducted into the Native American Music Hall of Fame on June 8, 2006.

XIT

XIT was a popular American Indian rock group from Albuquerque, New Mexico, that enjoyed a brief period of fame during the early 1970s. The band was an outgrowth of Lincoln St. Exit, a psychedelic-blues band made up of Sioux musicians A. Michael Martin (guitar and vocals), Leeja Herrera (drums), R. C. Gariss, Jr. (guitar), and Jomac Suazo (bass guitar). Lincoln St. Exit's first single, "Who's Been Driving My Little Yellow Taxi Cab," was released on Lance Records in 1966, with the song "Paper Lace" on the B side. The next year they released the 45-rpm single "The Bummer"/"Sunny Sunday Dream" on the Ecco label. Three more singles on three separate labels followed before they made the album *Drive It!* on Mainstream Records, released in 1970.

That same year, another Sioux, Tom Bee from Gallup, New Mexico, joined the band as a drummer alongside Herrera. Bee also became their manager and, with Mike Valvano, would become their principal songwriter. The band changed their name to XIT, which, according to Bee, stood for "Crossing of Indian Tribes," and became decidedly more political. Bee had written the song "We've Got Blue Skies," which was recorded by the Jackson Five. XIT was signed by a Motown Records subsidiary, Rare Earth, and their first album, *Plight of the Redman* (1972), was recorded at the historic Motown Hitsville studios in Detroit, Michigan. *Plight of the Redman*, a mix of Native chants and pop rock, was well received.

Very much a protest band, XIT hit a strong chord among Native youth coming under the influence of the RED POWER MOVEMENT of the day. Their next album, *Silent Warrior* (1973), also received critical acclaim. In 1974, they released the single "I Need Your Love (Give It to Me)" on Motown, but the label was in the process of folding Rare Earth and dropped the band. *Entrance (The Sound of Early XIT)*, released on Canyon Records in 1974, was a compilation, mostly of Lincoln St. Exit's earlier work. In 1977, XIT released *Relocation*, but by this time Herrera, Gariss, and Martin had left the band, and the album received little notice. XIT broke up shortly thereafter.

In 1988, Bee founded a successful recording company called Sound of America Records (SOAR). Bee eventually reconstituted XIT with new musicians, releasing *Entrance* in 1994, and a live album *Drums Across the Atlantic* in 1995, both on his SOAR label. Bee also bought back from Motown the earlier master recordings, and he has rereleased the older records, which were out of print and had become sought-after collector's items. After several successful tours, Bee decided to call it quits, and XIT performed a final farewell concert at the Mystic Lake Casino in Minnesota on May 20, 2000.

Further Reading

Murg, Wilhelm. "The Musicology of Tom Bee." *Indian Country Today*, 2 October 2003.
Rowlands, Lucinda. "'Without Reservation' by XIT." *Indian Country Today*, 20 November 2002.

Yazz, Beatien (Jimmy Toddy, "Little No Shirt")
(1928–   ) *Navajo (Dineh) painter*

Beatien Yazz was born Jimmy Toddy on March 5, 1928, near Wide Ruins, Arizona, to a traditional Navajo (Dineh) sheepherding family. As a child, he often drew pictures on the canyon walls with sharp stones to pass the time. His talent attracted the notice of the local trading post owners, Bill and Sally Lippincott, who gave him crayons and paper. He acquired his name Beatien Yazz (Little No Shirt) from his habit of not wearing a shirt, mimicking an artist he saw who was trying to get a tan.

Yazz had his first exhibition at age 10 at the Illinois State Museum in Springfield. The next year, he held a successful one-man show at the Art Center in La Jolla, California. When author Alberta Hannum visited the Southwest, she hired him to illustrate her book about the Wide Ruins trading post, *Spin a Silver Dollar* (1945).

Beatien Yazz attended the Santa Fe Indian School and later the Sherman Institute in Riverside, California. Before completing his coursework, he left to join the U.S. Marines. During World War II, he was a member of the famed Navajo CODE TALKERS, serving in China and the South Pacific. After the war, he enjoyed increasing fame, and collectors sought out his work. His paintings, original and personal, began to be influenced by the Studio School of DOROTHY DUNN, and later by the pan-Indian realism movement that developed in Oklahoma during the 1950s.

Yazz abandoned painting briefly to raise a family, but the 1958 release of another book by Hannum, *Paint the Wind*, which chronicled his life, led him to take up his paintbrush again. His most noted works include *Buffalo Hunt* (1977) and *The Yeibichei Gathering the Gift* (1980). Deteriorating eyesight eventually made it impossible for him to go on painting; his last work was completed in 1991. He was still living in Wide Ruins in December 2014, in good health except for his eye problem.

Further Reading
Brody, J. J. *Indian Painters and White Patrons*. Albuquerque: University of New Mexico Press, 1971.

Yellow Robe, Chauncey (Cano Wicakte, Kills in the Woods) (ca. 1868–1930) *hereditary Brulé Dakota Sioux chief, Indian rights activist*

Born around 1868 on the Rosebud Reservation in South Dakota (his tombstone gives his birth year as 1870), the son of Chief Yellow Robe (Tasinagi) and Tahcawin, Sitting Bull's niece, Chauncey Yellow Robe led the life of the traditional Dakota Sioux until, against his will, he was sent to the Carlisle Indian School in Pennsylvania in 1883. Although at first bewildered, he became a good student and played on the football team. Under Carlisle's outing system, Yellow Robe attended the Moody Institute summer school at Northfield, Massachusetts. In 1893, two years before leaving Carlisle, he was chosen to "represent" the North American Indians in the Congress of Nations at the opening of the Chicago Columbian Exposition (World's Fair), delivering a speech that was widely publicized at the time. After graduation, Yellow Robe taught at several government Indian schools. From about 1907 to 1909, he was an instructor in farming at the federal Indian boarding school in Rapid City, South Dakota. His non-Indian wife, Lillian Belle Springer, was the nurse there.

Yellow Robe was an ardent advocate of the intensely assimilationist educational methods of RICHARD HENRY PRATT. In 1911, he wrote:

> I entered Carlisle as a student in the fall of 1883, wearing long hair, feathers, blanket and a painted face, and above all not knowing one word of English. . . . I do not regret having been transformed from savagery to an independent American citizen. Through my

480

experiences, I believe there is only one way to educate the Indian—to take him away from his environment on the reservation and give him ample opportunity in the thickest atmosphere of civilization and he will become a worthy citizen.

Similarly, Yellow Robe was opposed to Wild West shows because he felt they glorified the Indian's "savage past." He was a prominent member of the SOCIETY OF AMERICAN INDIANS. At the same time, he was intensely proud of his culture. His children spoke their tribal language, and he taught them the lore, legends, and history of their people.

On August 4, 1927, when President Calvin Coolidge was officially adopted into the Sioux tribe at Deadwood City, South Dakota, Yellow Robe presented him with a war bonnet.

Yellow Robe starred in the film *The Silent Enemy* (1930), featuring MOLLY SPOTTED ELK and BUFFALO CHILD LONG LANCE (see LONGLANCE, SYLVESTER) produced by Douglas Burden and directed by Henry P. Carver, which was filmed in 1928–29 with a mostly Ojibwa cast in northern Ontario, the Northwest Territories, and Alaska. Yellow Robe was antipathetic to Long Lance's strong views favoring tribal culture. During the filming, he grew suspicious of his costar's claimed identification as a Blackfeet chief, prompting Paramount Pictures to conduct an investigation into Long Lance's background. Although a silent film, it was introduced by Yellow Robe in a short talking prologue. Ironically, after having survived months of subzero weather in the North, Yellow Robe caught cold while making this last piece of the film in New York City. It developed into pneumonia, and he died at the Rockefeller Institute Hospital in April 1930. His memory was honored in a tribute penned by President Coolidge.

Chauncey Yellow Robe's three daughters all had successful careers. Rosebud (1907–92), the eldest, was a noted actress, model, and educator. The middle sister, Chauncina White Horse (1909–1981) worked in advertising and sales; after her retirement, she was active in Indian affairs and served on the board of the National Indian Council on Aging. EVELYN YELLOW ROBE, the youngest daughter, became a noted speech pathologist and phonetician.

Further Reading

Yellow Robe, Chauncey. "The Menace of the Fraudulent Wild West Show." *Society of American Indians Quarterly Journal* 2 (July–September 1914): 224–225.
———. "My Boyhood Days." *Quarterly Journal of the Society of American Indians* 4, no. 1 (January–March 1916): 50–53.

Yellow Robe, Evelyn (Evelyn Yellow Robe Finkbeiner) (1919–) *Dakota–Brulé Lakota Sioux phonetician, laryngeal physiologist, speech pathologist*

Born on December 25, 1919, in South Dakota, Evelyn Yellow Robe was the youngest daughter of CHAUNCEY YELLOW ROBE and his wife, Lillian. When her mother died in 1922, she and her older sister, Chauncina, were looked after by Rosebud, the eldest sister. Around 1929, Rosebud married a journalist named A. E. Seymour and moved to New York. After their father died in 1930, Evelyn went to New York City to live with Rosebud. There she finished high school, where she was president of the honor society. Subsequently, she attended Mt. Holyoke College, where, in 1942, she became the first woman to receive a B.A. magna cum laude in speech and psychology. For excellence in scholarship she was named a Sarah Williston Scholar and a Mary Lyon Scholar. She also won a Gorse scholarship and an award from the government of France for excellence in French.

Also in 1942, Yellow Robe received a scholarship from the Illinois Federation of Women's Clubs and a university graduate fellowship to Northwestern University. There she won the newly created graduate Interpretation Award, receiving an M.A. in speech pathology in 1943. The following year, she won a second scholarship at Northwestern for postgraduate study, receiving a Ph.D. in 1947. She was awarded the Indian Achievement Medal of the Indian Council Fire in 1946.

Yellow Robe conducted research on the Dakota language, making extensive audio recordings of speakers (on 33 acetate discs) in 1947, now kept at the Library of Congress. In 1954, she was awarded a Fulbright fellowship to study the physiology of the larynx in Paris. She lectured at medical centers in London, Hamburg, Groningen, the Netherlands, and Padua, Italy. After returning to the United States, she was appointed lecturer in otolaryngology and assistant director of the Voice Clinic at Northwestern University Medical School.

Yellow Robe married Hans Finkbeiner, M.D. (1915–98), a cytologist and specialist in the early recognition of cancer, on December 26, 1959, and left the United States to live in Germany. She was interviewed in May 2001 by Theodore Sargent for his book *One Life of Elaine Goodale Eastman*. Her sister Rosebud, born on February 26, 1907, moved to New York City in 1927 and became an actress and radio star. Rosebud Yellow Robe died on October 5, 1992.

Further Reading

Weinberg, Marjorie. *The Real Rosebud: The Triumph of a Lakota Women.* Lincoln: University of Nebraska Press, 2004.

Yellowtail, Robert Summers (1889–1988) *Crow political leader*

Born in Lodge Grass on the Crow reservation in Montana on August 4, 1889, to Yellow Tail, a Crow, and Elizabeth Chienne, part Crow and French, Robert Summers Yellowtail began his education there in the Crow Agency boarding school. At age 13, he went to the Sherman Institute in Riverside, California, graduating in 1907. He studied for a while at the Extension Law School in Los Angeles and retained a keen interest in legal matters throughout his long life.

Though he belonged to the new generation of educated Indians, Yellowtail stood with traditional Chief Plenty Coups against efforts of Senator Thomas Walsh of Montana to open the Crow reservation, the third largest in the country, to homesteading. Between 1918 and 1920, Yellowtail spoke before

Crow leader Robert Yellowtail appeared before Congress in 1945. *(AP/Wideworld)*

the Indian Reorganization Act; yet ironically, though he was a popular figure on the reservation, the Crow voted almost unanimously against the act.

Yellowtail believed in the importance of Crow tradition. Through his efforts, during his first year as superintendent, 400 head of buffalo were transferred from Yellowstone Park to the Crow reservation. (The original herd had disappeared around 1883.) He supported the reintroduction of the Sun Dance in 1941, and his brother Thomas Yellowtail, a prominent Crow medicine man, became Sun Dance leader in 1969 (see TREHERO, JOHN).

By 1944, at the first convention of the NATIONAL CONGRESS OF AMERICAN INDIANS, and by 1945, among Northern Plains tribes, Yellowtail was actively campaigning to succeed John Collier as Indian commissioner. It would be another 20 years, however, before a Native American occupied this position (see BENNETT, ROBERT LAFOLLETTE). Yellowtail was instrumental in writing the first Crow tribal constitution of 1948 and was elected tribal chair in 1952. He led the opposition to the construction of a dam on the Bighorn River, and after it was built, fought for many years to get a settlement for the 6,846 acres of condemned land. Ironically, it was named the Yellowtail Dam.

Yellowtail owned a large ranch and raised stock part time for many years. After his retirement as tribal chair, he was able to devote more of his time to ranching. *Contrary Warriors: A Film of the Crow Tribe* (Rattlesnake Productions, 1988) is largely about his life and contains interviews with him. He died on June 18, 1988. His papers are housed at Little Big Horn College.

Further Reading

Bradley, Charles Crane, Jr. *The Handsome People: A History of the Crow Indians and the Whites.* Billings, Mont.: Council for Indian Education, 1991.

Hoxie, Frederick E. *Parading through History: The Making of the Crow Nation in America, 1805–1935.* New York: Cambridge University Press, 1995.

Poten, Constance J. "Robert Yellowtail, the New Warrior." *Montana The Magazine of Western History* 39, no. 3 (Summer 1989): 36–41.

various congressional committees to oppose a number of bills detrimental to the tribe, and he took a significant part in shaping the Crow Act of 1920, which allotted 640 acres of reservation land to every tribal member. The land could not be sold for 25 years unless the allottee died. Through his activities in Washington, Yellowtail won the respect of Montana senator Burton K. Wheeler, chair of the Senate Committee on Indian Affairs. Yellowtail was offered his choice of a superintendency at almost any agency he wanted, but he did not take the offer at that time; he also declined a position as inspector in the Department of the Interior.

During the hearings on the Wheeler-Howard bill (February–May 1934)—which became the INDIAN REORGANIZATION ACT—Yellowtail warned that factionalism was a danger to reorganization among the Crow. He also pointed out that the non-Indian owners, who had most of the best land on the heavily "checkerboarded" reservation, were not willing to sell the tribe back their parcels, and that, if forced to do so, they would demand grossly inflated prices.

Yellowtail accepted the superintendency of the Crow reservation in 1934, only the second Indian ever to be appointed a superintendent. His election was made possible by new civil service regulations that allowed Indian Commissioner JOHN COLLIER to give preference to Indians for jobs in the BUREAU OF INDIAN AFFAIRS (BIA). In this position, Yellowtail promoted

Yellow Thunder, Raymond (1920–1972)

Oglala Lakota Sioux murder victim

An Oglala Lakota cowboy from the Pine Ridge Reservation, Raymond Yellow Thunder lived in Gordon, Nebraska, for several years. He was born on the reservation in 1920 near Kyle, South Dakota, and was the grandson of American Horse, an Oglala chief. One of seven children, Yellow Thunder had grown up in poverty. Although he had once aspired to be an artist, he became a ranch hand in Gordon and trained horses on the side. By 1972, Yellow Thunder had been married and divorced, and he was known by his friends as a quiet, hardworking man with no enemies.

On the night of February 15, 1972, Yellow Thunder was beaten for sport by four white men: two brothers, Melvin and

Leslie Hare, Bernard Ludder, and Robert Bayless. He was then thrown into the trunk of a car and driven to the American Legion Post, where a dance was underway. Stripped naked, he was forced to dance for the crowd, beaten again, and thrown out into the cold. After a few days, when his family in Pine Ridge began to worry about him, they traveled to Gordon and found him on February 20, dead in his truck. Although the Hares were arrested, they were immediately freed on bail on a charge of second-degree manslaughter. Unable to get help from the Pine Ridge Tribal Council, the BUREAU OF INDIAN AFFAIRS, or private attorneys, the infuriated family and friends of Yellow Thunder turned to the AMERICAN INDIAN MOVEMENT (AIM) to seek a harsher penalty for the murder.

In March 1973, AIM led more than 1,400 Indians on a march through Gordon, Nebraska, shutting down the town for three days. The town capitulated, charging the murderers with manslaughter and false imprisonment and agreeing to form a human rights commission to monitor brutality and racism against Indians. The federal and state governments ordered their own investigation into Yellow Thunder's death, and the chief of police in Gordon was dismissed.

Three of the men arrested in connection with Yellow Thunder's death were found guilty of manslaughter, and the other, after cooperating with the authorities, was found guilty of false imprisonment. They were sentenced to imprisonment, with the longest term being six years. The convictions were considered a major victory by Indian advocates. During the 1980s, AIM established a camp in the Black Hills named Camp Yellow Thunder.

Youkioma (Yukioma, Yukiwma, "Almost Perfect")

(1835–1929) *traditional Hopi leader*

Born in Old Oraibi, Arizona, on the Third Mesa around 1835, Youkioma—meaning "Almost Perfect," and as with most Hopi names, spelled in various ways, including Yukioma and Yukiwma—was a member of the Kokop (Fire) Clan. By the end of the 19th century, the Hopi of Oraibi had begun to split into two factions, the "progressives," or "friendlies," under Bear Clan chief Lololma, who were willing to accommodate the federal government's forced ASSIMILATION policies, and the "traditionals" led by Lomahongyoma, head of the Spider Clan, who favored resistance. The split was also religious in nature, as the ancient Hopi culture was steeped in ceremony and prophesy. The progressives believed that the white Americans were the foretold "white brothers," or *bahanna*, Hopi who had migrated east in a distant past. The traditionals were skeptical, however, because the Americans spoke no Hopi, nor did they have the other half of a sacred stone tablet the Hopi had split before the migration.

The Kokop Clan, one of the most important in the Hopi clan system, was allied to Lomahongyoma and the traditionals. In 1890 and 1891, American government officials arrested and imprisoned a number of the hostile leaders, including Lomahongyoma, Youkioma, and his older brother Patupha, head of the Kokop Clan, for refusing to allow Oraibi children to be sent to school. These actions so inflamed the traditionals that they imprisoned Lololma—who had tried to convince the village to cooperate with the Americans—in a kiva until he was rescued by American soldiers.

In 1892, Congress authorized the ALLOTMENT of the Hopi reservation, an initiative both factions resisted by threatening to go to war. Adding fuel to the fire, the Hopi suffered from a plague of missionaries, anthropologists, and tourists, drawn by their closely guarded culture, and aggressively determined to invade the secret ceremonies and undermine the Hopi religion.

In 1894, Youkioma and other Hopi resistance leaders were arrested and imprisoned on Alcatraz Island. In 1902, Hopi superintendent Charles Burton, a zealous assimilationist, forced all Hopi men to have their hair cut short. Such heavy-handed tactics on the part of federal officials made the coexistence of the two factions untenable. After the retirement of Lomahongyoma in 1902, Youkioma became the leader of the traditionals, and he invited supporters from the Second Mesa town of Shongopovi to support his cause. In September 1906, the postponement of the important Snake Dance led to tensions between the two camps and the threat of violence. On September 7, after a few minor skirmishes, Youkioma drew a line on the ground and challenged the progressive faction, now led by WILSON TEWAQUAPTEWA, to a pushing match. If the progressives could push the traditionals across the line, the latter would vacate the town, but if the traditionals triumphed, they would stay.

The traditional side was defeated in the pushing match, and Youkioma and 300 of his followers gathered their belongings and moved to a site seven miles to the north, founding the village of Hotevilla on Third Mesa. Despite Youkioma's hope that he and his followers might be left alone by the *bahanna*, the government and missionaries followed them to the new town, even building a school there. For their continued resistance to education and Christianity, Commissioner of Indian Affairs FRANCIS ELLINGTON LEUPP had 101 of the Hotevilla men arrested in 1907. Most were sentenced to a year's hard labor at Keams Canyon, Arizona, and Youkioma himself was sent to the Carlisle Indian School in Pennsylvania for "rehabilitation." All of Hotevilla's children were rounded up and incarcerated in boarding schools, not to return until 1910. Hotevilla suffered severe hardship from cold weather and food shortages during its first years but continued to resist attempts at assimilation.

In 1911, Youkioma traveled to Washington, D.C., where he met with President William Taft in a vain attempt to lobby for Hopi self-determination. Youkioma spent much of the next decade in and out of prison, including three years in the local guardhouse, from 1916 to 1919, for resisting the opening of a day school in Hotevilla. As the nearby Hopi villages of Oraibi, Bakabi (Bacavi), and Kykotsmovi began to abandon their religious ceremonies under the repressive policies of Indian Commissioner CHARLES H. BURKE and Christian reformers, Youkioma's defiance made it possible to preserve these ceremonies at Hotevilla. Though Youkioma died there in 1929, Hotevilla remained a stronghold of Hopi traditionalism under the leadership of his son, DAN KATCHONGVA.

Further Reading

Wyckoff, Lydia L. "*Bacavi: Journey to Reed Springs* by Peter Whiteley." *American Indian Quarterly* 14, no. 3 (1990): 327–330.

Young Deer, James (James Johnson) (1878–1946)
Lenni Lenape (Delaware) actor, film director

James Young Deer was born James Johnson in Washington, D.C., on April 1, 1878 (his military records give the date as April 1, 1876), the son of George G. and Emma Young Johnson. In his publicity he claimed he was born in Lakota City, Nebraska, and many recent sources have designated him as Winnebago, but neither statement is correct. An item in the Carlisle *Arrow* from June 8, 1906, described him as "a young man of Indian and Spanish descent." According to his widow, Winnebago actress LILLIAN ST. CYR, in a *New York Times* article from May 16, 1958, he was Delaware (Lenni-Lenape).

Details of his actual origins are sketchy. In the 1860 and 1870 federal censuses, both his parents' families are designated "mulatto," a term simply meaning "mixed race." No doubt they were of mixed race, but in any case people of Indian ancestry in that period and in that part of the country were rarely designated as Indian on official documents, since they had no legal status as Indians. His father was from Pennsylvania; his mother and maternal grandmother, Anna Young, were from Washington, D.C. The second youngest of five children, he lost his father before he was four, and the family moved in with Emma's unmarried brother William P. Young, a lithographer by trade, who was at least 12 years older than Emma and had been a sailor in his younger days.

Young Deer later claimed to have toured the country in his youth with the Barnum and Bailey Circus. In October 1898, during the Spanish-American War, he enlisted in the U.S. Navy as James Y. Johnson but did not go to sea. He was discharged in October 1901. Some time later, Johnson adopted the name Young Deer. Contemporary news articles generally refer to him as James or Jim Youngdeer; in his film credits he is usually called James Young Deer. On April 9, 1906, on his marriage to Lillian St. Cyr in Washington, D.C., his name was entered as J. Younger Johnson.

Young Deer and St. Cyr, known as Princess Red Wing, began to work with Kalem, an independent film company established in New York City in 1907, and in 1908, Red Wing debuted in *The White Squaw*. Shortly afterward, they worked for Lubin Studios in Philadelphia, with Young Deer writing scenarios and assisting in production. His first film credit came as director of *The Falling Arrow*, released on May 3, 1909. Red Wing starred as Felice, the daughter of a Mexican farmer kidnapped by a white outlaw. Rescued by an Indian named Young Deer (played by Young Deer, though he is not credited), they fall in love. Felice's father opposes the romance, but after she is kidnapped again by the outlaw and rescued by Young

Deer, he finally consents to their marriage. *The Falling Arrow* explored themes that Young Deer would revisit time and again in his films: romance between an Indian and non-Indian, often leading to tragedy; the portrayal of American Indians as heroic and noble; and—remarkable for that day and age—the villain as a white man.

In 1909, the couple left Lubin and began appearing in films for Bison Motion Pictures. Based in Fort Lee, New Jersey, the company was a subsidiary of the New York Motion Picture Company (NYMP) and was led by legendary cameraman Fred Balshofer. Young Deer's first acting credit was for a Bison film, *The True Heart of an Indian*, released on July 2, 1909. He next appeared with Red Wing and served as technical adviser in a Biograph production *The Mended Lute* (1909), directed by D. W. Griffith. Young Deer directed two pictures for Vitagraph in 1909: *For Her Sake; or, Two Sailors and a Girl* and *Red Wing's Gratitude*, both featuring Red Wing. He returned to Bison to star in *Young Deer's Bravery* (1909), which the *Motion Picture Herald* described as "most entertaining, exciting and splendidly acted."

While continuing to work for Bison, Young Deer began a successful association with the French film company Pathé Frères. One of the earliest film studios and the dominant film company in Europe, Pathé had been exporting to the United States since 1896 but by 1909 saw its European-made films losing ground to the new American studios. Pathé's U.S. manager, J. A. Berst, persuaded the company to make movies in America. Eager to create Westerns with an emphasis on "realism," Berst immediately tapped Young Deer to manage the new Westerns division. *The Girl from Arizona* (1910), featuring Red Wing, became the first Pathé film made in America. The next, *White Fawn's Devotion: A Play Acted by a Tribe of Red Indians in America*, released in mid-1910, was directed by Young Deer and also starred Red Wing. Both were filmed near Bound Brook, New Jersey. In striving for realism, it appears that Young Deer hired the Miller Brothers 101 Ranch Wild West Show as extras—their brand can be spotted on one of the horses in the film *White Fawn's Devotion*. The Miller brothers, from Oklahoma, had started recruiting Indians from the plains to perform in their shows the previous year and a few years later would combine forces with Bison and become an important part of the film industry (see EAGLE SHIRT, WILLIAM).

In late November 1909, the Bison Company, along with Young Deer and Red Wing, relocated to Edendale, California, then a suburb of Los Angeles, where they built a studio at 1719 Allesandro Street (now Glendale Boulevard). He would star in 15 films for Bison from 1909 through 1911, including *Young Deer's Gratitude*, *The Indian and the Cowgirl*, *A True Indian Brave*, and *Young Deer's Return*, all released in 1910.

Some time in 1910, Young Deer began making films for Pathé in California. Among the first was the all-Indian *A Cheyenne Brave*, filmed on the S&M Ranch in Santiago Canyon, California, and released in August 1910. Other Pathé films directed by Young Deer in 1910 were *The Red Girl and the Child*, *Cowboy Justice*, *The Indian and the Maid*, the war drama *Under Both Flags*, and *The Yaqui Girl*, also filmed at the S&M Ranch, in which he also costarred with his protégé, Virginia Chester.

In September 1911, Young Deer and Red Wing starred in *Little Dove's Romance*, their last movie for Bison. The following month, director Thomas H. Ince arrived in California and reorganized the Bison Company. Joining forces with the Miller Brothers 101 Ranch, which was wintering in nearby Venice, California, Ince relocated to the Santa Ynez Canyon and began using the Miller Brothers' roster of Indian actors, including Oglala Lakotas Eagle Shirt and Luther Standing Bear.

In the meantime, Young Deer had convinced Pathé to relocate to Edendale, where he designed and supervised the construction of the new Pathé studios. In 1911, Young Deer invented a new process for photographing moonlight and firelight effects with exceptional clarity, which he subsequently used in his Westerns. In addition to being the studio head for Pathé, in 1911 Young Deer directed *The Cowboy's Devotedness*, *A Western Courtship* and *Lieutenant Scott's Narrow Escape*. He directed and starred alongside Red Wing in *Red Deer's Devotion* (1911) and directed and starred in *The Kid from Arizona* (1911). In 1912, he wrote and directed *The Squaw Man's Sweetheart*, starring Red Wing and George M. Gebhardt. His last directing credit for Pathé was *The Savage*, in 1913.

Young Deer's films were usually one- or two-reelers with running times of only 10 or 20 minutes each. At Pathé, he produced or directed more than 150 of these, for most of which he was not credited. Young Deer strove for realism, both in the sets and acting. He was once fined for mistreating a horse in a misguided attempt to make it appear dead.

His work did much to change the image of the Indian in the mainstream American media, which had typically portrayed them as senseless savages. In Young Deer's world, it was the white man who was almost invariably the savage; a shiftless, untrustworthy, drunken outlaw. By contrast, the Indians in his films were almost always honorable, trustworthy, and stoic regardless of their fate.

By this time, Young Deer and Red Wing were among the most famous actors in the country. Young Deer was one of the stars in the Tournament of Roses (Rose Bowl) parade in Pasadena in 1913. He was an ardent sportsman, promoting the fights of Jose Ybarra, known as "Mexican Joe Rivers," and managing fighters Bert Fagan and Johnny Schiff. He also apparently had a taste for the high life and was admitted to the hospital once for "alcohol hysteria" after a glass-eating stunt in a bar went awry.

On May 10, 1913, Young Deer was questioned by a grand jury investigating a white slavery ring and a string of brothels allegedly run by Los Angeles police officers. Later that year, on November 23, he was arrested in Los Angeles for "contributing to the delinquency" of a young woman, Marie Wilkerson, described as an actress. He protested his innocence and posted $1,500 bail. A few days later, he was named in a complaint by a 15-year-old girl, although the details were secret. In turn, on November 25, Wilkerson and her sister were caught trying to blackmail Young Deer and another defendant in the case, Frank Troxler, a businessman. The two girls had offered to drop the charges and leave town in return for $300, a large sum at the time. Wilkerson was arrested and charged with extortion, but her sister managed to get out of town.

Despite Wilkerson's arrest, Young Deer, fearing he would not get a fair trial, jumped bail and fled to England. In a letter to the presiding judge Fred H. Taft, parts of which were quoted in *The Los Angeles Times* of December 27, 1913, Young Deer stated that he believed he was "to be made the black sheep of the whole (white slave) happenings." He protested that his codefendant, Troxler, "was a white man and had no established business. He was released on his own personal bond. I had an established business. I was an Indian. I was held for $1,500." Fearing "the white man's justice," Young Deer had left Los Angeles to raise money and prepare his defense but promised to return as soon as he had raised the money. Remarkably, Judge Taft took him at his word and removed the case from the calendar until Young Deer was ready. Likewise the bondsmen did not forfeit Young Deer's bail, believing that he would return. In postponing the trial, Taft simply stated, "He is an Indian," and thus, according to a belief reinforced in part by Young Deer's own films, his word was good.

While in England, Young Deer directed several productions. The first three, from the popular "Lieutenant Daring" crime series, were *The Water Rats of London*, *Queen of the London Counterfeiters*, and *The Black Cross Gang*, which he also wrote. These were filmed at British and Colonial Films' one-stage studio at Hoe Street, Walthamstow, London. He also wrote and directed two films for Motograph, both produced by Joseph Bamberger. The first, *The Belle of Crystal Palace*, starring Babs Neville and Harry Lorraine, was filmed at Motograph's studio in the Crystal Palace at Sydenham, Kent. The second was not made until after Britain's declaration of war on Germany on August 4, 1914. This film, *The World at War*, featured Lorraine as Lieutenant Jack Daring, a pilot who catches spies and shoots down zeppelins with new skyguns.

In September 1914, before embarking on the SS *Cedric* bound for New York, Young Deer wrote Judge Taft from Liverpool, "I am returning to fulfill my promise to you." Young Deer had kept his word, and on December 4, 1914, Taft dismissed all charges against him when Wilkerson, the main witness against him, did not show up. Yet despite being absolved of all wrongdoing, Young Deer's career was in ruins. He had been dropped by Pathé in 1913, at the first hint of the scandal, and even Red Wing, who was unwavering in defense of her husband, had trouble finding movie roles.

By this time, the film industry was undergoing a major change. The short films that Young Deer had produced and directed were being replaced by longer, feature-length movies. In addition, Indian dramas of the kind that Young Deer made were played out. New corporations, such as Paramount and Universal, with the financial means to fund longer, more complex films, were coming on the scene, as were the first movie superstars, such as Charlie Chaplin, Mary Pickford, and Douglas Fairbanks, who would change the way movies were made and marketed.

In 1917, Young Deer appeared with Red Wing in *Under*

Handicap, a Western directed by Fred Balshofer for the Yorke Film Corporation. In 1918 and 1919, he worked as an actor at Universal Studios, but the only credit known for him there is as writer of the Western *Neck and Noose* (1919), directed by George Holt. Pathé brought him briefly to France, where he directed a few films. He came back to America in the winter of 1919, appearing in *Fighting Through*, directed by Christy Cabanne, then returned to England to direct his only known comedy, *Who Laughs Last* (1920) for Thespian Productions. In New York, he directed *The Stranger* (1920) for a small production company B. S. Moss.

Young Deer's last acting role was as a Mexican bandit in *Man of Courage* (1922). His last known film, and the last of the Lieutenant Daring series, was made in England the following year. *Lieutenant Daring RN and the Water Rats* (1924), released by British and Colonial, was a six-reel adventure about drug smugglers, starring Percy Moran, produced by J. B. McDowell, written by Young Deer and Moran, and directed by Edward R. Gordon, Young Deer, and Moran. The company went out of business later that year.

Young Deer's idealized vision of American Indians was going out of style. In part, this coincided with the end of the Progressive Era in Indian affairs and a crackdown on Indian culture by the federal government, which enacted new policies such as the DANCE ORDERS to try to stamp out Native religions. New filmmakers, such as John Ford, began to glamorize the conquest of the West, idealizing the pioneers, prospectors, and gunfighters, and relegating Indians to bit characters who, if anything, stood in the way of progress. Stories featuring interracial romance, a prominent theme in Young Deer's movies, became taboo as censorship began to take hold in Hollywood. His career floundering, Young Deer worked as an acting coach in San Francisco in 1930 and later opened an acting school in Hollywood. In the 1930s, he directed some low-budget B movies with studios from Hollywood's "Poverty Row," but no credits are known. Details of the last decade of his life are lacking. James Young Deer died of stomach cancer in New York City on April 6, 1946.

Despite the brevity of their fame, Young Deer and Red Wing were pioneers of the American cinema. They played an important role in the transition of movies from the simple, short films that were often under 10 minutes into the longer, feature-length films of today. They were among the first stars in the new medium, predating the golden era of silent film made famous by celebrities such as Tom Mix, Mary Pickford, Charlie Chaplin, and Rudolph Valentino. They successfully presented a sympathetic portrayal of Indians to the American public, a vision that, with few exceptions, would not reemerge in American films until the late 1960s.

See FILM, AMERICAN INDIANS AND.

Further Reading

Aleiss, Angela. *Making the White Man's Indian: Native Americans and Hollywood Movies*. Santa Barbara, Calif.: Praeger Publishers, 2005.
Wallis, Michael. *The Real Wild West: The 101 Ranch and the Creation of the American West*. New York: St. Martin's Griffin, 1999.

Yowlachie, Chief (Chief Yowlache, "Lucky Hand" Donald Simmons, Daniel Simmons,) (1891–1966)
Puyallup-Yakama actor, concert vocalist

Donald Simmons was born on August 15, 1891, on a farm on the Yakima (now Yakama) Reservation in Washington State, the son of John W. and Lucy Simmons (later Riddle). Though his given name was Donald, he used the name Daniel Simmons. He was an enrolled member of the Yakima Nation but actually a Puyallup by birth. To the public, he was "Chief Yowlachie" (Lucky Hand; earlier spelled Yowlache), but this was merely a stage name; he was not really a chief.

Simmons left the reservation in 1911 to learn the machinist's trade at the Cushman Indian Trade School in Tacoma, Washington. A fine, natural bass-baritone, he also studied singing. He was already using the name "Chief Yowlache" by December 1922 when he sang at the Pantages Theater in Portland, Oregon. Moving to southern California in 1923 to continue vocal studies, he initially got work as a film actor to finance his singing lessons.

In one of his earliest films, *Tonio, Son of the Sierras* (1925), Yowlachie played the title role as an army Indian scout unjustly accused of treachery. He had a leading role in *Moran of the Mounted* (Rayart, 1926); played "Iron Eyes" in the epic Western *War Paint* (MGM, 1926); and had the title role in *Sitting Bull at the Spirit Lake Massacre* (Sunset, 1927), a low-budget action film in which a fictitious Sitting Bull takes revenge on the whites. His first sound films were *The Invaders* (Syndicate, 1929, also released as a silent), *The Santa Fe Trail* (Paramount 1930, with Richard Arlen), and *The Girl of the Golden West* (First National, 1930).

During the 1920s, Yowlachie studied voice in Los Angeles and Pasadena with Alan Ray Carpenter and Otto Hummel, and in New York with Metropolitan Opera tenor Pasquale Amato. In the following decade, he had some success as a concert artist, giving his New York debut recital at the Barbizon-Plaza Hotel on November 18, 1930. The *New York Times* wrote of the "extraordinary range" of his voice, the "profound conviction and authority" of his delivery, and the "uncommon dignity" of his stage presence. For much of the 1930s, Yowlachie toured the country as a contract artist with Columbia Concerts Corporation. Among the highlights of this period were a performance of Indian songs arranged by Homer Grunn and S. Earle Blakeslie in which Yowlachie was accompanied by the Los Angeles Symphony Orchestra under Artur Rodzinski, and command performances at the White House for Presidents Herbert Hoover and Franklin Roosevelt. He did not work in films during the period 1931–38.

Yowlachie returned to the screen in 1939, playing mainly in serials and B Westerns, but also in such films as Cecil B. DeMille's color feature *Northwest Mounted Police* (Paramount, 1940) with Gary Cooper; the classic Western *Red River* (United Artists, 1948); and *Yellow Sky* (20th-Century Fox,

1948), with Gregory Peck and Anne Baxter. He acted and sang in the film *King of the Stallions* made by Monogram in 1942. A particularly notable B film was *The Cowboy and the Indians* (Columbia, 1949), which had a good script and in which Gene Autry introduced the song "Here Comes Santa Claus."

Yowlachie appeared in many other films during the 1950s and 1960s, still mainly Bs and serials but also including some features such as *A Ticket to Tomahawk* (20th-Century Fox, 1950), a lively musical comedy with Dan Dailey, Anne Baxter, Rory Calhoun, Walter Brennan, and Marilyn Monroe; *Winchester '73* (Universal, 1950), starring James Stewart and Shelley Winters, said to be one of the best Westerns of its time; and *Warpath* (Paramount, 1951), with a fine cast including Edmond O'Brien, Dean Jagger, and Wallace Ford. During this period, he also did considerable television work.

Chief Yowlachie died in Los Angeles on March 7, 1966. Curiously, his life span was almost exactly the same as screen actor NIPO STRONGHEART, who was also a Yakama.

Z

Zah, Peterson (1937–) *Navajo (Dineh) tribal chair, president*

Peterson Zah was born on December 2, 1937, the son of Henry and Mae (Multine) Zah, traditional Navajo (Dineh). The family lived in the disputed joint-use area of the Hopi reservation (see BIG MOUNTAIN), and Mae spoke only the Navajo language. Peterson attended the Phoenix Indian School, excelling in athletics, and after graduating in 1960, he studied at Arizona State University on a basketball scholarship.

Graduating from Arizona State in 1963 with a B.A. in education, Zah worked in the Arizona Vocational Education Department in Phoenix and later with VISTA, the domestic version of the Peace Corps. In 1965, he returned to Arizona State for two years to coordinate the training of volunteers assigned to work on INDIAN RESERVATIONS. He left that position in 1967 to become the executive director of a legal aid service in Window Rock on the Navajo Reservation. Over the next 14 years, the staff grew to more than 30 attorneys and some 100 employees spread over nine separate offices on the vast reservation, and the Dinebeiina Nahiilna Be Agaditahe (DNA), as the legal service was known, became an effective advocate for impoverished Navajo who had nowhere else to turn.

Beginning his political career with his election to the school board in Window Rock, Zah became its president the next year. In this position, he instituted an aggressive language-maintenance program, partly to preserve the language among the youth and partly because of his conviction that the Navajo language conveys important concepts that cannot be expressed in English. Zah helped develop Navajo curricula and textbooks, brought traditional medicine men and elders to lecture in the classrooms, and encouraged the hiring of Navajo teachers and the use of the Navajo language in all classes, including science and math.

In 1983, Zah defeated PETER MACDONALD in the race for the chair of the tribal council and leadership of the nation's largest and most populous reservation. His four-year term was fraught with difficulties, not the least of them the continued opposition of the MacDonald supporters. Moving away from MacDonald's emphasis on economic development, Zah tried to bolster the faltering Navajo education and health systems. However, he was hamstrung by the heavy budget cuts enacted by the new administration of President Ronald Reagan, whose commissioner of Indian affairs, KENNETH L. SMITH, slashed federal funds to the Navajo reservation by almost one-third. Zah was also unable to resolve the bitter Big Mountain dispute with the Hopi, despite campaign promises that he could sit down with his boyhood friend, Hopi chair IVAN SIDNEY, and forge a compromise. They did at least manage to call a truce in the war of lawsuits between the tribes. While Zah was in Washington, D.C., lobbying against federal cuts, an outbreak of the deadly hantavirus occurred on the reservation, causing widespread panic and concern.

Although Zah was defeated by MacDonald in 1987, MacDonald quickly became embroiled in a scandal surrounding his son's role in brokering a land purchase by the tribal government, and Zah regained leadership in 1990. He held the newly created position of tribal president until 1994. Since 1995, Zah has served at Arizona State University as adviser to the university president on American Indian affairs. His papers are housed at the Labriola Center, Arizona State University.

Zitkala-Sa *See* BONNIN, GERTRUDE.

APPENDIX: MAPS

Indian Activism in the United States, 20th–21st Century

Plymouth Capture of Mayflower II (1970)

Ganienkeh-Mohawk occupation (1974)

Kanesetake and Kanawake Mohawk barricades (1990)

Seige of Akwesasne (1979–81)

Montreal

North American Unity Caravans organized (1964)

Tuscarora stop the flooding on their reservation (1958)

Washington, D.C.

Occupation of BIA offices (1972)

The Longest Walk (1978)

The Longest Walk II (2008)

Walk for Justice (1994)

Trail of Broken Treaties caravan to Washington (1972)

Cornwall Bridge Blockade (1968)

Levi General travels to Geneva to state the case for Iroquois sovereignty at the League of Nations (1923)

Seneca block highway (1985)

Kinzua Dam protests (1964)

Columbus

Society of American Indians formed (1911)

Lumbee chase out Ku Klux Klan (1958)

Lumbee Eddie Hatcher and Timothy Jacobs seize newspaper office (1988)

Seminole Tribe of Florida v. Butterworth opens door to gaming (1981)

Wallace "Mad Bear" Anderson and a delegation of Miccosukee travel to Cuba and meet Fidel Castro (1959)

Menominee Warrior Society occupies church abbey (1975)

Great Lakes Indian Fish and Wildlife Commission founded (1984)

DRUMS founded (1970)

Gresham

Chicago

American Indian Chicago Conference (1961)

Kansas City

Huron cemetary dispute (1906)

Crazy Snake Rebellion (1900–09)

International Indian Treaty Council founded (1974)

Garrison Dam dispute (1946)

Leonard Peltier convicted (1977)

Fargo

Minneapolis

AIM founded (1968)

Mobridge

Rapid City

Pine Ridge

Occupation of Wounded Knee (1973, 1975)

National Congress of American Indians founded (1944)

Denver

Big Mountain land dispute begins (1960)

Taos

Blue Lake return (1970)

All-Pueblo Council reconstituted to oppose the Bursum Bill (1922)

Women of All Red Nations founded (1978)

Mt. Rushmore Prayer vigil (1971)

Custer Riot (1973)

Boulder

Native American Rights Fund founded (1970)

Occupation of Fairchild Instrument plant (1971)

Gallup

National Indian Youth Council founded (1961)

Mount Graham dispute (1988)

Battle Mountain disputes begin (1974)

Pyramid Lake disputes begin (1902)

Occupation of Alcatraz, (1964, 1969–71)

San Francisco

Box Canyon Murders (1974)

Hopi organize "meeting of religious people" to support their traditions (1956)

Indigenous Environmental Network founded (1990)

Fish-ins (1964)

David Sohappy arrested (1968) for fishing without license

Pit River Occupation (1970)

Columbia R.

- ● City
- ● Other important site

300 miles

300 km

© Infobase Learning

Mission Indians

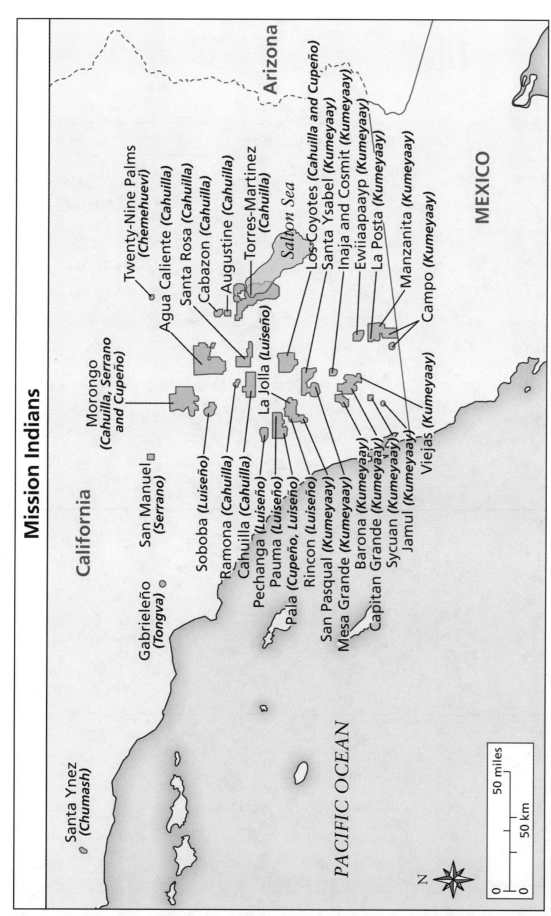

California

Santa Ynez
(Chumash)

Gabrieleño
(Tongva)

San Manuel
(Serrano)

Morongo
*(Cahuilla, Serrano
and Cupeño)*

Twenty-Nine Palms
(Chemehuevi)

Agua Caliente *(Cahuilla)*

Santa Rosa *(Cahuilla)*

Cabazon *(Cahuilla)*

Augustine *(Cahuilla)*

Torres-Martinez
(Cahuilla)

Salton Sea

Los Coyotes *(Cahuilla and Cupeño)*

Santa Ysabel *(Kumeyaay)*

Inaja and Cosmit *(Kumeyaay)*

Ewiiaapaayp *(Kumeyaay)*

La Posta *(Kumeyaay)*

Manzanita *(Kumeyaay)*

Campo *(Kumeyaay)*

MEXICO

Arizona

Soboba *(Luiseño)*

Ramona *(Cahuilla)*

Cahuilla *(Cahuilla)*

Pechanga *(Luiseño)*

Pauma *(Luiseño)*

Pala *(Cupeño, Luiseño)*

Rincon *(Luiseño)*

San Pasqual *(Kumeyaay)*

Mesa Grande *(Kumeyaay)*

Barona *(Kumeyaay)*

Capitan Grande *(Kumeyaay)*

Sycuan *(Kumeyaay)*

Jamul *(Kumeyaay)*

Viejas *(Kumeyaay)*

La Jolla *(Luiseño)*

PACIFIC OCEAN

N

50 miles

50 km

0

0

© Infobase Learning

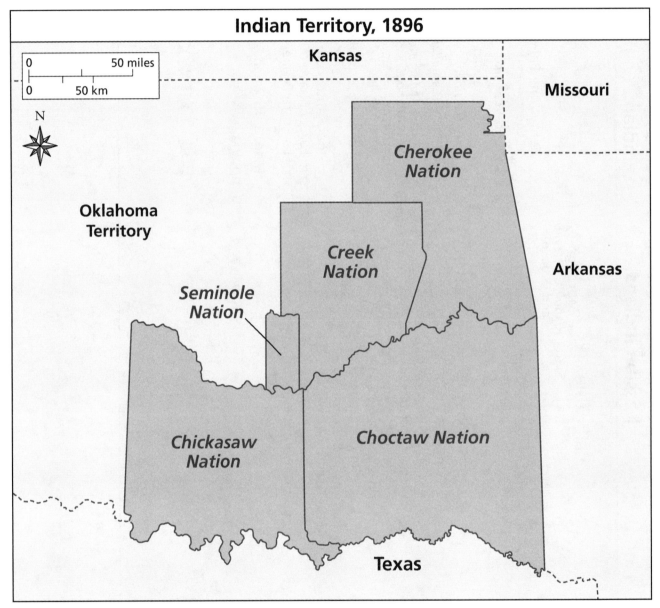

Indian Territory, 1896

0 ___ 50 miles
0 ___ 50 km

N

Kansas

Missouri

Oklahoma Territory

Cherokee Nation

Creek Nation

Seminole Nation

Arkansas

Chickasaw Nation

Choctaw Nation

Texas

© Carl Waldman and Infobase Learning

State of Oklahoma, 1907, and Earlier Locations of Its Indian Peoples

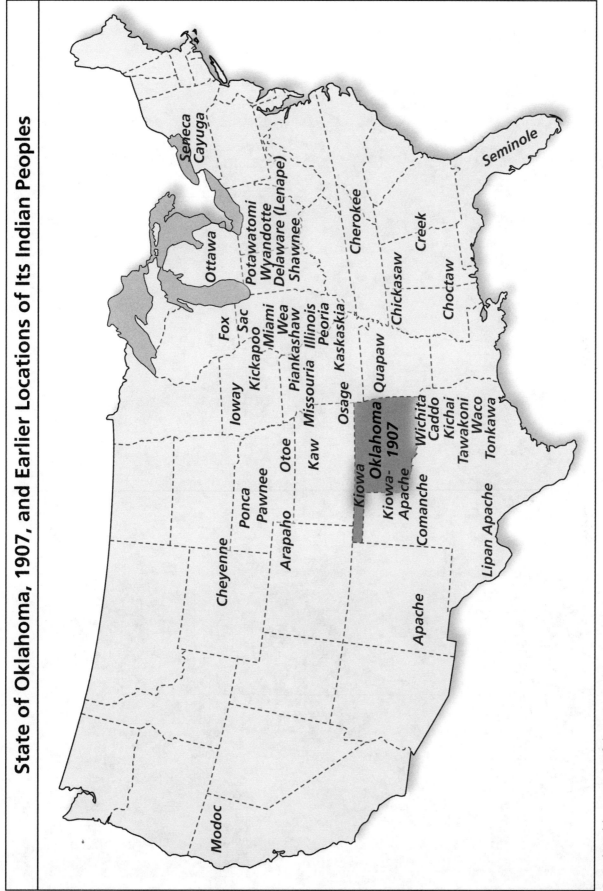

Seneca
Cayuga
Seminole
Ottawa
Potawatomi
Wyandotte
Delaware (Lenape)
Shawnee
Cherokee
Creek
Chickasaw
Choctaw
Fox
Sac
Miami
Wea
Kickapoo
Piankashaw
Illinois
Peoria
Kaskaskia
Quapaw
Ioway
Missouria
Osage
Oklahoma-1907
Wichita
Caddo
Kichai
Tawakoni
Waco
Tonkawa
Otoe
Kaw
Kiowa
Kiowa-
Apache
Ponca
Pawnee
Cheyenne
Arapaho
Comanche
Lipan Apache
Apache
Modoc

© Carl Waldman and Infobase Learning

Contemporary Federal and State Indian Lands in the United States

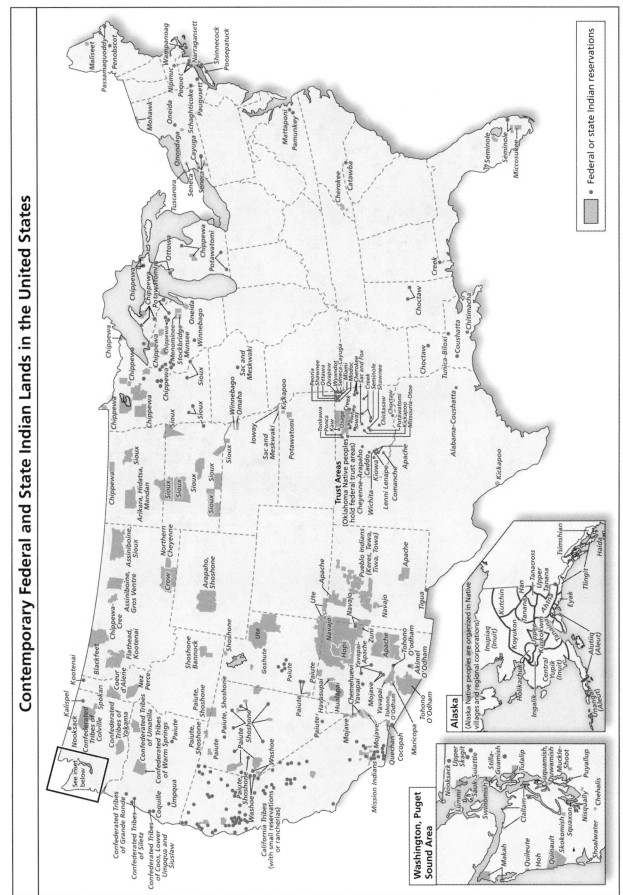

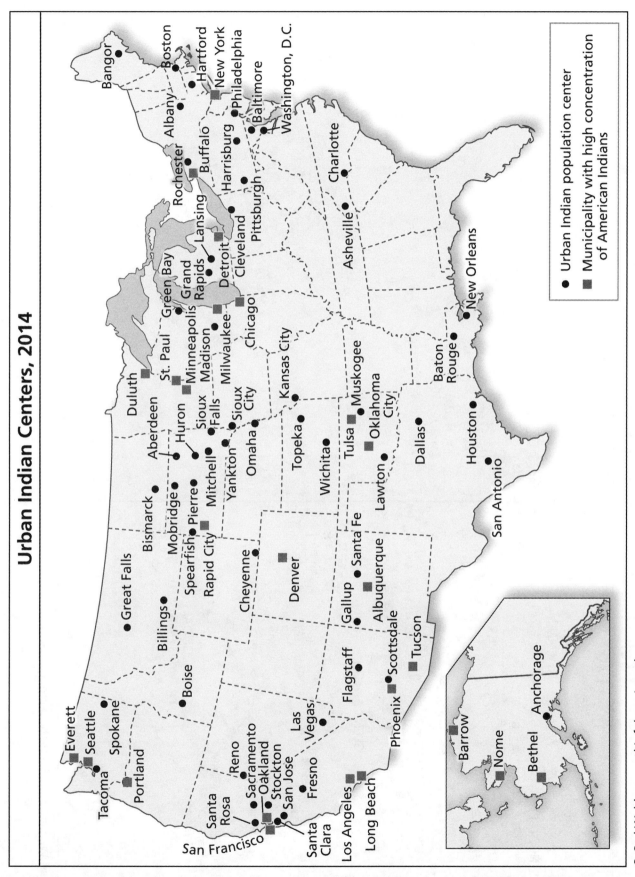

Urban Indian Centers, 2014

Bangor
Boston
Hartford
New York
Philadelphia
Baltimore
Washington, D.C.
Albany
Buffalo
Harrisburg
Pittsburgh
Charlotte
Rochester
Lansing
Cleveland
Asheville
Detroit
Green Bay
Grand Rapids
New Orleans
Duluth
St. Paul
Minneapolis
Madison
Milwaukee
Chicago
Baton Rouge
Aberdeen
Sioux Falls
Kansas City
Muskogee
Huron
Sioux City
Oklahoma City
Mitchell
Yankton
Omaha
Topeka
Tulsa
Houston
Bismarck
Mobridge
Spearfish
Pierre
Wichita
Lawton
Dallas
Rapid City
Cheyenne
Santa Fe
San Antonio
Great Falls
Denver
Gallup
Albuquerque
Billings
Scottsdale
Tucson
Boise
Flagstaff
Phoenix
Everett
Seattle
Spokane
Tacoma
Portland
Reno
Las Vegas
Sacramento
Oakland
Stockton
Santa Rosa
San Jose
Fresno
Los Angeles
Long Beach
Santa Clara
San Francisco

Barrow
Nome
Bethel
Anchorage

Legend:
● Urban Indian population center
■ Municipality with high concentration of American Indians

© Carl Waldman and Infobase Learning

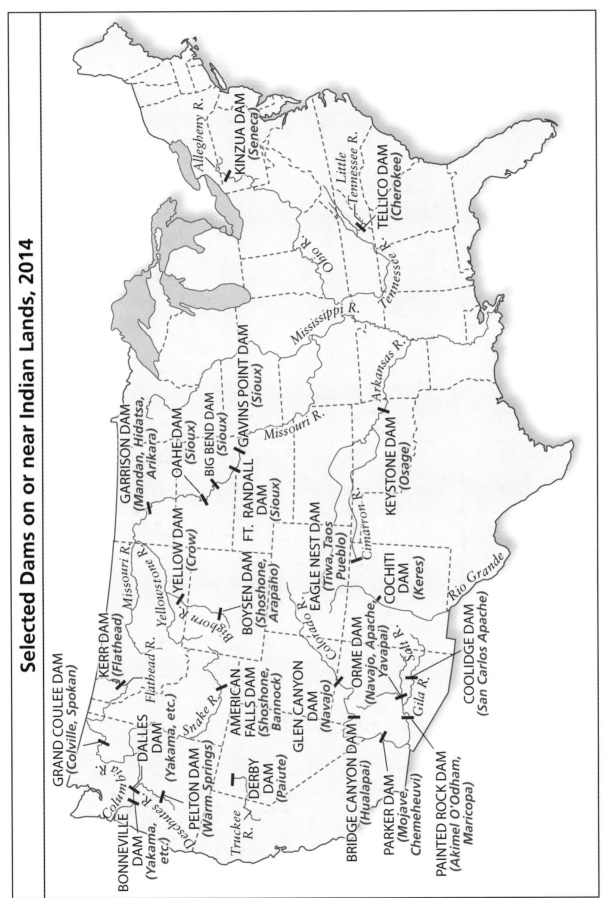

Selected Dams on or near Indian Lands, 2014

KINZUA DAM (Seneca)

Allegheny R.

Little Tennessee R.

TELLICO DAM (Cherokee)

Tennessee R.

Tennessee

Ohio R.

Mississippi R.

Arkansas R.

GARRISON DAM (Mandan, Hidatsa, Arikara)

OAHE DAM (Sioux)

BIG BEND DAM (Sioux)

GAVINS POINT DAM (Sioux)

FT. RANDALL DAM (Sioux)

Missouri R.

Missouri R.

KEYSTONE DAM (Osage)

Cimarron R.

KERR DAM (Flathead)

Flathead R.

Yellowstone R.

YELLOW DAM (Crow)

Bighorn R.

BOYSEN DAM (Shoshone, Arapaho)

EAGLE NEST DAM (Tiwa, Taos Pueblo)

COCHITI DAM (Keres)

Colorado R.

GRAND COULEE DAM (Colville, Spokan)

DALLES DAM (Yakama, etc.)

Snake R.

AMERICAN FALLS DAM (Shoshone, Bannock)

GLEN CANYON DAM (Navajo)

ORME DAM (Navajo, Apache, Yavapai)

Salt R.

COOLIDGE DAM (San Carlos Apache)

Rio Grande

Columbia R.

BONNEVILLE DAM (Yakama, etc.)

PELTON DAM (Warm Springs)

Deschutes R.

Truckee R.

DERBY DAM (Paiute)

BRIDGE CANYON DAM (Hualapai)

PARKER DAM (Mojave, Chemeheuvi)

Gila R.

PAINTED ROCK DAM (Akimel O'Odham, Maricopa)

© Carl Waldman and Infobase Learning

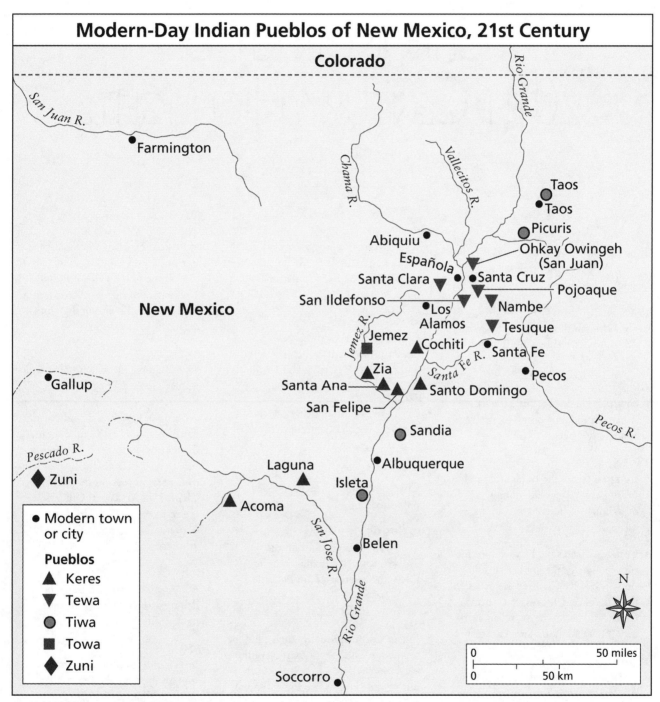

Modern-Day Indian Pueblos of New Mexico, 21st Century

Colorado

New Mexico

San Juan R.

Farmington

Chama R.

Vallecitos R.

Rio Grande

Taos

Taos

Picuris

Abiquiu

Española

Ohkay Owingeh
(San Juan)

Santa Clara

Santa Cruz

San Ildefonso

Pojoaque

Los
Alamos

Nambe

Jemez R.

Jemez

Tesuque

Cochiti

Santa Fe

Santa Fe R.

Zia

Gallup

Santa Ana

Santo Domingo

Pecos

San Felipe

Pecos R.

Pescado R.

Sandia

Zuni

Laguna

Albuquerque

Isleta

Acoma

San Jose R.

Belen

Rio Grande

- Modern town
  or city

Pueblos

▲ Keres

▼ Tewa

● Tiwa

■ Towa

◆ Zuni

N

Soccorro

0		50 miles
0	50 km	

© Carl Waldman and Infobase Learning

CHRONOLOGY OF 20TH-CENTURY HIGHLIGHTS

These are only some of the major events; the list is not intended to be comprehensive.

1887
- The General Allotment Act (Dawes Act) is passed to break up Indian reservations.

1889
- Susan La Flesche becomes the first American Indian woman to receive a medical degree.

1891
- Congress passes the Indian Mineral Leasing Act to regulate mining and oil drilling on Indian reservations.

1893
- Congress creates the Dawes Commission to manage the gradual dissolution of the Five Civilized Tribes, as the Cherokee, Chickasaw, Choctaw, Creek, and Seminole of Indian Territory (now Oklahoma) are known.

1898
- The Curtis Act extends the policy of Allotment to the Five Civilized Tribes.
- Nampeyo exhibits her pottery in Chicago and begins to cultivate an international reputation for her work.

1899
- Richard Henry Pratt hires Glenn "Pop" Warner to coach the Carlisle Indian School's football team; he will turn them into a national powerhouse.

1900
- Chitto Harjo leads the Creek resistance to Allotment, which becomes known as the Crazy Snake Rebellion.

1901
- Gertrude Bonnin, writing under the name Zitkala-Sa, publishes *Old Indian Legends*.

1902
- Charles Eastman's *Indian Boyhood* is published.

1903–1905
- The Derby Dam is built on the Truckee River, diverting water from the Paiute reservation on Pyramid Lake, Nevada.

1905
- Indian Commissioner Francis Ellington Leupp calls for a loosening of the harsh restrictions on Indian culture during the "Progressive Era" of Indian administration.

1906
- The Burke Act amends the Allotment policy.
- Blue Lake is seized by the federal government from Taos Pueblo in order to make the Carson National Forest, starting a long-standing land dispute.
- The village of Hotevilla is founded by Youkioma on the Hopi Reservation following a split among the Hopi regarding assimilation.

1907
- The Winters Doctrine protects Indian water rights.
- Robert Owen is elected senator from the state of Oklahoma, and Charles Curtis is appointed to fill a vacancy from Kansas, giving the Senate two Indian members for the first and only time in its history. In the same year, Charles David Carter (Chickasaw) is elected to the U.S. House of Representatives from Oklahoma's 4th District.

1908
- Actress Lillian St. Cyr makes her film debut in *The White Squaw* under the name Princess Red Wing.

1909
- Lyda Conley becomes the first Indian woman to plead before the U.S. Supreme Court.
- Willie Boy is tracked down after a celebrated manhunt and commits suicide rather than surrender over false charges of kidnapping and murder.

1910
- Henry Roe Cloud becomes the first Indian to graduate from Yale University.

1911
- The Society of American Indians, the first pan-Indian organization in the United States, is founded.

1912
- Jim Thorpe wins two gold medals and Louis Tewanima a silver medal in the Olympics in Sweden.
- The first Mohawk ironworker arrives in New York City.

1913
- Charles "Chief" Bender wins two World Series games to lead the Philadelphia Athletics to their third world championship in four years.

1914
- John Two Guns White Calf becomes the first Indian to fly in an airplane.
- The Cherokee Nation, the last of the Five Civilized Tribes governments, is dissolved.
- Red Fox St. James rides across the country to advocate for American Indian Day.

1915
- The Order of the Tipi, one of the first urban Indian organizations, in founded in New York City.

1917
- George E. Thomas becomes Tadadaho, or principal chief, of the Iroquois Confederacy in New York, a position he will hold for 40 years.

1918
- The Carlisle Indian School is closed.
- The Native American Church is incorporated.
- The worldwide influenza epidemic strikes Indian reservations, killing thousands.
- During World War I, Choctaw soldiers transmit telephone messages, in Choctaw, for the 142nd Infantry Regiment, 36th Division in the first use of Indian code talkers by the U.S. Army.

1919
- The first annual Crow Fair is held in Crow Agency, Montana.

1921
- Charles Burke replaces Cato Sells as Indian affairs commissioner, ending the Progressive Era of Indian administration.
- The Bursum bill limits the land rights of the New Mexico pueblos, leading to the revival of the All-Pueblo Council and the first modern Indian rights movement.
- The first of the dance orders, prohibiting Indian religious ceremonies, is enacted.
- The Snyder Act is passed in an attempt to improve the woeful medical conditions on Indian reservations.

1922
- An all-Indian football team, the Oorang Indian, joins the newly created National Football League (NFL).
- Joseph Strongwolf becomes the first Indian to make speeches over the radio.
- Alice Brown Davis is appointed chief of the Seminole Tribe of Oklahoma, the first woman to hold that position.
- The Everett Report upholds Indian claims to 6 million acres of land in New York State.

1923
- The Committee of One Hundred is established to review Indian policy.
- Levi General (Deskaheh) travels to Geneva, Switzerland, to plead the case for Iroquois sovereignty before the League of Nations.
- Navajo Tribal Council is set up, mainly to sign oil leases.

1924
- The American Indian Citizenship Act is passed.
- Congress passes the Indian Oil Leasing Act of 1924 in an attempt to cash in on the wealth of oil found on many Oklahoma Indian reservations.

1926
- William Hale is sentenced to life in prison for his role in the Osage Reign of Terror.

- Will Rogers hosts the first coast-to-coast radio broadcast on the newly formed National Broadcasting Network (NBC).
- The Six Nations Defense League, soon renamed the Indian Defense League of America (IDLA), is founded to protect treaty rights.
- The American Indian Association opens an urban Indian center in Manhattan.

1927
- Christine Quintasket (Mourning Dove) publishes her first novel, *Co-Ge-We-A, The Half-Blood: A Depiction of the Great Montana Cattle Drive.*
- Joe Guyon helps lead the New York Giants to their first NFL crown.

1928
- The Meriam Report harshly criticizes government Indian policy.
- Paintings by the "Kiowa Five" are featured in an international exposition in Prague, Czechoslovakia, that later travels throughout Europe, the first international showing of American Indian art.

1929
- Joe Shunatona stars in *The Moon Bride's Wedding*, one of the first sound films.

1930
- The film *The Silent Enemy*, featuring an all-Indian cast including Chauncey Yellow Robe, Sylvester Long Lance, and Molly Spotted Elk, is released.

1931
- In Connecticut, Harold and Gladys Tantaquidgeon open the first Indian museum in the United States run by Indians.

1932
- Dorothy Dunn encourages the Studio School (or Santa Fe School) of Indian art at the Santa Fe Indian School.

1933
- John Collier becomes Indian affairs commissioner.

- The Indian Emergency Work Program is established to help Indians cope with the Great Depression.
- Luther Standing Bear publishes *Land of the Spotted Eagle*.

1934
- The Indian Reorganization Act ends the policy of Allotment and the dismantling of Indian reservations.
- The Johnson-O'Malley Act is passed, ushering a change in Indian education.

1935
- The Indian Arts and Crafts Board is created.
- In Oklahoma, the Anadarko Indian Fair becomes the American Indian Exposition, the largest powwow in the country at the time.

1937
- The Association on American Indian Affairs is created.

1938
- Dr. Fred Loe discovers sulfanilamide, a remedy for trachoma, while practicing on the Rosebud Reservation in South Dakota.

1939
- Ellison "Tarzan" Brown wins his second Boston Marathon.

1941
- Henry Nolatubby is killed in the Japanese attack on Pearl Harbor, the first Indian casualty of World War II.

1942
- Supreme Court rules in *Tulee v. Washington* that Indians have the right to fish under preexisting treaties.

1944
- The National Congress of American Indians is formed.

1945
- War hero Ernest Evans is posthumously awarded the Medal of Honor.
- Ira Hayes and five other U.S. Marines plant an American flag on Mount Suribachi on the Pacific island of Iwo Jima, site of one of the bloodiest battles of World War II.

1946
- The Indian Claims Commission is established.
- Construction begins on the Garrison Dam, the first of the dams built under the Pick-Sloan Plan for flood control on the Missouri River. The Garrison Dam will flood the 153,000 acres of the most productive land of the Fort Berthold Reservation in North Dakota.

1949
- Maria Tallchief dances the lead in the premiere of George Balanchine's *The Firebird* at the New York City Ballet.

1950
- Indian Commissioner Dillon Myer calls for the Termination of Indians from federal services and the breakup of Indian reservations.

1951
- Allie Reynolds became the first American League pitcher to pitch two no-hitters in a single season.
- Raymond Harvey is awarded the Medal of Honor for bravery in the Korean War.

1953
- Congress passes Public Law 280, granting certain states criminal jurisdiction over Indian reservations.
- The American Indian Center of Chicago is founded.

1954
- The Menominee Termination Act is passed.

1955
- The Indian Health Service is transferred from the Bureau of Indian Affairs (BIA) to the Department of Health, Education, and Welfare.

1956
- The Indian Adult Vocational Training Act is passed to help encourage Indians to move from their reservations to large cities as part of the government policy known as Relocation.

1957
- The Bonneville Dam on the Columbia River floods Celilo Falls, one of the finest Indian salmon-fishing grounds on the continent.

1958
- Oscar Howe's paintings are rejected by the Philbrook Indian Art Annual, leading to a movement away from the Studio School.
- Link Wray releases "Rumble," introducing guitar distortion and power chords to rock and roll.
- Maurice Kenny's first collection of poetry, *Dead Letters Sent, and Other Poems*, is published.

1959
- The *Navajo Times* is founded on the Navajo Reservation.
- Dan Katchongva organizes the first of his "Meetings of Indian Brothers" on the Hopi Reservation, where the Hopi's traditional philosophy of resistance to assimilation begins to spread among other Indian tribes.

1961
- The American Indian Chicago Conference inaugurates the era of the Red Power movement.
- The National Indian Youth Council is formed.
- A paperback version of *Black Elk Speaks* is published, helping to inspire a revitalization of Indian religions.

1962
- The Institute of American Indian Arts is established in Santa Fe, New Mexico, and with its outstanding faculty, which includes Lloyd Kiva New, Alan Houser, and Fritz Scholder, revolutionizes Indian art.
- The *Tundra Times* is established in Fairbanks, Alaska.

1963
- William Rickard and George Heron organize the first North American Indian Unity Caravans, which carry the traditional Iroquois philosophy of resistance to assimilation.

1964
- Billy Mills captures the gold medal in the 10,000-meter race in the Japan Olympics.

- The National Indian Youth Council organizes "fish-ins" in the Northwest to protest the denial of Indian fishing rights.
- Buffy Sainte-Marie releases her first album, *It's My Way*.

1965
- The Kinzua Dam floods the Allegany Seneca reservation.

1966
- Robert LaFollette Bennett becomes the first American Indian to be named commissioner of the BIA in almost a century.

1967
- Betty Mae Tiger Jumper is elected chair of the Seminole Tribal Council in Florida, one of the first women to be elected to lead a federally recognized tribe.

1968
- The American Indian Movement (AIM) is founded.
- A group of Mohawk block the Seaway International Bridge to Cornwall Island over treaty rights.
- The periodical *Akwesasne Notes* makes its debut on the Akwesasne (St. Regis) Mohawk Indian Reservation.
- The Indian Civil Rights Act is passed.

1969
- The organization Indians of All Tribes occupies Alcatraz Island.
- The first tribal college, Navajo Community College (now Diné College), is opened at Many Farms, Arizona.
- The American Indian Community House is founded in New York City.
- N. Scott Momaday wins the Pulitzer Prize for *House Made of Dawn*.
- Vine Deloria, Jr., publishes his first book, *Custer Died for Your Sins: An Indian Manifesto*.

1970
- President Richard Nixon calls for the end of the Termination policy.
- AIM members seize the ship *Mayflower 2* in Massachusetts on Thanksgiving.

1971
- The Alaska Native Land Claims Settlement Act is passed.
- The Native American Rights Fund (NARF) is founded.
- Dan George is nominated for an Academy Award for his portrayal of a Cheyenne elder in the film *Little Big Man*.

1972
- Protesters occupy the BIA headquarters after the Trail of Broken Treaties protest in Washington, D.C.
- The murder of Raymond Yellow Thunder in Nebraska by non-Indians sparks outrage.
- The Indian Education Act, creating an Office of Indian Education under the U.S. Department of Education, is passed.

1973
- AIM members occupy the village of Wounded Knee.
- Astronaut William Pogue becomes the first Indian in space.
- R. C. Gorman becomes the first American Indian to be represented in the permanent collection of the Metropolitan Museum of Art in New York City.

1974
- The Navajo-Hopi Land Settlement Act is passed, igniting the Big Mountain Dispute.
- The Boldt Decision protects Indian fishing rights.
- "Come and Get Your Love" is a top 10 hit for the rock group Redbone.
- Will Sampson is nominated for an Academy Award for his role in *One Flew Over the Cuckoo's Nest*.

1975
- The American Indian Policy Review Commission is created.
- The Council of Energy Resource Tribes (CERT) is formed.
- The Indian Self-Determination and Education Assistance Act is passed.
- FBI agents battle AIM activists on the Pine Ridge Reservation in South Dakota. Two agents and an Indian man are killed.

- Kitty O'Neill becomes the "The Fastest Woman on Earth" when, traveling at a speed of 412 MPH, she sets the record for the quarter-mile in a race car.

1976
- AIM activist Anna Mae Aquash is found dead on the Pine Ridge Reservation in South Dakota.

1978
- The American Indian Religious Freedom Act is passed.
- The Indian Child Welfare Act is passed, regulating adoptions of Indian children by non-Indians.
- The Longest Walk, the last major demonstration of the Red Power era, is held in Washington, D.C.

1979
- In one of the largest nuclear accidents in the United States, a dam holding 100 million gallons of radioactive water and 1,100 tons of radioactive wastes bursts, contaminating the Rio Puerco on the Navajo Reservation.
- Robert J. Billings is one of the founders of the religious political group the Moral Majority, becoming its executive director.

1980
- LaDonna Harris becomes the first Native woman to run for the U.S. vice presidency, joining Barry Commoner on the ticket of the Citizen's Party.

1981
- A six-year occupation of the Black Hills in South Dakota at Camp Yellow Thunder begins.
- The *Lakota Times*, later renamed *Indian Country Today*, is established.

1982
- The Indian Mineral Development Act is passed.
- The U.S. Supreme Court, in *Seminole Tribe v. Butterworth*, rules that tribes, not states, regulate gambling establishments on Indian reservations.
- Passage of the Nuclear Waste Policy Act put pressure on tribes to allow the federal government to store radioactive wastes on their lands.

1983

- Supreme Court rules, in *New Mexico v. The Mescalero Apache Tribe*, that reservation hunting and fishing regulations apply to non-Indians as well as Indians on Indian reservations.
- Joy Harjo publishes her acclaimed book of poetry, *She Had Some Horses*.

1984

- The Native American Press Association—now known as the Native American Journalists Association (NAJA)—is formed.
- Louise Erdrich releases her first novel, *Love Medicine*.

1986

- The Mashantucket Pequot open a high-stakes bingo operation on their lands in Connecticut, soon to become the most successful casino in the world.

1987

- The Supreme Court, in the landmark decision *California v. Cabazon Band of Mission Indians*, affirms and expands the right of Indians to conduct gambling on their reservations.
- The cult classic film *Powwow Highway* is released.

- Hanay Geiogamah forms the successful Native American Dance Theater troupe.

1988

- The Indian Gaming Regulatory Act is passed.
- The Supreme Court hands down a decision limiting Indian religious freedom in *Lyng v. Northwest Indian Cemetery Association*.

1989

- The National Museum of the American Indian Act establishes an Indian Museum as part of the Smithsonian Institution.
- Michael Dorris wins the National Book Award for *The Broken Cord*.

1990

- The Native American Graves Protection and Repatriation Act is passed.
- The Supreme Court limits the ceremonial use of peyote by members of the Native American Church in *Employment Division of Oregon v. Smith*.
- The Iroquois National Lacrosse Team competes as representative of a sovereign nation in the World Championship Games in Australia.

1991

- Graham Greene is nominated for an Academy Award for his role in *Dances with Wolves*.

1993

- Ada Deer becomes the first woman to head the BIA.

1994

- The American Indian Religious Freedom Act is amended to strengthen protection of sacred sites and the ceremonial use of peyote.
- The United Nations declares the next 10 years to be the International Decade of the World's Indigenous Peoples.

1998

- Chris Eyre directs *Smoke Signals*, a film adaptation of *The Lone Ranger and Tonto Fistfight in Heaven*, a collection of stories by Sherman Alexie.

2004

- The National Museum of the American Indian opens on the Mall in Washington, D.C.

BIBLIOGRAPHY

Note: This list is intended as a basic bibliography. Specific references are provided in the **Further Reading** section at the end of most articles, including many sources not listed here.

GENERAL REFERENCE

Champagne, Duane. *Native America: Portrait of the Peoples.* Detroit, Mich.: Visible Ink Press, 1994.

Davis, Mary, ed. *Native America in the Twentieth Century: An Encyclopedia.* New York: Garland, 1994.

Deloria, Philip J. *Indians in Unexpected Places.* Lawrence: University Press of Kansas, 2004.

Hamlin-Wilson, Gail. *Biographical Dictionary of Indians of the Americas.* Newport Beach, Calif.: American Indian Publishers, 1991.

Hoxie, Frederick E. *The Encyclopedia of North American Indians.* Boston and New York: Houghton Mifflin, 1996.

Klein, Barry T. *Reference Encyclopedia of the American Indian.* West Nyack, N.Y.: Todd Publications, 1997.

Malinowski, Sharon, and George H. J. Abrams, eds. *Notable Native Americans.* New York: Gale, 1995.

Olson, James Stuart. *Encyclopedia of American Indian Civil Rights.* Westport, Conn.: Greenwood, 1997.

SOURCES BY TIME PERIODS

General 20th Century

Calloway, Colin G., ed. *New Directions in American Indian History.* Norman and London: University of Oklahoma Press, 1992.

Deloria, Vine, Jr., ed. *American Indian Policy in the Twentieth Century.* Norman: University of Oklahoma Press, 1985.

Gridley, Marion E., ed. and comp. *Indians of Today.* 4th ed. Sponsored by the Indian Council Fire. Chicago: M. E. Gridley, 1971.

James, M. Annette. *The State of Native America: Genocide, Colonization, and Resistance.* Boston: South End Press, 1992.

Liberty, Margot, ed. *American Indian Intellectuals.* 1976 Proceedings of the American Ethnological Society. St. Paul, Minn.: West Publishing, 1978.

Olson, James Stuart, and Raymond Wilson. *Native Americans in the Twentieth Century.* Urbana: University of Illinois Press, 1986.

Parman, Donald L. *Indians and the American West in the Twentieth Century.* Bloomington: Indiana University Press, 1994.

Wollock, Jeffrey. "On the Wings of History: American Indians in the 20th century." *Native Americas* 20 (Spring 2003): 14–31.

The Progressive Era

Debo, Angie. *And Still the Waters Run: The Betrayal of the Five Civilized Tribes.* Princeton, N.J.: Princeton University Press, 1991.

Hertzberg, Hazel W. *Search for an American Indian Identity: Modern Pan-Indian Movements.* Syracuse, N.Y.: Syracuse University Press, 1982.

Hoxie, Frederick E. *A Final Promise: The Campaign to Assimilate the Indians, 1820–1920.* Lincoln: University of Nebraska Press, 1984.

Larner, John W. et al., eds. *The Papers of the Society of American Indians.* Wilmington, Del.: Scholarly Resources, 1987.

MacDonald, Janet A. *Dispossession of the American Indian, 1887–1934.* Bloomington: Indiana University Press, 1991.

Trump, Eric Krenzen. "The Indian Industries League and Its Support of American Indian Arts, 1893–1922: A Study of Changing Attitudes towards Indian Women and Assimilationist Policy." Ph.D. dissertation, Boston University, 1996. UMI Microform 9621683.

Unrau, William E. *Mixed-Bloods and Tribal Dissolution: Charles Curtis and the Quest for Indian Identity.* Kansas City: University Press of Kansas, 1989.

Wilson, Raymond. *Ohiyesa: Charles Eastman, Santee Sioux.* Urbana: University of Illinois Press, 1999.

Between World War I and the Great Depression

Hertzberg, Hazel W. *Search for an American Indian Identity: Modern Pan-Indian Movements.* Syracuse, N.Y.: Syracuse University Press, 1982.

Jones, Carter. "Hope for the Race of Man: Indians Intellectuals, and the Regeneration of Modern America, 1917–1934." Ph.D. dissertation, Brown University, 1991. UMI Microform 9204889.

Kelly, Lawrence C. *The Navajo Indians and Federal Indian Policy 1900–1935.* Tucson: University of Arizona Press, 1968.

MacDonald, Janet A. *Dispossession of the American Indian 1887–1934.* Bloomington: Indiana University Press, 1991.

Philp, Kenneth R. *John Collier's Crusade for Indian Reform, 1920–1954.* Tucson: University of Arizona Press, 1977.

Stratton, David H. *Tempest over Teapot Dome: The Story of Albert Fall.* Norman: University of Oklahoma Press, 1998.

Unrau, William E. *Mixed-Bloods and Tribal Dissolution: Charles Curtis and the Quest for Indian Identity.* Kansas City: University Press of Kansas, 1989.

Wilson, Terry P. *The Underground Reservation: Osage Oil.* Lincoln: University of Nebraska Press, 1985.

Indian New Deal

Buffalohead, W. Roger. "The Indian New Deal: A Review Essay." *Minnesota History* 48, no. 8 (Winter 1983): 339–341.

Hauptman, Laurence M. *The Iroquois and the New Deal.* Syracuse, N.Y.: Syracuse University Press, 1981.

Hecht, Robert A. *Oliver La Farge and the American Indian: A Biography.* Metuchen, N.J., and London: Scarecrow Press, 1991.

Kelly, Lawrence C. *The Assault on Assimilation: John Collier and the Origins of Indian Policy Reform.* Albuquerque: University of New Mexico Press, 1983.

———. *The Navajo Indians and Federal Indian Policy 1990–1935.* Tucson: University of Arizona Press, 1968.

Parman, Donald H. *The Navajo Indians and the New Deal.* New Haven, Conn.: Yale University Press, 1976.

Philp, Kenneth R. *John Collier's Crusade for Indian Reform, 1920–1954.* Tucson: University of Arizona Press, 1977.

Rickard, Clinton. *Fighting Tuscarora.* Syracuse, N.Y.: Syracuse University Press, 1994.

Taylor, Graham D. *The New Deal and Al Tribalism: The Administration of the Indian Reorganization Act, 1934–45.* Lincoln: University of Nebraska Press, 1980.

Termination

Drinnon, Richard. *Keeper of the Concentration Camps: Dillon S. Myer and American Racism.* Berkeley: University of California Press, 1989.

Hauptman, Lawrence M. *The Iroquois Struggle for Survival: World War II to Red Power.* Syracuse, N.Y.: Syracuse University Press, 1986.

Hecht, Robert A. *Oliver La Farge and the American Indian: A Biography.* Metuchen, N.J., and London: Scarecrow Press, 1991.

Lawson, Michael L. *Dammed Indians: The Pick-Sloan Plan and the Missouri River Sioux, 1944–1980.* Norman: University of Oklahoma Press, 1982.

Parker, Dorothy R. *Singing an Indian Song: A Biography of D'Arcy McNickle.* Lincoln and London: University of Nebraska Press, 1992.

Peroff, Nicholas C. *Menominee Drums: Tribal Termination and Restoration, 1954–1974.* Norman: University of Oklahoma Press, 1982.

Philp, Kenneth R. *Termination Revisited: American Indians on the Trail to Self-Determination, 1933–1953.* Lincoln: University of Nebraska Press, 2002.

Red Power to the Present

Barreiro, Jose, and Robin M. Wright, eds. *Native Peoples in Struggle: Russell Tribunal and Other Forums.* Bombay, N.Y.: E.R.I.N. Publications, 1982.

Burnette, Robert, with John Koster. *The Road to Wounded Knee.* New York: Bantam Books. 1974.

Churchill, Ward, and Jim Vander Wall. *Agents of Repression: The FBI's Secret Wars against the Black Panther Party and the American Indian Movement.* Boston: South End Press, 1988.

Deloria, Vine, Jr. *Behind the Trail of Broken Treaties: An Indian Declaration of Independence.* Austin: University of Texas, 1985.

Josephy, Alvin M., et al. *Red Power: The American Indians' Fight for Freedom.* Lincoln: University of Nebraska Press, 1999.

Lurie, Nancy Oestreich, and Stuart Levine, eds. *The American Indian Today.* Baltimore: Penguin Books, 1968.

Matthiessen, Peter. *Indian Country.* New York: Viking, 1979.

———. *In the Spirit of Crazy Horse.* New York: Viking, 1992.

Shreve, Bradley G., and Shirley Hill Witt. *Red Power Rising: The National Indian Youth Council and the Origins of Native Activism.* Norman: University of Oklahoma Press, 2011.

Smith, Paul Chaat, and Robert Allen Warrior. *Like a Hurricane: The American Indian Movement from Alcatraz to Wounded Knee.* New York: New Press, 1996.

Steiner, Stan. *The New Indians.* New York: Harper and Row, 1968.

Trahant, Mark N. *The Last Great Battle of the Indian Wars: Henry M. Jackson, Forrest J. Gerard, and the Campaign for the Self-Determination of America's Indian Tribes.* Fort Hall, Idaho: The Cedars Group, 2010.

Voices from Wounded Knee. Mohawk Nation via Rooseveltown, N.Y.: Akwesasne Notes, 1974.

Weyler, Rex. *Blood of the Land: The Government and Corporate War against the American Indian Movement.* New York: Everest House, 1982.

SOURCES ON TOPICS

Agriculture and Ranching

Buskirk, Winfred. *The Western Apache: Living with the Land before 1950*. Norman: University of Oklahoma Press, 1986.

Carlson, Leonard A. *Indians, Bureaucrats, and Land: The Dawes Act and the Decline in Indian Farming*. Westport, Conn.: Greenwood Press, 1981.

Getty, Harry. *The San Carlos Apache Cattle Industry*. Tucson: University of Arizona Press, 1963.

Harvey, Cecil L. *Agriculture of the American Indian–A Select Bibliography*. Washington, D.C.: U.S. Department of Agriculture, Science and Education Administration, Technical Information Systems, 1979.

Hurt, R. Douglas. *Indian Agriculture in America: Prehistory to the Present*. Lawrence: University Press of Kansas, 1987. Reviewed by Henry C. Dethloff, *American Historical Review* 94, no. 5 (December 1989): 1,464–1,465.

Iverson, Peter. *When Indians Became Cowboys: Native Peoples and Cattle Ranching in the American West*. Norman: University of Oklahoma Press, 1994.

Kipp, Henry W. *Indians in Agriculture: An Historical Sketch*. Washington, D.C.: U.S. Department of the Interior, Bureau of Indian Affairs, 1988.

Nabhan, Gary Paul. *Enduring Seeds: Native American Agriculture and Wild Plant Conservation*. San Francisco: North Point Press, 1989.

American Indian Policy

Deloria, Vine, Jr., ed. *American Indian Policy in the Twentieth Century*. Norman: University of Oklahoma Press, 1985.

Kvasnicka, Robert M., and Herman J. Viola, eds. *The Commissioners of Indian Affairs, 1824–1977*. Lincoln: University of Nebraska Press, 1980.

Prucha, Francis Paul. *The Great Father: The United States Government and the American Indians*. 2 vols. Lincoln and London: University of Nebraska Press, 1995.

Anthropologists

Biographical Directory of Anthropologists Born before 1920. New York: Garland, 1988.

Chandler, Joan Mary. "Anthropologists and US Indians, 1928–1960." Ph.D. dissertation, University of Texas at Austin, 1972.

Architecture and Building

Mitchell, Joseph. "The Mohawks in High Steel." In Wilson, Edmund. *Apologies to the Iroquois*, 3–36. Syracuse, N.Y.: Syracuse University Press, 1992.

Nabokov, Peter, and Robert Easton. *Native American Architecture*. New York and Oxford: Oxford University Press, 1989.

The Arts

Henke, Robert. *Native American Painters of the 20th Century*. Jefferson, N.C.: McFarland, 1995.

Lester, Patrick D. *The Biographical Directory of Native American Painters*. Norman: University of Oklahoma Press, 1995.

Livingston, Lili Cockerille. *American Indian Ballerinas*. Norman: University of Oklahoma Press, 1997.

McBride, Bunny. *Molly Spotted Elk: A Penobscot in Paris*. Norman and London: University of Oklahoma Press, 1995.

Perison, Harry D. "Charles Wakefield Cadman: His Life and Works." Ph.D. dissertation, Eastman School of Music, 1978.

Reno, Dawn E. *Contemporary Native American Artists*. Brooklyn, N.Y.: Alliance Publishing, 1995.

Assimilation and Identity

Acculturation in the Americas: Proceedings and Selected Papers. New York: 29th International Congress of Americanists, 1949.

Bolt, Christine. *American Indian Policy and American Reform: Case Studies of the Campaign to Assimilate the American Indians:* London and Boston: Allen & Unwin, 1987.

Hertzberg, Hazel W. *Search for an American Indian Identity: Modern Pan-Indian Movements*. Syracuse, N.Y.: Syracuse University Press, 1982.

Hirschfelder, Arlene B. *American Indian Stereotypes in the World of Children*. Metuchen, N.J.: Scarecrow Press, 1982.

Hoxie, Frederick E. *A Final Promise: The Campaign to Assimilate the Indians, 1820–1920*. Lincoln: University of Nebraska Press, 1984.

Mantell, Harold. "Counteracting the Stereotype: A report on the Association's National Film Committee." *The American Indian* 5, no. 2 (Fall 1950): 16–20.

Mihesuah, Devon A. *American Indians: Stereotypes and Realities*. Atlanta: Clarity Press, 1996.

Raymond, William Stedman. *Shadows of the Indian: Stereotypes in American Culture*. Norman: University of Oklahoma Press, 1982.

Strickland, Rennard. *Tonto's Revenge: Reflections on American Indian Culture and Policy*. Albuquerque: University of New Mexico Press, 1997.

Unrau, William E. *Mixed-Bloods and Tribal Dissolution: Charles Curtis and the Quest for Indian Identity*. Kansas City: University Press of Kansas, 1989.

Crime and Criminality

French, Laurence. *Indians and Criminal Justice*. Totowa, N.J.: Allanheld, Osmun, 1982.

Lester, David. *Crime and the Native American*. Springfield, Ill.: Charles C. Thomas, 1999.

Silverman, Robert A., et al. *Native Americans, Crime, and Justice*. Boulder, Colo.: Westview Press, 1996.

The Curtis Act and Oklahoma

Bolster, Mel H. *Crazy Snake and the Smoked Meat Rebellion.* Boston: Brandon Press, 1976.

Carter, Kent. *The Dawes Commission and the Allotment of the Five Civilized Tribes, 1893–1914.* Orem, Utah.: Ancestry, 1999.

Debo, Angie. *And Still the Waters Run: The Betrayal of the Five Civilized Tribes.* Princeton, N.J.: Princeton University Press, 1991.

———. *The Road to Disappearance.* Princeton, N.J.: Princeton University Press, 1941.

Hendrix, Janey B. *Redbird Smith and the Nighthawk Keetoowahs.* Welling, Okla.: Cross-Cultural Education Center, 1983.

Hogan, Lawrence J. *The Osage Indian Murders: The True Story of a 21-Murder Plot to Inherit the Headrights of Wealthy Osage Tribe Members.* Frederick, Md.: Amlex, 1998.

Education

Adams, David Wallace. *Education for Extinction: American Indians and the Boarding School Experience, 1875–1928.* Lawrence: University Press of Kansas, 1995.

Coleman, Michael C. *American Indian Children at School, 1850–1930.* Jackson: University Press of Mississippi, 1993.

Szasz, Margaret. *Education and the American Indian: The Road to Self-Determination Since 1928.* 3rd. ed. Albuquerque: University of New Mexico Press, 1999.

Witmer, Linda F. *The Indian Industrial School: Carlisle Pennsylvania, 1979-1918.* Carlisle, Pa.: Cumberland Historical Society, 1993.

Wollock, Jeffrey. "Protagonism Emergent: Indians and Higher Education." *Native Americas* 14, no. 4 (Winter 1997–98): 12–23.

Environment, Environmentalism, and Industrial Development

Eichstaedt, Peter H. *If You Poison Us: Uranium and Native Americans.* Santa Fe, N.Mex.: Red Crane Books, 1994.

Gifford, Eli, and Michael R. Cook, eds. *How Can One Sell the Air? Chief Seattle's Vision.* Revised ed. Summertown, Tenn.: Book Publishing Co. (Native Voices), 2005.

Grinde, Donald A., and Bruce Johansen. *Ecocide of Native America: Environmental Destruction of Indian Lands and Peoples.* Santa Fe, N.Mex.: Clear Light, 1995.

Johansen, Bruce. *Wasi'chu: The Continuing Indian Wars.* New York: Monthly Review Press, 1979.

Jorgensen, Joseph G., ed. *Native Americans and Energy Development.* Cambridge, Mass.: Anthropology Resource Center, 1978.

———. *Native Americans and Energy Development II.* Cambridge, Mass.: Anthropology Resource Center and Seventh Generation Fund, 1984.

Lawson, Michael L. *Dammed Indians: The Pick-Sloan Plan and the Missouri River Sioux, 1944–1980.* Norman: University of Oklahoma Press, 1982.

Parlow, Anita. *Cry, Sacred Ground: Big Mountain USA.* Washington, D.C.: Christic Institute, 1988.

Standing Bear, Luther. *Land of the Spotted Eagle.* Lincoln: University of Nebraska Press, 1978.

Weyler, Rex. *Blood of the Land: The Government and Corporate War against the American Indian Movement.* New York: Everest House, 1982.

Whaley, Rick, with Walter Bresette. *Walleye Warriors: An Effective Alliance against Racism and for the Earth.* Philadelphia, Pa.: New Society Publishers, 1994.

Wilson, Terry P. *The Underground Reservation: Osage Oil.* Lincoln: University of Nebraska Press, 1985.

Health

Joe, Jennie R., and Robert S. Young. *Diabetes as a Disease of Civilization: The Impact of Culture Change on Indigenous Peoples.* New York: Mouton de Gruyter, 1994.

Leland, Joy. *Firewater Myths: North American Indian Drinking and Alcohol Addiction.* New Brunswick, N.J.: Publications Division, Rutgers Center of Alcohol Studies, 1976.

Young, T. Kue. *The Health of Native Americans: Toward a Biocultural Epidemiology.* New York: Oxford University Press, 1994.

Indigenous Economics

Barreiro, Jose, ed. *Indigenous Economics: Towards a New World Order.* Ithaca, N.Y.: Akwe:kon Press, 1992.

Blackburn, Thomas Carl, and Kat Anderson, eds. *Before the Wilderness: Environmental Management by Native Californians.* Menlo Park, Calif.: Ballena Press, 1993.

Cajete, Gregory, ed. *A People's Ecology: Explorations in Sustainable Living.* Santa Fe, N.Mex.: Clear Light, 1999.

Mohawk, John. "Development through Appropriate Technology." *Native Self-Sufficiency* 7, no. 1 (1984): 7.

Posey, Darrell, and Graham Dutfield. *Beyond Intellectual Property: Toward Traditional Resource Rights for Indigenous Peoples and Local Communities.* Ottawa: International Development Research Center, 1996.

Land Tenure and Allotment

Carlson, Leonard A. *Indians, Bureaucrats, and Land: The Dawes Act and the Decline in Indian Farming.* Westport, Conn.: Greenwood Press, 1981.

MacDonald, Janet A. *Dispossession of the American Indian, 1887–1934.* Bloomington: Indiana University Press, 1991.

Sutton, Imre. *Indian Land Tenure: Bibliographic Essays and a Guide to the Literature.* New York and Paris: Clearwater, 1975.

———, ed. *Irredeemable America: The Indians' Estate and Land Claims.* Albuquerque: University of New Mexico Press, 1985.

Washburn, Wilcom E. *The Assault on Indian Tribalism: The General Allotment Law (Dawes Act) of 1887.* Philadelphia: Lippincott, 1975.

Language Use

Campbell, Lyle, and Marianne Mithun. *The Languages of Native America: Historical and Comparative Assessment.* Austin: University of Texas Press, 1979.

Diamond, Jared. "Speaking with a Single Tongue." *Discover* 14, no. 2 (1993): 78–85.

Ewen, Alexander, and Jeffrey Wollock. "The Survival and Revival of American Indian Languages." *Daybreak Magazine* (Winter 1994): 16–17.

Reyhner, Jon. "American Indian Language Policy and School Success." *Journal of Educational Issues of Language Minority Students* (12 Special Issue), 1993.

Wollock, Jeffrey. "Linguistic Diversity and Biodiversity: Some Implications for the Language Sciences." In *On Biocultural Diversity: Linking Language, Knowledge and the Environment,* edited by L. Maffi, 248–262. Washington, D.C.: Smithsonian Institution, 2001.

Zepeda, Ofelia, and Jane H. Hill. "The Condition of Native American Languages in the United States." In *Endangered Languages,* edited by R. H. Robins and E. M. Uhlenbeck, 135–155. Oxford and New York: Berg, 1991.

Literature

Allen, Paula Gunn, ed. *Voice of the Turtle: American Indian Literature 1900–1970.* New York: Ballentine, 1995.

Bruchac, Joseph, ed. *Songs from This Earth on Turtle's Back: Contemporary American Indian Poetry.* Greenfield Center, N.Y.: Greenfield Review Press, 1983.

Niatum, Duane. *Harper's Anthology of 20th Century Native American Poetry.* San Francisco: Harper, 1988.

Ortiz, Simon. *Earth Power Coming: Short Fiction in Native American Literature.* Tsaile, Ariz.: Navajo Community College Press, 1983.

Velie, Alan R. *The Lightning Within: An Anthology of Contemporary Indian Fiction.* Lincoln: University of Nebraska Press, 1991.

Wiget, Andrew, ed. *Dictionary of Native American Literature.* New York and London: Garland, 1991.

Witalec, Janet, ed. *Native North American Literature.* New York: Gale, 1994.

Military

Bernstein, Alison R. *American Indians and World War II.* Norman: University of Oklahoma Press, 1991.

Britten, Thomas A. *American Indians in World War I: At War and at Home.* Albuquerque: University of New Mexico Press, 1997.

Hemingway, Albert. *Ira Hayes, Pima Marine.* Lanham, Md.: University Press of America, 1988.

Holm, Tom. "Fighting a White Man's War: The Extent and Legacy of American Indian Participation in World War II." *Journal of Ethnic Studies* 9 (1981): 69–81.

———. *Strong Hearts, Wounded Souls: Native American Veterans of the Vietnam War.* Austin: University of Texas Press, 1996.

Paul, Doris A. *Navajo Code Talkers.* Philadelphia, Pa.: Dorrance, 1973.

Philosophy

A Basic Call to Consciousness. Rooseveltown, N.Y.: Akwesasne Notes, 1981.

Churchill, Ward, ed. *Marxism and Native Americans.* Boston: South End Press, 1983.

Deloria, Vine, Jr. *The Metaphysics of Modern Existence.* San Francisco: Harper & Row, 1979.

———. *Red Earth, White Lies: Native Americans and the Myth of Scientific Fact.* New York: Scribner, 1995.

Mohawk, John. *Utopian Legacies: A History of Conquest and Oppression in the Western World.* Santa Fe, N.Mex.: Clear Light, 1999.

Religion and Spirituality

Deloria, Vine, Jr. *God Is Red: A Native View of Religion.* Santa Fe, N.Mex.: Clear Light, 1994.

Fools Crow, and Thomas Mails. *Fools Crow.* Lincoln: University of Nebraska Press, 1990.

Hirshfelder, Arlene, and Paulette Fairbanks Molin. *The Encyclopedia of Native American Religions,* updated edition. New York: Facts On File, 1999.

Neihart, John Gneisenau. *Black Elk Speaks: Being the True Life of a Holy Man of the Oglala Sioux.* Lincoln: University of Nebraska Press, 1988.

Vecsey, Christopher, ed. *Handbook of American Indian Religious Freedom.* New York: Crossroad, 1991.

Voget, Fred W. *The Shoshone-Crow Sun Dance.* Norman: University of Oklahoma Press, 1998.

Waters, Frank, and Oswald White Bear Fredericks. *The Book of the Hopi.* New York: Viking, 1985.

Sovereignty and Treaty Rights

A Basic Call to Consciousness. Rooseveltown, N.Y.: Akwesasne Notes, 1981.

Cohen, Fay. *Treaties on Trial: The Continuing Controversy over Northwest Indian Fishing Rights.* Seattle and London: University of Washington Press, 1986.

Cohen, Felix S. *Handbook of Federal Indian Law.* Charlottesville, Va.: Michie Bobbs-Merrill, 1982.

Deloria, Vine, Jr., and Clifford Lytle. *The Nations Within: The Past and Future of American Indian Sovereignty.* New York: Pantheon Books, 1984.

Lyons, Oren, and John Mohawk, eds. *Exiled in the Land of the Free: Democracy, Indian Nations, and the U.S.* Santa Fe, N.Mex.: Clear Light, 1998.

O'Brien, Sharon. *American Indian Tribal Governments.* Norman: University of Oklahoma Press, 1989.

Sports

Oxendine, Joseph B. *American Indian Sports Heritage.* Champaign, Ill.: Human Kinetics, 1988.

Wheeler, Robert W. *Jim Thorpe: World's Greatest Athlete.* Norman: University of Oklahoma Press, 1979.

Transportation

Smith, Dowell Harry. "Old Cars and Social Productions among the Teton Lakota." Ph.D. dissertation, University of Colorado, 1973. UMI Microform 7332591.

Urbanization

Fixico, Donald L. *Urban Indians.* New York: Chelsea House, 1991.

Lauer, Tammy. *American Indian Urbanization and Assimilation: A Bibliography.* St. Paul, Minn.: AI Research and Policy Institute, 1995.

Women

Farley, Ronnie. *Women of the Native Struggle. Portraits and Testimony of Native Women.* New York: Crown, 1993.

Sonneborn, Liz. *A to Z of American Indian Women.* Rev. ed. New York: Facts On File, 2007.

Writers

Littlefield, Daniel F. *A Biobibliography of Native American Writers, 1772–1924.* Native American Bibliography series, no. 2. Metuchen, N.J.: Scarecrow Press, 1981.

Littlefield Daniel F., and James W. Parins. *A Biobibliography of Native American Writers: A Supplement.* Native American Bibliography Series, no. 5. Metuchen, N.J.: Scarecrow Press, 1985.

Parker, Dorothy R. *Singing an Indian Song: A Biography of D'Arcy McNickle.* Lincoln and London: University of Nebraska Press, 1992.

Witalec, Janet, ed. *Native North American Literature.* New York: Gale, 1994.

Entries by Tribe or Group

Abenaki
Bruchac, Joseph

Acoma Pueblo
Ortiz, Simon J.
Paytiamo, James

Apache
Chino, Wendell
Cleghorn, Mildred
Houser, Allan

Arapaho
Coolidge Sherman
Heap of Birds, Edgar

Assiniboine
Adams, Hank
Akers, Dorothy

Athabaskan
Thompson, Morris

Bannock
LaVatta, George P.

Blackfeet
Gerard, Forrest J.
Old Person, Earl
Sanderville, Richard
Spopee

Welch, James P., Jr.
White Calf, James
White Calf, John

Cahuilla
Costo, Rupert
Meyers, John Tortes

Cayuga
Bomberry, Daniel
Farmer, Gary Dale
General, Alexander
General, Levi

Cayuse
Halfmoon, Frank L.

Chemehuevi
Willie Boy

Cherokee
Ballard, Louis Wayne
Blackstone, Tsianina Evan
Bronson, Ruth Muskrat
Churchill, Ward
Clark, Joseph
Crow, John Orien
Durham, Jimmie
Evans, Ernest Edwin
George, Charles
Grass, Luther Burbank
Hastings, William Wirt
Horn, Michael Hastings
Junaluska, Arthur Smith

Keeler, William Wayne
Lewis, Robert E.
Mankiller, Wilma Pearl
Montgomery, Jack Cleveland
New, Lloyd Kiva
Oskison, John Milton
Owen, Robert Latham
Reese, John N., Jr.
Rider, Iva Josephine
Rogers, William Penn Adair
Rogers, William Penn Adair, Jr.
Ross, Mary Golda
Smith, Redbird
Starr, Emmet
Strickland, Rennard
Swimmer, Ross O.
Teehee, Houston Benge
Thomas, Robert Knox
Thornton, Joe Tindle
Wheat, Zack
Wilkinson, Gerald

Cheyenne
Campbell, Ben Nighthorse
Harjo, Suzan Shown
Heap of Birds, Edgar
Henderson, James Youngblood
Peterson, Helen White
Storm, Hyemeyohsts
West, Walter Richard, Sr.

Chickasaw
Carewe, Edwin
Carter, Charles David
Fox, Finis
Fox, Wallace W.
Harvey, Raymond

Henderson, James Youngblood
Hogan, Linda
Maytubby, Floyd Ernest
McLendon, Mary Stone
Redwing, Roderic
Te Ata

CHIPPEWA (ANISHINABE)

Anderson, Cora Reynolds
Baldwin, Marie Louise Bottineau
Banks, Dennis James
Beaulieu, Gus H.
Beaulieu, Theodore H.
Bellecourt, Clyde Howard
Bender, Charles Albert
Boucha, Henry Charles
Bresette, Walt
Bruce, Robert Emil
Burns, Mark L.
Cloud, Elizabeth Bender Roe
DeMain, Paul
Fortunate Eagle, Adam
Gordon, Philip B.
Graves, Peter
Guyon, Joe
Hallett, William E.
Jourdain, Roger
Kidwell, Clara Sue
LaDuke, Winona
Northrup, Jim
Peltier, Leonard
Strongwolf, Joseph (?)
Sun Bear
Vizenor, Gerald Robert
Welch, Gustavus
Williamson, James S.

CHOCTAW

Barfoot, Van T.
Durant, William Alexander
Dwight, Ben
Farver, Peru
Hightower, Rosella
Kidwell, Clara Sue
Martin, Phillip
McLendon, Mary Stone
Muldrow, Hal R.
Parker, Gabe Edward
Parker, Gabe Edward, Jr.
Pogue, William Reid
Robertson, Wesley Leroy
Steigler, William G.
Victor, Wilma L.

COEUR D'ALENE

Alexie, Sherman
Garry, Joseph Richard

COLVILLE

Quintasket, Christine

COMANCHE

Harris, LaDonna
Ottipoby, James Collins

CREE

McNickle, D'Arcy
Sainte-Marie, Buffy
Smith, Jaune Quick-to-See

CREEK

Barnett, Jackson
Blackstone, Tsianina Evan
Blue Eagle, Acee
Childers, Ernest
Deere, Phillip
Harjo, Chitto
Harjo, Joy
Harjo, Suzan Shown
Pepper, Jim
Posey, Alex
Reynolds, Allie
Sampson, Will, Jr.

CROW

Old Coyote, Barney
Red Star, Kevin
Yellowtail, Robert Summers

DELAWARE (SEE LENNI LENAPE)

ESKIMO (SEE INUPIAT)

FLATHEAD

McNickle, D'Arcy

FOX (SEE ALSO SAC AND FOX)

Jones, William

GROS VENTRE (ATSINA)

Welch, James P., Jr.

HOPI

Banyacya, Thomas
Dukepoo, Frank Charles
Kabotie, Fred
Katchongva, Dan
Loloma, Charles, and Otellie Loloma
Mofsie, Louis
Nampeyo
Qöyawayma, Alfred H.
Rose, Wendy
Sekaquaptewa, Abbott
Sekaquaptewa, Emory
Sidney, Ivan
Tewanima, Louis
Tewaquaptewa, Wilson
Youkioma

INUPIAT

Beltz, William E.
Butler, Nilak
Rock, Howard

IROQUOIS CONFEDERACY (HODENOSAUNEE)

See under Cayuga, Mohawk, Oneida, Onondaga, Seneca, Tuscarora

ISLETA PUEBLO

Abeita, Jim

KAW

Curtis, Charles
Pepper, Jim

KICKAPOO

Wahpepah, Bill

KIOWA

Davis, Jesse Ed
Geiogamah, Hanay
Kickingbird, K. Kirke
Kiowa Five
Momaday, N. Scott
Poolaw, Horace

LAGUNA PUEBLO

Allen, Paula Gunn
Dukepoo, Frank Charles
Silko, Leslie Marmon

LENNI LENAPE (DELAWARE)

Exendine, Albert Andrew
Forbes, Jack D.
Geiogamah, Hanay
Young Deer, James

LUISEÑO

Calac, Pete
Luna, James
Scholder, Fritz

LUMBEE

Hatcher, Eddie
Long Lance, Sylvester
Williams, Robert A.

MAIDU

Fonseca, Harry

MASHANTUCKET PEQUOT

Hayward, Richard Arthur

MENOMINEE

Deer, Ada
Frechette, Evelyn
Washinawatok, Ingrid
Washinawatok, James A.

MIAMI

Cardin, Fred

MICCOSUKEE

Tiger, William Buffalo

MICMAC

Aquash, Anna Mae
Dillon, Patti

MODOC

Dorris, Michael

MOHAWK

Billings, Robert J.
Bruce, Louis Rook, Jr.
Fadden, Ray
Kenny, Maurice
Minoka-Hill, Lillie Rosa
Oakes, Richard
Porter, Tom
Richmond, Rosemary
Robertson, Robbie
Silverheels, Jay Smith
Swamp, Jake
Witt, Shirley Hill

MOHEGAN

Tantaquidgeon, Gladys
Tantaquidgeon, Harold

NARRAGANSETT

Brown, Ellison Myers

NAVAJO (DINÉ, DINEH)

Begay, Harrison
Blackgoat, Roberta
Blatchford, Herbert
Dodge, Henry Chee
Dodge, Thomas H.
Gorman, R. C.
Jones, Paul
MacDonald, Peter
Morgan, Jacob Casimera
Nakai, Raymond
Nakai, R. Carlos
Scott, O. Tacheeni
Tapahonso, Luci
Wauneka, Annie Dodge
Yazz, Beatien
Zah, Peterson

NEZ PERCE

Halfmoon, Frank L.
Phinney, Archie

NISQUALLY

Frank, Billy, Jr.
McCloud, Janet

OJIBWA, OJIBWAY (SEE CHIPPEWA)

OKANAGAN

Quintasket, Christine

OMAHA

La Flesche, Francis
La Flesche, Susan
Sloan, Thomas L.

ONEIDA

Bennett, Robert LaFollette
Charles, Wilson D.
Cornelius, Chester Poe
General, Alexander
General, Levi
Greene, Graham
Hill, Charlie
Hill, Norbert S., Jr.
Kellogg, Laura Miriam Cornelius
Schanandoah, Chapman
Wheelock, Dennison

ONONDAGA

Hill, David Russell
Lyons, Oren, Jr.
Shenandoah, Leon
Thomas, George E.
Thomas, George A.

OSAGE

Bacon Rind
Lookout, Fred
Mathews, John Joseph
Revard, Carter Curtis
Strickland, Rennard
Tallchief, Maria
Tallchief, Marjorie
Tinker, Clarence Leonard

OTOE

Shunatona, Joseph Bayhylle

OTTAWA

Williams, Scott T.

PAIUTE

Thom, Mel

PAPAGO

See Tohono O'odham

PASSAMAQUODDY

Gardipe, Carol
Stevens, John W.

PAWNEE

Blue Eagle, Acee
Echohawk, Brummett
Echohawk, John E.
Gover, Kevin
Murie, James R.
Shunatona, Joseph Bayhylle

PENOBSCOT

Gardipe, Carol Metcalf
Poolaw, Lucy Nicola
Sockalexis, Andrew
Spotted Elk, Molly

PEORIA

Dagenett, Charles Edwin
Larkin, Moscelyne

PEQUOT (SEE MASHENTUCKET PEQUOT)

PIMA (AKIMEL O'ODHAM)

Hayes, Ira Hamilton
Moore, Russell

PONCA

Warrior, Clyde

POTAWATOMI

Coulter, Robert
Crumbo, Woody

POWHATAN

Forbes, Jack D.

PUEBLO

See specific pueblos (Acoma Pueblo, Isleta Pueblo, Laguna Pueblo, San Ildefonso Pueblo, Santa Clara Pueblo, Taos Pueblo, Zuni Pueblo)

PUYALLUP

Yowlachie, Chief

QUAPAW

Ballard, Louis Wayne
Cardin, Fred

QUINAULT

DeLaCruz, Joseph

SAC AND FOX

Thorpe, Grace
Thorpe, Jim
Wahpepah, Bill
Whistler, Don

SALISH

Bomberry, Daniel
Smith, Jaune Quick-to-See

SAN ILDEFONSO PUEBLO

Martinez, Maria Montoya

SANTA CLARA PUEBLO

Dozier, Edward P.
Stroud-Lee, Agnes Naranjo
Velarde, Pablita

SEMINOLE

Billie, James
Billy, Josie
Davis, Alice Brown
Jumper, Betty Mae Tiger

SENECA

Big Tree, John
Cornplanter, Edward
Cornplanter, Jesse
Lyons, Lee H.
Mohawk, John
Parker, Arthur C.

SHAWNEE

Alford, Thomas Wildcat
Chouteau, Yvonne
Larkin, Moscelyne
Wray, Lincoln

SHOSHONE

LaVatta, George P.
Ridley, Jack R.
Smith, Jaune Quick-to-See
Trehero, John

SIOUX (DAKOTA, LAKOTA, OR NAKOTA)

Adams, Hank
Allen, Paula Gunn
Bissonette, Pedro
Black Elk
Black Elk, Wallace Howard
Bonnin, Gertrude
Brave, Benjamin
Brave Bird, Mary
Burnette, Robert Phillip
Catches, Peter
Crow Dog, Leonard
Deloria, Ella Cara
Deloria, Vine, Jr.
Deloria, Vine, Sr.
Dietz, William Henry
Eagleshirt, William
Eastman, Charles Alexander
Eastman, Irene
Fools Crow, Frank
Giago, Tim
Howe, Oscar
Lame Deer, John Fire
Looking Horse, Arvol
Means, Russell
Means, William
Medicine, Beatrice
Mills, Billy
Peltier, Leonard
Red Bow, Buddy
Reifel, Benjamin
Standing Bear, Luther
Trudell, John
Westerman, Floyd Red Crow
Wilson, Richard
Yellow Robe, Chauncey
Yellow Robe, Evelyn
Yellow Thunder, Raymond

S'KLALLAM

Niatum, Duane

SPOKANE

Alexie, Sherman

SUQUAMISH

George, Dan

TAINO

Barreiro, José

TAOS PUEBLO

Pop Chalee
Romero, Juan de Jesús

TEWA

Cajete, Gregory
Dozier, Edward P.
Nampeyo
Ortiz, Alfonso

TLINGIT

Shotridge, Louis

TOHONO O'ODHAM (FORMERLY PAPAGO)

Daniels, Victor
Segundo, Thomas

TULALIP

McCloud, Janet

TURTLE MOUNTAIN CHIPPEWA (SEE ALSO CHIPPEWA)

Baldwin, Marie Louise Bottineau
Bruce, Robert Emil
Erdrich, Louise

TUSCARORA

Anderson, Mad Bear
Gansworth, Howard Edward
Hewitt, John Napoleon Brinton
Marsh, Lucille Johnson
Mt. Pleasant, Jane
Rickard, Clinton
Rickard, William

UTE

Nakai, R. Carlos

WANAPUM

Sohappy, David

WASCO

Smith, Kenneth L.

WINNEBAGO (HO-CHUNK)

Cloud, Henry Clarence Roe
DeCora, Angel
Mofsie, Louis
Mountain Wolf Woman
Red Cloud, Mitchell
Snake, Reuben
St. Cyr, Lillian

WYANDOT, WYANDOTTE

Bearskin, Leaford
Bearskin, Leyland S.
Conley, Eliza Burton

YAKAMA

French, Richard
LaCourse, Richard Vance
Strongheart, Nipo
Yowlachie, Chief

YAVAPAI

Montezuma, Carlos

YUCHI

Brown, Samuel William, Jr.

ZUNI PUEBLO

Lewis, Robert E.

NON-INDIANS

Barsh, Russel Lawrence
Bates, Erl Augustus Caesar
Boas, Franz
Boyden, John Sterling
Brophy, William Aloysius
Brown, Dee
Burke, Charles Henry
Castañeda, Carlos
Chinquilla, Mary
Cody, Iron Eyes
Cohen, Felix Solomon
Collier, John
Colton, Harold Sellers
Du Bois, Constance Goddard
Dunn, Dorothy
Emmons, Glenn Leonidas
Fall, Albert Bacon
Garland, Hamlin
Gilmore, Melvin Randolph
Grinnell, George Bird
Hagerman, Herbert James
Jones, William Arthur
Josephy, Alvin M., Jr.
La Farge, Oliver
Leupp, Francis Ellington
Macleod, William Christie
McKenzie, Fayette Avery
Moorehead, Warren King
Myer, Dillon Seymour
Nash, Philleo
Nichols, John Ralph
Perry, Ted
Powers, Mabel
Pratt, Richard Henry
Red Thunder Cloud
Reel, Estelle
Rhoads, Charles James
Ryan, Will Carson, Jr.
Scattergood, Joseph Henry
Sells, Cato
Seton, Ernest Thompson
Speck, Frank Gouldsmith
St. James, Red Fox
Tax, Sol
Valentine, Robert Grosvenor
Warner, Pop
Watkins, Arthur Vivian

ENTRIES BY AREA OF ACTIVITY

*Denotes non-Indian

ACTIVIST

Abeita, Jim
Adams, Hank
Anderson, Mad Bear
Aquash, Anna Mae
Banks, Dennis James
Banyacya, Thomas
Barreiro, José
Bates, Erl Augustus Caesar
Bellecourt, Clyde Howard
Bissonnette, Pedro
Blackgoat, Roberta
Blatchford, Herbert
Bomberry, Daniel
Bonnin, Gertrude
Brave Bird, Mary
Bresette, Walt
Bronson, Ruth Muskrat
Butler, Nilak
Churchill, Ward
Conley, Eliza Burton
Cornelius, Chester Poe
Costo, Rupert
Crow Dog, Leonard
Deer, Ada Elizabeth
Deere, Phillip
Deloria, Vine, Jr.
Echohawk, John E.
Fortunate Eagle, Adam
Frank, Billy, Jr.
Garry, Joseph Richard
Gordon, Phillip B.
Harjo, Chitto
Harjo, Suzan Shown
Harris, LaDonna
Hatcher, Eddie
LaDuke, Winona

Lyons, Lee A.
Lyons, Oren, Jr.
Mankiller, Wilma Pearl
McCloud, Janet
McNickle, D'Arcy
Means, Russell
Means, William
Oakes, Richard
Peltier, Leonard
Peterson, Helen White
Phinney, Archie
Quintasket, Christine
Richmond, Rosemary
Rickard, Clinton
Rickard, William
Sohappy, David
Thom, Mel
Thorpe, Grace
Trudell, John
Wahpepah, Bill
Warrior, Clyde
Washinawatok, Ingrid
Washinawatok, James A.
Wauneka, Annie Dodge
Wilkinson, Gerald
Witt, Shirley Hill
Yellow Robe, Chauncey

ACTOR, ACTRESS, COMEDIAN, STORYTELLER

Banks, Dennis James
Big Tree, John
Carewe, Edwin
Chinquilla, Mary*
Cody, Iron Eyes*
Cornplanter, Jesse
Daniels, Victor
Eagleshirt, William
Farmer, Gary Dale
George, Dan
Greene, Graham
Hill, Charlie
Junaluska, Arthur Smith
Long Lance, Sylvester
Means, Russell
Powers, Mabel*
Redwing, Roderic
Rogers, William Penn Adair
Sainte-Marie, Buffy
Sampson, Will, Jr.
Shunatona, Joseph Bayhylle
Silverheels, Jay Smith
Spotted Elk, Molly
Standing Bear, Luther
St. Cyr, Lillian
Strongheart, Nipo
Sun Bear
Te Ata
Westerman, Floyd Red Crow
White Calf, John
Williams, Scott T.
Young Deer, James
Yowlachie, Chief

514

ADVOCATE AND REFORMER

Collier, John*
Colton, Harold Sellers*
Du Bois, Constance Goddard*
Garland, Hamlin
Kellogg, Laura Miriam Cornelius
La Farge, Oliver*
Leupp, Francis Ellington*
McKenzie, Fayette Avery
Montezuma Carlos
Moorehead, Warren King*
Parker, Arthur C.
Seton, Ernest Thompson*
St. James, Red Fox*
Strongwolf, Joseph

ANTHROPOLOGIST

Bates, Erl Augustus Caesar
Boas, Franz*
Castañeda, Carlos*
Deloria, Ella Cara
Dozier, Edward P.
Grinnell, George Bird*
Jones, William
La Farge, Oliver*
Medicine, Beatrice
Moorehead, Warren King*
Nash, Philleo
Ortiz, Alfonso
Parker, Arthur C.
Phinney, Archie
Red Thunder Cloud*
Shotridge, Louis
Speck, Frank Gouldsmith*
Tantaquidgeon, Gladys
Tax, Sol*
Thomas, Robert K.
Witt, Shirley Hill

ARTIST (VISUAL)

Begay, Harrison
Blue Eagle, Acee
Bresette, Walt
Cornplanter, Jesse
Crumbo, Woody
DeCora, Angel
Dietz, William Henry
Durham, Jimmie
Echohawk, Brummett
Fonseca, Harry
Fortunate Eagle, Adam
Gorman, R. C.
Heap of Birds, Edgar

Houser, Allan
Howe, Oscar
Kabotie, Fred
Kiowa Five
Loloma, Charles, and Otellie Loloma
Luna, James
Lyons, Oren, Jr.
Martinez, Maria Montoya
McLendon, Mary Stone
Mofsie, Louis
Nampeyo
New, Lloyd Kiva
Poolaw, Horace
Pop Chalee
Red Star, Kevin
Rider, Iva Josephine
Sampson, Will, Jr.
Scholder, Fritz
Smith, Jaune Quick-to-See
Velarde, Pablita
West, Walter Richard, Sr.
Yazz, Beatien

ASTRONAUT

Pogue, William Reid

ATHLETE OR COACH

Bender, Charles Albert
Bissonnette, Pedro
Boucha, Henry Charles
Brown, Ellison Myers
Calac, Pete
Campbell, Ben Nighthorse
Charles, Wilson D.
Dietz, William Henry
Dillon, Patti
Exendine, Albert Andrew
Guyon, Joe
Lyons, Oren, Jr.
Meyers, John Tortes
Mills, Billy
Reynolds, Allie
Silverheels, Jay Smith
Sockalexis, Andrew
Tewanima, Louis
Thorpe, Jim
Warner, Pop*
Welch, Gustavus
Wheat, Zack

ATTORNEY

Baldwin, Marie Louise Bottineau
Barsh, Russel Lawrence*

Boyden, John Sterling*
Cohen, Felix Solomon*
Conley, Eliza Burton
Cornelius, Chester Poe
Coulter, Robert
Curtis, Charles
Echohawk, John E.
Henderson, James Youngblood
Kickingbird, K. Kirke
Sloan, Thomas L.
Stigler, William G.
Teehee, Houston Benge
Wheelock, Dennison

AVIATOR

Bearskin, Leaford
Bearskin, Leyland S.
Clark, Joseph
Pogue, William Reid
Tinker, Clarence Leonard

BROADCASTER

Cornplanter, Jesse
Nakai, R. Carlos
Rogers, William Penn Adair
Shunatona, Joseph Bayhylle
Wauneka, Annie Dodge
Whistler, Don

BUSINESSPEOPLE

Beaulieu, Gus H.
Beaulieu, Theodore, H.
Gansworth, Howard Edward
Keeler, William Wayne
Parker, Gabe Edward

CHOREOGRAPHER

Geiogamah, Hanay
Junaluska, Arthur Smith
Mofsie, Louis

COMMISSIONER OR ASSISTANT SECRETARY FOR INDIAN AFFAIRS

Bennett, Robert LaFollette
Brophy, William Aloysius*
Bruce, Louis Rook, Jr.
Burke, Charles Henry*
Collier, John*
Crow, John Orien
Deer, Ada Elizabeth
Emmons, Glenn Leonidas*

Gerard, Forrest J.
Gover, Kevin
Hallett, William E.
Jones, William Arthur*
Leupp, Francis Ellington*
Myer, Dillon Seymour*
Nash, Philleo*
Nichols, John Ralph*
Reifel, Benjamin
Rhoads, Charles James*
Sells, Cato*
Smith, Kenneth L.
Swimmer, Ross O.
Thompson, Morris
Valentine, Robert Grosvenor*

CRIMINAL, SUSPECT, OR CRIME VICTIM

Frechette, Evelyn
Willie Boy
Yellow Thunder, Raymond

DANCER

Chouteau, Yvonne
Geiogomah, Hanay
Hightower, Rosella
Junaluska, Arthur Smith
Larkin, Moscelyne
Mofsie, Louis
Shunatona, Joseph Bayhylle
Spotted Elk, Molly
Tallchief, Maria
Tallchief, Marjorie

EDUCATOR

Anderson, Cora Reynolds
Ballard, Louis Wayne
Barreiro, José
Bates, Erl Augustus Caesar*
Blue Eagle, Acee
Bronson, Ruth Muskrat
Cajete, Gregory
Cloud, Elizabeth Bender Roe
Cloud, Henry Clarence Roe
DeCora, Angel
Dorris, Michael
Dunn, Dorothy*
Fadden, Ray
Farver, Peru
Forbes, Jack D.
Heap of Birds, Edgar
Hill, Norbert S., Jr.
Horn, Michael Hastings

Howe, Oscar
Kabotie, Fred
Kickingbird, K. Kirke
Kidwell, Clara Sue
LaDuke, Winona
Lyons, Oren, Jr.
McLendon, Mary Stone
Means, William
Mofsie, Louis
Mohawk, John
Morgan, Jacob Casimera
Mt. Pleasant, Jane
New, Lloyd Kiva
Old Coyote, Barney
Ottipoby, James Collins
Parker, Gabe Edward
Perry, Ted
Pratt, Richard Henry*
Reel, Estelle*
Ridley, Jack R.
Ryan, Will Carson, Jr.*
Seton, Ernest Thompson*
Standing Bear, Luther
Tantaquidgeon, Harold
Tapahonso, Luci
Thomas, Robert K.
Victor, Wilma L.
West, Walter Richard, Sr.

ENGINEER

MacDonald, Peter
Qöyawayma, Alfred H.
Ross, Mary Golda
Schanandoah, Chapman
Thompson, Morris

ETHNOLOGIST ETHNOGRAPHER

Baldwin, Marie Louise Bottineau
Du Bois, Constance Goddard*
Hewitt, John Napoleon Brinton
La Flesche, Francis
Murie, James R.

FILMMAKER

Alexie, Sherman
Carewe, Edwin
Fox, Finis
Fox, Wallace W.
Young Deer James

FORESTER

Burns, Mark L.
French, Richard

HISTORIAN

Barsh, Russell Lawrence*
Brown, Dee*
Deloria, Vine, Jr.
Forbes, Jack D.
Henderson, James Youngblood
Josephy, Alvin M., Jr.*
Kidwell, Clara Sue
Kickingbird, K. Kirke
Macleod, William Christie*
Mathews, John Joseph
McNickle, D'Arcy
Powers, Mabel*
Starr, Emmet
Strickland, Rennard
Williams, Robert A.

HEALER, HERBALIST, MEDICINE MAN

Billy, Josie
Black Elk
Black Elk, Wallace Howard
Catches, Peter
Crow Dog, Leonard
Deere, Phillip
Fools Crow, Frank
Lame Deer, John Fire
Looking Horse, Arvol
Red Thunder Cloud*
Tantaquidgeon, Gladys
Trehero, John

HUMORIST

Hill, Charlie
Northrup, Jim
Posey, Alex
Rogers, William Penn Adair

INDIAN BUREAU EMPLOYEE

Baldwin, Marie Bottineau
Burns, Mark L.
Dagenett, Charles Edwin
Farver, Peru
LaVatta, George P.
Phinney, Archie

JOURNALIST, EDITOR, PUBLISHER

Barreiro, José
Beaulieu, Theodore H.
Blatchford, Herbert
Bresette, Walt
DeMain, Paul
Durham, Jimmie
Giago, Tim
LaCourse, Richard Vance
Long Lance, Sylvester
Mohawk, John C.
Owen, Robert Latham
Posey, Alex
Rock, Howard
Rogers, William Penn Adair, Jr.

LEGAL SCHOLAR

Barsh, Russel Lawrence*
Cohen, Felix Solomon*
Deloria, Vine, Jr.
Henderson, James Youngblood
Kickingbird, K. Kirke
Strickland, Rennard
Williams, Robert A.

LINGUIST, LANGUAGE EXPERT

Boas, Franz*
Deloria, Ella Cara
Hewitt, John Napoleon Brinton
Jones, William
Phinney, Archie
Red Thunder Cloud*
Sanderville, Richard
Speck, Frank Gouldsmith*
Strongheart, Nipo
Yellow Robe, Evelyn

MARKSMAN, ARCHER

Redwing, Roderic
Thornton, Joe Tindle
Williams, Scott T.

MEMBER OF THE MILITARY, WAR HERO

Barfoot, Van T.
Bearskin, Leaford
Bearskin, Leyland S.
Childers, Ernest
Clark, Joseph
Echohawk, Brummett
Evans, Ernest Edwin

George, Charles
Harvey, Raymond
Hayes, Ira Hamilton
Lyons, Lee A.
Montgomery, Jack Cleveland
Muldrow, Hal R.
Old Coyote, Barney
Parker, Gabe Edward, Jr.
Red Cloud, Mitchell
Reese, John N., Jr.
Tantaquidgeon, Harold
Tinker, Clarence Leonard

MINISTER AND MISSIONARY

Alford, Thomas Wildcat
Billings, Robert J.
Brave, Benjamin
Chino, Wendell
Cloud, Henry Clarence Roe
Coolidge, Sherman
Davis, Alice Brown
Deloria, Vine, Sr.
Gordon, Phillip B.
Morgan, Jacob Casimera
Ottipoby, James Collins

MUSEUM CURATOR

Colton, Harold Sellers*
Fadden, Ray*
Shotridge, Louis
Tantaquidgeon, Gladys
Tantaquidgeon, Harold

MUSICIAN, SINGER, AND COMPOSER

Blackstone, Tsianina Evan
Bonnin, Gertrude
Bruce, Robert Emil
Cardin, Fred
Davis, Jesse Ed
Eastman, Irene
Harjo, Joy
Hill, David Russell
McLendon, Mary Stone
Moore, Russell
Nakai, R. Carlos
Paytiamo, James
Pepper, Jim
Poolaw, Lucy Nicola
Pop Chalee
Red Bow, Buddy
Rider, Iva Josephine
Robertson, Robbie

Robertson, Wesley Leroy
Sainte-Marie, Buffy
Shunatona, Joseph Bayhylle
Trudell, John
Westerman, Floyd Red Crow
Wheelock, Dennison
Wray, Link
Yowlachie, Chief

NOVELIST

Alexie, Sherman
Allen, Paula Gunn
Barreiro, José
Bruchac, Joseph
Deloria, Ella Cara
Dorris, Michael
Du Bois, Constance Goddard*
Erdrich, Louise
Hogan, Linda
LaDuke, Winona
La Farge, Oliver*
Mathews, John Joseph
McNickle, D'Arcy
Momaday, N. Scott
Oskison, John Milton
Quintasket, Christine
Silko, Leslie Marmon
Storm, Hyemeyohsts
Vizenor, Gerald Robert
Welch, James P., Jr.

PHILANTHROPIST, FOUNDATION ORGANIZER

Barnett, Jackson
Bomberry, Daniel
Mills, Billy
Rogers, William Penn Adair, Jr.
Scattergood, Joseph Henry*
Washinawatok, Ingrid

PHILOSOPHER

Cajete, Gregory
Cohen, Felix Solomon*
Deloria, Vine, Jr.
Eastman, Charles Alexander
Mohawk, John C.
Momaday, N. Scott
Thomas, Robert K.

PHOTOGRAPHER

Cody, Iron Eyes
Poolaw, Horace

PHYSICIAN

Bates, Erl Augustus Caesar*
Eastman, Charles Alexander
La Flesche, Susan
Marsh, Lucille Johnson
Minoka-Hill, Lillie Rosa
Montezuma, Carlos
Starr, Emmet

POET

Alexie, Sherman
Allen, Paula Gunn
Bruchac, Joseph
Durham, Jimmie
Erdrich, Louise
Harjo, Joy
Harjo, Suzan Shown
Hogan, Linda
Kenny, Maurice
Momaday, N. Scott
Niatum, Duane
Northrup, Jim
Ortiz, Simon J.
Posey, Alex
Revard, Carter Curtis
Rose, Wendy
Silko, Leslie Marmon
Tapahonso, Luci
Trudell, John
Vizenor, Gerald Robert
Welch, James P., Jr.

POLITICIAN

Akers, Dorothy
Anderson, Cora Reynolds
Beltz, William E.
Billings, Robert J.
Campbell, Ben Nighthorse
Carter, Charles David
Curtis, Charles
Durant, William Alexander
Fall, Albert Bacon*
Hagerman, Herbert James*
Hastings, William Wirt
Owen, Robert Latham
Posey, Alex
Reifel, Benjamin
Rogers, William Vann
Stigler, William G.
Watkins, Arthur Vivian*

POTTER

Du Bois, Constance Goddard*
Martinez, Maria Montoya
Nampeyo
Qöyawayna, Alfred H.

PRISONER

Spopee

RANCHER

Akers, Dorothy
Mathews, John Joseph
Sekaquaptewa, Emory

SCHOLAR

Barsh, Russel Lawrence*
Boas, Franz*
Cohen, Felix Solomon*
Costo, Rupert
Deloria, Ella Cara
Deloria, Vine, Jr.
Forbes, Jack D.
Henderson, James Youngblood
Hewitt, John Napoleon Brinton
Kickingbird, K. Kirke
Kidwell, Clara Sue
Macleod, William Christie*
McKenzie, Fayette Avery*
Medicine, Beatrice
Mohawk, John C.
Moorehead, Warren King*
Ortiz, Alphonso
Parker, Arthur C.
Phinney, Archie
Revard, Carter Curtis
Starr, Emmet
Strickland, Rennard
Thomas, Robert K.
Warrior, Clyde
Williams, Robert A.

SCIENTIST

Dukepoo, Frank Charles
Gardipe, Carol Metcalf
Gilmore, Melvin Randolph*
Grass, Luther Burbank
Halfmoon, Frank L.
Horn, Michael Hastings
Mt. Pleasant, Jane
Ridley, Jack R.
Schanandoah, Chapman

Scott, O. Tacheeni
Stroud-Lee, Agnes Naranjo
Williamson, James S.

SPIRITUAL LEADER (NATIVE RELIGIONS)

Black Elk
Black, Elk, Wallace Howard
Catches, Peter
Crow Dog, Leonard
Deere, Phillip
Fools Crow, Frank
Fortunate Eagle, Adam
General, Alexander
General, Levi
Lame Deer, John Fire
Looking Horse, Arvol
Shenandoah, Leon
Snake, Reuben
Sun Bear
Swamp, Jake
Tewaquaptewa, Wilson
Thomas, George A.
Thomas, George E.
Trehero, John
Youkioma

THEATER DIRECTOR, PLAYWRIGHT, AND PERFORMANCE ARTIST

Geiogamah, Hanay
Junaluska, Arthur Smith
Kenny, Maurice
Luna, James

TRADITIONAL LEADER AND CHIEF

Banyacya, Thomas
Billy, Josie
Blackgoat, Roberta
Catches, Peter
Cornplanter, Edward
Cornplanter, Jesse
Fools Crow, Frank
General, Alexander
General, Levi
Graves, Peter
Harjo, Chitto
Katchongva, Dan
Lyons, Oren, Jr.
Paytiamo, James
Porter, Tom
Rickard, Clinton
Rickard, William
Romero, Juan de Jesús

Shenandoah, Leon
Shunatona, Joseph Bayhylle
Smith, Redbird
Sohappy, David
Strongheart, Nipo
Swamp, Jake
Tewaquaptewa, Wilson
Thomas, George A.
Thomas, George E.
White Calf, James
Yellow Robe, Chauncey
Youkioma

TRADITIONAL WOMAN

Blackgoat, Roberta
Martinez, Maria Montoya
Mountain Wolf Woman
Nampeyo

TRIBAL LEADER

Abeita, Jim
Akers, Dorothy

Alford, Thomas Wildcat
Bacon Rind
Billie, James
Brown, Samuel William, Jr.
Burnette, Robert Phillip
Chino, Wendell
Cleghorn, Mildred
Davis, Alice Brown
DeLaCruz, Joseph
Dodge, Henry Chee
Dodge, Thomas H.
Durant, William Alexander
Dwight, Ben
Garry, Joseph Richard
Graves, Peter
Hastings, William Wirt
Hayward, Richard Arthur
Hill, David Russell
Jones, Paul
Jourdain, Roger
Jumper, Betty Mae Tiger
Keeler, William Wayne
Lewis, Robert E.
Lookout, Fred

MacDonald, Peter
Mankiller, Wilma Pearl
Martin, Phillip
Maytubby, Floyd Ernest
Morgan, Jacob Casimera
Nakai, Raymond
Old Person, Earl
Phinney, Archie
Sanderville, Richard
Segundo, Thomas
Sekaquaptewa, Abbott
Sekaquaptewa, Emory
Shotridge, Louis
Sidney, Ivan
Smith, Kenneth L.
Snake, Reuben
Stevens, John W.
Swimmer, Ross O.
Thom, Mel
Tiger, William Buffalo
Whistler, Don
Wilson, Richard
Yellowtail, Robert Summers
Zah, Peterson

Entries by Year of Birth

*Denotes non-Indian

1830–1839
Youkioma

1840–1849
Barnett, Jackson
Grinnell, George Bird*
Harjo, Chitto
Jones, William Arthur*
Leupp, Francis Ellington*
Pratt, Richard Henry*

1850–1859
Beaulieu, Gus H.
Beaulieu, Theodore H.
Boas, Franz*
Cornplanter, Edward
David, Alice Brown
Dodge, Henry Chee
Du Bois, Constance Goddard*
Eastman, Charles Alexander
Hewitt, John Napoleon Brinton
La Flesche, Francis
Owen, Robert Latham
Sells, Cato*
Smith, Redbird
Spopee
White Calf, James

1860–1869
Alford, Thomas Wildcat
Bacon Rind
Baldwin, Marie Louise Bottineau
Black Elk

Brave, Benjamin
Burke, Charles Henry*
Carter, Charles David
Chinquilla, Mary
Coolidge, Sherman
Cornelius, Chester Poe
Curtis, Charles
Durant, William Alexander
Fall, Albert Bacon*
Garland, Hamlin
Gilmore, Melvin Randolph*
Hastings, William Wirt
Katchongva, Dan
La Flesche, Susan
Lookout, Fred
Montezuma, Carlos
Moorehead, Warren King*
Murie, James R.
Nampeyo
Reel, Estelle*
Seton, Ernest Thompson*
Sloan, Thomas L.
Standing Bear, Luther
Yellow Robe, Chauncey

1870–1879
Abeita, Jim
Big Tree, John
Bonnin, Gertrude
Brown, Samuel William, Jr.
Burns, Mark L.
Conley, Eliza Burton
Dagenett, Charles Edwin
DeCora, Angel
Eagle Shirt, William
Gansworth, Howard Edward

General, Levi
Graves, Peter
Hagerman, Herbert James
Hill, David Russell
Jones, William
McKenzie, Fayette Avery*
Minoka-Hill, Lillie Rosa
Morgan, Jacob Casimera
Oskison, John Milton
Parker, Gabe Edward
Posey, Alex
Powers, Mabel*
Rogers, William Penn Adair
Romero, Juan de Jesús
Rhoads, Charles James*
Sanderville, Richard
Scattergood, Joseph Henry*
Schanandoah, Chapman
Starr, Emmet
Teehee, Houston Benge
Tewanima, Louis
Valentine, Robert Grosvenor*
Warner, Pop*
Wheelock, Dennison
White Calf, John
Young Deer, James

1880–1889

Anderson, Cora Reynolds
Bates, Erl Augustus Caesar
Bender, Charles Albert
Billy, Josie
Blackstone, Tsianina Evan
Carewe, Edwin
Cloud, Elizabeth Bender Roe
Cloud, Henry Clarence Roe
Collier, John*
Colton, Harold Sellers*
Cornplanter, Jesse
Deloria, Ella Cara
Dietz, William Henry
Exendine, Albert Andrew
Fox, Finis
Fox, Wallace W.
General, Alexander
Gordon, Phillip B.
Kellogg, Laura Miriam Cornelius
Martinez, Maria Montoya
Meyers, John Tortes
Mountain Wolf Woman
Parker, Arthur C.
Poolaw, Lucy Nicola
Quintasket, Christine
Rickard, Clinton
Ryan, Will Carson, Jr.*

Shotridge, Louis
Speck, Frank Gouldsmith*
St. Cyr, Lillian
St. James, Red Fox*
Tewaquaptewa, Wilson
Thomas, George E.
Thorpe, James Francis
Tinker, Clarence Leonard
Trehero, John
Watkins, Arthur Vivian*
Wheat, Zack
Willie Boy
Yellowtail, Robert Summers

1890–1899

Bronson, Ruth Muskrat
Bruce, Robert Emil
Calac, Pedro
Cardin, Fred
Clark, Joseph
Daniels, Victor
Dwight, Ben
Eastman, Irene
Emmons, Glenn Leonidas*
Farver, Peru
Fools Crow, Frank
Fox, Wallace W.
George, Dan
Guyon, Joe
Jones, Paul
LaVatta, George P.
Long Lance, Sylvester
Macleod, William Christie*
Marsh, Lucille Johnson
Mathews, John Joseph
Maytubby, Floyd Ernest
McLendon, Mary Stone
Myer, Dillon Seymour*
Nichols, John Ralph*
Ottipoby, James Collins
Paytiamo, James
Rider, Iva Josephine
Sekaquaptewa, Emory
Sockalexis, Andrew
Steigler, William G.
Strongheart, Nipo Tach
Strongwolf, Joseph
Tantaquidgeon, Gladys
Te Ata
Welch, Gustavus
Whistler, Don
Williams, Scott T.
Yowlachie, Chief

1900–1909

Akers, Dorothy
Banyacya, Thomas
Blue Eagle, Acee
Boyden, John Sterling*
Brophy, William Aloysius*
Brown, Dee*
Bruce, Louis Rook, Jr.
Charles, Wilson D.
Cody, Iron Eyes*
Cohen, Felix Solomon*
Costo, Rupert
Deloria, Vine, Sr.
Dodge, Thomas H.
Dunn, Dorothy*
Evans, Ernest Edwin
Frechette, Evelyn
Kabotie, Fred
Keeler, William Wayne
Kiowa Five
La Farge, Oliver*
Lame Deer, John Fire
McNickle, D'Arcy
Muldrow, Hal R.
Nash, Philleo
Parker, Gabe Edward, Jr.
Phinney, Archie
Poolaw, Horace
Pop Chalee
Redwing, Roderic
Reifel, Benjamin
Robertson, Wesley Leroy
Ross, Mary Golda
Shunatona, Joseph Bayhylle
Spotted Elk, Molly
Tantaquidgeon, Harold
Tax, Sol*

1910–1919

Barfoot, Van T.
Begay, Harrison
Beltz, William E.
Bennett, Robert LaFollette
Blackgoat, Roberta
Brown, Ellison
Catches, Peter
Childers, Ernest
Cleghorn, Mildred
Crow, John Orien
Crumbo, Woody
Dozier, Edward P.
Fadden, Ray*
Garry, Joseph Richard
Houser, Allan

Howe, Oscar
Josephy, Alvin M., Jr.*
Jourdain, Roger
Junaluska, Arthur Smith
Lewis, Robert E.
Montgomery, Jack Cleveland
Moore, Russell
Nakai, Raymond
New, Lloyd Kiva
Peterson, Helen White
Red Thunder Cloud*
Reynolds, Allie
Rickard, William
Rock, Howard
Rogers, William Penn Adair, Jr.
Shenandoah, Leon
Silverheels, Jay Smith
Thomas, George A.
Thornton, Joe Tindle
Velarde, Pablita
Victor, Wilma L.
Wauneka, Annie Dodge
West, Walter Richard, Sr.

1920–1929

Anderson, Wallace
Bearskin, Leaford
Bearskin, Leyland S.
Billings, Robert J.
Black Elk, Wallace Howard
Burnette, Robert Phillip
Castañeda, Carlos*
Chino, Wendell
Chouteau, Yvonne
Deere, Phillip
Echohawk, Brummett
Fortunate Eagle, Adam
Gardipe, Carol Metcalf
Gerard, Forrest J.
Grass, Luther Burbank
Halfmoon, Frank L.
Harvey, Raymond
Hayes, Ira Hamilton
Hightower, Rosella
Jumper, Betty Mae
Kenny, Maurice
Larkin, Moscelyne
Loloma, Charles, and Otellie Loloma
MacDonald, Peter
Martin, Phillip
Medicine, Beatrice
Old Coyote, Barney
Old Person, Earl
Red Cloud, Mitchell
Reese, John N., Jr.

Segundo, Thomas
Sekaquaptewa, Abbott
Sohappy, David
Stroud-Lee, Agnes Naranjo
Sun Bear
Tallchief, Maria
Tallchief, Marjorie
Thomas, Robert K.
Thorpe, Grace
Tiger, William Buffalo
Washinawatok, James A.
Yazz, Beatien
Yellow Robe, Evelyn
Yellow Thunder, Raymond

1930–1939

Allen, Paula Gunn
Ballard, Louis Wayne
Banks, Dennis James
Bellecourt, Clyde Howard
Campbell, Ben Nighthorse
Deer, Ada Elizabeth
DeLaCruz, Joseph
Deloria, Vine, Jr.
Forbes, Jack D.
Frank, Billy, Jr.
French, Richard
George, Charles
Giago, Tim
Gorman, R. C.
Harris, LaDonna
LaCourse, Richard Vance
Lyons, Lee A.
Lyons, Oren, Jr.
McCloud, Janet
Means, Russell
Mills, Billy
Mofsie, Louis
Momaday, N. Scott
Niatum, Duane
Ortiz, Alfonso
Perry, Ted*
Pogue, William Reid
Qöyawayma, Alfred H.
Revard, Carter Curtis
Richmond, Rosemary
Ridley, John R.
Sampson, Will, Jr.
Scholder, Fritz
Smith, Kenneth L.
Snake, Reuben
Storm, Hyemeyohsts
Stevens, John W.
Thom, Mel
Thompson, Morris

Vizenor, Gerald Robert
Wahpepah, Bill
Warrior, Clyde
Westerman, Floyd Red Crow
Wilkinson, Gerald
Wilson, Richard
Witt, Shirley Hill
Wray, Lincoln
Zah, Peterson

1940–1949

Adams, Hank
Aquash, Anna Mae
Barreiro, José
Billie, James
Bissonnette, Pedro
Blatchford, Herbert
Bomberry, Daniel
Bresette, Walt
Bruchac, Joseph
Churchill, Ward
Coulter, Robert
Crow Dog, Leonard
Davis, Jesse Ed
Dorris, Michael
Dukepoo, Frank Charles
Durham, Jimmie
Echohawk, John E.
Fonseca, Harry
Geiogamah, Hanay
Hallett, William E.
Harjo, Suzan Shown
Hayward, Richard Arthur
Henderson, James Youngblood
Hill, Norbert S., Jr.
Hogan, Linda
Horn, Michael Hastings
Kickingbird, K. Kirke
Kidwell, Clara Sue
Mankiller, Wilma Pearl
Means, William
Mohawk, John C.
Nakai, R. Carlos
Northrup, Jim
Oakes, Richard
Ortiz, Simon J.
Peltier, Leonard
Pepper, Jim
Porter, Tom
Red Bow, Buddy
Red Star, Kevin
Robertson, Robbie
Rose, Wendy
Sainte-Marie, Buffy
Scott, O. Tacheeni

INDEX

Note: This index is not meant to be exhaustive; it is one of several ways to find information in this book. Persons are also listed by tribe (see pp. 509–13) as well as by occupations or areas of activity (pp. 514–19). In addition, persons and topics are thoroughly cross-referenced in the articles.